# Proceedings

# 2004 International Conference on Parallel Processing

# ICPP 2004

# Proceedings

## 2004 International Conference on Parallel Processing

# *ICPP 2004*

15-18 August 2004 • Montreal, Quebec, Canada

**Sponsored by**
The International Association for Computers and Communications (IACC)

**In cooperation with**
Ohio State University, USA
McGill University, Canada

**Edited by**
Rudolf Eigenmann

Los Alamitos, California

Washington • Brussels • Tokyo

IEEE Computer Society Order Number P2197
ISBN 0-7695-2197-5
ISSN 0190-3918

*Additional copies may be ordered from*:

IEEE Computer Society
Customer Service Center
10662 Los Vaqueros Circle
P.O. Box 3014
Los Alamitos, CA 90720-1314
Tel: + 1 800 272 6657
Fax: + 1 714 821 4641
http://computer.org/cspress
csbooks@computer.org

IEEE Service Center
445 Hoes Lane
P.O. Box 1331
Piscataway, NJ 08855-1331
Tel: + 1 732 981 0060
Fax: + 1 732 981 9667
http://shop.ieee.org/store/
customer-service@ieee.org

IEEE Computer Society
Asia/Pacific Office
Watanabe Bldg., 1-4-2
Minami-Aoyama
Minato-ku, Tokyo 107-0062
JAPAN
Tel: + 81 3 3408 3118
Fax: + 81 3 3408 3553
tokyo.ofc@computer.org

*Individual paper REPRINTS may be ordered at*: reprints@computer.org

Editorial production by Stephanie Kawada
Cover art production by Joe Daigle/Studio Productions
Printed in the United States of America by Victor Graphics, Inc.

# Proceedings

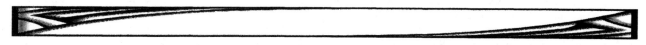

# ICPP 2004

# Table of Contents

## Keynote Address

## Session 1A: Scheduling Tools

## Session 1B: P2P Architecture

## Session 3B: Performance Evaluation I

## Session 3C: OS/Resource Management

## Keynote Address

## Session 4A: Architecture I

## Session 4B: Performance Evaluation II

## Session 4C: Cluster I

## Session 5A: Architecture II

## Session 5B: Network Services

## Session 5C: Cluster II

## Panel Session: Grids: Hype, Substance, or Renaissance?

**Moderator:** *Wu-chun Feng, Los Alamos National Laboratory*

## Keynote Address

## Session 6A: Applications

## Session 6B: Grid: Resource Management

## Session 6C: Wireless: Mobile Systems

## Session 7A: Algorithms

## Session 7B: Embedded Systems

## Session 7C: Wireless: Ad Hoc Networks

## Session 8A: Programming Methodologies

## Session 8B: Multimedia

## Session 8C: Proxy in Wireless Systems

## Author Index

# Preface

The 2004 International Conference on Parallel Processing is in its 33rd year. If parallel processing has been a small, individual research area in its early days, after a third of a century it has permeated almost every conceivable aspect of computing and its applications. The 2004 program includes traditional topics, such as computer architecture, embedded systems, operating systems, compilers, tools, programming methodologies, performance evaluation, algorithms, and applications. It also contains a growing range of topic areas that deal with parallelism in an increasingly internetworked world, such as network services, wireless systems, peer-to-peer technology, cluster and grid computing.

ICPP2004 has received 190 original paper submissions, presenting novel research contributions in the above areas. Each paper has been reviewed by three or more referees. Based on these reviews, the Program committee has selected 65 papers to be presented at the conference and to be included in these proceedings. In addition to the paper presentations, the conference program features three keynote speakers: Mark Hill, Andrew Chien, and Wolfgang Giloi. Furthermore, a panel discussion on "Grids: Hype, Substance, or Renaissance?" is moderated by Wu-chun Feng. Complementing the conference program, there are a number of workshops on emerging topics, the papers of which are compiled in a separate volume.

A large number of people have contributed to the success of ICPP 2004. Their names and functions are many and are listed on the following pages. Without their hard volunteer work, the ICPP conference would simply have been impossible.

**Tarek Abdelrahman,** *General Chair, University of Toronto*
**Rudi Eigenmann,** *Program Chair, Purdue University*

# Organizing Committee

### General Chair
Tarek Abdelrahman, *University of Toronto, Canada*

### Program Chair
Rudolf Eigenmann, *Purdue University, USA*

### Program Vice-Chairs

**Architecture**
José Moreira, *IBM, T. J. Watson, USA*

**Compilers and Languages**
Chen Ding, *University of Rochester, USA*

**Algorithms and Applications**
Ananth Grama, *Purdue University, USA*

**OS/Resource Management**
Peter Keleher, *University of Maryland, USA*

**Programming Methodologies & Tools**
Duane Szafron, *University of Alberta, Canada*

**Tools**
Allen Malony, *University of Oregon, USA*

**Performance Evaluation**
Jeff Vetter, *Oak Ridge National Lab, USA*

**Network Services**
Tao Yang, *UCSB / Ask Jeeves, USA*

**Wireless and Mobile Computing**
Albert Zomaya, *University of Sydney, Australia*

**Network-Based/Grid Computing**
Pratap Pattnaik, *IBM, T. J. Watson, USA*

**Multimedia**
Ashfaq Khokhar, *University of Illinois, Chicago, USA*

**Cluster Computing**
Xian-He Sun, *Illinois Inst. of Technology, USA*

**Peer-to-Peer Technology**
Charlie Hu, *Purdue University, USA*

**Parallel Embedded Systems**
Riccardo Bettati, *Texas A&M University, USA*

# Program Committee

Kevin Almeroth, *University of California at Santa Barbara, USA*
Jose Nelson Amaral, *University of Alberta, Canada*
Dan Andresen, *Kansas State University, USA*
Bill Arbaugh, *University of Maryland, USA*
Eduard Ayguade, *Universitat Politècnica de Catalunya, Spain*
David A. Bader, *University of New Mexico, USA*
Henri E. Bal, *Vrije Universiteit, Netherlands*
Suman Banerjee, *University of Wisconsin, USA*
Suchi Bhandarkar, *University of Georgia, USA*
Ricardo Bianchini, *Rutgers University, USA*
Gianfranco Bilardi, *University of Padova, Italy*
Angelos Bilas, *University of Crete, USA*
Azzedine Boukerch, *University of Ottawa, Canada*
Graça Bressan, *University of São Paulo, Brazil*
Kirk W. Cameron, *University of South Carolina, USA*
Jiannong Cao, *Hong Kong Polytechnic University, China*
Tzi-cker Chiueh, *State University of New York at Stony Brook, USA*
Alok N. Choudhary, *Northwestern University, USA*
Michal Cierniak, *Microsoft, USA*
Marcelo Cintra, *University of Edinburgh, UK*
Cliff Click, *Azul Systems, USA*
Marco Danelutto, *University of Pisa, Italy*
Sajal Das, *University of Texas, USA*
Amitava Datta, *University of Western Australia, Australia*
Eyal de Lara, *University of Toronto, USA*
Luiz De Rose, *IBM, USA*
Pedro Diniz, *ISI, University of Southern California, USA*
Don Dossa, *Lawrence Livermore National Laboratory, USA*
Richard J. Enbody, *Michigan State University, USA*
Thomas Fahringer, *University of Innsbruck, Austria*
Alan D. George, *University of Florida, USA*
Anshul Gupta, *IBM T. J. Watson, USA*
John L. Gustafson, *Sun Microsystems, Inc., USA*
Tim Harris, *University of Cambridge, UK*
Hossam Hassanein, *Queens University, Canada*
Mike Hicks, *University of Maryland, USA*
Adriana Iamnitchi, *University of Chicago, USA*
Liviu Iftode, *Rutgers University, USA*
Vijay Karamcheti, *New York University, USA*
Hironori Kasahara, *Waseda University, Japan*
Kate Keahey, *Argonne National Laboratory, USA*
Eun Jung Kim, *Texas A&M University, USA*
Hyoung Joong Kim, *Kangwon National University, Korea*
Chung-Ta King, *National Tsing Hua University, R.O.C.*
Kath Knobe, *Cambridge Lab, Hewlett Packard, USA*
Vipin Kumar, *University of Minnesota, USA*
Tei-Wei Kuo, *National Taiwan University, ROC*
Bjorn Landfeldt, *Sydney University, Australia*

# Reviewers

Kevin Almeroth
Jose Nelson Amaral
Ping An
Henrique Andrade
Dan Andresen
Bill Arbaugh
Eduard Ayguade
David A. Bader
Henri E. Bal
Hariharan Balakrishnan
Ramesh Balasubramanian
Vicençs Beltran
Suman Banerjee
Christopher Barton
Paul Berube
Riccardo Bettati
Suchi Bhandarkar
Praveen Bhojwani
Laxmi Bhuyan
Ricardo Bianchini
Gianfranco Bilardi
Angelos Bilas
Aniruddha Bohra
Jacir L. Bordim
Azzedine Boukerch
Graça Bressan
Ron Brightwell
Jose Brunheroto
Holger Brunst
Kirk W. Cameron
Chun Cao
Jiannong Cao
David Carrera
Jen-Yeu Chen
Li Chen
Wanli Chen
Yifeng Chen
Zhifeng Chen
Tzi-cker Chiueh
Soohyun Cho
Jon Crowcroft
Alok N. Choudhary
Michal Cierniak
Marcelo Cintra
Cliff Click
Benjamin Collins
Jon Crowcroft
Daniela Cunha

Marco Danelutto
Sajal Das
Amitava Datta
Francis David
Frank Dehne
Eyal de Lara
Luiz De Rose
Pedro DeRose
Marco Di Natale
Chen Ding
Pedro Diniz
Fangpeng Dong
Don Dossa
Jialin Dou
Cong Du
Mahmoud Elhaddad
Richard J. Enbody
Mark Fahey
Thomas Fahringer
Andriy Fedorov
Ronaldo Ferreira
Xinwen Fu
Alan D. George
Paolo Giaccone
Ian Glendinning
Bryan Graham
Ananth Grama
Jose A. Gregorio
Liliana Grigoriu
Laura Grit
Zhuang Guo
Anshul Gupta
John L. Gustafson
Tim Harris
Hossam Hassanein
Xiaoshan He
Taliver Heath
Philip Heidelberger
Mike Hicks
Jen-Wei Hsieh
Y. Charlie Hu
Chih-Yuan Huang
Adriana Iamnitchi
Liviu Iftode
Ciji Isen
Kazuhisa Ishizaka
Suresh Jagannathan
Song Jiang

Xuxian Jiang
Gokul B. Kandiraju
Jaewon Kang
Vijay Karamcheti
Hironori Kasahara
Kate Keahey
Peter Keleher
Ashfaq Khokhar
Thilo Kielmann
Dongkeun Kim
Eun Jung Kim
Ho Gil Kim
Hyoung Joong Kim
Keiji Kimura
Chung-Ta King
Kath Knobe
Andreas Knüpfer
Takeshi Kodaka
Simon Koo
Evangelos Kotsovinos
Mehmet Koyuturk
Dieter Kranzlmüller
Barbara Kreaseck
Vipin Kumar
Tei-Wei Kuo
Byung Kyu
Bjorn Landfeldt
Michael Laurenzano
Aleksandar Lazarevic
Doug Lea
Heung Ki Lee
Manhee Lee
Keqin Li
Xiaoyan Li
Zhiyuan Li
Shih-Wei Liao
Jyh-Ming Lien
Chu-Cheow Lim
Xiaomei Liu
Yunhao Liu
Zhanglin Liu
Shi-Wu Lo
Honghui Lu
Paul Lu
Yi Lu
Xiaoxing Ma
Steve MacDonald
Rabi Mahapatra

Hemant Mahawar
Allen Malony
Biju T. Maniampadavathu
Rich Martin
John Mellor-Crummey
Michael McCracken
Sam Midkiff
José Moreira
Amy Murphy
Matt Mutka
Shailabh Nagar
Wolfgang E. Nagel
Koji Nakano
Nidal Nasser
Esmond G. Ng
Lionel Ni
Jason Nieh
Robert Niewiadomski
Dimitris Nikolopoulos
Stephan Olariu
Sarp Oral
Benno Overeinder
David Padua
Vivek Pai
Yi Pan
Santosh Pande
Pratap Pattnaik
Fabrizio Petrini
Gian Pietro Picco
Luo Ping
Keshav Pingali
Eduardo Pinheiro
Müller-Pfefferkorn
Stefan Podlipnig
Naren Ramakrishnan
Muralikrishna Ramanathan
Sanjay Ranka
Sangig Rho

Paul Ruth
Silvius Rus
Ahmed Sameh
José Carlos Sancho
Oliverio Santana
Vivek Sarin
Selvakennedy Selvadurai
Kai Shen
Xipeng Shen
Wennie Wei Shu
Beth Simon
Ambuj Singh
Anand Sivasubramaniam
Allan Snavely
Andreas Stathopoulos
Michael Steinbach
Burkhard D. Steinmacher-burow
Ivan Stojmenovic
Michelle Mills Strout
Rajagopal Subramaniyan
Xian-He Sun
Yudong Sun
Alan Sussman
Duane Szafron
Abdelhamid Taha
Anthony Tam
Gabriel Tanase
Hong Tang
Rajeev Thakur
Parimala Thulasiraman
Jordi Torres
Ian Troxel
Hong-Linh Truong
Gopinath Vageesan
Jeffrey Vetter
Kees Verstoep
Michael J. Voss
Chen Wang

Cho-Li Wang
Guojun Wang
Quanhong Wang
San-Yuan Wang
Shengquan Wang
Jianbin Wei
Michael Welzl
Liz White
Marek Wieczorek
Manuela Winkler
Patrick Worley
Chengyong Wu
Chin-Hsien Wu
Jie Wu
Jun Wu
Li Xiao
Zhen Xiao
Hui Xiong
Chengzhong Xu
Dongyan Xu
Zhichen Xu
Yuanyuan Yang
Tao Yang
Kamen Yotov
Mohamed Younis
Kun Zhang
Pusheng Zhang
Tao Zhang
Xiaodong Zhang
Yanyong Zhang
Xiliang Zhong
Yuanyuan Zhou
Ye Zhu
Xiaotong Zhuang
Zhenyun Zhuang
Albert Zomaya

# Keynote Address

# A Future of Parallel Computer Architectures

Mark D. Hill
*University of Wisconsin*

# Session 1A:
# Scheduling Tools

# A Runtime System for Autonomic Rescheduling of MPI Programs*

Cong Du, Sumonto Ghosh, Shashank Shankar, and Xian-He Sun
*Department of Computer Science*
*Illinois Institute of Technology*
*{ducong, ghossum, shankar, sun}@iit.edu*

## Abstract

*Intensive research has been conducted on dynamic job scheduling, which dynamically allocates jobs to computing systems. However, most of the existing work is limited to redistribute independent tasks or at the algorithm design level. There is no runtime system available to support automatic redistribution of a running process in a heterogeneous network environment. In this study, we present the design and implementation of a system that dynamically reschedules running processes over a network of computing resources via automatic decision-making and process migration. The system is implemented on top of MPI-2 and HPCM (High Performance Computing Mobility) middleware. Experimental and analytical results show that the runtime system works well. It makes dynamic rescheduling of running tasks possible and improves system performance considerably. While the implementation is for MPI programs and using HPCM, the design of the system is general and can be extended to other distributed environments as well.*

## 1. Introduction

Runtime dynamic scheduling is a fundamental issue of parallel and distributed computing. The emergence of Grid [9], provides a promising platform for large-scale and resource intensive applications. The Grid provides the basic software infrastructure with mechanisms for resource sharing over a distributed heterogeneous network. The job scheduling and management system is an integrated component of Grid computing. When one system encounters some difficulties, such as a system failure, temporary resource unavailability, network outrage, system reconfiguration, or just performance degradation caused by preemption from high priority local jobs, the Grid jobs need to be rescheduled to another host to continue. In traditional job scheduling systems, task allocation is static. Once a task is assigned, it will stay where it is until it finishes or restarts at another site from the beginning. In these systems, a reassignment means the loss of all partial results. The nature of static allocation may cause dramatic performance loss in practice. Also, jobs may have to be rejected when a certain host cannot satisfy the jobs for required resources. However, if the mobility is supported and the decision is made automatically at runtime, a job can move from one host to another for both resource availability and performance gain. In this study, we intend to develop a novel system enabling dynamical reschedule of running processes over a network of computing resources, via automatic decision-making and process migration. We present the design and implementation of a runtime support system, which enables dynamic re-allocation of processes in a heterogeneous distributed environment. We also present a highly configurable and extensible rule-based mechanism for policy making that supports various system conditions in such environment.

Process migration is the act of transferring an active process from one computer to another. The process retains its execution sequence and memory state during a migration. The process is interrupted on the source machine and then is resumed at the break point with the same memory state on the destination machine [8]. HPCM is a heterogeneous process migration middleware [5, 6, 8].

The Message Passing Interface (MPI) is a standard library specification for message passing. It is proposed, developed broadly by vendors, implementers, and users. MPI-2 includes an extension to MPI-1 standard. It supports process creation and management, one-sided communications, extended collective operations, external interfaces, I/O, and additional language bindings [17].

In this study, we design and implement a runtime system on top of HPCM and MPI-2, providing resource registration, resource monitoring, process registration, and soft-state management to support dynamic rescheduling of MPI tasks. The system has a rule-based decision-making component that coordinates with other components of HPCM as a commander, and invokes the migration when it reaches a migration decision according to a highly configurable and extensible rule-based mechanism. Though the system is implemented on top of the MPI and HPCM middleware, it is general and can be extended for

* This research was supported in part by National Science Foundation under NSF ACI-0130458, ANI-0123930, and EIA-0130673.

checkpointing-based or mobile computing systems, and for other distributed environments.

This paper is organized as follows. In Section 2, we give an overview of related works on process migration and job scheduling. In Section 3, we present the features of the rescheduler and describe the implementation details. We present the rule-based decision-making mechanism in Section 4. Section 5 shows the performance results and analysis. Section 6, finally, concludes this paper and presents future works.

## 2. Related Works

The existing computation and data Grid do not support dynamic task re-allocation in general. Traditional static task scheduling requires that before scheduling, the arrival time and execution time of tasks and their dependencies be known to the scheduling system. Usually their relationships are defined by a DAG [12]. Clearly, this condition cannot be met in Grid computing. Some researchers have developed new algorithms for dynamic scheduling with limitations. Some algorithms duplicate the tasks and issue them simultaneously on multiple computing resources [14], [16]. Some issue multiple copies of tasks to idle computing resources [10]. These algorithms have limitations on the usage of resources. They provide dynamic features at the expense of resources and performance. They may also cause mutual exclusion problems when utilized in the tasks requiring non-duplicable resources. Some of them are based on performance prediction. In this case, the system may pay a penalty in terms of prediction error or system failure. Once performance degradation or system failures occur, a reassignment is necessary. In practice, this can cause the loss of all partial results and dramatic performance degradation.

Due to its importance, intensive research has been done in process migration. Some of the early works, such as MOSIX [3], V [4] and Sprite [7], combine the migration functionality to cluster operating systems. Because these systems work on clusters with specific operating systems, they do not use or provide a general runtime re-allocating function. These systems cannot be used in a Grid environment.

There are several other systems implemented for widely used operating systems at user-level, e.g. Condor [15], or at kernel-level, e.g. Linux Zap [21] to support homogeneous process migration. Condor is geared towards High Throughput Computing, through resource and job matching. A centralized broker uses a Class-Ads mechanism to match jobs to resources and then, schedule jobs on the Condor machines. Condor uses a checkpointing-based mechanism to implement process migration at the user-level. It only supports homogeneous process migration. Although several job scheduling policies are proposed [1, 2], they do not support heterogeneous runtime process rescheduling. The Zap system supports migration of legacy applications through the use of loadable kernel modules and virtualization of both the hosts and processes with respect to each other [21]. It uses a checkpointing-based mechanism to support process migration and cannot migrate over heterogeneous environments. However, the Zap system has not implemented the mechanism for scheduling and re-allocation. Heterogeneous process migration has been studied by a few researchers [22, 24] who address several important problems and discuss how to build their prototype systems. They also propose some triggering conditions, but they do not develop those simple triggers into a runtime rescheduling system.

There are some other applications that obtain mobility via mobile agents or mobile codes. Compared to process migration, mobile agents are modularly designed applications that inherently need to "jump" or "goto" other machines. They are scheduled by the execution workflow itself. They work under certain predefined virtual environments, and work well only for certain special purpose applications [13].

## 3. System Design and Features

The basic functionalities of our rescheduler include resource monitoring and registration; process registration;

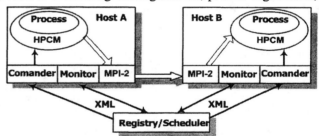

**Figure** 1. System Model

soft-state management; and a rule-based decision-making mechanism. It provides services that enable: effective communication between and within the hosts; transparent sharing, resources discovery and usage; and rule-based intelligent monitoring and decision-making.

Our system model consists of system state monitoring entities, commander entities and a process registration and decision-making entity. Figure 1 shows the system model.

A monitor and a commander entity reside on each host, including candidate destination hosts. There is also a central or hierarchical registry/scheduler, which can reside on any host with or without other entities. As shown in Figure 1, the monitor registers the host static information to the registry/scheduler and periodically gathers and updates the system status to it. The monitor determines the status of its local system resources as *free*, *busy*, *overloaded* or *unavailable*. It then reports its system status and other information to the registry/scheduler. The registry/scheduler analyzes the data from monitors and makes a decision regarding which process to migrate and where to migrate it. The registry/scheduler sends a message to the source machine's local commander to initialize the migration. After receiving the message, the source machine's local commander issues a command to the migrating process to start the process migration. The migrating process, in turn, initializes a process at the destination machine through the dynamic process creation, and creates a communication channel between the migrating process and the initialized process. The initialized process, then, is ready to take over the computation on the destination machine. The migrating process transfers the execution, memory, and communication states to the initialized process on the destination host at the nearest poll-point (pre-defined possible point in the execution sequence where a migration can occur). The details of the process migration mechanisms can be found in [5, 6, 8].

## 3.1 Monitoring and Decision-Making

At each host, the monitor gathers system information and manages local system state based on the information. Local decisions of the system state are made and are reported to its registry/scheduler. Monitoring can be performed periodically or only when necessary. We chose the former for a better reaction time. Based on the rules used in monitoring, the monitor can be very light-weighted.

System information consists of static and dynamic information. Static information, such as host name, IP address, operating system, and memory size, is not likely to change during the lifetime of the specific monitoring entity. The static information is used only for one-time registration. On the other hand, dynamic information from computational resources, memory, networks, disks or applications is quite likely to change with time. We gather dynamic information either through the use of scripts (such as UNIX shell-scripts on *NIX, or batch-files on Windows), or through APIs provided (such as *sysinfo* on LINUX platform, or the *WMI* on Windows platform). We chose to implement a script-based mechanism, partially for the ease of implementation, and partially for its portability. We implemented the shell scripts using utilities like 'vmstat', 'prstat', 'ps' etc, on Sun Solaris 5.8 to gather system information. These mechanisms could be easily ported to LINUX where the shell scripts could read the system parameters from '/proc',

The monitors collect various types of information. They are:
- Processor utilization and load: parameters include the load average, CPU utilization and the number of processes per processor.

- Memory state: available memory and percentage of available memory for both virtual and physical memory, and the memory statistics regarding the process.
- Disk usage: parameters include disk space used, disk space available. It gathers the disk usage parameters of the various mount points.
- Communication: parameters include latency, and bandwidth.

Based on the information, the monitor determines the system status according to a rule-based mechanism. This decision is made locally and specifically according to the rules defined for a specific local system. We can accommodate our system into a large number of heterogeneous systems with very large gaps in both performance and resource availability.

## 3.2 Registry/Scheduler

Registry/scheduler is an entity that resides on any host in the HPCM system. It can also reside on a host without any other entities configured, and it is a global system state manager and decision-making entity. Although conceptually it is a centralized entity in the system, we can extend it as a service in hierarchy. Each local system has its own registry/scheduler and each registry/scheduler has its own upper level registry/scheduler. We can configure a local registry/scheduler on a local cluster and its upper level registry/scheduler to a specific organization, such as a Virtual Organization in a Grid environment. The lower level registry/scheduler has its own health condition, which indicates its overall workload and availability of each kind of resource. Usually, it is preferred that the migration destination is chosen inside one's control domain, which includes the systems registered to the same registry/scheduler entity. This hierarchical design solves the problem of a centralized bottleneck, thereby improving the performance and the system scalability.

Registration mechanisms can be either *pull* or *push* based. The good thing about the *pull* based registration mechanisms is that the registry/scheduler can decide when it needs the information and status of each host. It then queries the current information to make more optimized decisions. But, this also leads to the registry/scheduler having to make a query at runtime when a decision is expected, thus slowing down the process.

The other side is the *push* model where all the registrants are expected to refresh their status every once in a while. This model forces the clients to maintain timers and to constantly keep querying the status of the registry, thus guaranteeing a certain amount of traffic. In this model there are chances of flooding the registry, if all the registrants become synchronized.

In our system, the registration of resources is based on a soft-state mechanism, wherein clients have to regularly update their presence and state information to the registry/scheduler through the *push* model, otherwise the registry/scheduler will consider them as *unavailable*.

Scheduling involves decision-making utilizing static information and runtime data. The registry/scheduler makes a decision on where to migrate a process based on "first fit" policy. From the machine list, the registry/scheduler chooses the first host, which is ready and owns all the resources required, as the migration destination host.

## 3.3 Communication

The monitor, commander and registry/scheduler of our system are components of communication. In addition to these, the migrating process and the initialized process are also involved in communication during process migration. Altogether, five kinds of communication parties coordinate and communicate with each other to form an automatic migration system as shown in Figure 1. We have developed several communication mechanisms, so that we can achieve high performance, scalability and extensibility. We discuss these mechanisms as follows:

- Migrating process and initialized process: The communication data between the migrating process and initialized process include the execution state and memory state. The amount of communication highly depends on the application. We have built up mechanisms to reduce the communication cost in process state transfer. We still need faster communication to improve the migration performance. In the following discussions, we use the communication channel of LAM MPI-2 [18] in process state transfer. Currently, we have tested several communication channels for the process state transfer including TCP/IP, MPI and PVM. We take advantage of the MPI-2 standard dynamic communicator management to support communication state migration over MPI-2. To enable process migration over MPI-2, we need to dynamically create a process with a communicator and join the communicators together, so that the migrating process and initialized process can communicate in one communicator. Fortunately, dynamic process management is defined in MPI-2 standard and LAM is one of the few MPI environments that support these functions. We cannot use other MPI such as MPICH-2 [19] and Sun MPI [20] because they do not support the dynamic process management, and the implementation is in their future schedule.

- Rescheduler, migrating and initialized process: The commander needs to issue a migration command to the migrating process. Then the address and the port of the destination machine are written to a temporary file and are read by the migrating process. We defined this command as a user-defined signal, which is simple, efficient and easy to bind to most systems and communication environments. The detailed application information, parameters, and resource requirements are encapsulated in an *application schema* in a XML format and sent to the destination machine to initialize the process on the destination machine. The *application schema* contains information such as: application characteristics, which include data, communication, or computing intensive; estimated communication data size; resources requirement; and estimated execution time on workstation with certain computing power. The *application schema* is initially provided by the users and is updated according to the statistics of actual executions.

- Entities of rescheduler: We combine a custom XML based protocol with TCP/IP sockets to form the communication subsystem of the rescheduler. The XML based protocol is used for communications between the monitor, registry/scheduler and commander entities. We chose this combination because its implementation can be easily extended, its protocol is simple to implement, and it is easy to debug. As its name suggests, XML is extensible and is transmitted using plain ASCII format and it is also transport independent. Even though we have chosen TCP/IP as our transport protocol, it could be changed in the future to another communication channel, such as various channels of MPI.

## 4. Rule-based Decision-Making Mechanism

We established a rule to describe the requirement of the system based on one or some specific performance or availability parameters. A rule is built to define the resource status of a system. We defined a policy as a group of rules. The policy defines the transformation mechanism of hosts or resources states. We classify the system states with a fine granularity using a series of numbers to support more complex migration rules and policies. Here we use a simplified three-state representation to introduce our mechanisms, which can be easily reconfigured to a finer granularity representation.

The relationship between the actions and the states is shown in Table 1. We define the system states as:

*free*: The host is willing and able to accept incoming HPCM-enabled applications.

*busy*: The host is no longer accepting any incoming applications. It is a state of "as is". The host does not try to migrate the migration-enabled applications out.

*overloaded*: This host needs to offload its applications onto other host, in order to switch either to *busy* or to *free*.

**Table 1. System State Description**

| System state | Loaded | Migrate in | Migrate out |
|--------------|--------|------------|-------------|
| *Free* | No | Yes | No |
| *Busy* | Yes | No | No |
| *Overloaded* | Yes | No | Yes |

We configure a time interval as Monitoring Frequency for each state. It indicates how often the system information is to be gathered. According to the established protocol, when a host reaches an *overloaded* state in the monitor, it consults the registry/scheduler to get a recommended candidate of destination machine. At the moment this registry/scheduler simply checks for host environments that are in the *free* state, and if there is one, it recommends it as the move-to host. The registry/scheduler then sends this message to the commander of the *overloaded* host, thus ensuing the migration.

In our system architecture, a monitoring entity resides on each host. A monitoring entity is composed of system information gathering engines, the process selector, the monitoring information database, and the rule-evaluator. Each of these modules is configurable, thus it is possible to change the internal architecture of gathering information, process selection etc. A flow representation of the monitoring architecture is shown in Figure 2. The registry/scheduler selects the process to be migrated. In the current system, we selected a migration-enabled process based on the start time of the process and the application description information provided in the *application schema* for each application. We get the estimated execution time of the application from the *application schema*, and the start time of the application from the *pid* file time-stamp. The registry/scheduler tends to migrate a process that has the latest completing time to reduce the possibility of migrating multiple processes.

A rule file contains the rule name (*rl_name*), the command to be fired to retrieve the system information (*rl_script*), description of the rule (*rl_desc*), the logic operator to evaluate the rule (*rl_operator*), a list of parameters to be passed to the shell script to retrieve the system information (*rl_param*), and the conditions for the system to be in *busy* state (*rl_busy*), and *overloaded* state (*rl_overLd*). The rules are shown in figure 3.

Rule 1 [processorStatus]: Makes decisions based on the process status, i.e. the idle time of the processor, and amount of time spent in executing idle process. It uses the Unix utility 'vmstat' to determine the processor status. This rule does not require any parameter. If the processor's idle time is higher than 45 but lower than 50 then the system is kept in *busy* state; if the processor's idle

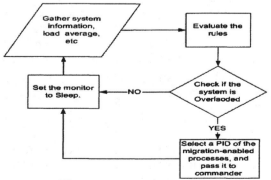

**Figure** 2. Rule Evaluation

time is lesser than 45 then the system is kept in *overloaded* state; otherwise the system is put into *free*.

Rule 2 [ntStatIpv4]: Determines the number of Ipv4 sockets currently open in the system. It uses the Unix utility 'netstat' to determine the number of sockets in a specified state. The rule takes as input a parameter

| rl_number: 1 | rl_number: 2 |
|---|---|
| rl_name: processorStatus | rl_name: ntStatIpv4 |
| rl_type: simple | rl_type: simple |
| rl_script: processorStatus.sh | rl_script: ntStatIpv4.sh |
| rl_desc: This rule determines the processor status i.e. the idle time. | rl_desc: This rule determines the number of sockets in a give state. |
| rl_operator: < | rl_operator: > |
| rl_param: | rl_param: ESTABLISHED |
| rl_busy: 50 | rl_busy: 700 |
| rl_overLd: 45 | rl_overLd: 900 |

**Figure** 3. Simple Rules

rl_number: 5
rl_name: cmp_rule
rl_type: complex
rl_desc: A Complex Rule.
rl_ruleNo: 4 1 3 2
rl_script: ( 40% * r 4 + 30% * r1 + 30% * r3 ) & r2

**Figure** 4: A Complex Rule

specifying the state of the socket to be monitored, such as the sockets in the *ESTABLISHED* state.

A complex rule evaluation determines the state of the system on the basis of a combination of rules. Figure 4 shows a Complex Rule. The *rl_type* determines the type of the rule to be complex. The *rl_script* specifies how the decision is made based on individual rules evaluated. It can be represented in an expression or a file name containing the expression. The *rl_param*, *rl_busy*, *rl_operator* and *rl_overLd* need not be specified in a complex rule.

Thus, as shown in Figure 4, rule numbers 4, 1, 3 and 2 are fired in sequence and the system is in *busy* state if both rule 2 and a combination evaluation of rule 4, 1 and 3 are in *busy* or one of them is in *busy* and the other is in *overloaded*. We can also define a complex rule as a weighted sum of several simple rules.

## 5. Evaluation

We implemented and tested the rescheduler working with other components of the HPCM system on a platform of 64-node cluster running on SunOS 5.8. Each workstation is a Sun Blade 100 with 1 UltraSparc-IIe 500MHz CPU, 256K L2 cache, and 128MB memory. We used the LAM/MPI [18] version 6.5.9 as the MPI-2 communication platform. The communication between the workstations is a 100Mbps internal Ethernet with exclusive use. We also used a computational intensive migration-enabled application named "test_tree", which creates 250 binary trees with specified number of levels, 100 levels in these tests, assigns a random number to each node of the trees, sorts the trees and computes the sum of all the tree nodes. We used NTP (Network Time Protocol) to synchronize the timing on workstations. The maximum error range is no more than 0.02 second.

## 5.1 Rescheduler Overhead

We monitor the host performance with or without the rescheduler using a standalone performance sensor, named *"sysinfo"*, for performance data collection. We configure the monitor, the commander and the registry/scheduler on one workstation. Another workstation is configured with a monitor and a commander and is registered to the registry/scheduler. Several performance parameters, including load average, CPU utilization, and communication cost, are collected. The comparisons of the measured results are shown in Figure 5 and Figure 6.

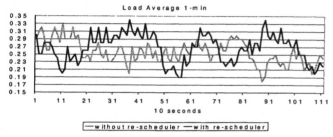

**Figure** 5. Overhead – Load Average 1-min

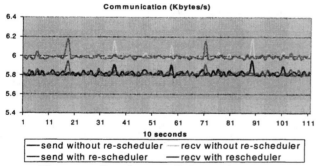

**Figure** 6. Overhead – Communication

The performance data is gathered at an interval of 10 seconds. The load average value is 0.256 for 1-minute without the rescheduler and 0.266 with the rescheduler. The overhead is 3.9%. The load average value is 0.262 for 5-minute without the rescheduler and 0.263 with the rescheduler. The overhead is 0.4%. The 1-minite load average is shown in Figure 5. The CPU utilization average is 0.263 and 0.260 for with and without the rescheduler and the overhead is 3.46%. The communication load with or without rescheduler is 5.82 KB/s for sending and 5.99KB/s for receiving as illustrated in Figure 6. The upper two curses are for receiving and the lower two curves are for sending. We can see clearly that there is almost no overhead for communication. Through the testing, we see that the overhead of the rescheduler operation is usually less that 4%. This testing is to explore only the overhead of the rescheduler. The overhead of

process migration is also small. Details of the migration overhead on both homogeneous and heterogeneous platforms can be found at our prior publication [8].

## 5.2 System Efficiency

Figure 7 and Figure 8 illustrate the efficiency of our system by another experiment. The tests are performed on two workstations and the whole duration is recorded in a 10-second time interval.

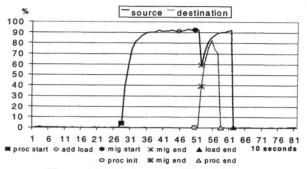

**Figure** 7. Efficiency – CPU Utilization

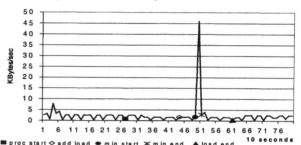

**Figure** 8. Efficiency – Communication

We start a migration-enabled process at the time point 28 (280 seconds from the beginning of test). We then add an additional application, which causes a dramatic load increase on this workstation and the rescheduler decides to migrate the migration-enabled process to another workstation. The migration decision is made at point 50. It takes 72 seconds, from the time that additional task is loaded, for the system to warm up and for the monitor to find out that this is a long task and determine that the system is overloaded. If the additional load is a short task, this period of time can avoid the fault migration caused by small system performance variations. It is a configurable parameter of the rescheduler and can be optimized for different type of workstations. We did not configure the system to be more sensitive because we tried to avoid false migration, which may reach a wrong decision. Then it takes 0.002 second to make a migration decision and within 0.3 seconds, the initialized process is started on the destination machine. The initialization is performed using the LAM/MPI dynamic process management. Though the LAM/MPI dynamic process management operations are slow, currently we do not have other choice because

MPICH-2 [19] and Sun MPI [20] do not support dynamic process management operations at this time. We can use other MPI-2 implementation in future to reduce the initialization time. We can also choose to improve this performance by pre-initializing the processes on the candidate destination machines. In this example, we do not use pre-initialization because we want to show clearly the entire process of the decision-making and migration. It takes the migrating process 1.4 seconds to reach its nearest poll-point. The initialized process starts data restoration and then resumes its execution within 1 second. After of 7.5 seconds, the process is migrated to another system completely, the CPU utilization drops down as shown in Figure 7, and the CPU begins to serve the addition task until it exits. Figure 8 illustrates the communication caused by the migration. The migration occurs when source machine is quite busy. The data restoration is started almost at the same time on the destination machine, and the initialized process resumes execution in parallel with the data collection and restoration. That is, the process resumes execution at the destination before the migration ends. This testing is to explore the time consuming on each phrase of process migration in decision-making and rescheduling.

## 5.3 Rescheduling and Policies

We defined 3 migrating policies to examine the effectiveness of the rescheduler. Table 3 compares the performance of the application under these 3 different migration policies, which are described as follows:
- Policy 1: No Migration.
- Policy 2: Migrate when any of the following conditions are met: 1) 1-min load average is greater than 2; 2) the number of active processes is greater than 150. The destination machine must meet all of the following conditions: 1) 1-min load average is lower than 1; 2) the number of active processes is less than 100.
- Policy 3: Migrate when any of the following conditions are met: 1) 1-min load average is greater than 2; 2) number of active processes is greater than 150; 3) the current incoming/outgoing communication flow is no more than 5MB/s. The destination machine must meet all of the following conditions: 1) 1-min load average is lower than 1; 2) the number of active processes is less than 100; 3) the current incoming/outgoing communication flow is no more than 3MB/s.

We performed the tests using 5 workstations. The 1st is the source machine where the process is originally started. The 2nd is busy in communication with the 5th machine. The communication speed is from 6.71MB/s to 7.78MB/s when applying policy 2 and policy 3. The 3rd workstation has a CPU workload of 2.52. The 4th workstation is free. As shown by Table 2, for each policy, we start the same MPI application on the 1st workstation. Then additional tasks are loaded to the 1st workstation and the system

becomes busy. Under Policy 1, the application does not migrate and it takes 983.6 seconds to finish. Under Policy 2, the rescheduler does not consider the communication state of each workstation. At that time the load of the 2nd workstation is 0.97, which is below the threshold, so the rescheduler chooses the 2nd workstation as the destination machine. The total execution time for the application is 433.27 seconds. Under Policy 3, the rescheduler chooses the 4th workstation as the destination machine, and the total execution time is 329.71 seconds.

**Table** 2. Comparison of Policies

| Policy | total exec time (sec) | start at | migrate to | source (sec) | destination (sec) | migration time (sec) |
|---|---|---|---|---|---|---|
| 1 | 983.6 | 1st | - | 983.6 | 0 | - |
| 2 | 433.27 | 1st | 2nd | 242.68 | 198.98 | 8.31 |
| 3 | 329.71 | 1st | 4th | 221.28 | 115.13 | 6.71 |

The rescheduler improves the performance of an application by choosing a good destination host. In this case, the execution time is reduced to 33.5%. The migration policy of the rescheduler is very important. The communication cost is also an important factor in the decision-making. Similarly, data access locality is another important issue that should be considered in the process of decision-making. If a process involves a lot in a local data access, the process is not to be migrated for slight performance degradation. These features have been enclosed in the *application schema*. An optimized policy can greatly improve the accuracy of migration decision.

## 6. Conclusion

Runtime dynamic scheduling is a fundamental issue of parallel and distributed computing. In parallel computing, it is conventionally instigated by load balancing and performance optimization. In a distributed Grid environment, it becomes more essential and can be applied for fault tolerance (reschedule when the machine will shut down, intrusion is detected, etc.); resources availability (reschedule when special hardware and software are required); data locality (reschedule the process close to the data); etc. in addition to load balance. In this study, we have successfully designed and implemented a runtime rescheduling support system, which triggers rescheduling automatically, and carries the dynamic rescheduling via process migration for MPI programs. We have addressed the technical hurdles of integrating rescheduling decision-making methodology with the heterogeneous process migration mechanisms, and verified the feasibility of MPI-2 [17] and HPCM (High Performance Computing Mobility) middleware [11] in supporting runtime dynamic scheduling. With the assistance of the runtime system and the support of HPCM, a MPI subtask, written in traditional languages such as C or Fortran, can automatically migrate from one machine to another, searching for required computing resources or for a better performance. By setting up a rule-based decision-making and scheduling mechanism, the system is extensible and flexible to various heterogeneous computing platforms. We experimentally tested the system for overhead and efficiency, as well as autonomics under MPI environments. Experimental and analytical results show that the rescheduling system works well and is a complement of existing work on dynamic scheduling, which mostly focuses on redistribution of independent new tasks instead of reschedule of running tasks.

HPCM is supported by the NSF Middleware Initiative (NMI) program and is released under NMI software release [11]. The current prototype implementation of the runtime system, as well as HPCM, is only for the proof of concept. Many issues remain open. We plan further improving the reschedule supported system with the ability of self-configuring and self-adjustment, so that the system can take feedbacks from the scheduling and performance history, and automatically improve its accuracy and efficiency. This study focuses on system and technical support to carry dynamic scheduling. It provides a system that can carry different decision-making and rescheduling algorithms, but does not intend to introduce any new algorithm. Interested readers may refer to [23, 25] for newly proposed rescheduling algorithms.

# References

[1] J. H. Abawajy, "Job scheduling policy for high throughput computing environments", in the *Proceedings of 9th conference of Parallel and Distributed Systems*, pp. 605-610, Dec. 2002.

[2] J. Basney and M. Livny, "Managing Network Resources in Condor", In the *Proceedings Of the HPDC9*, pp. 298-299, 2000.

[3] A. Barak and R. Wheeler, "Mosix: An Integrated Multiprocessor UNIX", in the *Proceedings of Winter 1989 USENIX Conference*, pp. 101-112, San Diego, CA, Feb. 1989.

[4] D. Cherton, "The V Distributed System", *Communications of the ACM*, 31(3): 314-333, March 1988.

[5] K. Chanchio and X.-H. Sun, "Communication State Transfer for Mobility of Concurrent Heterogeneous Computing", in the Proceedings of *the International Conference on Parallel Processing* (ICPP 2001, Best Paper Award), Sep. 2001.

[6] K. Chanchio and X.-H. Sun, "Data collection and restoration for heterogeneous process migration", *SOFTWARE--PRACTICE AND EXPERIENCE*, 32:1-27, April 15, 2002.

[7] Frederick Douglis, "Transparent Process Migration in the Sprite Operating System", *PhD thesis*, University of California, Berkeley, Sep. 1990.

[8] C. Du, X.-H. Sun and K. Chanchio, "HPCM: A Pre-compiler Aided Middleware for the Mobility of Legacy Code", in the *Proceedings of IEEE Cluster Computing Conference*, Hong Kong, Dec. 2003

[9] Ian Foster, Carl Kesselman, "The Grid 2: Blueprint for a New Computing Infrastructure," *Morgan-Kaufman*, ISBN 1558609334, Nov 2003.

[10] N. Fujimoto and K. Hagihara, "Near-Optimal Dynamic Task Scheduling of Independent Coarse-Grained Tasks onto a Computational Grid", in the *Proceedings of IEEE International Conference on Parallel Processing*, Kaohsiung, Oct. 2003.

[11] HPCM: High Performance Computing Mobility, http://meta.cs.iit.edu/~hpcm/.

[12] Y. K. Kwok and I. Ahmad, "Static Scheduling Algorithms for Allocating Directed Task Graphs to Multiprocessors", *ACM Computing Surveys* Vol.31, No.4, 1999, pp.406-471.

[13] Danny B. Lange and Mitsuru Oshima, "Seven Good Reasons for Mobile Agents", *Communications of the ACM*, Vol.42, No.3, March 1999.

[14] G. Li, D. Chen, D. Wang and D. Zhang, "Task Clustering and Scheduling to Multiprocessors with Duplication", in the *Proceedings of 2003 IEEE International Parallel and Distributed Processing Symposium* (IPDPS 2003), Nice, France, April 2003.

[15] M. Lizkow, M. Livny, and T. Tannenbaum. "Checkpoint and Migration of UNIX Processes in the Condor Distributed Environment", Technical Report 1346. University of Wisconsin-Madision, April 1997.

[16] G. Manimaran and C. Siva Ram Murthy, "A Fault-Tolerant Dynamic Scheduling Algorithm for Multiprocessor Real-Time Systems and Its Analysis", *IEEE Transactions on Parallel and Distributed Systems*, vol 9, No. 11, p137, 1998.

[17] The Message Passing Interface (MPI) standard, http://www-unix.mcs.anl.gov/mpi/.

[18] LAM/MPI Parallel Computing, http://www.lam-mpi.org.

[19] MPICH2, MPI-2 Home Page, http://www-unix.mcs.anl.gov/mpi/mpich2/.

[20] Sun MPI-2, Sun MPI 6.0 Software Programming and Reference Manual. http://www.sun.com/products-n-solutions/hardware/docs/html/817-0085-10/index.html

[21] Steven Osman, Dinesh Subhraveti, Gong Su, and Jason Nieh, "The Design and Implementation of Zap: A System for Migrating Computing Environment", in the *Proceedings of the 5th Operating System Design and Implementation OSDI'02*, Dec. 2002.

[22] P. Smith and N. Hutchinson, "Heterogeneous Process Migration: The Tui System", *Software -Practice and Experience*, Vol 28, No.6, pp.611-639, 1998.

[23] X.-H. Sun and M. Wu, "GHS: A Performance Prediction and Task Scheduling System for Grid Computing," in the *Proceedings of 2003 IEEE International Parallel and Distributed Processing Symposium* (IPDPS 2003), Nice, France, April 2003.

[24] M. M. Theimer and B. Hayes, "Heterogeneous Process Migration by Recompilation", in Proceedings of *the 11th IEEE International Conference on Distributed Computing Systems*, Jun. 1991.

[25] M. Wu and X.-H. Sun, "A General Self-adaptive Task Scheduling System for Non-dedicated Heterogeneous Computing", in the *Proceedings of IEEE Cluster Computing Conference*, Hong Kong, Dec. 2003.

# POSE: Getting Over Grainsize in Parallel Discrete Event Simulation

Terry L. Wilmarth and Laxmikant V. Kalé
*Department of Computer Science*
*University of Illinois at Urbana-Champaign*
*{wilmarth, kale}@cs.uiuc.edu*

## Abstract

*Parallel discrete event simulations (PDES) encompass a broad range of analytical simulations. Their utility lies in their ability to model a system and provide information about its behavior in a timely manner. Current PDES methods provide limited performance improvements over sequential simulation. Many logical models for applications have fine granularity making them challenging to parallelize. In POSE, we examine the overhead required for optimistically synchronizing events. We have designed an object model based on the concept of virtualization and new adaptive optimistic methods to improve the performance of fine-grained PDES applications. These novel approaches exploit the speculative nature of optimistic protocols to improve single-processor parallel over sequential performance and achieve scalability for previously hard-to-parallelize fine-grained simulations.[1]*

## 1. Introduction

Simulation makes it possible to analyze systems that would be expensive, dangerous or impossible to construct prototypes for. Some simulations are too complex for sequential simulation due to space and time limitations. Parallelization partitions large problems to fit in memory on many processors and should reduce execution time, but this has proved to be a challenging problem. Fujimoto suggests that a "sufficiently general solution to the PDES problem may lead to new insights in parallel computation as a whole" [6].

We present POSE, a Parallel Object-oriented Simulation Environment in which we have studied the major obstacles to effective parallelization of discrete event models. In particular, we have focused our study on fine-grained simulations which have exhibited the poorest performance.

---
[1]This work was supported in part by the National Science Foundation (NGS 0103645) and the local Department of Energy ASCI center, CSAR (B341494).

### 1.1. Parallel discrete event simulation

A discrete event simulation has a *state* that changes at discrete points in time (*timestamps*) via *events*. An *event list* is a queue of events to be performed on the state. A discrete *global clock* keeps track of progress in simulated time. Events are selected from the event list for execution based on the smallest timestamp. When an event is executed, it may schedule future events that are added to the event list. Thus there exist *causality* relationships between the events in the list.

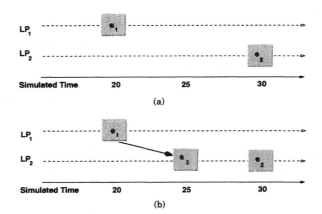

**Figure 1. Causality error**

In parallel, a discrete event model of a system maps physical processes to logical processes (LPs), each with access to a local portion of the state. A local clock keeps track of the progress of the LP. Errors arise when a causality relationship crosses the boundary of an LP.

For example, consider $LP_1$ and $LP_2$ with events $e_1$ and $e_2$ as in Figure 1. Let $T(e)$ be the timestamp of an event $e$. It would seem to be safe to execute the two events simultaneously. Suppose, however, that $e_1$ issues an event $e_3$ for $LP_2$, and $T(e_3) < T(e_2)$. Then $e_3$ must execute before $e_2$ because it may modify the local state which is later accessed by $e_2$.

## 1.2. Synchronization methods

An LP, on its own, cannot know if the earliest available event is *the* earliest event it will ever have. Methods for synchronizing the execution of events across LPs are necessary for ensuring the correctness of the simulation. There are two categories of such mechanisms.

The *conservative* approach avoids causality errors by determining the safety of processing the earliest event on an LP. An event is safe to process when no other event can generate earlier events on the same LP. Determining safety could lead to deadlocks, so deadlock avoidance or detection and recovery must be employed. Because an unsafe earliest event causes an LP to block, conservative methods are limited in the degree to which they can utilize the available parallelism.

The *optimistic* approach allows LPs to process the earliest available event with no regard to safety. Causality errors are detected and handled. When a *straggler* event arrives with a timestamp less than the LP's local clock, the LP is *rolled back* to the point where the straggler should have been executed. To recover state, we *checkpoint* it during *forward execution*. Events spawned by the events we rolled back are sent *cancellation messages* which remove events from an LP's event list. If a canceled event has already been executed, further rollbacks are required. This can cause a *cascade* of rollbacks throughout the simulation.

Optimistic simulations periodically estimate a global virtual time (GVT), the smallest timestamp of all events in the simulation at some point in time. Nothing earlier than the GVT can be rolled back or canceled, so it is safe to dispose of any checkpoints with an earlier timestamp. The process of reclaiming this memory and *committing* the event to history is called *fossil collection*.

We feel that optimistic mechanisms have greater potential for utilizing available parallelism than conservative mechanisms. Rather than blocking to wait for an event to be safe, optimistic approaches perform *speculative computation* that may not need to be rolled back.

## 1.3. Related Work

Much progress has been made in PDES over the last two decades but major problems remain[5]. Simulations developed by parallel computing experts with a deep understanding of the underlying parallel environment (usually those who developed it) perform well while those developed by non-experts perform poorly. The problem of fine-grained simulations (where synchronization overhead overwhelms computation) remains unsolved.

The most well-studied optimistic mechanism is Time Warp, as used in the Time Warp Operating System[7].

Time Warp was notable as it was designed to use process rollback as the primary means of synchronization. Georgia Tech Time Warp (GTW)[4] was developed for small granularity simulations such as wireless networks and ATM networks and designed to be executed on a cache-coherent, shared memory multiprocessor. GTW features a *simulated time barrier* which imposes a limit on how far into the future LPs can advance. POSE has a similar *speculative window*. GTW achieved speedups of 38 using 42 processors for simulating a PCS network.

The Synchronous Parallel Environment for Emulation and Discrete Event Simulation (SPEEDES)[15] was developed with an optimistic approach called *breathing time buckets*. SPEEDES has evolved to include various strategies for comparison purposes and has been used for a variety of applications including military simulations.

Many PDES systems are combinations or hybrids of existing mechanisms. Yaddes[13] allowed a program to be run sequentially, or in parallel using one of three mechanisms with no changes. Maisie[3] requires minor modifications to render a program executable as a sequential simulation, or parallel using conservative or optimistic synchronization mechanisms. Maisie's successor, Parsec[1], also allows for a mix of synchronization protocols amongst the LPs of a program. The best speedup reported for Parsec was nearly 8 on 16 processors for simulating a 3000-node wireless network using the conservative null message protocol.

## 1.4. Performance goals

Let $T_P$ denote single-processor parallel time. Let $T_S$ be the time obtained by our sequential simulator. $T_I$ or *ideal sequential time* is a lower bound on the sequential time. This is the time it would take to execute the simulation if we knew the events and their order in advance. This measure is useful when the program requires more memory than is available on a single processor. To obtain $T_I$, we run the program in parallel, compute the average grainsize and multiply by the number of events executed. As we shall see in Section 3, this is a lower bound on $T_S$ because of an interesting effect of our approach on event grainsize.

Our goal is to improve the scalability of problems with fine granularity. In particular, we seek to reduce *per event overhead* by making efforts to handle single events apply to *groups* of events. We have three subgoals for POSE. First, to achieve a lower *break-even point*, which is the number of processors required to better $T_S$. This improves the applicability of PDES in small parallel computing environments. Second, we wish to achieve near-linear speedups relative to $T_P$. Finally, we should obtain greater *maximum speedups*.

## 2. Fine Granularity and Overhead in PDES

For every event, there is overhead to handle the event in parallel. If the work performed by the event is small, the overhead will far outweigh it. Bagrodia[2] specifies three primary sources of overhead in PDES: partitioning-related, target architecture, and synchronization protocol overheads. We focus on the overhead of optimistic synchronization and have categorized the types of overhead encountered. Figure 5 in Section 4 charts overhead in a POSE program and illustrates the difficulties to overcome.

**Forward Re-execution Overhead** is forward execution time spent *re-executing* events that were previously rolled back.

**Checkpointing Overhead** is the time it takes to checkpoint an object's state. The simplest approach is *full checkpointing* which makes a copy of the state before *every* event. This can be wasteful if the state is large and complex. *Partial checkpointing* checkpoints only the portion of state that may have changed which is difficult to determine in practice. *Periodic checkpointing* only checkpoints before some events. This requires more overhead to reconstruct a state between two checkpoints and makes GVT estimation more challenging.

**Simulation Overhead** is the time it takes to orchestrate the execution, rollback and cancellation of events according to the synchronization strategy. It includes the time spent receiving events, inserting them in the event queue, determining when and what events can be executed, determining if a rollback is necessary or if a cancellation is pending, etc. Simulation overhead is proportional to the number of events in the simulation. Thus, if the number of events is high but the granularity is very fine, the simulation overhead will be large relative to the forward execution time. **Rollback Overhead** occurs when a straggler arrives and we must undo events, send cancellation messages to spawned events and restore a checkpointed state prior to the straggler's timestamp. **Cancellation Overhead** includes the time taken to issue cancellation messages as well as receiving and handling them. POSE prioritizes a cancellation slightly higher than the message to be canceled and performs cancellations before forward execution steps. **Commit Overhead** is fossil collection time and is performed whenever a new GVT estimate is available.

**GVT Overhead** is the time spent gathering, organizing and using data to compute the GVT estimate. GVT computation is especially likely to overwhelm forward execution time in less than ideal simulations. This is probably why there are so many algorithms for GVT calculation in the literature[11, 16, 12]. The algorithm used in POSE operates asynchronously, allowing the simulta-

neously execution of events. Its execution will dominate in situations where the degree of parallelism is low, but it doesn't force idle time on processors with plenty of work to do, and has resulted in less average overhead per processor than other strategies.

**Communication Overhead** includes message packing/unpacking and prioritized scheduling. This overhead naturally increases with the number of processors, since the percentage of non-local communication rises.

## 3. POSE

We have chosen to implement our PDES environment in CHARM++[8], a C++-based parallel programming system that supports the *virtualization* programming model. Virtualization involves dividing a problem into a large number $N$ of components that will execute on $P$ processors [9]. $N$ is independent of $P$, though ideally $N >> P$. The user's view of the program consists of these components and their interactions; the user need not be concerned with how the components map to processors. The underlying run-time system takes care of this and any remapping that might be done at run-time.

In CHARM++, these components are known as *chares*. Chares are C++ objects with special *entry* methods that may be invoked asynchronously from other chares. Since many chares can be mapped to a single processor, CHARM++ uses *message-driven execution* to determine which chare executes. A dynamic scheduler running on each processor that has a pool of *messages* (entry method invocations), selects one, determines the object it is destined for and invokes the corresponding method on the object. Different scheduling policies are available and the user can attach priorities to messages. The advantage of this approach is that no chare can hold a processor idle while it is waiting for a message. Since $N > P$, there may be other chares that can run in the interim. The logical processes (LPs) of PDES (called *posers* in POSE) are mapped onto CHARM++'s chares in a straightforward manner. Similarly, we use timestamps on messages as priorities and the CHARM++ scheduler serves as an event queue.

CHARM++ also provides generalized arrays of migratable parallel objects which allows us to implement our own load balancing strategies in POSE. Another benefit of using CHARM++ is its communication libraries[10]. POSE uses a streaming communication strategy to collect and periodically deliver messages by grouping them together into a single send operation. A last but not least reason for using CHARM++ to implement POSE is its highly portable nature and the existence of ports to most available parallel architectures and distributed environments.

## 3.1. Posers

*Posers* are CHARM++ chares representing entities in the simulation model. Each poser has a data field for *object virtual time* (OVT). This is the simulated time that has passed since the start of the simulation relative to the object. Posers have *event methods* which are CHARM++ *entry methods* that have a data field for *timestamp* in all messages sent to invoke them.

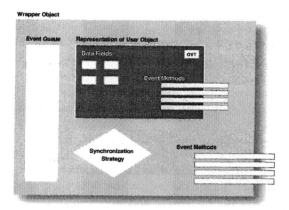

**Figure 2. Components of a *poser***

Posers have two methods for passing simulated time. The first is the *elapse* function. This is used in a poser when a certain amount of local time is passed (presumably performing some activity). It advances the OVT of the poser in which it is called. The second means is by an *offset* added to event invocations. This can be used as a means of scheduling a future activity or to indicate *transit time* in a simulation.

Posers have *plug-in behaviors* for their underlying implementation. These behaviors control the queuing of events, the synchronization of their execution and access to and modification of poser state. We refer to these respectively as the **wrapper** behavior, the **synchronization strategy** behavior, and the **representation** behavior. Different approaches or *plug-ins* can be used for each of these. Figure 2 illustrates how these components fit together. The simulation developer can concentrate on modeling entities (the representation). For more control over simulation behavior and performance, the developer can later look into trying different synchronization strategies.

Using virtualization allows us to maximize the degree of parallelism. Including an event queue in the object means that the scope of simulation activity resulting from a straggler is limited to the entity on which the straggler arrives. Since different entities may have dramatically different behaviors, we are also limiting the effects of those behaviors to a smaller scope. In particular, if one small data structure is a constantly updating

part of a larger, more static entity, we want to separate it from the larger structure to avoid checkpointing the larger state. Further, encapsulating the relevant data in an object makes migration of that object much simpler.

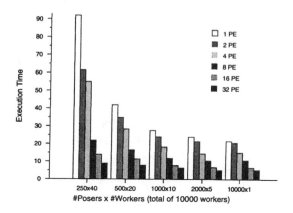

**Figure 3. Effects of virtualization**

Figure 3 shows the effects of virtualization. This is a simple simulation with 10000 worker entities. We organized the workers into teams. Each team is a poser object that encapsulates all the data associated with its workers. The simulation starts with each team giving each worker some work to do. Each worker performs its computation, then generates a few events for other workers. Some work is generated for a neighboring worker (likely to be on the same team) and some is generated for a distant worker. A random placement of posers on processors was used. We ran this simulation up to 32 processors for several team configurations. As the figure shows, we achieved the best performance for the case with 10000 team posers, each with a single worker. It would seem that larger posers should have benefited from the fact that some of their communication was guaranteed to be local, but instead overhead from checkpointing, fossil collection and rollback dominated.

### 3.2. Speculative synchronization mechanisms

In POSE, an object gets control of a processor when it either receives an event or cancellation message via the scheduler, or when another component of the simulation (typically the GVT after a new estimate has been calculated) awakens the object. In the first case, the object's synchronization strategy is immediately invoked and in the second case, we perform fossil collection before invoking the strategy.

Our optimistic strategy checks for cancellation messages and handles as many as possible. Note that a cancellation may arrive before the corresponding event. Next, the strategy checks for any stragglers that may have arrived and rolls back to the earliest. Finally, it is ready to perform forward execution steps.

This is where the opportunity to perform speculative computation arises. All optimistic strategies perform some amount of speculative computation. In traditional approaches, an event arrives and is sorted into the event list and the earliest event is executed. The event is the earliest on the processor, but may not be the earliest in the simulation, so its execution is speculative. In our approach, we have a *speculative window* that governs how far into the future beyond the GVT estimate an object may proceed. Speculative windows are similar to the time windows[14] of other optimistic variants, except in how events within the window are processed.

**Figure 4. Speculative event re-ordering**

Our strategy moves events from the CHARM++ scheduler to the event queues on the objects they are destined for in timestamp order. Each object gets a chance at forward execution for each event it gets and is allowed to speculate whenever it has control. If there are events with timestamp greater than or equal to the GVT estimate but within the speculative window, it executes *all* of them. The later events are probably not the earliest in the simulation and it is very likely that they are not even the earliest on that processor. We are allowing the strategy to speculate that those events are the earliest that the *object* will receive.

By handling events in bunches, we reduce scheduling and context switching overhead and benefit from a warmed cache, but risk additional rollback overhead. Figure 4 shows how events arriving on a processor might be reordered for better cache performance and fewer context switches (events of the same shade are intended for the same object). Table 1 compares the locality of reference for a simulation run sequentially versus the same simulation run with a speculative strategy. This shows that our speculative strategy is doing extra work, but benefiting dramatically from locality of reference.

**Table 1. Locality of reference comparison**

|  | Sequential | Speculative |
|---|---|---|
| References | 4,597,178,671 | 8,536,026,179 |
| Cache Misses | 2,371,769,619 | 610,132,131 |
| Miss Rate | 0.515919 | 0.071477 |

The locality of reference benefit is exhibited in our performance analysis by a smaller average grainsize for the same events as compared to that of the sequential and best-first orderings of events. It is this smaller grainsize that we use to compute $T_I$ as described in Section 1.4.

### 3.3. Adaptive synchronization mechanisms

We have described the concepts of poser virtualization and speculative strategies as implemented in POSE and they have improved performance in new and novel ways. Next, we use these approaches to get at the heart of the general-purpose PDES problem.

We want POSE to perform well on any type of model. One model may differ in its behavior from another and the approaches described so far handle a wide variety of behaviors. However, a model itself may have different components that differ dramatically in behavior. In this case, the best way to speculate about which events to execute on one object may not be the best on another. To handle this situation, we have developed speculative synchronization mechanisms that can adapt to differing behaviors on a per object basis.

Consider two extreme cases. One poser receives many events from all over the system being simulated. It is very likely to receive stragglers that lead to rollbacks. It also has a large state that might be cumbersome to checkpoint, restore and commit. We would like to keep a short leash on such an object to limit how much speculative computation it performs. Within the same simulation, we have another object with a small state. The object also receives a large number of events to execute, but the nature of the simulation results in those events arriving in order most of the time. For this type of object, we would like to allow it to speculate more than the first object, especially if there is idle time on its processor.

Our adaptive strategy takes some of these issues into consideration. It adjusts the speculative window size on a per object basis, according to the recent past rollback behavior of the object. The more successful speculative computation an object performs, the further into the future the object is allowed to speculate. Conversely, objects that receive stragglers are reined in and restricted in the amount of speculation they can do. This strategy effectively pushes our speedup curves for simulation closer to the near-linear goal discussed earlier.

Adding adaptivity at the object-level to a synchronization strategy collects data about object behavior that is useful for several other aspects of PDES. This information is useful for load balancing and communication optimization as well as GVT estimation. It has led to the development of adaptive load balancers, adaptive communication optimization frameworks and adaptive checkpointing strategies in POSE.

## 4. Performance of POSE

To better illuminate the problems with overhead in fine-grained simulations, we have designed a synthetic benchmark parameterized to exhibit the wide variety of behaviors found in PDES simulations. The benchmark creates objects placed on processors according to an initial distribution (uniform, random or imbalanced) and each object initially sends work to itself. A work event consists of performing computation for a time specified by a granularity (fine, medium, coarse, mixed, or a constant), then elapsing time according to a behavior pattern, spawning more work events for other objects.

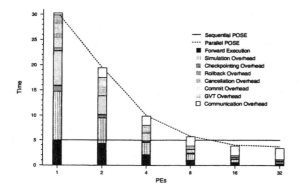

**Figure 5. Synthetic benchmark overhead**

We ran this benchmark with POSE using a parameter set with 5000 objects, high parallelism and fine granularity. The measured granularity was 0.00006s on average and the simulation executed about 81000 events. Figure 5 illustrates the overhead for this problem. This chart shows the average time per processor for each type of overhead in a simulation. The communication overhead represents all unaccounted for time between the maximum time spent in POSE on any processor and the simulation execution time. Thus it is a rough measure of time spent on communication and scheduling.

The black section of the bars represents the time spent in the forward execution of events. The sequential time (shown as a solid horizontal line) is ideal sequential time $T_I$ and it corresponds to the single processor forward execution time. The next section of the bar represents all synchronization overhead. The grey sections are dominated by checkpointing (the darker) and fossil collection (the lighter) for this example. Above those we show the GVT overhead topped off by a white bar indicating communication overhead. For this simulation, we see that the break even point occurs between 8 and 16 proces-

sors. With all the overhead represented here, it is easy to see how hard it is to handle fine-grained events.

In spite of the small size of this example, we achieved near-linear speedups relative to single processor parallel time. Between 16 and 32 processors, the work was distributed too much to maintain a high degree of parallelism versus communication overhead.

### 4.1. Performance of synchronization strategies

To illustrate how these approaches perform in fine-grained simulations, we ran a small instance (5000 objects, high communication) of our synthetic benchmark with three synchronization strategies. The first is a simple optimistic approach with a time window, the second is speculative with a speculative window of the same size as the time window of the first strategy. The third approach is the adaptive strategy with a starting window of the same size as the other two strategies, but with freedom to adjust to the behavior of each object.

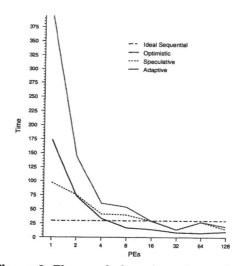

**Figure 6. Fine-grain benchmark run-time**

The simulation we ran had a very small grainsize averaging 23 $\mu s$ per event, with nearly 1,300,000 events executed. The comparative behavior of the three approaches appears in almost every experiment we run. Optimistic performs poorly compared to speculative initially, but the difference dwindles as the number of processors increases. The adaptive approach has more overhead than speculative on fewer processors but eventually adaptive performs much better on higher numbers of processors. This behavior is shown in Figure 6.

Speedup was difficult to achieve with such a small problem with small grainsize, but the adaptive strategy achieved a break even point at roughly 5 processors. The other strategies broke even at 16. The adaptive approach

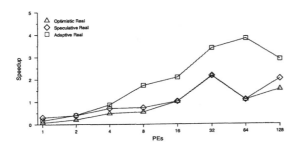

**Figure 7. Fine-grain benchmark speedup**

achieved a maximum speedup very near 4 on 64 processors as shown in Figure 7.

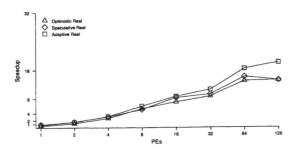

**Figure 8. Medium-grain benchmark**

Contrast this example with the speedup for the same simulation executed with a larger grainsize of 262 $\mu s$ on average in Figure 8. The adaptive strategy achieves a speedup of 18 on 128 processors. The adaptive approach gets some of its gains as the number of processors increases because it is less susceptible to rollback overhead and achieves better locality of reference than the other strategies. However, another major reason for the performance improvement is that the speculative behavior allows the GVT algorithm to come up with higher estimates each time it is invoked, thereby requiring fewer GVT algorithm invocations than the other strategies.

### 4.2. Big machine simulation

BigSim[17] simulates performance of applications on very large parallel computers. It operates in two modes: an on-line mode which correctly predicts performance based on some preset message latencies, and an emulator-only mode which logs the tasks that were performed and their dependencies. In this second mode, the logged tasks have not been ordered in time with respect to each other and need to be timestamp-corrected in order to obtain performance results about the original program run on the BigSim emulator. We use POSE to perform timestamp correction. BigNetSim is an additional POSE module that plugs into the timestamp correction

simulation and simulates the same application over a detailed network model. The behavior of the network model can be varied by its input parameters to model a variety of situations without ever needing to re-run the original program emulation. We discuss and present results for the timestamp correction phase of BigSim. The BigNetSim phase is in the preliminary performance analysis stage.

The timestamp correction simulation reads the trace log files generated by the BigSim emulator and creates posers to model the processors and nodes of the emulation. We start the first task at virtual time zero and let the tasks "execute" and record the virtual time at which each task starts, taking into account task dependencies and durations. We have an estimate of network latency which we use to determine how much time generated tasks spend in transit to the processor on which they will be executed. When all tasks have been executed, they will have correct timestamps and the final GVT should represent a correct runtime for the emulated application.

This simulation has very little computation taking place in events and mostly involves the exchange and update of information. Thus it serves as a challenging fine-grained problem for POSE.

We used the BigSim emulator on 32 processors to run a 2D Jacobi program on 8000 simulated processors. We show a speedup plot for the correction from 1 to 64 processors in Figure 9. The simulator processed 5,085,836 events and had an average grainsize of 198 $\mu s$.

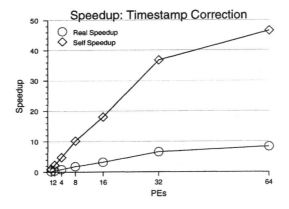

**Figure 9. Timestamp Correction Speedup**

The figure plots real speedup relative to ideal sequential time $T_I$ and self speedup relative to single processor POSE time. As the figure shows, self speedup is nearly linear to 32 processors, while real speedup shows a modest but correspondingly steady speedup improvement as we add processors. This problem did not achieve any speedup with traditional optimistic mechanisms.

## 5. Conclusions and Future Research

POSE has laid the foundation for a study of scalability in optimistically synchronized PDES. POSE incorporates the notion of virtualization from CHARM++, resulting in LPs being modeled by objects known as posers, several of which can be mapped to the same physical processor transparent to the user. The poser contains an instance of a synchronization strategy and its own event queue. This decentralization makes it possible to reduce the scope of overhead to just the objects directly affected. It also makes it possible for the synchronization strategy to react to the behavior of each object differently.

POSE expands the notion of speculation in optimistic synchronization. We have developed strategies that execute several fine-grained events on a single object with no intervening overhead. Not only does this reduce the per-event overhead, but it also has the effect of executing the events with a warmed cache and avoids the frequent context switching between objects that we would do if adhering to a strict timestamp ordering. Our strategy adapts to the behavior of each object by adjusting the speculative window, trying to obtain the largest set of events to execute speculatively on a single object while avoiding an increase in rollback overhead.

Future research will involve developing adaptive speculative strategies further to automatically react to simulation behavior. We will attempt to discern patterns in the forward execution behavior of objects and adjust speculation according to the pattern. Checkpointing frequency will also adapt to checkpoint only when state restoration is most likely to be needed. We are also developing improved strategies for communication in PDES. We use the priorities of messages to determine when they should be delivered. Finally, we have identified many factors affecting the load in a parallel discrete event simulation and are developing lightweight strategies for load balancing in POSE.

Ultimately, we hope to move the field of parallel discrete event simulation forward by developing techniques that allow parallel implementations of the most natural models to outperform their sequential implementations. Our results show much promise for improving the performance of general purpose PDES systems.

## References

[1] R. Bagrodia, R. Meyer, T. M, Y. Chen, X. Zeng, J. Martin, B. Park, and H. Song. Parsec: A parallel simulation environment for complex systems. *Computer*, 31(10):77–85, October 1998.

[2] R. L. Bagrodia. Perils and pitfalls of parallel discrete event simulation. In *Winter Simulation Conference*, 1996.

[3] R. L. Bagrodia and W.-T. Liao. Maisie: A language for the design of efficient discrete-event simulation. *IEEE Transactions on Software Engineering*, 20(4):225–237, April 1994.

[4] S. R. Das, R. Fujimoto, K. S. Panesar, D. Allison, and M. Hybinette. GTW: a time warp system for shared memory multiprocessors. In *Winter Simulation Conference*, pages 1332–1339, 1994.

[5] R. Fujimoto. Parallel Discrete Event Simulation: Will the Field Survive? *ORSA Journal on Computing (feature article)*, pages 213–230, 1993.

[6] R. M. Fujimoto. Parallel discrete event simulation. *Communications of the ACM*, 33(10):30–53, October 1990.

[7] D. Jefferson, B. Beckman, F. Wieland, L. Blume, and M. Diloreto. Time warp operating system. In *Proceedings of the eleventh ACM Symposium on Operating systems principles*, pages 77–93. ACM Press, 1987.

[8] L. Kalé and S. Krishnan. CHARM++: A Portable Concurrent Object Oriented System Based on C++. In A. Paepcke, editor, *Proceedings of OOPSLA'93*, pages 91–108. ACM Press, September 1993.

[9] L. V. Kalé. The virtualization approach to parallel programming: Runtime optimizations and the state of art. In *Los Alamos Computer Science Institute Annual Symposium*, October 2002.

[10] L. V. Kale, S. Kumar, and K. Vardarajan. A Framework for Collective Personalized Communication. In *Proceedings of IPDPS'03*, Nice, France, April 2003.

[11] Y.-B. LIN and E. LAZOWSKA. Determining the global virtual time in a distributed simulation. In *Proceedings of the International Conference on Parallel Processing*, pages 201–209, August 1990.

[12] F. Mattern. Efficient algorithms for distributed snapshots and global virtual time approximation. *Journal of Parallel and Distributed Computing*, 18(4):423–434, 1993.

[13] B. R. Preiss. Performance of discrete event simulation on a multiprocessor using optimistic and conservative synchronization. In *International Conference on Parallel Processing*, 1990.

[14] L. M. Sokol, J. B. Weissman, and P. A. Mutchler. Mtw: an empirical performance study. In *Proceedings of the 23rd conference on Winter simulation*, pages 557–563. IEEE Computer Society, 1991.

[15] J. S. Steinman. Breathing time warp. In *Proceedings of the seventh workshop on Parallel and distributed simulation*, pages 109–118. ACM Press, 1993.

[16] A. I. Tomlinson and V. K. Garg. An algorithm for minimally latent global virtual time. In *Proceedings of the Seventh Workshop on Parallel and Distributed Simulation*, pages 35–42. ACM Press, 1993.

[17] G. Zheng, T. Wilmarth, O. S. Lawlor, L. V. Kalé, S. Adve, and D. Padua. Performance modeling and programming environments for petaflops computers and the blue gene machine. In *NSF Next Generation Systems Program Workshop, 18th International Parallel and Distributed Processing Symposium(IPDPS)*, page 197, Santa Fe, New Mexico, April 2004. IEEE Press.

# Session 1B:
# P2P Architecture

# TAP: A Novel Tunneling Approach for Anonymity in Structured P2P Systems

Yingwu Zhu
Department of ECECS
University of Cincinnati
zhuy@ececs.uc.edu

Yiming Hu
Department of ECECS
University of Cincinnati
yhu@ececs.uc.edu

## Abstract

*In this paper we present **TAP**, a novel **T**unneling approach for **A**nonymity in structured **P**2P systems. An important feature of TAP is that anonymous tunnels are fault-tolerant to node failures. Relying on P2P routing infrastructure and replication mechanism, the basic idea behind TAP is to decouple anonymous tunnels from "fixed" P2P nodes and form anonymous tunnels from dynamic tunnel hop nodes. The primary motivation of TAP is to strike a balance between functionality and anonymity in dynamic P2P networks. We have implemented the tunneling mechanism in Java on FreePastry 1.3. An analysis of its anonymity and performance was evaluated via detailed simulations.*

## 1. Introduction

With the rapid growth and public acceptance of the Internet as a means of communication and information dissemination, *anonymity* is becoming a big concern for many Internet applications, such as anonymous web browsing, anonymous e-mail, and private P2P file sharing. The ultimate goal of anonymization is to protect a participant in a networked application in such a manner that *nobody* can determine his/her identity.

Many anonymous systems (e.g., [1, 18]) have been proposed to protect the identity of the participants. They use a small, fixed core set of *mixes* [3] to form an anonymous path (or tunnel). Such systems, however, have several limitations. First, if a corrupt entry mix receives traffic from a non-core node, it can identify that node as the origin of the traffic. Also, colluding entry and exit mixes can use timing analysis to disclose both source and destination. Secondly, traffic analysis attacks are difficult to counter. Cover traffic has been proposed to deal with such attacks, but it hurts performance and introduces a big bandwidth cost. Thirdly, the drastic imbalance between the relatively small number of mixes and the potential large number of users might pose a capacity problem. Lastly, law enforcement could force the

operator of a mix to disclose the identities of its users; and an authoritarian regime can block the network access to the small number of mixes.

To overcome the aforementioned drawbacks, peer-to-peer (P2P) based systems such as Crowds [10], MorphMix [11] and Tarzan [7] have been recently introduced to provide anonymity by having messages route through anonymous paths involving a randomly chosen sequence of P2P nodes. In such systems, each node is a mix and an anonymous path can follow any possible path through the system. Unfortunately, such P2P-based environment introduces a new problem: the mixes in a P2P system can join and leave at any time, anonymous paths therefore tend to be less stable. A path fails if one of its mixes leaves the system. Put another way, the dynamic nature of P2P systems renders anonymous tunnels vulnerable to node leaves/failures. If a node on a tunnel is down, the request/reply message is not able to route through the tunnel to the destination/originator. Thus, the dynamism of P2P systems poses a *functionality* problem for anonymous tunnels.

In this paper we present TAP, a novel tunneling approach for anonymity in structured P2P systems [12, 17, 9, 20]. The basic idea is to decouple anonymous tunnels from "fixed" nodes. Leveraging the P2P routing infrastructure and replication mechanism [12, 13], as will be shown later, TAP can make anonymous tunnels fault-tolerant to node failures. For example, current tunneling techniques [10, 11, 7] have a problem in maintaining long-standing remote login sessions, if a node on a tunnel fails. However, TAP can support long-standing remote login sessions in the face of node failures. Another application is anonymous email systems. Current tunneling techniques may fail to route the reply email back to the sender due to node failures along the tunnel, while TAP can route the reply back to the sender thanks to its robustness (as will be shown in Section 4 by using a reply tunnel $T_r$).

The rest of the paper is structured as follows. Section 2 describes TAP's system architecture and design. Section 3 details TAP's tunneling approach. Section 4 demonstrates how to use TAP to anonymously retrieve a file in structured P2P systems. Section 5 discusses the tunneling perfor-

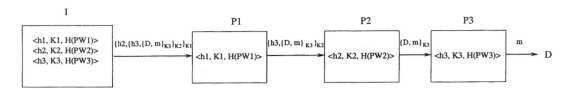

**Figure 1. Tunneling mechanism.** $h_i$ **represents the** $hopId$ **for the** $i$**th hop.** $P_i$ **represents the tunnel hop node whose** $nodeId$ **is numerically closest to the hopId** $h_i$**.** $K_i$ **represents the associated symmetric key for the** $i$**th hop.** $< h_i, K_i, H(PW_i) >$ **is the tunnel hop anchor related to the** $i$**th hop.**

mance enhancement. Section 6 gives TAP's security analysis. Section 7 evaluates TAP's anonymity and performance. Section 8 describes related work, and we finally conclude on Section 9.

## 2. Architecture and Design

TAP aims to use an Internet-wide pool of nodes, numbered in thousands, to relay each other's traffic to gain anonymity. To access the outside world anonymously, a user sets up an anonymous tunnel, which starts at his own node, via some other nodes. We call the node that is setting up the anonymous tunnel the *initiator*. The last node of the tunnel is called the *tail node*. We also distinguish between *benign nodes*, which are nodes that do not try to break the anonymity of other users and *malicious nodes*, which may collude with each other to compromise others' anonymity.

The basic idea behind TAP is to decouple anonymous tunnels from "fixed" nodes. Unlike current tunneling techniques, TAP defines an anonymous tunnel by a sequence of tunnel hops, each of which is specified by a *hopId* (hop identifier) instead of a IP address. A *hopId* is similar to a *fileId* and represents a peer node whose *nodeId* is numerically closest to the *hopId*. We call such a node a *tunnel hop node*. Leveraging the P2P routing infrastructure and replication mechanism [1], a tunnel hop node for a given *hopId* can be located despite the arrival and failure of nodes, unless all $k$ nodes (one node is the tunnel hop node and the other $k - 1$ nodes are tunnel hop node candidates for such a *hopId*. $k$ is the replication factor.) have failed simultaneously. Therefore, an anonymous tunnel in TAP is composed of a set of tunnel hops, each of which is mapped into a tunnel hop node *adaptively* as nodes join and leave.

A message routes through an anonymous tunnel using mix-style layered encryption: each hop of the tunnel removes or adds a layer of encryption depending on the direction of traversal of the message. We denote by $\{m\}_K$ encryption of the message $m$ with a symmetric key $K$. Figure 1 depicts an anonymous tunnel from the initiator $I$ via

tunnel hops $h_1$, $h_2$, and $h_3$. When the initiator $I$ sends a message $m$ to the destination server $D$ through the anonymous tunnel, it encrypts the message in a layered manner from the last hop of the tunnel with the symmetric keys, which results in $\{h_2, \{h_3, \{D, m\}_{K_3}\}_{K_2}\}_{K_1}$. Then $I$ sends the encrypted message to $P_1$, which is the tunnel hop node for $h_1$. When $P_1$ receives the message, it removes one layer of encryption using $K_1$, determines the next hop according to the identifier in the header, and sends it to $P_2$, which is the tunnel hop node for $h_2$. This process repeats until the tail node $P_3$ is reached, which relays the message $m$ to $D$. As will be discussed later, the corresponding reply is sent back to $I$ using a different anonymous tunnel (called the *reply tunnel*) which is included in message $m$ by $I$.

An important feature of TAP is that anonymous tunnels are fault-tolerant to node failures. This is because the $k$ replicas for the tunnel hop anchor $< h_i, K_i, H(PW_i) >$ of each tunnel hop are maintained on $k$ different nodes whose *nodeIds* are numerically closest to $h_i$ in spite of node joins and leaves. For example, consider the case when $P_1$ receives the message from $I$ and is going to send the message to $P_2$, which has already failed. Relying on the P2P routing infrastructure and replication mechanism, $P_1$ is able to route the message to $P_2'$, which has become the tunnel hop node for $h_2$ after $P_2$ fails. $P_2'$ then removes one layer of encryption using the symmetric key $K_2$ and sends the message to $P_3$, allowing the message to continue on the anonymous tunnel.

Having anonymous tunnels consist of an open-ended set of peer nodes, however, introduces a new challenge. An adversary can easily operate several malicious nodes in the system and try to break the anonymity of legitimate users by getting full control of their anonymous tunnels. With the replication of the tunnel hop information (i.e., the tunnel hop anchor as will be shown in Section 3.1), the probability for colluding nodes to compromise other users' anonymity becomes higher. However, the main motivation of TAP is to strike a balance between functionality and anonymity, and our goal is not to provide perfect anonymity in P2P systems.

TAP does not employ cover traffic due to the following reasons. First, cover traffic is very expensive in terms of

---

[1]Due to space constraints, we refer readers to [12, 13] for more details.

bandwidth overhead and it does not protect from internal attackers (malicious nodes who act as mixes in our system). Secondly, the number of potential mixes in our system is large (numbered in thousands or more) and they are probably spread across several countries and ISPs, rendering global eavesdropping very unlikely.

## 3. Tunneling Approach

In this section we detail TAP's tunneling mechanism. Without loss of generality, we take Pastry/PAST as an example for structured P2P systems. However, we believe that our tunneling approach can be easily adapted to other systems [17, 9, 20, 5, 8].

### 3.1. Tunnel Hop Anchor (THA)

A tunnel hop is "anchored" in the system through a *tunnel hop anchor*. A tunnel hop anchor is in the form of $< hopId, K, H(PW) >$, where $hopId$ uniquely identifies the tunnel hop and functions as a DHT (distributed hash table) key for the THA's storage and retrieval, $K$ is a symmetric key for encryption/decryption, and $H(PW)$ is the hash of a password $PW$. It can be envisioned a small file stored on the system, where $hopId$ is the $fileId$, and $K + H(PW)$ is the file content.

A THA is stored on $k$ nodes whose $nodeIds$ are numerically closest to its associated $hopId$. The $k$ nodes are the *replica set* for the THA and $k$ is the *replication factor*. The node with $nodeId$ numerically closest to $hopId$ in the replica set is the tunnel hop node and the other $k - 1$ nodes are the tunnel hop node candidates. If the tunnel hop node fails, one of the candidates will take its place, thus making an anonymous tunnel fault-tolerant to node failures.

The security of THAs is critical to anonymous tunnels in TAP. The nodes who have the right to access a THA must be *restricted*. Only its owner (the initiator who has deployed it) and the nodes in its replica set have the right to access it. Any node who wants to access a THA must be verified that it is either the owner or one of the nodes in the replica set. The identity of an owner can be verified by presenting the corresponding $PW$ of a THA as will be shown later, while the identity of the nodes in the replica set can be verified due to the verifiable constraint that these nodes' $nodeIds$ must be numerically closest to the $hopeId$ of the THA.

### 3.2. Generating THAs

Any node seeking anonymity has to generate and deploy a number of THAs before using anonymous tunnels. In order to avoid collision in generating THAs, we propose a THA generating mechanism which allows a node to generate node-specific THAs without revealing the node's identity. Note that the uniqueness of a THA is determined by its $hopId$. So the $hopId$ for a given node can be computed from a node-specific identifier $node\_ID$ (which could be, for example, the node's IP address, its private key or its public key), a secret bit-string $hkey$, and a time $t$ at which the $hopId$ is created. The purpose of the $hkey$ and $t$ is to prevent other nodes from linking the $hopId$ with a particular node by performing recomputation of the $hopId$ upon each node in the system, and revealing that node's identity. The following equation presents the generation more formally: $hopId \leftarrow H(node\_ID, hkey, t)$, where $H$ is a uniform collision-resistant hash function, e.g., SHA-1. After generating the $hopId$ for a THA, the node then generates a random bit-string as the symmetric key $K$ and another random bit-string as the $PW$.

With the THA generating approach described above, we can see that, the THAs a node generates not only avoid collision with those of other nodes, but also prevent other nodes from linking them with the node.

### 3.3. Deploying THAs

Before forming a tunnel, a node seeking anonymity must deploy a number (e.g., 3-5) of THAs into the system. More importantly, the node must deploy them anonymously such that nobody else can link a THA with itself. Thus, the node needs a bootstrapping anonymous tunnel to deploy the THAs for the *first* anonymous tunnel. Relying on a public key infrastructure on a P2P system by assuming each node has a pair of private and public keys, the node can use Onion Routing [18] as the bootstrapping tunnel by choosing a set of nodes [2], to deploy the THAs for its first anonymous tunnel. It creates an onion carrying instructions for each node on the Onion path to store a THA on the system. For example, a node $I$ creates an onion for the path $P_0$, $P_1$, $P_2$ is $\{P_1, THA_0, \{P_2, THA_1, \{D, THA_2\}_{K_2}\}_{K_1}\}_{K_0}$. It then sends the onion to $P_0$. Each node on the path removes one layer of encryption and stores the corresponding THA on the system. Or a node can deploy only one THA during each Onion Routing session.

It is worth pointing out that Onion Routing is just used to bootstrap a node's first anonymous tunnel. Once the node is able to form the first tunnel using the deployed THAs, it will use this tunnel to deploy other THAs if necessary. Without doubt, if a node on the bootstrapping Onion path fails, the deploying process will be aborted. We argue this is not a problem because the deploying process is not performance critical. A node can always try to use another Onion path to deploy its initial THAs until the first anonymous tunnel is able to be formed. A node can also rent a trusted node's anonymous tunnels to deploy its initial THAs. We leave this approach to our future work.

---

[2] We can employ the peer selection technique used in Tarzan by considering the chosen nodes' IP address prefixes.

Note that malicious nodes can simply try to flood the system with random THAs so that "real" THAs cannot be inserted. This sort of data flooding is a form of denial of service, as it prevents other nodes from deploying THAs to form anonymous tunnels and gaining anonymity. The usual way of counteracting this type of attack is to charge the node for deploying a THA. This charge can take the form of anonymous e-cash or a CPU-based payment system that forces the node to solve some puzzles before deploying a THA.

## 3.4. Deleting THAs

Our system provides a mechanism for a node to delete the THAs which it previously deployed. But any node cannot delete other nodes' deployed THAs by using this mechanism. Recall that when a node deploys a THA, a $PW$ is generated and the $H(PW)$ is included in the THA. The reason this value is stored as opposed to just the $PW$ is that it prevents a malicious node from learning the password $PW$ and deleting the THA. To delete a THA, a node has to present the secret $PW$ as a proof of ownership. The nodes which store the THA will hash the received $PW$, compare the hash value with the stored $H(PW)$, and if they match, remove the THA from their local storage.

## 3.5. Forming Tunnels

When forming a tunnel, a node selects a set of THAs it has already deployed. The chosen THAs must scatter in the DHT identifier space as far as possible (i.e., with different $hopId$'s prefixes) to minimize the probability that a single node has the information of multiple or all tunnel hops of the tunnel to be formed.

## 4. A Sample Application: Anonymous File Retrieval

In this section we demonstrate how to use TAP for an initiator $I$ to retrieve a file (with $fid$ as its $fileId$) in structured P2P systems like Pastry/PAST.

In the forward path, the initiator $I$ creates a forward tunnel $T_f$, and performs a layered encryption for each tunnel hop. More precisely, consider a forward tunnel $T_f$ that consists of a sequence of 3 hops $(h_1, h_2, h_3)$, where $h_i = < hid_i, K_i, H(PW_i) >$. Then $I$ produces the message $M = \{hid_2, \{hid_3, \{fid, K_I', T_r\}_{K_3}\}_{K_2}\}_{K_1}$, where $K_I'$ is a temporary public key for $I$ and $T_r$ is a reply tunnel for the requested file to route back. $T_r$ is a different tunnel from $T_f$. More precisely, it consists of a sequence of 3 hops $(h_1', h_2', h_3')$, where $h_i' = < hid_i', K_i', H(PW_i') >$. So $T_r = \{hid_1', \{hid_2', \{hid_3', \{bid, fakeOnion\}_{K_3'}\}_{K_2'}\}_{K_1'}\}$,

where $fakeOnion$ is introduced to confuse the last hop in $T_r$. $bid$ is an identifier subject to a condition that $I$ is the node whose $nodeId$ is numerically closest to it. Therefore, it guarantees that the reply will route back to $I$.

To retrieve the file, the initiator $I$ sends the message $M$ to the first tunnel hop node corresponding to $hid_1$. The first tunnel hop node retrieves the symmetric key $K_1$ from its local storage, removes one layer of encryption using $K_1$, determines the next tunnel hop node of $h_2$ and sends the extracted message to the next tunnel hop node. This process continues until the message reaches the tail tunnel hop node of $h_3$. The tail node strips off the innermost layer of encryption, revealing $I$'s request for file $fid$. Then it sends the request together with the reply tunnel $T_r$ and $K_I'$ to the responder node $R$ who stores such a file $f$ corresponding to $fid$.

Upon receiving the message, the responder node $R$ retrieves the file $f$ from its local storage, encrypts the file with a symmetric key $K_f$ ($\{f\}_{K_f}$), encrypts $K_f$ with $K_I'$ ($\{K_f\}_{K_I'}$), and sends the $\{f\}_{K_f}$, $\{K_f\}_{K_I'}$ and the reply tunnel $T_r$ with $hid_1$ removed to the tunnel hop node of $h_1'$. On the reply path, each successive tunnel hop node removes one layer of encryption from the reply tunnel $T_r$, revealing the next tunnel hop, and sends $\{f\}_{K_f}$, $\{K_f\}_{K_I'}$ and the stripped reply tunnel to the next tunnel hop node. This process repeats until the reply message reaches $I$, which decrypts $K_f$ using the corresponding temporary private key $K_I^{-1}$, and then decrypts the file $f$. Note that each tunnel hop performs only a single symmetric key operation per message that is processed.

It is also worth pointing out that a request tunnel is different from a reply tunnel in our design. This makes it harder for an adversary to correlate a request with a reply.

## 5. Tunnel Performance Enhancement

Note that in a P2P system (e.g., Pastry/PAST) consisting of $N$ nodes, it can route to the numerically closest node for a given $fileId$ in $\lceil \log_{2^b} N \rceil$ hops ($b$ is a system parameter, with a typical value of 4). As a result, the anonymous tunnel of $l$ hops might involve $l * \lceil \log_{2^b} N \rceil$ hops, introducing a big performance overhead.

In this section we propose a performance enhancement scheme for the basic tunneling mechanism. More precisely, consider a tunnel $T = (h_1, h_2, h_3)$, where $h_i = < hid_i, K_i, H(PW_i) >$. For each tunnel hop $h_i$, the initiator gets the IP address $ip_i$ of the corresponding tunnel hop node [3]. Then it creates an encrypted message in the form of $\{hid_2, ip_2, \{hid_3, ip_3, \{D, M\}_{K_3}\}_{K_2}\}_{K_1}$, by embedding the IP address of each tunnel hop node.

---

[3] The initiator can maintain a cache of the mappings between a tunnel hop $hopId$ and the IP address of its tunnel hop node, and it can periodically refresh the cache.

The initiator first attempts to send the message directly to the node with the IP address $ip_1$. If this node does not exist or it is not the tunnel hop node of $h_1$ any more, it routes to the tunnel hop node of $h_1$ by resorting to the P2P routing infrastructure. Each successive tunnel hop node on the tunnel removes a layer of encryption, revealing the next hop with a IP address and $hopId$. It first tries the IP address, if it fails, then routes the message to the tunnel hop node corresponding to the $hopId$. This process repeats until the message reaches the tail node, which in turn routes the message $M$ to the destination node $D$. Obviously, the tunneling approach with the IP address embedded as a hint at each hop provides a shortcut to the next tunnel hop along the path, resulting in great performance improvement (as will be shown in Section 7).

## 6. Security Analysis

In this section we analyze how our tunneling approach can defend against attacks from the various parties in the P2P system. In particular, we focus the analysis on initiator anonymity.

**A global eavesdropper**: As discussed earlier, TAP does not employ cover traffic due to its expensive bandwidth overhead. So if a global eavesdropper can observe every single node in the system, it should be able to break the anonymity of all participants by means of timing analysis at the node along anonymous tunnels or end-to-end timing analysis at the first and tail nodes. However, we argue that such an attacker is not realistic in the P2P environment with thousands of nodes distributed in the Internet. First, in our design each node is a mix and the number of mixes is very large and they are spread across several countries and ISPs, therefore a global attacker is very unlikely in such a P2P environment. Secondly, the dynamism of P2P systems due to node joins and leaves makes it virtually impossible for anyone to get knowledge of the whole network at any time.

**A local eavesdropper**: An adversary can monitor all local traffic to and from an initiator. Although the eavesdropper will reveal the initiator's traffic patterns (both sent and received), it cannot figure out the initiator's destination or message content without the cooperation from other nodes.

**The responder**: The probability that the responder correctly guesses the initiator's identity is $\frac{1}{N-1}$ ($N$ is the number of nodes in system), since all other nodes have the same likelihood of being the initiator.

**A malicious node**: The mix homogeneity (each node is a potential mix) of our design prevents an adversary from deterministically concluding the identity of an initiator: all nodes both originate and forward traffic. Thus, a malicious node along the tunnel cannot know for sure whether it is the first hop in the tunnel. It can only guess that its immediate predecessor is the initiator with some confidence.

**Colluding malicious nodes**: We consider the case that an adversary operates a portion of nodes which collude with each other to compromise the anonymity of legitimate users. It can read messages addressed to nodes under its control; it can analyze the contents of these messages. The adversary can use timing analysis to determine whether messages seen at different hops belong to the same tunnel. In TAP, each THA is replicated on a replica set of $k$ nodes. If one of these $k$ nodes is malicious, it can disclose the THA to other colluding nodes. As such, malicious nodes can pool their THAs to break the anonymity of other users. With some probability, the adversary can (1) have the THAs for all the hops following the initiator along a tunnel, or (2) control at least the first tunnel hop node and the tail tunnel hop node of a tunnel (the adversary can use timing analysis attack to compromise the tunnel). Thus, if a message belonging to these two cases reaches a malicious node, the adversary can have a chance to compromise the anonymity. But, it is worth pointing out that the adversary attack on the second case is very limited. This is because, first and most importantly, the adversary does not know if the first hop is really the first hop, which implies he cannot determine who the initiator is. Secondly, the network connection heterogeneity of P2P networks complicates the task of timing analysis attacks. As a result, in Section 7 we mainly focus on the first case.

Note that the primary motivation of TAP is to strike a balance between functionality and anonymity in very dynamic P2P networks. The adversary may occasionally break the anonymity of a user by using the THAs he has accumulated, but a user can form another tunnel anyway to protect its future anonymity once its current tunnel is found to be compromised.

## 7. Experimental Results

We have implemented TAP in Java on FreePastry 1.3 [2]. FreePastry 1.3 is a modular, open source implementation of the Pastry P2P routing and location substrate. It also includes an implementation of the PAST storage system and the replication manager, which provides application-independent management of replicas by replicating data on the set of $k$ nodes closest to a given key. To be able to perform experiments with large networks of nodes, we implemented TAP on a network emulation environment, through which the instances of the node software communicate. In all experiments reported in this paper, the peer nodes were configured to run in a single Java VM.

### 7.1. Simultaneous Node Failures/Leaves

In this experiment, we evaluate the ability of TAP to function after a fraction of nodes fail/leave simultaneously.

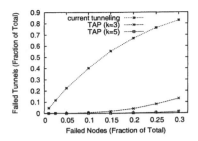

**Figure 2. The fraction of tunnels that fail as a function of the fraction of nodes that fail.**

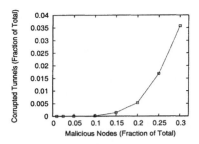

**Figure 3. The fraction of tunnels that are corrupted as a function of the fraction of nodes that are malicious. The replication factor $k$ is 3.**

We consider a $10^4$ node network that forms $5,000$ tunnels, and randomly choose a fraction $p$ of nodes that fail/leave. After node failures/leaves, we measure the fraction of tunnels that could not function. Note that we define the number of tunnel hops per tunnel as the *tunnel length*. In this experiment, the tunnel length is 5.

Figure 2 plots the mean tunnel failure rate as a function of $p$ for the current tunneling, TAP with the replicator factor $k = 3$, and TAP with $k = 5$, respectively. Note that in TAP, there is no significant tunnel failure. A higher replication factor $k$ makes tunnels more fault-tolerant to node failures. However, in the current tunneling approach, the tunnel failure rate increases dramatically as the node failure fraction increases.

## 7.2. Colluding Malicious Nodes

We now evaluate the anonymity of TAP against colluding malicious nodes in the system. We again consider a $10^4$ node network, where some of them are malicious and in the same colluding set. We assume the system has $5,000$ tunnels and randomly choose a fraction $p$ of nodes that are malicious. The tunnel length is 5 by default, unless otherwise specified.

We first measure the fraction of tunnels that can be corrupted by malicious nodes. Figure 3 plots the mean corrupted tunnel rate as a function of $p$. As $p$ increases, the corrupted tunnel rate increases. However, there is no significant tunnels corrupted even if $p$ is large enough (e.g., 0.3).

In the following experiments, the value of $p$ is fixed to be 0.1. We then evaluate the impact of the replication factor and the tunnel length on anonymity. Figure 4 (a) shows the fraction of tunnels that are corrupted as a function of the replication factor. As the replication factor increases, the fraction of tunnels that are corrupted increases. This is because a bigger replication factor allows malicious nodes to be able to learn more THAs, increasing the probability of compromising other users' anonymity. Figure 4 (b) shows the fraction of tunnels that are corrupted as a function of

the tunnel length. Note that the fraction decreases with the increasing tunnel length, and the tunnel length of 5 catches the knee of the curve.

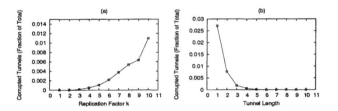

**Figure 4. The fraction of tunnels that are corrupted as a function of the replication factor (a) and the tunnel length (b).**

So far our experiments have not considered the dynamism of P2P systems that nodes enter and leave the system at will. In the presence of node leaves, malicious nodes instead can try to stay in system as long as possible so that they can accumulate more THAs to break others' anonymity. For example, if a benign node leaves, its responsible THAs are taken by another node, which might happen to be a malicious node. Moreover, the replication mechanism of P2P systems might happen to make malicious nodes to become the members of some THAs' replica sets as nodes leave. As such, malicious nodes can take advantage of the leaves of other nodes to learn more THAs. We assume there are $5,000$ tunnels in the beginning of the system. During each time unit, we simulate that a number of 100 benign nodes leaves and then another set of 100 benign nodes joins the system. So the fraction of malicious nodes $p$ is kept on 0.1 after each time unit. Then we measure the fraction of tunnels that are corrupted after each time unit. Figure 5 plots the mean corrupted tunnel rate. "unrefreshed" means that the original $5,000$ tunnels are used throughout the experiment, while "refreshed" means that a new set of 5,000 tunnels are created to replace the old tunnels after each time unit. Note that the corrupted rate of "unrefreshed" increases steadily as time goes, while that of "refreshed" keeps almost constant. We conclude that in such dynamic P2P systems, users should refresh their tunnels periodically to reduce the risk of having their anonymity compromised.

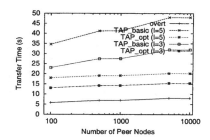

**Figure 6. Transfer latency.** $l$ **is the tunnel length.**

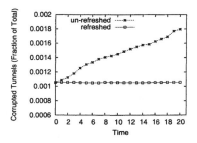

**Figure 5. The fraction of tunnels that are corrupted. The replication factor** $k$ **is 5.**

## 7.3. Performance

In this section we evaluate the performance of TAP in terms of transfer latency between peer nodes. Our performance analysis focuses on the overhead introduced by TAP. We simulated the size of a P2P network from 100 to 10,000 nodes. Each link in the network had a random latency from 10 ms to 2300 ms, randomly selected in a fashion that approximates an Internet network [14]. All links had a simulated bandwidth of 1.5 Mb/s. A randomly chosen initiator transferred a 2Mb file with a random $fileId$ to a node whose $nodeId$ is numerically closest to the $fileId$ in the following three ways: (1) overt transfer relying on the P2P routing infrastructure ("overt"), (2) anonymous transfer using TAP's basic tunneling mechanism ("TAP_basic"), and (3) anonymous transfer using TAP's performance optimized tunneling mechanism ("TAP_opt") (as discussed in Section 5). We ran 30 simulations for each network size, and each of the simulations involved 100,000 file transfers.

Figure 6 shows the transfer latency. Note that TAP's basic tunneling mechanism introduces a significant latency penalty in the file transfer. A longer tunnel introduces bigger performance overhead, thought it provides better anonymity. However, TAP's performance optimized tunneling mechanism can dramatically reduce the latency penalty, thus greatly improving the tunneling performance. It is also worth pointing out that the overhead introduced by symmetric encryption/decryption in tunneling is negligible in this experiment.

## 8. Related Work

In this section we present the research work related to anonymity and P2P systems.

Many systems such as Anonymous Remailer [1] and Onion Routing [18] achieve anonymity by having anonymous paths route through a small, fixed core set of *mixes* [3]. Recently, anonymous systems where every node is a mix have been proposed, such as Crowds [10], Hordes [16], Tarzan [7], MorphMix [11], and $P^5$ [15]. Recent work [19, 14] aims at mutual anonymity between an initiator and a responder. However, all these systems have not addressed the functionality problem of anonymous paths.

Structured P2P systems [12, 17, 9, 20], provide a P2P routing and lookup infrastructure. And P2P storage and file systems (e.g., [13]) layer their storage on top of such structured P2P systems. Currently, we implement TAP in Pastry/PAST, but our tunneling approach can be easily adapted to other systems [17, 9, 20, 5, 8]. There are two anonymous storage systems that deserve mentioning. Freenet [4] uses probabilistic routing to achieve anonymity, and FreeHaven [6] uses both cryptography and routing to provide anonymity.

## 9. Conclusions and Future Work

Via detailed simulations, we have arrived the following conclusions: (1) Leveraging the P2P routing infrastructure and replication mechanism, TAP is fault-tolerant to node failures. (2) By carefully choosing the replication factor and tunnel length, TAP can strike a balance between functionality and anonymity. (3) TAP's performance optimized tunnel mechanism can greatly improve tunneling performance. (4) Users seeking anonymity should reform their tunnels periodically against colluding malicious nodes in dynamic P2P networks to reduce the risk of having their anonymity compromised.

The ability of TAP in making anonymous tunnels fault-tolerant to node failures is to rely on the P2P routing infrastructure and replication mechanism. A big concern is how a message can be *securely* routed to a tunnel hop node given a *hopId* in P2P overlays where a fraction of nodes are malicious to pose a threat. Due to space constraints, we refer readers to our extended report [21] for the details of secure routing.

TAP currently has its own limitations. First, unlike MorphMix [11] and Tarzan [7], TAP lacks the ability to control future hops along a tunnel. It trades this ability for functionality. Secondly, TAP does not have a mechanism to detect corrupted/malicious tunnels. It requires users to reform their tunnels periodically against colluding malicious nodes. In our next steps, we hope to address these issues. Nevertheless, we believe that TAP is a first step towards understanding the construction of anonymous tunneling from P2P nodes in dynamic systems, and it provides a balance point between functionality and anonymity.

## 10. Acknowledgments

This work is supported in part by National Science Foundation under Career Award CCR-9984852 and ACI-0232647, and the Ohio Board of Regents.

## References

[1] Anonymous remailer. http://www.lcs.mit.edu/research/.

[2] Freepastry. http://www.cs.rice.edu/CS/Systems/Pastry/FreePastry/.

[3] D. L. Chaum. Untraceable electronic mail, return addresses, and digital pseudonyms. *Communications of the ACM*, 24(2):422–426, Feb. 1981.

[4] I. Clarke, O. Sandberg, B. Wiley, and T. W. Hong. Freenet: A distributed anonymous information storage and retrieval system. In *Workshop on Design Issues in Anonymity and Unobservability*, pages 331–320, Berkeley, CA, July 2000.

[5] F. Dabek, M. F. Kaashoek, D. Karger, R. Morris, and I. Stoica. Wide-area cooperative storage with CFS. In *Proceedings of the 18th ACM Symposium on Operating Systems Principles (SOSP '01)*, pages 202–215, Banff, Canada, Oct. 2001.

[6] R. Dingledine, M. J. Freedman, and D. Molnar. The free haven project: Distributed anonymous storage service. In *Workshop on Design Issues in Anonymity and Unobservability*, pages 67–95, Berkeley, CA, July 2000.

[7] M. J. Freedman and R. Morris. Tarzan: A peer-to-peer anonymizing network layer. In *Proceedings of the 9th ACM Conference on Computer and Communications Security (CCS 2002)*, pages 193–206, Washington, D.C., November 2002.

[8] J. Kubiatowicz, D. Bindel, Y. Chen, S. Czerwinski, P. Eaton, D. Geels, R. Gummadi, S. Rhea, H. Weatherspoon, W. Weimer, C. Wells, and B. Zhao. Oceanstore: An architecture for global-scale persistent storage. In *Proceedings of the Ninth international Conference on Architectural Support for Programming Languages and Operating Systems (ASPLOS)*, pages 190–201, Cambridge, MA, Nov. 2000.

[9] S. Ratnasamy, P. Francis, M. Handley, R. Karp, and Shenker. A scalable content-addressable network. In *Proceedings of ACM SIGCOMM*, pages 161–172, San Diego, CA, Aug. 2001.

[10] M. K. Reiter and A. D. Rubin. Crowds: anonymity for Web transactions. *ACM Transactions on Information and System Security*, 1(1):66–92, Nov. 1998.

[11] M. Rennhard and B. Plattner. Introducing morphmix: Peer-to-peer based anonymous internet usage with collusion detection. In *Proceedings of the Workshop on Privacy in the Electronic Society*, Washington, DC, November 2002.

[12] A. Rowstron and P. Druschel. Pastry: Scalable, decentralized object location, and routing for large-scale peer-to-peer systems. In *Proceedings of the 18th IFIP/ACM International Conference on Distributed System Platforms (Middleware)*, pages 329–350, Heidelberg, Germany, Nov. 2001.

[13] A. Rowstron and P. Druschel. Storage management and caching in PAST, a large-scale, persistent peer-to-peer storage utility. In *Proceedings of the 18th ACM Symposium on Operating Systems Principles (SOSP '01)*, pages 188–201, Banff, Canada, Oct. 2001.

[14] V. Scarlata, B. N. Levine, and C. Shields. Responder anonymity and anonymous peer-to-peer file sharing. In *Proceedings of IEEE International Conference on Network Protocols (ICNP 2001)*, Riverside, CA, Nov. 2001.

[15] R. Sherwood, B. Bhattacharjee, and A. Srinivasan. P5: A protocol for scalable anonymous communication. In *Proceedings of 2002 IEEE Symposium on Security and Privacy*, pages 58–70, Berkeley, CA, May 2002.

[16] C. Shields and B. N. Levine. A protocol for anonymous communication over the internet. In *ACM Conference on Computer and Communications Security*, pages 33–42, Athens, Greece, Nov. 2000.

[17] I. Stoica, R. Morris, D. Karger, M. Kaashoek, and H. Balakrishnan. Chord: A scalable peer-to-peer lookup service for internet applications. In *Proceedings of ACM SIGCOMM*, pages 149–160, San Diego, CA, Aug. 2001.

[18] P. F. Syverson, D. M. Goldschlag, and M. G. Reed. Anonymous connections and onion routing. In *IEEE Symposium on Security and Privacy*, pages 44–54, Oakland, California, May 1997.

[19] L. Xiao, Z. Xu, and X. Zhang. Mutual anonymity protocols for hybrid peer-to-peer systems. In *Proceedings of the 23rd International Conference on Distributed Computing Systems*, pages 68–75, Providence, Rhode Island, May 2003.

[20] B. Y. Zhao, J. D. Kubiatowicz, and A. D. Joseph. Tapestry: An infrastructure for fault-tolerance wide-area location and routing. Technical Report UCB/CSD-01-1141, Computer Science Division, University of California, Berkeley, Apr. 2001.

[21] Y. Zhu and Y. Hu. TAP: A novel tunneling approach for anonymity in structured P2P systems. Technical report, Department of ECECS, University of Cincinnati, Sept. 2003.

# Dynamic Layer Management in Super-peer Architectures

Zhenyun Zhuang, Yunhao Liu, Li Xiao
*Department of Computer Science and Engineering,*
*Michigan State University, East Lansing, MI 48824, USA*
*{zhuangz1, liuyunha, lxiao}@cse.msu.edu*

## Abstract

The emerging peer-to-peer (P2P) model has recently gained a significant attention due to its high potential of sharing various resources among networked users. Super-peer unstructured P2P systems have been found very effective by dividing the peers into two layers, super-layer and leaf-layer, in which message flooding is only conducted among super-layer. However, current super-peer systems do not employ any effective layer management schemes, which means the transient and low-capacity peers are allowed to act as super-peers. Moreover, the lack of an appropriate size ratio maintenance mechanism on super-layer to leaf-layer makes the system's search performance far from being optimal. We propose a Dynamic Layer Management algorithm, DLM, which can maintain the optimal layer size ratio, and adaptively adjust peers between super-layer and leaf-layer. DLM is completely distributed in the sense that each peer decides to be a super-peer or a leaf peer independently without the global knowledge. DLM could effectively help a super-peer P2P system maintain the optimal layer size ratio, and designate peers with relatively long lifetime and large capacities as super-peers, and the peers with short lifetime and low capacities as leaf-peers under highly dynamic network situations. We demonstrate that the quality of a super-peer system is significantly improved under DLM scheme by comprehensive simulations.

## 1. Introduction

Since the development of Napster, millions of peers join the network by connecting to at least one active peer in the peer-to-peer overlay network. Each peer acts as both a client who requests information and services, and a server who produces and/or provides information and services.

This work was partially supported by the US National Science Foundation (NSF) under grant ACI-0325760, by Michigan State University IRGP Grant 41114.

Today, both unstructured P2P systems, such as Gnutella [5], and structured P2P systems, such as Chord [16] and Cycloid [14], are under intensive study [3] [4] [7] [19]. While unstructured P2P systems are most commonly used in today's Internet, an early generation is *pure* unstructured P2P system. Gnutella is an example of pure P2P systems, where all the peers are involved in query flooding process. In these systems, any peer could be a query source issuing queries to its neighbors, and the peers receiving the queries may check its local storage, and response or further relay queries to their neighbors.

However, peers can be very different from each other in bandwidth, CPU power, duration times, shared files, and interests [6]. In pure P2P systems, all peers, regardless of their capacities, act equal roles and take the same responsibilities on all the operations. As the network size increases, the weak peers will seriously limit the scalability of P2P systems.

To address this problem, super-peer architectures were proposed, which have been attracting more and more users in unstructured P2P community. For example, KaZaA and early Morpheus, based on FastTrack P2P stack, have dominated the top downloads lists for most of 2001 and are still increasing in popularity in 2002 [6] [10]. Schemes are also proposed to introduce Ultra-peers into Gnutella protocol [2].

The advantages of super-peer systems are well discussed in [17]. However, current super-peer systems do not exploit any effective layer management schemes; thereby leave the following two problems unsolved. First, assume an optimal value of layer size ratio is given for a network, how to maintain this layer size ratio? Current super-peer approaches lack an appropriate size ratio maintenance mechanism, and make the system's search performance far from being optimal. Second, what types of peers should be elected to super-layer? As far as we know, no efficient algorithm is given to ensure that the super-peers have large-capacity and long-lifetime. Since no global knowledge exist in distributed P2P systems, it is impossible to tell what values can be "high" or "long" enough, especially under highly dynamic environments. This problem is even more difficult to solve when the network needs to consider more metrics besides capacity and duration-time.

In this paper, we propose a dynamic layer management algorithm to solve these two problems, called DLM, which is a fully distributed dynamic layer management algorithm; it can adaptively elect peers and adjust them between super-layer and leaf-layer. DLM is completely distributed in the sense that each peer determines to be a super-peer or a leaf-peer independently without global knowledge. DLM could effectively help a super-peer P2P system maintain an given layer size ratio, and designate peers with relatively long lifetime and large capacities as super-peers, and the peers with short lifetime and low capacities as leaf-peers under highly dynamic network situations.

The rest of this paper is organized as follows. In Section 2, we discuss the related work. In Section 3, we describe the importance of layer size ratio in super-peer systems and network assumptions. We then present the design rational of DLM in Section 4. In Section 5, we evaluate the effectiveness of DLM through simulations. In Section 6, we discuss the side effects of DLM, and we conclude this paper in Section 7.

## 2. Related Work

Applications based on Super-peer architectures are consuming a large portion of Internet traffic. For example, in June 2002, KaZaA consumed approximately 37% of all TCP traffic, which was more than twice the Web traffic on the University of Washington campus network [6]. Sandvine also estimates that 76% of P2P file sharing traffic is KaZaA/FastTrack traffic and only 8% is Gnutella traffic in the US [9]. Thus, super-peer architectures are attracting more and more attentions in P2P research communities.

To well understand the behavior of super-peer systems, authors in [17] examined the performance tradeoffs in super-peer systems by considering super-peer redundancy and topology variations. They also studied the potential drawbacks of super-peer networks and reliability issues. To make Gnutella network more scalable, Singla and Rohrs [2] describe how Ultrapeers work in an ideal network with a static topology and a handshaking mechanism based on Gnutella v0.6 protocol. Some requirements for super-peers were proposed, such as not fire walled, suitable operating system, sufficient bandwidth and sufficient uptime. Authors in [15] present some incentives to deploy super-peers and propose a topic-based search scheme to increase the effectiveness of super-peers.

However, because KaZaA, the most popular application based on super-peer architectures, is proprietary and uses encryption, little has been known about the protocols, architectures, and behaviors of KaZaA. With over millions of users at anytime, KaZaA has neither been documented nor analyzed. Since super-peers and leaf-peers take different responsibilities, peers need to be assigned to appropriate layers through some well-designed layer management mechanism. But as far as we know, no such mechanism is proposed to date.

## 3. Impact of Layer Size Ratio

We first discuss the importance of maintaining an appropriate layer size ratio in a super-peer network.

In a super-peer network, the search tasks are mainly performed by super-peers, which actually form the "backbone" of the P2P network. Indeed, super-peer systems take advantage of peers' heterogeneity by dividing peers into two layers- *super-layer* and *leaf-layer*, thereby scale better by reducing the number of query paths [17].

The peers in super-layer are called super-peer*s* and are responsible for processing and relaying the queries from the leaf-peers and other super-peer neighbors. Each super-peer behaves like a proxy or agent of its leaf-peers, and keeps an index of its leaf-peers' shared data. The peers in leaf-layer are called *leaf-peers*, and keep a small number of connections to super-peers for the purpose of reliability.

In super-peer systems, both super-peers and leaf-peers can submit queries, but only super-peers relay queries and query responses. A super-peer may forward an incoming query to its neighboring super-peers. When receiving a query, a super-peer first checks if the queried data is stored in local or in its leaf-peers (by checking the index of its leaf-peers' objects). If some results are found in a peer, it will send a *QueryHit* message back to the query source along the inverse query path.

Compared with pure P2P systems, super-peer systems have higher search efficiency because instead of all the peers, only super-peers are involved in search processes. Intuitively, an appropriate layer size ratio, i.e. the ratio of the number of leaf-peers to the number of super-peers, is of great importance in the sense that, on one extreme, if most of the peers are in the super-layer, the system will be more like a pure P2P system since too many peers take part in searching; on the other extreme, if too few super-peers are available, the system is more like a centralized P2P system. A major drawback of a centralized P2P system is single point of failure.

Some layer management mechanisms use pre-configured values as the thresholds to select super-peers. For example, the Ultra-peer Proposal in Gnutella 0.6 [1] recommends at least 15KB/s downstream and 10KB/s upstream bandwidth. We argue that this approach cannot maintain an appropriate size ratio. Let us look at the example shown in Figure 1.

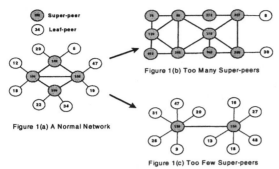

Figure 1(b) Too Many Super-peers

Figure 1(a) A Normal Network

Figure 1(c) Too Few Super-peers

**Figure 1 Inappropriate Layer Size Ratio**

Suppose that a system sets the bandwidth threshold to 50KB/s. Peers with bandwidths larger than 50KB/s can be selected as super-peers. A network with good size ratio is shown in Figure 1(a), where the number inside a peer denotes its bandwidth value. However, after a certain time period, if most new joining peers have high bandwidths, the system will soon have too many super-peers, as shown in Figure 1(b). Or if most joining peers are weak ones with low bandwidths, the system will be more like a centralized P2P as shown in Figure 1(c).

Consider a P2P network with $n$ participating peers, in which $n_s$ peers are super-peers and $n_l$ peers are leaf-peers. Assume each leaf-peer connects to $m$ super-peers and each super-peer connects to $k_s$ other super-peers and $k_l$ leaf-peers, on the average. We use $\eta$ to denote the layer size ratio of a super-peer network, and it is given by:

$$\eta = \frac{n_l}{n_s}.$$

Consider all the connections between super-layer and leaf-layer. The out-degree from super-layer to leaf-layer is $n_s k_l$, and the out-degree from leaf-layer to super-layer is $n_l m$. Since these two out-degrees are equal, so we have,

$$k_l = \frac{n_l m}{n_s} = m\eta.$$   **(Equation a)**

Also, since $n_s + n_l = n$, we have

$$n_s = \frac{n}{1+\eta}.$$   **(Equation b)**

Therefore, in a network with n, $n_s$, $n_l$, m defined above, on the average each super-peer connects to $k_l = m\eta$ leaf-peers, and $n_s = \frac{n}{1+\eta}$.

The size ratio of these two layers depends on the specific systems and applications, since each specific P2P system has its own targets and functions. Due to page limit, we leave the discussion of the appropriate size ratio to our other papers. In this paper, we just assume that the value of $\eta$ is given by the protocol, and every participating peer of the network knows this value.

We also assume that new peers randomly select active peers as neighbors based on the bootstrapping and joining mechanisms currently used, although this randomness does not necessarily lead to totally random topology [11]. Some studies also show that keeping high-capacity peers with high degree can make the system more scalable [18], but it also imports unfairness among peers, and thereby hinders the peers accurately report the capacities, as well. In this paper, we assume that all the peers in the same layer prefer to be treated equally.

## 4. Design of DLM

We propose a Dynamic layer management algorithm (DLM) that intends to deal with the two problems described in Section 1. These problems are not trivial to deal with, since no peer knows the global knowledge of the network. In other words, DLM should achieve two goals: (1) maintains the size ratio of super layer to leaf layer; (2) keeps the peers with larger lifetimes and capacities as super-peers, and keeps the peers with shorter lifetimes and capacities as leaf-peers.

Unfortunately, these two goals are not always compatible. For example, at some time, the system may have a highly skewed layer size ratio, and more super-peers are heavily needed, but all the joining peers have low bandwidths. In this case, DLM needs to consider the two goals simultaneously, and adaptively promote some leaf-peers, though not "powerful" enough, to super-layer. Moreover, to perform well under both stable and highly changeable network situations, DLM needs to dynamically adjust the promotion and demotion policies according to the changing environments.

Ideally, the super-peers should be more powerful and with longer lifetime. To measure the eligibility of a peer, we define two metrics, *capacity* and *age*.

**Definition 1:** We define *capacity* as the ability of a peer to process and relay queries and query responses.

We use *capacity(d)* to refer to the capacity value of a peer $d$. The value of capacity can be computed as,

$$capacity(d) = \sum_{i=1}^{r} w_i * v_i(d),$$

where $r$ is the number of metrics affecting the peer's capacity, $v_i(d)$ is the value of $i_{th}$ metric, and $w_i(d)$ is the weight of the corresponding metric. Examples of the metrics affecting the capacity are bandwidth, CPU powerfulness and storage space. We assume that a peer's capacity value does not change throughout its session and can be known when it connects the network. For simplicity, we omit the computation details of a peer's capacity, and just use the bandwidth of a peer as its capacity, which does not affect the presentation of DLM algorithm.

**Definition 2:** We define *age* as the length of time up to now since a peer joins the network up to present.

The lifetime of a peer is the time the peer participates in the P2P network. It is the gap from the time the peer joins the network to the time it leaves the network. The a*ge* is less or equal to the lifetime of a peer by the definition. DLM will automatically promote the leaf peers with larger ages to super layer, and demote the super-peers with smaller ages to leaf layer. Although the *capacity* value can be set at the time when the peer joins the system, there are no means to know the lifetime of a peer, since a peer may leave the network at any time. One practical way to infer the lifetime is by monitoring its *age*: the longer the peer lives, more likely the peer will lives in the future. So we use the *age* of a peer in DLM to denote its lifetime. We use *age(d)* to denote peer *d*'s *age* value.

In DLM, each peer first collects its neighboring peers' information, which includes the *capacities*, *ages*, and the number of neighboring leaf-peers (for a super-peer neighbor). After processing the collected information, the peer will determine its own status. We describe DLM in four phases.

- **Phase 1: Information Collection**

Peers first exchange information with its neighbors using messages. We design two pairs of messages, which are employed by a pair of leaf-peer and super-peer. The formats of these two pairs of messages are shown in Table 1.

**Table 1 Message Formats**

| Messages | Value | |
|---|---|---|
| Neigh_num_request | Null | |
| Neigh_num_response | $l_{nn}$ | |
| Value_request | Null | Null |
| Value_response | capacity | age |

The first pair of the messages includes *neighbor_num_request* and *neighbor_num_response* Messages; *neighbor_num_request* is sent from a leaf-peer *d* to a super-peer *s* to request the leaf neighbor number of *s*, and we use $l_{nn}(s)$ to refer to this number. Message *neighbor_num_response* is the response from the super-peer. The second pair of the messages is *value_request* and *value_response*, which are sent between a super-peer and a leaf peer to query and respond the latter peer's *capacity* and a*ge*. Note that these two pairs of messages can also be piggybacked in other messages in some P2P protocols.

One issue deserves some words here is how often that the peers exchange this information. Obviously, higher

frequency means higher accuracy, while more traffic overhead as well. In this design we employ an event-driven policy, in which information exchange is invoked whenever a peer finds that a new connection is created. In simulation, we have also evaluated other policies, such as time interval based policy where peers exchange information periodically. Our results show that event-driven performs the best in the sense that it incurred smaller overhead when having the same performance. Also, the amount of this overhead is trivial compared with other traffic costs in P2P systems, which we will discuss in Section 6.

- **Phase 2: Maintaining Appropriate Layer-Size-Ratio**

One of the goals of DLM is to maintain appropriate layer size ratio. To achieve this goal, DLM first needs to estimate the extent of appropriateness of current layer size ratio.

The basic idea of DLM is based on three observations. First, current layer size ratio can be easily calculated if the global knowledge is known, but in reality no peer knows this global knowledge. Second, it is trivial for a peer to collect its neighbors' information. Third, due to the randomness of the neighbor selection mechanism in super-peer systems, to some extent, the current numbers of leaf neighbors of super-peers can reflect the current layer size ratio. That is, if the super-layer size is too small, the average number of leaf neighbors of a super-peer will be larger than $k_l$, the "optimal" leaf neighbor number; otherwise it will be less than $k_l$. Since each peer knows the optimal value of $\eta$, then the value of $k_l$ can be computed using Equation a. Therefore, $l_{nn}$, the leaf neighbor number of some super-peer, can be used as a flag of the current layer size ratio when compared with the value of $k_l$.

To illustrate the comparison method, we now define the *related set* of a peer.

**Definition 3:** we use $G$ to represent the *related set* of a peer in the other layer. For a super-peer *s*, we define $G(s)$ as the set of its current neighboring leaf-peers. While for a leaf-peer *l*, we define $G(l)$ as the set of super-peers that it has connected within a period of time $T_l$.

The definitions of $G$ on super-peers and leaf-peers are different as a super-peer normally keeps connections to many leaf-peers, while a leaf-peer normally only connects to a few super-peers. To more accurately estimate the network condition, we hope that the size of $G$ is large enough, so that we consider all the super-peers that a leaf-peer has contacted in a recent period of time. In simulation, G contains all the super-peers that a leaf-peer has connected since it joins the network.

For a super-peer $s$, since it connects to some leaf-peers, it can directly use $l_{nn}(s)$. While for a leaf-peer $l$, it uses the average $l_{nn}$ value of the super-peers in $G(l)$. We let $\mu$ to denote the extent of inappropriateness of current layer size ratio compared to the optimal layer size ratio $\eta$, and it is computed as,

$\mu = log(l_{nn}/k_1)$.

We can see that a positive value of $\mu$, where $l_{nn}$ is larger than $k_1$, means that there are too few super-peers in the system, since super-peers have more leaf-peer neighbors than normal. While a negative value of $\mu$, where $l_{nn}$ is smaller than $k_1$, means that there are too many super-peers. Furthermore, a larger absolute value of $\mu$ means a larger degree of inappropriateness. Thereby the value of $\mu$ reflects the system requirement, and it is used to adjust some other parameters, which determine the possibility of a peer's being promoted or demoted.

- **Phase 3: Scaled Comparisons of Capacity and Age**

DLM automatically promotes the *leaf-peers* with large capacities and longer lifetimes to super-layer, and demotes the super-peers with small capacities and shorter lifetimes to leaf-layer. The decision of promotion or demotion is based on the comparison results with other peers.

One straightforward way of comparison is directly comparing the metric values of a peer with other peers. However, comparing in such a direct way may fail to maintain the layer size ratio successfully. Consider a scenario in which the system needs more super-peers, but the leaf-peers all have larger metric values than the current super-peers. The results of simple comparisons would forbid any leaf-peer to be promoted; thereby the system cannot adjust the layer size ratio at all.

DLM improves the direct comparison by using "scaled-comparison". Since the capacity and age metrics are disjoint, that is, a peer with high-capacity not necessarily has larger age and vice versa, we analyze these two metrics individually. In scaled-comparison, DLM introduces two scale parameters, $X_{capa}$ and $X_{age}$, corresponding to the two metrics respectively. These two scale parameters are adjusted dynamically by DLM based on the value of $\mu$ to reflect the system requirements.

For each peer that runs DLM, it uses two counting variables, $Y_{capa}$ and $Y_{age}$, corresponding to Capacity and Age metrics, respectively. A peer sets the value of these two counting variables by comparing its metric values with the peers in its related set, $G$. For a peer $d$, the pseudo codes of the scaled-comparison are listed below.

**for** all peer $d_i$ in *G(d)*
    **if** (capacity($d_i$)* $X_{capa}$ >capacity(*d*))
        $Y_{capa}$ +=1/ *(size of G(d))*;

    **if** (age($d_i$)* $X_{age}$ >age(*d*))
        $Y_{age}$ +=1/ *(size of G(d))*;

We can see that $Y_{capa}$ and $Y_{age}$ store the fractions of peers that have "larger" metric values than those of $d$ in $G(d)$. $Y_{capa}$ reflects the relative capacity value of a peer compared to the peers in the other layer; while $Y_{age}$ reflects the relative *age* value of one peer compared to the peers in the other layer. These two variables will be used to determine the eligibility of the peer's promotion or demotion.

The values of $X_{capa}$ and $X_{age}$ are adjusted according to the value of $\mu$. For a super-peer, if it finds that the system needs more super-peers, it will decrease the possibility of its demotion by decreasing the two scale parameters. Otherwise, it will increase the possibility of its demotion by increasing the scale parameters. While for a leaf-peer, if it finds that more super-peers are needed, it will decrease the scale parameters in hoping to increase the promotion possibility; otherwise it will increase the scale parameters to decrease the promotion possibility.

- **Phase 4: Promotion or Demotion**

For a leaf-peer $l$, if $Y_{capa}$ and $Y_{age}$ are small enough, it means that many super-peers in $G(l)$ have metric values "smaller" than it. Thus, $l$ may assume that it has comparatively large metric values and may decide to be promoted to super-layer. While for a super-peer $s$, if $Y_{capa}$ and $Y_{age}$ are large enough, it means that many leaf-peers in $G(l)$ have metric values "larger" than it. Thus, $s$ may assume that it has comparatively small metric values and may decide to be demoted to leaf-layer.

We use two threshold variables, $Z_{capa}$ and $Z_{age}$, in the determination. For a leaf-peer $l$, if $Y_{capa}$ and $Y_{age}$ are smaller than $Z_{capa}$ and $Z_{age}$, respectively, it will be promoted to be a super-peer. In promotion, the leaf-peer keeps its current connections to other super-peers. The scenarios before and after peer $l$'s promotion are illustrated in Figure 2(a) and 2(b).

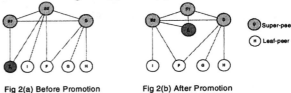

Fig 2(a) Before Promotion    Fig 2(b) After Promotion

**Figure 2 Promotion of a Leaf Peer**

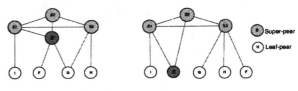

Fig 3(a) Before Demotion    Fig 3(b) After Demotion

**Figure 3 Demotion of a Super-peer**

## 5. Performance Evaluation

For a super-peer $s$, if $_{capa}$ and $Y_{age}$ are larger than $Z_{capa}$ and $Z_{age}$, respectively, it will be demoted to be a leaf-peer. In demotion, the super-peer only keeps $m$ of its current connections to other super-peers and drops the connections to leaf-peers. The scenarios before and after peer $s$'s demotion are illustrated in Figure 3(a) and 3(b).

The values of threshold variables, $Z_{capa}$ and $Z_{age}$, are also adjusted according to the value of $\mu$. When more super-peers are needed, super-peers will increase the values of the threshold variables to reduce the demotion tendencies, and leaf-peers will reduce the values of the threshold variables to increase the promotion tendencies. For the cases that there are too many super-peers, inverse measures will be taken accordingly.

Essentially, to achieve the two goals we set in the beginning of Section 4, DLM needs to consider two factors: the layer-size-ratio factor ($\mu$), and the capacity-age factor. The first factor reflects the requirement of keeping the optimal layer size ratio, and the second factor reflects the requirement of keeping large-capacity and large-age peers in the super-layer. Since the two scale parameters, $X_{capa}$ and $X_{age}$, are adjusted based on the values of the first factor, DLM can achieve the first goal: maintaining the optimal layer size ratio. Similarly, by using scaled comparisons method, DLM achieves the second goal: keeping large-capacity and large-age peers on the super-layer.

We use simulation to evaluate DLM and compare it to preconfigured algorithms. To collect real data, we implement two Gnutella clients based on the publicly available Mutella [8]. One client participates into the network as an ultra-peer, and the other acts as a leaf-peer. Using these two clients we collect some first-hand data, such as the lifetimes of ultra-peers and leaf-peers, the number of open connections and average query frequencies of peer The collected data are consistent with the data presented in previous studies [6, 12, 13]. We configure our simulation environments based on these observations. The values of the parameters are shown in Table 2.

**Table 2. Simulation Parameters**

| Parameter | Value | Description |
|---|---|---|
| $n$ | 50000 | # of peers in the network |
| $n_l$ | 48780 | # of preferred leaf-peers |
| $n_s$ | 1220 | # of preferred super-peers |
| $\eta$ | 40.0 | Layer size ratio |
| $m$ | 2 | Super-peer neigh. # of a leaf-peer |
| $k_l$ | 80 | Aver. leaf neigh. # of super-peers |
| $k_s$ | 3 | Aver super neigh. # of super-peers |

We evaluate DLM under various simulation environments. We first simulate a *stable* network by assigning new peers with capacity and lifetime values based on previous studies [12]. We then simulate a *dynamic* network with dynamic means of the distributions. For these two cases, the network sizes are not changed. We also evaluate DLM on networks with different sizes. The results are consistent, so we only present the results in dynamic environments, in Figures 4, 5, and 6.

In a *stable* network, the simulation starts "cold", i.e. without any peer. The size of the network increases with new peers joining until reaches the designated size. Then with time going, whenever a peer dies, a new peer is created and joins the network, thereby the network size does not change. The new peer is always assigned to leaf layer first, and DLM will promote eligible leaf peers to super layer. The lifetime and capacity values of a new peer are generated based on the distributions we observed and shown in previous studies.

We simulate the *dynamic* networks by varying the means of the capacity and age distributions for new joining peers. Starting from the 300th time unit, the lifetime values of new joining peers are generated using the method as before, but with half mean values. Thus from that time, the new peers have smaller lifetime values. Figure 4 plots the average ages of each layer. As expected, the age of super-layer is much larger than that of leaf-layer, regardless the changing environments.

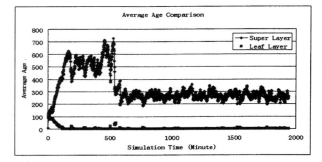

**Figure 4 Average Age**

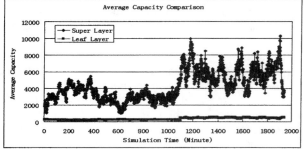

**Figure 5 Average Capacity**

34

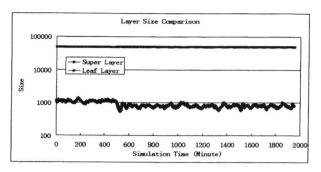

**Figure 6 Layer Sizes**

Starting from the $1,000^{th}$ time unit, the capacities of new joining peers are generated with doubled mean values; thereby the new peers are more powerful than previous peers. The results in Figure 5 indicate that DLM adaptively promotes the peers with large-capacities to super-layers and the average capacity value of super-layer is always larger than that of leaf-layer.

The layer sizes of the network are shown in Figure 6, we can see that an almost constant ratio is maintained throughout the simulation process, even the network environment is changing. Note that the Y-axis of Figure 6 is logarithmic.

We also compare DLM with pre-configured algorithms under dynamic network situations where the new peers' mean capacity values are periodically changed. We compare the sizes and ages of two layers in DLM and a preconfigured algorithm.

The results are shown in Figures 7 and 8. We can see that the DLM maintains the layer size ratio very well, while in the preconfigured algorithm, the layer size ratio changes periodically. For the average ages of super-layer and leaf-layer, in DLM, they are sharply divided and the average age of super-layer is much larger than that of the preconfigured algorithm, as shown in Figure 8. The comparisons of capacity values show similar results.

## 6. Discussion on Side Effects of DLM

Introducing DLM to super-peer systems does incur some traffic overhead, such as the traffic overhead for information exchanging among neighbors, and the peer adjustment overhead. In this section we discuss these issues in details.

- **Overhead for Information Exchanging**

To implement DLM, we propose to add two pairs of messages described in Section 4 to the existing super-peer P2P protocol. We argue that the additional overhead on delivering these two pairs of messages is negligible compared to the search traffic costs in a P2P system for two reasons. First, these messages are only transferred between directly connected neighbors, so they can have very simple formats and only need few bytes. As a result, these two pairs of messages are quite light-weighted. Second, these messages are only sent when new connections are created. Moreover, these two pairs of messages may be piggybacked in other messages available, thus reducing the traffic overhead even more. Our collected data and studies in [12] found that each connection can keep active for at least several minutes on the average. Therefore, the frequency of DLM message transferring is quite low compared with that of other messages.

- **Peer Adjustment Overhead**

When a super-peer is demoted to be a leaf-peer, it needs to cut the connections to the leaf-peers and some super-peers because a leaf-peer only keeps a small number (m) of links to super-peers. The leaf-peers disconnected by the demoted super-peer need to connect to another super-peer instead. We call this kind of connection overhead as *Peer Adjustment Overhead (PAO)*. Note that the promotion process does not cause PAO because no peers are disconnected during the process. We analyze this overhead and find that the peer adjustment overhead is quite small. The results are shown in Table 3.

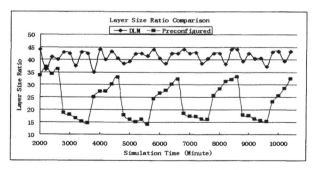

**Figure 7 Layer Size Ratios on Same Success Rate**

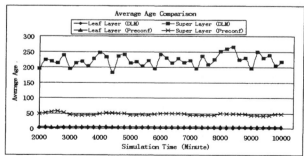

**Figure 8 Average Age Comparisons**

### Table 3 Peer Adjustment Overhead Analysis

| Network size | # of new leaf-peers | # of demoted super-peers | # of disconnected leaf-peers | PAO/NLCO (%) |
|---|---|---|---|---|
| 5,000 | 21.19 | 0.55 | 44.56 | 104.65% |
| 20,000 | 84.76 | 1.19 | 95.26 | 56.19% |
| 80,000 | 339.21 | 2.06 | 157.73 | 23.25% |

We count the number of new peers, the number of super-peers demoted as leaf-peers, and the number of disconnected leaf-peers caused by the demotions per unit time. The disconnected leaf-peers need to connect other super-peers and incur the PAO. This process behaves like a new joining leaf-peer making connections to super-peers. The difference is that each disconnected leaf-peer only needs to create one new connection to another super-peer, while each new joining leaf-peer needs to create $m$ new connections to super-peers. Thus, the PAO for a disconnected leaf peer is only $1/m$ of the connection overhead for a new joining peer. We call the connection overhead caused by new leaf-peers as *New Leaf-initiated Connection Overhead (NLCO)*. We also calculate the ratio of PAO and NLCO in Table 3.

In Table 2, we can see that as the network size increases, the ratio of PAO to NLCO decreases. The reason is that as the network size increases, the number of leaf-peers each super-peer connects to is more close to $k_l$ due to the randomness of connections between peers. Therefore, the probability of misjudgments is also decreased. It is safe to expect that in the real-world P2P networks with millions of peers, the ratio of PAO to NLCO is even smaller.

## 7. Conclusion

In this paper, we propose a dynamic layer management algorithm, DLM, which can adaptively elect peers and adjust them between super-layer and leaf-layer. Our simulation results show that DLM can maintain a given size ratio of super-layer to leaf-layer. It also designates peers with long lifetime and large capacities as super-peers, and the peers with short lifetime and low capacity as leaf-peers under highly dynamic network situations. With wide deployment of DLM, the quality of a super-peer system can be significantly improved.

## References

[1] The Gnutella protocol specification 0.6. 2002.

[2] Anurag Singla, C.R., Ultrapeers: Another Step Towards Gnutella Scalability, in *Working draft, available from the Gnutella Developers Forum at http://groups.yahoo.com/group/the_gdf/*.

[3] Bustamante, F.E. and Y. Qiao. Friendships that last: Peer lifespan and its role in P2P protocols. In Proceeding of *International Workshop on Web Content Caching and Distribution*. 2003. NY, USA.

[4] Ganesan, P., K. Gummadi, and H. Garcia-Molina. Canon in G Major: Designing DHTs with Hierarchical Structure. In Proceeding of *the 24th International Conference on Distributed Computing Systems (ICDCS 2004)*. 2004. Tokyo, Japan.

[5] Gnutella, http://gnutella.wego.com/.

[6] Gummadi, K.P., et al. Measurement, Modeling, and Analysis of a Peer-to-Peer File-Sharing Workload. In Proceeding of *the 19th ACM Symposium on Operating Systems Principles (SOSP)*. October 2003. Bolton Landing, NY.

[7] Liu, Y., et al. A Distributed Approach to Solving Overlay Mismatching Problem. In Proceeding of *IEEE ICDCS 2004*. 2004. Tokyo, Japan.

[8] Mutella, http://mutella.sourceforge.net/. 2003.

[9] P2P, R.c.o., http://www.sandvine.com.

[10] Peter Backx, T.W., Bart Dhoedt, Piet Demeester. A comparison of peer-to-peer architectures. In Proceeding of *Eurescom Summit*. 2002. Heidelberg, Germany.

[11] Ripeanu, M., A. Iamnitchi, and I. Foster, Mapping the Gnutella Network. IEEE Internet Comput-ing, 2002.

[12] Saroiu, S., P. Gummadi, and S. Gribble. A measurement study of peer-to-peer file sharing systems. In Proceeding of *Multimedia Computing and Networking (MMCN)*. 2002.

[13] Sen, S. and J. Wang. Analyzing peer-to-peer traffic across large networks. In Proceeding of *ACM SIGCOMM Internet Measurement Workshop*. 2002.

[14] Shen, H., C.-Z. Xu, and G. Chen. Cycloid: A Constant-Degree and Lookup-Efficient P2P Overlay Network. In Proceeding of *the International Parallel and Distributed Processing Symposium (IPDPS)*. 2004. Santa Fe, New Mexico.

[15] Singh, S., et al. The Case for Service Provider Deployment of Super-Peers in Peer-to-Peer Networks. In Proceeding of *the Workshop on Economics of Peer-to-Peer Systems*. 2003. Berkeley.

[16] Stoica, I., et al. Chord: A scalable peer-to-peer lookup service for Internet applications. In Proceeding of *ACM SIGCOMM*. 2001.

[17] Yang, B. and H. Garcia-Molina. Designing a super-peer network. In Proceeding of *the 19th International Conference on Data Engineering (ICDE)*. March 2003. Bangalore, India.

[18] Yatin Chawathe, et al. Making Gnutella-like P2P Systems Scalable. In Proceeding of *ACM SIGCOMM*. 2003.

[19] Zhuang, Z., et al. Hybrid Periodical Flooding in Unstructured Peer-to-Peer Networks. In Proceeding of *Proceedings of International Conference on Parallel Processing ICPP'03*. 2003.

# Session 1C:
# Compiler I

# Improving Load/Store Queues Usage in Scientific Computing

Christophe LEMUET    William JALBY    Sid-Ahmed-Ali TOUATI
PRiSM Laboratory, University of Versailles, France

## Abstract

*Memory disambiguation mechanisms, coupled with load/store queues in out-of-order processors, are crucial to increase Instruction Level Parallelism (ILP), especially for memory-bound scientific codes. Designing ideal memory disambiguation mechanisms is too complex because it would require precise address bits comparators; thus, modern microprocessors implement simplified and imprecise ones that perform only partial address comparisons. In this paper, we study the impact of such simplifications on the sustained performance of some real processors such that Alpha 21264, Power 4 and Itanium 2. Despite all the advanced features of these processors, we demonstrate in this article that memory address disambiguation mechanisms can cause significant performance loss. We demonstrate that, even if data are located in low cache levels and enough ILP exist, the performance degradation can be up to 21 times slower if no care is taken on the order of accessing independent memory addresses. Instead of proposing a hardware solution to improve load/store queues, as done in [1, 6, 5, 7, 4], we show that a software (compilation) technique is possible. Such solution is based on the classical (and robust) ld/st vectorization. Our experiments highlight the effectiveness of such method on BLAS 1 codes that are representative of vector scientific loops.*

## 1. Introduction

Memory system performance is essential to today's processors. Therefore, computer architects have spent, and are still spending, large efforts in inventing sophisticated mechanisms to improve data access rate, in terms of latency and bandwidth: multi-level and non-blocking caches, ld/st queues for out-of-order execution, prefetch mechanisms to tolerate/hide memory latencies, banking and interleaving to increase bandwidth, etc.

One key mechanism to tolerate/hide memory latency is the out-of-order processing of memory requests. With the advent of superscalar processors, the concept of ld/st queues has become a standard. The basic principle is simple: consecutive issued memory requests are stored in a queue and simultaneously processed. This allows the requests with shorter processing time (in the case of cache hits) to bypass requests with a longer processing time (in the case of cache misses for example). Unfortunately, data dependences may exist between memory requests: for instance, a load followed by a store (or vice-versa) addressing both exactly the same memory location have to be executed strictly in order to preserve program semantics. This is done on-the-fly by specific hardware mechanisms whose task is, first, to detect memory request dependences and, second, to satisfy such dependences (if necessary). These mechanisms are under high pressure in memory-bound programs, because numerous "in-flight" memory requests have to be treated.

In order to satisfy this high request rate, memory dependence detection mechanisms are simplified at the expense of accuracy and performance [3]. To be accurate, the memory dependence detection must be performed on complete address bits; this might be complex and expensive. In practice, the comparison between two accessed memory locations is carried out on a short part of the addresses: usually, few low order bits. If these low order bits match, the hardware takes a conservative action, i.e., it considers that the whole addresses match and triggers the procedure for a collision case (serialization of the memory requests).

In this article, we study in details the dynamic behavior of memory request processing on three modern processors (Alpha 21264, Power 4, Itanium 2). Because of the high complexity of such analysis, our work is focused on the different memory hierarchy levels (L1, L2, L3), excluding the main memory. Our benchmarking codes are simple floating point vector loops (memory-bound) which account for a large fraction of execution time in our scientific computing target area. Additionally, the structure of their address streams is regular, making it possible a detailed performance analysis of the interaction between these address streams with the dependence detection mechanisms and bank conflicts. Our aim is not to analyze or optimize a whole program behavior, but only small fractions that consist of simple scientific computing loops (libraries). One of the reasons is that the ld/st queue conflicts that we are interested in are *local* phenomena because, first, they strictly involve in-flight instructions (present in the instruction window). Second, they are not influenced by the context of a whole application as other events such as caches activities. So, there is no need to run complete complex applications to isolate these local events that we can highlight with micro-benchmarking (explained in Sect. 3). Third and last, the number of side effects and pollution of the cache performance in whole complex applications (such as SPEC codes) makes the potential benefits smoothened. We will show that our micro-benchmarks are a good diagnostic tool. We can precisely quantify the effects of load/store vectorization on poor memory disambiguation. It allows us to reveal the limitations of the dynamic memory dependences check ; they may lead to severe performance loss and make the code performance very dependent on the order of independent memory accesses.

We organize our article as follows. Sect. 2 presents some related work about the problem of improving ld/st queues and memory disambiguation mechanisms. Sect. 3 gives a description of our experimental environment. Then, Sect. 4 shows the most important results of our experiments that highlight some problems in modern cache systems, such that memory dependence detection mechanisms and bank conflicts. We propose in Sect. 5 an optimization method that groups the memory requests in a vectorized way. We demonstrate by our experiments that this method is effective, then we conclude.

## 2. Related Work

Improving ld/st queues and memory disambiguation mechanisms is an issue of active research. Chrysos and Emer in [1] proposed store sets as a hardware solution for increasing the accuracy of memory dependence prediction. Their experiments were conclusive by demonstrating that they can nearly achieve the peak performance with the context of large instruction windows. Park *et al* in [5] proposed an improved design of ld/st queues that scale better, that is, they have improved the design complexity of memory disambiguation. Another similar hardware improvement has been proposed by Sethumadhavan *et al* in [5]. A speculative technique for memory dependence prediction has been proposed by Yoaz *et al* in [7]: the hardware tries to predict colliding loads, relying on the fact that such loads tend to repeat their delinquent behavior. Another speculative technique devoted to superscalar processors was presented by S. Onder [4]. The author presented a hardware mechanism that classifies the loads and stores to an appropriate speculative level for memory dependence prediction.

All the above sophisticated techniques are hardware solutions. In the domain of scientific computing, the codes are often regular, making it possible to achieve effective compile time optimizations. Thus, we do not require such costly dynamic techniques. In this paper, we show that a simple ld/st vectorization is useful (in the context of scientific loops) to solve the same problems tackled in [1, 5, 7, 4]. Coupling our costless software optimization technique with the actual imprecise memory disambiguation mechanisms is less expensive than pure hardware methods, giving nonetheless good performance improvement.

## 3. Experimental Environment

In order to analyze the interaction between the processors (typically the cache systems) with the applications, we have designed a set of micro-benchmarks, as presented in the following section.

### 3.1. Our Micro-Benchmarks

Our set of micro-benchmarks consists of simple vector loops (memory-bound) which consume large fractions of execution times in scientific applications. Besides their representativity, these vector loops present two key advantages : first, they are simple, and second they can be easily transformed since they are fully parallel.

We divide our micro-benchmarks into two families:

1. *memory stress kernels* are artificial loops which aim to only send consecutive bursts of independent loads and stores in order to study the impact of memory address streams on the peak performance.[1] Such loops do not contain any data dependences.

    (a) the first one, called *LxLy*, corresponds to a loop in which two arrays X and Y are regularly accessed with only loads : Load X(0),

---

[1]In this paper, the peak performances refers to the ideal one, i.e., the maximal theoretical performance as computed from hardware specifications.

Load Y(0),Load X(1),Load Y(1),Load X(2),Load Y(2), etc.

   (b) the second one, called *LxSy* corresponds to a loop in which one array X is accessed with loads, while the Y one is accessed with stores: Load X(0),Store Y(0),Load X(1), Store Y(1), Load X(2), Store Y(2), etc.

2. *BLAS 1 kernels* are simple vector loops that contain flow dependences. In this article, we use three simple loops:

   - copy : Y(i) ← X(i);
   - vsum : Z(i) ← X(i) + Y(i);
   - daxpy : Y(i) ← Y(i) + a × X(i);

Despite the fact that we have experimented other BLAS 1 codes with various number of arrays, we chose these simple ones as illustrative examples, since they clearly exhibit the pathological behavior that we are interested in.

### 3.2. Experimentation Methodology

The performance of our micro-kernels are sensitive to several parameters that we explore. We focus in this paper on two major ones which are:

1. **Absolute Array Offsets**: the impact of the exact starting address of each array[2] is analyzed. This is because varying such offsets changes the accessed addresses of the vector elements, and thus it has a significant impact on ld/st queues behavior: we know that the memory address of the double floating point element X(i) is $\text{Offset}(X) + 8 \times i$.

2. **Data Location**: since we are interested in exploring the cache performance (L1, L2, L3), we parameterize our micro-kernels in order to lock all our arrays in the desired memory hierarchy level. By choosing adequate vector lengths, and by using dummy loops that flush the data from the non desired cache levels, we guarantee that our array elements are located exactly in the experimented cache level (checked by hardware performance counters).

Some other parameters, such that prefetch distances, have been carefully analyzed. However, because of the

---

[2]It is the address of the first array element that we simply call the array offset. The address zero is the beginning of a memory page.

lack of space, we restrict ourselves in this paper to the two parameters described above. Prefetch distances are fixed to those that produce the best performances. Note that in all our experiments, the number of TLB misses is extremely negligible.

After presenting the experimental environment, the next section studies the performance of the memory hierarchy levels in various target processors.

### 4. Experimental Study of Cache Behavior

This section presents a synthesis of our experimental results on three micro-processors: Alpha 21264, Power 4 and Itanium 2. Alpha 21264 and Power 4 are two representative ones of out-of-order superscalar processors, while Itanium 2 represents an in-order processor (an interesting combination between superscalar and VLIW).

In all our experiments, we focus on the performance of our micro-benchmarks expressed in terms of number of clock cycles (execution time), reported by the hardware performance counters available in each processor. Our measurements are normalized as follows:

- in the case of memory stress kernels, we report the minimal number of clock cycles needed to perform two memory accesses: depending on the kernel, it might be a pair of loads (LxLy kernel), or a load and a store (LxSy kernel);

- in the case of BLAS 1 kernels, we report the minimal number of clock cycles needed to compute one vector element. For instance, the performance of the vsum kernel is the minimal time needed to perform one instruction Z(i)←X(i)+Y(i). Since all our micro-benchmarks are memory-bound, the performance is not sensitive to any floating point computations.

One of the major point of focus is the impact of array offsets on the performance. Since most of our micro-benchmarks access only two arrays (except vsum that accesses three arrays), we explore the combination of two dimensions of offsets (offset X vs. offset Y). Therefore, 2D plots (ISO-surface) are used. A *geographical* color code is used: light colors correspond to the best performance (lowest number of cycles) while dark colors correspond to the worst performance. The legends show the discrete scales of the performances (minimal number of clock cycles). For instance, [1-3] means that the number of clock cycles belongs to this interval.

In the following sections, we detail the most important and representative experiments that allow to make a clear synthesis on each hardware platform.

## 4.1. Alpha 21264 Processor

The plot in Fig. 1 uses intensity to encode the performance of the LxSy kernel for each combination of array offsets. The lighter regions of the graph represent 1.3 cycle per iteration. In the darkest diagonal in the figure, the performance degradation is greater than 23 times when compared with the best one. This main diagonal corresponds to the effects of the interactions between a stream of a load followed by a store, both accessing two distinct memory locations (Load X(i) followed by Store Y(i)). However, the hardware assumes that these memory operations are dependent because they have the same $k$ address lower-bits. This diagonal is periodic (not reported in this figure) and arises when the offset of X (resp. Y) is a multiple of 32 KB, which means that $k = 15$ bits. The magnitude of performance degradation depends on the frequency of the false memory collisions, and the distance between them : the nearer is the issue time of two false colliding memory addresses, the higher is the penalty. The degradation in the secondary diagonal on the upper left of Fig. 1 corresponds to 11 cycles per iteration. It is due to the effects of interactions between the prefetch instructions of the X elements and the stores of Y elements. The periodicity of this diagonal is 32 KB too.

These performance penalties occur for all BLAS 1 kernels. This is due to the compiler optimization strategy. Indeed, the Compaq compiler (version 6.3) generates a well optimized code (loop unrolling with fine-grain scheduling) but keeps the same order of memory access as described by the C program (Load X(i) followed by Store Y(i)). This code generation allowed to reach peak performance only with ideal combination of array offsets, that are not controlled by the compiler.

## 4.2. Power 4 Processor

For this processor, we show the performance of some BLAS 1 kernels. The IBM compiler (version 5.02) generates also a well optimized code. The loops are unrolled and optimized at the fine-grain level, but they perform the same order of the memory accesses as described by the source program (Load X(i) followed by Store Y(i) for copy kernel, and Load X(i), Load Y(i) followed by Store Z(i) for vsum). Prefetch instructions are not inserted by the compiler, since data prefetching is automatically done by hardware.

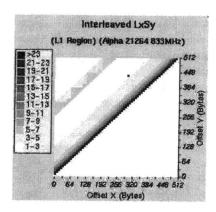

**Figure 1. Cache Behavior of Alpha 21264**

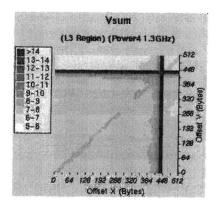

**Figure 2. Cache Behavior of Power 4**

Fig. 2 plots the performance of vsum code when the operands are located in L3. This figure is more complex:

- along the main diagonal, a stripe is visible with a moderate performance loss (around 17 %). This is due to the interaction between the two load address streams (loads of X and Y elements).

- a vertical (resp. horizontal) stripe can be observed where the execution times are larger (25 cycles instead of 7). This is due to the interaction between the loads of X elements (resp. Y elements) with the stores of Z elements.

In all cases, the "bad" vertical and diagonal zones appear periodically every 4 KB offset. It confirms that the processor performs partial address comparison on 12 low-order bits.

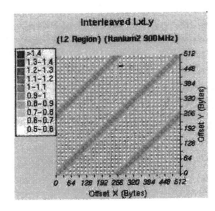

(a)

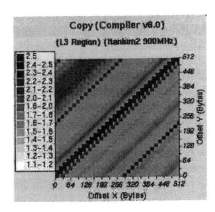

(b)

**Figure 3. Cache Behavior of Itanium 2**

## 4.3. Itanium 2 Processor

Contrary to the two previous processors, Itanium 2 is in-order. The instruction level parallelism is expressed by the program using instruction groups and bundles. Thus, analyzing the behavior of the memory operations is little easier. In this section, we show that the banking architecture of the L2 cache level and the memory disambiguation mechanisms may cause significant performance degradation. While the memory stress kernels are coded at low level, we use the Intel compiler (version version 7.0 beta) to generate optimized codes for our BLAS 1 loops. Software pipelining, loop unrolling and data prefetching are used to enhance the fine-grain parallelism. The experiments are performed in L2 and L3, since on Itanium 2, L1 cannot contain floating point

| Processor | L1 | L2 | L3 |
|-----------|-------|------|------|
| Alpha 21264 | 21.54 | 12 | - |
| Power 4 | 2.11 | 3.64 | 2.57 |
| Itanium 2 | - | 2.17 | 1.5 |

**Table 1. Performance Degradation Factors**

operands (this is a design choice of the Itanium family architecture).

First, let us examine the impact of L2 banking architecture. Fig. 3(a) plots the performance of the LxLy kernel (two streams of independent loads). The best execution time is 0.6 cycle, which is the optimal one. However, some regions exhibit performance loss, depending on the array offsets. Basically, two types of phenomenon can be observed:

1. three diagonals separated by 256 B in which the performance is 1.2 cycle instead of 0.6 cycle;

2. a grid pattern (crossed by the three diagonal stripes). Inside this grid, the execution times in some points are 0.6 cycle, but 1 cycle in others.

Both phenomena can be easily attributed to bank conflicts resulting from the interactions between the L2 interleaving scheme and the address streams.

All the performance troubles observed in L2 still exist in L3 level. Fig. 3(b) shows the performance of the copy kernel. The memory disambiguation problem is accentuated (wider diagonal stripes) because of the interaction between independent loads and stores. Another problem is highlighted by the upper-left diagonal zone, which is in fact due to the interferences between prefetch instructions (that behave as loads) and the store instructions.

**Summary** This section presented the behavior of the cache systems in Alpha 21264, Power 4 and Itanium 2 processors. We showed that the effectiveness of an enhanced instruction scheduling is not sufficient to sustain the best performance even in very simple codes, when we expect a maximal ILP extraction. We demonstrated that memory disambiguation mechanisms cause significant performance loss depending on array offsets. Bank conflicts in Itanium 2 are also an important source of performance troubles. Tab. 1 recapitulates the performance degradation factors[3] caused by these micro-architectural restrictions.

We can use many code optimization techniques to reduce the performance penalties previously exposed (for

---

[3]Counted as the ratio between the best and worst performance.

instance, array padding, array copying and code vectorization). In the next section of this article, we investigate the impact of vectorization.

## 5. The Effectiveness of Ld/St Vectorization

The performance degradation depicted in the last section arises when a program performs parallel accesses to distinct arrays. Theoretically, if the underlying processor has enough functional units (FUs), and if the different caches have enough ports, such memory operations can be executed in parallel. Unfortunately, for implementation reasons (design complexity), memory disambiguation mechanisms in actual ILP processors do not perform complete comparisons on address bits. Furthermore, some caches, as those implemented on Itanium 2, contain several banks and do not allow to sustain full access bandwidth. Thus, parallel memory operations are serialized during execution, even if enough FUs and ILP exist, and even if data are located in low cache levels.

Let us think about new ways to avoid the dynamic conflicts between memory operations. One of the ways to reduce these troubles is ld/st vectorization. This is not a novel technique, and we do not aim to bring a new one; we only want to demonstrate that the classical vectorization is a simple and yet elegant solution to a difficult problem. We schedule memory access operations not only according to data dependences and resources constraints, but we must also take into account the accessed address streams (even if independent). Since we do not know the exact array offsets at compile time, we cannot determine precisely all memory locations (physical addresses) that we access. However, we can rely on their relative address locations as defined by the arrays. For instance, we can determine at compile time the relative address between X(i) and X(i+1), but not between X(i) and Y(i) since array offsets are determined at linking time in the case of static arrays, or at execute time in the case of dynamically allocated arrays. Thus, we are sure at compile time that the different addresses of the elements X(i), X(i+1),..., X(i+k) do not share the same lower-order bits. This fact makes us group memory operations accessing to the same vector since we know their relative address. Such memory access grouping is similar to vectorization, except that only loads and store are vectorized. The other operations, such that the floating point ones, are not vectorized, and hence they are kept free to be scheduled at the fine-grain level to enhance the performance.

Vectorization is a complex technology, and many studies have been performed on this scope. In our frame-

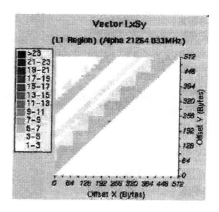

**Figure 4. Vectorization on Alpha 21264**

work, the problem is simplified since we tackle fully parallel innermost loops. We only seek a convenient vectorization degree. Ideally, the higher is this degree, the higher is the performance, but the higher is the register pressure too. Thus, we are constrained by the number of available registers. We showed in [2] how we can modify the register allocation step by combining ld/st vectorization at the data dependence graph (DDG) level without hurting ILP extraction. This previous study [2] shows how we can seek a convenient vectorization degree which satisfies register file constraints and ILP extraction. To simplify the explanation, if a non-vectorized loop consumes $r$ registers, then the vectorized version with degree $k$ requires at most $k \times r$ registers. Thus, if the processor has $\mathcal{R}$ available registers, a trivial valid vectorization degree is $k = \left\lfloor \frac{\mathcal{R}}{r} \right\rfloor$. The next sections explore the effectiveness of ld/st vectorization.

### 5.1. Alpha 21264 Processor

Fig. 4 shows the impact of vectorization on the LxSy kernel (compare it to Fig. 1). Even if all the troubles do not disappear, the worst execution times in this case are less than 7 cycles instead of 28 cycles previously. The best performance remains the same for the two versions, i.e., 1.3 cycle. This improvement is confirmed for all BLAS 1 kernels and in all cache levels. Tab. 2 presents the speedup resulted from vectorization. It is counted as the gain ratio between the worst performance of the vectorized codes and the worst performance of the original codes. The best performance of all the microbenchmarks are not altered by vectorization.

| Cache | LxLy | LxSy | Copy | Vsum | Daxpy |
|-------|------|------|------|------|-------|
| L1 | 0% | 53.57% | 45.83% | 80% | 29.17% |
| L2 | 26.32% | 75% | 48.15% | 80% | 30.77% |

**Table 2. Worst-Case Performance Gain on Alpha 21264**

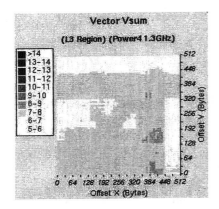

**Figure 5. Vectorization on Power 4**

## 5.2. Power 4 Processor

Fig. 5 shows the performance of vectorized vsum kernel when the operands are located in L3 (compare it to Fig. 2). As it can be seen, all the stripes of bad performance disappear. Vectorizing memory operations improves the worst performance of all our micro-benchmarks in all cache levels by reducing the number of conflicts between the memory operations. The best performance of all the micro-benchmarks are not degraded by vectorization.

## 5.3. Itanium 2 Processor

The case of Itanium 2 processor needs more efforts since there are bank conflicts in addition to imprecise memory disambiguation. Thus, the ld/st vectorization is not as naive as for the previous out-of-order processors. In order to eliminate bank conflicts, memory access operations are packed into instruction groups that access even or odd indexed vector elements. For instance `Load X(i)`, `Load X(i+2)`, `Load X(i+4)`,...and `Load X(i+1)`, `Load X(i+3)`, `Load X(i+5)`, etc. Thus, each instruction group accesses a distinct cache bank. Since each bank can contain 16 bytes of consecutive data, two consecutive double FP el-

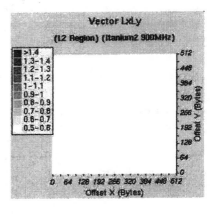

(a)

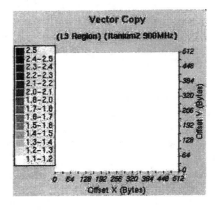

(b)

**Figure 6. Vectorization on Itanium 2**

ements may be assigned to the same bank. This fact prohibits accessing both elements at the same clock cycle (bank conflict). This is why we grouped the accesses in an odd/even way. Fig. 6(a) plots the performance of the vectorized LxLy kernel (compare it to Fig. 3(a)). As it can be seen, all bank conflicts and memory disambiguation problems disappear. The sustained performance is the peak one (ideal) for any vector offsets. When stores are performed, Fig. 6(b) shows the L3 behavior for the vectorized copy kernel (compare it to Fig. 3(b)). The original grid patterns are smoothed.

This improvement occurs for all our micro-benchmarks and in all cache levels. Tab. 3 shows the speedup resulted from vectorization, counted as the gain ratio between the worst performance of the vectorized codes and the worst performance of the original codes.

| Cache | LxLy | LxSy | Copy | Daxpy |
|-------|-------|-------|-------|--------|
| L2 | 45.45% | 18.18% | 47.62% | 40.91% |
| L3 | 28.57% | 18.75% | 54.55% | 33.33% |

**Table 3. Worst-Case Performance Gain on Itanium 2**

Again, ld/st vectorization does not alter the peak performance in all cases.

## 6. Conclusion and Future Work

Memory-bound programs rely on advanced compilation techniques that try to keep data into the cache levels, hoping to fully utilize a maximal amount of ILP on the underlying hardware functional units. Even in ideal cases when operands are located in lower cache levels, and when compilers generate codes that can statically be considered as "good", our article demonstrates that it is not sufficient for sustaining the peak performance.

First, the memory disambiguation mechanisms in modern ILP processors do not perform comparisons on whole address bits. If two memory operations access two distinct memory locations but share the same lower-order bits in their addresses, the hardware detects a false dependence and triggers a serialization mechanism. Consequently, ld/st queues cannot be fully utilized to re-order the independent memory operations.

Second, the banking structure of some caches prevent from sustaining entire access bandwidth. If two elements are mapped to the same bank, independent loads are restricted to be executed sequentially, even if enough FUs are idle. This fact is a well known source of troubles, but current compilers still does not take it into account (even with highly optimized, hand tuned, libraries provided by vendors), and the generated codes can be 2 times slower on Itanium 2.

Our study demonstrates that a simple existing compilation technique can help to generate faster codes that reduce the ld/st queue conflicts. Consecutive accesses to the same array are grouped together since we know at compile time their relative addresses. Coupling our simple vectorization technique with other classical ILP scheduling ones is demonstrated to be effective to sustain the peak performance. Even if we do not avoid all situations of bad relative array offsets in all hardware platforms, and thus few memory disambiguation penalties persist, we showed that we still get high speedups in all experimented processors (up to 54% of perfor-

mance gain). This simple software solution coupled with imprecise memory disambiguation mechanisms are less expensive than sophisticated totally hardware approaches such as [1, 6, 5, 7, 4].

Vectorization is not the only way that may solve the performance penalties highlighted in this paper. Array padding for instance can change the memory layout in order to produce ideal array offset combinations. However, array padding requires to analyze the whole application. In the case of scientific libraries on which we are focusing, we cannot apply this technique since the arrays are declared outside the functions (not available at the compilation time of the library).

In a future work, we will explore the main memory behavior with the same methodology. Already, some preliminary tests have confirmed us with the good performance capabilities of the vectorization strategy. A second future work may be devoted to generalize our vectorization methodology to take into account more complex scientific codes.

## References

[1] G. Chrysos and J. Emer. Memory Dependence Prediction using Store Sets. In *Proceedings of the 25th Annual International Symposium on Computer Architecture (ISCA-98)*, volume 26,3 of *ACM Computer Architecture News*, pages 142–154, New York, June 1998. ACM Press.

[2] W. Jalby, C. Lemuet, and S.-A.-A. Touati. An Efficient Memory Operations Optimization Technique for Vector Loops on Itanium 2 Processors. *Conurrency and Computation: Practice and Experience*, 2004 (to appear). Wiley Interscience.

[3] M. Johnson. *Superscalar Microprocessor Design*. Prentice-Hall, Englewood Cliffs, New Jersey, 1991.

[4] S. Onder. Cost Effective Memory Dependence Prediction using Speculation Levels and Color Sets. In *2002 International Conference on Parallel Architectures and Compilation Techniques (PACT'02)*, Virginia, Sept. 2002. IEEE.

[5] I. Park, C. L. Ooi, and T. N. Vijaykumar. Reducing Design Complexity of the Load/Store Queue. In *Proceedings of the 36th International Symposium on Microarchitecture (MICRO-36 2003)*, San Diego, Dec. 2003. IEEE.

[6] S. Sethumadhavan, R. Desikan, D. Burger, C. R. Moore, and S. W. Keckler. Scalable Hardware Memory Disambiguation for High ILP Processors. In *Proceedings of the 36th International Symposium on Microarchitecture (MICRO-36 2003)*, San Diego, Dec. 2003. IEEE.

[7] A. Yoaz, M. Erez, R. Ronen, and S. Jourdan. Speculation Techniques for Improving Load Related Instruction Scheduling. In *26th Annual International Symposium on Computer Architecture (26th ISCA'99), Computer Architecture News*, volume 27, pages 42–53. ACM SIGARCH, May 1999.

# Applying Array Contraction to A Sequence of DOALL Loops

Yonghong Song
Sun Microsystems, Inc.
4150 Network Circle
Santa Clara, CA 95054
yonghong.song@sun.com

Zhiyuan Li
Department of Computer Sciences
Purdue University
West Lafayette, IN 47907
li@cs.purdue.edu

## Abstract

*Efficient program execution on multiprocessor computers requires both sufficient parallelism and good data locality. Recent research found that, using a combination of loop shifting, loop fusion, and array contraction, one can reduce the memory required to execute a sequence of serial loops, thereby to improve the cache locality. This paper studies how to extend such a memory-reduction scheme to a sequence of DOALL loops which are executed in parallel on multiprocessors. Two methods are proposed to overcome difficulties caused by loop-carried dependences.* Data copy-in *is performed to remove anti-dependences between different parallel threads, and* computation duplication *is performed to remove flow dependences. Experiments performed on a number of benchmark programs show that the proposed technique improves both cache locality and parallel execution speed for the DOALL loops. The scheme achieves an average speedup of 1.41 for 17 programs on a 4-processor SUN machine.*

## 1 Introduction

Efficient program execution on multiprocessor computers requires both sufficient parallelism and good data locality. Recent research introduced a scheme (called *SFC*) that combines loop shifting (*S*), loop fusion (*F*) and array contraction (*C*) to transform a sequence of loop nests into a single loop nest such that the required total memory space is minimized [15, 14]. This reduction in memory requirement improves both the cache locality and the sequential execution speed of the program. It is then natural to ask whether the SFC can be used to improve the cache locality of a sequence of DOALL loops. (A DOALL loop is an indexed loop, e.g. a Fortran DO loop, which has no loop-carried data dependences, i.e., data dependences between different iterations, except those in a parallelizable reduction operation such as a vector summation.)

```
L1: DO I = 1, N
  A(I) = E(I)+E(I-1)
END DO
L2: DO I = 1, N
  E(I) = A(I)
END DO
```

(a)

```
a2 = E(1) + E(0)
DO I = 2, N
  a1 = a2
  a2 = E(I) + E(I - 1)
  E(I - 1) = a1
END DO
E(N) = a2
```

(b)

```
!$OMP PARALLEL DO
   DO I = 1, N
     A(I) = E(I) + E(I - 1)
   END DO
!$OMP PARALLEL DO
   DO I = 1, N
     E(I) = A(I)
   END DO
```

(c)

```
!$OMP PARALLEL PRIVATE(P,C,L,U,t)
    P = OMP_GET_NUM_THREADS()
    C = (N + P - 1)/P
    L = 1 + OMP_GET_THREAD_NUM() * C
    U = MIN(L + C - 1, N)
    t = E(L - 1)
!$OMP BARRIER

    DO I = L, U
      IF (I.EQ.L) THEN
        A(I) = E(I) + t
      ELSE
        A(I) = E(I) + E(I - 1)
      END IF
    END DO
    DO I = L, U
      E(I) = A(I)
    END DO
!$OMP END PARALLEL
```

(d)

```
!$OMP PARALLEL PRIVATE(P,C,L,U,t,a1,a2)
    P = OMP_GET_NUM_THREADS()
    C = (N + P - 1)/P
    L = 1 + OMP_GET_THREAD_NUM() * C
    U = MIN(L + C - 1, N)
    t = E(L - 1)
!$OMP BARRIER

    a2 = E(L) + t
    DO I = L + 1, U
      a1 = a2
      a2 = E(I) + E(I - 1)
      E(I - 1) = a1
    END DO
    E(U) = a2
!$OMP END PARALLEL
```

(e)

**Figure 1. Example 1**

In this paper, we shall show experimental results which demonstrate improved cache locality and execution speed of a number of benchmark programs as a result of applying a parallel version of SFC. Some of these programs require only straightforward loop fusion and array contraction. But for others, straightforward loop fusion (even with loop shifting) introduces loop-carried data dependences, which makes the resulting loop nest no longer DOALL. Hence, such programs require additional transforms in order to preserve the parallelism while allowing array contraction.

Figure 1 shows an example. Figure 1(a) lists a sequence of two loops, L1 and L2. Suppose array $A$ is dead after loop L2. Using the SFC technique [15, 14], one can first shift the loop limits in L2, then fuse both loops before contracting the array A into two scalars (Figure 1(b)). On the other hand, to execute the loops in Figure 1(a) on a multiprocessor computer, one can convert L1 and L2 into parallel loops, since they are both DOALL. Figure 1(c) shows how to use OpenMP directives to mark these two loops as paral-

0190-3918/04 $20.00

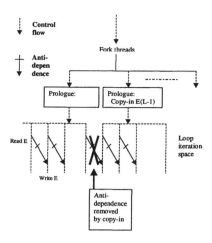

**Figure 2. Illustration of Data Copy-In**

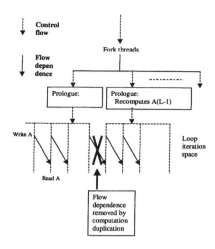

**Figure 3. Illustration of Computation Duplication**

lel. Unfortunately, the SFC technique cannot be applied in a straightforward way to these parallel loops, because they cannot be legally fused with or without loop shifting. (The fused loop in Figure 1(b) is not DOALL, since the shifting of L2 has created a loop-carried anti-dependence due to array E.) What we need is an alternative way to parallelize the given sequence of DOALL loops such that the SFC technique can be applied.

Our solution takes advantage of the fact that the number of available processors, $P$, is usually much smaller than the iteration counts of the parallel loops. We partition the iterations into $P$ blocks of consecutive iterations. By letting each processor executes one of such blocks, we confine the potential data races (due to the loop-carried data dependences) to the array elements that are accessed in those iterations on the partition boundary. We can then remove such boundary dependences by two kinds of duplication. The anti-dependences are removed by *data copy-in*, which duplicates the array elements in contention. The flow-dependences are removed by *computation duplication*, which makes the reader of an array element recompute the data value instead of taking the value computed by a different processor. Note that, based on the assumptions made in Section 2, output dependences will not exist between different threads.

Figure 1(d) shows the parallelization of the loops in Figure 1(a) using the idea of data copy-in. The parallel code, which uses OpenMP directives, is executed by each processor which participates in the execution of the loops. Depending on its assigned thread number, the processor gets to execute a certain block of the iterations. The variable $P$ represents the number of threads which, for the purpose of this paper, can be viewed as the number of available processors. The lower bound $L$ and upper bound $U$ define the range of the iterations executed in each thread. $E(L-1)$ is copied

in to remove the anti-dependence between the boundary iterations. Such copy-in operations are placed in the parallel loop's prologue, which is separated from the thread body by a synchronization barrier. Figure 2 illustrates how the copy-in removes the boundary anti-dependences. The SFC technique [15, 14] can now be applied to the thread body, producing the final array-contracted code in Figure 1(e).

To see how *computation duplication* works, consider an example which is produced by replacing the reference to $A(I)$ in loop L2 (see Figure 1(a)) by a reference to $A(I-1)$. In this example, if the parallel code were generated following the style of Figure 1(d), there would exist a flow dependence between different processors. Figure 3 illustrates how to use computation duplication to remove such a flow dependence.

In the rest of the paper, we shall present a scheme which a compiler may use to perform array contraction on DOALL loops as illustrated above. We present experimental results obtained by applying the scheme to the benchmark programs used in the previous study of the SFC technique [15, 14]. In Section 2, we present a program model for this study. In Section 3, we present the new compiler scheme for a sequence of DOALL loops. We show experimental results in Section 4, compare related work in Section 5 and conclude in Section 6.

## 2 Program Model and Loop Dependence Graph

We consider a collection of loop nests, $L_1, L_2, \ldots, L_m$, $m \geq 1$, as shown in Figure 4. Each label $L_i$ denotes a tight nest of loops with indices $L_{i,1}, L_{i,2}, \ldots, L_{i,n}, n \geq 1$, listed from the outermost level to the innermost. (For the exam-

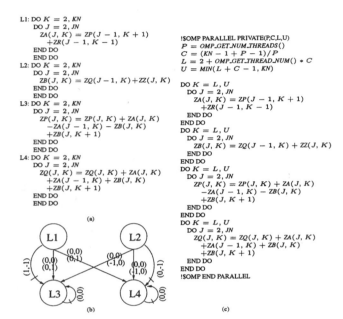

$$L_1 : \text{DO } L_{1,1} = l_{11}, l_{11} + b_1 - 1$$
$$\text{DO } L_{1,2} = l_{12}, l_{12} + b_2 - 1$$
$$\cdots$$
$$\text{DO } L_{1,n} = l_{1n}, l_{1n} + b_n - 1$$
$$\cdots$$
$$L_i : \text{DO } L_{i,1} = l_{21}, l_{21} + b_1 - 1$$
$$\text{DO } L_{i,2} = l_{22}, l_{22} + b_2 - 1$$
$$\cdots$$
$$\text{DO } L_{i,n} = l_{2n}, l_{2n} + b_n - 1$$
$$\cdots$$
$$L_m : \text{DO } L_{m,1} = l_{m1}, l_{m1} + b_1 - 1$$
$$\text{DO } L_{m,2} = l_{m2}, l_{m2} + b_2 - 1$$
$$\cdots$$
$$\text{DO } L_{m,n} = l_{mn}, l_{mn} + b_n - 1$$

**Figure 4. The program model**

```
L1: DO K = 2, KN
     DO J = 2, JN
        ZA(J, K) = ZP(J - 1, K + 1)
              +ZR(J - 1, K - 1)
     END DO
   END DO
L2: DO K = 2, KN
     DO J = 2, JN
        ZB(J, K) = ZQ(J - 1, K) + ZZ(J, K)
     END DO
   END DO
L3: DO K = 2, KN
     DO J = 2, JN
        ZP(J, K) = ZP(J, K) + ZA(J, K)
              - ZA(J - 1, K) - ZB(J, K)
              +ZB(J, K + 1)
     END DO
   END DO
L4: DO K = 2, KN
     DO J = 2, JN
        ZQ(J, K) = ZQ(J, K) + ZA(J, K)
              +ZA(J - 1, K) + ZB(J, K)
              +ZB(J, K + 1)
     END DO
   END DO
             (a)
```

```
!$OMP PARALLEL PRIVATE(P,C,L,U)
P = OMP_GET_NUM_THREADS()
C = (KN - 1 + P - 1)/P
L = 2 + OMP_GET_THREAD_NUM() * C
U = MIN(L + C - 1, KN)

DO K = L, U
   DO J = 2, JN
      ZA(J, K) = ZP(J - 1, K + 1)
            +ZR(J - 1, K - 1)
   END DO
END DO
DO K = L, U
   DO J = 2, JN
      ZB(J, K) = ZQ(J - 1, K) + ZZ(J, K)
   END DO
END DO
DO K = L, U
   DO J = 2, JN
      ZP(J, K) = ZP(J, K) + ZA(J, K)
            - ZA(J - 1, K) - ZB(J, K)
            +ZB(J, K + 1)
   END DO
END DO
DO K = L, U
   DO J = 2, JN
      ZQ(J, K) = ZQ(J, K) + ZA(J, K)
            +ZA(J - 1, K) + ZB(J, K)
            +ZB(J, K + 1)
   END DO
END DO
!$OMP END PARALLEL
                          (c)
```

**Figure 5. Example 2, its original loop dependence graph and intermediate result before computation duplication and data copy-in**

ple in Figure 1(a), we have $m = 2$ and $n = 1$.) All the outermost loops are assumed to be DOALL, with the possible presence of parallelizable reduction operations as mentioned before. We make a number of assumptions which are the same as in the previous study of the SFC technique for sequential execution [15, 14]. These assumptions are restated below.

Loop $L_{i,j}$ has the lower bound $l_{ij}$ and the upper bound $l_{ij} + b_j - 1$ respectively, where $l_{ij}$ and $b_j$ are loop invariants. All loops at the same level, $j$, are assumed to have the same trip count $b_j$. We assume that none of the given loops can be partitioned into smaller loops by *loop distribution* [18]. Otherwise, we apply maximum loop distribution [18] to the given collection of loops first. The purpose of maximum loop distribution is for optimal memory-space reduction [15].

The array regions referenced in the given collection of loops are divided into three categories. An *input array region* is upwardly exposed to the beginning of $L_1$. An *output array region* is live after $L_m$. A *local array region* does not intersect with any input or output array regions. Only the local array regions are amenable to array contraction. In the example in Figure 1(a), $A(1 : N)$ is the only local array region. Figure 5(a) shows a more complex example which resembles one of the well-known Livermore loops. In this example, where $m = 4$ and $n = 2$, each declared array is of dimension $[1 : JN + 1, 1 : KN + 1]$. ZA(2:JN,2:KN) and ZB(2:JN,2:KN) are local array regions.

To describe the dependence between a collection of loop nests, we extend the definitions of the traditional dependence distance vector [6] as follows.

**Definition 1** *Given a collection of loop nests, $L_1, \ldots, L_m$, as in Figure 4(a), if a data dependence exists from the source iteration $\vec{i} = (i_1, i_2, \ldots, i_n)$ of loop $L_{k_1}(1 \le k_1 \le m)$ to the destination iteration $\vec{j} = (j_1, j_2, \ldots, j_n)$ of loop $L_{k_2}(1 \le k_2 \le m)$, we say the* distance vector *of this dependence is $\vec{j} - \vec{i} = (j_1 - i_1, j_2 - i_2, \ldots, j_n - i_n)$.*

For simplicity of discussion, we assume that there exist no output dependences between different loop nests. Furthermore, we assume constant dependence distance vectors in this paper. In certain cases, one can replace non-constant distance vectors by constant ones without suffering the optimality of the solution [14].

Figure 5(b) illustrates the data dependences in the code example in Figure 5(a). The array regions associated with the dependence edges can be inferred from the program, and they are omitted in the figure. For instance, the flow dependence from $L_1$ to $L_3$ with $\vec{d} = (0, 0)$ is due to array region $ZA(2 : JN, 2 : KN)$. In Figure 5(b), where multiple dependences of the same type (flow, anti- or output) exist from one node to another, all these dependences are represented by a single arc. All associated distance vectors are then marked on this single arc.

## 3 The New SFC for DOALL Loops

The SFC technique relies on the fact that, given a sequence of loops shown in Figure 4(a), the number of simultaneously live array elements in the local array regions can be reduced by fusing the given $m$ loop nests into a single loop nest. Through Figure 1, we have illustrated how to make loop fusion legal by loop shifting and how to contract arrays after loop fusion. The details of these steps and the optimal loop-shifting choice are discussed in previous studies [15, 14]. In this paper, we focus on the new aspects of SFC when applied to DOALL loops.

In our new scheme, the compiler first creates a parallel region around the given sequence of loop nests. The iterations of each loop nest are divided evenly among the

```
procedure find_comp_dup()
    /* Let R_i be the input array region and R_d the array region which needs to be recomputed. */
    R_d = φ.
    for i = m to 1 by -1 do
        for (each flow dependence whose destination is in L_i) do
            Let L_p (1 ≤ p < i) be the loop containing the dependence source.
            Determine the array region, R_w, written by the dependence source.
            Determine the array region, R_r, used by the dependence destination.
            R_d = R_d ∪ (R_r - R_w - R_i). /* Only the needed values that are computed
                by a different processor must be recomputed locally by duplication. */
        end for
    end for
end procedure
```

```
procedure find_copy_in()
    /* Let R_o be the read-only input array region and R_d the array region which needs to be copied in. */
    R_d = φ.
    for i = 1 to m do
        for (each anti-dependence whose source is in L_i) do
            Determine the dependence destination L_j, j > i.
            Determine the array region, R_r, read by the dependence source in loop L_i.
            Determine the array region, R_w, written by the dependence destination in loop L_j.
            R_d = R_d ∪ (R_r - R_w - R_o).
        end for
    end for
end procedure
```

**Figure 6. The algorithm for determining duplicated computation**

**Figure 7. The algorithm for computing copy-in array regions**

processors. Figure 5(c) shows the code for Figure 5(a) after this intermediate step. A synchronization barrier separates the prologue of the parallel region from the thread body, and the latter contains the original loop nests whose loop bounds are modified according to the partitioning. We then apply computation duplication and data copy-in to the loop nests in the thread body, if they are needed. Array contraction follows afterwards, regardless whether computation duplication and data copy-in are applied or not. Next, we discuss how to determine whether computation duplication and data copy-in are needed in order to perform array contraction and, if needed, how to apply them.

## 3.1 Computation Duplication

Computation duplication may have a ripple effect that must be handled systematically. A duplicated computation in loop $L_i$ may require the values computed in another loop, say $L_j$, by a different processor. A new case of boundary flow dependence hence may arise. Note that loop $L_j$ must precede $L_i$ lexically in the given sequence of loops, hence $j < i$. A flow dependence from $L_i$ to $L_i$ will not require computation duplication because it cannot be loop-carried in $L_{i,1}$ which is a DOALL loop. Figure 6 shows the algorithm that formalizes the handling of the ripple effect. This algorithm visits the loop nests in the reversed lexical order. It determines all array regions whose computation must be duplicated because of the boundary flow dependences.

The inserted computation-duplication code recomputes the values of certain array elements that are used in the thread. The storage for such recomputed values deserves a careful consideration. In order to reduce the required memory size, it is beneficial to store these values in the original arrays. However, there are cases in which we are forced to allocate new variables that are private to the thread in order to store the recomputed values. Suppose an array element is written more than once in one of the original loop nests. It then has different values, at different time, that are used by different read references. Further suppose that, after loop parallelization, the same array element needs to be recomputed (by computation duplication) in the prologue

of the parallel region in order to remove flow dependences between different threads. Without allocating private variables, the single storage for the original array element obviously cannot hold multiple values, even though all of these values are used by some read references in the same loop executed by the same thread. Private variables must therefore be allocated to store all these values. The read operations will then read the corresponding private variables.

For the example in Figure 5(c), we can easily find that the array region which needs recomputation is $ZB(2 : JN, U + 1)$. This is due to the flow dependence from the reference to $ZB(J, K)$ in L2 to the reference to $ZB(J, K + 1)$ in L3 and due to the flow dependence from the reference to $ZB(J, K)$ in L2 to the reference to $ZB(J, K + 1)$ in L4.

## 3.2 Data Copy-in

After using computation duplication to remove boundary flow dependences, we use data copy-in to remove boundary anti-dependences. It is possible for an array to be both written (for computation duplication) and read in the prologue, which creates data races. When this happens, we place all data copy-in code ahead of the computation duplication code in the prologue, and we use an additional synchronization barrier to separate these two parts.

Figure 7 shows the procedure for finding array regions which need to be copied in, where $R_o$ represents the portion of input array regions which are read but not written in the given code segment. For each anti-dependence, the array region to be copied will be copied to variables that are private to the thread. Therefore such an anti-dependence no longer exists between different threads when the thread body is executed.

For the example in Figure 5(c), the array region which needs copy-in is $ZP(2 : JN, U + 1)$, which is due to the anti-dependence from the reference to $ZP(J - 1, K + 1)$ in L1 to the reference to $ZP(J, K)$ in L3.

## 3.3 Contracting the Arrays

After all necessary computation duplication and data copy-in are inserted in the parallel code region. The SFC

49

```
!$OMP PARALLEL PRIVATE(P,C,L,U,t)
P = OMP_GET_NUM_THREADS()
C = (KN - 1 + P - 1)/P
L = 2 + OMP_GET_THREAD_NUM() * C
U = MIN(L + C - 1, KN)
t(1 : JN - 1) = ZP(1 : JN - 1, U + 1).
IF (U.NE.KN) THEN
    DO J = 2, JN
        ZB(J, U + 1) = ZQ(J - 1, U + 1)
        +ZZ(J, U + 1)
    END DO
END IF
!$OMP BARRIER

DO K = L, U
    DO J = 2, JN
        IF (K.EQ.U) THEN
            ZA(J, K) = t(J - 1)
            +ZR(J - 1, K - 1)
        ELSE
            ZA(J, K) = ZP(J - 1, K + 1)
            +ZR(J - 1, K - 1)
        END IF
    END DO
END DO
DO K = L, U
    DO J = 2, JN
        ZB(J, K) = ZQ(J - 1, K) + ZZ(J, K)
    END DO
END DO
DO K = L, U
    DO J = 2, JN
        ZP(J, K) = ZP(J, K) + ZA(J, K)
        -ZA(J - 1, K) - ZB(J, K)
        +ZB(J, K + 1)
    END DO
END DO
DO K = L, U
    DO J = 2, JN
        ZQ(J, K) = ZQ(J, K) + ZA(J, K)
        +ZA(J - 1, K) + ZB(J, K)
        +ZB(J, K + 1)
    END DO
END DO
!$OMP END PARALLEL

              (a)
```

```
!$OMP PARALLEL PRIVATE(P,C,L,U,t,ZB1,a1,a2,b)
P = OMP_GET_NUM_THREADS()
C = (KN - 1 + P - 1)/P
L = 2 + OMP_GET_THREAD_NUM() * C
U = MIN(L + C - 1, KN)
t(1 : JN - 1) = ZP(1 : JN - 1, U + 1).
IF (U.NE.KN) THEN
    DO J = 2, JN
        ZB(J, U + 1) = ZQ(J - 1, U + 1)
        +ZZ(J, U + 1)
    END DO
END IF
!$OMP BARRIER

DO J = 2, JN
    ZB1(J) = ZQ(J - 1, L) + ZZ(J, L)
END DO

DO K = L, U - 1
    a1 = ZA(1, K)
    DO J = 2, JN
        a2 = ZP(J - 1, K + 1)
        +ZR(J - 1, K - 1)
        b = ZQ(J - 1, K + 1) + ZZ(J, K + 1)
        ZP(J, K) = ZP(J, K) + a2 - a1
        -ZB1(J) + b
        ZQ(J, K) = ZQ(J, K) + a2 + a1
        +ZB1(J) + b
        a1 = a2
        ZB1(J) = b
    END DO
END DO

a1 = ZA(1, K)
DO J = 2, JN
    a2 = t(J - 1) + ZR(J - 1, K - 1)
    ZP(J, K) = ZP(J, K) + a2 - a1
    -ZB1(J) + ZB(J, U + 1)
    ZQ(J, K) = ZQ(J, K) + a2 + a1
    +ZB1(J) + ZB(J, U + 1)
    a1 = a2
END DO
!$OMP END PARALLEL

              (b)
```

**Figure 8. Parallelized code for Example 2**

technique [15, 14] is applied to the new loop nests $L_1$ though $L_m$ in the thread body.

For the example in Figure 5(a), Figure 8(a) shows the code after automatic parallelization by applying computation duplication and data copy-in techniques. The only write reference to *shared* data is $ZB(J, U + 1)$ in the computation duplication code and the data copy-in code. Since there exists no other read references to array *ZB* in those codes, there exists no data race between different threads.

Figure 8(b) shows the code after array contraction. For arrays *ZA* and *ZB* in Figure 8(a), the local array regions accessed are $ZA(1 : JN, L : U)$ and $ZB(2 : JN, L : U + 1)$ respectively. After array contraction (Figure 8(b)), *ZA* is contracted to $ZA(1, L : U)$ plus two scalars, $a_1$ and $a_2$. Array *ZB* is contracted to $ZB(2 : JN, U + 1)$, $ZB1(2 : JN)$ and a scalar $b$.

We do not apply the extended SFC, including computation duplication and data copy-in, unless we determine that the predicted performance after final array contraction is better than that of the original code segment. For simplicity, we assume that the synchronization overhead is the same before and after the transformation. (Although we introduce new barriers in the prologue of the parallel region, we may also remove certain barriers because of loop fusion.) With such an assumption, we predict the profitability of the extended SFC by examining whether it reduces the

number of cache misses [15]. To estimate cache misses, we estimate the reuse distance [19] for each dependence and compare it to the cache size. If it is equal to or smaller than the cache size, the memory access at the dependence destination is assumed to be a cache hit. Otherwise, it is assumed to be a cache miss. We illustrate using Example 2 as follows.

Let $C_s$ represent the cache size and $C_b$ the cache line size, both measured in the number of data elements. We estimate the total number of cache misses in the original code of Example 2 (Figure 5(a)) by $x_1 = (KN - 1) * (JN - 1) * 12/C_b$. The total number of cache misses in the copy-in and computation duplication codes (accumulated over all threads) is estimated by $x_2 = (JN - 1) * 5 * P/C_b$, where $P$ represents the number of OpenMP threads. The number of cache misses in the code generated after array contraction (accumulated over all threads) is estimated by $(JN - 1) * 2 + (U - L + 1) * (JN - 1) * 4 * P/C_b$, which is equivalent to $x_3 = ((JN - 1) * 2 * P + (KN - 1) * (JN - 1) * 4)/C_b$. The condition $x_2 + x_3 < x_1$ holds if and only the condition $7 * P < (KN - 1) * 8$ holds, which is the case for large *KN*. We can let the compiler generate two versions of code such that only under the condition $7 * P < (KN - 1) * 8$ does the parallelized version with array contraction get executed.

## 4  Experimental Results

To evaluate the effectiveness of the array contraction technique discussed in this paper, we examine their applicability to the test programs used in the previous study of the SFC technique [15]. Among those 20 test programs, we find that the technique in this paper is not suitable for LL14, lucas and laplace-gs. This is because these three programs contain loops which are not DOALL but whose fusion is required in order to perform array contraction. For the experimentation in this paper, therefore, we exclude these three programs.

Table 1 lists the remaining 17 programs used in our experiments. In the listed programs, the loop nests fused for array contraction are all DOALL loops. In this table, "m/n" represents the number of loops in the loop sequence (m) and the maximum loop nesting level (n). For each of the benchmarks in Table 1, all $m$ loops are fused together. For swim95, swim00 and hydro2d, where $n = 2$, only the outer loops are fused. For all other benchmarks, all $n$ loop levels are fused. Further details concerning the program descriptions and input parameter selections can be found in the previous SFC study [15].

Among the 17 programs, the DOALL loops in combustion, climate, and all those purdue-set programs can be directly fused into a single DOALL loop without inserting data copy-in and computation duplication, as shown in Table 1. Optimal array contraction can be applied

## Table 1. Test Programs

| Benchmark Name | Description | Input Parameters | m/n | Comp. duplication and copy-in |
|---|---|---|---|---|
| LL18 | Livermore Loop No. 18 | N = 400, ITMAX = 100 | 3/2 | Computation Duplication |
| Jacobi | Jacobi Kernel w/o convergence test | N = 1100, ITMAX = 1050 | 2/2 | Both |
| tomcatv | A mesh generation program from SPEC95fp | reference input | 5/1 | Both |
| swim95 | A weather prediction program from SPEC95fp | reference input | 2/2 | Computation Duplication |
| swim00 | A weather prediction program from SPEC2000fp | reference input | 2/2 | Computation Duplication |
| hydro2d | An astrophysical program from SPEC95fp | reference input | 10/2 | Both |
| mg | A multigrid solver from NPB2.3-serial benchmark | Class 'W' | 2/1 | Neither |
| combustion | A thermochemical program from UMD Chaos group | N1 = 10, N2 = 10 | 1/2 | Neither |
| purdue-02 | Purdue set problem02 | reference input | 2/1 | Neither |
| purdue-03 | Purdue set problem03 | reference input | 3/2 | Neither |
| purdue-04 | Purdue set problem04 | reference input | 3/2 | Neither |
| purdue-07 | Purdue set problem07 | reference input | 1/2 | Neither |
| purdue-08 | Purdue set problem08 | reference input | 1/2 | Neither |
| purdue-12 | Purdue set problem12 | reference input | 4/2 | Neither |
| purdue-13 | Purdue set problem13 | reference input | 2/1 | Neither |
| climate | A two-layer shallow water climate model from Rice | reference input | 2/4 | Neither |
| laplace-jb | Jacobi method of Laplace from Rice | ICYCLE = 500 | 4/2 | Both |

without hurting the parallelism. In program `mgrid`, the sequence of DOALL loops fused for array contraction are all immediately embedded in an outermost DOALL loop. The remaining programs, i.e. `LL18`, `Jacobi`, `tomcatv`, `swim95`, `swim00`, `hydro2d` and `laplace-jb`, require computation duplication and/or data copy-in in order to keep the loops parallelized while allowing array contraction.

We manually apply the technique described in Section 3 to parallelize the loops using data copy-in and computation duplication. We then apply the tool developed in previous work [15] to perform loop shifting, loop fusion and array contraction (i.e. SFC). For comparison, we also run the parallelized code with computation duplication and data copy-in inserted, and then with loops fused. These versions, however, do not have arrays contracted. Altogether, thus, we have five versions of code to compare, including the original sequential code and the sequential code produced by the SFC technique. All these codes are run on a 4-processor SUN multiprocessor computer. Each processor is a SUN UltraSPARC II 248MHz processor with a 16KB L1 data cache and a 1MB L2 cache. The L1 cache is directly-mapped with a line size of 16 bytes. The L2 cache is directly-mapped with a line size of 64 bytes.

To generate the machine code, we use SUN's native Fortran compiler which has a version of Sun Workshop 6 update 1. All sequential codes are compiled with the "-fast" option. All parallel (OpenMP) codes are compiled with the "-fast -openmp -autopar" option. To measure the parallel performance of the original codes, we take the better execution time from two versions of codes. In one version, we manually add OpenMP pragmas to the original codes, which are compiled with the "-fast -openmp -autopar" option. The other version is parallelized automatically by the native compiler using its "-fast -autopar" option. The automatic parallelization facility of the compiler may re-arrange

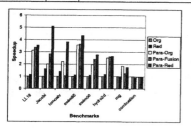

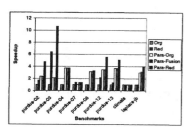

## Figure 9. Execution results

loop nests for better performance. We add "-autopar" to the compilation flag such that the loops not fused by our technique can be examined by the native compiler for automatic parallelization. For programs `purdue-07` and `climate`, we turn off parallelization for both the original loop nests and the loop nests transformed by our technique. This is because of small trip counts and small amount of work in the loop body.

### 4.1  Execution Results

Figure 9 compares the execution speed. The label "Org" stands for the sequential execution of the original codes, which is used as the normalization base. The label "Red" stands for the serial execution of the codes transformed by SFC. The label "Para-Org" stands for the parallel execution of the original codes. "Para-Fusion" stands for the parallel execution of the code transformed by the new technique

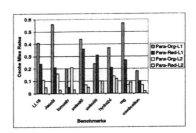

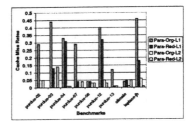

**Figure 10. Cache miss rate**

except that the arrays are not yet contracted after loop fusion. "Para-Red" stands for the parallel execution of the final codes transformed by the new technique.

According to Figure 9, the parallelized codes transformed by our technique perform better than the parallelized original codes in all 17 programs except mg, with a speedup ranging from 0.95 to 5.0 and a geometric means of 1.41. For mg, the original codes perform better than memory-reduction codes in both single-processor and multiprocessor runs. We suspect that this abnormal behavior is caused by the instruction scheduling performed by the native compiler's back-end. We will investigate this behavior further in the future study.

According to Figure 9, for all those listed programs, the parallelized code with array contraction also performs better than the parallelized code after loop fusion but before array contraction. The speedup ranges from 1.01 to 5.0 with a geometric mean of 1.42. For tomcatv, the performance of the parallelized version after loop fusion but before array contraction is particularly poor. This is because, for this program, loop interchange is performed to enable loop fusion. Before array contraction, the loop interchange spoils the spatial locality of most of the arrays.

Figure 10 shows the L1 and L2 cache miss rates. We measure the cache miss rate by using the **perfmon** package. We only measure the cache miss rate for the main thread, since we have not found a reliable way to measure the cache miss rates for the entire parallel programs on the computer system used in the experiments. In this figure, "Para-Org-L1" and "Para-Org-L2" stand for the L1 and the L2 cache miss rates of the original codes parallelized in the straightforward fashion. "Para-Red-L1" and "Para-Red-L2" stand for the L1 and the L2 cache miss rates of the parallel codes with array contraction. From this figure, we see that for most of the programs, array contraction indeed reduces cache miss rate for either the L1 or the L2 cache, or both. For swim00 and climate, although the miss rates are not reduced, the number of array references are reduced significantly because of several arrays being contracted to scalars. For swim00, the number is reduced from 9.2B to 6.3B. For climate, it is reduced from 6.9M to 1.5M.

## 5 Related Work

Several authors have considered a single perfect nest of loops. For such a single loop nest, they have studied the relationship between loop schedules (including parallel schedules) and storage optimization [17, 16, 11]. Unlike the SFC technique and its parallel extension discussed in this paper, the previous studies consider neither loop fusion nor loop shifting to enable array contraction. Among these studies, Strout et al. first propose the use of a universal occupancy vector (UOV) to derive schedule-independent stor-

age mapping for loops [16]. When such a mapping is found, arrays may be contracted along a single dimension without imposing new constraints on permissible loop schedules. Thie et al. study several problems concerning schedule and storage optimization [17], including the problems of finding the minimum storage under a given schedule, finding an optimal schedule (if possible) given an amount of storage, and finding the minimum storage that do not impose any new constraints on loop schedules. Pike et al. give a detailed study of the relationship between loop tiling and array contraction, given a perfect loop nest that is executed sequentially [11].

The computation duplication to avoid synchronization is not new. Mellor-Crummey et al. have used a similar computation duplication technique in dHPF compiler for effectively parallelization of HPF codes [9]. They target a single loop nest while we target a collection of loop nests. For cross-iteration anti-dependences, we use data copy-in while they use *selective* loop distribution to minimize synchronization overhead.

The SFC technique is first used to improve the performance of sequentially executed loops [15]. A closely related work is presented for the purpose of reducing the storage requirement in embedded systems [3]. Both of these techniques utilize network flow algorithms to compute the optimal shifting to minimize the required memory space, but the work in [3] targets a single-level loop only. The SFC technique [15] handles a collection of multi-level loop nests.

For loop fusion and array contraction, Kennedy and McKinley prove that maximizing data locality by loop fusion for registers is NP-hard [5]. Ding and Kennedy prove that loop fusion for maximum cache reuse is Np-hard [2]. Singhai and McKinley present *parameterized loop fusion* to improve parallelism and cache locality simultaneously [13].

Manjikian and Abdelrahman present a *shift-and-peel* technique to increase opportunities for loop fusion [8], which is first presented as *peel-and-jam* by Porterfield [12]. Allen *et al.* first combine loop distribution and loop fusion for parallelization purpose [1]. Gao *et al.* combine loop fusion and array scalarization to improve register utilization [4]. Lim *et al.* combine loop blocking, loop fusion and array contraction to exploit parallelism [7]. The above two works do not use loop shifting. Ng *et al.* combine loop fusion, array contraction and array rotation in a production compiler [10], which mostly focuses on single processor performance.

# 6 Conclusion

In this paper, we have presented a technique to apply array contraction to a sequence of DOALL loops. Previous studies have examined the relationship between parallel loop schedules and storage optimization for a single perfectly-nested loop. Our work presents a new method to combine array contraction with loop parallelization when given a sequence of DOALL loops. For loops that cannot be fused in a straightforward way to allow array contraction, we present two techniques, i.e. data copy-in and computation duplication, to remove fusion-preventing data dependences. Experimental results show that our technique obtain performance that is superior to the straightforward method which parallelizes the original loop nests without fusion and array contraction.

# Acknowledgment

This work is sponsored in part by National Science Foundation through grants ITR/ACR-0082834 and CCR-0208760. The authors thank the reviewers for their careful reviews and useful suggestions.

# References

[1] Allen, Callahan, and Kennedy. Automatic decomposition of scientific programs for parallel execution. In *Proceedings of the 14th ACM SIGACT-SIGPLAN Symposium on Principles of Programming Languages*, pages 63–76, January 1987.

[2] C. Ding and K. Kennedy. Improving effective bandwidth through compiler enhancement of global cache reuse. *Journal of Parallel and Distributed Computing*, 64(1):108–134, January 2004.

[3] A. Fraboulet, G. Huard, and A. Mignotte. Loop alignment for memory accesses optimization. In *Proceedings of the Twelfth International Symposium on System Synthesis*, Boca Raton, Florida, November 1999.

[4] G. R. Gao, R. Olsen, V. Sarkar, and R. Thekkath. Collective loop fusion for array contraction. In *Proceedings of the Fifth Workshop on Languages and Compilers for Parallel Computing*. Also in No. 757 in *Lecture Notes in Computer Science*, pages 281–295, Springer-Verlag, 1992.

[5] K. Kennedy and K. S. McKinley. Maximizing loop parallelism and improving data locality via loop fusion and distribution. In *Springer-Verlag Lecture Notes in Computer Science, 768. Proceedings of the Sixth Workshop on Languages and Compilers for Parallel Computing*, Portland, Oregon, August, 1993.

[6] D. J. Kuck. *The Structure of Computers and Computations*, volume 1. John Wiley & Sons, 1978.

[7] A. W. Lim, S.-W. Liao, and M. S. Lam. Blocking and array contraction across arbitrarily nested loops using affine partitioning. In *Proceedings of 2001 ACM Conference on PPOPP*, pages 103–112, Snowbird, Utah, June 2001.

[8] N. Manjikian and T. Abdelrahman. Fusion of loops for parallelism and locality. *IEEE Transactions on Parallel and Distributed Systems*, 8(2):193–209, February 1997.

[9] J. Mellor-Crummey, V. Adve, B. Broom, D. Chavarria-Miranda, R. Fowler, G. Jin, K. Kennedy, and Q. Yi. Advanced optimization strategies in the rice dhpf compiler. *Concurrency - Practice and Experience*, 1:1–20, 2001.

[10] J. Ng, D. Kulkarni, W. Li, R. Cox, and S. Bobholz. Interprocedural loop fusion, array contraction and rotation. In *Proceedings of the 12th International Conference on Parallel Architectures and Compilation Techniques*, pages 114–124, New Orleans, Louisiana, September 2003.

[11] G. Pike and P. N. Hilfinger. Better tiling and array contraction for compiling scientific programs. In *Proceedings of the IEEE/ACM SC 2002 Conference*.

[12] A. Porterfield. *Software Methods for Improving Cache Performance*. PhD thesis, Department of Computer Sciences, Rice University, May 1989.

[13] S. K. Singhai and K. S. McKinley. A parameterized loop fusion algorithm for improving parallelism and cache locality. *The Computer Journal*, 40(6), 1997.

[14] Y. Song, R. Xu, C. Wang, and Z. Li. Improving data locality by array contraction. *IEEE Transactions on Computers*. To appear in vol 53 no. 8, August 2004.

[15] Y. Song, R. Xu, C. Wang, and Z. Li. Data locality enhancement by memory reduction. In *Proceedings of the 15th ACM International Conference on Supercomputing*, Naples, Italy, June 2001.

[16] M. M. Strout, L. Carter, J. Ferrante, and B. Simon. Schedule-independent storage mapping for loops. In *Architectural Support for Programming Languages and Operating Systems*, pages 24–33, 1998.

[17] W. Thies, F. Vivien, J. Sheldon, and S. P. Amarasinghe. A unified framework for schedule and storage optimization. In *SIGPLAN Conference on Programming Language Design and Implementation*, pages 232–242, 2001.

[18] M. Wolfe. *High Performance Compilers for Parallel Computing*. Addison-Wesley Publishing Company, 1995.

[19] Y. Zhong, C. Ding, and K. Kennedy. Reuse distance analysis for scientific programs. In *Proceedings of the Sixth Workshop on Languages, Compilers, and Run-time Systems for Scalar Computers*, March 2002.

# Session 2A:
# Performance Tools

# StreamGen: A Workload Generation Tool for Distributed Information Flow Applications

Mohamed Mansour, Matthew Wolf, Karsten Schwan

*College of Computing*
*Georgia Institute of Technology*
*Atlanta, GA 30332-0280*
*{mansour, mwolf, schwan}@cc.gatech.edu*

## Abstract

*This paper presents the StreamGen load generator, which is targeted at distributed information flow applications. These include the event streaming services used in wide-area publish/subscribe systems or in operational information systems, the data streaming services used in remote visualization or collaboration, and the continuous data streams occurring in download services. Running across heterogeneous distributed platforms, these services are implemented by computational component that capture, manipulate, and produce information streams and are linked via overlay topologies. StreamGen can be used to produce the distributed computational and communication loads imposed by these applications. Dynamic application behaviors can be created with mathematical specifications or with behavior traces collected from application-level traces. An interesting set of traces presented in this paper is derived from long-term observations of the FTP download patterns observed at the Linux mirror site being run by the CERCS research center at the Georgia Institute of Technology.*

*Two different flow-based applications are created and evaluated with StreamGen. The first emulates the data streaming behavior in a distributed scientific collaboration, where a scientific simulation (i.e., a molecular dynamics code) produces simulation data sent to and displayed for multiple, interactive remote users. The second emulates portions of the event-streaming behavior of an operational information system used by a large U.S. corporation. Parametric studies with StreamGen's FTP traces applied to these applications are used to evaluate different load balancing strategies for the cluster machines manipulating these applications' data streams.*

## 1. Introduction

**Motivation.** Benchmarks are a common tool for assessing the performance of distributed computational platforms and their runtime infrastructures. Evaluations may focus on systems' end-to-end performance, compare different hardware architectures or middleware implementations, or assess individual subsystems' capabilities. A classification of benchmark types for parallel systems appears in [2]. From such previous work, it is well-known that microbenchmarks or macro benchmarks like TPC-x [8] are not sufficient for providing rigorous insights into the capabilities and behaviors of distributed hardware and software infrastructures. As a result, it is common practice to test and evaluate them with actual applications [3]. A general technique used in such cases is trace-based benchmarking, which involves the creation of a parameterized model of the actual or anticipated system workload, which is then used to conduct performance evaluations of the systems under consideration.

**The StreamGen workload generator.** This paper describes a workload generator, termed StreamGen, which may be used to create a set of distributed services interacting via an application-level overlay network. StreamGen is targeted at distributed information-flow applications, which are composed of computational kernels interconnected with communication links structured as graphs, such as pipelines or data distribution trees. Each kernel performs computations on units of data received as inputs and produces outputs as units of data sent to other kernels. End results are output at leaf nodes and/or at intermediate nodes.

Two concrete instances of information flow benchmarks are the NAS Parallel Benchmark (NPB) [4] and SPEC HPC2002 [7], which address the domain of high performance applications. Both are composed of computationally intensive interconnected kernels that implement specified target applications. StreamGen can be used to create such interconnected computational structures, and its workload generation facilities can implement the parameter and configuration settings proscribed by their benchmark specifications. StreamGen has additional capabilities, however. First, in contrast to the well-defined goals of NPB, StreamGen does not prescribe the use of certain computational kernels, since that would make it difficult to create meaningful emulations of the wide range of applications for which StreamGen is intended. Second, StreamGen can emulate the dynamic departures or arrivals of benchmark participants, where each participant's behavior may change at runtime, as her interests change or as the data being manipulated changes its nature.

StreamGen addresses commercial workloads in a fashion that complements transactional benchmarks like TPC-C [8] and ECPerf [9]. TPC-C is an OLTP benchmark that specifies a complex transactional workload, including initial database seeds and the amounts of work generated at the database level. The purpose of TPC-C is to compare the performance/value offered by different hardware/software systems. ECPerf is similar, but is designed to benchmark alternative implementations of J2EE servers. Both benchmarks are well suited for OLTP applications, but neither defines or operates with the dynamic behaviors of today's distributed information-flow applications. StreamGen's role in this context is to permit users to create distributed information flows and kernels that operate on those flows, sample kernels ranging from the complex business rules applied in operational information systems [11] to the simpler event filters or fusion expressions used in wide area event system [10].

The StreamGen workload generator has multiple components. Its workload generation tool, termed StreamGen-Gen, is derived from HttPerf [1]. This tool permits end users to generate workloads in which multiple data sources can impose loads on a single sink, or where a single source can impose workloads on multiple sinks. The link topologies used are defined by end users, but the APIs exposed by StreamGen permit a linked node to act as a sink, source, or both. The middleware used to implement such links is also determined by end users. The specific infrastructure used in this paper's evaluations of StreamGen's utility is the ECho publish/subscribe middleware, which is focused on interactive high performance applications like real-time collaboration.

An important attribute of StreamGen is its ability to generate and use typed information flows, i.e., flows that are comprised of typed data units. The efficient structured binary data representations [16] used for this purpose permit diverse computational kernels to interact via a single, uniform data representation. This is important for two reasons: (1) to conveniently implement the many diverse data formats typically found in heterogeneous distributed applications, and (2) to explicitly model (and measure) the data conversion actions necessary across different application components, the latter important both in the domain of large-data applications like scientific collaboration and commercial codes like operational information systems.

**Dynamic workload behaviors.** StreamGen explicitly supports *dynamic* information flow behaviors, via a library for traffic generation and a facility for traffic replay from captured traces. The particular traces used in this paper were obtained from analyses of FTP traffic to the Georgia Tech Linux FTP mirror server. This site houses many different Linux distributions, including multiple RedHat, SuSE, Mandrake, and Debian Linux releases, with the combined repository resources supporting close to 2 TB of data. The site is updated whenever new releases appear. It is used by end users to download or update Linux sources and binaries, and it collaborates with other mirror sites to maintain consistent data across multiple mirrors (note that there are 53 major Linux mirrors in the US). The popularity of the Linux operating system makes the GT/CERCS mirror site a popular destination. The total traffic experienced by the site is substantial, averaging 2500 hits/hour and peaking at 300,000 hit/hour during periods of high activity. The total traffic traces collected over two years are almost 13GB in size. Previous work [14] presents an algorithm for reconstructing user FTP sessions from low-level ftp traces.

Apart from providing us with sample dynamic traces, two outcomes of mirror measurements relevant to this paper are that this site experiences (1) high degrees of concurrency in file retrieval and (2) substantial burstiness of retrievals, the latter correlated with the arrival of new Linux releases. Namely, this information-flow-based application experiences levels of burstiness for relatively long-lived flows (i.e., entire Linux downloads) that are similar to those seen for web sites that contain dynamic information, as with the Mars Rover data, results of sports events, etc. We hypothesize that this is also the case for scientific data repositories accessed non-programmatically (i.e., directly accessed by end users) or programmatically (by mirror sites), thereby making our work relevant to the broad domains of high performance and grid computing.

**Using StreamGen.** This paper uses StreamGen and the dynamic traffic traces measured for the Linux mirror to better understand two classes of distributed applications. The first class concerns interactive scientific collaborations in which multiple end users define and use their own views on dynamically generated, shared simulation data. The StreamGen implementation generalizes the SmartPointer collaboration system first presented in [5], where output data is streamed from a large parallel computational science code (molecular dynamics) to a series of annotation and visualization services (see Figure 3). An individual end user can dynamically change this data, by way of various service components, to customize data representation and display to fit his or her current needs. End users range from high-end clients using display facilities like Immersive Desks to clients with small screens and very limited computational (e.g., handheld devices) and communication (e.g., wireless links) abilities. Parametric studies performed with **StreamGen** evaluate different load balancing strategies when clients are associated with visualization services, using multiple visualization servers.

The second class of applications evaluated with StreamGen concerns operational information systems. The StreamGen implementation captures some of the dynamic behaviors observed in and relevant to such systems. Here, a major airline carrier uses a distributed system to capture, analyze and store different business events as well as make business decisions and disseminate such decisions to their office and airport terminals. The StreamGen setup exercises enterprise servers with two distinct traffic patterns. In one pattern, thousands of clients are connected to these servers, each with a low rate of requests per second. This emulates airport terminals, where requests are generated as fast as operators can type. In the other pattern, a few clients connect to the enterprise server, each generating a high rate of requests per second. This is typical of e-commerce web front-ends connecting to legacy back-end systems. Requests could be processed by one server, or can result in a chain of internal requests propagating through the enterprise system and generating multiple database requests.

In the remainder of this paper, Section 2 describe the architecture and implementation of StreamGen. Section 3 presents the two application codes generalized with StreamGen. Section 4 presents experimental results attained with these applications on representative hardware platforms. Conclusions and future work appear last.

## 2. Architecture and Implementation

StreamGen emulates distributed applications structured as distributed services operating on data streams. Services merge items from multiple streams, apply data transformations, personalize or annotate data items, or apply business rules to them. The links between services are described by directed acyclic graphs (DAGs). These graphs are dynamic in nature, as nodes can enter or leave the system at any time and as services can choose to change how they interact.
StreamGen can be used in two modes. First, it can be applied at the `periphery' of a system, where a client built using the StreamGen library generates or injects data streams/requests against service node(s). Request rates can be based on statistical distributions, or they can be derived from realistic workload models like the ones described in [14]. Second, and as shown in Figure 1, StreamGen can also be incorporated within individual service nodes. In this mode, StreamGen enables users to couple outgoing to incoming traffic using its Virtual Connection module (described later). Users can define arbitrarily complex conditions on incoming events.

Service code is executed when conditions are satisfied, which may in turn generate outgoing messages.

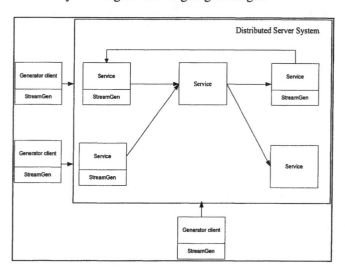

**Figure 1 StreamGen in a Distributed System.**

## 2.1. The StreamGen Library

The StreamGen library available for download from our website has the following components: (1) a C library with APIs for workload generation and monitoring, and (2) traces for generating realistic dynamic workloads [14]. The library consists of several modules. The *Scheduler* module is a one-shot timer API. Using the scheduler requires users to incorporate the timer_tick() call in the program's main loop. The *Transport* module provides objects to abstract basic transport concepts such as connections, sessions, and calls. This module also defines a set of basic events that correspond to different transport activities. For example, EV_CONN_CONNECTED is an event that, when fired, indicates that a new connection has been established. Similar events exist for connection closing, failure, message receipt, message transmission, etc. The Transport module implements HTTP, but other transports are added easily. To demonstrate how the different modules can be used, a user can log every outgoing call by simply registering a log_outgoing_call() function to execute whenever an EV_CALL_SEND_STOP event is fired. The *Statistics* module implements data collection and analysis functions. The *Generator* module contains pre-packaged APIs for generating workloads based on statistical distributions, but it is straightforward to program additional generators. Finally, the *Virtual Connection* module provides an implementation of a virtual connection. A virtual connection is built from one or more basic transport connections. Virtual connections can be set up to raise a

Virtual Event when an arbitrary combination of events occurs on the underlying transport connections. A Virtual Connection is an abstraction that monitors N input channels. The user can programmatically define a Virtual Event for this virtual connection that is fired (published) when the associated monitor condition evaluates to TRUE. This enables us to specify and control the information flow not just on the periphery on the system, but at any computational node. For example, we can create a virtual connection that is composed of input channels 1 and 2 (see Figure 2) and define a virtual event to be fired when three input messages have accumulated on input channel 1 and two on the input channel 2. A handler can be registered for this virtual event, which generates an output event on an output when the virtual event is fired.

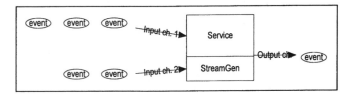

**Figure 2: A Virtual Connection Example.**

## 2.2. Library Implementation

The StreamGen library is derived from HttPerf [1], a tool for measuring web server performance. APIs have been added to the HttPerf code for generating workloads derived from FTP traces (explained below), in addition to the Virtual Connection module. HttPerf uses HTTP as the default transport protocol; to use a different transport protocol, new protocol bindings have to be created. This simply means generating (publishing) the appropriate events on the respective protocol events.

Table 1 lists the new APIs for Virtual Connections. Our current implementation limits monitor conditions to simple event counters. In the future, we will add native support for the ECho publish/subscribe event delivery system as the main transport and also extend monitor condition to take advantage of PBIO (ECho's data representation library). With these extensions in place, we will be able to build complex monitor conditions and virtual event handlers that can apply application-specific transformations, personalize and annotate event data, or apply business rules to information streams.

The experiments presented in this paper use ECho as the underlying communication mechanism. In these cases, StreamGen is simply used to inject trace-based workloads into the systems being evaluated. Since we do not use virtual connections or their APIs, StreamGen can be used

with a Transport Module into which ECho has not yet been integrated.

**Table 1: Virtual Connection APIs.**

| API | Description |
| --- | --- |
| typedef struct VCMonitorCondition { Conn* _connection; Event_Type _ev_type; int _num_events; } VCMonitorCondition; | Typedef for one element of the monitor condition |
| VCKey* add_virtual_connection(char* expression, VCMonitorCondition *list, int n) | Define a new virtual connection based on data in *list, which* has *n* entries. *expression* is a Boolean expression that we use to combine the conditions in *list* |
| Void remove_virtual_connection(VCKey* vc) | Cancel a previously defined connection |

The following programming actions are required when using StreamGen as a standalone workload generator. A *main()* function generates traffic patterns based on the supplied traces [14], by calling the *ftplog_parse()* API. This API schedules a user-specified callback to be executed for each selected trace, and such traces can be scaled via additional specified arguments. Arguments may be passed programmatically or from command lines. StreamGen also supports statistical workloads (e.g. random, uniform, etc.), by simply using one of the generators supplied with HttPerf. In these generators, each user callback generates some amount of traffic and then schedules its next execution time based on some statistical distribution.

## 3. Overview of Sample Applications

This section briefly describes the two classes of applications emulated with StreamGen. The first class is real-time scientific collaboration, represented by generalizing the `SmartPointer' application framework. The second class emulates a server subsystem of an operational information system, termed REDE, derived from the server clusters used by an airline with which we are familiar.

### 3.1. SmartPointer

SmartPointer is a framework for scientific collaboration first presented in [5]. Output data is streamed from a large parallel computational science code (molecular dynamics -MD) to a series of annotation and visualization services (see Figure 3). Two facts determine the application's operation. First, current end user needs determine the way in which services are applied to the data produced by the MD code. Second, the resources available to stream data and apply services are subject to dynamic variation. The purpose of using StreamGen, then, is to exercise the framework with different user behaviors, modeled via different request traces, services applied to request traces, and topologies linking such services. Different resource availabilities correspond to different configurations of the underlying hardware testbed.

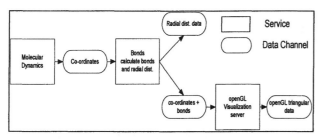

Figure 3: The SmartPointer System.

## 3.2. Replicated EDE (REDE)

The Replicated Enterprise Data Engine (REDE) system shown in Figure 4 was first described in [13]. The primary server applies business logic to an incoming stream of FAA data events and produces business data events. The system must operate within strict limits on output delays. In addition to FAA data processing, the server also maintains internal state, where new clients connecting to the system request a copy of this state. Since the internal state can be substantial, a large number of initial state requests can impact the server-based delay experienced by other clients. A new mirroring technique addressing this problem is evaluated in Gavrilovska et al. for different levels of constant rates of initial state requests. This paper refines these results, by studying the performance of the REDE cluster under more realistic workloads of initial state requests, generated with StreamGen's dynamic traffic traces. The hope is to gain insights about system performance under transient loads.

## 4. Using StreamGen for Performance Studies

### 4.1. Parametric Studies: EDE Enterprise System

To demonstrate the utility of the StreamGen generator, we first turn to the EDE enterprise system. The system's use in previous research [12][13] provides a reasonable initial testing configuration. As in that paper, we study the performance under loads imposed by additional initial state requests. The flexible infrastructure provided by StreamGen, however, permits us to use more realistic transients for the failures and arrivals of external clients. This results in two different experiments, highlighting the ease with which StreamGen can be reconfigured to test applications that stream information under different data assumptions. The desired rate for the "main" output data event is as in our previous work, but we utilize data access patterns for the full initial state requests that are based on the Linux ftp traces provided with StreamGen.

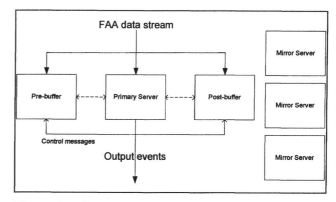

Figure 4: REDE Cluster.

A key parameter in evaluating the ability of a server to efficiently handle imposed load is the ratio of the sizes of the two event types: basic update events and the large, initial state events. The first experiment utilizing the StreamGen implementation for the EDE system uses a basic update event size of 500KB and a large initial state request size of 10MB. The particular traffic pattern chosen for the initial state perturbation is based on the access pattern of the RedHat 7.1 ISO image from the StreamGen library. Figure 5 shows the histogram of this arrival frequency, scaled to an appropriate size. The resulting delay in delivery of the main output data to those clients is shown in Figure 6.

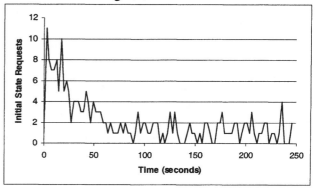

Figure 5 Histogram of Initial State Requests (bin size = 10 seconds)

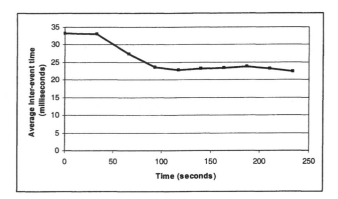

**Figure 6 Average Inter-event Delay – each data point averaged over 1000 events.**

The experiment was then reconfigured for a run where the main output data size is 500B and the initial state data event is 1MB in size. The hardware is changed to a Sun UltraSparc II platform with a Fast Ethernet (100Mb) interconnect, rather than a Pentium III platform with gigabit Ethernet of the first case. Due to this network bandwidth limitation, the server is able to send 12 initial state events per second. Figure 7 shows the distribution of initial state requests. The resulting delay in delivery of output data to those clients is shown in Figure 8.

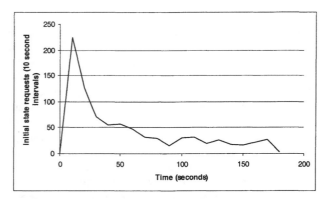

**Figure 7 Histogram of Initial State Requests (bin size = 10 sec)**

The ease of reconfiguration for these experiments is one advantage of using the StreamGen system: it is straightforward to change client access pattern, including duration, size, and time of processing of each data field (not all of which were fully explored in this example). This improves the experimenter's ability to explore the potential state space. In these experiments, for example, a qualitative difference exists between the reactions of the same server system to the two different access message size regimes. This can have profound impacts on the design and implementation of a distributed business information service. Another interesting insight from these experiments is derived from comparing them to our

previous results reported in [13]. Specifically, we can see that the initial spike in state requests causes clients of data events to experience increased delays of up to 62%, and that this effect lasts well beyond the duration of the spike. Furthermore, the perturbation measured in this paper's experiments is significantly less severe than the one reported in [13] when a less realistic, constant full state request rate was used.

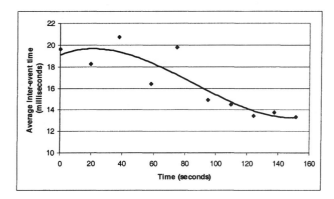

**Figure 8 Average Inter-event Delay – each data point averaged over 1000 events.**

## 4.2. Parametric Studies: Scientific Collaboration

A second demonstration of the capabilities of StreamGen uses the SmartPointer [5] distributed visualization and steering system for computational molecular modeling applications. It has a series of component services that annotate, personalize, and transform the scientific data flow. As described above, the system is based on a publish-subscribe semantic to allow transparent data access.

A limitation of the original implementation of SmartPointer is a lack of scalability in the graphics-rendering pipeline. In response, this experiment extends the basic SmartPointer architecture with a cluster of visualization servers and a simple load balancing algorithm to direct new connections to the appropriate server. Using StreamGen we utilize the client request modules to study the resulting system's scalability. The actual software architecture appears in Figure 9. The load-balancing algorithm samples queue lengths and delays at each server. It reacts to server overload by directing new client requests to the channel of the least loaded server. Existing requests are not migrated; they are serviced by the primary server until canceled.

Of particular interest is the following usage scenario: SmartPointer should scale to support wide-area collaborations across multiple researchers. Given the very long-running nature of many computational codes, we expect to see periodic bursts in interest in their output (i.e., visualization) data. For example, we should see a peak early in the morning as scientists check on the night's results, then similar peaks after lunch and right before leaving for the night. Some scientists will find interesting output results and continue observing and annotating data for long periods of time, while others will wait until sufficient data has accumulated for their needs before viewing it again.

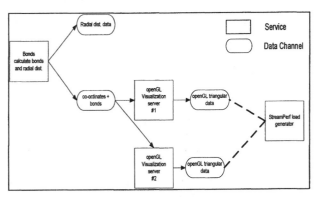

**Figure 9 Load Balancing Algorithm Setup**

To create a reasonable emulation of such a usage scenario, we utilize an observed traffic pattern from the StreamGen trace library, selecting a trace based on the RedHat 7.3 release data. For this trace, each rpm data download session is mapped to the behavior of some collaborator, and in the StreamGen extension of SmartPointer, it results in the creation of a new channel with a bounded-area specialization filter that represents the client's interests. Filter code represents each participant's choices of personalization and annotation and also associates some computational overhead with each additional stream. Further, each new channel lasts for N number of events, where N is the number of files in the FTP download session. This is analogous to some users watching for short periods of time and others watching for extended periods of time.

From these experiments, it is clear that to handle surges in demand; the openGL servers must be replicated. The question we aim to answer is how many replicates are needed for a certain load.

The experiments conducted use a cluster of seventeen 8-way Pentium III Xeon servers at the Georgia Tech IHPC laboratory. Each of the distributed service processes runs on a separate machine, as well as the client code generator. Figure 10 shows the total number of concurrent connections against the clustered visualization service as a function of time. This reflects both the number of new connections being initiated and the persistence of long-running connections.

As apparent in Figure 11, adaptive load balancing is clearly insufficient in the one- and two-server

implementations, but the three-server implementation has sufficient 'cycles' to prevent the queue overruns that make the previous two cases untenable. However, note that under the heaviest load, the delay is still considerably larger than desired by the soft real-time constraints the SmartPointer system tries to attain in the single, constant-rate client case.

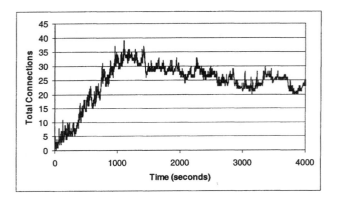

**Figure 10 Connections vs.. Visualization Server(s)**

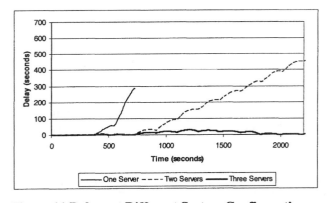

**Figure 11 Delays at Different System Configurations**

## 5. Conclusions

This paper describes a workload generation tool, termed StreamGen, for distributed information flow applications. The tool has three major components: a workload generation library derived from the HttPerf tool, support for structured data event types, and traces derived from traffic analyses at the Georgia Tech Linux mirror site. When applying StreamGen to two applications, one from the high-performance scientific domain and the other is an enterprise-scale application, some interesting insights are attained, particularly addressing the behavior of these applications under bursty load conditions. We also show that these insights are more realistic than those derived in earlier work that did not benefit from StreamGen's dynamic traffic traces.

While our current implementation of the Virtual Connection module still relies on the HTTP transport code provided in the HttPerf tool, StreamGen is easily generalized to other transport methods. This will be demonstrated in our future work by integrating it with our own ECho publish/subscribe communication library and by applying it to the data exchange middleware used by some of our industry partners. In addition, we intend to generalize the condition matching facilities in the current implementation of StreamGen to support arbitrary data transformations, annotations, and stream merging actions, similar to those offered by the Gryphon system [10].

# 6. References

[1] D. Mosberger and T. Jin, "httperf: A tool for measuring web server performance", WISP, ACM, Madison, WI, June 1998, pp. 59-67

[2] H. Pfneiszl and G. Kotsis, "Benchmarking Parallel Processing Systems - A Survey", Institute of Applied Computer Science and Information Systems, University of Vienna, Technical Report No. TR-96103

[3] M. Seltzer, et. al., "The Case for Application-Specific Benchmarking", In Proceedings of the 1999 Workshop on Hot Topics in Operating Systems

[4] M. Frumkin and R. F. Van der Wijngaart, "NAS Grid Benchmarks: a tool for Grid space exploration", in Proc. 10th Intl. Symp. on High Performance Distributed Computing, August, 2001, pp. 7-9

[5] M. Wolf, Z. Cai, W. Huang and K. Schwan, "SmartPointers: personalized scientific data portals in your hand." In Proc. of the 2002 ACM/IEEE conference on Supercomputing, Baltimore, Maryland, 2002

[6] G. Eisenhauer, F. Bustamente and K. Schwan, "Event Services for High Performance Computing," In Proc. of High Performance Distributed Computing (HPDC-2000), August 1-4, 2000

[7] Standard Performance Evaluation Corporation, "SPEC HPC2002 V1.0" [online], [cited November 2003], available from World Wide Web: <www.spec.org/hpc2002/>

[8] Transaction Processing Performance Council, "TPC V5" [online], [cited November 2003], available from World Wide Web: <http://www.tpc.org/tpcc/>

[9] Sun Microsystems, "ECPerf" [online], [cited November 2003], available from World Wide Web: <http://java.sun.com/j2ee/ecperf/>

[10] R. Strom, et.al.,. "Gryphon: An information flow based approach to message brokering." In International Symposium on Software Reliability Engineering, 1998

[11] V. Oleson, et. al., "Operational information systems - an example from the airline industry." In First Workshop on Industrial Experiences with Systems Software (WIESS)

[12] A. Gavrilovska, K. Schwan and V. Oleson, "Adaptable Mirroring in Cluster Servers", In Proc. of the 10th IEEE Intl. Symp. on High Performance Distributed Computing (HPDC-10'01), August 2001

[13] A. Gavrilovska, K. Schwan and V. Oleson, "A Practical Approach for Zero' Downtime in an Operational Information System", In Proc. of the 22nd Intl. Conf. on Distributed Computing Systems (ICDCS'02), July 2002

[14] M. Mansour, M. Wolf and K. Schwan, "Dynamic Traffic Behaviors - The GT Mirror Trace," High Performance Grid Computing workshop of IPDPS '04

[15] A. Snavely et. al., "Benchmarks for grid computing: a review of ongoing efforts and future directions", ACM SIGMETRICS Performance Evaluation Review, vol. 30 , no. 4, March 2003

[16] F. Bustamante, G. Eisenhauer, K. Schwan, and P. Widener, "Efficient Wire Formats for High Performance Computing," in Proc. of Supercomputing 2000 (SC 2000), Dallas, Texas, November 4-10, 2000

# An Algebra for Cross-Experiment Performance Analysis*

Fengguang Song, Felix Wolf, Nikhil Bhatia, Jack Dongarra, and Shirley Moore

University of Tennessee, ICL
1122 Volunteer Blvd Suite 413
Knoxville, TN 37996-3450, USA
{song, fwolf, bhatia, dongarra, shirley}@cs.utk.edu

## Abstract

*Performance tuning of parallel applications usually involves multiple experiments to compare the effects of different optimization strategies. This article describes an algebra that can be used to compare, integrate, and summarize performance data from multiple sources. The algebra consists of a data model to represent the data in a platform-independent fashion plus arithmetic operations to merge, subtract, and average the data from different experiments. A distinctive feature of this approach is its closure property, which allows processing and viewing all instances of the data model in the same way - regardless of whether they represent original or derived data - in addition to an arbitrary and easy composition of operations.*

**Keywords:** performance tool, multiexperiment analysis, tool interoperability, performance algebra, visualization

## 1  Introduction

Performance optimization of parallel applications usually involves multiple experiments to compare the effects of different code versions, different execution configurations, or different input data. For example, the experiments may reflect different algorithms, different domain decompositions, or different problem sizes. In addition, hardware characteristics may limit the availability of certain performance data, such as performance counters, in a single run, requiring multiple experiments to obtain a full set of data. Other than that, a user may wish to combine the results obtained using different monitoring tools that cannot be applied simultaneously. Also, the influence of system noise often creates a need to run the same experiment more than

once in order to smooth the effect of random errors. Finally, data coming from analytical models or simulations constitute another class of data that need to be compared to those already mentioned.

The traditional practice of comparing different experiments is to put multiple single-experiment views side by side or to plot overlay diagrams, which is limited in its ability to draw a differentiated picture of performance changes because the hierarchical structures of the performance space, as they exist between performance metrics or program and system entities are typically ignored. A comprehensive and generic approach to extract important cross-experiment information along resource hierarchies is the framework for multi-execution performance tuning by Karavanic and Miller [11], which includes an operator to calculate a list of resources showing a significant discrepancy between different experiments. However, this difference operator maps from its input space containing entire experiments into a smaller representation (i.e., a list of resources). A repeated application is not possible, further processing would require a logic or a display different from one suitable for the original input data.

The key idea of our approach is that the output of cross-experiment analysis can be represented just like its input, which allows us to use the same set of tools to process and, in particular, display it. This article describes an algebra named CUBE (CUBE Uniform Behavioral Encoding) that can be used to compare, integrate, and summarize performance data of message-passing and/or multithreaded applications from multiple experiments including results obtained from simulations and analytical modeling. CUBE instantiates and extends the aforementioned framework by Karavanic and Miller and consists of a data model to represent the data in a platform-independent fashion plus arithmetic operations to subtract, merge, or average the data from multiple experiments. Our main contribution is that all operations are closed in that their results are mapped into the same space, yielding an entire "derived" experiment including data and

---

*This work was supported by the U.S. Department of Energy under Grants DoE DE-FG02-01ER25510 and DoE DE-FC02-01ER25490 and is embedded in the European IST working group APART under Contract No. IST-2000-28077

metadata. As an important consequence of the closure property, we have been able to build an interactive viewer that allows convenient browsing through all elements of this space - regardless of whether they represent original experiments or derived experiments obtained by applying operations to original data. In addition, we can easily define composite operations, for example, in order to compute the difference of averaged data.

The article is organized as follows: In Section 2, we discuss the CUBE data model, followed by a description of the algebraic operations that can be performed on its instances in Section 3. After introducing the CUBE display component in Section 4, we demonstrate our method's usefulness using two practical examples in Section 5. Finally, we consider related work in Section 6 and present our conclusion plus future work in Section 7.

## 2   Data Model

Most performance data sets representing experiments, models, or simulations have a similar structure in that they are essentially mappings of program and system entities, such as functions and processes, onto a domain defined by one or more performance metrics, such as time and floating-point operations. The purpose of the CUBE data model was to give those commonalities a formal frame suitable for the definition of complex arithmetic operations.

The CUBE *data model* describes entity types to which performance data can refer, relationships between entities, and constraints that must be satisfied by a valid model instance. It consists of three different dimensions: a metric dimension, a program dimension, and a system dimension. Motivated by the need to represent performance behavior on different levels of granularity as well as to express natural hierarchical relationships among program and system resources, each dimension is organized in a hierarchy. A severity function determines how the different entities are mapped onto the actual metric values.

The metric dimension is represented as a forest consisting of multiple trees. Each metric has a name and a unit of measurement, which can either be seconds, bytes, or number of event occurrences. Within each tree, all metrics must have the same unit of measurement. To qualify for parentship of another metric, a metric must include the child metric. For example, execution time includes communication time and cache accesses include cache misses. Making a tool aware of this inclusion relationship by arranging metrics in a tree has the advantage that exclusive metrics can be computed automatically, for example, cache hits can be computed by subtracting misses from accesses.

The program dimension describes the static and dynamic program structure. Entities that can be defined include modules, regions, call sites, and call-tree nodes (i.e., call paths).

A region is a general code section representing a function, a loop, or another type of basic block. Regions must be properly nested. Although a call site is called as such, it is more general and denotes a source-code location where the control flow may move from one region into another region. For example, a loop entry point is a call site according to our definition. The region that can be reached by executing the call site is called its callee. The set of all call-tree nodes may form a forest with multiple root nodes, but in most cases there will be a single root node representing the invocation of the main function. A parallel program with different executables, however, may need more than one root. Every call-tree node points to the call site from where the node was entered. Note that there may be multiple nodes pointing to the same call site. Recursive programs, whose call structure is a possibly cyclic graph and not a tree, must be mapped onto a tree, for example, by collapsing loops in the graph into a single leaf node.

The system dimension defines hard- and software entities of the system on which the program is executed. It is a forest consisting of the levels machine, node, process, and thread from top to bottom. A machine is a collection of nodes and can be a cluster or a massively parallel processor, such as the CRAY T3E. A node may host multiple processes, which can be split up into multiple threads. To simplify the merging of system hierarchies, the model more or less disregards the physical characteristics of machines and nodes and considers them mainly as a logical grouping of processes for the purpose of aggregating performance data. Nested thread-level parallelism is currently not supported. Since the thread level is mandatory, pure message-passing applications are represented as a collection of single-threaded processes.

**Experiments.**   A valid instance of this data model is called a CUBE *experiment* and consists of two parts: metadata and data. The metadata part defines a set of metrics plus sets of program and system resources, as prescribed by the data model. As the data model allows a hierarchical arrangement of the different dimensions, ordering relations between their elements are included as well. The data part includes a *severity* function that maps tuples (metric $m$, call path $c$, thread $t$) onto the accumulated value of the metric $m$ measured while the thread $t$ was executing in call path $c$.

The severity function requires that data are mapped onto the call tree. Many performance tools, however, generate data referring to regions instead of call paths, that is, they generate flat profiles. This is not really a restriction, since every flat profile can be represented using multiple trivial call trees (one for each region) consisting only of a single node. Also, the severity of a certain tuple may be negative if it represents a difference between two experiments.

**Data Format.** CUBE experiments can be stored in the CUBE XML format. The format is specified using the XMLSchema language. A file representing a CUBE experiment consists of two parts: the metadata and the severity function values. The severity values are stored as a three-dimensional array with one dimension for the metric, one for the call path, and one for the thread. We have implemented a C++ API to read experiments from a file and to create experiments and write them to a file. The API is a simple class interface with fewer than fifteen methods.

## 3 Operations

In addition to reading and writing experiments, we allow experiments to be transformed by applying certain operators. The domain of all operators is the set of valid CUBE experiments. The range is always a subset of the domain so that the domain is never left. That is, the output of an operator can always be used as input for another operator, enabling the simple specification of complex operations by creating composite operators. To distinguish original data that has been collected during a real experiment from data that is the result of an operator we call the latter experiment a *derived* experiment as opposed to an *original* experiment.

**Operators.** We have defined three algebraic operators that we deem most useful for performance analysis. Others may follow in the future.

- Difference
- Merge
- Mean

The mean operator takes an arbitrary number of arguments, whereas the difference and merge operator are binary operators. However, since their range is a subset of the domain, a user can construct composite operators involving far more than two operands.

The difference operator takes two experiments and computes a derived experiment whose severity function reflects the difference between the minuend's severity and the subtrahend's severity. This feature is useful to compare the effects of code or parameter changes along the different dimensions of the data model.

The merge operator's purpose is the integration of performance data from different sources. Often a certain combination of performance metrics cannot be measured during a single run. For example, certain combinations of hardware events cannot be counted simultaneously due to hardware resource limits. Or the combination of performance metrics requires using different monitoring tools that cannot be deployed during the same run. The merge operator

takes two CUBE experiments with a different or overlapping set of metrics and yields a derived CUBE experiment with a joint set of metrics.

On parallel systems, unrelated system activities often perturb performance experiments in a way that lets results vary across multiple executions. For example, the execution time of a program can be different for separate runs even if all user-controlled execution parameters remain stable. Also, a user might want to combine several execution parameters in an overall picture in order to make a single statement about the performance for a range of execution parameters. The mean operator is intended to smooth the effects of random errors introduced by unrelated system activity during an experiment or to summarize across a range of execution parameters. To summarize in this manner, the user can conduct several experiments and create one derived experiment from the whole series.

**Implementation.** The actions performed by the operators can be divided into two subtasks: metadata integration followed by the actual arithmetic operation. It is obvious that if the metadata of the two operands are equal (i.e., if the structure of the metric, the program, and the system dimension is the same) the operation is reduced to a simple arithmetic operation on corresponding elements of the three-dimensional severity arrays. In the case of the difference operator this corresponds to an element-wise subtraction and in the case of the mean operator to an element-wise mean operation. As the merge operator is intended to join experiments involving different metrics, there is no simple case for this one.

However, the general case we have to deal with is two experiments with different metadata. In most cases the operators make sense only if there is at least some similarity between them. For example, computing the mean of experiments that test entirely different programs is generally not helpful. On the contrary, the difference between program runs with slightly different call trees can help in comparing the performance of alternative program versions. The next subsection deals with the task of integrating two different metadata sets.

**Metadata Integration.** Before executing the actual arithmetic operation when applying an operator to multiple experiments, we first need to integrate their metadata sets. The integration of one or more metadata sets consists of three separate parts: merging the metric dimension, the program dimension, and the system dimension. Merging metric trees and call trees can be more or less reduced to the task of merging arbitrary trees. Except for a different equality relation to compare the nodes in a tree, the procedure is very similar. To do this, we use the multi-execution framework's [11] structural merge operator. While traversing from the roots to the leaves, we try to match up the nodes from the two metadata sets using the equality relation. The equality relation is based on node attributes, such as name and unit of measurement for a metric or the callee for a node in the call tree. Nodes that cannot be matched are separately included in the new metadata set, whereas nodes that can be successfully matched become shared nodes, that is, they appear as a single node in the new metadata. The matching occurs in a top-down fashion with the consequence that once two nodes are considered different, the entire subtrees rooted at these nodes will both become part of the new metadata set even if they contain matching child nodes. When matching nodes in a call tree we have to take into account that certain call site attributes, such as line numbers, can change across different code versions but still refer to the "same" call site, a problem we have not addressed yet and which requires further consideration.

Integrating the system dimension is slightly different. Here, we have four levels with different meanings: machine, node, process, and thread. First, processes and threads are matched based on their application-level identifiers, for example, their global MPI rank and OpenMP thread number. The upper levels of the system hierarchy are not matched. Instead, CUBE either copies the entire node and machine hierarchy including the corresponding process-node mapping of one of the operand experiments into the result experiment or it collapses the hierarchy to a single machine and a single node. If not specified otherwise, the latter option is the default if the partitioning of processes into nodes is not compatible among the operands.

The focus of CUBE is to provide automatic merging mechanisms that follow simple rules and create predictable results without requiring manual intervention. As the default behavior might not satisfy the user in all possible situation, switches have been included to change the default according to a user's needs.

**Arithmetic Operation.** After the metadata have been integrated, a new severity function is computed whose domain is defined by the integrated metadata. This happens by an element-wise operation on the two input arrays. To be able to perform an element-wise operation, the operand's severity function needs to be extended with respect to the integrated metadata so that it is defined for every tuple (metric, call path, thread) of the new metadata. This is done by assigning zero to previously undefined tuples. For example, a call path occurring in one metadata set might not occur in another. If this happens the resulting value for this call path will be set to zero in those experiments that didn't contain the call path before.

In the case of the difference or the mean operators, the element-wise operation is just a subtraction or mean operation, respectively. In the case of the merge operator we make a simple case distinction. Recall that the purpose of the merge operator was to integrate performance experiments with different metrics. For example, one experiment counts floating point operations, and another one counts cache misses, since we might not be able to count both of them simultaneously. So, if the metric is provided only by one experiment we take the data from that experiment. If it is provided by both experiments we take it from the first one without loss of generality.

Note that all operators return a complete (albeit derived) CUBE experiment consisting of an integrated metadata set and a severity function with the integrated metadata as its domain.

## 4 Display Component

A natural application of the CUBE performance algebra is visual presentation. The closure property allows us to treat derived experiments just like original ones. For this purpose, we have implemented the CUBE display, a generic viewer that provides the ability to interactively browse through the multidimensional performance space defined by any valid CUBE experiment, whether it is derived or original.

As acceptance of performance tools among program developers is often limited by their complexity [14], our design emphasizes simplicity by combining a small number of orthogonal features with a limited set of user actions. Similar to Paradyn, CUBE displays the different dimensions of the performance space consistently using tree browsers (Figure 1). More than that, CUBE allows the user to interactively explore the severity mapping of metric/resource combinations onto the corresponding values. Since the space of all such combinations is large, CUBE provides the ability to select a view representing only a subset of the mapping plus flexible aggregation mechanisms to control the level of detail. In addition, the GUI includes a source-code display that shows the exact position of a performance problem in the source code. The CUBE display is implemented in C++ using the wxWidgets GUI toolkit and libxml2 to parse the CUBE XML format. Currently, CUBE supports most UNIX platforms and a Windows version is in preparation.

**Basic Principles.** The CUBE display consists of three tree browsers, representing the metric, the program, and the system dimension from left to right (Figure 1). The user can switch between a call tree or a flat-profile view of the program dimension. The call-tree view, as shown in the figure, is the default. The nodes in the metric tree represent performance metrics, the nodes in the call tree represent call paths, and the nodes in the system tree represent machines, nodes, processes, and threads from top to bottom. The thread level of single-threaded applications is hidden.

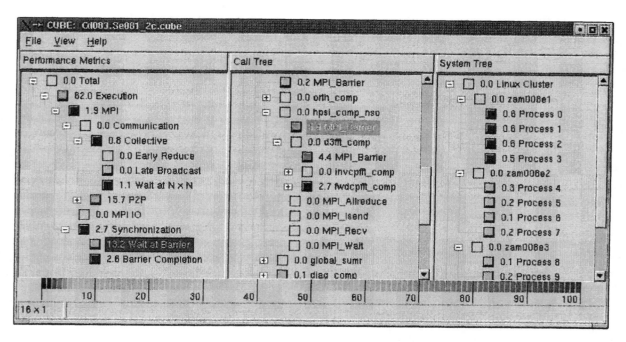

**Figure 1. The CUBE display showing the metric tree, the call tree, and the system tree from left to right. The selected node in the metric tree indicates large waiting times in front of MPI barriers.**

A user can perform two types of actions: selecting a node or expanding/collapsing a node. At any time, there are two nodes selected, one in the metric tree and another one in the call tree. Currently, it is not possible to select a node in the system tree. Each node is labeled with a severity value (i.e., a metric value). A value shown in the metric tree represents the sum of a particular metric for the entire program, that is, across all call paths and the entire system. A value shown in the call tree represents the sum of the selected metric across the entire system for a particular call path. A value shown in the system tree represents the selected metric for the selected call path and a particular system entity. All numbers can be displayed either as absolute values or as percentages of a maximum value. Percentages can be normalized with respect to other experiments to simplify the comparison. To help identify metric/resources combinations with a high severity more quickly, all values are ranked using colors. While the color indicates the severity's absolute value, its sign is indicated by giving the square a relief: a raised relief for positive values and a sunken relief for negative values. Depending on the severity representation, a color legend shows a numeric scale mapping colors onto values.

Note that all hierarchies in CUBE are inclusion hierarchies, meaning that a child node represents a subset of the parent node. For instance, in Figure 1 Wait-at-Barrier, which denotes the waiting time in front of barriers, is a subset of Synchronization. The severity displayed in CUBE follows the principle of *single representation*, that is, within a

tree each fraction of the severity is displayed only once. The purpose of this display strategy is to have a particular performance problem to appear only once in the tree and, thus, help identify it more quickly. In Figure 1, the value at Synchronization refers only to those synchronization times that are not covered by descendant nodes, that is, those that are neither waiting times in front or completion times after the barrier. After collapsing the Synchronization node, the label would show the entire time spent in MPI barriers. Thus, the display provides two aggregation mechanisms: aggregation across dimensions by selecting a node, and aggregation within a dimension by collapsing a node.

The emphasis of CUBE was not the invention of a new display in a technical sense. After all, the use of tree browsers is not revolutionary and even the coloring of nodes in the tree to symbolize a numeric value has been previously applied, for example, in the xlcb [15] corefile browser. However, CUBE demonstrates that the simplicity of the data model can be transferred into an interactive display with flexible view-selection capabilities by restricting the design to a very small number of orthogonal mechanisms.

## 5 Examples

This section demonstrates the advantages of our approach using two realistic examples. We illustrate how to conduct a before-after comparison by browsing through the difference of two experiments in the same way a user would browse through original data. We also show how CUBE can create a very comprehensive picture of performance behavior by combining data sets with different performance metrics recorded by different tools and using different modes of the same tool into one highly-integrated view.

CUBE is currently used by two performance tools: CONE [21] and EXPERT [22, 23]. As CUBE provides a generic API, every tool producing performance data matching the very general CUBE data model can take advantage of the CUBE algebra and display.

**CONE.** CONE is a call-graph profiler for MPI applications on IBM AIX Power4 platforms which maps hardware-counter data onto the full call graph including line numbers. CONE is based on a run-time call-graph tracking technique [7] developed at IBM. CONE automatically traverses and instruments the executable in binary form using DPCL [6] and causes the target application to make calls to a probe module responsible for performance monitoring. The performance data collected include wall-clock time as well as different hardware counters accessible via the PAPI library [4]. CONE supports several event sets that can be selected for measurement. Each of them forms a hierarchy of more general and more specific events, such as cache accesses and cache misses or instructions and floating-point instructions, respectively.

**EXPERT.** EXPERT is a post-mortem performance analysis tool for automatic analysis of MPI and/or OpenMP traces. Time-stamped events, such as entering a function or sending a message, are recorded as the target application runs and are later written to a trace file in the EPILOG format. After program termination, the trace is searched for execution patterns that indicate inefficient behavior. The performance problems addressed include inefficient use of the parallel programming model and low CPU and memory performance. EXPERT transforms event traces into a compact representation of performance behavior, which is essentially a mapping of tuples (performance problem, call path, location) onto the time spent on a particular performance problem while the program was executing in a particular call path at a particular location. Depending on the programming model, a location can be either a process or a thread. The performance problems are organized in a specialization hierarchy that contains general problems, such as large communication overhead, and very specific problems, such as a receiver waiting for a message as a result of an inefficient acceptance order. After the analysis has been finished, the mapping is stored in the CUBE format.

## 5.1 Subtracting Performance Data

Changing a program can alter its performance behavior. Altering the performance behavior means that different results are achieved for different metrics. Some might increase while others might decrease. Some might rise in certain parts of the program only, while they drop off in other parts. Finding the reason for a gain or loss in overall performance often requires considering the performance change as a multidimensional structure. With CUBE's difference operator, a user can view this structure by computing the difference between two experiments and rendering the derived result experiment like an original one.

As an example, we show how the CUBE difference operator can help track the effects of an optimization applied to PESCAN [5], a nano-structure simulation computing interior eigenvalues nearest to a given point of a (large) Hermitian matrix. The core of the application consists of an iterative eigensolver based on the preconditioned conjugate gradient method applied to the folded spectrum. The type of computation performed is a matrix-vector products done via FFT.

We conducted the experiments on a Intel Pentium III Xeon 550 MHz cluster with eight 4-way SMP nodes connected through Myrinet. We ran the application with 16 processes on four of the nodes to compute a medium-sized particle model. Figure 1 shows the CUBE display with a data set obtained from the unoptimized code version. The numbers reflect percentages of the overall execution time. The selected metric in the left tree represents a major performance problem: A large fraction of the execution time is spent waiting in front of barriers (13.2 %).

Wait-at-Barrier denotes the time a process waits inside the barrier function for another process to reach it as opposed to the time spent in the barrier function after the first process has left it (i.e., Barrier-Completion) or to collectively execute it (i.e., everything in between). Note that the distinction between these aspects of barrier synchronization requires measuring temporal displacements within individual barrier instances as they are recorded in trace files. Since Wait-at-Barrier is selected, the call tree shows the locations of barriers with excessive waiting times highlighted by colors.

The barriers have originally been introduced to avoid buffer overflow related to the asynchronous point-to-point communication when computing with large processor counts on an IBM platform. However, since they are not needed on a Linux cluster with smaller processor counts, such as those used in this experiment, we were able to speed up the application by removing them.

Waiting time at a barrier is caused by reaching the barrier at different points in time, for example as a result of load or communication imbalance or other delays. Some of the factors introducing temporal displacements are antipo-

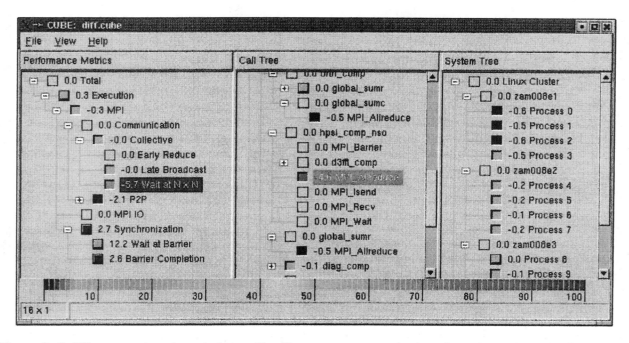

**Figure 2. A difference experiment shows the disappearance and migration of waiting times for application PESCAN.**

dal and cancel each other out if they are not materialized at a barrier or another synchronizing event. If they are materialized, the time that a process reaches the barrier earlier is turned into waiting time, which is effectively lost because after the synchronizing event the processes have caught up with each other. Worse than that, the contrary displacement might be materialized as well instead of neutralizing the previous one. So removing the barriers can save the actual barrier overhead needed to perform the synchronization as well as allow contrary displacements to cancel each other out. Those delays or imbalances that do not have an antipodal counterpart are usually materialized at the next synchronization point following the removed barrier, which can be a message exchange or a collective operation.

Figure 2 shows a difference experiment obtained by subtracting the optimized version from the original one. Performance gains are represented by raised reliefs, performance losses by sunken reliefs. The numbers are normalized with respect to the old version and show improvements in percent of the previous execution time. Whereas nearly all the negative performance effects of barrier synchronization have been eliminated including waiting time, barrier execution, and barrier completion, point-to-point communication (i.e., P2P) and inherent synchronization of collective all-to-all operations (i.e., Wait-at-NxN) have been increased, presumably as a result of waiting-time migration.

However, the gross performance balance is clearly positive. We measured the performance gain for the central

solver routine only without any trace instrumentation. We created two series of ten experiments for either configuration and took the minimum of each series as a representative. The speedup obtained for the solver by removing the barriers was about 16 %.

The waiting time still present in the application reflects to some extent a computational load imbalance as can be seen when viewing how execution time without MPI calls is distributed across the different processes (not shown here).

### 5.2 Integrating Performance Data

An integration of trace-based analysis to target parallel performance with counter-based analysis to target memory performance has proved to be a useful strategy [24] in order to define bounds for the runtime penalty of cache misses. An above average cache miss rate was found in MPI calls of the SWEEP3D benchmark code [2] using EXPERT. At the same time, those MPI call were identified as the source of Late-Sender problems with the result that most of the time spent in those calls was waiting time anyway, rendering the cache-miss problem insignificant. The monitoring method applied was recording the number of cache misses as part of individual trace records. However, recording one or more hardware-counter values as part of nearly every event record can increase trace-file size dramatically, a side-effect that severely limits the scalability of this approach. In this particular case, the timestamped storage of hardware-counter data was even unnecessary, since EXPERT did nothing other than accumulating the counters for every call path.

Taking advantage of the CUBE merge operator, it is now possible to record hardware-counter and trace data separately. In this way, counter data can be collected as a less space-intensive call-graph profile from the very beginning using CONE, thereby avoiding the undesired trace file enlargement in addition to dividing the overall measurement overhead between two program runs. Since both CONE and EXPERT produce CUBE-compliant output, we can use the merge operator to obtain a single derived CUBE experiment integrating the output from two different sources.

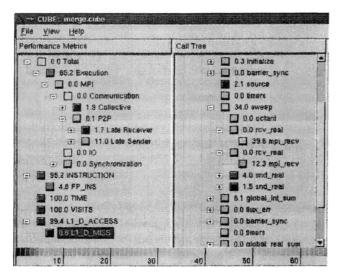

**Figure 3. Merge of outputs from CONE and EXPERT.**

If we want to consider multiple counters in our analysis, we might have to deal with a hardware restriction limiting the number and type of counters to be monitored in parallel. POWER4, for example, does not permit the combination of floating-point instructions with level 1 data-cache misses in the same run. The solution above can, of course, be applied to different outputs from the same tool as well. In this case, we can perform different measurements with CONE using different event sets and merge the results into a single experiment. To alleviate the effects of random errors, we can summarize multiple outputs from every single tool by applying the mean operator before we perform the merge operation.

Figure 3 shows a derived experiment obtained by merging one EXPERT output with two CONE outputs referring to different event sets. It includes metrics from two tools for the same application. The first tree from the top is the root of EXPERT's metric hierarchy. It is expanded and shows different trace-based metrics. Below are the

counter-based metrics from CONE including level 1 data cache misses (L1_D_MISS) and floating-point instructions (FP_INS), which have been collected during two different runs. The numbers represent percentages of their corresponding root metric's total amount. The call tree shows the percentage distribution of cache misses with a high concentration at MPI_Recv calls which are at the same time sources of Late-Sender problems (not shown).

## 6  Related Work

This work builds upon the framework for multi-execution performance tuning by Karavanic et al. [11], which was used in the Paradyn project [13] for an optimization strategy based on using historical performance data to guide the search for performance bottlenecks. Similar to CUBE, the framework defines operations on performance data stored in accordance with a specific data model. Whereas the framework's data model defines experimental data in terms of arbitrary resource hierarchies, CUBE favors interoperability over flexibility by adding more semantics and exactly specifying the type of program and system resources that can be described. Also, the framework does not consider any relationships between performance metrics, whereas CUBE models specialization relationships between metrics in the style of dependence relationships between the search hypotheses in Paradyn. The most significant difference between CUBE and the framework is that all operations in CUBE are closed in that an operator always maps its operands back into its domain. The framework includes a structural merge and a structural difference operator which, however, is defined only for experiment metadata as opposed to the actual performance numbers. In contrast, the performance difference operator, which computes the discrepancy between the actual performance data of two experiments, returns a list of foci (i.e., combination of resources from different hierarchies) where this discrepancy is significant. CUBE's difference operator and all other operators are defined for entire experiments and return entire (albeit derived) experiments including actual performance numbers that can be processed and displayed like original ones. For example, mechanisms aimed at finding hotspots can be applied to the original and the difference data likewise. Also, the framework does not include a mean operator. Another difference is that CUBE offers an API to transfer data from arbitrary sources into its specific input representation.

The problem of multiexperiment analysis has been addressed by many other groups as well. Projects such as ILAB [25], NIMROD [1], Tuner's Workbench [10], and ZENTURIO [17] provide an infrastructure for planning and conducting a series of experiments with different parameters. ZENTURIO can be combined with the AKSUM [19] performance tool to automatically analyze the evolution of higher-level performance problems across multiple experiments. Scalability-analysis features can also be found in the latest release of SvPablo [18].

There are a multitude of interactive browsers, such as AKSUM [19], HPCView [12], and SvPablo [18], that correlate the program structure with different performance metrics. The CUBE display's distinctive feature is the combination of a generic API that makes it available for third-party tools with a set of operations that can be performed on the data. In addition, CUBE's presentation logic achieves simplicity by relying on a single type of widget (i.e, a tree browser) regardless of the performance-space dimension displayed. Historically, CUBE emerged from the KOJAK [23] project, where a similar browser was used to present the results of event-trace analysis.

The CUBE algebra is based on a generic model of performance data providing a foundation for many postprocessing tools. The ASL [9] specification language, which provides language constructs to specify potential performance problems in parallel applications, is based on a similar data model with emphasis on automatic problem detection.

As CUBE focuses on automatic postprocessing of a wide range of performance data, it is also closely related to performance database projects, such as PerfDBF [8] and PPerfDB [16]. In fact, implementing the CUBE algebra on top of a database management system in addition to a pure XML file representation would be a natural extension, and interfacing to an existing performance database might open a large amount of performance data to our approach. On the other hand, CUBE - by relying on XML files only - provides cross-experiment capabilities without the burden of maintaining a whole database-management system.

## 7 Conclusion

The CUBE performance algebra addresses the problem of analyzing multiple performance data sets by defining a data model to represent a wide range of performance experiments plus operations to compare, integrate, and summarize them. The closure property of the algebra enables a new level of tool interoperability by combining the views provided by different experiments and performance tools into a single one and making this integrated view available to visualization and other postprocessing tools.

We have implemented a library to read and write experiments and to perform arithmetic operations on them, which is currently used by CONE and EXPERT. A generic display component illustrates the enriched view provided by derived experiments. Browsing through a difference experiment allows us to analyze the effects of optimizations in a very differentiated manner. Also, merging tracing output with profiling output can help reduce trace-file size signifi-

cantly. Finally, hardware restrictions limiting the number of hardware counters measured simultaneously can now be circumvented by merging the outputs of separate experiments.

We believe that our approach is especially well suited to support performance analysis on large-scale systems. As parallel machines grow larger, monitoring becomes much more complicated. Given the enormous amount of data generated even for a single metric during a single run, the ability to automatically integrate data from different runs becomes more and more important. New operators which perform data reduction, for example, based on multivariate statistical techniques [3], might further help manage size when applied to the integrated data. Also, the integration of topology information, for example obtained from instrumented MPI topology routines, into our data model could open the way for new automatic analysis and visualization tools. Finally, as the processing logic of CUBE relies entirely on an XML-centric data model, CUBE can be easily integrated with an Grid environment by exposing its functionality as an OGSI-compliant Grid service [20].

**Acknowledgment.** We would like to thank Andrew Canning and Lin-Wang Wang from Lawrence Berkeley National Lab for giving us access to their application. We are also grateful to Julien Langou for helping us run the PESCAN code and explaining to us the mathematics behind it.

## References

[1] D. Abramson, R. Sosic, J. Giddy, and B. Hall. Nimrod: A Tool for Performing Parameterised Simulations Using Distributed Workstations. In *Proc.of the 4th IEEE Symposium on High Performance Distributed Computing (HPDC)*, pages 112–121, 1995.

[2] Accelerated Strategic Computing Initiative (ASCI). *The ASCI sweep3d Benchmark Code.* http://www.llnl.gov/asci_benchmarks/.

[3] D. H. Ahn and J. S. Vetter. Scalable Analysis Techniques for Microprocessor Performance Counter Metrics. In *Proc. of the Conference on Supercomputers (SC2002)*, Baltimore, November 2002.

[4] S. Browne, J. Dongarra, N. Garner, G. Ho, and P. Mucci. A Portable Programming Interface for Performance Evaluation on Modern Processors. *The International Journal of High Performance Computing Applications*, 14(3):189–204, Fall 2000.

[5] A. Canning, L.W. Wang, A. Williamson, and A. Zunger. Parallel empirical pseudopotential electronic structure calculations for million atom systems. *Journal of Computational Physics*, 160(29), 2000.

[6] L. A. DeRose, T. Hoover Jr., and J. K. Hollingsworth. The Dynamic Probe Class Library - An Infrastructure for Developing Instrumentation for Performance Tools.

[7] L. A. DeRose and F. Wolf. CATCH – A Call-Graph Based Automatic Tool for Capture of Hardware Performance Metrics for MPI and OpenMP Applications. In *Proc. of the 8th International Euro-Par Conference*, number 2400 in LNCS, pages 167–176, Paderborn, Germany, August 2002. Springer.

[8] J. Dongarra, A. Malony, S. Moore, P. Mucci, and S. Shende. Scalable Performance Analysis Infrastructure for Terascale Systems. *Future Generation Computer Systems*, 2004. To appear.

[9] T. Fahringer, M. Gerndt, B. Mohr, G. Riley, J. L. Träff, and F. Wolf. Knowledge Specification for Automatic Performance Analysis. Technical Report FZJ-ZAM-IB-2001-08, ESPRIT IV Working Group APART, Forschungszentrum Jülich, August 2001. Revised version.

[10] A. Hondroudakis and R. Procter. The Tuner's Workbench: A Tool to Support Tuning in the Large. In P. Fritzson, editor, *Proc. of the ZEUS-95 Workshop on Parallel Programming and Computation*, pages 212–221. IOS Press, May 1995.

[11] K. L. Karavanic and B. Miller. A Framework for Multi-Execution Performance Tuning. *Parallel and Distributed Computing Practices*, 4(3), September 2001. Special Issue on Monitoring Systems and Tool Interoperability.

[12] J. Mellor-Crummey, R. Fowler, and G. Marin. HPCView: A Tool for Top-down Analysis of Node Performance. *The Journal of Supercomputing*, 23:81–101, 2002.

[13] B. P. Miller, M. D. Callaghan, J. M. Cargille, J. K. Hollingsworth, R. B. Irvine, K. L. Karavanic, K. Kunchithapadam, and T. Newhall. The Paradyn Parallel Performance Measurement Tool. *IEEE Computer*, 28(11):37–46, 1995.

[14] C. M. Pancake. Applying Human Factors to the Design of Performance Tools. In *Proc. of the 5th International Euro-Par Conference*, number 1685 in LNCS, pages 44–60. Springer, August/September 1999.

[15] Parallel Tools Consortium. *xlcb Graphical Browser: User Manual*. http://web.engr.oregonstate.edu/~pancake/ptools/lcb/xlcb.html.

[16] Portland State University. *PPerfDB*. http://www.cs.pdx.edu/~karavan/research.html.

[17] R. Prodan and T. Fahringer. On Using ZENTURIO for Performance and Parameter Studies on Cluster and Grid Architectures. In *Proc. of 11th Euromicro Conf. on Parallel Distributed and Network based Processing (PDP 2003)*, Genua, Italy, February 2003.

[18] L. A. De Rose, Y. Zhang, and D. A. Reed. SvPablo: A Multi-Language Architecture-Independent Performance Analysis System. In *Proc. of the International Conference on Parallel Processing (ICPP'99)*, Fukushima, Japan, September 1999.

[19] C. Seragiotto Júnior, M. Geissler, G. Madsen, and H. Moritsch. On Using Aksum for Semi-Automatically Searching of Performance Problems in Parallel and Distributed Programs. In *Proc. of 11th Euromicro Conf. on Parallel Distributed and Network based Processing (PDP 2003)*, Genua, Italy, February 2003.

[20] S. Tuecke, K. Czajkowski, I. Foster, J. Frey, S. Graham, C. Kesselman, T. Maguire, T. Sandholm, P. Vanderbilt, and D. Snelling. *Open Grid Services Infrastructure (OGSI) Version 1.0*. Global Grid Forum, June 2003. Draft Recommendation.

[21] University of Tennessee. *CONE*. http://icl.cs.utk.edu/kojak/cone/.

[22] F. Wolf. *Automatic Performance Analysis on Parallel Computers with SMP Nodes*. PhD thesis, RWTH Aachen, Forschungszentrum Jülich, February 2003. ISBN 3-00-010003-2.

[23] F. Wolf and B. Mohr. Automatic performance analysis of hybrid MPI/OpenMP applications. *Journal of Systems Architecture*, 49(10-11):421–439, 2003. Special Issue "Evolutions in parallel distributed and network-based processing".

[24] F. Wolf and B. Mohr. Hardware-Counter Based Automatic Performance Analysis of Parallel Programs. In *Proc. of the Minisymposium "Performance Analysis", Conference on Parallel Computing (ParCo)*, Dresden, Germany, September 2003.

[25] M. Yarrow, K. M. McCann, R. Biswas, and R. F. Van der Wijngaart. An Advanced User Interface Approach for Complex Parameter Study Process Specification on the Information Power Grid. In *Proc. of GRID*, pages 146–157, 2000.

# Clustering Strategies for Cluster Timestamps

Paul A.S. Ward, Tao Huang, and David J. Taylor
Shoshin Distributed Systems Group
University of Waterloo
Waterloo, Ontario N2L 3G1, Canada
{pasward,t6huang,dtaylor}@shoshin.uwaterloo.ca

## Abstract

*Visualization tools that illustrate communication in parallel programs use Fidge/Mattern timestamps to efficiently answer precedence queries. These timestamps have poor execution efficiency when the number of processes is large, limiting the scalability of the tool. Self-organizing hierarchical cluster timestamps can scale if the clusters they use capture communication locality. However, no clustering algorithm has been presented that enables these timestamps to work. In this paper we evaluate two clustering strategies for such timestamps, one static and one dynamic. The static algorithm was chosen to demonstrate an unproven assumption of cluster timestamps, namely that good clustering will always yield significant space saving, and to demonstrate that it is possible to select a range of cluster sizes that provide such a savings. We then assessed the merge-on-$N^{th}$-communication approach. In all but two cases it provides a timestamp size that is with 20% of the best achievable. We present detailed results for the strategies evaluated.*

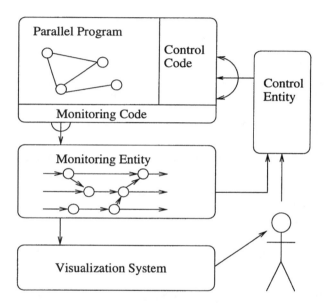

**Figure 1. Communication-Visualization Tool Architecture**

## 1 Motivation

Tools that provide communication visualizations for parallel programs, such as ATEMPT [12, 13], Object-Level Trace [8], and POET [14], can be broadly characterized as having the architecture shown in Figure 1. The parallel program is instrumented with monitoring code that captures significant event data. The information collected will include the event's process[1] identifier, number, and type, as well as partner-event identification, if any. This event data is forwarded from each process to a central monitoring entity which, using this information, incrementally builds and maintains a data structure of the partial order of events

that form the computation [15]. That data structure may be queried by a variety of systems, the most common being visualization engines and control entities that enable features such as parallel breakpoints (*e.g.* [24]) and program steering (*e.g.* [1]). The efficient representation of this partial-order data structure is the focus of this paper.

Communication-visualization tools we are aware of maintain the transitive reduction of the partial order, typically accessed with a B-tree-like index. This enables the efficient querying of events given a process identifier and event number. It does not, however, enable efficient event-precedence querying, which is one of the most common query types on such structures. To enable such testing, a vector timestamp is computed for each event and stored with that event in the data structure. While a variety of such timestamps have been proposed, the Fidge/Mattern time-

---

[1]Throughout this paper we will use the term "process" to indicate any sequential entity. It might be a single-threaded process, a thread, a semaphore, an EJB (in the case of Object-Level Trace), a TCP stream, *etc.*

stamp [2, 17] is the one used. Its use is dictated by its ability to answer precedence queries in constant time and the fact that it is dynamic (that is, computable without requiring complete knowledge of the event set). Unfortunately, this timestamp requires a vector of size equal to the number of processes in the computation. Such a requirement does not allow the data structure to scale with the number of processes.

## 1.1 The Vector-Timestamp-Size Problem

To illustrate this scalability problem consider a thousand-process system, where each process generates a thousand events that are sent to the observation tool. Such a system is by no means extravagant. Indeed there are many systems that already exceed this capacity, and Object-Level Trace has the capacity to monitor such a number of concurrent objects [8]. In such a case, a million events will be generated which will be stored in the partial-order data structure. The Fidge/Mattern vector timestamps for these events must then either be stored with the data structure, or calculated as needed.

If the Fidge/Mattern timestamps are pre-computed and stored with the data structure, we can expect the size of the structure to exceed four gigabytes (a million events times 1000-element vector per process, where each vector element is a 32-bit integer). In such a case the structure will spill into virtual memory. Virtual memory behaves very poorly when dealing with Fidge/Mattern timestamps because their most common use is for precedence testing. Such tests require just a single value from the vector. However, virtual memory systems presume spatial and temporal locality, and thus will read in an entire 4 KB page, or in other words, the complete vector. The rest of the vector typically has no further value. Ward has shown that to do something as simple as computing the greatest-concurrent elements of an event would require about 12,000 pages of virtual memory to be read, only to be discarded [20]. In summary, the virtual-memory system will thrash. The processor cache is similarly of little value with such timestamps.

The alternate solution, and the one adopted by both Object-Level Trace and POET, is to calculate timestamps as required. More precisely, these systems implement their own caching scheme for some timestamps, and calculate forward as needed. The effect is that the precedence-test cost when using such timestamps is $O(N)$, with the size of the constant being a function of the caching approach and the size of the cache (though in all instances it is large). Ward has shown that this approach, while superior to the pre-calculated method, remains quite poor. Elementary operations, such as partial-order scrolling, take several minutes as the vector size approaches 1000 [20], where they take negligible time when the number of processes is small.

This remains true even if the number of events is the same in both instances.

The key point that we wish to emphasize here is that the vector-timestamp size is a critical scalability bottleneck. The amount of space consumed by Fidge/Mattern timestamps is sufficiently large as to substantially affect the execution time of systems that use it for precedence determination.

## 1.2 A Possible Solution

In an attempt to reduce the space-consumption of vector timestamps, Ward and Taylor proposed self-organizing hierarchical cluster timestamps [20, 21, 22]. These timestamps are also dynamic and can efficiently answer precedence queries, but require up to an order-of-magnitude less space than do Fidge/Mattern timestamps. A critical design issue with these cluster timestamps is that the space consumption, and hence efficiency, is heavily dependent on whether or not the clusters used accurately capture locality of communication. If they do not, then the space-consumption saving is substantially impaired. The timestamp algorithm described by Ward and Taylor does not address the issue of cluster selection. Rather, it either assumes that a set of clusters have been pre-determined [21], or it allows for the dynamic clustering of timestamps [20, 22]. In the former case, any clustering strategy can be used, though the only one evaluated was fixed contiguous clusters. In the latter case, the strategy must dynamically cluster processes. In doing so, it can only look at events once, and once a process is placed in a cluster, that placement never changes. Only a trivial clustering algorithm, merge-on-1st-communication, has been evaluated.

The evaluation by Ward and Taylor of their cluster-timestamp algorithm showed that it is possible to substantially reduce the space-consumption using these timestamps. However, they also showed that such a reduction is critically dependent on the cluster size selected. Cluster size is the only parameter that is adjustable for their chosen clustering strategies. Ward subsequently determined that there is no single cluster size that worked well for all computations for the given clustering strategy [20]. The purpose of this paper is to address those two critical problems. Specifically, in this paper we demonstrate three things. First, we show that it is possible to select a single maximum cluster size which produces significant space-savings for all computations we have evaluated to date. Second, we show that for most computations it is possible to select a static clustering algorithm that is not significantly sensitive to the choice of maximum cluster size, and that there exists a large range of maximum cluster sizes which produce near-optimal results for the timestamp. Third, we evaluate some dynamic clustering approaches, and comment on the requirements for such an algorithm.

In the remainder of this paper we first briefly review the operation of the Fidge/Mattern and Ward/Taylor timestamps, and other work that has been developed to address the problem of efficient precedence determination. In Section 3 we describe our clustering algorithm and justify it. We then present experimental results that confirm the value of our cluster-timestamp approach. We conclude by noting what work is still required to make dynamic clustering strategies fully practical.

## 2 Background

In this section we first briefly describe our parallel computation model. We review the operation of the Fidge/Mattern timestamp. We then describe the self-organizing hierarchical cluster timestamp, taking particular note of how clusters might be selected for these timestamps. Finally, we discuss other approaches to the problem of space consumption, and how they relate to our work.

### 2.1 Computation Model

We presume a message-passing model of parallel computing: the computation comprises multiple sequential processes communicating *via* message passing. The sequential processes consist of three types of events: send, receive and unary, totally ordered within the process. A *parallel computation* is the partial order formed by the "happened before" relation over the union of all of the events across all of the processes, defined as follows:

**Definition 1 (happened before: $\rightarrow \subseteq E \times E$)** *"happened before" is the smallest transitive relation satisfying*

1. *$e \rightarrow f$ if $e$ and $f$ are in the same process and $e$ occurs before $f$*

2. *$e \rightarrow f$ if $e$ is a send event and $f$ is the matching receive event*

Concurrency between events is then defined as the events not being in the "happened before" relation:

$$e \parallel f \iff e \nrightarrow f \wedge f \nrightarrow e$$

We note that this model has been used successfully to capture far more than its simple description implies. In particular, it has been used to model threads, semaphores, concurrent objects, *etc.*

### 2.2 The Fidge/Mattern Timestamp

The Fidge/Mattern vector timestamp was designed as a fully-distributed algorithm, in which vectors are appended

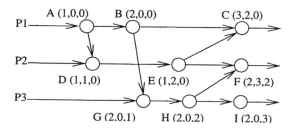

**Figure 2. Fidge/Mattern Timestamps**

to messages within the computation. In our context these timestamps are computed centrally in the monitoring entity, rather than within the parallel computation. As such, their calculation is somewhat different from that described by Fidge and Mattern. First, each process $p$ is assigned a unique identifier $p_i$, where $0 < p_i \leq N$ and $N$ is the number of processes in the computation. Each event $e$ is then assigned a vector timestamp $\mathcal{FM}(e)$ of size $N$ as follows. Define $\mathcal{FM}'(f)$ for event $f$, thus:

$$\mathcal{FM}'(f)[i] = \begin{cases} \mathcal{FM}(f)[i] + 1 & \text{if } i = p_f \\ \mathcal{FM}(f)[i] & \text{otherwise} \end{cases} \quad (1)$$

where $\mathcal{FM}(f)$ is the Fidge/Mattern timestamp of event $f$ and $p_f$ is the process in which event $f$ occurred. Then the Fidge/Mattern timestamp of event $e$ is the element-wise maximum of $\mathcal{FM}'(f)$ of all events $f$ that are immediate predecessors of $e$:

$$\mathcal{FM}(e) = \max_{f <: e} \left( \mathcal{FM}'(f) \right) \quad (2)$$

where $f <: e$ denotes $f$ is an immediate predecessor of $e$ and max is an element-wise maximum computation. The precedence test is then:

$$e \rightarrow f \iff \mathcal{FM}(e)[p_e] < \mathcal{FM}(f)[p_e] \quad (3)$$

An example of the Fidge/Mattern timestamp is shown in Figure 2.

### 2.3 Self-Organizing Hierarchical Cluster Timestamps

The self-organizing hierarchical cluster timestamp is based on the idea of grouping processes into clusters. Clusters in turn are grouped hierarchically into clusters of clusters, and so on recursively, until one large cluster encompasses the entire computation. It must be clearly emphasized at this point that these clusters are not in any way under the control of the user, nor do they (explicitly) represent any clustering that is a part of the parallel computation. Rather, these clusters are simply a mechanism by which processes are grouped with the intent of creating more efficient vector timestamps.

The efficacy of this timestamp is based on two observations. First, events within a cluster can only be causally dependent on events outside that cluster through receive events from transmissions that occurred outside the cluster. Such events are called "cluster receives." By identifying such cluster-receive events, it is possible to shorten the timestamp of all other events within the cluster to the number of processes in the cluster. Second, in many parallel and distributed computations, most communication of most processes is with a small number of other processes. If the clusters capture this communication locality, then there should be few cluster-receive events, and so the average space-consumption per timestamp will be significantly less than with the Fidge/Mattern timestamp.

Cluster-timestamp creation is the point at which the clustering strategy intersects with the timestamp algorithm. We therefore briefly describe the timestamp-creation algorithm. The algorithm first computes the Fidge/Mattern timestamp for the event. If the event is not a cluster receive, it is assigned a cluster timestamp that is the projection of the Fidge/Mattern timestamp over the processes in the cluster. If the event is a cluster receive, the algorithm acts according to whether the two clusters may be merged or not. This determination of mergeability is a function of the clustering strategy chosen, and is thus the point of intersection of the two algorithms. We discuss it further in Section 3. For events that are non-mergeable cluster receives, the timestamp assigned is the Fidge/Mattern timestamp. A note is made that this is the greatest cluster receive within this process at this point. For an event that is a mergeable cluster receive, the algorithm merges the clusters, thus making the event no longer a cluster receive. The cluster timestamp assigned is the projection of the Fidge/Mattern timestamp over the processes of the newly-merged cluster. The algorithm deletes Fidge/Mattern timestamps that are no longer needed.

The space consumption of this algorithm is $O(N)$ for cluster-receive events, where $N$ is the number of processes in the computation. All other events have a timestamp size of $O(c)$, where $c$ is the number of processes in the cluster (hereafter referred to as the cluster size). Clearly the efficacy of the algorithm is a function of the ability of the clustering strategy to minimize the number of cluster receive events.

## 2.4 Related Work

Finally, before describing the clustering strategies we have employed, we briefly summarize related approaches to the problem of efficient precedence determination, and in particular, methods for space-reduction for encoding partial orders.

There are various other approaches that have been taken to the problem of reducing the size of vector timestamps. Fowler and Zwaenepoel [4] create direct-dependency vectors. While these vectors can be substantially smaller than Fidge/Mattern timestamps, precedence testing requires a search through the vector space, which is in the worst case linear in the number of messages. Jard and Jourdan [9] generalize the Fowler and Zwaenepoel method, but have the same worst-case time bound. Singhal and Kshemkalyani [18] take the approach of transmitting just the information that has changed in the vector between successive communications. While not directly applicable in our context, it is possible to use a differential technique between events within the partial-order data structure. However, when we evaluated such an approach we were unable to realize more than a factor of three in space saving. Ward [19] has an approach based on Ore timestamps [16], though it is only applicable to low-dimension computations. There is also some amount of work on dynamic transitive closure (*e.g.*, [11]), though the problem being addressed is more general than is our problem, and the results are not as good for our application.

More recently, Garg and Skawratananond developed a technique for timestamping synchronous computations [5]. Their method results in timestamps that have size equal to the vertex cover of the communication graph of the computation. Since the communication graph is rarely known *a priori*, this technique would in practice only be applicable as a static algorithm, and then only for synchronous systems. Finally, their method requires unary events to have timestamps that are twice the size of those for synchronous events, and the timestamp for such unary events cannot be fixed until a subsequent synchronous event occurs in the same process.

## 3 Clustering Strategies

We now describe the clustering strategies we employed. While the approaches are fairly standard (see Kaufman and Rousseeuw [10] for various clustering methods), there are three significant issues that we focus on. First, we discuss the algorithm choice. Second, we indicate how we measure similarity and dissimilarity between processes. Finally, we specify how we deal with synchronous events.

### 3.1 Static Clustering

We initially considered and implemented variations on the $k$-means and $k$-medoid methods. We found, however, that the problem with the $k$-means approach was that determining a centroid is not obvious when dealing with communication events between processes. There is no clear definition for an abstract process that represents the centre of a cluster of processes. The $k$-medoid method was similarly problematic, in that the clusters created required one process to specifically be considered to be the central process for the cluster. Again, this does not match the reality of parallel computations well. Finally, the results of these approaches were poor, as they select the number of clusters to be created, rather than bounding the size of the desired clusters. The effect was that many processes were grouped within a single cluster, while the remaining clusters were sparse. The result of such a clustering would be that the cluster-timestamps would have little benefit over Fidge/Mattern timestamps, as most events would have a timestamp that was little smaller than the Fidge/Mattern one.

We therefore adopted a hierarchical clustering method. The reader should be careful to distinguish the hierarchical cluster approach used here from the hierarchical cluster-timestamp algorithm. The cluster-timestamp algorithm has a hierarchy of clusters, though in this paper, we are just exploring two levels of clusters. The hierarchical clustering method, as we use it here, produces a single level of clusters. It does so by progressively merging smaller clusters into larger ones. The number of processes that are permitted in any given cluster is limited to a maximum cluster size, for the reason described above.

To describe the precise algorithm we implemented, we first describe our method for determining similarity, and how we deal with synchronous events. Since we are concerned with minimizing the number of cluster-receive events, this is the key element for deciding to merge two clusters. We therefore pairwise compare all current clusters to determine the number of communication occurrences between the clusters. There is a communication occurrence between two clusters if there is a send event in one cluster and its corresponding receive event is in the other cluster. In practice, we examine the receive events in each cluster in the pair, and check to see if the corresponding send event is in the other cluster of the pair. This count represents the number of cluster-receive events that will be required if the cluster pair in question are not merged.

A naive approach at this point would be to simply select that pair of clusters that had the greatest pairwise communication and to merge those two clusters (subject to the constraint of limiting the maximum cluster size). This is probably a poor choice. The problem with this approach is that as clusters increase in size, they are likely to have more communication with other clusters, purely by virtue of their size. Rather than take this approach, we normalize the communication count based on the combined size of the pair of clusters. We then select the cluster pair with the highest normalized communication count for merging (again, subject to the maximum cluster size limit), thus taking a greedy algorithm approach. The reader should note that considering all possible combinations of processes in clusters would

```
 1: do
 2:    CRMax ← 0
 3:    c_1^m ← 0
 4:    c_2^m ← 0
 5:    ∀c_i ∈ clusters
 6:        ∀c_j ≠ c_i ∈ clusters
 7:            if (((|c_i| + |c_j|) > maxCS) continue
 8:            else
 9:                CR_{ij} ← communication (c_i, c_j)
10:                CR ← CR_{ij}/(|c_i| + |c_j|)
11:                if (CR > CRMax)
12:                    CRMax ← CR
13:                    c_1^m ← c_i
14:                    c_2^m ← c_j
15:    clusters ← clusters − c_1^m
16:    clusters ← clusters − c_2^m
17:    c_3 ← c_1^m ∪ c_2^m
18:    clusters ← clusters ∪ c_3
19: while (CRMax > 0);
```

**Figure 3. Static Clustering Algorithm**

be computationally too expensive to perform.

Finally, we note that synchronous events present a small additional complication. A synchronous event is effectively both a transmit and a receive. Thus, each synchronous communication is treated as two communication occurrences, rather than a single communication occurrence, since the benefit of merging the two clusters in question would be to remove two cluster-receive events, not one.

The formal algorithm we implemented is as shown in Figure 3. Lines 2–4 set the cluster pair that has maximum similarity to the unselected pair. In particular, line 2 sets the current maximum normalized cluster-receive count to zero. If it remains zero during the pairwise comparison, the algorithm terminates (line 19), as this indicates that there is no pair of clusters that can merge (i.e. the resultant cluster does not exceed the maximum cluster size permitted ($maxCS$)) that have a communication occurrence between them.

Lines 5–14 perform the pairwise comparison to select the most similar pair of clusters. Specifically, lines 5 and 6 form the nested loop over all clusters. Line 7 automatically rejects any cluster pair whose merger would exceed the maximum permitted cluster size, $maxCS$. Line 9 determines the number of communication occurrences between the cluster pairs for those cluster pairs whose merger is permitted by the cluster-size constraint. Line 10 normalizes that communication count, while line 11 determines if it exceeds the current best pair. If it does, this pair is set as the current best pair (lines 12–14).

After all pairwise comparisons have been performed, the pair of clusters with the most similarity is known. Lines 15–16 remove that pair from the set of clusters, and add in the new merged cluster that resulted from merging the selected pair (line 17–18).

The algorithm terminates when there are no two clusters that can merge, because the size restriction prevents it or there is no communication occurrence between two mergeable clusters. We follow this approach because no matter how poor a cluster might seem, if it reduces the number of cluster receives at all, it is better than if it were not formed. In particular, we presume that any implementation of the cluster-timestamp algorithm will use vectors of size equal to the maximum cluster size, since any variation in sizing of the vectors is likely to have a detrimental impact on the performance of the memory-allocation system.

Finally, we note that the algorithm is initialized by placing each process within its own cluster. The algorithm will operate in $O(N^3)$ time, as the outer while loop can iterate at most $N$ times, since each iteration will reduce the number of clusters by one. Since this is a static algorithm, this performance is acceptable. Further, when implemented, we observed that the performance was more than sufficient. The results for this algorithm are presented in Section 4.

## 3.2 Dynamic Clustering

A static clustering implies the overall timestamp algorithm must be static. Indeed, a simple approach wherein the static clustering algorithm might be used with the hierarchical cluster timestamp would be to perform two passes over the event data. The first pass would cluster the data, and the second pass would timestamp it.

In general such a static timestamp algorithm is not sufficient to the task of parallel-program communication visualization. Rather, what is required is a dynamic algorithm, since the observation tool is expected to operate while the computation is executing. The hierarchical cluster timestamp is dynamic, provided that it is paired with a dynamic clustering strategy. There is currently only one dynamic clustering strategy that has been explored for that timestamp, namely the merge-on-1st-communication approach. There are two key problems with that algorithm. First, while it is capable of producing excellent space reduction over Fidge/Mattern timestamps, it is only capable of so-doing if the maximum cluster size is selected appropriately. The problem with such a selection is that is it not known *a priori* what is an appropriate value for this parameter. It is only after execution of the algorithm that it is known if it was a good choice or not. When a poor value is chosen, the space consumption can approach that of Fidge/Mattern timestamps. As such, the algorithm cannot be reliably used as a dynamic timestamp algorithm.[2] The second problem,

which is in effect the cause of the first problem, is that there is no single value, or range of values, of maximum cluster size that is appropriate for all computations.

As a result of these problems we have started to investigate other dynamic clustering strategies. In this paper we investigate the merge-on-Nth-communication approach, as it is a fairly natural extension of the merge-on-1st-communication approach. Rather than merge on first communication between clusters, we keep a matrix that identifies the total number of cluster receives that have occurred thus far between the two clusters. This is then normalized by the size of the clusters, as was the case in the static algorithm. The decision to merge is then made when this normalized cluster-receive value passes a threshold. The algorithm thus degenerates to merge-on-1st-communication if that threshold is set to 0. We now present our results for these two algorithms.

## 4 Experimental Results

We have evaluated our algorithms over more than 50 different parallel and distributed computations covering a variety of different environments, including Java [7], PVM [6] and DCE [3], with up to 300 processes in each computation. The PVM programs tended to be SPMD style parallel computations, and included the programs from the Cowichan benchmark [23]. A number of them exhibited close neighbour communication and scatter-gather patterns. The Java programs were web-like applications, including various web-server executions. The DCE programs were sample business-application code. While space limitations prevent the publication of the code used, it is available for evaluation, together with the complete raw results, on our website at http://www.ccng.uwaterloo.ca/~pasward/-ClusterTimestamp.

For our experiments we compared the space requirements for four algorithms: Fidge/Mattern timestamps, cluster timestamps using merge-on-1st-communication, cluster timestamps using the static clustering algorithm described in Section 3.1, and cluster timestamps using the merge-on-Nth-communication algorithm described in Section 3.2. We cannot compare our work with the Garg and Skawratananond algorithm as their method is limited to synchronous computations and none of our computations contain exclusively synchronous communication. The comparison to Fidge/Mattern timestamps is appropriate as existing observation tools use it.

With the exception of the Fidge/Mattern algorithm, all of the algorithms under comparison have a single tunable parameter: the maximum cluster size. We therefore varied this value from 2 to 50 processes and observed the ratio

---

[2]The algorithm can, however, be used in a static mode. The approach taken is to iterate over the event data multiple times, using different values of maximum cluster size, until one is found that provides a suitable space

saving. It should be noted, however, that there is no guarantee that such a cluster-size choice will be found.

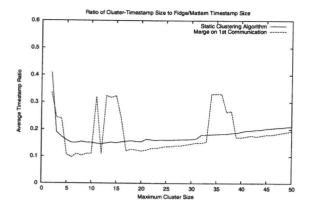

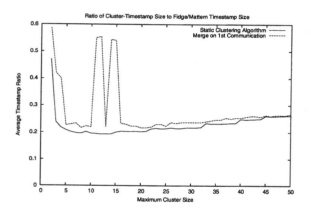

**Figure 4. Ratio of Static Cluster to Fidge/Mattern Sizes**

of the average cluster-timestamp size to the Fidge/Mattern-timestamp size. We followed the POET and OLT approach of assuming that the observation tool encodes timestamps using a fixed-size vector. By default this is 300. The cluster timestamps were assumed to be encoded using a vector of size equal to the maximum cluster size. These assumptions are consistent with the current behaviour of existing observation tools.

A couple of sample results for the static cluster algorithm for two distinct computations are shown in Figure 4. The figure shows the ratio of the cluster timestamp size to the Fidge/Mattern timestamp size. It illustrates the effect of two clustering algorithms, the static one and the merge-on-1st-communication, used in the initial evaluation of the cluster-timestamp algorithm. The Fidge/Mattern timestamp would have a ratio of 1, and is thus not shown in the figure since it is off the scale. These results are typical of the behaviour we observed for the various computations.

Several comments must be made about these results. First, we note that the static algorithm does not always pro-

duce the least space consumption. In particular, as can be seen in the upper figure (which shows the worst case we observed), in some instances the static algorithm was as much as 5% worse than the merge-on-1st-communication approach. We note that this is a small space-cost difference, and not relevant for the purpose of this paper. What is relevant is that these results clearly illustrate our second claim, namely that there exist cluster algorithms that are not significantly sensitive to the maximum cluster size selected. The static clustering algorithm we created produces relatively smooth ratio curves, demonstrating that it does not have the sensitivity to maximum cluster size that merge-on-1st-communication exhibits.

A couple of sample figures do not necessarily show the whole picture. We therefore examined all computations over the three different environments. In doing so we found that if the maximum cluster size is any value between 9 and 17 (inclusive) the resulting timestamp was within 20% of the best timestamp size achieved for all but one computation. This clearly demonstrates our second claim over all of our extant event data. We must emphasize at this point that such a range of maximum cluster sizes that produce an acceptable space reduction simply does not exist for either the merge-on-1st-communication strategy or for fixed contiguous clusters. Further, we must reiterate that this maximum-cluster-size parameter must, in general, be selected prior to the timestamping, and thus this lack of such an ideal in the merge-on-1st-communication case renders that technique of limited value.

To confirm our first claim, for all computations studied, we computed the range of maximum cluster sizes for which the timestamp size was within 20% of the best timestamp size achieved. The result of this was that we determined that for all computations a cluster size of 13 or 14 resulted in a timestamp size that was within 20% of the best achievable. By way of comparison, in Ward's analysis [20] of merge-on-1st-communication it was observed that there was no single maximum cluster size that was suitable for all computations. Indeed, for all but a couple of cases, less than 80% of the computations were within 20% of the best for any given maximum cluster size.

The results of our static clustering algorithm must be emphasized and reiterated: this work has shown that there exists a maximum cluster size that will result in cluster timestamps whose size is within 20% of the best size. Further, there is a significant range over which the vast majority of computations exhibit very good timestamp size reduction as compared with the Fidge/Mattern timestamp. Ward's original work on this timestamp algorithm did not demonstrate that such an ideal maximum cluster size existed, and in fact pointed strongly to the possibility that such an ideal did not exist. These results for the static clustering algorithm clearly demonstrate that this ideal does in fact exist, and

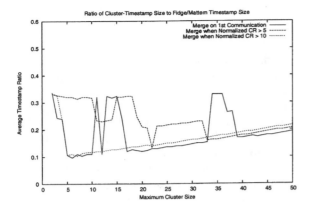

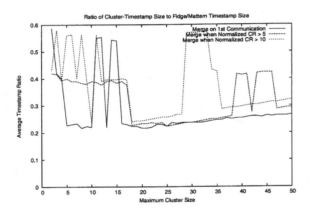

**Figure 5. Ratio of Static Cluster to Fidge/Mattern Sizes**

that it is simply a question of developing a suitable dynamic clustering strategy so as to capture that ideal.

With this in mind, we now turn our attention to the dynamic clustering algorithm. In this case we expected the results to be a gradual smoothing of the ratio curve, from that of merge-on-1st-communication. In addition, we expected the overall curve to rise, as the number of events that needed full Fidge/Mattern timestamps would increase because cluster merging was being deferred.

Sample results using the dynamic clustering algorithm are presented in Figure 5. The sample computations represented in this figure are the same as those computations shown in Figure 4. Several observations can be made about these results. First, we note that the upper graph indicates that this dynamic clustering method offers a lot of promise. In particular, we note that as the normalized cluster-receive threshold increased, the result was indeed the flatter curve that we had hoped for. More surprisingly, however, is the fact that the curve is not substantially higher than the merge-on-1st-communication curve at its best. This appears to be

because the computation has a very large number of events, but the number of cluster-receive events becomes fixed once the maximum cluster size reaches 22. This may be because the algorithm ceases to cluster processes, as the threshold is too large.

The second point of note is that the algorithm does not always smooth the curve as much as might be desired, and sometimes when it does so, it smooths it at a significantly higher timestamp size. Thus, the lower figure clearly exhibits the problem that, while smoothed at the CR > 5 point, it is smoothed at the 40% mark, not the 20% mark. Further, as the merging criteria was raised, the curve became less predictable. It is clear, therefore, that more work is required to achieve a suitable dynamic clustering algorithm.

As with the static algorithm, sample results do not present the full picture. We therefore looked at the raw results to determine over what range of maximum cluster size the computations exhibited a timestamp space reduction that was within 20% of the best achieved. We did this for a normalized cluster-receive threshold of 10, since that appeared to be the most promising based on visual inspection of the graphs. We were not able to find such a range that covered all computations for this dynamic clustering algorithm. However, we did find that when the maximum cluster size permitted was between 22 and 24 processes (inclusive), all but two computations had a timestamp size that was within 20% of the best size. The two that exceeded 20% of their best size over that range still had an average timestamp size that was less than one-third of their Fidge/Mattern timestamp size.

The full raw-result information for our experiments is available on our web site at http://www.shoshin.-uwaterloo.ca/~pasward/ClusterTimestamp.

## 5 Conclusions and Future Work

In this paper we have evaluated clustering algorithms for self-organizing hierarchical cluster timestamps. We have seen that a simple static clustering algorithm demonstrates that the cluster-timestamp technique can work well, and is not inherently sensitive to cluster-size selection. Further, we have shown that it is possible to create clustering strategies that work well with a large range of computations, rather than having parameters that are specific to each individual computation.

Third, we have evaluated a simple extension to the dynamic merge-on-1st-communication clustering strategy. We call this extension "merge-on-Nth-communication" though this is a normalized count. This approach allows for the selection of a maximum cluster size that produced very good results for all but two computations, and satisfactory results for those two cases where it was not ideal.

We are therefore investigating two lines of development.

First, we are exploring alternate dynamic clustering strategies. Second, we are developing two variants of the cluster timestamp. The first variant will collect a significant number of events before performing a static clustering and subsequent timestamp operation. Such an approach will require a mechanism for precedence determination for those events that have yet to receive a cluster timestamp. The second variant we are examining is one in which processes will be permitted to migrate between clusters in the event that it is apparent that the clustering initially selected is a poor one. We expect to report on these methods in the near future.

## Acknowledgments

The authors would like to thank IBM for on-going support of this work, and the various reviewers for their comments, which have helped to improve this paper.

## References

[1] G. Eisenhauer and K. Schwan. An object-based infrastructure for program monitoring and steering. In *Proceedings 2nd SIGMETRICS Symposium on Parallel and Distributed Tools (SPDT'98)*, pages 10–20, 1998.

[2] C. Fidge. Logical time in distributed computing systems. *IEEE Computer*, 24(8):28–33, 1991.

[3] O. S. Foundation. *Introduction to OSF/DCE*. Prentice-Hall, Englewood Cliffs, New Jersey, 1993.

[4] J. Fowler and W. Zwaenepoel. Causal distributed breakpoints. In *Proceedings of the 10th IEEE International Conference on Distributed Computing Systems*, pages 134–141. IEEE Computer Society Press, 1990.

[5] V. K. Garg and C. Skawratananond. Timestamping messages in synchronous computations. In *Proceedings of the 22nd IEEE International Conference on Distributed Computing Systems*, pages 552–559. IEEE Computer Society Press, 2002.

[6] A. Geist, A. Begulin, J. Dongarra, W. Jiang, R. Manchek, and V. Sunderam. *PVM: Parallel Virtual Machine*. MIT Press, Cambridge, Massachusetts, 1994.

[7] J. Gosling, B. Joy, and G. Steele. *The Java Language Specification*. Addison-Wesley, 1996. Available at http://java.sun.com/docs/books/jls/.

[8] IBM Corporation. IBM distributed debugger for workstations. Online documentation available at: http://-www-4.ibm.com/software/webservers/-appserv/doc/v35/ae/infocenter/olt/-index.html.

[9] C. Jard and G.-V. Jourdan. Dependency tracking and filtering in distributed computations. Technical Report 851, IRISA, Campus de Beaulieu – 35042 Rennes Cedex – France, August 1994.

[10] L. Kaufman and P. J. Rousseeuw. *Finding Groups in Data : An Introduction to Cluster Analysis*. John Wiley and Sons, 1990.

[11] V. King and G. Sagert. A fully dynamic algorithm for maintaining the transitive closure. In *Proceedings of the Thirty-First Annual ACM Symposium on Theory of Computing*, pages 492–498. ACM, 1999.

[12] D. Kranzlmüller. *Event Graph Analysis for Debugging Massively Parallel Programs*. PhD thesis, GUP Linz, Linz, Austria, 2000.

[13] D. Kranzlmüller, S. Grabner, R. Schall, and J. Volkert. ATEMPT — A Tool for Event ManiPulaTion. Technical report, Institute for Computer Science, Johannes Kepler University Linz, May 1995.

[14] T. Kunz, J. P. Black, D. J. Taylor, and T. Basten. POET: Target-system independent visualisations of complex distributed-application executions. *The Computer Journal*, 40(8):499–512, 1997.

[15] L. Lamport. Time, clocks and the ordering of events in distributed systems. *Communications of the ACM*, 21(7):558–565, 1978.

[16] O. Ore. *Theory of Graphs*, volume 38. Amer. Math. Soc. Colloq. Publ., Providence, R.I., 1962.

[17] R. Schwarz and F. Mattern. Detecting causal relationships in distributed computations: In search of the holy grail. *Distributed Computing*, 7(3):149–174, 1994.

[18] M. Singhal and A. Kshemkalyani. An efficient implementation of vector clocks. *Information Processing Letters*, 43:47–52, August 1992.

[19] P. A. Ward. A framework algorithm for dynamic, centralized dimension-bounded timestamps. In *Proceedings of the 2000 CAS Conference*, November 2000.

[20] P. A. Ward. *A Scalable Partial-Order Data Structure for Distributed-System Observation*. PhD thesis, University of Waterloo, Waterloo, Ontario, 2002.

[21] P. A. Ward and D. J. Taylor. A hierarchical cluster algorithm for dynamic, centralized timestamps. In *Proceedings of the 21st IEEE International Conference on Distributed Computing Systems*, pages 585–593. IEEE Computer Society Press, April 2001.

[22] P. A. Ward and D. J. Taylor. Self-organizing hierarchical cluster timestamps. In R. Sakellariou, J. Keane, J. Gurd, and L. Freeman, editors, *EuroPar'01 Parallel Processing*, volume LNCS 2150 of *Lecture Notes in Computer Science*, pages 46–56. Springer-Verlag, August 2001.

[23] G. V. Wilson and R. B. Irvin. Assessing and comparing the usability of parallel programming systems. Technical report, University of Toronto, 1995.

[24] Y. M. Yong. Replay and distributed breakpoints in an OSF DCE environment. Master's thesis, University of Waterloo, Waterloo, Ontario, 1995.

# Session 2B:
# P2P Information Sharing

# Group-based Cooperative Cache Management for Mobile Clients in a Mobile Environment*

Chi-Yin Chow     Hong Va Leong     Alvin T. S. Chan

Department of Computing, Hong Kong Polytechnic University, Hong Kong
{cscychow, cshleong, cstschan}@comp.polyu.edu.hk

## Abstract

*Caching is a key technique for improving data retrieval performance of mobile clients. The emergence of robust and reliable peer-to-peer (P2P) communication technologies now brings to reality what we call "cooperating caching" in which mobile clients not only can retrieve data items from mobile support stations, but also can access them from the cache in their neighboring peers, thereby inducing a new dimension for mobile data caching. This paper extends a COoperative CAching scheme, called COCA, in a pull-based mobile environment. Built upon the COCA framework, we propose a GROup-based COoperative CAching scheme, called GroCoca, in which we define a tightly-coupled group (TCG) as a set of peers that possess similar movement pattern and exhibit similar data affinity. In GroCoca, a centralized incremental clustering algorithm is used to discover all TCGs dynamically, and the MHs in same TCG manage their cached data items cooperatively. In the simulated experiments, GroCoca is shown to reduce the access latency and server request ratio effectively.*

## 1. Introduction

A mobile system is formed with a wireless network connecting mobile hosts (MHs) to mobile support stations (MSSs). The MHs correspond to mobile clients equipped with portable devices and MSSs represent stationary servers providing information access for the MHs residing in their service areas. This kind of network topology, with the presence of MSSs, is known as an *infrastructure network*. It is a commonly deployed architecture. In this paper, we consider the infrastructure network as a pull-based mobile environment. In a pull-based mobile system, an MH sends a request to the MSS via an uplink channel, and the MSS processes the request and sends the required data item back to the requesting MH via a downlink channel. As mobile environments are characterized by asymmetric communication, in which the downlink channels are of much higher bandwidth than the uplink channels, the MSS would poten-

tially be a scalability bottleneck in the system, as it serves an enormous number of MHs [1].

The other network topology in a mobile environment is called a *mobile ad hoc network* (MANET). In MANETs, an MH can directly communicate with other MHs residing in its transmission range; however, it has to communicate with other MHs who are not residing in the range through multi-hop routing. MANET is practical with many environments with no fixed infrastructure, such as battlefield, rescue operation, etc. In MANETs, the MHs can move freely, and disconnect themselves from the network at any instant. These two characteristics lead to dynamic network topology changes. As a result, the MHs may suffer from long access latency or access failure, when the peers holding the required data items are far way or unreachable. The latter situation may be caused by network partition [16].

The inherent shortcomings of a pull-based and MANET mobile system lead to a result that systems adopting these architectures would not be as appropriate in most real commercial environments. In reality, long data access latency or access failure could possibly cause the abortion of valuable transactions or the suspension of critical activities, so that it is likely to reduce user satisfaction and loyalty, and potentially bring damages to the enterprises involved.

COCA is a mobile cooperative caching framework that combines the P2P communication technology with a conventional pull-based mobile system, wherein the MHs can obtain the required data items either from the MSS or its neighboring peers [6].

In the recent years, cooperative caching in mobile environments has been drawing increasing attention [8, 9, 12, 14, 15]. Our work is different from previous works in that we extend COCA with a GROup-based COoperative CAching scheme (GroCoca), which can take into account the specific communication topology of the "tightly-coupled groups". We propose the formation of *tightly-coupled groups* (TCGs) that respect the geographical vicinity property of *communication groups*, as well as the operational vicinity property of *computation groups*. It is not difficult to define whether two peers are geographically close, based upon their locations. Geographically close peers can communicate in ad hoc mode. Two peers are said to be operationally close, if they perform similar operations and

*Research supported in part by the Research Grant Council and the Hong Kong Polytechnic University under grant numbers PolyU 5084/01E and H-ZJ86.

access similar set of data items. Since we are more interested in data management and caching issues in GroCoca in this paper, we consider two peers to be operationally close based on the set of data items they access. Operationally close peers can share data items with minimal help of MSS. To determine the membership of TCGs, we propose an incremental clustering algorithm to construct the TCGs dynamically, making use of information about the MHs' mobility and data access patterns.

Several distributed mobility-based clustering algorithms have been proposed for MANETs [3, 11, 13]. The algorithms cluster the MHs into groups by considering only their mobility patterns. Our work is unique in that we propose an incremental clustering algorithm that not only considers the client mobility pattern, but also the data access pattern. We study the communication overheads incurred by our clustering algorithm in terms of access latency and power consumption as well.

The advantages of COCA are twofold. First, as some of client requests can be handled by the peer, it reduces the number of requests sent to the MSS. Thus, the system workload, can be shared among the MHs. This desirable feature can be considered as a load sharing technique in mobile environments. The reduction on the number of server requests eases the traffic load in the scarce uplink channel. Second, when an MH that is not residing in the service area of the system encounters a local cache miss, it still has a chance to obtain the required data item from its peers before constituting an access failure. Our simulation results show that GroCoca can further improve the system performance by increasing data accessibility in TCGs identified dynamically.

The rest of this paper is organized as follows. Section 2 gives an overview of the COCA model. Section 3 delineates the group-based COCA extension, GroCoca, based on an incremental clustering algorithm. Section 4 describes the simulation model of COCA and GroCoca. Section 5 studies the performance of COCA and GroCoca through a number of simulated experiments. Finally, Section 6 offers brief concluding remarks on this work.

## 2. COCA

We assume that each MH is equipped with two wireless network interface cards (NICs) with a transmission range ($TranRange$), in which one is dedicated for communicating with the MSS, while the other one is devoted to communicate with other MHs via their wireless NICs. When an MH cannot find the required data item in its local cache, i.e., a *local cache miss*, it broadcasts a *request* message to its neighboring peers via P2P broadcast communication. The peers caching the required data item replies to the MH with a *reply* message via P2P point-to-point communication. After a timeout period, if the MH receives replies from some neighboring peers, i.e., a *global cache hit*, it selects the closest peer as a target peer. The MH then sends a *retrieve* request to the target peer via P2P point-to-point communica-

tion. Finally, the target peer receiving the *retrieve* request sends the requested data item to the MH also via P2P point-to-point communication. On the other hand, if no neighboring peer turns in a *reply* message throughout the timeout period, i.e., a *global cache miss*, the MH has to obtain the required data item from the MSS.

The timeout period is initially set to a default value that is defined as a round-trip time of a P2P communication scaled up by a congestion factor ($\varphi$), i.e., $\frac{size\ of\ request + size\ of\ reply}{BW_{P2P}} \times \varphi$, where $BW_{P2P}$ is the bandwidth of the P2P communication channel. For each search in the peers' cache, an MH records the time duration, $\tau$, spent, i.e., the time when the MH broadcasts a *request* message to the time when a *reply* message is received. Then, the timeout period is set to the average time duration $\overline{\tau}$ plus another system parameter $\varphi'$ times the standard deviation of $\sigma_\tau$, i.e., timeout period $= \overline{\tau} + \varphi'\sigma_\tau$.

## 3. GroCoca

In this section, we present the group-based cooperative caching scheme, GroCoca, extended from COCA. Client mobility is a key factor to the system performance of cache management in mobile environments. In a cooperative cache environment, if an MH arbitrarily forwards its cached data items to its neighboring peers for cooperative cache replacement, there may not be much benefit to the receiving MH, since the data items may not be useful to the latter. Furthermore, it does not make good use of the cache space of the receiving MH, since it may well have moved far away from the original MH after a while. Likewise, if an MH does not cache the data item returned by a neighboring peers in order to conserve its cache, thinking that the peer would still be accessible in the future, it may have regretted if the peer moves far away. In addition, when an MH forwards a data item to another peer and they possess different data access patterns, the action will reduce the peer's local cache hit ratio, and the "alien" data item will be removed very soon, as the peer is not interested in that data item. The decision of whether a data item should be cached thus depends on both factors of the access affinity on the data items and the mobility for each MH. To develop an effective cooperative caching scheme, GroCoca is proposed which defines and makes use of TCG which is defined as a group of MHs that are geographically and operationally close, i.e., sharing common *mobility* and *data access* patterns. In GroCoca, the common mobility pattern is discovered with an incremental clustering algorithm and the similarity of access patterns is captured by frequency-based similarity measurement.

### 3.1. Mobility Pattern

The MSS performs the incremental clustering algorithm to cluster the MHs into TCGs based on their mobility patterns. The mobility pattern is modeled by a weighted average distance between any two MHs. The MHs need not explicitly update their locations, but they embed the location information in the request sent to the MSS for the requesting data items. The location information is represented by a coordinate $(x, y)$ that can be obtained by global positioning system (GPS) or indoor sensor-based positioning system. For two MHs, $m_i$ and $m_j$, the distance between them is calculated as the Euclidean distance, $|m_i m_j| = \sqrt{(x_j - x_i)^2 + (y_j - y_i)^2}$, where $(x_i, y_i)$ and $(x_j, y_j)$ are the coordinates of $m_i$ and $m_j$ respectively. An exponentially weighted moving average (EWMA) [5] is used to forecast the future distance of each pair of MHs based on their mobility histories. The weighted average distance between two MHs, $m_i$ and $m_j$, is denoted by $\|m_i m_j\|$. It is initially set to $+\infty$. After the MSS receives both the location information of $m_i$ and $m_j$, $\|m_i m_j\|$ is set to $|m_i m_j|$. Then $\|m_i m_j\|$ is updated when either $m_i$ or $m_j$ sends their new location to the MSS, based on the equation: $\|m_i m_j\|^{new} = \omega \times |m_i m_j| + (1-\omega) \times \|m_i m_j\|^{old}$, where $\omega$ $(0 \leq \omega \leq 1)$ is a parameter to weight the importance of the most recent distance. The weighted average distance of each pair of MHs is stored in a two-dimensional matrix, called a *distance matrix* (DM).

## 3.2. Data Access Pattern

Other than the mobility pattern of the MHs, the incremental clustering algorithm also considers the similarity of their accesses to the data items. In the MSS, each data item is associated with an identifier from 1 to $n$, where $n$ is the number of data items stored in the server. The MSS maintains a counter vector $(V)$ with a length $n$ for each MH to store the access frequency of every data item. When an MH accesses a data item, the MSS increments the corresponding counter for the MH. The similarity score of two MHs, $m_i$ and $m_j$, is calculated by the equation: $\text{sim}(m_i, m_j) = \frac{\sum_{k=1}^{n} V_i(k) \times V_j(k)}{\sqrt{\sum_{k=1}^{n} V_i(k)^2} \times \sqrt{\sum_{k=1}^{n} V_j(k)^2}}$, where $V_i(k)$ is the total number of times that an MH, $m_i$, accesses the data item $k$. Note that $0 \leq \text{sim}(m_i, m_j) \leq 1$. The similarity score of each pair of MHs is stored in a two-dimensional matrix, called an *access similarity matrix* (ASM).

Since the uplink channel is scarce, a passive approach is adopted for collecting the data access pattern. An MH does not send any data access information actively to the MSS, but the MSS learns its data access pattern from the received requests sent by the MH. If the measured similarity score of two MHs is larger than or equal to a threshold $\delta$, they are considered to possess a similar access pattern. The threshold $\delta$ is set to the average non-zero similarity score in ASM, and adjusted with the standard deviation to adapt to client access behavior in different types of systems, i.e., $\bar{s} = \frac{\sum_{i=1}^{k-1} \sum_{j=i+1}^{k} \text{sim}(m_i, m_j)}{\sum_{i=1}^{k-1} \sum_{j=i+1}^{k} \lceil \text{sim}(m_i, m_j) \rceil}$, $\delta = \bar{s} + \phi \sigma_s$, where $\phi$ is a system parameter. Since the measured similarity score only takes into consideration a sample of the access pattern of each MH, it is smaller than the actual similarity score. The MSS would not start the clustering algorithm until $\delta$ grows up to non-zero.

## 3.3. Incremental Clustering Algorithm

The incremental clustering algorithm clusters the MHs into TCGs by considering their mobility and access patterns. The MHs in the same TCG possess a tight relationship because they share the common mobility and data access patterns.

In the clustering algorithm, a distance threshold $\Delta$ is adopted to determine whether an MH should be assigned to one of existing clusters or a new cluster should be created. The two matrices DM and ASM are used as input to the algorithm. In a TCG, any two MHs, $m_i$ and $m_j$, possess two properties: $\|m_i m_j\| \leq \Delta$ and $\text{sim}(m_i, m_j) \geq \delta$. The first MH classified into a new cluster is considered as a leader of that cluster, called the *cluster leader*. Each cluster has only one leader, and the cluster leader may be changed when a new MH is classified into the cluster.

The clustering algorithm considers the MHs one at a time and either assigns them to the existing clusters or creates new clusters for them. Let there be $NumClient$ MHs in the system, $\mathcal{M} = \{m_1, m_2, \ldots, m_{NumClient}\}$, in $c$ existing clusters, $\mathcal{C} = \{C_1, C_2, \ldots, C_c\}$ with $c$ corresponding cluster leaders, $\mathcal{L} = \{l_1, l_2, \ldots, l_c\}$. Initially, a new cluster $C_1$ is created for the first MH, $m_1$, and $m_1$ becomes the cluster leader of $C_1$. Then, the other MHs are considered one by one for admission. For each newly admitted MH, $m$, the algorithm finds out the closest cluster leader by looking up the weighted average distance in DM. $m$ is assigned to the closest cluster on condition that the two properties hold, i.e., the weighted average distance between the MH and the cluster leader is less than or equal to $\Delta$ and their similarity scores are larger than or equal to $\delta$; otherwise, the algorithm finds out the next closest cluster leader. This procedure is repeated until an appropriate cluster is found or no existing cluster satisfies the conditions. If there is no suitable cluster for the MH, the MH becomes the cluster leader of a new cluster.

When an MH is assigned to one of the existing clusters, the algorithm has to decide whether the newly admitted MH should be the leader of that cluster. The decision is based on their connectivity. The connectivity of an MH, $m$, as denoted by $\text{Conn}(m)$, is defined as the number of MHs whose weighted average distance between the MH and $m$ is less than or equal to $\Delta$. For instance, assume that $m$ is assigned to an existing cluster $C_h$. If $\text{Conn}(m) > \text{Conn}(l_h)$, $m$ takes over the role as the cluster leader from $l_h$; otherwise, no transition is required.

When a transition of cluster leader occurs, the algorithm checks whether any neighboring clusters should be merged together. If an MH, $m$, becomes the cluster leader of a cluster, $C_h$, the algorithm finds out the closest cluster leader, $l_k$. If the weighted average distances between $l_h$ and all MHs, including the leader, in cluster $C_k$ are less than or equal to $\Delta$ and their similarity scores are larger than or equal to $\delta$, $C_h$ and $C_k$ are merged together. The cluster leader of the merged cluster is the one with the highest connectivity. If

**Algorithm 1** The continuous clustering algorithm

1: **ClusterUpdate**(Cluster $\mathcal{C}$, Leader $\mathcal{L}$, MH $\mathcal{M}$)
2: **while** true **do**
3:   **for all** $m \in \mathcal{M}$ **do**
4:     $cid \leftarrow$ ClusterID($m$); // returns the ID of the assigned Cluster of an MH.
5:     $classified \leftarrow$ false;
6:     **if** $l_{cid} = m$ **then**
7:       **CheckClusterMerge**($\mathcal{C}$, $\mathcal{L}$, $m$);
8:     **else**
9:       **while** $\min_{C_j \in \mathcal{C}} \|ml_j\| \leq \Delta$ **do**
10:         **if** $sim(m, l_j) \geq \delta$ **then**
11:           **if** $m \notin C_j$ **then**
12:             // reassign $m$ to $C_j$
13:             $C_{cid} \leftarrow C_{cid} - \{m\}$; $C_j \leftarrow C_j \cup \{m\}$;
14:           **end if**
15:           **if** Conn($m$) > Conn($l_j$) **then**
16:             // change leadership
17:             $l_j \leftarrow m$;
18:             **CheckClusterMerge**($\mathcal{C}$, $\mathcal{L}$, $m$);
19:           **end if**
20:           $classified \leftarrow$ true;
21:         **end if**
22:       **end while**
23:       **if** not $classified$ **then**
24:         // form a new cluster for $m$
25:         $k \leftarrow$ newClusterID(); // returns a new ID
26:         $C_{cid} \leftarrow C_{cid} - \{m\}$;
27:         $C_k \leftarrow \{m\}$; $\mathcal{C} \leftarrow \mathcal{C} \cup \{C_k\}$;
28:         $l_k \leftarrow m$; $\mathcal{L} \leftarrow \mathcal{L} \cup \{l_k\}$;
29:       **end if**
30:     **end if**
31:   **end for**
32: **end while**

---

**Algorithm 2** The MH join algorithm

1: **MHJoin**(Cluster $\mathcal{C}$, Leader $\mathcal{L}$, MH $m$)
2: $classified \leftarrow$ false;
3: **if** $\mathcal{C} \neq \phi$ **then**
4:   **while** $\min_{C_j \in \mathcal{C}} \|ml_j\| \leq \Delta$ **do**
5:     **if** $sim(m, l_j) \geq \delta$ **then**
6:       $C_j \leftarrow C_j \cup \{m\}$;
7:       **if** Conn($m$) > Conn($l_j$) **then**
8:         $l_j \leftarrow m$;
9:         **CheckClusterMerge**($\mathcal{C}$, $\mathcal{L}$, $m$);
10:       **end if**
11:       $classified \leftarrow$ true;
12:     **end if**
13:   **end while**
14: **end if**
15: **if** not $classified$ **then**
16:   // form a new cluster for $m$
17:   $k \leftarrow$ newClusterID(); // returns a new ID
18:   $C_k \leftarrow \{m\}$; $\mathcal{C} \leftarrow \mathcal{C} \cup \{C_k\}$;
19:   $l_k \leftarrow m$; $\mathcal{L} \leftarrow \mathcal{L} \cup \{l_k\}$;
20: **end if**

---

**Algorithm 3** The MH leave algorithm

1: **MHLeave**(Cluster $\mathcal{C}$, Leader $\mathcal{L}$, MH $m$)
2: $cid \leftarrow$ ClusterID($m$);
3: $C_{cid} \leftarrow C_{cid} - \{m\}$;
4: **if** $C_{cid} = \phi$ **then**
5:   $\mathcal{C} \leftarrow \mathcal{C} - \{C_{cid}\}$; $\mathcal{L} \leftarrow \mathcal{L} - \{l_{cid}\}$;
6:   return;
7: **end if**
8: **if** $l_{cid} = m$ **then**
9:   $k \leftarrow arg_j \max_{m_j \in C_{cid}}(\text{Conn}(m_j))$; $l_{cid} \leftarrow m_k$;
10: **end if**

---

**Algorithm 4** The cluster merge algorithm

1: **ClusterMerge**(Cluster $\mathcal{C}$, Leader $\mathcal{L}$, MH $m$)
2: $cid \leftarrow$ ClusterID($m$);
3: **while** $\min_{C_j \in \mathcal{C} \wedge cid \neq j} \|l_{cid}l_j\| \leq \Delta$ **do**
4:   **if** $sim(l_{cid}, l_j) \geq \delta$ **then**
5:     $merge \leftarrow$ true;
6:     **for all** $m_h \in C_j$ **do**
7:       **if** $\|l_{cid}m_h\| > \Delta$ or $sim(l_{cid}, m_h) < \delta$ **then**
8:         $merge \leftarrow$ false; break;
9:       **end if**
10:     **end for**
11:     **if** $merge$ **then**
12:       **if** Conn($l_{cid}$) < Conn($l_j$) **then**
13:         $l_{cid} \leftarrow l_j$;
14:       **end if**
15:       $C_{cid} \leftarrow C_{cid} \cup \{C_j\}$;
16:       $\mathcal{C} \leftarrow \mathcal{C} - \{C_j\}$;
17:       $\mathcal{L} \leftarrow \mathcal{L} - \{l_j\}$;
18:     **end if**
19:   **end if**
20: **end while**

there is a tie, the initiator, $l_h$, becomes the leader. The algorithm repeats the checking to the next closest cluster, until the weighted average distance between the next closest cluster and $m$ is larger than $\Delta$.

The MSS postpones the announcement of any changes in the cluster, e.g., an MH is assigned to a new cluster or an MH joins/leaves, to any affected MH until the MH sends a request. The MSS then piggybacks the up-to-date member list to the MH along with the required data item. In the member list, the first MH is the cluster leader. In effect, we are performing an asynchronous group view change, without enforcing stringent consistency among group members.

The incremental clustering algorithm consists of four components. Algorithm 1 is a continuous clustering algorithm that is periodically executed to keep track of any changes in the MH mobility and data access patterns and hence the TCG properties. Algorithm 2 is executed when the system detects a new MH. Algorithm 3 is invoked when an MH leaves the system. Algorithm 4, which is invoked by Algorithm 1, is dedicated for performing cluster merging operations.

In the incremental clustering algorithm, $\Delta$ is a key factor to the clustering result. If we consider a case that all MHs in a cluster can connect to each other in single or two-hop communication, the required distance set to $\Delta$ is now derived. Figure 1 illustrates a cluster wherein $m_1$ is the leader of the cluster, and $m_2$ and $m_3$ are two MHs classified into $m_1$'s cluster. Let the distance between $m_2$ or $m_3$ and $m_1$ be equal to $\Delta$. The distance $l$ between $m_1$ and $m_2$ can be computed as: $l = \sqrt{\Delta^2 + \Delta^2 - 2\Delta^2 \cos\gamma} = \Delta\sqrt{2(1 - \cos\gamma)}$, where $0 < \gamma \leq \pi$. When $\gamma = \pi$, $l = 2\Delta$, i.e., $l$ is maximal. To ensure a single-hop communication for the peers in a cluster, $l$ should be less than or equal to $TranRange$, i.e., $2\Delta \leq TranRange$; hence, $\Delta = \frac{TranRange}{2}$. If $\Delta$ is set to $TranRange$, all MHs

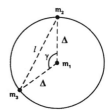

**Figure 1. Threshold $\Delta$ selection**

in a cluster can connect to one another in single- or two-hop communication. After presenting the clustering algorithm, the cooperative cache management scheme will be described in the next section.

### 3.4. Cooperative Cache Management Scheme

For every TCG, the MHs work together to manage their cache space as a whole, i.e., *global cache*. When an MH encounters a local cache miss, it sends a request to its neighboring peers. If one of its peers can turn in the required data item and the local cache is not full, the MH caches the data item, no matter it is returned by a peer in the same TCG or not. However, if the local cache is full, the MH does not cache the data item when it is supplied by a peer in the same TCG, on the belief that the data item can be readily available from the peer if needed. Finally, if the cache is full but the data item comes from a peer outside of its TCG, the MH would rather cache the data item in its local cache by removing the least valuable data item, since the providing peer may move away in future. After a peer sends the required data item to the requesting MH, if they are in the same TCG, the peer updates the last accessed time stamp of the data item, so that the data item can have a longer time-to-live (*TTL*) in the cache.

In GroCoca, the least valuable data item should be first removed from the global cache. To avoid incurring more communication overheads on forwarding data items among the MHs in TCG, an approximate LRU is implemented to perform cache replacement for peers in a TCG. The MH removes the data item with the least utility value from its local cache. The delay on removing the least valuable data item in TCG can be bounded by the time when each MH in the same TCG replaces its least valuable data item from their local cache once.

## 4. Simulation Model

In this section, we present the simulation model that is used to evaluate the performance of COCA and GroCoca. The simulation model is implemented in C++ using CSIM. The simulated mobile environment is composed of an MSS and *NumClient* MHs. The MHs move in a 1000 m × 1000 m (*Area*) space, which constitutes the service area of the MSS. There are 20 wireless communication channels between the MSS and the MHs with a total bandwidth 10 Mbps in downlink channels and 100 kbps in uplink channels. If all the point-to-point communication channels are busy, the MH has to wait until one of them is available

for transmission. Also, there is a wireless communication channel for an MH to communicate with other MHs with a bandwidth 2 Mbps and with a transmission range of *TranRange*. When an MH sends a message to another peer, it has to wait if either its channel or the peer's channel is busy.

### 4.1. Client Model

The mobility of the MHs is based on "reference point group mobility" model [10] which is a random mobility model for a group of MHs and for an individual MH within its group. Each group has a logical center which represents a motion reference point for the MHs belonging to the group. The group mobility is defined according to the "random waypoint" model [4]. The group randomly chooses its own destination in *Area* with a randomly determined speed $s$ from a uniform distribution $U(v_{min}, v_{max})$. It then travels with the constant speed $s$. When it reaches the destination, it comes to a standstill for one second to determine its next destination. It then moves towards its new destination with another random speed $s' \sim U(v_{min}, v_{max})$. All groups repeat this movement behavior during the simulation. In the simulation, the MHs are divided into several motion groups, and each group has *GroupSize* MHs.

The MHs generate accesses to the data items following a Zipf distribution with a skewness parameter $\theta$. If $\theta$ is set to zero, MHs access the data items uniformly. By increasing $\theta$, we are able to model a more skewed access pattern to the data items. The time interval between two consecutive accesses generated by an MH follows an exponential distribution with a mean of one second. The MHs in the same group share a common access range *AccessRange*. The access range of each group is randomly selected.

#### 4.1.1. Power Consumption Model

All MHs are assumed to be equipped with the same type of wireless NICs with an omnidirectional antenna so that all MHs within the transmission range of a transmitting MH can receive its transmission. The wireless NICs of the non-destination MH operates in an idle mode during the transmission. Furthermore, when an MH communicates with other MHs, it is able to adjust the transmission range by controlling the transmission power to the minimum range that can cover the target peers [2, 17].

In the power control mechanism, the transmission power is divided into several discrete levels. Each discrete level is

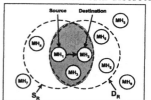 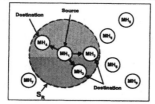

(a) P2P point-to-point communication  (b) P2P Broadcast communication

**Figure 2. Power consumption model.**

associated with a predefined equi-width transmission range. The minimum and maximum power levels produce the shortest transmission range $R_{min}$ and the longest transmission range $R_{max}$ respectively. The distance of each equi-width transmission range is $R_{range}$. When an MH, $m_i$, establishes a P2P point-to-point connection to another MH, $m_j$, the distance between them is $d$, $d = |m_i m_j|$. The required minimum transmission range can be calculated by:

$$R_{ij} = \begin{cases} R_{min}, & \text{for } d \leq R_{min} \\ \lceil d/R_{range} \rceil \times R_{range}, & \text{for } R_{min} < d \leq R_{max} \end{cases} \quad (1)$$

The communication power consumption measurement is based on [7], which uses linear formulas to measure the power consumption of the source MH, $S$, the destination MH, $D$ and other *remaining* MHs residing in the transmission range of the source MH, $S_R$ and the destination MH, $D_R$, Figure 2(a). The P2P point-to-point power consumption is measured by Equation 2.

$$P_{p2p} = \begin{cases} (v_{send} \times |msg|) + f_{send}, & \text{for } m = S \\ (v_{recv} \times |msg|) + f_{recv}, & \text{for } m = D \\ (v_{sd\_disc} \times |msg|) + f_{sd\_disc}, & \text{for } m \in S_R \wedge m \in D_R \\ (v_{s\_disc} \times |msg|) + f_{s\_disc}, & \text{for } m \in S_R \wedge m \notin D_R \\ (v_{d\_disc} \times |msg|) + f_{d\_disc}, & \text{for } m \notin S_R \wedge m \in D_R \end{cases} \quad (2)$$

where $f$ is the fixed setup cost for a transmission, and $v$ is the variable power consumption based on the size of a message $msg$ in byte ($|msg|$).

Power consumption of source MH, $S$, and other MHs residing in $S_R$ of a broadcast communication, as depicted in Figure 2(b), can be measured by Equation 3.

$$P_{bc} = \begin{cases} (v_{bsend} \times |msg|) + f_{bsend}, & \text{for } m = S \\ (v_{brecv} \times |msg|) + f_{brecv}, & \text{for } m \in S_R \end{cases} \quad (3)$$

Although the power consumption model in [7] is based on an ad hoc network mode, it is also used to approximate the power consumption in the communication between the MH and the MSS. When an MH communicates with the MSS, the surrounding MHs are not affected by the transmission so that no power is consumed by their wireless NICs.

### 4.2. Server Model

There is a single MSS in the simulated mobile environment. A database connected to the MSS contains 10000 equal-sized ($DataSize$) data items. It processes the request sent by all MHs residing in $Area$ with a first-come-first-serve policy. An infinite queue is used to buffer the requests from the MHs when the processor is busy.

Table 1 shows the default parameter settings used in the simulated experiments. Table 2 and Table 3 show the parameter settings for MHs playing different roles, as used in power consumption measurement for P2P point-to-point and broadcast communication respectively [7].

**Table 1. Default parameter settings.**

| Parameters | Default Values | Parameters | Default Values |
|---|---|---|---|
| NumClient | 100 | $R_{min}, R_{max}$ | 10, $TranRange$ |
| GroupSize | 5 | $R_{range}$ | 10 m |
| DataSize | 1 kbytes | $\Delta$ | $\frac{1}{2} TranRange$ |
| AccessRange | 1000 items | $\varphi, \varphi'$ | 10, 3 |
| CacheSize | 100 items | $\theta$ | 0.5 |
| TranRange | 100 m | $\omega$ | 0.25 |
| Speed ($v_{min} \sim v_{max}$) | $1 \sim 5$ m/s | $\phi$ | -1 |

**Table 2. Parameter settings for power consumption measurement in P2P point-to-point communication.**

| Conditions | $\mu W \cdot s/byte$ | $\mu W \cdot s$ |
|---|---|---|
| $m = S$ | $v_{send} = 1.9$ | $f_{send} = 454$ |
| $m = D$ | $v_{recv} = 0.5$ | $f_{recv} = 356$ |
| $m \in S_R \wedge m \in D_R$ | $v_{sd\_disc} = 0$ | $f_{sd\_disc} = 70$ |
| $m \in S_R \wedge m \notin D_R$ | $v_{s\_disc} = 0$ | $f_{s\_disc} = 24$ |
| $m \notin S_R \wedge m \in D_R$ | $v_{d\_disc} = 0$ | $f_{d\_disc} = 56$ |

**Table 3. Parameter settings for power consumption measurement in P2P broadcast communication**

| Conditions | $\mu W \cdot s/byte$ | $\mu W \cdot s$ |
|---|---|---|
| $m = S$ | $v_{bsend} = 1.9$ | $f_{bsend} = 266$ |
| $m \in S_R$ | $v_{brecv} = 0.5$ | $f_{brecv} = 56$ |

## 5. Simulated Experiments

In our simulated experiments, we compare the performance of COCA with a conventional caching scheme that does not involve any cooperation among MHs. This serves as a base case for comparison. LRU cache replacement policy is adopted in the base case (non-COCA or NC) and COCA (CC). Likewise, the performance of GroCoca (GC) is evaluated by comparing against the standard COCA. A perfect static knowledge of group classification (SK) is used as a yardstick to evaluate the effectiveness of GC in dynamically determining the TCG membership through incremental clustering. In the perfect static knowledge case, each MH knows the predefined mobility and data access patterns of *all* MHs so that it can correctly identify all the members in its TCG. All simulation results are recorded after the system reaches a stable state. Each MH generates about 20000 requests, where 2000 are treated as warm-up requests in order to avoid a transient effect. We conduct the experiments by varying several parameters: cache size, number of MHs and group size. The performance metrics are the access latency, server request ratio and power consumption on communication. The access latency is defined as a sum of the transmission time and the time spent on waiting for a required communication channel, if it is busy.

### 5.1. Effect of Cache Size

Our first experiment studies the effect of cache size on the system performance by varying the ratio of cache size to databases size from 1 percent to 20 percent. The results are shown in Figure 3.

Figures 3(a) and 3(b) show that all schemes exhibit better access latency and server request ratio with increasing cache size. This is because more required data items can be found in the local cache as the cache gets larger. In terms of the access latency and server request ratio, COCA schemes outperform the non-COCA scheme. For an MH adopting

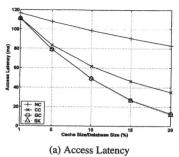
(a) Access Latency

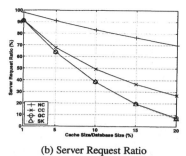
(b) Server Request Ratio

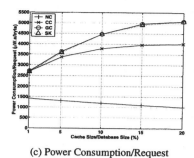
(c) Power Consumption/Request

**Figure 3. Performance studies on various cache size.**

COCA schemes, other than achieving a higher local cache hit ratio as the cache size gets higher, it also enjoys a higher global cache hit ratio because the chance of some neighboring peers turning in the required data item increases with the larger cache size. GC can further improve the access latency and the server request ratio, as it can effectively increase the data availability in TCG. Thus, the MHs adopting GC can achieve a higher global cache hit ratio than COCA.

The cost of adopting CC and GC is higher power consumption, as depicted in Figure 3(c). When the MHs enjoy higher local cache hit ratio, they can reduce the power consumption in broadcasting request to their neighboring peers. However, when the global cache hit ratio increases, more peers turn in the required data item to the requesting MHs. Therefore, the MHs have to consume much more power for sending the data item to their neighboring peers, and discarding unintended messages as they are residing in the transmission range of a source MH, destination MH or both. It would have saved much power if there is a mechanism for MHs to filter off unintended messages early on.

The performance difference between GC and SK increases as the server request ratio decreases. In GC, the accuracy of the clustering algorithm depends on the update rate of the mobility and data access information that is embedded to the request sent to the MSS. The update rate reduces with decreasing server request ratio so that the precision of the clustering algorithm is reduced.

### 5.2. Effect of Number of MHs

This experiment studies the effect of system workload on the system performance by varying the number of MHs in the system from 100 to 500 with the same default *GroupSize*. The results are depicted in Figure 4.

The system workload becomes higher with increasing number of MHs in the system, so that access latency increases in NC, as depicted in Figure 4(a). On the other hand, performance of CC and GC improves slightly as the number of MHs increases because there is a higher chance for the MHs to obtain the required data items from their neighboring peers. In other words, the system workload caused by increasing number of MHs is distributively shared by the group of MHs. The COCA schemes can thus be used as a load sharing technique in a heavily-loaded mobile environment. However, CC and GC are power intensive protocols,

as depicted in Figure 4(c), the power consumption of the MHs increases with the increasing number of MHs.

In this series of experiment, the client density of the system gets higher, as the number of MHs increases. In a high density situation, the chance of multiple motion groups possessing common mobility and data access patterns increases. Since GC is able to take such dynamic mobility behavior into consideration, the performance of GC is better than SK, when the number of MHs in the system is larger than 100. This result shows that the incremental clustering algorithm is effective in determining the proper TCG dynamically. The server request ratio is slightly reduced as the number of MHs increases, so the MSS can obtain sufficient location and data access information from the MHs via the server requests.

### 5.3. Effect of Group Size

In this series of simulated experiment, we examine the influence of system performance on various group size: 1, 2, 4, 5, 10, 20 and 25 and the results are illustrated in Figure 5.

In Figures 5(a) and 5(b), it can be observed that CC and GC outperform NC as the group size increases. Since there is no collaboration among peers in NC, its performance is not affected by varying the group size. Similar to the study of the cache size, GC performs better than CC in this series of simulated experiments. Since GC can improve the data availability in a TCG, the probability that the MHs can obtain the required data items from their neighboring peers is higher. Thus, access latency and server request ratio can be reduced. However, in CC and GC, the MHs have to consume much more power to communicate with other peers, as depicted in Figure 5(c). As the group size increases, the MHs spend more power to receive broadcast requests and to discard unintended messages sent by their neighboring peers. GC performs worse than SK when the server request ratio is less than 5 percent, due to the fact that the MSS does not have sufficient information to maintain the accuracy of the clustering algorithm.

### 6. Conclusion

In this paper, we have described a cooperative caching scheme, called COCA, in a pull-based mobile environment, and proposed a group-based cooperative caching scheme, called GroCoca, which adopts a centralized incremental

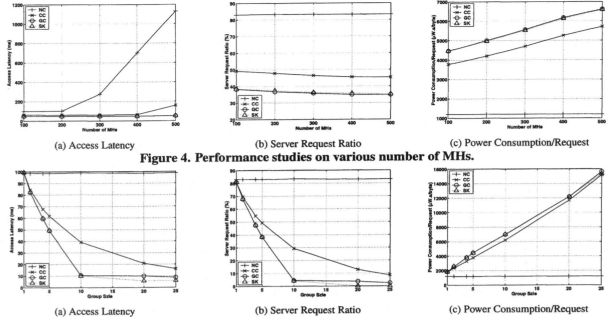

(a) Access Latency      (b) Server Request Ratio      (c) Power Consumption/Request

**Figure 4. Performance studies on various number of MHs.**

(a) Access Latency      (b) Server Request Ratio      (c) Power Consumption/Request

**Figure 5. Performance studies on various group size.**

clustering algorithm to determine all *tightly-coupled groups* (TCGs) by considering the combination of MHs' mobility and data access patterns. In a TCG, the MHs work together to make cache placement decision to improve data availability. The performance of COCA and GroCoca is evaluated through a number of simulated experiments, which show that COCA substantially reduces the access latency and the server request ratio, but it consumes much more power than a conventional caching scheme. GroCoca further improves the access latency and the server request ratio, but with extra power consumption.

## References

[1] S. Acharya, M. Franklin, and S. Zdonik. Balancing push and pull for data broadcast. In *Proc. of the SIGMOD*, pages 183–194, May 1997.

[2] S. Agarwal, S. V. Krishnamurthy, R. H. Katz, and S. K. Dao. Distributed power control in ad-hoc wireless networks. In *Proc. of the 12th PIMRC*, pages 59–66, September 2001.

[3] B. An and S. Papavassiliou. A mobility-based clustering approach to support mobility management and multicast routing in mobile ad-hoc wireless networks. *International Journal of Network Management*, 11(6):387–395, November 2001.

[4] J. Broch, D. A. Maltz, D. B. Johnson, Y.-C. Hu, and J. Jetcheva. A performance comparison of multi-hop wireless ad hoc network routing protocols. In *Proc. of the 4th MobiCom*, pages 85–97, October 1998.

[5] J. H. P. Chim, M. Green, R. W. H. Lau, H. V. Leong, and A. Si. On caching and prefetching of virtual objects in distributed virtual environments. In *Proc. of the 6th ACM International Conference on Multimedia*, pages 171–180, September 1998.

[6] C.-Y. Chow, H. V. Leong, and A. Chan. Peer-to-peer cooperative caching in mobile environments. In *Proc. of the 24th ICDCS Workshops on MDC*, pages 528–533, March 2004.

[7] L. M. Feeney and M. Nilsson. Investigating the energy consumption of a wireless network interface in an ad hoc networking environment. In *Proc. of the 20th INFOCOM*, pages 1548–1557, April 2001.

[8] T. Hara. Effective replica allocation in ad hoc networks for improving data accessibility. In *Proc. of the 20th INFOCOM*, pages 1568–1576, April 2001.

[9] T. Hara. Cooperative caching by mobile clients in push-based information systems. In *Proc. of the 11th CIKM*, pages 186–193, November 2002.

[10] X. Hong, M. Gerla, G. Pei, and C.-C. Chiang. A group mobility model for ad hoc wireless networks. In *Proc. of the 2nd MSWiM*, pages 53–60, August 1999.

[11] J.-L. Huang, M.-S. Chen, and W.-C. Peng. Exploring group mobility for replica data allocation in a mobile environment. In *Proc. of the 12th CIKM*, pages 161–168, November 2003.

[12] W. H. O. Lau, M. Kumar, and S. Venkatesh. A cooperative cache architecture in support of caching multimedia objects in MANETs. In *Proc. of the 5th ACM WoWMoM*, pages 56–63, September 2002.

[13] C. R. Lin and M. Gerla. Adaptive clustering for mobile wireless networks. *IEEE JSAC*, 15(7):1265–1275, September 1997.

[14] M. Papadopouli and H. Schulzrinne. Effects of power conservation, wireless coverage and cooperation on data dissemination among mobile devices. In *Proc. of the 2nd MobiHoc*, pages 117–127, October 2001.

[15] F. Sailhan and V. Issarny. Cooperative caching in ad hoc networks. In *Proc. of the 4th MDM*, pages 13–28, January 2003.

[16] K. H. Wang and B. Li. Efficient and guaranteed service coverage in partitionable mobile ad-hoc networks. In *Proc. of the 21st INFOCOM*, pages 1089–1098, June 2002.

[17] J. E. Wieselthier, G. D. Nguyen, and A. Ephremides. Energy-efficient broadcast and multicast trees in wireless networks. *MONET*, 7(6):481–492, December 2002.

# Mitigating Information Asymmetries to achieve Efficient Peer-to-Peer Queries

Jiang Guo, Baochun Li
Department of Electrical and Computer Engineering
University of Toronto
{jguo,bli}@eecg.toronto.edu

## Abstract

*Querying for a particular data item is perhaps the most important feature to be supported by peer-to-peer network infrastructures, and receives the most research attention in recent literature. Most existing work follows the line of designing decentralized algorithms to maximize the performance of peer-to-peer queries. These algorithms often have specific rules that peer nodes should adhere to (e.g., placement of data items on particular nodes), and thus assumes that peers are strictly cooperative. However, in realistic peer-to-peer networks, selfish and greedy peer nodes are the norm, and query strategies degenerate to random or flooding based searches. In this paper, we explore the design space with respect to query efficiency in selfish peer-to-peer networks where nodes have asymmetric information, and apply the signaling mechanism from microeconomics to facilitate the sharing of private information and thus improve search efficiency. We extensively simulate the signaling mechanism in the context of other alternative solutions in selfish networks, and show encouraging results with respect to improving query performance.*

## 1  Introduction

Querying for a particular data item is perhaps the most important feature to be supported by peer-to-peer network infrastructures, and receives the most research attention in recent literature. Most existing work seeks to design decentralized algorithms to maximize the performance of peer-to-peer queries. These algorithms often have specific rules that peer nodes should adhere to. Examples of such rules include all research proposals in the area of *structured* peer-to-peer networks, which specify the mandatory placement of data items on particular nodes (e.g., the Chord protocol [10]), and thus assist to achieve querying performance in the order of $\log N$, $N$ being the size of the peer-to-peer network. Obviously, these proposals assume that peers are strictly *cooperative* when it comes to implementing these

rules. However, in realistic peer-to-peer networks, selfish and greedy peer nodes are the norm, and query strategies unfortunately degenerate to random or flooding based searches (e.g., Gnutella). In such scenarios (often referred to as *unstructured* peer-to-peer networks), either the search performance is not satisfactory ($O(N)$) when doing random searches, or the message exchange overhead is high, when performing flooding-based searches.

Various previous work [1, 4, 6, 11] have been attempting to address such problem of querying performance in unstructured peer-to-peer networks. As one example, Cohen *et al.* [4] resort to the approach of requiring peer nodes to *collaboratively replicate* the actual data items in demand. We observe that all previous proposals have resorted to the introduction of a certain degree of *structure* or *discipline* (e.g., required replications) to an unstructured peer-to-peer network, and with this measure they have been successful in achieving better querying performances. Furthermore, we emphasize the following key observation: Introducing a certain degree of structure or discipline in unstructured networks has imposed the unwarranted assumption of *cooperation*, which is against the observation that leads to the study of such networks in the first place: *selfishness of nodes*. For one example, selfish peer nodes may not even be willing to share its own *private information* to others (the case of *asymmetric information*), not to mention the cooperation required to implement protocols that introduce structure (e.g., replications).

In this paper, we explore the following questions: What may occur if peer nodes do not share their private information, such as shortcuts to existing data items? What may be possibly proposed to incentivize selfish nodes to share their private information for the common good? Ultimately, what may be possibly proposed to improve query efficiency in selfish peer-to-peer networks where nodes hold asymmetric information? In light of all these questions, we propose to apply the *signaling* mechanism from microeconomics to facilitate the sharing of private information and thus improve search efficiency and avoid the phenomenon of adverse selection. We extensively simulate the signaling mechanism

91

in the context of other alternative solutions in selfish networks, and show encouraging results with respect to improving query performance.

The remainder of the paper is organized as follows. We formulate the problem in Sec. 2. In Sec. 3 we begin by discussing the case of asymmetrical information, and propose mechanisms to signal those private information, which can significantly improve the system equilibrium. In Sec. 4 we propose a set of distributed algorithms and present simulation results. Sec. 5 concludes the paper.

## 2 Problem Formulation

In this paper, we consider an *unstructured peer-to-peer network* that consists of $N$ selfish nodes. Each node can create shortcuts (*i.e.*, pointers) to any data items on any nodes. In addition, each node also has a set of *neighbors*, which generally includes all the other nodes in the network that this node is aware of. Since on each node $u$ the table to contain shortcuts is of limited size which is smaller than the number of items in the network, when node $u$ wishes to access an item that is not in its own shortcut table, node $u$ has to turn to its neighbors to forward the query until a node that owns such item is found or certain maximum query limits are imposed. We illustrate the nodes and their roles in the peer-to-peer network in Fig. 1.

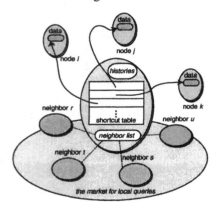

**Figure 1. Nodes in a peer-to-peer network.**

Provided that nodes are selfish and always seek to maximize their own gains, it is natural that nodes have to be rewarded in some way for providing the service of processing incoming queries. For convenience of our analysis, we model such queries in a *market*. At each query hop, the node that initiates the query and its neighbors constitute the market. In such market, the querying node, referred to as a *consumer*, is interested in the *commodity*, which is the information on the item's location. As a consumer, the querying node can purchase the commodity from its neighbors, also referred to as *producers*.

The nodes that initiate the queries wish to access the item as quickly and efficiently as possible — they benefit or *gain* from such successful queries. We introduce $\theta$ to quantitatively model such gains, and to reflect the quality of the purchased commodity. A commodity is said to have a quality of $\theta$, if the consumer receives a gain of $\theta$ when the consumer purchases such a commodity. A higher $\theta$ implies that the producer providing such a commodity is more likely to find the item. Without loss of generality and for convenience of our analysis, the producer that provides a commodity of $\theta$ gain is considered to have a *type* of $\theta$ (using microeconomics terms). We let $[\underline{\theta}, \overline{\theta}] \subset \mathbb{R}$ denote the set of possible quality levels, where $0 \le \underline{\theta} < \overline{\theta} < \infty$. $\overline{\theta}$ implies that the producer is most likely to locate the item, *i.e.*, it has the item in its possession or a shortcut to the item in its shortcut table. On the contrary, $\underline{\theta}$ implies that the producer is most unlikely to find the item, *i.e.*, it has no idea with respect to the whereabouts of the item. When selecting a neighbor to forward the query, it is clear that the neighbor of the highest type is always preferred.

The proportion of producers with $\theta$ or less is given by the distribution function $F(\theta)$. For simplicity, we assume that $F(\cdot)$ is nondegenerate and has an associated density function $f(\cdot)$, with $f(\theta) > 0$ for all $\theta \in [\underline{\theta}, \overline{\theta}]$. To produce a commodity of quality $\theta$ (to obtain the information on the position of the item, *e.g.*, entries in the shortcut table with a limited size), a producer incurs certain costs, denote as $r(\theta)$. We make the following assumptions with respect to such costs:

1. $r(\theta) \le \theta$, for all $\theta \in [\underline{\theta}, \overline{\theta}]$;

2. $r(\cdot)$ is a strictly increasing function.

The first assumption implies that every producer has a chance to accept queries, so that we disregard the case when $r(\theta)$ is larger than $\theta$. The second assumption implies that the producers with higher types are more likely to cost more to produce the commodity, *i.e.*, to obtain the information of the item. This assumption is mainly for the simplicity of our theoretical analysis. We relax such an assumption in our simulation experiments in Sec. 4.2.

Consider a producer $v$ of type $\theta$, $\theta$ is proprietary to $v$ itself, and not known by other nodes, including its neighbors. We refer to such information as *private information*. Such a scenario where nodes keep private information from other nodes is economically known as a system with *asymmetric information*. The opposite case is the system with *symmetric information*. Asymmetric information significantly impairs query performance in peer-to-peer networks. For example, suppose a consumer $u$ chooses to purchase the commodity at a price $p$ from a set of producers with different types. In the case of symmetric information, the consumer $u$ chooses the producer with the highest type $\overline{\theta}$ and receives the profit of $\pi_u = \overline{\theta} - p$. However, in the case of asymmetric information, the consumer can not tell the producers of high types apart from the producers of low types, *i.e.*, the consumer may not be able to choose the producer with $\overline{\theta}$.

In this paper, we are interested in exploring the effects of asymmetric information, as well as different alternatives of mitigating asymmetries in order to improve peer-to-peer queries.

# 3 Mitigating Information Asymmetries

For comparison purposes, we first consider the case of symmetric information, the ideal case where the types of the neighbors are *publicly observable*. In this case, since the consumer $u$ knows the quality of all commodities, it is clear that $u$ will simply choose the commodity of the highest quality. By choosing the neighbor that has the highest type $\theta$, the consumer $u$ will maximize its payoff.

To study the price $p^*$ at the equilibrium, we study the market where multiple consumers compete for one commodity by setting different prices, and the one with the highest price obtains the commodity. Following the *Bertrand model* [3], this is a simple case of an oligopolistic market, where we have $p^* = \overline{\theta}$ at equilibrium. The consumer $u$ earns zero profit due to the competition from other consumers. The producer of the highest type $\overline{\theta}$ wins the offer and obtains a welfare of $\overline{\theta} - r(\overline{\theta})$. It is clear that upon this query the market is efficient. However, such an ideal case is unrealistic in unstructured peer-to-peer networks, where such type information is not publicly observable, belonging to the case of asymmetric information.

## 3.1 Information asymmetries: microeconomics

We proceed to study the equilibrium in the case of asymmetric information and the welfare at such equilibrium.

The problem is modeled as a dynamic game $\mathcal{G}$. The steps of the game are as follows: (1) the consumer $u$ claims a price $p$; (2) each producer chooses to accept it or not and replies its choice to $u$; and (3) $u$ randomly chooses one of the set of neighbors who accept the price.

Due to asymmetric information, the consumer $u$ does not have any knowledge about its producers except $\underline{\theta}$ and $\overline{\theta}$. We note that when the types of producers are not observable, the price $p$ must be independent of such types.

From the perspective of a producer with type $\theta$, its strategy is straightforward: it chooses to serve $u$ only if $r(\theta)$ is equal to or smaller than $p$.

Let the inverse function of $x = r(\theta)$ be $\theta = g(x)$, the average commodity quality that the consumer $u$ receives when price is $p$ will be $D(p) = \int_{\underline{\theta}}^{g(p)} x f(x) dx$, where $f(\cdot)$ is the density function of producers' type.

Particularly, for any $p \in [r(\overline{\theta}), \overline{\theta}]$, all producers will choose to accept the price. For simplicity, we let $E[\theta]$ represent the expected commodity quality that the consumer

$u$ receives when all the producers are willing to accept the price, *i.e.*, $E[\theta] = \int_{\underline{\theta}}^{\overline{\theta}} x f(x) dx$.

To examine the consumer's strategy, we introduce the notion of a *competitive equilibrium* presented in Definition 3.1 1.

**Definition 1:** When producer types are unobservable, a *competitive equilibrium* is an operating point, where $p^* = D(p^*)$.

We call this a microeconomic approach, in which case the consumer $u$ will choose to be at the competitive equilibrium.

**Proposition 1:** There exists at least one competitive equilibrium, where $p^* = D(p^*)$.

*Proof:* Let function $\phi(p)$ represent $D(p) - p$. Since $D(p)$ is continuous on $p \in [r(\underline{\theta}), \overline{\theta}]$, $\phi(p)$ is continuous on the same range as well. When $p = r(\underline{\theta})$, $D(p) = \underline{\theta}$; hence, $\phi(r(\underline{\theta})) = \underline{\theta} - r(\underline{\theta})$. When $p = \overline{\theta}$, $D(p) = E[\theta]$ and $\phi(\overline{\theta}) = E[\theta] - \overline{\theta}$. With assumption 1, we have $r(\theta) \leq \theta, \forall \theta \in [\underline{\theta}, \overline{\theta}]$. Therefore, we have $\phi(r(\underline{\theta})) \geq 0$. On the other hand, it is not difficult to find out $E[\theta] \leq \overline{\theta}$, such that we have $\phi(\overline{\theta}) \leq 0$. According to the *intermediate value theorem* [5], there exists at least one $p^*$ that satisfy $\phi(p^*) = 0$, *i.e.*, $p^* = D(p^*)$. $\square$

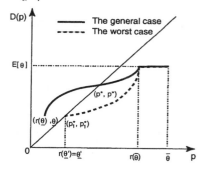

**Figure 2. General competitive equilibrium and the worst case**

Fig. 2 illustrates how Definition 1 helps to determine competitive equilibria. The solid curve is the general case of function $D(p)$, which has a competitive equilibrium $p^*$. Furthermore, from Fig. 2, we have two observations:

1. Competitive equilibria are actually those intersecting points between the curve $D(p)$ and the line of $D(p) = p$;

2. The competitive equilibrium price $p^*$ is upper bounded by $E[\theta]$ and lower bounded by $\underline{\theta}$.

The first observation is straightforward, according to the definition of competitive equilibrium. From the second observation, we notice that the competitive equilibrium may not be efficient and may be much smaller than $E[\theta]$. The problem is that to get the producers of the highest type to

93

accept the query, we need $p$ to be at least $r(\overline{\theta})$. However, the consumer $u$ can not reach even at this price because doing so will bring $u$ a negative payoff of $E[\theta] - r(\overline{\theta})$. Therefore, the consumer will choose to lower the price $p$ until the competitive equilibrium is encountered. In microeconomics term, such phenomenon is known as *adverse selection*. In the present context, adverse selection arises when only the commodities of lower quality are chosen, *i.e.*, only the neighbors that have worse path to the item are willing to accept the query. The worst case occurs, which is depicted as the dotted curve in Fig. 2, when we have $r(\underline{\theta}) = \underline{\theta}$ and $r(\theta) < \theta$ for all other $\theta$. The equilibrium price is $p^* = \underline{\theta}$, which is the lower bound.

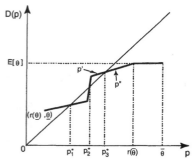

**Figure 3. The case of multiple competitive equilibria**

Depending on the distribution of neighbors/producers of different types $F(\theta)$, multiple competitive equilibria may exist, *e.g.*, Fig. 3 depicts a case in which there are three equilibria. Unfortunately, the lowest competitive equilibrium is always chosen by such microeconomic approach. In microeconomics, this is called *coordination failure*. The reason is straightforward: the price $p$ is too low because the consumer $u$ expects that the average quality of the commodities is low and, at the same time, only low type producers accept the query precisely because the price $p$ is low.

To summarize, based on the concept of competitive equilibrium, the microeconomic approach is inefficient due to *adverse selection* and *coordination failure*. Because of adverse selection, the average quality of commodity that the consumer $u$ receives can not reach the upper bound $E[\theta]$, while coordination failure causes the consumer $u$ to choose to stay at the lowest competitive equilibrium.

### 3.2 Information asymmetries: games

We propose an alternative approach based on game theory to address the problem of coordination failure. In such a game-theoretic model, the consumer $u$ could change the price $p$ and choose not to enter an equilibrium, if it observes that deviating from such equilibrium can yield higher payoff. In other words, in the game-theoretic model, consumer

$u$ is more sophisticated: If the price is too low, the consumer $u$ will find it in its interest to offer a higher price and attract better neighbors until the highest-price competitive outcome is obtained.

Furthermore, we will show that the consumer $u$ chooses to stay at the highest competitive equilibrium, which is actually the unique subgame perfect Nash equilibrium defined by Proposition 2.

**Proposition 2:** Let $p^*$ be the highest competitive equilibrium. If there is an $\epsilon > 0$ such that $D(p') > p'$ for all $p' \in (p^* - \epsilon, p^*)$, then $p^*$ is the unique pure strategy subgame perfect Nash equilibrium of the game-theoretic model.

*Proof:* We observe that Proposition 2 is exactly the first case of Proposition 13.B.1 in [7]. Refer to [7] for a detailed proof. □

For example, in Fig. 3, consider the equilibria $p_1^*$ and $p_2^*$, which are obviously dominated by the equilibrium $p_3^*$. In equilibrium $p_3^*$, for any $p'' > p_3^*$, the consumer $u$ will choose $p_3^*$ due to adverse selection, *i.e.*, $p''$ is dominated by $p_3^*$. On the other hand, for any $p' \in (p_2^*, p_3^*)$, the consumer $u$ earns positive profit on $p'$. However, due to the competition from other consumers, the consumer $u$ will finally choose $p_3^*$ instead and earn zero profit. Therefore, the consumer $u$ will arrive at the highest equilibrium $p_3^*$ and will no longer deviate.

The game-theoretic model solves the issue of coordination failure and achieves the highest competitive equilibrium. However, the game-theoretic model still suffers from adverse selection that is originated from asymmetric information. Consequently, the outcome of the game-theoretic model is also upper bounded by $E[\theta]$.

### 3.3 Mitigating Information asymmetries: signaling

*Signaling* [2, 9], as a branch of microeconomics, has been proposed to solve the problem of asymmetric information. In this paper, we apply the *signaling* mechanism to accomplish this objective. The basic idea is that the producers (neighbors) of high types may have actions they can take to distinguish themselves from their low type counterparts.

We model the problem as a *signaling game*, also a dynamic game of asymmetric information. As an extreme example to simply our analysis, we ask the producers to *signal their types by actually finding the item*. Obviously, this approach results in much overhead, since in some cases a number of producers would like to perform the query. In Sec. 4, we introduce a refined approach whose overhead is more moderate. We adapt the model discussed above as follows. The steps of the dynamic game is as follows: (1) the consumer $u$ claims a price $p$ and asks the producers — all its neighbors — to find the item; (2) each neighbor (producer) chooses whether or not it should *exactly* locate the item and replies the result to the consumer $u$; and (3) $u$ randomly choose one of the neighbors which has reported positive results to process the query.

In the analysis that follows, we examine the possible equilibrium of the signaling model and the welfare of each producer and consumer. Compared with the model discussed in Sec. 3.1, the significant extension of our signaling model is that the producers can infer their types by executing the signaling action. The cost incurred by such an action for a type $\theta$ producer is given by the function $c(\theta)$, which is assumed to be lower for high type producers, *e.g.*, $c(\overline{\theta}) < c(\underline{\theta})$. Since in most cases $r(\theta) \ll c(\theta)$, to keep things simple, we concentrate on the special case in which $r(\theta) = 0, \forall \theta \in [\underline{\theta}, \overline{\theta}]$.

From the perspective of a producer $v$ with type $\theta$, its strategy is as follows:

- $v$ chooses to take the signaling action, if $c(\theta) \leq p$;
- otherwise, $v$ chooses not to take the signaling action:

  - if there exists another producer that takes signaling action, $v$ is considered by the consumer $u$ as low type producer; therefore, $v$ receives zero profit.
  - if none of producers take signal action, the model degenerates to the microeconomic model discussed in Sec. 3.1.

For convenience of analysis, We further assume that $c(\overline{\theta}) < \overline{\theta} < c(\underline{\theta})$, so that only part of producers take the signaling action. Let the inverse function of $x = c(\theta)$ be $\theta = h(x)$, the average commodity quality that the consumer $u$ receives when price is $p$ will be $D'(p) = \int_{h(p)}^{\overline{\theta}} x f(x) dx$, where $p \in [c(\overline{\theta}), c(\underline{\theta})]$.

Similar to Sec. 3.1, we have the following definition and proposition.

**Definition 2:** When producers are eligible to take signaling actions, a *signaling equilibrium* is an operating point, where $p^* = D'(p^*)$.

**Proposition 3:** If there exists at least one producer that takes the signaling action, there exists at least one signaling equilibrium, where $p^* = D'(p^*)$.

Due to space constraints, we omit the proof that is similar to the proof of Proposition 1.

Since the consumer $u$ should earn at least zero profit, $p^*$ can not be larger than $\overline{\theta}$. Such an upper bound can be achieved when $c(\overline{\theta}) = \overline{\theta}$. Therefore, $p^*$ is upper bounded by $\overline{\theta}$.

We then discuss two extreme cases: (1) all producers take the signaling action; (2) none of producers take the action. In the former case, $c(\underline{\theta}) \leq p$, *i.e.*, the signaling action is so inexpensive that each producer takes the action

attempting to distinguish itself from other producers; on the contrary, in the latter case, $c(\overline{\theta}) > p$, meaning that the signaling action is too costly for any producer to take. However, in both cases, since we assume $r(\theta) = 0$, all producers accept the offer $p$. Furthermore, since the consumer $u$ can not distinguish high type producers from low type ones, the expected commodity quality that the consumer $u$ receives is $E[\theta]$ in both cases. If we consider both cases as extreme cases of the signaling game, the signaling equilibrium price $p^*$ is lower bounded by $E[\theta]$.

In most cases when only part of producers takes the signaling action, the signaling approach is efficient: the signaling approach can distinguish the producers of higher types and consequently improve the system query efficiency. However, signaling also incurs costs. For example, the proposed signaling approach may be costly in term of overhead. Consider a case when most neighbors have high types and would like to distinguish themselves, most neighbors would choose to complete the query; therefore, this approach becomes a flooding style query, which results in significant message overhead.

## 4 Algorithm Design and Performance Evaluation

### 4.1 HU algorithm: type estimation

In previous sections, in the case of a query, we assume that each producer has a type $\theta$, which reflects the extent to which the neighbor knows the position of the item being queried. Obviously, such type does not exist in reality. For the purpose of providing type information, we introduce HU algorithm, which is required before any microeconomics-based approaches may be implemented.

In HU algorithm, each node is required to keep a history of the queries. The history contains pair values of the following information: (1) the identifier of an item; (2) the timestamp of the last query to this item. When a node has just performed a query on an item, or forwarded a query on such item, the node updates the timestamp of this item. The intuition behind such mechanism is that a node that has recently performed or forwarded a query on an item is more likely to have an advantage over another node that has not recently encountered a query on such an item. Since the size of the history is limited, when a new entry is about to be inserted and the history is full, the history entry with the lowest timestamp is evicted.

Given the history of queries, we can obtain the type $\theta$ from the timestamp $t$ of the query. Consider an incoming query on item $i$, the producer $v$ checks its local storage as well as its history of queries. In the case that item $i$ has an entry in the query history with timestamp $t$, a larger $t$ means higher probability to achieve a successful query, indicating a higher type $\theta$. Formally, we can assume that producer $v$ associates $\theta$ with $t$ through a mapping function $\theta = \sigma(t)$, which increases on $t$. In the case that item $i$ is possessed by $v$, we can consider $t$ to be the current time $t_{now}$. Another extreme case occurs when item $i$ is in neither local storage nor the query history, we let $t$ be zero in this case.

Similarly, we can estimate $r(\theta)$ and $c(\theta)$. The production cost $r(\theta)$ has two parts: (1) the occupation cost of the entry in the query history; (2) the cost to update the entry. We model the production cost $r(\theta)$ by the function $r(\theta) = \tau(L_v, x, \theta)$, where $L_v$ is the size of the query history of $v$, and $x$ is the number of times that item $i$'s history entry has been updated during last time period $T$. A larger history size leads to lower $r(\theta)$, while a higher updating frequency means higher $r(\theta)$.

In order to estimate $c(\theta)$, we require that the current producer needs to know the number of hops $h$ that current query has covered so far. This can easily be done by allocating an entry in the message header of such a query message and asking intermediate producers to increment such entry. We model the signaling cost $c(\theta)$ by the function $c(\theta) = \chi(h, \theta)$. Intuitively, $c(\theta)$ becomes lower when $h$ increases.

## 4.2 Performance Evaluation

We have conducted simulation-based experiments using a packet-level, event-based C++ simulator to evaluate the effects of asymmetric information and to reveal the strengths of the signaling algorithm (SG) (Sec. 3.3), in the context of three approaches: (1) The ideal case of symmetric information (SI); (2) the microeconomic approach illustrated in Sec. 3.1 (ME); and (3) the game-theoretic approach outlined in Sec. 3.2 (GT).

SI is the ideal case that can always find the producer that has the highest type. In the other algorithms, transactions occur among nodes during the query. The difference is that in ME the consumer always adheres to the lowest competitive equilibrium while in GT the highest competitive equilibrium is chosen. In SG, the producers are offered an opportunity to complete specific actions in order to signal their types.

The signaling approach proposed in Sec. 3 is effective to enable high type producers to distinguish themselves. However, such approach may lead to significant message overhead, especially in the case that most producers are of high type. Instead, we introduce a slightly different version of such a signaling method. The consumer incrementally increases the price $p$ until one or more producers accept to process the query or $p_{max}$ is reached (obviously $p_{max} \leq \bar{\theta}$); the consumer randomly chooses one of them and pay the price $p$ until the query completes. Such refined approach does not qualitatively change the purpose of the signaling

method and, meanwhile, significantly reduces the message overhead brought by signaling.

Initially, each node is given a set of peer nodes as neighbors, which consists of an initial topology. To focus on the effect of shortcuts, we fix the neighbor set during the simulation. We have performed most of our simulations in a ring-like initial topology. We have also performed the simulation in the cases of other initial topologies such as (1) two-dimensional grids; (2) random graphs with Zipf-like node degree distributions; and (3) random graph with Gnutella-like node degree distributions, and have obtained qualitatively similar results. We omit the figures of these settings due to the space constraints.

The network consists of 1000 homogeneous nodes and 100 items. Each node has a shortcut table of 20 and a history [1] of size 40, i.e., $L = 40$. All items have uniform popularity. The network generates queries using a Poisson process with an average query rate $\lambda$ of 100 queries per time unit. The life time of each item follows the exponential distribution with the average life time of $\mu = 100$ time units. Each simulation runs 1000 time units which is sufficient for each algorithm to reach a stable state.

We assume that initially each item only has one copy in the network, and each consumer never replicates the item that has been queried and supposedly retrieved. The querying process progresses until the desired item is located or the maximum hops limit of 40 is reached.

We list the estimation functions that we use in the simulations as follows [2].

$$\theta = \frac{\max(t - t_0, 0) * 1000}{T} \quad (1)$$

$$r(\theta) = \frac{\min(x + 1, 20) * \theta}{20 * L} \quad (2)$$

$$c(\theta) = \frac{(40 - h) * 500 * T}{40 * \max(1, t - t_0)} \quad (3)$$

where $t$ is the timestamp of the history entry, $t_0$ is the beginning moment of every time period of $T$ ($T = 50$).

### 4.2.1 Simulation Results: Query Efficiency

With respect to the efficiency of queries, we compare all four algorithms in both the average query resolution hops and the query success ratios.

Fig. 4(a) shows that none of the algorithms has succeeded to resolve all the queries[3]. This is reasonable since the network is *strictly* unstructured with a query hop limit

---

[1]In case when an item is not in the history, it means the node has no idea on the whereabout of such item, i.e., it has the lowest type.

[2]We believe that substituting the constants in the functions with different values does not qualitatively effect our conclusions

[3]Since the type information we use here is not accurate and just an approximation, the SI algorithm in our simulation cannot always resolve queries.

of 40. The uniformly distributed item popularity and the approximation of type information also contribute to such results. SI always outperforms all the other alternatives, for the reason that a node in SI can always select the neighbor with the best knowledge of the desired item. SG is the second best, which solves about 40% compared to about 50% of SI. Compared with ME (about 18%) and GT (about 20%), the signaling approach significantly improves the query efficiency. This validates our analysis in previous sections that signaling can distinguish the advantageous neighbors from the neighbors that are less so. GT is worse than SG, but is still slightly better than ME. This confirms our analysis that, due to the coordination failure in ME, the market often fails and behaves inefficiently. Obviously, according to the figure, GT overcomes the issue of coordination failures, but still suffers from the asymmetric information.

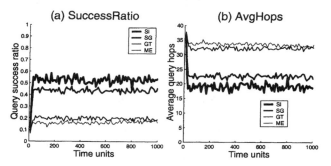

Figure 4. Query performance under uniform data popularity: (a) query success ratios; (b) average number of hops

Further, we evaluate the efficiency of queries in terms of the average number of query hops. As is evident in Fig. 4(b), the performance of SG approaches that of SI and results in much fewer query hops in average than GT and ME.

### 4.2.2 Simulation Results: Query Overhead

In order to evaluate the message passing overhead when performing queries, we compare all four algorithms with respect to the number of messages transmitted. Fig. 5 shows that SI causes the lowest amount of message overhead, due to the fact that the queries in SI can always find the best path to the item (*i.e.*, the shortest query path), and that there exist no transaction costs. GT and ME lead to nearly the same level of message overhead and ranks the second among the alternatives. Since in each query hop the current node needs to perform transactions with all neighbors, such an action results in additional overhead compared with that of SI. SG is evidently the worst, and causes worse levels of message passing overhead than GT and ME. This is because that, in our implementation of the signaling approach, the consumer

needs to incrementally increase the price $p$ until a producer of a high type accepts the query, which results in additional overhead. Considering the performance we have acquired by introducing signaling, the extra overhead is the cost that we have to pay, and we believe that SG has reached a better point of tradeoff between query performance and overhead.

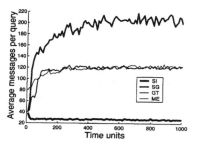

Figure 5. Query overhead in terms of the average number of messages per query under uniform data popularity

### 4.2.3 The case of heterogeneous item popularity

We have also evaluated all four algorithms under the assumption that the popularity of data items — the rate at which queries are issued — conforms to the *Zipf* distribution[4]. We use $\alpha = 1.2$ in our simulations, based on measurements from Saroiu *et al.* [8] on popular peer-to-peer file sharing systems.

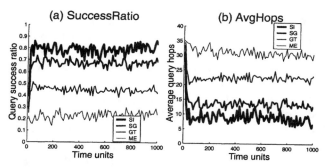

Figure 6. Query performance under Zipf-like data popularity: (a) query success ratios; (b) average number of hops

Fig. 6(a) shows that the Zipf distribution can be exploited by all four algorithms to improve query success rates, although the ranking with respect to query efficiency is still identical to that of the uniform popularity case. All four algorithms perform much more efficiently, for the reason that Zipf distribution always favors popular items and the queries on popular items encourage more nodes to create

---

[4]With a Zipf distribution, the popularity of the $i$th most popular item is proportional to $i^{-\alpha}$.

shortcuts on them. Consequently, upon one of such popular items, the number of neighbors which has the highest type $\bar{\theta}$ becomes larger and the expected type $E[\theta]$ also increases. It is encouraging to observe that, the signaling algorithm SG achieves the highest query success ratio after SI and in some cases even achieves the same success ratio as that of SI. The Zipf distribution also benefits ME and GT, whose query success ratios have nearly doubled. One interesting phenomenon is that GT performs much better in such a setting and separates itself from ME. The reason may be that, in such a setting, types of neighbors become much more diverse, multiple competitive equilibria exist in the game and GT has the advantage over ME to achieve the dominant equilibrium and to find more neighbors of high types. In addition, with respect to the average number of query hops, Fig. 6(a) shows that the same ranking is maintained as that of the uniform popularity case in Fig. 4(a).

To summarize, the ideal case of symmetric information (SI) shows that without asymmetric information, the query in a strictly unstructured peer-to-peer network should have performed much better. The signaling algorithm we have proposed (SG) encourages the nodes of high types to perform signaling actions and to reveal their private information, and therefore achieves much more efficient query performance. Another advantage of our proposed signaling algorithm is that the algorithm only incurs moderate signaling overhead compared with the ME and GT algorithms.

### 4.3 Discussions

We now discuss a few open but orthogonal problems with respect to our algorithms and implementations, that may possibly be addressed in future work.

First, it may require additional work to deploy our proposal to wide-area peer-to-peer network environments, most of which are beyond the scope of this paper. For example, we implicitly assume that a particular micro-payment mechanism exists as an underlying layer, which is still an open problem in the literature.

Second, it is clear that the performance of all our algorithms depends on the accuracy of type estimations, which are provided by the HU algorithm. In our simulation, we simply adopt a regular *Least Recently Used* cache replacement algorithm in the HU algorithm. We believe any improvements on the accuracy of type estimations will effectively improve the query performance of our algorithms, and they do not affect the general conclusions we have reached with respect to the nature of these algorithms.

## 5 Concluding remarks

Efficient peer-to-peer queries are essential to the success of unstructured peer-to-peer networks. Our observation is

that, if a node can always find the best neighbor as the next hop, the query should be as efficient as flooding and at the same time causes only acceptable message overhead. Unfortunately, when selecting the next hop to forward the query, the node often suffers from the fact that the node cannot distinguish the better neighbors from the inferior candidates. This is the phenomenon of information asymmetries in selfish peer-to-peer networks, a key observation and focus of our paper. We have thoroughly examined the system behavior in asymmetric information and proposed a signaling mechanism to overcome the problem, associated with a decentralized algorithm. Our analytical and simulation results have led to and established an efficient peer-to-peer query algorithm with moderate message overhead. We believe that our studies presented in this paper form a first step towards a thorough understanding of the behavior of peer nodes in strictly selfish overlay networks, where algorithms have to be carefully designed to avoid unwarranted assumptions of cooperative behavior.

## References

[1] L. Adamic, B. Huberman, R. Lukose, and A. Puniyani. Search in power law networks. In *Physical Reviews*, volume E64, pages 46135–46143, 2001.

[2] G. Akerlof. The market for 'lemons': Quality uncertainty and the market mechanism. In *Quately Journal of Economics*, volume 89, pages 488–500, 1970.

[3] J. Bertrand. Theorie Mathematique de la Richesse Sociale. In *Journal des Savants*, pages 499–508, 1883.

[4] E. Cohen and S. Shenker. Replication Strategies in Unstructured Peer-to-Peer Networks. In *Proc. of ACM SIGCOMM 2002*.

[5] R. Finney. *Calculus: A complete course*. Addison-Wesley Press, 2000.

[6] Q. Lv, P. Cao, E. Cohen, K. Li, and S. Shenker. Search and Replication in Unstructured Peer-to-Peer Networks. In *Proceedings of the 16th annual ACM International Conference on Supercomputing*, 2002.

[7] A. Mas-colell, M. D. Whinston, and J. R. Green. *Microeconomic theory*. Oxford University Press, New York, 1995.

[8] S. Saroiu, P. Gnummadi, and S. Gribble. A Measurement Study of Peer-to-Peer File Sharing Systems. In *Proc. of SPIE/ACM Conference on Multimedia Computing and Networking (MMCN 2002)*.

[9] A. M. Spence. Job market signaling. In *Quately Journal of Economics*, volume 87, pages 355–374, 1973.

[10] I. Stoica, R. Morris, D. Karger, F. Kaashoek, and H. Balakrishnan. Chord: A Scalable Peer-to-Peer Lookup Service for Internet Applications. In *Proc. of ACM SIGCOMM 2001*.

[11] H. Zhang, A. Goel, and R. Govindan. Using the Small-World Model to Improve Freenet Performance. In *Proceedings of IEEE Infocom*, 2002.

# Session 2C:
# Compiler II

# Non-uniform dependences partitioned by recurrence chains

Yijun Yu
CS Department, University of Toronto, Canada

Erik H. D'Hollander
EE Department, Ghent University, Belgium

## Abstract

*Non-uniform distance loop dependences are a known obstacle to find parallel iterations. To find the outermost loop parallelism in these "irregular" loops, a novel method is presented based on recurrence chains. The scheme organizes non-uniformly dependent iterations into lexicographically ordered monotonic chains. While the initial and final iterations of monotonic chains form two parallel sets, the remaining iterations form an intermediate set that can be partitioned further. When there is only one pair of coupled array references, the non-uniform dependences are represented by a single recurrence equation. In that case, the chains in the intermediate set do not bifurcate and each can be executed as a WHILE loop. The independent and the initial iterations of monotonic dependence chains constitute the outermost parallelism. The proposed approach compares favorably with other treatments of non-uniform dependences in the literature. When there are multiple recurrence equations, a dataflow parallel execution can be scheduled using the technique to find maximum loop parallelism.*

**Keywords** *non-uniform dependences, loop parallelization, recurrence chains, iteration space partitioning, imperfectly nested loop*

## 1. Introduction

Data dependences of a program lead to maximal parallelism by a data flow execution. A more restricted parallelism is implemented in common parallel programming languages because the loop control limits the traversal of the iteration space to regular patterns. Common language support for parallelism is parallel DO loops (DOALL). It is one of the most important goals for parallelizing compilers to reveal loop parallelism [1, 16, 30, 8, 27]. The loop can run in parallel when no data dependences exist between any two iterations with different index values. This is judged by various dependence tests [29, 14, 18, 22]. Moreover, some loop nests being tested as sequential can still be parallelized after suitable loop transformations.

Existing DOALL loop transformation methods focus on loops with uniform distance dependences [2, 9]. Many loops, however, are with non-uniform distance dependences where these transformations can not be applied. For instance, we found that more than 46% of the nested loops in the SPECfp95 benchmark contain non-uniform data dependences. Furthermore, coupled array subscripts, i.e. indices that appear in both dimensions, often cause non-uniform distances. Another study of 12 benchmarks [21] found out 45% of two dimensional array reference pairs with coupled linear subscripts. Including one-dimensional arrays, about 12.8% of the coupled subscripts in the SPECfp95 benchmarks generate non-uniform dependences. The percentage of loops with non-uniform dependences is higher because a single pair of non-uniform coupled subscripts will cause non-uniform dependences.

A way to catch all dependences by sequential linear steps through the iteration space is to find a set of vectors whose linear combinations compose all distance vectors [23, 26, 6]. To enable DOALL partitioning, a previous scheme in [27] replaces the non-uniform distance vectors with a set of pseudo distance vectors. They allow DOALL loop transformations to work as if they are uniform distance vectors because an integer linear combination of these lexicographically positive (LP) vectors covers all the non-uniform dependences. It finds maximal parallelism when the dependences are uniform, but may generate artificial dependences in the non-uniform case.

To avoid introducing artificial dependences into the loop, another way of treating the non-uniform dependences is based on exact solution of the dependence equations [11]. Although it is generally impossible to enforce data flow scheduling at compile time, recurrence chain partitioning makes it possible when there is only one pair of coupled subscripts or there is no compile-time unknown variable in the loop bounds. The recurrence chain partitioning separates the iteration space into three sequential partitions. The first and the last sets are fully parallel. When there is only one pair of coupled subscripts, the intermediate set is partitioned as disjoint monotonic recurrence chains that can be executed as WHILE loops. When there are multiple coupled subscripts and loop bounds are known at compile time, the intermediate set is successively partitioned into subsets following the dataflow until it is empty.

The remainder of the paper is organized as follows. Section 2 presents the program model for non-uniform distance dependences. Section 3 illustrates the recurrence chain partitioning scheme by showing what kinds of dependences form the recurrence chains and how to generate the parallel partitions. Section 4 presents the results of applying

100

different schemes on some program examples and section 5 compares it with related work.

## 2. Program model

Consider the coupled array subscripts occur in $m$ nested loops: $L_1, \ldots, L_m$. For $l = 1, \ldots, m$, every loop $L_l$ is normalized to have a unit stride and each loop index variable $I_l$ is constraint by a lower bound $p_l$ and an upper bound $q_l$. The loop bounds are affine functions of the index variables in the outer loops. The *iteration space* $\Phi$ of the loop is a vector set of all values taken by the integer loop indices

$$\{\mathbf{i} = (i_1 \ldots i_m) \mid p_l \leq i_l \leq q_l, 1 \leq l \leq m, \mathbf{i} \in \mathbb{Z}^m\}. \quad (1)$$

Loop carried dependences occur when the same array-element is addressed in two different iterations, where at least one of them is a write. Assume an array $\mathbf{X}$ is referred with affine index expressions: $X[\mathbf{IA} + \mathbf{a}]$ and $X[\mathbf{IB} + \mathbf{b}]$ where $\mathbf{I}$ denotes the vector of loop indexing variables, integer matrices $\mathbf{A}, \mathbf{B}$ and vectors $\mathbf{a}, \mathbf{b}$ are constants. A *direct dependence* occurs between iterations $\mathbf{i}$ and $\mathbf{j}$ if 1) the diophantine equation has a solution

$$\mathbf{i}\,\mathbf{A} + \mathbf{a} = \mathbf{j}\,\mathbf{B} + \mathbf{b} \quad (2)$$

2) and the solution is within the loop bounds: $\mathbf{i}, \mathbf{j} \in \Phi$.

A solution of the diophantine equations results in a pair of directly dependent iterations $(\mathbf{i}, \mathbf{j})$, also noted as $(\mathbf{i} \to \mathbf{j})$. The union of these pairs is called the *direct dependences set* of the loop, $\Delta$. An *indirect dependence* between $\mathbf{i}$ and $\mathbf{j}$ occurs when there exists a chain of $M > 1$ direct dependences: $(\mathbf{i}_k, \mathbf{i}_{k+1}) \in \Delta$ for $1 \leq k \leq M, \mathbf{i}_1 = \mathbf{i}$ and $\mathbf{i}_M = \mathbf{j}$. Including both direct and indirect dependences, the *dependence set* is $\Delta^+ = \{(\mathbf{i}, \mathbf{j}) \mid (\mathbf{i}, \mathbf{j}) \in \Delta \vee \exists\, \mathbf{k} : (\mathbf{i}, \mathbf{k}), (\mathbf{k}, \mathbf{j}) \in \Delta\}$. The *dependence distance* between two dependent iterations $\mathbf{i}$ and $\mathbf{j}$ is $\mathbf{d} = \mathbf{j} - \mathbf{i}$. The union of all distances in a dependence set is called *the dependence distance set*. Therefore the direct dependence set $\Delta$ gives rise to the *direct distance set* $\mathcal{D}$. Likewise the dependence distances in a loop are represented by the *distance set* $\mathcal{D}^+$. For any two direct dependent iterations $(\mathbf{i}, \mathbf{j}) \in \Delta$ and any non-zero vector $\mathbf{c} \in \mathbb{Z}^m$, if $(\mathbf{i} + \mathbf{c}, \mathbf{j} + \mathbf{c}) \in \Delta$ as long as $\mathbf{i} + \mathbf{c}, \mathbf{j} + \mathbf{c} \in \Phi$, then the loop has *uniform* dependences. In all other cases, the dependences of the loop are *non-uniform*.

Consider an example from [27], as listed in figure 1. The iteration space of this loop is: $\Phi = \{(i_1, i_2) \mid 1 \leq i_1 \leq N_1, 1 \leq i_2 \leq N_2, i_1, i_2 \in \mathbb{Z}\}$. A dependence equation is established as a system of diophantine equations:

$$\begin{cases} 3i_1 & +1 = j_1 & +3 \\ 2i_1 & +i_2 & -1 = & j_2 & +1 \end{cases} \quad (3)$$

The solutions of (eq.3) are a set of direct dependences. When $N_1 = N_2 = 10$, the dependences are non-uniform because e.g. $(1, 2) \to (3, 4)$ does not imply $(1, 1) \to (3, 3)$. The detection of parallelism in uniform dependence loops has received widespread attention, e.g. by unimodular

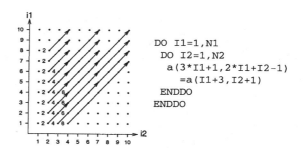

**Figure 1. An example loop and its iteration space. The direct dependences are shown as arrows with direct distance $(d, d)$ where $d = 2, 4, 6$ are marked to the left of the arrow tails.**

transformations[4, 24], partitioning[9] and others [15]. Unfortunately, many loops contain non-uniform dependences, for which no general mathematical approach is available to detect the parallel iterations. A number of alternatives have been proposed for the case of affine index expressions, e.g. uniformization oriented techniques [23, 26, 6, 19, 27] and dataflow oriented techniques [20, 11].

In this paper, the loops with non-uniform dependences are parallelized using WHILE loops with irregular strides. Dataflow oriented code in the cases where the uniformization method such as PDM [27] allows for extra parallelism, a recurrence chain partitioning in section 3 constructs WHILE loops with irregular strides to follow the non-uniform dependences.

## 3. Recurrence chain partitioning

To avoid artificial dependences introduced by uniformization methods [27], our recurrence partitioning scheme discovers dataflow parallelism by solving exact dependences. Using exact dependences, each step of *dataflow* partitioning puts the iterations without lexicographically predecessors into an initial fully parallel set and partitions the remaining iterations successively until no more iteration is left. Besides the initial set, a three-sets dataflow partitioning also separates the iterations without lexicographically successors as a fully parallel final set. When the dependences can be solved as dependence convex hulls, however, the dataflow partitioning may not terminate at compile-time for unknown loop bounds. Therefore a special treatment is proposed here to allow partitioning for loops with unknown bounds and a single pair of coupled subscripts. In one step, it separates the intermediate set of the three-set dataflow partitioning into disjoint monotonic dependence chains.

**Definition 1. Monotonic dependence chain.** *A monotonic dependence chain is a sequence of lexicographically ordered iterations in which each iteration directly depends on a unique immediate predecessor iteration.* □

For example, the loop in figure 2 has non-uniform dependences. The dependences are separated into monotonic

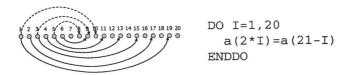

```
DO I=1,20
    a(2*I)=a(21-I)
ENDDO
```

**Figure 2. The loop dependences are solved as** $\{i \rightarrow j \mid 2i = 21 - j\}$ **where** $i < j$ **or** $i > j$ **are respectively solid or dashed arrows.**

chains. A solution chain $6 \rightarrow 9 \rightarrow 3 \rightarrow 15$ is separated into three monotonic chains: $6 \rightarrow 9, 3 \rightarrow 9$ and $3 \rightarrow 15$. Each monotonic chain has only two iterations, thus the iteration space is partitioned into two sets. The first set is the union of the initial iterations $\{1, 2, 3, 4, 5, 6\}$ and the independent iterations $\{7, 12, 14, 16, 18, 20\}$.

The dependences can be specified as a relation in the iteration space. Consider a dependence equation $\mathbf{i} A + \mathbf{a} = \mathbf{j} B + \mathbf{b}$ established from two references in two iterations with index vectors $\mathbf{i}$ and $\mathbf{j}$ respectively. If $\mathbf{i} \prec \mathbf{j}$, iteration $\mathbf{i}$ is called a *predecessor* of iteration $\mathbf{j}$ and $\mathbf{j}$ a *successor* of $\mathbf{i}$. The exact dependences are the union of the predecessor and successor relations:

$$R_d = R_{pred} \cup R_{succ} = \{\mathbf{j} \rightarrow \mathbf{i} \mid \mathbf{i} A + \mathbf{a} = \mathbf{j} B + \mathbf{b}, \mathbf{j} \prec \mathbf{i}\}$$
$$\cup \{\mathbf{i} \rightarrow \mathbf{j} \mid \mathbf{i} A + \mathbf{a} = \mathbf{j} B + \mathbf{b}, \mathbf{i} \prec \mathbf{j}\} \tag{4}$$

For multiple coupled subscripts, the combined dependence relation unions all the dependence relations of each dependence equation. An accurate solution to a union of integer convex sets can be found by the algorithm [18] implemented in an integer programming tool, the Omega library.

### 3.1. Partitioning the iteration space into three sets

Intuitively, the iteration space can be partitioned into separate monotonic chains. Starting from an initial iteration, i.e. an iteration without predecessors, a WHILE loop can be formed for each monotonic chain by updating the iteration index iteratively until it exceeds the border of iteration space. However, even when the dependent iterations are on separate recurrence chains, the lexicographical order is not always followed by a WHILE loop. In that case, several monotonic dependence chains may intersect at the same iteration, e.g. figure 2 shows that a WHILE loop updating indices successively by $i' = 21 - 2i$, forms chain $6 \rightarrow 9 \rightarrow 3 \rightarrow 15$ which violates the lexicographical ordering, whereas monotonic chains $6 \rightarrow 9, 3 \rightarrow 9, 3 \rightarrow 15$ intersect, such that iterations $3, 9$ will be executed twice.

The recurrence chain partitioning only executes the initial and final iterations once. The iteration space is separated into two fully parallel sets and one intermediate set so that the monotonic chains in the intermediate set are separate, or as in the above example, the monotonic chains in the intermediate set are empty. For the monotonic chains in the

intermediate set to be disjoint, it requires a single pair of coupled subscripts. According to the dependence relation in (eq.4), an *independent* iteration that has neither predecessor nor successor; otherwise it is a *dependent* iteration with predecessors or successors. A dependent iteration that has no predecessor is an *initial* iteration, a dependent iteration that has no successor is a *final* iteration, otherwise a dependent iteration that has both predecessors and successors is an *intermediate* iteration. Therefore the whole iteration space is composed of independent, initial, intermediate and final iterations. Using *dom* $(R)$ and *ran* $(R)$ respectively to denote the relation $R$'s domain dom $R \equiv \{\mathbf{x} \mid (\mathbf{x} \rightarrow \mathbf{y}) \in R\}$ and range ran $R \equiv \{\mathbf{y} \mid (\mathbf{x} \rightarrow \mathbf{y}) \in R\}$, the sets are calculated from the dependence relation $R_d$ and the iteration space $\Phi$ as: dep $= (\text{dom } R_d \cup \text{ran } R_d)$, initial $= \text{dep} \setminus \text{ran } R_d$, intermediate $= \text{dom } R_d \cap \text{ran } R_d$ and final $= \text{dep} \setminus \text{dom } R_d$. The independent and initial iterations are in an *initial set* $P_1$ of the iteration space, the intermediate iterations are in an *intermediate set* $P_2$ and the final iterations are in an *final set* $P_3$. They are calculated as

$$P_1 = \Phi \setminus \text{ran } R_d, \qquad P_2 = \text{ran } R_d \cap \text{dom } R_d$$
$$P_3 = \text{ran } R_d \setminus \text{dom } R_d \tag{5}$$

A dependence occurs only from an initial iteration to an intermediate one, from an intermediate iteration to another, or from an intermediate iteration to a final one. Thus the three sets can be executed in the order of $P_1 \rightarrow P_2 \rightarrow P_3$. The intermediate set $P_2$ needs to be further partitioned for dependences that occur inside $\{\mathbf{i} \rightarrow \mathbf{j} \mid (\mathbf{i} \rightarrow \mathbf{j}) \in R_d, \mathbf{i}, \mathbf{j} \in P_2\}$.

### 3.2. Partitioning the intermediate set

Starting from dependence equation (eq.2): $\mathbf{i} A + \mathbf{a} = \mathbf{j} B + \mathbf{b}$, when both $A$ and $B$ are full rank square matrices, there is an one-to-one recurrence relation between the dependent iterations.

**Lemma 1.** *When there is only one pair of coupled references with full rank coefficient matrices* $A$ *and* $B$*, the monotonic dependence chains in the intermediate set* $P_2$ *are disjoint, i.e., there is only one predecessor and one successor for each iteration in* $P_2$*.*

*Proof.* Each iteration in $P_2$ has at least one predecessor and one successor because $P_2$ is the intersection of the domain and range of the dependence relation. Since $A$ and $B$ are full rank, let $T = BA^{-1}, \mathbf{u} = (\mathbf{b} - \mathbf{a})A^{-1}$. The dependence (eq.2) is rewritten as: $\mathbf{i} = \mathbf{j} T + \mathbf{u}$. Suppose $\exists \mathbf{j} \in P_2$ such that there are two different predecessors $\mathbf{i}_1$ and $\mathbf{i}_2$, thus $\mathbf{i}_1 = \mathbf{j} T + \mathbf{u}$ and $\mathbf{i}_2 = \mathbf{j} T + \mathbf{u}$. However, $\mathbf{i}_1 = \mathbf{i}_2$. Thus there is only one predecessor for all iteration $\mathbf{j} \in P_2$. Similarly only one successor follows each iterations $\mathbf{i} \in P_2$ by replacing $T$ with $AB^{-1}$ and $\mathbf{u}$ with $(\mathbf{a} - \mathbf{b})B^{-1}$. $\square$

Since the monotonic chains are disjoint in the intermediate set, a compile-time recurrence chain partitioning is applicable to the intermediate set instead of doing unlimited steps of dataflow partitioning when loop bounds contain unknown variables.

The dependence relation is $R_d = \{\mathbf{j} \to \mathbf{i} \mid \mathbf{i} = (\mathbf{j} - \mathbf{u})\mathbf{T}^{-1}, \mathbf{j} \prec \mathbf{i}\} \cup \{\mathbf{i} \to \mathbf{j} \mid \mathbf{j} = \mathbf{i}\mathbf{T} + \mathbf{u}, \mathbf{i} \prec \mathbf{j}\}$. The initial iterations $\mathbf{i}_0$ are those without preceding solution in the iteration space $\Phi$ (either is not integer or is outside the bounds): $(\mathbf{i}_0 - \mathbf{u})\mathbf{T}^{-1} \notin \Phi$. The sequence of the recurrent dependent iterations is on a *dependence recurrence chain*. The general solution of an iteration on the recurrence chain beginning with $\mathbf{i}_0$ is $\mathbf{i}_k = \mathbf{i}_0\mathbf{T}^k + \mathbf{u}(\mathbf{T}^{k-1} + \cdots + \mathbf{T}^0)$. The distance vector between the dependent iterations $\mathbf{i}_{k+1}$ and $\mathbf{i}_k$ is

$$
\begin{aligned}
\mathbf{d}_k &= \mathbf{i}_{k+1} - \mathbf{i}_k = (\mathbf{i}_0(\mathbf{T} - \mathbf{I}) + \mathbf{u})\mathbf{T}^k = \mathbf{d}_0\mathbf{T}^k \\
\mathbf{d}_0 &= \mathbf{i}_0(\mathbf{T} - \mathbf{I}) + \mathbf{u}.
\end{aligned}
\tag{6}
$$

Removing the initial and final iterations, a recurrence chain will be separated into disjoint monotonic chains. WHILE loops are constructed to sequentially execute these monotonic chains. If initially $\mathbf{i}_0 \in R_{pred}$, the WHILE loop changes index by $R_{pred}$ i.e. $\mathbf{I} = (\mathbf{I} - \mathbf{u})\mathbf{T}^{-1}$, otherwise the WHILE loop changes index by $R_{succ}$ i.e. $\mathbf{I} = \mathbf{I}\mathbf{T} + \mathbf{u}$. Each WHILE loop starts at an iteration that depends on an initial iteration in $P_1$. The starting iterations are in the following set: $W = \{\mathbf{j} \mid (\mathbf{i} \to \mathbf{j}) \in R_d, \mathbf{i} \in P_1, \mathbf{j} \in P_2\}$ and the WHILE loop stops when the successor becomes a final iteration. Thus the condition for the WHILE loop to continue is $\mathbf{i} \in (\Phi \setminus final) = \mathbf{i} \in (\Phi \cap dom\, R_d)$.

Only $\cap, \cup, \setminus, dom, ran$ operations are applied to the union of convex sets $\Phi$ and $R_d$ to obtain the fully parallel sets $P_1, W, P_3$. Therefore each of them can be specified by a union of convex sets which is the logical conjunctive normal form where each logical operand is a linear inequality. Although Fourier-Motzkin elimination can be used to generate a DO loop nest for each convex set, it is first necessary to make the convex sets disjoint. An algorithm exists [13] to generate loops from a lexicographically ordered union of convex sets. The lexicographical order of the convex sets is not necessary here because they are fully independent.

## 3.3. Extending the iteration space to statement-level

To reveal statement-level parallelism in case of imperfectly nested loops or multiple statements in a loop body, each instance of a statement $S(\mathbf{I})$ with loop index vector $\mathbf{I} = \mathbf{i}$ needs to be associated with a unique index vector $\mathbf{s_i}$ such that 1) the lexicographical ordering of $\mathbf{s_i}$ reflects the statement instances execution order; 2) the set of statement index vectors forms a union of convex sets.

An example of such extension has been proposed by the affine mapping framework in [12]. Assume there are $l$ surrounding loops for a statement $S(\mathbf{I})$. For any instance $S(\mathbf{i})$, a statement index $s_k$ is inserted after each loop index $i_k$ for $k = 1, \cdots, l$ and $s_0$ is given before the outermost loop index $i_1$ to indicate the position of the whole loop nest in the program. A unique index vector $\mathbf{s_i} = (s_0, i_1, s_1, \cdots, i_l, s_l)$ is thus formed. In order to apply lexicographical ordering on the statement index vectors, dummy zeroes are appended

to the unique index vectors for statements outsides the innermost loop. To make sure the set of statement index vectors forms a union of convex sets, the statements in the same loop are associated with a sequence of numbers with unit increment. The first statement in the loop $L_k$ is associated with $s_k = 1$ for convenience. Both the unified iteration space with statement instances and the iteration space with loop body instances are a union of convex sets. Thus the partitioning method for them are inherently the same, the only difference is that we calculate statement-level dependences from the following relations for any two instances of statements $S_1(\mathbf{I}; \mathbf{I}^1)$ and $S_2(\mathbf{I}; \mathbf{I}^2)$ with unique index vectors $\mathbf{s_i}$ and $\mathbf{t_j}$:

$$
\begin{aligned}
R_d = \{\mathbf{t_j} \to \mathbf{s_i} \mid \mathbf{i}A + \mathbf{a} = \mathbf{j}B + \mathbf{b}, \mathbf{t_j} \prec \mathbf{s_i}\} \\
\cup\{\mathbf{s_i} \to \mathbf{t_j} \mid \mathbf{i}A + \mathbf{a} = \mathbf{j}B + \mathbf{b}, \mathbf{s_i} \prec \mathbf{t_j}\}
\end{aligned}
\tag{7}
$$

## 3.4. The recurrence partitioning algorithm

Algorithm 1 summarizes the recurrence chains partitioning scheme. Initially the unified iteration space $\Phi$ and the dependence relation $R_d$ are calculated. If there is a single pair of coupled subscripts with full rank coefficient matrices $\mathbf{A}$ and $\mathbf{B}$, the recurrence chain partitioning is applied to the intermediate set after a three-set dataflow partitioning according to $\Phi$ and $R_d$. WHILE loops are generated for each monotonic chain in the intermediate set. Otherwise, if the loop bounds are known at compile-time, the dataflow partitioning is successively done to the iteration space $\Phi$ and the dependence sub-relation $R_d$ until $\Phi$ is empty.

**Algorithm 1.** The recurrence partitioning scheme
**Input:** *A sequential loop nest with a single pair of coupled linear array subscripts or with compile-time known loop bounds. The loop body is denoted as $S(\mathbf{I})$.*
**Output:** *A sequence of DOALL loop nests.*

*let $\Phi$ be the unified iteration space, calculate dependences as:*

$$
R_d = \bigcup \{\mathbf{s_i} \to \mathbf{t_j} \mid \begin{array}{l} (\mathbf{i}A + \mathbf{a} = \mathbf{j}B + \mathbf{b} \vee \mathbf{i}A + \mathbf{a} \\ = \mathbf{j}B + \mathbf{b}) \wedge \mathbf{s_i} \prec \mathbf{t_j} \wedge \mathbf{s_i}, \mathbf{t_j} \in \Phi \end{array} \}
$$

**if** $X(\mathbf{I}A + \mathbf{a})$, $X(\mathbf{I}B + \mathbf{b})$ *are the single reference pair in $S(\mathbf{I})$*
 *and $\mathbf{A}, \mathbf{B}$ are full rank* **then**
  $P_1 = \Phi \setminus (ran\, R_d)$; $P_2 = (ran\, R_d) \cap (dom\, R_d)$;
  $P_3 = (ran\, R_d) \setminus (dom\, R_d)$;
  $W = \{\mathbf{j} \mid (\mathbf{i} \to \mathbf{j}) \in R_d \wedge \mathbf{i} \in P_1 \wedge \mathbf{j} \in P_2\}$;
  **call** *DOALLCodeGeneration($P_1$, $S(\mathbf{I})$)*;
  **call** *DOALLCodeGeneration($W$, $S'(\mathbf{I})$)*

*where $S'(\mathbf{I}) \equiv$*
$\begin{cases} \text{if } (\mathbf{I} \in R_{pred}) \text{ then} \\ \quad \mathbf{T} = \mathbf{A}\mathbf{B}^{-1}; \mathbf{u} = (\mathbf{a} - \mathbf{b})\mathbf{B}^{-1} \\ \text{else} \\ \quad \mathbf{T} = \mathbf{B}\mathbf{A}^{-1}; \mathbf{u} = (\mathbf{b} - \mathbf{a})\mathbf{A}^{-1} \\ \text{end if} \\ \text{do while}(\mathbf{I} \in (\Phi \cap dom\, R_d)) \\ \quad S(\mathbf{I}); \mathbf{I} = \mathbf{I}\mathbf{T} + \mathbf{u}; \\ \text{end do while} \end{cases}$

  **call** *DOALLCodeGeneration($P_3$, $S(\mathbf{I})$)*;
**else if** *the loop bounds are constant* **then**

```
  do while (Φ is not empty)
    P₁ = Φ \ (ran R_d); Φ = Φ \ P₁;
    R_d = {i → j | (i → j) ∈ R_d ∧ i, j ∈ Φ};
    call DOALLCodeGeneration(P₁, S(I))
  enddo while
endif
subroutine DOALLCodeGeneration(Set, Body)
  separate Set into N disjoint convex sets CH₁, · · · , CH_N [13];
  do i=1, N
    generate a DOALL loop nest with the body Body
      bounded by CH_i [3];
  enddo
  return
```

If there are multiple coupled subscripts and the loop bounds are unknown at compile-time, the recurrence partitioning can not apply. In that case, the pseudo distance partitioning in [27] is used instead.

The theoretical speedup of the partitioning is determined by the execution time of the critical path in proportion to the number of iterations on the critical path. The following theorem states the lower bound of the speedup when the monotonic chains do not bifurcate. Consequently the theoretical parallel speedup is at least $\frac{|\Phi|}{l}$ on $O(|\Phi|)$ parallel processors, where $|\Phi|$ denotes the number of iterations in iteration space $\Phi$.

**Theorem 1.** *Given a recurrence equation* $\mathbf{i}_{k+1} = \mathbf{i}_k \mathbf{T} + \mathbf{u}$ *with non-singular matrix* $\mathbf{T}$*, let* $a = \max(|det(\mathbf{T})|, |det(\mathbf{T}^{-1})|)$*. In the iteration space* $\Phi$*, the critical path found by algorithm 1 contains at most* $l = \lfloor \log_a(L) + 1 \rfloor$ *iterations, where* $L$ *is the maximum Euclid distance between any two iterations:* $L = \max_{\mathbf{i}_1, \mathbf{i}_2 \in \Phi} ||\mathbf{i}_2 - \mathbf{i}_1||$*.*

*Proof.* For each distance vector $\mathbf{d} = \mathbf{i}_2 - \mathbf{i}_1$, the Euclid distance is $||\mathbf{d}|| = \sqrt{d_1^2 + \cdots + d_m^2}$. Suppose $n$ is the length of a recurrence chain by (eq.6), $||\mathbf{d}_n|| = ||\mathbf{d}_0||a^n$ or $a^n = \frac{||\mathbf{d}_n||}{||\mathbf{d}_0||} \leq ||\mathbf{d}_n|| \leq L$. Since $a > 1$, the length of the critical path is $n + 1 \leq \lfloor \log_a(L) + 1 \rfloor$. □

## 4. Results

This section applies the recurrence partitioning on several examples and compares their speedups with other schemes.

**Example 1** The example in figure 1 after our recurrence chain partitioning is:

```
1  C initial partition
2   DOALL i1=1,min(N1,3)
3    DOALL i2=1,N2
4     s(i1,i2)
5    ENDDOALL
6   ENDDOALL
7   DOALL i1=4,N1
8    DOALL i2=1,min((2*i1)/3,N2)
9     s(i1,i2)
10   ENDDOALL
11   DOALL i2=(2*i1+3)/3,N2
12    IF (i1-3.1e.3*((i1-2)/3)) THEN
13     s(i1,i2)
```

```
14     ENDIF
15    ENDDOALL
16   ENDDOALL
17  C intermediate partition and while start
18   DOALL i1=4,min((3*N2+5)/8,min((N1+2)/3,7)),3
19    DOALL i2=(2*i1+3)/3,N2-2*i1+2
20     chain(i1,i2)
21    ENDDOALL
22   ENDDOALL
23   DOALL i1=10,min((3*N2+5)/8,(N1+2)/3),3
24    DOALL i2=(2*i1+3)/3,min(N2-2*i1+2,(8*i1-2)/9)
25     chain(i1,i2)
26    ENDDOALL
27    DOALL i2=(8*i1+9)/9,N2-2*i1+2
28     IF (i1-7.1e.9*((i1-4)/9)) THEN
29      chain(i1,i2)
30     ENDIF
31    ENDDOALL
32   ENDDOALL
33  C final partition
34   DOALL i1=4,min((N1+2)/3,(3*N2-1)/2),3
35    DOALL i2=max(N2-2*i1+3,(2*i1+3)/3),N2
36     s(i1,i2)
37    ENDDOALL
38   ENDDOALL
39   DOALL i1=3*(((N1+5)/3+1)/3)+1,
40  *      min(N1,(3*N2-1)/2),3
41    DOALL i2=(2*i1+3)/3,N2
42     s(i1,i2)
43    ENDDOALL
44   ENDDOALL
45   ...
46   SUBROUTINE chain(i,j)
47    DO WHILE (2.1e.i.and.3*i.le.2+N1
48  *      .and.1.1e.j.and.2*i+j.le.2+N2)
49     s(i,j);
50     IF (i.mod.3.ne.1) RETURN;
51     ip = 3*i-2
52     jp = 2*i+j-2
53     i = ip
54     j= jp
55    ENDDO
56   END
```

The original loop body is represented as an inlined function $s(i, j)$. The first partition index set splits as a union of convex sets without dependences. Similarly no dependence is within the intermediate set and the final set. The monotonic recurrence chains in the intermediate set are executed by a WHILE loop in the subroutine "chain" that can be inlined. Since $det(\mathbf{T}) = 3$, the largest partition has at most $\lfloor 1 + log_3(\sqrt{N_1^2 + N_2^2}) \rfloor$ iterations by theorem 1.

**Example 2** Consider another non-uniform dependence example used by Ju et al [11].

```
DO I=1,N
  DO J=1,N
    a(2*I+3,J+1) = a(I+2*J+1,I+J+3)
  ENDDO
ENDDO
```

The PDM partitioning can only find a parallelism of two in the innermost loop, thus the recurrence chain partitioning is applied using algorithm 1:

```
1  DOALL i=1,12
2   IF(mod(i,2).eq.1)THEN
3    DOALL j=1,min(-i+10,(i-1)/2)
```

```
4     a(2*i+3,j+1)=a(i+2*j+1,i+j+3)
5     ENDDOALL
6   ENDIF
7   DOALL j=(i+2)/2,min(i+3,-i+10)
8     a(2*i+3,j+1)=a(i+2*j+1,i+j+3)
9   ENDDOALL
10  DOALL j=max(-i+11,1),min(i+3,12)
11    a(2*i+3,j+1)=a(i+2*j+1,i+j+3)
12  ENDDOALL
13  DOALL j=(3*i+8)/2,12
14    a(2*i+3,j+1)=a(i+2*j+1,i+j+3)
15  ENDDOALL
16 ENDDOALL
17 i=2
18 j=6
19 a(2*i+3,j+1)=a(i+2*j+1,i+j+3)
20 DOALL i=2,8
21   IF(mod(i,2).eq.0)THEN
22    DOALL j=1,min(-i+10,i/2)
23      a(2*i+3,j+1)=a(i+2*j+1,i+j+3)
24    ENDDOALL
25   ENDIF
26   IF(i.eq.3)a(2*i+j,i+1)=a(i+2*j+1,i+j+3)
27   IF(i.ge.4)THEN
28    DOALL j=i+4,min((3*i+6)/2,12)
29      a(2*i+3,j+1)=a(i+2*j+1,i+j+3)
30    ENDDOALL
31   ENDIF
32 ENDDOALL
```

For this N=12 case, there is only a single iteration in the intermediate set, particularly iteration $(2,6)$. Therefore the WHILE loop is simplified away. For general N the WHILE loop can not be removed. When $n > 1$, the maximum distance between any two iterations in the iteration space is $L = \sqrt{2}n$. Let $a = |det(\mathbf{T})| = 2$, thus the longest critical path has at most $\lfloor \log_a(L)+1 \rfloor = \lfloor \log_2(n)+0.5 \rfloor$ iterations by theorem 1.

**Example 3** Consider the previous imperfect nested loop example from Chen et al [6]:

```
DO I=1,N
  DO J=1,I
    DO K=J,I
      ... = a(I+2*K+5,4*K-J)
    ENDDO
    a(I-J,I+J)= ...
  ENDDO
ENDDO
```

Our recurrence chain partitioning is applied to find an empty intermediate set $P_2$, the result code is generated as follows (a visualization can be seen in [28]).

```
1  DOALL I=1,N
2    DOALL J=1,I
3      DOALL K=J,I
4        ... = a(I+2*K+5,4*K-J)
5      ENDDOALL
6      IF (I-J-7.LE.3*((I+J)/4)) THEN
7        a(I-J,I+J)=...
8      ENDIF
9    ENDDOALL
10 ENDDOALL
11 DOALL I=30,N
12   DOALL J=1,(I-23)/7
13     IF (I+J+1.LE.4*((I-J-5)/3)) THEN
14       a(I-J,I+J)=...
```

```
15   ENDIF
16 ENDDOALL
17 ENDDOALL
```

Lines 1-10 are $P_1$ and 11-17 are $P_3$. Compare with the DOACROSS loop generated in [6], this code has only DOALL loops and theoretically can finish in two iteration time.

**Example 4** Cholesky is a kernel in the NASA benchmarks, in which two imperfectly nested loops contain non-uniform dependences.

```
  DO 1 J=0, N
    I0=MAX( -M, -J)
    DO 2 I=I0, -1
      DO 3 JJ=I0-I, -1
        DO 3 L=0, NMAT
3         a(L,I,J)=a(L,I,J)-a(L,JJ,I+J)*a(L,I+JJ,J)
        DO 2 L=0, NMAT
2         a(L,I,J)=a(L,I,J)*a(L,0,I+J)
    DO 4 L=0, NMAT
4     epss(L)=EPS*a(L,0,J)
    DO 5 JJ=I0, -1
      DO 5 L=0, NMAT
5       a(L,0,J)=a(L,0,J)-a(L,JJ,J)**2
    DO 1 L=0, NMAT
1     a(L,0,J)=1./SQRT(ABS(epss(L)+a(L,0,J)))
  DO 6 I=0, NRHS
    DO 7 K=0, N
      DO 8 L=0, NMAT
8       b(I,L,K)=b(I,L,K)*a(L,0,K)
      DO 7 JJ=1, MIN(M, N-K)
        DO 7 L=0, NMAT
7         b(I,L,K+JJ)=b(I,L,K+JJ)
*           -a(L,-JJ,K+JJ)*b(I,L,K)
    DO 6 K=N, 0, -1
      DO 9 L=0, NMAT
9       b(I,L,K)=b(I,L,K)*a(L,0,K)
      DO 6 JJ=1, MIN(M, K)
        DO 6 L=0, NMAT
6         b(I,L,K-JJ)=b(I,L,K-JJ)
*           -a(L,-JJ,K)*b(I,L,K)
```

When parameters NMAT=250, M=4, N=40, NHRS=3, it takes 238 partitioning steps for the compiler to finish the recurrence dataflow partitioning (the result code is not shown here to save space). Because there are multiple coupled subscripts and generally compile-time unknown parameters NMAT, M, N, NHRS, the PDM partitioning is applied:

```
1    DOALL 6 L=0, NMAT
2      DO 1 J=0, N
3        I0=MAX(-M,-J)
4        DO 2 I=I0, -1
5          DO 3 JJ=I0-I, -1
6  3        A(L,I,J)=A(L,I,J)-A(L,JJ,I+J)*A(L,I+JJ,J)
7  2        A(L,I,J)=A(L,I,J)*A(L,0,I+J)
8  4        EPSS(L)=EPS*A(L,0,J)
9          DO 5 JJ=I0, -1
10 5        A(L,0,J)=A(L,0,J)-A(L,JJ,J)**2
11 1      A(L,0,J)=1./SQRT(ABS(EPSS(L)+A(L,0,J)))
12       DOALL 6 I=0, NRHS
13         DO 7 K=0, N
14 8        B(I,L,K)=B(I,L,K)*A(L,0,K)
15         DOALL 7 JJ=1, MIN(M, N-K)
16 7        B(I,L,K+JJ)=B(I,L,K+JJ)
17 *          -A(L,-JJ,K+JJ)*B(I,L,K)
```

```
18        DO 6 K=N, 0, -1
19 9        B(I,L,K)=B(I,L,K)*A(L,0,K)
20        DOALL 6 JJ=1, MIN(M, K)
21 6        B(I,L,K-JJ)=B(I,L,K-JJ)
22 *          -A(L,-JJ,K)*B(I,L,K)
```

**Experiments** To observe the performance results, one has to take the parallel loop overhead and loop granularity into considerations. The experiments have been performed on a SMP Linux system with 4 identical Itanium CPU's. The back-end Intel compiler accepts OpenMP directives [7] to generate light-weighted threads. A code region is indicated as parallel by a directive pair: `c$omp parallel` and `c$omp end parallel`. Nested outermost DOALL loops are coalesced into a single parallel loop. Barrier synchronization is only necessary at the borders of the partition sets P1/P2 and P2/P3, directive `c$omp end do nowait` is used between the DOALL nests that are generated from a fully parallel set. The speedup is given as the ratio between the original sequential execution time and the multi-threads execution time where environment variable `OMP_NUM_THREADS` specifies the number of CPU used. The four examples subjected to the partitioning methods are shown in figure 3. For Example 1 with parameters N1=300, N2=1000, the PL [9], PDM [27] and REC speedups are compared. The REC speedup is better than linear when the number of threads is smaller than 3 because array subscripts calculations are simplified in the recurrence WHILE loop. However, it drops below linear when number of threads is larger than 3 because the loop bounds calculation gets more overhead. For Example 2 with parameter N=300, the UNIQUE [11] and REC speedups are compared. They both outperforms linear speed when executed on single CPU because the convex loop index calculations are optimized by Omega calculator. REC outperforms UNIQUE because it generates shorter sequence of fully parallel regions. For Example 3 with parameter N=300, speedups of the REC partitioning, inner loop J, K parallelization [25], and the DOACROSS parallelization [6] are compared. REC performs the best because it has least synchronizations. For Example 4 with parameters NMAT=250, M=4, N=40 and NRHS=3, PDM [27] and REC dataflow partitioning speedup results are shown. REC partitioning outperforms PDM and even linear program when nthread is smaller than three because of the loop bounds optimization by Omega calculator. When the number of threads is larger than 3, however, the simpler PDM partitioning performs better because it has better load balance.

## 5. Related work

To test loop parallelism for non-uniform dependences, the *range test* [5] is based on intersection of the value range of non-linear expressions to mark a loop parallel for an empty range. Since the dependence range is less exact, our recurrence chain partitioning uses the *Omega* test [17] to solve

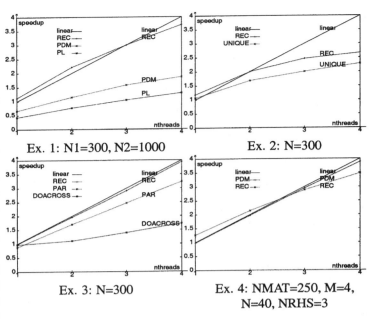

Ex. 1: N1=300, N2=1000        Ex. 2: N=300

Ex. 3: N=300        Ex. 4: NMAT=250, M=4, N=40, NRHS=3

**Figure 3. Speedup on Itanium multiprocessor**

the dependence relation based on exact integer programming. The zero columns of pseudo distance matrix (PDM) are first used to test for parallel loops, then the Omega test is used for those loops with non-zero columns in the PDM.

Wolf et al [24] extend the uniform distance vectors to *dependence vectors*, i.e., each element of the dependence vector is either a constant or a direction sign. Both distance and direction vectors are treated in the same framework of dependence vectors. This leads to outermost loop parallelization as well as innermost loop parallelization by unimodular transformations. For non-uniform dependences, however, the direction vector representation introduces more artificial distance vectors than dependence uniformization: it is equivalent to use the basis of the vector space as pseudo distance vectors which may have a higher rank and a smaller determinant than the PDM derived from distance vectors. An algorithm in [24] can find a legal unimodular transformation that reduces the outermost columns of a distance matrix to zero. However, this algorithm can not be used for the pseudo distance matrix because the unimodular transformation found are not always legal when there are non-uniform dependences.

Shang et al [26] represent the non-uniform distances as an affine (*non-negative* linear) combination of the basic dependence vectors (BDV), which are not lexicographically positive. The Basic Ideas I and III generate a set of full-rank BDV which inhibits parallelizing the outermost loops by a unimodular transformation, while the Basic Idea II searches for a set of *cone-optimal* BDV, i.e., the BDV are minimal in rank. Because the lexicographical positiveness is not carried by the BDV, an additional *linear scheduling* [10] is needed to maintain the lexicographical order.

Tzen et al [23] and Chen et al [6] implement the BDV linear scheduling by DO-ACROSS loops synchronization. DOACROSS loops allow the iterations to be asynchronously executed within a delay, which is enforced by P/V synchronization on the loop index. DOACROSS synchronization is more complex than the barrier synchronization of DOALL loops. Though no parallelism is obtained using PDM partitioning for their example shown in example 3, two perfectly nested DOALL loops can be obtained using recurrence chain partitioning.

Punyamurtula et al [19] propose the minimum distance tiling that runs the adjacent iterations in parallel as long as their distance is smaller than the minimum dependence distances. After making the minimum distances tiling of the iteration space, Tzen or Chen's method is used for the inter-tile dependences. This method creates innermost parallelism whereas PDM partitioning creates outermost parallelism. Theoretically, it speedups Example 2 by 4 times.

Ju et al [11] propose unique-set oriented partitioning to exploit exact non-uniform dependences: The dependence convex hulls are separated into head or tail sets by lexicographical order. The first recurrence equation is called "flow" and the second is called "anti", which split the head or tail sets. The intersections among the (head, tail) $\times$ (flow,anti) sets yield 5 individual cases. The method also applies only to one pair of subscripts with non-singular $A, B$ matrices, otherwise their coefficients calculation will divide by zero. Using their approach on Example 2, 5 perfectly nested DOALL loops were obtained in sequence [11]p.334. The number of iterations is not 144 due to apparent errors in the loop bounds of the 3rd and 4th loop nests. We recalculated the example with their method and found that two of the 5 unique sets can not be written as perfectly nested loops because they are not convex sets. Among the five unique sets, the third one is sequential. Whereas applying the recurrence chain partitioning, only 3 fully parallel partitions are obtained, resulting in more parallelism.

## 6. Conclusion

This paper presents two partitioning schemes, based on recurrence chains, to find outermost parallelism for loops with non-uniform dependences. Comparing to the previously discovered pseudo distance matrix (PDM) method [27], recurrence chains partitioning is an enhancement when the loops has a single pair of coupled subscripts or with symbolic affine bounds. When the loop has non-linear bounds and multiple pairs of coupled subscripts, PDM can still be applied. The advantage of REC lies in the dataflow partitioning for non-uniform dependences.

## References

[1] R. Allen and K. Kennedy. Automatic translation of Fortran programs to vector form. *TOPLAS*, 9(4):491–542, Oct 1987.

[2] U. Banerjee. Unimodular transformations of double loops. In *Advances in Languages and Compilers for Parallel Computing, 1990 Workshop*, pages 192–219, Aug. 1990.

[3] U. Banerjee. *Loop transformations for restructuring compilers: the foundations*. Kluwer Academic, 1993. 305 p.

[4] U. Banerjee, R. Eigenmann, A. Nicolau, and D. A. Padua. Automatic program parallelization. *Proc. of the IEEE*, 81(2):211–243, Feb 1993.

[5] W. Blume and R. Eigenmann. The Range test: a dependence test for symbolic, non-linear expressions. In *Proceedings, Supercomputing '94*, pages 528–537. IEEE, 1994.

[6] D. Chen and P. Yew. On the effective execution of nonuniform DOACROSS loops. *TPDS*, 7(5):463–476, May 1996.

[7] D. Clark. OpenMP: A parallel standard for the masses. *IEEE Concurrency*, 6(1):10–12, JAN-MAR 1998.

[8] E. D'Hollander, F. Zhang, and Q. Wang. The Fortran parallel transformer and its programming environment. *Journal of Information Sciences*, 106:293–317, 1998.

[9] E. H. D'Hollander. Partitioning and labeling of loops by unimodular transformations. *TPDS*, 3(4):465–476, Jul 1992.

[10] P. Feautrier. Some efficient solutions to the affine scheduling problem. I. One-dimensional time. *International Journal of Parallel Programming*, 21(5):313–347, Oct 1992.

[11] J. Ju and V. Chaudhary. Unique sets oriented parallelization of loops with non-uniform dependences. *The Computer Journal*, 40(6):322–339, 1997.

[12] W. Kelly and W. Pugh. Minimizing communication while preserving parallelism. In *Supercomputing'96*, pages 52–60. ACM, 1996.

[13] W. Kelly, W. Pugh, and E. Rosser. Code generation for multiple mappings. In *The 5th Symposium on the Frontiers of Massively Parallel Computation*, 1995.

[14] X. Kong, D. Klappholz, and K. Psarris. The I-test - an improved dependence test for automatic parallelization and vectorization. *TPDS*, 2(3):342–349, jul 1991.

[15] A. W. Lim and M. S. Lam. Maximizing parallelism and minimizing synchronization with affine partitions. *Parallel Computing*, 24(3-4):445–475, May 1998.

[16] D. A. Padua and M. J. Wolfe. Advanced compilers optimizations for supercomputers. *CACM*, 29(12):1184–1201, Dec 1986.

[17] P. M. Petersen and D. A. Padua. Static and dynamic evaluation of data dependence analysis techniques:. *TPDS*, 7(11):1121–1132, Nov 1996.

[18] W. Pugh. A practical algorithm for exact array dependence analysis. *CACM*, 35(8):102–114, Aug 1992.

[19] S. Punyamurtula, V. Chaudhary, J. Ju, and S. Roy. Compile time partitioning of nested loop iteration spaces with non-uniform dependences. *Journal of Parallel Algorithms and Applications*, 13(1):113–141, Jan. 1999.

[20] L. Rauchwerger, N. M. Amato, and D. A. Padua. A scalable method for run-time loop parallelization. *International Journal of Parallel Programming*, 23(6):537–576, 1995.

[21] Z. Shen, Z. Li, and P.-C. Yew. An empirical study of Fortran programs for parallelizing compilers. *TPDS*, 1(3):356–364, July 1990.

[22] J. Subhlok and K. Kennedy. Integer programming for array subscript analysis. *TPDS*, 6(6):662–668, June 1995.

[23] T. Tzen and L. Ni. Dependence uniformization: A loop parallelization technique. *TPDS*, 4:547–558, May 1993.

[24] M. E. Wolf and M. S. Lam. A loop transformation theory and an algorithm to maximize parallelism. *TPDS*, 2(4):452–471, Oct 1991.

[25] M. Wolfe and C. Tseng. The POWER test for data dependence. *TPDS*, 3(5):591–601, sep 1992.

[26] W.Shang, E.Hodzic, and Z.Chen. On uniformization of affine dependence algorithms. *IEEE Trans. Computers*, 45(7):827–40, 1996.

[27] Y. Yu and E. D'Hollander. Partitioning loops with variable dependence distances. In *ICPP'00*, pages 209–218. IEEE, Aug 2000.

[28] Y. Yu and E. D'Hollander. Loop parallelization using the 3D iteration space visualizer. *Journal of Visual Languages and Computing*, 12(2):163–181, April 2001.

[29] C.-Q. Zhu and P.-C. Yew. A scheme to enforce data dependence on large multiprocessor systems. *TSE*, 13(6):726–739, Jun 1987.

[30] H. Zima, H. Bast, and M. Gerndt. SUPERB - a tool for semi-automatic MIMD SIMD parallelization. *Parallel Computing*, 6(1):1–18, Jan 1988.

# Global Partial Replicate Computation Partitioning[1]

Yiran Wang     Li Chen     Zhao-Qing Zhang*

*Institute of Computing Technology, CAS*
*{wyr, lchen, zqzhang}@ict.ac.cn*

## Abstract

*Early parallelizing compilers use the owner-computes rule to partition computation. Partial replication is then introduced to eliminate near-neighbor communication at the cost of some replicated computation, hence improves the performance and scalability. Current exploration of partial replicate computation partitioning is limited within a single loop nest. In this paper, we present a formal description of the global partial replicate computation partitioning problem, a simplified cost model and a heuristic solution. Experimental results show that the solution is superior to local approaches.*

*Keywords: parallelizing compiler, partial replicate computing partitioning, data dependence, distributed memory systems, data parallel.*

## 1. Introduction

In data parallel programs, the computation partition specifies which processors must execute each dynamic instance of statements. The selection of good computation partition can have a dramatic impact on performance. In parallelizing compilers, the owner-compute rule is usually adopted to derive computation partition from data partition. Its philosophy is to reduce communications by placing the computation on the owner of the involved data.

However, array references not aligned with the computation partition would incur communications between neighboring processors. If these communications are deeply nested thus frequently executed, they can severely degrade performance.

Researchers have found a better partitioning method, *Partial Replicate Computation Partitioning* (PRCP). Its main idea is to partially replicate the computation of the source statement of a flow-dependence so that the communication incurred by the dependence can be eliminated.

Two approaches of partial replicate computation partitioning have been proposed. The dHPF [1] compiler replicates the computation of localized or new arrays within a loop nest. The compiler relies on user directives and manual code transformation to direct the PRCP.

The Autopar [4, 3, 9] compiler finds a communication-free computation partition for a loop

nest automatically. This approach can only deal with situations where all communications in a loop nest can be eliminated.

The rest of this paper is organized as follows. We begin by introducing some related work on partial replicate computation partitioning and some motivating examples in section 2. Section 3 then presents a formal representation of the computation partitioning problem. As it is hard to find an optimal PRCP, we develop a heuristic automatic approach under a simplified cost model described in section 3.2 and a prototype implementation in Autopar [4]. Our approach is described in section 3.4 and illustrated through an example in section 3.5. Our prototype achieves on average 31 percent of reduction of communication volume in BT, LU and SP in NPB serial. The experimental result is presented in section 4. We conclude and discuss some future work in section 5.

## 2. Related Work and Motivation

The section first introduces the definition of partial replicate computation partitioning, then surveys some existing approaches, and finally presents the goal of our research.

### 2.1. Partial Replicate Computation Partition

Partial replicate computation partition is a decomposition of the computation. Compared to traditional computation partition, it is not a partition of the computation space but a cover of it, i.e. the execution of the same dynamic instance of a statement may be replicated on multiple processors.

In this paper, a computation partition (CP) is donated as a union of home processors of multiple array references. As an example, *ON_HOME* $a(...,i,...),a(...,i+1,...)$ denotes the union of the home processors of $a(...,i,...)$ and $a(...,i+1,...)$.

We illustrate the concept of PRCP with an example in Figure 1. It is a fragment extracted from SP of NPB2.3 serial. Under the owner-compute rule, communications for $cv(k-1)$, $cv(k+1)$, $rhos(k-1)$, and $rhos(k+1)$ will be introduced inside loop i. These communications are costly due to their high frequency.

A computation partitioning is described by the underlined text in the figure. It partially replicate computation of S1, S2, and S3 and avoids the communications for rho_i and cv. As can be seen, after partial replicate computation partitioning, references

1 This research is supported in part by National Natural Science Foundation China (69933020) and by National 863 Hitech project 2002AA1Z2104.

$rho\_i(i,j,k)$ and $ws(i,j,k)$ in S1 and S2 become non-local. However the needed communication is much more coarse grained and cheaper than the original ones.

```
CHPF$ INDEPENDENT NEW(ru1,cv,rhoq)
do    j = 1, grid_points(2)-2
  do    i = 1, grid_points(1)-2
    do    k = 1-1, grid_points(3)-1
S1:     ru1 = c3c4*rho_i(i,j,k)
                    ON HOME lhs(i,j,k-1,*),(lhs(i,j,k+1,*)
S2:     cv(k) = ws(i,j,k)
                    ON HOME lhs(i,j,k-1,*),(lhs(i,j,k+1,*)
S3:     rhos(k) = dmax1(dz4 + con43 * ru1,
        dz5 + c1c5 * ru1, dzmax + ru1, dz1)
                    ON HOME lhs(i,j,k-1,*),(lhs(i,j,k+1,*)
    do    k =    1, grid_points(3)-2
    lhs(i,j,k,1) =    0.0d0
                    ON HOME lhs(i,j,k,1)
    lhs(i,j,k,2) = -dttz2 * cv(k-1) - dttz1 * rhos(k-1)
                    ON HOME lhs(i,j,k,2)
    lhs(i,j,k,3) =    1.0 + c2dttz1 * rhos(k)
                    ON HOME lhs(i,j,k,3)
    lhs(i,j,k,4) =    dttz2 * cv(k+1) - dttz1 * rhos(k+1)
                    ON HOME lhs(i,j,k,4)
    lhs(i,j,k,5) =    0.0d0
                    ON HOME lhs(i,j,k,5)
```

**Figure** 1: Partial replicate computation partitioning, an example

Generally, a PRCP eliminates communications at the cost of some newly introduced communications, so PRCP needs an effective cost evaluation.

## 2.2. A Survey of Existing Approaches

In the computation partition phase of dHPF [1], computation partition of primary computation [1] is determined first, and then the computation of scalars, localized and new arrays is assigned to processors that need the result. Therefore their computation may be partially replicated. In this scheme, the burden of ensuring the profitability of PRCP is put on the user. The user directive on loop j in the figure is needed by this scheme to achieve the desired PRCP.

In Autopar [3], partial replicate computation partition is regarded as an adjustment to the original computation partition. For each complex loop nest, the compiler tries to find a communication-free computation partitioning by applying partial replicate computation partitioning. The partition is deduced from a Relative Partial Redundant Computation Relation Graph constructed from the program data dependence [3].

The latter is completely automatic while the former is easier to be integrated with other computation partition optimizations. To handle more general situations, both methods need users adding directives and applying manual code transformation.

In Figure 1, the problem of profitability is trivial. Communications inside the deeper loop i are eliminated at the cost of the newly introduced communications outside loop *j* and a little amount of replicate computation. But there are other situations for which the

profitability problem is not trivial. Such a case is given in Figure 2, which is extracted from BT of NPB2.3 serial.

*Rho_i*, *square* and some other arrays are private variables of outer loop indexed by step. If partial replicate partitioning *ON_HOME rhs(\*,i,j,k-1)*, *rhs(\*,i,j,k+1)* is applied to S1, S2 and S3, non-local reference to array *u* will be introduced. Since the corresponding definition of *u* is inside loop step, the communication to be eliminated and generated is at the same loop level, the gains and penalty must be evaluated under a global communication optimization framework. In this example, there exists a communication which makes this newly introduced communication redundant, so the PRCP is profitable as long as the cost of communication to be eliminated is greater than the cost of replicated computation.

```
CHPF$INDEPENDENT LOCALIZE (rho i, us, vs, ws,
square, qs)
do onetrip =1,1
  do k = 0, grid_points(3)-1
    do j = 0, grid_points(2)-1
      do i = 0, grid_points(1)-1
S1:     rho_inv = 1.0d0/u(1,i,j,k)
S2:     rho_i(i,j,k) = rho_inv
S3:     us(i,j,k) = u(2,i,j,k) * rho_inv
        ......
  do k = 1, grid_points(3)-2
    do j = 1, grid_points(2)-2
      do i = 1, grid_points(1)-2
        ......
      up1    = us(i+1,j,k)
      rhs(2,i,j,k) = rhs(2,i,j,k) + dx2tx1 * (u(2,i+1,j,k) −
          2.0d0 * u(2,i,j,k) + u(2,i-1,j,k)) + xxcon2 *con43
          * (up1 − 2.0d0 *uijk + um1) − tx2 *
          (u(2,i+1,j,k)*up1 − u(2,i-1,j,k) *um1 +
          (u(5,i+1,j,k)- square(i+1,j,k) - u(5,i-1,j,k)+
          square(i-1,j,k)) * c2)
```

**Figure** 2: Partial replicate computation partition for a program fragment

By adding a user directive into the source code and some manual code transformation as shown by underlined text in Figure 2, the expected PRCP can be obtained in dHPF.

## 2.3. Another Motivating Example

PRCP schemes are usually derived from the corresponding USE-DEF relation [1, 3]. But in some situations, considerations on available regions may provide better PRCP schemes.

Available regions come from definitions and communications primitives for non-local uses. An *Enhanced Available Section Descriptors* [9] is introduced to record available regions under PRCP, which is a variation to ASD [8]. We illustrate it through the example in Figure 3, which is extracted from BT of NPB2.3 Serial.

In the figure, PRCP1 is attained from USE-DEF relation of *u*, eliminating the communication incurred by DEP1 and incurring communication on DEP2. While PRCP2 is derived from the available region *rhs*, decreasing the communication volume incurred by DEP1 without no new communication.

On the entry of L1, the available regions are *rhs(m,i,j,k:k+1)* generated by subroutine *z_solve*, and *u(m,i,j,k-2:k+2)* generated by subroutine *compute_rhs*.

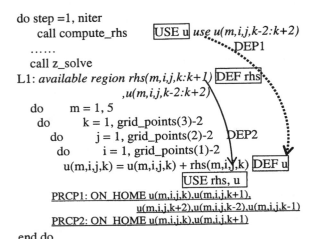

```
do step =1, niter
    call compute_rhs        USE u  use u(m,i,j,k-2:k+2)
    ......                                       DEP1
    call z_solve
L1: available region rhs(m,i,j,k:k+1)  DEF rhs
                       ,u(m,i,j,k-2:k+2)
    do    m = 1, 5
      do      k = 1, grid_points(3)-2
        do      j = 1, grid_points(2)-2   DEP2
          do      i = 1, grid_points(1)-2
            u(m,i,j,k) = u(m,i,j,k) + rhs(m,i,j,k)  DEF u
                                        USE rhs, u
    PRCP1: ON  HOME u(m,i,j,k),u(m,i,j,k+1),
                     u(m,i,j,k+2),u(m,i,j,k-2),u(m,i,j,k-1)
    PRCP2: ON  HOME u(m,i,j,k),u(m,i,j,k+1)
end do
```

**Figure 3**: Example of PRCP derived from available regions

So, under PRCP1, communication for *rhs(m,i,j,k,k-1)*, *rhs(m,i,j,k,k+1)*, and *rhs(m,i,j,k,k+2)* are needed. While under PRCP2, the necessary communication is those acquiring *u(m,i,j,k,k-1)*, *u(m,i,j,k,k+1)*, and *u(m,i,j,k,k+2)* for *compute_rhs*. As can be seen, the volumes are the same.

Under such a restrained candidate set, we prefer PRCP2 to PRCP1 for its lesser computation volume.

Available regions, provides more alternatives for a heuristic implementation of replicate computation partition.

## 2.4. Goal of Our Research

The previous sections illustrate the following two points. First, an effective global cost model is crucial to an automatic PRCP framework. Second, beside USE-DEF relations, DEF-USE relations (based on available regions analysis) should be used in searching for an optimal PRCP scheme.

The problem of global PRCP is more complex if partition tuning occurs at different loop levels. We solve the whole problem hierarchically, starting from the sub-problems at the deepest loop levels in a bottom-up manner. The reason is that deeper nested communication is more costly.

The goal of our research is to carry out a formal representation for global partial replicate computation partition and to provide a heuristic algorithm.

## 3. Automatic CP Framework

In our scheme, the computation partition phase is split into two steps in our. First, an initial computation partition is generated following the owner-compute rule. Second, PRCP is applied as an adjustment after the communication optimization phase.

This section is composed of several parts: first, we give a formal description of the problem; second, we describe our heuristic algorithm, its cost model and the prototype implementation in Autopar and at last we illustrate the algorithm through an example.

In our framework, computation partition is performed at the granularity of an iterations i.e. all statements in a loop share the same computation partition.

### 3.1. Formal Representation of the Problem

The global PRCP problem is represented in a hierarchical fashion. Each sub-problem is the PRCP problem for all loops and statements nested in a same loop. Sub-problems are solved bottom up. The solution process is quite similar to interval analysis. We use a condensed program dependence graph (CPDG) to denote a sub-problem, where each node is an interval, extra entry and exit vertices are added to record information needed by the parent problem.

Definition: A Program Fragment is denoted as a CPDG, G=<V, E, s, e>.

V is a set of vertices. Each vertex denotes a fragment of the program.

E is a set of edges. Each edge denotes the DEF-USE relation between a pair of vertices.

In V, s and e are two special elements that denote the entry and exit vertex respectively.

A computation partition, P, is a function on V: $P: v \mapsto r, \forall v \in V$ , where r is a partial replicate computation vector [3]. It denotes the partial replication of the computation.

A trivial computation partition uses the owner-computes rule for each vertex.

The cost of a computation partition is the execution time of the result program. An optimal computation partition has the minimal cost.

The PRCP Problem is to find an optimal and satisfying computation partition for a given CPDG.

### 3.2. Some Related Issues

```
do j = 2, ny - 1
   do i = 2, nx - 1
      do k = 2, nz – 1
         ...
         f(m,i,j,k) = f(m,i,j,k) - tmp1 * f(m,i,j,k-1)
         ...
         f(m,i,j,k+1)  =   f(m,i,j,k+1)  -  tmp2  *
f(m,i,j,k-1)
```
**Figure 4**: A complicated DOACROSS loop for PRCP

In the Autopar compiler, DOACROSS loops may be parallelized by coarse-grain pipelining.

If PRCP is applied to a pipeline loop, it is necessary to split the loop for inserting communications in some situation. The code generation is complicated and an extra cost is introduced in such situations. It is even worse if the compiler tries to adjust the granularity of the pipeline loop by strip-mining outer loops.

To simplify the PRCP solution, we exclude DOACROSS loops from consideration. In fact, it is not substantial obstacles to PRCP.

Figure 4 is such an example, the output dependence within the loop body, makes loop splitting necessary when exploiting inter-node pipelining.

### 3.3. A Simplified Cost Model

As the cost of PRCP for a program fragment is hard to estimate, we develop a simple linear cost model. In this model, the cost of a solution is:

$$C = \sum_{v \in V \wedge v \notin \{s,e\}} \left( C_c(v) + C_n(v) \right)$$

For a vertex v, $C_c(v)$ denotes the computation cost and $C_n(v)$ denotes the communication cost.

The computation cost of a vertex v is:

$$C_c(v) = \frac{(1+r)}{p} \times C_v(v)$$

In which, $C_v(v)$ is the estimated time to execute a serial version, r is the ratio of replicate computation executed and p is the number of processors participating in parallel computing.

The communication cost of a vertex v is:

$$C_n(v) = \sum_{m \in C(v)} Vol(m) * b_0 + l_0$$

In which, $C(v)$ is the set of messages on v and $b_0$ and $l_0$ are predefined machine parameters corresponding to the bandwidth and latency of the network respectively.

This model does not consider the influence of communication and computation overlapping, network resource constraints and imperfect load balance. Though simple, we found our cost model effective to direct CP algorithms for many real applications.

### 3.4. Our Heuristic Method

In this section, we will introduce a framework to find satisfying solutions to global PRCP problems. The framework contains several algorithms, such as global problem decomposition, single PRCP solving and local PRCP propagation.

As described in 3.2, we do not consider the PRCP of DOACROSS loops in our approach. A vertex representing a DOACROSS loop is *un-adjustable*.

We begin by introducing the data structures employed. Then we define some operations on the graph and data structure. Finally we give the algorithm.

**Data Structures:**

A vertex is structured hierarchically. Vertices in a graph are stored as a forest. Each non leaf node in the forest represents the summary of all its child nodes.

On each vertex, we record 1) the coefficient of the computation cost, 2) the PRCP vector, 3) the available regions and use regions, 4) the DEF regions 5) communication placed after it and 6) a flag showing whether it is an *un-adjustable* Vertex.

The communication is placed at the definition point for the convenience of redundant communication elimination and communication merging. The computation partitioning of each leaf vertex is denoted by the sum of PRCP vectors of itself and its parent.

A Completely Aligned Cycle is a circle in the CPG in which no edge incurs communication.

**Operations:**

**Vertex Merging**: Generate a new vertex as the parent of all input vertices. PRCP vector of the new vertex is <0, 0>. The available region, use region and the coefficient of computational cost must be recomputed for the new vertex.

The merging of normal vertices and un-adjustable vertices results in an un-adjustable vertex; if there exist communications between vertices to be merged, the result vertex will be un-adjustable.

**Partial Replicate Computation Partition Tuning**: PRCP vector of the corresponding vertex is adjusted in this operation. Its def array regions, use regions and communications are adjusted at the same time. Communication on predecessors of the vertex should be adjusted as well.

For a vertex, if partial replicate computation vector is r=<n,p> and one of its original array region (definition or use) is (…,i+a:i+b,…), the new region is (…,i+a-n:i+b+p,…).

**Algorithm.** Search for a PRCP adjustment, and apply a corresponding vertex merging

Detailed process is shown in Figure 5. The supporting functions and denotations are explained as follows.

**Function** *Required*(edge, rgn): gives a PRCP vector with the least replication for vertex u, which makes array a's DEF region equal to *rgn*, where edge=<u, v>.

**Function** *Allowed*(v, a): gives a PRCP vector with the largest replication for vertex v, under which array a's use region on v is still a subset of the its available region.

**Function** *Benefit* computes the cost difference between new and old PRCP solution.

**Denotations**: R is a candidate set of PRCP adjustment schemes. s=<v1, e, v2, r ,b> is a candidate PRCP adjustment scheme, where e is the edge in question, v1 is the vertex to be partitioned, v2 is a related vertex, r is the PRCP vector, and b is the benefit.

**Algorithm 1**. Local Elimination:

1. The trivial solution is generated. For each node, its PRCP vector is set to <0, 0>. Preliminary communication is generated at the corresponding definition point. Then perform redundant communication elimination and communication

merging;

    2. Merge all adjacent un-adjustable vertices;

    3. If there are some groups of un-adjustable vertices that share the same set of successors and shares the same set of predecessors, merge each group;

    4. Constructs a set of candidate PRCP schemes, and applies a best scheme (see Figure 5)

    If the algorithm returns true, go to step 2;

    5. Search for a Completely Aligned Circle with the shortest length in the graph. If such a circle is found, contract it to a single vertex, go to step 2;

    6. Now, there are no more opportunity of optimization, record the USE array regions of exit vertex $e$ and communication of entry vertex $s$. These two attributes will be used in the outer PRCP problem.

**Algorithm 3.** Local Propagation:

This simple algorithm computes the final PRCP vector of all leaf vertices in the graph top down.

The most costly step of the local algorithm is step 4. The complexity to find all PRCP adjustment candidates is $O(N*E*A)$, where N, E and A are the number of vertices, edges and arrays in the graph respectively. For a candidate, the complexity to compute its benefit is $O(E*A)$ since all array references of all connected edges should be considered. This step would be repeated N times at most. So the time complexity of the algorithm is $O(N2E2A2)$. Its space complexity is $O(N*E*A)$.

**Algorithm 2.** Search for a PRCP adjustment, if successful, apply the corresponding scheme

```
R=Φ
step 1:For each vertex v in the graph
        For each outgoing edge e, let e=<v, u>
            For each array a, let rgn be its use region on v
                s.v₁=v; s.v₂=u; s.r=Required(e, rgn);
                Determine if there is a r in R satisfies
                    ( r.v₁==s.v₁ and r.r==s.r)
                If no such r is found, add s to R
            For each array a
                s.v₁=v; s.v₂=0; s.r=Allowed(v, a);
                Determine if there is a r in R satisfies
                    ( r.v₁==s.v₁ and r.r==s.r)
                If no such r is found, add s to R
step 2:For each PRCP scheme vector r in R
        r.b= Benefit(r);
        If (r.b <= 0) R=R-{r};
step 3:
    If (R == Φ)
            return .false.;
    else
    Choose a candidate r with the greatest profit in R
        Partial_Replicate_Computation_Partition_Tuning(G, r)
        /*Apply the scheme*/
        if (r.v₂!=0)  Merge(r.v₁, r.v₂);
            /*it is generated by Allowed*/
        return .true.;
    else return .false.
```

**Figure** 5: Algorithm 2, try applying a PRCP adjustment

A concise proof to the algorithm is given below.

In the final PRCP, the computation on each processor is a superset of that of the initial solution, so a correct parallel program can be derived from the solution. Second, the number of vertices of the graph would monotonically decreases, so the algorithm terminates. At last, as each PRCP tuning is profitable, the cost of final solution is no more than that of the initial one.

The global PRCP algorithm is described in Figure 6.

**Algorithm 4.** Global PRCP.

Pre-processing: Decompose the global PRCP problem to hierarchical sub-problems and generate trivial solution to the global problem;

    Elimination: while there are still unsolved problems

      Find a leaf problem;

        Call Local Elimination Algorithm;

        /*propagate info. on entry/exit vertex to its parent*/

        In the parent problem:

          Modify the communication incurred by

            use in the child;

          Modify the available region of the child and

            its if_adjustable attribute;

    Propagation:

      Traverse the tree top down, for each vertex

        Accumulate the PRCP vector of it to

           all its children;

        For each child of it

            Call Local propagation Algorithm;

    Translation:

      Translate all PRCP vectors into computation partition

**Figure** 6: Global PRCP algorithm

### 3.5. Prototype Implementation in Autopar

Autopar [4] is a parallelizing compiler targeting distributed memory systems. It translates FORTRAN programs annotated by "Distributed OpenMP" [10] directives into hybrid OpenMP/MPI programs. The middle end of Autopar performs data distribution, computation partitioning, initial communication placing, and computation partition tuning and communication optimization in turn.

A prototype of our algorithm has been implemented in the computation partition tuning phase of Autopar.

### 3.6. Illustration through an Example

The example in Figure 7 is the ADI loop of APPSP of NPB 1.0. The PRCP adjustment of JACZ and RHSZ are already performed previously according to our global algorithm.

All non local references are annotated on the edge in the figure. Based on one dimensional block data distribution of Autopar, only offset in zeta direction in array reference are considered and computation in xi and eta direction are condensed. Actually our algorithm also works on other block data distribution modes, multi-dimensional block distribution and multi-partition [5, 6, 7, 2].

In Figure 7, A(n,p) represents reference to A(i-n:i+p). In particular, RSD123, RSD4 and RSD5 represent reference to *rsd(1:3,...)* , *rsd(4,...)* and *rsd(5,...)*

respectively.

The dashed vertices in the graph are un-adjustable. As entry and exit vertices do not participant in the kernel part of the algorithm and edges related to them are numerous, we omitted them in the following figures.

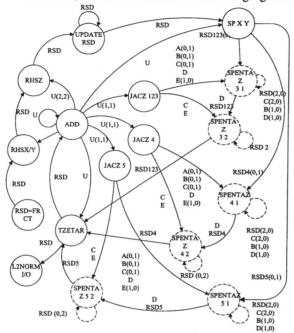

**Figure 7:** Example problem from APPSP of NPB1.0

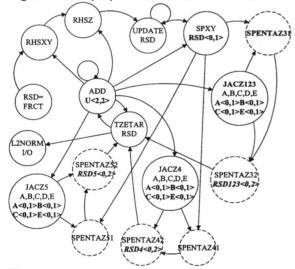

**Figure 8:** Initial solution to the problem

Figure 8 shows the initial solution of the problem. On each vertex, communications are intensified in the bold text while def regions are present in italic text.

The first PRCP adjustment is applied on vertex "JACZ123", the related vertex is "SPENTAZ31".

Figure 9 describes the intermediate solution after three steps of PRCP tuning and vertex union.

The status after merging all three un-adjustable vertices and contract the cycle consists of vertex "ADD"

and "TZETAR" is shown in Figure 10. Regions of RSD123, RSD4 and RSD5 are merged to a region of RSD.

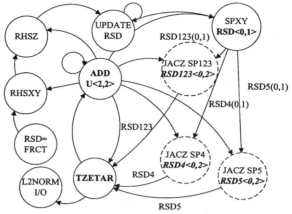

**Figure 9:** An intermediate result

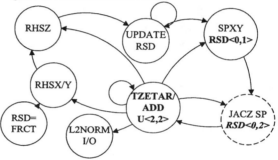

**Figure 10:** Another intermediate result

In Figure 10, another opportunity of PRCP tuning is spotted i.e. on the vertex "TZETAR/ADD". According to the available array region generated by vertex "JACZ SP", the PRCP vector of "TZETAR/ADD" is adjusted to<0, 2>. It is applied as it is profitable. Another tuning on vertex "SPXY" is not profitable on any machine because volume of communication is not reduced. We contract all the vertices and the final result is showed in Figure 11. The communication needed by the program fragment is marked on entry vertex s.

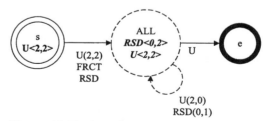

**Figure 11:** Final result

Let *adjacent*(array, l, u) represent the communication satisfying a non-local reference as array(...,i - l: i + u,...).

In the final computation partition, residual communications are adjacent(U,0,2) and adjacent(RSD, 0, 1) besides the communications introduced by wave front and reduction loops. In contrast, communication in initial solution are adjacent(U,2,2), adjacent(RSD,0,1), three adjacent(A,0,1), three adjacent(B,0,1), three adjacent(C,0,1) and three adjacent(E,1,0).

## 4. Experimental Results and Evaluation

We carried out experiments on six scientific computing programs. The result of BT, LU and SP of NAS Parallel Benchmark serial is shown in Figure 12 and Figure 13. Each benchmark is applied one-dimensional partitioning. In these experiments, aggressive inlining of subroutines is activated.

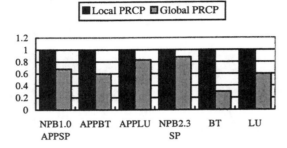

**Figure** 12: Comparison of communication volume

Figure 12 shows the reduction of communication volume under global PRCP over local solution. One should notice that the proportion will not vary with different numbers of processors. The referenced program is generated by AutoPar3.2 where local communication-free PRCP is adopted [3].

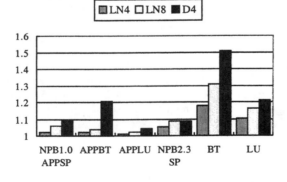

**Figure** 13 Relative speedup of global PRCP over local PRCP

Our experiments were performed on two different high performance clusters, Dawning3000 and Shenteng 6800. The Dawning 3000, developed by National Research Center for Intelligent Computing Systems, CAS, is a 4-way SMP cluster connected with Myrinet or 1000 Mb Ethernet. Only Ethernet is available in our experiments. Its processors are 375 MHz Power3-II with 64KB L1 D-cache, 32KB I-cache and 8MB L2 cache. The Shenteng 6800 is developed by *the Lenovo Corp*. It is a 4-way SMP cluster with 1.3 GHz Itanium2

processors. Each processor has 32 KB L1 cache, 256 KB L2 cache, and 3 MB L3 cache. The SMPs are connected by *QsNet*.

Figure 13 shows the speedup of the global PRCP programs over the local PRCP ones. The label D4 stands for experimental results on 4 nodes of Dawning 3000. The labels LN4 and LN8 stand for 4 and 8 nodes on Shenteng 6800 respectively.

*IBM xlf 7.1* and *Intel efc 8.0* serves as the native compilers on Dawning 3000 and Shenteng 6800 respectively. All programs are compiled with –O3 option.

On Dawning 3000, the speedup is greater. The reason may lie in its lower network performance. As for the result of LN4 and LN8, the relative speedup is greater on more nodes. An explanation can be given in our cost model, the absolute volume of partial replicate computation and communications reduction on each single node do not vary with the number of participating processors. So the execution time saving is similar in two situations. As the total execution time decreases on more nodes, the speedup goes up.

## 5. Summary and Future Work

Partial Replicate Computation Partition is a computation decomposition technique that trades a little amount of replicated computation for the elimination of costly communications. Automatic exploration of partial replicate computation partition globally is an untouched area.

In this paper, we provide a formal representation of the PRCP problem, give a global PRCP framework and show encouraging results.

Our cost model and heuristic algorithm can be improved in future work. Loop distribution during computation partitioning is helpful to improve the performance of the result parallel program [1]. The problem of PRCP tuning and loop transformations can be combined. An integrated framework is needed to further improve computation partitioning.

## 6. References

[1] Vikram Adve, Guohua Jin, John Mellor-Crummey and Qing Yi. Design and Evaluation of a Computation Partitioning Framework for Data-Parallel Compilers, *http://www-sal.cs.uiuc.edu/~vadve/publications.html*, submitted for publication.

[2] J. Mellor-Crummey, V. Adve, B. Broom, D. Chavarria-Miranda ,R. Fowler, G. Jin, K. Kennedy and Q. Yi. Advanced Optimization Strategies in the Rice dHPF Compiler. Concurrency: Practice and Experience,1:1-20,March 2001.

[3] Li Chen, Zhao-Qing Zhang and Xiao-Bing Feng. Redundant computation partition on distributed-memory systems. Algorithms and Architectures for Parallel Processing, 2002. Proceedings.

Fifth International Conference on , 23-25 Oct. 2002 Pages:252 – 260

[4] Xiao-Bing Feng, Global Automatic Data Distribution, PhD thesis, Institute of Computing Technology, Chinese Academy of Science, 1999, page 100

[5] J. Bruno and P. Cappello. Implementing the beam and warming method on the hypercube. In Proceedings of 3<sup>rd</sup> Conference on Hypercube Concurrent Computers and Applications; pages 1073-1087, Pasadena, CA, January 1988.

[6] S. Lennart. Johnsson, Youcef Saad, and Martin H. Schultz. Alternating direction methods on multiprocessors. SIAM Journal of Scientific Computing, 8(5):686-700, 1987

[7] N.H. Naik, V, Naik and M. Nicoules. Parallelization of a class of implicit finite difference schemes in computational fluid dynamics. International Journal of High Speed Computing, 5(1):1-50, 1993

[8] Manish Gupta, Edith Schonberg, Harini Srinivasan: A Unified Data-Flow Framework for Optimizing Communication. LCPC 1994: 266-282

[9] Li Chen, Optimization of Parallel Codes on SMP Clusters, PhD thesis, Institute of Computing Technology, Chinese Academy of Science, 2002

[10] J. Merlin, D. Miles, V. Schuster, Distributed OpenMP: Extensions to OpenMP for SMP Clusters, Second European Workshop on OpenMP (EWOMP2000), Edinburgh, U.K. 2000

# Low-cost Register-pressure Prediction for Scalar Replacement Using Pseudo-schedules*

Yin Ma
Steve Carr
Michigan Technological University
Department of Computer Science
Houghton MI 49931-1295
{*yinma,carr*}@*mtu.edu*

Rong Ge
Simon Fraser University
School of Computing Science
Burnaby BC Canada V5A 1S6
*rge@cs.sfu.ca*

## Abstract

*Scalar replacement is an effective optimization for removing memory accesses. However, exposing all possible array reuse with scalars may cause a significant increase in register pressure, resulting in register spilling and performance degradation. In this paper, we present a low cost method to predict the register pressure of a loop before applying scalar replacement on high-level source code, called Pseudo-schedule Register Prediction (PRP), that takes into account the effects of both software pipelining and register allocation. PRP attempts to eliminate the possibility of degradation from scalar replacement due to register spilling while providing opportunities for a good speedup.*

*PRP uses three approximation algorithms: one for constructing a data dependence graph, one for computing the recurrence constraints of a software pipelined loop, and one for building a pseudo-schedule. Our experiments show that PRP predicts the floating-point register pressure within 2 registers and the integer register pressure within 2.7 registers on average with a time complexity of $O(n^2)$ in practice. PRP achieves similar performance to the best previous approach, having $O(n^3)$ complexity, with less than one-fourth of the compilation time on our test suite.*

## 1. Introduction

Traditional optimizing compilers have effective global register allocation algorithms for scalars. Now, many commercial compilers extend register allocation by replacing multiple array references to the same memory location with references to scalars to allow global register allocation to put these values in registers. This replacement of

arrays with scalar temporaries is called *scalar replacement* [2, 3, 4, 5, 6, 8].

Because traditional scalar register allocation algorithms cannot allocate array elements to registers, scalar replacement becomes a bridge to expose the opportunities for allocating array elements to registers using traditional algorithms. Consequently, scalar replacement reduces the number of memory accesses and improves performance. Unfortunately, converting all possible array reuse to scalars may dramatically increase the register pressure in short fragments of code, resulting in performance degradation in loops due to increased register spilling [6]. Aggressive scheduling techniques such as software pipelining are sensitive to register demands, magnifying the change in register pressure from scalar replacement. If the extent of scalar replacement can be controlled precisely, those risks are likely to be eliminated and scalar replacement may always provide a positive speedup. To achieve this goal, we present a new algorithm, called *Pseudo-schedule Register Prediction* (PRP), that predicts the register pressure of a given loop before scalar replacement and software pipelining are applied. PRP achieves good performance with $O(n^2)$ complexity in practice.

PRP determines register pressure directly from the source code by estimating the effects of optimization and software pipelining without actually performing optimization and complete software pipelining. Performing scalar replacement on unoptimized source allows the compiler to retain the structure of the original code, making it easier to gather loop and array information. By avoiding optimization and full software pipelining, PRP becomes significantly cheaper since the code is not fully compiled both to predict pressure and to generate the final code. While these simplifications lower the accuracy of PRP, we show that on average PRP produces register pressure estimations usually within 0, 1 or 2 registers of the actual pressure.

*This research has been partially supported by NSF grant CCR-0209036.

116

We begin this paper with a brief discussion of previous work on register-pressure prediction. Then, we give a review of scalar replacement and software pipelining. Next, we present PRP and our experimental results. Finally, we give our conclusions and discuss future work.

## 2. Previous Work

Wolf, et al. [13], present a technique for ensuring that unroll-and-jam, scalar replacement and software pipelining do not use too many registers. They consider the effects of the pipeline filling requirements and the number of scalars needed for scalar replacement when modeling the floating-point register requirement before loop transformations. Their method defines pipeline filling requirements of a processor as the number of floating-point registers required to keep the pipeline running at full speed. To get the total register pressure of a loop, the number of scalars needed for scalar replacement is added to the pipeline filling requirements. This technique will overestimate the number of registers required since the registers reserved for pipeline filling may not all be needed.

Carr, et al. [3, 5], estimate register pressure before applying scalar replacement by reserving an experimentally determined number of registers for scheduling and adding that amount to the number of scalars used in a loop by scalar replacement. As in Wolf's method, this technique may reserve more registers than necessary to allow for the increased register pressure due to scheduling.

Huff [10] presents a scheduling method to apply software pipelining with minimum register pressure. Huff defines, two metrics, *MaxLive* and *MinAvg*, to measure the register pressure. MaxLive represents the lower bound on the number of registers required by a software pipelined loop. It is very accurate but available only after a software pipeline has been created, making it too costly and too late for prediction. MinAvg also represents a lower bound on register pressure, but its computation occurs before pipelining. MinAvg is defined as the sum of minimum lifetimes of all variables divided by the initiation interval (II), where II is the number of cycles between the initiations of two consecutive iterations in a loop. Unfortunately, MinAvg ignores the effects of overlapping lifetimes. In addition, MinAvg assumes all variables can be scheduled such that minimum lifetimes are achieved. Under high resource constraints minimum lifetimes are often not achieved, resulting in a highly inaccurate register pressure estimation.

Ding [7] proposes a different approach that uses MinDist to compute register pressure. MinDist is a two dimensional array used to compute software pipelining dependence constraints that contains information about the minimum lifetime of each variable. Ding claims that the overlapping in software pipelining requires additional registers only when the lifetime of a variable is longer than II. Since MinDist

gives the lower bound of the lifetime of a variable, the number of registers for this variable can be directly predicted as $\left\lceil \frac{Lifetime}{II} \right\rceil$. MinDist, however, ignores resource constraints, resulting in an imprecise prediction under high resource constraints.

Recently, Ge [9] described a new method that uses the information in MinDist to build a schedule as an approximation of the real schedule for predicting register pressure. DU chains are computed based on the approximate schedule. The maximum number of DU chains overlapped in a cycle will be the number of registers predicted. By her observation, long DU chains and aggregated short DU chains reflect the effect of high resource conflicts. She presents two heuristic algorithms to handle these two types of chains.

Ge's method predicts register pressure more accurately than MinAvg and MinDist methods at the intermediate language level. However, our objective is to predict register pressure at the source level before applying scalar replacement. Ge's method can give imprecise prediction on source code because it relies on a complete DDG. Moreover, computing MinDist and the length of recurrences takes $O(n^3)$ time. This cost is higher than desired for our purposes.

## 3. Scalar Replacement and Software Pipelining

In this section, we review scalar replacement and software pipelining, motivating the need to predict register pressure to limit potential performance degradation in the presence of high register pressure.

### 3.1. Scalar Replacement

*Scalar replacement* is a loop transformation that uses scalars, later allocated to registers, to replace array references to decrease the number of memory references in loops. In the code shown below, there are three memory references and one floating-point addition during an iteration.

```
for ( i = 2; i < n; i++ )
    a[i] = a[i-1] + b[i];
```

The value defined by a[i] is used one iteration later by a[i-1]. Using scalar replacement to expose this reuse, the resulting code becomes

```
T = a[1];
for ( i = 2; i < n; i++) {
    T = T + b[i];
    a[i] = T;
}
```

Here the number of memory references decreases to two with the number of arithmetic operations remaining the same. If the original loop is bound by memory accesses, scalar replacement improves performance. On the other hand, more scalars are used, demanding more registers to hold their values. The resulting increased register pressure may cause excessive register spilling and degrade performance [6].

## 3.2. Software Pipelining

Software pipelining [1, 11, 12] is an advanced scheduling technique for modern processors. One popular method for software pipelining, modulo scheduling [12], tries to create a schedule with the minimum number cycles used for one iteration of a loop such that no resource and dependence constraints are violated when this schedule is repeated.

The *initiation interval* (II) of a loop is the number of cycles between the initiation of two consecutive iterations. The initiation interval gives the number of cycles needed to execute a single iteration of a loop and determines the loop's performance. Given a loop and a target architecture, compilers can predict the lower-bound on II. The resource initiation interval (ResII) gives the minimum number of cycles needed to execute the loop based upon machine resources such as the number of functional units. The recurrence initiation interval (RecII) gives the minimum number of cycles needed for a single iteration of the loop based upon the length of the cycles in the DDG. The maximum value between RecII and ResII, called the minimum initiation interval (MinII), represents a lower bound on the minimum value of an II.

Software pipelining can significantly improve loop performance. Consider a loop $L$ that iterates $n$ times and contains three instructions we call A, B, and C. Assume that dependences in the loop require a sequential ordering of these operations within a single loop iteration. Thus, even if our target architecture allows 3 operations to be issued at once, a schedule for a single loop iteration would require 3 instructions due to dependences among the operations. The resulting loop would execute in $3 * n$ cycles on a machine with one-cycle operations.

A software pipelined version of $L$ might well be able to issue all three operations in one instruction by overlapping execution from different loop iterations. This might under ideal circumstances, lead to a single-instruction loop body of $A^{i+2}B^{i+1}C^i$ where $X^j$ denotes operation $X$ from iteration $j$ of the loop [1]. The cost of the software pipelined loop is about one-third of the cost of the original loop, namely $n + 2$ cycles including the prelude and postlude. So software pipelining can, by exploiting inter-iteration concurrency, dramatically reduce the execution time required for a loop.

Unfortunately, overlapping of loop iterations also leads to additional register requirements. For illustrative purposes, assume that operation A computes a value, $v$, in a register and that operation C uses $v$. In the initial sequential

version of a loop body one register is sufficient to store $v$'s value. In the software pipelined version, we need to maintain as many as three different copies of $v$ because we have different loop iterations in execution simultaneously. In this particular case, the register holding the value from iteration $i$ can be used by operation C and defined by operation A in the same instruction since reads from registers occur before writes to registers in the pipeline. Thus, we would need 2 registers for $v$.

Since software pipelining and scalar replacement can demand a larger number of registers, we must predict register pressure before applying them, or risk degrading performance. In the next section, we detail our register-pressure prediction algorithm.

## 4. Pseudo-schedule Register Prediction (PRP)

To predict the number of registers used by software pipelining directly from high-level source code, we must build a sufficiently detailed DDG to represent the loop body, approximate the RecII and approximate the final software pipeline. This section describes our approach, PRP, that attempts to balance the detail needed for an accurate prediction with the desire to make the prediction as efficient as possible.

### 4.1. Constructing the DDG

In this section, we present a low-cost algorithm to generate a sufficiently precise DDG directly from high-level source code. This algorithm only applies to innermost loops that contain only assignment statements with array references, scalars and arithmetic operators. The construction algorithm presented in this section is based on an *abstract syntax tree (AST)*. In addition to an AST, the algorithm utilizes the array data dependence graph to predict the effects of scalar replacement.

Nodes in the DDG represent intermediate operations and edges between nodes represent data dependences. The label on an edge is a vector ⟨Delay,Diff⟩, where Delay represents the minimum number of cycles that must occur between the two operations incident on this edge and Diff represents the number of loop iterations between the two adjacent nodes.

Before construction, we prune the original array dependence graph to represent the flow of values between array references as is done in scalar replacement [3]. After analyzing the pruned graph, we build a reuse map, called *reuseMap*, from each array reference to one of three states: *generator*, *replaced*, and *move-out-of-loop*. *Generator* marks an array reference that will be kept after scalar replacement. *Replaced* indicates references eliminated during scalar replacement, and *move-out-of loop* indicates those references that are loop invariant. Any array reference marked as *replaced* or *move-out-of-loop* will not be put in the DDG. Besides array references, reuse may also happen in index addressing and scalars. In our algorithm, reuse maps for index addressing and scalars are updated during DDG generation.

The approximate DDG construction algorithm must remain consistent with the expected output of the optimizer. We have found that optimization results are quite predictable for loops amenable to scalar replacement. While the DDG construction is tailored to the optimizer we are using, we expect that the concepts are more widely applicable since the optimization passes are standard and generally predictable. The algorithm reads each element in an AST in execution order and generates the corresponding DDG nodes. Any specialized instruction generation should be reflected in the DDG generation. Because constants and scalars defined outside loops don't need new registers, no DDG nodes are generated for them. For array references, scalars and index subscripts, we always use old nodes if reuse is available; otherwise, we add this node to *reuseMap*. Edges are added if two nodes have a dependence. The Delay and Diff on edges are determined by the targeted architecture. Loads and stores have dependences if they may access the same memory location. To represent the dependences in the AST and model the backend scheduler that we use, we assume that a store has dependences with all loads generated in the same statement and a load has a dependence only with the latest generated store.

The key to generating a good DDG for prediction is to consider reuse thoroughly. Each reuse critically impacts the shape of a DDG because reused operations share a set of nodes. This, in turn, affects the prediction of register pressure. Without a precise DDG, PRP produces an inaccurate register-pressure prediction. Figure 2A gives an example DDG constructed by our algorithm.

## 4.2. RecII Approximation

After generating a DDG, PRP generates a pseudo-schedule used for register-pressure prediction. Scheduling fills out a table where each column corresponds to one available functional unit in the target architecture, and each row represents an execution cycle. The number of rows in the table is the MinII, the maximum value of RecII and ResII. An accurate register pressure prediction requires a precise estimation of MinII. Unfortunately, traditional methods for computing RecII, such as using MinDist, are $O(n^3)$ where $n$ is the number of nodes in a DDG. This is too expensive to use in prediction. To limit the cost of PRP, we present a heuristic algorithm that is close to the $O(n^2)$ in most situations.

In practice, a DDG generated by a compiler is not an arbitrary graph but one with a certain topological order already. If we give each node a sequence number in the order of being generated, the node numbers obey the order of execution. So we define a forward edge as an edge from a node with a smaller sequence number to one with a larger number and a backward edge as an edge from a source node sequence number greater than or equal to the sink node sequence number. With this order, our algorithm approximately computes RecII in three steps.

The first step converts a DDG from a directed graph to an undirected graph called the *SimpleDDG*, in which there is only one edge between each pair of nodes. This is shown in Figure 1A. Then, for each pair of nodes, we merge the vectors of one forward edge with the largest Delay and one backward edge with the smallest Diff together to be forward and backward vectors of a new undirected edge, as shown in Figure 1A. In Figure 1A, the first vector is the forward vector and the second vector is the backward vector. If there are only forward edges or backward edges, we leave the corresponding vector blank or give special values, such as [1,0][-10000,-10000], where -10000 means there is no edge between the two nodes.

After creating the undirected graph, in the second step we simplify it using four transformations. The algorithm visits each node and applies transformations repeatedly until no more simplifying is possible. A detailed description of the four transformations is given below.

**Transformation 1:** If there is an edge having the same source and sink, compute the potential RecII as if both the forward vector and backward vector have valid values using the equation below.

$$\text{Potential RecII} = \frac{D_f + D_b}{F_f + F_b}$$

where $D_f$ is delay in the forward vector, $D_b$ is delay in the backward vector, $F_f$ is diff in the forward vector and $F_b$ is diff in the backward vector. Then, remove this edge. See Figure 1B for an example where the potential RecII is 3 by applying the equation $\frac{2+1}{0+1}$.

**Transformation 2:** If a node only has one edge connecting it to other nodes, then remove this node and the edge with it, as shown in the Figure 1C.

**Transformation 3:** If a node has degree two, merge its two edges by adding the values in the matching elements in their vectors, as shown in the Figure 1D.

**Transformation 4:** If there are two edges between a pair of nodes, merge the two edges. The forward vectors with the largest Delay/Diff ratio will be the forward vector of the new edge. The same is true of the backward vector. Two potential RecIIs are computed if a cycle can go clockwise and counterclockwise. For the clockwise cycle, we use the forward vector of the first edge

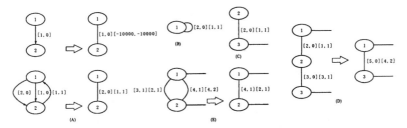

**Figure 1. DDG Simplification Transformations**

and the backward vector of the second edge to compute the RecII. For the counterclockwise cycle, we use the backward vector of the first edge and the backward vector of the second edge to compute another RecII, as shown in the Figure 1E. In the example, one potential RecII is $\frac{7}{3}$ computed by $\frac{3+4}{1+2}$ and another potential RecII is 3 computed by $\frac{4+2}{1+1}$.

After graph simplification, the graph may be empty. In this case, we take the maximum potential RecII computed during simplification as the approximate RecII. However, if nodes remain in the graph, such as the simplification from Figure 2A to Figure 2B, we apply a third step using the algorithm in Figure 3 to compute one more potential RecII on the simplified graph. The maximum of all computed potential RecIIs is our approximate RecII.

### 4.3. Register-pressure Prediction

PRP uses the standard kernel scheduling algorithm to fill out a schedule table but ignores all backward edges in the *SimpleDDG*[12]. The ResII is computed from the approximate DDG and the target architecture. Once the compiler generates a pseudo-schedule, it computes the lifetime for each potential virtual register. In the *SimpleDDG*, the definition of a virtual register is implicit because multiple nodes may map to one expression in the source, indicating they share one virtual register. If a node has at least one forward edge, this node represents the definition of a virtual register. The last use of this virtual register is the latest-generated sink node on the forward edge with the largest lifetime (LT), where LT = Diff * II + Delay. For instance, if an edge has the vector $\langle 3, 1 \rangle$ and the II is 9, its LT will be $9 * 1 + 3 = 11$ cycles.

| Def | 1(0) | 2(0) | 3(0) | 5(1) | 7(1) | 9(2) | 11(0) |
|-----|------|------|------|------|------|------|-------|
| Use | 2(0) | 9(2) | 4(1) | 6(1) | 8(2) | 12(2) | 12(2) |

#### Table 1. The Define-Use List for Figure 2A

To compute LT for each virtual register, we consider the DU-chains in the DDG. Consider the def-use table for Figure 2 in Table 1. Each column in the table is a def-use pair. The first number is the node number and the second one is

the cycle in which this node is scheduled. With the Def-Use table and the schedule table, we will use the DU-Chain technique introduced by Ge to predict the final register pressure [9]. The idea behind this technique is if there are two def-use pairs, $A \to B$ and $B \to C$, we consider the chain $A \to B \to C$. If there is a branch such as $A \to B$ with $B \to C$ and $B \to D$, we choose the chain $A \to B \to C$ instead of $A \to B \to D$ if $B \to C$ has a longer LT or $C$ is generated later than $D$ if both LTs are equal. So the integer DU chains for Figure 2A are $1 \to 2 \to 11$, $3 \to 4 \to 10$, $6 \to 7$, $8 \to 9$, and $12 \to 13$. After drawing all chains into the schedule table, we apply Ge's adjustment methods on long DU chains. A long chain is defined as any chain whose length is greater than or equal to the II. A node may be delayed in real schedules for resource conflicts or backward edges, causing inaccuracies in the pseudo-schedule. A delay in one node of a chain will result in the delay of successor nodes. The longer the chain, the more likely its last node may be delayed. To handle long chains, we increase the iteration number of the last node of the chain by one. Our experiments show that the register-pressure prediction after this adjustment is closer to the actual register pressure. Finally, the predicted register pressure is the maximum number of DU chains passing through a cycle after adjustments.

### 4.4. The Effects of Loop Unrolling

Some scalar replacement algorithms use unrolling to eliminate register-to-register copies. The unroll factor of scalar replacement is determined by the maximum distance of a dependence edge leaving a generator in the DDG. Our experiments have shown there is only a small change in the number of floating-point registers used after unrolling. The integer register pressure is strongly correlated with the unroll factor. In our method, we use the equation below to handle the effects of unrolling:

$$I_a = I_b * \left( 1 + \frac{2}{3} * \text{unroll factor} \right)$$

where $I_a$ is the integer pressure after unrolling and $I_b$ is the integer pressure before unrolling. For floating-point register pressure prediction, we make no adjustments.

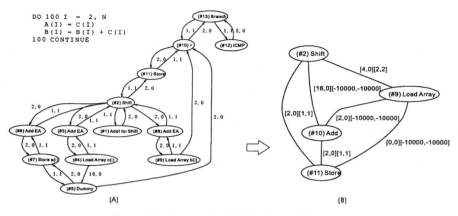

**Figure 2. Example DDG Simplification**

## 4.5. The Effects of Software Pipelining

Software pipelining aims at fully utilizing the idle functional units. It schedules using information in a DDG, including backward edges, that is ignored by our method. When the RecII is larger than the ResII, the algorithm will underestimate the register pressure. To compensate for the underestimation, we update the prediction using the following equations:

$$I_a = \lceil I_b + c \times (T - I_b) \rceil$$
$$F_a = \lceil F_b + c \times (T - F_b) \rceil$$

where

$$c = 0 \quad \text{if } \frac{RecII}{ResII} < 1.5$$
$$c = 0.3 \quad \text{if } 1.5 \leq \frac{RecII}{ResII} < 2$$
$$c = 0.6 \quad \text{if } \frac{RecII}{ResII} \geq 2$$

The values of $c$ come from observation. $F_a$ and $I_a$ are the floating-point and integer register pressure after adjustment, respectively. $F_b$ and $I_b$ are the floating-point and integer pressure before adjustment, respectively. $T$ is the total number of registers used. The larger the difference between RecII and ResII, the greater the impact on register pressure by software pipelining. The coefficient $c$ may have other values for other software pipelining algorithms.

## 5. Experiment

We have implemented PRP in Memoria, a source-to-source Fortran transformer. Memoria performs scalar replacement, unroll-and-jam and a number of other loop transformations. After scalar replacement, we use Rocket to generate the software pipeline using iterative modulo scheduling [12] and determine the register pressure of the final loop. The machine-independent optimization passes used include constant propagation, global value numbering, partial redundancy elimination, strength reduction and dead code elimination.

For our experiments, we have chosen a target architecture that has two integer functional units and two floating-point functional units. Both integer and floating-point instructions have a latency of two cycles. In this experiment, we investigate 162 loops extracted from the SPEC95 benchmark suite on which both scalar replacement and iterative modulo scheduling are applicable. Each loop is saved into an individual file. The register pressure of a loop is the sum of registers defined in a loop body and live-in registers.

We compare the performance of PRP to the method described in Ge's thesis [9]. Our implementation of Ge's method uses our DDG generation algorithm in Memoria. Ge's method has been shown to be superior to the MinAvg approach developed by Huff [10] and the MinDist technique proposed by Ding [7]. Ge reports that MinAvg and MinDist give an average register mis-prediction of 4–5 registers on an exact low-level DDG. PRP achieves much better results on an approximate DDG as reported in the next section.

### 5.1. Accuracy of Register-pressure Prediction

Table 2 reports the accuracy of our register-pressure prediction algorithm. The column "Avg Err" reports the average of the absolute value of the difference between the predicted register pressure and the actual register pressure obtained by Rocket. "Rel Err" gives the average relative error of the prediction.

PRP gives the highest prediction accuracy. This algorithm predicts the floating-point register pressure within 1.99 registers and the integer register pressure within 2.65 registers, on average. Ge's method predicts floating-point pressure within 2.53 registers and integer register pressure within 3.32 registers on average. Theoretically, Ge's method should be better than PRP, or at least equivalent to it since the DDGs are the same and Ge's method does a better job of scheduling and predicting RecII. The problem is that in Memoria we do not have enough information in the approximate DDG to compute Ge's method accurately. For example, information regarding outer-loop induction vari-

| Benchmark | #Loops | PRP | | | | Ge | | | |
|---|---|---|---|---|---|---|---|---|---|
| | | Integer | | Floating-Point | | Integer | | Floating-Point | |
| | | Avg Err | Rel Err | Avg Err | Rel Err | Avg Err | Rel Err | Avg Err | Rel Err |
| 101.tomcatv | 4 | 0.50 | 0.04 | 1.50 | 0.23 | 1.50 | 0.10 | 1.00 | 0.10 |
| 102.swim | 10 | 2.80 | 0.13 | 2.50 | 0.27 | 3.60 | 0.16 | 3.40 | 0.28 |
| 103.su2cor | 36 | 3.44 | 0.21 | 1.44 | 0.25 | 3.81 | 0.22 | 3.06 | 0.36 |
| 104.hydro2d | 55 | 1.82 | 0.16 | 1.67 | 0.38 | 2.36 | 0.19 | 1.84 | 0.37 |
| 107.mgrid | 2 | 3.00 | 0.50 | 1.00 | 0.25 | 2.00 | 0.33 | 1.00 | 0.25 |
| 110.applu | 31 | 2.52 | 0.18 | 2.35 | 0.22 | 3.90 | 0.22 | 3.16 | 0.27 |
| 125.turb3d | 16 | 3.38 | 0.18 | 3.00 | 0.32 | 5.69 | 0.26 | 2.88 | 0.33 |
| 141.apsi | 8 | 4.63 | 0.39 | 3.00 | 0.84 | 1.63 | 0.12 | 1.88 | 0.67 |
| All Loops | 162 | 2.65 | 0.19 | 1.99 | 0.20 | 3.32 | 0.33 | 2.53 | 0.35 |

**Table 2. Prediction Accuracy**

ables is not present in the approximate DDG. Ge's method relies heavily on an exact DDG and, thus, achieves accuracy less than PRP when predicting register pressure on an approximate DDG.

PRP performs better on applications such as 101.tomcatv and 104.hydro2d than on applications such as 125.turb3d and 141.apsi. The reason has to do with the complexity of the DDG. 125.turb3d and 141.apsi have a higher percentage of loops with a more complex DDG, increasing the errors in the total effect of the approximation algorithms. Benchmarks like 101.tomcatv and 104.hydro2d have less complex DDGs and experience less error.

To compare the savings in compilation time due to the approximate RecII computation (the most computationally expensive portion of prediction), we evaluate the total compilation time of PRP using the RecII approximation algorithm and the total compilation time of PRP using MinDist to compute the RecII on a 2.4GHz AMD Athlon XP. PRP with the RecII approximation algorithm requires $389ms$ of compilation time over the set of benchmark loops while PRP with MinDist requires more than four times the compilation time, $1808ms$.

PRP is approximate. Impreciseness in DDG construction, RecII computation and scheduling brings errors into the final results. Generally, the prediction is worse than average in loops with unrolling in scalar replacement and loops with their RecII much larger than their ResII because we use equations as a simple model of their effects. To make a detailed analysis on the process of error accumulation, we tested the accuracy of each step separately below.

### 5.2. Accuracy of DDG Construction

A precise DDG provides an essential foundation for good register-pressure prediction. To measure the preciseness of our approximate DDG, we recorded the absolute value of the difference between the number of integer/floating-point virtual registers predicted from that DDG and the number of integer/floating-point virtual registers used in the low-level intermediate after optimization. We predict the number of integer virtual registers within an average of 1.35 registers and within an average of 0.65 reg-

ister for floating-point virtual registers. Table 3 give the distribution of the error. The absolute error is computed by taking the absolute value of the difference between the number of virtual registers required by the approximate DDG and the number of virtual registers found in the actual intermediate code after optimization. The entries for each benchmark indicate the number of loops whose absolute error matches the column heading.

| Benchmark | Absolute Error | | | | | | |
|---|---|---|---|---|---|---|---|
| | 0 | 1 | 2 | 3 | 4 | 5 | >5 |
| #Loops(Int) | | | | | | | |
| 101.tomcatv | 4 | 0 | 0 | 0 | 0 | 0 | 0 |
| 102.swim | 4 | 1 | 3 | 0 | 1 | 0 | 1 |
| 103.su2cor | 12 | 10 | 7 | 5 | 1 | 1 | 0 |
| 104.hydro2d | 35 | 9 | 5 | 0 | 3 | 1 | 2 |
| 107.mgrid | 0 | 2 | 0 | 0 | 0 | 0 | 0 |
| 110.applu | 17 | 3 | 7 | 2 | 1 | 0 | 1 |
| 125.turb3d | 7 | 1 | 3 | 2 | 0 | 1 | 2 |
| 141.apsi | 1 | 4 | 2 | 1 | 0 | 0 | 0 |
| Total | 111 | 26 | 16 | 1 | 5 | 0 | 3 |
| #Loops(FP) | | | | | | | |
| 101.tomcatv | 4 | 0 | 0 | 0 | 0 | 0 | 1 |
| 102.swim | 8 | 1 | 1 | 0 | 0 | 0 | 0 |
| 103.su2cor | 24 | 5 | 5 | 0 | 0 | 0 | 2 |
| 104.hydro2d | 33 | 13 | 7 | 0 | 2 | 0 | 0 |
| 107.mgrid | 1 | 0 | 1 | 0 | 0 | 0 | 0 |
| 110.applu | 25 | 2 | 2 | 0 | 0 | 0 | 2 |
| 125.turb3d | 10 | 2 | 1 | 0 | 3 | 0 | 0 |
| 141.apsi | 5 | 1 | 0 | 1 | 1 | 0 | 0 |
| Total | 79 | 30 | 28 | 9 | 7 | 3 | 6 |

**Table 3. Virtual Register Errors**

PRP predicts the number of virtual registers exactly for over half of the test cases. In the rest of them, most of the errors are caused by the failure to identify reuse on scalars because our method only scans innermost loop bodies and doesn't utilize reuse from outside of loops. However, in general, our algorithm can directly and quite precisely construct an approximate DDG graph for loops before scalar replacement and global optimization.

### 5.3. Accuracy of RecII Approximation

To measure the effectiveness of our RecII approximation, we implemented the algorithm in Rocket and compared the predicted RecII to the actual RecII computed by

```
algorithm Approximation_Process( graph )
    Node n = FindNodeWithMaxDegree( graph )
    int #f = n.theNumberofForwardEdges
    int #b = n.theNumberofBackwardEdges
    Vector F = <0,0>
    Vector B = <0,0>
    if #f >= #b then
        do breadth-first search along all forward edges
            foreach node visited do
                traverse the edge E with the max Delay/Diff ratio
                    in forward vectors
            endforeach
            F = E.forwardVector
        enddo
        do breadth-first search along all forward edges
            foreach node visited do
                traverse the edge E with the min Delay/Diff ratio
                    in backward vectors
            endforeach
            B = E.forwardVector
        enddo
    else
        do breadth-first search along all backward edges
            foreach node visited do
                traverse the edge E with the max Delay/Diff ratio
                    in forward vectors
            endforeach
            F = E.forwardVector
        enddo
        do breadth-first search along all backward edges
            foreach node visited do
                traverse the edge E with the min Delay/Diff ratio
                    in backward vectors
            endforeach
            B = E.forwardVector
        enddo
    endif
    MaxRecII = ComputeRecII( F, B )
```

**Figure 3. RecII Approximation**

Rocket's software pipelining algorithm. Table 4 gives the results of this experiment. The "Abs Err" row indicates the absolute value of the difference between the predicted RecII and the actual RecII. For 113 out of 162 loops, our algorithm computed the RecII exactly, with an average error of 2.51. For loops with many DDG nodes having a degree more than three, our algorithm usually gives inaccurate results because simplification cannot reduce the complexity of the graphs significantly.

Because simplification uses an iterative algorithm, the number of passes before the algorithm halts becomes a critical factor to measure the efficiency of the entire algorithm. On average, Memoria simplifies the DDG in 2.86 iterations, while Rocket simplifies the graph in an average of 3.59 iterations. Table 5 gives the distribution of the iteration counts. Simplification halts within 5 iterations on 94% of the loops. In practice, we can consider it to be a constant without relation to the number of nodes in graphs. The conversion from a directed graph to an undirected graph only travels each node and read values once for each edge. Therefore, the

| Benchmark | Abs Err | | | | Percentage | | Avg Err |
|---|---|---|---|---|---|---|---|
| | 0 | 1 | 2 | >2 | <=2 | >2 | |
| 101.tomcatv | 1 | 0 | 2 | 1 | 75 | 25 | 3.00 |
| 102.swim | 7 | 0 | 1 | 2 | 80 | 20 | 1.60 |
| 103.su2cor | 21 | 2 | 1 | 12 | 67 | 33 | 3.36 |
| 104.hydro2d | 50 | 1 | 0 | 4 | 92 | 8 | 0.44 |
| 107.mgrid | 1 | 0 | 0 | 1 | 50 | 50 | 2.00 |
| 110.applu | 18 | 6 | 0 | 7 | 77 | 23 | 1.94 |
| 125.turb3d | 9 | 0 | 0 | 7 | 56 | 44 | 8.63 |
| 141.apsi | 6 | 0 | 0 | 2 | 75 | 25 | 4.00 |
| All Loops | 113 | 9 | 4 | 36 | 78 | 22 | 2.51 |

**Table 4. Accuracy of RecII Approximation**

| Iterations | 2 | 3 | 4 | 5 | 6 | 7 | 8 |
|---|---|---|---|---|---|---|---|
| Rocket | 0 | 87 | 55 | 6 | 3 | 6 | 0 |
| Memoria | 90 | 37 | 21 | 8 | 0 | 1 | 3 |

**Table 5. Distribution of RecII Iterations**

time complexity of simplification becomes $O(n^2)$, where $n$ is the number of nodes.

By observation, simplification effectively eliminated the nodes in the DDG and reduced DDG complexity. The result gives us a very good estimation of RecII with a significantly lower cost than computing RecII on the original DDG.

### 5.4. Accuracy of Scheduling

We tested our scheduling algorithm along with RecII approximation in Rocket. We compute an approximate schedule to predict register pressure from the exact DDG of Rocket before software pipelining. Table 6 details the performance comparison. The columns labeled "Rel Err" report the relative error of the predicted register pressure from the pseudo-schedule compared to the actual register pressure from the actual schedule.

PRP achieves a floating-point register pressure prediction within 1.42 registers and an integer register pressure prediction within 2.03 registers on average. This predictions is better than PRP achieved on the approximate DDG; however, Ge's method achieves the best performance on an exact DDG. With an exact DDG, Ge's method outperforms PRP using the precise RecII and the consideration of backward edges in scheduling. The increased accuracy is a trade-off with speed since Ge's method requires $O(n^3)$ time while PRP runs in close to $O(n^2)$ time.

### 6. Conclusion

We have presented a method, called Pseudo-schedule Register Prediction (PRP), for predicting the register pressure of loops considering both scalar replacement and software pipelining directly from source code without the need to perform intermediate code optimization or full software pipelining. By performing the prediction directly on source code, we retain high-level information needed in loop optimizations with a significantly lower cost than doing full compilation in order to compute exact register pressure.

| Benchmark | PRP | | | | Ge | | | |
|---|---|---|---|---|---|---|---|---|
| | Integer | | Floating-Point | | Integer | | Floating-Point | |
| | Avg Err | Rel Err | Avg Err | Rel Err | Avg Err | Rel Err | Avg Err | Rel Err |
| 101.tomcatv | 1.00 | 0.07 | 0.40 | 0.05 | 0.80 | 0.05 | 0.60 | 0.08 |
| 102.swim | 2.90 | 0.13 | 1.90 | 0.18 | 1.30 | 0.06 | 1.00 | 0.07 |
| 103.su2cor | 2.75 | 0.16 | 1.13 | 0.14 | 2.30 | 0.12 | 0.83 | 0.09 |
| 104.hydro2d | 0.84 | 0.07 | 1.05 | 0.17 | 0.67 | 0.05 | 0.96 | 0.14 |
| 107.mgrid | 1.67 | 0.20 | 1.00 | 0.23 | 0.67 | 0.03 | 1.67 | 0.37 |
| 110.applu | 1.64 | 0.11 | 1.50 | 0.15 | 1.56 | 0.08 | 1.25 | 0.10 |
| 125.turb3d | 3.82 | 0.18 | 2.47 | 0.14 | 2.76 | 0.09 | 2.65 | 0.11 |
| 141.apsi | 1.92 | 0.17 | 1.17 | 0.14 | 1.67 | 0.17 | 0.42 | 0.07 |
| All Loops | 2.03 | 0.15 | 1.42 | 0.12 | 1.52 | 0.08 | 1.12 | 0.11 |

**Table 6. Prediction Accuracy on Exact DDG**

PRP includes three approximation algorithms: one for constructing the data dependence graph at the intermediate language level, one for computing RecII and one for building a schedule. The time complexity is $O(n^2)$ in practice compared to the $O(n^3)$ complexity of previous approaches. In addition our experiments show this method has the best performance when predicting register pressure directly from the source code.

We are currently engaged in embedding this prediction algorithm into a standard scalar replacement algorithm and trying to build a model describing the relationship between register pressure and the final speedup scalar replacement can provide. We hope with this model and the prediction algorithm shown in this paper, we can replace only a selected subset of array references to achieve good speedup. We wish to precisely control the register pressure after transformation with our prediction method; consequently, eliminating the possibility of performance degradation caused by excessive replacement.

Only predicting for scalar replacement is not enough because unroll-and-jam is often applied before scalar replacement in order to create more opportunities for reducing the number of memory references and improving parallelism. Unroll-and-jam may increase the demand on registers and cause significant performance degradation. Therefore, we must predict register pressure for unroll-and-jam and scalar replacement accurately.

PRP, as a fast prediction algorithm, is a cornerstone of promising solutions for making the performance of scalar replacement predictable. Without performance degradation, scalar replacement will be not only an efficient optimization but also a feasible and effective one given its low cost and potential high gain.

# References

[1] V. Allan, R. Jones, and R.Lee. Software pipelining. *ACM Computing Surveys*, 7(3), 1995.

[2] R. Bodik, R. Gupta, and M. L. Soffa. Load-reuse analysis: Design and evaluation. In *Proceedings of the ACM SIG-PLAN 1990 Conference on Programming Language Design and Implementation*, pages 64–76, Atlanta, GA, 1999.

[3] D. Callahan, S. Carr, and K. Kennedy. Improving register allocation for subscripted variables. In *Proceedings of the ACM SIGPLAN 1999 Conference on Programming Language Design and Implementation*, pages 53–65, White Plains, NY, 1990.

[4] D. Callahan, J. Cocke, and K. Kennedy. Estimating interlock and improving balance for pipelined architectures. *Journal of Parallel and Distributed Computing*, 5(4):334–358, 1988.

[5] S. Carr and K. Kennedy. Scalar replacement in the presence of conditional control flow. *Software – Practice and Experience*, 24(1):51–77, 1994.

[6] S. Carr and P. Sweany. An experimental evaluation of scalar replacement on scientific benchmarks. *Software – Practice and Experience*, 33(15):1419–1445, 2003.

[7] C. Ding. Improving software pipelining with unroll-and-jam and memory-reuse analysis. Master's thesis, Michigan Technological University, 1996.

[8] E. Duesterwald, R. Gupta, and M. L. Soffa. A practical data flow framework for array reference analysis and its use in optimizations. In *Proceedings of the ACM SIGPLAN 1993 Conference on Programming Language Design and Implementation*, pages 68–77, Albuquerque, NM, 1993.

[9] R. Ge. Predicting the effects of register allocation on software pipelined loops. Master's thesis, Michigan Technological University, 2002.

[10] R. A. Huff. Lifetime-sensitive modulo scheduling. In *Proceedings of the ACM SIGPLAN 1993 Conference on Programming Language Design and Implementation*, pages 258–267, 1993.

[11] M. Lam. Software pipelining: An effective scheduling technique for VLIM machines. In *Proceedings of the ACM SIGPLAN 1988 Conference on Programming Language Designe and Implementation*, pages 318–328, Atlanta, GA, June 1988.

[12] B. R. Rau. Iterative modulo scheduling: An algorithm for software pipelining loops. In *the 27th International Symposium on Microarchitecture ( MICRO-27)*, pages 63–74, San Jose, CA, 1994.

[13] M. E. Wolf, D. E. Maydan, and D.-K. Chen. Combining loop transformations considering caches and scheduling. In *Proceedings of the 29th Annual ACM/IEEE International Symposium on Microarchitecture*, pages 274–286, Paris, France, 1996.

# Session 3A:
# Grid: High Performance

# Effects of Spatial and Temporal Heterogeneity of Channel Bandwidth on Performance of Individual Messages in Heterogeneous Communication Networks

Soo-Young Lee and Jun Huang
Department of Electrical and Computer Engineering
Auburn University
Auburn, AL 36849
sylee@eng.auburn.edu

## Abstract

*Channel bandwidth available for a message on a communication network varies with time and link. This variation (heterogeneity) can have a significant effect on performance of an individual message and also that of the network as a whole. Therefore, it is necessary to understand effects of bandwidth heterogeneity on the network performance in order to optimally utilize a heterogeneous communication network. The ability to use such a network optimally is highly desirable in many applications such as network-based data-intensive high performance computing. The main goal of this study, as the first step toward developing effective schemes to utilize heterogeneous communication networks, is to analyze effects of temporal and spatial heterogeneity on performance of individual messages in detail via an extensive simulation, in terms of throughput, end-to-end delay, etc. Also, the problems of path selection and multi-path data transfer are considered to illustrate how the analysis results may be used in the future effort of optimizing the network performance by taking channel bandwidth heterogeneity into account.*

*Key Words:* Channel bandwidth, End-to-end delay, Multi-path data transfer, Path selection, Spatial heterogeneity, Temporal heterogeneity, Throughput

## 1. Introduction

A communication network, wired or wireless is normally shared by multiple users who submit their requests at any time. Therefore, the available bandwidth (just "bandwidth" hereinafter) of a channel or link for a request (message) varies with time, i.e., a channel is *temporally heterogeneous*. Also, different channels would have different characteristics in terms of bandwidth, i.e., channels in a network are *spatially heterogeneous*. The concept of temporal and spatial heterogeneity in the bandwidth is applicable to various levels of a communication network, i.e., not only the channel level but also higher levels. For example, temporal heterogeneity may be considered for each sub-network and spatial heterogeneity among sub-networks. These two types of heterogeneity can have a significant effect on QoS of an individual request, such as delay and transfer time, and also network wide performance measures such as utilization, system throughput, queue length, etc.

Realization of an overlay network involves mapping its topology onto the base (physical) network [1][2]. This mapping requires finding a "path" in the base network for each "edge" in the overlay network. Here, a path may consist of one or more channels or links. The path is to be selected such that it satisfies requirements (bandwidth, e.g.) of the corresponding edge. Also, multiple paths may be employed for an edge when a single path cannot meet the requirements of the edge. Heterogeneity must be considered in mapping of an overlay network and scheduling of messages in the network, in order to optimize its performance.

In an effort to minimize communication overhead in high performance computing, multiple communication paths between computing nodes were employed [3]. The main issues are how to choose a path over others and how to partition a large size of data (message) among multiple paths. They considered "characteristics" of paths such as latency in path selection and aggregation. However, only spatial heterogeneity in terms of the average characteristics have been considered. That is, temporal variation of the characteristics was not taken into account.

The idea of utilizing multiple paths was also employed for video streaming in the "path diversity" framework [4]. The objectives are to minimize packet loss caused by congestion due to time-varying bandwidth and to provide sufficient bandwidth for media streaming, by using more than one path simultaneously from a source to a destination. A quantitative measure of temporal heterogeneity in the bandwidth has not been considered in their algorithms.

In order to quantify (temporal) heterogeneity of channel bandwidth, one may consider a second order measure of the bandwidth in addition to its mean. Earlier, heterogeneity in the available computing powers of computing nodes on a cluster or Grid was studied in terms of load balancing [5],[6]. It has been shown that average parallel execution time of a task can be substantially reduced by taking the standard deviation of available computing power on each node into account when partitioning the task over multiple nodes. The similar approach must be applicable to a communication network.

Most of the previous work on communication bandwidth managements utilized either the average or instant bandwidth. Nevertheless, there were some research efforts on scheduling and allocation problems under varying channel conditions [7],[8],[9]. Basically, they took heuristic approaches which compensate variation of channel conditions in order to satisfy certain QoS requirements. Another load-aware routing protocol [10] also considers only the average load at intermediate nodes without taking heterogeneity explicitly into account. More specifically, the second order moment of available channel bandwidth was not quantitatively utilized to optimize network performance.

As shown in this study, it is possible to improve network performance significantly by considering both types of heterogeneity in channel bandwidth explicitly. Such improvement is highly desirable also in high performance computing applications involving large-scale data exchange among computing nodes through a communication network, such as data-intensive Grid computing. In this paper, effects of heterogeneity on end-to-end delay and throughput (transfer time) of individual requests (messages) are analyzed in detail in order to provide a base for an effective scheme to be developed for utilizing heterogeneous communication networks. Also, the applications of path selection and multipath communication are considered to illustrate how heterogeneity can be exploited to improve QoS of individual messages.

In Section 2, a network model to be employed for analysis is described. In Section 3, performance measures used to quantify the QoS of individual messages are defined. In Section 4, effects of heterogeneity on the QoS are analyzed in detail via simulation. Two examples of applications are considered in Section 5, followed by a summary in Section 6.

## 2. Network Model

A communication network employed in this study is represented by a graph where a node may be a user, a switch, a router, etc. and an edge is a wired or wireless channel

or link. In this paper, bandwidth of a channel refers to the bandwidth that is available for or can be allocated to an individual message (request) on the channel. A *path* is a set of consecutive edges (links) from a node to another. Two types of paths are of interest, *serial* path and *parallel* path.

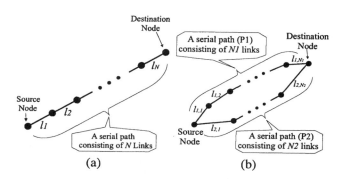

**Figure 1. Illustration of (a) a serial path and (b) a parallel path where $N_p = 2$.**

A serial path consists of $N$ serially connected links from a source node to a destination node through $N - 1$ intermediate nodes (routers) as illustrated in Figure 1-(a). The bandwidth $B_i$ of link $i$ ($l_i$ in the figure), specified in terms of packets-per-second (*pps*), is assumed to be randomly distributed between $\beta_i^{min}$ and $\beta_i^{max}$ with the mean of $b_i$ and the standard deviation of $\sigma_{B_i}$, where $1 \leq i \leq N$. $B_i$ remains constant over a period of time, referred to as an *interval*, $T_{interval}$, as illustrated in Figure 2. Also, the normalized standard deviation, $\frac{\sigma_{B_i}}{b_i}$, is denoted by $\bar{\sigma}_{B_i}$.

A parallel path is composed of $N_p$ serial paths which are independent of each other, as illustrated in Figure 1-(b). Path $j$ of a parallel path consists of $N_j$ links where $1 \leq j \leq N_p$. Link $i$ on path $j$ may be denoted by $l_{ij}$ along with the associated bandwidth parameters $B_{ij}$, $\beta_{ij}^{max}$, $\beta_{ij}^{min}$, $b_{ij}$, and $\sigma_{B_{ij}}$. For a parallel path where all links on each path are identical, $b_j$, $\sigma_{B_j}$, and $\bar{\sigma}_{B_j}$ will be used to denote the mean, standard deviation, and normalized standard deviation of bandwidth of all links on path $j$, respectively.

Transmission rate at the source node follows the bandwidth of the bottle-neck link (the link with the minimum bandwidth) of the path. Note that a higher transmission rate would lead to a higher throughput, but at the expense of a longer (queueing) delay. The source node is informed of any change in $B_i$ with a delay of $T_{feedback}$, and updates its transmission rate at the interval of $T_{update}$. Practically, the value of $T_{update}$ should not be shorter than the average one-way-trip-time from the destination node to the source node.

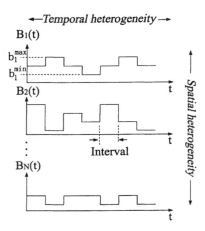

←—Temporal heterogeneity—→

**Figure 2. Temporal bandwidth heterogeneity on each channel and spatial bandwidth heterogeneity among channels.**

Temporal heterogeneity of bandwidth is defined for each channel or link $i$ and is quantified by $\bar{\sigma}_{B_i}$. That is, it indicates the temporal fluctuation of bandwidth (available for a message) about its mean. Spatial heterogeneity is defined for a group of channels or links and may be quantified by a measure of variation among the members in the set $\{\bar{\sigma}_{B_i}\}$, such as the difference between the maximum and minimum.

There are other factors in addition to channel bandwidth, which can be considered in a network model. They include routing protocol, medium access control, buffer size, bandwidth allocation strategy, source rate control, etc. However, the main focus of this paper is on analyzing effects of temporal and spatial variation in the bandwidth allocated to a message on its QoS. Therefore, those factors are not explicitly considered in the model (they will be included in the future model). Equivalently, the model takes only their combined "net" effect on the allocated bandwidth into account.

## 3. Performance Measures (QoS)

The main focus of this study is on analyzing and optimizing performance of individual messages, and the QoS considered for each message in this paper includes *end-to-end delay* and *throughput* (equivalently *transfer time*).

End-to-end delay, $T^d$, is defined to be the time it takes to transfer a packet from a source to a destination, i.e., it is a *per-packet* end-to-end delay. It is a real-time measure and, in general, consists of 4 components, i.e., $T^d = T_p^d + T_t^d + T_q^d + T_o^d$, where $T_p^d$, $T_t^d$, $T_q^d$, and $T_o^d$ represent propagation delay, transmission delay, queueing delay, and other overhead, respectively. $T_p^d$ relates to the physical

property of the network, which is determined by the speed of the electro-magnetic wave on a certain medium (copper, fiber, etc.); $T_t^d$ is inversely proportional to the channel bandwidth; $T_q^d$ is the waiting time that a packet spends in queueing into and dequeuing from the buffers of routers on the path, and reflects the mismatching of bandwidth between the incoming and outgoing links of a router; $T_o^d$ represents all other overheads including system processing time, packet assembling or dissembling time. This study mainly considers $T_t^d$ and $T_q^d$ because they contribute most of $T^d$ and, more importantly, depend on channel bandwidth and its variation. The mean, standard deviation, and normalized standard deviation of $T_d$ are denoted by $t_d$, $\sigma_{T_d}$, and $\bar{\sigma}_{T_d}$, respectively.

Transfer time, $T_{trans}$, is the time it takes to send a given size of data from a source to a destination. Throughput is defined to be the size of data ($S$) that a path is able to transfer in a unit time and is measured in terms of packet-per-second (*pps*). This measure basically reflects the effective bandwidth of a path. It is a long-term measure which is evaluated at the destination node over a relatively long period.

## 4. Effects of Heterogeneity

In this section, effects of heterogeneity on QoS of an individual message are analyzed using simulation results. The bandwidth of each channel, $B_i$, is assumed to be independently and uniformly distributed between $\beta_i^{min}$ and $\beta_i^{max}$. Other distributions such as a truncated Gaussian distribution have been considered, but lead to the qualitatively similar results. Therefore, the results for the uniform distribution only are provided in this paper.

### 4.1. Feedback Latency

In Figure 3 where the notation $T_{interval} = [X, Y]$ indicates that $T_{interval}$ is uniformly distributed between $X$ and $Y$, effects of $T_{feedback}$ on throughput and end-to-end delay are analyzed for a serial path of 4 links. It is seen that throughput is almost independent of $T_{feedback}$ while it decreases as $\bar{\sigma}_B$ increases (refer to Figures 3-(a)). This is because throughput is mainly determined by the average bandwidth of the path as will be discussed later on. However, $T_{feedback}$ has a significant effect on the end-to-end delay as can be seen in Figure 3-(b). The longer the feedback latency is, the longer the end-to-end delay results. When the feedback latency is longer, the duration of mismatch between the source rate and the bandwidth of the bottleneck link is longer leading to a longer end-to-end delay per packet due to longer queues.

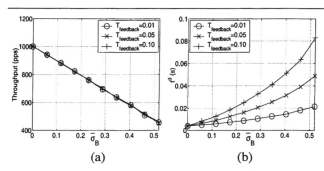

(a)                          (b)

**Figure 3. Effects of $T_{feedback}$ on (a) throughput and (b) end-to-end delay.** $T_{interval}$=[0.01,5.00] s, $T_{update}$=0.01 s, $N = 4$, $b_i$=1000 pps, and $\bar{\sigma}_{B_i} = \bar{\sigma}_B$ for all $i$.

### 4.2. Temporally Heterogeneous and Spatially Homogeneous

**4.2.1. Serial Path** For a serial path of a single link, it is not difficult to show that the average transfer time, $t_{trans}$, and the normalized standard deviation of transfer time, $\bar{\sigma}_{t_{trans}}$, can be derived as $t_{trans} = \frac{S}{b}$ and $\bar{\sigma}_{t_{trans}} = \frac{\sigma_{t_{trans}}}{t_{trans}} = \frac{\bar{\sigma}_B\sqrt{b}}{\sqrt{S}}$, respectively, where $S$ is the size of data. Now, consider a serial path of $N$ links where $b_i = b$ and $\sigma_{B_i} = \sigma_B$ for all $i$. The source transmission rate follows the bandwidth of the bottle-neck link along the path in the simulation. Therefore, *effective* bandwidth, $B_{effective}$, of the serial path can be approximated as that of the bottle-neck link. The average effective bandwidth, $b_{effective}$, which is equivalent to throughput, can be derived as follows (for the uniform distribution).

$$
\begin{aligned}
b_{effective} &= E\{B_{effective}\} = E\{min_i\{B_i\}\} \\
&= b - \frac{N-1}{N+1}\frac{\beta^{max} - \beta^{min}}{2} \\
&= b(1 - \frac{N-1}{N+1}\sqrt{3}\bar{\sigma}_B) \quad (1)
\end{aligned}
$$

From Equation 1, one can see that the average effective bandwidth decreases as $\bar{\sigma}_B$ (temporal heterogeneity) increases, and the decrease is larger (as large as $\sqrt{3}\bar{\sigma}_B$) for a longer path (a larger $N$). The more links are involved in a path, the higher the probability that $min\{B_i\}$ is smaller is. This is verified by the simulation results in Figure 4-(a) where it is also seen that the simulation results well match with the theoretical ones.

The end-to-end delay is the sum of delays on $N$ links. The delay on an individual link includes the transmission and queueing delays (refer to Section 3). The queueing delay increases as $\bar{\sigma}_B$ increases since the probability and degree of bandwidth mismatch between adjacent links increase leading to longer queues. Therefore, the end-to-end

delay increases as $\sigma_b$ and/or $N$ increase as shown in Figure 4-(b).

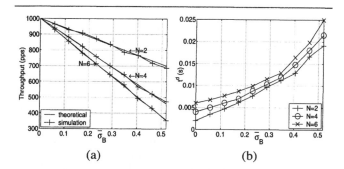

(a)                          (b)

**Figure 4. (a) Throughput and (b) end-to-end delay on a temporally heterogeneous serial path of $N$ links.** $S = 10^6$ **packets.** $b_i = 1000\ pps$ and $\bar{\sigma}_{B_i} = \bar{\sigma}_B$ for $i = 1, \cdots, N$.

**4.2.2. Parallel Path** In Figure 5, transfer time and throughput achieved on a parallel path are plotted. In this parallel path, each path is composed of a single link. $S_j = 10^5$ packets for $j = 1, \cdots, N_p$ where $S_j$ is the size of data transferred over path $j$, i.e., the total size of data is $N_p S^o$ packets transferred over $N_p$ paths. It can be seen in Figure 5-(a) that transfer time increases up to 16% as $\bar{\sigma}_B$ increases when $N_p > 1$. The increase in transfer time is larger for a larger $N_p$. In Figure 5-(b), the aggregated throughput over $N_p$ paths is plotted as a function of $N_p$. Ideally, it is to increase linearly proportional to $N_p$. However, the throughput is degraded from the ideal one as $N_p$ increases, with a larger degradation for a larger $\bar{\sigma}_B$ (up to more than 40 % when $N_p = 19$ and $\bar{\sigma}_B$=0.4).

Note that the results in Figure 5 are for the cases where each path is a single link. By referring to Figure 4, it should not be difficult to see that effects of $\bar{\sigma}_B$ and/or $N_p$ are larger on a parallel path when the number of links per path is greater than one as verified in the simulation.

### 4.3. Temporally and Spatially Heterogeneous

In addition to temporal heterogeneity on each link, different links may exhibit different characteristics, i.e., $b_i \neq b_j$ and/or $\bar{\sigma}_{B_i} \neq \bar{\sigma}_{B_j}$ for $i \neq j$. In this section, only the results for cases where $b_i = b$ for all $i$, but $\bar{\sigma}_{B_i} \neq \bar{\sigma}_{B_j}$ for $i \neq j$, are presented. However, in practice, even when $b_i \neq b_j$, it is often the case that the allocated average bandwidth is the same for all links. For instance, it would not be optimal to allocate different average bandwidths on different links along a serial path since the overall effective band-

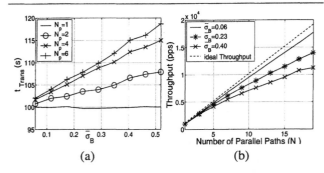

**Figure 5. (a) Transfer time and (b) throughput on a temporally heterogeneous parallel path consisting of $N_p$ paths with one link per path. $S_j=10^5$ packets and $b_j=1000$ pps for $j = 1, \cdots, N_p$.**

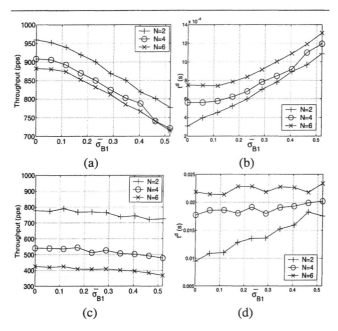

**Figure 6. Throughput and end-to-end delay on a temporally and spatially heterogeneous serial path with $b_i=1000$ pps for $i = 1, \cdots, N$: (a) & (b) $\bar\sigma_{B_i} = 0.1$ for $i = 2, \cdots, N$, and (c) & (d) $\bar\sigma_{B_i} = 0.52$ for $i = 2, \cdots, N$.**

width of the path mainly depends on the bottle-neck link, i.e., the link with the lowest (average) bandwidth. Note that a link with a large $\bar\sigma_B$ may become a bottle-neck link even though its average bandwidth is not the lowest. Nevertheless, cases where $b_i \neq b_j$ are considered for the application examples in Section 5.

**4.3.1. Serial Path** In Figure 6, $b_i = 1000$ pps for all $i$ and $\bar\sigma_{B_1}$ is varied with $\bar\sigma_{B_i}$ fixed for $i = 2, \cdots, N$. In Figures 6-(a) and (b), $\bar\sigma_{B_i}$ for $i = 2, \cdots, N$ is fixed at 0.1, and $\bar\sigma_{B_1}$ is varied from 0 to 0.52. It is clear that throughput is degraded significantly (close to 20%) due to spatial heterogeneity in $\{\bar\sigma_{B_i}\}$. The relative degradation in end-to-end delay is larger as shown in Figure 6-(b). As spatial heterogeneity among links increases, the probability and degree of bandwidth mismatch between adjacent links increase, which causes a longer end-to-end delay for each packet as discussed in Section 4.2.1. When $\bar\sigma_{B_i}$ for $i = 2, \cdots, N$ is fixed at 0.52, the change of spatial heterogeneity in $\{\bar\sigma_{B_i}\}$ is smaller as $\bar\sigma_{B_1}$ increases from 0 to 0.52. Therefore, the relative degradation in throughput and end-to-end delay is less as can be seen in Figures 6-(c) and (d).

**4.3.2. Parallel Path** In Figure 7, the average bandwidth is the same for all links, but $\bar\sigma_{B_j}$ is distributed linearly among $N_p$ paths such that its mean among the paths is unchanged. In quantifying spatial heterogeneity, $\Delta\bar\sigma_B = \bar\sigma_{B_1} - \bar\sigma_{B_{N_p}}$ is adopted. Over each of the $N_p$ paths, the same size of data ($S_j = S^o$ for all $j$) is transmitted, and transfer time is determined by the "slowest" path. Transfer time increases substantially as $\Delta\bar\sigma_B$ increases. The increase in transfer time is larger when each path becomes longer. This is because the temporal (effective) bandwidth heterogeneity of each path increases as the path length increases.

It is also seen that transfer time is longer for a larger $N_p$. As more paths are involved in a parallel path, the proba-

bility that the variation of effective bandwidth among the paths is larger increases, which makes the (average) transfer time longer. Note that transfer time of a message transmitted over multiple paths depends on the "slowest" path, i.e., the path which finishes its transfer last.

## 5. Applications

In this section, two examples where effects of heterogeneity in channel bandwidth may be taken into account in order to improve (optimize) certain performance measures (QoS) are discussed.

### 5.1. Path Selection

In Figure 8-(a), a parallel path is shown, where each path consists of 4 links. Note that the average bandwidth of links on path 3 is higher than those on paths 1 and 2, but $\bar\sigma_{B_j}$ (heterogeneity) is also larger for links on path 3 than those on paths 1 and 2. $\bar\sigma_{B_j}$ is constant for all links on path 1 while it is linearly distributed over links on path 2 (note that the mean of $\bar\sigma_{B_i}$ for all links on each path is the same for both paths 1 and 2). In Figure 9, the three paths are compared in terms of end-to-end delay and transfer time. First, it is seen that path 3 performs worst among the three in both per-

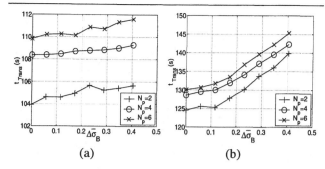

(a)     (b)

**Figure 7. Transfer time on a temporally and spatially heterogeneous parallel path: (a) each path is a single link, and (b) each path consists of 2 links where $\Delta\bar{\sigma}_B = \bar{\sigma}_{B_1} - \bar{\sigma}_{B_{N_p}}$. $b_j = 1000$ pps and $S_j = 10^5$ packets for $j = 1, \cdots, N_p$. $\bar{\sigma}_{B_j}$ is varied linearly over $N_p$ paths for $j = 1, \cdots, N_p$ such that its mean is fixed at 0.26.**

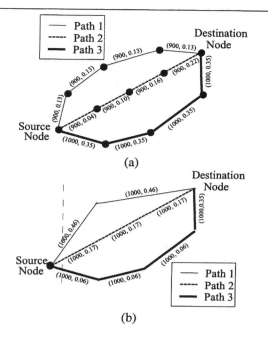

(a)

(b)

**Figure 8. (a) A parallel path where the number of links is the same for all paths, and (b) a parallel path where the number of links varies with path. The pair of numbers on each link is $(b_i, \bar{\sigma}_{B_i})$.**

formance measures though its average bandwidth is higher than that on the other paths. This is due to its high temporal heterogeneity in bandwidth. Comparing paths 1 and 2 which have the identical $b_j$, one can see that path 1 performs better than path 2 since spatial heterogeneity (among links) is higher on path 2 than on path 1. Therefore, one should consider $\{\bar{\sigma}_{B_i}\}$ in addition to $\{b_i\}$ in selecting a path, in order to optimize the performance measures.

In Figure 8-(b), another example of parallel path where the number of links varies with path, i.e., 2, 3, and 4 links on paths 1, 2, and 3, respectively, is considered. All links have the same average bandwidth, but $\bar{\sigma}_{B_j}$ is largest on path 1 and smallest on path 3. In Figure 10, the same performance measures, end-to-end delay and transfer time, are used to compare the three paths. The smallest delay and transfer time are achieved on path 3 which is the "longest" (the largest number of links) among the three paths. Path 1 performs worst due to its highest (temporal) heterogeneity though it is the "shortest." Therefore, one should not simply select the shortest path even when the average bandwidth is the same on all links.

**Implementation** Two cases may be considered: $(i)$ a source has the information on the behavior $(b_i, \bar{\sigma}_{B_i})$ of each link, and $(ii)$ a source doesn't have. In the case $(i)$, an analytic formula or look-up table which relates a given QoS to the set $\{b_i, \bar{\sigma}_{B_i}\}$ characterizing a path is to be derived. If a path is temporally heterogeneous but spatially homogeneous, an analytic formula may be obtained for certain distributions as shown in Section 4.2.1 for the QoS of throughput which is proportional to the effective bandwidth of a path. However, for a temporally and spatially heteroge-

neous path, it is much more challenging. With such an analytic formula or look-up table available, a source refers to it in order to select a path when there are more than one possible path. In the case $(ii)$, a source needs to estimate a given QoS by measuring it for each possible path before the selection process.

## 5.2. Multi-Path Data Transfer

Consider cases where multiple paths (or a parallel path) are available for transferring a large size of data. That is, data is partitioned for simultaneous transfers over multiple paths. In order to minimize the overall transfer time, one needs to determine how much data is to be transferred over each path (or equivalently transmission rate for each path), considering bandwidth heterogeneity on the multiple paths. Let's define percentage *reduction* in transfer time as $\frac{t_{trans} - t'_{trans}}{t_{trans}} \times 100$ where $t_{trans}$ is the transfer time achieved when the partitioning is done considering only the means of link bandwidths, and $t'_{trans}$ is the transfer time obtained by considering the normalized standard deviations (heterogeneity) of link bandwidths also (in addition to their means). Similarly, percentage reduction in end-to-end delay may be defined as $\frac{t^d - t'^d}{t^d} \times 100$.

131

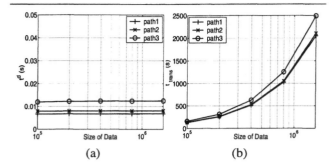

(a)                  (b)

**Figure 9. Comparison of the three paths in Figure 8-(a) in terms of (a) end-to-end delay and (b) transfer time.**

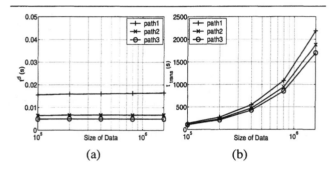

(a)                  (b)

**Figure 10. Comparison of the three paths in Figure 8-(b) in terms of (a) end-to-end delay and (b) transfer time.**

Recall that $S$ denotes the (total) size of data and $S_j$ the size of data to be transferred over path $j$, i.e., $S = \sum_j S_j$. In Figure 11, cases where 2 paths are employed for data transfer and all links have the same average bandwidth ($b = 1000$) are considered. Note that one would normally partition $S$ so that $S_1 = S_2$ since $b_1 = b_2$. However, that does not lead to the optimal performance. In Figure 11-(a), both paths have the same number of links ($N$). It can be seen that a significant reduction (up to 28%) in transfer time is achieved by assigning more data to the path with lower (temporal) heterogeneity (path 1 in this graph). Also, the reduction becomes larger when there is a larger difference (spatial heterogeneity) between $\bar{\sigma}_{B_1}$ and $\bar{\sigma}_{B_2}$ and when each path is longer (a larger $N$). In Figure 11-(b), cases where the number of links is different for a different path ($N_1 \neq N_2$) are considered. The similar observations can be made in this graph. However, reduction is larger since $N_1 \neq N_2$ leads to higher spatial heterogeneity (between the two paths).

It is also shown in Figure 11 that the simulation results well match with the theoretical ones (optimum).

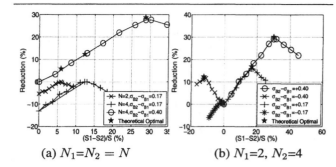

(a) $N_1 = N_2 = N$       (b) $N_1 = 2$, $N_2 = 4$

**Figure 11. Reduction in transfer time on a parallel path ($N_p = 2$). $b_j = 1000$ pps for $j = 1, 2$. $S = S_1 + S_2 = 2 \times 10^6$ packets.**

Now, consider cases where $b_1 \neq b_2$, i.e., two paths have different average link bandwidths (refer to Figure 12). $S_j$ is the size of data to be transferred over path $j$ when only $\{b_j, j = 1, 2\}$ is taken into account (i.e., $S_j$ is linearly proportional to $b_j$). Let $S'_j$ denote the size of data to be transferred over path $j$ when considering $\{\bar{\sigma}_{B_j}, j = 1, 2\}$ in addition to $\{b_j, j = 1, 2\}$. In Figures 12-(a) and (b), it can be seen that the minimum transfer time (maximum reduction) is obtained by assigning a size of data more than $S_1$ to path 1 on which temporal heterogeneity ($\bar{\sigma}_{B_1}$) is lower than on path 2. The larger the difference in temporal heterogeneity between two paths is (i.e., the larger the spatial heterogeneity is), the larger the reduction is. Also, a larger reduction is possible when the path with lower temporal heterogeneity (path 1) has a higher average bandwidth. In addition, there exists an optimal point at which the reduction is maximized, and the value of $\frac{S'_1 - S_1}{S}$ for the optimal point depends on $b_1$ and $b_2$.

In Figures 12-(c) and (d), it is seen that the reduction in end-to-end delay shows a monotonic behavior, i.e., always increasing as $\frac{S'_1 - S_1}{S}$ increases. This is the case since the per-packet delay is reduced as a larger fraction of message is transmitted over the path with lower temporal heterogeneity (path 1 in this case: note that $\bar{\sigma}_{B_1} < \bar{\sigma}_{B_2}$). Therefore, one is to select a proper value of $\frac{S'_1 - S_1}{S}$ depending on which QoS is to be optimized.

As $N_p$ increases, it is more likely that heterogeneity (variation of effective bandwidth) among paths increases. This would lead to a larger maximum reduction in transfer time by taking spatial heterogeneity into account.

**Implementation** The main issue in multi-path data transfer is how to divide a given large size of message over the multiple paths to be utilized simultaneously for the message, given the effective bandwidth and its variation ($b_j, \bar{\sigma}_{B_j}$) for each path $j$. Consider the QoS of transfer time of a message. How the message is to be divided to minimize its overall transfer time is equivalent to dividing a computational task over multiple temporally heterogeneous computers for minimizing the parallel execution time. An effective load balancing strategy has been designed and its performance has been demonstrated in one of our previous work [6]. The strategy consists of two steps where a task is partitioned proportional to the average computing power available on computing nodes in the first step and the partitioning is adjusted considering the standard deviations of the available computing powers in the second step. A similar scheme can be employed for balancing communication load over temporally heterogeneous paths.

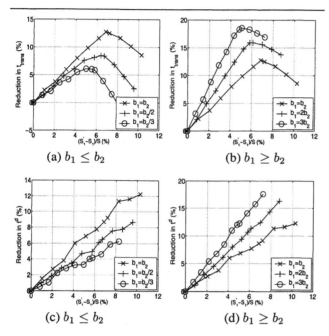

(a) $b_1 \leq b_2$    (b) $b_1 \geq b_2$

(c) $b_1 \leq b_2$    (d) $b_1 \geq b_2$

**Figure 12. Reduction in transfer time ($(a), (b)$) and end-to-end delay ($(c), (d)$) on a parallel path with $N_p = 2$. $N_j = 2$ for $j = 1, 2$. $S = S_1 + S_2 = S'_1 + S'_2 = 2 \times 10^6$ packets, $\bar{\sigma}_{B_1}$=0.06, $\bar{\sigma}_{B_2}$=0.46, and $b_1 + b_2 = 2000$ pps.**

## 6. Summary

In this study, effects of heterogeneity in communication link bandwidth on certain performance measures (QoS) of individual messages have been analyzed through an extensive simulation. The performance measures adopted in this paper are end-to-end delay and throughput (or transfer time).

It has been shown that temporal heterogeneity (temporal variation of bandwidth) on each link alone can have significant effects on the performance measures. The effects become even larger when there also exists spatial heterogene-

ity among links or paths. For the two applications, it has been demonstrated that significant improvements in end-to-end delay and transfer time are possible by considering the standard deviation of link bandwidth as well as its mean. One can achieve a larger improvement when ($i$) heterogeneity of bandwidth is higher, ($ii$) the number of links in a path is larger , or ($iii$) the number of paths involved is greater.

The analysis results obtained in this study are applicable to not only path selection and multi-path data transfer, but also other applications such as mapping an overlay network onto an existing network, finding an optimal multicast tree, data-intensive Grid computing, etc.

## References

[1] J. Touch, "Dynamic Internet Overlay Deployment and Management Using the X-Bone," *Computer Networks*, pp117-135, July 2001.

[2] D. Anderson, H. Balakrishnan, F. Kaashoek, and R. Morris, "Resilient Overlay Networks," *Proceedings of the 18th ACM Symposium on Operating Systems Principles*, October 2001.

[3] J. Kim and D. Lilja, "Multiple Path Communication," *High Peformance Cluster Computing*, vol. 1, pp364-382, Prentice Hall, 1999.

[4] T. Nguyen and A. Zakhor, "Path Diversity with Forward Error Correction System for Packet Switched Networks," in *IN-FORCOM*, San Francisco, CA, April 2003.

[5] J. Huang and S.-Y. Lee, "Effects of Spatial and Temporal Heterogeneity on Performance of a Target Task in Heterogeneous Computing Environments," *ISCA 15th International Conference on Parallel and Distributed Computing Systems*, pp301-306, September 2002.

[6] S.-Y. Lee and J. Huang, "A Theoretical Apporach to Load Balancing of a Target Task in Temporally and Spatially Heterogeneous Grid Computing Environment," *the 3rd International Workshop on Grid Computing*, pp70-81, November 2002.

[7] Matthew Andrews, Sem Borst, Francis Dominique, Predrag Jelenkovic, Krishnan Kumaran, K.G. Ramakrishnan, Phil Whiting. Dynamic bandwidth allocation algorithms for high-speed data wireless networks. Bell Labs Technical Journal, July-September, 1998.

[8] T. Nandagopal, T. Kim, X. Gao and V. Bharghavan, "Achieving MAC Layer Fairness in Wireless Packet Networks." ACM Mobicom 2000, Boston, MA, August 2000.

[9] X. Liu, E. Chong, and N. Shroff, "Transmission Scheduling for Efficient Wireless Utilization", Proceedings of the 2001 IEEE INFOCOM, Alaska, April 2001, pp. 776-785. [Infocom.pdf]

[10] S. Lee, M. Gerla, "Dynamic Load-Aware Routing in Ad Hoc Network," Proceedings of ICC 2001, Helsinki, Finland, June 2001.

[11] S. Lee, M. Gerla, "Split Multipath Routing with Maximally Disjoint Paths in Ad Hoc Networks," Proceedings of ICC 2001, Helsinki, Finland, June 2001.

# Evaluating the Scalability of Java Event-Driven Web Servers

Vicenç Beltran, David Carrera, Jordi Torres and Eduard Ayguadé
{vbeltran, dcarrera, torres, eduard}@ac.upc.es

European Center for Parallelism of Barcelona (CEPBA)
Computer Architecture Department, Technical University of Catalonia (UPC)
C/ Jordi Girona 1-3, Campus Nord UPC, Mòdul C6, E-08034
Barcelona (Spain)

## Abstract

*The two major strategies used to construct high-performance web servers are thread pools and event-driven architectures. The Java platform is commonly used in web environments but up to the moment it did not provide any standard API to implement event-driven architectures efficiently. The new 1.4 release of the J2SE introduces the NIO (New I/O) API to help in the development of event-driven I/O intensive applications. In this paper we evaluate the scalability that this API provides to the Java platform in the field of web servers, bringing together the majorly used commercial server (Apache) and one experimental server developed using the NIO API. We study the scalability of the NIO-based server as well as of its rival in a number of different scenarios, including uniprocessor, multiprocessor, bandwidth-bounded and CPU-bounded environments. The study concludes that the NIO API can be successfully used to create event-driven Java servers that can scale as well as the best of the commercial native-compiled web server, at a fraction of its complexity and using only one or two worker threads.*

## 1 Introduction

The development of Web Servers is always a challenging task because it implies the creation of high performance I/O strategies. Servers attending requests from thousands of clients simultaneously need to perform really efficiently if they want to offer a good Quality of Service. Two major strategies are commonly used to confront the service of requests in a Web Server. The first approach is based on a multithread or multiprocess strategy, assigning a different thread or process to the service of each incoming request. The second strategy, referred to as event-driven model, is based on the division of the request servicing process into a set of stages. One or more threads are in charge of each stage and make use of non-blocking I/O operations to respond simultaneously to a number of requests coming from different clients. At the moment, the multithreaded approach to the problem of attending to multiple concurrent client requests is widely used on commercial Web Servers.

The Java platform has been traditionally considered a low-performance environment to develop I/O intensive applications. Even on J2EE[10] environments, Java is only used as far as it is required by the standard and in general the entry point to a J2EE server, which is usually a Web Server, is delegated to native compiled applications. This is the case of many commercial J2EE Application Servers, such as the WebSphere Application Server[6] from IBM, which choose Apache[12] Web Server as its web entry point server. But this situation can change if the new API for efficient I/O operations included in the J2SE platform since its 1.4 release really comes to offer a high-performance I/O infrastructure. This new API, called NIO[11] (New I/O), provides the Java platform with a number of features traditionally available in most native compiled environments but still lacking in the the J2SE APIs. These features include the memory mapping of files and the availability of non-blocking I/O operations.

In this paper we evaluate the scalability of an experimental event-driven Java web server in a number of scenarios, bringing it together with the widely used Apache HTTP Server in our testing platform to compare their scalability on uniprocessor, multiprocessor, bandwidth-bounded and CPU-bounded environments. The obtained results demonstrate that the NIO API can be used to create Java web servers scaling (with the load and with the

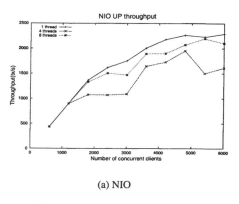

(a) NIO

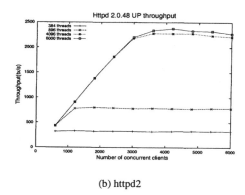

(b) httpd2

**Figure 1. Throughput comparison on a uniprocessor (UP) system**

number of available processors) as well as the best of the native-compiled commercial servers and at a fraction of their complexity and resource-consumption, independently of the execution scenario.

The use of event-driven architectures for web servers is an already explored area. Flash[9] is an asymmetric multi-process event-driven web server which exploits the creation of a set of helper processes to avoid thread-blocking in the main servicing process. Haboob[14] is also an event-driven web server, based on the concepts of staged event-driven servers introduced by SEDA[14]. JAWS[5] web server uses the Proactor[4] pattern to easily construct an event-driven concurrency mechanism. In [15], the authors propose a design framework to construct concurrent systems based on the combination of threading and event-driven mechanisms to achieve both high throughput and good parallelism. Some advanced topics about performance issues involving event-driven architectures have been studied in [7], [16] and [3]. The introduction of a non-blocking I/O API in the J2SE was preceded by the development of an extensively used API called NBIO[13] (Non-Blocking I/O), which was used to create the standard API NIO. None of the previously commented articles evaluate the causes of performance scalability, with respect to the workload intensity and the number of processors, of the event-driven architectures for Java web servers in comparison to the more commonly used multithreaded servers. This is the main contribution of this paper.

The remaining of the paper is as follows: section 2 remarks some important aspects about the operation and design of Web Servers and present some of the new features introduced in the Java platform with the Java NIO API. In section 3 we describe the execution environment used for these experiments. Next, in section 4 a performance evaluation of the studies web servers is performed for monoprocessor environments. Section

5 evaluates the nio web server and the Apache 2 web server on multiprocessors environments. Finally, section 6 give some concluding remarks derived from this work. An extended version of this paper containing more results can be found at [2].

## 2 Web Server architectures

The action of accepting new incoming requests on the server is usually performed by a thread which is always listening at a concrete port. When a new request arrives to the server, the request is read and then the server can mainly behave in two different ways depending on the underlaying I/O capabilities available on the execution environment: it can use one thread performing blocking I/O operations for each active socket or it can use one thread performing non-blocking I/O operation among all the active sockets. What really makes difference between these two possibilities is the fact that in the first case the thread which performs the blocking I/O operation is no longer available for processing new incoming requests until the service is completed, while in the second case the thread can continue attending other clients through other sockets. This difference of concept results in a completely different way of implementing servers: if the first version is chosen, a number of threads must be created in the server in order to give response to a high number of clients. If the second version is chosen, just one thread could (theoretically) attend a high number of clients simultaneously. Once a request have been read from the client socket, the web server has to provide the client with the data requested through the connection socket.

The 1.4 release of the Java 2 Standard Edition includes a new set of I/O capabilities created to improve the performance and scalability of intense I/O applications. The classic Java I/O mechanisms don't offer the

135

desired level of efficiency to run applications with high I/O requirements. Some widely existing I/O capabilities implemented on most of operating systems such as mapping files to memory, readiness selection of channels and non-blocking I/O operations, were not supported by previous versions of the J2SE and have been included in the 1.4 release. The NIO package includes a readiness selection operation on channels (SocketChannels and FileChannels). This select operation is used in the implementation of the main loop to detect which web clients have sent requests to the server or which sockets have more data available. The non-blocking features of the NIO API have been used to create a web server core, based on the event-driven strategy, which is is used in the scope of this paper to evaluate the capabilities of a server based on this technology. This experimental web server will be referred to as nio server from now.

## 3 Testing environment

To perform the experiments, a 4-way 1.4Ghz Xeon machine with 2GB of memory was used to run the servers, and two 2-way 2.4Ghz Xeon system with 2GB of memory were used to run the workload generators. All them were running Linux as the operating system with a 2.6.2 kernel. The Java Runtime Environment (JRE) 1.4.1 from IBM was the chosen J2SE environment to run the Java servers. The commercial server chosen for the comparison is Apache 2.0.48 and it configured using a multithread schema instead of a multiprocess strategy.

We used three different configurations for the network connection between the System under Test (SUT) and the workload generators. The first configuration connected the server machine to one client machine through a 100 Mbits ethernet interface. The second configuration connected each one of the two client machines to the SUT through a 100 Mbit/s ethernet interface, so we obtained an accumulated bandwidth between the server and the clients of 200 Mbit/s. Finally, the third configuration connected the SUT with a client machine through a 1 Gbit/s ethernet interface. Each connection between each client machine and the SUT used a crossed-link wire to avoid collisions.

### 3.1 Benchmark

The benchmark used to generate the workload for the experiments was Httperf[8]. This workload generator and web performance measurement tool allows the creation of a continuous flow of HTTP requests issued from one or more client machines and processed by one Web server machine: the SUT (System Under Test). The con-

figuration parameters of the benchmarking tool used for the experiments presented in this paper were set to create a realistic workload, with non-uniform reply sizes, and to sustain a continuous load on the web server. One of the parameters of the tool represents the number of emulated clients on the client machine. Each emulated client issues a number of requests, some of them pipelined, over a persistent HTTP connection.

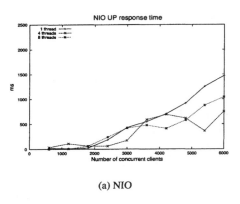

(a) NIO

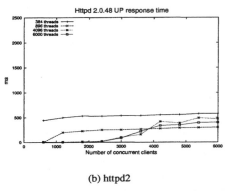

(b) httpd2

## Figure 2. Response time comparison on a uniprocessor (UP) system

The workload distribution generated by the Httperf benchmark was extracted from the Surge[1] workload generator. The distributions produced by Surge are based on the observation of some real web server logs, from where it was extracted a data distribution model of the observed workload. This fact guaranties than the used workload for the experiments follows a realistic load distribution.

## 4 Scalability on uniprocessors

The objective of this experiment was to compare the behavior of the NIO web server to the Apache 2 server. As a previous sub-objective of this task, we had to determine which configuration for each server, experimental or commercial, offered the best results so we could compare the best configuration of each server. For this experiment the SMP support for the kernel of the SUT was disabled, so the system ran as an uniprocessor environment.

## 4.1 Configuration effects

For this test, each server, the nio server and the httpd2 (Apache 2.0.48), was tested under a number of settings. From these configurations it was derived which one produced the best performance for each Web Server. The nio server was tested with 1, 4 and 8 worker threads and the httpd2 server was configured with 500, 1000, 4000 and 6000 threads. Each test was run for a time period of 5 minutes, with the Httperf benchmark configured to produce a constant workload intensity equivalent to having a range of 600 to 6000 concurrent clients, and each connected client producing an average of 6,5 requests grouped in a session. For this first experiment, the workload was entirely produced on one client machine connected to the SUT through the 1 Gbit/s link, so it was ensured that the test was not bandwidth-bounded.

The obtained throughput for each server can be seen in figure 1. The response time for the nio and httpd2 servers can be seen in figure 2.

Observing the throughput results in figure 1, httpd2 seems to scale better than nio when the load increases. Its throughput raises linearly respect to the intensity of the generated workload whereas the obtained results for the nio server indicate that on a uniprocessor system it has more problems to be adapted to the increasing workload intensity.

Concerning to the configurations of the servers, it is remarkable for the httpd2 server that the size for the thread pool offering a best result for this experiment was 4096. According to our experiments, configuring the httpd2 server with a pool size of 6000 threads offered a slight performance increase with respect to the 4096 threads configuration but reduced significantly the stability of the system, even hanging the system several times. About the nio configurations, it is specially noticeable that with only one or two worker threads (with an additional acceptor thread) it can achieve the same throughput than the httpd2 server with 4096 threads. This characteristic of the nio server is specially important on a Java server, which is commonly limited to spawn a maximum of 1000 threads for the JVM.

For the test, it was ensured that the network bandwith was not a limiting factor because the observed bandwidth usage was always under 40MB/s (results on bandwidth usage can be found in [2]), which is less than the maximum achievable bandwidth for a 1 Gbit link, which was the used connection between the SUT and the client.

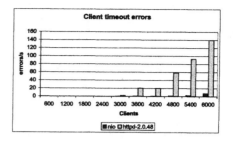

(a) Client timeout

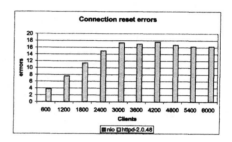

(b) Connection reset

**Figure 3. Connection errors**

The client is not the bounding factor on this test either, because as it will be seen in section 5, higher throughputs are obtained when running the same tests with the SMP support activated in the kernel. As it was expected, there is a linear relation between the achieved throughput of each server and the bandwidth required by each test.

## 4.2 Considerations about connection errors, throughput and response time

The response time observed for the httpd2 server, as it can be seen in figure 2, was surprisingly low in average in comparison with the results obtained for the nio server for all the configurations. As it seemed a suspicious result, we studied the number of connection errors detected on the benchmark client. At first glance it seemed that with the httpd2 server a higher amount of connection errors were detected on the client machine. These errors can be divided on client timeouts and connection resets.

A client timeout error happens when the socket timeout defined by the client expires. This timeout value is used when establishing a TCP connection, when sending a request, when waiting for a reply, and when receiving a reply. If during any of those activities a request fails to make forward progress within the alloted time, httperf considers the request to have died, closes the associated connection or session and increases the client-timeout error count. For our tests, the emulated clients established a 10 seconds socket timeout value.

A connection reset error takes place when a server socket timeout expires, and it is seen from the client side of the connection as an unexpected socket close. Typically, it is detected when the client attempts to send data to the server at a time the server has already closed its end of the connection.

The results for both client timeout and connection reset errors observed in the nio and httpd2 experiments can be seen in figure 3. They are expressed in number of errors per second. An interesting conclusion about connection reset errors can be extracted from figure 3(b). On it, it can be seen that while the nio server never produces connection reset errors, the amount of this kind of errors observed for the httpd2 server is not negligible and in a phase of the test even increases linearly with respect to the workload intensity. The cause for this difference is that because the multithreaded architecture of httpd2 binds one client connection to one server thread, it needs to free threads from their assigned clients to be able to process new client connections. This forces the server to automatically disconnect clients after an inactivity period. The inactivity time before closing a connection is the server socket timeout and is usually set to low values, depending on the expected workload intensity. For our experiments, we set up htppd2 with a timeout value of 15 seconds. Each client emulated by the workload generator, httperf, produced a workload based on the alternation of activity periods and think time periods. When the think time of a client exceeds the server timeout, a connection reset error takes place. As far as the nio server doesn't associate connected clients with server threads, it does not need to apply disconnection policies to its clients.

With respect to the client timeout errors, it can be observed that the number of errors of this type present in the tests for the httpd2 server is much higher than for the nio server. The explanation to this fact originates from the way clients are attended. In a multithreaded server, such as httpd2, each thread is binded to a client connection. When a request is received, the requested resource is located and a blocking I/O operation on the client socket is performed. This operation is not finished upon all the response is sent to the client. This virtually sequences the way in which responses are sent to clients and propitiates that waiting clients see their timeouts expire. On the other hand, in an event-driven server, such as nio, one or more worker threads attend a number of clients each one but never perform blocking operations on the socket sharing in a more fair way the

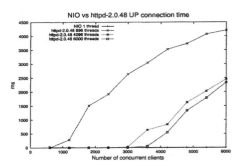

**Figure 4. Connection time for the best configuration of nio and httpd2**

network resource between clients. Individual responses are not sent as fast as with a multithreaded server (i.e. they obtain higher response times) but socket inactivities are less usual, avoiding timeouts to expire. When a socket send buffer is full, the in course operation gets blocked and the nio server starts attending another connected client which has room in its socket buffer for the data to be sent. This effect can be observed in figures 2(b) and 2(a).

Another noticeable fact is that the event-driven architecture makes possible to reach shorter waiting times for each connection to be established, as it can be seen in figure 4. This situation is explained because the multithreaded schemes use one thread for each client, and it implies that when the number of simultaneous clients exceeds the number of available threads for the server, contention to access the web server appears and provokes a fast increase of the time needed to establish connection with the server. In the scope of an event-driven server, the number of concurrent clients has nothing to do with the number of worker threads running on it and all clients can be attended without causing contention. The connection time value for the nio server on our experiments has been always below 10 ms. It is also a matter of fact that for the httpd server the point at which the connection time starts growing exponentially is not always directly related to the size of the pool of threads. When it is set up with a pool size of 896 threads, the connection time starts degrading when the workload intensity exceeds the maximum number of available concurrent connections for the server (i.e. the number of threads). On the other hand, when the overload introduced in the system caused by the costs of managing higher pool sizes (4096 or 6000 threads) causes that the connection time starts degrading before reaching the maximum number of available concurrent connections for the server. The high load provoked by the workload intensity and the overhead caused by the management of a high number of threads present in the system is what will finally limit the maximum achievable throughput for a multithreaded server.

## 4.3 Performance effects of limiting factors

With this experiment we wanted to study the two servers in different conditions: when the system was bandwidth-bounded and when it was CPU-bounded. As it was said in section 4.1, the SUT kernel was configured without SMP support. For the client machines, three configurations were used: one client with a 100Mbit/s link, two clients with a 100Mbit/s link each one and one client with a 1 Gbit/s link.

The throughput observed in this experiment for the three network configurations can be seen in figure 5, and the resulting response times are shown in figure 6. When the most limiting factor in the system is bandwidth availability (in the 100 and 200 Mbit/s configurations, as it is presented in [2]), both httpd2 and nio servers have similar behaviors. Their throughput scales linearly with the workload intensity up to the moment when the maximum available bandwidth is reached. In that point, nio advances the httpd2 server. This difference is hardly appreciable with a 100 Mbit/s bandwidth, and more obvious when it is increased to 200 Mbit/s. The reason of the better performance of the nio server with respect to the httpd2 server is that the httpd2 server is obligated to apply a socket activity timeout to its clients to sustain an acceptable quality of service, and it is translated to the ethernet level as an increase in the experienced network congestion. As it is shown in section 4.2, the number of connection reset errors is considerable for the httpd2 server and inexistent for the nio server. This additional network load for the httpd2 server is more obvious as higher is the limiting bandwidth, and loses relevance when the computing capacity of the system becomes the limiting factor for the web server. On the other hand, when the bottleneck is the computing capacity of the system, the httpd2 server scales better with the workload intensity up to the moment when the overhead of rejecting a huge number of connections per second starts degrading its performance, moment at which the nio server advances it with a higher observed throughput.

Observing the obtained response times in figure 6, it can be seen that when the limiting factor in the system is the bandwidth, the response time for both servers is very close because it is determined by the network capacity. When the bottleneck is the CPU (in the 1 Gbit/s connection), the response time observed for the servers is clearly different. The nio server response time, as ex-

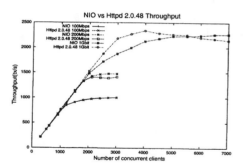

**Figure 5. Throughput scalability on a uniprocessor (UP)**

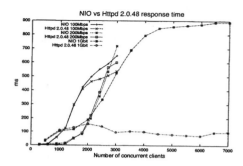

**Figure 6. Response time scalability on a uniprocessor (UP)**

plained in section 4.2, increases with the workload intensity because thanks to its event-driven architecture all connected clients are attended concurrently without allowing the client connection timeouts to expire. This forces the server to dedicate a part of the bandwidth to each client and enlarging on this way the response time for all them. The httpd2 server responds to one client at a time, seen from the network viewpoint, and it reduces the response time for successful connections (those whose timeout does not expire). As far as the httperf benchmark only takes into account successful connections, the observed average response time for the server is kept low.

## 5 Scalability on multiprocessors

Once the scalability for each web server under different workload intensities was determined with the experiments presented on section 4, it was time to explore how well each server could scale with respect to the number of available processors in the system. The procedure for the experiment was analogous to the followed one on section 4. First of all, some different configurations for each tested web server were studied on the SUT, now configured with full SMP support (4 processors available on the system). After that, the most performing-configuration observed for httpd2 web server and the most performing-configuration of the nio-server were brought together on a SMP environment with the objective of comparing their scalability properties.

## 5.1 Best-performing configurations for a SMP system

For this test, each server was tested under a number of settings to evaluate their performance trends on a multiprocessor environment. The nio server was tested with 2, 3 and 4 worker threads and the httpd2 server was configured with 2000, 4000 and 6000 threads. Each test was run for a time period of 5 minutes, with the Httperf benchmark configured to produce a constant workload intensity equivalent to having a range of connected clients from 600 to 6000, and each client producing an average of 6,5 requests grouped in a session. The workload was entirely produced on one client machine connected to the SUT through the 1 Gbit/s link. So it was ensured that the test was not bandwidth-bounded (more results on bandwidth usage can be found in [2]).

The obtained throughput for each server can be seen in figure 7. The response time for the nio and httpd2 servers can be seen in figure 8. Observing at the obtained results for the nio and httpd2 servers' throughput, it can be seen that their behavior is very similar. The httpd2 server gets higher throughputs than nio, but the difference is pretty short.

The response time observed for the nio server is worse than the results obtained for the httpd2 server, but it could be explained again by the connection errors introduced by httpd2, as it has been explained in section 4.2. The obtained values for both nio and httpd2 are shown in figure 8.

The best configuration for the nio server is that one involving two worker threads. For a uniprocessor kernel, best results were obtained with one simple worker thread, so the availability of more processors on the system favors the use of more worker threads attending clients in parallel.

## 5.2 Scaling with the number of processors

The objective of the following experiment was to explore the scalability properties of the two servers when the execution environment is moved from an uniprocessor system to a multiprocessor.

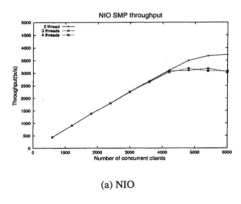

(a) NIO

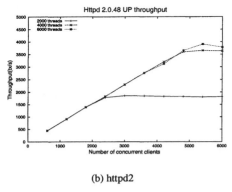

(b) httpd2

**Figure 7. Throughput comparison on a 4-way SMP system**

For the tests, we used one client machine connected to the SUT through the 1Gbit/s link. For 1-CPU configurations, a kernel without SMP support was used. For the SMP experiments, a kernel supporting the 4-way SMP system was used, so 4 processors were available in the system. The results for the uniprocessor (UP) system are obtained from the experiments presented on section 4.3. The servers' settings for the uniprocessor and multiprocessor tests were extracted from results obtained on section 4.1 and 5.1 respectively. Thus, the best settings for each environment were used, resulting in 2 worker threads for the nio server and 4096 threads for the http2 server.

The obtained results reveal that the nio server scales with the number of processors as well as the native-compiled and multithreaded httpd2 server for the response time, shown in figure 10, and for the throughput, shown in figure 9. The throughput obtained by both servers on the SMP environment doubles the value obtained on the uniprocessor when it is stabilized. The values reached by the nio and httpd2 servers are equivalents and can be considered to be in the same range of

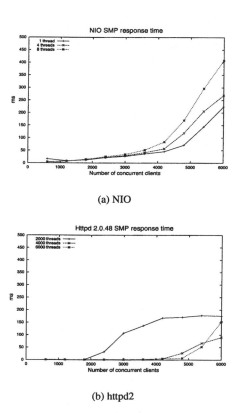

(a) NIO

(b) httpd2

**Figure 8. Response time comparison on a 4-way SMP system**

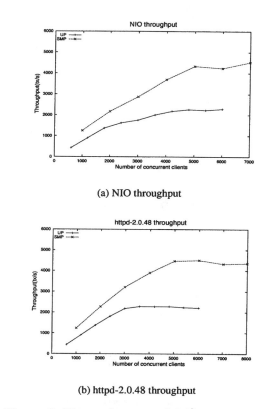

(a) NIO throughput

(b) httpd-2.0.48 throughput

**Figure 9. Throughput scalability from 1 to 4 CPUs**

results. The observed response time for the two servers on the SMP environment is significantly lower than the obtained values for the uniprocessor configuration.

## 6  Conclusions and Future Work

In this paper we have presented the potential benefits of using event-driven architectures on web servers. Concretely, we have studied how the new non-blocking I/O API (NIO) included in the J2SE platform since its 1.4 release can help in the development of high-performance event-driven Java web servers. It has been probed that our experimental NIO-based server can outperform a widely used commercial native-compiled web server but reducing the complexity of the code and the system resources required to run it.

The NIO API applied to the creation of event-driven Web Servers scales well when changing the workload intensity and when changing the number of processors and it makes it at least as well as the Apache 2 server.

Choosing a Java event-driven architecture to implement next-generations high-performance web servers

can be an option, but the really interesting conclusion of this study is that Java Application Servers can no more need to use native-compiled Web Servers as their web interfaces. Many commercial application servers choose Apache as their web interface because it is supposed to offer a better performance than Java Web Servers. But these decisions compromises the portability of the entire middleware. Choosing a Java event-driven architecture as the web interface for a Java Application Server can facilitate the integration of both elements, Web Server and Application Server, without paying the price of low performance.

A derived conclusion obtained from the results presented in this paper is that the event-driven architecture can be widely exploited on multiprocessors. Although it is an already proposed idea in the literature referring to staged servers, it has not been applied to application servers yet. Dividing the server in pipelined stages, adding one or more threads to each stage and assigning a processor affinity to each thread can convert a multiprocessor running an staged event-driven Java application server in a real high-scalable request processing pipeline.

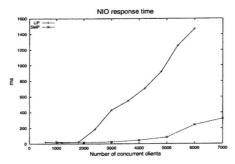

(a) NIO Response time

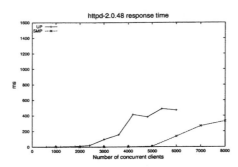

(b) httpd-2.0.48 response time

**Figure 10. Response time scalability from 1 to 4 CPUs**

## Acknowledgments

We are grateful to our colleague Josep Solé-Pareta and to his team, whose support in the configuration of the network for the testing platform has made possible this work. This work is supported by the Ministry of Science and Technology of Spain and the European Union (FEDER funds) under contract TIC2001-0995-C02-01 and by the CEPBA-IBM Research agreement.

## References

[1] P. Barford and M. Crovella. Generating representative web workloads for network and server performance evaluation. In *Measurement and Modeling of Computer Systems*, pages 151–160, 1998.

[2] V. Beltran, D. Carrera, J. Torres, and E. Ayguadé. Evaluating the new java 1.4 nio api for web servers. Technical Report UPC-DAC-2004-18 / UPC-CEPBA-2004-4, Technical University of Catalonia (UPC), 2004.

[3] S. Harizopoulos and A. Ailamaki. Affinity scheduling in staged server architectures. Technical Report CMU-CS-02-113, Carnegie Mellon University, 2002.

[4] J. Hu, I. Pyarali, and D. Schmidt. Applying the proactor pattern to high-performance web servers. In *Proceedings of the 10th International Conference on Parallel and Distributed Computing and Systems. IASTED*, October 1998.

[5] J. Hu and D. Schmidt. *Domain-Specific Application Frameworks: Frameworks Experience by Industry*. Wiley & Sons, 1999.

[6] IBM Corporation. WebSphere Application Server. http://www.ibm.com/websphere.

[7] J. R. Larus and M. Parkes. Using cohort scheduling to enhance server performance (extended abstract). In *LCTES/OM*, pages 182–187, 2001.

[8] D. Mosberger and T. Jin. httperf: A tool for measuring web server performance. In *First Workshop on Internet Server Performance*, pages 59–67. ACM, June 1998.

[9] V. S. Pai, P. Druschel, and W. Zwaenepoel. Flash: An efficient and portable Web server. In *Proceedings of the USENIX 1999 Annual Technical Conference*, 1999.

[10] Sun Microsystems, Inc. Java 2 Platform, Enterprise Edition (J2EE). http://java.sun.com/j2ee.

[11] Sun Microsystems, Inc. *New I/O APIs. 2002. http://java.sun.com/j2se/1.4.2/docs/guide/nio*.

[12] The Apache Software Foundation. *Apache HTTP Server Project. http://httpd.apache.org*.

[13] M. Welsh. *NBIO: Nonblocking I/O for Java. http://www.eecs.harvard.edu/ mdw/proj/java-nbio*.

[14] M. Welsh, D. E. Culler, and E. A. Brewer. SEDA: An architecture for well-conditioned, scalable internet services. In *Symposium on Operating Systems Principles*, pages 230–243, 2001.

[15] M. Welsh, S. Gribble, E. Brewer, and D. Culler. A design framework for highly concurrent systems. Technical Report UCB/CSD-00-1108, UC Berkeley, April 2000.

[16] N. Zeldovich, A. Yip, F. Dabek, R. Morris, D. Mazières, and F. Kaashoek. Multiprocessor support for event-driven programs. In *Proceedings of the 2003 USENIX Annual Technical Conference (USENIX '03)*, San Antonio, Texas, June 2003.

# LYE: a high-performance caching SOAP implementation

Daniel Andresen*, David Sexton, Kiran Devaram, Venkatesh Prasad Ranganath,
Department of Computing and Information Sciences
Kansas State University
{dan, dms3333, kiran, rvprasad}@cis.ksu.edu

## Abstract

*The Simple Object Access Protocol (SOAP) is a dominant enabling technology in the field of web services. Web services demand high performance, security and extensibility. SOAP, being based on Extensible Markup Language (XML), inherits not only the advantages of XML, but its relatively poor performance. This makes SOAP a poor choice for many high-performance web services. In this paper, we present a new approach to implementing the SOAP protocol using caching on the SOAP server. This approach has significant performance advantages over current approaches while maintaining complete protocol compliance. We demonstrate its practicality by implementing a demonstration system under Linux, giving speedups of over 250% in our sample applications.*

## 1. Introduction

Recently, there has been tremendous development in the area of web services in eCommerce, high-performance computing, and Computational Grid. In response to the need for a standard to support web services, SOAP became the standard binding for the emerging Web Services Description Language (WSDL) [12, 13]. SOAP is based on XML [2] and thus achieves high interoperability when it comes to exchange of information in a distributed computing environment. While carrying the advantages that accrue with XML, it has several disadvantages that restrict its usage. SOAP calls have a large overhead due to the considerable execution time required to process XML messages. In this paper, we partially mitigate a primary negative of SOAP: its speed of execution. We do this through the selective implementation of caching on the server side, feeling that a number of applications repetitively send the same information, often in a structured form. Examples might include "stock tickers," game broadcasts, or airline ticket pricing. Each of these is likely to send the same information multiple times, yet the information is also continuously changing, so a simple reverse proxy cache is inadequate.

In our previous work, we implemented caching on the client-side SOAP engine, and achieved speedups of over 800% for the client [8, 7]. In this paper, we optimize the server-side processing of a SOAP request, achieving speedups of 250% for structured datatypes and achieving at least a small optimization for all transactions. We use the Java implementation of in Tomcat 5.0.14, and choose the most normal model of SOAP that is used in distributed software, the RPC-style. This choice is common among Web developers, as it closely resembles the method-call model.

Detailed information about SOAP and how it is used in web services is presented in Section 2, as well as a discussion of other efforts in the field. In Section 3, we present our analysis on the factors and potential of caching within the SOAP architecture. We then discuss our implementation in Section 4, which is followed by the results of the experiments we conducted to compare performance of several variations of our algorithm. We will present our conclusions and future work to extend/improve these algorithms in Section 6.

## 2. Background and related work

We use HTTP as the underlying protocol for transporting SOAP XML payloads, although it is not mandatory according to the SOAP specification. Binding SOAP to HTTP provides the advantage of being able to use the formalism and decentralized flexibility of SOAP with the rich feature set of HTTP. To send a request to the server, the SOAP RPC client creates an instance of org.apache.soap.rpc.Call, a Java class that encapsulates a SOAP RPC method call. After specifying the name of the service and the method being invoked, we set the parameters, which in this case are the names of the two cities, using the setParam() method of the Call object. The actual communication with the server is done with the use of the invoke() method of the Call object to make a method call to the server. Fig. 1 shows the SOAP payload that the client generates. Being in ASCII text, this message is very large in size when compared to a similar request of a JavaRMI client. Note that the source and the destination cities are stored in the *From* and the *To* tags of the SOAP payload.

Upon examination of the profile data of this SOAP RPC client, it is found that, about 50% of the execution time is spent in XML encoding and creating a HTTP connection[7]. XML encoding involves preparation of the SOAP payload, which is basically serializing and marshalling of the payload before it is transmitted to the server.

```
POST /soap/servlet/rpcrouter HTTP/1.0
Host: hostname
Content-Type: text/xml;charset=utf-8
Content-Length:
SOAPAction: ""
Accept-Encoding: gzip

<?xml version="1.0" encoding=UTF-8?>
<SOAP-ENV:Envelope
xmlns:xsi="http://www.w3.org/2001/XMLSchema-instance"
xmlns:xsd="http://www.w3.org/2001/XMLSchema"
xmlns:SOAP-ENV="http://schemas.xmlsoap.org/soap/envelope/">
<SOAP-ENV:Body>
<ns1:getFlightInfo xmlns:ns1="urn:FlightInfoService"
SOAP-ENV:encodingStyle="http://schemas.xmlsoap.org/soap/encoding/">
<From xsi:type="xsd:string">Madison</From>
<To xsi:type="xsd:string">Las Vegas</To>
</ns1:getFlightInfo>
</SOAP-ENV:Body>
</SOAP-ENV:Envelope>
```

**Figure 1. SOAP payload generated by SOAP RPC client.**

Comparing several such requests from the client, it is found that the SOAP payloads differ only in the values of the *From* and the *To* tags (Figure 1). For each such request, the client has to prepare the SOAP payload, which takes significant amount of processing time involving XML encoding. From this observation, we figure out that, there can be a better way to handle similar multiple calls made from our clients.

There have been several studies comparing SOAP with other protocols, mainly binary protocols such as Java RMI and CORBA. All of this research has proven that SOAP, because of its reliance on XML, is inefficient compared to its peers in distributed computing. In this section we examine studies [3, 6, 4] which explain where SOAPs slowness originates and consider various attempts to optimize it.

SOAP, relying heavily on XML, requires its wire format to be in ASCII text. This is the greatest advantage of using SOAP, as the applications need not have any knowledge about each other before they communicate. However, since the wire format is ASCII text, there is a cost of conversion from binary form to ASCII form before it is transmitted. Along with the encoding costs, there are substantially higher network-transmission costs, because the ASCII encoded record is larger than the binary original [3]. Refer-

ence [3] shows that there is a dramatic difference in the amount of encoding necessary for data transmission, when XML is compared with the binary encoding style followed in CORBA.

Extreme Lab at Indiana University [4] developed an optimized version of SOAP, namely XSOAP. Its study of different stages of sending and receiving a SOAP call has resulted in building up of a new XML parser that is specialized for SOAP arrays, improving the deserialization routines. This study employs HTTP 1.1, which supports chunking and persistent connections.

Reference [11] states that XML is not sufficient to explain SOAPs poor performance. SOAP message compression was one attempt to optimize SOAP; it was later discarded because CPU time spent in compression and decompression outweighs any benefits [11]. Another attempt in [11] was to use compact XML tags to reduce the length of the XML tag names. This had negligible improvement on encoding, which suggests that the major cost of the XML encoding and decoding is in the structural complexity and syntactic elements, rather than message data [11].

In Reference [1], O. Azim and A. K. Hamid, describe client-side caching strategy for SOAP services using the Business Delegate and Cache Management design patterns. Each study addressed pinpoints an area where SOAP is slow compared to its alternatives. Some present optimized versions of SOAP using such mechanisms as making compact XML payload and binary encoding of XML. While said mechanisms achieved better efficiency, none could match Java RMIs speed and simultaneously preserve compliance to the SOAP standard.

## 3. Cost Analysis

The previous section provides numbers that indicate that marshalling incurs the highest cost while processing a SOAP message processing. In this section we shall consider various steps involved in processing a SOAP message, associate cost functions to these steps, and illustrate the impact of possible caching-based optimizations based on the changes to the cost functions. These can be broken down into the following steps.

1. Reception of the request by the router,

2. Identification of the provider and the dispatch of the call to the provider

3. Dispatch of the call to the actual service and reception of the subsequent response,

4. Marshalling of the envelope, and

5. Marshalling of the response.

Of these steps, 1 and 3 cannot be optimized, while the rest can be optimized via caching. If there are multiple requests for the same data then Step 2 can be optimized by caching the marshalled form of the response or marshalled response [1] for each distinct request. A request is *distinct* from another request if either the service differs or any of the arguments in the request differ in value. However, *staleness* of response has a major impact on the correctness of the approach and the performance of cache. Hence, in this exposition we assume that there is suitable logic to ensure staleness constraints on the cached data is honored[2]. We introduce 3 variables to capture the performance cost incurred in step 2 and beyond.

$bCacheLT$ is the time taken to lookup the marshalled data for a given response object,

$t_{dispatch}$ is the time taken to dispatch the call to the provider,

$t_{marshall}$ is the time taken to prepare the marshalled response based on the response, and

$bCacheMiss$ is the probability of cache misses.

Hence, the total cost of processing per message is given by $cost(1) = bCacheLT + (t_{dispatch} + t_{marshall}) \times bCacheMiss$ as the dispatch and marshalling cost are only incurred when there is a cache miss in step 2.

We have observed that the envelope for a service is independent of the request, hence, it is possible to cache the envelope in it's marshalled form and avoid redundant marshalling operations in step 4. This leads us to a cost function $cost4(1) = envelopeMT \times (1 - cacheEnabled)$ where $cacheEnabled$ ranges over *0* indicating caching in step 4 is disabled and *1* indicating caching in step 4 is enabled.

In step 5, we have identified 2 possible caching strategies given below.

**Marshalled response caching** If marshalled response is cached, upon receiving a response from the provider the router checks if there is a marshalled form of the given response in the cache. If so, the marshalled form is used. If not, a new marshalled response is generated from the given response and cached.

**Marshalled response template caching** For a service, the structure of the marshalled response does not change between any two similar responses[3]. Also, marshalling of response involves wrappers that wrap the serialized form of primitive data types. Hence, it is possible to create and cache a template of the marshalled response that contains the required wrappers with "holes" in

them and the serialized form of the primitive data components of response can be injected into the "holes" while instantiating the template. When compared to the previous strategy, this strategy *should* incur more cost in terms of template instantiation.

As both the above strategy involve cache lookups based on responses and as responses are in general complex data types, the cost associated with lookup is non-negligible when compared with lookup based on primitive data type. The cost is incurred by "walking/visiting" each component of the response in order to check if it exists as a key in the cache. The situation would be similar even if we were to resort to hash-based cache lookups but the cost would probably increase by a multiplicative constant when there are collisions during hashing. This cost is also incurred while marshalling a response in non-cached scenario. Hence, we capture the cost of exploring the response as $t_{explore}$ and the sum of cost of marshalling each component of a response as $t_{responseMTime}$. Let $eCacheMiss$ be the probability of cache misses in step 5 and $t_{instantiateTime}$ be the cost of instantiating a template of a marshalled response. From these, the total cost of processing per message in step 5 can be calculated as $cost5(1) = t_{explore} + t_{responseM}$ when no caching (NC) is used, $cost5(1) = t_{explore} \times (c_1 + eCacheMiss) + t_{responseM} \times eCacheMiss$ when *marshalled response caching(MRC)* is used and $c_1 \geq 1$, and $cost5(1) = t_{explore} + t_{instantiate}$ when *marshalled response template caching(MRTC)* is used.

Upon substituting *cost5* and *cost4* in *cost1* we get the following cost functions for processing $n$ messages.

$$
\begin{aligned}
cost1_{NC}(n) = & \ (bCacheLT + (t_{dispatch} + cost4(1) \\
& +t_{explore} + \underline{t_{responseMTime}}) \\
& \times bCacheMiss) \times n \\
cost1_{MRC}(n) = & \ (bCacheLT + (t_{dispatch} + cost4(1) \\
& +t_{explore} \times (c_1 + eCacheMiss) \\
& +\underline{t_{responseMTime} \times eCacheMiss}) \\
& \times bCacheMiss) \times n \\
cost1_{MRTC}(n) = & \ (bCacheLT + (t_{dispatch} + cost4(1) \\
& +t_{explore} + t_{instantiate}) \\
& \times bCacheMiss) \times n \\
& +\underline{t_{marshall}}
\end{aligned}
$$

In the above functions, the underlined factors of the equation strongly influence the overall cost. Hence, we shall compare each of these equations based on the underlined terms.

**NC vs MRC** When $eCacheMiss \ll 1$, MRC outperforms NC. This happens in cases when the request is fixed over time in terms of the values of its components. Hence, approach MRC should scale elegantly with support to enforce staleness constraints or well tuned

---

1  From here on, we will refer to the marshalled from of the response as *marshalled response*.

2  This is part of our future work.

3  Responses are similar if the termination condition of the dispatch is the same.

cache flushing logic. Either of these two features is required to control the growth rate of the cache as it is directly proportional to the number of distinct responses.

**NC vs MRTC** In this case MRTC should outperform NC with marginal memory overhead when $t_{instantiate} \ll t_{responseM}$, since the cost of instantiating a template should be relatively smaller than marshalling the entire response.

**MRC vs MRTC** In this case $eCacheMiss$ decides the validity of the pivotal relation $t_{instantiate} \ll t_{responseM} \times eCacheMiss$. Assuming $t_{instantiate}$ and $t_{responseM}$ are comparable, the relation holds in case of services in which the high rate of change of response leads to increased $eCacheMiss$ value. In such situations MRTC is bound to outperform MRC. If the rate of repetition of response is high then it leads to decreased $eCacheMiss$ value, hence, MRC is bound to outperform MRTC. However, if $t_{instantiate}$ is considerably smaller than $t_{responseM}$ then the performance of MRC may be comparable that of MRTC. Independent of the relation, MRTC has a better memory cost when compared MRC as MRTC' cache growth rate is proportional to the number of services used in a period of time while MRC' cache growth rate is proportional to the number of distinct responses in a period of time.

From the above inferences, we can conclude that caching of responses at various stages can improve the performance of a SOAP server. We can also conclude, and verify in Section 5, that *marshalled response template caching* can provide in improvements in both, time and space, when compared to *marshalled response caching*.

## 4. Implementation

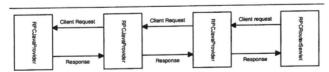

**Figure 2. Standard SOAP RPC flow of control**

Our intent was to create multiple SOAP caching implementations with minimal changes to the current SOAP architecture. We were able to use the flexibility of the current SOAP architecture with slight modifications to develop our caching strategies. As per design, the client request processing is controlled by the provider implementation. The provider can be grouped with 4 other classes that constitute

the flow of a request as it passes through the server (See Figure 2).

The first stage of execution is related to the RPCRouterServlet. This class accepts a client request message and transforms it into Java objects. The client request contains the provider name along with the service method name and parameters. The provider is then located using the information supplied by the client request.

The client request is then passed to the provider who forwards the request to the RPC router, the second stage of execution. The router is responsible for finding and executing the service requested by the client.

The third stage of execution is the service implementation. The service is a custom implementation not associated with the server. In our experiment, the available services consisted of generating and returning simple and complex data types. The value returned from the service is wrapped in an org.apache.soap.Response object and returned to the provider.

The provider is the last stage of execution. The provider controls the request processing and response generation and, therefore, a majority of the execution time required to complete process the client request is within the provider. The provider interface allowed us to use the existing org.apache.soap.provider.RPCJavaProvider as a model to develop our own providers for each of the three caching strategies. There was a need for some slight modifications and additions, but all the existing method signatures remained the same.

The RPCJavaProvider implementation itself can be broken into four different sections. These sections consist of invoking the service, building an envelope, marshalling the envelope and setting resulting xml into the current context. The profiled data from the RPCJavaProvider showed a large percentage of the time spent by the provider was in the XML encoding or marshalling process. If there was a scenario where the service was to produce the same response multiple times, this would prove costly and inefficient. The same response xml would need to be regenerated for every client request.

To avoid the regeneration of the same response xml, a cache was constructed for use with every new provider implementation. This cache implementation is based on a java.util.Hashtable. The specifics on how the cache was used and the modifications required to support the cache is stated with each provider implementation.

### 4.1. Complete Caching

The first of three caching implementations consists of complete caching of the response object. In this implementation, a unique client request is received and a response

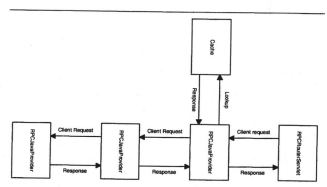

**Figure 3. Complete Caching flow of control**

generated. Once the response has been marshaled into xml form, it is cached using the client request as the key. This will ensure the response will be correct for an identical client request. This will also negate the time required to generate a response for a non unique client request.

The cache exists within the provider and is keyed by the client request encapsulated in a Call object generated from the client request. The Call object is used as the key to provide that every aspect of the client request is used to identify the correct response stored in the cache. In addition to other objects used to encapsulate the client request, have the equals and the hashkey methods overwritten from to allow the cache to function correctly. The complete caching strategy allowed the server to skip several stages, including the service execution and the response marshalling.

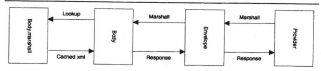

**Figure 4. Body Caching flow of control**

## 4.2. Body Caching

For the next implementation, we started to focus on the sections of the response xml message. We noticed that the body element within the response did not change for the same values returned by the service. If the Body element was cached, there would be no need to remarshaling or serialization of any repeated values returned from the service.

The body section of the xml message was cached using the response from the service as the key. The Response object returned from the RPCRouter will be used as the key. This will guarantee the cached body element is correct for the response value.

There were several object modified in this implementation. For the Hashtable to function correctly, the equals and hashkey methods were added to Response and org.apache.soap.rpc.Parameter. The Parameter object contains the return value from the service. The hashkeys returned by the Response object were the hashkeys of the return values of the service.

The objects in the envelope hierarchy also needed to be modified to contain the cache. The cache existed within the Response node, but also required a modification to the Body element.

### 4.3. Envelope and Body Caching (Template)

In the last implementation, we also realized that for every request message sent by our clients, the envelope element of the response did not change. This allowed us to keep a static copy to avoid the process of marshalling the envelope object. We continued to cache the Body element as with the Body Caching implementation described above. We are again focused on avoiding the remarshaling of any part of the response message that will not change from an identical response.

The Envelope object required the only additional modification in this implementation. The marshalling code was removed and replaced with a static envelope header definition.

## 5. Experimental results

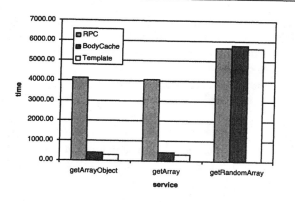

**Figure 5. Relative times to marshal array objects for an array of objects, a repeated array of integers, and an array of random integers. (Pentium 4 system, time in ticks)**

Our experimental results are positive. We were able to reduce the amount of time to generate a response in each of

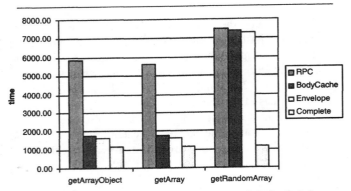

**Figure 6. Relative times to completely fetch array objects for an array of objects, a repeated array of integers, and an array of random integers. (Pentium 4 system, time in ticks)**

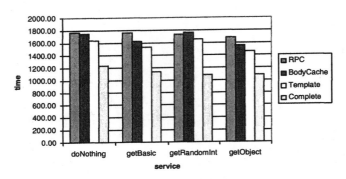

**Figure 8. Relative times to completely fetch simple and compound objects. Responses include a simple compound object, random integer, null response, and integer. (Pentium 4 system, time in ticks)**

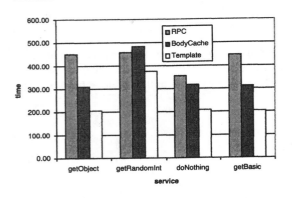

**Figure 7. Relative times to marshall simple and compound objects. Responses include a simple compound object, random integer, null response, and integer. (Pentium 4 system, time in ticks)**

the caching implementations. The different provider implementation performed as expected with the complete caching strategy providing the largest speedup followed by the envelope plus body caching and body caching only.

**Environment** For each provider test, the same client configuration was used. The only difference between each of the client requests was the provider name in the envelope payload. For each test run, the different service calls were grouped together. Each provider client was allowed to make a request for a single service. This was repeated 25 times for each service. Before starting a new service grouping, the cache was cleared for each of the caching provider implementation.

The services provided in our experiment were designed to return a variety of different values. The values returned where void, int, string, an array of ints and an array of objects (See Figures 8 and 7). The arrays returned always contained 100 elements.

Our software environment was Tomcat 5.0.14, J2SDK 1.4.2_02, and J2EE 1.3.1 running under Linux 2.4.x kernels on a 500Mhz. Pentium III, 1.8Ghz. Pentium 4, and dual Athlon MP 1800+. Each machine had sufficient RAM that paging was not an issue. All results are from the Pentium 4 system unless otherwise noted.

We used the sun.misc.Perf timer included in the j2sdk 1.4.2. This timer gave us a resolution of 1,000,000 per second. The time between sequential calls to the timer was less than 5 ticks on all machines.

**Caching strategies** The four providers used in the experiment where the RPCJavaProvider, BodyCacheProvider, TemplateCacheProvider and CompleteCacheProvider. Each of the last three providers included a Caching strategy as mentioned in Section 4. The RPCJavaProvider was provided by the original SOAP implementation. All of the caching strategies provided in this experiment provided positive results with all producing faster response times, with the exception of the random services, where in one case a small (¡2%) performance slowdown was noted.

- *CompleteCache* There was no need for work within the server for the complete caching provider implementation, with the exception of a cache lookup and retrieval. There client request message was service in an average of around 65% of the time required by the RPCProvider for basic response types and an average of around 20% for an array, for a speedup of over 500% (Table 1). This caching strategy, however, blocks com-

148

| | null | Basic | Random int | Object | Array Object | Array | Random Array |
|---|---|---|---|---|---|---|---|
| SOAP/RPC | 1767 | 1760 | 1732 | 1689 | 5860 | 5608 | 7485 |
| Body | 1750 | 1629 | 1759 | 1553 | 1783 | 1780 | 7382 |
| Template | 1633 | 1533 | 1656 | 1454 | 1637 | 1643 | 7290 |
| Complete | 1234 | 1136 | 1085 | 1082 | 1164 | 1149 | 1149 |

**Table 1. Average response time for retrieving various types of objects under different caching strategies (Pentium 4 system, time in ticks).**

munication with the service and ignores of any possible changes that might have occurred with the service response.

- *Envelope & body caching* The Envelope and Body caching strategy show the next best performance gain. In this implementation, there was no need to regenerate the Envelope and Body elements for the xml response message. However, this strategy was sensitive to the changes in any changes in a response from the service and the service was allowed to execute normally. The time required by this provider was 75 – 92% of the RPCProvider profile for basic response types and around 28% for an array. The Random services are not included in these numbers because they negate the use of a cache. They still show a small performance gain, however, because of the Envelope caching.

- *Body only* Our last implementation consisted of a Body only caching strategy. As the name suggests, the Envelope element is not cached. Our interest was the caching the serialized value returned from a service. The time required by this provider was 91 – 99% of the RPCJavaProvider profile for basic response types and around 31% for an array. The random services in this implementation produced times that were higher than expected, exceeding the time required by the RPC-JavaProvider by a small percentage. This is as expected since the only time difference between this provider implementation and the RPCJavaProvider implementation is the addition of a cache lookup and adding the body element to the cache (Figures 9 and 10).

The numbers mentioned above was the total time required to service each client request. In theory, the only values that should have changed in each implementation should have been the time required to marshal the data. If you compare the marshalling time (Figures 5, 6, 7, and 8) required by the Body only and Envelope and Body caching strategies to the RPCJavaProvider marshalling, you will see a performance gain of around 10% and 15% respectively for basic values and around 250% for arrays.

**Scalability** We can also see from Figure 11 that, as might be expected, the scalability of the server is significantly en-

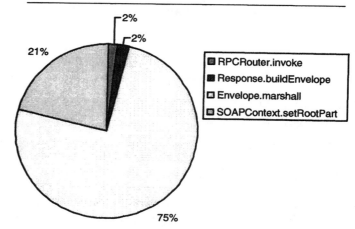

**Figure 9. Time distribution for fetching an array under SOAP RPC. (Pentium 4 system)**

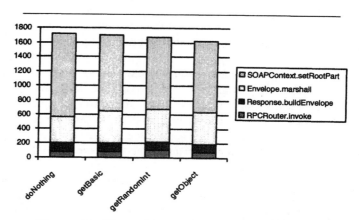

**Figure 10. Time distribution for fetching simple objects. (Pentium 4 system)**

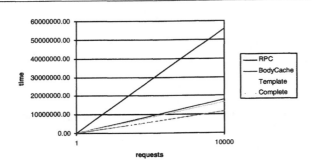

**Figure 11. Response times of various algorithms over varying loads servicing a burst of simple requests.**

hanced through lower processing loads. The overhead imposed by the cache lookup times has been measured to be practically negligable, so almost the full benefit of reduced XML data handling is available to improve overall server performance.

## 6. Future Work and Conclusion

We are currently working to enhance our system in two major areas. First, we plan to implement subelement-level caching, allowing partial caching to occur even if a subset of the subelements in a reply have been modified from a previous call. We anticipate this will give significant improvements for SOAP communication in which many elements are constant, but a few change regularly. Second, we plan to explore applying partial evaluation (aka program specialization) to produce optimized response modules for SOAP-based web services [10, 9, 5]. We are also exploring various cache management options, and the possibility of submitting our code for inclusion into the primary Apache code base.

In this paper we have presented a new approach for accelerating the performance of a vital portion of the eCommerce infrastructure through the use of directed caching of responses. Our theoretical analysis predicts, and experimental results confirm, that this approach can give substantial speedups (250%+) for many practical applications, while exacting no performance penalty for applications unsuited to the architecture beyond the memory devoted to the cache.

## Acknowledgments

This material is based in part upon work supported by the National Science Foundation under the award numbers CCR-0082667 and ACS-0092839. Any opinions, findings, and conclusions or recommendations expressed in this publication are those of the author(s) and do not necessarily reflect the views of the National Science Foundation.

## References

[1] O. Azim and A. Hamid. Cache SOAP services on the client side. *JavaWorld: IDG's magazine for the Java community*, Mar. 2002. http://www.javaworld.com/javaworld/jw-03-2002/jw-0308-soap.html.

[2] T. Bray, J. Paoli, and C. Sperberg-McQueen. Extensible Markup Language (XML) 1.0. *W3C*, Feb. 1998. http://www.w3.org/TR/1998/REC-xml-19980210.

[3] F. E. Bustamante, G. Eisenhauer, K. Schwan, and P. Widener. Efficient wire formats for high performance computing. In *Proceedings of Supercomputing 2000*, pages 64–64, 2000.

[4] K. Chiu, M. Govindaraju, and R. Bramley. Investigating the limits of SOAP performance for scientific computing. In *Proceedings of the 11th IEEE International Symposium on High Performance Distributed Computing HPDC-11 2002 (HPDC'02)*, page 246. IEEE Computer Society, 2002.

[5] J. C. Corbett, M. B. Dwyer, J. Hatcliff, S. Laubach, C. S. Păsăreanu, Robby, and H. Zheng. Bandera: extracting finite-state models from java source code. In *Proceedings of the 22nd International Conference on Software Engineering*, pages 439–448, June 2000.

[6] D. Davis and M. Parashar. Latency performance of SOAP implementations. In *Proceedings of the 2nd IEEE/ACM International Symposium on Cluster Computing and the Grid*, pages 407–412, 2002.

[7] K. Devaram and D. Andresen. SOAP optimization via client-side caching. In *Proceedings of the First International Conference on Web Services (ICWS 2003)*, pages 520–524, Las Vegas, NV, June 2003.

[8] K. Devaram and D. Andresen. SOAP optimization via parameterized client-side caching. In *Proceedings of the IASTED International Conference on Parallel and Distributed Computing and Systems (PDCS 2003)*, pages 785–790, Marina Del Rey, CA, Nov. 2003.

[9] M. B. Dwyer and J. Hatcliff. Slicing software for model construction. In *Proceedings of the 1999 ACM Workshop on Partial Evaluation and Semantic-Based Program Manipulation*, pages 105–118, Jan. 1999.

[10] J. Hatcliff and O. Danvy. A computational formalization for partial evaluation. *Mathematical Structures in Computer Science*, 7(5):507–541, 1997.

[11] C. Kohlhoff and R. Steele. Evaluating SOAP for high performance business applications: Real-time trading systems. In *Proceedings of WWW2003*, Budapest, Hungary, 2003.

[12] Simple object access protocol (soap) 1.1, Feb. 2003. http://www.w3.org/TR/SOAP/.

[13] Web Services Description Language (WSDL), 2001. http://www.w3.org/TR/wsdl.

# Session 3B:
# Performance Evaluation I

# The Impact of MPI Queue Usage on Message Latency

Keith D. Underwood        Ron Brightwell

Sandia National Laboratories*
P.O. Box 5800 MS-1110
Albuquerque, NM 87185-1110
E-mail: {kdunder,rbbrigh}@sandia.gov

## Abstract

*It is well known that traditional micro-benchmarks do not fully capture the salient architectural features that impact application performance. Even worse, micro-benchmarks that target MPI and the communications subsystem do not accurately represent the way that applications use MPI. For example, traditional MPI latency benchmarks time a ping-pong communication with one send and one receive on each of two nodes. The time to post the receive is never counted as part of the latency. This scenario is not even marginally representative of most applications. Two new micro-benchmarks are presented here that analyze network latency in a way that more realistically represents the way that MPI is typically used. These benchmarks are used to evaluate modern high-performance networks, including Quadrics, InfiniBand, and Myrinet.*

## 1 Introduction

A significant challenge in the assessment of parallel computers is the poor correlation of micro-benchmarks and the way that applications use the system. This is particularly prevalent in benchmarks that assess the performance of the network subsystem and the MPI library. A particularly egregious example of this is a standard ping-pong latency benchmark. in which one node sends a single message to another. After receiving the message, the second node sends a reply. This is repeated several times to obtain an average latency. On both nodes, the receive is posted outside of the time measurements.

Recent work[6] indicates that applications deviate from this behavior in two significant ways: they have numerous receives that are pre-posted and many unexpected messages[1]. Increasing the number of posted receives increases the amount of work that must be performed when a message is received because the list of posted receives must be searched to find a matching receive. In turn, unexpected messages increase the amount of work that must be done when a receive is posted. Standard MPI micro-benchmarks do not measure either scenario. Indeed, these micro-benchmarks do not even measure the time required to perform an MPI_Irecv or MPI_Recv as part of the latency path. This fails to represent real applications in what is measured (receives are a part of each computation/communication phase) and in how MPI queues are used.

This paper presents two new micro-benchmarks that analyze the behavior of an MPI implementation over a given network in the presence of longer posted receive queues and longer unexpected message queues. These micro-benchmarks are then used to analyze four networks: Quadrics[16], Myrinet[4], Infiniband[9], and the custom network on ASCI Red[20]. Each of these systems takes a slightly different approach to the integration of the network with the node and a slightly different approach to MPI offloading. The results show that both the weight of the protocol and the speed of the processor have significant impacts on message latency when the queues are heavily utilized. This suggests that more processing capability needs to be allocated to MPI processing — particularly for networks that offload a portion of MPI.

The remainder of this paper is organized as follows. Section 2 presents related work. Section 3 describes the benchmarks used while Section 4 covers the experimental platforms. Results are presented in Section 5 followed by conclusions in Section 6 and future work in Section 7.

---

*Sandia is a multiprogram laboratory operated by Sandia Corporation, a Lockheed Martin Company, for the United States Department of Energy's National Nuclear Security Administration under contract DE-AC04-94AL85000.

[1]Unexpected messages are MPI messages which arrive at a node before a matching receive is posted using an MPI_Recv or MPI_Irecv

## 2  Related Work

The ping-pong latency benchmark has become a standard by which all high-performance networks are evaluated. NetPIPE[19] and Netperf[1] are benchmarks that are commonly used to mesaure ping-pong latency, but it is almost as common for individuals (or network vendors) to write their own. With the advent of MPI, there has been surprisingly little published research on more realistic latency measurements. Our preliminary work in [17] presented a new latency micro-benchmark that includes the variance in transmission time, which the standard ping-pong benchmark does not reveal.

Overall, there have been some attempts at providing a more complete set of micro-benchmarks that better characterize the behavior of real applications and/or expose potential performance advantages that applications may leverage. Our work in [10] is a micro-benchmark suite that measures the potential for overlap that an MPI implementation offers. Recent work in [11] contains results that use micro-benchmarks to measure overhead, overlap potential, the impact of buffer re-use, and memory consumption. Other work has studied the impact of LogP[8] parameters on application performance[14] as well as the LogGP[2] parameters of modern networks[3]. All of these provide a more complete picture of the interaction of the application and the network. This paper differentiates itself by focusing on the impact of MPI queue usage scenarios that can occur in applications. The new benchmarks presented here illustrate how various queue usage scenarios can serve to increase the overhead (or gap, depending on where queue processing occurs) of the baseline hardware as defined by the LogP model.

## 3  Benchmarks

Studying the impacts of MPI queue length on message latency required two new benchmarks. Each is based on a standard ping-pong benchmark with some modifications. The first benchmark varies both the length of the pre-posted receive queue and the portion of that queue that is traversed. Ping-pong message latency is then measured in that context. The second benchmark varies the length of the unexpected queue and also measures the impact on message latency.

### 3.1  Pre-posted Receive Queue Impact

The benchmark designed to measure the impact of changes in the pre-posted receive queue length provides three degrees of freedom: the length of the pre-posted receive queue, the portion of the pre-posted receive queue that is traversed, and the size of the message. This enables the user to measure the impacts of both the receive queue length and the impact of actual queue traversal.

Pseudo-code describing the benchmark on each of two nodes is shown in Figure 1. Each node must first post the number of receives that are to be traversed when the actual latency measuring message arrives. These receives use tags that do not match the latency measuring message. This must occur on both nodes since the ping-pong latency will be divided by two to determine the one-way latency. Next, the receive that matches the latency message is posted, followed by the remaining queue entries that are requested (which will not be traversed when the latency message is received). Both nodes then enter a barrier operation that is designed to insure that node 1 exits first (this is not the standard MPI_Barrier) so that the barrier does not inadvertently interfere with the latency measurement. Following this, the standard ping-pong latency is measured and then the extra receives that were posted are cleared out of the queue (by sending a matching stream of messages).

Measurements for this paper use the average time from 1000 iterations of the core routine shown in Figure 1. The inner loop iterates 1000 times and sums the times from all of the iterations. The time is divided by 1000 and then divided by two to obtain a one-way latency measure.

### 3.2  Unexpected Message Queue Impact

The benchmark created to assess the impact of unexpected message queue length on message latency only allows the length of the unexpected message queue and the size of the message to be varied. It deviates from the traditional way of measuring latency in that it includes the time to post the receive for the latency measuring message as part of the latency. This better reflects the way that MPI is actually used by applications, which typically have some number of iterations and posts receives in each iteration.

Figure 2 shows pseudo-code for the benchmark that measures the impact of a long unexpected queue. The requested number of unexpected messages is first sent to each processor. The processors barrier in such a way that node 1 is guaranteed to exit first. Then, node 0 does a non-blocking send while node 1 waits on the message. The posting of the receive (and thus traversal of the unexpected queue) on node 0 is overlapped with this send. On node 1, a send is performed as soon as the receive completes. When the ping-pong latency timing is complete, the unexpected messages are cleared by posting matching receives. The inner loop is timed for 1000 iterations to obtain an average, and this value is divided by two to obtain the one-way latency.

This benchmark required a number of design decisions. First, node 1 exits the barrier first allowing some of the time traversing the unexpected queue to be hidden. This was an attempt to be as fair as possible in measuring the time. Oth-

```
prepost_traversed_receives();
post_latency_receive();
prepost_untraversed_receives();
barrier();
begin_timer();
send_message();
wait_for_response();
end_timer();
clear_receives();
                 (a)
```

```
prepost_traversed_receives();
post_latency_receive();
prepost_untraversed_receives();
barrier();
wait_for_message();
send_response();
clear_receives();
                 (b)
```

**Figure 1. Pseudo-code for pre-posted queue impact benchmark: (a) node 0, and (b) node 1**

```
send_unexpected_messages();
barrier();
begin_timer();
nonblocking_send_message();
post_latency_receive();
wait_for_response();
end_timer();
clear_unexpected_messages();
                 (a)
```

```
send_unexpected_messages();
barrier();
wait_for_message();
send_response();
clear_unexpected_messages();
                 (b)
```

**Figure 2. Pseudo-code for unexpected queue impact benchmark: (a) node 0, and (b) node 1**

erwise, the extra time for node 1 to exit the barrier would also be counted against the unexpected message behavior of the network. The second design choice made was to perform the non-blocking send on node 0 so that the post of the receive could be overlapped with it. Again, since this benchmark deviates from the standard ping-pong test by including the time to post a receive, a conservative choice was made to allow the network as much opportunity for overlap as possible.

## 4  Experimental Platforms

A number of platforms were evaluated using the newly developed micro-benchmarks. In the commodity space, Myrinet (Lanai-9), Quadrics (Elan3), and InfiniBand network hardware was evaluated. Myrinet (Lanai-X) and Quadrics (Elan4) hardware evaluations will be added as soon as hardware becomes available. To constrast the commodity networks, the custom network on ASCI Red was also evaluated. In addition to differences in hardware, differences in programming models were considered for both Quadrics and the ASCI Red network.

The Myrinet[4] Lanai9 evaluation platform contains dual processor, 2.4 GHz Pentium-4 nodes, but only one processor per node was used for testing. Each node has 2 GB of memory. The network used Lanai-9 (Myrinet 2000) adapters running GM[15]. The software used was

MPICH-GM on RedHat 7.3 with a Linux 2.4.20 kernel. InfiniBand[9] testing was done using dual processor, 3.06 GHz Pentium-4 nodes, and again, only one processor per node was used for testing. The network uses Voltaire HCAs and switches to provide 4× InfiniBand. The software stack consists of MVAPICH[12] on RedHat 9.0 with a Linux 2.4.22 kernel.

The Myrinet[4] LanaiX evaluation platform contains dual processor, 3.06 GHz Pentium-4 nodes, but only one processor per node was used for testing. Each node has 2 GB of memory. The network used Lanai-X adapters running GM[15]. The software used was MPICH-GM on SuSE Linux 9.0 with a Linux 2.4.25 kernel.

Quadrics[16] Elan3 hardware was tested on dual processor, 1 GHz Pentium-III nodes with 1 GB of memory. Elan3 network hardware was used with a RedHat 7.3 distribution and a Linux 2.4.20 kernel. Two versions of MPI software were used: the default MPICH variant from Quadrics using the TPorts API and a variant of MPICH 1.2.5 built at Sandia[5] using the Cray SHMEM API[7].

Quadrics Elan4 hardware was tested on dual processor, 2 GHz Opteron nodes with 2 GB of memory. Elan4 network hardware was used with a SuSe Linux Enterprise 8.0 distribution and a modified Linux 2.4.21 kernel. Two versions of MPI software were used: the default MPICH variant from Quadrics using the TPorts API and a variant of MPICH 1.2.5 built at Sandia[5] using the Cray SHMEM

API[7].

Compared to the commodity platforms discussed, ASCI Red[20] is a relatively unique system. It is a large-scale supercomputer comprised of more than 4500 dual-processor nodes connected by a high-performance custom network fabric. Each compute node has two 333 MHz Pentium II Xeon processors. Each compute node has a network interface, called a CNIC, that resides on the memory bus and allows for low-latency access to all of physical memory on a node. The CNIC interface connects each node to a 3-D mesh network that provides a 400 MB/s uni-directional wormhole-routed connection between the nodes. The CNIC interface is capable of sustaining the 400MB/s node-to-node transfer rate to and from main memory across the entire machine.

The software environment on ASCI Red is also significantly different from the standard commodity model. The compute nodes run Cougar, a variant of the Puma lightweight kernel that was designed and developed by Sandia and the University of New Mexico for maximizing both message passing throughput and application resource availability [18].

Cougar uses a simple network protocol built around the Portals message passing interface [18]. Portals are data structures in an application's address space that determine how the kernel should respond to message passing events. Portals allow the kernel to deliver messages directly from the network to the application's memory.

Cougar is not a traditional symmetric multi-processing operating system. Instead, it supports four different modes that allow different distributions of application processes on the processors. The following provides an overview of two of these processor modes that are relevant to this paper. More details can be found in [13].

The simplest processor usage mode is to run both the kernel and application process on the system processor. This mode (proc 0 mode) is commonly referred to as "heater mode" since the second processor is not used and only generates heat. In this mode, the kernel runs only when responding to network events or in response to a system call from the application process.

In the second mode, message co-processor mode (or proc 1 mode), the kernel runs on the system processor and the application process runs on the user processor. When the processors are configured in this mode, the kernel runs continuously waiting to process events from external devices or service system call requests from the application process. Because the time to transition from user mode to supervisor mode and back can be significant, this mode offers the advantage of reduced network latency and faster system call response time.

# 5   Results

Each benchmark was used to measure each of the systems in question. These measurements highlight differences in network hardware and system integration. They also highlight distinct differences between the relative complexities of the communication APIs that are used by the MPI implementation on the networks by measuring more than one API on a number of the platforms.

## 5.1   Pre-posted Queue Impacts

The length of the pre-posted receive queue has two distinct impacts on the latency of messages. First, a long pre-posted receive queue has implications for resource usage and resource management. Thus, even if most incoming messages match the first entry, a long posted receive queue can have a negative impact on message performance. Second, each item traversed in the pre-posted queue takes many processor cycles. This can significantly increase the time to handle an incoming message. Graphs in this section show message latency as the number of receives pre-posted is varied from 0 to 1000 and the percent of that queue traversed is varied from 0 to 100 to show both of these effects.

Figures 3(f) and 4(e) and (f) show the impact of the length of the pre-posted receive queue on InfiniBand, Myrinet Lanai9, and Myrinet LanaiX, respectively. Even with a 2.4 GHz (or greater) Pentium-4 handling the pre-posted receive queue traversal, the latency impact of a long queue is quite noticeable. Simply having a long queue has no impact on latency; however, latency can be increased by as much as 60% when a large fraction of that queue is traversed. These increases in latency manifest themselves as an increase in overhead (from the LogP model) when queue traversal is handled on the host. This indicates a need for a better data structure than a simple linear list, even when a fast processor is handling the list traversal.

Figure 3(a) and (b) compare the impact of the length of the pre-posted receive queue on Quadrics Elan3 using the TPorts and SHMEM APIs. This provides a direct comparison between APIs that offload many of the MPI semantics and APIs that do not on a single hardware platform. The impact of the pre-posted receive queue on MPI over SHMEM on Quadrics Elan3 (Figure 3(b)) is comparable to the behavior of MPI on InfiniBand and Myrinet (when adjusted for differences in host processor performance). The impact on MPI over the TPorts API, however, is much more drastic. At the baseline, increasing the length of the pre-posted receive queue to 1000 entries (even if the first entry matches the incoming message) doubles the latency of messages. Since TPorts offloads this queue onto the network interface, this is likely due to a resource management issue. As more items in that queue must be traversed to find

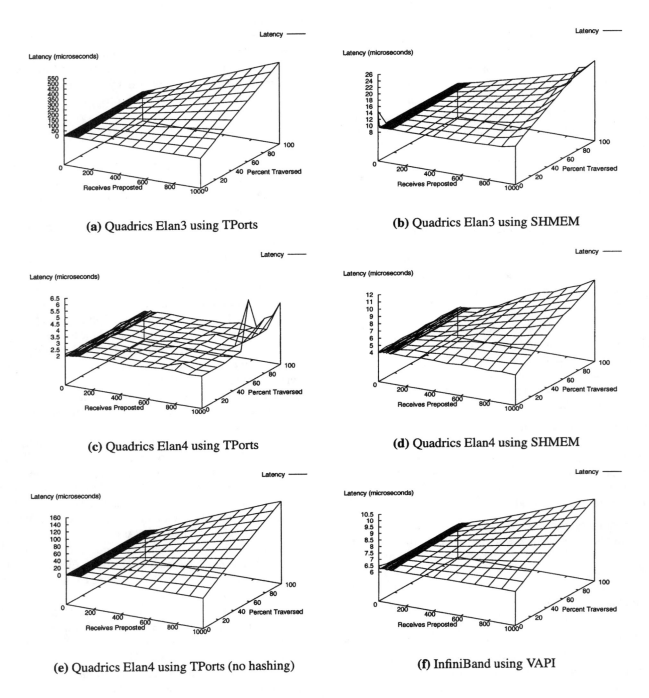

**(a)** Quadrics Elan3 using TPorts

**(b)** Quadrics Elan3 using SHMEM

**(c)** Quadrics Elan4 using TPorts

**(d)** Quadrics Elan4 using SHMEM

**(e)** Quadrics Elan4 using TPorts (no hashing)

**(f)** InfiniBand using VAPI

**Figure 3. Latency impacts as the pre-posted receive queue is varied**

a match, we see the impacts of the slow network interface processor. Each item in the queue that is traversed adds approximately 0.49 $\mu s$ to the latency of the message. These are effectively increases in the gap because the queue traversal is handled on the NIC. Results from the newest Quadrics hardware (Elan4, Figures 3(c) and (d)) show a completely different picture. The TPorts interface appears to be much faster than the SHMEM interface, even in the presence of long queues. This inconsistency was traced to an apparent addition of a hashing algorithm based on the MPI envelope information. Since different MPI tags were used to select the message, the hash algorithm effectively prevented traversing the entire queue; however, a simple change to the benchmark (wildcarding the source address, which is a relatively common application behavior) produced the graph in Figures 3(e). While the performance of the embedded microprocessor has greatly improved (dropping the penalty to approximately 0.1 $\mu s$ per queue element for small queues and 0.15 $\mu s$ per queue element for long queues), it still shows a significant performance degradation when the entire list must be traversed.

Figure 4(a) and (b) compare the Portals and SHMEM communication APIs on ASCI Red in Proc 0 mode. In Proc 0 mode, all of the communication API processing is handled on the application processor. This comparison highlights the impact of the complexity of the pre-posted receive queue list traversal on message latency when the length of that queue is varied. Portals, which has semantics that are designed to handle MPI as well as other supercomputer message traffic such as I/O, provides a rich set of queue traversal and matching semantics. These matching semantics cannot be disabled; thus, each match list item that must be traversed adds significant overhead. For SHMEM, the semantics are very simple and MPI must implement all of the queue traversal and matching semantics. This allows MPI to customize the queue traversal and matching operations to match its needs. The penalty is that features such as independent progress and matching offload are lost. The ultimate result is that Portals has significantly lower latency when a small number of queue items are traversed. When a large number of queue items are traversed, the robustness of the portals matching semantics causes it to have a higher overall latency.

Comparing Figure 4(c) and (d) to Figure 4(a) and (b) illustrates the impact of Proc 1 mode. Proc 1 mode offloads the communication API onto a second processor in an SMP configuration. Thus, all application (and MPI) processing occur on one processor in a node while all Portals or SHMEM processing occur on a second, equivalent processor in the same node. When MPI uses the SHMEM API, it sees a consistent benefit from this offloading ability. In contrast, when MPI uses the Portals API, it sees a significant benefit when a small number of elements are traversed

in the posted receive queue, but pays an extremely large penalty when a large number of posted receive queue elements are traversed. This is clearly a performance bug in the software that handles offloading for Portals; however, it points out the complexities in properly handling such offloading.

## 5.2 Unexpected Message Queue Impacts

Unexpected message queue length impacts latency in a slightly different way than the pre-posted queue length. The entire unexpected message queue must be traversed each time a receive is posted, whereas the pre-posted queue only needs to be traversed until a match is found. Another difference is that the posting of a receive can be overlapped with a send (and therefore partially hidden by the latency of the physical layer) if non-blocking operations are used for both (and the send is initiated first).

Figure 5(a) shows the increase in latency as the length of the unexpected message queue is increased for Myrinet and InfiniBand. Note that Myrinet is relatively unaffected by the length of the unexpected message queue. This is because, as with the pre-posted queue traversal, all of the "work" in MPI is performed on the host processor. For these tests, the host processor is a multi-gigahertz Intel Pentium-4. Such a processor is capable of traversing the unexpected message queue quickly; thus, virtually all of the added latency is hidden in the message transfer time. InfiniBand behaved similarly, but, unfortunately, the InfiniBand results were cut short at 100 unexpected messages due to an apparent bug in the MPI library. Although the queue traversal times are hidden from these latency tests, they are serving to increase the overhead (from the LogP model) of the communications beyond that required by the baseline hardware.

Figure 5(b) shows the increase in latency as the length of the unexpected message queue is increased for Quadrics Elan3 and the custom network on ASCI Red. For Quadrics Elan3 using MPI over the TPorts API, latency increases by approximately 0.1 $\mu s$ for each additional item in the unexpected queue (with large numbers of unexpected messages — at small numbers of unexpected messages, much of this increase is hidden by message transfer time). This is because Quadrics offloads unexpected message handling and must traverse the unexpected queue with the relatively slow embedded processor on the card each time a receive is posted. This leads to an increase in the LogP "gap" while the card is busy processing the incoming message. The curve for Quadrics using MPI over the SHMEM API shows a striking difference from the TPorts results. When unexpected queue processing occurs on the host, relatively little impact is seen on the latency — even with 1000 unexpected messages in the unexpected message queue. This is simply a matter of using a faster processor with a larger

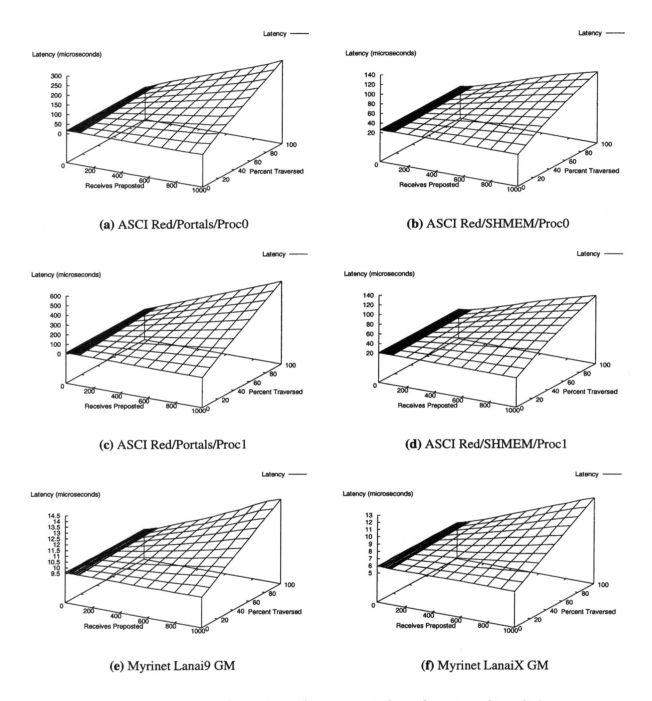

(a) ASCI Red/Portals/Proc0

(b) ASCI Red/SHMEM/Proc0

(c) ASCI Red/Portals/Proc1

(d) ASCI Red/SHMEM/Proc1

(e) Myrinet Lanai9 GM

(f) Myrinet LanaiX GM

**Figure 4. Latency impacts as the pre-posted receive queue is varied**

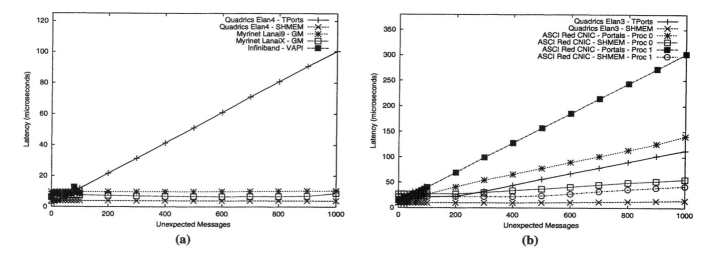

**Figure 5. Latency impacts as the unexpected queue is varied**

cache to perform the exact same list processing. This behavior changes little when moving to Quadrics Elan4 (Figure 5(a)); however, minimum latencies were used for the Quadrics Elan4 TPorts data due to unexplained variability in our current hardware platform. This is simply an issue with a new system that has not been fully brought up yet.

Results from ASCI Red, shown in Figure 5(b), explore issues of both protocol complexity and network integration. ASCI Red makes available two communication APIs — Portals, which provides a rich set of semantics including much of the queue processing needed by MPI, and the lightweight Cray SHMEM interface. Comparing Portals performance to SHMEM performance, it is clear that the rich semantics of Portals come at a cost. Although Portals performs better when there is a small number of unexpected messages, the robust matching semantics provided by Portals cause it to yield higher latency when there is a large number of unexpected messages. The second interesting feature of this graph is the comparison of Proc 0 and Proc 1 modes. When offloading the communications API to a second (equally fast) processor in an SMP node (Proc 1 mode), both Portals and SHMEM have better performance with small numbers (under 100) of unexpected messages. As the number of unexpected messages grows large, however, Portals (which offloads matching to the second processor) ramps up to significantly higher latencies than Proc 0 mode while SHMEM (which performs queue processing on the application processor) continues to see an advantage from Proc 1 mode. For Portals, there seems to be a detrimental impact from the interaction of the two processors for longer unexpected message queues. While this is clearly a performance bug in Portals offloading software, it highlights an issue that is easy to implement badly in offloading

scenarios.

## 6 Conclusions

Two new benchmarks were introduced to evaluate MPI latency in more realistic usage scenarios. These benchmarks highlight the key weakness in networks that offload protocol processing onto the network interface: the network interface processor is typically much slower than the host processor. Thus, under some usage scenarios, they have much poorer performance than competing networks that use the host processor for these tasks. Specifically, InfiniBand and Myrinet perform as much as an order of magnitude better than Quadrics when MPI queues are lengthy. Similarly, the weight of the protocol underlying MPI can significantly increase latency when longer MPI queues occur. When combined with application analysis[6] that indicates that longer queues sometimes occur, this suggests that more processing power needs to be allocated to network functions.

## 7 Future Work

This work is part of a broader overall effort to characterize applications and to develop successful benchmarking techniques. Future efforts will include further analysis of application codes to explore how MPI is used. In addition, these benchmarks will be enhanced and other benchmarks will be designed to test systems under typical usage scenarios. New benchmark development efforts will include a focus on key network features such as measuring the ability to overlap communications and computation. In addition, network bandwidth under typical loads (e.g. receiving from multiple simultaneous sources) will be tested. Finally, the benchmarking of collective operations will be investigated. Collective benchmarks are particularly unrealistic in that they measure the time to perform a large number of consecutive operations. This is yet another benchmarking scenario that never occurs in practice.

# References

[1] *Netperf.* http://www.netperf.org.

[2] A. Alexandrov, M. F. Ionescu, K. E. Schauser, and C. Sheiman. LogGP: Incorporating long messages into the LogP model. *Journal of Parallel and Distributed Computing*, 44(1):71–79, 1997.

[3] C. Bell, D. Bonachea, Y. Cote, J. Duell, P. Hargrove, P. Husbands, C. Iancu, M. Welcome, and K. Yelick. An evaluation of current high-performance networks. In *17th International Parallel and Distributed Processing Symposium (IPDPS'03)*, Apr. 2003.

[4] N. J. Boden, D. Cohen, R. E. F. A. E. Kulawik, C. L. Seitz, J. N. Seizovic, and W.-K. Su. Myrinet: A gigabit-per-second local area network. *IEEE Micro*, 15(1):29–36, Feb. 1995.

[5] R. Brightwell. A new MPI implementation for Cray SHMEM. Technical report, Sandia National Laboratories. Work in progress.

[6] R. Brightwell and K. D. Underwood. An analysis of NIC resource usage for offloading MPI. In *Proceedings of the 2002 Workshop on Communication Architecture for Clusters*, Santa Fe, NM, April 2004.

[7] Cray Research, Inc. *SHMEM Technical Note for C, SG-2516 2.3*, October 1994.

[8] D. E. Culler, R. M. Karp, D. A. Patterson, A. Sahay, K. E. Schauser, E. Santos, R. Subramonian, and T. von Eicken. Logp: Towards a realistic model of parallel computation. In *Proceedings 4th ACM SIGPLAN Symposium on Principles and Practice of Parallel Programming*, pages 1–12, 1993.

[9] Infiniband Trade Association. *http://www.infinibandta.org*, 1999.

[10] W. Lawry, C. Wilson, A. B. Maccabe, and R. Brightwell. COMB: A portable benchmark suite for assessing MPI overlap. In *IEEE International Conference on Cluster Computing*, September 2002. Poster paper.

[11] J. Liu, B. Chandrasekaran, J. Wu, W. Jiang, S. Kini, W. Yu, D. Buntinas, P. Wyckoff, and D. K. Panda. Performance comparison of MPI implementations over Infini-Band, Myrinet and Quadrics. In *The International Conference for High Performance Computing and Communications (SC2003)*, November 2003.

[12] J. Liu, J. Wu, S. P. Kini, P. Wyckoff, and D. K. Panda. High performance RDMA-based MPI implementation over Infini-Band. In *Proceedings of the 2003 International Conference on Supercomputing (ICS-03)*, pages 295–304, New York, June 23–26 2003. ACM Press.

[13] A. B. Maccabe, R. Riesen, and D. W. van Dresser. Dynamic processor modes in Puma. *Bulletin of the Technical Committee on Operating Systems and Application Environments (TCOS)*, 8(2):4–12, 1996.

[14] R. P. Martin, A. M. Vahdat, D. E. Culler, and T. E. Anderson. Effects of communication latency, overhead, and bandwidth in a cluster architecture. In *Proceedings of the 24th Annual International Symposium on Computer Architecture*, June 1997.

[15] Myricom, Inc. The GM Message Passing System. Technical report, Myricom, Inc., 1997.

[16] F. Petrini, W. chun Feng, A. Hoisie, S. Coll, and E. Frachtenberg. The Quadrics network: High-performance clustering technology. *IEEE Micro*, 22(1):46–57, January/February 2002.

[17] R. Riesen, R. Brightwell, and A. B. Maccabe. Measuring MPI latency variance. In J. Dongarra, D. Laforenza, and S. Orlando, editors, *Recent Advances in Parallel Virtual Machine and Message Passing Interface: 10th European PVM/MPI Users' Group Meeting, Venice, Italy, September/October 2003 Proceedings*, volume 2840 of *Lecture Notes in Computer Science*, pages 112–116. Springer-Verlag, 2003.

[18] L. Shuler, C. Jong, R. Riesen, D. van Dresser, A. B. Maccabe, L. A. Fisk, and T. M. Stallcup. The Puma operating system for massively parallel computers. In *Proceeding of the 1995 Intel Supercomputer User's Group Conference*. Intel Supercomputer User's Group, 1995.

[19] Q. Snell, A. Mikler, and J. Gustafson. NetPIPE: A Network Protocol Independent Performance Evaluator . In *Proceedings of the IASTED International Conference on Intelligent Information Management and Systems*, June 1996.

[20] S. R. W. Timothy G. Mattson, David Scott. A TeraFLOPS Supercomputer in 1996: The ASCI TFLOP System. In *Proceedings of the 1996 International Parallel Processing Symposium*, 1996.

# A Case Study in Exploiting Temporal Uncertainty in Parallel Simulations

Margaret L. Loper and Richard M. Fujimoto
*College of Computing, Georgia Institute of Technology*
*Atlanta, GA 30332-0832*
*<margaret, fujimoto>@cc.gatech.edu*

## Abstract

*Approximate Time (AT) has been proposed as a means for expressing temporal uncertainty in distributed simulation applications in order to enhance parallel performance. This is accomplished by specifying time intervals rather than precise values to indicate when an event might occur. This paper describes a case study in applying AT to a queueing simulation application in order to assess the performance and accuracy that can be obtained using this technique. Up to an order of magnitude speedup was obtained, with error in throughput statistics less than 3%, although somewhat larger error was reported in delay statistics.*

## 1. Introduction

A consistent notion of time is an important quality in parallel and distributed simulations. Simply put, time is a set of "instants" with a temporal precedence order. In simulation time, the "instants" are traditionally precise values that represent time in the physical system and the temporal precedence order is a total order on the set of values. The total ordering of time values in simulations is known as time stamp order.

A new type of simulation time has been proposed [1] [2] in which the simulation's knowledge about the values that represent time is uncertain. This new approach is called Approximate Time and it uses intervals rather than precise time values to represent time. Temporal uncertainty is ubiquitous in simulation modeling, stemming from the fact that virtually any simulation is only an approximation of the real world. Thus, there is no a priori reason to believe there is only one correct ordering of events that is acceptable during the execution of the simulation model.

Previous AT research has defined the mechanism for time stamping events, maintaining the simulation's notion of time with intervals, and ordering events according to intervals. This paper addresses how temporal uncertainty affects the accuracy of the simulation. The size of the time interval defines the uncertainty that can be tolerated for the event, the larger the time interval the less certain the occurrence of the event. For a specific event this may have little affect on the simulation. However, over the course of a simulation's execution, the uncertainty could cause events to happen in different orders as compared to the precise execution. While this may be a valid outcome for some simulations, for others it could invalidate the results of the execution.

This paper begins by providing an overview of Approximate Time, giving a brief description of approximate clocks and approximate time event ordering. Next, related temporal uncertainty work is described. The relationship of accuracy and uncertainty is then discussed and illustrated using a queuing simulation. The last section of the paper presents experimental data, which shows how uncertainty affects the performance and accuracy of a simulation.

## 2. Approximate Time

Approximate Time is based on temporal uncertainty and uses time intervals rather than precise time values to represent time. An interval is a closed bounded set of "real" numbers [3] [ET, LT] = {t: ET ≤ t ≤ LT}, where ET denotes the earliest time (or E-time) in the interval and LT the latest time (or L-time). This section defines Approximate Clocks, the mechanism for time stamping events and maintaining the simulation's notion of approximate time and Approximate Time Causal (ATC) order, the temporal precedence order used in approximate time. The synchronization algorithm required to ensure the interval values that represent time are causally and totally ordered will not be presented. The details of this algorithm can be found in [1] and [2].

### 2.1. Approximate Clocks

The definition of approximate clocks has three parts: how the simulation manages its local clock and updates the clock based on its view of global time, how the simulation

161

assigns time stamps to events based on its notion of simulation time, and how events are processed by the simulation.

The local simulation clock of each logical process (LP) is defined as an interval $[C_E, C_L]$, indicating the LP's current time is greater than or equal to $C_E$, but no larger than $C_L$. Before executing an event, each LP computes the time to which it would like to advance. This local clock interval is submitted to the synchronization algorithm. The synchronization algorithm returns a global clock interval that is used as the LPs current simulation time.

If an LP's current simulation time is $[C_E, C_L]$ and that LP schedules a new event X, then $ET(X) \geq C_E$. (however if the lookahead of an LP is L, then $ET(X) \geq C_E. + L$). If X and Y are events generated by a single LP, and X causally precedes Y, then it must be the case that $ET(X) \leq ET(Y)$. An LP can process an event if the event's time stamp intersects the clock interval [CE, CL]. Each LP processes the set of current events in E-time order. For any two events X and Y residing within a single LP, if $ET(X) < ET(Y)$ then X must be processed before Y. If $ET(X) = ET(Y)$, and there is no other ordering information known by the LP (e.g., FIFO or sequence numbers), then X and Y may be processed in any order.

## 2.2. Approximate Time Event Ordering

Approximate time causal (ATC) order assumes each event is assigned a time interval to indicate when the event *could* occur and defines a partial ordering among events [4]. Time intervals are assigned to the event by the simulation model, typically based on uncertainty regarding when the event occurs. If the time intervals of two events do not overlap, then the event with the earlier time interval must be processed before the one with the later time interval (e.g., events X and Z in Figure 1).

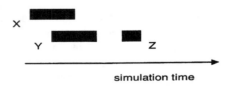

**Figure 1 Time intervals for events X, Y, and Z. X and Y are concurrent events (X ‖ Y) while X precedes Z (X~>Z) in ATC-order.**

If the two events have overlapping intervals and there is a causal relationship between these events, as defined by Lamport's happens before relationship [5], the two events must also be processed in causal order [6]. For example, in

Figure 2 the "fire" event happens before the "target hit," so the fire event must be processed by the observer before the target hit event. Two events with overlapping time intervals but no causal relationship between them may be processed in any order, e.g., events X and Y in Figure 1.

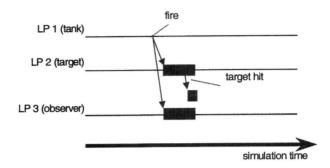

**Figure 2 Example of approximate time causal order of events.**

## 3. Related Work

Temporal uncertainty is inherent in simulation modeling, and exploiting this uncertainty may provide an approach for increasing concurrency. The literature indicates that several mechanisms have been used to represent temporal uncertainty. In fuzzy logic, the first notion of fuzzy time was suggested by [10] who proposed representing the lack of knowledge about events with fuzzy sets of time intervals. This idea was later modeled by [11], who created a temporal logic to deal with the uncertainty of when an event occurred in a given interval of time. In [12], an approach based on Zadeh's possibility theory [13] was proposed for the representation and management of imprecision and uncertainty in temporal knowledge. For the most part, this work is concerned with creating a temporal logic for designing fuzzy systems and natural language understanding of time. This work does not consider requirements of simulation or distributed applications.

Time intervals have also been recognized as a means for representing temporal uncertainty. Interval orders were introduced by [14] as a new time stamp technique. Interval orders extend Lamport time [5] by making the time stamp an interval. This approach preserves causality, but requires vector time stamps to determine "on-line" the relationship between two events. On-line recognition of interval orders were proposed by [15] but requires the whole order be known in advance. This is an unrealistic assumption for distributed simulation scenarios.

In [16], an interval-based temporal logic was introduced that used intervals as the basic unit of time. Allen also described a method of representing the relationship between intervals so that one could reason about events. His rationale for using intervals as a temporal representation is similar to characteristics we can exploit in distributed simulation.

# 4.    Uncertainty and Accuracy

Accuracy is defined in [17] as "the degree of exactness of a model or simulation, with high accuracy implying low error. Accuracy equates to the quality of a result." In this research, accuracy is defined by a set of metrics that characterize the state and behavior of the simulation. These metrics are defined by the simulation developer as a measure of the realism of the model when compared to the real world. According to [18], uncertainty establishes a boundary on the accuracy with which something can be known. In this research, interval size (uncertainty) is varied in order to determine the bounds on accuracy. This is accomplished using a methodology described in [1].

The remainder of this section illustrates the relationship between accuracy and uncertainty using a simulation of a queueing system. First a simulation called ASim is described followed by an example computation showing how uncertainty can affect accuracy.

## 4.1.    Queueing Simulation

A simulation of jobs arriving and departing at queues was developed to evaluate Approximate Time. The simulation, called ASim, models two types of objects: queues and jobs. A queue creates jobs during initialization and the jobs travel between all queues during the course of the execution. A single ASim can model multiple queues. There is no limit to the number of jobs that can be supported, provided adequate memory is available on the machine(s) running the simulation.

Each queue and job in ASim is modeled as a separate process. The process defines the life cycle of the job as it moves through time at the queue. The passage of time is accomplished using *Hold* and interval Hold (*iHold*) [1] primitives. The *Hold* primitive is used by the jobs and queues to wait for a specific type of message to arrive. The *iHold* primitive is used only by the jobs to advance time by some interval time value. There are two types: iHold(Arrive) is used to advance time while a job arrives at a queue and iHold(Queue) is used to advance time for a job sitting at the queue. The iHold primitive is also called an internal event since it is an event the job schedules for itself.

There are three types of external events sent between the queue and job. The first event sent is an *Arrival*. This event indicates the job is ready to arrive at the queue. Once the queue is clear, it sends the job a *QueueFree* (QF) event indicating it is safe to arrive. When the job has cleared the queue, it sends a *QueueClear* (QC) event back to the queue indicating it is safe for another job to arrive. The job then goes to the queue. When it completes its queue activity, it

schedules an *Arrival* at the next queue it will visit and it leaves its current queue. These events can have either a precise or interval time stamp.

The interaction between the queue and job is shown in Figure 3.

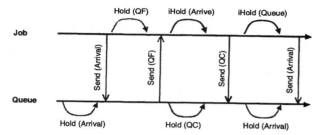

**Figure 3   Interaction between a job and the queue**

## 4.2.    Accuracy Example

A computation is composed of two jobs (J1 and J2) and one arrival queue (AQ) in shown in Figure 4. The behavior of the jobs with respect to the queue is as follows. When a job departs a queue it schedules its arrival at its destination queue by sending an "Arrival" event. When the job arrives at the destination queue, the queue determines if it is busy or clear for the job to arrive. If it is busy, the arriving job is put into the arrival queue and waits for the queue to clear. If the queue is clear, the job is sent a QF event. The job then executes an iHold(Arrive) event to arrive. Once the job completes the arrival, it sends the queue a QC event indicating that it has cleared the queue. Upon receiving the QC event, the queue then sends the next job in the arrival queue a QF event indicating approval to start the arrival process.

This computation using precise time stamps is shown in Figure 4 using solid lines. As can be seen, J1 arrives just before J2 and therefore J2 waits in the queue. Once J1 clears the queue, J2 can arrive at the queue. When the events use interval time stamps, it is possible for the uncertainty to change the behavior of the execution. The modified execution is shown in Figure 4 in dashed lines.

Due to the uncertainty of the Arrive event time, J2 arrives before J1 in this execution. The dashed line after the Arrive events shows that beyond this point, the behavior of the execution can change. This means that J1 will wait in the queue while J2 arrives. Subsequent behaviors may also change based on the change in the event sequence.

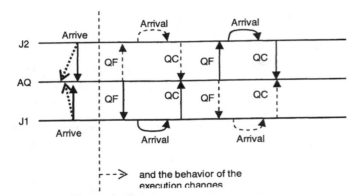

**Figure 4  How uncertainty can change the outcome of an execution**

One might initially think this error completely invalidates the results of the execution (as compared to the execution using precise time stamps). And in fact, this may be true for some models. However, in others this new sequence of events may be perfectly valid. In fact, the uncertainty associated with the Arrive event maybe an accurate reflection of the travel time between queues. Therefore, the uncertainty the time interval introduces to the Arrive event may be a better reflection of the interaction being modeled.

## 5.  Experiments

A series of experiments were performed to evaluate performance and accuracy when using time intervals. The experiments were run on the process-oriented queueing simulation called ASim. A distributed simulation system implementing the approximate time mechanisms was developed utilizing an HLA-based Run Time Infrastructure (RTI) software package called RTI-Kit. The details of the experiments are described in the following sections.

### 5.1.  Execution Environment

A distributed operating system, which implements the approximate time mechanisms [1], was developed for these experiments. The distributed operating system is called the Approximate Time-Run Time Infrastructure (AT-RTI). The AT-RTI was developed utilizing an HLA-based software package called the Federated Simulation Development Kit (FDK) developed by the Parallel and Distributed Simulation group at Georgia Tech [19]. The AT-RTI provides a minimal set of services similar to those defined in the HLA specification [20], but are accessed using a simplified application programming interface. The AT-RTI was run on the SGI Origin 2000 shared memory multiprocessor with 16 CPUs running IRIX 6.2. The Origin 2000 is a MIPS R10000 195 MHz machine with 4096 MB of main memory.

For the AT experiments, ASim modeled two types of queues: Pacing queues that act as "hubs" and have considerable job traffic (arrivals and departures), and Satellite queues that service pacing queues and have some job traffic. Each Pacing queue had 17 Satellite queues associated with it and each CPU modeled 3 Pacing queue "clusters." A total of 810 jobs were modeled on each CPU, each queue was initialized with 15 jobs.

The computation was distributed across a variable number of processors. The four cases investigated were 1, 4, 8, and 16 processors. When the computation was run on 1 processor, ASim modeled 3 Pacing queues or 54 total queues. When ASim was run on 16 processors, a total of 48 Pacing queues were modeled or a total of 864 queues.

All messages sent between queues (Arrival, Queue Free, Queue Clear) have interval time stamps and all simulations have zero lookahead. The iHold events (Arrive and Queue) also use intervals. All intervals are centered on the precise timestamp. Each ASim run was 1440 simulated minutes. For each interval size, the simulation was executed five times and the statistics averaged. The results presented are the arithmetic mean of the data collected.

Two types of statistics were gathered in these experiments: performance and accuracy. Performance statistics measure the execution speed of the AT algorithm within the AT-RTI. Specifically, statistics on run time, lower bound on time stamp (LBTS) computations[1], and scalability are presented. Accuracy statistics look at the effect of AT on the application. As described in the previous section, accuracy metrics are used to evaluate model behavior. The accuracy statistics are presented in terms of throughput, delays, and timestamp assignment. The performance and accuracy data are discussed in the following sections.

### 5.2.  Performance Data

Two types of performance statistics were gathered during the experiments. The first is performance improvement, which includes the speed up of run time and reduction of LBTS computations. Speed up is defined as the execution time using precise time stamps divided by the execution time using intervals. The second performance statistic is scalability. Scalability is defined in this research as the cost of scaling a computation from 1 CPU to 4, 8 or 16 CPUs. In other words, the run time cost of increasing the problem size in proportion to the number of CPUs. Each statistic is discussed in turn.

---

[1] LBTS is the smallest timestamp of any event a process will receive in the future; if simulations have zero lookahead, it is equivalent to the minimum time stamp of any unprocessed or partially processed event in the system. The time stamp of any unprocessed event is a lower bound on future events that may be produced after processing that event.

**5.2.1 Performance Improvement.** For all experimental data presented in this chapter, the x-axis of the graphs show the increasing interval size from 0 to 1 minute. However, not all intervals varied as large as 1 minute. In order to cleanly graph the data a simplification was made in the x-axis label. For interval size 0, all intervals were zero, which is the same as using precise time stamps. The next interval size plotted is 0.2 minutes, where all event intervals were 0.2 minutes (or 12 seconds). Following this data point, the Queue Free (QF) and Queue Clear (QC) event intervals remained constant at 0.2 minutes while the Arrival, iHold(Arrive) and iHold(Queue) intervals increased to 0.6 and 1.0 minutes. Even though the x-axis label states 0.6 and 1.0 minutes, the largest interval used by the QF and QC events was 0.2 minutes. The QF and QC event intervals did not exceed 0.2 minutes in order to ensure there would be a separation time between job arrivals.

The run time speedup of ASim using AT is shown in Figure 5. The graph shows the speedup for 4, 8, and 16 CPUs as compared to precise time stamps. As can be seen, the run time performance of ASim speeds up as the size of the interval increases.

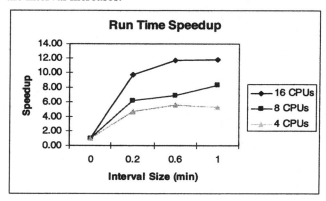

**Figure 5  Run time speedup of ASim using AT**

When the interval size was 1.0 minute, a maximum speed up of approximately 5.6 was achieved on 4 CPUs; on 8 CPUs the speed up was 8.3; and an 11.7 speedup was achieved on 16 CPUs. Run time improved due to increased concurrency in processing events. When precise time stamps are used, one event is processed per LBTS computation. When interval time stamps are used, the number of events processed per LBTS computation ranged from 22.6 on 4 CPUs to 70.4 on 16 CPUs, thereby increasing concurrency.

With the maximum interval size, the number of LBTS computations required to synchronize the simulation was reduced by a factor of 23 on 4 CPUs, 40 on 8 CPUs, and 73 on 16 CPUs. In other words, using AT greatly reduced the number of LBTS computations required during the

execution since more events are being processed concurrently. This is shown in Figure 6.

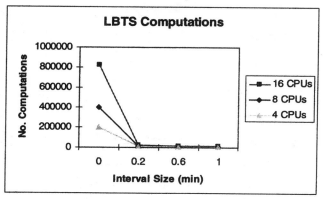

**Figure 6  Run time speedup of ASim measured by LBTS computations**

In both these graphs, it is noticeable that most of the performance improvement was achieved with small interval sizes, and performance improves only slightly as the interval size increases beyond 0.2 minutes. This is an important point as will be discussed in the section on accuracy.

**5.2.2 Scalability.** The next statistic to be presented is called scalability. These experiments increase the size of the problem in proportion with the number of CPUs. For example, a simulation containing 3 Pacing clusters that runs on 1 CPU is scaled to a computation simulating 48 Pacing clusters on 16 CPUs. The term scale factor is defined as the additional time required to run the scaled problem or

$$\text{Scale Factor} = \frac{\text{Execution Time of Scaled Problem}}{\text{Execution Time of Problem on 1 CPU}}$$

Figure 7 shows the scalability of ASim using AT when the computation is scaled to 4, 8, and 16 CPUs. The x-axis of this graph is the number of CPUs the computation was scaled to and the y-axis is the resulting scale factor. The individual lines plotted on the graph are the results for different interval sizes. Ideally, scale factor should stay fixed at 1 (smaller values indicate better performance).

As can be seen from the figure, the computation does not scale well when precise time stamps are used. On 4 CPUs the scale factor is 6.7, on 8 CPUs the scale factor is 17 and on 16 CPUs the scale factor is 51. In other words, with precise time stamps it will take 51 times longer to run an execution on 16 CPUs than it did on 1 CPU. As can be seen in Figure 5, AT improves the scalability of a computation. The scale factor is reduced to 1.2, 2, and 4.4 for 4, 8 and 16 CPUs respectively. In other words, an AT computation scaled to 16 CPUs takes 4.4 times longer to execute, as compared to 51 times longer with precise time stamps. Therefore, AT improved the scalability of the execution by as much as 11.6 times.

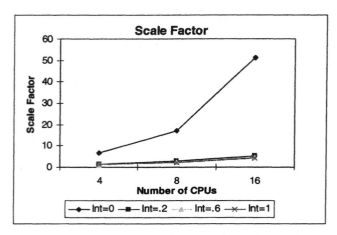

Figure 7  Scalability of ASim using AT

## 5.3.    Accuracy Statistics

Accuracy is the degree of exactness of a simulation, with high accuracy implying low error. A set of metrics that characterize the state and behavior of the simulation were used to define accuracy. The accuracy statistics look at the effect of AT on the application using these metrics. Two types of accuracy statistics are presented: throughput and delay. Throughput refers to the number of jobs traveling through a queue per unit time. Delay refers to the wait time experienced by a job. Each statistic is described in more detail in the following sections.

**5.3.1  Throughput.** There are two types of accuracy metrics presented for throughput category. The first metric is Number of Arrivals, which indicates the average number of jobs arriving at a queue during the simulation run. If interval time stamps cause the number of arrivals to either increase or decrease as compared to the same execution using precise time stamps, then the throughput of the queue changes.

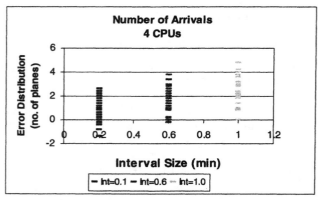

Figure 8  Number of arrivals for ASim on 4 CPUs

Figure 8 shows the Number of Arrivals for ASim running on 4 CPUs. The graph is an error distribution plot showing the difference in the average number of jobs arriving at a queue in the presence of uncertainty as compared to the same execution using precise time stamps.

Observe in Figure 8 that the number of arrivals increase as interval size increases. This is expected. Since intervals are centered on the precise time stamp, the leading edge of the interval (ET) occurs earlier in time as the interval size increases. In this execution, the iHold events are consistently processed at the leading edge of the interval. As a result, events following the iHold events also occur earlier. Therefore, jobs arrive and depart earlier than in the simulation that uses precise time stamps. This causes jobs to visit more queues. This results in an increase in the number of arrivals for a queue.

Another observation is the size of the error distribution. For an interval size of 0.2 minutes, the error ranged from –1.4 to 2.6 arrivals. For interval size 0.6 minutes, the error ranged from –0.2 to 3.8; and for interval size 1.0 the error ranged from 0 to 4.8. So the maximum error of 4.8 (or 258.8 arrivals) out of an expected 254 arrivals gives an approximate error of 2%.

The next metric presented for throughput is *Time in Queue*. This metric indicates the average amount of time a job waits in the queue before it departs. This metric is for a queue, i.e. wait time is averaged over all jobs in the queue. If introducing uncertainty causes the wait time to increase or decrease from the expected wait time (i.e., wait time in the precise timestamp execution), it can affect the rate at which jobs depart from the queue.

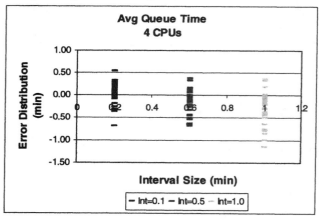

Figure 9  Queue time for ASim on 4 CPUs

As can be seen in Figure 9, the error distribution graph for average queue time decreases as the interval size increases, which is opposite from the previous throughput statistics presented. The reason is quite simple. As the interval size increases, the iHold(Queue) event tends to be processed at the leading edge (or ET) of the interval. As this happens, jobs spend less time waiting in the queue and therefore the error becomes negative. The largest error observed for queue time was with an interval size of 1.0, ranging from –1.15 to 0.36. The lower bound of –1.15 minutes is equal to an error of 2.59%.

**5.3.2 Delay.** The next category of statistics is delay. Delay refers to the wait time experienced by jobs as they arrive and depart queues. The accuracy metrics presented for delay are Block Time and Wait for Queue. Each is discussed in detail below.

The first metric, *Block Time*, refers to the end-to-end travel time observed by a job. Specifically, it's the time that a job departs the queue until it arrives at its destination queue. Unlike previous graphs, this statistic is gathered per job, not per queue. Figure 10 shows the error distribution for block time. As can be seen in the graph, the error ranged from –3.67 to 2.41 minutes when the interval size was 1.0. This translates to a block time of 73.55 minutes with intervals compared to the expected block time of 77.22 minutes or a maximum error of 4.75%.

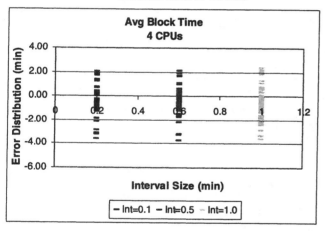

**Figure 10  Block time in ASim on 4 CPUs**

The next delay metric is *Wait for Queue*. This is the time that a job waits at the queue to arrive. As discussed previously, temporal uncertainty can cause a job to arrive at its destination queue earlier or later than if it had a precise time stamp. A different arrival time can cause the state of the queue to be different which, in turn, can cause a job to wait more or less time to arrive (as illustrated in section 4.2).

Figure 11 shows the average wait time for a queue when ASim was run on 4 CPUs. The graph has an interesting shape as the majority of the data points fall between ±0.5 minutes. However there are a few data points that fall between –1.5 and –2.0 minutes. The outlying data points are associated with Pacing queues and the points closely grouped together come from Satellite queues. This behavior is a result of model design. ASim is designed so that Pacing queues receive more jobs than Satellite queues. Therefore, as uncertainty is introduced into the simulation and jobs depart/arrive earlier from/at queues, the Pacing

queues become even busier and the wait for the queue increases. If the Pacing queues received the same number of jobs as Satellite queues, the Wait Time for Queue may not be as affected as much by uncertainty.

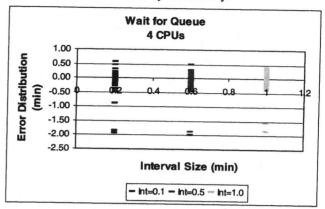

**Figure 11  Average wait for queue on 4 CPUs**

Even though the error is within ± 30 seconds for all of the Satellite queues that does not translate into a small percentage of error for the wait time as compared to precise time stamps. In fact, for all interval sizes there are approximately 14 out of 54 queues on a CPU that exceed 10% and approximately 5 queues that exceed 15%. For example, the average wait time at one queue was 1.49 minutes using precise time stamps (i.e., the expected behavior) but when uncertainty was introduced the wait time was 1.21 minutes or a difference of –0.28 minutes. This translates to a –18.61% error. While this is a large percentage, the error is less than 30 seconds in magnitude.

## 5.4.  Observations

The error distribution graphs presented in this section are representative of the data gathered on 8 and 16 CPUs. The shapes of the distributions are very similar and the maximum and minimum values vary only small amounts. The data for all CPUs can be found in [1].

In each of the accuracy statistics, the least amount of error was observed when the interval size was 0.2 minutes or less. As discussed in the performance statistics, most performance gain was also realized when the interval was 0.2 minutes. Therefore, small interval sizes can yield a large performance improvement with a small loss in accuracy. This is an important observation as it shows that accuracy does not have to be significantly degraded in order to improve the performance of the simulation. The simulation developer must evaluate these statistics in concert in order to select the interval size that best meets the needs of the simulation.

# 6.    Conclusion

Experiments assessing the performance and accuracy of AT have been described. Several types of statistics are presented to fully understand the effect uncertainty has on the execution. The first set of statistics show that an order of magnitude performance improvement is achieved using AT. Specifically, a run time speed up ranged from 5-12 was realized (depending on number of CPUs) and the number of LBTS computations was reduced by a factor of 22-73. Further, the number of events processed per LBTS was increased from 1 in the precise time stamp case to 22.6 on 4 CPUs to 70.4 on 16 CPUs. AT also enabled the execution to be scaled to increasing numbers of CPUs. With precise timestamps the scale factor of the execution ranged from 6.7-51 and with AT the scale factor was reduced to 1.2-4.4. For all statistics, the majority of the improvement was achieved with an interval size of 0.2 minutes and improvement reached a plateau with an interval of 0.6 minutes.

The second set of statistics show that the accuracy of the AT execution remains comparable with the precise time stamp execution. Each throughput metric had less than 3% error, even with the maximum interval size. For the delay statistics, error had a larger range. The Block time error was within 4.75% regardless of the interval size, while Wait for Queue, had the largest range of results. Regardless of interval size, 75% of the queues had an error less than 10% and 90% of the queues had an error less than 15%. Further research is required to understand whether the error observed in Wait for Runway is due to AT or the job routing algorithm implemented in ASim.

The research presented here focused on developing the theory and algorithms for exploiting temporal uncertainty in parallel and distributed simulations. The authors have implemented AT in air traffic control and military simulations and are currently investigating its applicability to agent-based simulations.

## Acknowledgements

Funding for this research was provided by the National Science Foundation Grant ATM-0326431, the Link Foundation Fellowship in Advanced Simulation and Training, the NASA Office of Space Science GSRP Fellowship, and the GTRI graduate assistance program.

## References

[1] Loper, M.L., *Approximate Time and Temporal Uncertainty in Parallel and Distributed Simulation*, Ph.D. Thesis, 2002, p. 205.

[2] Fujimoto, R.M., *Exploiting Temporal Uncertainty in Parallel and Distributed Simulations*. in *Proceedings of the 13th Workshop on Parallel and Distributed Simulation*. 1999.

[3] Moore, R.E., *Methods and Applications of Interval Analysis*. SIAM Studies in Applied Mathematics, ed. W. Ames. 1979, Philadelphia, PA: SIAM. 190.

[4] Birman, K., A. Schiper, and P. Stephenson, *Lightweight Causal and Atomic Group Multicast*. ACM Transaction on Computer Systems, 1991. **9**(3): p. 272-314.

[5] Lamport, L., *Time, Clocks, and the Ordering of Events in a Distributed System*. Communications of the ACM, 1978. **21**(7): p. 558-565.

[6] Raynal, M. and M. Singhal, *Logical Time: Capturing Causality in Distributed Systems*. IEEE Computer, 1996. **29**(2): p. 49-56.

[7] Sokol, L.M. and B.K. Stucky. *MTW: Experimental Results for a Constrained Optimistic Scheduling Paradigm*. in *Proceedings of the SCS Multiconference on Distributed Simulation*. 1990.

[8] Porras, J., J. Ikonen, and J. Harju. *Applying a Modified Chandy-Misra Algorithm to the Distributed Simulation of a Cellular Network*. in *Proceedings of the 12th Workshop on Parallel and Distributed Simulation*. 1198: IEEE Computer Society Press.

[9] Rao, D., et al. *Unsynchronized Parallel Discrete Event Simulation*. in *Proceedings of the 1998 Winter Simulation Conference*. 1998.

[10] Vitek, M. *Fuzzy Information and Fuzzy Time*. in *IFAC Fuzzy Information*. 1983. Marseille, France.

[11] Dutta, S. *An Event Based Fuzzy Temporal Logic*. Proceedings of the 18th IEEE International Symposium on Multiple-Valued Logic. 1988. Palma de Mallorca, Spain.

[12] Dubois, D. and H. Prade, *Processing Fuzzy Temporal Knowledge*. IEEE Transactions on Systems, Man, and Cybernetics, 1989. **19**(4): p. 729-744.

[13] Zadeh, L.A., *Fuzzy Sets as a Basis for a Theory of Possibility*. Fuzzy Sets and Systems, 1978. **1**: p. 3-28.

[14] Diehl, C. and C. Jard. *Interval Approximations and Message Causality in Distributed Systems*. Proceedings of the 9th Annual Symposium on Theoretical Aspects of Computer Science (STACS '92). 1992: Springer.

[15] Bouchitte, V., R. Jegou, and J.-X. Rampon, *On-Line Recognition of Interval Orders*. 1993, INRIA. p. 18.

[16] Allen, J., *Maintaining Knowledge about Temporal Intervals*. Communications of the ACM, 1983. **26**(11): p. 832-843.

[17] IST, *A Glossary of Modeling and Simulation Terms for Distributed Interactive Simulation (DIS)*. 1995, Institute for Simulation and Training, University of Central Florida: Orlando.

[18] Pace, D. *Issues Related to Quantifying Simulation Validation*. 1991.

[19] Fujimoto, R., et al., *FDK Users Guide*. 2001, Parallel and Distributed Simulation Group, College of Computing, Georgia Tech: Atlanta, GA. p. 81.

[20] IEEE, *IEEE Standard for Modeling and Simulation (M&S) High Level Architecture (HLA) - Federate Interface Specification*. 2001, IEEE: New York, NY. p. 466.

# Performance Models for Evaluation and Automatic Tuning of Symmetric Sparse Matrix-Vector Multiply

Benjamin C. Lee, Richard W. Vuduc, James W. Demmel, Katherine A. Yelick
University of California, Berkeley
Computer Science Division
Berkeley, California, USA
{blee20, richie, demmel, yelick}@cs.berkeley.edu

## Abstract

*We present **optimizations** for sparse matrix-vector multiply SpMV and its generalization to multiple vectors, SpMM, when the matrix is symmetric: (1) symmetric storage, (2) register blocking, and (3) vector blocking. Combined with register blocking, symmetry saves more than 50% in matrix storage. We also show performance speedups of $2.1\times$ for SpMV and $2.6\times$ for SpMM, when compared to the best non-symmetric register blocked implementation.*

*We present an approach for the selection of tuning parameters, based on **empirical modeling and search** that consists of three steps: (1) Off-line benchmark, (2) Run-time search, and (3) Heuristic performance model. This approach generally selects parameters to achieve performance with 85% of that achieved with exhaustive search.*

*We evaluate our implementations with respect to **upper bounds** on performance. Our model bounds performance by considering only the cost of memory operations and using lower bounds on the number of cache misses. Our optimized codes are within 68% of the upper bounds.*

## 1 Introduction

We present optimizations, an approach for tuning parameter selection, and performance analyses for sparse matrix-vector multiply (SpMV), $y \leftarrow y + A \cdot x$, where $A$ is a symmetric, sparse matrix (*i.e.*, $A = A^T$) and $x,y$ are dense column vectors called the *source* and *destination*. We also consider the generalization of SpMV to multiple vectors where $x,y$ are replaced by matrices $X,Y$, referring to this kernel as SpMM. Symmetry is traditionally exploited to reduce storage, but performance gains are also possible since the cost of memory accesses dominates the cost of flops on most modern cache-based superscalar architectures.

The challenge in efficient performance tuning for sparse

computational kernels is the considerable variation in the best choice of sparse matrix data structure and code transformations across machines, compilers, and matrices, the latter of which may not be known until run-time. This paper describes a new implementation space for the symmetric case, considering symmetric storage (Section 3), register blocking (Section 3), and vector blocking (Section 4).

We present an empirical modeling and search procedure to select optimal tuning parameters that characterize a SpMM code for a given matrix and machine (Section 5). Our approach extends models of the SPARSITY system [7, 5]. To evaluate the measured performance of our best implementations, we formulate upper bounds on performance (Section 6). We bound execution time from below by considering only the cost of memory accesses and by modeling data placement in the memory hierarchy for a lower bound on cache misses.

The following summarizes experimental results from four different computing platforms (Table 1) and a test suite of twelve sparse symmetric matrices (Table 2):

1. **Symmetric register blocking** achieves up to $2.1\times$ speedups for SpMV and $2.6\times$ speedups for SpMM over non-symmetric register and vector blocking.

2. Combining **symmetry, register and vector blocking** achieves up to $9.9\times$ speedups for a dense matrix in sparse format and up to $7.3\times$ for a true sparse matrix when compared to a naïve code (no optimizations).

3. The **empirical modeling and search procedure** generally selects parameters that yield within 85% of the best performance achieved by an exhaustive search over all possible parameter values. [1]

4. Measured performance achieve 68% of the **performance upper bound**, on average.

---

[1]"All possible values" subject to constraints that consider the characteristics of practical applications and architectural parameters.

| Property | Sun Ultra 2i | Intel Itanium 1 | Intel Itanium 2 | IBM Power 4 |
|---|---|---|---|---|
| Clock rate (MHz) | 333 | 800 | 900 | 1300 |
| Peak Main Memory Bandwidth (MB/s) | 664 | 2.1 | 6400 | 8000 |
| Peak Flop Rate (Mflop/s) | 667 | 3200 | 3600 | 5200 |
| DGEMM $n = 1000$ (Mflop/s) | 425 | 2200 | 3500 | 3500 |
| DGEMV $n = 2000$ (Mflop/s) | 58 | 345 | 740 | 915 |
| DSYMV $n = 1000$ (Mflop/s) | 92 | 625 | 1400 | 1600 |
| DSPMV $n = 2000$ (Mflop/s) | 62 | 115 | 356 | 1700 |
| DSYMM $n = 2000$ (Mflop/s) | 383 | 1900 | 3400 | 3500 |
| STREAM Triad Bandwidth (MB/s) | 250 | 1100 | 3800 | 2100 |
| L1 total size (KB) | 16 | 16 | 32 | 32 |
| L1 line size (B) | 16 | 32 | 128 | 128 |
| L1 latency (cy) | 2 | 2 (int) | 0.34 | 0.7 |
| L2 total size (KB) | 2048 | 96 | 256 | 1536 |
| L2 line size (B) | 64 | 64 | 128 | 128 |
| L1 latency (cy) | 7 | 6-9 | 0.5 | 12 |
| L3 total size (KB) | n/a | 2 | 1.5 | 16 |
| L3 line size (B) | n/a | 64 | 128 | 512 |
| L3 latency (cy) | n/a | 21-24 | 3 | 45 |
| Memory latency (cy, $\approx$) | 36 | 36 | 11 | 167 |
| Compiler | Sun C v6.1 | Intel C v5.0.1 | Intel C v7.0 | IBM XLC |

**Table 1. Evaluation platforms.**

| | Name | Application Area | Dimension | Nonzeros |
|---|---|---|---|---|
| 1 | dense1600 | Dense Matrix | 1600 | 1280800 |
| 2 | bcsstk35 | Stiff matrix automobile frame | 30237 | 1450163 |
| 3 | crystk02 | FEM Crystal free vibration | 13965 | 968583 |
| 4 | crystk03 | FEM Crystal free vibration | 24696 | 1751178 |
| 5 | nasasrb | Shuttle rocket booster | 54870 | 2677324 |
| 6 | 3dtube | 3-D pressure tube | 45330 | 3213332 |
| 7 | ct20stif | CT20 Engine block | 52329 | 2698463 |
| 8 | gearbox | ZF aircraft flap actuator | 153746 | 4617075 |
| 9 | finan512 | Financial portfolio optimization | 74752 | 596992 |
| 10 | pwt | Structural engineering problem | 36519 | 326107 |
| 11 | vibrobox | Structure of vibroacoustic problem | 12328 | 342828 |
| 12 | gupta1 | Linear programming matrix | 31802 | 2164210 |

**Table 2. Matrix benchmark suite. 1 is a dense matrix stored in sparse format; 2–8 arise in finite element applications; 9–11 come from assorted applications; 12 is a linear programming example. For each matrix, we show the number of non-zeros in the upper-triangle.**

This paper summarizes the key findings of a recent technical report [3]. We refer the reader to the report for further details. The empirical modeling and search procedure for tuning parameters does not appear in the report.

## 2 Experimental Methodology

We conducted experiments on machines based on the microprocessors in Table 1. Latency estimates were obtained from a combination of published sources and experimental measurements using the Saavedra-Barrera memory system microbenchmark [10] and MAPS benchmarks [11].

Table 2 summarizes the size and application of each symmetric matrix in the matrix benchmark suite used for evaluation. Most of the matrices are available from either the collections at NIST (MatrixMarket [12]) or the University of Florida [13]. The size of these matrices exceed the largest cache size for the evaluation platforms.

We use the PAPI v2.1 library for access to hardware counters on all platforms [14] except Power 4; not all PAPI counters are available for the Power 4 and HPM counters overcount memory traffic. We use the cycle counters, reported as the median of 25 consecutive trials, as timers.

Presented performance in Mflop/s always uses "ideal" flop counts. That is, if a transformation of the matrix requires filling in explicit zeros (*e.g.* register blocking), arith-

metic with these extra zeros are *not* counted as flops when determining performance.

## 3 Optimizations for Matrix Symmetry

The baseline implementation stores the full matrix in compressed sparse row (CSR) format and computes SpMV using a non-symmetric kernel.

### 3.1 Symmetric Storage

Matrix symmetry enables storing only half of the matrix and, without loss of generality, our implementation stores the upper-triangle. Although the symmetric code requires the same number of floating point operations as the baseline, symmetry halves the number of memory accesses to the matrix: a symmetric implementation simultaneously applies each element and its transpose, processing only the stored half of the matrix. In both cases, stores to the destination are indirect and potentially irregular.

### 3.2 Symmetric Register Blocking

SPARSITY's *register blocking* is a technique for improving register reuse [7]. The sparse $m \times n$ matrix is logically divided into aligned $r \times c$ blocks, storing only those blocks containing at least one non-zero. SpMV computation proceeds block-by-block. For each block, we can reuse the corresponding $c$ elements of the source by keeping them in registers to increase temporal locality to the source, assuming a sufficient number are available.

Register blocking uses the blocked variant of compressed sparse row (BCSR) storage format. Blocks within

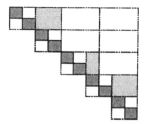

**Figure 1. Square diagonal blocking.** A $10 \times 10$ matrix with $2 \times 3$ **register blocks.**

the same block row are stored consecutively, and the elements of each block are stored consecutively in row-major order. When $r = c = 1$, BCSR reduces to CSR. BCSR potentially stores fewer column indices than CSR implementation (one per block instead of one per non-zero). The effect is to reduce memory traffic by reducing storage overhead. Furthermore, SPARSITY implementations fully unroll the $r \times c$ submatrix computation, reducing loop overheads and exposing scheduling opportunities to the compiler.

A uniform block size may require filling in explicit zero values, resulting in extra computation. We define the *fill ratio* to be the number of stored values (original non-zeros plus explicit zeros) divided by the number of non-zeros in the original matrix. The profitability of register blocking depends highly on the fill and the non-zero pattern of the matrix.

In our symmetric implementation of $r \times c$ register blocking, we use the following *square diagonal blocking* scheme (Figure 1). Given a row-oriented storage scheme and $r \times c$ register blocks, the diagonal blocks are implemented as square $r \times r$ blocks. We align the register blocks from the right edge of the matrix, which may require small degenerate $r \times c'$ blocks to the right of the diagonal blocks, where $c' < c$ and $c'$ depends on the block row.

## 4 Optimizations for Multiple Vectors

The baseline implementation, given $k$ vectors, applies the unblocked symmetric SpMV kernel once for each vector. This implementation requires $k$ accesses to the entire matrix and, for large matrices, brings the entire matrix through the memory hierarchy once for each vector.

Vector blocking is a technique for reducing memory traffic for the SpMM kernel, $Y = Y + A \cdot X$, where $A$ is a symmetric sparse $n \times n$ matrix, and $X, Y$ are dense $n \times k$ matrices. [2] The $k$ vectors are processed in $\lceil \frac{k}{v} \rceil$ groups of

---

[2] $X, Y$ are collections of $k$ dense column vectors of length $n$.

the *vector width* $v$ and multiplication of each element of $A$ is unrolled by $v$. The computation of SpMM proceeds sequentially across matrix elements or register blocks, computing results for the corresponding elements in each of the $v$ destinations in the vector block. When $v = 1$, the subroutine is effectively a single vector implementation of SpMV.

Thus, the matrix is accessed at most $\lceil \frac{k}{v} \rceil + 1$ times in contrast to the $k$ times required by the baseline. The effect is to reduce memory traffic and increase temporal locality to $A$ by amortizing the cost of accessing a matrix element for $v$ vectors. Furthermore, unrolling the multiply for the $v$ vectors reduces loop overhead and exposes scheduling opportunities to the compiler.

## 5 Automated Empirical Tuning

A register and vector blocked SpMM code is characterized by the parameters $(r, c, v)$, indicating optimal register block size $r \times c$ and vector width $v$. The optimal parameters vary significantly across machines and matrices and are difficult to choose by purely analytic modeling [2].

Our approach to selecting $(r, c, v)$ is based on *empirical modeling and search*, executed partly off-line and partly at run-time. Given a machine, a symmetric matrix $A$, and a number of vectors $k$, our tuning parameter selection procedure consists of the following 3 steps:

1. **Off-line benchmark**: Once per machine, measure the performance (in Mflop/s) of symmetric SpMM for a dense matrix stored in sparse format, for all $(r, c, v)$ such that $1 \leq r, c \leq b_{\max}$ and $1 \leq v \leq v_{\max}$, where $k$ is set equal to $v$. In practice, we use $b_{\max} = 8$ and $v_{\max} = 10$. Denote this *symmetric register profile* by $\{ P_{rcv}(\text{dense}) \, | \, 1 \leq r, c \leq b_{\max}, 1 \leq v \leq v_{\max} \}$.

2. **Run-time "search"**: When the matrix $A$ is known at run-time, compute an estimate $\hat{f}_{rc}(A)$ of the true fill ratio for all $1 \leq r, c, \leq b_{\max}$. Estimating this quantity is a form of empirical search over possible block sizes, and depends only on the matrix non-zero structure.

3. **Heuristic performance model**: Choose $(r, c, v)$ that maximizes the following *estimate* of register blocking performance $\hat{P}_{rcv}(A)$,

$$\hat{P}_{rcv}(A) = \frac{P_{rcv}(\text{dense})}{\hat{f}_{rc}(A)}, \qquad (1)$$

for all $1 \leq r, c \leq b_{\max}$ and $1 \leq v \leq \min\{v_{\max}, k\}$. Intuitively, $P_{rcv}(\text{dense})$ is an empirical estimate of expected performance, and $\hat{f}_{rc}(A)$ reduces this value according to the extra flops per non-zero due to fill.

The key idea is to decouple machine-specific aspects of performance which can be measured off-line (Step 1) from matrix-specific aspects determined at run-time (Step 2), combining these aspects with a heuristic model of performance evaluated at run-time (Step 3). This procedure adapts our prior technique for non-symmetric SpMV [1, 2, 4].

Trying all or even a subset of block sizes is infeasible if the matrix is known only at run-time, due to the cost of converting the matrix to blocked format. In contrast, the fill can be estimated accurately and cheaply [2], while the total run-time cost of executing Steps 2 and 3, followed by a single conversion to $r \times c$ blocked format, is not much greater than the cost of only the conversion [2].

# 6 Bounds on Performance

We present performance upper bounds to estimate the potential payoff from low-level tuning given a matrix and a data structure, but independent of instruction mix and ordering. These bounds extend prior bounds for non-symmetric SpMV [4]. The performance model consists of a lower bound model of execution time and a lower bound model on cache misses at each level in the memory hierarchy. The following are underlying assumptions for these bounds:

1. Our lower bound model of execution time considers only the cost of memory operations, taking SpMV and SpMM to be memory bound. Assuming write-back caches and sufficient store buffer capacity, we account only for the cost of loads and ignore the cost of stores.

2. For a hit in cache level $i$, we assign a cost $\alpha_i$ to access the data at that level, as determined by microbenchmarks on streaming workloads likely to represent the fastest memory access patterns.

3. We further bound time from below by obtaining a lower bound on cache misses that considers only compulsory misses, accounts for cache line sizes, and assumes full associativity.

4. We further bound time from below by ignoring TLB misses. This assumption is justified by the predominantly streaming behavior of SpMV [2], but may lead to an optimistic bound in the multiple vector case.

## 6.1 Lower Bound Execution Time Model

If the total execution time is $T$ seconds, the performance $P$ in Mflop/s is

$$P = \frac{4kv}{T} \times 10^{-6} \qquad (2)$$

where $k$ is the number of stored non-zeros in the $n \times n$ sparse matrix $A$ (excluding any fill) and $v$ is the vector

width in the vector blocked implementation. To get an upper bound on performance, we require a lower bound on $T$.

Consider a machine with $\kappa$ cache levels, where the access latency at cache level $i$ is $\alpha_i$ in cycles, and the memory access latency is $\alpha_{\mathrm{mem}}$. Let $H_i$ and $M_i$ be the number of cache hits and misses at each level $i$, respectively. Also, let $L$ be the total number of loads. The execution time $T$ is

$$
\begin{aligned}
T &= \sum_{i=1}^{\kappa} \alpha_i H_i + \alpha_{\mathrm{mem}} M_\kappa \\
&= \alpha_1 L + \sum_{i=1}^{\kappa-1} (\alpha_{i+1} - \alpha_i) M_i + (\alpha_{\mathrm{mem}} - \alpha_\kappa) M_\kappa \qquad (3)
\end{aligned}
$$

where $H_1 = L - M_1$ and $H_i = M_{i-1} - M_i$ for $2 \leq i \leq \kappa$. According to Equation (3), we can minimize $T$ by minimizing $M_i$, assuming $\alpha_{i+1} \geq \alpha_i$.

## 6.2 Counting Load Operations

Let $A$ be an $m \times m$ symmetric matrix with $k$ stored non-zeros. Let $D_r$ be the number of $r \times r$ non-zero diagonal blocks, $B_{rc}$ be the number of $r \times c$ non-zero register blocks, and $f_{rc}$ be the fill ratio given these blocks. Let $\|D_r\|$ and $\|B_{rc}\|$ denote the total number of matrix elements (including filled zeros) stored in the diagonal and non-diagonal blocks, respectively.

The upper bound on $D_r$ is $\lceil \frac{m}{r} \rceil$ with at most $\|D_r\| = \lceil \frac{m}{r} \rceil \cdot \frac{r(r+1)}{2} \approx \frac{m(r+1)}{2}$ diagonal blocked elements in the matrix, since a diagonal block has at most $\frac{r(r+1)}{2}$ elements. Furthermore, we estimate the number of non-diagonal blocks $B_{rc}$ by counting the stored elements excluded from the diagonal blocks so that $B_{rc} = \frac{\|B_{rc}\|}{rc}$ where $\|B_{rc}\| \approx k f_{rc} - \frac{m(r+1)}{2}$ and each register block contains $rc$ elements. In the case of $1 \times 1$ register blocking, $\|D_r\| + \|B_{rc}\| = k$.

The matrix requires storage of $\|D_r\| + \|B_{rc}\|$ double precision values, $D_r + B_{rc}$ integer column indices, and $\lceil \frac{m}{r} \rceil + 1$ integer row indices. Since the fill ratio is defined as the number of stored elements (fill included) divided by the number of non-zeros (fill excluded), $f_{rc} \approx \frac{\|D_r\| + \|B_{rc}\|}{k}$ and is always at least 1.

Every matrix element, row index, and column index must be loaded once. We assume that SpMM iterates over block rows in the stored upper triangle and that all $r$ entries of the destinations can be loaded once for each of $D_r$ block rows and kept in registers for the duration of the block row multiply. We also assume that all $c$ destination elements can be kept in registers during the multiplication of a given transpose block, thereby requiring $B_{rc}c$ additional loads from the destination. A similar analysis for the block columns in the transpose of the stored triangle yields $rD_r + cB_{rc}$ loads. Thus, the number of loads, scaled for multiple vectors, is [3]

---

[3] where $D_r$ and $B_{rc}$ can be represented in terms of $f_{rc}, m, r, c,$ and $k$.

$$\text{Loads}(r,c,v) = \underbrace{B_{rc}rc + D_r\left(\frac{r^2+r}{2}\right) + B_{rc} + D_r + \left\lceil\frac{m}{r}\right\rceil + 1}_{\text{matrix}} +$$

$$\underbrace{vrD_r + vcB_{rc}}_{\text{source}} + \underbrace{vrD_r + vcB_{rc}}_{\text{destination}} \quad (4)$$

## 6.3 Lower Bounds on Cache Misses

Beginning with the L1 cache, let $l_1$ be the L1-cache line size, in double-precision words. One compulsory L1 read miss per cache line is incurred for every matrix element (value and index) and each of the $mv$ destination elements. In considering the vectors, we assume the vector size is less than the L1 cache size, so that in the best case, only one compulsory miss per cache line is incurred for each of the $2mv$ source and destination elements. Thus, a lower bound $M_{lower}^{(1)}$ on L1 misses is

$$M_{lower}^{(1)}(r,c,v) = \frac{1}{l_1}\left[kf_{rc} + \frac{1}{\gamma}\left(D_r + B_{rc} + \left\lceil\frac{m}{r}\right\rceil + 1\right) + 2mv\right] \quad (5)$$

where the size of one double precision floating point value equals $\gamma$ integers. In this paper, we use 64-bit double-precision floating point data and 32-bit integers, so that $\gamma = 2$. The factor of $\frac{1}{l_1}$ accounts for the L1 line size. An analogous expression applies at other cache levels by substituting the appropriate line size.

## 7 Evaluation

Figures 2–5 summarize the performance of our optimizations on the four platforms in Table 1 and the matrices in Table 2. We compare the following nine implementations and bounds.

1. **Non-Symmetric Unoptimized Reference**: The unblocked $(1,1)$ single vector implementation with non-symmetric storage. Represented by *crosses*.

2. **Symmetric Reference**: The unblocked $(1,1)$ single vector implementation with symmetric storage. Represented by *five-pointed stars*.

3. **Non-Symmetric Register Blocked**: The blocked single vector implementation with non-symmetric storage where $r$ and $c$ are chosen by exhaustive search to maximize performance. Represented by *asterisks*.

4. **Symmetric Register Blocked**: The blocked single vector implementation with symmetric storage where $r$ and $c$ are chosen by exhaustive search to maximize performance. Represented by *plus signs*.

5. **Non-Symmetric Register Blocked with Multiple Vectors**: The blocked multiple vector implementation with non-symmetric storage where $r$, $c$, and $v$ are chosen by exhaustive search to maximize performance. Represented by *upward pointing triangles*.

6. **Symmetric Register Blocked with Multiple Vectors**: The blocked multiple vector implementation with symmetric storage where $r$, $c$, and $v$ are chosen by exhaustive search to maximize performance. We refer to these parameters as $r_{opt}$, $c_{opt}$, and $v_{opt}$. Represented by *six-pointed stars*.

7. **Tuning Parameter Selection Heuristic**: The blocked multiple vector implementation with symmetric storage where $r$, $c$, and $v$ are chosen by the tuning parameter selection heuristic described in Section 5. We refer to these parameters as $r_{heur}$, $c_{heur}$, and $v_{heur}$. Represented by *hollow circles*.

8. **Analytic Upper Bound**: The analytic upper bound on performance implementation 6. We use Equation (4) and Equation (5) to compute the numbers of loads and cache misses. Represented by *solid lines*.

9. **PAPI Upper Bound**: An upper bound on performance for implementation 6. The number of loads and cache misses are obtained from PAPI event counters. Represented by *dashed lines*.

## 7.1 Effects of Symmetry on Performance

Considering all four platforms, the maximum performance gain from symmetry is $2.08\times$ for register blocked SpMV over the non-symmetric register blocked kernel (4 versus 3). The median speedup is $1.34\times$. The maximum performance gain from symmetry is $2.58\times$ for register and vector blocked SpMM over the non-symmetric register and vector blocked kernel (6 versus 5). However, the median speedup of $1.09\times$ is appreciably slower. Furthermore, symmetry can reduce performance in the rare worst case. The chosen register block sizes, shown in the appendices, suggest these performance decreases are due to block sizes in the symmetric case that lead to significantly more fill than those in the non-symmetric case.

An implementation optimized for symmetry, register and vector blocking achieves maximum, median, minimum performance gains of $7.32\times$, $4.15\times$, and $1.60\times$ compared to the naïve code (6 versus 1) over all platforms and matrices. Given symmetric storage, the other two optimizations almost always improve and never reduce performance. The increasing performance gains as optimizations are incrementally applied suggest cumulative performance effects of these optimizations.

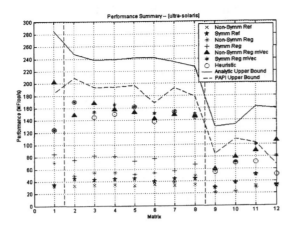

**Figure 2. Performance Summary – Sun Ultra 2i. Performance (MFlop/s) of various optimized implementations compared to upper bounds on performance.**

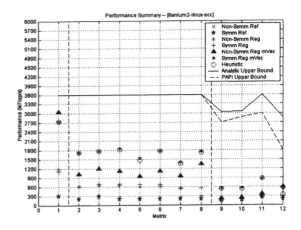

**Figure 4. Performance Summary – Intel Itanium 2. Performance data and upper bounds shown in a format analogous to the format in Figure 2. The model predicts machine peak (3.6 Gflop/s) for matrices 1–7.**

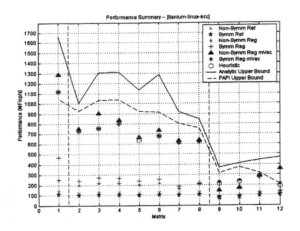

**Figure 3. Performance Summary – Intel Itanium 1. Performance data and upper bounds shown in a format analogous to the format in Figure 2.**

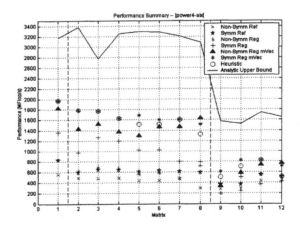

**Figure 5. Performance Summary – IBM Power 4. Performance data and upper bounds shown in a format analogous to the format in Figure 2. The analytic upper bound is omitted due to the unavailability of hardware counters.**

| | Overall | Ultra 2i | Itanium 1 | Itanium 2 | Power4 |
|---|---|---|---|---|---|
| I. Symmetry Register Blocking | | | | | |
| minimum | -9.89 | 35.48 | -9.89 | -9.89 | 31.97 |
| median | 58.33 | 60.94 | 47.64 | 57.98 | 61.09 |
| maximum | 64.79 | 64.79 | 64.79 | 64.79 | 64.79 |
| II. Symmetry Register and Vector Blocking | | | | | |
| minimum | -4.17 | 28.57 | -4.17 | 12.28 | 28.57 |
| median | 53.70 | 53.70 | 50.25 | 59.51 | 53.70 |
| maximum | 64.79 | 57.08 | 64.79 | 64.79 | 64.79 |

**Table 3. Percentage savings in matrix storage.**

## 7.2 Accuracy of Automatic Tuning Parameter Selection

On the Ultra 2i, Itanium 1, and Itanium 2, the block size selection procedure generally chooses $(r, c, v)$ whose performance is 93% or more of the best by exhaustive search. On Power4, the predictions are somewhat less accurate, at 85% of the best or greater. Nevertheless, in nearly all cases the selected implementation yields at least some speedup over the symmetric register blocked single vector case (7 versus 4).

The heuristic does not select near-optimal implementations in the case of Matrix 12 (a linear programming matrix). We discuss this case in detail in the full report [3].

## 7.3 Proximity of Performance to Upper Bounds

To evaluate our performance models, we consider the proximity of the upper bounds to the measured performance of the symmetric, register and vector blocked code. The finite element matrices (FEM Matrices 2–8) achieve 72% to 90% of the PAPI bound, but only 53% to 73% of the analytic bound on the Ultra 2i and Itanium 1 . This difference suggests that further performance improvements on these platforms will require reducing the gap between the number of predicted and measured cache misses. The measured performance of these matrices on the Itanium 2 and Power 4 were 38% to 63% of the analytic bound. [4]

The non-FEM matrices realize relatively lower measured performance, achieving 65% to 120% of the PAPI bound and 44% to 62% of the analytic bound on the Ultra 2i and Itanium 1. Cases in which the measured performance exceeds the PAPI upper bound (Matrix 12 on Ultra 2i and Matrix 1 on Itanium 1) may be caused by limitations in the PAPI counters. The realized performance of these matrices on the Itanium 2 is 29% to 38% and 23% to 32% of the PAPI and analytic bounds, respectively, and 38% to 54% of the analytic bound on the Power 4.

---

[4]Note that no PAPI data was available for a bound on the Power 4.

## 7.4 Effects of Symmetry on Storage

Symmetry can significantly save storage . We show maximum and median savings of 64.79% and 56.52%, respectively, for symmetric register blocking (Table 3, I). Symmetry may also use almost 10% more memory in the case of matrix 12 on the Itanium 1 and 2. We show maximum and median savings of 64.79% and 53.70%, respectively, when adding multiple vectors (Table 3, II).

A large register block size in a symmetric code can save more than 50% of storage because the memory for matrix indices decreases by up to a factor of $r \times c$, augmenting the savings from storing half the matrix. An increase in storage from symmetric storage is also possible, however, if the chosen register block size results in significant fill.

## 8 Related Work

Temam and Jalby [18] and Fraguela, *et al.*, [19] developed probabilistic cache miss models for SpMV, but assumed a uniform distribution of non-zero entries. In contrast, our lower bounds account only for compulsory misses. Gropp, *et al.*, use similar bounds to analyze and tune a computational fluid dynamics code [17] on Itanium 1. However, we tune for a variety of architectures and matrix domains. Work in sparse compilers (*e.g.* Bik *et al.* [20], Pugh and Spheisman [21], and the Bernoulli compiler [22]) complements our own work. These projects consider expressing sparse kernels and data structures for code generation. In contrast, we use a hybrid off-line, on-line model for selecting transformations.

## 9 Conclusions and Future Directions

Symmetry significantly reduces storage requirements, saving as much as 64.79% when combined with register blocking. Symmetry, register and vector blocking, improves performance by as much as 7.3× (median 4.15×) over a naïve code, 2.08× (median 1.34×) over non-symmetric register blocked SpMV, and 2.6× (median 1.1×) over non-symmetric register and vector blocked SpMM. Moreover, the performance effects of these optimizations appear to be cumulative, making the case to combine these techniques.

Our heuristic, based on an empirical performance modeling and search procedure, is reasonably accurate, particularly for matrices arising from FEM applications. Heuristic chosen tuning parameters yield performance within 85% of the performance achieved from exhaustive search. Additional refinements may improve the accuracy on matrices with little or no block structure.

The performance of our optimized implementations are, on average, within 68% of the performance bounds, smaller

175

than previously observed for non-symmetric SpMV. Additional refinements to explicitly model low-level code generation and employing automated low-level tuning techniques (*e.g.*, ATLAS/PHiPAC [8, 9]) may close the gap.

Sparse kernels may be optimized for other forms of *symmetry* (*e.g.* structural, skew, hermitian, skew hermitian). Symmetric *cache blocking* may mitigate the effects of increasing matrix dimensions and vectors that do not fit in cache, grouping the matrix into large blocks whose sizes are determined by cache size. Optimizations for sparse kernels may also be implemented and evaluated for *parallel systems*, such as SMPs and MPPs [6]. Lastly, performance optimized kernels will be distributed to *application end-users*.

# References

[1] E.-J. Im., K. Yelick, R. Vuduc. SPARSITY: Framework for Optimizing Sparse Matrix-Vector Multiply. *International Journal of High Performance Computing Applications, 18(1), 2004*.

[2] R. Vuduc. Automatic Performance Tuning of Sparse Matrix Kernels. PhD thesis, U.C. Berkeley, Dec. 2003.

[3] B. Lee, R. Vuduc, J. Demmel, K. Yelick, M. de Lorimier, L. Zhong. *Performance Optimizations and Bounds for Sparse Symmetric Matrix-Multiple Vector Multiply*. Technical Report UCB/CSD-03-1297, University of California, Berkeley, November 25, 2003.

[4] R. Vuduc, J. Demmel, K. Yelick, S. Kamil, R. Nishtala, B. Lee. *Performance Optimizations and Bounds for Sparse Matrix-Vector Multiply*. In *Supercomputing*, Baltimore, MD, November 2002.

[5] E.-J. Im. *Optimization the Performance of Sparse Matrix–Vector Multiplication*. PhD thesis, U.C. Berkeley, May 2000.

[6] E.-J. Im and K. Yelick. Optimizing sparse matrix vector multiplication on SMPs. In *Proc. of the 9th SIAM Conf. on Parallel Processing for Sci. Comp.*, March 1999.

[7] E.-J. Im and K. A. Yelick. Optimizing sparse matrix–vector multiplication for register reuse. In *Proceedings of the International Conference on Computational Science*, May 2001.

[8] J. Bilmes, K. Asanović, C. Chin, and J. Demmel. Optimizing matrix multiply using PHiPAC: a Portable, High-Performance, ANSI C coding methodology. In *Proc. of the Int'l Conf. on Supercomputing, Vienna, Austria*, July 1997.

[9] C. Whaley and J. Dongarra. Automatically tuned linear algebra software. In *Proc. of Supercomp.*, 1998.

[10] R. H. Saavedra-Barrera. *CPU Performance Evaluation and Execution Time Prediction Using Narrow Spectrum Benchmarking*. PhD thesis, U.C. Berkeley, February 1992.

[11] A. Snavely, N. Wolter, and L. Carrington. *Modeling Application Performance by Convolving Machine Signatures with Application Profiles*. In *Proceedings of the IEEE 4th Annual Workshop on Workload Characterization, Austin, TX*, December, 2001.

[12] R. F. Boisvert, R. Pozo, K. Remington, R. Barrett, and J. J. Dongarra. The Matrix Market: A web resource for test matrix collections. In R. F. Boisvert, editor, *Quality of Numerical Software, Assessment and Enhancement*, pages 125–137, London, 1997. Chapman and Hall. math.nist.gov/MatrixMarket.

[13] T. Davis. UF Sparse Matrix Collection. www.cise.ufl.edu/research/sparse/matrices.

[14] S. Browne, J. Dongarra, N. Garner, K. London, and P. Mucci. A scalable cross-platform infrastructure for application performance tuning using hardware counters. In *Supercomputing*, November 2000.

[15] R. Barrett, M. Berry, T. F. Chan, J. Demmel, J. Donato, J. Dongarra, V. Eijkhout, R. Pozo, C. Romine, and H. V. der Vorst. *Templates for the Solution of Linear Systems: Building Blocks for Iterative Methods, 2nd Edition*. SIAM, Philadelphia, PA, 1994.

[16] K. Remington and R. Pozo. NIST Sparse BLAS: User's Guide. Technical report, NIST, 1996. gams.nist.gov/spblas.

[17] W. D. Gropp, D. K. Kaushik, D. E. Keyes, and B. F. Smith. High performance parallel implicit CFD. *Parallel Computing*, 27(4), March 2001.

[18] O. Temam and W. Jalby. Characterizing the behavior of sparse algorithms on caches. In *Proceedings of Supercomputing 92*, 1992.

[19] B.B. Fraguela, R. Doallo, and E.L. Zapata. Memory hierarchy performance prediction for sparse blocked algorithms. *Parallel Processing Letters*, 9(3), March, 1999.

[20] A.J.C. Bik and H.A.G. Wijshoff. Automatic nonzero structure analysis. *SIAM Journal on Computing*, 28(5):1576-1587, 1999.

[21] W. Pugh and T. Spheisman. Generation of efficient code for sparse matrix computations. In *Proceedings of the 11th Workshop on Languages and Compilers for Parallel Computing*, LNCS, August 1998.

[22] P. Stodghill. *A Relational Approach to the Automatic Generation of Sequential Sparse Matrix Codes*. PhD thesis, Cornell University, August 1997.

# Session 3C:
# OS/Resource Management

# Robust Resource Allocation for Sensor-Actuator Distributed Computing Systems

Shoukat Ali[†], Anthony A. Maciejewski[‡], Howard Jay Siegel[‡§], and Jong-Kook Kim[◇]

[†]University of Missouri-Rolla
Dept. of Electrical and Computer Engineering
Rolla, MO 65409-0040 USA
shoukat@umr.edu

Colorado State University
[‡]Dept. of Electrical and Computer Engineering
[§]Dept. of Computer Science
Fort Collins, CO 80523-1373 USA
{hj, aam}@colostate.edu

[◇]Purdue University
School of Electrical and Computer Engineering
West Lafayette, IN 47907-1285 USA
jongkook@purdue.edu

## Abstract

*This research investigates two distinct issues related to a resource allocation: its robustness and the failure rate of the heuristic used to determine the allocation. The target system consists of a number of sensors feeding a set of heterogeneous applications continuously executing on a set of heterogeneous machines connected together by high-speed heterogeneous links. There are a number of quality of service (QoS) constraints that must be satisfied. A heuristic failure occurs if the heuristic cannot find an allocation that allows the system to meet its QoS constraints. The system is expected to operate in an uncertain environment where the workload, i.e., the load presented by the set of sensors, is likely to change unpredictably, possibly invalidating a resource allocation that was based on the initial workload estimate. The focus of this paper is the design of a static heuristic that: (a) determines a robust resource allocation, i.e., a resource allocation that maximizes the allowable increase in workload until a run-time reallocation of resources is required to avoid a QoS violation, and (b) has a very low failure rate.*

*This study proposes a heuristic that performs well with respect to the failure rates and robustness to unpredictable workload increases. This heuristic is, therefore, very desirable for systems where low failure rates can be a critical requirement and where unpredictable circumstances can lead to unknown increases in the system workload.*

This research was supported by the DARPA/ITO Quorum Program through the Office of Naval Research under Grant No. N00014-00-1-0599, and by the Colorado State University George T. Abell Endowment. Some of the

## 1. Introduction

This paper investigates the problem of robust resource allocation in a class of heterogeneous computing (HC) systems. An HC system in this class consists of heterogeneous sets of sensors, continuously executing applications, machines, network links, and actuators, and has a number of quality of service (QoS) constraints that must be satisfied during the operation of the system. The system is configured with an initial mapping (i.e., allocation of resources to applications) that is used when the system is first started. The initial mapping attempts to optimize a robustness criterion while ensuring that all QoS constraints will be met for a given initial system workload (i.e., the load associated with the set of initial sensor outputs).

For the particular kind of HC system being considered here, robustness of the initial mapping is an important concern. Generally, these systems operate in an environment that undergoes unexpected changes, e.g., in the system workload, which may cause a QoS violation. Therefore, even though a good initial mapping of applications may ensure that no QoS constraints are violated when the system is first put in operation, dynamic mapping approaches may be needed to reallocate resources during execution to avoid QoS violations.

The general goal of this paper is to delay the *first remapping* of resources required at run time to prevent QoS violations due to variations in the amount of workload generated by the changing sensor outputs. This paper uses a generalized performance metric that is suitable for evalu-

equipment used was donated by Intel and Microsoft.

ating an initial mapping for such "robustness" against increases in the workload (a formal definition of robustness and a general procedure to derive it are given in [3]). The initial mapping problem is defined as finding a static mapping (i.e., one found in an off-line planning phase) of a set of applications onto a suite of machines to maximize the robustness against workload, where robustness is defined as the maximum allowable increase in system workload until run-time re-mapping of the applications is required to avoid a QoS violation. The contributions of this research include quantifying a metric for robustness, designing and developing heuristics for mapping the applications so as to optimize the robustness, and evaluating the relative performance of these heuristics for the intended dynamic distributed HC system. The mapping problem has been shown, in general, to be NP-complete [12, 13, 16]. Thus, the development of heuristic techniques to find near-optimal mappings is an active area of research, e.g., [5, 6, 9, 14, 19, 20, 21].

The remainder of this paper is organized in the following manner. Section 2 develops models for the applications and the hardware platform. Section 3 presents a quantitative measure of the robustness of a given mapping of applications to machines. Three heuristics to solve the initial mapping problem are described in Section 4. The simulation experiments and the evaluation of the heuristics are discussed in Section 5. A sampling of some related work is presented in Section 6. Section 7 concludes the paper.

## 2. System Model

The system consists of heterogeneous sets of sensors, applications, machines, and actuators. Each machine is capable of multi-tasking, executing the applications allocated to it in a round robin fashion. Similarly, a given network link is multi-tasked among all data transfers using that link. Each sensor produces data periodically at a certain rate, and the resulting data streams are input into applications. The applications process the data and send the output to other applications or to actuators. The applications and the data transfers between them are modeled with a directed acyclic graph, shown in Figure 1.

The figure also shows a number of *paths* (enclosed by dashed lines) formed by the applications. A path is a chain of producer-consumer pairs that starts at a sensor (the driving sensor) and ends at an actuator (if it is a trigger path) or at a multiple-input application (if it is an update path). In the context of Figure 1, path 1 is a trigger path, and path 2 is an update path. In a real system, application $d$ could be a missile firing program that produces an order to fire. It needs target coordinates from application $b$ in path 1, and an updated map of the terrain from application $c$ in path 2. Naturally, application $d$ must respond to any output from $b$, but must not issue fire orders if it receives an out-

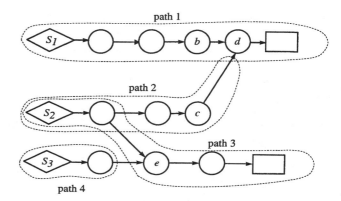

**Figure 1. The DAG model for the applications (circles) and data transfers (arrows). The diamonds and rectangles denote sensors and actuators, respectively. The dashed lines enclose each path formed by the applications.**

put from $c$ alone; such an output is used only to update an internal database. So while $d$ is a multiple input application, the rate at which it produces data is equal to the rate at which the "trigger" application $b$ produces data. That rate, in turn, equals the rate at which the driving sensor, $S_1$, produces data. The problem specification indicates the path to which each application belongs, and the corresponding driving sensor.

Let $\mathcal{P}$ be the set of all paths, and $\mathcal{P}_k$ be the list of applications that belong to the $k$-th path. Note that an application may be present in multiple paths. Let $\mathcal{A}$ be the set of applications.

The sensors constitute the interface of the system to the external world. Let the maximum periodic data output rate from a given sensor be called its output data rate. The minimum throughput constraint states that the computation or communication time of any application in $\mathcal{P}_k$ is required to be no larger than the reciprocal of the output data rate of the driving sensor for $\mathcal{P}_k$. For application $a_i \in \mathcal{P}_k$, let $R(a_i)$ be set to the output data rate of the driving sensor for $\mathcal{P}_k$. In addition, let $T_{ij}^c$ be the computation time for application $a_i$ allocated to machine $m_j$. The "c" in the superscript denotes "computation." Also, let $T_{ip}^t$ be the time to send data from application $a_i$ to application $a_p$. The "t" in the superscript denotes "transfer." Because both machines and communications are assumed to be multi-tasked, $T_{ij}^c$ and $T_{ip}^t$ will depend on the level of multi-tasking (i.e., the number of applications assigned to a machine or the number of communications assigned to a link). See [1] for further details of the computation and communication models used here.

The maximum end-to-end latency constraint states that, for a given path $\mathcal{P}_k$, the time taken between the instant the driving sensor outputs a data set until the instant the actuator or the multiple-input application fed by the path receives the result of the computation on that data set must be no greater than a given value, $L_k^{\max}$. Let $L_k$ be the actual (as opposed to the maximum allowed) value of the end-to-end latency for $\mathcal{P}_k$. The quantity $L_k$ can be found by adding the computation and communication times for all applications in $\mathcal{P}_k$ (including any sensor output or actuator input communications). Let $\mathcal{D}(a_i)$ be the set of successor applications of $a_i$. Then,

$$L_k = \sum_{\substack{i:\, a_i \in \mathcal{P}_k \\ p:\, (a_p \in \mathcal{P}_k) \wedge (a_p \in \mathcal{D}(a_i))}} \left[ T_{ij}^c + T_{ip}^t \right]. \quad (1)$$

Let $\lambda_z$ be the output from the $z$-th sensor in the set of sensors, and be defined as the number of objects present in the most recent data set from that sensor. This system is expected to operate under uncertain outputs from the sensors, requiring that the resource allocation be robust against unpredictable increases in the sensor outputs. The system workload, $\lambda$, is the vector composed of the load values from all sensors. Let $\lambda^{\text{init}}$ be the initial value of $\lambda$, and $\lambda_i^{\text{init}}$ be the initial value of the $i$-th member of $\lambda^{\text{init}}$.

The computation times of different applications (and the communication times of different data transfers) are likely to be of different complexities with respect to $\lambda$. Assume that the dependence of $T_{ij}^c$ and $T_{ip}^t$ on $\lambda$ is known (or can be estimated) for all $i, p$. Then, $T_{ij}^c$ and $T_{ip}^t$ can be re-expressed as functions of $\lambda$ as $T_{ij}^c(\lambda)$ and $T_{ip}^t(\lambda)$, respectively. In general, $T_{ij}^c(\lambda)$ and $T_{ip}^t(\lambda)$ will be functions of the loads from all those sensors that can be traced back from $a_i$. For example, the computation time for application $d$ in Figure 1 is a function of the loads from sensors $S_1$ and $S_2$, but that for application $e$ is a function of the $S_2$ and $S_3$ loads (but each application has just one driving sensor: $S_1$ for $d$ and $S_2$ for $e$). Then Equation 1 can be used to express $L_k$ as a function of $\lambda$.

## 3. Performance Goal

This section quantifies the robustness of a mapping [3]. To simplify the presentation, but without loss of generality, it is assumed that $\lambda$ is a continuous variable, and that computation and communication times are continuous functions of $\lambda$. The change in $\lambda$ can occur in different "directions" depending on the relative changes in the individual components of $\lambda$. For example, $\lambda$ might change so that all components of $\lambda$ increase in proportion to their initial values. In another case, only one component of $\lambda$ may increase while all other components remain fixed. Figure 2 illustrates some possible directions of increase in $\lambda$. In Figure 2, $\lambda^{\text{init}} \in \mathbf{R}^2$

is the initial value of the system load. The region enclosed by the axes and the curve $C$ gives the feasible values of $\lambda$, i.e., all those values for which the system does not violate a given QoS constraint. The element of $C$ marked as $\lambda^*$ has the feature that the Euclidean distance from $\lambda^{\text{init}}$ to $\lambda^*$, $||\lambda^* - \lambda^{\text{init}}||$, is the smallest over all such distances from $\lambda^{\text{init}}$ to a point on $C$. (The symbol $|| \cdot ||$ stands for the Euclidean norm.) An important interpretation of $\lambda^*$ is that the value $||\lambda^* - \lambda^{\text{init}}||$ gives the largest Euclidean distance that the variable $\lambda$ can move in *any* direction from an initial value of $\lambda^{\text{init}}$ without incurring a QoS violation. *This paper defines* $\Delta\Lambda = ||\lambda^* - \lambda^{\text{init}}||$ *to be the robustness of a mapping, against the system workload, with respect to satisfying the QoS constraints.*

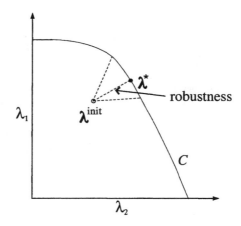

**Figure 2. Some possible directions of increase of the system load $\lambda$, and the degree of robustness.**

A conceptual way of determining $\Delta\Lambda$ is now given. Let $\mathcal{L}_i^{\text{T}}$ be the set of all those $\lambda$ values at which application $a_i$ equals its throughput constraint, i.e., $\mathcal{L}_i^{\text{T}} = \{\lambda : T_{ij}^c(\lambda) = 1/R(a_i)\} \cup \{\lambda : \forall a_p \in \mathcal{D}(a_i), T_{ip}^t(\lambda) = 1/R(a_i)\}$. The "T" in the superscript denotes "throughput." Let $\mathcal{L}^{\text{T}}$ be the set of $\lambda$ values at which *any* application equals its throughput constraint, i.e., $\mathcal{L}^{\text{T}} = \bigcup_{a_i \in \mathcal{A}}(\mathcal{L}_i^{\text{T}})$.

Similarly, let $\mathcal{L}_k^{\text{L}}$ be the set of those $\lambda$ values at which path $\mathcal{P}_k$ equals its latency constraint, i.e.,

$$\mathcal{L}_k^{\text{L}} = \{\lambda : \sum_{\substack{i:\, a_i \in \mathcal{P}_k \\ p:\, (a_p \in \mathcal{P}_k) \wedge (a_p \in \mathcal{D}(a_i))}} \left[ T_{ij}^c(\lambda) + T_{ip}^t(\lambda) \right] = L_k^{\max}\}.$$

The "L" in the superscript denotes "latency." Let $\mathcal{L}^{\text{L}}$ be the set of $\lambda$ values at which *any* path equals its latency constraint, i.e., $\mathcal{L}^{\text{L}} = \bigcup_{\mathcal{P}_k \in \mathcal{P}}(\mathcal{L}_k^{\text{L}})$.

Finally, let $\mathcal{L}$ be the set of $\boldsymbol{\lambda}$ given by $\mathcal{L}^T \bigcup \mathcal{L}^L$. One can then determine $\Delta\boldsymbol{\Lambda}$ by determining the smallest value of $||\boldsymbol{\lambda} - \boldsymbol{\lambda}^{\text{init}}||$ over all $\boldsymbol{\lambda} \in \mathcal{L}$. That is,

$$\Delta\boldsymbol{\Lambda} = \min_{\boldsymbol{\lambda} \in \mathcal{L}} ||\boldsymbol{\lambda} - \boldsymbol{\lambda}^{\text{init}}||. \quad (2)$$

This research assumes that the optimization problem given in Equation 2 can be solved to find the global minimum. An optimization problem of the form $x^* = \text{argmin}_x f(x)$, subject to the constraint $g(x) = 0$, where $f(x)$ and $g(x)$ are convex and linear functions, respectively, can be solved easily to give the global minimum [8]. Because all norms are convex functions, the optimization problem posed in Equation 2 reduces to a convex optimization problem if $T_{ij}^c(\boldsymbol{\lambda})$ and $T_{ip}^t(\boldsymbol{\lambda})$ are linear functions. If $T_{ij}^c(\boldsymbol{\lambda})$ and $T_{ip}^t(\boldsymbol{\lambda})$ functions are not linear, then it is assumed that heuristic techniques could be used to find near-optimal solutions.

# 4. Heuristic Descriptions

This section develops three greedy heuristics for the problem of finding an initial static allocation of applications onto machines to maximize $\Delta\boldsymbol{\Lambda}$. Greedy techniques perform well in many situations, and have been well-studied (e.g., [16]). One of the heuristics, Most Critical Task First (MCTF), is designed to work well in heterogeneous systems where the throughput constraints are more stringent than the latency constraints. The other heuristic, the Most Critical Path First (MCPF) heuristic, is designed to work well in heterogeneous systems where the latency constraints are more stringent than the throughput constraints.

It is important to note that these heuristics use the $\Delta\boldsymbol{\Lambda}$ value to guide the heuristic search; however, the procedure given in Section 3 for calculating $\Delta\boldsymbol{\Lambda}$ assumes that a complete mapping of all applications is known. During the course of the execution of the heuristics, not all applications are mapped. In these cases, for calculating $\Delta\boldsymbol{\Lambda}$, the heuristics assume that each such application $a_i$ is mapped to the machine where its computation time is smallest over all machines, and that $a_i$ is using 100% of that machine. Similarly for communications where one or two of the applications is unmapped, it is assumed that the data transfer occurs over the highest speed communication link, and that the link is 100% utilized by the data transfer. With these assumptions, $\Delta\boldsymbol{\Lambda}$ is calculated and used in any step of a given heuristic.

Before discussing the heuristics, some additional terms are now defined. Let $\Delta\boldsymbol{\Lambda}^T$ be the robustness of the resource allocation when only throughput constraints are considered, i.e, all latency constraints are ignored. Then, $\Delta\boldsymbol{\Lambda}^T = \min_{\boldsymbol{\lambda} \in \mathcal{L}^T} ||\boldsymbol{\lambda} - \boldsymbol{\lambda}^{\text{init}}||$. Similarly, let $\Delta\boldsymbol{\Lambda}^L$ be the robustness of the resource allocation when only latency constraints are considered. Then, $\Delta\boldsymbol{\Lambda}^L = \min_{\boldsymbol{\lambda} \in \mathcal{L}^L} ||\boldsymbol{\lambda} - \boldsymbol{\lambda}^{\text{init}}||$. In addition, let $\Delta\boldsymbol{\Lambda}_{ij}^T$ be the robustness of the assignment of $a_i$ with respect to the throughput constraint, i.e., it is the largest increase in load in any direction from the initial value that does not cause a throughput violation for application $a_i$, either for the computation of $a_i$ on machine $m_j$ or for the communications from $a_i$ to any of its successor applications. Then, $\Delta\boldsymbol{\Lambda}_{ij}^T = \min_{\boldsymbol{\lambda} \in \mathcal{L}_i^T} ||\boldsymbol{\lambda} - \boldsymbol{\lambda}^{\text{init}}||$. Similarly, let $\Delta\boldsymbol{\Lambda}_k^L$ be the robustness of the assignment of applications in $\mathcal{P}_k$ with respect to the latency constraint, i.e., it is the largest increase in load in any direction from the initial value that does not cause a latency violation for the path $\mathcal{P}_k$. It is given by $\min_{\boldsymbol{\lambda} \in \mathcal{L}_k^L} ||\boldsymbol{\lambda} - \boldsymbol{\lambda}^{\text{init}}||$.

***Most Critical Task First Heuristic***: The MCTF heuristic makes one application to machine assignment in each iteration. Each iteration can be split into two phases. Let $\mathcal{M}$ be the set of machines in the system. Let $\Delta\boldsymbol{\Lambda}^*(a_i, m_j)$ be the value of $\Delta\boldsymbol{\Lambda}$ if application $a_i$ is mapped on $m_j$. Similarly, let $\Delta\boldsymbol{\Lambda}^{T*}(a_i, m_j)$ be the value of $\Delta\boldsymbol{\Lambda}_{ij}^T$ if application $a_i$ is mapped on $m_j$. In the first phase, each unmapped application $a_i$ is paired with its "best" machine $m_j$ such that

$$m_j = \underset{m_k \in \mathcal{M}}{\text{argmax}}(\Delta\boldsymbol{\Lambda}^*(a_i, m_k)). \quad (3)$$

(Note that $\text{argmax}_x f(x)$ returns the value of $x$ that maximizes the function $f(x)$. If there are multiple values of $x$ that maximize $f(x)$, then $\text{argmax}_x f(x)$ returns the set of all those values.) If the RHS in Equation 3 returns a set of machines, $G(a_i)$, instead of a unique machine, then $m_j = \text{argmax}_{m_k \in G(a_i)}(\Delta\boldsymbol{\Lambda}^{T*}(a_i, m_k))$, i.e., the individual throughput constraints are used to break ties in the overall system-wide measure. If $\Delta\boldsymbol{\Lambda}^*(a_i, m_j) < 0$, this heuristic cannot find a mapping. The first phase does not make an application to machine assignment; it only establishes application-machine pairs $(a_i, m_j)$ for all unmapped applications $a_i$.

The second phase makes an application to machine assignment by selecting one of the $(a_i, m_j)$ pairs produced by the first phase. This selection is made by determining the most "critical" application (the criterion for this is explained later). The method used to determine this assignment in the first iteration is totally different from that used in the subsequent iterations.

Consider the motivation for the special first iteration. Let $\Delta\boldsymbol{\Lambda}_g$ be the value of $\Delta\boldsymbol{\Lambda}$ at the end of the $g$-th iteration. Before the first iteration of the heuristic, all applications are unmapped, and the system resources are entirely unused. With the system in this state, the heuristic selects the pair $(a_x, m_y)$ such that

$$(a_x, m_y) = \underset{\substack{(a_i, m_j) \text{ pairs from} \\ \text{the first phase}}}{\text{argmin}} (\Delta\boldsymbol{\Lambda}^*(a_i, m_j)).$$

The application $a_x$ is then assigned to the machine $m_y$. It is likely that if the assignment of this application is postponed, it might have to be assigned to a machine where its maximum allowable increase in the system load is even smaller. (The discussion above does not imply that an optimal mapping must contain the assignment of $a_x$ on $m_y$.) Experiments conducted in this study have shown that the special first iteration significantly improves the performance.

The criterion used to make the second phase application to machine assignment for iterations 2 to $|\mathcal{A}|$ is different from that used in iteration 1, and is now explained. The intuitive goal is to determine the $(a_i, m_j)$ pair, which if not selected, may cause the most future "damage," i.e., decrease in $\Delta\Lambda$. Let $\mathcal{M}^{a_i}$ be the ordered list, $\langle m_1^{a_i}, m_2^{a_i}, \cdots, m_{|\mathcal{M}|}^{a_i} \rangle$, of machines such that $\Delta\Lambda^*(a_i, m_x^{a_i}) \geq \Delta\Lambda^*(a_i, m_y^{a_i})$ if $x < y$. Note that $m_1^{a_i}$ is the same as $a_i$'s "best" machine. Let $v$ be an integer such that $2 \leq v \leq |\mathcal{M}|$, and let $r(a_i, v)$ be the percentage decrease in $\Delta\Lambda^*(a_i, m_j)$ if $a_i$ is mapped on $m_v^{a_i}$ (its $v$-th best machine) instead of $m_1^{a_i}$, i.e.,

$$r(a_i, v) = \frac{\Delta\Lambda^*(a_i, m_1^{a_i}) - \Delta\Lambda^*(a_i, m_v^{a_i})}{\Delta\Lambda^*(a_i, m_1^{a_i})}.$$

Additionally, let $T(a_i, 2)$ be defined such that,

$$T(a_i, 2) = \frac{\Delta\Lambda^{\mathrm{T}*}(a_i, m_1^{a_i}) - \Delta\Lambda^{\mathrm{T}*}(a_i, m_2^{a_i})}{\Delta\Lambda^{\mathrm{T}*}(a_i, m_1^{a_i})}.$$

Then, in all iterations other than the first iteration, MCTF maps the most critical application, where the most critical application is found using the pseudo-code in Figure 3. The technique shown in Figure 3 builds on the idea of the Sufferage heuristic given in [19].

***Two-Phase Greedy Heuristic***: This research also proposes a modified version of the Min-min heuristic. Variants of the Min-min heuristic (first presented in [16]) have been studied, e.g., [1, 9, 19, 21], and have been seen to perform well in the environments for which they were proposed. Two-Phase Greedy (TPG), a Min-min style heuristic for the environment discussed in this research, is shown in Figure 4.

***Most Critical Path First Heuristic***: The MCPF heuristic explicitly considers the latency constraints of the paths in the system. It begins by ranking the paths in the order of the most "critical" path first (defined below). Then it uses a modified form of the MCTF heuristic to map applications on a path-by-path basis, iterating through the paths in a ranked order. The modified form of MCTF differs from MCTF in that the first iteration has been changed to be the same as the subsequent iterations.

The ranking procedure used by MCPF is now explained in detail. Let $\hat{\Lambda}^{\mathrm{L}}(\mathcal{P}_k)$ be the value of $\Delta\Lambda_k^{\mathrm{L}}$ assuming that each application $a_i$ in $\mathcal{P}_k$ is mapped to the machine $m_j$ where it has the smallest computation time, and that $a_i$

(1) **initialize**: $v = 2$; $\mathcal{F}$ = the set of $(a_i, m_j)$ pairs from the first phase
(2) **for** $v = 2$ to $|\mathcal{M}|$
(3)      **if** $\mathrm{argmax}_{(a_i, m_j) \in \mathcal{F}}(r(a_i, v))$ is a unique pair $(a_x, m_y)$
(4)          **return** $(a_x, m_y)$
(5)      **else**
(6)          $\mathcal{F}$ = the set of pairs returned by $\mathrm{argmax}_{(a_i, m_j) \in \mathcal{F}}(r(a_i, v))$
(7) **end for**
/* program control reaches here only if no */
/* application, machine pair has been */
/* selected in Lines 1 to 7 above. */
/* $\mathcal{F}$ is now the set of $(a_i, m_j)$ pairs from */
/* the last execution of Line 6*/
(8) **if** $\mathrm{argmax}_{(a_i, m_j) \in \mathcal{F}}(T(a_i, 2))$ is a unique pair $(a_x, m_y)$
(9)      **return** $(a_x, m_y)$
(10) **else**
(11)      arbitrarily select and return an application, machine pair from the set of pairs given by $\mathrm{argmax}_{(a_i, m_j) \in \mathcal{F}}(T(a_i, 2))$

**Figure 3. Selecting the most critical application to map next given the set of $(a_i, m_j)$ pairs from the first phase of MCTF.**

(1) **do** until all applications are mapped
(2)      **for** each unmapped application $a_i$, find the machine $m_j$ such that $m_j = \mathrm{argmax}_{m_k \in \mathcal{M}}(\Delta\Lambda^*(a_i, m_k))$; resolve ties arbitrarily
(3)      **if** $\Delta\Lambda^*(a_i, m_j) < 0$, this heuristic cannot find a mapping
(4)      from the $(a_i, m_j)$ pairs found above, select the pair(s) $(a_x, m_y)$ such that $(a_x, m_y) = \mathrm{argmax}_{(a_i, m_j)\, \text{pairs}}(\Delta\Lambda^*(a_i, m_j))$; resolve ties arbitrarily
(5)      map $a_x$ on $m_y$
(6) **enddo**

**Figure 4. The TPG heuristic.**

can use 100% of $m_j$. Similarly for the communications between the consecutive applications in $\mathcal{P}_k$, where one or two of the applications is unmapped, it is assumed that the data transfer between the applications occurs over the highest speed communication link, and that the link is 100% utilized by the data transfer. The heuristic ranks the paths in an ordered list $\langle \mathcal{P}_1^{\text{crit}}, \mathcal{P}_2^{\text{crit}}, \cdots, \mathcal{P}_{|\mathcal{P}|}^{\text{crit}} \rangle$ such that $\hat{\Lambda}^{\text{L}}(\mathcal{P}_x^{\text{crit}}) \le \hat{\Lambda}^{\text{L}}(\mathcal{P}_y^{\text{crit}})$ if $x < y$.

For an arbitrary HC system, one is not expected to know if the system is more stringent with respect to latency constraints or throughput constraints. In that case, this research proposes running both MCTF and MCPF, and taking the better of the two mappings. The Duplex heuristic executes both MCTF and MCPF, and then chooses the mapping that gives a higher $\Delta\Lambda$.

*Other Heuristics*: To compare the performance of the heuristics proposed in this research (MCTF and MCPF), five other greedy heuristics were also implemented. These included: TPG, Two-Phase Greedy X (TPG-X), and two fast greedy heuristics. TPG-X is an implementation of the Max-min heuristic [16] for the environment discussed in this research. TPG-X is similar to the TPG heuristic except that in Line 4 of Figure 4, "argmax" is replaced with "argmin." The first fast greedy heuristic, denoted FGH-L, iterates through the unmapped applications in an arbitrary order, assigning an application $a_i$ to the machine $m_j$ such that (a) $\Delta\Lambda^*(a_i, m_j) \ge 0$, and (b) $\Delta\Lambda^{\text{L}}$ is maximized (ties are resolved arbitrarily). The second fast greedy heuristic, FGH-T, is similar to FGH-L except that FGH-T attempts to maximize $\Delta\Lambda^{\text{T}}$.

*An Upper Bound*: An upper bound, UB, on the $\Delta\Lambda$ value is also calculated for comparing the absolute performance of a given heuristic. The UB is equal to the $\Delta\Lambda$ for a system where the following assumptions hold: (a) the communication times are zero for all applications, (b) each application $a_i$ is mapped on the machine $m_j$ where $\Delta\Lambda_{ij}^{\text{T}}$ is maximum over all machines, and (c) that each application can use 100% of the machine where it is mapped. These assumptions are, in general, not physically realistic.

## 5. Simulation Experiments and Results

In this study, several sets of simulation experiments were conducted to evaluate and compare the heuristics. Experiments were performed for different values of $|\mathcal{A}|$ and $|\mathcal{M}|$, and for different types of HC environments. For all experiments, it was assumed that an application could execute on any machine.

The following simplifying assumptions were made for performing the experiments. Let $n_s$ be the total number of sensors. The computation time function, $T_{ij}^{\text{c}}(\lambda)$, was assumed to be of the form $\sum_{1 \le z \le n_s} b_{ijz}\lambda_z$, where $b_{ijz} = 0$ if there is no route from the $z$-th sensor to application $a_i$. Otherwise, $b_{ijz}$ was sampled from a Gamma distribution with a given mean and given values of "task heterogeneity" and "machine heterogeneity." (See [4] for a description of the method used in this study for generating random numbers with given mean and heterogeneity values.) The

communication time functions, $T_i^{\text{t}}(\lambda)$, were similarly generated. The mean and heterogeneity parameters for communication times were kept the same as those for the computation times, because communication times in the particular target HC system [2] are of the same order as computation times.

For a given set of computation and communication time functions, the experimental set-up allowed the user to change the values of output rates and end-to-end latency constraints so as to change the "tightness" of the throughput and latency constraints. The reader is directed to [1] for details.

An experiment is characterized by the set of system parameters (e.g., $|\mathcal{A}|$, $|\mathcal{M}|$, application and machine heterogeneities) it investigates. Each experiment was repeated 90 times to obtain good estimates of the mean and standard deviation of $\Delta\Lambda$. Each repetition of a given experiment will be referred to as a trial. For each new trial, a DAG with $|\mathcal{A}|$ nodes was randomly regenerated, and the values of $T_{ij}^{\text{c}}(\lambda)$ and $T_i^{\text{t}}(\lambda)$ were regenerated from their respective distributions.

Results from a typical set of experiments are shown in Figure 5. The first bar for each heuristic, titled "$\Delta\Lambda^{\text{N}}$," shows the normalized $\Delta\Lambda$ value averaged for all those trials in which the given heuristic successfully found a mapping. The normalized $\Delta\Lambda$ for a given heuristic is equal to $\Delta\Lambda$ for the mapping found by that heuristic divided by $\Delta\Lambda$ for the upper bound defined in Section 4. The second bar, titled, "$\delta\lambda^{\text{N}}$," shows the normalized $\Delta\Lambda$ averaged only for those trials in which every heuristic successfully found a mapping. These figures also show, in the third bar, the value of the failure rate for each heuristic. The failure rate or FR is the ratio of the number of trials in which the heuristic could not find a mapping to the total number of trials. The interval shown at the tops of the first two bars is the 95% confidence interval [17].

Figure 5 shows the relative performance of the heuristics for the given system parameters. In this figure, FGH-T and FGH-L are not shown because of their poor failure rate and $\Delta\Lambda$, respectively. It can be seen that the $\Delta\Lambda$ performance difference between MCTF and MCPF is statistically insignificant. The traditional Min-min and Max-min like heuristics, i.e., TPG and TPG-X, achieve $\Delta\Lambda$ values significantly lower than those for MCTF or MCPF. To make matters worse, the FR values for TPG and TPG-X are significantly higher than those for MCTF or MCPF. Even though Duplex's $\Delta\Lambda$ value is statistically no better than that of MCTF or MCPF, its FR value, 12%, is about half that of MCTF or MCPF (23%).

Additional experiments were performed for various other combinations of $|\mathcal{A}|$, $|\mathcal{M}|$, and tightness of QoS constraints, and the relative behavior of the heuristics was similar to that in Figure 5. Note that all communication times were set to zero in Figure 5 (but not in all experiments). Given the formulation of UB, it is expected that if the communication times are all zero in a given environment, then UB will be closer to the optimal value, and will make it easier to evaluate the performance of the heuristics with respect to the upper bound.

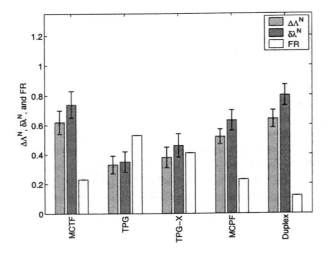

**Figure 5. The relative performance of heuristics for a system where $|\mathcal{M}| = 6$, $|\mathcal{A}| = 50$. Number of sensors = number of actuators = 7. Task heterogeneity = machine heterogeneity = 0.7. All communication times were set to zero. A total of 90 trials were performed.**

## 6. Related Work

A number of papers in the literature have studied the issue of robustness in distributed computing systems (e.g., [2, 7, 10, 11, 15, 18]). These studies are compared below with our paper.

The study in [2] is similar to the one in this paper. However, the robustness measure used in [2] makes a simplifying assumption about the way changes in $\lambda$ can occur. Specifically, it is assumed that $\lambda$ changes so that all components of $\lambda$ increase in proportion to their initial values. That is, if the output from a given sensor increases by $x\%$, then the output from all sensors increases by $x\%$. Given this assumption, for any two sensors $\sigma_p$ and $\sigma_q$, $(\lambda_p - \lambda_p^{\text{init}})/\lambda_p^{\text{init}} = (\lambda_q - \lambda_q^{\text{init}})/\lambda_q^{\text{init}} = \Delta\lambda$. For this particular definition of an increase in the system workload, any function of the vector $\lambda$ is in reality only a function of the single scalar parameter, $\Delta\lambda$ (because $\lambda^{\text{init}}$ is a constant vector). This research does not make this simplifying assumption; as a result, the approach taken in this paper is quite different from that in [2].

Given an allocation of a set of communicating applications to a set of machines, the work in [7] investigates the robustness of the makespan against uncertainties in the estimated execution times of the applications. The paper discusses in detail the effect of these uncertainties on the value of makespan, and how to find more robust resource allocations. Based on the model and assumptions in [7], several theorems about the properties of robustness are proven. The robustness metric in [7] was formulated for errors in the estimation of application execution times; our measure is formulated for unpredictable increases in the system load. Additionally, the formulation in [7] assumes that the execution time for any application is at most $k$ times the estimated value, where $k \geq 1$ is the same for all applications. In our work, no such bound is assumed on the system workload.

The research in [10] considers a single-machine scheduling environment where the processing times of individual jobs are uncertain. The system performance is measured by the total flow time (i.e., the sum of *completion* times of all jobs). Given the probabilistic information about the processing time for each job, the authors determine the normal distribution that approximates the flow time associated with a given schedule. A given schedule's robustness is then given by 1 minus the risk of achieving substandard flow time performance. The risk value is calculated by using the approximate distribution of flow time. Our problem domain considers multiple machines and communication links.

The studies in [11] and [15] explore slack-based techniques for producing robust resource allocations. While [11] focusses on a job-shop environment, [15] focusses on real-time systems. The central idea is to provide each task with extra time (defined as slack) to execute so that some level of uncertainty can be absorbed without having to reallocate. However, it has been shown that when application times are known as a function of the workload, slack is not a good measure of robustness [3].

The work in [18] develops a mathematical definition for the robustness of makespan against machine breakdowns in a job-shop environment. The authors assume a certain random distribution of the machine breakdowns and a certain rescheduling policy in the event of a breakdown. Given these assumptions, the robustness of a schedule $s$ is defined to be a weighted sum of the expected value of the makespan of the rescheduled system, $M$, and the expected value of the schedule delay (the difference between $M$ and the original value of the makespan). However, the problem domain in [18] is different from ours.

## 7. Conclusions

Two distinct issues related to a resource allocation are investigated: its robustness and the failure rate of the heuristic used to determine the allocation. The system is expected to operate in an uncertain environment where the workload is likely to increase unpredictably, possibly invalidating a resource allocation that was based on the initial workload estimate. The focus of this work is the design of a static heuristic that: (a) determines a maximally *robust* resource allocation, i.e., a resource allocation that maximizes the allowable increase in workload until a run-time reallocation of resources is required to avoid a QoS violation, and (b) has a very low *failure rate*. This study proposes a heuristic, called Duplex, that performs well with respect to the failure rate and the robustness towards unpredictable workload increases. Duplex was compared under a variety of simulated heterogeneous computing environments, and with a number of other heuristics taken from the literature. For all of the cases considered, Duplex gave the lowest failure rate, and a robustness value much better than that of TPG or TPG-X. Duplex is, therefore, very desirable for systems where low failure rates can be a critical requirement and where unpredictable circumstances can lead to unknown increases in the system workload.

*Acknowledgments*: The authors thank Sameer Shivle for his valuable comments.

# References

[1] S. Ali. *Robust Resource Allocation in Dynamic Distributed Heterogeneous Computing Systems*. PhD thesis, School of Electrical and Computer Engineering, Purdue University, Aug. 2003.

[2] S. Ali, J.-K. Kim, Y. Yu, S. B. Gundala, S. Gertphol, H. J. Siegel, A. A. Maciejewski, and V. Prasanna. Greedy heuristics for resource allocation in dynamic distributed real-time heterogeneous computing systems. In *The 2002 International Conference on Parallel and Distributed Processing Techniques and Applications (PDPTA 2002), Vol. II*, pages 519–530, June 2002.

[3] S. Ali, A. A. Maciejewski, H. J. Siegel, and J.-K. Kim. Measuring the robustness of a resource allocation. *IEEE Transactions on Parallel and Distributed Systems*, 15(7):630–641, July 2004.

[4] S. Ali, H. J. Siegel, M. Maheswaran, D. Hensgen, and S. Sedigh-Ali. Representing task and machine heterogeneities for heterogeneous computing systems. *Tamkang Journal of Science and Engineering*, 3(3):195–207, invited, Nov. 2000.

[5] I. Banicescu and V. Velusamy. Performance of scheduling scientific applications with adaptive weighted factoring. In *10th IEEE Heterogeneous Computing Workshop (HCW 2001)* in the proceedings of 15th International Parallel and Distributed Processing Symposium (IPDPS 2001), Apr. 2001.

[6] H. Barada, S. M. Sait, and N. Baig. Task matching and scheduling in heterogeneous systems using simulated evolution. In *10th IEEE Heterogeneous Computing Workshop (HCW 2001)* in the proceedings of 15th International Parallel and Distributed Processing Symposium (IPDPS 2001), Apr. 2001.

[7] L. Bölöni and D. C. Marinescu. Robust scheduling of metaprograms. *Journal of Scheduling*, 5(5):395–412, Sept. 2002.

[8] S. Boyd and L. Vandenberghe. *Convex Optimization*, available at http://www.stanford.edu/class/ee364/index.html.

[9] T. D. Braun, H. J. Siegel, N. Beck, L. L. Bölöni, M. Maheswaran, A. I. Reuther, J. P. Robertson, M. D. Theys, B. Yao, D. Hensgen, and R. F. Freund. A comparison of eleven static heuristics for mapping a class of independent tasks onto heterogeneous distributed computing systems. *Journal of Parallel and Distributed Computing*, 61(6):810–837, June 2001.

[10] R. L. Daniels and J. E. Carrillo. $\beta$-Robust scheduling for single-machine systems with uncertain processing times. *IIE Transactions*, 29(11):977–985, 1997.

[11] A. J. Davenport, C. Gefflot, and J. C. Beck. Slack-based techniques for robust schedules. In *6th European Conference on Planning (ECP-2001)*, pages 7–18, Sept. 2001.

[12] E. G. Coffman, Jr. (ed.). *Computer and Job-Shop Scheduling Theory*. John Wiley & Sons, New York, NY, 1976.

[13] D. Fernandez-Baca. Allocating modules to processors in a distributed system. *IEEE Transaction on Software Engineering*, SE-15(11):1427–1436, Nov. 1989.

[14] I. Foster and C. Kesselman, editors. *The Grid: Blueprint for a New Computing Infrastructure*. Morgan Kaufmann, San Fransisco, CA, 1999.

[15] S. Ghosh. *Guaranteeing Fault Tolerance Through Scheduling in Real-Time Systems*. PhD thesis, Faculty of Arts and Sciences, Univ. of Pittsburgh, 1996.

[16] O. H. Ibarra and C. E. Kim. Heuristic algorithms for scheduling independent tasks on nonidentical processors. *Journal of the ACM*, 24(2):280–289, Apr. 1977.

[17] R. Jain. *The Art of Computer Systems Performance Analysis*. John Wiley & Sons, Inc., New York, NY, 1991.

[18] V. J. Leon, S. D. Wu, and R. H. Storer. Robustness measures and robust scheduling for job shops. *IEE Transactions*, 26(5):32–43, Sept. 1994.

[19] M. Maheswaran, S. Ali, H. J. Siegel, D. Hensgen, and R. F. Freund. Dynamic mapping of a class of independent tasks onto heterogeneous computing systems. *Journal of Parallel and Distributed Computing*, 59(2):107–131, Nov. 1999.

[20] Z. Michalewicz and D. B. Fogel. *How to Solve It: Modern Heuristics*. Springer-Verlag, New York, NY, 2000.

[21] M.-Y. Wu, W. Shu, and H. Zhang. Segmented min-min: A static mapping algorithm for meta-tasks on heterogeneous computing systems. In *9th IEEE Heterogeneous Computing Workshop (HCW 2000)*, pages 375–385, May 2000.

# Job Fairness in Non-Preemptive Job Scheduling

Gerald Sabin        Garima Kochhar *        P. Sadayappan
Dept. of Computer Science and Engineering
The Ohio State University
395 Dreese Lab., 2015 Neil Ave.
Columbus, OH 43210–1277, USA
{sabin,saday}@cis.ohio-state.edu
garima_kochhar@dell.com

## Abstract

*Job scheduling has been a much studied topic over the years. While past research has studied the effect of various scheduling policies using metrics such as turnaround time, slowdown, utilization etc., there has been little research on how fair a non-preemptive scheduling policy is. In this paper, we propose an approach to assessing fairness in non-preemptive job scheduling. Our basic model of fairness is that no later arriving job should delay an earlier arriving job. We quantitatively assess the fairness of several job scheduling strategies and propose a new strategy that seeks to improve fairness.*

## 1  Introduction

There has been much research evaluating various non-preemptive job scheduling strategies [1, 11, 17, 4, 20, 7, 6, 18, 20, 22, 12, 19, 2, 15, 16, 9]. These papers focus on the user or system benefits of a particular scheduling policy by studying metrics such as turnaround time, slowdown and utilization. The conclusions drawn from these papers have been slow to make an impact in production schedulers. One of the concerns expressed by site administrators is that even though overall average metrics may improve, some jobs may starve or suffer inordinate delays [17]. For example, it is generally the case that a Shortest-Job-First (SJF) scheduling policy achieves better average job slowdown than a First-Come-First-Serve (FCFS) policy [17], but has worse worst-case behavior. Since short jobs are prioritized over long jobs, there is the possibility of long delays or even starvation for some of the very long jobs.

So system administrators generally prefer some variant of an FCFS policy and are reluctant to implement new policies promoted by simulation-based research studies, because of their concerns over issues such as job starvation and fairness. A standard conservative backfilling scheme with an FCFS priority queue is a well known and well understood scheduling policy. It might be reasonable to expect that non-FCFS scheduling strategies would be "less fair" than FCFS-based approaches because they do not schedule jobs based on their arrival order. However, we are unaware of any published research on quantitatively assessing different non-preemptive scheduling policies in regards to fairness, using real job workloads.

In this paper, we present a trace-based simulation study that quantitatively characterizes different non-preemptive, space-shared scheduling strategies with regard to job fairness. The basic notion of fairness we consider is that a job has been treated unfairly if its start time is delayed because of a later arriving job. We use simulation to determine each job's "fair-start" time - the time at which the job would have started under the same scheduling policy if no more jobs were to arrive (i.e. if all later arriving jobs in the workload trace were removed). This fair-start time is compared with the "actual-start" time for the job, i.e. the job's start time in a simulation involving all jobs in the workload trace (i.e. including all later arriving jobs also). A job is considered to be unfairly treated if its actual-start time is greater than its fair-start time. The study provides some surprising conclusions - that an FCFS scheduling policy is not really always superior in fairness to other policies that have been shown to provide better response times.

This paper is organized as follows. Section 2 gives some background on job scheduling, backfilling and the metrics used. Section 3 describes the simulation setup. Section 4 elaborates on our quantitative approach to characterizing fairness. Sections 5 and 6 examine the relative fairness of different scheduling schemes under the scenarios of perfect estimates of job run times and real user runtime estimates from the workload traces, respectively. Section 7 describes a dynamic conservative scheduling policy that is proposed to enhance fairness. Section 8 summarizes related work and

---

*This work was performed at the Ohio State University, where Garima Kochhar obtained her Masters degree. She is currently a member of the High Performance Computing Clusters Group at Dell Inc.

Section 9 provides conclusions.

## 2 Background

Job scheduling is usually viewed in terms of a 2D chart with time along one axis and the number of processors along the other. Each job can be thought of as a rectangle whose width is the user estimated run time and height is the number of processors required. The simplest way to schedule jobs is to use a strict First Come First Served (FCFS) policy. With such a policy, no job starts before the preceding job has stared. Therefore jobs run in queue order and the scheme is absolutely fair. However, this approach suffers from low system utilization, since processors may be idle even when jobs requiring fewer processors are waiting in the queue. Backfilling [10, 11] was proposed to improve the system utilization and has been implemented in most production schedulers [5, 14]. With backfilling, "holes" are identified in the 2D chart and smaller jobs are moved forward to fill those holes. There are two common variations to backfilling - conservative and aggressive. In conservative backfilling, a smaller job is moved forward in the queue as long as it does not delay any previously queued job. In aggressive backfilling, a smaller job is allowed to move forward as long as it does not delay the job at the head of the queue. The job queues can be sorted by different priority orders depending on the scheduling policy. A simple queuing order is First Come First Serve (FCFS). Other strategies attempt to sort the queue in a way intended to reduce common performance metrics, e.g. Shortest Job First (SJF), which orders the queue by job runtime, or Largest eXpansion Factor (LXF) [7], which orders jobs based on the ratio of their expected response time to their runtime.

## 3 Simulation Setup

We use an event-based simulator to perform our experiments. The simulator takes as its input a subset of a trace from a real supercomputer center, in the Standard Workload Format Version 2.0 [3]. It generates a schedule using the information in the trace, for a specified scheduling policy.

The input traces can be altered to increase the relative load of a system. To increase load, the job run times (and user estimates of the job's run time) are increased by a constant factor for all jobs. For example, increasing the run time of every job by 60% corresponds to a load of 1.6, assuming a load of 1.0 to represent the base case. We use traces with the altered loads to evaluate policies under higher load conditions since the relative merits of alternate scheduling schemes tends to be accentuated under high load conditions. Under low loads, the choice of the scheduling policy may not have much impact on the generated schedule. This is very evident under extremely light loads - all jobs would start as soon as they arrive, irrespective of the

queue ordering policy and whether conservative or aggressive backfilling were used.

For our simulations we use 5000 job subsets of the Cornell Theory Center (CTC) trace and the San Diego Supercomputer Center (SDSC) trace, both obtained from the publicly available workload achieve [3]. We used these two traces because most of the other traces in the archive do not contain information about user estimates of job runtime. The subset traces represent roughly a one month's subset of the original traces. We first ran simulations under the idealized assumption that all users estimated the actual job run times perfectly. Although this is unrealistic and users in practice tend to overestimate their jobs, it is useful to first perform simulations under the idealized assumption of perfect runtime estimates. This allows us to seek insights into inherent differences between alternate scheduling policies, without the variability introduced by inaccurate user estimates of runtime. We then repeated all the simulation experiments using the actual user estimates of job run times from the workload traces. Increasing the load of a trace via runtime expansion, will provably give an identical schedule (in terms of the order the jobs start) as shrinking the interarrival time of the jobs. Another option for increasing the offered load is to duplicate jobs. We have run simulations using duplication as well as runtime expansion. The trends and results from the simulations using both techniques are consistent with each other. We ran simulations for loads varying from 1.0 to 1.8 in increments of 0.2. Due to space limitations, we only present data in this paper for a load of 1.0 (Low Load) and a load of 1.4 (High Load) using runtime expansion, since they are representative of the observed trends and adding the additional data does not provide any additional insight into the problem.

## 4 Fairness

As we have previously stated, fairness has not been much studied in the context of job scheduling. Where as several "performance" metrics such as response time, wait time, slowdown, utilization, loss of capacity etc. have been used to compare job scheduling strategies, a standard metric to evaluate fairness does not exist. In this section we present the approach that we propose to characterize fairness.

In order to motivate our approach, we use an analogy. Consider a deli line, having many workers, each performing only one task. Would it be fair for a person who arrived later to have access to the cashier earlier than the first person in the line? In general, this would be considered unfair. But if the later person is only ordering a soda, and arrives at the cashier in time to have the sale completed before the earlier person's sandwich order is ready, everything is still fair. The later person obtained a resource "out of order", but did not delay the earlier arriving person. This is analogous to a later arriving job that backfills but has no negative effect on the start time of earlier arriving jobs. We will refer to this situation as a "benign backfill".

Informally, how fairly a job is treated depends on whether the job could have run at an earlier time had no later arriving job been serviced. If it is delayed because of a later arriving job, it is considered to be treated unfairly. This is analogous to the deli line, and answers the question "did any later arriving job affect my start time". Based on the previous discussion, benign backfilling is obviously possible, and is in fact the desired result of backfilling. This makes it difficult to measure whether a particular job was delayed by a backfill, or if the backfill was benign. Therefore, simply counting how many jobs leap-frogged ahead of a particular job is not an adequate metric to characterize unfairness.

Instead, to assess fairness, we assign a "fair start time" to each job. The fair start time is used to determine whether a job was treated unfairly. Any job which starts after its "fair start time" is considered to have been treated unfairly. We can also measure how unfair this treatment was by taking the ratio of fair turnaround time to actual turnaround time

Using the fair start time, a Fair Turnaround Time is computed (similar to the job turnaround time)

$$Fair\ TurnaroundTime = Fair\ WaitTime + RunTime$$

The crux to measuring fairness is in determining a fair start time for each job. Conceptually, to determine a fair start time for job j, we remove all jobs whose queue time is greater than that of j. We then perform a complete simulation for all the remaining queued jobs including job j. When j starts in this simulation we have the "fair start time". This schedule is computed using the same scheduling policy implemented by the scheduler under test. The start time of job j under this schedule, where there are no jobs that arrived after j, is called the "fair start time" of j. This gives us the time a job would start, if no later arriving job unfairly delayed it. In the real schedule this allows all jobs arriving after j to backfill as long as they do not delay j.

An issue that warrants further discussion with the above approach for assessing fairness is that a job may move forward significantly through backfilling during the simulation to compute its fair-start time. On the one hand, this represents exactly what would have happened if no later jobs had arrived in the system. But on the other hand, since the job is getting a "lucky" break and moving ahead of earlier jobs, it would seem unreasonable for the job's owner to insist that any later actual start time for the job would represent unfair treatment of the job. Due to this, we also define a second fair-start time for each job, where no backfilling is allowed for the job when computing its fair-start time. With this alternate approach, in the simulation to determine fair-start time, we force the job in question to wait until all previously queued jobs have started. For the remainder of this paper we will call the time obtained with the first option as the "strict" fair start time, and that with the second option as the "relaxed" fair start time, indicative of the fact that the second option delays the fair start time of the job in question.

A consequence of the proposed approach to characterizing fairness is that the fair-start time of a particular job in a trace will generally be different under different scheduling strategies. Consider a job X that arrives at t=60 minutes. It is possible for it to have a fair-start time of 100 minutes and an actual start time of 120 minutes with scheduling strategy A, and a fair-start time of 200 minutes and an actual start time of 180 minutes with scheduling scheme B. Under our model of fairness, the job is unfairly treated by scheduling scheme A, but is fairly treated by scheduling scheme B, although the actual start time for scheme B is much worse. Is this reasonable? We believe that the conclusion regarding fairness is not inappropriate, since fairness and performance are rather orthogonal considerations. Although the user might prefer scheduling scheme A because it provides a better response time, it does not mean that it is a fairer scheme.

Is it possible to use a common "reference" fair-start time for each job when comparing the fairness of different scheduling schemes? We believe not, since the relative performance of the "base scheme" would confound the evaluation. A strict FCFS policy (i.e. with no backfilling) is a completely fair scheduling scheme. So this might seem to be a logical choice for a reference scheme. However, FCFS-no-backfill generates an inherently poor schedule with very high average response time due to low utilization. Therefore, backfilling scheduling schemes would likely result in most jobs having better response times than that with FCFS-no-backfill. This would be true even with schedules that are blatantly unfair. For example, consider an FCFS-aggressive schedule on a trace with many pairs of identically shaped jobs that arrive in close proximity. With most implementations of aggressive backfilling, these pairs of identical, close proximity jobs would start in arrival order, i.e. be treated fairly. Now consider a modified schedule where we swap the positions of the job pairs in the aggressive backfill schedule - i.e. have the later job run in the earlier job's slot and vice versa. This modified schedule is unquestionably unfair with respect to these job pairs. But in the corresponding FCFS-no-backfill schedule, it is very likely that all jobs would have later start times than the FCFS-aggressive schedule. So if we just compare a job's start-time with its reference start-time under the FCFS-no-backfill schedule, all jobs would be considered to be fairly treated for this contrived schedule that is obviously unfair.

Thus it is problematic to use a single reference schedule in comparing fairness of different scheduling schemes. The metric for fairness should be independent of the performance (from the classical user/system metrics) of the scheduling policies. The goal with characterizing fairness is not to determine whether one policy is more effective than another with respect to user/system performance metrics. Fairness and performance are both important in determining the attractiveness of a scheduling strategy, but they are independent factors.

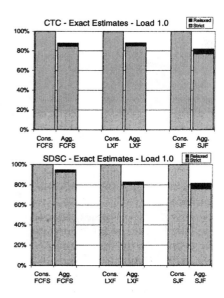

**Figure 1. Fraction of fairly treated load: low load, exact estimates**

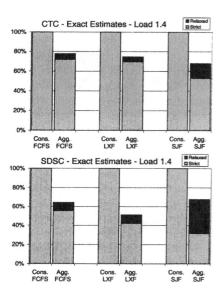

**Figure 2. Fraction of fairly treated load: high load, exact estimates**

## 5   Evaluation With Exact Runtime Estimates

In this section we evaluate several job scheduling policies with respect to fairness. Although in practice users tend to over-estimate job run times, it is often useful to perform evaluations first under the idealized assumption of exact estimates of runtime, before studying the case with actual runtime estimates from the job logs. We consider conservative and aggressive backfilling, with three queuing policies: FCFS, LXF and SJF. For each of these six scheduling strategies, simulations were run with both the CTC-subset trace and SDSC-subset trace. Results are reported for load of 1.0 and 1.4. In comparing how the different scheduling strategies compare with respect to fairness, we show the fractional system load (CPU-hours) that was treated fairly. Not surprisingly, conservative backfilling is far superior to aggressive backfilling. This is the expected result because each job receives its reservation when it arrives at the scheduler. This reservation is fixed, and no other job can push it backwards. Further, if all job run times are assumed to be accurately estimated, no job completes early and no new "holes" are created in the schedule when a job completes.

This is not the case with aggressive backfilling. Here, all jobs do not receive a reservation upon submission to the scheduler. Only the job at the head of the queue of waiting jobs receives a reservation. This allows jobs to run out of order, presenting the possibility for unfairness. Fig. 2 show that greater than 60% of the job load can be treated unfairly. Further, Fig. 1 and 2 show that a higher percentage of the load is being treated unfairly when the load is increased.

Under high load, it may be seen that the difference in

fairly treated load under the strict and relaxed metrics for aggressive backfill is more significant for SJF than for FCFS or LXF. This is due to starvation of long jobs. In very highly loaded situations, long jobs tend to starve when using an SJF policy. Since a newly arriving job is not allowed to receive a relaxed fair start time before the long job starts in the simulation, short jobs end up being assigned a large fair start time that is easily met. This situation does not arise when starvation does not occur. We address this situation in sections 6 and 7.

## 6   Inaccurate Actual user Estimates

We now examine the fairness of the different schemes under the realistic scenario of inaccurate user estimates of job runtime. In these simulations, the scheduler uses the user runtime estimate available in the workload log. However, the simulator causes job termination based on log information about the job's actual runtime. The estimates given by users of supercomputer centers are known to be quite inaccurate [11, 22].

As seen in Fig. 4, aggressive backfilling is fairer than conservative backfilling when real user estimates of job runtime are used, especially when comparisons are made using the strict fair-start time metric. This trend is in surprising contrast to the previous exact estimate scenario. This suggests that the poor user estimates make conservative backfilling an unfair scheme. Conservative backfilling is no longer as fair as when using exact estimates. Suppose that a running job (A) using 16 processors creates a backfill window with 16 processors, that a 24-processor job at the head

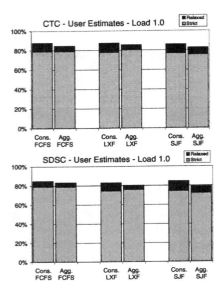

**Figure 3. Fraction of fairly treated load: low load, user estimates**

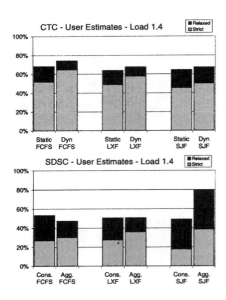

**Figure 4. Fraction of fairly treated load: high load, user estimates**

of the queue (B) cannot use, but a later 10-processor job (C) can. Let A terminate early, releasing its 16 processors. However, since C has already backfilled and used up 10 processors, only 22 free processors are available instead of 32. In this situation, the later arriving job C causes job B to miss its fair-start time. With conservative backfilling this phenomena can also occur in intermediate backfilling stages. This is because once a job moves forward in the schedule, it does not move back. The processors that it has reserved (earlier in the schedule) may prevent a higher priority job from backfilling into that hole at a later backfilling event.

From the graphs in Figures 3 and 4 we see that the above trend is more pronounced when the load offered to the system is higher. In the case of a conservative backfilling scheme we also see that SJF is usually more unfair than FCFS and LXF (with the exception of the SDSC high load case, in saturation), especially in low load situations using the strict fair start time.

It is interesting to note that using an FCFS queuing policy does not always lead to the most fair schedule. This is surprising because we are considering jobs in the arrival order, yet backfilling is causing much of the load to miss it's fair start time.

We see that the results in this section are very different from the case of exact runtime estimates. Conservative backfilling schemes, which were seen to be completely fair under exact estimates, are now seen to introduce a significant amount of unfairness when evaluated under the realistic scenario of inaccurate user runtime estimates. They are actually worse in many instances than the corresponding aggressive backfilling schemes. This motivates us to explore a

**Table 1. Data showing the time needed to perform a scheduling iteration in ms**

|  | **CTC 1.0** | **CTC 1.4** | **SDSC 1.0** | **SDSC 1.4** |
|---|---|---|---|---|
| **Agg** | 0.72 | 0.83 | 0.63 | 0.77 |
| **Static** | 0.97 | 1.62 | 0.72 | 2.55 |
| **Dyn** | 1.00 | 1.87 | 0.77 | 2.48 |

new scheme - dynamic conservative backfilling - which updates reservations as jobs complete, thus attempting to alleviate the unfairness introduced because of the inaccuracy of user estimated job run times. The details of this scheme are presented in the next section.

## 7 Dynamic Reservations

The discussion of the previous section suggested that the poor fairness results for conservative backfilling are a consequence of the backfilling of lower priority jobs, moving ahead of existing reservations for higher priority jobs in the schedule when early job termination occurs. In this section, we propose a "dynamic conservative" backfill scheduling policy, intended to improve fairness. The difference from standard (static) conservative backfilling is that the schedule is recomputed from scratch when using dynamic reservations. Before making a scheduling decision, all reservations are removed and the schedule is then recomputed, considering all jobs in queue priority order. This is intended to address the problem with standard (static) conservative back-

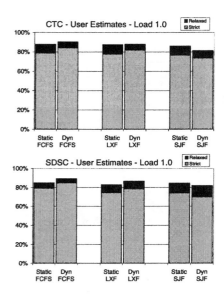

**Figure 5. Fraction of fairly treated load: low load, user estimates**

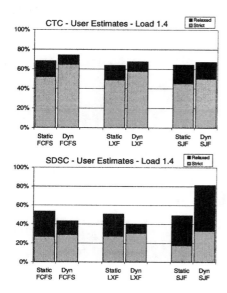

**Figure 6. Fraction of fairly treated load: high load, user estimates**

fill schedules, where a lower priority job can move ahead in the reservation schedule and cause an earlier job to miss its fair-start time. By redoing the reservations at each scheduling event, every attempt is made to prevent a lower priority job from getting and keeping an "unfair" reservation ahead of higher priority jobs. If a lower priority job gets a reservation by backfilling ahead of the existing reservation of a higher priority job, the high priority job will have a chance to move ahead of the lower priority job at every scheduling event reservation, as long as the lower priority job has not started. It is impossible to completely avoid unfairness, because it is not possible to reverse any damage done by lower priority jobs that have already started execution after backfilling, but all unfairness caused by intermediate unfair backfills is prevented. It should be noted that changing from a static conservative scheduling policy to a dynamic conservative scheduling policy does not have a major impact on the time needed to compute a schedule, as can be see from Table 1. Furthermore, the time needed to compute a schedule is on the order of milliseconds, while scheduling iterations are typically on the order of minutes. Therefore, the time to compute a dynamic conservative schedule is not an issue.

Fig. 5 and 6 show that for most cases shown (excluding SJF) the dynamic conservative scheme is fairer than static conservative backfilling. Also, the graphs show that there is less of a difference between the strict and the relaxed fair start time when using a dynamic conservative scheme.

So far we have used the unfairly treated fraction of job load as the means of characterizing unfairness. However, the fractional load that misses the fair start time provides

no information on the extent by which jobs are unfairly delayed. In order to quantify the extent of unfairness to jobs, we next present data on the average per-job miss time for the various schemes: the metric we use is the average per-node miss time. It is obtained by accumulating a processor-width-weighted sum of the extent by which unfairly treated jobs miss their fair-start time, and dividing by the sum of processor widths of all jobs (fairly as well as unfairly treated). The rationale behind this measure is that in regards to unfairness, a ten-processor job that misses by an hour should count ten times as much as a sequential job that misses by the same amount. Further, jobs that complete much earlier than their fair-start time should not decrement and offset the accumulated processor-seconds corresponding to unfairly treated jobs. Finally, to obtain a per-processor measure (so that different sites with different number of processors and different traces can be compared), the accumulated missed processor-seconds is divided by the total number of processors used by all the jobs combined.

$$AveragePerNodeMissTime =$$
$$\frac{\sum_{i \in jobs} max(ActualStartTime_i - FairStartTime_i, 0) * Nodes_i}{\sum_{i \in jobs} Nodes_i}$$

From Fig. 7 and 8 it can be seen that standard (static) conservative backfilling is better than aggressive backfilling, and dynamic conservative backfilling is even better than static conservative backfilling. Considering the different queue priority schemes, SJF performs very poorly using this metric.

Tables 2 and 3 show worst case data for user estimates. These results further show that aggressive backfilling is not a fair scheme, even if many jobs make their fair start time.

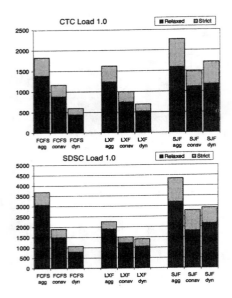

Figure 7. Average miss time (in seconds) per processor: low load, user estimates

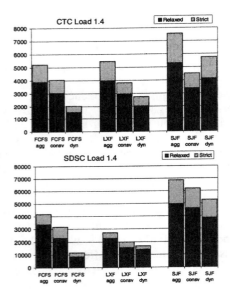

Figure 8. Average miss time (in seconds) per processor: high load, user estimates

The worst case fairness ratio is much worse for aggressive backfilling than for static or dynamic conservative backfilling. This suggests that there are a few users who miss their fair start time very badly with aggressive backfilling, making it a less attractive scheme from the viewpoint of fairness. The table also shows that dynamic backfilling often has a

**Table 2. Worst case fair turnaround rime ratio: Actual user estimates, CTC trace**

| Load/Category | Dyn | Static | Agg |
|---|---|---|---|
| 1.0/Very Short | 2.59 | 4.38 | 32.4 |
| 1.0/Short | 1.78 | 3.38 | 8.51 |
| 1.0/Long | 2.94 | 2.19 | 3.12 |
| 1.0/Very Long | 1.57 | 1.78 | 1.59 |
| 1.4/Very Short | 16.57 | 10.91 | 65.42 |
| 1.4/Short | 2.43 | 6.84 | 8.58 |
| 1.4/Long | 4.90 | 5.64 | 4.48 |
| 1.4/Very Long | 2.25 | 1.51 | 3.07 |

Very Short: < 15 min, Short: > 15 min and < 1 hr
Long: > 1 hr and < 4 hrs, Very Long: 4+ hrs

**Table 3. Worst case fair turnaround time ratio: Actual user estimates, SDSC trace**

| Load/Category | Dyn | Static | Agg |
|---|---|---|---|
| 1.0/Very Short | 6.43 | 7.76 | 8.87 |
| 1.0/Short | 4.06 | 5.72 | 4.07 |
| 1.0/Long | 1.72 | 1.80 | 3.91 |
| 1.0/Very Long | 1.49 | 1.60 | 1.92 |
| 1.4/Very Short | 12.51 | 14.32 | 16.08 |
| 1.4/Short | 12.34 | 4.89 | 5.98 |
| 1.4/Long | 5.09 | 3.21 | 4.10 |
| 1.4/Very Long | 2.01 | 3.86 | 12.79 |

Very Short: < 15 min, Short: > 15 min and < 1 hr
Long: > 1 hr and < 4 hrs, Very Long: 4+ hrs

better worst-case ratio than static conservative, for almost all job lengths.

Overall, the data clearly suggests that the dynamic conservative strategy is best in terms of job fairness. But what about the standard performance metric of average job turnaround time? Fig. 9 and 10 shows the average job turnaround time for the different scheduling policies, under low and high load, for both traces. It can be seen that dynamic conservative backfilling generally has the highest average turnaround time, with aggressive backfilling having the lowest. Standard (static) conservative backfilling fares in between. So we find a trade-off between maximizing fairness and maximizing performance: dynamic conservative backfilling is fairest, but is the worst performer; aggressive backfilling is the least fair, but is the best with respect to performance.

## 8 Related Work

Although there is a plethora of publications on the topic of job scheduling, the topic of fairness in job scheduling has

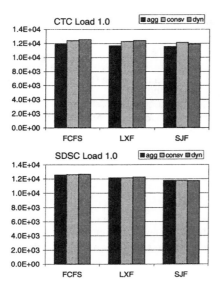

Figure 9. Average turnaround time: low load, user estimates

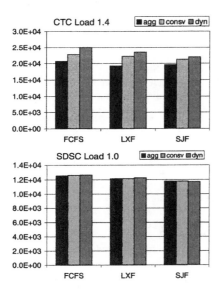

**Figure 10. Average turnaround time: high load, user estimates**

been little explored. The few studies that we are aware of, that consider fairness are [8, 13, 21, 16, 9].

The notion of quantitatively characterizing fairness in job scheduling was addressed in [16, 9]. The approach to characterizing fairness that we present in this paper is similar in spirit to that used in [16, 9], but has differences - our current approach in this paper represents a progressive refinement of the ideas presented in those two theses.

The study in [8] examines a fair share strategy i.e. fairness from a user perspective. At many DOE supercomputer centers, the queue priority policies often involves user fairshare, which is a measure of the aggregate weighted recent system resource usage by each user. The effectiveness of such fair-share based policies are examined in relation to performance metrics. Fairness is examined with respect to users, and not with respect the individual jobs. This is tangential to our work which focuses on fairness with respect to individual jobs.

In [13] , the issue of fairness is examined in an online preemptive scheduler. The authors define a schedule to be lambda-fair if no later arriving job increases the turnaround time of an earlier arriving job by more than a factor of lambda. Their experiments are run with a gang scheduler and the main basis for achieving fairness lies in keeping track of job resource consumption and in preempting a running job if some queued job is in danger of being treated unfairly. In this work, we consider non-preemptive job scheduling, the dominant form of job scheduling deployed at supercomputer centers. While it is feasible to create algorithms in the preemptive scheduling context to achieve guaranteed fairness, it is impossible in the non-preemptive context. However, different scheduling strategies differ in the extent of unfairness they cause. Our work has focused on assessing alternative scheduling strategies with respect to fairness, and to develop a strategy that improves fairness.

In [21], a variety of scheduling approaches are considered in a theoretical queuing framework. The notion of fairness used there is in a statistical steady-state sense - for example, a scheme would be classified as guaranteeing lambda-fairness in that the expected response time of a stream of jobs could be related to some lambda defined as a function of the average load. In contrast, our goal has been to develop an approach to concretely assess the fairness of scheduling schemes using real workload traces.

## 9  Discussion and Conclusion

Fairness is an important issue that has generally been overlooked by research on job scheduling. This is an important reason why system administrators have been reluctant to deploy new scheduling strategies even if simulation studies show benefits in terms of standard user/system metrics. In this paper, we have used a quantitative trace-based simulation approach for evaluating the fairness of scheduling policies. The basic idea which we use to assess fairness is "did a later arriving job delay an earlier arriving job?"

In light of the surprising amount of unfairness in conservative backfilling schedules, we attempted to improve upon the scheme by implementing a dynamic conservative backfilling strategy. The results show that dynamic reservations do improve on fairness over a static reservation policy.

The study generated several interesting results:

- In a real-world setting where user estimates of runtime are often inaccurate, conservative backfilling has a surprisingly amount of unfairness. This is contrary to the common belief that conservative backfilling is extremely fair.

- FCFS backfilling is not necessarily the most fair queue priority policy, even though the jobs are considered for backfilling in arrival order.

- If fairness is a main priority, dynamic reservations can be used to improve the scheduler

## Acknowledgment

We thank the referees for their comments and questions that helped us improve the paper.

## References

[1] S.-H. Chiang, A. Arpaci-Dusseau, and M. Vernon. The impact of more accurate requested runtimes on production job scheduling performance. In *Job Scheduling Strategies for Parallel Processing*. Springer Verlag, 2002.

[2] S. H. Chiang and M. K. Vernon. Production job scheduling for parallel shared memory systems. In *Proceedings of International Parallel and Distributed Processing Symposium*, 2002.

[3] D. G. Feitelson. Logs of real parallel workloads from production systems. URL: http://www.cs.huji.ac.il/labs/parallel/workload/.

[4] D. G. Feitelson, L. Rudolph, U. Schwiegelshohn, K. C. Sevcik, and P. Wong. Theory and practice in parallel job scheduling. In D. G. Feitelson and L. Rudolph, editors, *Job Scheduling Strategies for Parallel Processing*, pages 1–34. Springer Verlag, 1997. Lect. Notes Comput. Sci. vol. 1291.

[5] D. Jackson, Q. Snell, and M. Clement. Core algorithms of the Maui scheduler. In D. G. Feitelson and L. Rudolph, editors, *Job Scheduling Strategies for Parallel Processing*, pages 87–102. Springer Verlag, 2001. Lect. Notes Comput. Sci. vol. 2221.

[6] J. Jones and B. Nitzberg. Scheduling for parallel supercomputing: A historical perspective of achievable utilization. In *5th Workshop on Job Scheduling Strategies for Parallel Processing*, 1999.

[7] R. Kettimuthu, V. Subramani, S. Srinivasan, T. B. Gopalsamy, D. K. Panda, and P. Sadayappan. Selective preemption strategies for parallel job scheduling. In *Proc. of Intl. Conf. on Parallel Processing*, 2002.

[8] S. D. Kleban and S. H. Clearwater. Fair share on high performance computing systems: What does fair really mean? *3rd International Symposium on Cluster Computing and the Grid*, 2003.

[9] G. Kochhar. Characterization and enhancements of backfill scheduling strategies. Master's thesis, Ohio State University, 2003.

[10] D. Lifka. The ANL/IBM SP scheduling system. In D. G. Feitelson and L. Rudolph, editors, *Job Scheduling Strategies for Parallel Processing*, pages 295–303. Springer-Verlag, 1995. Lect. Notes Comput. Sci. vol. 949.

[11] A. W. Mu'alem and D. G. Feitelson. Utilization, predictability, workloads, and user runtime estimates in scheduling the ibm sp2 with backfilling. In *IEEE Transactions on Parallel and Distributed Systems*, volume 12, pages 529–543, 2001.

[12] D. Perkovic and P. J. Keleher. Randomization, speculation, and adaptation in batch schedulers. *Cluster Computing*, 3(4):245–254, 2000.

[13] U. Schwiegelshohn and R. Yahyapour. Fairness in parallel job scheduling. *Journal of Scheduling, 3(5):297-320. John Wiley.*, 2000.

[14] J. Skovira, W. Chan, H. Zhou, and D. Lifka. The EASY - LoadLeveler API project. In D. G. Feitelson and L. Rudolph, editors, *Job Scheduling Strategies for Parallel Processing*, pages 41–47. Springer-Verlag, 1996. Lect. Notes Comput. Sci. vol. 1162.

[15] Q. Snell, M. Clement, D. Jackson, , and C. Gregory. The performance impact of advance reservation meta-scheduling. In D. G. Feitelson and L. Rudolph, editors, *Workshop on Job Scheduling Strategies for Parallel Processing*, volume 1911 of *Lecture Notes in Computer Science*. Springer-Verlag, 2000.

[16] S. Srinivasan. Selective reservation strategies for backfill job scheduling. Master's thesis, Ohio State University, 2002.

[17] S. Srinivasan, R. Kettimuthu, V. Subramani, and P. Sadayappan. Characterization of backfilling strategies for job scheduling. In *2002 Intl. Workshops on Parallel Processing*, August 2002. held in conjunction with the 2002 Intl. Conf. on Parallel Processing, ICPP 2002.

[18] S. Srinivasan, R. Kettimuthu, V. Subramani, and P. Sadayappan. Selective reservation strategies for backfill job scheduling. In *8th Workshop on Job Scheduling Strategies for Parallel Processing*, July 2002.

[19] S. Srinivasan, V. Subramani, R. Kettimuthu, P. Holenarsipur, and P. Sadayappan. Effective selection of partition sizes for moldable scheduling of parallel jobs. In *HiPC*, pages 174–183, 2002.

[20] D. Talby and D. Feitelson. Supporting priorities and improving utilization of the ibm sp scheduler using slack-based backfilling. In *Proceedings of the 13th International Parallel Processing Symposium*, 1999.

[21] A. Wierman and M. Harchol-Balter. Classifying scheduling policies with respect to unfairness in an m/gi/1. In *Proceedings of the 2003 ACM SIGMETRICS international conference on Measurement and modeling of computer systems*, pages 238 – 249, 2003.

[22] D. Zotkin and P. Keleher. Job-length estimation and performance in backfilling schedulers. In *Proceedings of the 8th High Performance Distributed Computing Conference*, 1999.

# Dynamic Load Balancing of MPI+OpenMP applications

Julita Corbalán, Alejandro Duran, Jesús Labarta
CEPBA-IBM Research Institute
Departament d'Arquitectura de Computadors
Universitat Politècnica de Catalunya
Jordi Girona, 1-3, Barcelona, Spain.
{*juli, aduran, jesus*}*@ac.upc.es*

## Abstract

*The hybrid programming model MPI+OpenMP are useful to solve the problems of load balancing of parallel applications independently of the architecture. Typical approaches to balance parallel applications using two levels of parallelism or only MPI consist of including complex codes that dynamically detect which data domains are more computational intensive and either manually redistribute the allocated processors or manually redistribute data. This approach has two drawbacks: it is time consuming and it requires an expert in application analysis. In this paper we present an automatic and dynamic approach for load balancing MPI+OpenMP applications. The system will calculate the percentage of load imbalance and will decide a processor distribution for the MPI processes that eliminates the computational load imbalance. Results show that this method can balance effectively applications without analyzing nor modifying them and that in the cases that the application was well balanced does not incur in a great overhead for the dynamic instrumentation and analysis realized.*

**Keywords**: MPI, OpenMP, load balancing, resource management, parallel models, autonomic computing

## 1  Introduction

A current trend in high performance architecture is clusters of shared memory (SMP) nodes. MPP manufacturers are replacing single processors in their existing systems by powerful SMP nodes (small or medium SMPs are more and more frequent due to their affordable cost). Moreover, large SMPs are limited by the number of CPUS in a single system. Clustering them seems the natural way to reach the same scalability as distributed systems.

MPI and MPI+OpenMP are the two programming models that programmers can use to execute in clusters of SMP.

When application is well balanced pure MPI programs usually results in a good application performace. The problem appears when application has internal static or dynamic load unbalance. If the load unbalance is static, there exists approaches that consist of statically analyze the application and perform the data distribution accordingly. If load unbalance is dynamic, complex code lines to analyze and redistribute data must be inserted in the application to solve this problem. In this case, programmers must spent a lot of time analyzing the application code and their behavior at run time. Moreover, it is not only a question of time, analyzing a parallel application is a complicated job.

In this work, we propose to exploit the OpenMP malleability to solve the load unbalance of irregular MPI applications. The goal is do that automatic and dynamically by the system (resource manager and runtime libraries) without *a priori* application analysis.

One of the key points of our proposal is to be conscious that there are several MPI processes, with OpenMP parallelism inside, that are collaborating to execute a single MPI+OpenMP job. Since resources are allocated to jobs, one processor initially allocated to a MPI process that compounds the job can be reallocated to another MPI process of the same job, as long as they are in the same SMP node, *helping* it to finish the work.

We present a Dynamic Processor Balancing (DPB) approach for MPI+OpenMP applications. The main idea is that the system dynamically measures the percentage of computational load imbalance presented by the different MPI processes and, according to that, it redistributes OpenMP processes among them. We have developed a runtime library that dynamically measures the percentage of load imbalance per MPI process and informs to the resource manager who controls the processor allocation in the SMP node. The resource manager redistributes processors trying to balance the computational power. Moreover, since the resource manager has a global view of the system, it could decide to move processors from a job to another if this would increase the system throughput.

In this paper we present a preliminary study of the potential of this technique. Evaluations have been done assuming that there is only one MPI+OpenMP application simultaneously running and limiting the resource manager to only one SMP node.

In the next section we will introduce the related work. In section 3 the proposed technique is presented and its components explored. In section 4 some results are presented showing the potential of the technique. Finally, section 5 concludes the paper and shows future directions of research.

## 2 Related work

The proposal presented by Huang and Tafti [1] is the closest one to our work. They advocate for the idea of balancing irregular applications by modifying the computational power rather than using the typical mesh redistribution. In their work, the application detects the overloading of some of its processes and tries to solve the problem by creating new threads at run time. They observe that one of the difficulties of this method is that they do not control the operating system decisions which could opposite their own ones.

Henty [2] compares the performance achieved by the hybrid model with the one achieved by a pure MPI, when executing a discrete element modeling algorithm. In that case they conclude that its hybrid model does not improve the pure MPI. Shan et al. [3] compare the performance between two different kinds of adaptive applications under the three programming models: MPI, OpenMP and Hybrid. They observe similar performance results for the three models but they also note that the convenience of using a particular model should be based on the application characteristics. Capello and Etiemble [4] arrive to the same conclusion. Dent et al. [11] evaluate the hybrid model and they conclude it is an interesting solution to applications such as IFS, where exists load balancing problems and a lot of overhead due the cost of the message passing when using a great number of processors. Smith , after evaluating the convenience of an hybrid model[5], believes such a model could contribute with the best from MPI and OpenMP models and it seems a good solution to those cases where MPI model does not scale well. He also concludes that the appropriate model should be selected depending of the particular characteristics of the application. Finally, some authors such as Schloegel et al [12] and Walshaw et al. [13][14] have been working on the opposite approach. They have been working of solving the load-balancing problem of irregular applications by proposing mesh repartitioning algorithms and evaluating the convenience of repartition the mesh or just adjust them.

## 3 Dynamic Processor Balancing

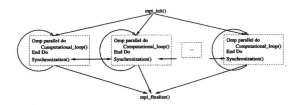

**Figure 1. Basic MPI+OpenMP structure**

MPI+OpenMp jobs are composed by a set of MPI processes that periodically synchronize. Each one of these processes opens loop parallelism, with OpenMP, inside them. Figure 1 shows the main structure of a two level MPI+OpenMP application. Computational loops can consume different time depending on the data each MPI process calculates. If the application is irregular, the amount of data to process can also vary during the application life for each MPI process.

Rather than redistributing data, processor balancing consists of redistributing computational power, that is the number of allocated processors, among collaborative MPI processes. Processor balancing can be done by the application itself or by the system. If the application performs this work itself three main problems arise: **(1)** the system can take decisions that unauthorize application decisions (this problem is also mentioned by Tafti in [6] ), **(2)** the programmer has to introduce a complex implementation to dynamically evaluate the different computational percentages of each MPI group and redistribute OpenMP processes, and **(3)** power balancing could be runtime dependent and not *a priori* calculated. In any case, this is a complicated process that must be done by an expert and that requires to spent a lot of time.

Our proposal is that processor balancing can be done dynamically by the system transparently to the application and without any previous analysis. This approach has the advantage that it is totally transparent to the programmer, applications must not be modified depending neither on the architecture nor the data, and rescheduling decisions are taken considering not just the job but also the system workload. In this paper we will show that information extracted automatically at runtime is enough to reach a good balancing without modifying the original application at all.

Processor balancing is performed in several steps: Initially, the resource manager applies an Equipartition [15] policy. Once decided the initial distribution, each MPI process, while running normally, will measure the time dedicated to execute code and the time spent by communication such as barriers or sending/receiving messages. This computation will be automatically done by a run time library. This information will be sent periodically to the resource manager, who will adjust the job allocation, moving processors from low loaded MPI processes to high loaded MPI processes (from the point of view of computation). This process will be repeated until a stable allocation is found.

Moreover, since the system has a global overview, it can detect situations such as applications that cannot be balanced, reallocating some of its processors to other running jobs where they could produce more benefit. Obviously, the final implementation should include some filters to avoid undesirable job behavior as ping-pong effects.

In next subsections the main elements introduced in the system are presented: the run time profiling library, the modifications done in the OpenMP run time to give support to this mechanism, and the Dynamic Processor Balancing policy (DPB) implemented inside the resource manager.

## 3.1 Profiling libray

Most scientific applications have the characteristic that they are iterative, that is, they apply the same algorithm several times to the same data. Data is repeatedly processed until the number of iterations reaches a fixed value, or until the value of some parameters reaches a certain value (for instance, when the error converges to a certain value). The profiling library exploits this characteristic to accumulate meaningful times for computation and communication usage.

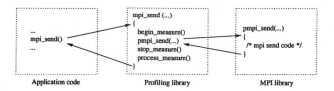

**Figure 2. MPI profiling mechanism**

MPI defines a standard mechanism to instrument MPI applications that consist of providing a new interface that it is called before the real MPI interface[16]. Figure 2 shows how the standard MPI profiling mechanism works. The application is instrumented using this profiling mechanism. When a MPI call is invoked from the application the library measures the time spent in the call and add its to a total count of time spent in MPI calls.

The iterative structure of the application is detected using a Dynamic Periodicity Detector library (DPD) [8]. DPD is called from the instrumented MPI call and it is fed with a value that is a composition of the MPI primitive type ( send, receive, ... ), the destination process and the buffer address. With this value DPD will try to detect the pattern of the periodic behavior of the application. Once, a period is detected the profiling library keeps track of the time spent in executing the whole period.

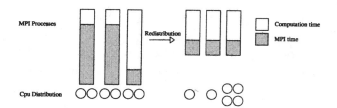

**Figure 3. DPB example**

These two values, mpi execution time and period execution time, are averaged from the values of a few periods and passed to the resource manager for feeding the allocation policy.

## 3.2 Dynamic Processor Balancing policy

The goal of the Dynamic Processor Balancing (DPB) policy is generating a processor distribution where all the MPI process spend the same amount of time in computation, reducing the computation imbalance as much as possible based on the data gathered by the profiling library.

Figure 3 shows an example of how DPB works. In the figure there is one process with more computation time than the others. This produces that global execution time increases as the other two processes ( the ones in the left) are spending their time waiting at the synchronization point ( send/receive, barrier, ... ). In this case, DPB will take the decision of stealing a processor to each of the left processes and give them to the loaded one. This decision makes the two victim processes go slower but the global time is reduced due to a better utilization of the resources.

The policy is not working constantly but is only invoked when the resource manager has collected enough information for the policy to work ( computation and MPI time from all processes of a job ). Each time the policy is invoked it tries to improve one of the processes of the job, the one with highest computation time, by increasing its processor allocation. Those processors are stolen from a victim process. The chosen victim is the process with minimum computation time of those that have more than one processor ( a process needs always at least one ). Once the victim is selected, an ideal execution time for next allocation, $t_{i+1}$ is computed for that process using the formula:

$$t_{i+1}(highest) = t_i(highest) - (t_{mpi}(victim) - t_{mpi}(highest))/2$$

This heuristic assumes that the MPI time of the process that has more computation time is the minimum MPI time that any of the process can have. Then, with this *future* time, the number of cpus that should be moved between the processes to obtain that time based on the last execution time, is calculated as follows:

$$cpus = \frac{cpus_i(highest)*t_i(highest)}{t_{i+1}(highest)} - cpus_i(highest)$$

Some restriction apply to the above:

- No process can have allocated less than one processor. So this means that sometimes the calculated cpus will not be possible. This case is treated giving the maximum possible.

- If the time $t_{i+1}$ is estimated that will be worst that actual time the current allocation is maintained.

Even with this checks, sometimes a decision will lead to an increase in execution time. To recover from those situations the last allocation is always saved. When the policy detects that the last execution time was worst than the previous, it recovers the saved allocation. After there is any change in the allocation, the mpi and period time counters of theprofiling library are reset to zero to obtain new data from the job.

### 3.3 OpenMP runtime library modifications

When the policy decides a new allocation the resource manager informs the processes of their new processor availability, by leaving the new information in a shared memory zone of the process. After that, the OpenMP run time library should adjust it parallelism level ( number of running threads ) to comply with the system policy.

From the application point of view this can be done in two ways:

**Synchronously** Two rendezvous points are defined at the entrance and exit of parallel regions. When an application arrives at a synchronization point, it checks for changes in its allocation and adjusts its resources properly. So, this means that while the application is inside the parallel region could potentially run with more (or less) resources than those actually allocated to it.

**Asynchronously** In this version, the resource manager does not wait for the application to make the changes but it preempts immediately the processor stopping the running thread on it. As this can happen inside a parallel region, the run time needs the capability to recover the work that was doing or it has assigned that thread in order to exit the region. This is not an easy task as available resources can change several time inside a parallel region leading to deadlocks if not carefully planed. Further information of this approach can be found at Martorell et al. [10].

Our implementation, in the IBM's XL library, uses the first approach. As the parallel regions our work focuses are small enough, the time a process does not comply the allocation is so small that there are no significative difference between the results obtained with both approaches. So, the results obtained will be applicable to both scenarios as long as this restriction is maintained.

## 4 Evaluation

### 4.1 Architecture

The evaluation has been performed in a single node of an IBM RS-6000 SP with 8nodes of 16 Nighthawk Power3 @375Mhz (192 Gflops/s) with 64 Gb RAM of total memory. A total of 336Gflops and 1.8TB of Hard Disk are available. The operating system was AIX 5.1. MPI library was configured to use shared memory for message passing inside the node.

### 4.2 Synthetic case

Firstly, a synthetic application was used to discover the potential of the technique presented. The synthetic application includes a simple external loop with two internal loops. Two MPI processes execute the external loop and internal loops are parallelized with eigth OpenMP threads. At the beginning and the end of each external iteration there is a message interchange to synchronize MPI processes. So, it is a simple case that follows the structure shown in Figure 1. This synthetic job allows giving a specific workload to each of the MPI processes, allowing to use different imbalance scenarios.

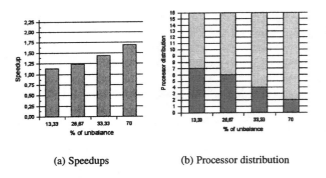

(a) Speedups      (b) Processor distribution

**Figure 4. Results for synthetic imbalances**

Four different scenarios have been tested: 13,33%, 26,67%, 33,33% and 70% of imbalance. The speedups obtained ( the version without the balancing mechanism was taken as reference) are summarized in the Figure 4(a). This results show that the technique is able to cope perfectly with different imbalance situations so it can becoming interesting policy in order to balance, in a transparent way, hybrid applications. It obtains, at least, the same gain that the imbalance that has been introduced. In figure 4(b) the processor distribution that DPB used is shown. There it can be seen that, in fact, the percentage of processor unbalance of the allocation closely reassembles the imbalance of the scenario.

## 4.3 Applications

To verify our approach in a more complex situation we executed some MPI+OpenMP applications in a single SMP node. Each job made use of all the processors of a node distributed among the different MPI processes.

The applications, selected from the NAS Multizone benchmark suite [9], were: BT, LU and SP with input data classes A and B. These benchmarks solve discretized versions of the unsteady, compressible Navier-Stokes equations in three spatial dimensions. BT zone partition is done asymmetrically so an equipartition of the zones (the default approach in all benchmarks) will result in an unbalanced execution. SP and LU on the other hand do the zone partition in a symmetric way so their execution are expected to be balanced.

All the NAS-MZ benchmarks come with two load balancing algorithms, which can be selected at compile time. This algorithms represent slightly more than a 5% of the total code. Their objective is to overcome the possible imbalances from the default equipartion of the zones. First one, maps zones to MPI process trying that all them have a similar amount of computational work. It also, tries to minimize communication between MPI processes by taking into account zone boundaries. Second one, assigns a number a processors to each MPI process based on the computational load of the zones assigned to it from the initial equipartition. Both methods are calculated before the start of the computation based on knowledge of the data shape and computational weight of the application so we will refer to the first one as Application Data Balancing and to the second as Application Processor Balancing. Our objective is to obtain a similar performance to Application Processor Balancing but done in a dynamic and application independent way without modifiying the source code at all.

We have executed the NAS-MZ benchmarks with these two approaches, with DPB, and with a simple equipartition version, which has been used as reference value for the calculation of the speedup in the following sections.

### 4.3.1  Irregular zones (BT-MZ)

The situation that the data domain is irregular either in its geometry or in its computational load is very frequent on scientific codes mainly because of the nature of the entities being modelled ( weather forecasting, ocean flow modelling, ... ). So the BT-MZ benchmark will evaluation will help to see if DPB can help to improve those codes.

Figure 5(a) shows the speedup for the different load balancing strategies with data class A. As it can be seen DPB is closely tied with the Application Processor Balancing algorithm. For a two MPI processes execution, DPB gets some more performance ( 1,26 vs 1,18 of speedup), with four MPI

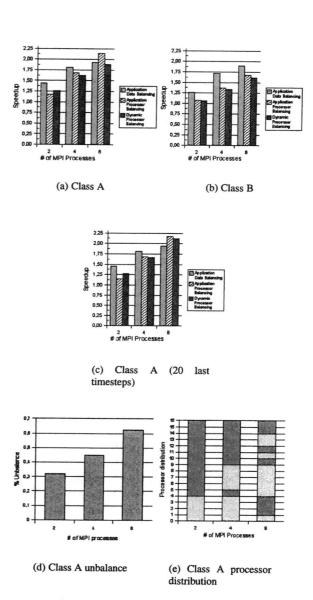

(a) Class A          (b) Class B

(c)  Class  A  (20  last timesteps)

(d) Class A unbalance     (e) Class A processor distribution

**Figure 5. Results for BT-MZ**

processes DPB is just a 4% behind. For the eight processes execution this difference is really high (14%). This is due to the warmup time of DPB ( time to detect the application structure, obtain the first measures, find a stable allocation, . . . ). So, for longer executions DPB will be as good option as the Application Processor Balacing algorithm. This hypothesis is confirmed if we take a look at the speedups obtained for the last 20 time steps of the benchmark ( figure 5(c)). There, not only the difference for the eight processes case decreases until a 2%, that is due to the dynamic profiling, but also the difference in the two processes case is bigger. For further confirmation, if we look the speedups of the data class B, which have a longer execution time, we can see that the differences between the two method remain similar.

When comparing with Application Data Balancing, this method obtains better performance in most cases. This is because data distribution allows finer movements than processor distribution. Even so, for the class A with 8 MPI processes both processor balancing techniques obtain better speedup (see figure 5(c)) so it is not a clear option in all the situations and worst of all it can not be performed transparently as DPB.

In figure 5(d) shows the processor distribution that DPB chooses for the different MPI processes configuration for data class A. It can be seen that the distributions found by the algorithm are quite complex.

### 4.3.2  Regular domains (LU-MZ, SP-MZ)

Evaluating a benchmark that is already balanced will show the overheads introduced by the profiling and constant monitoring of DPB.

Figure 6 shows the different speedups obtained for the LU-MZ and for the SP-MZ benchmarks for both, data class A and B. Surprisingly enough, DPB seems to improve the execution for both data classes of the LU-MZ benchmark with two MPIs (1,13 of speedup) when the benchmark was supposed not be unbalanced. Actually, the improvement is not due to a better processor distribution but because the implementation of the original benchmark spent to much time yielding and that affected their execution time. The same thing happens for the two MPIs case of the SP-MZ class B (see figure 6(d)) but here the reference execution was not affected by the yielding effect and the other seem to scale down.

If we concentrate on the other cases, we can see that none of the methods gets an improvement. And most important we can see that DPB doesn't have an important impact on their executions (a maximum of a 3% overhead) which it means it has a fairly good instrumentation method that it is almost negligible.

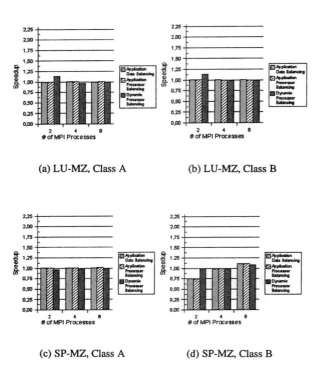

(a) LU-MZ, Class A          (b) LU-MZ, Class B

(c) SP-MZ, Class A          (d) SP-MZ, Class B

**Figure 6. Speedups for LU-MZ and SP-MZ**

### 4.4  Effect of node size

We have evaluated the effect in the improvement achieved by DPB when varying the node size. Results presented in the previous sub-sections have been calculated with a single node with 16 cpus. Since we don't have a distributed version of the resource manager, we have performed some experiments to give an idea about the reduction in the speedup introduced when node size are small.

These experiments consist of the concurrent execution of two and four instances of the resource manager, each one managing a subset of the node: eight processors when sim-

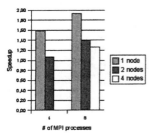

**Figure 7. BT-MZ Class A for different nodes sizes**

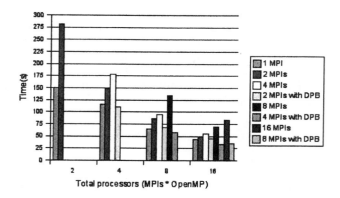

**Figure 8. BT Class A. MPI vs MPI+OpenMP**

ulating two nodes and four processors when simulating four nodes.

Figure 4.4 shows the speedup achieved by BT.A when executing in 1 node with 16 cpus, 2 nodes with eight cpus each one, and 4 nodes with 4 cpus. In all the experiments there are 16 cpus. The speedup is calculated comparing with the execution time of BT.A without load balancing.

With small nodes, DPB has less chances to move processors between MPI processes and this results in a reduction in the speedup. For instance, in the case of 8 mpi processes, the speedup goes from 1.9 when running in a node with 16 cpus to 1.3 when executing in 4 nodes (2 mpi processes per node).

## 4.5   Comparing MPI vs MPI+OpenMP

In figure 4.5 is shown a comparative of the execution times for different processor availability of combinations of MPI and Openmp: ranging from pure OpenMP ( only one MPI process ) to pure MPI ( only one OpenMP in each ) going throught hybrid combinations. There it can be seen than using more MPIs only increases the execution time while using just one gets the lowest time. When our dynamic policy is used even lowest execution times are achieved with hybrid configurations.

These results show point that when an application is unbalanced is better to use and hybrid approach that allows to overcome the unbalance either with a hardcoded algorithm, as those shown in 4.3.1, or ,even better, automatically like the proposal of this paper. When the application is well balanced, on the other hand, it may be worth it to use a pure MPI approach [4].

## 5   Conclusions and Future work

This papers investigates the feasibility of having a Dynamic Processors Balancing algorithm that helps to reduce the imbalance presented on MPI+OpenMP applications. Our proposal works at the system level changing the resource allocation of the jobs for improving their utilization and reducing total execution time. We have shown, as with a simple low overhead profiling mechanism, enough information can be collected to perform this task properly. In fact, results show close performance (sometimes even better) with some other application specific handcrafted techniques. Those other techniques require a good knowledge of the data geometry of the application and spending a considerable effort in analyzing and tuning of the applications. Also, the fact that our proposal does not need any modification in the application combined with the low impact that has on already balanced applications, because of its low overhead, makes it a good candidate for a default system component.

Future work will follow three directions. First of all, the developed technique will be used to evaluate a broader range of benchmarks and applications, and also evaluate them in bigger configurations. The second line of work it is to expand the current platform for using it for workloads. This means researching policies to maximize some system metric (like throughput) as well as application specific metrics. This new platform will be distributed, dealing with jobs that span through more than one SMP node. And the last line will be trying to get better resource usage by allowing processor sharing between processes. To be able to achieve that coordination between the three levels (system,MPI and OpenMP) will required.

## 6   Acknowledgements

This work has been supported by the Spanish Ministry of Education under grant CYCIT TIC2001-0995-C02-01, the ESPRIT Project POP (IST -2001-33071) and by the IBM CAS Program. The research described in this work has been developed using the resources of the European Center for Parallelism of Barcelona (CEPBA).

## References

[1] W. Huang and D. Tafti. "A parallel Computing Framework for Dynamic Power Balancing in Adaptive Mesh Refinement Applications". Proceedings of Parallel Computational Fluid Dynamics 99.

[2] D.S. Henty. "Performance of Hybrid Message-Passing and Shared-Memory Parallelism for Discrete Element Modeling". Proc. of the Supercomputing (SC). 2000.

[3] H. Shan, J.P. Shingh, L. Oliker and R. Biswas. "A comparison of Three Programming Models for Adaptive Applications on the Origin2000". Proc. Of Supercomputing (SC) 2000.

[4] F. Cappello and D. Etiemble. "MPI versus MPI+OpenMP on the IBM SP for the NAS Benchmarks". Proc. of the Supercomputing (SC). 2000

[5] L.A. Smith. "Mixed Mode MPI/OpenMP Programming" . Edimburg Parallel Computing Centre, Edinburgh, EH9 3JZ

[6] D.K.Tafti. "Computational Power Balancing, Help for the overloaded processor". http://www.me.vt.edu/people/faculty/tafti.html

[7] D.K. Tafti, G. Wang. "Application of Embedded Parallelism to Large Scale Computations of Complex Industrial Flows". http://www.me.vt.edu/people/faculty/tafti.html

[8] F. Freitag, J. Corbalan, J. Labarta. "A Dynamic Periodicity Detector: Application to Speedup Computation". IPDPS 2001.

[9] R.F. Van der Wijngaart, H.Jin, "NAS Parallel Benchmarks, Multi-Zone Versions". NAS Technical Report NAS-03-010. July 2003.

[10] X. Martorell, J. Corbalan, D. Nikolopoulos, N. Navarro, E. Polychronopoulos, T. Papatheodorou and J. Labarta. "A Tool to Schedule Parallel Applications on Multiprocessors: the NANOS CPU Manager". Proc. of the 6th Workshop on Job Scheduling Strategies for Parallel Processing (JSSPP'2000), in conjunction with the 14th IEEE International Parallel and Distributed Processing Symposium (IPDPS'2000), May 2000.

[11] D. Dent, G. Mozdzynski, D. Salmond and B. Carruthers. "Implementation and Performance of OpenMP in ECMWF's IFS Code". Fifth European SGI/Cray MPP Workshop, September 1999.

[12] K. Schloegel, G. Karypis and V. Kumar. "Parallel multilevel algorithms for multi-constraint graph partitioning". Technical Report #99-031. 1999. University of Minnesota, Minneapolis.

[13] C. Walshaw, A. Basermann, J. Fingberg, G. Lonsdale, B. Maerten."Dynamic multi-partitioning for parallel finite element applications". In Proc. of Parallel Computing: Fundamentals & Applications, Proceedings of the International Conference ParCo'99. August 1999. Imperial College Press. pages 259-266, 2000.

[14] C. Walshaw and M. Cross. "Dynamic Mesh Partitioning and Load-Balancing for Parallel Computational Mechanics Codes". In Computational Mechanics Using High Performance Computing, pages 79-94. Saxe-Coburg Publications, Stirling, 2002.

[15] C. McCann, R. Vaswani, and J. Zahorjan. "A dynamic processor allocation policy for multiprogrammed, shared memory multiprocessors". ACM Transactions on Computer Systems, 11(2):146–178, May 1993.

[16] Message Passing Interface Forum. "The MPI message-passing interface standard". http://www.mpiforum.org, May 1995.

# Keynote Address

# Taming Lambda's for Applications:
# The OptIPuter System Software

Andrew A. Chien

*Computer Science and Engineering
and Center for Networked Systems
University of California, San Diego*

Dense wavelength-division multiplexing (DWDM), dark fiber, and low-cost optical switches provide the technological capability for private, high bandwidth communication in shared distributed computing environments. These emerging environments are often called lambda grids. However, at present, knowledge and control cutting across many traditional systems and network abstractions are needed for applications to benefit from these dynamic optical connections. This hurdle is dauntingly complex and error prone, and too great to surmount for most applications.

We are developing application abstractions called Distributed Virtual Computers (DVC), which simplify application use of dynamic optical resources. DVC descriptions naturally express communication and computation resource requirements, enabling coordinated resource binding. In addition, DVCs provide shared namespace provides a natural vehicle for incorporating a range of novel capabilities, including novel transport protocols which expose and exploit the capabilities DWDM environment, including efficient multi-point to point (GTP), optical multicast, real-time communication, and fast point to point transports. DVCs also provide a convenient model for integrating a wide array of network-attached instruments and storage.

We will describe initial experience with DVCs and how they provide an integrating architecture for lambda grids.

The OptIPuter project is a large multi-institutional project led by Larry Smarr at the University of California, San Diego (UCSD) and Tom DeFanti at the University of Illinois at Chicago (UIC). Other software efforts include optical signaling software, visualization, distributed configuration management, and two driving applications involving petabytes of data (in conjunction with the Biomedical Informatics Research Network and the Scripps Institute of Oceanography). We are also constructing a high-speed OptIPuter testbed. www.optiputer.net

Supported in part by the National Science Foundation under awards NSF EIA-99-75020 Grads and NSF Cooperative Agreement ANI-0225642 (OptIPuter), NSF CCR-0331645 (VGrADS), NSF ACI-0305390, and NSF Research Infrastructure Grant EIA-0303622. Support from Hewlett-Packard, BigBangwidth, Microsoft, and Intel is also gratefully acknowledged.

# Session 4A:
# Architecture I

# The $k$-valent Graph: A New Family of Cayley Graphs for Interconnection Networks

Sun-Yuan Hsieh* and Tien-Te Hsiao
Department of Computer Science and Information Engineering
National Cheng Kung University, Tainan, Taiwan

## Abstract

*This paper introduces a new family of Cayley graphs, named the k-valent graphs, for building interconnection networks. It includes the trivalent Cayley graphs (Vadapalli and Srimani, 1995) as a subclass. These new graphs are shown to be regular with the node-degree k, to have logarithmic diameter subject to the number of nodes, and to be k-connected as well as maximally fault tolerant. We also propose a shortest path routing algorithm and investigate some algebraic properties like cycles or cliques embedding.*

## 1 Introduction

Design of interconnection networks is an important issue of the parallel processing or distributed system. The choice of network topologies significantly determines the performance of these kinds of systems. Many such networks have been proposed in the literature [1,2,4–11,13,15,16,19,21]. The network structure is often modelled as an undirected graph, in which the vertices correspond to the processors and the edges correspond to the communication channels. Several fundamental properties of an interconnection network are its node degree, connectivity, diameter, symmetry, and fault tolerance [24]. They will be discussed for measuring the new networks introduced in this paper.

There is a class of graphs called Cayley graphs which is very suitable for designing interconnection networks [2]. This class is based on permutation groups and includes quite a few well-known families of graphs like hypercubes [4], star graphs [1, 2], pancake graphs [2], etc. All of these graphs are regular, i.e., each node has the same degree and symmetric. In the above networks, however, the node degree, a number of neighbors for each node, increases with the size of the graph. It makes the use of these graphs prohibitive for the networks with large number of nodes.

Therefore, the fixed node degree networks are concerned in the point view of VLSI (Very Large Scale Integration) implementation [16]. There are applications where the computing nodes in the network can have only a fixed number of I/O ports [5].

P. Vadapalli and P. K. Srimani [19] proposed the trivalent Cayley graphs with the fixed node-degree 3. This class of graphs was shown to be regular, to have logarithmic diameter, and to be maximally fault-tolerant. Several topological properties and shortest path routing algorithm were discussed in [14, 18–20, 22]. However, both the node-degree and the node-connectivity of trivalent Cayley graphs are limited by 3. It is weakness that makes the network disconnected easily when more faulty nodes appear with large size of the graph. Besides, higher connectivity is desirable because of its lower contention for communication resources. So we generalize the work of [19] to propose a new family of Cayley graphs, named the $k$-valent graphs $G_{k,n}$. It possesses a flexible property that the degree of each node is fixed by $k$ without regarding the size of the network. In fact, the trivalent Cayley graphs are in the subclass of the $k$-valent graphs. The $k$-valent graphs are also maximally fault tolerant ($k$-connected) and have logarithmic diameter.

This paper is organized as follows: In the next section, the $k$-valent graphs are introduced, including the definition, basic properties and the relation to the trivalent Cayley graphs. In Section 3, a shortest path routing algorithm is proposed to establish the diameter. Some topological properties, embeddings and node-connectivity (fault tolerance), are discussed in Section 4 and Section 5 respectively.

## 2 The $k$-valent Graph

**Definition 1.** A *$k$-valent graph* $G_{k,n}$ is an undirected graph with $N = n(k-1)^n$ vertices for any integers $n \geq 2$ and $k \geq 3$. Each node $v$ of $G_{k,n}$ has the form $s_0 s_1 \ldots s_{m-1} \tilde{s}_m s_{m+1} \ldots s_{n-1}$ corresponding to a string of $n$ symbols selected from $\{0, 1, \ldots, k-2\}$ such that exactly one symbol $\tilde{s}_m$ is in *marked* form and the others are in *unmarked* form. We sometimes use $v^m$ for representing a node

*Corresponding author. Email: hsiehsy@mail.ncku.edu.tw

$v$ with the marked symbol on position $m$, and thus the notations $v^m$ and $v$ are used interchangeably throughout this paper. Let $s_i^* = s_i$ or $\tilde{s}_i$. Each edge is of the type $(v, \delta(v))$, where $\delta \in \{f, f^{-1}, g_1, g_2, \ldots, g_{k-2}\}$ is a *generator* defined as follows:

- $f(u^m) = v^{(m-1) \bmod n}$, where $u^m = s_0^* s_1^* \ldots s_{n-1}^*$, $v^{(m-1) \bmod n} = s_1^* s_2^* \ldots s_{n-1}^* \alpha^*$ and $\alpha = (s_0 + 1) \bmod (k-1)$;

- $f^{-1}(u^m) = v^{(m+1) \bmod n}$, where $u^m = s_0^* s_1^* \ldots s_{n-1}^*$, $v^{(m+1) \bmod n} = \beta^* s_0^* s_1^* \ldots s_{n-2}^*$ and $\beta = (s_{n-1} - 1) \bmod (k-1)$;

- $g_i(u^m) = v^m$, where $u^m = s_0^* s_1^* \ldots s_{n-1}^*$, $v^m = s_0^* s_1^* \ldots s_{n-2}^* \gamma^*$ and $\gamma = (s_{n-1} + i) \bmod (k-1)$ for $1 \le i \le k-2$.

For example, $\{\tilde{0}0, \tilde{0}1, \tilde{1}0, \tilde{1}1, 0\tilde{0}, 0\tilde{1}, 1\tilde{0}, 1\tilde{1}\}$ is the node set of $G_{3,2}$; $f(\tilde{0}0) = 0\tilde{1}$; $g_1(\tilde{0}0) = \tilde{0}1$. Since $f$ (respectively $f^{-1}$) is the inverse of $f^{-1}$ (respectively $f$), and the inverse of $g_i$ equals $g_{k-i-1}$ for $1 \le i \le k-2$, the edges of $G_{k,n}$ are bidirectional. Moreover, according to Definition 1, it is clear that $G_{k,n}$ belongs to Cayley graphs.

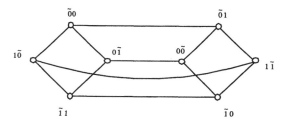

**Figure 1. An example graph $G_{3,2}$.**

P. Vadapalli and P. K. Srimani [19] defined the *trivalent Cayley graphs* $TC_n$ as the following definition.

**Definition 2.** [19] Each node of a *trivalent Cayley graph* $TC_n$, $n \ge 2$, corresponds to a circular permutation in lexicographic order of $n$ symbols, $t_1, t_2, \ldots, t_n$, complemented or uncomplemented. The node set of $TC_n$ is defined as $V(TC_n) = \{t_j^* t_{j+1}^* \ldots t_n^* t_1^* t_2^* \ldots t_{j-1}^* | t_i^* = t_i$ or $\bar{t}_i$ for all $i, j \in \{1, \ldots, n\}\}$. Let $\bar{\bar{j}} = j$. Each edge is of the type $(v, \delta(v))$, where $\delta \in \{f_{TC}, f_{TC}^{-1}, g_{TC}\}$, defined in the following way:
$$f_{TC}(t_j^* t_{j+1}^* \ldots t_n^* t_1^* t_2^* \ldots t_{j-1}^*) = t_{j+1}^* \ldots t_n^* t_1^* t_2^* \ldots t_{j-1}^* \bar{t}_j^*$$
$$f_{TC}^{-1}(t_j^* t_{j+1}^* \ldots t_n^* t_1^* t_2^* \ldots t_{j-1}^*) = \bar{t}_{j-1}^* t_j^* \ldots t_n^* t_1^* t_2^* \ldots t_{j-2}^*$$
$$g_{TC}(t_j^* t_{j+1}^* \ldots t_n^* t_1^* t_2^* \ldots t_{j-1}^*) = t_j^* t_{j+1}^* \ldots t_n^* t_1^* t_2^* \ldots \bar{t}_{j-1}^*$$

Two graphs $G_1$ and $G_2$ are *isomorphic* if there is a one-to-one function $\pi$ from $V(G_1)$ onto $V(G_2)$ such that $(u, v) \in E(G_1)$ if and only if $(\phi(u), \phi(v)) \in E(G_2)$ [23].

**Theorem 1.** *$G_{3,n}$ and $TC_n$ are isomorphic.*

*Proof.* Let $t_1, t_2, \ldots, t_n$ be a lexicographic order of $n$ symbols for $TC_n$. For each node $s_0 s_1 \ldots s_{m-1} \tilde{s}_m s_{m+1} \ldots s_{n-1}$ of $G_{3,n}$, where $s_i \in \{0, 1\}$, we define a function $\pi$ mapping $V(G_{3,n})$ to $V(TC_n)$ as follows:

$$\pi(s_0 s_1 \ldots s_{m-1} \tilde{s}_m s_{m+1} \ldots s_{n-1}) = t'_{n-m+1} t'_{n-m+2} \ldots t'_n t'_1 \ldots t'_{n-m}, \quad (1)$$

where $t'_i = t_i$ if $s_{(m+i-1) \bmod n} = 0$ and $t'_i = \bar{t}_i$ if $s_{(m+i-1) \bmod n} = 1$, for $i \in \{1, \ldots, n\}$. The function $\pi$ is obviously one-to-one and onto. And we get $f = \pi^{-1} \circ f_{TC} \circ \pi$; $f^{-1} = \pi^{-1} \circ f_{TC}^{-1} \circ \pi$; $g_1 = \pi^{-1} \circ g_{TC} \circ \pi$. It is checked that $\pi(u)$ and $\pi(v)$ are adjacent in $TC_n$ if and only if $(u, v)$ path exists for all $u$ and $v$ in $G_{3,n}$. $\square$

## 3  Shortest path routing and diameter

A graph is said to be *simple* if it contains no loops and multiple edges. A *path* is a simple graph whose vertices can be ordered so that two vertices are adjacent if and only if they are consecutive in the list. The distance of $u$ and $v$ is defined by the length of a shortest $(u, v)$ path. Since $G_{k,n}$ is a Cayley graph, it is node-symmetric [2], that is, the graph viewed from any vertex is the same. The distance between two arbitrary nodes is equal to the distance between some node (source node) and the identity node ($\tilde{0}0 \ldots 0$) by suitably renaming the symbols representing the strings. Thus, our shortest path routing algorithm aims at constructing a shortest path from a given source node to the identity node. The following definitions are prepared for calculating the length of the shortest path. For a given node $v = s_0^* s_1^* \ldots s_{n-1}^*$, let $v[i] = s_i^*$, $0 \le i \le n-1$ and $v[i, j] = s_i^* s_{i+1}^* \ldots s_j^*$, $0 \le i < j \le n-1$. A *0-substring* is a continued substring whose symbols are all zero.

**Definition 3.** Consider an arbitrary node $v = s_0 s_1 \ldots s_{m-1} \tilde{s}_m s_{m+1} \ldots s_{n-1}$ in $G_{k,n}$. The marked symbol $\tilde{s}_m$ divides the string into two parts: the *left part* $s_0 s_1 \ldots s_{m-1}$ and the *right part* $\tilde{s}_m s_{m+1} \ldots s_{n-1}$. We also define the following notations for $v$:

- $NSL_v[x] = |\{s_i : s_i \equiv x \pmod{k-1}$ for $0 \le i \le m-1\}|$.

- $NSR_v[x] = |\{s_i : s_i \equiv x \pmod{k-1}$ for $m \le i \le n-1\}|$.

- Let $LZL_v$ be the length of a longest 0-substring in the left part, i.e. $LZL_v = \max\{l \ge 0 : s_j = s_{j+1} = \cdots = s_{j+l-1} = 0, 0 \le j \le m-1\}$. Also let $j_{L_v}$ indicate the position of the left-end of the leftmost longest 0-substring in the left part. In particular, define $j_{L_v} = 0$ if $LZL_v = 0$.

- Let $LZR_v$ be the length of a longest 0-substring in the right part, i.e. $LZR_v = \max\{l \geq 0 : s_j = s_{j+1} = \cdots = s_{j+l-1} = 0, m \leq j \leq n-1\}$. Also let $j_{R_v}$ indicate the position of the left-end of the left-most longest 0-substring in the right part. In particular, define $j_{R_v} = m$ if $LZR_v = 0$.

Throughout this paper, the subscript $v$ can be omitted from the notations $NSL_v[x]$, $NSR_v[x]$, $LZL_v$, $LZR_v$, $j_{L_v}$, and $j_{R_v}$ if no ambiguity aries.

**Definition 4.** Consider an arbitrary node $v$ in $G_{k,n}$. Define:

1. $DIST_1(v) =$
$$\begin{cases} 2n + m - 2LZL - NSL[0] - NSR[1] - 2 \\ \quad \text{if } (m - j_L - LZL) > 0 \\ 2n + m - 2LZL - NSL[0] - NSR[1] \\ \quad \text{otherwise.} \end{cases}$$

2. $DIST_2(v) =$
$$\begin{cases} 3n - m - 2LZR - NSR[0] - NSL[-1] - 2 \\ \quad \text{if } (n - j_R - LZR) > 0 \\ 3n - m - 2LZR - NSR[0] - NSL[-1] \\ \quad \text{otherwise.} \end{cases}$$

3. $DIST_3(v) = 2n + m - NSL[-2] - NSR[-1].$

4. $DIST_4(v) = 3n - m - NSR[2] - NSL[1].$

The *distance function of $v$* is defined as

$$DIST(v) = \min_{1 \leq i \leq 4}\{DIST_i(v)\}.$$

---

**Algorithm 1** OPTMAL_ROUTE

1: compute the value $l \in \{1, 2, 3, 4\}$ such that $DIST_i(v)$ is the minimum of $DIST_i(v)$'s for all $1 \leq i \leq 4$.
2: execute Algorithm DIST_$l$

---

The four terms $DIST_1(v)$–$DIST_4(v)$, defined in Definition 4 represent the lengths of four possibly shortest paths of $G_{k,n}$ from $v$ to the identity node. Those paths of the lengths $DIST_1(v)$–$DIST_4(v)$ are constructed by the algorithms DIST_1–DIST_4 respectively. Algorithm 1 is our optimal routing algorithm. It simply selects the shortest one from the four possible pathes as the routing path. As shown later, the distance function $DIST(v)$ computes the length of a shortest path from $v$ to the identity node.

**Lemma 2.** *For an arbitrary node $v$ in $G_{k,n}$, $DIST(v) - DIST(v') = \pm 1$ or $0$, where $v' = \delta(v)$ and $\delta \in \{f, f^{-1}, g_1, g_2, \ldots, g_{k-2}\}$.*

*Proof.* Assume that $v = s_0 s_1 \ldots s_{m-1} \tilde{s}_m s_{m+1} \ldots s_{n-1}$ and $\delta(v) = v' = t_0 t_1 \ldots t_{m'-1} \tilde{t}_{m'} t_{m'+1} \ldots t_{n-1}$. Let $NSL'$, $NSR'$, $LZL'$, and $LZR'$ be the corresponding

---

**Algorithm 2** DIST_1$(v, n, m, LZL, j_L)$

1: **for** $i = 0$ to $(j_L - 1)$ **do**
2: $\quad v \leftarrow f(v)$
3: **end for**
4: **for** $i = 0$ to $(j_L - 1) + (n - m)$ **do**
5: $\quad$ **if** $v[n-1] \neq 1$ **then**
6: $\quad\quad v \leftarrow g_{k-v[n-1]}(v)$
7: $\quad$ **end if**
8: $\quad v \leftarrow f^{-1}(v)$
9: **end for**
10: **if** $(m - j_L - LZL) > 0$ **then**
11: $\quad$ **for** $i = 1$ to $(m - j_L - LZL - 1)$ **do**
12: $\quad\quad v \leftarrow f^{-1}(v)$
13: $\quad$ **end for**
14: $\quad v \leftarrow g_{k-v[n-1]-1}(v)$
15: $\quad$ **for** $i = 1$ to $(m - j_L - LZL - 1)$ **do**
16: $\quad\quad v \leftarrow f(v)$
17: $\quad\quad$ **if** $v[n-1] \neq 0$ **then**
18: $\quad\quad\quad v \leftarrow g_{k-v[n-1]-1}(v)$
19: $\quad\quad$ **end if**
20: $\quad$ **end for**
21: **end if**

---

parameters (defined in Definition 3) of $v'$. By the definition of the distance function, we can utilize the fact that $\min_{1 \leq i \leq 4}\{DIST_i(v)\} - DIST_p(v') \leq DIST(v) - DIST(v') \leq DIST_q(v) - \min_{1 \leq i \leq 4}\{DIST_i(v')\}$, for some $1 \leq p, q \leq 4$, to simplify the computation.

**Case 1.** $\delta \in \{g_1, g_2, \ldots, g_{k-2}\}$. In this case, we have that $m' = m$, $NSL'[x] = NSL[x]$, and $LZL' = LZL$. According to Definition 4, the following equations can be obtained to get $DIST(v) - DIST(v') = \pm 1$ or $0$.

$$\begin{aligned} DIST_1(v) - DIST_1(v') &= \pm 1 \text{ or } 0 \\ DIST_2(v) - DIST_2(v') &= \pm 1 \text{ or } 0 \\ DIST_3(v) - DIST_3(v') &= \pm 1 \text{ or } 0 \\ DIST_4(v) - DIST_4(v') &= \pm 1 \text{ or } 0 \end{aligned}$$

**Case 2.** $\delta = f$.
**Case 2.1.** $m \neq 0$. In this case, we have that $m' = m - 1$. The following equations can be obtained to get $DIST(v) - DIST(v') = \pm 1$.

$$\begin{aligned} DIST_1(v) - DIST_1(v') &= \pm 1 \\ DIST_2(v) - DIST_2(v') &= \pm 1 \\ DIST_3(v) - DIST_3(v') &= 1 \\ DIST_4(v) - DIST_4(v') &= -1 \end{aligned}$$

**Case 2.2.** $m = 0$. In this case, we have that $m' = n - 1$, $NSL[x] = 0$, and $LZL = 0$. Hence, $DIST_4(v) \geq 2n$; $DIST_3(v') \geq 2n - 1 \geq DIST_2(v')$. These two terms can be ignored respectively in $DIST(v)$ and $DIST(v')$.

**Algorithm 3** DIST_2($v, n, m, LZR, j_R$)

1: **for** $i = 0$ to $(n - 2 - j_R - LZR)$ **do**
2:    $v \leftarrow f^{-1}(v)$
3: **end for**
4: **if** $(n - j_R - LZR) > 0$ **then**
5:    $v \leftarrow g_{k-v[n-1]-1}(v)$
6:    **for** $i = 0$ to $(n - 2 - j_R - LZR)$ **do**
7:      $v \leftarrow f(v)$
8:      **if** $v[n-1] \neq 0$ **then**
9:        $v \leftarrow g_{k-v[n-1]-1}(v)$
10:      **end if**
11:    **end for**
12: **end if**
13: **for** $i = 0$ to $(m - 1)$ **do**
14:    $v \leftarrow f(v)$
15:    **if** $v[n-1] \neq 0$ **then**
16:      $v \leftarrow g_{k-v[n-1]-1}(v)$
17:    **end if**
18: **end for**
19: **for** $i = 0$ to $j_R - m - 1$ **do**
20:    $v \leftarrow f(v)$
21: **end for**
22: **for** $i = 0$ to $j_R - m - 1$ **do**
23:    **if** $v[n-1] \neq 1$ **then**
24:      $v \leftarrow g_{k-v[n-1]}(v)$
25:    **end if**
26:    $v \leftarrow f^{-1}(v)$
27: **end for**

---

**Algorithm 4** DIST_3($v, n, m$)

1: **for** $i = 0$ to $(m - 1)$ **do**
2:    $v \leftarrow f(v)$
3:    **if** $v[n-1] \neq k - 2$ **then**
4:      $v \leftarrow g_{k-2-v[n-1]}(v)$
5:    **end if**
6: **end for**
7: **for** $i = m$ to $(n - 1)$ **do**
8:    $v \leftarrow f(v)$
9:    **if** $v[n-1] \neq 0$ **then**
10:      $v \leftarrow g_{k-1-v[n-1]}(v)$
11:    **end if**
12: **end for**
13: **for** $i = 0$ to $(m - 1)$ **do**
14:    $v \leftarrow f(v)$
15: **end for**

---

**Algorithm 5** DIST_4($v, n, m$)

1: **for** $i = m$ to $(n - 1)$ **do**
2:    **if** $v[n-1] \not\equiv 2 \pmod{k-1}$ **then**
3:      $v \leftarrow g_{k-v[n-1]+1}(v)$
4:    **end if**
5:    $v \leftarrow f^{-1}(v)$
6: **end for**
7: **for** $i = 0$ to $(m - 1)$ **do**
8:    **if** $v[n-1] \neq 1$ **then**
9:      $v \leftarrow g_{k-v[n-1]}(v)$
10:    **end if**
11:    $v \leftarrow f^{-1}(v)$
12: **end for**
13: **for** $i = m$ to $(n - 1)$ **do**
14:    $v \leftarrow f^{-1}(v)$
15: **end for**

---

The following equations can be obtained to get $DIST(v) - DIST(v') = \pm 1$.

$$DIST_1(v) - DIST_4(v') = -1$$
$$DIST_2(v) - DIST_1(v') = \pm 1$$
$$DIST_3(v) - DIST_2(v') = 1$$

**Case 3.** $\delta = f^{-1}$. This case is symmetric to Case 2 because $v' = f^{-1}(v) \Leftrightarrow f(v') = v$. $\qquad\square$

**Lemma 3.** *For the identity node $I$ in $G_{k,n}$, $DIST(I) = 0$ and $DIST(\delta(I)) = 1$ for any $\delta \in \{f, f^{-1}, g_1, g_2, \ldots, g_{k-2}\}$.*

*Proof.* Straightforward. $\qquad\square$

**Theorem 4.** *Given an arbitrary node $v$ in $G_{k,n}$, Algorithm* OPTIMAL_ROUTE *correctly generates an optimal (shortest) path of length $DIST(v)$ from $v$ to the identity node.*

*Proof.* Clearly, Algorithm OPTIMAL_ROUTE constructs a path of length $DIST(v)$ for a given node $v$. By Lemma 2, since an application of any one generator can decrease the value of $DIST(v)$ at best by one, the algorithm does construct a shortest path from $v$ to the identity node. $\qquad\square$

The diameter of a graph $G$, defined as $diam(G)$, is the maximum distance between every two vertices in $G$. We utilize our shortest path routing algorithm to compute the diameter $diam(G_{k,n})$ for $k \geq 6$ in the following theorem.

**Theorem 5.** *For an arbitrary node $v$ in $G_{k,n}$, $DIST(v) \leq \max\{2n, \frac{5n}{2} - 2\}$. Moreover, $diam(G_{k,n}) = \lfloor \frac{5n}{2} \rfloor - 2$ when $k \geq 6$ and $n \geq 4$; and $diam(G_{k,n}) = 2n$ when $k \geq 6$ and $n = 2, 3$.*

*Proof.* By Definition 4, we have that $DIST(v) \leq \min\{2n + m - 2, 3n - m - 2, 2n + m, 3n - m\} = \min\{2n + m - 2, 3n - m - 2\} \leq \frac{5n}{2} - 2$ for $m > 0$, and $DIST(v) \leq \min\{2n, 3n - 2\} \leq 2n$ for $m = 0$. Hence the upper bound of the diameter is $\max\{\frac{5n}{2} - 2, 2n\}$. Note that it is $\frac{5n}{2} - 2$ for $n \geq 4$.

We next show the lower bound. For $k \geq 6$ and $n \geq 4$, consider the node $v$ in $G_{k,n}$ such that $v[i] \notin \{0, 1, k - 2, k - 3\}$ and $m = \lfloor n/2 \rfloor$. Thus $NSL[0] = NSL[1] = $

$NSL[-1] = NSL[-2] = NSR[0] = NSR[1] =$ $NSR[-1] = NSR[-2] = 0$ and $LZL = LZR = 0$. By Definition 4, $DIST(v) = \min\{2n + \lfloor \frac{n}{2} \rfloor - 2, 3n - \lfloor \frac{n}{2} \rfloor - 2\} = \lfloor \frac{5n}{2} \rfloor - 2$. Therefore, $\lfloor \frac{5n}{2} \rfloor - 2 \leq diam(G_{k,n}) \leq \frac{5n}{2} - 2$ and $diam(G_{k,n}) = \lfloor \frac{5n}{2} \rfloor - 2$. The case of $k \geq 6$ and $n = 2, 3$ can be shown similarly. □

## 4  Topological properties

A *cycle* is a graph with an equal number of nodes and edges whose nodes can be placed around a circle so that two vertices are adjacent if and only if they appear consecutively along the circle [23]. Two cycles are *node-disjoint* if they have no common node. An edge defined by the generator $f$ (or $f^{-1}$) is an *F-edge*. Any cycle in $G_{k,n}$ consisting of only *F*-edges is an *F-cycle*. For non-negative integer $i$, we recursively define $f^i(v) = \begin{cases} v & \text{if } i = 0, \\ f(f^{i-1}(v)) & \text{if } i > 0. \end{cases}$ The notation $f^{-i}(v)$ is defined in the same way.

**Theorem 6.** $G_{k,n}$ *can embed* $(k-1)^{n-1}$ *node-disjoint F-cycles of length* $n(k-1)$.

*Proof.* Given an arbitrary node $v$ in $G_{k,n}$, it is not difficult to verify that $f^{n(k-1)}(v) = v$ and $f^i(v) \neq f^j(v)$, where $1 \leq i, j \leq n(k-1)$ and $i \neq j$. Thus, from an arbitrary node $v$, a cycle of length $n(k-1)$ in $G_{k,n}$ can be generated by a functional iteration $f^{n(k-1)}(v)$. Since $G_{k,n}$ has $n(k-1)^n$ nodes, there are totally $(k-1)^{n-1}$ *F*-cycles of each length $n(k-1)$ can be generated. These cycles are node-disjoint by the fact that $f(u) = f(v)$ if and only if $u = v$. □

Each *F*-cycle has a unique node $v$ such that $v[i] = s$ and $m = 0$ for two given integers $0 \leq i \leq n - 1$ and $0 \leq s \leq k - 2$. Therefore, for each *F*-cycle $C$, we can define $C$-leader (*leader* for short if no ambiguity aries) to be the unique node $v$ of $C$ satisfying that $v[0] = 0$ and $m = 0$. Note that each leader uniquely determines a specific *F*-cycle. Two *F*-cycles $C_1$ and $C_2$ are said to be *adjacent* if there exists a node $v_1 \in C_1$ and a node $v_2 \in C_2$ such that $v_1 = g_i(v_2)$ for some $1 \leq i \leq k - 2$.

**Theorem 7.** *Each F-cycle of* $G_{k,n}$ *is adjacent to* $n(k-2)$ *(respectively,* $k-2$*) different F-cycles for* $n > 2$ *(respectively,* $n = 2$*).*

*Proof.* We first consider $n > 2$. For an arbitrary *F*-cycle $C$ with the $C$-leader $v = \bar{0}s_1s_2 \dots s_{n-1}$,

$$f^{-i} \circ (g_j \circ f^i(v)) = \bar{0}s_1s_2 \dots s' \dots s_{n-1}, \quad (2)$$

where $\circ$ means function composition and $s' = (s_{i-1} + j) \bmod (k-1)$ for all $i \neq 1$ and $1 \leq j \leq k - 2$. Thus $(n-1)(k-2)$ leaders of $(n-1)(k-2)$ distinct *F*-cycles can be arrived from $v$. This implies that the given *F*-cycle is adjacent to $(n-1)(k-2)$ distinct *F*-cycles. Moreover, the other $(k-2)$ leaders can be arrived from $v$ by

$$f^{-1-jn} \circ (g_j \circ f(v)) = \bar{0}s'_1s'_2 \dots s'_{n-1}, \quad (3)$$

where $s'_i = (s_i - j) \bmod (k-1)$. Therefore, each *F*-cycle is adjacent to $n(k-2)$ different *F*-cycles. The case of $n = 2$ can also be shown using either Equation 2 or Equation 3. □

An edge of $G_{k,n}$ defined by the generator $g_i$ is called *G-edge*. A *clique* in a graph is a set of pairwise adjacent nodes. A clique is said to be *maximal* if it is not contained in another clique. A *G-clique* is a maximal clique in $G_{k,n}$ such that each pair of adjacent nodes is connected by a *G*-edge. For example, $\{\bar{0}0, \bar{0}1\}$ is a *G*-clique in $G_{3,2}$. Note that a *G*-clique contains $k - 1$ nodes. Given some fixed $0 \leq s \leq k - 2$, each *G*-clique has a unique node $v$ satisfying that $v[n-1] = s$. Therefore, for a *G*-clique $K$, we can define the $K$-leader (*leader* for short if no ambiguity aries) to be the unique node $v \in K$ satisfying that $v[n-1] = 0$. We use such a node to represent its corresponding *G*-clique for convenience. Two *G*-cliques are *node-disjoint* if they have no common node.

**Theorem 8.** $G_{k,n}$ *can embed* $n(k-1)^{n-1}$ *node-disjoint G-cliques of size* $k - 1$.

*Proof.* Clearly, there are $n(k-1)^{n-1}$ leaders in $G_{k,n}$, which correspond to $n(k-1)^{n-1}$ *G*-cliques. It is not difficult to verify that these *G*-cliques are pairwise node-disjoint. Moreover, since each *G*-clique contains $k - 1$ nodes, the $n(k-1)^{n-1}$ *G*-cliques form a partition of the vertices of $G_{k,n}$. □

Two *G*-cliques $K_1$ and $K_2$ are said to be *adjacent* if there exists a pair of vertices $u \in K_1$ and $v \in K_2$ such that either $v = f(u)$ or $v = f^{-1}(u)$.

**Theorem 9.** *Each G-clique in* $G_{k,n}$ *is adjacent to* $2(k-1)$ *(respectively,* $k-1$*) different G-cliques when* $n > 2$ *(respectively,* $n = 2$*).*

*Proof.* We first consider that $n > 2$. Given an arbitrary *G*-clique with its leader $v = s_0^* s_1^* \dots s_{n-2}^* 0^*$, we can apply $f^i \circ g_j(v)$ for $i = \pm 1$ and $1 \leq j \leq k - 2$, to reach $2(k-2)$ distinct *G*-cliques, and apply $f^{\pm 1}(v)$ to reach another two distinct *G*-cliques. Therefore, each *G*-clique is adjacent to $2(k-1)$ distinct *G*-cliques.

When $n = 2$, we can apply $f^1 \circ g_j(v)$ and $f^1(v)$ (or $f^{-1} \circ g_j(v)$ and $f^{-1}(v)$) to reach $k - 1$ distinct *G*-cliques. Note that the *G*-cliques reached by $\{f^1 \circ g_j(v), f^1(v)\}$ are the same with those reached by $\{f^{-1} \circ g_j(v), f^{-1}(v)\}$. □

# 5 Maximal fault tolerance

The node fault tolerance of an undirected graph is measured by the node-connectivity of the graph [24]. The node-connectivity of a graph $G$, written $\kappa(G)$, is the minimum size of a node set $S$ such that $G - S$ is disconnected or has only one node [23]. A graph $G$ is $\xi$-connected if its node-connectivity is at least $\xi$. Obviously, the node-connectivity of a graph $G$ cannot exceed the minimum degree of a node in $G$; thus $\kappa(G_{k,n}) \leq k$ since $G_{k,n}$ is $k$-regular. A graph is said to be *maximally fault-tolerant* if node-connectivity equals the minimum node-degree of the given graph. A set of paths from $u$ to $v$ are *pairwise internally disjoint* if any two of them have no common internal nodes. In this section, we show that $\kappa(G_{k,n}) = k$ and hence this class of graphs is maximally fault-tolerant. For convenience, the notation $P[x, y]$ is used to denote a path from $x$ to $y$.

**Lemma 10.** [19] $\kappa(G_{3,n}) = 3$ *for* $n \geq 2$.

**Definition 5.** For a given $G_{k,n}$ construct the reduced graph $RG_{k,n}$ in the following way: condense each $\mathcal{F}$-cycle with its leader $\bar{0}s_1 s_2 \ldots s_{n-1}$ into a single node (super node) and label it with $s_1 s_2 \ldots s_{n-1}$; connect two arbitrary super node if and only if the corresponding $\mathcal{F}$-cycles are adjacent in $G_{k,n}$.

**Lemma 11.** $\kappa(RG_{k,n}) \geq k$ *for* $k \geq 4$ *and* $n \geq 3$.

*Proof.* Consider a subgraph $R_{k,n}$ of $RG_{k,n}$ defined as follows: The node set of $R_{k,n}$ is the same with $RG_{k,n}$; and two node $x_1 x_2 \ldots x_{n-1}$ and $y_1 y_2 \ldots y_{n-1}$ of $R_{k,n}$ are adjacent iff there is exactly one $i$ such that $x_i \neq y_i$ and $x_j = y_j$ for all $j \neq i$.

We show the lemma by showing that there are $k$ pairwise internally disjoint paths between two arbitrary distinct nodes in $R_{k,n}$. The proof is by induction on $n$.

BASIS: Prove that the result is true for $n = 3$. Consider two arbitrary nodes $u$ and $v$ in $R_{k,3}$.

**Case 1.** $u$ and $v$ have exactly one different symbol. Without loss of generality, assume that $u = 0x$ and $v = 0y$. According to Corollary **??** and the construction of $R_{k,n}$, $k$ pairwise internally disjoint paths from $u$ to $v$ can be constructed as follows: $(0x, 0y)$, $(0x, 1x, 1y, 0y)$, $\ldots$, $(0x, (k-2)x, (k-2)y, 0y)$ and $(0x, 0z, 0y)$ for $z \in \{0, 1, \ldots, k-2\} \setminus \{x, y\}$.

**Case 2.** $u$ and $v$ have two different symbols. Assume that $u = u_1 u_2$ and $v = v_1 v_2$. Then, according to Corollary **??** and the construction of $R_{k,n}$, $2k - 4$ ($\geq k$ when $k \geq 4$) pairwise internally disjoint paths from $u$ to $v$ can be constructed as follows: $(u_1 u_2, u_1 v_2, v_1 v_2)$, $(u_1 u_2, v_1 u_2, v_1 v_2)$, $(u_1 u_2, x u_2, x v_2, v_1 v_2)$, and $(u_1 u_2, u_1 x, v_1 x, v_1 v_2)$ for all $x \in \{0, 1, \ldots, k-2\} \setminus \{u_1, v_1\}$.

INDUCTION STEP: Assume that the result is true for $n-1$ and then show it is true for $n \geq 4$. It is not difficult to

verify that $R_{k,n}$ has a recursive structure which can be decomposed into $k - 1$ copies of $R_{k,n-1}$. Each $R_{k,n-1}$ is a subgraph of $R_{k,n}$ induced by nodes in $x_1 x_2 \ldots x_{n-2} y$ for some fixed symbol $y$ and $x_i \in \{0, 1, \ldots, k-2\}$. Consider two arbitrary node $u$ and $v$. If $u$ and $v$ are in the same $R_{k,n-1}$, then there are $k$ pairwise internally disjoint paths from $u$ to $v$ by induction hypothesis. Otherwise, $u$ and $v$ are in different $R_{k,n-1}$'s. Assume that $u = u_1 u_2 \ldots u_{n-2} 0$ and $v = v_1 v_2 \ldots v_{n-2} 1$. By the induction hypothesis, there are $k$ pairwise internally disjoint paths $P_1, P_2, \ldots, P_k$ from $u$ to the node $v' = v_1 v_2 \ldots v_{n-2} 0$ because $u$ and $v'$ are in the same $R_{k,n-1}$. Let $n_1, n_2, \ldots, n_k$ be the neighbors of $v'$ which belong to paths $P_1, P_2, \ldots, P_k$, respectively. According to Corollary **??** and all $n_i$'s are in the same $R_{k,n-1}$, we have that $n_i = t_1^i t_2^i \ldots t_{n-2}^i 0$ in which $t_j^i \neq v_j$ for some $j$ and $t_l^i = v_l$ for all $1 \leq l \leq n - 2$ and $l \neq j$. Let $n_i'$ be the neighbor of $n_i$ which is located in the same $R_{k,n-1}$ with $v$, that is, $n_i' = t_1^i t_2^i \ldots t_{n-2}^i 1$. Note that $n_i'$, for all $1 \leq i \leq k$, are adjacent to $v$. Also let $P_i[u, n_i]$ be the subpath of $P_i$ from $u$ to $n_i$, $1 \leq i \leq k$. Then, $k$ pairwise internally disjoint paths from $u$ to $v$ can be constructed as $P_i[u, n_i] + (n_i, n_i') + (n_i', v)$ for all $i = 1, 2, \ldots, k$, where "$+$" means the path-concatenation operation[1]. $\square$

**Lemma 12.** [12] *Given two sets of nodes $V_1$ and $V_2$ such that $|V_1| = |V_2| = \xi$ in a $\xi$-connected graph, there are $\xi$ node disjoint paths connecting the nodes form $V_1$ to $V_2$.*

**Lemma 13.** $\kappa(G_{k,n}) \geq k$ *for* $k \geq 4$ *and* $n \geq 2$.

*Proof.* We show the lemma by showing that there are $k$ pairwise internally disjoint paths between two arbitrary nodes $u$ and $v$ in $G_{k,n}$. There are two cases.

**Case 1.** $n = 2$. Recall that in this case, $RG_{k,2}(= R_{k,2})$ is a complete graph on $k - 1$ nodes. Thus there are totally $k - 1$ $\mathcal{F}$-cycles in $G_{k,2}$.

**Case 1.1.** $u$ and $v$ are in the same $\mathcal{F}$-cycle $C$. This cycle is a concatenation of two internally disjoint paths from $u$ to $v$, denoted by $P_1$ and $P_2$, which contribute two paths. Let $C_1, C_2, \ldots C_{k-2}$ be the other $\mathcal{F}$-cycles of $G_{k,2}$. Then, the other $k - 2$ paths can be constructed using the following three steps:

1. For each $C_i$, identify the *entry node* $g_{j_i}(u) \in C_i$ and the *exit node* $g_{l_i}(v) \in C_i$, where $1 \leq j_i, l_i \leq k - 2$. [2]

2. For each $C_i$, construct a path $Q_i$ from $g_{j_i}(u)$ to $g_{l_i}(v)$ using the $\mathcal{F}$-edges of corresponding $\mathcal{F}$-cycle.

3. Construct the desired $k$ internally disjoint paths: $P_1$, $P_2$, $(u, g_{j_1}(u)) + Q_1 + (g_{l_1}(v), v)$, $(u, g_{j_2}(u)) + Q_2 + (g_{l_2}(v), v)$, $\ldots$, $(u, g_{j_{k-2}}(u)) + Q_{k-2} + (g_{l_{k-2}}(v), v)$.

---

[1] In the remainder of this paper, the notation "+" is used to mean the path-concatenation.

[2] It is not difficult to show that there exist $j_i$ and $l_i$ such that $g_{j_i}(u)$ and $g_{l_i}(v)$ are in the same $\mathcal{F}$-cycle $C_i$.

**Case 1.2.** $u$ and $v$ are in different $\mathcal{F}$-cycles. Let $F_1$ and $F_2$ be the $\mathcal{F}$-cycles to which $u$ and $v$ belong, respectively. We first construct three pairwise internally disjoint paths from $u$ to $v$ using $F_1$ and $F_2$. If $u$ and $v$ are adjacent, then the desired paths can be constructed as follows:

A. Find two nodes $u_1$ and $u_2$ (respectively, $v_1$ and $v_2$) different from $u$ (respectively, $v$) in $F_1$ (respectively, $F_2$) such that $g_i(u_1) = v_1$ and $g_i(u_2) = v_2$ for some $1 \leq i \leq k - 2$.

B. Let $P[u, u_1]$ and $P[u, u_2]$ (respectively, $Q[v_1, v]$ and $Q[v_2, v]$) be two paths in $F_1$ (respectively, $F_2$) whose nodes are all different but $u$ (respectively, $v$). Then, $(u, v)$, $P[u, u_1] + (u_1, v_1) + Q[v_1, v]$, and $P[u, u_2] + (u_2, v_2) + Q[v_2, v]$ form the desired three paths.

Otherwise, if $u$ and $v$ are not adjacent, then the desired three paths can be constructed as follows:

I. Find two nodes $u_1$ and $u_2$ (respectively, $v_1$ and $v_2$) different from $u$ (respectively, $v$) in $F_1$ (respectively, $F_2$) such that $g_i(u_1) = v$, $g_j(u_2) = v_1$, and $g_l(u) = v_2$, where $1 \leq i, j, l \leq k - 2$.

II. Let $P'[u, u_1]$ and $P'[u, u_2]$ (respectively, $Q'[v_1, v]$ and $Q'[v_2, v]$) be two paths in $F_1$ (respectively, $F_2$) whose nodes are all different but $u$ (respectively, $v$). Then, $P'[u, u_1] + (u_1, v)$, $(u, v_2) + Q'[v_2, v]$, and $P'[u, u_2] + (u_2, v_1) + Q'[v_1, v]$ form the desired three paths.

The other $k - 3$ internally disjoint paths from $u$ to $v$ can be constructed from the other $k - 3$ $f$-cycles using the method similar to that of Case 1.1.

**Case 2.** $n \geq 3$. If $u$ and $v$ are in the same $\mathcal{F}$-cycle, there exist $k$ internally disjoint paths from $u$ to $v$: two paths are constructed in the same $\mathcal{F}$-cycle, and the other $k - 2$ paths are constructed from adjacent $k - 2$ $\mathcal{F}$-cycles based on the method similar to that of Case 1. If $u$ and $v$ are in different $\mathcal{F}$-cycles, then the set of nodes $\{g_1(u), g_2(u), \ldots, g_{k-2}(u), g_1(f(u)), g_1(f^{-1}(u))\}$ (respectively, $\{g_1(v), g_2(v), \ldots, g_{k-2}(v), g_1(f(v)), g_1(f^{-1}(v))\}$) which are in $k$ different $\mathcal{F}$-cycles, denoted by $\{\mathcal{C}_1, \mathcal{C}_2, \ldots, \mathcal{C}_k\}$ (respectively, $\{\mathcal{C'}_1, \mathcal{C'}_2, \ldots, \mathcal{C'}_k\}$), and can be reached from $u$ (respectively, $v$). By Lemma 11 and Lemma 12, there are $k$ node-disjoint paths connecting $\{\mathcal{C}_1, \mathcal{C}_2, \ldots, \mathcal{C}_k\}$ and $\{\mathcal{C'}_1, \mathcal{C'}_2, \ldots, \mathcal{C'}_k\}$ in $RG_{k,n}$. This implies that there exist $k$ pairwise internally disjoint paths from $u$ to $v$ in $G_{k,n}$. $\square$

**Theorem 14.** $\kappa(G_{k,n}) = k$ for $k \geq 3$ and $n \geq 2$.

*Proof.* By Lemma 10 and Lemma 13, we have that $\kappa(G_{k,n}) \geq k$. By the fact that $G_{k,n}$ is a $k$-regular graph, we have that $\kappa(G_{k,n}) \leq k$. Thus the result holds. $\square$

## 6 Conclusion

We generalize the concept of the trivalent graph and propose a new family of $k$-valent graphs $G_{k,n}$ for designing interconnection networks. The proposed graph is regular with the node-degree $k$, for all $k \geq 3$. We also show that $G_{k,n}$ has logarithmic diameter subject to the number of nodes and is maximally fault tolerant. Besides, a shortest path routing algorithm is also presented.

## References

[1] S. B. Akers and B. Krishnamurthy, "The star graph: an attractive alternative to $n$-cube," in *Proceedings of International Conference on Parallel Processing*, St. Charles, IL, pp. 555–556, 1987.

[2] S. B. Akers and B. Krishnamurthy, "A group-theoretic model for symmetric interconnection networks," *IEEE Transactions on Computers*, 38(4):555–556, 1989.

[3] S. G. Akl, *Parallel Computation: Models and Methods*. Prentice Hall, 1997.

[4] L. Bhuyan and D. P. Agrawal, "Genereated hypercube and hyperbus structure for a computer network," *IEEE Transactions on Computers*, bf33:323–333, 1984.

[5] C. Chen, D. P. Agrawal, and J. R. Burke, "dBCube: a new calss of hierarchical multiprocessor interconnection networks with area efficient laylot," *IEEE Transactions on Parallel and Distributed Systems*, 4:1332-1344, 1993.

[6] G. H. Chen, J. S. Fu, and J. F. Fang, "Hypercomplete: a pancyclic recursive topology for large-scale distributed multicomputer systems," *Networks*, 35(1):56–69, 2000.

[7] K. Day and A. Tripathi, "Arrangement graphs: a class of generated star graphs," *Information Processing Letters*, 42:235–241, 1992.

[8] K. Ghose and K. R. Desai, "Hierarchical cubic networks," *IEEE Transactions on Parallel and Distributed Systems*, 6:427–435, 1995.

[9] W. J. Hsu, "Fibonacci cubes: a new interconnection topology," *IEEE Transactions on Parallel and Distributed Systems*, 4:3–12, 1993.

[10] K. Hwang and J. Ghosh, "Hypernet: a communication-efficient architecture for constructing massively parallel computers," *IEEE Transactions on Computers*, C-36:1450–1466, 1987.

[11] Q. M. Malluhi and M. A. Bayoumi, "The hierarchical hypercube: a new interconnection topology for massively parallel systems," *IEEE Transactions on Parallel and Distributed Systems*, 5:17–30, 1994.

[12] K. Menger, "Zur allgemeinen Kurventheorie," *Fund. Math.*, 10:95–115, 1927.

[13] S. Öhring and S. K. Das, "Folded petersen cube networks: new competitors for the hypercubes," *IEEE Transactions on Parallel and Distributed Systems*, 7:151–168, 1996.

[14] S. Okawa, "Correction to the diameter of trivalent Cayley graphs," *IEICE Transactions on Fundamentals*, E84-A:1269–1272, 2001.

[15] F. P. Preparata and J. Vuillemin, "The cube-connected cycles: a versatile network for parallel computation," *Communication of the ACM*, 24:300–309, 1981.

[16] M. R. Samatham and D. K. Pradhan, "The de Bruijn multiprocessor network: a versatile parallel processing and sorting networks for VLSI," *IEEE Transactions on Computers*, C-38:567–581, 1989.

[17] G. Tel, *Topics in Distributed Algorithms*. Cambridge Int'l Series on Parallel Computation, Cambridge University Press, 1991.

[18] C.-H. Tsai, C.-N. Hung, L.-H. Hsu, and C.-H. Chang, "The correct diameter of trivalent Cayley graphs," *Information Processing Letters*, 72:109–111, 1999.

[19] P. Vadapalli and P. K. Srimani, "Trivalent Cayley graphs for interconnection networks," *Information Processing Letters*, 54:329–335, 1995.

[20] P. Vadapalli and P. K. Srimani, "Shortest routing in trivalent Cayley graph network," *Information Processing Letters*, 57:183–188, 1996.

[21] P. Vadapalli and P. K. Srimani, "A new family of Cayley graph interconnection networks for constant degree four," *IEEE Transactions on Parellel and Distributed Systems*, 7:26–32, 1996.

[22] M. D. Wagh and J. Mo, "Hamilton cycles in Trivalent Cayley graphs," *Information Processing Letters*, 60:177–181, 1996.

[23] Douglas B. West, *Introduction to graph theory*, Prentice-Hall, Upper Saddle River, NJ 07458, 2001.

[24] Junming Xu, *"Topological structure and analysis of interconnection networks,"* Kluwer Academic, 2001.

# Parallel Routing and Wavelength Assignment for Optical Multistage Interconnection Networks

Enyue Lu and S. Q. Zheng
Department of Computer Science
Erik Jonsson School of Engineering and Computer Science
University of Texas at Dallas
Richardson, TX 75083-0688, USA
{enyue, sizheng}@utdallas.edu

## Abstract

*Multistage interconnection networks (MINs) are among the most efficient switching architectures in terms of the number of switching elements (SEs) used. For optical MINs (OMINs), two I/O connections with neighboring wavelengths cannot share a common SE due to crosstalk. In this paper, we focus on the wavelength dilation approach, in which the I/O connections sharing a common SE will be assigned different wavelengths with enough wavelength spacing. We first study the permutation capacity of OMINs, then propose fast parallel routing and wavelength assignment algorithms for OMINs. By applying our permutation decomposition and graph coloring techniques, the proposed algorithms can route any permutation without crosstalk in wavelength-rearrangeable space-strict-sense Banyan networks and wavelength-rearrangeable space-rearrangeable Benes networks in polylogarithmic time using a linear number of processors.*

## 1. Introduction

The explosive growth of Internet is driving an increased demand for transmission rate and faster switching technologies. Optical communications with photonic switching promise to meet high bandwidth, low error probability, and large transmission capacity. The networks using optical transmission and maintaining optical data paths can be used to remove the expensive optic-electro and electro-optic conversions. The electronic parallel processing for controlling such networks are capable, in principle, of meeting future high data rate requirements.

Nonblocking networks have been favored in switching systems since they can set up any one-to-one I/O mapping. For a nonblocking space-division-multiplexing network, it can be *strictly nonblocking (SNB)*, or *rearrangeable nonblocking (RNB)* [2, 8]. In SNB networks, a connection can be established from any idle input to any idle output without disturbing existing connections while in RNB networks the connection can be established if the rearrangement of existing connections is allowed. With wavelength-division-multiplexing (WDM) technology, the concept of SNB and RNB in space-division switching can be extended to wavelength-division switching. Depending on whether wavelengths can be reassigned, this extension results in four combinations: wavelength-rearrangeable space-rearrangeable *(WRSR)*, wavelength-rearrangeable space-strict-sense *(WRSS)*, wavelength-strict-sense space-rearrangeable *(WSSR)*, and wavelength-strict-sense space-strict-sense *(WSSS)*. It has been shown that using both wavelength and space multiplexing techniques in a fully dynamic manner, networks can achieve higher bandwidth and higher connectivity [19].

To build a large IP router with capacity of 1 Tb/s and beyond, optical multistage interconnection networks (OMINs) will be used. An OMIN usually comprises a number of $2 \times 2$ switching elements (SEs) grouped into several stages interconnected by a set of optical links (e.g. [6, 7, 22]). One of the problems with such OMINs is *crosstalk* at optical SEs, i.e., if more than one signal with the neighboring wavelengths share the same SE, they interfere with each other[1]. In electronic switching networks, there is only link conflict, i.e., two active inputs intend to be connected with the same output. The crosstalk in photonic switching networks adds a new type of blocking, called *wavelength conflict*.

In order to minimize wavelength conflicts in photonic switching networks, three approaches, *space dilation*, *time*

---

1  In this paper, we only consider non-filterable first-order SE crosstalk[12, 13], and different wavelengths are referred to the wavelengths with enough wavelength spacing so that no crosstalk will be generated when such wavelengths passing through the same SE

*dilation* and *wavelength dilation*, have been proposed. In space and time dilations, crosstalk can be avoided by ensuring at most one connection passing through an SE. More specifically, in space dilation crosstalk can be avoided by increasing the number of SEs in a switching network (e.g. [14, 23, 24]), while in time dilation a set of conflicting connections is partitioned into subsets so that the connections in each subset can be established simultaneously without conflicts (e.g. [15, 17, 21, 26]). In wavelength dilation, the crosstalk between two signals passing through the same SE is suppressed by routing to ensure the wavelengths to be far apart (e.g. [5, 20, 25]), or by using wavelength converters (e.g. [18]). Since the connections with neighboring wavelengths do not share any SE, the wavelength dilation approach is also useful for establishing a set of connections that would normally cause link conflicts in blocking space-division-multiplexing OMINs such as Banyan networks.

In this paper, we focus on the wavelength dilation approach, and consider the problem of quickly configuring an OMIN and assigning each connection a wavelength for realizing a permutation without crosstalk. In wavelength dilation, if there are wavelength converters available, we can convert the input signals with the neighboring wavelengths entering into the same SE to different ones. Thus, two wavelengths are necessary plus the costs of the wavelength converters. The use of wavelength converters will increase hardware cost and configuration time. If there is no wavelength converter available, i.e. each connection will be assigned the same wavelength, then we need to find a wavelength assignment for connections plus a setting of SEs so that there is no crosstalk in OMINs.

Through this paper, we assume that no wavelength converter is available in OMINs and assure the wavelengths in the same SE to be different by routing. The switch model used in this paper follows [16, 20]. The OMINs under such switch model can be built up using $2 \times 2$ multi-wavelength SEs, in which each input/output is capable of receiving/transmitting optical signals of a set of wavelengths and each wavelength is switched independently in SEs [20]. Such a multi-wavelength SE has an independently controllable state, straight or cross as shown in Fig. 1 (a), for each wavelength. Figure 1 (b) shows a signal transmission in a multi-wavelength SE, where the connections for the wavelength $\lambda_2$ in the upper input and the wavelength $\lambda_2'$ in the lower input are in cross state and all other connections are in straight state.

If an SE can only receive/transmit one wavelength for each input/output, it is called a *basic* SE. The OMINs considered in this paper are WRSS Banyan networks and WRSR Benes networks, where the WRSR Benes networks only contain basic SEs. For an I/O permutation, if there is a setting of SEs to realize the permutation and a wavelength assignment of connections so that no two connections with the same wavelength share any SE or link, we called this

setting and wavelength assignment a *crosstalk-free configuration* of the OMIN for the permutation. An algorithm that can find a crosstalk-free configuration for any permutation of an OMIN is called a *crosstalk-free routing and wavelength assignment* algorithm for the OMIN. In this paper, by applying graph edge and vertex coloring techniques, we present crosstalk-free routing and wavelength assignment algorithms that can route any permutation without crosstalk in $O(\log^2 N)$ time for a WRSS Banyan network using at most $2^{\lfloor \frac{\log N + 1}{2} \rfloor}$ wavelengths and in $O(\log^3 N)$ time for a WRSR Benes network using at most $2 \log N$ wavelengths, on a completely connected multiprocessor system of $N$ processing elements (PEs). We also show that both routing and wavelength assignment algorithms can be implemented on a hypercube of $N/2$ PEs in $O(\log^4 N)$ time.

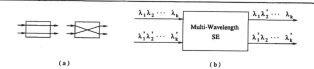

**Figure 1. A $2 \times 2$ multi-wavelength SE. (a) Two states. (b) Signal transmission.**

## 2. Definitions and Notations

Let $I = \{I_0, I_1, \cdots, I_{N-1}\}$ and $O = \{O_0, O_1, \cdots, O_{N-1}\}$ be the sets of inputs and outputs, respectively, of an $N \times N$ OMIN. Let $\pi : I \longmapsto O$ be a one-to-one *I/O mapping* that indicates connection requests from inputs to outputs. $I_i$ and $O_j$ are *active* if and only if there is a connection request from $I_i$ to $O_j$, and in this case, $\pi(i) = j$ and $\pi^{-1}(j) = i$. The connection from input $i$ to output $\pi(i)$ is denoted by $i$ since it is a one-to-one mapping.

A one-to-one I/O mapping involving $K(\leq N)$ active inputs is called a *partial permutation*. A partial permutation with $K = N$ active inputs is also called a *permutation*. We are interested in a type of partial permutations that can be simultaneously connected through OMIN without crosstalk. Such partial permutations are called *crosstalk-free (CF) partial permutations*.

A special type of partial permutation, named *semi-permutation*, which ensures only one active input in every SE of the first and last stages of an OMIN at the same time, has the maximum potential to be simultaneously realized in OMIN without crosstalk. It was shown that any permutation can be decomposed into two semi-permutations and each semi-permutation can be routed in one pass in an optical Benes network without crosstalk [26]. In [10], we presented a parallel permutation decomposition algorithm to decompose a partial permutation into two partial semi-permutations and proved the following lemma[2].

**Lemma 1** *For any partial permutation with $K(\leq N)$ active inputs, two partial semi-permutations can be computed in $O(\log K)$ time on a completely connected multiprocessor system of $N$ PEs.*

The parallel decomposition algorithm of [10] is equivalent to an algorithm that finds a 2-edge coloring of a bipartite graph $G$ with $\Delta(G) \leq 2$, where $\Delta(G)$ is the *degree* of $G$, the maximum number of edges incident at a vertex.

## 3. Parallel Routing and Wavelength Assignment in WRSS Banyan Networks

### 3.1. Banyan-type Networks

A class of multistage self-routing networks, *Banyan-type* networks, has received considerable attention. A network belonging to this class satisfies the following three properties:

i. It has $N = 2^n$ inputs, $N = 2^n$ outputs, $n$-stages and $N/2$ SEs in each stage.

ii. There is a unique path between each input and each output.

iii. Let $u$ and $v$ be two SEs in stage $i$, and let $S_j(u)$ and $S_j(v)$ be two sets of SEs to which $u$ and $v$ can reach in stage $j$, $0 < i + 1 = j \leq n$. Then $S_j(u) \cap S_j(v) = \emptyset$ or $S_j(u) = S_j(v)$ for any $u$ and $v$.

Because of the above properties (short connection diameter, unique connection path, uniform modularity, etc.), Banyan-type networks are very attractive for constructing switching networks. Several well-known networks, such as *Banyan*, *Butterfly*, *Omega*, and *Baseline*, belong to this class. It has been shown that these networks are topologically equivalent [1]. In this paper, we use Baseline network as the representative of Banyan-type networks.

An $N \times N$ Baseline network, denoted by $BL(N)$, is constructed recursively. A $BL(2)$ is a $2 \times 2$ SE. A $BL(N)$ consists of a switching stage of $N/2$ SEs, and a shuffle connection, followed by a stack of two $BL(N/2)$'s. Thus a $BL(N)$ has $\log N$ stages labeled by $0, \cdots, n - 1$ from left to right[3], and each stage has $N/2$ SEs labeled by $0, \cdots, N/2 - 1$ from top to bottom. Every SE has two inputs/outputs, each

2   The algorithms discussed in this paper are all based on a completely connected multiprocessor system consisting of a set of $N$ PEs connected in such a way that there is a direct connection between every pair of PEs. We assume that each PE can communicate with at most one processor during a communication step. The presented algorithms run on a completely connected multiprocessor system can be easily transformed to algorithms on more realistic multiprocessor systems as talked in Section 5.

3   In this paper, we assume $N = 2^n$ ($n = \log N$) and all logarithms are in base 2.

named *upper input/output* or *lower input/output* according to its relative position. The $N$ links interconnecting two adjacent stages $i$ and $i + 1$ are called *output links* of stage $i$ and *input links* of stage $i + 1$ and labeled by $0, \cdots, N - 1$ from top to bottom. The input (resp. output) links in the first (resp. last) stage of $BL(N)$ are connected with $N$ inputs (resp. outputs) of $BL(N)$. To facilitate our discussions, the labels of stages, links and SEs are represented by binary numbers. Let $a_l a_{l-1} \cdots a_1 a_0$ be the binary representation of $a$. We use $\bar{a}$ to denote the integer that has the binary representation $a_l a_{l-1} \cdots a_1 (1 - a_0)$. Fig. 2 shows a $BL(16)$.

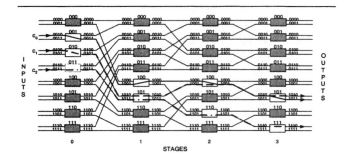

**Figure 2. The self-routing of connections $c_0$, $c_1$, and $c_2$ in $BL(16)$.**

Self-routing in $BL(N)$ is decided by the destination of each connection. Routing from inputs to outputs of $BL(N)$, if the $(n - i)$-th bit, $d_{n-i-1}$, of the destination equals to 0 (resp. 1), the input of the SE through which the connection passes in stage $i$ is connected to the SE's upper (resp. lower) output. Fig. 2 shows three connection paths for connections $c_0$, $c_1$ and $c_2$. Connections $c_0$ and $c_1$ share two links, output link 1001 in stage 2 and input link 1010 in stage 3, and two SEs, SE 4 in stage 2 and SE 5 in stage 3; connections $c_1$ and $c_2$ share SE 5 in stage 1. Clearly, Banyan networks are blocking space-division-multiplexing networks. In the next subsection, we will show by using wavelength dilation, Banyan networks can be WRSS networks.

### 3.2. Routing and Wavelength Assignment algorithm

The idea of our crosstalk-free routing and wavelength assignment algorithm for WRSS Banyan networks is as follows. We partition a set of connections into subsets so that the connections in the same subset don't share any SE or link, and then assign the connections in different subsets with different wavelengths and the connections in the same subset with the same wavelength. Each of these subsets is called a *crosstalk-free (CF) subset*. Clearly, this wavelength assignment will not cause crosstalk in any SEs. Since

$BL(N)$ is a self-routing network, the routing for each connection can be easily done following the self-routing rule. We only need to consider how to partition a set of connections into CF subsets and assign the connections in different subsets with different wavelengths.

In order to find CF subsets, we need to study the permutation capacity of $BL(N)$ first. For $BL(N)$, the $k$-th *modulo-g input group* comprises inputs $I_{(k-1)g}, I_{(k-1)g+1}, \cdots, I_{kg-1}$, and the $k$-th *modulo-g output group* comprises outputs $O_{(k-1)g}, O_{(k-1)g+1}, \cdots, O_{kg-1}$, where $g = 2^i$ with $0 \leq i \leq n$ and $1 \leq k \leq N/g$. We say that two connections *share* a modulo-$g$ input (resp. output) group if their sources (resp. destinations) are in the same modulo-$g$ input (resp. output) group. The following lemma is proved in [13].

**Lemma 2** *Given a partial permutation $\pi$ of $BL(N)$, if any two connections in $\pi$ do not share any modulo-$2^{\lfloor \frac{n+1}{2} \rfloor}$ input group and also do not share any modulo-$2^{\lfloor \frac{n+1}{2} \rfloor}$ output group, then $\pi$ can be routed in $BL(N)$ simultaneously without crosstalk.*

We assume $g = 2^{\lfloor \frac{n+1}{2} \rfloor}$ in the rest of this section. By Lemma 2, if we assign different wavelengths to the connections in $\pi$ with sources (resp. destinations) sharing the same modulo-$g$ input (resp. output) group, then we can route $\pi$ in $BL(N)$ without crosstalk. This wavelength assignment problem can be reduced to the edge coloring of a bipartite graph as follows.

Given any partial permutation $\pi$ with $K$ active inputs for $BL(N)$, we construct a graph $G(\pi, g)$, named *I/O mapping graph*, as follows. The vertex set consists of two parts, $V_1$ and $V_2$. Each part has $N/g$ vertices, i.e., each modulo-$g$ input (resp. output) group is represented by a vertex in $V_1$ (resp. $V_2$). There is an edge between vertex $\lfloor i/g \rfloor$ in $V_1$ and vertex $\lfloor j/g \rfloor$ in $V_2$ if $j = \pi(i)$. Thus, $G(\pi, g)$ is a bipartite graph with $N/g$ vertices in each of $V_1$ and $V_2$ and $K$ edges, where at most $g$ edges are incident at any vertex, and the degree of $G(\pi, g)$ equals to $g$. Since there may be more than one connection from a modulo-$g$ input group to the same modulo-$g$ output group, $G(\pi, g)$ may have parallel edges between two vertices.

It has been proved that any bipartite graph $G$ has a $\Delta(G)$-edge coloring [3]. Hence, $G(\pi, g)$ has a $g$-edge coloring since $G(\pi, g)$ is bipartite and $\Delta(G(\pi, g)) = g$. Thus, if we can find a $g$-edge coloring of $G(\pi, g)$, then we can assign wavelength $i$ to the connections corresponding to the edges with the color $i$, $0 \leq i \leq g - 1$. By Lemma 2, we know this wavelength assignment will not cause any crosstalk in $BL(N)$.

An efficient algorithm for finding a $g$-edge coloring of a bipartite graph can be found in [11], from which we have the following lemma.

**Lemma 3** *For any partial permutation $\pi$ with $K$ active inputs, a $g$-edge coloring of the I/O mapping graph $G(\pi, g)$ can be found in $O(\log g \cdot \log K)$ time using a completely connected multiprocessor system of $N$ PEs.*

By the above discussion and Lemma 3, the following Theorem is clear since $O(\log g) = O(\log N)$.

**Theorem 1** *For any partial permutation $\pi$ with $K (\leq N)$ active inputs, a crosstalk-free routing and wavelength assignment of $\pi$ for a WRSS $BL(N)$ can be found in $O(\log N \cdot \log K)$ time using at most $2^{\lfloor \frac{n+1}{2} \rfloor}$ wavelengths on a completely connected multiprocessor system of $N$ PEs.*

It is easy to verify that $2^{\lfloor \frac{n+1}{2} \rfloor}$ wavelengths are also necessary for a WRSS $BL(N)$ since there exist permutations with $2^{\lfloor \frac{n+1}{2} \rfloor}$ connections sharing a common SE.

# 4. Parallel Routing and Wavelength Assignment in WRSR Benes Networks

## 4.1. Benes Networks

The Benes network [2] is one of the most efficient switching architectures in terms of the number of $2 \times 2$ SEs used. We denote an $N \times N$ Benes network by $B(N)$, which can be constructed from $BL(N)$ by concatenating the mirror image of the first $\log N - 1$ stages of a $BL(N)$ to the back of the $BL(N)$. Thus, a $B(N)$ consists of $2 \log N - 1$ stages labeled by $0, 1, \cdots, 2n - 2$ from left to right. Each $B(N)$ contains 2 $B(N/2)$s from stage 1 to stage $2n - 3$, respectively named *upper subnetwork* and *lower subnetwork*, each having 2 $B(N/4)$s from stage 2 to $2n - 4$, named upper subnetwork and lower subnetwork of $B(N/4)$ respectively, and so on. Fig. 3 shows a $B(8)$, which contains 2 $B(4)$s within dashed boxes, each containing 2 $B(2)$s within dotted boxes.

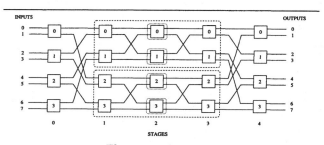

**Figure 3. A $B(8)$.**

Benes networks are space-division-multiplexing rearrangeable nonblocking. By [10, 26], we know that each permutation can be decomposed into two crosstalk-free partial permutations so that each CF partial permutation can be routed in an optical Benes network simultaneously. Hence, if we assign the same wavelength to the connections in the same CF partial permutation and assign the different wavelengths to the connections in different CF partial permutations, two wavelengths are sufficient for a WRSR $B(N)$ in which SEs may contain non-basic states. In the following two subsections, we will show the case that WRSR Benes networks only contain basic SEs, which has the reduced hardware complexity [16].

## 4.2. Upper Bound for the Number of Wavelengths

In order to find an upper bound for the number of wavelengths needed for crosstalk-free routing, we need to consider routing a permutation in an OMIN. We model the wavelength assignment for a permutation in an OMIN as the vertex coloring of a graph $G_\omega$, where the vertex set $V(G_\omega) = \{connections\}$ and the edge set $E(G_\omega) = \{\{u, v\}|$two connections $u$ and $v$ conflict with each other$\}$. We call $G_\omega$ a *wavelength conflict graph*. Although finding the minimum number of wavelengths and assigning the wavelengths to the connections are equivalent to finding the minimum number of colors and assigning the colors to the vertices respectively, which are both NP-complete for general graphs, we can find an upper bound for the number of wavelengths needed for realizing any permutation in WRSR Benes networks.

**Theorem 2** *For any permutation of a WRSR $B(N)$,*

$$\omega \leq \begin{cases} 2 \log N, & \text{if } N \leq 4 \\ 2 \log N - 1, & \text{otherwise} \end{cases}$$

*where $\omega$ is the number of wavelengths needed for the crosstalk-free routing of a permutation in $B(N)$.*

*Proof.* Each connection conflicts with at most $2 \log N - 1$ connections since it passes through total $2 \log N - 1$ basic SEs. Thus $\Delta(G_\omega) \leq 2 \log N - 1$. By Brooks theorem (see a proof in [3]), if $G_\omega$ is neither a complete graph nor an odd cycle, then we need at most $\Delta(G_\omega)$ colors to color $V(G_\omega)$ such that any two adjacent vertices have different colors; otherwise $\Delta(G_\omega) + 1$ colors are sufficient. Clearly, for any permutation of an OMIN with $N > \Delta(G_\omega) + 1$, $G_\omega$ is neither a complete graph nor an odd cycle since $\Delta(G_\omega) < N - 1$ and $N$ is even. Therefore, the theorem holds. $\square$

The simple proof of an upper bound on the number of required wavelengths does not directly lead to a wavelength assignment algorithm. In the next subsection, we utilize the properties of our permutation decomposition and the structure of Benes network to obtain a fast parallel crosstalk-free routing and wavelength assignment algorithm for a WRSR $B(N)$ using no more than $2 \log N$ wavelengths.

## 4.3. Routing and Wavelength Assignment Algorithm

Our routing and wavelength assignment algorithm uses the permutation decomposition algorithm of [10] as a subalgorithm and the vertex coloring technique similar to that of [4]. Conceptually, this algorithm has $\log N$ iterations from iteration 0 to iteration $\log N - 1$. In each iteration $i$, if $i < \log N - 1$, the algorithm decides the setting of SEs in stage $i$ and stage $2 \log N - 2 - i$ and uses at most $2i + 3$ wavelengths to ensure that there is no wavelength conflict in stage $j$ for any $j \in \{0, \cdots, i\} \cup \{2 \log N - 2 - i, \cdots, 2 \log N - 2\}$; if $i = \log N - 1$, the algorithm decides the setting of SEs in stage $\log N - 1$ and uses at most $2 \log N$ wavelengths to ensure that there is no wavelength conflict in $B(N)$.

We define a *wavelength class* as the set of connections assigned the same wavelength. A wavelength $\lambda$ is called a *free* wavelength for a connection $c$ if $\lambda$ is not assigned to any connection conflicting with $c$.

Each $PE_i$ is associated with connection $i$, and maintains one variable $\lambda(i)$, and two arrays $C_i$ and $W_i$, $0 \leq i < N - 1$. For any $0 \leq i \leq N - 1$, $C_i$ consists of $2 \log N - 1$ entries $C_i[j]$, $0 \leq j \leq 2 \log N - 2$, and $W_i$ consists of $2 \log N$ entries $W_i[k]$, $0 \leq k \leq 2 \log N - 1$. $\lambda(i)$, $C_i[j]$, and $W_i[k]$ are used to record the assigned wavelength, the new conflicting connections generated in iteration $\lfloor j/2 \rfloor$, and the number of conflicting connections with wavelength $k$, respectively, for connection $i$. We call $C_i$ and $W_i$ *connection conflict array* and *wavelength conflict array* of connection $i$, respectively. The other variables are all working variables. Initially, let $\lambda(i) := 0$, $C_i[j] := \infty$, and $W_i[k] := 0$, for $i \in \{0, \cdots, N - 1\}$, $j \in \{0, \cdots, \leq 2 \log N - 2\}$, and $k \in \{0, \cdots, 2 \log N - 1\}$, respectively. We use operator ":=" to denote an assignment local to a PE or to the control unit, and use operator "←" to denote an assignment requiring some interprocessor communication. In our parallel routing and wavelength assignment algorithm, each iteration $i$ consists of the following steps:

*Step 1-Permutation Decomposition*: decompose a (partial) permutation of each subnetwork $B(N/2^i)$ into two parts, each named upper or lower partial permutation, satisfying that two active inputs (resp. outputs) in an SE in the first (resp. last) stage of $B(N/2^i)$ are in different parts.

*Step 2-Setting SEs*: set the SEs in the first and last stages of each $B(N/2^i)$ in such a way that (i) if $i \neq \log N - 1$, the active inputs and outputs in the upper (resp. lower) partial permutation are connected with an upper (resp. lower) subnetwork $B(N/2^{i+1})$; (ii) if $i = \log N - 1$, each active input is connected with its mapped output.

The above two steps decide the routing for the given permutation. The following steps are used to find a wavelength assignment for the routing solution. For all $PE_c$, $0 \leq c \leq N - 1$, do in parallel:

*Step 3-Recording Conflicting Connections*: (i) if there is

a connection $c'$ so that $c$ and $c'$ pass through the same SE in stage $i$ and $c' \neq C_c[j]$ for all $0 \leq j < 2i$, then $C_c[2i] := c'$; (ii) if $i \neq \log N - 1$ and there is a connection $c''$ so that $c$ and $c''$ pass through the same SE in stage $2 \log N - 2 - i$ and $c'' \neq C_c[j]$ for all $0 \leq j < 2i + 1$, then $C_c[2i + 1] := c''$.

*Step 4-Reassigning Wavelengths*: if connection $c$ is in a lower partial permutation, $\lambda'(c) := \lambda(c)$ and $\lambda(c) := \lambda(c) + (2i + 1)$.

*Step 5-Updating Conflicting Wavelengths*: update wavelength conflicts by (i) adding new conflicts and (ii) updating existing conflicts, where (ii) consists of two substeps: (ii-1) clearing old wavelengths and (ii-2) adding updated wavelengths. The detailed implementation of this step is given in Algorithm 1.

---

if $i \neq \log N - 1$, $j' := 2i + 1$; otherwise, $j' := 2i$;
for all $PE_c$, $0 \leq c \leq N - 1$, do
  $t(c) := \infty$;
  for $j = 2i$ to $j'$ do
    if $C_c[j] \neq \infty$ and $\lambda(c) \leq 2 \log N - 1$ then
      $t(C_c[j]) \leftarrow \lambda(c)$;
    end if
    if $t(c) \neq \infty$ then
      $W_c[t(c)] := W_c[t(c)] + 1$;  /* (i): adding new conflicts */
      $t(c) := \infty$;
    end if
  end for
  if connection $c$ is in a lower partial permutation and $i \neq 0$ then
    for $j = 0$ to $2i - 1$ do
      if $C_c[j] \neq \infty$ then
        $t(C_c[j]) \leftarrow \lambda'(c)$;
      end if
      if $t(c) \neq \infty$ then
        $W_c[t(c)] := W_c[t(c)] - 1$;    /* (ii-1): clearing old wavelengths */
        $t(c) := \infty$;
      end if
      if $C_c[j] \neq \infty$ and $\lambda(c) \leq 2 \log N - 1$ then
        $t(C_c[j]) \leftarrow \lambda(c)$;
      end if
      if $t(c) \neq \infty$ then
        $W_c[t(c)] := W_c[t(c)] + 1$;  /* (ii-2): adding updated wavelengths */
        $t(c) := \infty$;
      end if
    end for
  end if
end for

**Algorithm 1:** Updating Conflicting Wavelengths

By the above five steps, it is easy to know the wavelength assignment in each iteration will not result in any conflict in the SEs that have been set up so far. However, we can reduce the number of wavelengths by reassigning new wave-

lengths in $\{0, \cdots, 2(i+1)\}$ to the connections with wavelengths in $\{2(i+1) + 1, \cdots, 2(2i+1) - 1 = 4i + 1\}$ without resulting in any wavelength conflict. (The correctness for the reassignment of wavelengths will be proved in Lemma 4.) This is done as follows: for $\lambda^* = 2(i+1) + 1$ to $4i + 1$, if $\lambda(c) = \lambda^*$, then perform the following two steps:

*Step 6-Adjusting Wavelengths*: find a free wavelength $j \in \{0, 1, \cdots, j' + 1\}$ such that $W_c[j] = 0$ by checking the values in $\{W_c[0], \cdots, W_c[j' + 1]\}$, and $\lambda'(c) := \lambda(c)$ and $\lambda(c) := j$. (The value of $j'$ in this step and next step is the same as that in Algorithm 1.)

*Step 7-Updating Conflicting Wavelengths*: for $k = 0$ to $j'$, do (i) if $C_c[k] \neq \infty$ and $\lambda'(c) \leq 2 \log N - 1$, then decrease $W_{C_c[k]}[\lambda'(c)]$ by 1; and (ii) if $C_c[k] \neq \infty$, then increase $W_{C_c[k]}[\lambda(c)]$ by 1. (The detailed implementation is similar to Algorithm 1)

**Lemma 4** *After iteration $i$, $0 \leq i \leq \log N - 1$, of our parallel routing and wavelength assignment algorithm, there is no wavelength conflict in stage $j$, for any $j \in \{0, \cdots, i\} \cup \{2 \log N - 2 - i, \cdots, 2 \log N - 2\}$, and at most $\omega_i$ wavelengths are used, where*

$$\omega_i \leq \begin{cases} 2(i+1), & \text{if } i = 0, \log N - 1 \\ 2(i+1) + 1, & \text{otherwise} \end{cases}$$

*Proof.* The proof is done by induction on iteration $i$. If $i = 0$, it is true since two connections passing though the same SE in the first or last stage are assigned different wavelengths and $\omega_0 = 2$. Now we assume that it is true for any $i < k \leq \log N - 1$. In iteration $k$, by assumption, we know that there is no wavelength conflict in stage $j$, for any $j \in \{0, \cdots, k-1\} \cup \{2 \log N - 1 - k, \cdots, 2 \log N - 2\}$, using $\omega_{k-1}$ wavelengths. By Step 4, two connections passing though the same SE in stage $k$ and stage $2 \log N - 2 - k$ are assigned different wavelengths using $2 \cdot \omega_{k-1}$ wavelengths. Hence, there is no wavelength conflict in stage $j$ for any $j \in \{0, \cdots, k\} \cup \{2 \log N - 2 - k, \cdots, 2 \log N - 2\}$, using $2 \cdot \omega_{k-1}$ wavelengths. In the following, we show that $2 \cdot \omega_{k-1}$ wavelengths are too much for the case that $2 \cdot \omega_{k-1} > 2(k+1) + 1$ if $k \neq \log N - 1$ or the case that $2 \cdot \omega_{k-1} > 2 \log N$ if $k = \log N - 1$. For iteration $k$, each connection conflicts with at most $2(k+1)$ connections if $k \neq \log N - 1$ and at most $2 \log N - 1$ if $k = \log N - 1$. This is because for iteration $j$, if $j \leq k < \log N - 1$, we need to consider wavelength conflicts in two stages, stages $j$ and $2 \log N - 2 - j$; if $j = k = \log N - 1$, we only need to consider wavelength conflict in stage $\log N - 1$ since stage $j$ and stage $2 \log N - 2 - j$ are the same. Thus, in Step 6, a free wavelength of index no greater than $2(k+1)$ for $k < \log N - 1$ and $2 \log N - 1$ for $k = \log N - 1$ can always be found. Furthermore, the connections in the same wavelength class have no wavelength conflict so that we can do wavelength adjustment for these connections at the same time without resulting in any new conflict. □

**Theorem 3** *For any (partial) permutation, a routing and wavelength assignment for a WRSR $B(N)$ can be found in $O(\log^3 N)$ time using at most $2 \log N$ wavelengths on a completely connected multiprocessor system of $N$ PEs.*

*Proof.* By the recursive structure of $B(N)$ and by applying our permutation decomposition algorithm recursively, we can find a setting of SEs in $B(N)$ so that any permutation can be realized. By Lemma 4, we know that the wavelength assignment assures no wavelength conflict for the routing solution. Now, we analyze the time complexity. In each iteration, Steps 2 and 4 take $O(1)$ time and each of other steps takes $O(\log N)$ time. Iteration $i$ has at most $\omega_{i-1}(\leq 2i+1)$ wavelength classes to be adjusted, and thus, Steps 6 and 7 in iteration $i$ are executed at most $\omega_{i-1}(\leq 2i+1) = O(\log N)$ times. Since there are $\log N$ iterations, the total time complexity of our routing and wavelength assignment algorithm is $O(\log^3 N)$. $\square$

## 5. Implementation on Realistic Multiprocessor Systems

The presented algorithms running on a completely connected multiprocessor system can be easily transformed to algorithms on more realistic multiprocessor systems. As an example, in this section, we show how to implement our algorithms on a hypercube of $N/2$ PEs such that any (partial) permutation can be routed without crosstalk in a WRSS $BL(N)$ and a WRSR $B(N)$ in $O(\log^4 N)$ time.

In our presentation, the Benes network $B(N)$ is the back-to-back concatenation of two $BL(N)$'s. A *Butterfly network* (also known as Banyan-type network) of $N$ inputs and $N$ outputs, denoted by $BF(N)$, is isomorphic to $BL(N)$ (see Fig. 4 (a) and (b)). An $n$-dimensional *hypercube*, denoted by $H(2^n)$, is constructed recursively. $H(2)$ is an edge with two nodes. $H(2^n)$ is constructed from $2$ $H(2^{n-1})$'s by adding $2^{n-1}$ edges, named *n-dimension edges*, that connect the corresponding $2^{n-1}$ nodes in $2$ $H(2^{n-1})$'s. Butterfly networks are in the family of the hypercube [9] because $H(N/2)$ can be obtained from $BF(N)$ by merging all SEs in row $i$ of $BF(N)$ as a node $i$ of $H(N/2)$ and merging all links connecting SEs contained in two different nodes as an edge of $H(N/2)$. Fig. 4 (c) shows a $H(4)$, where $k$-dimension edges are labeled by $k^*$. Since each PE can communicate with at most one other PE in every communication step of our algorithms, in the following, we show how to implement one communication step of a completely connected multiprocessor system of $N$ PEs by a set of one-to-one communications on a $H(N/2)$, in which each PE is responsible for a pair of connections $i$ and $\bar{i}$.

The time complexity of our routing and wavelength assignment algorithm for a WRSS $BL(N)$ depends on $g$-edge coloring algorithm, which can be implemented in $O(\log^4 N)$ time on $H(N/2)$ [11], Thus, the rout-

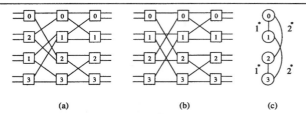

**Figure 4. The relationship of Baseline network, Butterfly network and hypercube (a)** $BL(8)$ **(b)** $BF(8)$ **(c)** $H(4)$

ing and wavelength assignment algorithm for a WRSS $BL(N)$ takes $O(\log^4 N)$ on $H(N/2)$.

Considering our routing and wavelength assignment algorithm for a WRSR $B(N)$, we can see that the total time for routing on $H(N/2)$ only depends on the decomposition algorithm [10], which can be implemented in $O(\log^3 N)$ time on $H(N/2)$ since each pointer jumping step on a completely connected multiprocessor system can be implemented on $H(N/2)$ by a sorting operation, which takes $O(\log^2 N)$ time. Consequently, the routing on $H(N/2)$ takes $O(\log^4 N)$ time. For wavelength assignment, communications among PEs only occur in Step 5 and Step 7, in which $PE_c$ needs to talk to $PE_d$ if $d$ is recorded in $C_c$ (see "$\leftarrow$" operations in Algorithm 1). Fortunately, all conflicting connections of $c$ are recorded in connection conflict array $C_c$ in the order of SEs through which $c$ passes from both sides, i.e. from a pair of outside stages $i$ and $2 \log N - 2 - i$ towards the center stage, stage $\log N - 1$. Thus, these conflicting connections can be located using this ordering via interstage connections in $B(N)$. Since the interstage interconnection pattern between stage $i$ (resp. $2 \log N - 2 - i$) and stage $i+1$ (resp. $2 \log N - 3 - i$) of $B(N)$ corresponds to $(\log \frac{N}{2} - i)$-dimension edges of $H(N/2)$, the communication ordering defined by connection conflict arrays directly corresponds to a classic hypercube communication technique called *dimension ordering*. Thus, the total time for wavelength assignment on $H(N/2)$ remains unchanged. Therefore, when our routing and wavelength assignment algorithm for a WRSR $B(N)$ is implemented on $H(N/2)$, it has a slowdown factor of $O(\log N)$ and its time complexity is $O(\log^4 N)$.

## 6. Conclusion

In this paper, we studied the crosstalk problem in OMINs using wavelength dilation approach. We proposed parallel routing and wavelength assignment algorithms to route a partial permutation in optical WRSS Banyan networks and WRSR Benes networks so that there is no crosstalk in these networks. For an arbitrary partial permutation, it can be routed without crosstalk in a WRSS $BL(N)$ in $O(\log^2 N)$

time using at most $2^{\lfloor \frac{\log N + 1}{2} \rfloor}$ wavelengths and in a WRSR $B(N)$ with only basic SEs in $O(\log^3 N)$ time using at most $2 \log N$ wavelengths, on a completely connected multiprocessor system with $N$ PEs. The proposed algorithms run on a completely connected multiprocessor system can be easily transformed to algorithms on more realistic multiprocessor systems. For example, our routing and wavelength assignment algorithms for a WRSS $BL(N)$ and a WRSR $B(N)$ take $O(\log^4 N)$ time on a hypercube with $N/2$ PEs.

# References

[1] D.P. Agrawal, "Graph Theoretical Analysis and Design of Multistage Interconnection Networks", *IEEE Transactions on Computers*, vol. C-32, no. 7, pp. 637-648, July 1983.

[2] V.E. Benes, *Mathematical Theory of Connecting Networks and Telephone Traffic*, Academic Press, New York, 1965.

[3] J.A. Bondy and U.S.R. Murty, *Graph Theory with Applications*, Elsevier North-Holland, 1976.

[4] A.V. Goldberg, S.A. Plotkin, and G.E. Shannon, "Parallel Symmetry-Breaking in Sparse Graphs," *Proceedings of the Nineteenth Annual ACM Symposium on Theory of Computing*, pp. 315-323, 1987.

[5] Q.P. Gu and S. Peng, "Wavelengths Requirement for Permutation Routing in All-Optical Multistage Interconnection Networks", *Proceedings of 14th International Parallel and Distributed Processing Symposium (IPDPS)*, pp. 761-768, May 2000.

[6] H. Hinton, "A Non-Blocking Optical Interconnection Network Using Directional Couplers", *Proceedings of IEEE Global Telecommunications Conference*, pp. 885-889, Nov. 1984.

[7] D.K. Hunter, P.J. Legg, and I. Andonovic, "Architecture for Large Dilated Optical TDM Switching Networks", *IEE Proceedings on Optoelectronics*, vol. 140, no. 5, pp. 337-343, Oct. 1993.

[8] F.K. Hwang, *The Mathematical Theory of Nonblocking Switching Networks*, World Scientific, 1998.

[9] F.T. Leighton, *Introduction to Parallel Algorithms and Architectures: Arrays · Trees · Hypercubes*, Morgan Kaufmann Publishers, 1992.

[10] E. Lu and S.Q. Zheng, "High-Speed Crosstalk-Free Routing for Optical Multistage Interconnection Networks", *Proceedings of the 12th IEEE International Conference on Computer Communications and Networks*, pp. 249-254, Oct. 2003.

[11] E. Lu and S.Q. Zheng, "Parallel Routing Algorithms for Nonblocking Electronic and Photonic Multistage Switching Networks", *Proceedings of IEEE International Parallel and Distributed Processing Symposium (IPDPS 2004), Workshop on Advances in Parallel and Distributed Computing Models*, April, 2004.

[12] G. Maier, A. Pattavina, and S.G. Colombo, "Control of Non-filterable Crosstalk in Optical-Cross-Connect Banyan Architectures", *Proceedings of IEEE Global Telecommunications Conference GLOBECOM*, vol. 2, pp. 1228-1232, Nov.-Dec. 2000.

[13] G. Maier and A. Pattavina, "Design of Photonic Rearrangeable Networks with Zero First-Order Switching-Element-Crosstalk", *IEEE Transactions on Communications*, vol. 49, no. 7, pp. 1268-1279, Jul. 2001.

[14] K. Padmanabhan and A. Netravali, "Dilated Network for Photonic Switching", *IEEE Transactions on Communications*, vol. COM-35, no. 12, pp. 1357-1365, Dec. 1987.

[15] Y. Pan, C. Qiao, and Y. Yang, "Optical Multistage Interconnection Networks: New Challenges and Approaches", *IEEE Communications Magazine*, vol. 37, no. 2, pp. 50-56, Feb. 1999.

[16] G. Pieris and G. Sasaki, "A Linear Lightwave Benes Network", *IEEE/ACM Transactions on Networking*, vol. 1, no. 4, pp. 441-445, Aug. 1993.

[17] C. Qiao, R. Melhem, D. Chiarulli, and S. Levitan, "A Time Domain Approach for Avoiding Crosstalk in Optical Blocking Multistage Interconnection Networks", *IEEE Journal Lightwave Technology*, vol. 12, no. 10, pp. 1854-1862, Oct. 1994.

[18] X. Qin and Y. Yang, "Nonblocking WDM Switching Networks with Full and Limited Wavelength Conversion", *IEEE Transactions on Communications*, vol. 50, no. 12, pp. 2032-2041, Dec. 2002.

[19] J. Sharony, S. Jiang, T.E. Stern, and K.W. Cheung, "Wavelength Rearrangeable and Strictly Nonblocking Networks", *IEEE Electronics Letters*, vol. 28, no. 6, pp. 536-537, Mar. 1992.

[20] J. Sharony, K.W. Cheung, and T.E. Stern, "The Wavelength Dilation Concept in Lightwave Networks-Implementation and System Considerations", *IEEE Journal of Lightwave Technology*, vol. 1, no. 5/6, pp. 900 -907, May-Jun. 1993.

[21] X. Shen, F. Yang, and Yi Pan, "Equivalent Permutation Capabilities between Time-Division Optical Omega Networks and Non-Optical Extra-Stage Omega Networks", *IEEE/ACM Transactions on Networking*, vol. 9, no. 4, pp. 518-524, Aug. 2001.

[22] G.H. Song and M. Goodman, "Asymmetrically-Dilated Cross-Connect Switches for Low-Crosstalk WDM Optical Networks", *Proceedings of IEEE 8th Annual Meeting Conference on Lasers and Electro-Optics Society Annual Meeting*, vol. 1, pp. 212-213, Oct. 1995.

[23] F.M. Suliman, A.B. Mohammad, and K. Seman, "A Space Dilated Lightwave Network-a New Approach", *Proceedings of IEEE 10th International Conference on Telecommunications (ICT 2003)*, vol. 2, pp. 1675 -1679, 2003.

[24] M. Vaez and C.T. Lea, "Strictly Nonblocking Directional-Coupler-Based Switching Networks under Crosstalk Constraint", *IEEE Transactions on Communications*, vol. 48, no. 2, pp. 316-323, Feb. 2000.

[25] T.S. Wong and C.T. Lea, "Crosstalk Reduction Through Wavelength Assignment in WDM Photonic Switching networks", *IEEE Transactions on Communications*, vol. 49, no. 7, pp. 1280-1287, Feb. 2001.

[26] Y. Yang, J. Wang, and Y. Pan, "Permutation Capability of Optical Multistage Interconnection Networks", *Journal of Parallel and Distributed Computing*, vol. 60, no. 1, pp. 72-91, Jan. 2000.

# An Effective Fault-Tolerant Routing Methodology for Direct Networks *

M.E. Gómez, J. Flich, P. López, A. Robles, and J. Duato
Dept. of Computer Engineering
Universidad Politécnica de Valencia
Camino de Vera, 14, 46071–Valencia, Spain
E-mail: megomez@gap.upv.es

N.A. Nordbotten, O. Lysne, and T. Skeie
Simula Research Laboratory
P.O. Box 134, N-1325 Lysaker, Norway

E-mail: nilsno@simula.no

## Abstract

Current massively parallel computing systems are being built with thousands of nodes, which significantly affects the probability of failure. In [14], we proposed a methodology to design fault-tolerant routing algorithms for direct interconnection networks. The methodology uses a simple mechanism: for some source-destination pairs, packets are first forwarded to an intermediate node, and later, from this node to the destination node. Minimal adaptive routing is used along both subpaths. For those cases where the methodology cannot find a suitable intermediate node, it combines the use of intermediate nodes with two additional mechanisms: disabling adaptive routing and using misrouting on a per-packet basis. While the combination of these three mechanisms tolerates a large number of faults, each one requires adding some hardware support in the network and also introduces some overhead. In this paper, we will perform an in-depth detailed analysis of the impact of these mechanisms on network behaviour. We will analyze the impact of the three mechanisms separately and combined. The ultimate goal of this paper is to obtain a suitable combination of mechanisms that is able to meet the trade-off between fault-tolerance degree, routing complexity, and performance.

## 1  Introduction

There exist many compute-intensive applications that require a huge amount of processing power, only achieved with massively parallel computers, such as the Earth Simulator [12], the ASCI Red [1], and the BlueGene/L [3].

The high running times of applications require to keep such systems running even in the presence of failures. However, the huge number of processors and associated devices (memories, switches, links, etc.) significantly increases the probability of failure. In this paper, we deal with failures in the interconnection network. These failures may isolate a large fraction of the machine, wasting many healthy processors that otherwise could have been used.

There exist several approaches to tolerate faults in the interconnection network. The most frequently used technique in commercial systems consists of replicating components, swapping the faulty and the spare components in case of failure. The main drawback of this approach is the extra cost of the spare components. Another powerful technique is based on reconfiguring the routing tables in the case of failure, adapting them to the new topology after the failure [4]. This technique is extremely flexible but this flexibility may also kill performance. However, most of the solutions proposed in the literature are based on designing fault-tolerant routing algorithms able to find an alternative path when a packet meets a fault along the path to its destination. Most of them require a significant amount of extra hardware resources (e.g., virtual channels) to route packets around faulty components depending on either the number of tolerated faults [8] or the number of dimensions of the topology [19]. Alternatively, there exist some fault-tolerant routing strategies that use none or a very small number of extra resources to handle failures, at the expense of providing a lower fault-tolerance degree [8, 13], disabling a certain number of healthy nodes (either in blocks (fault regions) [5, 6] or individually [9, 10]), preventing packets from being routed adaptively [15], or drastically increasing the latencies for some packets [21]. Moreover, when faults occur, link utilization may become significantly unbalanced when using these fault-tolerant routing strategies, thus leading to premature network saturation and consequently degrading network performance.

From our point of view, a fault-tolerant strategy for the interconnection network should not degrade performance at all in the absence of faults but should also tolerate a reasonably large number of faults without significantly degrading performance, without disabling any healthy node, without requiring too many extra hardware resources, and without introducing any significant penalty (e.g., extra latency) when routing packets in a faulty network. In

*This work was supported by the Spanish MCYT under Grant TIC2003-08154-C06-01.

[14], we proposed a fault-tolerant routing methodology that satisfies all the properties mentioned above. It allows the use of fully adaptive routing in the absence of failures and does not sacrifice any healthy node. In order to avoid network failures, packets are first forwarded to an intermediate node, and then, from this node to the destination node. Minimal adaptive routing is used in both subpaths. The methodology requires the use of, at least, three virtual channels (one adaptive and two escape) per physical channel. In order to avoid deadlocks, two virtual networks are defined, each one relying on a different escape channel but both using the same adaptive channel(s).

However, for some fault combinations and some source-destination pairs, the methodology proposed in [14] could not provide a suitable intermediate node. In these cases, two additional mechanisms were used. The first one is disabling adaptive routing for some paths (i.e., deterministic routing is used). The second one is using misrouting for some paths to circumvent some special fault combinations. In some cases, it may even be necessary to combine the three mechanisms in order to tolerate a given fault combination.

The effectiveness of a given fault-tolerant solution for a system should be measured by taking into account three aspects: (i) fault-tolerance degree, (ii) cost and the additional resources required, and (iii) performance achieved by the system when using the selected solution (both in the absence and presence of failures).

The methodology proposed in [14] is 7-fault tolerant in a 3D torus network. However, the implementation cost and the performance degradation of the proposed solution were not analyzed and compared to the mechanism used in the BlueGene/L supercomputer. Most important, the relationship among cost, performance, and fault tolerance were not obtained. As commented before, the proposed solution relies on the use of intermediate nodes for routing plus two additional mechanisms in order to tolerate more fault combinations. Every additional mechanism affect fault tolerance but also performance and implementation cost in a different way, and it is therefore desirable to analyze this trade-off.

In this paper, we take on this challenge. We will perform a detailed analysis of the different mechanisms used by the fault-tolerant routing methodology proposed in [14]. To this end, we will analyze the three mechanisms individually and in a combined way when applied to 3-D tori. In particular, we will analyze the pros and cons of each mechanism, trying to obtain a suitable mechanism combination that is able to meet the trade-off between fault-tolerance degree, routing complexity, and performance.

The rest of the paper is organized as follows. Section 2 briefly describes the methodology proposed in [14] to make the paper self-contained. In Section 3, we analyze in detail the different mechanisms that could be applied by the methodology, also showing their performance evaluation results. Finally, in Section 4, some conclusions and future work are drawn.

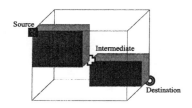

**Figure 1. Routing through an intermediate node.**

## 2 Fault-Tolerant Methodology

A static fault model[1] is assumed for the methodology Therefore, it only focuses on the computation of the routing info for every source-destination pair, knowing in advance where the failures are located. The methodology assumes at least three virtual channels (at least one adaptive and two escape) per physical channel. The adaptive channel(s) enable(s) routing through any minimal path, whereas the escape channels guarantee deadlock freedom based on the bubble flow control [20] and the dimension order routing.

A fault-free path will be computed by the methodology for each source-destination $(S - D)$ pair. In the presence of faults, the problem arises with the paths that may reach at least one faulty component. The methodology avoids these faults by using intermediate nodes for routing. For these source-destination pairs, packets will be first forwarded to an intermediate node ($I$), and later, from this node to the destination node. Notice that packets are not ejected and reinjected at the intermediate nodes. Minimal adaptive routing will be used in both subpaths.

The intermediate node $I$ is selected inside the minimal adaptive cube defined by $S$ and $D$. Thus, both subcubes defined by $S$ and $I$, and by $I$ and $D$, will be inside this cube, but they will be smaller and will avoid the failure. Figure 1 shows these subcubes for a given source, destination, and intermediate node.

At the intermediate node, some special actions must be performed in order to avoid deadlocks. We simply use two different escape channels. One of them will be used as escape channel for the $S$-$I$ stretch and the second one for the $I$-$D$ stretch. Therefore, we define two virtual networks. Each one will rely on a different escape channel but both will use the same adaptive channel(s).

Different intermediate nodes can be used for a particular $S - D$ pair. The general rules used to select the intermediate nodes in a 3D-torus network are the following:

(i) The intermediate node must overcome or leave behind the failure in one of the dimensions. This allows overriding the failure in the path between the intermediate node and

[1]In a static fault model, all the faults are known in advance when the machine is (re)booted. This fault model needs to be combined with checkpointing techniques.

the destination.

(ii) The intermediate node in one of the other dimensions must not overcome the failure. This allows overriding the failure in the cube defined between the source and the intermediate node.

(iii) In the remaining dimension, the coordinate of the intermediate node can vary between the coordinates of the source and the destination.

There are some particular faulty situations, where minimal routing is not possible. In particular, if the source, destination, and failure are in the same ring and the latter is located along the minimal path between the source and destination. The solution consists of selecting an intermediate node in the non-minimal path (along the ring in the opposite direction) from $S$ to $D$, in such a way that both subpaths $S - I$ and $I - D$ are minimal.

By using intermediate nodes, all the fault combinations for one fault are tolerated by the methodology, also using minimal paths in most cases.

In order to deal with more than one fault at a time, the methodology defines an area where all the failures are confined and uses intermediate nodes (computed following the aforementioned rules) to avoid this area. Figure 2.(a) shows the area that contains the faults that affect the path and possible intermediate nodes for a 2D Torus network, for a given source-destination pair and with several failures in the network.

With more than one failure it is sometimes necessary to use additional mechanisms. For instance, Figure 2.(b) shows a combination of 7 faults that is impossible to solve only with the use of intermediate nodes. In particular, there is no $I$ node that can be reached from $S$ that can reach $D$ (by using adaptive routing in both stretches).

Figure 2.(b) shows a possible path that could be used from $S$ to $D$, using the node located at $X_S - 1, Y_S + 1$ as the intermediate node. In order to reach $I$ from $S$, adaptive routing can not be used, because some faults could be encountered. In order to properly reach $I$ from $S$, misrouting and disabling adaptive routing is used. Misrouting allows us to force the routing of packets along several directions at the beginning of the path to the intermediate node or/and at the beginning of the path to the destination. Once misrouting is finished, normal routing is resumed.

When using misrouting, an appropriate deadlock-free deterministic routing algorithm is required. The methodology uses the direction order-routing ($X + Y + Z + X - Y - Z-$) instead of the dimension-order routing ($X \pm Y \pm Z\pm$). This routing is deadlock-free and allows routing through useful non-minimal paths, since it allows routing packets in both directions of a dimension. In the example (Figure 2.(b)), by using direction-order routing, misrouting, and disabling adaptive routing, the packets will be misrouted one hop in the $X+$ direction, and then forwarded by using direction-order routing to the intermediate node along the $Y+$ and $X-$ direction. Notice

that disabling adaptive routing is required after misrouting in order to avoid all the faults. In order to reach $D$ from $I$, misrouting must also be used in order to avoid faults. The packet will be misrouted seven hops in the $Y+$ direction to reach the destination node.

To sum up, in a scenario with more than one failure, the methodology will try to override the faults by using all the strategies we have shown so far. Basically, for a given source-destination pair and a set of failures which compromises the set of minimal paths between them, the methodology:

- Searches for a minimal path:

- It will look for a valid *intermediate node* along any minimal path. If there are several valid intermediate nodes, one of them will be randomly selected.

- If it is not possible to avoid faults using only an intermediate node along a minimal path, then *deterministic routing* will be computed with or without an *intermediate node*.

- If routing through minimal path is not found, then it tries non-minimal paths:

- This non-minimal path can be obtained by using one or both of the *Intermediate node* and *Misrouting* mechanisms.

- The mechanism of *disabling adaptive routing* can be applied to one or both subpaths, S-I and I-D.

- The combination that provides the shortest path is always selected, giving priority to the one that does not disable adaptive routing.

In order to support the methodology, packets that use an intermediate node for routing will have two headers, the first one for routing the packet towards the intermediate node, and the second one for routing the packet towards the final destination. Additional info is required in both packet headers. In particular, some packets will include control fields about misrouting (direction and hops) and about switching off adaptive routing. Assuming that up to three misroutings can be used, each packet header will include the directions to misroute (six directions are possible in a 3D Torus, two on each dimension, so 3 bits are needed) and the number of hops to misroute along each direction. An extra bit in both headers indicates if adaptive routing is disabled for the packet. We have reserved 3 bytes in the packet header in order to indicate the three directions to misroute and their hops. In this way, up to eight hops can be done in each direction.

## 3 Evaluation of the Methodology

In this section we will evaluate the impact of the different mechanisms proposed in the methodology, both separately and considering possible combinations among them. First, we are interested in analyzing their fault-tolerant properties, that is, how many faults each mechanism is able to tolerate. Only link faults are considered. A node failure can be modeled by the failure of all the links connected to it

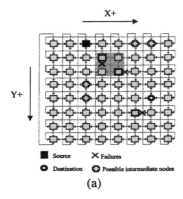

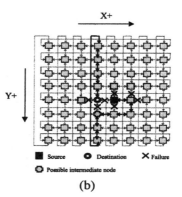

(a)                                                    (b)

**Figure 2. Examples of 2D Tori with more than one failure. (a) A faulty region is defined and intermediate nodes are computed. (b) Misrouting and disabling adaptive routing is required.**

We will say that the methodology is $n$−fault tolerant, if it is able to tolerate any combination of $n$ failures. Indeed, we will say that a given combination of failures is tolerated if the mechanism is able to provide routing info to communicate every source-destination pair in the network. If, for a combination of $n$ faults, there is at least one source-destination pair whose path is not fault-free, then the combination is not tolerated, and the methodology will not be $n$-fault tolerant. Faults can disconnect some nodes in the network. As these nodes can no longer send or receive messages, this situation is not considered as a non-tolerated combination.

Second, we will analyze the percentage of routing paths that use each of the mechanisms. Next, we will analyze the complexity of the methodology in terms of the number of resources and the hardware support that is required by each one of the mechanisms that can be used by the methodology.

Finally, we are interested in analyzing how the different mechanisms and their combinations influence network performance. It is desirable that the network performance does not degrade significantly in the presence of failures. So, we will analyze network performance for different number of failures. Moreover, we are interested in comparing the proposed methodology with real fault-tolerant mechanisms used in nowadays systems. In particular, we will compare performance degradation of the proposed methodology with the one obtained when using a mechanism similar to the one used in the IBM BlueGene/L supercomputer.

### 3.1 BlueGene/L Supercomputer

The BlueGene/L supercomputer [3] is a jointly funded research partnership between IBM [16] and Lawrence Livermore National Laboratory [17] as part of the United States Department of Energy ASCI Advanced Architecture Research Program. This massively parallel system of $65,536$ nodes is based on a new architecture that exploits

system-on-a-chip technology to get target peak processing power of 360 teraFLOPS. The machine is expected to be operational in 2004-2005. BlueGene/L is configured as a 3D Torus of $64 \times 32 \times 32$ compute nodes, constructed with point-to-point serial links between the routers.

The torus network uses virtual cut-through [18] and provides both adaptive and deterministic minimal-path routing. Physical channels are multiplexed into four virtual channels. Two[2] virtual channels are used for adaptive minimal routing [11]. The remaining two virtual channels are used for deterministic minimal routing. The first one is used to implement the escape paths for the adaptive routing, whereas the second one is reserved for high priority packets. In the deterministic virtual channels, the bubble flow control mechanism [20] is used to avoid deadlocks inside a ring, whereas the dimension order routing is used to avoid deadlocks when routing through different dimensions.

The BlueGene/L supercomputer uses a static fault model with checkpointing. Fault-tolerance is achieved by marking healthy nodes as faults in order to preserve its topology and routing scheme. The number of marked nodes is quite large: all the nodes included in four planes (4,096 or 8,192 nodes) that contain the faulty node/link are marked as faulty. A special hardware bypasses the four planes and, therefore, the topology is the same and routing is not changed.

### 3.2 Simulation Tool

A detailed event-driven simulator has been implemented to model the performance behavior exhibited by the proposed methodology and a mechanism similar to the one used in the BlueGene/L supercomputer. The simulator models a direct interconnection network with point-to-point bidirectional serial links. Each router has a non-multiplexed

---

[2]It is expected that most of the traffic will use adaptive routing, so, in order to reduce the head-off-line blocking effect, two virtual channels are used.

crossbar with queues only at the input ports. Each physical input port uses four virtual channels. Each virtual channel provides buffering resources in order to store two packets. The crossbar has an input for each input queue and an output for each output port. A round-robin policy has been used to select among packets contending for the same output port.

Packets are adaptively routed through minimal paths by using the two adaptive virtual channels. In the two escape channels, packets are deterministically routed following the $X+Y+Z+X-Y-Z-$ ordering when misrouting is available. Otherwise, dimension-order routing ($X \pm Y \pm Z\pm$) is applied. The bubble flow control mechanism is used in both escape channels. When a packet arrives at an input port, the corresponding escape queue will be used only if the adaptive queues are full. The output port selected for each routed packet will take into account the information located in the packet header (destination node, adaptive routing disabled/enabled, and misrouting info), the status of available output ports, and the status of the queues at the neighbor nodes.

In all the presented simulation results, the network topology is a 3D Torus, since it is the one adopted in the BlueGene/L and other commercial multicomputers. Four internal ports connects the router to the processing node. We will present results for $3 \times 3 \times 3$ (27 nodes) and $8 \times 8 \times 8$ (512 nodes) torus networks. Although current systems are built with large topologies (e.g. a $32 \times 32 \times 64$ Torus for BlueGene/L), smaller networks can be exhaustively evaluated from a fault-tolerant point of view and the results can be then transferred to larger networks.

In order to make the performance results independent of the relative positions of the faults, a large number of simulations (for every number of fault combinations analyzed) has been performed. When applicable, confidence intervals will be shown. For each simulation run, we assume that the packet generation rate is constant and equal for all the nodes. The destination of a message is randomly chosen (with the same probability for all the nodes). This pattern has been widely used in other evaluation studies [2, 7]. In all the simulations, the packet length is set to 128 bytes.

## 3.3 Combinations of Fault Tolerant Mechanisms Evaluated

In this paper, we are interested in identifying the mechanism, or the combination of them, that best meet the trade-off among cost, performance, and fault-tolerance degree. The proposed fault-tolerant methodology combines the use of three mechanisms: intermediate nodes, disabling adaptive routing, and misrouting. We will refer to them as I, D, and M, respectively. These mechanisms will be evaluated separately (I, D, M) and all together (I+D+M). The combinations of I+D, I+M, and M+D will be also evaluated. In what follows, we summarize each mechanism and their possible combinations

- I: All the packets are adaptively routed. To avoid faults, an intermediate node is used if needed.
- D: To avoid faults, packets can disable adaptive routing if needed (i.e., deterministic routing is applied). Otherwise, adaptive routing is applied.
- M: To avoid faults, packet routing is forced along up to three directions at the beginning of the path to the destination (following minimal or non-minimal paths). Then, packets are adaptively routed. Notice that this mechanism also could be used, in a particular case, to route packets through minimal paths in a deterministic way.
- I+D: To avoid faults, packets can use an intermediate node and/or disable adaptive routing. In the case of using an intermediate node, deterministic routing could be applied either just along a subpath or along the entire path. Packets are adaptively routed unless adaptivity is disabled for that packet.
- I+M: If an intermediate node is used, misrouting (M) can be applied, if needed, at the beginning of one subpath or both subpaths (S-I, I-D). Otherwise, misrouting (M) can be applied, if needed, at the beginning of the path to destination. In all cases, packets are adaptively routed after misrouting.
- D+M: To avoid faults, packet routing can be forced along up to three directions at the beginning of the path to destination. Then, packets can disable adaptive routing if needed to avoid faults (following non-minimal paths). Otherwise, adaptive routing is applied after misrouting.
- I+D+M: It was already described in Section 2.

## 3.4 Fault Analysis Models

For a reduced number of faults in the network, all the possible combinations of faults will be explored. However, as the number of faults increases, the number of possible fault combinations increases exponentially. Therefore, from a particular number of faults, it is impossible to explore all the fault combinations in a reasonable amount of time. We will tackle this problem with two approaches. In the first approach, we will focus on faults bounded into a limited region of the network. Notice that, the worst combinations of faults to be solved by the methodology are those where they are closely located. This is because the number of fault-free paths among the nodes that are surrounded by the faults will be reduced. As the number of fault combinations within this region is much lower than the one for the entire network, all the fault combinations can be evaluated. Although the results obtained cannot be directly extended to the generic case, where the faults are located over the entire network, it will give us an approximation of the effectiveness of the methodology in the worst case.

For this, we must define the region where the faults will be located. The region will be formed by all the links in the positive direction of dimensions of the nodes that are one hop away from a node (the center node). The center node will be randomly selected[3]. The region will be referred to as *distance 1* region and will be formed by 21 links. Notice that for a high number of faults and for a large number of fault combinations, the center node will be hardly accessible, as very few links will be non-faulty.

In the second approach, a statistical analysis will be performed, analyzing a subset of fault combinations randomly located over the entire network. From the obtained results, statistical conclusions can be extracted about the fault-tolerance degree of our methodology.

## 3.5 Evaluation Results

### 3.5.1 Fault-tolerance

Table 1 shows the percentages of fault combinations not tolerated by the different mechanisms and their possible combinations in a $3 \times 3 \times 3$ torus network. Results for the three models of fault analysis (exhaustive, *distance 1*, and probabilistic) are shown. In the probabilistic results, the error is always less than 1%. As can be observed, if the methodology uses all the mechanisms (I+D+M) a very good fault-tolerance degree is achieved. In particular, I+D+M is able to tolerate all the evaluated fault combinations with up to 7 faults[4]. Notice that all the fault combinations with six and seven faults have been only analyzed by using the *distance 1* analysis model. As this represents a worst-case analysis, it seems very probable that the mechanism is 7-fault tolerant. Moreover, for the probabilistic fault analysis model, all the fault combinations analyzed (up to 14 faults) are tolerated. However, in the *distance 1* analysis model some fault combinations are not tolerated from 8 faults upwards. In particular, with 14 faults up to 7% of the fault combinations are not tolerated in the *distance-1* analysis.

Table 1 also shows the fault tolerance of the mechanisms when used individually. The D mechanism is not able to tolerate any fault. This result was expected, since the deterministic routing used (DOR routing) is not even 1-fault tolerant. Regarding the I mechanism alone, we can observe that it is 1-fault tolerant. Moreover, the number of fault combinations not tolerated by the mechanism increases significantly as the number of the faults in the network increases. Finally, the M mechanism obtains a better fault-tolerance degree than the I mechanism. It is 3-fault tolerant. However, for a larger number of fault combinations, the percentage of not tolerated combinations also increases significantly. Therefore, in the light of these results, it must be noticed that by using each mechanism separately an acceptable fault-tolerant degree can not be achieved, requiring additional support to be effective.

Looking at possible combinations of mechanisms, we can observe that disabling adaptive routing is effective when it is combined with I. In fact, I+D obtains a very good fault-tolerance degree. It is 5-fault tolerant and the percentage of non-tolerated fault combinations remains low as the number of faults in the network increases. 7 faults (100 % tolerated by I+D+M) are tolerated with a number of singular cases lower than 0.5%. These results are obtained thanks to the use of $X \pm Y \pm Z \pm$. However, when using direction order routing, as applied by I+D+M, only 3 faults were tolerated by I+D. $X \pm Y \pm Z \pm$ provides more flexibility in the entire path when an intermediate node is used (i.e., taking into account the $S - I$ stretch and the $I - D$ stretch), since the dimensions are always travelled in the same order regardless of the direction (+ or -).

On the other hand, we can observe that D together with M does not help much. D+M exhibits fault-tolerance capabilities similar to those obtained with M. I+M seems to be 7 fault-tolerant as I+D+M, but in the *distance 1* region it has a slightly higher percentage of non-tolerated combinations. This is due to the fact that misrouting can be used in the same way as deterministic routing.

These results are obtained for a $3 \times 3 \times 3$ Torus. For larger tori and for the same number of faults, they will generally be located further apart and then it will be easier to find fault-free paths for each source-destination pair. Hence, it is expected that the same or better fault-tolerance degree will be achieved.

Table 2 shows (in the third column) the percentage of paths (source-destination pairs) that require using at least one of the mechanisms in order to avoid the faults in a $3 \times 3 \times 3$ torus network, for different numbers of injected faults[5]

As can be seen, for one fault, 6.85% of the paths require at least one mechanism. This percentage increases as the number of faults increases. We can notice that almost half the paths in the network would require using at least one of the mechanisms in order to deal with 14 faults in the network (17% of links failed).

Additionally, Table 2 shows the percentage of paths that use each mechanism or any combination of them. It can be noticed that the most frequently used mechanism is the intermediate node (I). In particular, for all the combinations of mechanisms that use intermediate nodes (I+D+M and I+D), more than 98% of the paths that require some mechanism use only the intermediate node, when the injected faults is lower than 6. The rest of the paths that could not be computed by using only intermediate nodes, were computed by using the alternative mechanisms, either separately or jointly. Remember that when several mechanisms are able to avoid the faults, we select the one that provides a shorter path. Also, adaptive routing is preferred. The percentages for I+M (not shown) are similar to the ones obtained for I+D+M, taking into account that minimal deterministic routing can be enforced when using misrouting.

---

[3]The selection of the center node will not affect the results due to the symmetry property of the torus network.

[4]Note that from 6 link faults upwards, some nodes may become disconnected in a 3D-Torus.

[5]The percentage of affected paths differs when applying different combinations of mechanisms, because only tolerated fault combinations are included when calculating the percentage of affected paths.

| Link failures | Analysis Type | # of combinations | D | I | M | D+M | I + D | I+M | I+D+M |
|---|---|---|---|---|---|---|---|---|---|
| 1 | Exhaustive | 81 | 100% | 0% | 0% | 0% | 0% | 0% | 0% |
| 2 | | 3,240 | 100% | 2.5% | 0% | 0% | 0% | 0% | 0% |
| 3 | | 85,320 | 100% | 7.44% | 0% | 0% | 0% | 0% | 0% |
| 4 | | 1,663,740 | 100% | 14.67% | 0.95% | 0.84% | 0% | 0% | 0% |
| 5 | | 25,621,596 | 100% | 24.06% | N/A | N/A | 0% | 0% | 0% |
| 5 | dist. 1 | 20,349 | 100% | 38.70% | 20.71% | 17.41% | 0% | 0% | 0% |
| 6 | | 54,264 | 100% | 54.70% | 43.99% | 38.53% | 0.073% | 0% | 0% |
| 7 | | 116,280 | 100% | 70.0% | 67.93% | 62.33% | 0.43% | 0% | 0% |
| 8 | | 203,490 | 100% | N/A | N/A | 81.54% | 1.41% | 0.00638% | 0.0054% |
| 9 | | 293,930 | 100% | N/A | N/A | 92.75% | 3.47% | 0.052% | 0.046% |
| 10 | | 352,716 | 100% | N/A | N/A | 97.57% | 7.07% | 0.24% | 0.22% |
| 11 | | 352,716 | 100% | N/A | N/A | 99.21% | 12.52% | 0.757% | 0.72% |
| 12 | | 293,930 | 100% | N/A | N/A | 99.73% | 18.85% | 1.956% | 1.89% |
| 13 | | 203,490 | 100% | N/A | N/A | 99.91% | 28.73% | 4.213 | 4.11% |
| 14 | | 116,280 | 100% | N/A | N/A | 99.98% | 38.38% | 7.8% | 7.65% |
| 5 | Probabilistic | > 14,000,000 | 100% | 24.07% | 4.23% | 2.11% | 0% | 0% | 0% |
| 6 | | > 6,000,000 | 100% | 35.46% | 11.22% | 8.11% | 0% | 0% | 0% |
| 7 | | > 4,500,000 | 100% | 48.72% | 22.55% | 19.33% | 0% | 0% | 0% |
| 8 | | > 3,400,000 | 100% | 62.98% | 41.04% | 37.60% | 0% | 0% | 0% |
| 9 | | > 2,700,000 | 100% | 76.51% | 54.14% | 47.82% | 0.00008% | 0% | 0% |
| 10 | | > 2,200,000 | 100% | 87.40% | 70.29% | 69,71% | 0.48% | 0% | 0% |
| 11 | | > 1,700,000 | 100% | 94.47% | 83.08% | 74.47% | 1.063% | 0% | 0% |
| 12 | | > 1,500,000 | 100% | 98.05% | 91.69% | 90.12% | 2.79% | 0% | 0% |
| 13 | | > 1,300,000 | 100% | 99.46% | 96.60% | 93.67% | 3.16% | 0% | 0% |
| 14 | | > 1,000,000 | 100% | 99.88% | 98.86% | 98.17% | 8.47% | 0% | 0% |

**Table 1. Percentages of link fault combinations not tolerated by each mechanism and their possible combinations. Exhaustive, distance-1 region and probabilistic results are shown.**

### 3.5.2 Cost

In what follows, we present the pros and cons of each mechanism used by our fault-tolerant methodology related to its implementation cost:

- Intermediate nodes

- Pros: Easy to compute paths. Adaptive routing is usually allowed in both subpaths.

- Cons: Increases the size of the packet header: two headers are required for some packets. Routing algorithm must take into account the existence of intermediate nodes. Tables at the source nodes returning the intermediate node for a given destination are required. Extra escape channel must be used.

- Misrouting

- Pros: More flexibility to avoid routing through faulty paths.

- Cons: Increases the size of the packet header: directions and hops to misroute are required. Routing algorithm is more complex. It is tedious to compute paths. Non-minimal paths are used. Deterministic routing is applied at the beginning of the path by forcing packet routing along certain directions.

- Disabling adaptive routing

- Pros: Avoids paths that encounter the faults. Easy to compute paths.

- Cons: Slight increment in the packet header: adaptive routing enable/disable bit. Routing algorithm must take into account the adaptive routing enable/disable bit. Routing is restricted, as deterministic routing is used.

### 3.5.3 Performance

Now, we focus on the impact of the mechanisms on performance. For this, we will analyze the performance of the following combinations of mechanisms: I+D, I+D+M, I+M, and D+M. The evaluation will be performed taking into account the different packet headers that are required when using each combination of mechanisms. That is, when intermediate nodes are used, for some packets (those that use an intermediate node) a second header is needed. When misrouting is used, extra bits (3 bytes) in the header are added in order to indicate the directions to misroute and the number of hops in each direction. If adaptivity is disabled, an extra bit will be used in the packet header. In order to make the results independent of the relative positions of the faults, we have run 50 simulations (for each number of faults and each combination of mechanisms), each of them corresponding to a different randomly-selected fault combination or fault scenario.

Figure 3 shows the mean overall network throughput for different numbers of failures in a 8 × 8 × 8 torus network. The confidence interval is always lower than ±5. As can be seen, D+M provides the lowest throughput. Indeed, once a fault is present in the network, the throughput achieved is decreased by 31.6%. This is due to several factors, such as the use of deterministic routing for a large number of paths (see Table 2), the use of non-minimal paths, and a larger

| Mechanism Combination | # faults | Affected %Paths | Percentage of utilization of the available mechanisms | | | | | | |
|---|---|---|---|---|---|---|---|---|---|
| | | | M | I | I+M | D | I+D | D+M | I+D+M |
| I+D+M | 1 | 6.85% | 0% | 100% | 0% | 0% | 0% | 0% | 0% |
| | 2 | 13.0287% | 0% | 99.7% | 0.036% | 0.0667% | 0.138% | 0% | 0.0714% |
| | 3 | 18.5968% | 0% | 99.264% | 0.0715% | 0.16% | 0.341% | 0% | 0.165% |
| | 4 | 23.621% | 0% | 98.68% | 0.11% | 0.258% | 0.601% | 0% | 0.508% |
| | 5 | 28.157% | 0% | 98.05% | 0.1775% | 0.415% | 0.916% | 0% | 0.426% |
| D+M | 1 | 6.85% | 23.36% | - | - | 64.077% | - | 12.68% | - |
| | 2 | 13.0287% | 24.38% | - | - | 62.40% | - | 13.20% | - |
| | 3 | 18.5968% | 25.38% | - | - | 60.817% | - | 13.766% | - |
| | 4 | 23.63% | 25.645% | - | - | 59.24% | - | 15.108% | - |
| I+D | 1 | 6.85% | - | 100% | - | 0% | 0% | - | - |
| | 2 | 13.0287% | - | 99.703% | - | 0.0706% | 0.2456% | - | - |
| | 3 | 18.5968% | - | 99.26% | - | 0.167% | 0.575% | - | - |
| | 4 | 23.621% | - | 98.725% | - | 0.275% | 1.003% | - | - |
| | 5 | 28.157% | - | 98.057% | - | 0.39% | 1.527% | - | - |
| I+D+M | 6 | 28.282% | 0% | 95.927% | 0.502% | 0.36% | 1.944% | 0% | 1.44% |
| | 7 | 30.951% | 0% | 94.60% | 0.7431% | 0.617% | 2.323% | 0% | 2.0708% |
| | 8 | 33.46% | 0% | 93.28% | 0.99% | 0.692% | 2.859% | 0% | 2.859% |
| | 9 | 35.606% | 0% | 90.85% | 1.34% | 0.758% | 3.359% | 0% | 3.69% |
| | 10 | 37.5% | 0% | 89.04% | 1.733% | 0.7733% | 3.84% | 0% | 4.6139% |
| | 11 | 39.2% | 0% | 87.19% | 2.20% | 0.775% | 4.28% | 0% | 5.536% |
| | 12 | 40.73% | 0% | 85.416% | 2.74% | 0.772% | 4.667% | 0% | 6.39% |
| | 13 | 42.067% | 0% | 83.77% | 3.311% | 0.736% | 5.00% | 0% | 7.164% |
| | 14 | 43.204% | 0% | 82.32% | 3.92% | 0.68% | 5.27% | 0% | 7.78% |
| I+D | 6 | 28.339% | - | 95.70% | - | 0.632% | 3.673% | - | - |
| | 7 | 31.07% | - | 94.24% | - | 0.77% | 4.99% | - | - |
| | 8 | 33.51% | - | 92.63% | - | 0.925% | 6.446% | - | - |
| | 9 | 35.59% | - | 91.17% | - | 1.011% | 8.063% | - | - |
| | 10 | 37.62% | - | 89.23% | - | 1.143% | 9.641% | - | - |
| | 11 | 39.36% | - | 87.52% | - | 1.245% | 11.23% | - | - |
| | 12 | 40.88% | - | 85.91% | - | 1.32% | 12.77% | - | - |
| | 13 | 42.163% | - | 84.43% | - | 1.38% | 14.18% | - | - |
| | 14 | 43.128% | - | 83.18% | - | 1.412% | 15.41% | - | - |

**Table 2. Percentage of paths that make use of at least one mechanism, to avoid the faults, in a $3 \times 3 \times 3$ Torus network. Percentages of utilization of each mechanism for the paths affected by the faults. For up to 5 faults, exhaustive analysis. From 6 faults upwards** *distance 1* **analysis.**

packet header. For more injected faults, the throughput decreases very slowly.

The I+D and I+D+M mechanisms obtain a highly stable throughput regardless of the number of faults in the network. In the presence of the only one first fault in the network, the throughput is only slightly degraded. This is because the affected paths use most of the time only intermediate nodes (see Table 2) and, therefore, adaptive routing is not seriously limited. As the number of injected faults increases, the throughput slightly decreases. This behavior is due to the normal traffic unbalance that the faults progressively introduce into the network. Anyway, even with 14 faults present in the network, throughput decreases on average only by 8%. The differences between I+D and I+D+M are due to the use of non-minimal paths and the extra space required in the packet headers when misrouting is applied. However, although I+D+M provides a slightly worse performance, note that it tolerates a larger number of faults (up to 7 faults). Although results for I+M are not shown, I+M provides performance results very similar to I+D+M.

Finally, we will compare the performance degradation when using our methodology against the performance degradation that would be obtained by a fault-tolerant mechanism similar to the one used in the BlueGene/L supercomputer. The BlueGene/L system disables four planes of nodes in order to deal with a fault. As we are using a smaller torus network, we will model the mechanism of the BlueGene/L system by only disabling one plane. Figure 3 shows the network throughput obtained with three combinations of mechanisms (I+D, I+M+D, D+M) and a mechanism similar to the one used in the BlueGene/L supercomputer when there are up to 7 faults in a $8 \times 8 \times 8$ Torus. Error bars are not shown as they are too small.

Notice that this is a worst case for the mechanism similar to the BlueGene/L fault-tolerant mechanism because it assumes that the seven faults are located in different planes. If the seven faults were located in the same plane, only one plane would be disconnected for all the seven faults. Anyway, as shown in Figure 3, our mechanism obtains a higher network throughput for seven faults even if only one plane is disconnected for all the seven faults. Network

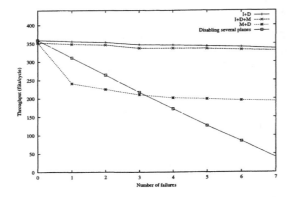

**Figure 3. Throughput (flits/cycle) degradation for several mechanisms (I+D, I+D+M and M+D), and for the mechanism used in the BlueGene/L supercomputer.** $8 \times 8 \times 8$ **Torus.**

throughput degrades only by 6.4% and 6.25% for I+M+D and I+D, respectively, with 7 random faults. On the other hand, when using the mechanism similar to the BlueGene/L, the network performance drops by 13.65% and 88.85% when disabling one plane and seven planes, respectively. However, these results must be put in context, that is, they are obtained in a $8 \times 8 \times 8$ torus. For larger networks, in particular for the $32 \times 32 \times 64$ torus used in the BlueGene/L supercomputer, the BlueGene/L mechanism would reduce performance by a lower percentage. In particular, a fault would disconnect four planes of at least $32 \times 32$ nodes (4,096 out of 65,536 nodes). So, network performance would decrease, in the presence of seven faults, at least by a 6.25%, if all the 7 faults are located in the same set of four planes. For our mechanism, in a larger network, performance degradation in the presence of seven faults would be significantly lower than 6.4% as well, because the traffic unbalance introduced by the faulty links will be lower, in relative terms, in a larger network.

### 3.6 Discussion

In the light of the analysis results, we observe that routing through an intermediate node is the fault-tolerant mechanism most widely used by the methodology. This is good, because it allows packets to continue being routed adaptively in the presence of faults, thus avoiding an excessive degradation in performance. However, it is necessary to combine it with other mechanisms to guarantee an acceptable fault-tolerant degree. In particular, we have observed that just disabling adaptivity in some cases, is enough to increase the fault-tolerance degree of the methodology from 1 fault up to 5 faults. Furthermore, this combination of mechanisms (I, D) is able to tolerate up to 14 faults with a high probability (less than 9% of fault

combinations are not tolerated). This is an interesting result, especially if we take into account that the improvement in the fault-tolerance degree is achieved without hardly increasing the implementation cost of the methodology.

Moreover, if we want to improve the fault-tolerance degree of the methodology, an alternative mechanism, such as misrouting, should be applied. In particular, the methodology becomes 7-fault tolerant when combining the I and M mechanisms (I+M). However, the application of misrouting leads to an increase in the packet header that slightly degrades the network performance. Also, the computation time of the fault-free routing paths is increased. Notice that this is the price to pay if we want to guarantee high fault-tolerance degree. On the other hand, we have observed that it is not worth combining the three mechanisms (I+D+M), because it roughly achieves the same fault-tolerance degree and performance level as I+M but at the expense of a slightly higher cost.

Finally, it is observed that by applying only misrouting and disabling adaptive routing (i.e., without using intermediate nodes), either separately or jointly, is not enough to provide a cost-effective fault-tolerant routing methodology. In fact, the network performance degrades dramatically from the first fault upwards because a lot of packets have to follow non-minimal paths and many of them cannot be routed adaptively.

## 4 Conclusions

In this paper, we have explored all the fault-tolerant capabilities offered by the methodology proposed in [14] for direct networks. In this sense, we have analyzed in depth the different mechanisms that can be applied by the methodology, looking for the suitable combination of them to meet the trade-off between the provided fault-tolerance degree, the required implementation cost, and the achieved performance level.

The analysis carried out in this paper has been particularized to a 3D-torus network with $3 \times 3 \times 3$ nodes. Among the analyzed mechanisms, routing through intermediate nodes (I) is the only mechanism able to maintain a high network performance in the case of failure, at the expense of adding an extra escape channel and a second packet header (if required). This is the price to pay in order to provide high performance. However, the fault-tolerance capabilities of this mechanism are poor. Fortunately, we have shown that by combining it with a simple mechanism, such as disabling adaptive routing (D) on a per-packet basis, it is possible to guarantee an acceptable fault-tolerance degree (up to 5 link faults are tolerated) without hardly increasing the implementation cost or degrading performance. Therefore, the resulting mechanism (I+D) is a cost-effective mechanism.

Despite the fact that in current systems it is not realistic to assume the possible existence of a large number of faults, it may be that a designer prefer to guarantee a higher fault-tolerance degree at expense of a lower performance level. In this case, an alternative mechanism, such as misrouting (M), should be used. The resulting mechanism (I+M) is 7-fault tolerant with very high probability and exhibits a network performance slightly lower than that of I+D. Therefore, if providing high fault-tolerance degree is the primary concern, this mechanism should be the choice.

Therefore, we can conclude stating that routing through intermediate nodes is the key mechanism to to provide a cost-effective fault-tolerant routing methodology for direct networks.

# References

[1] ASCI Red Web Site. http://www.sandia.gov/ASCI/Red/.

[2] R. Bopana, D. Cohen, R. Felderman, A. Kulawik, C. Seitz, J. Seizovic and W. Su. A Comparison of Adaptive Wormhole Routing Algorithms. *Proc. 20th Annual Int. Symp. Comp. Architecture, May 1993.*

[3] IBM BG/L Team. An Overview of BlueGene/L Supercomputer. *ACM Supercomputing Conf.*, 2002.

[4] R.Casado, A Bermudez, J Duato, F.J. Quiles, and J.L. Sanchez. A protocol for deadlock-free dynamic reconfiguration in high speed local area networks. *IEEE Trans. on Parallel and Distributed Systems*, Vol. 12, No. 2, pp. 115-132, 2001.

[5] A. A. Chien and J. H. Kim. Planar- adaptative routing: Low-cost adaptive networks for multiprocessors. *Proc. of the 19th Int. Symp. on Computer Architecture*, pp. 268-277, May 1992.

[6] S.Chalasani and R.V. Boppana. Communication in multicomputers with nonconvex faults. *IEEE Trans. on Computers*, vol. 46, no. 5, pp. 616-622, May 1997.

[7] W. J. Dally. Virtual-channel flow control. *IEEE Trans. on Parallel and Distributed Systems*, vol. 3, no. 2, pp. 194-205, March 1992.

[8] W.J. Dally and H. Aoki. Deadlock-free adaptive routing in multicomputer networks using virtual channels. *IEEE Trans. on Parallel and Distributed Systems*, vol 4, no 4. pp 466-475, April 1993.

[9] W. J. Dally et al., The Reliable Router: A Reliable and High-Performance Communication Substrate for Parallel Computers. *Proc. Parallel Computer Routing and Communication Workshop*, 1994.

[10] J. Duato. A theory of fault-tolerant routing in wormhole networks. *Proc. of the Int. Conf. on Parallel and Distributed Systems*, pp. 600-607, Dec. 1994.

[11] J. Duato. A Necessary and Sufficient Condition for Deadlock-Free Outgoing in Cut-Through and Store-and-Forward Networks. *IEEE Trans. on Parallel and Distributed Systems*, vol. 7, no. 8, pp. 841-854, Aug. 1996.

[12] Earth Simulator Center. http://www.es.jamstec.go.jp/esc/eng/index.html.

[13] G.J. Glass, and L.M. Ni. Fault-Tolerant Wormhole Routing in Meshes without Virtual Channels. *IEEE Trans. on Parallel and Distributed Systems*, vol. 7, no. 6, pp. 620-636, 1996.

[14] M.E. Gómez, J. Duato, J. Flich, A. Robles, P. López, N.A. Nordbotten, O. Lysne, T. Skeie. A New Fault-Tolerant Mechanism for Direct Networks. *Techn. Report* http://www.gap.upv.es/ir200.pdf.

[15] C.T. Ho and L. Stockmeyer. A New Approach to Fault-Tolerant Wormole Routing for Mesh-Connected Parallel Computers. *Proc. of 16th Int. Parallel and Distributed Processing Symp.*, Apr. 2002.

[16] IBM homepage, http://www.ibm.com.

[17] Lawrence Livermore National Lavoratory homepage, http://www.llnl.gov

[18] P. Kermani and L. Kleinrock. Virtual cut-through: A new computer communication switching technique. *Computer Networks*, vol. 3, pp. 267-286,1979.

[19] D.H. Linder and J.C. Harden. An Adaptive and fault tolerant wormhole routing strategy for k-ary n-cubes. *IEEE Trans. on Computers*, vol. C-40 no 1, pp.2-12, Jan. 1991.

[20] V. Puente, J.A. Gregorio, J.M. Prellezo, R. Beivide, J. Duato, and C. Izu. Adaptive Bubble Router: A Design to Balance Latency and Throughput in Networks for Parallel Computers. *Proc. of the 22nd Int. Conf. on Parallel Processing*, September 1999.

[21] Y.J. Suh, B.V. Dao, J. Duato, and S.Yalamanchili. Software-based rerouting for fault-tolerant pipelined communication. *IEEE Trans. on Parallel and Distributed Systems*, vol. 11, no. 3, pp. 193-211, 2000.

[22] L.G. Valiant A Scheme for Fast Parallel Communication. *SIAM J. Comput.* 11, pp. 350-361, 1982.

# Session 4B:
# Performance Evaluation II

# Probabilistic Real-Time Guarantees
## for Component-Oriented Phased Array Radars *

Chin-Fu Kuo, Ya-Shu Chen, Tei-Wei Kuo, Phone Lin and Cheng Chang[†]
Department of Computer Science and Information Engineering,
National Taiwan University, Taipei, Taiwan 106, ROC
[†]System Development Center, Chung Shan Institute of Science and Technology,
TaoYuan, Taiwan 325, ROC
{d89005,ktw}@csie.ntu.edu.tw

## Abstract

*In recent years, many modern phased array radars are built with commercial-off-the-shelf components, and the functions of many hardware components are also re-implemented by software modules. In such systems, radar tasks could be modelled as distributed real-time tasks which require end-to-end deadline guarantees and have precedence constraints. Different from most previous work on either algorithms with restrictions in resource utilization or heuristics without analytical ways for schedulability guarantees, the objective of this paper is to propose a joint real-time scheduling algorithm for both Transmitter/Receiver and Signal Processor workloads with an analytical framework for off-line probabilistic analysis and on-line admission control. The strength of our approach is verified by analysis results and a series of experiments based on a real phased array radar for air defense frigates [6].*

**Keywords: Phased Array Radar, Real-Time Task Scheduling, Probabilistic Performance Guarantee, Distributed Systems, Dwell Scheduling**

## 1 Introduction

How to efficiently schedule radar resource to achieve the maximum performance is one of the most essential and challenging problems in the design of a multi-function phased array radar. Due to hardware constraints, many traditional radar systems are designed with non-real-time resource scheduling mechanisms, such as FIFO scheduling [3]. As a result, much resource is wasted with a very limited guarantee on system performance.

In recent years, many modern phased array radars are no longer built in a complicated hardware system with every-thing wired. Instead, engineers are now building phased array radars with commercial-off-the-shelf (COTS) components, and the functions of many hardware components are now re-implemented by software modules [4]. The development of component-oriented signal processors is strongly influenced by the Rapid prototyping of Application Specific Signal Processors (RASSP) program lead by the Department of Defense, United States of America [11]. The RASSP program formalized an engineering process for developing a Signal Processor (SP) in order to reduce the total product development time and cost by a factor of four.

With the component-oriented phased array radar architecture, radar tasks could be modelled as distributed real-time tasks which require end-to-end deadline guarantees and have precedence constraints. The task scheduling problem for component-oriented phased array radars is often complicated by the existence of multiple processing units in some components, such as those in SP. Although real-time scheduling problems have been analyzed for different architectural assumptions, little work addresses the unique problem for real-time radar task (or dwell) scheduling, especially when complicated real-time resource allocation issues are mixed with reliability and cost issues. The task models and the work presented in [1, 6] are among the few closely related to dwell scheduling at the Radar Control Computer (RCC) level. Although researchers and engineers have started exploring real-time dwell scheduling at RCC, the proposed algorithms are mainly variations of the Partial Template algorithm [3]. Different from most previous work on either algorithms with restrictions in resource utilization or heuristics without analytical ways for schedulability guarantees, the objective of this paper is to propose a joint real-time scheduling algorithm for both Transmitter and Receiver (TR) and SP workloads with an analytical framework for off-line probabilistic analysis and on-line admission control.

While nonpreemptible task scheduling with end-to-end deadlines and precedence constraints is shown being NP-

*This research was supported in part by the National Science Council under grants NSC92-2213-E-002-091 and NSC-92-2213-E-002-093, and NSC92-2213-E-002-094.

233

hard in the literature [5], different heuristics on multi-stage scheduling (e.g., [13]) are proposed. Distinct from the past work, this paper aims at the proposing of a real-time scheduling algorithm at RCC to have joint considerations of TR and SP workloads. In addition to that, we would propose an analytical framework for off-line probabilistic analysis and on-line admission control to balance the hardware cost and the performance guarantee. We first present a task model for a typical phased array radar and then an abstraction of a component-oriented phased array radar. A priority-driven scheduling algorithm is proposed for TR workloads, and an analytic method is presented to derive deadlines for workloads in SP based on the given probabilistic guarantees of radar tasks. SP scheduling is proposed based on the well-known rate-based multi-processor algorithm [2], provided that no task migration or preemption is allowed. The schedulability test of the proposed joint scheduling algorithm (i.e., TR and SP scheduling) is presented for off-line probabilistic analysis and on-line admission control. The strength of our approach is verified by analysis results and a series of simulation experiments based on a real phased array radar for air defense frigates [6].

The rest of this paper is as follows: Section 2 defines the system architecture and formally defines the workload of a typical phased array radar. Section 3 proposes our TR and SP scheduling algorithm with probabilistic guarantees. In Section 4, the performance evaluation results based on a real example system are presented. Section 5 is the conclusion.

## 2 System Architecture and Workload Characteristics

### 2.1 System Architecture

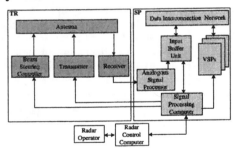

**Figure 1. The hardware architecture of a phased array radar**

A component-oriented phased array radar consists of several important modules: Radar Control Computer (RCC), Signal Processor (SP), Beam Steering Controller (BSC), Receiver, Antenna, and Transmitter, where an SP consists of an Analog Signal Processor (ASP), a Signal Processing Computer (SPC), and various processing units, as shown in Figure 1 [3, 6]. RCC schedules dwell transmissions in a real-time fashion by sending SPC commands. When SPC receives

commands from RCC for radar beam transmissions, it issues commands to BSC and Transmitter for radar beam transmissions in specified directions. Antenna and Receiver receive returned signals and pass them to ASP for analog-to-digital signal processing. The digital signals are saved at the input buffer unit (IBU) for later processing. Processing units of the SP are Vector Signal Processors (VSP) which conducts different types of data processing such as pulse compression, FFT, and other digital signal processing. Data Interconnection Network (DIN) is for data transmission between VSP's and IBU.

A *dwell* is defined as the process from the transmitting of a radar beam by Transmitter to the saving of the corresponding returned digital signals in IBU. RCC schedules tasks in units called *scheduling interval* (SI) [3]. In other words, RCC sends a sequence of commands to SP for dwell transmissions, and retrieves results from SP at the beginning of an SI. Besides, SP must read the output results of TR (in IBU) at the beginning of an SI. With the synchronization behavior among RCC, TR, and SP, radar tasks always consider to arrive at a multiple of SI and have deadlines as multiples of SI [1].

### 2.2 Workload Characteristics

A typical phased array radar could be modelled as a distributed system, where a radar task is decomposed into one TR subtask and one SP subtask. TR and SP subtasks must be executed in TR and SP, respectively. The execution time of a TR subtask is defined as the length of the corresponding dwell, where the *dwell length* is defined as the duration in executing a dwell. TR subtasks are nonpreemptible. Moreover, the returned signals of a dwell are processed by one of VSP's in SP. We say that the SP subtask corresponding to the dwell runs on one VSP and handles the returned signals. SP subtasks are nonpreemptible and could not be migrated among VSP's. The processing time of the returned signals for a dwell is referred to as the execution time of the corresponding SP subtask.

There exists a precedence constraint between a TR subtask and its corresponding SP subtask because the SP subtask processed the returned signals resulted from the execution of the TR subtask. An SP subtask could not start to execute until its precedent TR subtask finishes. A task $\tau_i$ in a phased array radar system has an end-to-end deadline, which is the time for the completion of its corresponding SP subtask (from the release of its corresponding TR subtask). Moreover, the TR and SP subtasks of $\tau_i$ have their worst execution times, depending on the characteristics of their corresponding dwell or radar task.

A phased array radar could have at least three kinds of works: Search, Track Confirmation, and Track.

- *Search*: A phased array radar must scan its surveillance space periodically for suspicious targets, e.g., in terms of

---

[1]Some implementations of radar systems ignore the SI constraints. However, the synchronization among RCC, TR, and SP will become complicated because synchronization might be needed virtually at any time.

Horizon Search or Long Range Search. This scan must be done in a hard real-time fashion. Such hard real-time searches are called *High-Priority Search (HS) tasks* in this paper. *Low-Priority Search (LS) tasks*, such as Normal Volume Search, are conducted when there are free system resources available after the servicing of highly critical tasks.

- *Track Confirmation*: When suspicious targets are detected at RCC (because of reflected signals), a Track Confirmation is issued for each detected target in the direction of the target to verify its presence. A Track Confirmation (TC) task must be done in a hard real-time fashion to *identify* suspicious targets.

- *Track*: Once a target is identified, a sequence of "semi-periodic" Normal Track (NT) dwells are issued to track the target. The word *semi-periodic* means "periodic" but with dynamically changing periods. The reason for tracking being semi-periodic is because the distance between every two consecutive tracking executions for a target depends on many factors, such as target type, target position, target speed, etc. The tracking of a target might need to go into a Precision Track (PT) task, which is also "semi-periodic", because the tracking of the target needs better precision. High Precision Track (HPT) tasks may be initiated by the operators for many purposes, such as missile guidance. They also need to be done in a hard real-time fashion.

| Task Types | Timing Constraints | Periodic | Deadline Type | Priority |
|---|---|---|---|---|
| High-Priority Search (HS) | $\{B_i^S, c_{S,1}, c_{S,2}, D_i^S, P_i^S\}$ | periodic | hard deadline | 1 |
| Track Confirmation (TC) | $\{c_{C,1}, c_{C,2}, D_C\}$ | aperiodic | hard deadline | 2 |
| High-Precision Track (HPT) Precision Track (PT) Normal Track (NT) | $\{c_{T,1}, c_{T,2}, P_T^H, P_T^L, D_T\}$ | semi-periodic | hard deadline | 3 |

**Table 1. Timing parameters of a typical phased array radar**

Different phased array radars have different system specifications and parameters, e.g., different search frame times for different search modes and different tracking rates for different tracking modes. A typical workload consists of High-Priority Search tasks, High Precision Track tasks, Precision Track tasks, Normal Track tasks, and Track Confirmation tasks, as shown in Table 1, where 1 is the highest priority, and 3 is the lowest priority [6].

An HS task must issue $B_i^S$ beams every $P_i^S$ time units, where $c_{S,1}$ is the dwell length, and $c_{S,2}$ is the execution time of a corresponding SP subtask. The relative end-to-end deadline of the HS task is $D_i^S$. HS or LS tasks are referred to as *search tasks* although we will focus our discussions on HS tasks in this paper (where the timing constraints of HS and LS tasks are similar). For each suspicious target, a TC task is issued with a relative end-to-end deadline $D_C$, a dwell length $c_{C,1}$, and an execution time $c_{C,2}$ of a corresponding SP subtask. Once the target is identified, a sequence of semi-periodic Track dwells are issued to track the target. For the reset of this

paper, NT, PT, or HPT tasks are referred to as *track tasks* for the simplicity of discussions for the rest of this paper. Each track task issues a sequence of semi-periodic Track dwells to track a target. The period of a track task is bounded by a lower bound $P_T^L$ and an upper bound $P_T^H$. Besides, a track task has a dwell length $c_{T,1}$ and requires the execution time $c_{T,2}$ of the returned signals in SP. The end-to-end relative deadline of track task is $D_T$.

## 3 Probabilistic Schedulability Guarantees under Two-Stage Scheduling

### 3.1 Overview

The purpose of this section is to propose a two-stage scheduling algorithm to provide different levels of guarantees for different radar tasks in a probabilistic fashion. It is to avoid unnecessary deployment of a large number of hardware equipments, due to some pessimistic performance analysis of radar systems.

The component-oriented phase-array radars under considerations have two major components, as shown in Figure 1: TR and SP. Each radar task $\tau_i$ is modelled as a sequence of two subtasks $\tau_{i,1}$ and $\tau_{i,2}$, where $\tau_{i,1}$ (referred to as a *TR subtask*) executes in TR for dwell transmission, and $\tau_{i,2}$ (referred to as an *SP subtask*) represents the processing of the returned signals in SP. The system architecture of a phased-array radar could be abstracted as a chain of two processor groups. TR must adopt nonpreemptible uniprocessor scheduling because dwell transmissions must be done one after another. We propose to schedule TR subtasks in a priority queueing model (Please see Section 3.2) on the first processor group (referred to as the *TR p-group*), where the TR p-group has only one processor. The returned signals of TR subtasks will be buffered at the IBU of SP for processing. We propose to schedule SP subtasks with returned signals in the IBU in a distributed rate-based real-time scheduling algorithm (Please see Section 3.3) on the second processor group (referred to as the *SP p-group*). Because signal processing on each VSP is also nonpreemptible, no migration of any task execution among processors (i.e., VSP's) in the SP p-group is allowed. The number of VSP's in SP varies, depending on the needs of a radar system for signal processing.

Let each task $\tau_i$ be given a probability threshold $\phi_i$ such that the phased-array radar must guarantee that a specified portion of its tasks will always complete before their deadlines if the task is admitted (the admission control policy will be presented later)! That is $\Pr[R_i \leq D_i] \geq \phi_i$, where $R_i$ is the completion time (relative to its arrival time) of a radar task $\tau_i$, and $D_i$ is a given deadline (relative to its arrival time). In this paper, we first assume that TR subtasks (and its corresponding radar tasks) have Poisson distributions on their arrivals (with a "control parameter" on the variance for analysis and performance evaluation). Let the inter-arrival times of each radar task $\tau_i$ in the system be generally distributed with a density function $f_i$ and a rate $\lambda_i$. Each task $\tau_i$ has a deadline $D_i$ relative to its arrival time, referred to as the *relative deadline*. The completion time of a task $\tau_i$ relative to its arrival time is referred to as the *relative completion time. The technical problem on the scheduling of TR and SP subtasks is how to assign TR and SP subtasks deadlines for real-time scheduling.*

We first propose an analysis framework in Section 3.2 to derive deadlines for SP subtasks. The analysis framework consists of two parts: The first part is on the analysis of the completion time of TR subtasks, and the second part is on the schedulability analysis of SP subtasks.

## 3.2 Probabilistic Guarantees for Beam-Transmission Scheduling

Given a probabilistic guarantee $\Pr[R_i \leq D_i] \geq \phi_i$ for a task $\tau_i$, the first thing is to derive a bound $D_{i,1}$ on the completion time of its TR subtask based on the priority queueing model. We shall first derive the average waiting time for a TR subtask and then do a Laplace transform and quadratic differentiation to obtain the variance of the waiting time distribution. The bound of the relative completion time of TR subtasks is obtained by a table lookup over the standard normal distribution table based on the derived mean and variance.

Different radar systems have different priority assignments for different radar tasks [6]. We assume that the priority of a TR subtask or an SP subtask inherits that of its corresponding radar task. When a TR subtask is under processing for a beam transmission, it is non-preemptable. We adopt a priority queueing model for TR-subtask scheduling, where the TR p-group services TR subtasks with higher priorities first. We assume that each priority queue has only TR subtasks belonging to the same task, and each queue is serviced in a first-in-first-out (FIFO) fashion.

Given a probabilistic guarantee $P_{TR+SP}(D_i) \geq \phi_i$ for a task $\tau_i$ (where $P_{TR+SP}(x)$ denotes $\Pr[R_i \leq x]$ for the completion time of a radar task), the objective of this section is to derive the average waiting time for a TR subtask and then $D_{i,1}$ that satisfies $P_{TR}(D_{i,1}) \geq \phi_i$ (where $P_{TR}(x)$ denotes $\Pr[R_i \leq x]$ for the completion time of a TR subtask) based on the priority queueing model. Note that the two functions $P_{TR}(D_{i,1}) = \Pr[R_i \leq D_{i,1}]$ and $P_{TR+SP}(D_i) = \Pr[R_i \leq D_i]$ are defined to simplify the presentation. Once $D_{i,1}$ is determined for TR subtasks of $\tau_i$, the deadline for SP subtasks of $\tau_i$ is set as $(D_i - D_{i,1})$, where $D_{i,1} = \lceil \frac{x}{SI} \rceil SI$ for the smallest $x$ that satisfies $P_{TR}(x) \geq \phi_i$, where $P_{TR}(x) = \Pr[R_i \leq x]$.

We model each radar task $\tau_i$ in the system with a Poisson arrival pattern with the rate $\lambda_i$. The service time of the TR subtask of $\tau_i$ has a general service time distribution with the mean $c_{i,1}$. Each task $\tau_i$ has a fixed relative deadline $D_i$. An M/G/1 nonpreemptible priority queueing system is adopted to model the behaviors of TR subtasks and to derive their average waiting time. Suppose that the queue with a smaller

index has a higher priority, and queue $Q_i$ is for radar task $\tau_i$ where $1 \leq i \leq N$, and $N$ is the number of radar tasks. We can derive the average waiting time for each task type, as follows, based on an M/G/1 nonpreemptive priority queueing system [8]:

Since the arrival of each TR subtask is a Poisson arrival, any TR subtask arrival (of the $N$ tasks) also forms a Poisson process with the rate $\Lambda = \lambda_1 + \lambda_2 + ... + \lambda_N$. Let $C$ be the service time of an arbitrary TR subtask (of the $N$ tasks). The expected value of $C$ (i.e., $E[C]$) and the second moment of $C$ (i.e., $E[C^2]$) can be derived by the following equations: $E[C] = \frac{\lambda_1}{\Lambda} c_{1,1} + \frac{\lambda_2}{\Lambda} c_{2,1} + ... + \frac{\lambda_N}{\Lambda} c_{N,1}$ and $E[C^2] = \frac{\lambda_1}{\Lambda} c_{1,1}^2 + \frac{\lambda_2}{\Lambda} c_{2,1}^2 + ... + \frac{\lambda_N}{\Lambda} c_{N,1}^2$. Let $W_{q_i}$ be the waiting time for a TR subtask of $\tau_i$ in the queue. We can obtain the expected value of $W_{q_i}$ as follows: $E[W_{q_i}] = \frac{\lambda E[C^2]}{2(1-u_{i-1})(1-u_i)}$ where $u_i = \lambda_1 \cdot c_{1,1} + \lambda_2 \cdot c_{2,1} + ... + \lambda_i \cdot c_{i,1}$. Consequently, the expected value of the time $W_i$ spent by a TR subtask of $\tau_i$ in the system is $E[W_i] = E[W_{q_i}] + \frac{1}{c_{i,1}}$, and the expected value of the time $W$ spent by an arbitrary TR subtask is $E[W] = E[W_q] + \frac{1}{E[C]}$.

The purpose of this section is to derive the deadline $D_{i,1}$ for TR subtasks of each radar task $\tau_i$ based on the distribution of the waiting time of $\tau_i$. Let $f_{q,i}(x)$ be the density function of the waiting time $W_{q_i}$ for each TR subtask of radar task $\tau_i$, and $f_{q,i}^*(s)$ the Laplace transform of $f_{q,i}(x)$. Based on the results in [8], $f_{q,i}^*(s)$ could be obtained as follows:

$$f_{q,i}^*(s) = \frac{(1-u_n)[s + \lambda_H - \lambda_H G_H^*(s)] + \lambda_L[1 - B_L^*(s + \lambda_H - \lambda_H G_H^*(s))]}{s - \lambda_j + \lambda_j B_j^*(s + \lambda_H - \lambda_H G_H^*(s))} \quad (1)$$

where $B_i^*(s)$ is the Laplace transform of the density function for the service time of each TR subtask of $\tau_i$, $\lambda_H = \sum_{i=1}^{j-1} \lambda_i$, $\lambda_L = \sum_{i=j+1}^{n} \lambda_i$, $B_H^*(s) = \sum_{i=1}^{j-1} \frac{\lambda_i}{\lambda_H} B_i^*(s)$, $B_L^*(s) = \sum_{i=j+1}^{n} \frac{\lambda_i}{\lambda_L} B_i^*(s)$, $G_H^*(s) = B_H^*(s + \lambda_H - \lambda_H G_H^*(s))$, and $u_i = \lambda_1 \cdot c_{1,1} + \lambda_2 \cdot c_{2,1} + ... + \lambda_i \cdot c_{i,1}$. Based on results in [14], we have $E[W_{q_i}^n] = (-1)^n \frac{d^n f_{w,i}^*(s)}{ds^n} \Big|_{s=o}$ and the variance $v_{q_i}$ of $W_{q_i}$ can be obtained by the following equation: $v_{q_i} = E[W_{q_i}^2] - (E[W_{q_i}])^2$. We use the normal distribution $N(.)$ with the mean $E[W_{q_i}]$ and the variance $v_{q_i}$ to estimate $D_{i,1}$ such that $P_{TR}(D_{i,1}) \geq \phi_i$ by a table lookup, where $P_{TR}(x) = \Pr[R_i \leq x]$.

## 3.3 Rate-Based Scheduling for Signal Processing

### 3.3.1 Reservation Ratios of SP Subtasks

The idea of generalized processor sharing (GPS) was first proposed by Parekh and Gallager [10] in the context of rate-based flow and congestion control at network gateway nodes. GPS-based scheduling is a work-conserving scheduling mechanism, in which each task $\tau_i$ is given a positive real number $\theta_i$ (called the *reservation ratio*) such that $\tau_i$ is guaranteed to be served at a rate of $g_i = \frac{\theta_i}{\sum_j \theta_j}$. In particular, Spuri, et al. [12] proposed an effective GPS-based mechanism called *TB server* to service tasks under the framework of the EDF scheduling. In [2], a distributed and revised version of the TB algorithm (called Multiprocessor Constant-Bandwidth Server (M-CBS)) was proposed for multi-processor environments, where preemption or migration is allowed.

In this section, we propose to adopt M-CBS for SP scheduling, however, under a more restricted constraint on preemption or migration. We shall determine the reservation ratio for a radar task and propose a scheduling mechanism for SP subtasks. A schedulability test of SP subtasks should also be derived on extending M-CBS for no preemption or migration. Note that results in the previous section derive an upper bound on the relative deadline of an SP subtask, i.e., $D_{i,2} = (D_i - D_{i,1})$, for a given probability to guarantee the schedulability of the corresponding radar task $\tau_i$.

The design of an SP scheduling algorithm must guarantee the processing of all of the returned signals of the TR subtasks of $\tau_i$ if they could arrive at IBU within their relative deadline $D_{i,1}$. As discussed in Section 2, the period of each track task $\tau_i$ has a lower bound $P_i^L$ and an upper bound $P_i^H$, depending on its corresponding track type. Once a radar task is admitted, a radar system should keep tracks of the corresponding target with a specified degree of guarantee. The reservation ratio of each radar task is set as $\theta_i = \frac{c_{i,2}}{D_{i,2}}$, where $c_{i,2}$ is the execution time of the SP subtask of $\tau_i$, if $P_i^L \geq D_{i,2}$. Otherwise, the reservation ratio of $\tau_i$ is $\theta_i = \frac{c_{i,2}}{P_i^L}$. The rationale behind the assignment is to provide the SP subtasks of $\tau_i$ an enough capacity to process its returned signals. Since the period of each search task is a fixed constant, the reservation ratio of a search task $\tau_i$ is $\theta_i = \frac{c_{i,2}}{D_{i,2}}$ if $P_i^S \geq D_{i,2}$, where $P_i^S$ is the period of the search task. Otherwise, the reservation ratio of $\tau_i$ is $\theta_i = \frac{c_{i,2}}{P_i^S}$. Note that since the tracking of an identified target starts with a Track Confirmation, then a sequence of Normal Tracks, and possibly a sequence of Precision Tracks, the reservation ratio needed to track a target must be the maximum of the reservation ratios for the corresponding radar tasks of the target (in the confirmation, normal tracking, and precision tracking states) if a guarantee on the tracking of the target is required.

### 3.3.2 SP Scheduling

SP scheduling is based on M-CBS [2], that is a work-conserving scheduling mechanism in which the schedulability of the SP subtasks of each radar task $\tau_i$ is guaranteed with a reservation ratio $\theta_i$. We say that an SP subtask arrives if its corresponding returned signals is in the IBU of SP. When an SP subtask arrives, its deadline is set based on M-CBS, except that no preemption or migration is allowed: Let $T = \tau_1, \tau_2, ...., \tau_n$ denote a collection of radar tasks under scheduling, where each radar task $\tau_i$ has a reservation ratio $\theta_i$ ($\leq 1$), for $1 \leq i \leq n$. Suppose that radar tasks in $T$ are indexed in a non-increasing reservation ratio order, i.e., $\theta_i \geq \theta_{i+1}$, for all $i$, $1 \leq i \leq n$, and $\theta(T) = \Sigma_{\tau_i \in T}\theta_i$. $T^{(i)}$ denotes the collection of radar tasks with the $(n-i+1)$ minimum reservation ratios in $T$, i.e., $T^{(i)} = \tau_i, \tau_{i+1}, ..., \tau_n$. (According to this notation, $T \equiv T^{(1)}$.)

Let $\kappa(T)$ denote the smallest value of $k$ that satisfies the following inequality (Please see Theorem 2 in the next section), where $M$ is the number of processors, i.e., VSP's, in the SP p-group. $Max(npb_i)$ and $Min(d_j)$ are the maximum execution time and the minimum relative deadline of all SP subtasks, respectively:

$$M(1 - \frac{Max(npb_i)}{Min(d_j)}) \geq min_{k=1}^{n}\{(k-1) + \frac{\theta(T^{(k+1)})}{1-\theta_k}\} \quad (2)$$

Radar tasks $\tau_1, \cdots, \tau_{(\kappa(T)-1)}$ are called *high-priority radar tasks*, and the rest are called *deadline-based radar tasks*. Let an SP subtask of an admitted radar task $\tau_i$ arrive at time $t$, the deadline of the SP subtask is set as $-\infty$ if $\tau_i$ is a high-priority radar task. (The admission control test will be explained in the next section.) Let the arriving SP subtask correspond to the $l_{th}$ instance of the SP subtasks of $\tau_i$ for some integer $l > 0$. If the corresponding radar task is a deadline-based radar task, then the deadline of the SP subtask is set as $d_{i,l} = \max\{t, d_{i,l-1}\} + \frac{c_{i,2}}{\theta_i}$, where $d_{i,l}$ denotes the absolute deadline of the $l_{th}$ instance of the SP subtasks of $\tau_i$, and $d_{i,0} = 0$. The scheduling of SP subtasks is based on the earliest-deadline-first algorithm [9], where the SP subtask with the earliest absolute deadline is scheduled first for any available processor. No preemption or migration is allowed. The SP scheduling algorithm is called *M-CBS without preemption and migration* (M-CBS-NPM). Note that $-\infty$ denotes the smallest possible absolute deadline such that SP subtasks of high-priority radar tasks are always scheduled first.

Since M-CBS is designed to schedule tasks with a reservation ratio $\theta_i \leq 1$, each search task $\tau_i$ that could have a reservation ratio $\theta_i$ larger than one is split into $\lceil \lceil \frac{1}{P_i^S/B_i^S} \rceil \cdot \theta_i \rceil$ corresponding radar tasks, i.e., $\tau_{i,1}, .., \tau_{i, \lceil \lceil \frac{1}{P_i^S/B_i^S} \rceil \cdot \theta_i \rceil}$.[2] The reservation ratio of each corresponding radar task is $\frac{\theta_i}{\lceil \lceil \frac{1}{P_i^S/B_i^S} \rceil \cdot \theta_i \rceil}$. Instances of TR subtasks of $\tau_i$ and their corresponding SP subtasks are assigned to the $\lceil \lceil \frac{1}{P_i^S/B_i^S} \rceil \cdot \theta_i \rceil$ corresponding radar tasks in a round robin fashion. Note that a search task $\tau_i$ must issue $B_i^S$ beams in each period $P_i^S$. Each radar task $\tau_{i,j}$ (split from $\tau_i$) is considered independently in TR and SP scheduling. The SP scheduling of all radar tasks (regardless of whether they are split or not) is as presented in the previous paragraph.

### 3.3.3 Properties

The purpose of this section is to provide a polynomial-time schedulability test for SP scheduling. It also serves for the admission control of new radar tasks. We shall first summarize related theorems of *M-CBS* in [2, 9]: Note that each *M-CBS* server in [2, 9] is a radar task in this paper.

**Theorem 1** *[2] Given a collection $T$ of M-CBS servers, let each server be associated with a reservation ratio $\theta_i$. $T$ is*

---

[2]Search tasks are radar tasks that could have a reservation ratio $\theta_i = \frac{c_{i,2}}{D_{i,2}}$ (or $\frac{c_{i,2}}{P_i^S/B_i^S}$ if $(P_i^S/B_i^S) < D_{i,2}$) larger than one.

schedulable by M-CBS with processor migration and preemption allowed if and only if there exists a value for $k$ that satisfies the following inequality, where $M$ is the number of processors: $M \geq min_{k=1}^{n}\{(k-1) + \frac{\theta(T^{(k+1)})}{1-\theta_k}\}$.

**Lemma 1** *[9] When a uni-processor system is scheduled with more than one M-CBS servers on the earliest-deadline-first basis, every server meets its deadlines if the sum of the total reservation ratio of all servers is no greater than $1 - \frac{Max(npb_i)}{Min(d_j)}$, where $Max(npb_i)$ and $Min(d_j)$ are the maximum execution time of any nonpreemptable portion and the minimum of the relative deadlines for all subtasks executed by servers, respectively.*

Since no M-CBS server could have a reservation ratio larger than one, we shall first provide a schedulability test for radar tasks if no radar task has a reservation ratio larger than one. We then show that the inequality of the schedulability test remains when we split radar tasks with a reservation ratio larger than one in a way presented in the previous section.

**Theorem 2** *Given a collection $T$ of radar tasks with reservation ratios no larger than 1, $T$ is schedulable by M-CBS-NPM if and only if there exists a value for $k$ that satisfies the following inequality:*

$$M(1 - \frac{Max(npb_i)}{Min(d_j)}) \geq min_{k=1}^{n}\{(k-1) + \frac{\theta(T^{(k+1)})}{1-\theta_k}\},$$

*where $Max(npb_i)$ and $Min(d_j)$ are the maximum execution time and the minimum of the relative deadlines of all SP subtasks, respectively.*

**Proof.** The correctness of this theorem follows from Theorem 1 and Lemma 1 by considering the worst-case blocking cost. □

According to M-CBS-NPM, any search task $\tau_i$ that has a reservation ratio $\theta_i$ larger than one must be first split into $\lceil \lceil \frac{1}{P_i^S/B_i^S} \rceil \cdot \theta_i \rceil$ corresponding radar tasks. We first show that the tasks split from a search task with $\theta_i \leq 1$ could provide enough processing power for the SP subtasks of the search task in meeting their deadline requirement:

**Lemma 2** *Given a radar task $\tau_i$ with a reservation ratio $\theta_i > 1$, $\tau_i$ could be split into $\lceil \lceil \frac{1}{P_i^S/B_i^S} \rceil \cdot \theta_i \rceil$ corresponding radar tasks, i.e., $\tau_{i,1}, .., \tau_{i,\lceil\lceil\frac{1}{P_i^S/B_i^S}\rceil\cdot\theta_i\rceil}$, and the reservation ratio of each corresponding radar task is $\frac{\theta_i}{\lceil\lceil\frac{1}{P_i^S/B_i^S}\rceil\cdot\theta_i\rceil}$. If instances of TR subtasks of $\tau_i$ and their corresponding SP subtasks are assigned to the $\lceil \lceil \frac{1}{P_i^S/B_i^S} \rceil \cdot \theta_i \rceil$ corresponding radar tasks in a round robin fashion, then the SP subtasks of the instances of $\tau_i$ will meet their deadlines under M-CBS-NPM.*

**Proof.** The correctness of the proof follows from the fact that the total execution time guaranteed by M-CBS-NPM for the corresponding radar tasks is no less than the maximum demanded execution time. □

**Theorem 3** *Given a collection $T$ of radar tasks (where radar tasks with reservation ratios larger one are split based on M-CBS-NPM), $T$ is schedulable by M-CBS-NPM if and only if*

there exists a value for $k$ that satisfies the following inequality: $M(1 - \frac{Max(npb_i)}{Min(d_j)}) \geq min_{k=1}^{n}\{(k-1) + \frac{\theta(T^{(k+1)})}{1-\theta_k}\}$, *where $Max(npb_i)$ and $Min(d_j)$ are the maximum execution time and the minimum of the relative deadlines of all SP subtasks, respectively.*

**Proof.** The correctness of this theorem follows from Theorem 2 and Lemma 2. □

Theorem 3 could be used for on-line admission control when the system considers to admit any new radar task, given the number of VSP's in SP. We must point out that Theorem 3 could also be used for the capacity estimation of SP when the (maximum) workload of a radar system and its characteristics are given! Engineers could estimate the minimum number of VSP's needed for a given workload in a more optimistic based on the following corollary:

**Corollary 1** *Given a collection $T$ of radar tasks (where radar tasks with reservation ratios larger one are split based on M-CBS-NPM), the number of VSP's needed for the radar tasks is no less than $M$ if $M \leq \sum \theta_i$, where $\theta_i$ is the reservation ratio of a radar task $\tau_i$.*

**Proof.** The correctness of this corollary follows from the fact that when the number of VSP's allocated for the radar tasks is $M$, the maximum processing time supplied by the VSP's is $M \cdot (t_2 - t_1)$ in a interval of time $[t_1, t_2]$. □

## 4 Performance Evaluation

The purpose of this section is to evaluate the performance of the proposed methodology, referred to as the Probabilistic Real-Time Scheduling algorithm (PRTS) in this section. A simulation model was constructed to investigate the performance of the proposed methodology. We compared the schedulability and the performance of PRTS with the Ultimate Deadline Algorithm (UD) [7, 9], the Proportional Deadline Algorithm (PD) [9], the Equal Deadline Algorithm (EQD), the Equal Flexibility Algorithm (EQF) [7], the Equal Slack Algorithm (EQS) [7], and the Effective Deadline Algorithm (ED) [7, 9][3]. The performance of PRTS proposed in this paper was verified and simulated under different probabilistic guarantees (i.e., 91%, 93%, 95%, 97%, and 99%). We used $PRTS_\phi$ to denote PRTS with a probabilistic guarantee $\phi$ in this section.

The system parameters for the experiments were based on a real phased array radar for air defense frigates [6]: Each tested task set had a search task and several track tasks. The search task issued 45 beams for every 40 SI (where 40 SI = 1 sec). We set the dwell length, the execution time in SP, and the relative deadline of each search (/track) task as

---

[3]Under UD, $D_{i,1} = D_i$ and $D_{i,2} = 0$. Under PD, $D_{i,1} = D_i \cdot \frac{c_{i,1}}{c_{i,1}+c_{i,2}}$ and $D_{i,2} = D_i \cdot \frac{c_{i,2}}{c_{i,1}+c_{i,2}}$. Under EQD, $D_{i,1} = D_i/2$ and $D_{i,2} = D_i/2$. Under EQF, $D_{i,1} = (D_i - c_{i,1} - c_{i,2}) \cdot \frac{c_{i,1}}{c_{i,1}+c_{i,2}} + c_{i,1}$ and $D_{i,2} = (D_i - c_{i,1} - c_{i,2}) \cdot \frac{c_{i,2}}{c_{i,1}+c_{i,2}} + c_{i,2}$. Under EQS, $D_{i,1} = \frac{D_i-c_{i,1}-c_{i,2}}{2}+c_{i,1}$ and $D_{i,2} = \frac{D_i-c_{i,1}-c_{i,2}}{2}+c_{i,2}$. Under ED, $D_{i,1} = D_i - c_{i,2}$ and $D_{i,1} = c_{i,2}$.

0.24 (/0.16) SI, 1.5 (/0.25) SI, and 8 (/6) SI, respectively. The time interval between two consecutive instance arrivals for a track task was exponentially distributed with a mean 4 SI. The number of the track tasks in a tested task set of the simulations was from 10 to 20. In other words, the total utilization of the corresponding TR subtasks (including the search task) varied from 0.67 to 1.07. When the total utilization of TR subtasks was over 1, TR was overloaded. Let $N_T$ denote the number of track tasks per SI. Each task set was simulated for 40,000 SI.

The primary performance metrics were the schedulability of the task sets and the number of VSP's (labelled as $N_{VSP}$) needed for different scheduling algorithms. The schedulability of a simulated task set for each algorithm had to be achieved. If an algorithm under simulation could schedule a task set, then we re-did the simulation with a smaller number $N_{VSP}$ of VSP's until some task in the task set missed its deadline. We should derive the minimum number of VSP's needed for a scheduling algorithm.[4] We did not show the minimum number of VSP's needed for a scheduling algorithm in figures if the scheduling algorithm could not schedule the task set, regardless of the number of adopted VSP's in SP.

## 4.1 Analysis Results and Experimental Results

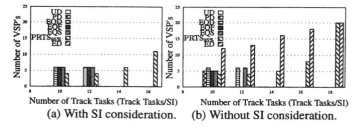

(a) With SI consideration.  (b) Without SI consideration.

**Figure 2. The number of VSP's needed for the algorithms with and without SI considerations.**

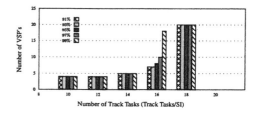

**Figure 3. The number of VSP's needed for PRTS without SI considerations.**

In this section, we showed the analysis results based on Theorem 3 and the results of the simulation. We first investigated the $N_{VSP}$ values for different algorithms based on

---

[4]Note that a smaller number of VSP's means a better system performance.

the calculation results by using Theorem 3. The algorithms under evaluation included UD, PD, EQD, EQF, EQS, ED, and PRTS$_{95\%}$. Let $U_{TR,i}(\mathbb{K})$ denote the total average utilization for the task set $TS_i$ (with $i$ track tasks) for Algorithm $\mathbb{K}$, where $\mathbb{K}$ can be UD, PD, EQD, EQF, EQS, ED, or PRTS. We first calculated $U_{TR,i}(\mathbb{K})$ for the algorithms. $TS_i$ could not be scheduled by Algorithm $\mathbb{K}$, if the calculated value $U_{TR,i}(\mathbb{K}) > (1 - \frac{Max(npb_i)}{Min(d_j)})$, where $Max(npb_i)$ and $Min(d_j)$ were the maximum execution time and the minimum of the relative deadlines of all TR subtasks, respectively. Otherwise (i.e., $U_{TR,i}(\mathbb{K}) \leq (1 - \frac{Max(npb_i)}{Min(d_j)})$), we could use Theorem 3 to calculate $N_{VSP}$ for Algorithm $\mathbb{K}$, and this algorithm could schedule the tested task set $TS_i$.

**The Performance Comparison for Different Algorithms with SI Considerations.** In Figure 2.(a), we compared $N_{VSP}$ for different algorithms where SI was considered. Obviously, UD, PD, and ED could not schedule any tested task set. The reason was that $D_{i,1}$ ($D_{i,2}$) of a task $\tau_i$ under ED (UD or PD) was too small to guarantee the scheduling of the TR (SP) subtasks. When $N_T \leq 12$, PRTS$_{95\%}$, EQD, EQS, and EQF could schedule the tested task sets, and the $N_{VSP}$ values for PRTS$_{95\%}$ were smaller than that for EQD, EQS, and EQF. The reason was that $D_{i,2}$ for PRTS$_{95\%}$ was larger than that for EQD, EQS, or EQF.

**The Performance Comparison for Different Algorithms without SI Considerations.** In Figure 2.(b), we compared $N_{VSP}$ for different algorithms where SI was not considered. We observed that UD could not schedule any tested task set. EQD and EQS could schedule the tested task sets when $N_T \leq 12$. EQF could schedule the tested task sets only when $N_T = 10$. Although ED and PRTS$_{95\%}$ could schedule the tested task sets when $N_T \leq 18$, PRTS$_{95\%}$ had smaller $N_{VSP}$ values. We knew that PRTS$_{95\%}$ outperformed the other algorithms in terms of $N_{VSP}$ and had the highest guarantee for schedulability.

**The Effects of Probabilistic Guarantees on PRTS without SI Considerations.** For PRTS, we might set up different probabilistic guarantees when a task set was scheduled. In Figure 3, we investigated the effects of the probabilistic guarantees on PRTS when SI was not considered. We set probabilistic guarantees as 91%, 93%, 95%, 97%, and 99% and re-run the experiments. For the situation when SI was considered, we observed similar phenomenons, so the results for PRTS with SI considerations were not shown in this paper. We observed the following phenomenons: (1) When $N_T \leq 14$, the effects of the probabilistic guarantees were insignificant (i.e., the $N_{VSP}$ values were almost the same). (2) When $N_T = 16$, PRTS with the higher probabilistic guarantee needed more VSP's. (3) When $N_T = 18$, the $N_{VSP}$ values for PRTS with different probabilistic guarantee setups were the same, which were close to

20. Phenomenon 1 was observed because TR utilization was relatively low so that the waiting time of a TR subtask was not very long even under different probabilistic guarantees. Phenomenon 1 indicated that when $N_T \leq 14$, we could set the probabilistic guarantee as 99% (i.e., no more than 1% task instances missed their deadlines), PRTS could provide the same schedulability as that the other algorithms provided, and the $N_{VSP}$ value for PRTS was the smallest among UD, PD, EQD, EQF, EQS, ED, and PRTS (Please see Figure 2.(b).). Phenomenon 2 showed that PRTS needed more VPS's to provide a higher probabilistic guarantee with the increasing of $N_T$ (i.e., $N_T = 16$). Note that when $N_T = 18$, the system utilization of TR was about 99%. Since TR was almost fully utilized, different probabilistic guarantees did not affect the $N_{VSP}$ values, as shown in Phenomenon 3. When $N_T = 20$ (i.e., the TR utilization = 1.06), TR might be overloaded, no scheduling algorithms could guarantee the schedulability of all tasks without any deadline violation.

In the experiments, PRTS always guaranteed the schedulability of search tasks and, at the same time, reduced the number of VSP's needed for phased array radars, compared to UD, PD, EQD, EQF, EQS, and ED. Even when the number of track tasks per SI was 20, 99.96% of the executions of track tasks would meet their deadline requirements (even though a 100% or even 95% guarantee was impossible), where PRTS without SI consideration was applied. The experimental results for PRTS with SI consideration were similar to those without SI consideation.

## 5  Conclusion

This paper addresses two important issues on radar scheduling: (1) schedulability guarantees for radar tasks (2) the system capacity estimation. While lots of existing work suffers from conservative resource allocation problems, we aims at the proposing of a joint real-time scheduling algorithm for TR and SP workloads with an analytical framework for off-line probabilistic analysis and on-line admission control. A priority-driven scheduling algorithm is proposed for TR workloads, and an analytic method is presented to derive deadlines for workloads in SP based on the given probabilistic guarantees of radar tasks. SP scheduling is then proposed based on the well-known rate-based multi-processor algorithm M-CBS, where no task migration or preemption is allowed. We provide different levels of schedulability guarantees in a probabilistic fashion for different radar tasks. The capability of the proposed scheduling algorithm is evaluated by a series of experiments based on a real phased array radar for air defense frigates [6].

For future research, we shall further extend the results to RCC scheduling with multiple TR's, especially when they are applied in a more structured way. We shall also apply the proposed two-stage scheduling algorithm to more general distributed real-time systems.

## References

[1] A. Barbato and P. Giustiniani. An improved scheduling algorithm for a naval phased array radar. In *Radar 92. International Conference*, pages 42–45, 1992.

[2] S. Baruah, J. Goossens, and G. Lipari. Implementing constant-bandwidth servers upon multiprocessor platforms. In *Eighth IEEE Real-Time and Embedded Technology and Applications Symposium*, 2002.

[3] R.A. Baugh. *Computer Control of Modern Radars*. RCAM&SR-Moorestown Library, 1973.

[4] C. Chang and T.-C. Wang. Use object-oriented paradigm to design a programmable radar digital signal processor. In *Third Workshop on Object-Oriented Technology and Applications*, 1997.

[5] M.R. Garey and D.S. Johnson. *Computers and Intractability: A guide to the Theory of NP-Completeness*. W. H. Freeman & Company, 1979.

[6] A.G. Huizing and A.A.F. Bloemen. An efficient scheduling algorithm for a multifunction radar. In *IEEE International Radar Conference*, pages 359–364, 1996.

[7] B. Kao and H. Garcia-Molina. Deadline assignment in a distributed soft real-time system. *IEEE Transactions on Parallel and Distributed Systems*, 8(12):1268–1274, 1997.

[8] L. Kleinrock. *Queueing Systems Volume II: Computer Applications*. Wiley-Interscience Publication, 1976.

[9] J. W. Layland. *Real-Time System*. Prentice Hall, 2000.

[10] A.K. Parekh and R.G. Gallager. A generalized processor sharing approach to flow control in integrated services networks: The single node case. In *The Proceedings of IEEE INFOCOM*, 1992.

[11] Rapid prototyping of Application Specific Signal Processors (RASSP). http://eto.sysplan.com/eto/rassp. 2000.

[12] M. Spuri, G. Buttazzo, and F. Sensini. Scheduling aperiodic tasks in dynamic scheduling environment. In *IEEE Real-Time Systems Symposium*, 1995.

[13] L.H. Su. A hybrid two-stage flowshop with limited waiting time constraints. *Computers and Industrial Engineering*, 44(3):409–424, 2003.

[14] E.J. Watson. *Laplace Transforms and Applications*. Birkhauserk, 1981.

# Using Hardware Operations to Reduce the Synchronization Overhead of Task Pools

Ralf Hoffmann      Matthias Korch      Thomas Rauber

*Department of Computer Science*
*University of Bayreuth, Germany*
*{ralf.hoffmann, matthias.korch, rauber}@uni-bayreuth.de*

## Abstract

*We consider the task-based execution of parallel irregular applications, which are characterized by an unpredictable computational structure induced by the input data. The dynamic load balancing required to execute such applications efficiently can be provided by task pools. Thus, the performance of a task-based irregular application is tightly coupled to the scalability and the overhead of the task pool used to execute it. In order to reduce this overhead this article considers the use of the hardware-specific synchronization operations* Compare & Swap *and* Load & Reserve/Store Conditional. *We present several different realizations of task pools using these operations. Runtime experiments on two shared-memory machines, a SunFire 6800 and an IBM p690, show that the new implementations obtain a significantly higher performance than implementations relying on the POSIX thread library for synchronization.*

## 1. Introduction

When executing irregular applications on multiprocessor machines, a static work distribution usually does not lead to an optimal load balance and, therefore, dynamic load balancing is required to execute such applications efficiently. One way to balance the load dynamically is the use of *task pools*. For that purpose, the application is split into several *types of tasks*. Every task type specifies a sequence of operations to be performed. At runtime, *tasks*, i.e., instances of these task types with corresponding arguments, are created dynamically and are stored in the task pool until they are scheduled onto a processor for execution. Typically, tasks can create new tasks during their execution. Thus, the visualization of the parent-child dependences between tasks during a typical run of a task-based application leads to an irregularly structured directed acyclic graph (DAG), the specific structure of which depends on the input data.

While the execution of the tasks directly contributes to the computation of the output data, the work required to manage the tasks represents an overhead reducing the efficiency of the parallel execution of the application. This overhead is composed of the time required to execute the instructions of the task pool operations, and waiting times resulting from synchronization and memory latencies. Many different approaches towards a reduction of this overhead are possible. In this article, we consider the application of efficient synchronization mechanisms [13, 14, 18] based on the hardware-specific synchronization operations *Compare & Swap* (CAS) and *Load & Reserve/Store Conditional* (LR/SC) to implement task pools on shared-memory parallel computers. Such operations are available on most modern parallel computer systems and thus enable the efficient implementation of task pools on many different hardware architectures. The task pools are implemented in assembler in order to use these synchronization operations efficiently and to obtain near maximum performance on the machines considered. In runtime experiments we investigate the performance gain in comparison to platform-independent task pools presented in [11], which are implemented in C and use synchronization operations provided by the POSIX thread library.

The rest of the paper is organized as follows: Section 2 introduces the hardware synchronization operations. Section 3 describes the evaluation strategy and the different versions of central and distributed task pools and their realization using hardware operations. Section 4 presents runtime experiments for the hierarchical radiosity application. Section 5 discusses related work, and Section 6 concludes the paper.

## 2. Synchronization operations

The first machine we consider is a Sun Fire 6800 server, a symmetric multiprocessor (SMP) equipped with 24 UltraSPARC III+ [18] CPUs at 900 MHz. To support synchronization between the processors in the system, the CPU provides three different atomic read-modify-write (RMW) operations. The most powerful operation is *Com-*

*pare & Swap* (CAS); it supports the conditional modification of a 32-bit or 64-bit value by writing a new value to a memory location if the current value of that memory location is equal to a value specified in a given register. This operation always returns the value originally read from the memory location. Typically, this operation is executed in a loop until the operation succeeds, i.e., until the value at the memory location is equal to the value in the register and the value at the memory location has been replaced with the new value.

The second SMP we consider is an IBM p690+ server equipped with 32 Power4+ CPUs at 1700 MHz. The Power4 processor does not support RMW operations as single atomic instructions. Instead, two separate read and write operations, *Load & Reserve* (LR) and *Store Conditional* (SC), are provided in a 32-bit and a 64-bit version. These operations are based on a similar pair of operations, *Load Linked* and *Store Conditional* (LL/SC), suggested in [8]. If a memory location is read to a general purpose register using LR, the executing Power4 processor sets a reservation on this memory location in a special register. This reservation is released as soon as any processor issues a write operation targeting this location or another memory location that shares the same cache line. After reading the value to a register, the register can be modified using arbitrary machine instructions. Writing the value back to the memory location using SC only succeeds if there exists a valid reservation on the respective address in the executing processor. Thus, the complete RMW cycle needs to be executed repeatedly until the SC operation succeeds if a behavior similar to the atomic RMW operations of other processors shall be emulated.

## 3. Task pool implementation and evaluation

### 3.1. Evaluation strategy

To evaluate the different task pool versions, we perform runtime experiments with a synthetic task-based application, which provides exact control of the number of tasks created and the granularity of the tasks. The application uses only one task type called $A$. A task of this type creates new tasks according to the following rule:

$$A(i) \rightarrow \begin{cases} \{100f\} & \text{for } i \leq 0, \\ \{10f\}\ A(i-2)\ \{50f\} \\ \quad A(i-1)\ \{100f\} & \text{for } i > 0. \end{cases} \quad (1)$$

The values in braces determine simulated computation times. The factor $f$ can be used to adjust the computation time of the tasks. According to (1), a task that is called with argument $i \leq 0$ just waits for 100 time units and returns. If the argument $i$ is greater than 0, the task waits for 10 time units, then creates a new task with argument $i-2$, waits for 50 time units, creates a task with argument $i-1$, and finally returns after waiting for another 100 time units

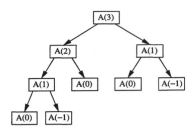

**Figure 1. Task creation scheme for one task of the synthetic application created with argument 3.**

(see also Figure 1). Shared variables are not used. Though no locality in the computations can be exploited, this approach has the benefit that no synchronization operations are necessary to protect shared variables and thus performance limitations that are due to synchronization are only caused by the task pools themselves.

When called with argument $k$, the application sequentially creates $k$ tasks with the arguments $k-1$ to 0 in the initialization phase. As a result of the task creation scheme (1), the total number of tasks processed by the application grows exponentially with $k$ as fast as the Fibonacci series. For the runtime experiments shown, we use the value $k = 35$ to ensure a runtime long enough to measure differences in the task pool implementations. The total number of tasks created is $78, 176, 299$.

This evaluation method is well suited to investigate the performance and the scalability of the task pools. It considers a highly unbalanced task graph and allows to observe the influence of the task granularity on the run time behavior of the task pools. By changing the parameter $f$, it is possible to decrease the computation time of the tasks to increase the share of time needed to execute the task pool operations. This helps to uncover bottlenecks in the task pool operations, which are otherwise difficult to observe.

### 3.2. Memory management

The memory management is an important part of a task pool implementation because each task creation and termination requires a data structure allocation and deallocation, respectively. Using system calls for each task operation may create a major bottleneck inside the task pool. Therefore, we have implemented a special purpose memory manager which takes advantage of the fixed data structure sizes and allocates several objects in advance to minimize the number of system calls. We re-use memory blocks and store objects already allocated but currently unused in private distributed free-lists. Later requests for objects can be satisfied from these lists without any system call. Due to the use of private lists, no synchronization is needed, and therefore the memory manager does not limit the scalability of the task pools. The memory manager of the Pthreads task pools is implemented platform-independently in C. In order to investigate the best performance possible, the memory manager of the new task pool implementations is implemented in assembler.

### 3.3. Central task pools

Central task pools use a single queue to store the tasks. This queue is accessed by all processors concurrently. All tasks are available to all processors and so this type of task pool offers a good load balance. Limitations to scalability are set by synchronization operations required for concurrent accesses to the queue. Therefore, an efficient implementation of the task pool can improve the performance significantly, particularly if the tasks are fine-grained and the queue must be accessed frequently.

All central task pools we investigate have in common that the tasks in the central task queue are processed in LIFO order (last in first out, stack). Depending on the application, the LIFO order can improve the data locality because newly created tasks often access parts of the data used by the creating task. Therefore, executing newly created tasks shortly after the parent task may reduce the number of cache misses. We consider the following three implementation variants:

**SQ-SL (single queue, simple lock):** This implementation uses a simple lock to realize the concurrent accesses to the queue. We assume that exactly one thread per processors is executed, and therefore the lock operations can use busy loops without deteriorating the performance.

We use a shared memory location as a global lock variable and the synchronization operations of the underlying hardware to guarantee mutual exclusion. On the SPARC system we use the CAS operation as described in [18] to implement an atomic access to the lock variable. On the Power4 processor we use the LR/SC operations to implement a behavior similar to CAS. These lock implementations are used to acquire a lock before inserting or removing a task into or from the task pool.

**SQ-TL (single queue, ticket lock):** To improve the scalability, the simple lock is replaced by the scalable and fair ticket lock (cf. [13]). Basically, the ticket lock uses two shared counters. The value of one of the counters is increased atomically by each processor requesting a lock. The second counter is only increased on lock release. A processor requesting a lock reads and stores the value of the first counter and enters the critical section when the value of the second counter reaches the value previously stored. On the SPARC processor we increment the counter atomically using CAS. On the Power4 system we use the LR/SC operations to implement the atomic increment.

The implementation uses busy loops to compare the local value previously read with the global second counter. The lock release is realized by a non-atomic increase of the second counter. In contrast to the simple lock, the repeated execution of the atomic operation is only necessary until the ticket increase succeeds. Waiting for the acquirement of the lock is implemented using a simple non-atomic load operation and therefore waiting does not affect any other processor.

**SQ-LF (single queue, lock-free):** This implementation modifies the task queue directly using a lock-free approach. The idea is to modify the head of the queue atomically while keeping the queue in a consistent state. This makes the implementation of lock-free task pools more complicated than lock-based task pools. Insertion of a task into the queue is done by storing the current head element in the data structure of the new element. The new task becomes the new head element if the current head element is equal to the element previously read. On the SPARC CPU this can be easily achieved by using the CAS operation. On the Power4 CPU the current head element is loaded with LR and written to the data structure. The memory location of the new element is not inside the cache line of the location of the head element and so we ensure that this store operation does not invalidate the reservation. Finally, the new element is written back using SC which only succeeds if no other processor has changed the head element.

The removal of an element from the list is more complicated. To determine the new head element, it is necessary to read the successor of the current head element. The new head element can only be stored if the head element and the successor have not been changed (this is called the ABA problem [14]). The CAS operation is not suitable for such a test because it can only test a single memory location at once. One possibility to overcome this problem is an additional counter which is stored together with the head element. With each change in the queue the counter is increased so that a change can be detected even if the actual value of the head element is still the same. The SPARC processor offers a 64-bit CAS so the atomic operation can be applied to the head element (first 32 bit) and the counter (second 32 bit).

Although the Power4 processor can emulate the CAS operation, the LR/SC operations can be used more efficiently to implement the lock-free behavior. The remove operation needs knowledge about the head element and the successor at the same time. As with CAS this is also impossible with the LR/SC operations. But unlike CAS the LR/SC operations can detect changes in the queue even if the head element is still the same. The LR operation loads the current head element and a normal load operation reads the successor. The successor is written as the head element using SC. Because any change in the queue (removal and insertion) involves a write access to the head element, the final SC operation would fail if any other processor had modified the queue.

| Task pool implementation | Best speedup SPARC | No. of threads SPARC | Efficiency SPARC | Best speedup Power4 | No. of threads Power4 | Efficiency Power4 |
|---|---|---|---|---|---|---|
| Pthreads-SQ | 3.1 | 4 | **0.78** | 0.95 | 2 | 0.47 |
| SQ-SL | 9.1 | 12 | 0.76 | 1.06 | 2 | 0.53 |
| SQ-TL | 8.98 | 16 | 0.56 | 1.13 | 2 | **0.57** |
| SQ-LF | **11.26** | 16 | 0.70 | **1.7** | 4 | 0.43 |

**Table 1. Speedup and efficiency of the central task pools for task size $f = 50$ on the SPARC and the Power4 system.**

**Runtime experiments:** As a comparison basis we use a Pthreads task pool which implements the same load balancing strategy. On the SPARC system, all new task pool implementations perform similarly well for one thread. For empty tasks ($f = 0$), the Pthreads implementation is almost 2.2 times slower than any task pool using hardware operations, but for larger tasks ($f = 50$), the difference is only marginal ($\approx 1\%$). For 20 threads, we can observe a different situation. For small task sizes ($f < 10$), no task pool implementation reaches the sequential execution time. With a factor $f = 0$ the Pthreads implementation is $\approx 2$ times slower than the best task pool, which uses the ticket lock. With increasing task sizes, the Pthreads implementation gets even slower and for $f = 50$ the task pool using the ticket lock is more than 16 times faster. Only with ten times larger tasks ($f = 500$) the Pthreads task pool achieves almost the same execution time as the new task pools. Although the ticket lock task pool performs very well and is the fastest implementation for 20 threads, the task pool using the lock-free approach can achieve the best speedup of 11.26 with 16 threads (Table 1).

On the Power4 system we can observe a greater improvement even for one thread. Our new implementations are up to three times faster than the Pthreads implementation while still achieving a 23% lower execution time for $f = 50$. In contrast to the SPARC system, our lock-free implementation is the fastest on the Power4. The reason for this is the more efficient implementation of the lock-free algorithm on the Power4 processor described above. For 32 threads, the implementations using the ticket lock and the lock-free approach are much faster than the Pthreads implementation. The lock-free approach performs best and is $\approx 1.6$ times faster for $f = 0$ and $\approx 1.8$ times faster for $f = 50$ than the Pthreads task pool. In contrast, the task pool using the simple lock is only slightly better than the Pthreads implementation. Although the new implementations are much faster than the Pthreads task pool, with 32 threads they are still much slower than the single thread version.

To investigate the speedup of our implementations, we compare the resulting execution time with the sequential execution time of a special single-queue task pool. This task pool does not use synchronization operations to protect the queue and can thus be used as a suitable reference

in the speedup calculation.

Table 1 presents the best speedups and the corresponding efficiencies for the central task pools with a task size of $f = 50$. On the SPARC system the lock-free implementation achieves the best speedup of 11.26 using 16 threads. On the faster Power4 system the tasks are executed faster with respect to the synchronization operations because the ratio of CPU speed and memory speed is larger. Thus, the speedups are much smaller. The best speedup is only 1.7 using 4 threads. The task pool using the ticket lock performs very well on both machines. The best speedup is achieved by the lock-free implementation but, in contrast to the SPARC system, the lock-free task pool performs generally best on the Power4 system due to the efficient implementation using LR/SC.

### 3.4. Distributed task pools

As the speedups measured for the central task pools indicate, using a single queue to store the tasks leads to a bottleneck if the tasks are small and the task pool is accessed by the processors frequently. The use of several queues distributed among the processors can improve the throughput of the task pool and reduces the overhead and the number of access conflicts. To achieve a good load balance, the processors need to search several queues for new work if their local queues are empty. Also, the data locality is often improved because new tasks can be stored locally and, as long as all task queues are filled, all processors can execute locally created tasks without stealing. The drawback of distributed queues may be an increased overhead generated by the search for new tasks which may involve checking other processors' queues.

Distributed task pools differ in the number of queues and in the access rules to the queues. Our distributed task pools assign one task queue to each processor and every processor adds new tasks only to its local queue. In the best case, when all queues are filled, all processors can work without any collisions. The search for new tasks is controlled by an array for each processor containing the permuted IDs of all processors. Using these arrays, every processor checks the queues in a different order.

### 3.4.1. Distributed task pools without grouping

We consider the following implementations using different synchronization operations.

**DQ-SL (distributed queue, simple lock):** This distributed task pool uses simple locks based on the hardware operations CAS or LR/SC, respectively, to protect the concurrent accesses to the task queues. New tasks are inserted immediately into the task queue assigned to the processor. The removal operation first checks the local queue and then searches the other queues following the order described in the permutation array. In both cases the processor needs to acquire and release one lock on each queue accessed.

**DQ-SL-PRIV (distributed queue, simple lock, private buffer):** In this implementation, newly created tasks are inserted into a private buffer and are only moved to the queue when the size of the private buffer exceeds a specified threshold. Access to the private buffer does not require any synchronization operations which can improve the performance significantly. The use of additional private buffers per processor improves the overall throughput of the task pool. However, because task stealing from private buffers is not possible, using too large buffers can negatively affect the load balance. We investigate the performance gain of the smallest buffer size, i.e., we store only a single task in the private buffer, in order to minimize the load imbalance.

Our experiments show that the approach with a single task leads to an improved performance without a noticeable load imbalance. Because of this, all task pool implementations described in the following use a private buffer that can store one single task.

**DQ-SL-PRIV-C (distributed queue, simple lock, private buffer, cache optimized):** Cache optimizations can improve the performance further. Exploiting the underlying memory system is often favorable, but for the use of synchronization operations it is even more important. Knowledge about the underlying realization of hardware synchronization operations can be used to improve the performance. For example, the reservation set by the LR operation on the Power4 system does not only cover the specified memory address. Instead, any write operation to the memory area corresponding to the cache line in which the address is located invalidates the reservation even if this write operation is totally unrelated to the synchronization operation.

Therefore, we align the data structures of the task pool to the cache line size of the actual processor. So the private buffer, the public queue, the lock variable and additional data for each processor are stored in different cache lines. This improves the performance by reducing unnecessary cache invalidations.

**DQ-SL-TRY-PRIV-C (distributed queue, simple lock, single try, private buffer, cache optimized):** The lock operation is modified so that it tries to acquire the lock only once. If the lock attempt fails, the processor immediately continues with the queue of the next processor in its search order. The processor does not need to wait for the lock release and can continue to search for tasks in other queues. This results in a semi-nonblocking task pool which leads to improved performance in situations where several processors are searching for new tasks in the same queue. In such a situation, these processors would have to be serialized if normal spinlocks were used.

**DQ-TL-PRIV-C (distributed queue, ticket lock, private buffer, cache optimized):** In this implementation, the simple lock is replaced by the ticket lock.

**DQ-CLH-PRIV-C (distributed queue, CLH lock, private buffer, cache optimized):** The simple lock is replaced by the CLH-lock as described in [13], which is another fair lock that reduces the required memory bandwidth further. The lock realizes an implicit list of the waiting processors. Each processor owns a memory location which stores a pointer to the previous processor in the list. The lock is represented by a pointer to the head element of this list initially pointing to a dummy element. To request the lock, the processor sets a waiting flag in its own element and swaps this element with the lock element atomically. Then, this processor waits for the waiting flag of the swapped element to be cleared. The subsequent processor waits for the previous element and so on. The hardware requirements are lower at the cost of a slightly higher memory usage. An atomic fetch-and-store (e.g., SWAP) is the only requirement. The SPARC processor offers this operation so this lock solves the starvation problem evoked by CAS when many processors try to acquire the lock and CAS fails more often. Although this method is more complicated than the simple lock, the actual code is only slightly larger.

**DQ-SL-SP-PRIV-C (distributed queue, simple lock with SINGLEPUT extension, private buffer, cache optimized):** In this implementation we exploit the fact that enqueuing of new tasks into a queue can only be performed by the processor assigned to the queue. The order of the task queue is changed from LIFO (stack) to FIFO (first in first out). Task removal is performed at the head of the queue and insertion is done at the tail. Because task stealing requires synchronization for the removal, the head of the queue is protected by the simple lock. By inserting a dummy element into the list, the queue owner can insert new tasks without synchronization. The new task order may lead to a decrease in the data locality because newly created tasks will be executed only after all previously created task have been executed. Thus, the input data of the task may no longer be in the cache.

| Task Pool implementation | Best speedup SPARC | No. of threads SPARC | Efficiency SPARC | Best speedup Power4 | No. of threads Power4 | Efficiency Power4 |
|---|---|---|---|---|---|---|
| Pthreads-DQ | 17.49 | 20 | 0.87 | 1.32 | 4 | 0.33 |
| DQ-SL | **18.09** | 20 | **0.90** | 1.47 | 32 | 0.05 |
| DQ-SL-PRIV | 16.04 | 20 | 0.80 | 2.68 | 32 | 0.08 |
| DQ-SL-PRIV-C | 17.22 | 20 | 0.86 | 3.07 | 8 | 0.38 |
| DQ-SL-TRY-PRIV-C | 17.07 | 20 | 0.85 | 3.1 | 4 | 0.78 |
| DQ-TL-PRIV-C | 16.83 | 20 | 0.84 | 2.91 | 4 | 0.73 |
| DQ-CLH-PRIV-C | 17.04 | 20 | 0.85 | 2.88 | 4 | 0.72 |
| DQ-SL-SP-PRIV-C | 16.86 | 20 | 0.84 | 2.91 | 8 | 0.36 |
| DQ-LF-PRIV-C | 16.55 | 20 | 0.83 | **3.25** | 4 | **0.81** |
| DQ-LF-SPARC2-PRIV-C | 15.86 | 20 | 0.79 | N/A | N/A | N/A |

**Table 2. Speedup and efficiency of the distributed task pools for task size $f = 50$ on the SPARC and the Power4 system.**

**DQ-LF-PRIV-C (distributed queue, lock-free, private buffer, cache optimized):** The lock-free approach described in Section 3.3 is also applied to the distributed task pools. On the SPARC system we implement an additional lock-free method. The approach using a counter needs an atomic operation which supports a data type that can store the head element and the counter. The idea of the following method is to supply a more general method to implement a lock-free task queue for processors with atomic synchronization operations. We simulate the task removal by a double insertion. At first, the whole queue is removed by the insertion of a NULL pointer (i.e., by swapping the head element with NULL, thus making the queue empty). The new modified queue is reinserted if the queue is still empty. If the queue already contains new elements, the queue will be removed and merged with the current (still removed) queue. The procedure is repeated until the local queue can be inserted successfully. This method needs more work and can take more time in the worst case but it has the advantage to work with any atomic operation which can store a memory address. Also the correctness is guaranteed (possible overflow problem with count method).

However, it is not reasonable to use this method in a central task pool. The insertion of new tasks while the queue is being modified is more likely because all processors can insert tasks into the central task queue. Thus, the removing processors more often have to repeat the removal operation. This is also true for distributed task pools but it is less likely because insertions are only performed by one processor. Only other processors which also try to remove tasks from the respective task queue, may interfere with this operation.

Because this method is not necessary on the Power4 processor, we implemented this second lock-free approach only on the SPARC system. The implementation is named **DQ-LF-SPARC2-PRIV-C (distributed queue, alternative lock-free for SPARC, private buffer, cache optimized).**

**Runtime experiments:** In general, the distributed task pools achieve a better performance than the central task pools (Table 2). On the SPARC system, the task pools using hardware operations can achieve a faster execution time than the Pthreads implementation by a factor up to 2.6 for one thread and a factor up to 1.91 for 20 threads.

The semi-nonblocking task pool performs best for $f < 50$. For bigger tasks, the Pthreads implementation is even slightly faster than most of the task pools which use hardware operations. But the task pool using the simple lock can still outperform the Pthreads implementation (Table 2). The ticket lock implementation, even though slower than the semi-nonblocking pool, is slightly faster than both lock-free task pools. The overhead of the additional work needed to realize a lock-free modification of the task queue is greater than the possible benefit of the removed lock operation.

The difference between the task pool implementations is significantly larger on the Power4 system. Even in the sequential run, the Pthreads implementation is significantly slower than the best new task pool by a factor of 4.47 for $f = 0$. For $f = 50$, the Pthreads task pool is still 39% slower. The task pool using the CLH lock is slightly slower than the SINGLEPUT implementation. The ticket lock is together with the semi-nonblocking task pool the fastest implementation that is based on locks. In contrast to the SPARC system, the lock-free task pool is clearly the fastest on the Power4 system. The LR/SC operations are more suitable for the lock-free modifications because of the non-atomic behavior.

With 32 threads on the Power4 system we observe a similar improvement. The task pool without a private buffer (DQ-SL) is already faster than the Pthread implementation by a factor of $\approx 1.45$ (for $f = 0$ and $f = 50$) but all other optimized task pool implementations are even faster. While most task pools achieve a similar performance, the lock-free implementation is also the best using 32 threads.

Table 2 shows the speedup and the efficiency of all dis-

| Task pool implementation | Best speedup SPARC | No. of threads SPARC | Efficiency SPARC | Best speedup Power4 | No. of threads Power4 | Efficiency Power4 |
|---|---|---|---|---|---|---|
| Pthreads-DQ-BL | 19.26 | 20 | 0.963 | 10.07 | 32 | 0.31 |
| DQ-BL-SL-C | 19.77 | 20 | 0.989 | 26.82 | 32 | 0.84 |
| DQ-BL-TL-C | 19.76 | 20 | 0.988 | 26.70 | 32 | 0.83 |
| DQ-BL-SP-C | **19.81** | 20 | **0.991** | **27.18** | 32 | **0.85** |

**Table 3. Speedup and efficiency of the block-distributed task pools for task size of $f = 50$ on the SPARC and the Power4 system.**

tributed task pools on the SPARC and the Power4 system. The speedups with respect to the sequential reference task pool on the SPARC system are similar reaching values from 15.86 to 18.09 with the best efficiency of 0.9. The more general lock-free implementation that uses double insertion is slower than the lock-free approach that uses a counter. As expected, the difference is only small. On the Power4 system the speedups differ from 1.33 for the Pthreads implementation to 3.25 for the best lock-free implementation which offers a good efficiency of 0.81 for 4 processors but the scalability is still much worse than on the SPARC system.

### 3.4.2. Block-distributed task pools

Task stealing is an expensive step for the task pool especially for a distributed task pool where several task queues must be searched for new tasks. In block-distributed task pools the tasks are stored in groups. The task stealing is organized similarly as before. The processor looks for a non-empty task queue on other processors but the queues do not store single tasks but groups of tasks. Stealing such groups reduces the overhead because several tasks can be transferred with a single task pool operation. Task groups may also improve the data locality because grouped tasks possibly access closely related data since they are likely to be created in a similar context. The disadvantage of this method is a possibly worse load balance. The number of tasks per group should depend on the application because the buffering of many large tasks in a group leads to load imbalance. On the other hand, buffering only a few small tasks will not use the full potential of the grouping strategy.

We choose a group size of four tasks to limit the load imbalance but still to be able to measure the performance gain. For efficient realization we store two groups in a private buffer. Tasks are always inserted into the private buffer. The second group of the private buffer is moved to the public queue when both groups are filled. All other parameters are chosen as for the distributed task pools.

We apply the grouping strategy to the following task pools: The **DQ-BL-SL-C (block-distributed queue, simple lock, cache optimized)** implementation uses cache-aligned data structures and protects concurrent accesses to the public queue by a simple lock. The semi-

nonblocking approach is used in the **DQ-BL-SL-TRY-C (block-distributed queue, simple lock, single try, cache optimized)** implementation. The **DQ-BL-TL-C (block-distributed queue, ticket lock, cache optimized)** task pool uses the ticket lock to realize mutual exclusion between the processors. Our SINGLEPUT approach that exploits the exclusive insertion strategy described above is realized in the task pool **DQ-BL-SP-C (block-distributed queue, simple lock with SINGLEPUT, cache optimized)**. Additionally, we use the semi-nonblocking method to protect the task removal.

**Runtime experiments:** Storing the tasks in groups highly improves the performance while it does not decrease the load balance noticeably for a group size of 4. Using one thread on the SPARC system we measure an execution time which is almost identical to the reference task pool and all task pool implementation have almost the same execution time. Using 20 threads, we observe an almost optimal scalability even for the Pthreads implementation. The optimized task pools are still slightly faster with only minor differences in the execution times.

On the Power4 system there is a similar situation for the sequential run. All task pools achieve almost the same execution time. The optimized task pools are only slightly faster but the overhead of the task pool is still noticeable for small task sizes ($f < 5$). For 32 threads, we observe a significantly better performance of the block-distributed task pools than for the distributed task pools without grouping. The overhead is only measurable for small task sizes ($f < 20$) but still relatively low. The Pthreads implementation is up to a factor of 5.06 slower (for $f = 20$) than the best optimized task pool. The SINGLEPUT implementation without synchronization for task insertion offers the best performance. The worse data locality created by using a FIFO queue order instead of the stack order used by all other task pools can be counterbalanced by the use of groups of tasks. The corresponding distributed task pool without grouping cannot achieve such a good performance because of this data locality problem.

Table 3 shows the speedups and the efficiencies for the block-distributed task pools with the task size $f = 50$. On the SPARC system the SINGLEPUT task pool also achieves the best speedup of 19.81 with an almost ideal efficiency of 0.99 while the speedup of the Pthreads implementation is only 19.26. The efficiency on the Power4 system is smaller. The Pthreads implementation only achieves a speedup of 10.07 while the best optimized task pool, which uses the SINGLEPUT method, achieves a speedup of 27.18 with a good efficiency of 0.85.

## 4. Experiments with a realistic application

In order to investigate the performance of the optimized task pools with a realistic application, we have also performed experiments with the hierarchical radiosity application from the SPLASH-2 suite [19]. We use the builtin scene 'largeroom' to investigate the performance of the task pools.

For the central task pools, the new task pools are significantly faster than the Pthreads task pools. For the SPARC system the ticket lock implementation is the fastest and achieves a speedup of 9.26. The speedup of the corresponding Pthreads task pool is 7.09. For the Power4 machine, the Pthreads task pool reaches a speedup of 9.14 whereas the task pool using the ticket lock already achieves a maximum speedup of 11.25. The lock-free task pool performs best achieving a speedup of 15.84.

For the distributed task pools, a different situation occurs on the SPARC system. None of the new task pools can achieve the same performance as the Pthreads implementation, and only few task pools (e.g., the ticket lock implementation) can reach approximately the maximum speedup of the Pthreads task pool (10.24 vs. 10.5). In contrast, on the Power4 machine all optimized task pools are faster than the Pthreads task pool, which achieves a maximum speedup of 12.08. While some implementations like the ticket lock task pool and the cache-optimized simple lock task pool are only slightly better, other task pools can achieve higher speedups. The distributed task pool with the SINGLEPUT extension and the task pool using the one-try lock even reach a speedup of 18.13 and 18.97. The speedup of the best implementation DQ-SL, which represents the non cache optimized variant, is 19.98.

For the block-distributed task pools we observe a similar situation on the Power4 system. The Pthreads task pool achieves a maximum speedup of 12.4. The task pool implementing the SINGLEPUT extension and the task pool using the simple lock are only slightly better. The semi-nonblocking task pool outperforms the other implementations and reaches a speedup of 19.61.

Figure 2 presents a summary of the best performing task pools for the radiosity application. The distributed Pthreads task pools are faster than the central task pools for both systems. The maximum speedup of the best Pthreads task pool on the Power4 system is 12.4 whereas the best new implementation achieves a speedup of 19.98. As for the synthetic application, we also measured a good performance of the lock-free central task pool for the radiosity application. On the Power4 system, one optimized

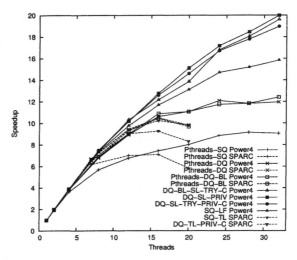

**Figure 2. Speedup of the best task pools for the radiosity application.**

central task pool implementation outperforms even the distributed Pthreads task pools with a speedup of 15.84.

## 5. Related work

Various approaches have been proposed towards the efficient parallel execution of irregular computations, including Dynamic Task Graphs [9], Symbolic Linear Clustering [4], hierarchical run queue organizations [5], automatic loop scheduling [3], and task pools distributed among the address spaces using special communication threads [7]. [16] considers computations on irregular adaptive grids, and [17] investigates different load balancing strategies for the computation of macroscopic thermal dispersion. There exist several programming environments dedicated to provide dynamic load balancing in irregular applications, e.g., Charm++ [10], DOTS [2] and Cilk [15].

Synchronization mechanisms for shared-memory systems have been studied extensively in the past. An overview of several lock-based algorithms for mutual exclusion can be found in [1, 13]. Non-blocking (also called lock-free) data structures have been proposed in, e.g., [6, 14]. [12] introduces obstruction-freedom as a new, weaker property that allows greater flexibility in the design of efficient implementations.

## 6. Conclusions and future work

We have presented several implementations of task pools, which offer a reduced synchronization overhead. The synchronization overhead of a task pool can be a major source of performance degradation if the number of tasks executed is large and the granularity of the tasks is small. The reduction of the synchronization overhead was possible using the hardware operations *Compare & Swap* and *Load & Reserve/Store Conditional*. Since modern microprocessors usually support at least one of these two synchronization mechanisms, our implementations can be adapted to most modern parallel computers. Especially for very small tasks, the reduced overhead of the new task pools leads to improved performance on multi-processor machines compared with task pools based on Pthreads synchronization operations.

As the runtime experiments show, the performance of the task-based execution of irregular applications is influenced by the task pool implementation as well as the underlying hardware architecture. The application of hardware operations greatly reduces the overhead of the task pools. Among the central task pools, which have the disadvantage of a high overhead, the new implementation are 3.6 (SPARC) and 1.8 (Power4) times faster than the Pthreads task pools for a selected task size. The new block-distributed task pools are 1.03 (SPARC) and 2.7 (Power4) times faster. For the radiosity application we observed a slight slowdown of 2.5% on the SPARC system, which points to a general scalability problem. On the Power4 system, the reduced overhead results in 61% higher speedup and an improved scalability.

The results also show that it is not possible to select one task pool implementation which is best for all situations. The ticket lock performs usually very well on both machines. In contrast to the SPARC system, the lock-free implementations can be even faster than lock-based implementations on the Power4 system. The experiments with the synthetic application showed that cache-optimized block-distributed task pools can obtain a high performance for different task granularities on the Sun Fire as well as the IBM system.

Our experiments show that the use of hardware operations in task pools has a high potential. Future research will investigate the use of the new task pools in different realistic irregular applications and the possible performance gain.

# References

[1] J. H. Anderson, Y.-J. Kim, and T. Herman. Shared-memory mutual exclusion: Major research trends since 1986. *Distributed Computing*, 16:75–100, 2003. Special issue celebrating the 20th anniversary of PODC.

[2] W. Blochinger, W. Küchlin, and A. Weber. The distributed object-oriented threads system DOTS. In A. Ferreira, J. Rolim, H. Simon, and S.-H. Teng, editors, *Fifth Intl. Symp. on Solving Irregularly Structured Problems in Parallel (IRREGULAR '98)*, number 1457 in LNCS, pages 206–217, Berkeley, CA, U.S.A., Aug. 1998. Springer.

[3] R. L. Cariño and I. Banicescu. A load balancing tool for distributed parallel loops. In *Proceedings of the International Workshop on Challenges of Large Application in Distributed Environments (CLADE) 2003*, pages 39–46. IEEE Computer Society Press, June 2003.

[4] M. Cosnard, E. Jeannot, and T. Yang. SLC: Symbolic scheduling for executing parameterized task graphs on multiprocesors. In *International Conference on Parallel Processing*, 1999.

[5] S. P. Dandamudi and S. Ayachi. Performance of hierarchical processor scheduling in shared-memory multiprocessor systems. *IEEE Transactions on Computers*, 48(11):1202–1213, 1999.

[6] M. Herlihy, V. Luchangco, and M. Moir. Space- and time-adaptive nonblocking data structures. In *CATS*, 2003.

[7] J. Hippold and G. Rünger. Task pool teams for implementing irregular algorithms on clusters of SMPs. In *Proc. of IPDPS*, Nice, France, 2003. CD-ROM.

[8] E. H. Jensen, G. W. Hagensen, and J. M. Broughton. A new approach to exclusive data access in shared memory multiprocessors. Technical Report UCRL-97663, Lawrence Livermore National Laboratory, Livermore, CA, Nov. 1987.

[9] T. Johnson, T. A. Davis, and S. M. Hadfield. A concurrent dynamic task graph. *Parallel Computing*, 22(2):327–333, 1996.

[10] L. V. Kale and S. Krishnan. CHARM++. In G. V. Wilson and P. Lu, editors, *Parallel Programming in C++*, chapter 5, pages 175–214. MIT Press, Cambridge, MA, 1996.

[11] M. Korch and T. Rauber. A comparison of task pools for dynamic load balancing of irregular algorithms. *Concurrency and Computation: Practice and Experience*, 16:1–47, Jan. 2004.

[12] V. Luchangco, M. Moir, and N. Shavit. Obstruction-free synchronization: Double-ended queues as an example. In *Proceedings of the 23rd International Conference on Distributed Computing Systems (ICDCS)*, 2003.

[13] J. M. Mellor-Crummey and M. L. Scott. Algorithms for scalable synchronization on shared-memory multiprocessors. *ACM Transactions on Computer Systems*, 9(1):21–65, 1991. Additional information at http://www.cs.rochester.edu/u/scott/synchronization/pseudocode/ss.html.

[14] M. M. Michael and M. L. Scott. Nonblocking algorithms and preemption-safe locking on multiprogrammed shared-memory multiprocessors. *Journal of Parallel and Distributed Computing*, 51(1):1–26, 1998.

[15] K. H. Randall. *Cilk: Efficient Multithreaded Computing*. PhD thesis, MIT Department of Electrical Engineering and Computer Science, June 1998.

[16] K. Schloegel, G. Karypis, and V. Kumar. A unified algorithm for load-balancing adaptive scientific simulations. In *Proc. Supercomputing 2000*, 2000.

[17] V. Thomé, D. Vianna, R. Costa, A. Plastino, and O. da Silveira Filho. Exploring load balancing in a scientific SPMD application. In *Proceedings of the 2002 ICPP Workshops*, pages 419–426, Aug. 2002.

[18] D. L. Weaver and T. Germond, editors. *The SPARC Architecture Manual Version 9*. PTR Prentice Hall, Englewood Cliffs, New Jersey, 2000.

[19] S. C. Woo, M. Ohara, E. Torrie, J. P. Singh, and A. Gupta. The SPLASH-2 programs: Characterization and methodological considerations. In *Proceedings of the 22nd International Symposium on Computer Architecture*, pages 24–36, Santa Margherita Ligure, Italy, 1995.

# Adaptive Data Partition for Sorting using Probability Distribution

Xipeng Shen and Chen Ding
Computer Science Department, University of Rochester
{xshen,cding}@cs.rochester.edu

## Abstract

*Many computing problems benefit from dynamic partition of data into smaller chunks with better parallelism and locality. However, it is difficult to partition all types of inputs with the same high efficiency. This paper presents a new partition method in sorting scenario based on probability distribution, an idea first studied by Janus and Lamagna in early 1980's on a mainframe computer. The new technique makes three improvements. The first is a rigorous sampling technique that ensures accurate estimate of the probability distribution. The second is an efficient implementation on modern, cache-based machines. The last is the use of probability distribution in parallel sorting. Experiments show 10-30% improvement in partition balance and 20-70% reduction in partition overhead, compared to two commonly used techniques. The new method reduces the parallel sorting time by 33-50% and outperforms the previous fastest sequential sorting technique by up to 30%.*

## 1 Introduction

Many types of dynamic data have a total ordering and benefit from partial sorting into sublists. Examples include N-body simulation in physics and biology studies, where particles are partitioned based on their coordinates, and discrete-event simulation in computer networking and economics, where events are ordered by their arrival time. Partial sorting or partition allows these large scale problems to be solved by massively parallel computers. Data partition is also important on machines with a memory hierarchy because it dramatically improves cache performance for in-core data and memory performance for out-of-core data. Therefore, the efficient and balanced data partition is critical to good parallelism and locality.

Most previous methods either have a high overhead or only apply to uniformly distributed data (as discussed in Section 2.) For example, Blelloch et al. showed that one of the fastest pivot-based methods, *over-sampling*, consumed 33-55% of the total sorting time [2]. It remained an open question whether we could find balanced partitions for non-uniform data in linear time.

In early 80s, Janus and Lamagna published a method that first samples the data and estimates its cumulative distribution function (CDF); it then assigns data into equal-size (not necessarily equal-length) buckets through direct calculation [10]. This simple idea achieves balanced data partition in linear time, even for non-uniform distributions. We call the partition method *PD-partition* and its use in sorting *PD-sort* in short. Janus and Lamagna implemented their algorithm using the PL/1 language and measured the performance on an IBM 370 machine. Since then, however, this method seems forgotten and is rarely mentioned by later studies of sorting performance on modern cache-based machines.

In search for a better sorting method for unbalanced data sets, we independently discovered the idea of using probability distribution. Compared to the method of Janus and Lamagna, this work makes three improvements. The first is a rigorous sampling method that ensures accurate estimate of the probability distribution. Janus and Lamagna did not address the sampling problem for non-standard distributions. They used a fixed number of samples (465) in their experiments [10]. Using the sampling theory, our method guarantees the statistical accuracy for a large class of non-uniform distributions [21], with the number of samples independent of the size of data and number of categories.

The second contribution is an efficient implementation of probability calculations on modern machines. It uses temporary storage to avoid repeated calculations. It uses scalar expansion to improve instruction-level parallelism and hide memory latency. The latter two problems did not exist on machines used by Janus and Lamagna. Our implementation is 19-28% faster than the base implementation of *PD-partition*.

Finally, we measure the effect of *PD-partition* in sequential and parallel sorting and compare it with the fastest sorting methods in the recent literature. Our *PD-partition* outperforms other partition methods in both efficiency and balance. Our sorting implementation outperforms quick-sort by over 10% and outperforms other cache-optimized algorithms by up to 30% [11, 22].

Furthermore, we designed a parallel sorting algorithm using *PD-partition*. It achieves 33-50% time saving compared to parallel sorting using *over-sampling* and *over-partitioning*, two techniques popular on modern systems (see Section 2).

In the rest of this paper, we review related work in Section 2 and describe PD-partition in Section 3, the statistical sampling in Section 4, and an optimized implementation in Section 5. We present an evaluation in Section 6, and conclude with a summary of our findings.

## 2 Related work

Data partition is a basic step in program parallelization on machines with distributed memory. Many applications use irregular data, for example, particles moving inside a space or a mesh representing a surface. Parallelization is often done by an approach called inspector-executor, originally studied by Saltz and his colleagues [5]. For example, in N-body simulation, the inspector examines the coordinates of particles and partitions them into different machines. Much later work used this model, including the language-based support by Hanxleden et. al. [8], the compiler support by Han and Tseng [7], the use on DSM [15], and many others that are not enumerated here. When data can be sorted, the partition problem in N-body simulation can be viewed as a sorting problem. Instead of finding balanced sublists, we need to find subspaces with a similar number of data. Mellor-Crummey et al. [16] and Mitchell et al. [17] used bucket sort to significantly improve the cache locality of N-body simulation programs. Bucket sort produces balanced partitions for uniformly distributed data, but may produce severely unbalanced partitions for highly skewed distributions.

Parallel sorting [1, 2, 3, 4, 6, 9, 13, 20] is an important application of data partition. Recent work includes NOWSort by Arpaci-Dusseau et al. [1], $(l; m)$-merge sort by Rajasekaran [18], an implementation of column-sort by Chaudhry et al. [4], and parallel sorting on heterogeneous networks by Cerin [3]. Most of these methods use pivots to partition data. Three main ways to pick pivots are as follows. The term $p$ represents the number of processors.

- *Regular-sampling (RS)* [20, 14]. Each processor sorts the initial local data. It picks $p$ equally spaced candidates. All $p^2$ candidates are then sorted to pick $(p-1)$ equally spaced pivots.

- *Over-sampling (OS)* [2, 9]. The $p * r$ random candidates are picked from the initial data, where $r$ is called the *over-sampling ratio*. The candidates are sorted to pick $(p-1)$ equally spaced ones as the pivots.

- *Over-partitioning (OP)* [13]. The $p * r * t$ candidates are picked randomly from the whole data set, where $t$ is called *over-partitioning ratio*, and $r$ is the same as in *Over-sampling*. The candidates are sorted, and $(pt-1)$ pivots are selected by taking $r^{th}, 2r^{th}, \cdots, (pt-1)r^{th}$ candidates. The whole data set is partitioned into $p * t$ sublists, which form a task queue for parallel processors.

Pivot-based methods have a significant time overhead. They sort candidates and use a binary search to find a suitable bucket for each data. To balance the partitions, they need a large number of candidates. As we will discuss later, *PD-partition* is more efficient for parallel sorting because it does not sort samples and calculates the bucket assignment with only a constant number of operations.

Instead of using pivots, Arpaci-Dusseau et al. partition data into even length buckets [1]. Xiao et al. used a similar algorithm—*inplaced flash quicksort* [22], which utilizes an additional array to reuse elements in a cache line. Both methods partition data in linear time, but both assume that the input data have a uniform distribution. For other distributions, the partitions may be severely unbalanced.

Our method provides a way to partition data efficiently and yields good balance even for non-uniform distributions. It extends the work by Janus and Lamagna [10] in three ways. *PD-partition* depends on the accurate estimation of the cumulative distribution function. Janus and Lamagna did not show how to ensure accurate estimation for non-standard input distribution. Our work solves this problem using the sampling theory [21]. Janus and Lamagna designed their algorithm for minimizing the total number of instructions in sequential sorting. We adapt the algorithm to maximize the parallelism and locality in dynamic data partition. We also give an optimized implementation that significantly reduces the partition overhead on modern machines. In addition, we evaluate dynamic data partition in the context of parallel sorting against popular parallel sorting methods. We also demonstrate fast sequential sorting of non-uniform inputs (faster than quick-sort and other cache-optimized sorting algorithms) on modern machines with a deep memory hierarchy.

## 3 Probability distribution-based partition algorithm

Probability Distribution-based partition (*PD-partition*), similar to the extended *distributive partitioned sorting* by Janus and Lamagna [10], has two steps: the selection of buckets (by estimating the *Cumulative Distribution Function or CDF*) and the assignment of data into buckets. The complexity of the two steps is linear to the size of the input.

## 3.1 CDF estimation

The estimation of $CDF$ includes three steps [10]:

1) Traverse data to find the range of data. Divide the range into $c$ equal-length *cells*. Select $s$ random samples from the data. Distribute the samples into the cells. Let $s_i$ be the number of samples in cell $i$. To make $s_i > 0$ (well-behaved), always add 1 to $s_i$. Let $sc = s + c$. Figure 1(b) shows the first step. The height of each bar is the number of samples contained in each cell.

2) Take $\frac{s_i}{sc}$ as the probability of a randomly picked data value belonging to cell $i$. The cumulative probability $p_1, \cdots, p_c$ is therefore a cumulation of $\frac{s_i}{sc}$ for $i = 1, 2, \cdots, c$. Figure 1(c) shows the cumulation step.

3) To get $CDF$, the third step fits a line between each adjacent pair of cumulative probabilities. It saves the $y$-intersect of each line to get an estimate of the $CDF$ of the total data. Figure 1(d) shows the final step.

The time cost of $CDF$ estimation is linear to the number of samples. This estimation requires *well-behaved* distributions, i.e. the CDF is continuous and monotonic increasing.

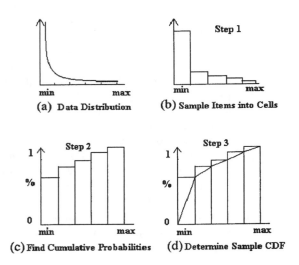

**Figure 1. Estimation of CDF**

## 3.2 Assignment of data into buckets

The second step assigns data into buckets. For each data element $x$, the algorithm finds the bucket assignment in three calculations. First it finds the cell number of $x$. Recall that during CDF estimation, the range between the maximum and minimum of the total data is divided into $c$ equal-length cells. The cell number of $x$ is therefore the floor of $(x - min)/lc$, where $lc$ is the cell length. The second step finds $p_x$, the cumulative probability or CDF of $x$. It equals to the cumulative probability of its preceding cell plus the cumulative probability of elements smaller than $x$ in this cell. The latter term is calculated based on the slope of the cell. The calculation assumes a uniform distribution within each cell.

Using the cumulative probability $p_x$, we can get the bucket number of $x$ in one calculation. Let $b$ be the number of buckets. Since we want balanced partitions, the buckets should have an equal size. In other words, each bucket has the equal probability, $1/b$, for $x$ to fall into. Thus, the bucket number of $x$ is $\lfloor p_x/\frac{1}{b} \rfloor$ or $\lfloor p_x * b \rfloor$. All three steps take a constant amount of time. Therefore, the time complexity of the bucket assignment is $O(n)$, where $n$ is the size of the input data. Figure 2 shows the algorithm for assigning data into buckets.

## 4 Statistical measurement of CDF estimation

The accuracy of CDF estimation strongly effects the partition balance of *PD-partition*. An inaccurate CDF estimation may result in severely unbalanced partition. In the worst case, most data fall into a single partition and the performance degrades to that of quick-sort plus the partition overhead. The accuracy of CDF estimation is determined by the number of samples used for the CDF estimation. Janus and Lamagna used 465 samples in their sequential sorting algorithm without formal statistic analysis. In our experiments, we found it too few to generate accurate estimations. Based on sampling theory [21], we provide a way to determine the sample size with high accuracy guarantee.

We model the problem as a multinomial proportion estimation [21]— a problem to find the smallest number, $s$, of random samples from a multinomial population (i.e. a population including multiple categories) such that with at least $1 - \alpha$ probability the estimated distribution is within a specified distance of the true population, that is,

$$Pr\{ \bigcap_{i=1}^{k} | p_i - \pi_i | \le d_i \} \ge 1 - \alpha \qquad (1)$$

where $k$ is the number of categories in the population, $p_i$ and $\pi_i$ are the observed and the actual size of category $i$, $d_i$ and $\alpha$ are the error bounds given. Thompson proposes the following formula for $s$ [21]:

$$s = \max_{m} z^2(1/m)(1 - 1/m)/d^2 \qquad (2)$$

where $m$ is an integer from 0 to $k$, $z$ is the size of the upper $(\alpha/2m) * 100$th portion of the standard normal distribution, and $d$ is the distance from the true distribution.

The $m$ that gives the maximum in Formula (2) depends on $\alpha$. Thompson shows, in the worst case, $m = 2$ for $0 \leq \alpha < .0344$; $m = 3$ for $.0344 \leq \alpha < .3466$; $m = 4$ for $.3466 \leq \alpha < .6311$; $m = 5$ for $.6311 \leq \alpha < .8934$; and $m = 6$ for $.8934 \leq \alpha < 1$ [21]. Note that for a given $d$ and $\alpha$, $s$ is independent to the size of data and the number of categories $k$.

In the CDF estimation, each cell is a category. The CDF value in a cell is the size of this and all other cells of smaller values. Formula (2) gives the minimal size of samples for a given confidence $(1 - \alpha)$ and distance $d$. Suppose we want the probability to be at least 95% that CDF values are within 0.01 distance of the true distribution, Formula (2) gives the minimal sampling size 12736. In our experiments, we use 40000 samples, which guarantees with 95% confidence that the CDF is within 0.0056 distance (i.e. 99.4% accurate).

## 5   Optimizations in implementation

It is important to make the bucket assignment as fast as possible. In our implementation, we make two optimizations. In the loop of Figure 2, there are four floating-point computations. Let $bucketNum[i]$ be the bucket number covered by the range from the minimal data to the end of cell $i$. Let $bucketNum1[i]$ be the number of buckets covered by cell $i$, which is equal to $bucketNum[i] - bucketNum[i-1]$. We store these two numbers for each cell instead of recomputing them. Using the stored numbers, the assignment of each datum can be simplified to two instead of four floating-point computations. The second optimization is scalar expansion inside the assignment loop to increase the parallelism and hide the calculation latency. For lack of space, we leave the detail algorithm in a technical report [19]. The evaluation section 6.2 will show that the optimizations accelerate the PD-sort by 19-28%.

**Notations:** in the following discussion, $n$ is the total number of data, $s$ the total number of samples, $c$ the number of cells, and $b$ the number of buckets. In parallel sorting, $b$ is the number of processors.

## 6   Evaluations

We first measure the efficiency and balance of *PD-partition* and compare them with those of other partition methods. We then use them as sorting methods by applying quick-sort within each bucket. We compare their speed in sequential and parallel sorting.

Our experiments were conducted on Linux machines with 2.0GHz Pentium 4 processors and 512MB main memory. The size of the second level cache was 512KB. All methods were compiled by $gcc\ -O3$. They sorted randomly generated integers of different distributions. For

```
/* data: the array of data, size is N;
    min,max: the minimum and maximum of data;
    C: number of cells in range [min, max];
    lc: the length of each cell;
    cdf[i]: the cdf of ith cell;
    cdf[0] = 0 and cdf[c] = 0.9999999;
    slope[i]: the slope of the fitting line in cell i;
    B: the number of buckets */
......
    lcR = 1/lc;
    for (int i=0;i<N;i++){
        /* find the cell number of data[i] */
        int n = (int)((data[i] - min)*lcR);
        /* find the cdf of data[i] */
        float l = data[i]-min-n*lc;
        float xcdf = cdf[n]+slop[n]*l;
        /* bucket number of data[i] */
        int bucketNum = (int)(xcdf*B);
        /* put data[i] into a new array corresponding to its bucket-
Num */
        ......}
```

**Figure 2. Assigning data to buckets**

*PD-partition* and sorting, unless otherwise noted, the cell number was 1000, sample size was 40000, bucket number was 128, and the input included 64 million integers. For each type of the distribution, the result is the average of 20 randomly generated data sets. The uniformly distributed data were generated by function $random()$ in the standard C library; the normally distributed data were generated by *problib*, a statistics library [12]. Our technical report includes the results of additional types of distributions [19].

### 6.1   Data partition

We show the partition results from *PD-partition*, *over-sampling* [2, 9] and *over-partitioning* [13]. *Regular sampling* [20, 14] has more overhead and is not included in the evaluation. In *over-sampling*, the over-sampling rate is 32 (as in [2]). In *over-partitioning*, the over-sampling rate is 3 and the over-partitioning rate is $log\ b$ (as in [13]), where $b$ is the number of buckets. Section 2 describes the three algorithms in more detail.

We measure their speed by the partition time, and measure the partition balance using a concept called *bucket expansion* (BE), which is the ratio of the largest size to the average size of all buckets. It measures the worst-case (im)balance. The ratio is equal to or greater than 1. A ratio of 1 means perfect balance because all buckets have the same size.

We use the relative balance and speed in the evaluation to compare all three methods in a single figure in Figure 3. The following factors affect the partition balance and cost.

**Effects of data distribution** We use uniform and three normal distributions to study the effects of data distribution, shown in Figure 3(a). Our method takes less than 80% and 60% time of *over-sampling* and *over-partitioning* and achieves better balance. The uniform distribution has the greatest gain because a uniform distribution is estimated better by samples than heavily skewed distributions are. A problem shown is that the bucket ratio of our method becomes worse when the distribution becomes less uniform. The problem can be significantly alleviated by using more samples as explained in Section 4.

**Effects of data size and bucket number** Figure 3(b,c) show the effect of the data size and bucket number on the uniform distribution. Our method reduces partition overhead from $O(N \log b)$ to $O(N)$. Thus, the time ratio is $\frac{O(N)}{O(N \log b)}$, which is independent of $N$ but proportional to $\frac{1}{\log b}$, consistent with Figure 3(b,c). Figure 3(c) also shows that PD-partition is more scalable and produces larger number of buckets faster with better balance than *over-sampling* and *over-partitioning*.

**Effects of the number of samples and cells** More cells allow the $CDF$ fitting at a finer granularity (see Figure 1.) More samples yields better estimation for each cell. The number of samples depend on the number of cells because more cells require more samples, as shown in Formula 2. In Figure 3(d), we use 1000 cells but vary the number of samples from 5000 to 80000. We show results on uniform distribution and other distributions have similar results. The figure shows that PD-based partition obtains greater improvement in balance from using more samples than the other two methods do. The time of PD-based sorting increases slightly faster than the other two methods as the number of samples increases. But the overhead is small even for a larger number of samples. The time ratios are still less than 0.6 and 0.4.

Figure 3(e) shows the changes of the number of cells. For a normal distribution (mean=3000,deviation=300.), the partition balance is improved when the number of cells is increased from 100 to 1600. It is worsened when the number of cells is increased from 1600 to 12800, because the samples in a cell become too few to estimate the probability. Figure 3(f) shows the effects using the uniform distribution. The balance ratio decreases monotonically as the number of samples increases, because a small number of samples is enough for estimating CDF in this case.

## 6.2 Comparison with sequential quick-sort

Quick-sort is believed by many to be the fastest internal (in-memory) sorting method. A recent study by Xiao et al. shows that for uniformly distributed input data, simple partition is faster. But for non-uniform data distributions,

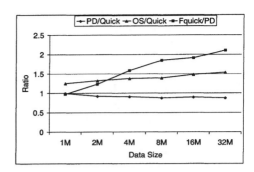

**Figure 4. Comparison of the sequential sorting time on normal distribution (mean=3000, std=1000). PD: PD-sort; Quick: quick-sort; OS:** *over-sampling.* **Fquick: inplaced flash quick-sort.**

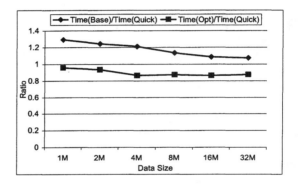

**Figure 5. The effect of algorithm and implementation improvement to** *PD-partition. Base* **is our basic data assignment algorithm.** *Opt.* **is the optimized version.** *Quick* **is quicksort. The input data are in normal distribution (mean=3000, std=1000).**

**Table 1. Time for Sequential Sorting (sec.)**

| Data Size | PD-sort | Quick-sort | Over-sampling sort |
|-----------|---------|------------|--------------------|
| 2M | 0.334 | 0.365 | 0.480 |
| 4M | 0.647 | 0.719 | 0.985 |
| 8M | 1.298 | 1.491 | 2.064 |
| 16M | 2.624 | 2.951 | 4.341 |
| 32M | 5.227 | 6.008 | 9.197 |

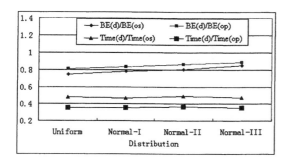

(a) Comparison on the uniform distribution, and three normal distributions (m=3000, d=3000,1000,300)

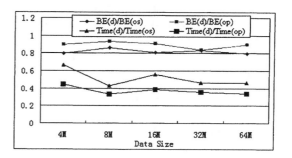

(b) Effect of data size on the uniform distribution

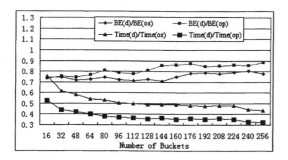

(c) Effect of the number of buckets on the uniform distribution

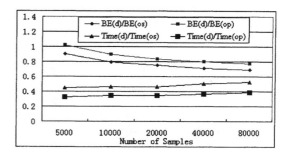

(d) Effect of the number of samples on the uniform distribution

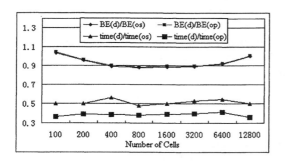

(e) Effect of the number of cells on the normal distribution (m=3000, d=300)

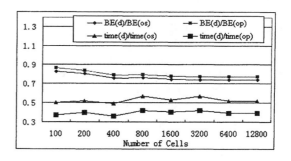

(f) Effect of the number of cells on the uniform distribution

**Figure 3. Evaluating the major factors in data partition. BE: Bucket Expansion; d:** *PD-partition*; **os:** *over-sampling*; **op:** *over-partitioning*. **The balance and speed ratios are lower than 1, showing that** *PD-partition* **is more balanced and efficient than the** *over-sampling* **and** *over-partitioning*.

quick-sort still gives the best performance because simple methods could not give balanced partitions [22]. We now show that PD-sort outperforms quick-sort for uniform and non-uniform distributions.

We use PD-partition to cut data into blocks smaller than the cache size and then sort each block. Since the block partition takes linear time, it has better cache locality than the recursive partition schemes like quicksort, when data size is much greater than the cache size.

We target buckets of the size 256KB in the partition methods. It is less than the real cache size (512K) to leave room for other data and to reduce cache interference. Figure 4 compares the speed on normal distribution with mean of 3000 and variance of 1000. Other distributions have similar results [19]. Table 1 shows the sorting time. We also show *over-sampling* for comparison. For sequential sorting, *over-partitioning* is similar to *over-sampling* except using more buckets.

When sorting more than four million data, PD-sort outperforms quicksort by more than 10%. In comparison, *over-sampling* is slower than quick-sort because of the high partition overhead. The speed gap widens on larger data inputs.

The algorithm and implementation improvement described in Section 5 are critical: without them the PD-sort is no faster than quicksort. Figure 5 shows 19-28% time reduction in the overall sorting time. The optimization is designed to speed up the probability calculation and therefore not applicable to quicksort.

We also compared our method with *Inplaced flash quick-sort*, proposed by Xiao et. al [22]. It partitions data assuming a uniform distribution and then sorts each bucket using quick-sort. It takes an additional array to reuse elements in a cache line. It was shown to be faster than many other sequential sorting methods [22]. Our method is slightly faster than the inplaced flash quick-sort for data sizes smaller than 4 million and about 30% faster when sorting larger data sets.

### 6.3 Parallel sorting

We compare the parallel performance of PD-sort with sorting methods using *over-sampling* and *over-partitioning*. In the absence of a large scale parallel computer, we analyze the communication costs and implement a simulator to measure the computation costs. All three algorithms perform data partition on a single processor and then sort each sub-list on a parallel processor. The communication cost has two parts: the cost to obtain pivots or CDF, and the cost to move data to their assigned processors. The second part is similar in all methods. The first part is negligible as shown in [19]. Assuming the same communication cost, we use the computation costs to measure the performance of parallel sorting.

Figure 6 compares the sorting speed on a normal dis-

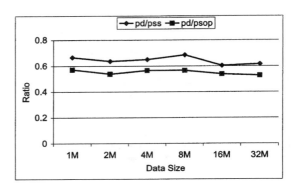

**Figure 6. Computation cost ratios of** *over-sampling* **(PSS) and** *over-partitioning* **(PSOP) to PD-sort on normal distribution (mean=3000, std=1000). PD-sort is represented by pd.**

tribution (mean=3000, std=1000.) The other distributions show similar results [19]. In the experiment, we assume that the data are perfectly partitioned by all three algorithms, so the computation time is the sorting time of D/P integers. Section 6.1 shows better partition balance by PD-sort than by *over-sampling* and *over-partitioning*. Since the actual computation time is determined by the size of the largest bucket, the perfect balance assumption grants higher benefits to *over-sampling*. For *over-partitioning*, the use of the task queue may lead to better load balance, but it also may increase the run-time overhead. Assuming the perfect data partition, Figure 6 shows over 33%-50% speed improvement by PD-sort for large data sets (> 4M) because of faster partitioning.

## 7 Conclusions

We have presented a new partition method, PD-partition, for sequential and parallel sorting. Through extensive comparisons with previous methods, we found that

- *PD-partition* consistently improves the partition efficiency for all types of distributions tested, while maintaining better partition balance than other methods do.

- The performance improvement is independent of the data size.

- Unlike pivot-based methods, the overhead of this approach does not increase with the number of buckets. In fact, the improvement is greater for more buckets, showing that it is suitable for use in large scale parallel sorting.

- Using more samples improves the partition balance

with a slight increase in the overhead. The effect from the number of cells depends on the number of samples.

Overall, *PD-partition* shows 10-30% improvement in the partition balance and 20-70% reduction in the partition speed. Our cache-optimized PD-sort method is over 10% faster than quick-sort, commonly believed to be the fastest sequential sorting method for unbalanced data inputs. It slightly outperforms other cache-optimized algorithms [11, 22] for data size smaller than 4 million and about 30% for large data sets. The corresponding parallel sorting method is 33% to 50% faster than two popular approaches in the recent literature.

Adaptive data partition has important uses in many application domains such as scientific simulation, sparse matrix solvers, computer network simulation, and distributed database and Web servers. We expect that *PD-partition* will significantly improve the partition balance and speed in problems with unbalanced data inputs.

# References

[1] A. C. Arpaci-Dusseau, R. H. Arpaci-Dusseau, D. E. Culler, J. M. Hellerstein, and D. A. Patterson. High-performance sorting on networks of workstations. In *Proceedings of ACM SIGMOD'97*, pages 243–254, 1997.

[2] G. E. Blelloch, C. E. Leiserson, B. M. Maggs, C. G. Plaxton, S. J. Smith, and M. Zagha. An experimental analysis of parallel sorting algorithms. *Theory of Computing Systems*, 31(2):135–167, 1998.

[3] C. Cerin. An out-of-core sorting algorithm for clusters with processors at different speed. In *16th International Parallel and Distributed Processing Symposium (IPDPS)*, Ft Lauderdale, Florida, USA, 2002.

[4] G. Chaudhry, T. H. Cormen, and L. F. Wisniewski. Column-sort lives! an efficient out-of-core sorting program. In *Proceedings of the Thirteenth Annual Symposium on Parallel Algorithms and Architectures*, pages 169–178, July 2001.

[5] R. Das, M. Uysal, J. Saltz, and Y.-S. Hwang. Communication optimizations for irregular scientific computations on distributed memory architectures. *Journal of Parallel and Distributed Computing*, 22(3):462–479, Sept. 1994.

[6] D. J. DeWitt, J. F. Naughton, and D. A. Schneider. Parallel sorting on a shared-nothing architecture using probabilistic splitting. In *Proceedings of the First International Conference on Parallel and Distributed Information Systems*, pages 280–291, 1991.

[7] H. Han and C.-W. Tseng. Improving compiler and runtime support for adaptive irregular codes. In *Proceedings of the International Conference on Parallel Architectures and Compilation Techniques*, Oct. 1998.

[8] R. v. Hanxleden, K. Kennedy, C. Koelbel, R. Das, and J. Saltz. Compiler analysis for irregular problems in Fortran D. In *Proceedings of the Fifth Workshop on Languages and Compilers for Parallel Computing*, New Haven, CT, Aug. 1992.

[9] J. S. Huang and Y. C. Chow. Parallel sorting and data partitioning by sampling. In *Proceedings of the IEEE Computer Society's 7th International Computer Software and Applications Conference*, pages 627–631, 1983.

[10] P. J. Janus and E. A. Lamagna. An adaptive method for unknown distributions in distributive partitioned sorting. *IEEE Transactions on Computers*, c-34(4):367–372, April 1985.

[11] A. LaMarca and R. Ladner. The influence of caches on the performance of sorting. In *Proceedings of 8th Ann. ACM-SIAM Symp. on Discrete Algorithms (SODA97)*, pages 370–379, 1997.

[12] A. Larrosa. http://developer.kde.org/ larrosa/otherapps.html.

[13] H. Li and K. C. Sevcik. Parallel sorting by overpartitioning. In *Proceedings of the 6th Annual Symposium on Parallel Algorithms and Architectures*, pages 46–56, New York, NY, USA, June 1994.

[14] X. Li, P. Lu, J. Schaeffer, J. Shillington, P. S. Wong, and H. Shi. On the versatility of parallel sorting by regular sampling. *Parallel Computing*, 19(10):543–550, October 1993.

[15] H. Lu, A. L. Cox, S. Dwarkadas, R. Rajamony, and W. Zwaenepoel. Compiler and software distributed shared memory support for irregular applications. In *Proceedings of 1997 ACM SIGPLAN Symposium on Principles and Practice of Parallel Programming*, 1997.

[16] J. Mellor-Crummey, D. Whalley, and K. Kennedy. Improving memory hierarchy performance for irregular applications. *International Journal of Parallel Programming*, 29(3), June 2001.

[17] N. Mitchell, L. Carter, and J. Ferrante. Localizing non-affine array references. In *Proceedings of International Conference on Parallel Architectures and Compilation Techniques*, Newport Beach, California, October 1999.

[18] S. Rajasekaran. A framework for simple sorting algorithms on parallel disk systems. In *Proceedings of the Tenth Annual Symposium on Parallel Algorithms and Architectures*, 1998.

[19] X. P. Shen, Y. Z. Zhong, and C. Ding. Adaptive data partitioning using probability distribution. Technical report 823, Computer Science, University of Rochester, Rochester, NY, 2003.

[20] H. Shi and J. Schaeffer. Parallel sorting by regular sampling. *Journal of Parallel and Distributed Computing*, 14(4):361–372, 1992.

[21] S. K. Thompson. Sample size for estimating multinomial proportions. *The American Statistician*, 1987.

[22] L. Xiao, X. Zhang, and S. A. Kubricht. Improving memory performance of sorting algorithms. *ACM Journal on Experimental Algorithmics*, 5:1–23, 2000.

# Session 4C:
# Cluster I

# Packet Size Optimization for Supporting Coarse-Grained Pipelined Parallelism

Wei Du
Department of Computer Science and
Engineering
Ohio State University, Columbus OH 43210
duw@cis.ohio-state.edu

Gagan Agrawal
Department of Computer Science and
Engineering
Ohio State University, Columbus OH 43210
agrawal@cis.ohio-state.edu

## ABSTRACT

The emergence of grid and a new class of *data-driven* applications is making a new form of parallelism desirable, which we refer to as *coarse-grained pipelined* parallelism. In this paper, we focus on the problem of choosing *packet size*, i.e., the unit of transfer between the pipeline units, in exploiting this form of parallelism.

We develop an analytical model for this purpose. Because the pipeline includes both communication and computation phases, the frequency and/or volume of communication between different phases can be different. We consider two models, fixed-frequency and fixed-size, and derive mathematical expressions for both.

We have carried out detailed evaluation of our models using three applications, executed with different parameters and datasets. Our experiments show that the choice of packet size makes a significant difference in the execution time, and the packet sizes suggested by the model result in the lowest or very close to the lowest possible execution time.

## 1. INTRODUCTION

The work presented in this paper is in the context of *coarse-grained pipelined parallelism*. Two recent trends are making this form of parallelism feasible and desirable. The first trend is the emergence of grid computing. A grid environment facilitates better sharing of data and computing resources. Particularly, the availability of data repositories and access to data collection instruments and sensors is creating a new scenario for execution of many applications.

The second trend is the emergence of a new class of data-driven or data-intensive applications. This class includes scientific data analysis, data mining, data visualization, and image analysis. These applications are typically both compute and data intensive, and require fast or even interactive response time. Therefore, these applications are a suitable target for parallelization.

Consider the execution of such data-driven applications in scenarios where the data is available on a repository or a data collection site on the internet, and the final results are required on a user's desktop. It is usually not possible to perform all analysis at the site hosting such a shared data repository or a data collection instrument. Similarly, networking and storage limitations make it impossible to download all data at a single site before processing. Thus, the application needs to be broken into a process or stage that executes on the site hosting or collecting the data, one or more stages that executes on clusters or SMP machines, and a final stage that executes on the user's local machine. We refer to such a model of execution as coarse-grained parallel pipelined execution.

One important factor that impacts the execution of applications with this model is *packet size*, i.e, the unit of data transfer from

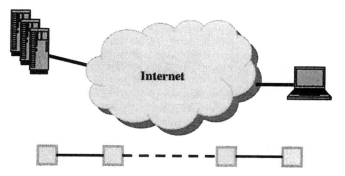

**Figure 1: A Simple Pipeline. The first stage is on the site hosting the data repository, the last stage is on the user's desktop, there are one or more stages in between performing transformation and processing.**

one pipeline stage to another. Clearly, a very large packet size may prevent the pipelined parallelism from being exploited. At the same time, a very small packet size could lead to high overheads because of communication latencies. Thus, choosing a suitable packet size is important for performance.

In this paper, we develop and validate analytical models for determining the packet size that will result in the lowest execution time. Our work builds on the work of Wang *et al.* on packet size optimization for multi-link communication pipeline [11]. The key difference in our work is that computation is involved in the pipeline and needs to be modeled. Moreover, because of computation, the frequency and/or the volume of communication at different stages can be different.

The rest of the paper is organized as follows. Background information on our target class of applications and the coarse-grained pipelined execution model is sketched in Section 2. The packet size problem and our basic approach are discussed in Section 3. The details of analytical model for the different cases are presented in Section 4. Section 5 focuses on the experimental validation of our models. We compare our work with related research efforts in Section 6 and conclude in Section 7.

## 2. TARGET APPLICATIONS AND COARSE-GRAINED PIPELINED PARALLELISM

In this section, we describe our target applications and the scenario for their execution in a distributed environment. We describe the *coarse-grained pipelined parallel* execution model and explain why it is a good match for our target applications.

Our focus is on a variety of data-driven applications, arising in domains like scientific data analysis, data mining, visualization, and image analysis, and spanning both scientific and commercial interests.

Processing and analyzing large volumes of data plays an increasingly important role in many domains of scientific research. In many applications, because of computational and storage requirements, and to ensure fault tolerance and high availability, datasets are stored on storage systems distributed across a wide area network, creating a science data grid [8, 7]. A variety of analysis and processing can be performed on these scientific datasets and images.

Business decisions today are increasingly driven by analysis of data. Various data mining and On Line Analytical Processing (OLAP) techniques are used in decision support systems. Grid technologies are driving the creation of *virtual organizations*, which comprise collections of institutions or entities sharing and analyzing information [5]. These virtual organizations can be expected to use a variety of business decision support functionalities that have been commonly used in centralized organizations. Thus, we expect that data mining and OLAP will be common operations performed in a grid environment.

Two obvious ways of executing an application that processes datasets available in grid-based data repositories are, downloading all data at the user's local machine, or performing all computations at sites hosting data repositories. However, neither of these two options is feasible in most situations. Sufficient storage space and/or network bandwidth is not likely to be available to download all data. At the same time, a node hosting a data repository is not likely to offer sufficient computing power to execute the entire application.

Therefore, a natural option for executing these applications is to use a pipeline of computing resources, where the site hosting the data repository is the first stage and the user's local machine where the results are required is the final stage. Typically, one or more clusters and/or SMP machines serve as the intermediate stage(s). An example pipeline is shown in Figure 1.

We refer to the above model of execution as the *coarse-grained pipelined parallelism*. The processing associated with an application is carried out in several stages. These stages are executed on a pipeline of computing units, each of which handles the intermediate results obtained from the previous stage. Typically, the first stage in this pipeline is the unit where the input data is available, and the last stage is where the final results are viewed. Many research groups have developed runtime support and scheduling techniques for this class of applications [1, 10, 13]. In our recent work, we have developed language and compiler support for this form of parallelism [4].

Our work is being implemented and evaluated using DataCutter, which is an existing runtime system for supporting pipelined parallelism in a grid environment [2, 1]. Specifically, DataCutter supports a *filter-stream* model of execution. Typically, one filter executes one stage of the pipeline, using one or more input *streams*. The results of the processing are packed and sent as one or more output *streams*.

# 3. PACKET SIZE OPTIMIZATION PROBLEM

This section formulates the packet size optimization problem that we are addressing in this paper. We also illustrate the various cases we are considering. Detailed results for each of these cases are presented in Section 4.

## 3.1 Overview of the Problem

As we had stated previously, in our target setting, the application is decomposed into several stages and mapped onto a pipeline of computing and communication units. The first stage of the pipeline is always on the site hosting the data repository and is responsible for reading, subsetting, and forwarding the data to the following stages. The last stage is typically on a user's desktop and in charge of collecting and viewing the results.

Suppose the entire operation involves reading and processing a data file of size $B$. One possibility is to transmit and process this file as one big packet. This option is likely to be impractical, because of the limited memory that may be available at different stages of the pipeline. Moreover, this option does not allow overlapping of the operations at different stages of the pipeline. Now, consider another extreme, where a single data-item is received, processed, and forwarded at each processing stage. Again, this option is likely to give poor performance, because of the high communication latency and the overhead involved in switching between communication and computation at each node. Thus, an important optimization parameter for getting high performance from the pipeline is the granularity at which packets are received, processed, and forwarded at each pipeline unit.

## 3.2 Solution Approach

Optimization of packet size in a multi-link communication pipeline has been researched by Wang *et al.* [11]. While their formulation can form the basis for our analysis, their results are not directly applicable to the problem we are considering. This is because of the following two reasons:

- Our pipeline includes both communication and computation stages. Both of them need to be modeled for determining the impact of packet size on the overall execution time.

- Because of computation, the volume and/or the frequency of communication between the different stages can vary. This is not directly handled by Wang *et al.*'s work.

Consider a pipeline with $m$ filters or computing stages. There are $m - 1$ streams connecting these stages. For our analysis, we consider it as a pipeline with $n = 2m - 1$ stages. Similar to Wang *et al.*, we consider the communication time to be an affine function of the size of the packet communicated, i.e., it comprises a fixed overhead per message and a per-byte cost. Based upon our experiences with our target class of applications, we find that the same model can be used for computation stages. There is usually a fixed overhead associated with receiving a packet and starting the processing. The remaining cost is usually linear in the size of the packet.

To present our analysis, we use the following terminology.

- n: the number of pipeline stages, including both computation and communication stages

- $G_i$: the fixed per-packet *overhead* for stage $i$

- $g_i$: the per-byte cost for stage $i$

- B: the size of the entire data file

- k: the number of packets

- $t_{i,j}$: the time the $i$th packet spends in the $j$th stage, $t_{i,j} = $ *size of packet* $i * g_j + G_j$

We still need to be able to handle the fact that the volume and/or the frequency of communication between different stages may not be the same. This is because an output packet of a computation stage is most likely different from its input packet, in both content and size. We introduce $\alpha_i$ as the ratio of output size to input size for the stage $i$. Obviously, this value is equal to 1 for all communication stages. We also assume that the value is same for all packets passing through stage $i$.

In our analysis, we will consider two models of execution. These models are *fixed-frequency* and *fixed-size* communication. In the fixed-frequency model, all computation stages except the last one send out one packet after getting one as input. The size of the output packet may be different from the size of the input packet. In the fixed-size model, the computation stages always communicate same size or almost same size packets. That is, the computation stages might need to wait for more than one input packets in order to prepare an output packet of the required size. Note that it is possible to execute the pipeline in a way that both the frequency and size of packets communicated may be different. We do not consider this possibility in this paper.

To choose the packet size to minimize the execution time, we need expressions for the total execution time. Before elaborating the different cases we are handling, we review the basic results from Wang *et al.* [11]. The expression for execution time is based upon the notion of a *bottleneck* stage. This is the stage which is always busy after the first packet is received, and before the last packet exits it. We assume that the $b^{th}$ stage is the bottleneck stage, and is characterized by the two-tuple $(G_b, g_b)$. Then the total execution time of a program can be stated as:

$$T = T_f + T_b + T_l \qquad (1)$$

where $T_f$, $T_b$, and $T_l$ are defined as follows:

- $T_f$: the time the first packet takes to reach the bottleneck stage.

- $T_b$: the time all packets spend in the bottleneck stage.

- $T_l$: the time the *last packet* takes to exit the pipeline after leaving the bottleneck stage.

Figure 2 shows the execution time-line of a pipeline consisting of three computing stages and two communication stages.

Note that the above formulation assumes that there is only a single bottleneck stage in the pipeline. However, this does not limit our analysis in any way. Suppose, there are two bottleneck stages in a pipeline. Then, the amount of time spent by all packets in these two stages will be identical. Therefore, we will derive the same expression by considering either of these two as the bottleneck.

## 4. CHOOSING OPTIMAL PACKET SIZES

In this section, we derive the expressions for choosing the optimal packet size. Recall that $B$ is the total size of input file, $k$ is the number of packets used, and $p = \lceil \frac{B}{k} \rceil$ is the size of each packet. We will aim at determining the value of $k$ in our analysis. In the next two subsections, we focus on fixed-frequency and fixed-sized communication patterns, respectively.

## 4.1 Fixed-Frequency Communication Pattern

The expression for minimizing the execution time depends upon which stage is the bottleneck stage. Here the bottleneck stage is defined as the pipeline stage which has the largest processing time for each incoming packet. Considering the packet size change pattern

| | Stage$_1$ | Stage$_2$ ... ... | Stage$_i$ | ... ... | Stage$_n$ |
|---|---|---|---|---|---|
| size of packet | $\frac{B}{k}$ | $\alpha_1 \frac{B}{k}$ | $\alpha_1 ... \alpha_{i-1} \frac{B}{k}$ | | $\alpha_1 ... \alpha_{n-1} \frac{B}{k}$ |

**Figure 4: Changing Size of the Packet Flowing Through the Pipeline Shown in Figure 3**

shown in Figure 4, the formal definition of bottleneck stage b under the fixed-frequency communication model is as follows.

$$b = \left\{ i \, \middle| \, \left(\prod_{j=1}^{i-1} \alpha_j\right) \frac{B}{k} g_i + G_i = \right.$$
$$\left. max \left\{ \left(\prod_{l=1}^{j-1} \alpha_l\right) \frac{B}{k} g_j + G_j \right\}, j = 1, \cdots, n \right\}.$$

We separately consider two different cases, corresponding to bottleneck at the first stage, and bottleneck at any of the other stages.

### 4.1.1 Bottleneck at the First Stage

Figure 3 shows the execution time-line for a 1st-stage bottleneck pipeline, and Figure 4 illustrates how the size of a packet changes in the pipeline. We rewrite $T_f$, $T_b$ and $T_l$ as follows.

$$T_f = 0 \qquad (2)$$

$$T_b = B * g_1 + k * G_1 \qquad (3)$$

$$T_l = (\alpha_1 \frac{B}{k} * g_2 + G_2) + (\alpha_1 \alpha_2 \frac{B}{k} * g_3 + G_3) + \cdots$$
$$(\alpha_1 \alpha_2 \cdots \alpha_{i-1} \frac{B}{k} * g_i + G_i) + \cdots +$$
$$(\alpha_1 \alpha_2 \cdots \alpha_{n-1} \frac{B}{k} * g_n + G_n) \qquad (4)$$

Substituting equations 2, 3 and 4 in the equation 1, we get

$$T = T_f + T_b + T_l$$
$$= B * g_1 + k * G_1 +$$
$$(\alpha_1 \frac{B}{k} * g_2 + G_2) + (\alpha_1 \alpha_2 \frac{B}{k} * g_3 + G_3) + \cdots$$
$$(\alpha_1 \alpha_2 \cdots \alpha_{i-1} \frac{B}{k} * g_i + G_i) + \cdots +$$
$$(\alpha_1 \alpha_2 \cdots \alpha_{n-1} \frac{B}{k} * g_n + G_n)$$
$$= B * g_1 + k * G_1 + \sum_{i=2}^{n} \left( \left(\prod_{j=1}^{i-1} \alpha_j\right) \frac{B}{k} * g_i + G_i \right) (5)$$

Since $\frac{d^2 T}{d^2 k} > 0$, to obtain the value of $k$ such that $T$ is minimized, we differentiate the above equation with respect to $k$, and set the result to 0.

$$\frac{dT}{dk} = -\frac{B \sum_{i=2}^{n} \left(\prod_{j=1}^{i-1} \alpha_j\right) g_i}{k^2} + G_1 = 0 \qquad (6)$$

Solving equation 6, we can get

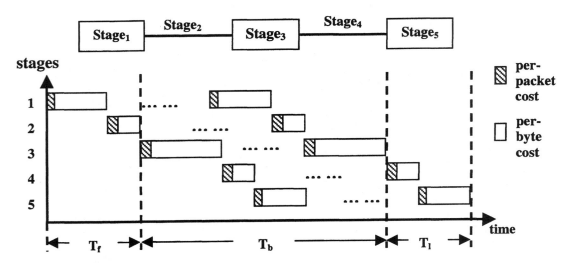

Figure 2: Execution Time-line of a Pipeline with Three Computation Stages and Two Communication Stages. $Stage_3$ is the bottleneck stage.

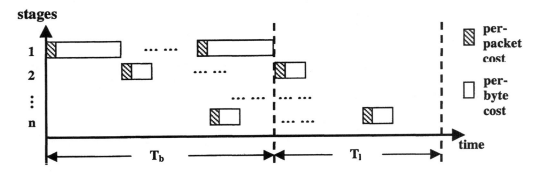

Figure 3: Execution Time-line of A *1st*-Stage Bottleneck Pipeline under Fixed-Frequency Communication Pattern

$$k = \left\lceil \sqrt{\frac{B \sum_{i=2}^{n} \left(\prod_{j=1}^{i-1} \alpha_j\right) g_i}{G_1}} \right\rceil . \quad (7)$$

### 4.1.2 Bottleneck at Second or Later Stages

The execution time-line of a pipeline with bottleneck at second or later stages is given in Figure 5. The change in the size of the packet is already depicted by Figure 4. Now $Stage_b$ is the bottleneck stage, where $b \neq 1$. We rewrite $T_f$, $T_b$ and $T_l$ as follows.

$$T_f = (\frac{B}{k} * g_1 + G_1) + (\alpha_1 \frac{B}{k} * g_2 + G_2) + \cdots + $$
$$(\alpha_1 \alpha_2 \cdots \alpha_{i-1} \frac{B}{k} * g_i + G_i) + \cdots + $$
$$(\alpha_1 \alpha_2 \cdots \alpha_{b-2} \frac{B}{k} * g_{b-1} + G_{b-1}) \quad (8)$$

$$T_b = \alpha_1 \alpha_2 \cdots \alpha_{b-1} B * g_b + k * G_b \quad (9)$$

$$T_l = (\alpha_1 \alpha_2 \cdots \alpha_b \frac{B}{k} * g_{b+1} + G_{b+1}) + \cdots + $$
$$(\alpha_1 \alpha_2 \cdots \alpha_{n-1} \frac{B}{k} * g_n + G_n) \quad (10)$$

Substituting equations 8, 9 and 10 in the equation 1, differentiating the resulting equation with respect to $k$, and setting the result to 0, then solving the equation, we get

$$k = \left\lceil \sqrt{\frac{B \left(g_1 + \sum_{i \neq b} \left(\prod_{j=1}^{i-1} \alpha_j\right) g_i\right)}{G_b}} \right\rceil . \quad (11)$$

## 4.2 Fixed-Size Communication Pattern

This scheme differs from the previous one in that there are fixed-size packets flowing on the communication links, except the last packet. Hence, communication frequency varies depending on the packet content and the filtering condition. Such pattern may save us some overhead. On the other hand, it can also introduce more idle time for later stages, which in turn increases the total runtime.

$$b = \left\{ i \left| \prod_{j=1}^{i-1} \alpha_j \left(\frac{B}{k} g_i + G_i\right) = \right. \right.$$
$$\left. max \left\{ \prod_{j=1}^{l-1} \alpha_j \left(\frac{B}{k} g_l + G_l\right) \right\}, l = 1, \cdots, n \right\} \quad (12)$$

As mentioned earlier, $\alpha_i$ is the ratio of output size with respect to input size for stage $i$. So to have an output packet whose size

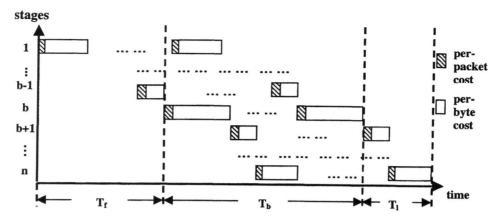

**Figure 5: Execution Time-line of a Pipeline With Bottleneck at Second or Later Stages: Fixed-Frequency Communication Pattern**

is same as that of the input, stage $i$ needs to process $\left\lceil \frac{1}{\alpha_i} \right\rceil$ packets before sending out a packet. Here, we define the bottleneck stage $b$ as in 12.

Intuitively, we compare the time spent at each stage to process the original packet, and the slowest one is the bottleneck stage. We again consider the two cases, corresponding to bottleneck at the first stage, and bottleneck at second or later stages. The detailed expressions for this class are presented in a related technical report [3].

We summarize results from all models in table 1.

### 4.3 Applicability to the Grid Environment

An obvious question is, how can the analytical models we have derived be used in a grid environment, given the variability of the resources in such an environment. Clearly, our models will need the fixed ($G_i$) and per-byte ($g_i$) cost for both computing and communication phases. We believe that the use of coarse-grained pipelined model will require the availability of dedicated computing resources. Thus, the fixed and per-byte cost for computing phases will not change during the execution of an application. These costs can be obtained during an initial execution of the application on the same or similar environment and used as part of our models.

The communication bandwidth and latency are more likely to vary dynamically in a grid environment. To obtain information about these, existing tools such as the Network Weather Service (NWS) [12] can be used. The closed-form expressions we have derived can be used with newly obtained parameters and optimal packet size can be computed without a significant runtime overhead.

## 5. EXPERIMENTAL RESULTS

This section reports a series of experiments we conducted for validating our work. Our experiments have focused on two aspects: 1) demonstrating that the choice of packet size can make a significant difference on the overall execution time of our target applications, and 2) showing that the packet sizes suggested by the expressions we have derived give best or very close to the best performance.

### 5.1 Experimental Setting and Applications

In the long run, we expect that pipelined parallelism can be exploited in wide-area networks. However, this is going to require high bandwidth networks and certain level of quality of service support. Recent trends are clearly pointing in this direction, for ex-

ample, the five sites that are part of the NSF funded Teragrid project expect to be connected with a 40 Gb/second network [9]. However, for our study, we did not have access to a wide-area network that gave high bandwidth and allowed repeatable experiments. Therefore, all our experiments were conducted within a single cluster. The cluster we used had 700 MHz Pentium machines connected through Myrinet LANai 7.0.

In the set of applications we have focused on, the following four computation stages are common:

- Read (R) stage, which is responsible for reading a chunk of points from the data file and prepares packets for sending to subsequent stages.

- A filtering or subsetting stage, denoted by F, which filters out points based upon a relatively inexpensive test.

- A local processing stage, denoted by L, which performs the processing independently on each packet.

- A global processing stage, denoted by G, which combines local results to compute the final results.

It is obvious that $\alpha_1 = 1$ since the R stage does not perform any processing on the input data before it forwards them to next stage. Similarly, for all communication stages $\alpha_i = 1, i = 2, 4, 6$.

We use three applications to test our model, two of which are algorithms implementing isosurface rendering. They are, z-buffer based isosurface rendering and active pixels based rendering, referred to as ZBUF and ACTP, respectively. Isosurface rendering is a key visualization problem. The inputs to the problem are a three-dimensional grid, a scalar isosurface value, and a two-dimensional viewing screen with an angle associated with it. The goal is to view a surface, as seen from the given viewing angle, which captures the points in the grid where the scalar value matches the given isosurface value.

Our third application is k-nearest neighbor search, referred to as KNN. It is one of the basic data mining problems [6]. Here, the training samples are described by an n-dimensional numeric space. Given a new point and a range, the goal is to find the $k$ training samples that are closest to the new point within the specific range. This application also involves four stages.

We created two versions for both KNN and ZBUF, based upon certain choices of parameters. KNN-1st, ACTP and ZBUF-1st are versions in which the first phase of the pipeline is the bottleneck stage, while in KNN-2nd and ZBUF-2nd, the second computation

| Communication Pattern | Bottleneck Stage $b$ | $k$ |
|---|---|---|
| fixed-frequency | $b=1$ | $k = \sqrt{\dfrac{B\sum(\prod_{j=1}^{i-1}\alpha_j)g_i}{G_1}}$ |
| | $b \neq 1$ | $k = \sqrt{\dfrac{B\left(g_1+\sum_{i\neq b}(\prod_{j=1}^{i-1}\alpha_j)g_i\right)}{G_b}}$ |
| fixed-size | $b=1$ | $k = \sqrt{\dfrac{B\sum g_i}{G_1}}$ |
| | $b \neq 1$ | $k = \sqrt{\dfrac{B\left(\sum_{i<b}\frac{g_i}{\alpha_i}+\sum_{i>b}g_i\right)}{(\prod_{i=1}^{b-1}\alpha_i)G_b}}$ |

**Table 1: Summary of All Models**

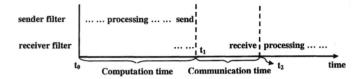

**Figure 6: A Time-line Illustrating the Division of Computation and Communication Time**

stage is the bottleneck stage. These versions allow us to validate expressions for different cases that we had listed in the previous section.

In our experiments, we have run these applications under both fixed-frequency and fixed-size communication schemes with various inputs sizes.

## 5.2 Measuring Pipeline Parameters

For using the expressions we have derived for optimal packet sizes, we need to know the fixed overhead and the per-byte cost associated with each stage of an application. We now describe how these values are obtained.

Note that we need to execute an application at least once to obtain these values. However, this is still a lot easier than iteratively finding the optimal packet size. Moreover, the values associated with a communication phase are independent of the application and can be determined just once for the target execution environment. Similarly, if some phases are common between multiple applications, the parameters can be determined once and used later.

To determine the fixed ($G_i$) and per-byte ($g_i$) cost for a computation phase, we identify the program components that represent these costs and instrument the code to measure these components. The parameters we obtained for the computational phases for all applications are summarized in Table 2.

We used the following procedure to determine the parameters associated with a communication phase. It is important to note that this is not strictly the time required over the communication link. The time spent in the middleware in preparing or receiving a message is also included in the communication time. This is illustrated through the Figure 6. The communication time starts when sender finishes the *send* operation, and ends when receiver finishes the *receive* operation, i.e. it is of duration $t_2 - t_1$ in Figure 6.

For the communication links in the cluster we used, $G_i$ was 32.6 $\mu$s and $g_i$ was 1.73 $\mu$s, for very communication phase $i$.

## 5.3 Evaluation of Fixed-Frequency Model

We now present experimental results validating the expressions

we have derived for the fixed-frequency model.

### 5.3.1 K-Nearest Neighbor Search

In this experiment, we test the KNN-1st with $K = 3$, $B = 108M$, and $\alpha_3 = 75.85\%$. In Figure 7, we show how the execution time of this application varies as the packet size is changed. As can be seen from the figure, execution time can vary by up to a factor of 3 as the packet size is changed. However, the lowest execution time can be achieved from choosing any packet size from a significant range of values.

The packet size suggested by our model can be calculated as follows. Using the parameters from Table 2 and the Equation 7, we get

$$k = \left\lceil \sqrt{\frac{108 * 10^6 (1.73 + 0.054 + 75.85\% * (1.73 + 0.013))}{2.41}} \right\rceil$$
$$= 11798$$

then

$$\left\lceil \frac{B}{k} \right\rceil = 9154 \text{ bytes}$$

From Figure 7, we can see that this value of packet size can give the lowest execution time. Thus, our model suggests a packet size that minimizes execution time.

### 5.3.2 Zbuffer Based ISO-Surface Rendering

We test the application ZBUF-2nd here. The size of data file $B$ is about 145M, the output image size is 512x512, and value of $\alpha_3$ is 3.42%. Calculating $k$ by taking parameters in Table 2 and using the Equation 11, we get

$$k = \left\lceil \sqrt{\frac{152729808 (0.1289 + 1.73 + 3.42\% * (1.73 + 0.7569))}{2.1606}} \right\rceil$$
$$= 11726$$

then

$$\left\lceil \frac{B}{k} \right\rceil = 13025 \text{ bytes}$$

The impact of packet size on the execution time is shown in Figure 8. Two things can again be observed from this Figure. First, the choice of the packet size can have a large impact on execution time. Second, the packet size suggested by our model minimizes the execution time.

### 5.3.3 ActivePixel Based ISO-Surface Rendering

| Communication Pattern | Applications | Parameters | | | |
|---|---|---|---|---|---|
| Fixed-frequency | KNN-1st | $G_1$ | $g_3$ | $g_5$ | $\alpha_3$ |
| | | 2.41 | 0.054 | 0.013 | 75.85% |
| | ZBUF-2nd | $G_3$ | $g_1$ | $g_5$ | $\alpha_3$ |
| | | 2.1606 | 0.1289 | 0.7569 | 3.42% |
| | ACTP | $G_1$ | $g_3$ | $g_5$ | $\alpha_3$ |
| | | 1.5338 | 0.1494 | 0.2191 | 2.95% |
| Fixed-size | KNN-2nd | $G_3$ | $g_1$ | $g_5$ | $\alpha_3$ |
| | | 2.4087 | 0.0872 | 0.0127 | 1 |
| | ZBUF-1st | $G_1$ | $g_3$ | $g_5$ | $\alpha_3$ |
| | | 1.3848 | 0.1207 | 1.0296 | 1 |
| | ACTP | $G_1$ | $g_3$ | $g_5$ | $\alpha_3$ |
| | | 1.4552 | 0.1356 | 0.1937 | 1 |

**Table 2: Parameters for Computational Phases for All Applications**

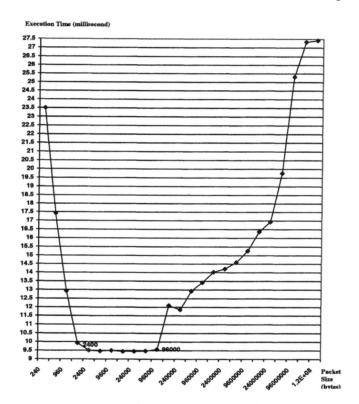

**Figure 7: Runtime of KNN-1st under Fixed-Frequency Scheme**

The size of data file $B$ is about 145M, the output image size is 2048x2048, and value of $\alpha_3$ is 0.0295. Calculating $k$ by taking parameters in Table 2 and using the Equation 7, we get

$$k = \left\lceil \sqrt{\frac{152729808(1.73 + 0.1494 + 0.0295 * (1.73 + 0.2191))}{1.5338}} \right\rceil$$
$$= 13888$$

then

$$\left\lceil \frac{B}{k} \right\rceil = 10997 \text{ bytes}$$

The variation in execution time as the packet size is changed is shown in Figure 9. Again, we see that execution time can vary significantly and the packet size suggested by our model achieves the lowest execution time.

## 5.4 Evaluation of Fixed-Size Model

Detailed evaluation of this model is presented in a related technical report [3].

## 6. RELATED WORK

Our work is closely related to the work on optimizing packet size in a multi-link communication pipeline by Wang *et al.* [11]. In comparison, our contributions are two fold. First, we have derived expressions for cases where computation is involved and as a result, frequency and/or the volume of communication across different links is different. Second, we have carried out a detailed validation of the model for our target applications and their execution scenario.

Several researchers have developed runtime, scheduling, or language/compiler support for coarse-grained pipelined parallelism. The Stampede project [10] has focused on interactive multimedia applications, which have several common characteristics with the applications we have targeted. The support offered is in the form of cluster-wide threads and shared objects. Yang *et al.* have developed a scheduler for vision applications which are executed in a pipelined fashion within a cluster [13]. They include support for meeting real-time constraints. Our previous work involved developing language support on top of DataCutter [4]. None of these efforts had, however, considered the packet size optimization problem in details.

## 7. CONCLUSIONS

The work presented here has been in the context of coarse-grained pipelined execution model. This model is very suitable for the execution of data-driven applications in an environment where the data is available on remote data repositories and the results are desirable on a user's desktop. Within this context, we have focused on determining packet size that will achieve the best performance.

We have derived analytical expressions for this purpose. Though our work builds on top of the work of Wang *et al.* on packet size for multi-link communication pipelines, we also addressed two new challenges. First, we had to model computation phases. Second, because of computation, the frequency and/or the volume of communication between the different communication stages can be different. We have considered two models, fixed-frequency and fixed-size communications, and derived expressions for choosing the packet size.

We have carried out detailed evaluation of our models using three

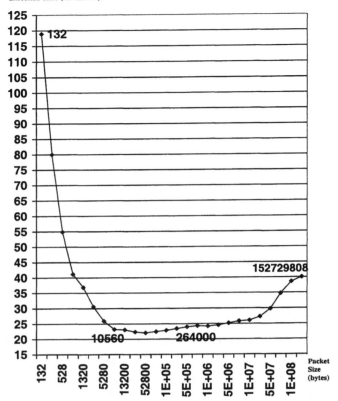

**Figure 8: Runtime of Zbuffer Based ISO-Surface Rendering (ZBUF-2nd) under Fixed-Frequency Scheme**

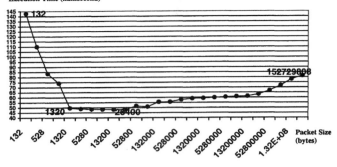

**Figure 9: Runtime of ActivePixels Based ISO-Surface Rendering (ACTP) under Fixed-Frequency Scheme**

applications, executed with different parameters and datasets. Our experiments have shown that the choice of packet size makes a significant difference in the execution time, and the packet sizes suggested by the model result in the lowest or very close to the lowest possible execution time. With a little extra effort, the models can be applied to applications running on the Grid environment.

# 8. REFERENCES

[1] Michael D. Beynon, Tahsin Kurc, Umit Catalyurek, Chialin Chang, Alan Sussman, and Joel Saltz. Distributed processing of very large datasets with DataCutter. *Parallel Computing*, 27(11):1457–1478, October 2001.

[2] Michael D. Beynon, Tahsin Kurc, Alan Sussman, and Joel Saltz. Optimizing execution of component-based applications using group instances. In *Proceedings of the Conference on Cluster Computing and the Grid (CCGRID)*, pages 56–63. IEEE Computer Society Press, May 2001.

[3] Wei Du and Gagan Agrawal. Packet size optimization for supporting coarse-grained pipelined parallelism. Technical Report OSU-CISRC-5/04-TR29, Department of Computer Science and Engineering, The Ohio State University, May 2004.

[4] Wei Du, Renato Ferreira, and Gagan Agrawal. Compiler Support for Exploiting Coarse-Grained Pipelined Parallelism. In *Proceedings of Supercomputing 2003*, November 2003.

[5] Ian Foster, Carl Kesselman, and Steven Tuecke. The Anatomy of Grid: Enabling Scalable Virtual Organizations.

*International Journal of Supercomputing Applications*, 2001.

[6] Jiawei Han and Micheline Kamber. *Data Mining: Concepts and Techniques*. Morgan Kaufmann Publishers, 2000.

[7] Grid Physics Network. GriPhyN. http://www.griphyn.org.

[8] Ron Oldfield. Summary of existing and developing data grids. White paper, Remote Data Access Group, Global Grid Forum, available from http://www.sdsc.edu/GridForum/RemoteData/Papers/papers.html.

[9] Teragrid project partners. The TeraGrid: A Primer, September 2002. Available at www.teragrid.org.

[10] U. Ramachandran, R. S. Nikhil, N. Harel, J. M. Rehg, and K. Knobe. Space-Time Memory: A Parallel Programming Abstraction for Interactive Multimedia Applications. In *Proceedings of the Conference on Principles and Practices of Parallel Programming (PPoPP)*, pages 183–192. ACM Press, May 1999.

[11] R. Y. Wang, A. Krishnamurthy, R. P. Martin, T. E. Abderson, and D. E. Culler. Modeling Communication Pipeline Latency. In *Proceedings of the ACM SIGMETRICS Conference*. ACM Press, June 1998.

[12] R. Wolski. Forecasting Network Performance to Support Dynamic Scheduling Using the Network Weather Service. In *Proceedings of the Conference on High Performance Distributed Computing (HPDC)*, 1997.

[13] M. T. Yang, R. Kasturi, and A. Sivasubramaniam. An Automatic Scheduler for Real-Time Vision Applications. In *Proceedings of the International Parallel and Distributed Processing Symposium (IPDPS)*, 2001.

# Complexity results and heuristics for pipelined multicast operations on heterogeneous platforms

O. Beaumont
LaBRI, UMR CNRS 5800
Bordeaux, France
Olivier.Beaumont@labri.fr

A. Legrand and L. Marchal and Y. Robert
LIP, UMR CNRS-INRIA 5668
ENS Lyon, France
{Arnaud.Legrand,Loris.Marchal,Yves.Robert}@ens-lyon.fr

## Abstract

*In this paper, we consider the communications involved by the execution of a complex application deployed on a heterogeneous platform. Such applications extensively use macro-communication schemes, such as multicast operations, where messages are broadcast to a set of predefined targets. We assume that there is a large number of messages to be multicast in pipeline fashion, and we seek to maximize the throughput of the steady-state operation. We target heterogeneous platforms, modeled by a graph where links have different communication speeds. We show that the problem of computing the best throughput for a multicast operation is NP-hard, whereas the best throughput to broadcast a message to every node in a graph can be computed in polynomial time. Thus, we introduce several heuristics to deal with this problem and prove that some of them are approximation algorithms. We perform simulations to test these heuristics and show that their results are close to a theoretical upper bound on the throughput that we obtain with a linear programming approach.*

## 1. Introduction

Multicasting is a key communication primitive in computer networks. Lin and Ni [7] have published a survey paper where they consider different multicast algorithms operating under several network models; they explain the close relationships between multicast algorithms and Steiner trees. Several authors have discussed optimized broadcast algorithms for a variety of parallel architectures, such as wormhole routed networks, cut-through routed networks, and networks of workstations. Recently, the design of multicast algorithms has been the focus of many papers, due to the advent of new technologies such as mobile, wireless, ad-hoc, and optical networks.

In this paper, we consider multicast algorithms for heterogeneous networks of workstations. We assume a realistic model of communications, namely the *one-port* model, where a given processor can simultaneously receive data from one of its neighbor, and send (independent) data to one of its neighbor at a given time-step. This is to be contrasted with the traditional *multi-port* model, where the number of simultaneous messages sent or received by a given processor is not bounded.

The traditional objective of multicast algorithms is to minimize the *makespan*, i.e. the time elapsed between the emission of the first message by the source and the last reception. In this paper, rather than concentrating on the implementation of a single multicast operation, we deal with the optimization of *a series of successive multicast operations* or equivalently of a single multicast operation of a very large message split into small chunks. Such series of multicasts typically occur in the execution of a complex application, deployed on a heterogeneous "grid" platform, and using macro-communication schemes intensively. In many cases, the application would perform a large number of instances of multicasts (for example if data parallelism is used), and the makespan is not a significant measure for such problems. Rather, we focus on the optimization of the steady-state mode, and we aim at optimizing the averaged throughput, i.e. the averaged number of multicasts which are initiated every time-step.

In previous papers, we have dealt with other communication primitives than the multicast operation. We have shown how to compute the optimal steady-state throughput for a series of scatter or reduce operations [6], and a series of broadcast operations [2].

The idea is to characterize the steady-state operation of each resource through a linear program in rational numbers (that can thus be solved with a complexity polynomial in the platform size), and then to derive a feasible periodic schedule from the output of the program (and to describe this schedule in polynomial size too). In this paper, we prove that surprisingly, multicast operations turns out to be more difficult than scatters or broadcasts: even characterizing the optimal throughput of a series of multicasts is shown to be NP-hard.

Following this negative result, we introduce several polynomial time heuristics to deal with the series of multicasts problem. These heuristics can be divided into two categories: the first category is based upon the linear programming approach, and some heuristics are in fact shown to be approximation algorithms (they have a guaranteed worst-case performance). The second category re-visits the traditional heuristics that aim at building "good" multicast trees, namely trees that minimize either the sum of the edge weights (Steiner trees) or the weight of the longest path in the tree (which is the makespan under the multiport model); we extend these heuristics to cope with the new objective, i.e. maximizing the throughput of the multicast tree. Due to lack of space, we do not survey related work: instead, we refer to the extended version of the paper [1].

## 2. Framework

The target architectural platform is represented by an edge-weighted directed graph $G = (V, E, c)$, as illustrated in Figure 1(a). Note that this graph may well include cycles and multiple paths. Let $p = |V|$ be the total number of nodes. There is a *source* node $P_{source}$, which plays a particular role: it is the source of all the messages to be sent; initially, it holds all the data to be multicast. There is a set of $N$ destination nodes, which we denote as $\mathcal{P}_{target} = \{P_{t_1}, \ldots, P_{t_N}\}$. If $\mathcal{P}_{target} = V \setminus \{P_{source}\}$, all nodes are receiving the messages, we have a succession of broadcast operations. Otherwise, there are some nodes that are neither source nor destination, but which may participate by forwarding the information.

There are several scenarios for the operation mode of the processors. In this paper, we concentrate on the *one-port model*, where a processor node can simultaneously receive data from one of its neighbor, and send (independent) data to one of its neighbor. At any given time-step, there are at most two communications involving a given processor, one in emission and the other in reception.

Each edge $e_{j,k} : P_j \to P_k$ is labeled by a value $c_{j,k}$ which represents the time needed to communicate one unit-size message from $P_j$ to $P_k$. The graph is directed: the time to communicate in the reverse direction, from $P_k$ to $P_j$, is $c_{k,j}$ (provided that this link exists). Note that if there is no communication link between $P_j$ and $P_k$ we let $c_{j,k} = +\infty$, so that $c_{j,k} < +\infty$ means that $P_j$ and $P_k$ are neighbors in the communication graph. We state the communication model more precisely: if $P_j$ sends a unit-size message to $P_k$ at time-step $t$, then (i) $P_k$ cannot initiate another receive operation before time-step $t + c_{j,k}$ (but it can perform a send operation); and (ii) $P_j$ cannot initiate another send operation before time-step $t + c_{j,k}$ (but it can perform a receive operation).

**Series of multicasts** We define the SERIES OF MULTICASTS problem as follows: the source processor emits a (potentially infinite) sequence of unit-size messages. Start-up costs are included in the values of the link capacities $c_{j,k}$. The optimization problem, which we denote as SERIES$(V, E, c, P_{source}, \mathcal{P}_{target})$, is to maximize the throughput, i.e. the average number of multicasts initiated per time-unit. We work out a little example in Section 3, using the platform represented in Figure 1(a).

## 3. Example

In this section, we work out a simple example. The platform graph is represented on Figure 1(a). The processor $P_{source}$ aims at multicasting a series of messages to the target processors $P_7, P_8, \ldots, P_{13}$ (which are shaded on the figure). Edges are labeled with the communication time needed to transfer one unit-size message. All edges between processors $P_7, P_8, P_9$, and $P_{10}$ have weight $1/5$, and edges between processors $P_{11}, P_{12}$, and $P_{13}$ have weight $1/10$.

Because the edge from $P_6$ to $P_7$ has weight 1, $P_7$ cannot receive more than one message per time-unit. This is an upper bound for the throughput that can be achieved with this platform for the SERIES OF MULTICASTS problem. In the following, we prove that this bound can be obtained, but only when using several multicast trees simultaneously.

Assume (by contradiction) that a single multicast tree $\mathcal{T}$ could deliver one message every time-unit. As $P_{11}$ belongs to the set of target processors, $P_1$ has to receive the messages and to transfer them to $P_{11}$, so at least one of the edges $(P_{source}, P_1)$ and $(P_2, P_1)$ belongs to $\mathcal{T}$. Since $\mathcal{T}$ is a tree, only one of these edges belongs to $\mathcal{T}$. We examine both cases:

- $(P_{\text{source}}, P_1) \in \mathcal{T}$: then $P_{\text{source}}$ sends a message to $P_1$ every time-unit, so it cannot perform any other sending operation. $P_3$ receives no message, and neither does $P_7$, hence a contradiction.

- $(P_2, P_1) \in \mathcal{T}$: then $P_2$ spends all its time sending messages to $P_1$. Therefore, $P_2$ has to receive its messages from $P_3$ at the same rate and $P_6$ has to receive its messages from $P_5$. As $P_3$ has to spend all its time sending data to $P_2$, $P_4$ (hence $P_5$ and $P_6$) cannot receive any message. Hence a contradiction.

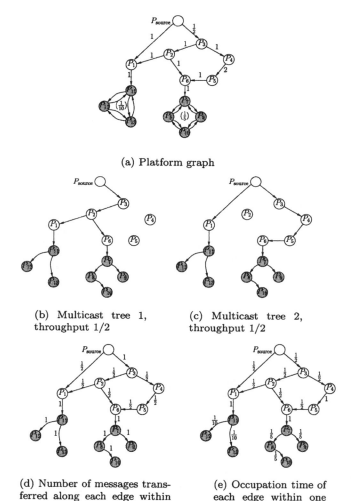

(a) Platform graph

(b) Multicast tree 1, throughput 1/2

(c) Multicast tree 2, throughput 1/2

(d) Number of messages transferred along each edge within one time-unit

(e) Occupation time of each edge within one time-unit

**Figure 1. Example for the Series problem.**

Hence a throughput of one message every time-unit is not achievable with a single multicast tree. However, we outline an optimal schedule which reaches such a throughput, using two multicast trees. These trees, whose throughputs are both 1/2, are shown on Figures 1(b) and 1(c). The number of messages sent along each edge during on time-unit with this optimal solution is presented on Figure 1(d). Figure 1(e) shows the corresponding communication times on each edge. We point out that the two multicast trees are not edge-disjoint, but all the communications induced by each of them can be orchestrated so as to take place within one time-unit, as outlined in Figure 1(e). We see that some processors reach their maximum sending capacity, such as $P_{\text{source}}, P_1, P_2, P_3, P_4, P_6$; also, some processors reach their maximum receiving capacity: $P_1, P_6, P_7, P_{11}$.

## 4. Complexity results

In this section, we derive complexity results for the Series of Multicasts problem. We first show that even the simple problem to determine the optimal throughput that can be achieved for a succession of multicast operations is NP-hard. Worst, we prove that this optimal throughput cannot be polynomially approximated up to a logarithmic factor (unless P=NP). The interested reader will find all the proofs of these results in the extended version of the paper [1].

### 4.1 Complexity of the Series of Multicasts problem

We formally state the decision problem associated to the determination of the optimal throughput for the Series problem. In the following, log denotes the logarithm in base 2:

**Definition 1 (COMPACT-MULTICAST).** *Given a weighted platform graph $G = (V, E, c)$, a source processor $P_{\text{source}}$, a set of destination processors $\mathcal{P}_{\text{target}}$, a rational bound for the throughput $\rho$, and a rational bound for the size $S$, is there a $K$-periodic schedule of period $T$, i.e. a schedule which performs $K$ multicast operations every $T$ units of time in steady-state, such that $K \leqslant \log S$ and $\frac{K}{T} \geqslant \rho$?*

**Theorem 1.** *COMPACT-MULTICAST($G$, $P_{\text{source}}$, $\mathcal{P}_{\text{target}}$, $\rho, S$) is NP-complete.*

We point out that the bound $S$ is introduced so that the description of a periodic schedule can be polynomial in the problem size. Informally, a $K$-periodic schedule is the superposition of $K$ multicast trees, and the condition $K \leqslant \log S$ ensures that all these trees can be encoded with a size polynomial in the input: each tree is at most the size of the platform graph, and there are no more than $\log S$ of them. We point out that similar difficulties hold for specifying cyclic schedules in general: see the survey paper of Hanen and Munier [4].

The proof of this result (available in [1]) can be used to derive an inapproximability result. The class APX is defined as the problems in NP which admit a polynomial-time $\lambda$-approximation algorithm, for some constant $\lambda$. Therefore, if we show that COMPACT-MULTICAST does not belong to this class, this will prove that, unless P=NP, no polynomial-time heuristic can approximate the best throughput, up to an arbitrary constant factor.

**Theorem 2.** *COMPACT-MULTICAST does not belong to the class APX.*

We can refine Theorem 1 by suppressing the restriction on the compactness of the solution. We first come to a formulation of the problem using weighted multicast trees:

**Definition 2 (COMPACT-WEIGHTED-MULTICAST).** *Given a weighted platform graph $G = (V, E, c)$, a source processor $P_{source}$, a set of destination processors $\mathcal{P}_{target}$, a rational bound for the throughput $\rho$, is there a periodic schedule consisting of $k \leqslant 2|E|$ multicast trees $\{T_1, \ldots, T_k\}$, where $\alpha_i$ is the average number of messages sent through tree $T_i$ within one time-unit, $\alpha_i = a_i/b_i$, where $a_i$ and $b_i$ are integers such that $\forall i = 1, \ldots, k$, $\log a_i + \log b_i \leqslant 4|E|(\log |E| + A = \log \max c_{i,j})$, and $\sum \alpha_i \geqslant \rho$?*

**Theorem 3.** *COMPACT-WEIGHTED-MULTICAST($G$, $P_{source}$, $\mathcal{P}_{target}$, $\rho$, $S$) is NP-complete.*

The following result states that restricting to compact weighted trees does not affect the optimality of the solution:

**Theorem 4.** *Given a weighted platform graph $G = (V, E, c)$, a source processor $P_{source}$, a set of destination processors $\mathcal{P}_{target}$, if there exists a periodic schedule that achieves a throughput $\rho$, then there also exists a solution of COMPACT-WEIGHTED-MULTICAST($G$, $P_{source}$, $\mathcal{P}_{target}$, $\rho$).*

The main two complexity results stated in this section should be compared to their equivalent for the broadcast problems.

|  | Broadcast | Multicast |
|---|---|---|
| The best tree | NP-hard [2] | NP-hard (Th. 1) |
| Combination of weighted trees | P [2] | NP-hard (Th. 3 and 4) |

In many situation (e.g. the broadcast problem), using a relaxation such as the steady-state mode renders the problem much more simple. This relaxation is not sufficient for the multicast problem since the resulting optimization problem is NP-hard and does not even belong to the class APX. In [1], we show that these complexity results can be extended to a similar problem, namely Parallel Prefix computations.

## 5. LP-based heuristics

### 5.1. Lower and upper bound for multicast completion time

We consider a unit size message that can be arbitrarily split in smaller parts to be multicast on the platform. We denote by $x_i^{j,k}$, $\forall P_i \in \mathcal{P}_{target}$, $\forall (P_j, P_k) \in E$ the fraction of the message (of total size 1) from $P_{source}$ to $P_i$ that transits on the edge between $P_j$ and $P_k$. For any node $P_j$, we denote by $\mathcal{N}^{out}(P_j)$ (resp. $\mathcal{N}^{in}(P_j)$) the set of nodes $P_k$ such that $(P_j, P_k) \in E$ (resp. $(P_k, P_j) \in E$).

#### 5.1.1 Set of general constraints

In what follows, we give a set of linear constraints that must be fulfilled by any solution.

- The first set of constraints states that the entire message has been sent from $P_{source}$ and has been received at $P_i$:

  (1) $\quad \forall i \in \mathcal{P}_{target}, \quad \displaystyle\sum_{P_j \in \mathcal{N}^{out}(P_{source})} x_i^{source,j} = 1$

  (2) $\quad \forall i \in \mathcal{P}_{target}, \quad \displaystyle\sum_{P_j \in \mathcal{N}^{in}(P_i)} x_i^{j,i} = 1$

- The second set of constraints states a conservation law at $P_j$, where $P_j \neq P_{source}$ and $P_j \neq P_i$ for the messages sent to $P_i$:

  (3) $\quad \forall j, \quad P_j \neq P_{source}$ and $P_j \neq P_i$,
  $$\sum_{P_k \in \mathcal{N}^{out}(P_j)} x_i^{j,k} = \sum_{P_k \in \mathcal{N}^{in}(P_j)} x_i^{k,j}$$

- The following set of constraints is related to the architectural framework of the platform. Let $n_{j,k}$ be the total fraction of packets that transit on the communication link between $P_j$ and $P_k$. Let us suppose (until next section) that we know how to compute $n_{j,k}$. Therefore, the occupation time $t_{j,k}$ of the link $(P_j, P_k)$ is given by

  (4) $\quad \forall (P_j, P_k) \in E, \quad t_{j,k} = n_{j,k} \times c_{j,k}$

270

We also need to write down the constraints stating that communication ports for both incoming and outgoing communications are not violated. The occupation time of the ports for incoming (resp. outgoing) communications will be denoted by $t_j^{(\text{in})}$ (resp. $t_j^{(\text{out})}$):

$$(5) \quad \forall j, \qquad t_j^{(\text{in})} = \sum_{P_k \in \mathcal{N}^{\text{in}}(P_j)} t_{k,j}$$

$$(6) \quad \forall j, \qquad t_j^{(\text{out})} = \sum_{P_k \in \mathcal{N}^{\text{out}}(P_j)} t_{j,k}$$

- The last set of constraint is related to the total multicast time $T^*$ for a unit size message. The constraints simply state that $T^*$ is larger than the occupation time of any incoming or outgoing communication port:

$$(7) \quad \forall j, \qquad T^* \geqslant t_j^{(\text{in})}$$

$$(8) \quad \forall j, \qquad T^* \geqslant t_j^{(\text{out})}$$

### 5.1.2 Total fraction of packets that transit on a communication link

We have denoted by $n_{j,k}$ the total fraction of packets that transit on the communication link between $P_j$ and $P_k$. We know that a fraction $x_i^{j,k}$ of the message sent to $P_i$ transit on this link. The main difficulty is that the messages transiting on this link and sent to different $P_i$'s may well be partly the same, since the same overall message is sent to all the nodes in $\mathcal{P}_{\text{target}}$. Therefore, the constraint

$$(9) \quad n_{j,k} = \sum_{P_i \in \mathcal{P}_{\text{target}}} x_i^{j,k}$$

that would hold true for a scatter operation, may be too pessimistic, but provides an upper bound for the completion time of the multicast. On the other hand, if our aim is to find a lower bound for the completion time of the multicast, we can make the optimistic assumption, stating that all the messages transiting between $P_j$ and $P_k$ are all sub-messages of the largest one, i.e.

$$(9') \quad n_{j,k} = \max_{i \in \mathcal{P}_{\text{target}}} x_i^{j,k}$$

Therefore, the following linear program provides a lower bound for the multicast time of an infinitely divisible message of unit size:

**Multicast-LB**$(\mathcal{P}, \mathcal{P}_{\text{target}})$ : MINIMIZE $T^*$, SUBJECT TO Equations (1, 2, 3, 4, 5, 6, 7, 8, 9')

and the following linear program provides an upper bound for the multicast time of an infinitely divisible message of unit size:

**Multicast-UB**$(\mathcal{P}, \mathcal{P}_{\text{target}})$ : MINIMIZE $T^*$, SUBJECT TO Equations (1, 2, 3, 4, 5, 6, 7, 8, 9)

In the extended version of the paper [1], we show that neither the upper bound nor the lower one are tight, but we use the solution of the **Multicast-LB**$(\mathcal{P}, \mathcal{P}_{\text{target}})$ linear program in order to find an heuristic that differs at most by a factor $|\mathcal{P}_{\text{target}}|$ from the optimal solution, where $|\mathcal{P}_{\text{target}}|$ is the number of targets in the platform.

### 5.1.3 Broadcast on the whole platform

Another simple heuristic consists in performing a broadcast on the whole platform. Broadcast is a special case of multicast where the set of target nodes is the whole platform. Surprisingly, it has been proved that the optimal throughput given by the linear program **Multicast-LB**$(\mathcal{P}, \mathcal{P})$ (denoted by **Broadcast**$(\mathcal{P})$) can be achieved in this case. The construction of a schedule achieving this throughput relies on non-trivial graph theorems (weighted versions of Edmond's and König's theorems), and will not be detailed here. The interested reader may refer to [2] to find the description of such a schedule. The following set of inequalities holds true:

$$\textbf{Multicast-LB}(\mathcal{P}, \mathcal{P}_{\text{target}}) \leqslant \textbf{Multicast-UB}(\mathcal{P}, \mathcal{P}_{\text{target}})$$

$$\textbf{Multicast-LB}(\mathcal{P}, \mathcal{P}_{\text{target}}) \leqslant \textbf{Broadcast}(\mathcal{P})$$

$$\textbf{Multicast-LB}(\mathcal{P}, \mathcal{P}_{\text{target}}) \geqslant \frac{\textbf{Multicast-UB}(\mathcal{P}, \mathcal{P}_{\text{target}})}{|\mathcal{P}_{\text{target}}|}$$

### 5.2. Refined Heuristics

In this section, we briefly present three different heuristics based on the solutions given by **Broadcast**$(\mathcal{P})$, **Multicast-LB**$(\mathcal{P}, \mathcal{P}_{\text{target}})$ and **Multicast-UB**$(\mathcal{P}, \mathcal{P}_{\text{target}})$. The interested reader can find the formal description of all heuristics in [1]. Since we know how to build schedule from the solutions of **Broadcast**$(\mathcal{P})$ and **Multicast-UB**$(\mathcal{P}, \mathcal{P}_{\text{target}})$, the heuristics that we propose are all based on those solutions, on restricted or extended platforms.

### 5.2.1 Reduce-Broadcast

We start from **Broadcast**$(\mathcal{P})$ and try to reduce the broadcast platform. At each step of the algorithm, we select the node whose contribution to the propagation of the message in the lowest, that is the node with the minimum $\sum_{i \in \mathcal{P}_{\text{target}}} \sum_{P_j \in \mathcal{N}^{\text{in}}(P_m)} x_i^{j,m}$ in the solution of **Broadcast**($\mathcal{P}$). This node is discarded and we compute the broadcast time on the remaining platform graph $\mathcal{P} \setminus P_m$. Note that in this new platform, there may well be no path from $P_{\text{source}}$ to a node in $\mathcal{P}_{\text{target}}$. In this case, we set **Broadcast**($\mathcal{P} \setminus P_m$)$= +\infty$. We stop pruning the platform graph when no improvement in the broadcast time can be found.

### 5.2.2 Augmented-Multicast

We start from **Multicast-LB**($\mathcal{P}, \mathcal{P}_{\text{target}}$) and aim at extending the set of target nodes $\mathcal{P}_{\text{target}}$ until broadcast is possible on the platform consisting of the nodes in $\mathcal{P}_{\text{target}}$. At each step of the algorithm, we select the node (not yet in $\mathcal{P}_{\text{target}}$) whose contribution to the propagation of the message is the largest. We stop adding nodes to $\mathcal{P}_{\text{target}}$ as soon as no improvement can be found.

### 5.2.3 Multisource-Multicast

The idea is to start from **Multicast-UB**($\mathcal{P}, \mathcal{P}_{\text{target}}$) and to augment the number of sources without changing the target nodes $\mathcal{P}_{\text{target}}$. The linear program **MulticastMultiSource-UB**($\mathcal{P}, \mathcal{P}_{\text{target}}, \mathcal{P}_{\text{source}}$) describes a multicast on the platform $\mathcal{P}$, with the set of target nodes $\mathcal{P}_{\text{target}}$ and the set of (ordered) intermediate sources $\mathcal{P}_{\text{source}} = \{P_{s_0}(= P_{\text{source}}), P_{s_1}, \ldots, P_{s_l}\}$. In the linear program, $x_{s_i,j}^{k,l}$ denotes the fraction of the message sent to $P_j$, that was initially sent by source $P_{s_i}$ and transiting on the communication link between $P_k$ and $P_l$. We measure the occupation of communication links by summing up the different messages transiting on this link (Equation (9), corresponding to a scatter operation). Thus, it is possible to reconstruct a schedule from the solution of the linear program that achieves exactly the throughput given by the linear program.

**MulticastMultiSource-UB**($\mathcal{P}, \mathcal{P}_{\text{target}}, \mathcal{P}_{\text{source}}$) :
MINIMIZE $T^*$,
SUBJECT TO
$$\begin{cases} 1, 2, 3, 9, 4, 5, 6, 7, 8, \text{ and} \\ (1b) \quad \forall i \in \mathcal{P}_{\text{target}} \setminus \mathcal{P}_{\text{source}}, \\ \quad \sum_{j<l} \sum_{P_k \in \mathcal{N}^{\text{out}}(P_{s_j})} x_{s_j,i}^{s_j,k} = 1 \\ (2b) \quad \forall i \in \mathcal{P}_{\text{target}} \setminus \mathcal{P}_{\text{source}}, \\ \quad \sum_{j<l} \sum_{P_k \in \mathcal{N}^{\text{in}}(P_i)} x_{s_j,i}^{k,i} = 1 \\ (3b) \quad \forall i, k, j \leqslant l \; P_k \neq P_{s_j} \text{ and } P_i, \\ \quad \sum_{P_l \in \mathcal{N}^{\text{in}}(P_k)} x_{s_j,i}^{l,k} = \sum_{P_l \in \mathcal{N}^{\text{out}}(P_k)} x_{s_j,i}^{k,l} \end{cases}$$

We start with $\mathcal{P}_{\text{source}} = \{P_{\text{source}}\}$. At each step of the algorithm, we select the node $P_m$ from $\mathcal{P} \setminus \mathcal{P}_{\text{source}}$ such that $\sum_{i \in \mathcal{P}_{\text{target}}} \sum_{P_j \in \mathcal{N}^{\text{in}}(P_m)} x_i^{j,m}$ is maximal in the solution of **MulticastMultiSource-UB**($\mathcal{P}, \mathcal{P}_{\text{target}}, \mathcal{P}_{\text{source}}$). Since the contribution of $P_m$ to the propagation of the message to the nodes of $\mathcal{P}_{\text{target}}$ is large, we can expect that adding it to the set of sources will decrease the multicast time. We stop adding new sources when no improvement in the multicast time can be found.

## 6. Tree-based heuristic

When targeting the problem of finding a good tree to multicast a message in a network, the most common goal is to optimize the resources consumed by the tree. Usually, a cost is associated to each communication link, and we aim at minimizing the cost of the multicast tree, that is the sum of the cost of its edges. This problem, called the *Minimum Steiner Tree*, is known to be NP-complete [5]. Several heuristics have been designed to approximate the solution of this problem, but none for the SERIES OF MULTICASTS problem. Indeed, in this case, the goal is to build up a spanning tree of minimal cost, containing all target nodes, where the cost of a tree is the maximum sum, over all nodes in the tree, of the cost of the outgoing edges of that node. Indeed, for each node, the sum of the weights of outgoing edges is the time needed to forward the message to all its children.

A classical heuristic to build a minimum Steiner tree is the Minimum Cost Path Heuristic (first introduced in [9] and adapted to directed networks in [8]). In this algorithm, a tree (consisting initially of the source node of the multicast) grows until it spans all the multicast target nodes: at each step, we determine which target is the closest to the current tree, and we add the minimum path from the current tree to this target into the new tree.

From this heuristic designed for the Minimum Steiner Tree problem, we can derive a heuristic to our problem, although the metric is not the same. Consider a platform graph $G = (V, E, c)$ and a set of target nodes $\mathcal{P}_{\text{target}} = \{P_{t_1}, P_{t_2}, \ldots, P_{t_{|T|}}\}$. We denote the multicast tree by *Tree*. The sketch of the algorithm is given in Figure 2.

We first choose the target node which is the closest, in the sense of our metric, to the current tree. This node, and the path to reach it, will be added to the tree. The only difficult part of the algorithm concerns the update of the cost of the edges (lines 13,14). On the resulting graph, the cost of any edge on the path from the source to any already added target node is equal to

```
MINIMUM-TREE(𝒫, 𝒫_target)
1:  c(i, j) ← c_{i,j};
2:  Tree ← ({P_source}, ∅);
3:  while 𝒫_target ≠ ∅; do
4:      NodeToAdd← ∅; path← ∅; cost← ∞;
5:      for each node P_t ∈ 𝒫_target do
6:          Compute the path P(P_t) from Tree to P_t
            such that c(P_t) = max_{(i,j)∈P(P_t)} c(i, j) is
            minimal
7:          if c(P_t) < cost then
8:              NodeToAdd← P_t
9:              path← P(P_t); cost← c(P_t);
10:     Add P(P_t) and P_t to the tree;
11:     𝒫_target ← 𝒫_target \ P_t
12:     for each edge (i, j) ∈ P(P_t) and all k such that
        (i, k) ∈ E do
13:         c(i, k) ← c(i, k) + c(i, j);
14:         c(i, j) ← 0;
```

**Figure 2. Tree-Based Heuristic**

zero: for the selection of the next target, choosing edges which have already been chosen in the multicast tree of the message will not incur any additional cost, since these edges already carry the message. To explain line 13, consider a graph where the path $P_{source} \rightarrow \cdots \rightarrow P_i \rightarrow P_j \rightarrow \cdots \rightarrow P_{t_1}$ already belongs to the multicast tree. Assume we want to add the new target $P_{t_2}$ to the multicast tree, using path $P_{source} \rightarrow \cdots \rightarrow P_i \rightarrow P_k \rightarrow \cdots \rightarrow P_{t_2}$. Since $P_{source}, \ldots, P_i$ already belong to the multicast tree, there is no additional cost for using the corresponding edges. However $P_i$ already spends $c(i, j)$ units of time sending data to $P_j$, so that $P_i$ needs $c(i, j) + c(i, k)$ units of time to send the message to both nodes $P_j$ and $P_k$. Thus, the potential cost induced by the edge $(i, k)$ must be updated as shown at line 13.

## 7. Experimental results

In this section, we compare the heuristics given in this paper using simulations on "realistic" topologies generated by Tiers, a random topology generator [3]. We perform the experiments for several numbers of nodes and targets. We use two types of configurations, one "small" platform type with 30 nodes and a "big" platform type with 65 nodes. For each type, 10 different platforms are generated using the same set of parameters. These platforms are used to test our heuristics with several densities of targets: the targets are randomly selected among the nodes belonging to the local area networks in the platforms. The results are presented on Figure 3. On these graphs, the name

of the heuristics have the following meaning:

**scatter** This corresponds to the upper bound for the multicast completion time, as if the messages sent to each node were different. Figures 3(a) and 3(c) present the ratio of the results of the heuristics over this value.

**lower bound** This corresponds to the lower bound for the multicast completion time, which is not always achievable. Figures 3(b) and 3(d) present the ratio of the results of the heuristics over this value.

**broadcast** This consists in broadcasting to the whole platform, as described in Section 5.1.3.

**MCPH** The tree-based heuristic, adapted from the Minimum Cost Path Heuristic, and described in Figure 2.

**Augm. MC, Red. MC** and **Multisource MC** are the LP based heuristics developed in Section 5

On Figure 3, we can see that the heuristics described in this paper are much closer to the lower bound than to the upper bound (scatter operation), except for the first experiment in a small platform, where the target nodes is reduced to one element. This is a very good result since the lower bound is not even guaranteed to be achievable.

The best results are given by the refined heuristics based on linear programming: **Augm. MC, Red. BC** and **Multisource MC**. However, the result of the tree-based heuristic **MCPH** is very close to their result, and its execution is shorter since it does not require to solve linear programs.

Surprisingly, we also notice that the result of the simple **broadcast** heuristic, included in our experiments for the sake of the comparison, performs well as soon as the density of targets among the local nodes is greater than 20%. To explain these good results, we recall that this heuristic does compute the optimal throughput of a broadcast on the whole platform. Moreover, the overall small size of the platform and the distribution of the target nodes leads to a platform graph such that there is almost one target node in each Local Area Network. That is a reason why the BROADCAST heuristic performs so well in this specific case.

## 8. Conclusion

In this paper, we have studied the problem of multicasting a series of messages on heterogeneous platforms. Our major objective was to maximize the

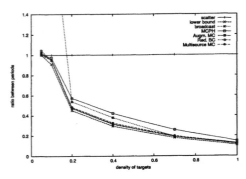

(a) Comparison with scatter on a small platform

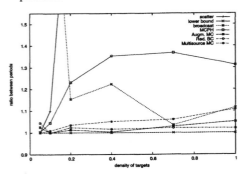

(b) Comparison with the lower bound on a small platform

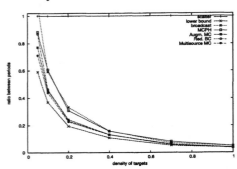

(c) Comparison with scatter on a big platform

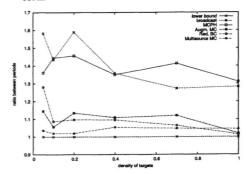

(d) Comparison with the lower bound on a big platform

**Figure 3. Comparison on the heuristics**

throughput that can be achieved in steady-state mode, when a large number of same-size multicasts are executed in a pipeline fashion. Achieving the best throughput may well require that the target platform is used in totality: we have shown that using a single spanning tree is not powerful enough. But the general problem is very difficult: we have proved that determining the optimal throughput is a NP-complete problem. This negative result demonstrates that pipelining multicasts is more difficult than pipelining broadcasts, scatters or reduce operations, for which optimal polynomial algorithms have been introduced [2, 6].

We have introduced several heuristics to solve the pipelined multicast problem, most based on linear programming, and one adapted from a Steiner tree heuristic. These heuristics perform very well: there are close to the theoretical lower bound.

## References

[1] O. Beaumont, A. Legrand, L. Marchal, and Y. Robert. Complexity results and heuristics for pipelined multicast operations on heterogeneous platforms. Technical report, LIP, ENS Lyon, France, Feb. 2004.

[2] O. Beaumont, A. Legrand, L. Marchal, and Y. Robert. Pipelining broadcasts on heterogeneous platforms. In *International Parallel and Distributed Processing Symposium IPDPS'2004*. IEEE Computer Society Press, 2004. Extended version available as Research Report of LIP, ENS Lyon, France, at www.ens-lyon.fr/LIP.

[3] K. L. Calvert, M. B. Doar, and E. W. Zegura. Modeling internet topology. *IEEE Communications Magazine*, 35(6):160–163, June 1997.

[4] C. Hanen and A. Munier. Cyclic scheduling on parallel processors: an overview. In P. Chrétienne, E. G. Coffman, J. K. Lenstra, and Z. Liu, editors, *Scheduling Theory and its Applications*, pages 193–226. John Wiley & Sons, 1994.

[5] R. M. Karp. Reducibility among combinatorial problems. In R. E. Miller and J. W. Thatcher, editors, *Complexity of Computer Computations*, pages 85–103, NY, 1972. Plenum Press.

[6] A. Legrand, L. Marchal, and Y. Robert. Optimizing the steady-state throughput of scatter and reduce operations on heterogeneous platforms. In *APDCM'2004, 6th Workshop on Advances in Parallel and Distributed Computational Models*. IEEE Computer Society Press, 2004.

[7] X. Lin and L. Ni. Multicast communication in multicomputer networks. *IEEE Trans. Parallel Distributed Systems*, 4(10):1105–1117, 1993.

[8] S. Ramanathan. Multicast tree generation in networks with asymmetric links. *IEEE/ACM Transactions on Networking*, 4(4):558–568, 1996.

[9] H. Takashami and A. Matsuyama. An approximate solution for the steiner tree problem in graphs. *Intl. J. Math Educ. in Sci. and Technol.*, 14(1):15–23, 1983.

# Efficient and Scalable All-to-All Personalized Exchange
## for InfiniBand-based Clusters*

Sayantan Sur      Hyun-Wook Jin      Dhabaleswar K. Panda

Computer and Information Science,
The Ohio State University,
Columbus, OH 43210
{surs,jinhy,panda}@cis.ohio-state.edu

## Abstract

*The All-to-All Personalized Exchange is the most dense collective communication function offered by the MPI specification. The operation involves every process sending a different message to all other participating processes. This collective operation is essential for many parallel scientific applications. With increasing system and message sizes, it becomes challenging to offer a fast, scalable and efficient implementation of this operation. InfiniBand is an emerging modern interconnect. It offers very low latency, high bandwidth and one-sided operations like RDMA write. Its advanced features like RDMA write gather allow us to design and implement All-to-all algorithms much more efficiently than in the past. Our aim in this paper is to design efficient and scalable implementations of traditional personalized exchange algorithms. In this paper we present two novel approaches towards designing All-to-all algorithms for short and long messages respectively. The Hypercube RDMA Write Gather and Direct Eager schemes effectively leverage the RDMA and RDMA with Write gather mechanisms offered by InfiniBand. Performance evaluation of our design and implementation reveals that it is able to reduce the All-to-All communication time by upto a factor of 3.07 for 32 byte messages on a 16 node InfiniBand cluster. Our analytical models suggest that the proposed designs will perform 64% better on InfiniBand clusters with 1024 nodes for 4k message size.*

## 1  Introduction

Cluster based computing systems are becoming popular for a wide range of scientific applications, owing to their cost-effectiveness. These systems are typically built from commodity PCs connected with high speed Local Area Networks (LANs) or System Area Networks (SANs). A majority of these scientific applications are written on top of the Message Passing Interface (MPI) [13, 4]. MPI provides both *point-to-point* and *collective* communication functions. Many parallel applications use collective communication functions to communicate either with all partic-

ipating processes or a subset of them. Many applications, such as IS and FT in the NAS Parallel Benchmark suite [2], almost use collective operations exclusively for communication. Thus, providing high performance and scalable collective communication support is critical for cluster based systems. One of the most important collectives is MPI_Alltoall. In MPI_Alltoall, every process sends distinct data to each of the other processes. As the number of processes participating in the MPI_Alltoall or the message sizes becomes larger, the All-to-All communication cost rapidly increases. Thus, it is a challenge to provide an efficient design and implementation for this collective. In this paper we focus on the design and implmentation issues regarding MPI_Alltoall for InfiniBand-based Clusters.

The current implementation [17] of the MPI collective functions, including MPI_Alltoall, is based on MPI level point-to-point operations. Thus, the collective operations are abstracted onto point-to-point primitives. This approach cannot fully utilize the advanced features offered by contemporary interconnects. There are several modern network interconnects that provide very low latency (less that $7\mu s$) and high bandwidth (in the order of 10.0Gbps) for cluster based systems. Two of the leading products are Myrinet [3] and Quadrics [12]. Recently InfiniBand [1] has entered the high performance computing market. InfiniBand offers a new model of data transport based on memory semantics. This operation is called *Remote Direct Memory Access* (RDMA). It allows transfer of data directly between user level buffers on remote nodes without the active participation of the receiver. This is a one-sided operation that does not incur a software overhead at the remote side. InfiniBand also allows Gather/Scatter RDMA operations.

In addition, the current MPI implementation [17] of MPI_Alltoall considers only the message size to decide the algorithm being used. However, we note that the total time taken for the All-to-All communication depends on two parameters - the message size and the number of processes participating in the exchange.

In this paper, we aim to provide answers to the following questions :

1. Can we identify the performance bottlenecks for the

---
*This research is supported in part by Department of Energy's grant #DE-FC02-01ER25506, National Science Foundation's grants #CCR-0204429 and #CCR-0311542 and by the Post-doctoral Fellowship Program of Korea Science and Engineering Foundation (KOSEF).

All-to-All communication operation?

2. Can we propose new designs so as to fully utilize the benefits of RDMA, Gather/Scatter RDMA and other features of InfiniBand?

3. Can we design a scalable All-to-all implementation that performs the best for any given message and system size?

This paper shows that replacing the point-to-point communication calls in the collective operations with faster lower-level primitives can provide significant performance gains. Our approach makes it possible to reduce the number of data copies, number of memory registration operations and rendezvous protocol overheads. We propose a Hypercube RDMA Write-Gather based scheme (HRWG) for optimizing the All-to-All communication time for small messages and a Direct Eager scheme (DE) for achieving better performance for larger messages. We provide performance evaluation on a 16 node InfiniBand cluster. We also provide analytical models to evaluate the performance of our design and implementation on large scale clusters.

The designs for MPI_Alltoall were implemented and integrated into the MVAPICH [10] implementation of MPI over InfiniBand. MVAPICH is an implementation of Abstract Device Interface (ADI) for MPICH [5]. MVAPICH is based on MVICH [9]. Compared to the current MPI_Alltoall implementation, our new designs demonstrate improvement in latency by a factor of upto 3.07 on a 16 node cluster. In addition, our analytical models show a benefit of upto 64% for an All-to-All exchange in a 1k node cluster for 4k message size.

The rest of the paper is organized as follows: In section 2, we provide an overview of the InfiniBand architecture. In section 3, we provide background on MPI_Alltoall and existing algorithms. In section 4, we describe the limitations of implementing collective operations using MPI level point-to-point functions. In section 5, we propose our designs for RDMA based MPI_Alltoall. We evaluate our designs using experiments and analytical models in section 6. Conclusions and future research directions are presented in Section 7.

## 2  InfiniBand Architecture Overview

The InfiniBand Architecture [1] defines a switched network fabric for interconnecting processing nodes and I/O nodes. It provides a communication and management infrastructure for inter-processor communication and I/O. In an InfiniBand network, processing nodes and I/O nodes are connected to the fabric by Channel Adapters (CA). Channel Adapters usually have programmable DMA engines with protection features.

InfiniBand Architecture supports both channel semantics and memory semantics. In channel semantics, send/receive operations are used for communication. In memory semantics, InfiniBand provides Remote Direct Memory Access (RDMA) operations, including RDMA write and RDMA read. RDMA operations are one-sided and do not incur software overhead at the remote side. Write Gather and

Read Scatter are supported in RDMA operations. RDMA write operation can gather multiple data segments together and write all data into a contiguous buffer at the receiver end. Gather/scatter features are very useful to transfer non-contiguous data. The Gather/Scatter facility not only reduces the startup costs, but also increases network utilization. RDMA Write with Immediate data is also supported. With Immediate data, a RDMA Write operation consumes a receive descriptor and then can generate a completion entry to notify the remote node of the completion of the RDMA Write operation.

## 3  Overview of MPI_Alltoall and Existing Algorithms

In this section, we provide a brief overview of the MPI_Alltoall collective function. We also describe the existing algorithms used in implementing MPI_Alltoall and their cost models.

### 3.1  MPI_Alltoall Overview

MPI supports both point-to-point and collective communication functions. MPI_Alltoall is a commonly used collective for achieving a complete exchange of data among all participating processes. MPI_Alltoall is a blocking operation. The call does not return until the communication buffer can be reused. MPI_Alltoall is used when all the processes have a fixed length of message to send to each of the other processes. The $j$th block of data sent from process $i$ is received by process $j$ and placed in the $i$th block of the receive buffer.

### 3.2  Existing Algorithms

In this section we provide an overview of existing algorithms and their cost models.

#### 3.2.1  Hypercube / Combining Algorithm

A hypercube is a multidimensional mesh of nodes with exactly two nodes in each dimension. A $d$-dimensional hypercube consists of $p = 2^d$ nodes. The All-to-All personalized communication algorithm for a $p$-node hypercube with store-forward routing is an extension of the two-dimensional mesh algorithm to $\log p$ steps [8]. Pairs of nodes exchange data in a different dimension in each step. In a $p$ node hypercube, there are a set of $p/2$ links in the same dimension connecting two subcubes of $p/2$ nodes each. At any stage in All-to-All personalized communication, every node holds $p$ packets of $m$ bytes each. While communicating in a particular dimension, every node sends $p/2$ of these packets (consolidated as one message, or as multiple messages). Thus, $mp/2$ bytes of data are exchanged along the bidirectional channels in each of the $\log p$ iterations. The resulting total communication time is:

$$T_{hypercube} = (t_s + 1/2 t_w mp) \log p \qquad (1)$$

Where,

$t_s$ = Message startup time, $t_w$ = Time to transfer one byte, $m$ = Message size in bytes, and $p$ = Number of processes.

### 3.2.2 Direct Virtual Ring

The direct algorithm is a straightforward way to exchange messages among all the processes. It assumes that all the processes have direct links connecting them. The processes are arranged in a virtual ring. Each process then sends its message to its neighbor. To avoid all the processes from sending to a single destination, the destinations are scattered among all of them, by using a modulus operation. Process $rank$ sends its message for process $(rank+i)\%p$, $\forall i, (0 \leq i \leq p)$. So, at every step, each process sends $m$ bytes of data and it does it for $(p-1)$ steps [8]. Thus, the total time for an All-to-All exchange is:

$$T_{direct-ring} = (p-1)t_s + t_w m(p-1) \qquad (2)$$

## 4 Limitations of Current MPI_Alltoall

In this section we analyze in detail, the problems associated with implementing the MPI_Alltoall collective by using MPI level point-to-point communication functions. The MPI point-to-point communication calls pass through many software layers before the actual communication takes place.

### 4.1 Small Messages

The All-to-All communication for small messages is often implemented by using a combining algorithm like Hypercube or Recursive Doubling. The current implementation of MPI_Alltoall is based on Recursive Doubling. In order to use combining algorithms, it is required to pack the messages into contiguous buffers. This necessitates one copy from the user buffer to the MPI layer buffer. In addition, there is one more copy induced by the implementation of the MPI send and receives. This is usually done to avoid on-the-fly memory registration and address exchange costs [11]. So, in total, there are four copies for the transfer of a single message across as shown in Figure 1. The copy

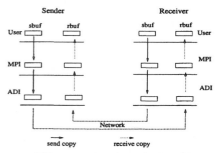

**Figure 1. MPI_Alltoall Message Path for Small Messages in current MPI implementation**

cost rises rapidly as the message size and the system size increase. This means that combining algorithms like Hypercube or Recursive Doubling cannot be efficiently implemented using MPI sends and receives.

### 4.2 Large Messages

In the current implementation of MVAPICH, the MPI point-to-point communication for large messages undergoes a *rendezvous* protocol as shown in Figure 2. The

sender registers the application buffer and sends a *rendezvous_start* message to the receiver. The receiver then tries to register the application receive buffer and if successful, sends a *rendezvous_ok* message to the sender along with the virtual address and the memory handle of the buffer. The sender then sends the data, followed by an ACK. On current generation InfiniBand hardware, the ad-

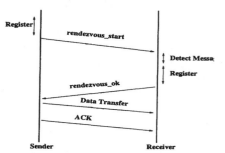

**Figure 2. The Rendezvous Protocol**

dress exchange phase costs around $10\mu s$. The sender cannot send the message until the receiver replies back to the sender with the virtual address and memory handles. When implementing high communication density collectives like MPI_Alltoall, this presents a critical *bottleneck* during each step of the collective algorithm. Thus, as the system size increases, the total cost due to the *rendezvous* protocol increases linearly. The point-to-point implementation requires individual memory registration of the sender and recieve buffer per message. In collective communication, often times one contiguous buffer is used as the sender buffer. The individual messages are specified as offsets from the beginning of this buffer. The multiple registration operations can be coalesced into one for improving performance. However, if the collectives are implemented using MPI point-to-point functions, registration coalescing is no longer possible.

### 4.3 Performance Limitations of the Current Implementation

Figure 3 shows the performance of the current MVAPICH implementation for MPI_Alltoall exchange for 4, 8 and 16 nodes. We observe that with increasing system and message size the total cost of the All-to-All communication increases sharply.

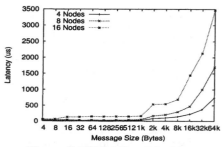

**Figure 3. MPI_Alltoall Latency**

# 5 Proposed RDMA based MPI_Alltoall Design

In this section we will take a detailed look into our designs, which fully utilize the RDMA Write and RDMA Write with gather for implementing MPI_Alltoall. In order to fully utilize the features provided by InfiniBand, we directly implement the collective operations on the InfiniBand Verbs Layer. Also, by directly implementing the collectives over the Verbs layer, we avoid software overheads such as copying and multiple registrations. The proposed implementation path is shown in Figure 4. It should be noted that MVAPICH uses the InfiniBand reliable connection transport. Since the network guarantees reliable delivery, we do not have to explicitly take into account message losses.

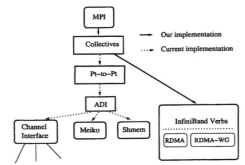

**Figure 4. Implementation path for All-to-all**

## 5.1 RDMA Based Design Issues

Before we can directly utilize the benefits provided by RDMA for implementing MPI_Alltoall, a few difficulties must be addressed:

**Memory Registration and Address Exchange:** There can be two design choices, either we copy over the message at the beginning of the All-to-All communication to specific pre-registered buffers, or we can perform an address exchange after registering both sender and receiver buffers. The registration operation is costly and is not feasible for smaller message sizes. Moreover, on current generation InfiniBand hardware, the address exchange phase costs around $10\mu s$. On the other hand, the copy-based approach avoids on-the-fly registration and address exchange costs. However, the cost for copying large sized buffers can be prohibitively high.

**Message Arrival Detection:** The RDMA Write operation in InfiniBand is totally transparent to the receiver process. The only way the receiver process can make out whether data has really arrived in the buffers is by polling the contents of a specific pre-defined memory location. For achieving this, there needs to be a persistent association of buffers at the sender and receiver end. Achieving a persistent association is relatively simple when pre-registered buffers are used. All the processes can implicitly decide on start and end buffer locations. Prior to the All-to-All communication the processes can reset the last bytes of the persistent

buffers. Marking the completion of a RDMA write for direct application buffers, which are registered on-the-fly, is impossible using the earlier technique. Here, there is no unique value of the memory location that the MPI implementation can poll on. The application may choose to send any data value of its choice. Usually, in such a case, completion of a RDMA write operation can only be determined by using an explicit ack. Hence, specific buffers need to be provided for collecting acks.

## 5.2 Design for Small Messages with HRWG scheme

For small messages, the message transfer startup time dominates the total cost of the operation. The message transfer startup time for the Hypercube algorithm is $t_s \log p$ and for that of the Direct Virtual Ring algorithm is $t_s(p-1)$. Currently, InfiniBand has very high bandwidth availability (850 MB/s). Thus the cost of transferring the data $t_w m$ for a small message is comparably less. So, our natural choice for smaller messages is the Hypercube algorithm. We implement the Hypercube algorithm using the RDMA Write Gather feature provided by InfiniBand. Hence, we call this scheme as HRWG.

Now we look closely at the startup time cost $t_s$. There are various costs associated with message startup based on the implementation mechanism. If we decide to have a zero copy implementation, then the address exchange phase will dominate the message startup time. Also, we would have to pay on-the-fly registration cost. This can be comparably costlier than copying the data over to a pre-registered buffer. Hence, we choose a copy-based approach, implementing the Hypercube algorithm for small message sizes. However, our copy-based mechanism has only two data copies bypassing the MPI-level buffer in Figure 1 instead of the four copies in the point-to-point based implementation.

**Collective Buffer Management:** We implement a buffer management scheme for the copy-based approach. In order to detect the arrival of an incoming message, we use memory polling. In our implementation, the collective communication buffer is created during the communicator initialization time. All processes in the communicator need to exchange addresses and memory handles for remote buffers. The collective communication buffer can then be divided into several parts. This can be done implicitly by all processes. There are two divisions of the buffer for supporting back-to-back collective calls. Also, we set up persistent associations with our $\log p$ neighbors of the hypercube. Figure 5 shows how these buffers are arranged.

The collective buffer is zeroed at the beginning. At the start of one All-to-All operation, the *tail* flags of the other buffer (for all of the $\log p$ peers) are cleared. However, we need to make sure that the flag cannot be set before the data is delivered. And to do this, we need to use some knowledge about the implementation of the InfiniBand hardware. On our current InfiniBand hardware, data is delivered in order (the last byte is written last). Thus, the arrival of the tail flag

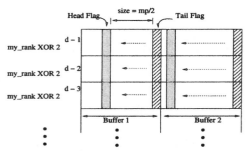

**Figure 5. Bufferring scheme for All-to-all**

does ensure that the entire message has arrived.

If a process is involved in an All-to-All operation and is still waiting for its completion, another process might have entered into a successive, back-to-back All-to-All. We must guarantee that the buffer space provided for an All-to-All operation will not be over-written until it is safe to do so. We observe that providing buffering for two back-to-back All-to-Alls is sufficient to make such a gurantee.

**Efficient Message Forwarding:** For implementing the Hypercube algorithm, we have to keep track of the buffers in transit and forward them correctly to the next dimension across which communication will take place. We can keep track of the buffers to send, by simply observing a pattern of communication within the hypercube. At every step of communication in the hypercube, a process sends $p/2$ messages. The number of contiguous buffers from the received buffer-pool per peer is, $2^{(d-(d-i))}$, $\forall i$ in 0 to $(d-1)$. The buffer to be forwarded can be easily found out by maintaining a set of pointers at the middle of the receive buffers. The number of *middle* pointers is equal to the number of contiguous buffers to be forwarded from the persistent buffer associated with that dimension. After each iteration, the middle pointers can be moved either backwards or forwards depending on whether the rank of the destination process is greater than the rank of the sending process and vice-versa. The amount of data to be sent per *middle* pointer is recursively halved. Figure 6 gives a detailed view of how the *middle* pointers are managed.

Collective Buffer of process 0 of 16 processes.

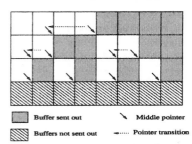

**Figure 6. Efficient message forwarding**

**RDMA Transfer Mechanisms:** For transferring the buffers over the network, two different methods can be adopted. We can either transmit the buffer as one single RDMA or we can send the buffers individually using

multiple RDMA writes. By using RDMA with gather list, we can reduce the message startup time. On the other hand by using multiple RDMAs we can achieve flexibility in the buffer management. Figure 7 [11] shows the performance of one RDMA Write versus RDMA write-gather with two segments and two RDMAs for small messages. We clearly note that the startup costs associated with RDMA write gather are comparably lower than using back-to-back RDMA Writes. Hence, we choose the RDMA with gather method for transferring small messages.

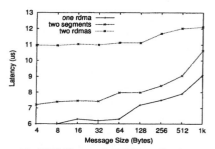

**Figure 7. RDMA and RDMA Gather Performance**

### 5.3 Design for Large messages with Direct Eager (DE) scheme

For large messages, the network latency is the major factor in determining the total time taken by the All-to-All operation. Hence, we choose the Direct virtual Ring based algorithm for implementing `MPI_Alltoall`. We implement the Direct virtual Ring based algorithm in an eager manner. We call our scheme Direct Eager (DE). We must consider message startup costs if we want to achieve a zero-copy implementation. In order to achieve zero copy, we have to :

- Register the user buffer
- Exchange addresses of the user buffer
- Mark the completion with an explicit ack

In order to avoid registering parts of the buffer multiple times, as done by the MPI point-to-point based implementation, we register the entire send buffer as one single buffer. This avoids generating unnecessary entries in the registration cache and needlessly filling it up. For long running applications which do a lot of message-passing, this is critical, so as to minimize the cache miss rate. Now, we take a look at the overall latency for the All-to-All operation for the Direct virtual ring based algorithm:

$$T_{direct-ring} = (2t_{pci}m + t_{overhead})(p-1)+$$

$$(t_{link} + t_{pci})m + (p-1)t_{rndz} \quad (3)$$

Where,

$t_{post}$ = Time to post address information, $t_{pci}$ = Time to transfer one byte over PCI bus, $t_{overhead}$ = Per packet overhead, $t_{link}$ = Time to transfer one byte over a link, and $t_{rndz}$ = Rendezvous exchange cost.

In this performance model, we reflect the fact that multiple RDMAs are in fact serialized on the local PCI bus. For calculating the per packet overhead we use the time taken to transfer a zero byte message. In addition, for the operation startup cost, we take into account the transfer cost of one message to the remote host. Subsequent messages are parallelized with other operations.

In addition to multiple memory registrations, the *rendezvous* protocol presents a bottleneck at each of the $(p-1)$ steps of the Direct virtual algorithm. Each message transfer has to be preceded by interaction of both sender and receiver. This takes away the advantage of RDMA, in that it is no longer truly one sided. The entire `MPI_Alltoall` is then bottlenecked.

Instead, we adopted a new *Direct Eager* mechanism for implementing the All-to-All operation. In this new scheme, every process sends its receive buffer address to its next nearest neighbor, then the next one and so on in a ring-like manner. That is, process $rank$ sends its address to $(rank + i)\%p, \forall i(0 \leq i \leq p)$. This phase is totally network parallelized as the addresses and memory handles are RDMA-ed to pre-registered buffers. Then, process $rank$ waits for address from process $(rank + p - 1 - i)\%p$, $\forall i(0 \leq i \leq p)$. We note that the time spent waiting for the first address is almost negligible since the process $i$ sends address to $j$ first and $j$ sends data to $i$ first. Hence, we name our scheme as *Direct Eager*.

With this mechanism, the cost for the entire All-to-All operation is:

$$T_{direct-eager} = t_{post}(p-1) + (2t_{pci}m + t_{overhead})(p-1) +$$

$$(t_{link} + t_{pci})m \qquad (4)$$

Where,

$t_{post}$ = Time to post address information.

## 6 Performance Evaluation

In this section, we evaluate performance of our All-to-All communication. We conducted our experiments on a 16 node cluster. The cluster consists of 8 each of two different types of machines, I and II.

- I : SuperMicro SUPER P4DL6 node. Dual Intel Xeon 2.4 GHz processors, 512 KB L2 cache, 512 MB memory, PCI-X 64-bit 133 MHz bus.
- II : SuperMicro SUPER X5DL8-GG node. Dual Intel Xeon 3.0 GHz processors, 512 KB L2 cache, 1 GB memory, PCI-X 64-bit 133 MHz bus.

All the machines had Mellanox InfiniHost MT23108 DualPort 4x HCAs. The nodes are connected using the Mellanox InfiniScale 24 port switch MTS 2400. The Linux kernel version used was 2.4.22smp. The InfiniHost SDK version is 3.0.1 and HCA firmware version is 3.0.1. It is to be noted that performance numbers for 4 and 8 nodes are on machines II.

The All-to-All latency was obtained by executing `MPI_Alltoall` 1000 times with the same buffer being used for communication. The average of the latencies from all the nodes was calculated. The calls to `MPI_Alltoall` were synchronized in each iteration using `MPI_Barrier`.

### 6.1 Evaluation for Small Messages

We implemented the Hypercube algorithm (HRWG) for performing the All-to-All communication for small messages. Figure 8 compares the performance of the current implementation and the proposed scheme. We observe that the proposed scheme (HRWG) has a 3.07 factor of improvement over the current implementation for 32 byte message size. Figure 9 shows the scalability of our implementation. We note that with increasing system size, it is indeed better to have a combining algorithm than a naive point-to-point based implementation.

### 6.2 Evaluation for Larger Messages

For medium and large messages we implement the Direct virtual Ring based algorithm with the Direct Eager(DE) mechanism. The DE mechanism performs better than the current implementation. Figures 10 and 11 show the performance of our implementation compared to the current one. We note that DE performs better for medium sized messages. This is mainly because the total cost for *rendezvous* is comparable to that of the message transfer latency. Figures 12 and 13 show the scalability of our designs. It is to be noted that the benefits offerred by the DE scheme increase as the number of processes increase.

### 6.3 Performance Estimation for Large Systems

In this section, we try to extrapolate the performance of our DE mechanism to find out how much performance improvement we can expect over larger scale clusters.

As shown in Equations (3) and (4), the DE mechanism avoids adding a cost of rendezvous that is linear according to the number of processes. This will show performance improvement when the All-to-All communication happens over a large cluster. In order to carry out performance estimation for large systems, we assumed the following: current generation nodes with PCI-X 64 bit 133 MHz interface, a non-blocking network with fat tree topology and InfiniBand 4X links. On such systems the values of the parameters in Equations (3) and (4) are: $t_{post} = 2\ \mu s$, $t_{pci} = 0.00093985\ \mu s$, $t_{overhead} = 5.8\ \mu s$, $t_{link} = 0.000745058\ \mu s$ and $t_{rndz} = 10\ \mu s$.

Figure 14 shows the comparison of our model with real data collected on our InfiniBand cluster I. It is to be noted that the error from the real experimental data is quite small.

Figure 15 shows the performance estimation. We observe a performance benefit of 64% for All-to-all communication between 1k nodes with 4k message size.

## 7 Related Work

Traditionally, study of algorithms for supporting efficient All-to-All communication has been an active area of research [7, 8]. Researchers have focused on a variety of algorithms, mainly based on the physical topology and architecture of highly parallel supercomputers [18, 16]. Recent research for clusters suggests that some algorithms perform better than others for a given message size than others and vice-versa [14, 6, 17]. However, none of these focus on clusters equipped with InfiniBand.

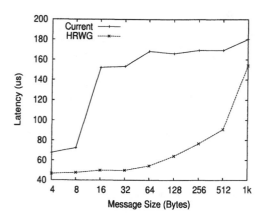

**Figure 8. Small Messages on 16 nodes**

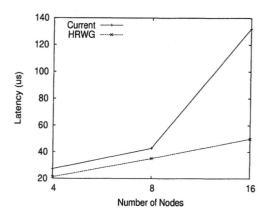

**Figure 9. 32 byte Message Scalability**

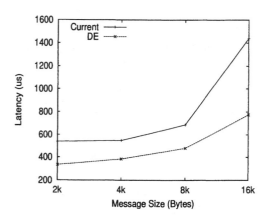

**Figure 10. Medium Messages (16 nodes)**

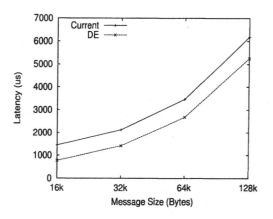

**Figure 11. Large Messages (16 nodes)**

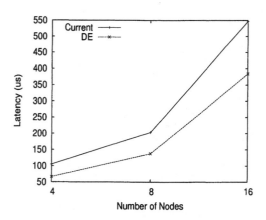

**Figure 12. Large Messages (4k) Scalability**

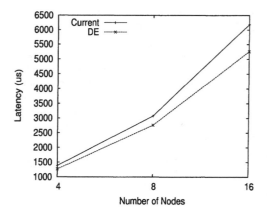

**Figure 13. Large Messages (128k) Scalability**

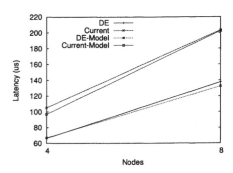

**Figure 14. Comparison of our Performance Model with Experimental Results**

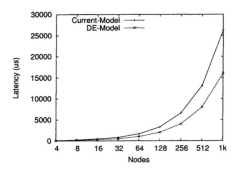

**Figure 15. Performance estimation for 4k message among 1k nodes**

## 8 Conclusions and Future Work

In this paper, we presented new designs to take advantage of the advanced features offered by InfiniBand in order to achieve scalable and efficient implementation of the `MPI_Alltoall` collective. We proposed that the implementation of collectives be done directly on the InfiniBand Verbs Interface rather than using MPI level point-to-point functions. We evaluated in detail why MPI send receive calls are a hindrance to achieving good performance from collective operations. We detailed our design challenges and proposed two different schemes for small and large messages, HRWG and DE respectively. Our performance evaluation on a 16 node cluster shows that we can get an improvement of upto a factor of 3.07 for 32 byte messages. We studied the analytical models of our implementation, and our investigation shows that for a 1k node cluster, we can get a performance improvement of upto 64% for 4k messages. We plan to continue our work in this direction. In this work we have focused on fully utilizing the RDMA and RDMA Write Gather for efficiently implementing `MPI_Alltoall`. We plan to explore the use of InfiniBand Hardware Multicast and Atomic operations for furthur improving our designs. Also, we plan to have an efficient `MPI_Alltoall` implementation for clusters equipped with SMP nodes. We intend to carry out application level evaluation of our designs on large scale clusters. We will continue to update our performance numbers as newer InfiniBand hardware and software are released. For a more updated version please refer to [15].

## References

[1] InfiniBand Trade Association. Infiniband architecture specification. Release 1.0, October 2000.

[2] D. H. Bailey, E. Barszcz, J. T. Barton, D. S. Browning, R. L. Carter, D. Dagum, R. A. Fatoohi, P. O. Frederickson, T. A. Lasinski, R. S. Schreiber, H. D. Simon, V. Venkatakrishnan, and S. K. Weeratunga. The NAS parallel benchmarks. volume 5, pages 63–73, Fall 1991.

[3] N. J. Boden, D. Cohen, R. E. Felderman, A. E. Kulawik, C. L. Seitz, J. N. Seizovic, and W. Su. Myrinet: A gigabit-per-second local area network. February 1995.

[4] W. Gropp, E. Lusk, N. Doss, and A. Skjellum. A high performance, portable implementation of the mpi message passing interface. In *Parallel Computing*, 1996.

[5] W. Gropp, E. Lusk, and A. Skjellum. MPICH-a portable implementation of MPI. http://www-unix.mcs.anl.gov/mpi/mpich/.

[6] M. Jacunski, P. Sadayappan, and D. K. Panda. All-to-all broadcast on switch based clusters of workstations. In *IPPS/SPDP*, 1999.

[7] S. Lennart Johnsson and C. T. Ho. Optimum broadcasting and personalized communication in hypercubes. *IEEE Transactions on Computers*, 38(9), September 1989.

[8] V. Kumar, A. Grama, A. Gupta, and G. Karypis. *Introduction to Parallel Computing : Design and Analysis of Algorithms*. Addison Wesley / Benjamin Cummings, 1993.

[9] Lawrence Berkeley National Laboratory. MVICH: MPI for Virtual Interface Architecture. http://www.nersc.gov/research/FTG/mvich/index.html.

[10] Network-Based Computing Laboratory. MVAPICH: MPI for InfiniBand on VAPI layer. http://nowlab.cis.ohio-state.edu/projects/mpi-iba/index.html, January 2004.

[11] J. Liu, J. Wu, S. P. Kini, P. Wyckoff, and D. K. Panda. High Performance RDMA-Based MPI Implementation over InfiniBand. In *International Conference on Supercomputing*, 2003.

[12] F. Petrini, W. Feng, A. Hoisie, S. Coll, and E. Frachtenberg. The quadrics network: High performance clustering technology. *IEEE Micro*, 2002.

[13] M. Snir, S. Otto, S. Huss-Lederman, D. Walker, and J. Dongarra. *MPI-The Complete Reference, Volume 1 - The MPI-1 Core, 2nd Edition*. The MIT Press, 1998.

[14] N. S. Sundar, D. N. Jayasimha, D. K. Panda, and P. Sadayappan. Hybrid algorithms for complete exchange in 2-d meshes. *IEEE Transactions on Computers*, 12(12), December 2001.

[15] S. Sur, H-W. Jin, and D. K. Panda. Efficient and scalable All-to-all personalized exchange for InfiniBand-based clusters. Technical report, Ohio State University, 2004.

[16] R. Thakur and A. Choudhary. All-to-all communication on meshes with wormhole routing. In *IPPS*, 1994.

[17] R. Thakur and W. Gropp. Improving the performance of collective operations in MPICH. In *Euro PVM/MPI conference*, 2003.

[18] Y. Yang and J. Wang. Efficient all-to-all broadcast in all-port mesh and torus networks. In *HPCA*, 99.

# Session 5A:
# Architecture II

# SPAL: A Speedy Packet Lookup Technique for High-Performance Routers

**Nian-Feng Tzeng**
Center for Advanced Computer Studies
University of Louisiana at Lafayette
Lafayette, Louisiana 70504, U.S.A.
tzeng@cacs.louisiana.edu

## Abstract

*This work introduces and evaluates a technique for speedy packet lookups, called SPAL, in high-performance routers, realized by fragmenting the BGP routing table into subsets. Such a router contains multiple line cards (LCs), each of which is equipped with a forwarding engine (FE) to perform table lookups locally based on its forwarding table (which is a fragmented subset). The number of table entries in each FE drops as the number of LCs in a router grows. This reduction in the forwarding table size drastically lowers the amount of SRAM (e.g., L3 data cache) required in each LC to hold the trie constructed according to the matching algorithm. SPAL calls for caching the lookup result of a given IP address at its home LC (denoted by $LC_{ho}$, using the LR-cache), such that the result can satisfy the lookup requests for the same address from not only $LC_{ho}$ but also other LCs quickly, when the switching fabric for interconnecting LCs has a low latency. Lookup results obtained from remote LCs are also held in the LR-cache of a local LC. Our trace-driven simulation reveals that SPAL indeed leads to substantial improvement in mean lookup performance. SPAL may possibly shorten the worst-case lookup time (thanks to fewer memory accesses during longest-prefix matching search) when compared with a current router without partitioning the routing table. It takes no specific traffic into consideration when selecting the partitioning bits, promising good scalability and a small mean lookup time per packet.*

## 1. Introduction

Rapid expansion of the Internet leads to sustained growth in the BGP routing tables held at backbone routers, and the table growth rate has expedited radically for the past two years [4], with certain routing tables now involving more than 120K prefixes (see AS1221, AS4637, AS6447 in [4]). As search in routing and forwarding tables is complex, usually based on *longest prefix matching search* to arrive at the most *specific* search result for a given IP address, prefixes are usually organized as a tree-like structure called a *trie*, with its nodes either corresponding to prefixes or forming paths to prefixes, for effective search. It is highly desirable to fit the trie within static RAM (SRAM) for good search performance, requiring a rather large amount of SRAM for the forwarding engine (FE) at each line card (LC), in

the form of an L3 data cache. When IPv6 addressing is dealt with, the SRAM amount needed is likely to be several times higher, further in need of strategies for effectively containing the SRAM size.

Most commercial backbone routers carry out table lookups independently and concurrently at multiple FEs situated in different LCs, each of which houses one or multiple ports for external links to terminate. To improve forwarding performance required by high-speed links operating up to the OC-768 (40 Gbps) rate in a router, one may employ a variety of approaches like enhanced routing/forwarding table lookup algorithms [7, 8, 12], hardware-based lookup designs [10], and hardware-assisted forwarding lookups [5, 16]. This work deals with a technique for accelerating packet lookups in a high-performance router with multiple LCs, each of which has one FE to carry out table lookups (see Fig. 1).

The latency of a small crossbar switch has fallen considerably, resulting from a steady decline in the switching time of crossbars. Recent crossbars enjoy consistently low latencies, as evidenced by the Pericom's P15X1018 crossbar switch, which features 10 ports (of 18-bit width each) running at 133 MHz [13]. One may expect to see a future crossbar with its switching time down to a few *ns*. Such crossbar switches make it possible to build a multistage-based switching fabric for interconnecting a moderate number of LCs in a router, with packet latency over the fabric being 10 *ns* or less.

The opportunity offered by fast switched crossbars plus ever expanding BGP routing tables at backbone routers with a push to handle IPv6 addressing motivates this study on fragmenting a routing table into subsets of roughly equal sizes for LCs, so that the number of prefixes maintained in each forwarding table is a small fraction of the number of total prefixes kept in the routing table. Fragmentation is based on selected bit positions of prefixes in the routing table, and most prefixes are in single partitions after fragmentation. Each partition constitutes a forwarding table housed at one LC. The number of partitions (i.e., LCs) can be of any integer, not necessarily a power of 2. A small on-chip cache is introduced to each LC for holding the lookup results of destination addresses of the packets arriving at the LC. Caching lookup results permits subsequent lookup requests for same addresses to be satisfied immediately without resorting to (time-consuming) prefix matching by FEs (situated at either local LCs or remote ones). This caching takes merely 4K blocks at each LC to effectively reduce both traffic over the switching fabric and the load

This work was support in part by NSF under Grants EIA-9871315 and CCR-0105529.

of requests for address lookups at each FE. Together, a hardware-assisted design for speedy packet lookups, called SPAL, is obtained for high-performance routers, with four salient features. First, SPAL drastically lowers the size of the trie (due to few prefixes) at each LC, making it possible to hold the whole trie (or a large portion of it) in the L3 data cache of the network processor at the LC for much faster matching algorithm execution. Second, the lookup result of an IP address cached at its home LC not only can satisfy forthcoming lookup requests from the home LC swiftly, but also can reply to the lookup requests from other LCs more quickly over a low-latency switching fabric than those LCs would otherwise have carried out prefix matching search themselves individually (taking hundreds of *ns*). Third, the cache introduced to an LC may also keep the lookup results obtained from other LCs (called remote LCs), so that requests for looking up same destination addresses of subsequent packets arriving at the LC can be satisfied locally more quickly, cutting down traffic over the switching fabric and reducing the request loads of those remote LCs. Finally, SPAL not only makes a router exhibit quicker mean lookups but also possibly shortens the worst-case lookup time as well.

The LR-cache equipped in each LC is on the same chip as the FIL (fabric interface logics, see Fig. 1), but it need not be very large to harvest almost full potential gains in performance; our extensive simulation studies have indicated that a cache with some 4K blocks is usually adequate. Therefore, SPAL is an effective hardware-assisted design for fast packet lookups in a router, usually reducing its overall SRAM at each LC (including the off-chip L3 data cache plus the LR-cache introduced to hold lookup results) tremendously.

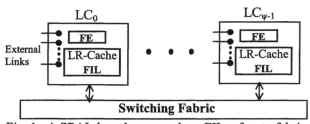

Fig. 1. A SPAL-based router, where FIL refers to fabric interface logics.

When compared with its existing counterpart, a router under SPAL exhibits far quicker lookups. Our trace-driven simulation indicates that a SPAL-based router with 16 LCs can forward, on an average, over 336 million of packets per second, if each LR-cache involves 4K blocks, when the Lulea trie [7] is adopted for longest prefix matching. This average forwarding ability is 4.2 times faster than that of an existing router, which keeps all prefixes of the routing table in each LC and has no LR-caches. A SPAL-based router may also shorten the worst-case lookup time, in comparison with a conventional router under the same longest prefix matching algorithm.

While IP lookup traffic streams present different characteristics than the data streams of typical computing applications, an independent investigation based on 1998 traces [5, 6] indicated the adequacy of 4K blocks in each cache to reach hit rates higher than 0.93. While the Internet has grown by more than 10 times from Jan. 1996 (with 14 million hosts) to July 2002 (with 162 million hosts), the locality of IP traffic over the Internet **does not drop** based on two separate, independent trace-driven simulation studies using 1998 traces and 2002 traces, perhaps due to the observed fact that a small percentage of flows between AS pairs (say, 9%) in the Internet accounts for a large percentage of total traffic (say, 90%) [9]. This SPAL-based solution is believed to be equally effective in greatly quickening packet lookups for future Internet traffic as it is for past 1998 WorldCup traffic [17] and 2002 backbone traffic [14] employed for our simulation. For a given cache size, the larger a SPAL-based router is, the higher lookup performance it attains; this results mainly from fragmenting the set of prefixes (and thus the IP addresses) into more partitions based on SPAL, yielding better address space coverage (thanks to fewer prefixes) by each LR-cache.

## 2. Background

### 2.1 Packet Lookups

Packet lookups in routers can be expedited by various approaches, generally classified as software-based or hardware-based ones. A software-based approach often intends to either lower the memory requirement of a routing/forwarding table (so as to fit the table into fast SRAM, in the form of L3 data cache of the FE processor) or reduce the number of memory accesses during each lookup. An enhanced trie implementation, called a *DP trie* (dynamic prefix trie), was considered to lower the average number of memory accesses upon search [8] and to yield a small code size and low storage requirements. Various algorithms resort to multiple-bit inspection at each search step (rather than single-bit inspection for the DP trie), and the number of bits inspected at each time (called the *stride*) affects the search speed and the memory amount needed for keeping the trie [15]. The Lulea algorithm constructs a 3-level compressed data structure, with the strides of 16, 8, and 8, respectively, for the first, the second and the third levels [7]. Another method replaces the largest full binary subtrie of a binary trie with a corresponding one-level multiple-bit subtrie recursively, starting with the root level, to produce an *LC-trie* (level-compressed trie) [12]. Search in an LC-trie requires an explicit comparison when arriving at a leaf to ensure a search match. While applicable to 128-bit IPv6 prefixes, software-based approaches often lead to far longer lookup times and bigger storage for the trie.

Hardware lookup designs have been proposed for high-speed routers under IPv4. In particular, a 2-level multi-bit trie with fixed strides was implemented in hardware to support IP lookups at the speed of memory accesses [10], with the first level realized by a table with $2^{24}$ entries addressed by the first 24 IP bits. Each sub-trie in the second level contains $2^8$ entries, and the total number of such sub-tries depends on the set of prefixes at hand. The memory requirement of this hardware design is huge (> 32 Mbytes). When a lookup hardware design is applied to 128-bits prefixes, it always takes a massive amount of memory.

## 2.2 Caching Lookup Results

A network processor equipped with hardware caches for capturing table lookup results has shown to improve overall packet forwarding performance significantly [5, 6]. The caching algorithm described in [5] mapped IP addresses carefully to virtual addresses so as to make use of CPU caches (both L1 and L2) for fast lookups. Separately, a technique for improving the effective coverage of the IP address space has been considered by caching a *range* of contiguous IP addresses in each entry [6]. It yields better performance when the address range cached in an entry is larger. Two steps of address range merging were considered and a greedy bit selection algorithm was introduced to minimize the total number of address ranges and the size differences among address ranges after mapping [6]. Simulation results have confirmed that address range merging after proper mapping may improve caching efficiency (in terms of mean lookup time) markedly.

While some routing tables might give rise to the minimum range sizes larger than $2^0 = 1$, a backbone router tends to contain a growing number of prefix exceptions in its routing/forwarding table [11, 15], making the minimum range size equal to 1 and thus nullifying the potential benefit of the first step of range merging. According to prefix length distribution results [2, 15], a number of prefixes in the routing table of a typical backbone router is of length 32, rendering the minimum range granularity equal to 1. Thus, cache hit rates using the network processor cache after address range merging may not be high usually.

## 2.3 Partitioning for Parallel Search

A technique has been considered recently [1] for partitioning the routing table into subsets, which can then be searched in parallel. It groups all prefixes of a given length in the routing table as one partition. Clearly, the size of each partitioned subset varies considerably, e.g., the length of size 24 typically accounts for about 50% of all prefixes [2]. Unlike our SPAL, the earlier technique keeps *all* partitioned subsets at each FE for search in parallel [1]; table lookups of all packets arriving at an LC are performed locally in the LC, and no lookup result obtained by one LC may be shared by any other LC. In addition, the sizes of forwarding tables in LCs are not reduced when the number of LCs grows.

## 3. SPAL-Based Routers

Each LC in any currently existing router maintains the entire set of prefixes, whose size grows steadily over time, no matter how many LCs are within the router. As the trie size typically is proportional to the number of prefixes, this certainly calls for large SRAM (in the form of an L3 data cache of the FE processor, for example) in order to hold the trie for fast lookups, in particular when IPv6 is concerned. The proposed SPAL aims to reduce the SRAM requirement while accelerating table lookups through fragmenting the BGP routing table into $\psi$ subsets (of roughly equal sizes), one for each LC (as its forwarding table) in a router with $\psi$ LCs. As depicted in Fig. 1, a low-latency switching fabric is employed to interconnect all LCs through fabric interface logics (FIL's), and the fabric can be a shared-bus (for a small $\psi$), a crossbar, or a multistage-based structure, among others. In this study, no emphasis on the fabric details will be placed, but the fabric latency (in terms of system cycles) is assumed to depend on the fabric size. Each LC also includes one small fast SRAM housed inside the FIL chip, referred to as the LR-cache, for holding the lookup results obtained by the local FE and by other remote FEs (as will be detailed in Sec. 3.2).

## 3.1 Table Partitioning

Partitioning is done using appropriately chosen bits in IP prefixes, and a subset of routing table prefixes is referred to as an *ROT-partition*. For a router with $\psi$ LCs, the key decision on partitioning its routing table is to choose appropriate bits for yielding $\psi$ ROT-partitions in the most desirable way, namely, (1) each ROT-partition involving *as few prefixes as possible*, and (2) the size difference between the largest ROT-partition and the smallest one being *minimum*. Any partitioning which satisfies these two criteria is deemed **optimum**. Let $\eta = \lceil \log_2\psi \rceil$, then the number of bits chosen for partitioning is $\eta$, where $\lceil x \rceil$ is the smallest integer $\geq x$. Note that $\psi$ doesn't have to be a power of 2 and can be any integer, say 3, 5, 6, 7, etc. For easy explanation in the following, we consider simplified prefixes of up to 8 bits, with the leftmost bit in a prefix denoted by $b_0$, the next bit by $b_1$, etc. Only the case of $\psi$ being a power of 2 is stated here.

Given 7 simplified prefixes in a routing table: $P_1 = 101*$, $P_2 = 1011*$, $P_3 = 01*$, $P_4 = 001110*$, $P_5 = 10010011$, $P_6 = 10011*$, $P_7 = 011001*$, if $b_2$ and $b_4$ are used for partitioning, we arrive at 4 ROT-partitions: $\{P_3, P_5\}$, $\{P_3, P_6\}$, $\{P_1, P_2, P_3, P_7\}$, $\{P_1, P_2, P_3, P_4\}$, where the first partition corresponds to $b_2b_4 = 00$, the second one corresponds to $b_2b_4 = 01$, and the third (or fourth) one, to $b_2b_4 = 10$ (or 11). With this partitioning, $\kappa^{th}$ ROT-partition resides in $LC_\kappa$, where $\kappa = 0, 1, 2, 3$. Any packet arriving at $LC_\kappa$ is called a *local* packet, if $b_2b_4$ of its destination address equals $\kappa$ since its lookup will be done by the local (accompanying) FE; otherwise, the packet is a remote one, with its *home* being $LC_h$ ($h = b_2b_4$). Each packet has one and only one *home LC*, which can be determined immediately upon arrival by examining the appropriate bit positions of the packet destination address. Non-local packets are delivered from their arrival LCs through the switching fabric to their respective home LCs for longest-prefix matching, if they miss in the LR-caches of their arrival LCs. Each such a packet is routed across the switching fabric using $b_2$ and $b_4$ of its destination address. Note that $P_3$ belongs to every partition, because both $b_2$ and $b_4$ of $P_3$ are "*" (which would match any IP address whose $b_2$ is 0 or 1 and whose $b_4$ is 0 or 1, requiring that $P_3$ should exist in each partition since a matched IP may arrive at any FE). Similarly, $P_1$ belongs to the third and the fourth partitions, as $b_4$ of $P_1$ is "*". On the other hand, the use of $b_0$ and $b_4$ for partitioning arrives at $\{P_3, P_7\}$, $\{P_3, P_4\}$, $\{P_1, P_2, P_5\}$, $\{P_1, P_2, P_6\}$, where each partition involves 2 or 3 prefixes. Obviously, the latter partitioning is superior to the former one, based on the two criteria listed above.

For a given set of prefixes, a chosen bit (say $b_v$) separates prefixes into two subsets with $(\Phi_0+\Phi_*)$ and $(\Phi_1+\Phi_*)$ prefixes, respectively, where $\Phi_0$ (or $\Phi_1$) is the number of prefixes whose $b_v$ bits equal "0" (or "1") and $\Phi_*$ is the number of prefixes with $b_v$ bits being "*" (since these prefixes are to appear in both subsets). According to Criterion (1) above, we need to find out the bit $b_v$ such that $(\Phi_0+\Phi_1+\Phi_*+\Phi_*) = \Phi+\Phi_*$ is smallest among all $0 \leq v \leq 31$, where $\Phi$ is the set size (a fixed number). This criterion is thus equivalent to locating the bit $b_v$ which leads to a minimum $\Phi_*$, ruling out a large $v$ (say $> 24$), since the vast majority of prefixes in a routing table (e.g., more than 83% for the set of prefixes obtained from [2]) have length no more than 24, and $b_v$ in a prefix is "*" for any $v$ larger than the prefix length. Criterion (2) requires the search of bit $b_v$ such that $|(\Phi_0+\Phi_*)-(\Phi_1+\Phi_*)| = |\Phi_0-\Phi_1|$ is minimum for all $0 \leq v \leq 31$. When examining bit $b_v$, this criterion calls for ignoring prefixes with bit $b_v$ = "*", counting only those with bit $b_v$ being "0" or "1". Notice that Criterion (1) considers only $\Phi_*$ whereas Criterion (2) deals with $\Phi_0$ and $\Phi_1$. In general, when multiple control bits are to be chosen for a set of prefixes, these two criteria are applied recursively, first to find one control bit $b_v$ among $0 \leq v \leq 31$, and then to find bit in each of the two subsets separately before deciding the bit for both subsets as the second control bit. Similarly, the third control bit is decided using the two criteria on the four subsets obtained using the two chosen control bits.

## 3.2 LR-Cache Operation and Organization

### Principle of Operation

Typically, the routing table of a backbone router gets updated some 20 times per second on an average (and possibly as many as 100 times), leading to one table update in $50 - 10$ *ms* [3, 15]. Once the routing table is updated, those changes should be reflected in the forwarding tables at all LCs. To ensure appropriate lookups, this study assumes that all entries in every LR-cache are *flushed after each table update*. (Note that this simple flushing will not work effectively if the routing table is updated incrementally and very frequently.) After flushing, the availability status bit of each cache entry is set to the *invalid state*. Once an entry is chosen to hold a lookup result, its availability status bit is set to the *shared state*. Two types of lookup results may exist in LR-cache entries: results homed locally (LOC,

obtained by the local FE) and results homed remotely (REM, obtained through remote FEs). An entry uses one bit, called the $M$ (short for "mix") status bit, to indicate its LOC/REM status. This bit is necessary for implementing an efficient cache replacement mechanism, realizing a suitable "mix" of LOC entries and REM entries within each set (of cache entries) under a given cache organization (i.e., a given cache size, block size, degree of set associativity) to achieve good performance.

When a lookup result is obtained through prefix matching by the FE in the home LC, the result is first placed in the LR-cache of the LC. If the cache has no free entry in the set of interest (decided by the destination IP address), one entry in the set has to be chosen for replacement. It chooses an entry with its $M$ bit being REM (or LOC), if the total number of entries with $M$ = REM (or LOC) in the set exceeds the predefined value, say 50%. The $M$ status bit is examined first to decide the candidate block(s) to replace. (Note that hardware logics can be employed to make this decision instantly, since the number of blocks in each set does not have to be larger, say $\leq 4$, to get nearly best performance, as revealed by our simulation results. Given 4 blocks in a set, for example, the logic can load the $M$ bits of the four blocks to check them against 16 possible values: $0000_2$, $0001_2$, ..., $1111_2$, in parallel via the "XOR" operation.) A conventional replacement strategy (such as LRU, FIFO, or random) is then applied to the candidate block(s) to choose the one for eviction.

To lower the load of an FE and cut down traffic over the switching fabric, the LR-cache records a packet immediately when a miss occurs at the arrival LC. This early cache block recording prevents subsequent packets with the same destination from proceeding beyond the LR-cache, enhancing SPAL performance. Since this recorded cache entry is not complete until its reply is back, a status bit (waiting bit, i.e., W-bit) is added to the cache entry, with the bit set until its reply is back and fills the entry. When a forthcoming packet hits an LR-cache entry whose W-bit is set, the packet is stopped from proceeding forward and held in the waiting list associated with the incomplete entry. The packet is allowed to advance after the W-bit of the hit cache entry is cleared (by a reply). Once a reply comes back and hits the cache entry recorded earlier, the entry is completed with the lookup result (i.e., filling its Next_hop_LC# field) and its W-bit is cleared. The reply is then moved back to the arrival LC of the packet, if it is not local.

### Cache Organization

An LR-cache is of on-chip SRAM and organized as a set-associative cache, with a block able to hold *one* lookup result (i.e., <IP address, Next_hop_LC#>). The reason for a small block size is due to weak spatial locality of IP addresses in practice since the devices with contiguous IP addresses usually have little direct temporal correlation of network activities; a larger block size leads to poorer lookup performance because of decreased cache space utilization [5]. The degree of set associativity for LR-caches is chosen 4, and this choice leads to nearly best performance, according to our simulation results and an earlier work [16]. The cache size ranges from 1K to 8K blocks.

A *victim cache* is for keeping blocks which are evicted from a cache due to conflict misses. It is a small fully-associative cache, aiming to hold those blocks which get replaced so that they are not lost. Entries in the victim cache follow a conventional mechanism for replacement (e.g., LRU, FIFO, random). When a packet is searched in an LR-cache, its associated victim cache is also examined simultaneously. In this study, each LR-cache is equipped with a victim cache of 8 blocks, which are found to yield effective lookup performance improvement by avoiding most conflict misses.

### 3.3 Overall Lookup Flows

To explain overall lookup flows, let us consider a packet arrival immediately after a table update (when all LR-cache entries are in the invalid state). The packet terminates at one LC (referred to as the *arrival LC*, denoted by $LC_{ar}$), where the packet header is extracted and delivered to the LR-cache in $LC_{ar}$. A cache miss will result, and a cache entry is created for the lookup result of this packet header (referred to as the packet hereinafter). Bits of appropriate positions in the destination address of the packet are then examined (by LR1, an LR detector composed of "XOR" logics, shown in Fig. 2) to decide if the packet lookup is to be done locally or remotely, and the bit positions used for examination are those selected for table partitioning (mentioned above). If a local lookup is to be carried out, the packet is moved to the FE of $LC_{ar}$ for longest-prefix matching (based on any software matching algorithm devised earlier for this purpose). After the lookup result is obtained, it is sent to the LR-cache to complete the corresponding block, with its $M$ bit set to LOC. This cached result will satisfy later lookup requests for an identical destination address much faster.

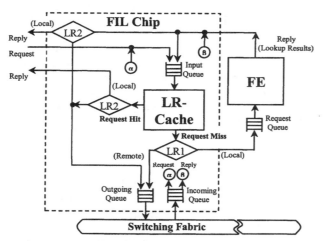

Fig. 2. LR-cache and relevant logics housed inside the FIL chip, where an LR1 (or LR2) detector examines the destination (or originator) address.

If a remote lookup is to be performed (by detector LR1), the packet is moved to the Outgoing Queue (see Fig. 2) ready for delivery over the switching fabric to its home LC, denoted by $LC_{ho}$, where the lookup flow then follows as if the packet had arrived there. Specifically, after received by $LC_{ho}$ and put in its Input Queue, the packet is first searched over the (on-chip) LR-cache therein. If a cache miss results, a block is reserved to hold the lookup result of this packet. The packet is then forwarded (through LR1) to the FE of $LC_{ho}$ for longest-prefix matching, whose result later finishes the reserved block, with its $M$ bit set to LOC. A reply is also produced (through LR2 at the upper left corner depicted in Fig. 2) and put in the Outgoing Queue of $LC_{ho}$ for transmission through the fabric back to $LC_{ar}$. This reply completes the cache block created previously in the LR-cache of $LC_{ar}$, with the $M$ bit of the block set to REM. The block created in the LR-cache of $LC_{ho}$ thereafter serves to quickly reply upcoming lookup requests (of the same address) originated from *any* LC, whereas the cache block created in $LC_{ar}$ takes care of forthcoming lookup requests from $LC_{ar}$. While multiple copies of the same lookup result, one in an LC, may be created in the router this way, those copies not only serve multiple packets (from different LCs) with the same destination address concurrently, but also effectively cut down traffic over the switching fabric and the load to the LR-cache in $LC_{ho}$. As a result, SPAL can yield high lookup performance, partly because of good parallelism in packet lookups.

As blocks with the LOC status and those with the REM status compete in each LR-cache, a proper mix of LOC blocks and REM blocks is necessary. Fortunately, the coverage of IP address space by each LR-cache under SPAL is improved substantially due to table partitioning, which leads to the forwarding table in each LC involving only a small fraction of the prefixes maintained in the routing table. The number of LOC blocks required to achieve a given performance level drops as $\psi$ (the number of LCs) increases, whereas at the same time, a bigger percentage of lookup requests at each LC will be homed remotely, urging more cache blocks for remote lookup results (i.e., more REM blocks). For a given $\psi$, fewer blocks should be allocated for REM blocks when the size of the LR-cache shrinks, in order to get the best lookup performance, since the cost is far smaller over the fabric than longest-prefix matching execution.

## 4. Results of Table Partitioning

Two routing tables were obtained for our evaluation use, one being the FUNET routing table with 41,709 prefixes given in [12] (called RT_1) and the other with 140,838 prefixes [2] (called RT_2). Unlike any existing router, a SPAL-based router calls for partitioning the routing table in accordance with the number of LCs (which can be of any integer, not necessary a power of 2) in the router. Following the two criteria for table partitioning stated in Sec. 3.1, we arrived at the two desired bit positions for fragmenting RT_1 (or RT_2) into

4 partitions: bits 12 and 14 (or 8 and 14). If RT_1 (or RT_2) is to be partitioned into 16 fragments, the preferred partitioning bit positions are found to be 12, 14, 15, 16 (or 11, 13, 14, 16).

Storage Sizes

Three distinct tries (namely, the DP trie [8], the Lulea trie [7], and the LC trie [12]) have been implemented to assess the storage sizes needed for all ROT-partitions after fragmenting RT_1 and RT_2. Under the DP trie for RT_1 (or RT_2) with $\psi = 4$, the storage sizes of the four tries built and held in LCs after partitioning are 209, 216, 217, and 220 Kbytes (or 1082, 1082, 1042, and 1027 Kbytes), respectively, assuming that each node in the trie consists of one byte for the index field plus 4 bytes for each of the five pointers. Since the trie size before partitioning is 859 (or 2827) Kbytes, the DP trie sees the amount of SRAM reduction in each LC caused by partitioning to exceed 638 (or 1745) Kbytes under RT_1 (or RT_2) with $\psi = 4$. The DP trie after partitioning for $\psi = 16$ reduces its size down to the range of 50 and 62 Kbytes (or of 279 and 335 Kbytes) with respect to RT_1 (or RT_2). As a result, storage reduction in each LC due to partitioning is no less than 795 (or 2492) Kbytes under RT_1 (or RT_2) when $\psi$ equals 16. Note that the reduction amount will be much larger under IPv6. Total SRAM amounts required for the DP trie after (or without) partitioning are depicted in Fig. 3 under DP_S (or DP_W).

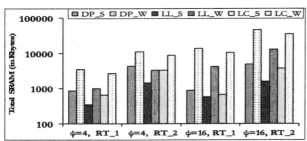

Fig. 3. Total SRAM (in Kbytes) required for different tries under IPv4.

For the Lulea trie [7] (whose storage requirement is often the lowest) with $\psi = 4$ under RT_1 (or RT_2), the partitioned tables in 4 LCs require 90, 91, 89, and 87 Kbytes (or 361, 358, 348, and 342 Kbytes), respectively, as opposed to roughly 260 (or 822) Kbytes in an LC of a conventional router without partitioning. This indicates an SRAM reduction in each LC caused by partitioning for $\psi = 4$ under the Lulea trie to be 169 (or 461) Kbytes or beyond, when RT_1 (or RT_2) is concerned. For $\psi = 16$, the Lulea trie sees its size to be no more than 39 (or 113) Kbytes in any LC after partitioning RT_1 (or RT_2), giving rise to a savings of at least 221 (or 709) Kbytes in each LC. Total SRAM amounts required for the Lulea trie after (or without) partitioning are depicted under LL_S (or LL_W) in Fig. 3. Similarly, the LC-trie [12] under RT_1 (or RT_2) enjoys storage reduction in any LC due to SPAL by no less than 815 (or 1345) Kbytes,

for $\psi = 4$ with a fill factor of 0.25. The storage saving amount in an LC increases to over 1025 (or 1927) Kbytes for RT_1 (or RT_2) under $\psi = 16$ with the same fill factor (of 0.25). Therefore, SPAL always leads to a far bigger SRAM savings in each LC than the size of the LR-cache incorporated therein (i.e., 24 Kbytes) under the three distinct tries we have implemented and examined.

## 5. Performance Evaluation

Trace-driving simulation was employed to evaluate the performance of SPAL-based routers under different LR-cache sizes and $\psi$ values. This includes simulation scenarios of different LC speeds and various longest prefix matching algorithms under many traces available to the public. Note that the LC speeds considered are those after link aggregations, if needed; for example, Cisco's 12000 Series routers allow multiple links of varying speeds (terminating at separate ports of an LC) to be aggregated in each LC for up to 10 Gbps.

### 5.1 Simulation Methodology

Our simulator takes as its input, the packet streams fed to all LCs and the mean longest prefix matching time per lookup in FEs. The packet streams were derived from various traces of actual packet destinations collected and posted [14, 17], one stream for each LC. For Abilene-I, Abilene-II, Bell Labs-I, and other data sets in the PMA long traces archive (details about where, when and how traces were collected and about the trace format can be found in [14]), the destinations of IP packet records (each consisting of 64 bytes) in the traces were employed as packet streams to drive our simulation studies. For the WorldCup98 data set (which contained all request logs from April 30th till July 26th, 1998 with more than 1.35 billions requests in total [17]), the clientID field of each request (i.e., a mapped IP address of the request originator or proxy) was employed to drive our simulator. Two different LC speeds were evaluated: 10 Gbps and 40 Gbps. Given a simulated LC speed of 10 (or 40) Gbps, packets of varying length are generated in a way that on an average, they together amount to the given speed, with the mean packet length assuming to be 256 bytes and the smallest packet size equal to 40 bytes. Under the clock cycle of 5 *ns* simulated for the LC speed of 40 (or 10) Gbps, one packet was generated in anywhere from 2 cycles to 18 cycles (or from 6 cycles to 74 cycles). Given a trace, once a packet is generated at an LC, its destination was supplied by the trace. Each LC in our simulation produces 300,000 packets, which correspond to a time period of roughly 15 (or 60) *ms* for the mean packet length of 256 bytes under the LC speed of 40 (or 10) Gbps. This duration is so chosen because prefix changes occur some 20 times on an average [3] and possibly up to 100 times [15] per second, and every prefix change leads to the cache contents in LR-caches being flushed entirely.

The LR-cache organization can be specified by its size (in terms of blocks), given that its degree of set associativity equals 4, the victim cache size is 8, and each cache block is set to hold only *one* lookup result. When a conventional replacement policy is needed, the LRU is applied. Likewise, the replacement policy in the victim cache follows the LRU. In a cycle (of 5 *ns*), at most one packet is checked against an LR-cache (see Fig. 2); if the check leads to a miss, the cache is then updated accordingly. Each table lookup consists of multiple memory accesses and the execution of the software code which realizes longest prefix matching. The mean number of memory accesses varies widely from one matching algorithm to another. We have implemented various tries to measure the average numbers of memory accesses per lookup under the two sets of prefixes utilized for this study, namely, RT_1 and RT_2. It is found that the Lulea trie [7] requires 6.2 (or 6.6) memory accesses per lookup on an average for RT_1 (or RT_2), while the DP trie [8] yields about 16 memory accesses per lookup for either set of prefixes. Since the trie is kept in off-chip SRAM (e.g., the L3 data cache, if existing), we assume the memory access time as 12 *ns* and the code execution time as 120 *ns* (for executing some 100 instructions per lookup) in our simulation. This assumption leads to a matching search time of roughly 40 cycles (of 5 *ns* each) in FEs under the Lulea trie and of 62 cycles or so under the DP trie. SPAL was evaluated under these search times in FEs.

## 5.2 Outcome and Discussion

Extensive simulation results for RT_1 and RT_2 were gathered and found to exhibit a similar trend; therefore, only the results for RT_2 are presented here. They confirm that typical packet streams indeed **have sufficient temporal locality** to make the LR-cache effective, according to traces collected in 1998 and 2002 available to the public [14, 17]. The results are for different cases: 10 Gbps & 40-cycle lookup, 10 Gbps & 62-cycle lookup, 40 Gbps & 40-cycle lookup, and 40 Gbps & 62-cycle lookup. Since those cases see their results follow a similar trend, in this article, we present the simulation outcomes only for *the case of 40 Gbps & 40-cycle lookup*, under two traces from WorldCup98, namely, D_75 (for July 9, 1998) and D_81 (for July 15, 1998), two traces from the Abilene-I data set in the PMA Long Traces Archive, namely, L_92-0 and L_92-1, and the Bell Labs-I trace from the same archive.

As the set of associativity degree is chosen to be 4 and blocks in a set can be employed to hold LOC and REM lookup results, we examined how the "mix" value ($\gamma$, reflecting % of blocks devoted for REM results) affected lookup performance under various LR-cache sizes ($\beta$, in blocks) for $\psi$ ranging from 1 to 16. The simulation outcomes all follow a trend similar to that signified in Fig. 4, where the mean lookup time (in cycles of 5 *ns* each) as a function of $\gamma$ under the five traces is depicted for $\psi = 4$ with $\beta$ equal to 4K. This figure reveals that $\gamma = 50\%$ typically yields best (or nearly best) performance. Note that if the LR-cache is small (like $\beta = $ 1K), $\gamma = 25\%$ may then be chosen, namely, only one cache block per set is for the REM results. Hence, we

present subsequently the outcomes only for $\gamma = 50\%$ (or 25%) under $\beta \geq 2K$ (or $\beta = 1K$).

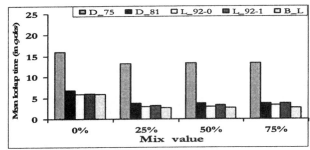

Fig. 4. Mean lookup time (in cycles) versus mix value ($\gamma$) for $\psi = 4$ and $\beta = 4K$.

We investigated the impact of the LR-cache size on SPAL performance, with simulation results under the five traces demonstrated in Fig. 5 – Fig. 6. The average lookup time (in cycles) as a function of the cache size ($\beta$) for $\psi = 16$ is depicted in Fig. 5, where a table lookup carried out at an FE (after a miss in the LR-cache) takes 40 cycles. For any given trace, a larger $\beta$ consistently yields a shorter lookup time; with $\beta = 4K$, the mean lookup times under SPAL sized $\psi = 16$ drop below 9.2 cycles for all the traces shown, translating to a lookup speed beyond 21 million packets per second for each LC. Therefore, a SPAL-based router sized 16 can forward over 336 million packets per second, provided that $\beta \geq$ 4K. In contrast, a current router without table partitioning nor LR-caches experiences the mean lookup time equal to 200 *ns* (i.e., 40 cycles) if the queuing time of the FE is ignored optimistically; that is equivalent to 5 million lookup per second per LC. Thus, a SPAL-based router with $\psi = 16$ accelerates packet lookups by 4.2 times, when compared with its commercial counterpart, despite its reduced total SRAM amount and a possibly shorter worst-case lookup time.

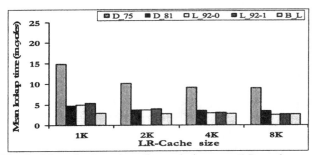

Fig. 5. Mean lookup time (in cycles) versus LR-cache size ($\beta$) under $\psi = 16$.

Mean lookup performance versus $\psi$ (i.e., the number of LCs) under $\beta = 4K$ and $\gamma = 50\%$ is illustrated in Fig. 6. According to the figure, a larger $\psi$ generally leads to a lower mean lookup time for any trace, because of better address space coverage in each LC (due to fewer prefixes in its forwarding table) and increased parallelism offered by more FEs (for longest-prefix matching execution).

Specifically, the mean lookup time for trace L92_0 drops from more than 6 cycles down to less than 3 cycles, if $\psi$ rises from 1 to 16, translating to a speedup factor of more than 2 as a result of finer routing table fragmentation (and thus partitioning the IP packet streams into more subsets) for larger parallelism. When the LR-cache is incorporated in each LC while the routing table is not partitioned (as treated in an earlier processor caching work [6]), the mean lookup time will be independent of $\psi$ and be always equal to that of $\psi = 1$ depicted in Fig. 6. The benefits due to incorporating LR-caches in LCs then drop substantially because (1) the LR-cache has a larger coverage of the address space (i.e., the whole routing table, instead of a small fraction of it, like SPAL) and (2) the lookups of same IP addresses have to be repeated in different LCs, discounting the purpose of caches. Note that the number of LCs can be of any integer, not limited to powers of 2 as mentioned earlier.

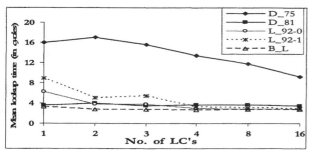

Fig. 6. Mean lookup time (in cycles) versus $\psi$ under $\beta = 4K$ and $\gamma = 50\%$.

## 6. Conclusion

A speedy packet lookup (SPAL) technique has been investigated for high-performance routers, realized by fragmenting the BGP routing tables and incorporating a small cache (say $4K \times 6$ bytes under IPv4, called the LR-cache) for keeping lookup results. The forwarding table housed in each LC (linecard) includes only a small subset of prefixes (in the routing table), leading to a significant drop in the SRAM requirement and a possibly improved worst-case lookup time. The number of LCs (i.e., fragments of a BGP table) can be an arbitrary integer, not necessarily a power of 2. The LR-cache enables quick replies to subsequent requests (for looking up same addresses) originated from the home LC as well as other LCs, greatly enhancing mean lookup performance of a SPAL-based router. Trace-driven simulation is adopted to assess the performance measures of interest, and the simulation outcomes under various traces demonstrate that SPAL exhibits over 4.2 times faster mean lookups in a router with $\psi = 16$ LCs under the LR-cache size of 4K blocks, when compared with any existing router whose forwarding tables are all identical and have the same number of prefixes as the core routing table. For a given LR-cache size and any trace, mean lookup performance typically improves for a larger $\psi$, as a result of finer routing table fragmentation so that each LR-cache in an LC then achieves a better address space coverage. The partitioning bits are chosen according to the prefixes in a given routing table and irrespective of packet streams, and the partitioning bits obtained this way often yield high lookup concurrency to arrive at a small mean lookup time. In addition, SPAL is feasibly applicable to IPv6. With its ability to speed up packet lookup performance while lowering overall SRAM substantially, SPAL is ideally suitable for future high-performance routers.

## References

[1] M. Akhbarizadeh and M. Nourani, "An IP Packet Forwarding Technique Based on Partitioned Lookup Table," *Proc. 2002 IEEE International Conf. on Communications*, Apr./May 2002.

[2] AS1221 BGP Table Data, URL – http://bgp.potaroo.net/as1221/bgp-active.html, routing table snapshot taken at 4:14pm, Jan 30, 2003.

[3] A. Basu and G. Narlikar, "Fast Incremental Updates for Pipelined Forwarding Engines," *Proc. IEEE Conf. on Computer Communications (INFOCOM '03)*, Apr. 2003.

[4] BGP Table Data, URL – http://bgp.potaroo.net, 2003.

[5] T. Chiueh and P. Pradhan, "High-Performance IP Routing Table Lookup using CPU Caching," *Proc. IEEE Conf. on Computer Communications (INFOCOM '99)*, Apr. 1999, pp. 1421-1428.

[6] T. Chiueh and P. Pradhan, "Cache Memory Design for Internet Processors," *IEEE Micro*, vol. 20, Jan./Feb. 2000.

[7] M. Degermark *et al.*, "Small Forwarding Tables for Fast Routing Lookups," *Proc. ACM SIGCOMM 1997 Conference*, Sept. 1997, pp. 3-14.

[8] W. Doeringer, G. Karjoth, and M. Nassehi, "Routing on Longest-Matching Prefixes," *IEEE/ACM Trans. on Networking*, vol. 4, no. 1, pp. 86-97, Feb. 1996.

[9] C. Estan and G. Varghese, "New Directions in Traffic Measurement and Accounting," *Proc. ACM SIGCOMM 2002 Conference*, Aug. 2002, pp. 323-336.

[10] P. Gupta, S. Lin , and N. McKeown, "Routing Lookups in Hardware at Memory Access Speeds," *Proc. IEEE Conf. on Computer Communications (INFOCOM '98)*, Apr. 1998, pp. 1240-1247.

[11] G. Huston, "Analyzing the Internet's BGP Routing Table," *The Internet Protocol Journal*, vol. 4, no. 1, Mar. 2001.

[12] S. Nilsson and G. Karlsson, "IP-Address Lookup Using LC-Tries," *IEEE J. on Selected Areas in Communications*, vol. 17, no. 6, pp. 1083-1092, June 1999.

[13] Pericom Semiconductor Corporation, "Throughput Expansion with FET-Based Crossbar Switching," Nov. 2001, URL – http://www.pericom.com/.

[14] PMA Long Traces Archive, URL – http://pma.nlanr.net/ Traces/long/, Passive Measurement and Analysis, National Laboratory for Applied Network Research, Sept. 2002.

[15] M. Ruiz-Sanchez, E. Biersack, and W. Dabbous, "Survey and Taxonomy of IP Address Lookup Algorithms," *IEEE Network*, vol. 15, pp. 8-23, Mar./Apr. 2001.

[16] N. Tzeng, "Hardware-Assisted Design for Fast Packet Forwarding in Parallel Routers," *Proc. 2003 International Conference on Parallel Processing*, Oct. 2003, pp. 11-18.

[17] WorldCup98 Dataset, URL – http://ita.ee.lbl.gov/html/ contrib/WorldCup.html, The Internet Traffic Archive, Lawrence Berkeley National Laboratory, Apr. 2000.

# Architectural Characterization of an XML-centric Commercial Server Workload

Padma Apparao, Ravi Iyer, Ricardo Morin, Naren Nayak, Mahesh Bhat
*Intel Corporation*
David Halliwell, William Steinberg
*Morgan Stanley*
*padmashree.k.apparao@intel.com*

## Abstract

*As XML (Extensible Markup Language) rapidly emerges as the standard for information storage and communication, it becomes increasingly important to understand its architectural characteristics and performance implications. In this paper, our goal is to characterize a representative XML-based server in a managed runtime environment such as Java\*. Based on detailed measurements on an Intel® XeonTM processor-based commercial server running a real-world XML-based server workload, we start by looking at symmetric multiprocessor (SMP) scaling characteristics and the benefits of Hyper-Threading Technology. Using performance monitoring events provided on the processor, we present an overview of the architectural characteristics (such as clocks per instruction (CPI), cache miss rates, memory/bus utilization, branch behavior and efficiency). Using profiling tools like Intel® VTuneTM Performance Analyzer, we map these architectural/performance characteristics to the various components of application execution -- helping us identify hot spots and propose potential enhancements to code generation and application software. We believe that the information presented in this paper will be useful in understanding the XML processing characteristics and may serve as a useful first step to identifying potential hardware/software optimizations for improved future performance.*

## 1. Introduction

The design and optimization of server platforms have been traditionally guided by the performance characterization of scientific and technical workloads [22]. However, for the last decade, there has been a significant emphasis on understanding the characteristics of commercial server workloads and influencing server architecture design for these workloads. As a result, several academic and industry projects [2, 3, 4, 5, 6, 9, 13, 14, 15, 18] have been concentrated on understanding the performance of front-end and back-end workloads. Front-end workloads used for these studies range from simplistic single-system web servers (like SPECweb99 [17]) to multi-node configurations for e-commerce (like TPC-W [19]). Recently, several useful characterization studies on mid-tier workloads [2, 6, 13, 14] have also

surfaced. While these workloads certainly serve as a useful starting point, the industry continues to move forward with emerging standards. For instance, XML (Extensible Markup Language) has become the de-facto standard for flexible information exchange (storage and communication) over the Internet. Furthermore, XML coupled with a platform-independent managed runtime environment based on Java\* makes the entire solution extremely attractive to application developers. In this paper, we analyze the performance characteristics of a realistic commercial workload that is developed in Java\* and is XML-centric.

The contribution of this paper is as follows. We study, in detail, the characteristics of an XML-centric Java-based message processing server application used by Morgan Stanley. We start by analyzing the multiprocessor scaling characteristics of the application by running it on state-of-the-art servers based on Intel® Xeon™ processors. We also study the performance improvements gained by Intel's Hyper-Threading Technology [23] (HT Technology) for this application. To understand the scaling behavior, we analyze detailed architectural data using in-built performance counters. We analyze the architectural performance characteristics such as Clocks Per Instruction (CPI), instructions retired, branch prediction ratios, cache performance and bus utilization statistics on our measurement platform. We then analyze the cache characteristics of this application by running trace-driven simulations using a cache simulator. Finally, we use detailed profiling tools to understand the hot spots in the workload and their impact on overall performance. Based on our analysis, we were able to identify the architectural characteristics on a per component basis.

Related work on this topic can only be found in the context of XML usage patterns [12], storage and relational databases [1, 7] and routing [16]. In [12], the author presents an overview of the usage patterns likely for XML and classifies them into specific categories such as a configuration pattern and a structure storage pattern. In [7], the authors discuss six different storage alternatives using XML. In [1], the authors discuss the potential of optimizing database queries using XML representation. Finally, in [16], XML representation is used to intelligently route messages (using application-level XML routers) over a mesh-based overlay network. To our knowledge, there has not yet been a study that has looked at the architectural impact of XML processing on client or server platforms. We believe that the detailed study presented in this paper is the first to actually quantify and analyze the impact of XML processing on server architectures as well as provide insights into the execution profile of such a workload.

## 2. XML-based Server Workload Description

Morgan Stanley has embraced XML as the standard data format for facilitating system communication and seamless exchange of information. XML is at the core of Morgan Stanley's message processing backbone, which interconnects a variety of applications and databases. XML provides not only a standardized mechanism for data exchange, but delivers unprecedented flexibility through easy to maintain document-centric data representation. The workload discussed in this paper is called Trade Completion (TC), and it is a key XML processing component that links front and back-end applications at Morgan Stanley. TC is a scalable Java*-based XML processing application deployed in a multi-tier configuration, using multiple Intel® Xeon™ processor-based servers running Linux: application servers, queue management servers and database servers. The application is layered on top of a generalized Java*-based workflow and XML processing framework, which provides message routing, transformation, transaction management, data caching, XML parsing, XML serialization, threading, and database persistence services. The TC application, depicted at a high level in Figure 1, is responsible for the automated processing of trade XML data sourced from front-end sales and trade systems and exchanges. Prior to entering the TC application, the data are converted from the Financial Information eXchange (FIX) protocol [8] data format into XML.

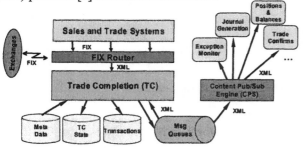

**Figure 1.** Trade Completion Application Overview

Through TC, trade data are "enriched" in support of payment and transfer of ownership (i.e., settlement) activities, via processing steps which include: validation, principal figuration, commissions, taxes and fees, settlement dates and instructions, and net figuration. The data is then made available to other systems such as Risk

and Settlement through a XML publish/subscribe engine called CPS, as well as through a relational database. In addition to storing enriched trade data for further use through queries and reporting, the relational database capability is also used as a meta-data repository and a mechanism to track processing state in a persistent and transactionally consistent fashion.

The TC application is built on top of the Java* XML Broker (JXB), a generalized workflow and XML processing engine, developed by Morgan Stanley. JXB is a comprehensive framework for the development and deployment of XML-based applications. Using JXB, developers employ an easy to use graphical user interface to define processing "flows" that are "wired" together via "transports," which can be configured to use asynchronous messaging services or "internal" reference-passing mechanisms. Processing flows encapsulate business rules, XML message enrichment operations and data persistence requirements. JXB applications such as TC, are deployed onto one or many JXB runtime servers, depending on the application transaction volume processing requirements. An important characteristic of JXB applications is their inherent scalability, because "flows" are multi-threaded, and as such, are capable of accessing and processing queued messages in parallel. This capability is critical, as TC needs to be able to process an ever-increasing volume of transactions: from approximately 1 million messages per day in early 2003, to about 2 million by the end of the same year.

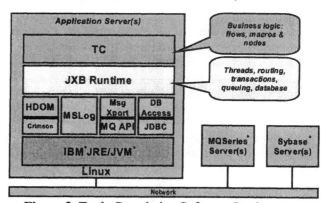

**Figure 2.** Trade Completion Software Stack

In TC, asynchronous messaging services are implemented using the IBM* WebSphere* MQSeries* product, which provides reliable messaging services, with guaranteed delivery. The application relies on the Sybase* Adaptive Server Enterprise* product for relational database services. Figure 2 depicts TC's software stack. A key component of the software stack is HDOM, which is a tree-based Application Programming Interface (API) for representing and manipulating XML documents in Java. HDOM is a Morgan Stanley enhancement to the JDOM

[31] open source package, which uses hash tables to speed up lookups within XML documents. Additional components include: Crimson* to support XML parsing and internal representation, MSLog to capture application-level logging information, a Java*-based interface to access MQSeries* queues, and the necessary JDBC* drivers to access the Sybase* database. All of these components run on top of the IBM* Java* Virtual Machine (JVM*) and Red Hat* Linux Advanced Server*.

## 3. XML Processing Phases and Requirements

In this section, we discuss the processing requirements of XML documents and the technologies generally used for each phase. The processing of XML documents typically involves the following types of operations:
- XML Document Parsing
- XML Serialization
- Querying/Updating (XPath) Operations
- Style-Sheet (XSLT) Processing

**XML Document Parsing:** An XML document has to be parsed first in order for any other query/update operations to take place on it. There are two main XML parsing technologies SAX (Simple API for XML) and DOM (Document Object Model). SAX is an event-based parser that reads an XML document from beginning to end, and each time it encounters a syntax construction, it notifies the application. Details of the SAX API can be found in [24]. DOM is a set of interfaces for building an in-memory representation of the parsed XML document. The object representation is in the form of a tree and one can traverse and manipulate the tree with DOM methods like insert, delete just like any other tree data structure. The DOM Level 1 specification can be found in [25]. SAX parsers are typically used when processing serial streams of, often large, documents and there is no updating/modifications being done to the documents. DOM on the other hand is limited to the use of smaller documents dependent on the memory available in the system, because it requires a memory representation of the entire document. Also DOM allows for random access to the document for searches, modifications and updates.

**XML Serialization:** Serialization is a process through which an object's state is transformed into some serial format, such as XML or a binary format, in order to be stored for some later use. This serialized format includes sufficient information to "deserialize" (or resurrect) the object (variables, code, and all objects reachable from this object). An XML-centric application, such as the workload used in this study, emphasizes the aspect of serializing binary objects (represented by XML documents in memory) into XML documents represented as sequences of bytes.

**Querying/Updating (XPath) Operations:** The workload used in this study performs a great deal of XPath operations on the XML documents. XPath is a fourth generation declarative language for processing XML and locating specific nodes in an XML document. To some extent XPath is to XML what SQL is to relational databases. XPath is a language for addressing, searching, and matching pieces of the document. It is a W3C Recommendation [26], and it is implemented in many programming languages and XML packages. The most common task is to traverse, or search, the document tree. The next most common task was to retrieve the value contained in an element. XPath uses a path notation, similar to that used in file systems and URLs, to specify and match pieces of the document. For example, the XPath: /x/y/z searches the document for a root node of x, under which resides the node y, under which resides the node z. This statement returns all nodes that match the specified path structure. Two of the most commonly performed operations are: (1) GetValue: The most commonly performed action when working with XML documents is looking up the value of a given node, and (2) SetValue: Another common action is to set the value of a node to a desired value. This function takes a starting node, an XPath statement (just like getValue) and a string to set the value of the matching node to. It finds the desired node, removes all of its children (thereby removing any text and other elements contained within it), and sets its text contents to the passed-in string.

**Style-sheet (XSLT) Processing:** When communicating XML documents between systems, both ends must be able to view the XML document in the format they choose. This is where XSLT comes into play. XSLT is W3C-recommended [27]. XSLT is a language for transforming XML documents. An XSLT processor or transformer converts an XML document into another document, which can be of any format such as XML, HTML, PDF, or any other format supported by the transformer.

## 4. Analysis Methodology & Tools

Performance analysis and tuning is a challenging process whose speed and effectiveness are primarily driven by the power and quality of the performance analysis tools available. We start by detailing the systems that we measured. This section also describes the rich set of event monitoring facilities available in many of Intel's processors, and a powerful performance analysis tool based on those facilities, called Intel® VTuneTM Performance Analyzer [21]. We also perform detailed cache simulations driven by hardware traces collected. A brief overview of our cache simulator called CASPER

[10, 11] and the methodology that it is based on is also discussed below.

## 4.1. Measurement Platforms and Configurations

The Morgan Stanley Trade application being evaluated requires 3 servers to be configured in our laboratory as shown in Figure 2. Table 1 shows the system configurations used for measurements of TC application.

| | TC Application Server | MQServer | Database Server |
|---|---|---|---|
| Processor | 4 P, Intel® Xeon™ MP 2.0GHz, 512K L2, 2MB L3 Cache (per proc) | 4 P, Intel® Pentium® III Xeon™ 900MHz | 4 P, Intel® Pentium® III Xeon™ 900MHz |
| Memory | 4GB DDR SDRAM | 4GB DDR SDRAM | 4GB DDR SDRAM |
| OS | Linux* RedHat*7.3 (Kernel 2.4.18-3 smp) | Linux* RedHat*7.3 (Kernel 2.4.18-3 smp) | Linux* RedHat* 7.3 (Kernel 2.4.18-3 smp) |
| Network | 100 Mb Ethernet | 100 Mb Ethernet | 100 Mb Ethernet |

**Table 1. System Configuration**

There was a significant effort spent on tuning the application for high performance [28]. The main parameters that were adjusted were number of threads that the application used, the number of JDBC connections and the heap size for JVM. We also tuned the garbage collection mechanism (by adjusting number of GC threads) to minimize mark times and the table locking mechanisms in the database to avoid synchronization problems. We tuned this workload for four processors, which is the production usage of the application. We left the application unchanged for rest of the configurations for comparability purpose.

We carried out the measurements by varying the number of processors. For each configuration, performance was measured with the default setting (with HT Technology), as well as disabling HT Technology. Thus, a total of six configurations were measured along the following two dimensions: (a) one (1P), two (2P) and four (4P) processors (b) single-threaded (HT Technology disabled) and multithreaded (with HT Technology). The stability of the workload, as well as some of the system-level performance indicators, were measured using the Linux* tools such as SAR and IOSTAT. All performance measurements and tracing was conducted when the application reached steady state. Multiple runs were performed to ensure that the application behavior was consistent and repeatable.

## 4.2. Hardware Events Used

The event monitoring hardware provides several facilities including simple event counting, time-based sampling, event sampling and branch tracing. A detailed explanation of these techniques is not within the scope of this paper. Here, we describe some the key hardware events that were used for our performance analysis, which are:

- *Instructions*: number of instructions retired by CPU.

- *Unhalted cycles*: number of CPU cycles that the workload took to execute, not counting when the CPU was halted.
- *Cache Misses*: the number of misses and its breakdown at each level of the cache hierarchy.
- *Bus traffic*: the number of memory requests placed on the front-side bus and the resulting utilization.

The reader is referred to the IA-32 Intel® Architecture Optimization Reference Manual [29], for more details on these events.

## 4.3. Intel® VTuneTM Performance Analyzer

The Intel® VTuneTM Performance Analyzer tool provides a rich set of features to aid in performance analysis and tuning:

- Time-based and event-based sampling.
- Attribution of events to code locations
- Call graph analysis
- Hot spot analysis

This tool provides the means for reporting the % contribution of a small instruction address range to the overall program performance, and for highlighting differences in performance among versions of applications and different hardware platforms. It does this through an Excel spreadsheet interface, which facilitates easy use manipulation. The tool has been a primary workhorse for a wide variety of applications which been tuned for the best possible performance on the Intel® Xeon™ processor.

## 4.4. Overview of CASPER

In order to understand the cache scaling characteristics for this workload, we collected and ran traces collected on real systems through a cache simulator called CASPER (Cache Architecture Simulation and Performance Exploration using Ref-streams) [10, 11]. CASPER provides a rich set of features for detailed cache evaluation studies such as the following:

- Uniprocessor cache hierarchies
- Multiprocessor cache hierarchies
- CMP cache simulations
- Chipset Cache simulations
- Coherence / Snoop Filters

CASPER exposes a variety of performance metrics and characterization statistics in order to evaluate an organization or understand the memory access properties of a workload. For more details on CASPER, the reader is referred to [11].

## 5. Measurement / Analysis of XML-Based TC

In this section, we present and analyze our detailed measurement, simulation and profiling data for the XML-centric application running on an Intel® Xeon™ processor-based server. We start by discussing the performance scaling with respect to number of processors and then number of threads. We also study the cache scaling and sharing characteristics of the application with respect to number of processors as well as with respect to basic cache organization parameters such as size, line size and associativity. Finally, we discuss the various architectural components (branch misprediction, cache misses, Translation Lookaside Buffer [TLB] misses, etc) and estimate how these may impact the overall cycles needed for each instruction executed and retired. Last, we present a detailed view of the application profile – the various components (XML processing, Just-In-Time compiled (JITed) code, kernel components, etc) that execute a large fraction of key processor events (e.g., instructions, misses) – to understand the hot spots.

## 5.1. Performance Scaling with Processors

We start by studying the application throughput and its sensitivity to the number of processors available in the server. In addition, we also evaluate the benefits attained by HT Technology. To do so, we measured the platform performance after disabling HT Technology in the microprocessor. The application throughput (in messages per second) was measured in a four-processor server with one, two and four processors enabled. Figure 3 presents the messages per sec as a function of number of processors. From the figure, it can be observed that the 1P to 2P speedup is quite significant (~1.9X). The improvement from 1P to 4P system is also quite good (~3.3X). We also found that the use of HT Technology improves the overall throughput from 24% (at 1P) to 19% (at 4P). As expected, the performance improvement reduces with more number of logical or physical processors (due to higher resource utilization, more synchronization issues and an increase in I/O rate). To understand the performance scaling better, we show the cycles per instruction (CPI) and pathlength for the measured configurations (Figure 4). The overall throughput is a function of CPI and pathlength and can be expressed as follows –

Thput (msgs / sec) = (#CPUs * Frequency) / (CPI * Pathlength)

With HT Technology disabled, the cycles per instructions increases by roughly 25% as we move from one to two processor systems. We will discuss the reasoning behind this overhead (as it relates to increase in cache misses and utilization) in subsequent sections. At the same time, the pathlength (the number of instructions executed and retired for each unit of operation [one message for this workload]) actually reduces by ~16%. The system data (SAR) shows that numbers of "context switches/sec" are same in the case of 1P and 2P, but the throughput (messages/sec) almost doubles going from 1P to 2P. This indicates that the "context switches/message" doubled in case of 1P resulting in more pathlength in case of 1P than 2P. As a result, the performance improvement (discussed

earlier) becomes somewhat lower than 2X. From two to four processor systems, the CPI increases by roughly 11% and the pathlength remains roughly constant. As a result the scaling from two to four processors reduces by about 11% (~1.75X as opposed to ~2X).

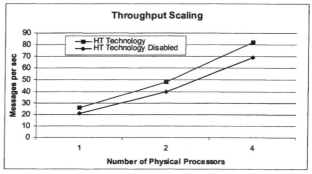

**Figure 3.** Application Performance Scaling

When the processor employs HT Technology, the increase in CPI with doubling of the number of processors is roughly 10%. The benefits of HT Technology are also clear from the reduction in CPI (up to 27% for 4P). The CPI reduction comes from overlapped execution that HT Technology makes possible – more instructions utilize the pipeline simultaneously and memory latency is hidden by useful computation.

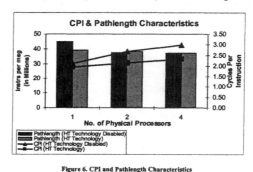

Figure 6. CPI and Pathlength Characteristics

**Figure 4.** CPI and Pathlength Characteristics

## 5.2. Measured Cache Performance

In order to understand the cache performance characteristics of an XML-centric workload, we measured the misses per instruction (MPI) on the measurement platform with the number of processors varied. Each processor employed a 2MB third-level (L3) cache. Figure 5a shows the measured L3 MPI data with and without HT Technology. We find that cache miss rate increases quite moderately with number of processors. From 1P to 2P, the increase in cache miss rate is roughly 5%, implying that the coherence overhead in this workload is relatively minimal. Additionally, we also found that the HT Technology-enabled MPI is roughly the same as the HT Technology-disabled cache MPI (except for 4P configurations in which case the difference is within 3%). This shows that the interference in the L3 cache due to multiple threads executing behind it is rather minimal.

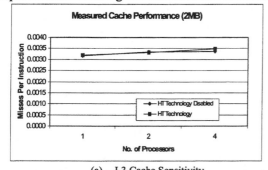

(a)  L3 Cache Sensitivity

| CPU config | L1i MPI | L1d MPI | L2 MPI | L3 MPI |
|---|---|---|---|---|
| 1P w/o HT | 0.0042 | 0.0241 | 0.0048 | 0.0032 |
| 1P w/ HT | 0.0049 | 0.0391 | 0.0061 | 0.0032 |
| 2P w/o HT | 0.0048 | 0.0288 | 0.0054 | 0.0033 |
| 2P w/ HT | 0.0045 | 0.0379 | 0.0059 | 0.0033 |
| 4P w/o HT | 0.0047 | 0.0302 | 0.0052 | 0.0034 |
| 4P w/ HT | 0.0044 | 0.0372 | 0.0055 | 0.0035 |

(b) Comparison across cache levels (L1, L2 and L3)

**Figure 5.** Measured Cache Performance

Figure 5b shows a comparison of the misses per instruction across the cache hierarchy (L1i, L1d, L2 and L3). From the figure, it can be noted that the use of multiple threads increases the cache miss rate for both L1d and L2, but not for L3 as mentioned above. An interesting observation is that the L1d and L2 cache misses reduce with increase in the number of processors if hyper-threading is enabled. This may be caused because the working set is reducing as the number of processors increase; in turn reducing the interference caused by multiple threads sharing the cache.

## 5.3. Simulated Cache Performance

Since the analysis of cache performance using measurements is limited to the configuration available, we collected traces on a one processor system and ran it through a cache simulator as described in Section 2. Now, we discuss the results obtained from the cache simulator. We started by evaluating the sensitivity of miss rate to first-level (L1) cache configuration in terms of cache size, line size and associativity. Additionally, we also studied the trade-offs of split L1 caches (instruction versus data) and unified L1 caches to see whether interference is significant to necessitate a separate instruction cache.

The L1 cache simulation results are illustrated in Figure 6 (a). In the figure, we show the cache miss rate sensitivity to cache size (from 8K to 128K). If the cache size is increased from 8K to 128K, we find that the miss rate

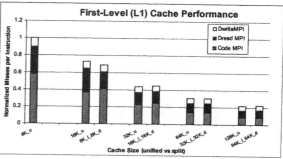

(a) Impact of Cache Size

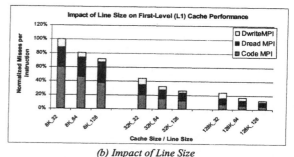

(b) Impact of Line Size

**Figure 6.** L1 Cache Performance

reduces to 24% of the smaller cache size (minor differences between unified and separate caches). The largest reduction comes from the code MPI component since it does not seem to fit in the available cache size and typically exhibits good spatial and temporal locality in memory access. Figure 6(b) also shows the benefits of larger line sizes in the L1 (separate instruction and data cache). We find that the miss rate reduces by 20% to 30% or more when the line size is increased from 32 bytes to 64 bytes. A higher benefit is obtained with a larger cache size. Increasing the line size from 64 to 128 bytes is not as effective as it was when increasing from 32 to 64 bytes. Also, we find that, for small caches, there is a benefit to having a split cache. Beyond 32K total cache size, the difference between the two is rather small.

Figure 7 shows second-level (L2) cache data in the same format as Figure 6. The L2 cache size is varied from 256KB to 2MB and the line size is varied from 64 bytes to 256 bytes. The associativity of the L2 cache is kept fixed at 8. We find a moderate reduction in miss rate with increased L2 cache size (20% or lower decrease with doubling of cache size). On the other hand, as the cache line size is doubled, the miss rate reduces by roughly 25 to 35% with more improvement at smaller line sizes and larger cache sizes. This indicates that the workload exhibits substantial spatial locality. It should be noted that the increase in line size comes at the expense of larger bandwidth required at the interconnect and the memory subsystem.

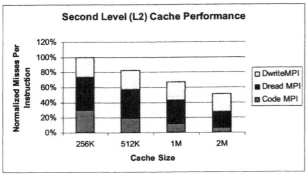

*(a) Impact of Cache Size*

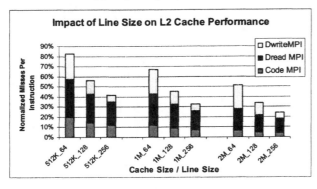

*(b) Impact of Line Size*

**Figure 7. L2 Cache Performance Characteristics**

## 5.4. Bus Bandwidth Characteristics

In this subsection, we discuss the bus traffic and performance/bandwidth characteristics when running the TC workload. Table 2 shows the utilization of the address and data bus under the twelve configurations – (1) one, two and four processor configurations and (2) with and without HT Technology enabled. As expected, we find that the utilization on the front-side bus (both address and data) increases considerably as we increase the number of processors. By enabling HT Technology however, the increase in utilization is not as substantial. Ultimately, these utilization statistics directly affect performance by increasing the queuing delay when requests need access to the bus. For one and two processor systems, the utilizations are low to moderate and as a result, the queuing delays (not presented here for brevity) were not found to be too high. However, with four processor systems, the utilizations begin to approach a significant value to where it starts affecting the latency considerably and therefore has an impact on scalability. As we discussed in the previous section, the two to four processor performance scalability is limited to 1.75X as a result of this latency increase in the platform.

## 5.5. Potential CPI Contributors

While looking at the overall performance scalability is certainly useful, another aspect that is also valuable is to

| #Procs | Address Bus Utilization | | Data Bus Utilization | |
|---|---|---|---|---|
| | HT Technology Disabled | HT Technology | Disabled | HT Technology |
| 1 | 13.2% | 14.9% | 15.0% | 17.6% |
| 2 | 22.5% | 27.8% | 26.6% | 34.2% |
| 4 | 40.0% | 49.0% | 45.7% | 56.1% |

Table 2. Bus Performance and Bandwidth Characteristics

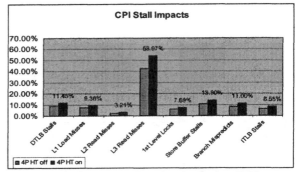

**Figure 8: CPI deconstruction for major CPU events**

understand the architectural events that contribute significantly to the overall CPI. It is rather difficult to accurately estimate the breakdown of CPI into each individual event since the events may actually be overlapped due to the superscalar processor architecture and the out-of-order execution engine. We estimate this contribution by counting the various events of interest and estimating the approximate stall time as a result of the event. In Figure 8, we show estimates of the % stall times caused for each of the following events (L1/L2/L3 Misses, TLB misses, branch misprediction and store buffer stalls). From the figure, it is easily noticeable that the maximum contributor to CPI is likely to be the L3 misses. Store buffer stalls, DTLB stalls and branch mispredicts are the next leading contributors to CPI. The purpose here is to understand the potential areas for architectural optimization that can improve the performance of XML-centric workloads.

## 6. Profiling the XML-centric Application

In this section, we start by providing a brief analysis of the TC workload and the following section uses the analysis to drive down under the covers of the HDOM layer. Profiling of the TC workload has shown that about 50% of the time is being spent in the application (JITed code) with the rest being spent in the JVM, Linux Kernel and other libraries (Figure 9). This data was collected on a four-processor system with HT Technology enabled.

**Kernel Time:** At the time of these measurements the application the processors were not 100% utilized, being about 10% idle and this idle time is reflected in the "vmlinux" module. The other functions in vmlinux include system_call that is the systemcall handler and do_anonymous_page that does memory management operations in the kernel.

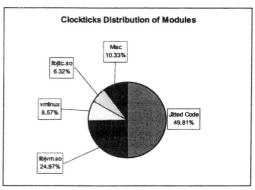

**Figure 9: Execution Breakdown of Modules**

**JVM Time:** The application spends about 25% in the JVM, doing memory management, garbage collection, threading and other functions (Figure 9). As shown in Table 3, garbage collection and memory management functions consume about 50% of the JVM time (12.5% of the total time). Of these memory management functions, cacheAllocWithInitialization is the major contributor, taking about 26% of the JVM time. This function allocates memory pages and initializes them with zeros before giving them to the application. As shown in Table 3, some of the memory management functions (e.g. parallelBitwiseSweepScan) exhibit high CPI.

| Function | % Module Clockticks | % Module Instructions Retired | % Total Clockticks | % Total Instructions | CPI |
|---|---|---|---|---|---|
| cacheAllocWithInitialization | 26.97% | 23.32% | 7.60% | 8.66% | 3.47 |
| LocalMark | 8.72% | 6.72% | 2.45% | 2.50% | 3.89 |
| atomicSetTLHAllocbits | 7.50% | 7.73% | 2.11% | 2.87% | 2.91 |
| JVM_Clone | 2.90% | 2.72% | 0.82% | 1.01% | 3.2 |
| parallelBitwiseSweepScan | 2.06% | 0.65% | 0.58% | 0.24% | 9.55 |
| XeFillStackTrace | 2.05% | 1.39% | 0.58% | 0.52% | 4.42 |
| Misc | 49.81% | 57.47% | 10.83% | 16.92% | |

**Table 3: Hot Functions in the JVM Module.**

**JITed Code:** The JITed code consists of all XML processing and other application code. Analysis of this reveals that about 15% time is spent in the XML processing package, with the main application taking about 6% of the total time. The rest of the time is spent in Java* library packages such as string operations, with java.lang. String taking 9% of the total time and list operations taking 15% of the time. The third column in Table 4 is showing the amount of time of the basic classes that is the result of being invoked by the HDOM code. For example, the application spends 9.2% in java.lang.String, but of that 5.71% is the cause of some HDOM functionality. Taking into account all the indirect calls from HDOM, we observe the 37% of the total application is the HDOM functionality that is doing XML processing. Table 5 shows the hot functions of the JITed code, with the string function charAt taking the most amount of time at the method level. The "% call count"

column shows the percentage of the total calls to this method.

| Packages | % of Total Clockticks | % From HDOM |
|---|---|---|
| msjava.HDOM | 14.95% | 14.95% |
| Java.lang.String | 9.20% | 5.71% |
| Java.util.AbstractList | 5.25% | 5.22% |
| Com.msdw.appmw.jxb. | 5.21% | |
| Java.util.ArrayList | 5.21% | 5.04% |
| Java.util.LinkedList | 4.59% | 0.36% |
| Java.util.HashMap | 2.97% | 2.73% |
| Java.lang.Object | 2.80% | 2.77% |
| Java.io | 2.63% | |
| msjava.mslog | 1.44% | |

**Table 4: Time Distribution of the JITed Code**

| Method | % of Total Clockticks | % Call Count |
|---|---|---|
| java.lang.String.charAt | 1.92% | 5.83% |
| java.lang.Object.<init> | 1.91% | 4.83% |
| java.util.HashMap.get | 1.57% | 3.03% |
| java.lang.String.equals | 1.48% | 2.62% |
| com.msdw.appmw.jxb.broker.JXBXPathMap._getPath | 1.38% | 2.50% |
| java.util.ArrayList.get | 1.34% | 2.47% |
| java.util.AbstractList$Itr.next | 1.12% | 2.36% |
| java.io.OutputStreamWriter.write | 1.05% | 2.32% |
| java.util.AbstractList$Itr.hasNext | 1.04% | 2.21% |
| java.util.AbstractList$Itr.<init> | 1.02% | 1.90% |
| java.lang.String.length | 0.97% | 1.84% |
| java.lang.String.hashCode | 0.96% | 1.78% |
| java.util.ArrayList.RangeCheck | 0.95% | 1.78% |
| msjava.hdom.Element.clone | 0.82% | 1.59% |
| java.util.ArrayList.size | 0.78% | 1.41% |
| java.util.LinkedList.access$100 | 0.77% | 1.39% |
| java.lang.String.getChars | 0.76% | 1.38% |

**Table 5: Time Distribution of the JITed Code**

Figure 10 shows the reverse callers of the primitive classes of Java obtained by post processing HPROF [30] output, e.g., we see that java.lang.String functions are invoked by the HDOM package 21% of the time and 25% of the time from the TC framework, another 29% from the java.util.Hashmap class and another 9% from other string functions. In this analysis we have accounted for 85% of the string operations and 90% of the Hashmap methods. We can safely say that all the Arraylist operations are a result of invocation from the HDOM package (namely XML processing). Similarly 50% of the hashmap operations are from the HDOM package.

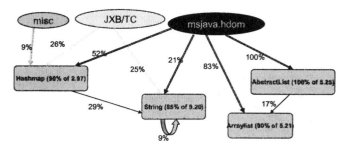

**Figure 10: Reverse Callers**

The analysis we have done in this section using Intel® VTune™ Performance Analyzer shows that about 37%

of the application time is spent in XML processing and that translates to a significant amount of String and list processing. So any optimizations we can do to enhance string performance will benefit XML processing.

## 7. Conclusions and Future Work

The purpose of this paper was to study an application that is heavily based on XML data representation. We used a commercial application and showed the characteristics of this workload through detailed measurements on the most current state-of-the-art Intel servers. We also performed cache simulations to show the cache characteristics of this workload. Finally we profiled the workload using a powerful tool (Intel® VTuneTM Performance Analyzer) and showed where most of the time is spent in the application. As far as we know, there has been no prior architectural study using XML-based Java* workloads. We uncovered some useful characteristics that will help us improve application performance through software improvements as well as system architecture improvements in the future.

Future work in this area is abundant. We have begun to understand XML-based workloads. It would be valuable to evaluate various optimizations in application software (through tuning and measurements) and architectural improvements using detailed microprocessor simulations. It would also be valuable to understand the portions of XML parsing that can be effectively implemented in a hardware accelerator (a programmable engine or an ASIC). Finally it would be very useful to better understand how XML-based data processing is similar to or differs from the processing of other data representations.

® is a trademark or registered trademark of Intel Corporation or its subsidiaries in the United States and other countries.
* Other names and brands may be claimed as property of others

## References

[1] A. Aboulnaga et al., "Estimating the Selectivity of XML path Expressions for Internet Scale Applications," VLDB 2001, http://www.cs.wisc.edu/niagara/papers/vldb01xmlsel.pdf
[2] C. Amza, et al. "Specification and Implementation of Dynamic Web Site Benchmarks", IEEE 5th Annual Workshop on Workload Characterization, Austin, Nov. 2002.
[3] L. Barroso, K. Gharachorloo, and E. Bugnion, "Memory System Characterization of Commercial Workloads," 25th International Symposium on Computer Architecture, June 1998.
[4] T. Bezenek, et al. "Characterizing a JAVA implementation of TPC-W," Workshop on Computer Architecture Evaluation Using Commercial Workloads (CAECW), Jan. 2000.
[5] H. Cain, et al. "An Architectural Evaluation of Java TPC-W," Proceedings of the 7th International Symposium on High-Performance Computer Architecture, January, 2001.
[6] K. Chow, et al. "Enterprise Java Performance: Best Practices." Intel Technology Journal. http://developer.intel.com/technology/itj/2003/volume07issue01/ , Feb. 2003.
[7] T. Fian et al., "The Design and Performance Evaluation of XML Storage Strategies," http://www.cs.wisc.edu/niagara/papers/xmlstore.pdf
[8] FiX Protocol, http://www.fixprotocol.org/
[9] R. Iyer, "Exploring the Cache Design Space for Web Servers" industrial track at the 15th International Parallel and Distributed Processing Symposium (IPDPS'01), May 2001.
[10] R. Iyer, "CASPER: Cache Architecture, Simulation and Performance Exploration using Re-streams," Intel's Design and Test Technology Conference (DTTC), 2001.
[11] R. Iyer, "On Modeling and Analyzing Cache Hierarchies using CASPER," 11th IEEE/ACM MASCOTS, Orlando, Oct 2003.
[12] E. Johnson, "XML Usage Patterns," XML Europe 2001, Berlin, Germany, May 2001.
[13] M. Karlsson, et al., "Memory System Behavior of Java-Based Middleware," Proc of 9th Int'l Symposium on High-Performance Computer Architecture (HPCA-9), Feb. 2003.
[14] M. Marden, et al., "Comparison of Memory System Behavior in Java and Non-Java Commercial Workloads," Proc. of Computer Architecture Evaluation using Commercial Workloads (CAECW-02), Feb. 2002.
[15] R Radhakrishnan and L. John, "A Performance Study of Modern Web Applications," EuroPar'99, 1999.
[16] A. Snoeren et al., "Mesh-based Content Routing using XML," 18th ACM Symposium on Operating System Principles, Banff, Canada Oct 2001.
[17] SPECweb99 Benchmark, http://www.specbench.org/osg/web99/
[18] R. Stets, K. Gharachorloo, and L. Barroso, "A Detailed Comparison of Two Transaction Processing Workloads," 5th Annual Workshop on Workload Characterization, November 2002.
[19] "TPC-W Benchmark" available at http://www.tpc.org/tpcw/
[20] XML (Extensible Markup Language), ver 1.0 (2nd edition), http://www.w3.org/TR/REC-xml
[21] "Intel® VTuneTM: Visual Tuning Environment," Intel Corp., http://developer.intel.com/design/perftools/vtune/
[22] Kimberly Keeton, Russell M. Clapp, Ashwini K. Nanda: Guest Editors' Introduction: Evaluating Servers with Commercial Workloads. IEEE Computer 36(2): 29-32 (2003)
[23] Deborah T. Marr, et al, "Hyper-Threading Technology Architecture and Microarchitecture", Intel Technology Journal. 2002, available at http://www.intel.com/technology/itj/
[24] SAX Project, http://www.saxproject.org/
[25] Document Object Model (DOM) Level 1 Spec, Ver 1.0, W3C Reco, 1998, http://www.w3.org/TR/REC-DOM-Level-1/
[26] XML Path Language (XPath), Ver 1.0, W3C Reco, Nov 16, 1999, http://www.w3.org/TR/xpath.html
[27] XSL Transformations (XSLT), Ver 1.0, W3C Reco, Nov 16, 1999, http://www.w3.org/TR/xslt
[28] David Halliwell, et al. "Java*-Based XML Processing Performs on Intel® Architecture", Intel® Developer Services, June 2003.
[29] IA-32 Intel® Architecture Optimization Reference Manual, http://developer.intel.com/design/pentium4/manuals/
[30] HPROF, http://java.sun.com/j2se/1.4.1/docs/guide/jvmpi/jvmpi.html
[31] JDOM Project, http://www.jdom.org/

# Distributed QoS-Aware Scheduling Algorithm for WDM Optical Interconnects with Arbitrary Wavelength Conversion Capability

Zhenghao Zhang and Yuanyuan Yang

Department of Electrical & Computer Engineering

State University of New York, Stony Brook, NY 11794, USA

*Abstract*—In this paper, we study scheduling problems in bufferless time slotted WDM optical interconnects with wavelength conversion ability. We consider the case when the connection requests have different priorities and give algorithms that are aware of the Quality of Service (QoS) requirements. The wavelength conversion considered in this paper is the general case of limited range wavelength conversion with arbitrary wavelength conversion capability, as limited range wavelength conversion is easier to implement and more cost effective than full range wavelength conversion, and it also includes full range wavelength conversion as a special case. We show that the problem of maximizing network throughput and giving service differentiation can be formalized as finding an optimal matching in a weighted bipartite graph. We then give an optimal distributed scheduling algorithm called *the Downwards Expanding Algorithm* that runs in $O(k^2)$ time to find such a matching, where $k$ is the number of wavelengths per fiber.

**Keywords:** Wavelength-division-multiplexing (WDM), optical interconnects, scheduling, wavelength conversion, limited range wavelength conversion, weighted bipartite graphs, matching.

## I. INTRODUCTION

Currently, there exists an enormous demand for bandwidth from many emerging computing and networking applications, such as data-browsing in the world wide web, video conferencing, video on demand, E-commerce and image distributing. Optical networking is a promising solution to this problem because of the huge bandwidth of optics. As optics become a major networking media in all communications needs, optical interconnects will inevitably play an important role in interconnecting processors in parallel and distributed computing systems.

*Wavelength Division Multiplexing (WDM)* is a technique that can better utilize the optical bandwidth by dividing the bandwidth of each fiber into multiple wavelength channels. In a WDM all-optical network, data is modulated on a selected wavelength channel and this information-bearing signal remains in the optical domain throughout the path from source to destination. *Wavelength converters* can be used to convert signal on one wavelength to another and make the

The research was supported by the U.S. National Science Foundation under grant numbers CCR-0073085 and CCR-0207999.

network more flexible. *Full range wavelength converter* is capable of converting a wavelength to any other wavelength in the optical system, but is quite difficult and expensive to implement due to current technological limitations [10], [5]. A realistic all-optical wavelength converter may only be able to convert a wavelength to several adjacent wavelengths, which is called *limited range wavelength converter*. It was shown [10], [5], [11] that limited range wavelength converters can achieve network performance similar to full range wavelength converters even when the conversion range is very small. Thus, we will focus on limited range conversion in this paper. However, it should be mentioned that our proposed algorithm is general enough to apply to all possible conversion abilities, including full range wavelength conversion which can be viewed as a special case of limited range wavelength conversion.

A *WDM optical interconnect* (also called WDM switch or crossconnect in the literature) provides interconnections between a group of input fiber links and a group of output fiber links, with each fiber link carrying multiple wavelength channels. Such an interconnect can be used to provide high-speed interconnections among a group of processors in a parallel and distributed computing system. It can also be used as an optical crossconnect (OXC) in an intermediate router or an edge router of a wide-area communication network. Figure 1 shows such an WDM interconnect. It has $N$ input fibers and $N$ output fibers. On each fiber there are $k$ wavelengths. Any input wavelength channel can be connected to any output fiber. In addition, there are limited range wavelength converters equipped on the input side of the switch, with the aid of which an input wavelength channel may be connected to all its adjacent channels on an output fiber. Since optical buffers are currently made of fiber delay lines and are very expensive and bulky [1], we consider bufferless WDM optical interconnects in this paper. It can be seen from the figure that an input fiber is first fed into a demultiplexer, where different wavelength channels are separated from one another. The signals are then fed into wavelength converters to be converted to proper wavelengths. The output of the wavelength converter can then be connected to one of the $N$ output fibers, controlled by the splitter. Before each output fiber there is an optical combiner to multiplex the signals on different wavelengths into the fiber. Apparently, it is required that all the signals fed to an optical combiner must be on different wavelengths.

We will study optimal QoS-aware scheduling in this WD-

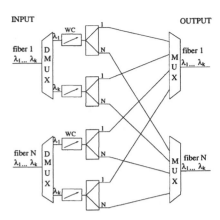

Fig. 1. A wavelength convertible WDM optical interconnect.

M optical interconnect. We assume the information is carried by optical packets arriving at the interconnect which can be one or several time slots long. We refer to an incoming packet as a connection request or simply a request. The traffic is unicast, i.e., each connection request is destined for one output fiber. The request may be of different priorities. To meet the QoS requirement, service differentiation should be given to connection requests such that the blocking probability is higher for lower priority connection requests than that for higher priority connection requests.

Since the traffic is unicast, connection requests arrived at the interconnect in one time slot can be partitioned into $N$ subsets according to their destinations. The decision of accepting a request or not in one subset does not affect the decisions in other subsets, as no connection request belongs to two subsets. Thus the scheduling algorithm can be run for each output fiber independently and in a distributed manner. The input to the scheduling algorithm is the connection requests destined to this fiber. The output of the algorithm is the decision whether a request is granted or not, and if granted, which wavelength channel it is assigned to. We will show that the scheduling problem can be formalized into a weighted bipartite graph matching problem and present an algorithm called the Downwards Expanding Algorithm to solve it.

Current approaches to meeting the QoS requirement in WDM networks are mainly based on reserving resources for higher priority connection requests, [18]. This approach is simple and easy to implement but may result in low resource utilization. As will be seen, our proposed method is more cost-effective in the sense that all resources (wavelength channels) can be assigned to all connection requests whenever possible. Extensive research has been conducted on scheduling algorithms for various electronic switches (which can be considered as a single wavelength switch). For example, [4] considered scheduling algorithms in input-buffered electronic switches under unicast traffic. Scheduling algorithms for WDM broadcast and select networks were also well studied in recent years, see, for example, [6], [7]. In this type of network, the source node broadcasts its information to all other nodes via a selected wavelength, and

only the destination node tunes into this wavelength to get the message, so that only one wavelength on the fiber is used at a time, both for the source and the destination node. It is a different type of network from the WDM interconnect considered in this paper. We consider a space-division switch where all wavelengths on a fiber can be utilized concurrently. There has also been some work in the literature on the performance analysis of WDM optical interconnects with limited range wavelength conversion in WDM wavelength routing networks (or optical circuit switching networks), e.g., [5], [10], [11]. Note that in this case there is no need for a scheduling algorithm since the connection requests arrive at the interconnect asynchronously and can be served in a "first come first served" manner. The only work on time slotted WDM interconnects with limited range wavelength conversion that we are aware of is [8], [13]. [8] only provided some rather preliminary simulation results. [13] gave an optimal algorithm for nonprioritized scheduling. In this paper we will consider prioritized scheduling.

## II. WAVELENGTH CONVERSION

As mentioned earlier, with limited range wavelength conversion, an incoming wavelength may be converted to a set of adjacent outgoing wavelengths. We define the set of these outgoing wavelengths as the *adjacency set* of this input wavelength. The cardinality of the adjacency set is the *conversion degree* of this wavelength. We assume the wavelength conversion has the following two properties:

*Property 1:* The wavelengths in the adjacency set can be represented by an interval of integers. The adjacency set of an input wavelength $\lambda_i$ is denoted by $[begin(i), end(i)]$, where $begin(i)$ and $end(i)$ are positive integers and $begin(i) \leq end(i)$.

*Property 2:* For two wavelengths $\lambda_i$ and $\lambda_j$, if $i < j$, then $begin(i) \leq begin(j)$ and $end(i) \leq end(j)$.

We can use a bipartite graph to visualize the wavelength conversion: the left side vertices represent input wavelengths and the right side vertices represent output wavelengths. If input wavelength $\lambda_i$ can be converted to output wavelength $\lambda_j$, they are connected by an edge. Figure 2 is such a conversion graph for $k = 8$. The adjacency set of $\lambda_2$, for example, can be represented as $[1, 4]$.

Note that under this type of wavelength conversion different wavelengths may have different conversion degrees. For example, the conversion degree of $\lambda_1$ is 3, while the conversion degree of $\lambda_2$ is 4. We therefore introduce the *conversion distance* which is defined as the largest difference between a wavelength and a wavelength that it can be converted to as a measure of the conversion ability. For example, the conversion distance for $\lambda_1$ is $3 - 1 = 2$. In fact the conversion distance is 2 for all the wavelengths in this example. However, in our scheduling algorithms it is not required that the conversion distances are the same for all wavelengths, as in some applications wavelengths may have different conversion distances.

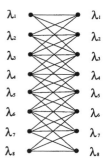

Fig. 2. Conversion graph for an 8-wavelength optical interconnect with conversion distance 2.

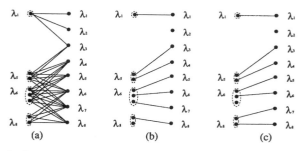

Fig. 3. Request graph and matchings in an 8-wavelength interconnect with conversion distance 2. (a) Request Graph. (b) A maximum matching. (c) An optimal matching.

## III. PROBLEM FORMALIZATION

In this section we show how the problem of optimal scheduling in the WDM interconnect can be formalized into a bipartite graph matching problem. We first consider the case that all connections hold for one time slot. The multi time slot case will be discussed at the end of Section V.

The relationship between the connection requests destined for an output fiber and the available wavelength channels on that output fiber can be described by a bipartite graph, called *request graph*. On the left side of the request graph, each node represents a connection request and on the right side of the graph, each node represents an output wavelength. We use $A$ to represent the set of the left side vertices and $B$ for the right side vertices. Let the vertices on the left side be sorted in a nondecreasing order according to their wavelength indexes. For example, a connection request on $\lambda_1$ is above a connection request on $\lambda_2$, a connection request on $\lambda_2$ is above a connection request on $\lambda_3$ and so on. If there are multiple connection requests on the same wavelength they can be in an arbitrary order. The vertices on the right side are also sorted according to their wavelength indexes. There is an edge connecting a left side vertex $a$ and a right side vertex $b$ if the wavelength of connection request $a$ can be converted to output wavelength $b$. Thus, the conversion graph discussed earlier can be simply considered as a special case of the request graph that there is exactly one connection request coming on each wavelength.

For convenience, we also define the *request vector*. A request vector is a $1 \times k$ row vector, with the $i_{th}$ element representing the number of connection requests arrived on wavelength $\lambda_i$. Figure 3(a) shows the request graph when the request vector is $[1,0,0,0,2,3,0,2]$.

In a request graph $G$, let $E$ denote the set of edges. Any wavelength assignment can be represented by a subset of $E$, $E'$, where edge $ab \in E'$ if wavelength channel $b$ is assigned to connection request $a$. Under unicast traffic, any connection request needs only one output channel and an output channel can be assigned to only one connection request. It follows that the edges in $E'$ are vertex disjoint, because if two edges share a vertex, either one connection request is assigned two wavelength channels or one wavelength channel is assigned to two connection requests. Thus, $E'$ is a *matching* in $G$.

For a given set of connection requests, to maximize network throughput, we should find a maximum matching in the request graph. This problem was studied and solved in [13]. A maximum matching for the request graph in Figure 3(a) is shown in Figure 3(b). If the connection requests have different priorities, we can assign weights to connection requests based on their priorities and then find a group of contention-free connection requests with maximum total weights. The problem can be formalized as: Given a request graph with weighted left side vertices, find a matching that maximizes both the number and the total weights of the covered left side vertices. Such a matching is called an *optimal matching*. As an example, Figure 3(c) shows an optimal matching for the request graph in Figure 3(c) when there are two different priorities and the two requests on $\lambda_8$ are of higher priority and the rest requests are of lower priority.

## IV. MAXIMUM MATCHINGS IN REQUEST GRAPHS

Before we move onto solving the problem formalized in the previous section, we first briefly discuss maximum matchings in request graphs. Based on the definition, it can be shown that the request graph has the following properties:

*Property 1:* The adjacency set of any left side vertex is an interval. In the following we use interval $[begin(a_i), end(a_i)]$ to represent the adjacency set of any left side vertex $a_i$.

*Property 2:* Let $[begin(a_i), end(a_i)]$ be the adjacency set of left side vertex $a_i$, and $[begin(a_j), end(a_j)]$ be the adjacency set of left side vertex $a_j$. If $i < j$ then $begin(a_i) \leq begin(a_j)$ and $end(a_i) \leq end(a_j)$.

*Property 3:* In request graph $G$, if edge $a_i b_u \in E$, $a_j b_v \in E$ and $i < j$, $u > v$, then $a_i b_v \in E$, $a_j b_u \in E$.

*Property 4:* In a request graph, edges $a_i b_u$ and $a_j b_v$ are a pair of *crossing edges* if $i < j$ and $u > v$. There exists a maximum matching of a request graph with no crossing edges. As a result, in this matching, the $i_{th}$ matched left side vertex is matched to the $i_{th}$ matched right side vertex.

*Property 5:* Properties 1 and 2 also hold for right side vertices. Namely, the adjacency set of any right side vertex $b_u$ is also an interval or can be represented by $[begin'(b_u), end'(b_u)]$, and for two right side vertices $b_u$ and $b_v$, if $u < v$ then $begin'(b_u) \leq begin'(b_v)$ and $end'(b_u) \leq$

TABLE 1

**First Available Algorithm**
**for** $i := 1$ **to** $n$ **do**
    let $b_j$ be the first vertex in $B$
    adjacent to $a_i$ and is not matched yet
    **if** no such $b_j$ exists
        $MATCH[i] := \Lambda$
    **else**
        $MATCH[i] := j$
    **end if**
**end for**

$end'(b_v)$.

*Property 6:* Removing any vertex from the request graph, all the above properties still hold.

As in [13], we can use a simple algorithm called the First Available Algorithm described in Table 1 for finding a maximum cardinality matching in a request graph. The input to this algorithm is: (1) The left side vertex set $A$ and the right side vertex set $B$; (2) For each left side vertex $a$, the set of vertices adjacent to it denoted by interval $[begin(a), end(a)]$. We call $begin(a)$ and $end(a)$ the begin value and end value of $a$, respectively. The output of the algorithm is array $MATCH[]$. $MATCH[i] = j$ means that the $i_{th}$ left side vertex is matched to the $j_{th}$ right side vertex. $MATCH[i] = \Lambda$ if the $i_{th}$ left side vertex is not matched to any left side vertex. In the description of the algorithm $n$ is the number of left side vertices. In this algorithm, left side vertex $a_i$ is matched to the first available right side vertex that is adjacent to it. We can image this as picking the "top" edge in the request graph and adding it to the matching in each iteration. [13] gave a proof for the following theorem.

*Theorem 1:* First Available Algorithm finds a maximum matching in a request graph.

Finding the first available vertex is easy and can be implemented in hardware. The time complexity of this algorithm is $O(n)$ (where $n$ is the number of left side vertices), since the loop is executed $n$ times.

## V. OPTIMAL MATCHINGS IN WEIGHTED REQUEST GRAPHS

### A. Matroid Greedy Algorithm

Optimal matching in an arbitrary bipartite graph can be found by the following simple greedy algorithm which can be called the *matroid greedy algorithm* [14]: Start with an empty list. In step $s$, let $a_i$ be the left side vertex with the $s_{th}$ largest weight. Check if there is a matching covering $a_i$ and all the previously selected vertices in the list. If yes, add $a_i$ to the list, otherwise leave $a_i$ uncovered. Set $s \leftarrow s + 1$ and repeat until all vertices have been checked.

The key operation of the matroid algorithm is to check if a matching covering the new vertex and all the previously selected vertices can be found. Suppose we are checking vertex $a_i$. Let the matching covering all the vertices in the list at this step be $M_i$. If there is an $M_i$ alternating path with one end being $a_i$ and the other end being an unmatched right side vertex, we can find such a matching. Otherwise no such matching exists and $a_i$ should be left unmatched.

A bipartite graph is convex if it has Property 1 defined in the previous section. Clearly, our request graph is a special case of a convex bipartite graph. It was shown in [17] how to find an optimal matching in a convex bipartite graph by using the matroid greedy algorithm and we will briefly explain their idea in the following. Define the set of the right side vertices that can be reached by $a_i$ using $M_i$ alternating paths as the *reachable set* of $a_i$ and denote it by $R$. $R$ can be found by expanding itself in a step by step manner, starting from the adjacency set of $a_i$. In each step the newly added vertices are checked to see if there is one still unmatched. If yes then stop and update the matching. Otherwise expand $R$ until it cannot be expanded further. If $R$ needs to be expanded, or no unmatched vertex is found in $R$, first pick a left side vertex that is matched to one of the vertices in $R$, say, $a_j$. Then add to $R$ the right side vertices adjacent to $a_j$ but not in $R$ yet, since these vertices can also be reached by $a_i$ using $M_i$ alternating paths. This is simply to take the unions of current $R$ and the adjacency set of $a_j$. Note that the adjacency set of $a_j$ is an interval. Thus if $R$ is also an interval the union of the two is still an interval, since they share at least one element, the vertex matched to $a_j$. Since $R$ is started as an interval, $R$ is always an interval during the expansion process. Hence, the expansion is simply to take the unions of two intervals which can be done in constant time. To find the entire reachable set, no more than $n(i)$ expansions are needed, where $n(i)$ is the number of the left side vertices in the list when checking $a_i$.

In a general bipartite graph, to find the reachable set or equivalently an $M_i$ augmenting path, we may also need only $n(i)$ expansions, but the work in each expansion may not be constant time. One might need to scan all the edges incident to a left side vertex which might take as much as $m$ operations, where $m$ is the number right side vertices. Therefore, we can see that finding the reachable set in a convex bipartite graph is considerably easier. Next we show that in a request graph the amount of work can be further reduced.

### B. The Downwards Expanding Algorithm

We now present a new algorithm, called the Downwards Expanding Algorithm, for finding an optimal matching in a request graph. As can be seen, we will gradually simplify the matroid algorithm by using the special properties of a request graph until the Downwards Expanding Algorithm is formed.

From the discussions in the previous section, we know that to see if $a_i$ can be covered along with all the previously selected left side vertices, we need to find the reachable set of $a_i$, which is defined as the set of the right side vertices that can be reached by $a_i$ using $M_i$ alternating paths, where $M_i$ is the current matching. If there is an unmatched right side vertex in the reachable set, $a_i$ will be added to the list, otherwise $a_i$ is unmatched. To find the reachable set $R$, at first we can set $R_0 = [begin(a_i), end(a_i)]$. If one of the vertices in $R_0$ is not covered by $M_i$, we can match $a_i$ to this vertex and we are done. Otherwise all the vertices in $R_0$ are matched to some other left side vertices in the list and we need to expand $R_0$. As explained earlier, the union of $R_0$ and the adjacency set of a left side vertex matched to a vertex in $R_0$ is still an interval, and the vertices belong to this interval all can be reached by $a_i$ using $M_i$ alternating paths. Of all the left side vertices matched to vertices in $R_0$, let $a_{u_0}$ and $a_{l_0}$ be the one with the smallest and the largest index, respectively. We claim that right side vertices in interval $R_1 = [begin(a_{u_0}), end(a_{l_0})]$ all can be reached by $a_i$ using $M_i$ alternating paths. This is because that the union of the adjacency set of $a_{u_0}$ and $R_0$ is $[begin(a_{u_0}), end(a_i)]$, the union of the adjacency set of $a_{l_0}$ and $R_0$ is $[begin(a_i), end(a_{l_0})]$ by Property 2 of the request graph, and these two intervals have some overlap. Furthermore, also by Property 2, the adjacency set of any other left side vertex matched to a vertex in $R_0$ is a subset of $R_1 = [begin(a_{u_0}), end(a_{l_0})]$. Therefore we need not take the union of $R_0$ with the adjacency set of these vertices.

We can check all the right side vertices in $R_1$ that have not been checked before. If there is an unmatched vertex we are done. Otherwise we can again find two left side vertices with the smallest index and the largest index matched to vertices in $R_1$, say, $a_{u_1}$ and $a_{l_1}$, respectively and expand $R_1$ to $R_2 = [begin(a_{u_1}), end(a_{l_1})]$. This process is repeated until we find a right side vertex that is not covered, or the interval cannot be expanded further which means after some $I_{th}$ expansion $R_{I-1} = R_I$. In this case we have found all the right side vertices reachable from $a_i$ via $M_i$ alternating paths.

We now show that by keeping the matching *non-crossing*, the work in each expansion can be reduced greatly. Recall Property 4 that in a request graph $G$, edge $a_ib_u$ and $a_jb_v$ cross each other if $i < j$ and $u > v$ and in a matching that does not have crossing edges, or is non-crossing, the $i_{th}$ matched left side vertex is matched to the $i_{th}$ matched right side vertex.

As explained earlier, when expanding $R_I$ to $R_{I+1}$, we need to find $a_{u_I}$ and $a_{l_I}$. Let $b_{u_I}$ and $b_{l_I}$ be the vertices in $R_I$ with the smallest index and the largest index, respectively. If there are no crossing edges in $M_i$ then $a_{u_I}$ must be matched to $b_{u_I}$ and $a_{l_I}$ must be matched to $b_{l_I}$. Thus there is no need to compare the indexes of all the left side vertices matched to $R_I$ to find $a_{u_I}$ and $a_{l_I}$. All that is needed is to find $b_{u_I}$ and $b_{l_I}$ which is very easy as they are simply the beginning and the end of interval $R_I$. If the matching needs to be updated, it can also be made non-crossing. The updating is needed when we find a right side vertex $b_w$ in $R_I$ that is not covered and $a_i$ can be added to the list. In this case, matching $M_i$ should be updated to $M_i'$, in which $a_i$ and $b_w$ both are covered. Consider the subgraph of $G$ with a vertex set containing all the left side vertices and right side vertices covered by $M_i$ plus $a_i$ and $b_w$ and call it $G_i$. There is a perfect matching in $G_i$ since all the vertices can be covered. Also, since $G_i$ is a subgraph

TABLE 2

DOWNWARDS EXPANDING ALGORITHM FOR FINDING AN OPTIMAL MATCHING

**Downwards Expanding Algorithm**
```
List := ∅;
for s := 1 to n do
      [x, y] := [begin(a_i), end(a_i)]
      while x ≤ y
            for w := x to y do
                  if b_w is not matched
                        exit the while loop;
                  end if;
            end for;
            let a_l be the vertex matched to b_y
            [x, y] := [y + 1, end(a_l)]
      end while;
      if b_w is found
            Find a_j in the list with a larger index than a_i
            and is closest to a_i
            if no such a_j
                  MATCH[i] := w
            else
                  u := MATCH[j]
                  if w < u
                        MATCH[i] := w
                  else
                        for t := u to w − 1 do
                              let a_h be the vertex matched to b_t
                              MATCH[h] := MATCH[h] + 1.
                        end for
                        MATCH[i] := u
                  end if
            end if
            List := List ∪ {i}
      end if
end for
```

of the request graph, there must be a maximum matching of $G_i$ with no crossing edges. $M_i'$ can simply be this matching. Note that at the first step the matching is empty and of course non-crossing. We will show that at each step the matching can be maintained non-crossing in an "augmenting" manner based on the matching at the previous step.

We are now in a position to present the Downwards Expanding Algorithm as described in Table 2. It is so named because we only expand the reachable set downwards.

In the algorithm, we start with $begin(a_i)$ and search downwards in interval $[x_0, y_0] = [begin(a_i), end(a_i)]$. If no unmatched right side vertex is found, we find a left side vertex matched to $end(a_i)$, say, $a_{l_0}$, and start the search from $x_1$ in interval $[x_1, y_1] = [y_0 + 1, end(a_{l_0})]$. Again, if no unmatched right side vertex is found, then start the search from $x_2$ in interval $[x_2, y_2] = [y_1 + 1, end(a_{l_1})]$, where $a_{l_1}$ is the vertex matched to $b_{y_1}$. This process is repeated until an unmatched vertex is found or at some step $I$ $x_I > y_I$, in the latter case the reachable set cannot be expanded.

If an unmatched right side vertex is found, say, $b_w$, we then search for the first matched left side vertex with an index greater than $a_i$. If no such vertex exists we simply match $a_i$ to $b_w$. Otherwise let this vertex be $a_j$, and suppose $a_j$ is matched $b_u$. If $w < u$, we also match $a_i$ to $b_w$. If not, suppose $a_i$ is the $l_{th}$ left side vertex in $G_i$, and $a_j$ will be the $(l+1)_{th}$ left side vertex in $G_i$. We match $a_i$ to $b_u$ and perform the following operation: for the $(l+1)_{th}$ to the $(l+w-u)_{th}$ left vertices in $G_i$, increment the indexes of their matching by 1. We call this "shifting" operation and illustrate it in Figure 4. The solid lines are the edges in the previous matching and the dashed lines are the edges in the new matching. The black nodes are covered by the matching, and the white nodes are not covered by the matching.

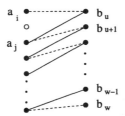

Fig. 4. When $b_w$ is found, we need to "shift" the matching.

Note that in the algorithm the expansion is equivalent to setting $R_{I+1}$ to $R_I \cup [begin(a_{l_I}), end(a_{l_I})]$, i.e., only expanding downwards. To find $a_{l_I}$ we assume that the current matching is non-crossing. The algorithm works if we can show: (1) There is indeed no need to expand the interval upwards, in other words, no unmatched right side vertex can be found by searching the vertices with smaller indexes than $begin(a_i)$; (2) The new matching is still non-crossing.

To prove the claims we need an invariant which is true throughout the execution of the algorithm. First, we define a *starting vertex*. A right side vertex $b_s$ is called a "starting vertex" with respect to a matching $M$ if $b_s$ is matched but $b_{s-1}$ is not.

*Lemma 1:* If a right side vertex $b_s$ is a starting vertex, it is matched to a left side vertex with begin value of $s$.

**Proof.** By induction. At the first step, the left side vertex with the largest weight was matched to the first right side vertex that is adjacent to it, since all the right side vertices are available at this time. (Here we do not consider isolated vertices because we can always delete them and work on a graph with no isolated vertices.) Since that right side vertex is the only matched right side vertex at this step the invariant holds.

Suppose it holds in all steps before $a_i$ is checked. When checking $a_i$, if no unmatched right side vertex can be found by the downwards searching, the matching is unchanged thus the invariant also holds. If an unmatched right side vertex $b_w$ is found, $a_i$ and $b_w$ will be matched. Consider the new matching given by the algorithm written as $M_i'$.

First, if $a_i$ is matched to $b_w$, we only added one edge to the matching and any starting vertex in $M_i$ is still matched to a vertex with begin value of it. The only possible change to them is that a starting vertex in $M_i$ may not be a starting vertex anymore in $M_i'$ (due to the addition of $b_w$). If $b_w$ is not a starting vertex in $M_i'$, the invariant will hold. Thus we only need to consider the case that $b_w$ is a starting vertex, or, $b_{w-1}$ exists and is unmatched in $M_i'$. But this implies that $b_w$ is the begin value of $a_i$, since if it is not, $b_{w-1}$ would be adjacent to $a_i$ and the algorithm would have found $b_{w-1}$ before $b_w$. Therefore, the invariant holds if $a_i$ is matched $b_w$.

If $a_i$ is matched to $b_u$, we need to perform the shifting operation to update the matching. (The notations here are the same as in the description of the algorithm.) Note that vertices from $b_{u+1}$ to $b_w$ are not starting vertices in $M_i'$, since their previous vertices are all matched in $M_i'$. We also do not need to be concerned with other matched right side vertices except $b_u$ for similar reasons mentioned earlier. For $b_u$, again if $b_u$ is not a starting vertex with respect to the new matching we are done. If it is a starting vertex, we know that $b_u$ can be matched to $a_i$, hence $u \in [begin(a_i), end(a_i)]$. We also know that $w > u$ from the algorithm. Since vertices from $begin(a_i)$ to $b_{w-1}$ are all matched, Hence $b_u$ is either not a starting vertex in $M_i'$ or is simply the begin value of $a_i$. ∎

Having seen that the invariant always holds, we now prove that the first claim is true. Suppose it is not. Then an unmatched vertex $b_w$ can be found by an upwards search. Suppose it is found after the $(I+1)_{th}$ expansion, in other words, $b_w$ is in the adjacency set of $a_{u_I}$ where $a_{u_I}$ is the left side vertex matched to $R_I$ with the smallest index, but $b_w$ is not in $R_I$. We can let $b_w$ be such a vertex with the largest index (closest to $begin(a_i)$) as can be seen in Figure 5. (In this figure, solid line are edges in the matching, dashed lines are edges not in the matching. Matched vertices are in black unmatched vertices are in white.) Thus $b_{w+1}$ is a starting vertex (with respect to $M_i$). Suppose it is matched to $a_j$. By our invariant, $w+1$ is the begin value of $a_j$. If $b_{w+1} \in R_I$ then $a_j$ is simply $a_{u_I}$, since $b_{w+1}$ is the vertex in $R_I$ with the smallest index, and $M_i$ has no crossing edges. If $b_{w+1} \notin R_I$ then $j < u_I$. In either case by Property 3 $a_j$ is adjacent to $b_w$. It contradicts with the fact that $w+1$ is the begin value of $a_j$.

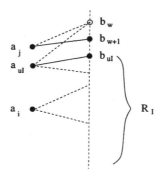

Fig. 5. $a_j$ will be adjacent to $b_w$.

We now show that the second claim is also true, that is,

the new matching $M_i'$ is also non-crossing. The first fact is that vertices in the list with smaller indexes than $a_i$ cannot be matched to vertices with larger indexes than $b_w$ in $M_i$. Suppose this is not the case. Let $a_j$ and $b_v$ be such a pair of vertices and let $b_v$ be the one closest to $b_w$. Note that vertices $b_{w+1}, b_{w+2}, \ldots, b_{v-1}$ cannot be matched to left side vertices with larger indexes than $a_j$, because otherwise edge $a_j b_v$ will cross these edges. Also, from the choice of $b_v$, vertices $b_{w+1}$, $b_{w+2}, \ldots, b_{v-1}$ cannot be matched to left side vertices with larger indexes than $a_j$. Hence $b_w$, $b_{w+1}$, $\ldots$, $b_{v-1}$ are all unmatched. Thus $b_v$ is a starting vertex, and by our invariant the begin value of $a_j$ is simply $v$. By Property 2 of the request graph, the begin value of $a_i$ is no less than $v$. Therefore, the algorithm could not have found $b_w$ in the downwards search because the search starts at $begin(a_i)$. The fact is thus true.

Now consider $G_i$. To make the new matching $M_i'$ non-crossing, we need to let the $j_{th}$ left side vertex in $G_i$ be matched to the $j_{th}$ right side vertex in $G_i$. As in the description of the algorithm, suppose $a_i$ is the $l_{th}$ left side vertex in $G_i$. If all the left side vertices in $G_i$ have smaller indexes than $a_i$, there would not be a left side vertex in $G_i$ that is matched to a vertex with a larger index than $b_w$, due to the fact we just proved. Thus $b_w$ is also the $l_{th}$ vertex, and the matching for other vertices is unchanged. Hence the new matching is still non-crossing. Now consider the case that an $a_j$ with a larger index than $a_i$ can be found and $a_j$ is matched to $b_u$. If $u > w$ $b_w$ is also the $l_{th}$ right side vertex, because all the $l - 1$ left side vertices with smaller indexes than $a_i$ are matched to vertices with smaller indexes than $b_u$. Thus we can safely add edge $a_i b_w$ in the matching without crossing any edges. If $u < w$, consider the old matching $M_i$. Since $a_j$ was the left side vertex with the $l_{th}$ largest index, $b_u$ was also the $l_{th}$ right side vertex. Thus, in $G_i$, $a_i$ was inserted before $a_j$ and becomes the $l_{th}$, but $b_w$ was inserted after $b_u$ and hence $b_u$ is still the $l_{th}$. Therefore, we can match $a_i$ to $b_u$. Thus, $b_{u+1}, b_{u+2}, \ldots, b_w$ will be the $(l+1)_{th}, (l+2)_{th}, \ldots,$ $(l+w-u)_{th}$ right vertices in $G_i$ (recall that vertices from $begin(a_i)$ to $b_{w-1}$ are all matched) and they are matched to the $(l+1)_{th}, (l+2)_{th}, \ldots, (l+w-u)_{th}$ left side vertices in $G_i$ by the algorithm.

Therefore, we have the following theorem.

*Theorem 2:* The Downwards Expanding Algorithm finds an optimal matching in the request graph.

Now we analyze the complexity of this algorithm. Note that when checking $a_i$, if there are $n(i)$ vertices in the list, to find an unmatched right side vertex, we need to scan no more than $n(i) + 1$ right side vertices, since if we have scanned $n(i) + 1$ right side vertices there will be at least one unmatched. Also, note that each right side vertex is scanned at most once. The expanding operation which takes constant time also needs to be performed no more than $n(i)$ times. To find the nearest vertex in the list ($a_j$ in the algorithm), one only needs do a search in the list which also takes $O(n(i))$ time. Finally, if an unmatched vertex is found, we need to modify the matching for at most $n(i)$ left side vertices and each sin-

gle modification is only an "add one" operation. Therefore, we conclude that in each round the running time is $O(n(i))$. In the worst case all the left side vertices can be covered, and the running time of the entire algorithm is $O(1 + 2 + \cdots + n)$ $= O(n^2)$, where $n$ is the number of left side vertices. Though the algorithm still has the same order of complexity as the algorithm designed for convex bipartite graphs [17], the work in each step of our algorithm is much simpler, which is critical for scheduling in high-speed interconnects where decisions must be made in real-time. In our applications, $n$ could be as large as $Nk$, where $N$ is the number of input fibers and $k$ is the number of wavelengths per fiber. However, the number of right side vertices is only $k$, and the number of left side vertices in the list can never exceed $k$. Thus, the running time for the Downwards Expanding Algorithm to find an optimal matching for an output fiber is $O(k^2)$.

### C. Discussions on Multi Time Slot Case

So far we have only considered the case that the durations of all connection requests are one time slot. However, it is easy to see that our algorithm can also be applied to the case that the connections hold for more than one time slots. Note that in this case, at the beginning of a time slot, some of the output wavelength channels may still be occupied by connections arrived earlier and cannot be assigned to the newly arrived requests. In this case, we can simply remove the right side vertices representing these channels from the request graph. By Property 6, we can use the same algorithm for finding optimal matchings for the request graph with the "incomplete" right side. The bounds for the running time of the algorithm is the same as before.

### VI. SIMULATION RESULTS

Besides giving proofs and analyses for the proposed scheduling algorithm, we also implemented the algorithm in software and tested them by simulations. We tested the interconnects of two sizes, one with 8 input fibers and 8 output fibers and with 8 wavelengths on each fiber, and the other with 16 input fibers and 16 output fibers and with 16 wavelengths on each fiber.

In the simulations, we assume that the arrivals of the connection requests at the input channels are bursty traffic: an input channel alternates between two states, the "busy" state and the "idle" state. When it is in the "busy" state, it continuously receives connection requests and all the connection requests go to the same destination; otherwise the input channel is in the "idle" state and does not receive any connection requests. The length of the busy and idle periods follows geometric distribution. The network performance is measured by the *blocking probability* which is defined as the ratio of the total number of blocked connection requests over the total number of arrived connection requests. The durations of the connections are one time slot and for each experiment the simulation program was run for 100,000 time slots.

In Figure 6 we plot the blocking probabilities for various

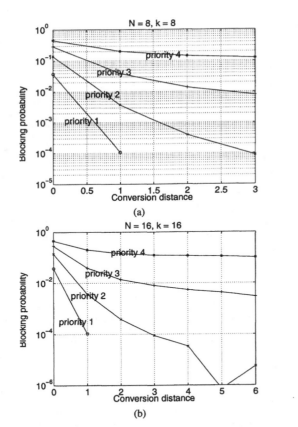

Fig. 6. Blocking probability. (a) $8 \times 8$ interconnect with 8 wavelengths per fiber. (b) $16 \times 16$ interconnect with 16 wavelengths per fiber.

In this paper we have presented an optimal QoS-aware scheduling algorithm in bufferless time slotted WDM optical interconnects with wavelength conversion ability. We have introduced the request graph and showed that the problem of maximizing network throughput and giving service differentiation is equivalent to finding an optimal matching in a weighted request graph. We then gave the Downwards Expanding Algorithm that runs in $O(k^2)$ time for finding such an optimal matching, where $k$ is the number of wavelengths per fiber. The proposed scheduling algorithm were also evaluated by simulations under bursty traffic. Our future work includes developing analytical models for performance evaluation of the interconnects under the scheduling algorithm.

## REFERENCES

[1] D. K. Hunter, M. C. Chia and I. Andonovic "Buffering in optical packet switches," *Journal of Lightwave Technology*, vol. 16 no. 12, pp. 2081-2094, 1998.

[2] M. Kovacevic and A. Acampora, "Benefits of wavelength translation in all-optical clear-channel networks," *IEEE Journal on Selected Areas in Comm.*, vol. 14, no. 5, pp. 868 -880, 1996.

[3] S.L. Danielsen, C. Joergensen, B. Mikkelsen and K.E. Stubkjaer, "Analysis of a WDM packet switch with improved performance under bursty traffic conditions due to tunable wavelength converters," *Journal of Lightwave Technology*, vol. 16, no. 5, pp. 729-735, May 1998.

[4] N. McKeown, "The iSLIP scheduling algorithm input-queued switch," *IEEE/ACM Trans. Networking*, vol.7, pp.188-201, 1999.

[5] T. Tripathi and K. N. Sivarajan, "Computing approximate blocking probabilities in wavelength routed all-optical networks with limited-range wavelength conversion," *IEEE Journal on Selected Areas in Communications*, vol. 18, pp. 2123–2129, Oct. 2000.

[6] M.S. Borella and B. Mukherjee "Efficient scheduling of nonuniform packet traffic in a WDM/TDM local lightwave network with arbitrary transceiver tuning latencies," *IEEE Journal on Selected Areas of Communications*, vol. 14, no. 5, pp. 923-934, 1996.

[7] G.N. Rouskas and V. Sivaraman "Packet scheduling in broadcast WDM networks with arbitrary transceiver tuning latencies," *IEEE/ACM Trans. Networking*, vol. 14, no. 3, pp. 359-370, 1997.

[8] G. Shen, et. al, "Performance study on a WDM packet switch with limited-range wavelength converters," *IEEE Comm. Letters*, vol. 5, no. 10, pp. 432-434, 2001.

[9] L. Xu, H.G. Perros and G. Rouskas, "Techniques for optical packet switching and optical burst switching," *IEEE communications Magazine*, pp. 136 - 142, Jan. 2001.

[10] R. Ramaswami and G. Sasaki, "Multiwavelength optical networks with limited wavelength conversion," *IEEE/ACM Trans. Networking*, vol. 6, pp. 744–754, Dec. 1998.

[11] X. Qin and Y. Yang, "Nonblocking WDM switching networks with full and limited wavelength conversion," *IEEE Trans. Comm.*, vol. 50, no. 12, pp. 2032-2041, 2002.

[12] Y. Yang, J. Wang and C. Qiao "Nonblocking WDM multicast switching networks," *IEEE Trans. Parallel and Distributed Systems*, vol. 11, no. 12, pp. 1274-1287, 2000.

[13] Z. Zhang and Y. Yang, "Distributed scheduling algorithms for wavelength convertible WDM optical interconnects," *Proc. of the 17th IEEE International Parallel and Distributed Processing Symposium*, Nice, France, April, 2003.

[14] E.L. Lawler, "Combinatorial Optimization:Networks and Matroids," *Holt, Rinehart and Winston*, 1976.

[15] J. Hopcroft and R. Karp "An $n^{\frac{5}{2}}$ algorithm for maximum matchings in bipartite graph," *SIAM J. Comput.*, 2(4):225-231, 1973.

[16] F. Glover "Maximum matching in convex bipartite graph," *Naval Res. Logist. Quart.*,14, pp. 313-316, 1967.

[17] W. Lipski Jr and F.P. Preparata "Algorithms for maximum matchings in bipartite graphs," *Naval Res. Logist. Quart.*, 14, pp. 313-316, 1981.

[18] A. Kaheel, T. Khattab, A. Mohammed and H. Alnuweiri, "Quality-of-service mechanisms in IP-over-WDM networks," *IEEE Communications Magazine*, vol. 40, no. 12, pp. 38 -43, Dec. 2002.

prioritized connection requests as a function of conversion distance. The Downwards Expanding Algorithm is used to maximize network throughput and give service differentiation. The tested traffic load is $\rho = 0.8$ (average busy period 40 time slots and average idle period 10 time slots). There are four priorities, with 10%, 20%, 30%, 40% of the total traffic, from the highest priority (priority 1) to the lowest priority (priority 4).

We can see that the blocking probability for all priorities decreases as the conversion distance increases. But when the conversion distance is larger than a certain value, the decease of blocking probability is marginal. In this case there is little benefit for further increasing the conversion degree, which is exactly the reason for using limited range wavelength converters other than the full range wavelength converters.

We can also see that the Downwards Expanding Algorithm achieves good service differentiation. For example, in Figure 6 (b) we can see that in a $16 \times 16$ interconnect with 16 wavelengths per fiber, the blocking probability of priority 4 is about $10^{-1}$, while the blocking probability of priority 2 is about $10^{-4}$ when the conversion distance is 3. The blocking probability of priority 1 should be even smaller but cannot be seen here because the reliable values of small blocking probability are extremely hard to obtain by simulations and we will use analytical models to find them in our future work.

# Session 5B:
# Network Services

# BUCS - A Bottom-Up Cache Structure for Networked Storage Servers

Ming Zhang and Qing Yang
Department of Electrical and Computer Engineering
University of Rhode Island
Kingston, RI 02881 USA
{mingz, qyang}@ele.uri.edu
Tel:1(401)874-2293
Fax:1(401)782-6422

## Abstract

*This paper introduces a new caching structure to improve server performance by minimizing data traffic over the system bus. The idea is to form a bottom-up caching hierarchy in a networked storage server. The bottom level cache is located on an embedded controller that is a combination of a network interface card (NIC) and a storage host bus adapter (HBA). Storage data coming from or going to a network are cached at this bottom level cache and meta-data related to these data are passed to the host for processing. When cached data exceed the capacity of the bottom level cache, some data are moved to the host RAM that is usually larger than the bottom level cache. This new cache hierarchy is referred to as **bottom-up cache structure (BUCS)** in contrast to a traditional CPU-centric top-down cache where the top-level cache is the smallest and fastest, and the lower in the hierarchy the larger and slower the cache. Such data caching at the controller level dramatically reduces bus traffic and leads to great performance improvement for networked storages. We have implemented a proof-of-concept prototype using Intel's IQ80310 reference board and Linux network block device. Through performance measurements on the prototype implementation, we observed up to 3 times performance improvement of BUCS over traditional systems in terms of response time and system throughput.*

***Key words:*** *cache structure, bus contention, networked storage, intelligent controller*

## 1. Introduction

Rapid technology advances have resulted in dramatic increase in CPU performance and network speed over the past decade. Similarly, throughput of data storages have also improved greatly due to technologies such as RAID and extensive caching. In contrast, the performance increase of system interconnects such as PCI bus have not kept pace with these improvements. As a result, it has become the major performance bottleneck for high performance servers. Extensive research has been done in addressing this bottleneck problem [2][4]. Most notable research efforts in this area aim at increasing the bandwidth of system interconnects by replacing PCI with PCI-X, PCI Express, or InfiniBand [1]. The InfiniBand technology uses a switch fabric as opposed to a shared bus thereby increasing bandwidth greatly [11].

It is interesting to recall the great amount of research efforts in designing various types of interconnection networks for multiprocessors for high communication bandwidth in the 80's and 90's, while at the same time there was also a great deal of research in minimizing communication by means of data caching. Both tracks of efforts contributed greatly to the architecture advance of parallel/distributed computing. We believe that it is both feasible and beneficial to build a cache hierarchy with an intelligent controller to minimize communication cost across the system interconnects.

Feasibility comes from the fact that embedded processor chips are becoming more powerful and less costly. This fact makes it cost-effective to offload many I/O and network functions at controller level [6][7] and to cache I/O and network data close to such embedded processors [12]. Table-1 lists performance parameters of three generation *I/O processors* (IOP) from Intel [10]. Compared to i960 processors that are still widely used in many RAID controllers, an IOP315 chip set has 6 times higher frequency and supports up to 12 GB on-board memory. Most Gigabit network adapters support checksum offloading by computing and checking packet checksums at the NIC level.

Potential benefit of such data caching is also fairly clear because data localities exist in many applications. Kim, Pai and Rixner have shown in their recent research [12] that

| I/O Processor | i960 | IOP310 | IOP315 |
|---|---|---|---|
| Bus Speed | 33 MHz | 66 MHz | 133 MHz PCI-X |
| Bus Width | 64/32-bit | 64-bit | 64-bit |
| CPU Speed | 100 MHz | 733 MHz | 733 MHz |
| Memory Type | 32/64-bit | 64-bit | 32/64-bit |
| Max Memory | 128 MB | 512 MB | 12 GB |

**Table 1.** *Performance parameters of three generations of I/O Processor.*

data locality exists in web applications and significant performance gain can be obtained with network interface data caching. The research work by Yocum and Chase [19] also showed the benefit of "payload caching" for network intermediary servers. By temporarily storing the payload of a packet in a NIC, they were able to improve system performance substantially. These existing research works indicate a great potential for reducing unnecessary data traffic across a system bus by means of data caching.

The above observations motivate us to introduce a new caching structure for the purpose of minimizing data traffic over a system bus. The idea is to form a bottom-up cache hierarchy in a server. The bottom level cache is located on an embedded controller that is a combination of a *network interface card* (NIC) and a storage *host bus adapter* (HBA). Storage data coming from or going to a network are cached at this bottom level cache and meta-data related to these storage data are passed to the host for processing. When cached data exceeds the capacity of the bottom level cache, some data are moved to the host RAM that is usually larger than the RAM on the controller. We call the cache on the controller *level-1* (L-1) cache and the host RAM *level-2* (L-2) cache. This new system is referred to as **bottom-up cache structure** (BUCS) in contrast to a traditional CPU-centric top-down cache where the top-level cache is the smallest and fastest, and the lower in the hierarchy the larger and slower the cache. BUCS tries to keep frequently-used data at a lower-level cache as much as possible to minimize data traffic over the system bus as opposed to placing frequently used data at a higher-level cache as much as possible in a traditional top-down cache hierarchy. For storage read requests from a network, most data are directly passed to the network through a L-1 cache. Similarly for storage write requests from the network, most data are directly written to the storage device through a write-back L-1 cache without copying them to the host RAM as being done in existing systems. Such data caching at a controller level dramatically reduces traffic on the system bus such as PCI bus and leads to a great performance improvement for networked storages. We have implemented a proof-of-concept prototype using Intel's IQ80310 reference board and Linux

NBD (network block device). Measured results show that BUCS improves response time and system throughput over traditional systems by as much as a factor of 3.

The research contributions of this paper are four fold. Firstly, we proposed a new concept of a bottom-up cache structure. This caching structure clearly minimizes data traffic over a PCI bus and increases throughput for networked storages. Secondly, we proposed a marriage between a storage HBA and a NIC with unified cache memory. Although there exist controller cards containing both a storage HBA and a NIC [13], these cards mainly concentrate on the direct data bypass rather than the functional marriage of the two that share RAM and other resources as we proposed here. Such a marriage is both feasible with high performance embedded processors and beneficial because of short circuit of data transfer between storage device and network interface. Third, we have implemented a proof-of-concept prototype BUCS using Intel's IQ80310 with Intel XScale$^{TM}$ IOP310 processor and embedded Linux. And finally, we have carried out performance measurements on the prototype to show that the BUCS system provides up to 3 times performance improvement in terms of response time and system throughput over a traditional server.

The paper is organized as follows. The next section gives a detailed description of BUCS architecture and designs. Section 3 presents the prototype implementation of BUCS and reports the performance results. Related work is discussed in Section 4. Section 5 concludes the paper.

## 2. Bottom-Up Cache Structure and Design

Data flow inside a normal storage server as results of read/write requests is shown in Figure 1. The server system consists of a system RAM, an HBA card controlling the storage device, and a NIC interconnected by a system interconnect typically a PCI bus. Upon receiving a read request over the NIC, the server host OS checks if the requested data are already in the host RAM. If not, the host OS invokes I/O operations to the storage HBA and loads the data from the storage device via the PCI bus. After the data are loaded to the host RAM, the host generates headers and assembles response packets to be transferred to NIC via the PCI bus. The NIC then sends the packets out to the requesting client. As a result, data are moved across the PCI bus at least once or even twice. Upon receiving a write request over the NIC, the host OS first loads the data from NIC to host RAM via the PCI bus and then stores the data into the attached storage device later, via the PCI bus again. Therefore, for write operations, one piece of data travels through the PCI bus twice. An important thing here is that the host never examines the data contents for either read operations or write operations except for moving data from one peripheral to another.

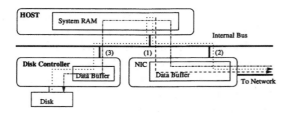

**Figure 1.** *Data flows in a traditional system for three cases: (1) A network read request finds data in the system RAM. Data go through bus once. (2) The requested data is not in the system RAM. Data goes through bus twice: one from storage device to the RAM and the other from the RAM to network. (3) A write request from the network goes through the bus twice: one from network to the system RAM and the other from the system RAM to the storage.*

The idea of BUCS is very simple. Instead of moving data back and forth every time between a peripheral device and host RAM across a PCI bus, we try to keep frequently used data in a cache at a controller level, the lowest level. Only meta-data that describe storage data and commands are transferred to the host system every time for necessary processing. Most of storage data do not travel through the PCI bus between host RAM and controllers because of effective caching at the low level. Since the lowest level cache (L-1 cache) is usually limited in size because of power and cost constraints, we use the host RAM as a L-2 cache to cache data replaced from the L-1 cache. The two level caches work together and are managed by a BUCS cache manager residing in the kernel of host OS.

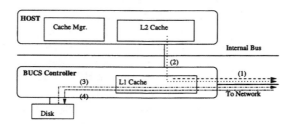

**Figure 2.** *Data flows in a BUCS system for four cases: (1) A read request finds data in L-1 cache. Data do not go through system bus. (2) The requested data is not in L-1 cache but in L-2 cache. Data go through bus once. (3) The requested data is missed from both L-1 cache and L-2 cache. Data is loaded from the storage, cached at L-1 cache, and sent out to the network. No bus transfer is necessary. (4) Written data goes to L-1 cache and the storage device.*

Figure 2 shows the data flow inside the server system as result of networked storage requests. For a read request, the BUCS cache manager checks if data are already in the L-1 or L-2 cache. If data is in the L-1 cache, the host prepares headers and invokes the BUCS controller to send data packets to the client over the network. If the data is in the L-2 cache, the cache manager moves the data from the L-2 cache to the L-1 cache. If the data is still in the storage device, the cache manager reads them out and puts them directly into the L-1 cache. In both cases, the host generates packet headers and transfers them to the BUCS controller. The controller then sends assembled packets including headers and data out to the client.

For a write request, the controller only generates a unique identifier for the data contained in a data packet and notifies the host of this id. The host then attaches this id with the meta-data in the corresponding previous command packet. The cache manager check if the old data are still in the L-1 cache or L-2 cache. If the data is in the L-1 cache, then new data will overwrite the old data directly. If the old data are in the L-2 cache, the old copy will be discarded and the actual data are stored in the L-1 cache directly. If old data are not found, the data are stored in the L-1 cache directly and later persisted into correct location in the attached storage device. The server simply responds the client with an acknowledge packet. Compared to the traditional system described above, BUCS does not transfer large bulk of data to host RAM but only related commands and meta-data via the PCI bus. As a result, the PCI bus is removed from the critical data path for most of operations.

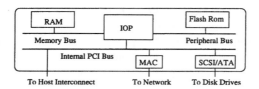

**Figure 3.** *Functional block diagram of a BUCS controller. It integrates a storage HBA and NIC with a unified RAM.*

BUCS controller is a marriage between a HBA and a NIC by integrating the functionalities of storage HBA and NIC, as shown in Figure 3. The firmware in the Flash ROM on-board contains the embedded OS code, the microcode of a storage controller, and some network protocol functions. Besides a high performance embedded processor, the BUCS controller has a storage controller chip that manipulates attached disks and a network *media access control* (MAC) chip that transmits and receives packets. An important component on the BUCS board is the on-board RAM, most of which is used as a L-1 cache except for some reserved space for on-board code. The BUCS controller is connected to a server host via a PCI or PCI-X interface.

**Data placement and Identifying a data item in the cache**: The basic unit for caching is a file block for file system level storage protocols or a disk block for block-level storage protocols allowing the system to maintain cache contents independently from network request packets. A special cache manager manages this two level cache hierarchy. All cached data are organized and managed by a single hashing table that uses the on-disk offset of a data block as its hash key. The size of each hash entry is around 20 bytes. If the average size of data represented by each entry is 4096 bytes, the hash entry cost is less than 5%, which is reasonable and feasible. When one data block is added to the L-1 or the L-2 cache, an existed hash entry is modified or a new hash entry is created by the cache manager, filled with meta-data about this data block, and inserted into the appropriate place in the hash table. Because the cache is managed by software, data mapping becomes trivial with addresses and pointers. We let a cache manager reside on the host and maintain meta-data in a host memory for both L-1 cache and L-2 cache. The cache manager sends different messages via APIs to the BUCS controller that acts as a slave to finish cache management tasks. The reason we choose this method is that network storage protocols are still processed at the host side, thus only the host can easily extract and acquire the meta-data about all cached data.

**Data replacement policy**: To make a room for new data to be placed in a cache upon cache full, we implement a LRU replacement policy in our cache manager while other replacement policies can be used as well. Most frequently used data are kept at L-1 cache. After the L-1 cache is full, least recently used data is replaced from the L-1 cache to the L-2 cache. The dirty data will be written to the storage device before being replaced to the L-2 cache. The cache manager updates the corresponding entry in the hash table to reflect such replacement. When a piece of data in the L-2 cache is accessed again and needs to be placed in the L-1 cache, it is prompted back to the L-1 cache. A hash entry is unlinked from the hash table and discarded by the cache manager when the data is discarded.

**Write operations**: Because a single cache manager manages the cache hierarchy, it is fairly easy to make sure that data in L-1 cache and L-2 cache are exclusive rather than inclusive. Data exclusivity not only makes efficient use of RAM space but also simplifies write operations because of no consistency issue between the two caches. Therefore, write operation is performed only at the cache where the data is located and there is no write-back or write-through issue between the two caches. Between cache and storage device, a write-back policy is used.

**Interfaces between BUCS and Host OS:** With a new integrated BUCS controller, interactions between host OS and controllers are changed and thus the interface between OS and BUCS has to be carefully designed. Our current design is to make the host system treat BUCS controller as a normal NIC with some additional functionalities. This greatly simplifies our implementation and keep changes to OS kernel minimum as opposed to introducing a whole new class of devices. In this way, interface design is similar to that of [12] with some modifications to satisfy our specific requirements. We add codes in the host OS to export several APIs that can be utilized by other parts of the OS and also add corresponding microcodes in BUCS controller. The APIs we have implemented include *bucs_cache_init()*, *bucs_append_data()*, *bucs_read_data()*, *bucs_write_data()*, *bucs_destage_l1()*, *bucs_prompt_l2()*, and etc. The detailed description of these APIs can be found in [20]. For each API, the host OS writes a specific command code and parameters to the registers of BUCS controller, and the command dispatcher invokes the corresponding microcode onboard to finish desired tasks.

## 3. Experimental Study

### 3.1. Prototype Implementation

We have implemented a proof-of-concept prototype of our BUCS using an Intel IQ80310 reference board driven by an IOP310 CPU. The board is plugged into a PCI slot of a host and is driven by an embedded Linux. We run the BUCS microcode as a kernel module running under this embedded Linux. The code uses the DMA engine and Message Unit provided by the hardware to communicate with the cache manager on the host. We modified the Linux kernel on the host to add a preliminary cache manager and to implement the APIs. Because of the time limitation, we did not finish the integration with the host OS and can not provide transparent support to all user space programs. Instead we reimplemented one of the data access protocols, NBD, to utilize our BUCS. We believe that fully integration with OS only need more programming work and our current prototype is sufficient to demonstrate the potential benefits of BUCS. The reason we choose NBD is that it is a simple protocol that can be easily modified and customized. A NBD client in Linux OS is a kernel module that exports a block device that can be partitioned, read, and written just like a normal disk device. It connects to a NBD server and redirects I/O requests to the server. We rewrite the user space NBD server to be a kernel module so that it can accept requests from clients in kernel and/or interact with the BUCS directly.

### 3.2. Experimental Environment and Workloads

Using the prototype implementation discussed above, we carried out performance measurements of BUCS compared to traditional servers. Five PCs are used in our experiments with one PC acting as a server and remaining 4 PCs acting as clients. All the PCs have single Pentium III 866 MHz CPU, 512 MB PC133 SDRAM, 64bit-33MHz PCI bus, and Maxtor 10 GB IDE Disk. They are interconnected by an Intel NetStructure 470T Gigabit Switch via Intel Pro1000 Gigabit NICs. An Intel IQ80310 board acts as a BUCS controller and is plugged into one of the PCI slots in the server PC. It has an Intel Pro1000T Gigabit NIC, an Adaptec 39160 Ultra 160 SCSI controller, and a Seagate Cheetah 15,000 rpm SCSI disk (ST318453LW) as storage device. We reserved 128 MB memory on IQ80310 as the L-1 cache and 256 MB memory in the host as the L-2 cache.

Two kinds of workloads are used in our measurements. The first one is a micro-benchmark that generates continuous storage requests with pre-specified data sizes. The purpose of the benchmark is to observe performance behaviors of the BUCS system under various request data sizes and request types. The second workload is a real block level trace downloaded from the Trace Distribution Center at Brigham Young University. They had run TPC-C benchmark with 20 data warehouses using Postgres database on Redhat Linux 7.1 and collected the trace using their kernel level disk trace tool, DTB. We ignored the time stamp values in the trace and sent one request immediately after the previous request is completed since we are interested in the response time value under two different systems. The trace file contains more than 3 million requests with size ranging from 4KB to 124KB. It has an average request size (mean value) about 92.4 KB and is read-dominated with 99% of its operations being read operations. The average request rate (mean value) is about 282 requests/second.

### 3.3. Numerical Results and Discussions

Our first experiment is to measure performances of the BUCS and the traditional server for read requests generated from one NBD client over the network using the micro-benchmark. Figure 4 shows our measured results for both BUCS and the traditional server. In this figure, response times and throughput speedup are plotted as functions of data sizes of read requests. Throughput speedup is defined as the ratio between the average throughput of the BUCS and the throughput of the traditional system with same speed network. For each system, two sets of data were collected corresponding to 100 Mbps network and 1Gbps network, respectively. As shown in Figure 4, performances of the BUCS are significantly better than that of the traditional system. As the data size increases, performance improvements of the BUCS increase. This result agrees well with our initial expectation. The larger data size is, the more data will travel through the PCI bus between host RAM and the NIC/HBA in the traditional system. As a result, BUCS

shows greater advantages because of effective data caching and minimization of PCI traffic. The performance improvement goes as high as a factor of 3. For example, the average response time of BUCS is 8.88 ms compared to 27.36 ms of the traditional system for data size of 128KB on the 1Gbps network. The throughput speedup goes as high as 3.09 with 1 Gbps network.

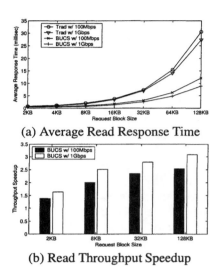

(a) Average Read Response Time

(b) Read Throughput Speedup

**Figure 4.** *Measured read performance of the traditional system and the BUCS system with single NBD client.*

The throughput speedup increases when we increase the network speed from 100 Mbps to 1 Gbps as shown in Figure 4. For example, with data block size being 128 KB, the speedup of BUCS is 2.53 with 100 Mbps network while it becomes 3.09 with 1 Gbps network. It is clearly shown that our BUCS benefits more from network improvement than the traditional system. While throughput speedup increases greatly as network bandwidth increases, the response time change is not as significant. This is because network latency does not reduce linearly with the increase of network bandwidth. For example, we measured average network latencies (mean value) over 100 Mbps and 1 Gigabit Ethernet switches to be 128.99 and 106.78 microseconds, respectively [9]. These results indicate that network latencies resulting from packet propagation delays do not change dramatically as Ethernet switches increase their bandwidth from 100 Mbps to 1 Gbps.

Similar performance results were observed for write operations as shown in Figure 5. Again, performance improvement of BUCS increases with the increase of data size. However, such increase is not monotonic. At size 32KB, the speedup of BUCS with 1Gbps network reaches a peak point and comes down for larger sizes. While analyzing this result, we noticed that the on-chip data cache of IOP310 is

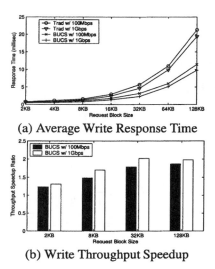

(a) Average Write Response Time

(b) Write Throughput Speedup

**Figure 5.** *Measured write performance of the traditional system and the BUCS system with single NBD client.*

32KB [10]. Our current implementation utilizes the TCP/IP stack of the embedded Linux that carries out more memory data copies when receiving data than sending out data. As a result, when write operations are performed the cache effects make a more difference in throughput. Such effects are not clearly shown for read operations and for lower speed network. Therefore, it further implies that there is room for additional performance improvement through code optimizations on the BUCS board.

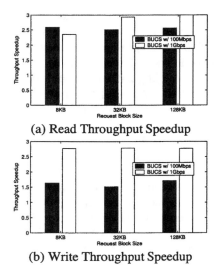

(a) Read Throughput Speedup

(b) Write Throughput Speedup

**Figure 6.** *Speedup measured using four clients.*

Our next experiment is to increase the number of clients

that generate networked storage requests in order to observe how BUCS performs with higher workloads. Figure 6 shows the server throughput speedup with four clients in the network. Three sets of bars were drawn for three different data sizes, 8KB, 32KB, and 128KB, respectively. It is observed that the throughput speedup of BUCS is similar to the one-client case implying that BUCS can handle higher load and scale fairly well with more clients. Similar to the single client case, up to a factor of 3 performance improvement was observed for the 4-client cases. Therefore, we can claim with experimental backing that BUCS effectively reduces bottleneck of the system bus.

Figure 7 shows the response time plots measured for TPC-C trace. Each dot in this figure represents the exact response time of one storage request. We plotted 10,000 requests randomly selected from the 3 million requests. It is clearly seen from this figure that BUCS dramatically reduces response time as compared to traditional systems. For the 100 Mbps network, most requests finish within about 12 ms with BUCS system as opposed to 30 ms with traditional systems. For 1Gbps network, similar performance differences are observed between BUCS and traditional systems with slightly lower response times. To further observe the distribution of response times, we summarized number of requests finished in different time intervals in Table-2. As shown in Table-2, BUCS can finish over 50% of storage requests within 10 ms and close to 100% remaining requests within 20 ms. With traditional system, only about 20% of requests can finish within 10 ms and over 58% of requests complete in longer than 20 ms. For 1Gbps network, 99.89% of requests complete within 10 ms with BUCS while only 24.29% of requests finish within 10 ms and majority take more than 20 ms with traditional systems. The average response time of BUCS is about three times faster than that of traditional systems. Performance results for TPC-C trace are fairly consistent with the results of the micro-benchmarks describe above. Although other researchers [21] had observed the poor temporal locality of TPC-C I/O accesses after being filtered by a large database buffer cache, our BUCS still provides a data "shortcut" to avoid extra PCI bus traffic.

## 4. Related Work

The bus contention problem is not new and was pointed out a few years ago by Arpaci-Dusseau et *al* [2] for streaming applications. Barve et *al* [4] found that the overall performance of the storage subsystem is bound by the performance of the I/O bus that connects multiple disks because all disk services are serialized due to bus contention.

An interesting work done by Krishnamurthy et *al* [13] offloads scheduling functions to network interface equipped with an i960 processor, improving greatly scalability in me-

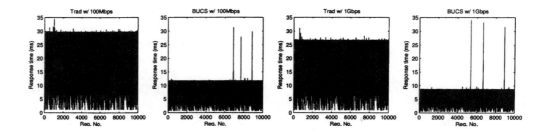

**Figure 7.** *Measured response times (millisecond) of the BUCS and the traditional system using TPC-C trace.*

| | Number of requests with response time t | | | | Avg. Response Time (mean value) |
|---|---|---|---|---|---|
| | t < 10 ms | 10 ≤ t < 20 ms | 20 ≤ t < 30 ms | 30 ms ≤ t | |
| Traditional w/ 100 Mbps | 2218 | 1856 | 5897 | 29 | 20.553 ms |
| BUCS w/ 100 Mbps | 5116 | 4879 | 4 | 1 | 8.207 ms |
| Traditional w/ 1 Gbps | 2429 | 2151 | 5419 | 1 | 18.513 ms |
| BUCS w/ 1 Gbps | 9989 | 8 | 0 | 3 | 6.103 ms |

**Table 2.** *The number of requests finished in different time intervals using TPC-C trace. We sampled 10000 requests randomly.*

dia services. Their approach allows direct data forwarding from a disk to network eliminating traffic from host CPU and host RAM by using the co-processor. Our work differs from this work in that we propose a general cache hierarchy for general storage servers as opposed to scalable scheduling for stream media applications.

There are several research projects that study data caching at network adapter level. The "payload caching" [19] by Yocum and Chase employs cache on a NIC as a short-term buffer for payloads of packets in a network intermediary to reduce bus traffic. It is shown in their research that substantial performance gains are obtained by caching part of incoming packet stream and directly forwarding them from the cache to the network. A research work by Kim et *al* [12] introduces a network interface data caching to reduce local interconnect traffic on networking servers. They have shown such caching reduces PCI traffic and increases web server throughput significantly because of high data locality that exists in web applications. Walton et *al* [17] combined two Myrinet cards on a same bus for efficient IP forwarding by transferring data directly from one card to another, called *peer DMA*, without involving the host processor. Although our BUCS shares some common objectives with the above work of network interface caching, the difference of our work from that of above is the integration of the storage controller cache and NIC cache eliminating data copy between storage subsystem and network subsystem via PCI bus. Furthermore, our two-level cache hierarchy and efficient management of the caches allow much larger cache size to be seen by clients than a single on-board cache that is usually limited because of cost

and power constraints.

Recently, there has been a great deal of research in offloading computation tasks to programmable and intelligent devices to improve system performance. Most of the modern Gigabit NICs can compute the checksum in hardware, which was proposed in RFC1936 [16]. By utilizing this feature and other optimizations, Trapeze/IP [8] yielded a TCP bandwidth of 988 Mbps on a Gigabit network. In order to reduce the CPU utilization and achieve wire speed in a Gigabit network environment, various TOE [18] products and iSCSI accelerators are under production. Buonadonna and Culler [5] proposed a new system area network architecture, Queue Pair IP, that provides a QP abstraction on existing inter-network protocols and effectively reduces the CPU utilization by offloading part of the network protocol to a programmable NIC. EMP [15] also provides a zero-copy OS-bypass message passing interface by offloading the protocol to programmable NICs. TCP Server [14] and Split-OS [3] decouple various OS functionalities and offload them to different intelligent devices. TCP Server achieves performance gains of up to 30% by using dedicated network processors on a symmetric multiprocessor server or dedicated nodes on a cluster-based server. Our intention is to improve the server performance by reducing bus traffics. Instead of offloading computation tasks, our work "offloads" frequently used data to an intelligent adapter.

## 5. Conclusions and Future Work

This paper has introduced a new caching structure, BUCS, to address the bus contention problem, which limits the further performance improvement of a storage server. In a BUCS system, a storage controller and a NIC are replaced by a BUCS controller that integrates the functionalities of both and has a unified cache memory. By placing frequently used data in the on-board cache memory, many requests can be satisfied directly in the L-1 cache thereby reducing bus traffic. The data in the L1 cache is replaced to the host memory, the L2 cache, when needed. With effective caching policy, this two level cache can provide a high speed and large size cache for networked storage data accesses. Through experiments on our prototype implementation using micro-benchmark and real world traces, we have observed up to 3 times performance improvement of BUCS over traditional systems in terms of response time and system throughput. We are currently working on our prototype and hope to have a fully functional and highly optimized implementation in the near future.

## Acknowledgments

This research is sponsored in part by National Science Foundation under grants CCR-0073377 and CCR-0312613. Any opinions, findings, and conclusions or recommendations expressed in this material are those of the author(s) and do not necessarily reflect the views of the National Science Foundation. We thank Dr. Xubin He at Tennessee Technological University and anonymous refererees for valuable suggestions and comments that improve the quality of the paper. We also thank Performance Evaluation laboratory at Brigham Young University for providing the TPC-C trace.

## References

[1] Infiniband$^{TM}$ specification. http://www.infinibandta.org, June 2001.

[2] R. H. Arpaci-Dusseau, A. C. Arpaci-Dusseau, D. E. Culler, J. M. Hellerstein, and D. A. Patterson. The architectural costs of streaming I/O: A comparison of workstations, clusters, and SMPs. In *Proceedings of The Fourth International Symposium on High-Performance Computer Architecture*, pages 90–102, Las Vegas, Nevada, Feb. 1998.

[3] K. Banerjee, A. Bohra, S. Gopalakrishnan, M. Rangarajan, and L. Iftode. Split-OS: An operating system architecture for clusters of intelligent devices. In *Work-in-Progress Session at the 18th Symposium on Operating Systems Principles*, Chateau Lake Louise, Banff, Canada, Oct. 2001.

[4] R. D. Barve, P. B. Gibbons, B. Hillyer, Y. Matias, E. A. M. Shriver, and J. S. Vitter. Round-like behavior in multiple disks on a bus. In *Proceedings of the Sixth Workshop on I/O in Parallel and Distributed Systems*, pages 1–9, Atlanta, GA, May 1999.

[5] P. Buonadonna and D. E. Culler. Queue Pair IP: A hybrid architecture for System Area Networks. In *Proceedings of the 29th Annual International Symposium on Computer Architecture*, pages 247–256, Anchorage, Alaska, May 2002.

[6] Y. Coady, J. S. Ong, and M. J. Feeley. Using embedded network processors to implement global memory management in a workstation cluster. In *The Eighth IEEE International Symposium on High Performance Distributed Computing*, Redondo Beach, CA, Aug. 1999.

[7] M. Fiuczynski, R. Martin, B. Bershad, and D. Culler. SPINE: An operating system for intelligent network adapters. Technical Report 98-08-01, University of Washington, Seattle, Aug. 1998.

[8] A. Gallatin, J. Chase, and K. Yocum. Trapeze/IP: TCP/IP at near-Gigabit speeds. In *Proceedings of the 1999 USENIX Annual Technical Conference (Freenix Track)*, Monterey, California, June 1999.

[9] X. He, Q. Yang, and M. Zhang. Introducing SCSI-To-IP Cache for Storage Area Networks. In *Proceedings of the 2002 International Conference on Parallel Processing*, pages 203–210, Vancouver, Canada, Aug. 2002.

[10] Intel. Intel I/O processor overview. http://www.intel.com/design/iio/index.htm.

[11] E. J. Kim, K. H. Yum, C. R. Das, M. Yousif, and J. Duato. Performance enhancement techniques for InfiniBand$^{TM}$ architecture. In *Preceedings of the Ninth International Symposium on High-Performance Computer Architecture*, pages 253–262, Anaheim, CA, Feb. 2003.

[12] H. Kim, V. S. Pai, and S. Rixner. Increasing web server throughput with network interface data caching. In *Proceedings of the Tenth International Conference on Architectural Support for Programming Languages and Operating Systems*, pages 239–250, San Jose, CA, Oct. 2002.

[13] R. Krishnamurthy, K. Schwan, R. West, and M.-C. Rosu. A network co-processor-based approach to scalable media streaming in servers. In *Proceedings of the 2000 International Conference on Parallel Processing*, pages 125–134, Toronto, Canada, Aug. 2000.

[14] M. Rangarajan, A. Bohra, K. Banerjee, E. V. Carrera, R. Bianchini, L. Iftode, and W. Zwaenepoel. TCP servers: Offloading TCP/IP processing in internet servers. design, implementation, and performance. Technical Report DCS-TR-481, Rutgers University, Department of Computer Science, Mar. 2002.

[15] P. Shivam. EMP: Zero-copy OS-bypass NIC-driven Gigabit Ethernet message passing. In *Proceedings of SC 01*, Denver, Colorado, Nov. 2001.

[16] J. Touch and B. Parham. RFC 1936: Implementing the Internet checksum in hardware. http://www.ietf.org/rfc/rfc1936.txt.

[17] S. Walton, A. Hutton, and J. Touch. Efficient high speed data paths for IP forwarding using host based routers. In *Proceedings of the 10th IEEE Workshop on Local and Metropolitan Area Networks*, Sydney, Australia, Nov. 1999.

[18] E. Yeh, H. Chao, V. Mannem, J. Gervais, and B. Booth. Introduction to TCP/IP Offload Engine (TOE). http://www.10gea.org/SP0502IntroToTOE_F.pdf.

[19] K. Yocum and J. Chase. Payload caching: High-speed data forwarding for network intermediaries. In *Proceedings of 2001 USENIX Annual Technical Conference*, pages 305–317, Boston, MA, June 2001.

[20] M. Zhang and Q. Yang. BUCS - a bottom-up cache structure for networked storage servers. Technical report, Dept. ECE, Univ. of Rhode Island, May 2004.

[21] Y. Zhou, J. F. Philbin, and K. Li. The multi-queue replacement algorithm for second level buffer caches. In *Proceedings of USENIX 2001 Annual Technical Conference*, pages 91–104, Boston, MA, June 2001.

# FIFO Based Multicast Scheduling Algorithm for VOQ Packet Switches

Deng Pan and Yuanyuan Yang

*Abstract*—Many networking/computing applications require high speed switching for multicast traffic at the switch/router level to save network bandwidth. However, existing queueing based packet switches and scheduling algorithms cannot perform well under multicast traffic. While the speedup requirement makes the output queued switch difficult to scale, the single input queued switch suffers from the head of line (HOL) blocking, which severely limits the network throughput. An efficient yet simple buffering strategy to remove the HOL blocking is to use the virtual output queueing (VOQ), which has been shown to perform well under unicast traffic. However, it is impractical to use the traditional virtual output queued (VOQ) switches for multicast traffic, because a VOQ multicast switch has to maintain an exponential number of queues in each input port. In this paper, we give a novel queue structure for the input buffers of a VOQ multicast switch by separately storing the address information and data information of a packet, so that an input port only needs to manage a linear number of queues. In conjunction with the multicast VOQ switch, we present a first-in-first-out based multicast scheduling algorithm, FIFO Multicast Scheduling (FIFOMS), and conduct extensive simulations to compare FIFOMS with other popular scheduling algorithms. Our results fully demonstrate the superiority of FIFOMS in both multicast latency and queue space requirement.

## I. INTRODUCTION AND BACKGROUND

Multicast is an operation to transmit information from a single source to multiple destinations, and is a requirement in high-performance networks. Many networking/computing applications require high speed switching for multicast traffic at the switch/router level to save network bandwidth. Scheduling multicast traffic on packet switches has received extensive attention in recent years, see, for example, [3] [4] [5] [6] [11]. Although there have been many scheduling algorithms proposed for different types of packet switches, how to efficiently organize and schedule multicast packets on the switches remains a challenging issue.

In general, packet switches can be divided into two broad categories: output queued (OQ) switches and input queued (IQ) switches, based on where the blocked packets are queued at the switch. A typical OQ switch, as shown in Fig.1(a), has a first-in-first-out (FIFO) queue at each output port to buffer the packets destined for that output port. O-Q switches are shown to be able to achieve unity throughput, and can easily meet different QoS requirements, such as delay, bandwidth and fairness, by applying various scheduling algorithms. However, in order for OQ switches to work at full throughput, the switching speed of the internal fabric and the receiving speed of the output port must be $N$ times faster than the sending speed of the input port, where $N$ is the number of the input ports of the switch. This deficiency makes OQ switches difficult to scale [12].

This research was supported by the U.S. National Science Foundation under grant numbers CCR-0073085 and CCR-0207999.

Deng Pan is with Dept. of Computer Science, State University of New York, Stony Brook, NY 11794, USA.

Yuanyuan Yang is with Dept. of Electrical and Computer Engineering, State University of New York, Stony Brook, NY 11794, USA.

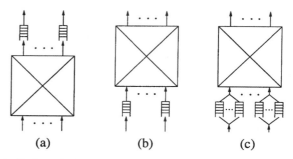

Fig. 1. Packet switches can be divided into two categories based on where the unserved packets are buffered. (a) Output queued switch. (b) Single input queued switch. (c) Multiple input queued Switch.

On the other hand, for IQ switches, the switching fabric and the output port only need to run at the same speed as that of the input port, and therefore IQ switches have been the main research focus of high speed switches. The single input queued switch, as shown in Fig.1(b), has a FIFO queue at each input port to store the incoming packets waiting for transmission. Since only the packet at the head of line (HOL) of each input queue can participate the packet scheduling, the packets behind the HOL packet suffer from the so called "head of line" blocking, which means that even though their destination output ports may be free, they cannot be scheduled to transfer because the HOL packet is blocked. Furthermore, it is proved in [13] that when $N$ is large, a single input queued switch running under the unicast i.i.d. Bernoulli traffic saturates at an offered load of approximately 0.586, and with correlated input traffic throughput can be even lower [8].

[6] proposed a multicast scheduling algorithm called TATRA based on the single input queued switch structure, by mapping the general multicast switching problem onto a variant of the popular block packing game, Tetris. However, the performance of TATRA is restricted by the HOL blocking with the single input-queued structure, especially when the incoming traffic has mixed multicast and unicast packets or the multicast packets have a relatively small average number of destinations (or fanout).

An efficient yet simple buffering strategy to remove the HOL blocking is to adopt the multiple input queued switch structure . A typical multiple input queued switch has a separate FIFO queue corresponding to each output port at each input port, resulting in a total of $N^2$ input queues, as shown in Fig.1(c). It is also called virtual output queue (VOQ) structure, since each queue stores those packets arrived from a given input port and destined for the same output port. HOL blocking is eliminated because a packet cannot be held up by a packet ahead of it that is destined for a different output. It is known that the VOQ switch structure can achieve

100% throughput for all independent arrival processes by using the maximum weight matching algorithm [2]. However, one problem for the traditional VOQ structure to be applied to multicast traffic is that a multicast packet has too many possible destinations, which is equal to $(2^N - 1)$ for a switch with $N$ output ports. This means that a VOQ switch for multicast traffic needs to maintain $(2^N - 1)$ separate queues at each of its input ports, which is obviously infeasible, especially for a large $N$.

Based on the VOQ switch structure, a lot of scheduling algorithms have been proposed, such as iSLIP [1], PIM [12], 2DRR [9] and SERENA [7], but most of them are mainly designed for unicast traffic, because, as stated above, the traditional VOQ switch cannot handle multicast traffic. Recently, [15] extended the VOQ unicast scheduling algorithm WSGS [14] to multicast scheduling, but it restricts the maximal forwarding fanout and therefore is not able to fully utilize the multicast capability of a crossbar switching fabric.

In order to eliminate the HOL blocking, and at the same time to make the VOQ structure practical for multicast traffic, in this paper we present a novel scheme to organize the packets in the input buffers of a VOQ switch by separately storing the address information and the data information of a packet. In conjunction with the new structure of the VOQ multicast switch, we present a first-in-first-out based multicast scheduling algorithm, called FIFO Multicast Scheduling (FIFOMS). As will be seen, FIFOMS can fully use the multicast capability of a crossbar fabric, does not suffer from the HOL blocking, and performs well under both multicast traffic and unicast traffic. It can provide fairness guarantee, and achieve 100% throughput under uniformly distributed traffic. Our simulation results show that FIFOMS outperforms other input queueing based scheduling algorithms in average packet delay and buffer space requirement.

In the following, we assume a switch model of $N$ input ports and $N$ output ports with a multicast-capable crossbar as its switching fabric. The switch runs in a synchronous time slot mode, and the incoming traffic includes fixed length unicast and multicast packets.

## II. QUEUE STRUCTURE FOR MULTICAST VOQ SWITCHES

As mentioned above, under the existing queueing scheme of a VOQ switch, each input port needs to maintain $(2^N - 1)$ separate queues, which makes the VOQ switch impractical for scheduling multicast traffic. In the following, we describe a new scheme for organizing packets in the input buffers of a multicast VOQ switch, so that the number of queues at each input port can be reduced to $N$.

In general, the main task of a switch includes two separate functions: 1) Scheduling - deciding for each input port which output port the packet should be sent to, and making arbitration when more than one input ports request for the same output port. 2) Data forwarding - sending the packet data from input ports to output ports according to the scheduling decision.

Accordingly, the information that a packet carries can be divided into two parts. The first part is the data content to be transferred. The second part is the destination address information of the packet, which is also used by the switch to make the scheduling decision. When the switch handles only unicast traffic, where the data content of a packet needs to be sent only once from an input port to a single output port, it is natural to combine the two functions into a single unit and use it for both scheduling and transmission. However, when multicast traffic is involved, a packet may need to be sent to multiple output ports. Although the destinations are different, the data content to be sent is the same. Therefore, there is no need to store multiple copies of the same data content. A more efficient way would be to store the address and data content of a packet separately: the data are stored once and used for all destination addresses of the packet. We use two different types of cells to store the two parts of a packet: the data cell to store the data content of the packet, and the address cell to store the destination information of the packet.

A new data cell is created to store the data content when a new packet arrives at the switch. Its data structure can be described as follows:

```
DataCell {
    binary dataContent;
    int fanoutCounter;
}
```

The dataContent field stores the data content of a packet. Since we assume the incoming traffic includes only fixed size packets, it can be implemented as a fixed size field. The fanoutCounter field records the number of destination output ports that the dataContent is going to be sent to. When a packet arrives at the switch, the fanoutCounter field of its data cell is equal to the fanout of the packet. As the dataContent is sent to part or all of the destinations of the packet, the number in the fanoutCounter field is decremented accordingly. When it becomes 0, it means that all the destination output ports have been served, and therefore the data cell can be destroyed so as to return the buffer space to the switch.

The address cell stores the destination address information of a packet. Specifically, an address cell represents one of the destination output port of the packet, and serves as a place holder in the virtual output queue corresponding to that output port. When a new packet with fanout $k$ enters the switch, $k$ address cells are created for these destination output ports. The data structure of an address cell can be described as follows:

```
AddressCell {
    int timeStamp;
    pointer pDataCell;
}
```

The timeStamp field records the arrival time of the packet that the address cell is related to. It will be used by the scheduling algorithm FIFOMS for two purposes: On the one hand, because all the address cells of the same packet have

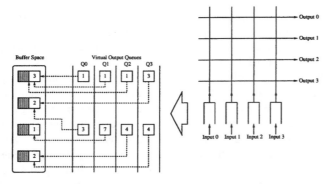

Fig. 2. An example of a $4 \times 4$ multicast VOQ switch. Left part shows the details of input port 0.

the same arrival time, the timeStamp field can be used to identify the address cells that belong to the same multicast packet. On the other hand, the time stamp value can be used as a scheduling criterion of the first-in-first-out principle, where the address cells of earlier arrived packets have smaller values. The pDataCell field is a pointer to the data cell that the address cell corresponds to. When an address cell is scheduled to transfer, the input port will actually send to the corresponding output port the dataContent of the data cell that the address cell's pDataCell field points to.

After explaining the two types of cells used, we now present the entire picture of the queue structure in a multicast VOQ switch. In each input port, there is a buffer used to store the data cells, and there are $N$ virtual output queues to store the address cells for the $N$ output ports. All the address cells in the same virtual queue are destined for the same output port, and only the address cells at the head of the queues can be scheduled.

Fig.2 gives an example of a $4 \times 4$ multicast VOQ switch. The input ports and output ports are connected by a crossbar fabric, and the incoming packets are buffered at the input side. The details of input port 0 are shown in the left part of the figure, in which there is a buffer for data cells and four virtual output queues for address cells. Input port 0 has four packets that have not been fully transferred, and the packets entered the switch at the 1st, 3rd, 4th and 7th time slots, respectively. The fanout of the first packet is 3, and the packet still needs to be sent to output ports 0, 1 and 2, the destinations of the third packet are output ports 0 and 3, the destinations of the fourth packet are output ports 2 and 3, and the seventh packet is a unicast packet to output port 1.

## III. FIRST-IN-FIRST-OUT MULTICAST SCHEDULING ALGORITHM (FIFOMS)

By using the modified queue structure, the VOQ switch now can efficiently handle multicast packets. However, no appropriate algorithms are available for scheduling multicast traffic on the VOQ switch. On the one hand, existing multicast scheduling algorithms, such as TATRA, are based on the single input queued switch structure, and therefore, suffer from the HOL blocking. On the other hand, current scheduling algorithms for VOQ switches, see, for example, [1] [12] [9], [7] were mainly designed for unicast traffic, because the

traditional VOQ switch queue structure is not suitable for multicast traffic. The scheduling principle of these scheduling algorithms is that an input port can only send its packet to one output port in a single time slot. Apparently, it does not take the characteristics of multicast traffic into consideration.

In this section, we propose a new multicast scheduling algorithm, called FIFO Multicast Scheduling (FIFOMS), for working with the multicast VOQ switch. As will be seen, the VOQ switch structure completely removes the HOL blocking, and enables FIFOMS to achieve 100% throughput under uniformly distributed traffic. And at the same time, FIFOMS utilizes the multicast capability of a crossbar switch to send a multicast packet to all its destination output ports in the same time slot whenever possible, which significantly reduces the multicast latency.

It should be mentioned that for any multicast scheduling algorithm, there is an inherent conflict in scheduling. In order to make use of the multicast characteristics and achieve short average cell delay, it is preferred for a multicast packet to be sent to all its destination output ports in the same time slot, or in other words, all the output ports should choose the same multicast packet in the scheduling arbitration. However, for the sake of fast scheduling, each output port should make arbitration concurrently. Then, the question is: How could the independently made decisions choose the same packet? FIFOMS solves this problem by adopting the first-in-first-out rule. It assigns every incoming packet a time stamp with the value equal to its arrival time, and uses the time stamp as a criterion in the scheduling arbitration. The time stamp criterion makes the multicast packets arrived earlier have better chance to be chosen by all its destination output ports when the output ports make scheduling decisions independently. Next, we will describe FIFOMS and its associated packet preprocessing algorithm.

### A. Preprocessing Incoming Packets

In order to fit into the multicast VOQ switch queue structure, a multicast packet needs to be preprocessed upon arriving. One data cell is generated in the data buffer to store the content of the packet. A separate address cell is generated for each of the destination output ports, with its timeStamp field assigned the value of current time slot, and is put at the end of the corresponding queue.

Details of the packet preprocessing algorithm are described in Table 1.

### B. First-In-First-Out Multicast Scheduling Algorithm (FIFOMS)

Similar to iSLIP [1] or PIM [12], FIFOMS is an iterative algorithm, and each iterative round consists of two steps: 1) Request - address cells at each input port make requests to their destination output ports for possible transmission. 2) Grant - each output port selects one request from all the requests it received, and grants the transmission to the corresponding address cell.

However, different from iSLIP and PIM, the accept step is not needed in FIFOMS, because in our request step, all the

## TABLE 1
### PACKET PREPROCESSING ALGORITHM

```
Input: A new packet with destination vector dest[N], in which
       dest[i] = true means output port i is one of its destinations.

Output: One data cell in the buffer, and k address cells in the virtual
        output queues, where k is the fanout of the multicast packet.

dc = new DataCell(); // generate a new data cell
dc.dataContent = new_ packet_ body; // copy the message body

for (int i = 0; i < N; i++) {
    // generate the address cell for output port i, and enqueue it
    if (newPacket.dest[i] == true) {
        ac = new AddressCell();
        ac.timeStamp = currentSlot;
        ac.pDataCell = dc;
        queue[i].enqueue(ac);
    }
}
```

## TABLE 2
### FIRST-IN-FIRST-OUT MULTICAST SCHEDULING ALGORITHM

```
Input: Input ports with address cell queues and data cell buffers.

Output: Scheduling decision.

do {
    // request step
    for all input ports do {
        if the input port is free {
            smallest_time_stamp = the smallest time stamp of all HOL
                address cells whose corresponding output port is free;

            for all HOL address cells {
                if address cell's corresponding output port is free AND
                    its time stamp is equal to smallest_time_stamp {
                    the address cell makes a request to the corresponding
                        output port, and sends its time stamp as weight;
                }
            }
        }
    }

    // grant step
    for all output ports do {
        select the smallest time stamp from all its requests;
        if there are more than one such requests, randomly select one;
        grant the address cell corresponding to the selected request;
        mark the output port and the granted address cell as reserved;
    }
} while some output port and input port pairs match in this round;

// data transmission
set the crosspoints of the switch fabric;
for all input ports do {
    find the data cell through the pointer field of the scheduled address cell;
    send the data cell to all the scheduled output ports;
}

// post-transmission processing
for all input ports do {
    for each scheduled address cell {
        decrease the fanoutCounter field of the data cell that
            the address cell points to by 1;
        if the data cell's fanoutCounter field becomes 0 {
            destroy the data cell;
        }
        remove the address cell from the head of queue;
    }
}
```

address cells that make requests must point to the same data cell. Therefore, only one of the data cells in an input port can be granted the transmission, and there is no potential conflict in which an input port needs to send more than one data cells in a single time slot. In a scheduling round, FIFOMS has one fewer operational step, and less data exchange between inputs and outputs. The FIFOMS scheduling algorithm is described in Table 2, and we will explain each step in more detail next.

### B.1 Request Step

In the request step, an input port finds the earliest HOL address cells, and give them priorities to send transmission requests. There are two possible cases. 1) If the input port is free in the current scheduling round (an input port or an output port is free if it has not been scheduled to send or receive a packet in the current round), it simply selects the HOL address cells whose time stamp is the smallest and corresponding output ports are free. Then the selected address cells send requests to their output ports with the scheduling weight being its time stamp. Note that there may be more than one such address cells with the same smallest time stamp in an input port, which came from the same multicast packet. 2) Otherwise, if some address cells have been scheduled to transfer in the earlier rounds of the current time slot, it means that all the other HOL address cells with the same time stamp, if there is any, must have made requests in the earlier rounds but were not selected by the output ports. Since one input port can send at most one data cell in a single time slot, the input port cannot make requests any more.

### B.2 Grant Step

After the request step, each output port has collected some requests with different weights. Following the first-in-first-out rule, an output port grants the request with the smallest time stamp. It is possible that several requests have the same smallest time stamp. In this case, the output randomly select one to grant.

The iterative rounds of the request and grant steps continue

until there are no possible matched pairs of free output ports and free input ports.

### B.3 Data Transmission

After the scheduling decisions are generated during the iterative rounds in the form of matched input and output pairs, the corresponding crosspoints connecting the scheduled input ports and output ports are set, and the input port begins to send the data cell. Note that an input port may be connected to more than one output ports simultaneously. Thus, the algorithm can fully use the built-in multicast capability of the crossbar switch fabric.

### B.4 Post Transmission Processing

After the transmission is completed, some post processing work needs to be performed to update the address cells and data cells that have been transferred. The served HOL

321

address cells are removed from the heads of their queues, and the fanoutCounter fields of the related data cells are decreased accordingly. If a data cell's fanoutCounter field becomes 0, i.e., it has been sent to all destination output ports, the data cell is destroyed to return the buffer space.

## IV. HARDWARE IMPLEMENTATION AND COMPLEXITY ANALYSIS OF THE FIFOMS SCHEDULING ALGORITHM

In this section, we discuss some implementation and performance issues of the newly proposed scheduling algorithm and analyze the complexity of the algorithm.

### A. Hardware Implementation

One important property of a practical scheduling algorithm is that it should be easy to implement. In the following, we briefly discuss the hardware implementation of the FIFOMS scheduler. As can be seen, FIFOMS can be fairly easy to implement in hardware and thus achieve high speed switching in practice.

The scheduler can be logically divided into two units as shown in Fig.3, corresponding to the scheduling functionality and data forwarding functionality, respectively.

In the control unit on the left, the input side consists of all the address cell queues, because the information provided by the address cells are used for making scheduling decisions. A comparator is used at each input port to select the HOL address cells with the smallest time stamp. Since the comparison operation of each input port does not depend on each other, it can be performed in parallel. The selected address cells send their requests with time stamps as weights to the corresponding output ports. Then each output port uses a comparator to select the request with the smallest time stamp and grants the transmission to the corresponding address cell. Finally, before the next iterative round of FIFOMS could start, the grant results of the current round are fed back to the input ports.

The data forwarding unit consists of the data cell buffer space and the crossbar switching fabric. The scheduling decisions made by the control unit are forwarded to the data forwarding unit as control signals. The output of the comparator of each input port is used to select from the buffer space which data cell should be sent. And the output of the comparator of each output port controls which crosspoint should be set to connect a particular input port with this output port.

### B. Space Complexity of the Algorithm

As has been seen, by separately storing the data and address information of a packet, a VOQ switch is able to handle multicast traffic efficiently. The multicast VOQ switch saves buffer space by storing only one copy of data content of a multicast packet. Compared to the single input queued switch, the multicast VOQ switch consumes slightly more storage space. The main cost comes from the separately stored multiple address cells of a packet, in which case a single packet may need up to $N$ times of the size of an address cell. Fortunately, the data structure of an address cell only

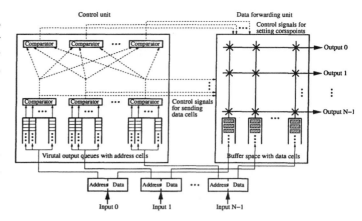

Fig. 3. The overall FIFOMS scheduler can be logically divided into two units, the control unit on the left and the data forwarding unit on the right.

includes an integer field and a pointer field, and a small constant number of bytes should be sufficient.

### C. Time Complexity of the Algorithm

The time complexity for preprocessing an arriving packet is $O(N)$, because when a multicast packet arrives at the switch, up to $N$ address cells may need to be created. [16] pointed out the potential memory speedup problem, but since the destinations of a packet are independent and an address cell comprises only several bytes, the operation can be done in parallel by hardware to achieve $O(1)$ complexity. Furthermore, the preprocessing of new packets can be overlapped with the scheduling and the switching in the switch. Thus it would not introduce extra time delay.

The most time-consuming operation in each round of FIFOMS is for an input port to find the smallest time stamp from those of all the HOL address cells, and for an output port to select the request with the smallest time stamp. If the operation is executed in a serial fashion, the time complexity is $O(N)$. If we use the parallel comparators as that in the WBA scheduler [10], the time complexity can be reduced to $O(1)$.

The convergence time has been a big concern for iterative matching algorithms like FIFOMS. In the worst case, FIFOMS runs $N$ rounds to converge, because in each round at least one output port is scheduled for receiving a data cell from an input port and will not be considered in the future rounds. But as will be seen later in the simulation results section in Fig.5, for the average case, the convergence rounds of FIFOMS is much smaller than $N$. And we have an interesting observation that FIFOMS and iSLIP require almost the same number of rounds to converge under relatively light traffic load.

## V. SIMULATION RESULTS

We have conducted extensive simulations to compare the performance of FIFOMS with other three scheduling algorithms: TATRA [6], iSLIP [1] and a simple FIFO scheduling algorithm on the output queued switch structure.

TATRA is a multicast scheduling algorithm based on the single input queued switch structure. By minimizing the number of input ports with the set of cells that lose contention for output ports and remain at the HOL of the input queues in each cycle, it achieves good performance as well as strict fairness. Through the comparison with TATRA, we demonstrate that FIFOMS successfully removes the HOL blocking, which restricts the maximum throughput TATRA can reach.

iSLIP is a scheduling algorithm mainly designed for unicast traffic based on the VOQ switch structure. In the simulation, iSLIP schedules a multicast packet as separate (independent) unicast packets. Through the comparison with iSLIP, we show that FIFOMS can make use of the characteristics of multicast traffic and take advantage of the multicast capability of the crossbar switch. As a result, FIFOMS has much shorter average cell delay than iSLIP for multicast traffic.

As discussed in the introduction section, the output queued switch structure is known to be superior to the input queued structure in performance but requires $N$ times fast switching ability. Despite its much stronger hardware requirement, in our simulations we also include a simple FIFO scheduling algorithm on the output queued structure as an ultimate performance benchmark for FIFOMS.

In the simulations, we collect the following four types of statistics:

- Average input oriented delay: Input oriented delay represents the transmission delay from the sender's point of view. Specifically, it is equal to the maximum delay that the last destination output port of a multicast packet receives the packet.
- Average output oriented delay: Average output oriented delay represents the transmission delay from the receiver's point of view. It can be computed as the average of the delay that the multicast packet is delivered to all its destination output ports.
- Average queue size: Average queue size tells how long a new incoming packet needs to wait before transmission, and it also represents the space requirement of the algorithm. For FIFOMS and iSLIP, the queue size is defined to be the number of data cells in the buffer of an input port, in the sense that how many unsent packets an input port needs to hold.
- Maximum queue size: Maximum queue size gives the maximum buffer space for an algorithm to work without loss of packets.

All the simulated switches are assumed to operate in a discrete time slot manner with fixed size packets. In each simulation run, there is a sufficient warmup period (typically half of the total simulation time) to obtain stable statistics. The simulation runs for a fixed amount of simulation time ($10^6$) unless the switch becomes unstable (i.e. it reaches a stage where it is unstable to sustain the offered load).

In order to compare the performance of the algorithms in various networking environments, we consider several different types of traffic, including Bernoulli traffic, uniform traffic, and burst traffic.

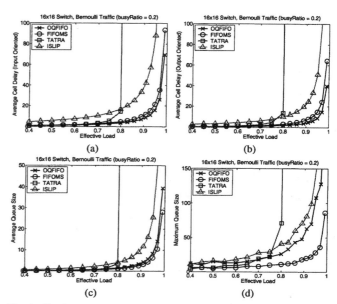

Fig. 4. Simulation results for a $16 \times 16$ switch under Bernoulli traffic with $b = 0.2$ (a) Average input oriented delay. (b) Average output oriented delay. (c) Average queue size. (d) Maximum queue size.

### A. Simulation Results Under Bernoulli Traffic

The Bernoulli traffic is one of the most widely used traffic models in the simulation of scheduling algorithms. A Bernoulli traffic can be described using two parameters $p$ and $b$. $p$ is the probability that an input port is busy at a time slot, i.e., the probability an input port has some packet to arrive at the beginning of a time slot. The destination of the incoming packet is uniformly distributed over all possible multicast destinations. To be precise, a packet has the probability of $b$ to be addressed to each output port. Therefore, for an $N \times N$ switch, the average fanout of a multicast packet is $b \times N$, and the effective load is $p \times b \times N$.

The simulation results for a $16 \times 16$ switch under the Bernoulli traffic with $b = 0.2$ and a series of different $p$ values are shown in Fig.4. As can be seen from the figure, in terms of input and output oriented average cell delays, FIFOMS closely matches OQFIFO, which has the best performance. In addition, FIFOMS outperforms all other three algorithms in terms of both average queue size and maximum queue size. On the other hand, due to the HOL blocking in the single input queued switch structure that TATRA is based on, when the effective load goes beyond 80%, the delay of TATRA increases dramatically and it becomes unstable. It can also be observed that iSLIP has much longer average cell delay than all the other algorithms. This is because iSLIP is a scheduling algorithm specially designed for unicast traffic.

Fig.5 compares the convergence rounds between FIFOMS and iSLIP. We can see that the convergence rounds of both FIFOMS and iSLIP are not sensitive to the increasing of the traffic. Also, it is interesting to notice that FIFOMS and iSLIP take roughly the same number of iterative rounds to converge. To be more specific, FIFOMS outperforms iSLIP until the effective load reaches above 90%, under which iSLIP has

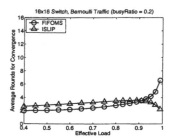

Fig. 5. Average convergence rounds of FIFOMS and iSLIP for a $16 \times 16$ switch under Bernoulli Traffic with $b = 0.2$.

already become unstable.

### B. Simulation Results Under Uniform Traffic

In real-world applications, the fanout of most multicast connections is limited by some upper bound value instead of being uniformly distributed over all the possible destinations. In this case, we can use the uniform traffic with a restricted maximum fanout to capture this characteristics.

A uniform traffic can be described using two parameters $p$ and $maxFanout$, in which $p$ is the probability that an input port has a packet to arrive at a time slot, and $maxFanout$ is the maximum possible fanout of any incoming packet. The fanout of a packet is uniformly distributed from 1 to $maxFanout$, and the individual destination output ports are randomly selected from all the $N$ output ports. Therefore, for an $N \times N$ switch, the average fanout is $(1 + maxFanout)/2$, and the effective load is $p \times (1 + maxFanout)/2$.

First, let's look at the simulation results when $maxFanout$ is set to 1, which is exactly the pure unicast traffic. There is no doubt that the well-known unicast scheduling algorithm iSLIP achieves short average cell delay. Although mainly designed for multicast traffic, FIFOMS manages to match and even surpass iSLIP on average cell delay, and is the best in terms of buffer requirement. On the contrary, the performance of TATRA is greatly affected by the HOL blocking, it can only reach a maximum effective load of about 55%, which is consistent with the theoretical analysis result of 0.586 in [13].

Simulations are also conducted under uniform traffic with $maxFanout = 8$ and the corresponding results are shown in Fig.7. FIFOMS consistently gives a satisfactory performance. It has the shortest average cell delay (both input oriented and output oriented) among the three input queued scheduling algorithms, and even excels OQFIFO on buffer requirement. It also can be observed that as the $maxFanout$ value becomes larger, TATRA has better performance, because it has more choices to move the cells in the Tetris box.

### C. Simulation Results Under Burst Traffic

In practice, network packets are usually highly correlated and tend to arrive in a burst mode. For a discrete time slot switch, we generally use a two state Markov process which alternates between off and on states to describe the burst nature. In the off state, there is no packet to arrive. In the on state, packets arrive at every time slot and all have the same destinations. At the end of each slot, the traffic can switch

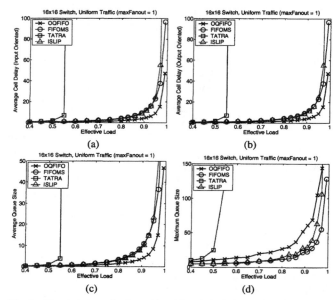

Fig. 6. Simulation results for a $16 \times 16$ switch under uniform traffic with maxFanout= 1. (a) Average input oriented delay. (b) Average output oriented delay. (c) Average queue size. (d) Maximum queue size.

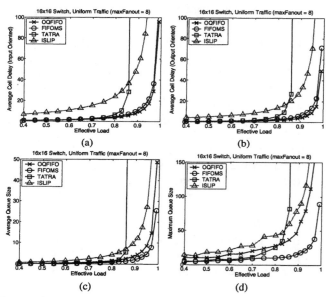

Fig. 7. Simulation results for a $16 \times 16$ switch under uniform traffic with maxFanout= 8. (a) Average input oriented delay. (b) Average output oriented delay. (c) Average queue size. (d) Maximum queue size.

between off and on states independently. A burst traffic can be described using three parameters $E_{off}$, $E_{on}$ and $b$. $E_{off}$ is the average length of the off state, or alternatively the probability to switch from the off state to the on state is $1/E_{off}$. $E_{on}$ is the average length of the on state, or the probability to switch from the on state to the off state is $1/E_{on}$. $b$ is the probability of a packet being addressed to a specific output port. Therefore, for an $N \times N$ switch, the average fanout is $p \times N$, the arrival rate is $E_{on}/(E_{off} + E_{on})$, and the effective load is $p \times N \times E_{on}/(E_{off} + E_{on})$. For easy comparison, we set $E_{on}$ to be the same value 16 as in [6].

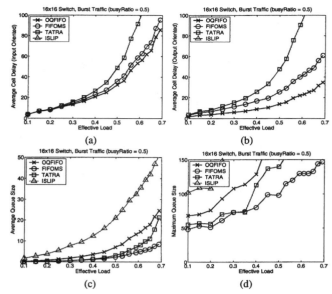

Fig. 8. Simulation results for a $16 \times 16$ switch under burst traffic with $q = 0.5$. (a) Average input oriented delay. (b) Average output oriented delay. (c) Average queue size. (d) Maximum queue size.

The simulation results for a $16 \times 16$ switch with $b = 0.5$ are shown in Fig.8. Due to the burst nature, the saturated throughput of all the algorithm becomes much lower. As to average cell delay, FIFOMS outperforms TATRA, but is not as good as OQFIFO. iSLIP saturates at a so small value that it cannot even be seen in the first two graphs, which is consistent with the theoretical analysis of [8]. As under other traffic modes, FIFOMS has the smallest queue space.

## VI. CONCLUSIONS

In this paper, we first gave a novel scheme to organize the multicast packets in input buffers of a VOQ switch. By separately storing the address and data of a packet, the new queue structure enables the VOQ switch to handle multicast traffic efficiently, because it decreases the number of queues an input port needs to manages from exponential to linear, and at the same time it keeps all existing advantages of the VOQ switch.

In conjunction with the multicast VOQ switch, we also designed a multicast scheduling algorithm, first-in-first-out multicast scheduling (FIFOMS). The main features of FIFOMS can be summarized as follows:

- Performs well under both multicast and unicast traffic: FIFOMS is designed for scheduling multicast traffic, and fully uses the inherent multicast capability of the crossbar switch. Furthermore, even under the pure unicast traffic, the performance of FIFOMS can also match the specifically designed unicast scheduling algorithms.
- Achieves 100% throughput under uniformly distributed traffic: Under uniform 100% offered load, all the $N \times N$ virtual output queues have sustaining backlogs. As a result, each output port can receive one data cell in each time slot, and therefore FIFOMS achieves 100% throughput.

- Starvation free: Because of the FIFO property, FIFOMS provides fairness guarantee. In other words, the time a packet can stay in the switch is bounded by a maximum value, since an address cell will definitely get scheduled after all its competitors are served, which include the earlier address cells in the other queues of the same input port and the earlier address cells in the virtual queues corresponding to the same output port of the other input ports.
- Enables fanout splitting: The destination output ports of a multicast packet can be served in separate time slots. It is allowed to send the data cell to some output ports in a slot, and leave others for later chances. Fanout splitting is necessary for an algorithm to achieve high throughput under multicast traffic.

We have conducted extensive simulations to compare the performance of FIFOMS with other popular scheduling algorithms. And the results fully demonstrate the superiority of FIFOMS in both the average cell delay and the queue space requirement.

## REFERENCES

[1] N. McKeown, "The iSLIP scheduling algorithm for input-queued switches," *IEEE/ACM Trans. Networking*, vol. 7, no. 2, pp. 188-201, Apr. 1999.
[2] N. McKeown, A. Mekkittikul, V. Anantharam, and J. Walrand, "Achieving 100% throughput in an input queued switch," *IEEE Trans. Commun.*, vol. 47, no. 8, pp. 1260-1267, Aug. 1999.
[3] W.-T. Chen, C.-F. Huang, Y.-L. Chang, and W.-Y. Hwang. "An efficient cell-scheduling algorithm for multicast ATM switching systems," *IEEE/ACM Trans. Networking*, vol. 8, no. 4, pp. 517-525, Aug. 2000.
[4] G. Han and Y. Yang, "A random graph approach for multicast scheduling and performance analysis," *Proc. of 12th IEEE International Conference on Computer Communications and Networks*, pp. 270-275, Dallas, Texas, October 2003.
[5] Z. Zhang and Y. Yang, "Multicast scheduling in WDM switching networks," *Proc. of IEEE 2003 International Conference on Communications (ICC '03)*, pp. 1458-1462, Anchorage, Alaska, May 2003.
[6] R. Ahuja, B. Prabhakar and N. McKeown, "Multicast Scheduling Algorithms for Input-Queued Switches," *IEEE J. Select. Areas Commun.*, vol. 15, no. 5, pp. 855-866, Jun. 1997.
[7] P. Giaccone, B. Prabhakar, and D. Shah, "Towards simple, high performance schedulers for high-aggregate bandwidth switches," *Proc. of IEEE INFOCOM '02*, New York, NY, June 2002.
[8] S.-Q. Li, "Performance of a nonblocking space-division packet switch with correlated input traffic," *IEEE Trans. Commun.*, vol. 40, no. 1, pp. 97-108, Jan. 1992.
[9] R. LaMaire and D. Serpanos, "Two dimensional round-robin schedulers for packet switches with multiple input queues," *IEEE/ACM Trans. Networking*, vol. 2, pp. 471-482, Oct. 1994.
[10] B. Prabhakar, N. McKeown and R. Ahuja, "Multicast scheduling for input-queued switches," *IEEE J. Select. Areas Commun.*, vol. 15, no. 5, pp. 855-866, June 1997.
[11] N. McKeown and B. Prabhakar, "Scheduling multicast cells in an input queued switch," *Proc. of IEEE INFOCOM '96*, San Francisco, CA, USA, vol. 1, pp. 261-278, Mar. 1996.
[12] T. Anderson, S. Owicki. J. Saxe, and C. Thacker, "High-speed switch scheduling for local-area networks," *ACM Trans. Comput. Syst.*, vol. 11, no. 4, pp. 319-352, Nov. 1993.
[13] M. J. Karol, M. J. Hluchyj, and S. P. Morgan, "Input versus output queueing on a space-division packet switch," *IEEE Trans. Commun.*, vol. 35, pp. 1347-1356, Dec. 1987.
[14] A. Smiljanic, "Flexible bandwidth allocation in high-capacity packet switches," *IEEE/ACM Trans. Networking*, vol. 10, no. 2, pp. 287-293, April 2000.
[15] A. Smiljanic, "Scheduling of multicast traffic in high-capacity packet switches," *Proc. of IEEE HPSR '02*, Kobe, Japan, pp. 72-77, May 2002.
[16] D. Stiliadis, "Efficient multicast algorithms for high-speed routers," *Proc. of IEEE HPSR '03*, Torino, Italy, pp. 117-122, Jun. 2003.

# RGB: A Scalable and Reliable Group Membership Protocol in Mobile Internet[*]

Guojun Wang[1,2], Jiannong Cao[1], Keith C. C. Chan[1]

[1]Department of Computing
Hong Kong Polytechnic University
Hung Hom, Kowloon, Hong Kong
{csgjwang,csjcao,cskcchan}@comp.polyu.edu.hk

[2]School of Information Science and Engineering
Central South University
Changsha, Hunan, P. R. China, 410083
gordon434@163.net

## Abstract

*We propose a membership protocol for group communications in mobile Internet. The protocol is called RGB, which is the acronym of "a Ring-based hierarchy of access proxies, access Gateways, and Border routers". RGB runs in a parallel and distributed way in the sense that each network entity in the ring-based hierarchy maintains local information about its possible leader, previous, next, parent and child neighbors, and that each network entity independently collects/generates membership change information, which is propagated by the one-round membership algorithm concurrently running in all the logical rings. We prove that the proposed protocol is scalable in the sense that the scalability of a ring-based hierarchy is as good as that of a tree-based hierarchy. We also prove that the proposed protocol is reliable, in the sense that, with high probability of 99.500%, a ring-based hierarchy with up to 1000 access proxies attached by a large number of mobile hosts will not partition when node faulty probability is bounded by 0.1%; if at most 3 partitions are allowed, then the Function-Well probability of the hierarchy is 99.999% accordingly.*

## 1. Introduction

Internet computing and wireless communications are two of the current most important network technologies. In recent years, these two network technologies are converging for mobile Internet computing. With the integration of heterogeneous wired Internet and different kinds of wireless access networks, such as wireless LANs, cellular networks, and satellite networks, more services such as multimedia services with QoS guarantee and personalized services with mobility support, will be deployed in mobile Internet in the near future.

Group communications systems provide communications services among groups of processes. A *group* consists of a set of processes called *members* of the group. A process may voluntarily *join* or *leave* a group, or cease to be a member due to *failure*. The *membership* of a group is a list of currently operational processes in the group. The task of *membership management* is to maintain membership in case of *Member-Join/Leave/Handoff/Failure* events. Typical applications using membership include replicated file systems, distributed database systems, peer-to-peer systems, video conferencing systems and distance learning systems.

Many existing group communications systems are mainly designed for generic LAN or WAN environment, which don't explicitly consider *Mobile Hosts* (MHs) as group members. Therefore, there is no guarantee that they can also work well in the presence of MHs. Our work deals with MHs as group members in mobile Internet. However, the design of a group membership protocol for mobile Internet is a challenging task. In fact, the intrinsic issues in WANs like *high message latency, frequent connectivity changes,* and *instability due to link failures or congestion* [15], still exist in mobile Internet. Furthermore, there are more difficult issues which need to be addressed due to in-

[*]This research is supported in part by the Hong Kong Polytechnic University Central Research Grant *G-YY41*, and in part by the University Grant Council of Hong Kong under the CERG Grant PolyU *5170/03E*.

troducing MHs as follows.

**Frequent disconnection.** MHs are often disconnected from their attached wireless networks. Disconnection can be categorized into three types: *temporary disconnection*, which may resume normal operation within a very short period of time; *voluntary disconnection*, which is initiated by the user, and after an arbitrary period of time may reconnect at any other cell and resume normal operation; *faulty disconnection*, which may be caused by any failure occurrences and may not be allowed to resume normal operation.

**Frequent handoff.** In order to accommodate requirements of mobile users, such as reducing power consumption and increasing moving speed, the trend is to build smaller wireless cells. With smaller cells, handoffs may occur more frequently. Therefore, fast handoff is needed to decrease service disruptions to mobile users.

**Frequent failure occurrence.** As is well known that Internet is unreliable in the sense that hosts, routers and communications links may become faulty, and that no communications latency bound can be guaranteed. With different kinds of wireless networks integrated into the wired Internet, it becomes more unreliable: MHs may become faulty more easily than stationary hosts; wireless communications links between MHs and their attached devices may be more unreliable than wired communications links. Therefore, frequent failures may occur in mobile Internet.

The rest of the paper is organized as follows. In Section 2, we introduce some related works. In Section 3, we propose a 4-tier integrated network architecture for mobile Internet computing. In Section 4, we propose a scalable and reliable group membership protocol called *RGB*, the acronym of "a *R*ing-based hierarchy of access proxies, access *G*ateways, and *B*order routers". In Section 5, we analyze the scalability and reliability of our ring-based hierarchy. We conclude this paper in Section 6.

## 2. Related Works

The work on membership problem in asynchronous systems has been pioneered by the *ISIS* system [6], and the work in synchronous distributed systems has been introduced in [8]. The asynchronous membership problem is later proved to be impossible to solve without additional assumptions on detection of crashed processes [7], which comes from a very famous Fischer-Lynch-Paterson *impossibility result* in asynchronous systems [12].

There are many researches on membership management problem targeted toward generic LAN or WAN environment. In [1, 2], some ring-based schemes are proposed for LANs or multiple LANs within a local area. There are some schemes for WANs with respect to scalability issues. In the *membership roles* scheme [5], *core members*, *client members* and *sink members* are distinguished. In the *Spread*

system [3], two levels of protocols are integrated: one for LANs called *Ring*, another for WANs connecting the LANs, called *Hop*.

There are some hierarchical schemes with multiple levels for more scalable solutions as follows. In the *Transis* system [11], a WAN is viewed as a hierarchy of *multicast clusters*, each of which represents a domain of machines capable of communicating via broadcast or multicast hardware. The clusters are arranged in a hierarchy, with representatives from each local domain participating in the next level up the hierarchy. Such a hierarchy is called a *cluster-based hierarchy with representatives*. In the *CONGRESS* system [4], a WAN is viewed as a hierarchy of *domains*, where each domain is serviced by a CONGRESS server: *Local Membership Server* (LMS) and *Global Membership Server* (GMS). LMS is placed in each host, and serves for each client running on its host. GMSs are placed in a tree-based hierarchy, and the higher-level logical GMSs are indeed the lowest-level physical ones. Such a hierarchy is called a *tree-based hierarchy with representatives*. In [14, 15], the *Moshe* membership servers schemes are proposed, which are generalization of the schemes in [4], but without explicitly stating how to organize the servers. In [16], an explicit *layered* scheme is proposed, which is similar to that in the *Transis* system [11].

There are some *one-round* algorithms. The algorithm in [9] terminates within one round in case of a single process crash or join. But in case of multiple faults, it may take a linear number of rounds. In each round, a token revolves around a virtual ring consisting of all the member processes. In [13], all the group members form one logical ring and a token is used to reach agreement. The algorithm in [15] terminates within one round of message communications over 98% of the running time. However, the algorithms are inefficient in case of large group.

There are also some works which explicitly consider MHs as group members. In [17], the authors extend their layered scheme in [16] by reducing the overhead of membership management and the number of messages exchanged to complete the membership change process in mobile Internet. Our work also deals with MHs as group members in mobile Internet. In mobile Internet communications environment, scalability and reliability are two major issues. In particular, different kinds of faults occur more frequently in mobile Internet than in their wired counterpart. As is well known that the tree-based structure has good scalability property and it is used in many communications protocols, for example in IP multicast [10] in wired Internet. The proposed protocol based on the ring-based hierarchy has comparable scalability property with that of the tree-based structure. More interestingly, we show that the proposed protocol based on the ring-based hierarchy is more reliable than that based on the tree-based hierarchy.

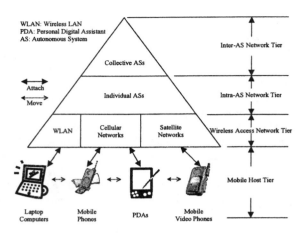

WLAN: Wireless LAN
PDA: Personal Digital Assistant
AS: Autonomous System

**Figure 1. The 4-Tier Integrated Network Architecture for Mobile Internet Computing**

## 3. The 4-Tier Mobile Internet Network Architecture

Different integration strategies for mobile Internet have been investigated by many researchers, such as *Unified Wireless Networks Architecture* [18], *System Architecture for Mobile Communications Systems* [20], *All-IP Wireless/Mobile Network Architecture* [22], and *FIT-MIP Global System Architecture* [19]. Based on these architectures, we propose a basic mobile Internet architecture called the *4-Tier Integrated Network Architecture for Mobile Internet Computing* in Figure 1, which are illustrated as follows.

**Mobile Host Tier** consists of different kinds of MHs which attach themselves to devices in upward wireless access networks tier. There are some traditional MHs like laptop computers, Personal Digital Assistants (PDAs) and mobile phones, which may be equipped with some new features like multi-mode operations. In addition, some forthcoming MHs like mobile video phones may also appear in the near future.

**Wireless Access Network Tier** comprises many different kinds of wireless access networks, such as local-area broadband wireless LANs, wide-area cellular networks, and world-wide satellite networks. MHs may attach to different kinds of wireless networks through devices like access points in wireless LANs, base stations in cellular networks, and satellites in satellite networks. We abstract all these devices as *Access Proxies* (APs).

**Intra-AS Network Tier** corresponds to individual *Autonomous Systems* (ASs) in Internet. As is well-known that Internet is organized as an interconnection of thousands of separate administrative domains called ASs. According to geographical and/or administrative factors, different wire-

less access networks may attach to different ASs through devices called *Access Gateways* (AGs).

**Inter-AS Network Tier** is the topmost tier in the hierarchy. As is well-known that *Border Gateway Protocol* (BGP) is the *de facto* standard for controlling routing of traffic across a collection of ASs among *Border Routers* (BRs) in these ASs. Usually AGs may communicate with BRs within the same ASs.

With the 4-tier architecture, we infer that in a mobile group communications system, group members may be highly dynamic, strongly heterogeneous, and size of the group may be potentially very large. In the following section, we propose a novel group membership protocol to manage such group with highly dynamic, strongly heterogeneous, and potentially very large characteristics in mobile Internet.

## 4. The Ring-based Hierarchical Group Membership Protocol

Based on the above 4-tier integrated network architecture for mobile Internet computing, we propose a *ring-based hierarchy* and associated protocol for membership management. The hierarchy is shown in Figure 2. In the proposed protocol, each mobile host can join or leave a group at will, or fail in the group due to the fact that some errors occur. The membership change information will firstly be captured in its attached access proxy, then propagated along the logical ring where the access proxy resides. The leader node in the logical ring will then propagate such information to its parent node. This process will continue until the leader node in the topmost logical ring is reached. Before presenting the *One-Round Token Passing Membership* algorithm and the *Membership-Query* algorithm, we firstly describe data structures maintained by *Mobile Hosts* (MHs), *Network Entities* (NEs) including *Access Proxies* (APs), *Access Gateways* (AGs) and *Border Routers* (BRs), and *Tokens* which circulate around the logical rings.

### 4.1. The Ring-based Hierarchy for Group Membership Management

Figure 2 shows different tiers of group membership hierarchy, namely, *Border Router Tier* (BRT), *Access Gateway Tier* (AGT), *Access Proxy Tier* (APT), and *Mobile Host Tier* (MHT), with the higher three tiers consisting of logically organized rings to form a ring-based hierarchy. Notice that only a portion of NEs configured to run the proposed protocol will be involved in the hierarchy.

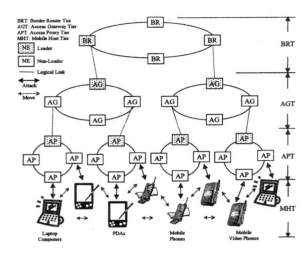

BRT: Border Router Tier
AGT: Access Gateway Tier
APT: Access Proxy Tier
MHT: Mobile Host Tier

NE: Leader

NE: Non-Leader

Logical Link

Attach

Move

Laptop Computers    PDAs    Mobile Phones    Mobile Video Phones

**Figure 2. The Ring-based Hierarchy for Group Membership Management**

## 4.2. The Data Structures of MHs, NEs and Tokens

**Data structure of MHs.** An MH as a group member records the following information.

- GID: GroupID. Group identity, available from some group addressing scheme, e.g. Class D address in IP multicast [10].

- AP: NodeID. Node identity of attached AP, e.g. its IP address.

- GUID: GloballyUniqueID. Globally unique identity of MH, available from some globally unique identity scheme, e.g. Mobile IP *Home Address* [21].

- LUID: LocallyUniqueID. Locally unique identity of MH, available from some locally unique identity scheme, e.g. Mobile IP *Care-of Address* [21].

- Status: Integer. Typical status like *operational*, *disconnected*, and *failed*.

**Data structure of NEs.** Different kinds of NEs may maintain slightly different information. Details of the data structure are as follows.

- GID: GroupID. See data structure of MHs.

- Current, Leader, Previous, Next, Parent, Child: NodeID. Node identity of the current, leader, previous, next, parent, and child node in the logical ring/hierarchy, e.g. its IP address.

- RingOK: Boolean. If the logical ring containing the current node is functioning well, i.e., a token can circulate normally along the logical ring, then TRUE, else FALSE.

- ParentOK: Boolean. If the parent node exists, and the logical ring containing the parent node functions well, then TRUE, else FALSE.

- ChildOK: Boolean. If the child node exists, and the logical ring containing the child node functions well, then TRUE, else FALSE.

- ListOfLocalMembers[ ]: MemberInfo. List of operational local members.

- ListOfRingMembers[ ]: MemberInfo. List of operational members within the union of coverage areas of all the nodes in the current logical ring for fast membership query.

- ListOfNeighborMembers[ ]: MemberInfo. List of operational members in neighboring nodes in the hierarchy for fast handoff.

- MQ: MessageQueue. Message queue which is self-optimized for aggregating some successive messages into one for further processing.

**Data structure of Tokens.** Each NE independently collects/generates membership change messages, which are propagated by using a *Token* as follows.

- GID: GroupID. See data structure of MHs.

- Holder: NodeID. Node identity of the holder of the Token, e.g. its IP address.

- OP: TypeOfAggregatedOperations. Type of aggregated Token operations, e.g. Member-Join/Leave/Handoff/Failure, NE-Join/Leave/Failure, Notification-to-Parent/Child, and Holder-Acknowledgement.

### 4.3. The One-Round Token Passing Membership Algorithm

For membership management, any membership change message such as Member-Join/Leave/Handoff/Failure, will be propagated in the hierarchy from bottom to top by using a *Token*. In each logical ring, after the Token successfully circulates the ring for one round, the control of the Token will be transferred to the next NE in the ring. Figure 3 shows the one-round algorithm on each logical ring.

One of the major functionalities of our one-round algorithm is to reach agreement within each logical ring. Another one is to maintain the status of the ring-based hierarchy. The *Function-Well* status within the current ring is set

```
01   Algorithm. One-Round Token Passing Membership
02   Input: The current node CurNode where a Token resides
03          and the logical ring where CurNode resides.
04   Output: Propagate membership change information
05          along the ring.
06
07   while TRUE do {
08     Execute Token.OP on CurNode;
09     Set CurNode.RingOK to TRUE;
10     if CurNode.Current == CurNode.Leader
11        and CurNode.ParentOK then
12        CurNode.Parent.MQ.Insert(CurNode,
13          Notification-to-Parent);
14     if CurNode.ChildOK then
15        CurNode.Child.MQ.Insert(CurNode,
16          Notification-to-Child);
17     if CurNode.Current == Token.Holder then
18        Send a corresponding Holder-Acknowledgement
19          message to its child(ren) which have sent
20          the original messages to the Holder's MQ;
21     if CurNode.Current == Token.Holder.Next then {
22        Prepare a fresh Token at an appropriate node;
23        Transfer control of the fresh Token to the node.}
24   }
```

**Figure 3. The One-Round Token Passing Membership Algorithm**

by *RingOK* of each node in the ring, and the *Function-Well* status of the parent node and the child node is set by *ParentOK* and *ChildOK* respectively. A logical ring *functions well* when the Token in the proposed algorithm can circulate around the logical ring normally. Furthermore, if all the logical rings in the ring-based hierarchy function well, then the hierarchy is a *Function-Well* hierarchy. Since at any time there is at most one membership change message propagated along a ring through our one-round algorithm, membership information maintained in the Function-Well hierarchy is consistent.

We illustrate how a membership change message is propagated from bottom to top along the ring-based hierarchy with the *Member-Join* message as an example. If an MH hopes to join a group, it firstly contacts with the AP it knows, which is either manually configured or dynamically acquired. If the MH successfully contacts with the AP, then it sends a Member-Join message to the AP, which is queued in the AP's MQ. If the AP happens to be a single one which is not in any AP logical ring, then it tries to join such a ring. If any *Access Proxy Ring* (APR) satisfies some locality/proximity criterion, then the AP joins the APR. In case that the contact procedure fails, an APR is built to include the single AP itself and make itself the ring leader. Notice that such an APR may merge with its neighboring AP ring or contact with upward tier AGs. Such a join process continues until the topmost logical ring in the hierarchy is reached.

The proposed protocol runs in a parallel and distributed way in the sense that each NE in the hierarchy maintains local information about its possible leader, previous, next, parent and child neighbors, and that each NE independently collects/generates membership change messages to be propagated by the one-round membership algorithm concurrently running in all the logical rings.

### 4.4. The Membership-Query Algorithm

With our ring-based hierarchy, there are many possible membership maintenance schemes. If only the nodes in the bottommost tier maintain local membership, we call it *Bottommost Membership Scheme* (BMS). If only the nodes in the topmost tier maintain global membership, we call it *Topmost Membership Scheme* (TMS). Since there may exist sub-tiers in each tier, some *Intermediate Membership Schemes* (IMSs) may be possible between BMS and TMS schemes.

For the Membership-Query algorithm with the TMS scheme, firstly the requesting application tries to find some NE with GID, then the NE sends global membership information to the application. For the BMS scheme, firstly the requesting application tries to find some NE with GID, then the NE forwards the request to each bottommost AP leaders, then the AP leaders send local membership back to the original NE or directly to the requesting application to generate global membership information.

The Membership-Query algorithm with the TMS scheme is more efficient than that with the BMS scheme with regard to the requesting application. However, to maintain membership information using the TMS scheme, it is both space- and time-consuming if the membership hierarchy becomes larger. Due to space restriction, we neglect algorithmic descriptions and analysis in this paper.

## 5. Scalability and Reliability Analysis of the Ring-based Hierarchy

Our proposed protocol uses a ring-based hierarchy, which has the properties of simplicity, scalability and reliability in designing membership and multicast protocols. In subsection 5.1, we show that the ring-based hierarchy has comparable scalability with the tree-based hierarchy, which has been widely used. In subsection 5.2, we argue that the ring-based hierarchy is more reliable than the tree-based hierarchy.

### 5.1. Comparative Analysis on Scalability Property

In [4], the authors propose a tree-based hierarchy of membership servers (LMSs and GMSs) with representatives called the *CONGRESS hierarchy*. Their one-round algorithm is documented in [14] and refined in [15]. In this section, we compare our ring-based hierarchy with the tree-based hierarchy.

The number $n$ of LMSs/APs in the tree/ring-based hierarchy is considered equivalent scalability parameter in the sense that it is more reasonable to consider the number of LMSs/APs, not that of clients/MHs, as the group size.

The one-round algorithm in [14] and [15] for fast membership agreement in a fault-free case is used to measure scalability criteria for both the tree-based hierarchy and the ring-based hierarchy.

We calculate the total number of message hops *HopCount* to propagate the membership change message. Since our major concern is the *proposal* message in [14] and [15], HopCount is approximate to $n$ times the number of the proposal message hops, or $n$ times the number of edges in the hierarchy.

Consider the tree-based hierarchy without representatives. In a tree-based hierarchy with height $h \geq 3$ and with branches $r \geq 2$ for each non-leaf node, the number of leaf nodes (LMSs) is $n = r^{h-1}$. Then HopCount is:

$$HopCount_{Tree-based}(n, h, r)$$

$$\stackrel{def}{=} n * \sum_{i=0}^{h-2} r^{i+1} \quad (1)$$

Then consider the tree-based hierarchy with representatives, where some hop counts should be removed from formula (1). For example, $h - 2$ should be removed for the root GMS, since there is no real message transfer between the root GMS and its representatives. Then the being removed and the final HopCounts are:

$$HopCountsRemoved_{Tree-based}(n, h, r)$$

$$\stackrel{def}{=} n * \sum_{i=0}^{h-3} ((h - i - 2) * (r^i - \sum_{j=0}^{i-1} r^j)) \quad (2)$$

$$HopCount_{Tree-based}(n, h, r) \stackrel{def}{=} n * (\sum_{i=0}^{h-2} r^{i+1} -$$

$$\sum_{i=0}^{h-3} ((h - i - 2) * (r^i - \sum_{j=0}^{i-1} r^j))) \quad (3)$$

We then normalize HopCount by dividing it with $n$, which stands for the "average" number of messages for one

Table I. Comparison on Scalability between the Tree-based Hierarchy and the Ring-based Hierarchy

| $n$ | $h$ | $r$ | $HC_{Tree}^N$ | $n$ | $h$ | $r$ | $HC_{Ring}^N$ |
|---|---|---|---|---|---|---|---|
| 25 | 3 | 5 | 29 | 25 | 2 | 5 | 35 |
| 125 | 4 | 5 | 149 | 125 | 3 | 5 | 185 |
| 625 | 5 | 5 | 750 | 625 | 4 | 5 | 935 |
| 100 | 3 | 10 | 109 | 100 | 2 | 10 | 120 |
| 1000 | 4 | 10 | 1099 | 1000 | 3 | 10 | 1220 |
| 10000 | 5 | 10 | 11000 | 10000 | 4 | 10 | 12220 |

membership change message. Notice that we simply denote it as $HC_{Tree}^N$.

$$HC_{Tree}^N \stackrel{def}{=} N\_HopCount_{Tree-based}(n, h, r)$$

$$\stackrel{def}{=} \sum_{i=0}^{h-2} r^{i+1} - \sum_{i=0}^{h-3} ((h - i - 2) * (r^i - \sum_{j=0}^{i-1} r^j)) = r^{h-1} +$$

$$\sum_{i=0}^{h-3} \frac{r^i(r^2 - (h - i - 1)r + 2(h - i - 2)) - (h - i - 2)}{r - 1} \quad (4)$$

We then calculate HopCount in the ring-based hierarchy with height $h \geq 2$ and with each ring containing exactly $r \geq 2$ nodes. The number of APs in the bottommost logical rings is $n = r^h$, and the total number of logical rings is $tn = \sum_{i=0}^{h-1} r^i$. Then HopCount is:

$$HopCount_{Ring-based}(n, h, r) \stackrel{def}{=} n*((r+1)*tn-1) \quad (5)$$

We then normalize HopCount by dividing it with $n$, which stands for the "average" number of messages for one membership change message. Notice that we simply denote it as $HC_{Ring}^N$.

$$HC_{Ring}^N \stackrel{def}{=} N\_HopCount_{Ring-based}(n, h, r)$$

$$\stackrel{def}{=} (r + 1) * tn - 1 = (r + 1) * \sum_{i=0}^{h-1} r^i - 1 \quad (6)$$

We then give numerical results according to formulae (4) and (6) in Table I. As we can see, the scalability property of the ring-based hierarchy is almost the same as that of the tree-based hierarchy. The two schemes are comparable with respect to scalability.

331

## 5.2. Comparative Analysis on Reliability Property

In order to compare reliability between the tree-based hierarchy with representatives [4] and our ring-based hierarchy, we define a *transformation* hierarchy called *a tree-based hierarchy without representatives*. In such a hierarchy: (A) nodes are physically different from each other; (B) nodes in the lowest level with the common parent are logically connected into a ring; and (C) nodes not in the lowest level but with the common parent are logically connected into a ring.

If we remove the root node and the associated edges from the transformation hierarchy and remove all the *parent-children* edges but the first one from such a relationship, then such a hierarchy becomes our ring-based hierarchy. Since we consider only node faults, we deduce that the tree-based hierarchy without representatives has similar reliability property as our ring-based hierarchy.

Since one representative node fault is indeed several logical node faults in the tree-based hierarchy with representatives, the tree-based hierarchy without representatives is more reliable than that with representatives. Thus, the ring-based hierarchy is more reliable than the tree-based hierarchy with representatives. Below we only analyze the reliability of the ring-based hierarchy.

We now present an analytical model for *Function-Well* (*fw*) probability of our ring-based hierarchy with the following parameters: $n$, $h$, $r$, which are previously mentioned; $f$, which denotes the node faulty probability with uniform and independent fault distribution in the hierarchy; and $k$, which is the maximal number of allowed partitions.

We assume only node fault in the hierarchy, while link fault will be simulated by node fault. We also assume that any single node fault in a logical ring can be detected quickly by *Token* retransmission schemes and be locally repaired by excluding the faulty node from the ring. If there are more than one fault in the ring, then the ring is considered to be partitioned, which will merge with other partitions later. In case that the hierarchy is partitioned into no more than $k$ partitions, the hierarchy is considered *Function-Well*.

We firstly present the Function-Well probability $t$ of each logical ring as:

$$t \stackrel{def}{=} Prob_{fw-ring}(r,f) \stackrel{def}{=} \sum_{i=0}^{1} \binom{r}{i}(1-f)^{r-i}f^i$$

$$= (1-f+rf)*(1-f)^{r-1} \quad (7)$$

We then suppose a full ring-based hierarchy for *worst-case* analysis: it contains maximal number of tiers; each tier contains maximal number of logical rings; and each logical

Table II. Function-Well Probability of the Ring-based Hierarchy (Left: $h$=3, $r$=5; Right: $h$=3, $r$=10)

| $n$ | $f(\%)$ | $k$ | $fw(\%)$ | $n$ | $f(\%)$ | $k$ | $fw(\%)$ |
|-----|---------|-----|----------|------|---------|-----|----------|
| 125 | 0.1 | 1 | 99.968 | 1000 | 0.1 | 1 | 99.500 |
| 125 | 0.1 | 2 | 99.999 | 1000 | 0.1 | 2 | 99.994 |
| 125 | 0.1 | 3 | 99.999 | 1000 | 0.1 | 3 | 99.996 |
| 125 | 0.5 | 1 | 99.211 | 1000 | 0.5 | 1 | 88.448 |
| 125 | 0.5 | 2 | 99.972 | 1000 | 0.5 | 2 | 99.215 |
| 125 | 0.5 | 3 | 99.975 | 1000 | 0.5 | 3 | 99.864 |
| 125 | 2.0 | 1 | 88.409 | 1000 | 2.0 | 1 | 16.094 |
| 125 | 2.0 | 2 | 98.981 | 1000 | 2.0 | 2 | 45.470 |
| 125 | 2.0 | 3 | 99.592 | 1000 | 2.0 | 3 | 72.038 |

ring contains maximal number of nodes. Such a hierarchy contains $tn = \sum_{i=0}^{h-1} r^i$ logical rings and less than $k$ logical rings may not function well. We present the Function-Well probability of the hierarchy as:

$$Prob_{fw-hierarchy}(n,h,r,f,k)$$

$$\stackrel{def}{=} \sum_{i=0}^{k-1} \binom{tn}{i}t^{tn-i}(1-t)^i \quad (8)$$

Numerical results from (7) and (8) are given in Table II with conclusions as follows.

(1) Our ring-based hierarchy is reliable in the sense that, with high probability of 99.500%, a ring-based hierarchy with up to 1000 APs directly attached by a large number of MHs will not partition when the node faulty probability is bounded by 0.1%; if at most 3 partitions are allowed, then the *Function-Well* probability of the hierarchy is 99.999% accordingly.

(2) Under the definition of Function-Well hierarchy with at most 3 partitions allowed, with high probability of 99.864%, a group with up to 1000 APs directly attached by a large number of MHs guarantees that the hierarchy still functions well when the node faulty probability is bounded by 0.5%.

(3) With the node faulty probability increasing to 2.0%, the small-scale hierarchy still functions well with very high probability. For example, the *Function-Well* probability is 99.592% for a small-scale hierarchy with up to 125 APs directly attached by MHs. However, the large-scale hierarchy with up to 1000 APs directly attached by MHs functions well with probability of only 72.038%.

## 6. Conclusions

The scalable and reliable properties of the RGB protocol are very important to provide reliable large-scale group communications services for a large number of applications in unreliable communications networks. As a final remark, we argue that the proposed protocol is efficient similar to tree-based protocols since only a sequence of logical rings from bottom to top, not all the rings in the hierarchy, will be involved with respect to any specific membership change message. In particular, the delay for propagating membership messages with small-scale logical rings is smaller compared with that with large-scale logical rings, while the small-scale logical rings are more common than large-scale ones. As our future work, we will extend RGB with *Membership-Partition/Merge* algorithms to provide *partitionable* and *self-organizable* group membership services to applications.

# References

[1] Y. Amir, L.E. Moser, P.M. Melliar-Smith, D.A. Agarwal, and P.Ciarfella, "The Totem single-ring ordering and membership protocol," *ACM Transactions on Computer Systems*, Vol. 13, Issue 4, pp. 311-342, November 1995.

[2] D.A. Agarwal, L.E. Moser, P.M. Melliar-Smith, and R.K. Budhia, "The Totem multiple-ring ordering and topology maintenance protocol," *ACM Transactions on Computer Systems*, Vol. 16, Issue 2, pp. 93-132, May 1998.

[3] Y. Amir and J. Stanton, "The Spread wide area group communication system," *Technical Report TR CNDS-98-4*, The Center for Networking and Distributed Systems, The Johns Hopkins University, Baltimore, MD, 1998.

[4] T. Anker, G.V. Chockler, D. Dolev, and I. Keidar, "Scalable group membership services for novel applications," *Networks in Distributed Computing (DIMACS Workshop)*, Vol. 45, American Mathematical Society, pp. 23-42, 1998.

[5] O. Babaoglu and A. Schiper, "On group communication in large-scale distributed systems," *Proc. the 6th workshop on ACM SIGOPS European workshop: Matching operating systems to application needs*, pp. 17-22, 1994.

[6] K.P. Birman and T.A. Joseph, "Reliable communication in the presence of failures," *ACM Transactions on Computer Systems*, Vol. 5, Issue 1, pp. 47-76, February 1987.

[7] T.D. Chandra, V. Hadzilacos, S. Toueg, and B. Charron-Bost, "On the impossibility of group membership," *Proceedings of the fifteenth annual ACM symposium on Principles of distributed computing*, pp. 322-330, 1996.

[8] F. Cristian, "Reaching agreement on processor-group membership in synchronous distributed systems," *Distributed Computing*, Vol. 4, pp. 175-187, 1991.

[9] F. Cristian and F. Schmuck, "Agreeing on processor group membership in timed asynchronous distributed systems," *UCSD Technical Report CSE95-428*, University of California, San Diego, 1995.

[10] S. E. Deering, "Host extensions for IP multicasting," *IETF RFC 1112*, SRI Network Information Center, August 1989.

[11] D. Dolev and D. Malki, "The Transis approach to high availability cluster communication," *Communications of the ACM*, Vol. 39, Issue 4, pp. 64-70, April 1996.

[12] M.J. Fischer, N.A. Lynch, and M.S. Paterson, "Impossibility of distributed consensus with one faulty process," *Journal of the ACM (JACM)*, Vol. 32, Issue 2, pp. 374-382, April 1985.

[13] M.A. Hiltunen and R.D. Schlichting, "A configurable membership service," *IEEE Transactions on Computers*, Vol. 47, Issue 5, pp. 573-586, May 1998.

[14] I. Keidar, J. Sussman, K. Marzullo, and D. Dolev, "A client-server oriented algorithm for virtually synchronous group membership in WANs," *Proc. the 20th International Conference on Distributed Computing Systems*, pp. 356-365, April 2000.

[15] I. Keidar, J. Sussman, K. Marzullo, and D. Dolev, "Moshe: A group membership service for WANs," *ACM Transactions on Computer Systems*, Vol. 20, Issue 3, pp. 191-238, August 2002.

[16] H. Kim, D. Lee, and H.Y. Youn. "A scalable membership service for group communications in WANs," *Proc. the 2000 Pacific Rim International Symposium on Dependable Computing*, pp. 59-66, 2000.

[17] B. Kim, D. Lee, and D. Nam, "Scalable group membership service for mobile Internet," *Proc. the Seventh International Workshop on Object-Oriented Real-Time Dependable Systems (WORDS 2002)*, pp. 295-298, 2002.

[18] W.W. Lu, "Compact multidimensional broadband wireless: The convergence of wireless mobile and access," *IEEE Communications Magazine*, Vol. 38, Issue 11, pp. 119-123, November 2000.

[19] L. Morand and S. Tessier, "Global mobility approach with Mobile IP in All IP networks," *IEEE International Conference on Communications (ICC 2002)*, Vol. 4, pp. 2075-2079, 2002.

[20] T. Otsu, N. Umeda, and Y. Yamao, "System architecture for mobile communications systems beyond IMT-2000," *Proc. the IEEE Global Telecommunications Conference (GLOBECOM 2001)*, Vol. 1, pp. 538-542, 2001.

[21] C. Perkins, "IP mobility support," *IETF RFC 2002*, October 1996.

[22] T.B. Zahariadis, K.G. Vaxevanakis, C.P. Tsantilas, N.A. Zervos, and N.A. Nikolaou, "Global roaming in next-generation networks," *IEEE Communications Magazine*, Vol. 40, Issue 2, pp. 145-151, February 2002.

# Session 5C:
# Cluster II

# Migration Decision for Hybrid Mobility in Reconfigurable Distributed Virtual Machines

Song Fu and Cheng-Zhong Xu
Department of Electrical & Computer Engg.
Wayne State University, Detroit, Michigan 48202
{oaksong, czxu}@wayne.edu

## Abstract

*Virtual machine (VM) is an important mechanism to multiplex computer resources. The increasing popularity of network computing has renewed research interests in the adaptive and distributed virtual machines. Service migration is a vital technique to construct reconfigurable VMs. By incorporating mobile agent technology, VM systems can improve their resource utilization, load-balancing and fault-tolerance significantly. This paper focuses on the decision problem of hybrid mobility for load-balancing in reconfigurable distributed VMs. We tackle this problem from three aspects: migration candidate determination, migration timing and destination server selection. The service migration timing and destination server selection are formulated as two optimization models. We derive the optimal migration policy for distributed and heterogeneous systems based on stochastic optimization theories. Renewal processes are applied to model the dynamics of migration. We solve the agent migration problem by dynamic programming and extend the optimal service migration decision by considering the interplay of the hybrid mobility. Our decision policy is complementary to the existing service and agent migration techniques. Its accuracy is verified by simulations.*

## 1 Introduction

A virtual machine (VM) presents an abstract view of the underlying physical machine or system software to programs that run with it. It allows multiple applications and even different operating systems to run concurrently and multiplex computer resources. These abstraction and isolation properties greatly simplify the development of applications and improve program portability. Since the classical VMs were first designed as a solution to multiplexing the shared mainframe resources in the early seventies, it has been an active research area. To support network-centric applications, research interests in VM are recently renewed. Systems like DVM [11], Collective [10], *etc* develop techniques to construct a distributed VM for networked computers or to migrate the state of a VM across a network. Besides, the widely used Java VM (JVM) middleware and MPI software package facilitate the construction of distributed and parallel applications.

A distributed virtual machine can be viewed as a set of virtual servers running on top of multiple physical servers. It is certainly possible to deploy its components as static computing units. However, this abstraction layer would not be fully exploited unless it is instantiated and managed dynamically. Virtual machine migration is one approach to its dynamic reconfiguration. It moves parts of or the entire VM from one computer to another for system adaptivity. Since VMs are usually created to provide services for programs running on top of them, we use the terms of VM migration and service migration interchangeable. Service migration techniques have been incorporated into many recently proposed systems. Examples include a VM-based architecture for grid computing in [3], *capsule* in Collective [10], M-DSA [4] in Traveler [15].

In addition to service migration, agent migration is another way to construct dynamic distributed systems [5]. An agent represents an autonomous computation that can migrate in a network to perform tasks on behalf of its creator. It provides a general approach to load-balancing, fault-tolerance, and data locality. MALD [2] is an example that uses mobile agents to balance the workload of distributed web servers. In [15, 4], we proposed a resource brokerage infrastructure, which assigns task agents to a distributed shared array (DSA), an application-level distributed virtual machine. Load-balancing is achieved via the agent migration. Furthermore, the DSA virtual machine can be reconfigured reactively or proactively by transferring the DSA virtual servers between physical servers.

In a reconfigurable distributed VM system with the hybrid mobility of services and agents, migration decision becomes a crucial performance issue. It deals with three aspects of the problem. First is migration candidate determination, concerning which server should transfer a service and/or which agent should exercise a migration. Another one is migration timing, determining when a migration should be performed. Finally, a destination server should be selected so that the performance gain from a migration won't be outweighed by its overhead. Literature is full of heuristic algorithms for either service or agent migration and lacks formal analyses of this decision problem. This paper provides a rigid stochastic optimization model to obtain the optimal migration policy for hybrid mobility.

In this paper, we investigate the hybrid migration decision problem in bulk synchronous computation, by assuming the workload change of an agent is a random process with arbitrary probabilistic distributions. Each agent carries out its tasks during its life span (corresponding to a *time domain*) and its execution may be performed on different virtual servers due to migrations (referring to this as a *space domain*). We formulate the migration issues as two stochastic optimization models, and obtain the optimal migration policy in both time and space domains. We derive the optimal phase for service migration with the objective of minimizing the migration frequency, and obtain the lower bound of the destination server capacity for an expected target gain value. We tackle the agent migration problem by dynamic programming and extend the optimal service migration decision by considering the interplay of the hybrid mobility. The simulation results verify the accuracy of our migration decisions. The decision policy provides a formal guidance to perform hybrid migrations for load-balancing and is complementary to the existing migration mechanisms.

The rest of the paper is organized as follows. In Section 2, we present the related work. Section 3 introduces the model of a reconfigurable distributed virtual machine. Section 4 and 5 describe the optimal decisions of service/agent migration, and their interplay. Simulation results are presented in Section 6. Section 7 concludes the paper.

## 2  Related Work

Research interests in applying the classical virtual machines to grid computing are recently revived. However, these systems are not easily reconfigurable, due to the enormous execution contexts. In contrast, application-level distributed virtual machines can be tuned to become more efficient for specific applications, and it is much easier to migrate these lightweight services in a network. The Global Object Space in JESSICA2 [17], and the Distributed Shared Array [4] in Traveler [15] are such examples.

Figueiredo *et al.* [3] proposed an architecture for grid computing based on dynamic virtual machines. It allows a VM to be created on any computer that has sufficient resource to support it, and enables service migrations among computers to pursue resource locality. Sapuntzakis *et al.* [10] tackled the problem of how to migrate OS-level VMs across the Internet. A virtual machine monitor is utilized to encapsulate the state of a running computer into a data structure, *capsule*. By serializing and transferring capsules between physical machines, a VM can resume running after migration. To support virtual machine reconfiguration in Traveler [15], we designed a mobile distributed shared array (M-DSA) [4], which supports the migration of a DSA service to a new physical server when the original one is overloaded or going to fail.

By utilizing mobile agents, a load scheduling and resource management scheme for network-centric applications was proposed in Traveler [15]. In that scheme, mobile agents can autonomously roam the network to find virtual servers with appropriate capacities to run on. A different approach was introduced in MALD [2], where web servers dispatch mobile agents to retrieve the system load information and redistribute load on all servers.

Although all of the works dealt with reconfigurable VMs, they focused on how to realize service and agent migrations by providing different mechanisms. In this paper, we concentrate on the migration decision in support of hybrid mobility. Although there are many reports in literature on mobile agent systems (see [13] for a review), there are few on agent scheduling for mobility. Moizumi and Cybenko [7] formulated a trav-

elling agent problem to find optimal agent migration sequence which minimizes the expected completion time of a task with unreliable networks and unpredictable nodal services. In [18], Zhuang *et. al* proposed an approach to optimize the number of agent migrations for a given task by utilizing compiler optimization techniques. They both focused on finding the optimal agent itinerary to complete its tasks. However, we are more interested in the decision problem as when and to which server an agent migration will be exercised. The objective is to balance system workload in a dynamic distributed environment supporting server reconfiguration.

## 3  Reconfigurable Distributed Virtual Machine Model

An agent-aware virtual machine is composed of a set of virtual servers spreading among distributed physical servers. Each virtual server can accommodate multiple agents to share resource and perform computation and communication. Each physical server can be run in two modes: *dedicated* or *multiprogrammed*. On a dedicated server, only virtual servers of the same application can reside, while a multiprogrammed server allows virtual servers of different applications to share its resources. On the other hand, a VM can be run on a single physical server or a cluster of servers. Correspondingly, on a *dedicated* or *multiprogrammed single-server* system, only service migration can be applied for its reconfigurability. In a *dedicated multi-server* VM, both service and agent migrations are useful to balance workload among multiple physical servers. The most general type is the *multiprogrammed multi-server* VMs. But the asynchrony among different applications makes multiprogrammed servers hard to analyze. In this paper, we confine our discussion to the dedicated multi-server reconfigurable virtual machines.

Consider a distributed application in a heterogeneous environment. A virtual machine $V = \langle s_1, s_2, \ldots, s_N \rangle$, formed by $N$ servers out of the available physical servers, is allocated to the application. Let a sequence $C = \langle c_1, c_2, \ldots, c_N \rangle$ denote their computational capacities and each $c_i$, $i = 1..N$, is a constant. The computation on the virtual machine comprises multiple agents, each of which executes a number of tasks that collectively determine its workload. We use a dynamic agent distribution sequence $M = \langle m_1, m_2, \ldots, m_N \rangle$ to represent the number of agents assigned to different servers. Due to a many-to-one mapping between agents and servers, we use a sequence $A_i = \langle a_{i,1}, a_{i,2}, \ldots, a_{i,m_i} \rangle$ to denote the set of agents residing on server $s_i$ in the VM.

We use the bulk synchronous computation as our execution model because of its popularity in scientific and engineering applications. In the bulk synchronous computation, agents proceed in phases. Let $l = 0, 1, \ldots$, be the phase index of the computation and $w_{i,k}(l)$ denote the workload of agent $a_{i,k}$ on server $s_i$ at phase $l$. Due to the heterogeneity of server capacities, we use scaled workload, $\tilde{w}_{i,k}(l)$, to denote the workload of agent $a_{i,k}$ normalized by its quota of server capacity. We assume the proportional share scheduling [12] among mobile agents of the same server. Multiple agents share the resource and each of them has an equal quota of the server capacity. That is, for server $s_i$ with capacity $c_i$, an residing agent $a_{i,k}$ is assigned a portion of capacity as $c_{i,k} = c_i/m_i$. Therefore, we have $\bar{w}_{i,k}(l) = w_{i,k}(l)/c_{i,k} = m_i w_{i,k}(l)/c_i$. For simplicity in notation, we will use $w_{i,k}(l)$ to denote the scaled workload henceforth.

As the computation proceeds, the scaled workload of each agent may evolve dynamically. Let $\delta_{i,k}(l-1)$ denote the net change of scaled workload $w_{i,k}(l)$ from phase $l-1$ to $l$ due to the workload generation and/or consumption by agent $a_{i,k}$ during the period. The overall scaled workload of server $s_i$ equals to the summation of its agents' scaled workload, i.e. $w_i(l) = \sum_{k=1}^{m_i} w_{i,k}(l)$. Similarly, its scaled workload change is defined as $\delta_i(l-1) = \sum_{k=1}^{m_i} \delta_{i,k}(l-1)$. Let sequences $w(l) = \langle w_1(l), w_2(l), \ldots, w_N(l) \rangle$ and $\delta(l-1) = \langle \delta_1(l-1), \delta_2(l-1), \ldots, \delta_N(l-1) \rangle$ denote the scaled workload distribution at phase $l$ and the scaled workload change distribution from phase $l-1$ to $l$ of the virtual machine, respectively. Then the bulk synchronous computation can be characterized by an additive dynamic system:

$$w(l) = w(l-1) + \delta(l-1) \qquad (1)$$

where the scaled workload change is independent of the server workload. The scaled workload is described by a Markov chain, which is assumed in many other studies on bulk synchronous computations [8, 16]. As a result of the agents' workload change between phases, the computation of a server becomes non-deterministic. Although this paper focuses on the additive scaled workload evolution model, our analysis can be extended to other dynamic models as discussed in [14].

During a service migration, the residing virtual servers on a physical server can be transferred as a whole. We treat the virtual servers on each physical server as a set and the two terms, physical and virtual servers will be used interchangeably. When a server decides to perform a service migration to another available server during the computation, the correspondent entry in the capacity sequence $C$ will be replaced by the destination server's capacity. Similarly, agent migration leads to a modification of the agent distribution sequence $M$, as agents land on or leave from servers of the virtual machine. So the migration decision problem can be tackled based on renewal processes. We use sequences $C^0 = \langle c_1^0, c_2^0, \ldots, c_N^0 \rangle$ and $M^0 = \langle m_1^0, m_2^0, \ldots, m_N^0 \rangle$ to represent the capacities and agent distribution on the *original servers*, i.e. the servers allocated to an application at its initiation. The scaled workload of an agent $a_i$ at phase $l$ and its scaled workload change from phase $l-1$ to $l$ on its original server are denoted by $w_{i,k}^0(l)$ and $\delta_{i,k}^0(l-1)$, respectively. We assume initially agents have equal scaled workload at phase $l = 0$.

To make the migration decision problem tractable, we make some simplifying assumptions.

**Assumption 1**: The initial scaled workload changes of different agents on a server, $\delta_{i,k}^0(\cdot)$, are independently distributed random variables and they are distribution-free. Agent autonomy makes the construction of independent agents easier by utilizing data locality and migration.

**Assumption 2**: Service/agent migration does not affect the probabilistic distribution of the scaled workload change of an agent. But it may have different mean after migration. This is reasonable because the scaled workload change equals to the

amount of agent workload change relative to its capacity quota. This quota is a constant during the agent execution on a server with a fair-share scheduling scheme.

# 4 Service Migration Decision

A virtual machine is composed of a set of servers executing tasks of their residing agents and synchronizing with each other by performing barrier operations between phases. By the dynamic system in (1), it is expected that the servers' scaled workload will change with time and cause overloaded states. Since the duration of a phase is determined by the heavily loaded servers, the overall system performance may deteriorate in phase. Service migrations aim to eliminate the performance bottleneck of a virtual machine by increasing capacities of the overloaded components. A service migration involves the tasks of transmitting service states and data along with the residing agents to a destination server with a higher capacity, continuing services and resuming agent execution there. Although we do not focus on the details of how to perform service migrations, it is clear that a migration operation would incur significant runtime overhead and the adaptive computation can not afford frequent migrations.

The objective of service migration decision is to obtain the optimal timing in phase to minimize the migration frequency, and the lower bound of the destination server capacity to guide the server selection. In the following, we suppose there are only service migrations during the execution of a virtual machine. The agent migration decision problem and its interplay with service migration will be tackled in Section 5.

## 4.1 Migration Candidate Determination and Service Migration Timing

Although servers of a virtual machine need to perform global barrier synchronization between phases, their executions within a phase can be assumed to be independent. This is particular the case in agent-based systems, where autonomous agents perform their own tasks with local services and data sets. A service migration decision is made by a server based on its overall workload relative to its capacity. In the following, we use a set of simplified notations, in which $s$ denotes any server in a virtual machine, $c$ and $m$ representing its capacity and number of agents, $\langle a_1, a_2, \ldots, a_m \rangle$ being the set of its agents, $w_i(l)$ and $\delta_i(l)$ denoting the scaled workload and workload change of a residing agent $a_i$ at phase $l$.

For a server, its overall workload at a phase is the summation of all its agents' workloads, if we do not consider their overlapping. We define the *expected relative workload* of server $s$ at phase $l$ as

$$r(l) = E\left[ \frac{\sum_{i=1}^m w_i(l)}{m} \right], \qquad (2)$$

The expected relative workload represents a server's overall workload, i.e. $\sum_{i=1}^m w_i(l) \cdot c/m$, w.r.t. its capacity, $c$. We use the scaled workload of each agent in order to ensure workload of different servers in a VM are comparable with each other.

Due to the non-negligible runtime overhead in a migration, certain degree of overload must be tolerated. We reformulate the decision problem as "Given a bound of overload, find the minimal migration frequency". Therefore, the optimal migration timing is obtained by finding the maximal phase $l^*$ for a given overload bound $R$, i.e.

$$r(l) \leq R. \tag{3}$$

$R$ reflects the degree to which a server is considered to be overloaded. In general, the server capacity refers to the amount of tasks that can be performed by the server in a time unit. In the multi-phase computations we considered in this paper, a conservative definition of the time unit is the sequential execution time of a phase. Since a multi-phase application may have different execution times in different phases, strictly, the time unit should be the maximum of the execution time in different phases. Other definitions may be possible, but we require that the time unit is fixed and large enough to cover any phase. The workload of an agent changes with phases, and represents the number of tasks to be carried out in a phase. So, each agent's workload occupies a percentage of the server capacity. The overall workload of a server in a time unit is less than its capacity, i.e. $0 < R < 1$.

Next, we will derive the expression of scaled workload $w_i(l)$ with reference to the value $w_i^0(l)$ on the original server. Consider server $s$ makes a service migration at certain phase $k$. Let $s'$ denote the server after migration, in the *space domain*. We use $(c', m')$ to represent its capacity and number of agents, respectively. For a residing agent, say $a_i$, its scaled workload and workload change after migration are denoted by $(w_i'(\cdot), \delta_i'(\cdot))$. The *workload conservation property* states the workload of an agent remains unchanged at the moment of migration. That is $w_i'(k)c'/m' = w_i(k)c/m$. In the *time domain*, with the additive scaled workload evolution model in Eq. (1), it is clear $w_i'(l) = w_i'(k) + \sum_{t=k}^{l-1} \delta_i'(t)$, for phases $l > k$. If there is no service migration at phase $k$, the scaled workload will become $w_i(l) = w_i(k) + \sum_{t=k}^{l-1} \delta_i(t)$, for $l > k$. By Assumption 2, we have $\delta_i'(t)c'/m' = \delta_i(t)c/m$. Thus, we derive $w_i'(l) = w_i(l)cm'/(c'm)$. Together with $(c^0, m^0)$ for the original server and $m = m^0$ due to no agent migration, the scaled workload of agent $a_i$ on server $s$ can be calculated as

$$w_i(l) = \frac{w_i^0(l)}{\tilde{c}}, \tag{4}$$

where $\tilde{c} = c/c^0$ is called the *relative capacity*. We can see that the scaled workload of an agent equals to its initial scaled workload relative to the ratio of capacities between the current server and original one. This is caused by service migrations in the space domain.

Let $\mu_i$ be the means of the scaled workload changes $\delta_i^0(\cdot)$, for $i = 1..m$. According to the additive workload evolution model, the scaled workload of agent $a_i$ on its original server at phase $l$ is $w_i^0(l) = w_0 + \sum_{t=0}^{l-1} \delta_i^0(t)$, where $w_0 = w_i^0(0)$ is the scaled workload at phase 0, i.e. the initial scaled workload of an agent on its original server. Since the scaled workload changes $\delta_i^0(\cdot)$ in different phases are independent random variables, we have the expected value of scaled workload $E[w_i(l)] = E[w_i^0(l)]/\tilde{c} = (w_0 + l\mu_i)/\tilde{c}$. Thus, the expected relative workload of server $s$ becomes

$$r(l) = \frac{\sum_{i=1}^{m}(w_0 + l\mu_i)}{m\tilde{c}} = \frac{w_0 + l\bar{\mu}}{\tilde{c}}, \tag{5}$$

where $\bar{\mu} = (\sum_{i=1}^{m} \mu_i)/m$ is the average change rate of the scaled workload. If $\bar{\mu} \leq 0$, then the overall scaled workload

of a server tends to remain unchanged or decrease, as the computational phase proceeds. It means there is no need to perform service migrations any more. So, we only consider the cases with $\bar{\mu} > 0$ in our discussion. With $r(l) \leq R$, we have the following theorem to determine the optimal timing for service migrations.

**Theorem 4.1** *For any server $s$ with capacity $c$ in a virtual machine, suppose the scaled workload changes of agents on the original server, $\delta_i^0(\cdot)$, $i = 1..m$, have the average mean $\bar{\mu} > 0$. The optimal service migration timing $l^*$ in phase, under Assumption 1 and Assumption 2, is*

$$l^* = \frac{\tilde{c}R - w_0}{\bar{\mu}}, \tag{6}$$

Intuitively, Theorem 4.1 states that the optimal service migration timing of a server equals to its available server capacity, apart from the initial workload, divided by the average rate of workload increase. Eq. (6) reflects the influence from both the time domain and the space domain. It shows the timing is proportional to the relative server capacity. This is because both $w_0$ and each $\mu_i$, are defined relative to the capacity of the original server. To reduce the service migration frequency, we can select the destination server with the highest capacity. But this greedy strategy may allocate more resource to less heavily-loaded virtual servers, which leads to resource imbalance in the virtual machine. We will discuss this tradeoff in Section 4.2.

## 4.2 Destination Server Selection

Servers in a virtual machine independently decide when to perform service migrations based on Theorem 4.1. As we have discussed in the previous subsection, the selection of a destination server is a tradeoff between the local and global performance optimizations. From an individual server's perspective, it is preferable to obtain an available server with the highest capacity as its destination so that its service migration frequency becomes minimal. But from the perspective of the entire virtual machine, it'd better allocate more powerful servers to more heavily-loaded virtual servers. In this section, we introduce a migration gain function and try to find the lower bound of capacity, that a prospective destination server must have, for a given target gain value.

For server $s$ in a VM, the execution time of its agent $a_i$ at phase $l$, $t_i(l)$, is proportional to its workload relative to the capacity quota, i.e. its scaled workload, as $t_i(l) \propto w_i(l)$. The duration of a computational phase on a server is determined by its agent with the longest completion time, i.e. $t(l) = \max_{i=1..m} t_i(l)$. Consider server $s$ makes a service migration to an available server, denoted by $s'$, with capacity $c'$ at the optimal migration timing $l^*$ according to Theorem 4.1. We require $c' > c$, otherwise this migration is meaningless w.r.t. the system performance improvement. Thus the execution time of each agent on server $s'$ will be reduced. We define the *expected migration gain* for this service migration as

$$g(c') = E[\sum_{l=l^*}^{k-1}(t(l) - t'(l))] - E[O(w(l^*))], \tag{7}$$

where $k$ is the prospective optimal migration timing for server $s'$ with its supposed capacity $c'$ according to Theorem 4.1. The execution time on server $s'$ is $t'(l) \propto \max_{i=1..m} w_i'(l)$, and $O(\cdot)$ returns the migration overhead for a given scaled workload. The expected migration gain function describes the performance improvement, in terms of agents' execution time on the two servers until the next service migration, compared with the migration overhead. We do not use the execution time of the entire virtual machine as a metric to express performance gain, due to the unpredictable behaviors of other servers in the VM and the independency of server execution. We expect the performance benefits in terms of a value $G$ from a service migration. The target gain, $G$, is measured relative to the migration overhead. So, the selection of a destination server in a service migration is guided by finding the lower bound of the server capacity for a given non-negative target gain value $G$ of the migration gain function, i.e.

$$g(c') \geq G. \tag{8}$$

By increasing $G$, capacities of the destination servers will become higher accordingly. But to avoid resource allocation imbalance in the virtual machine, we need to choose the value of $G$ appropriately. Since the state information of services on a server is usually maintained by a relatively limited number of variables, the main portion of the service migration overhead is caused by transferring codes and data of services. The size of data set is likely to change little since its initial assignment to a server and the code of services are immutable. So, the migration overhead of a server can be represented by a constant, denoted by $H$. However, our optimization approach is still applicable with the general overhead function, $O(\cdot)$. Since the execution time of an agent, $t_i(l)$, is solely determined by its scaled workload $w_i(l)$, we will use these two terms interchangeably. Next, we transform the migration gain function to find the minimal capacity of the destination server for a given target gain value.

With the expressions of $t(l)$, $t'(l)$ and $w_i(l)$, the expected migration gain (7) becomes

$$
\begin{aligned}
g(c') &= E[\sum_{l=l^*}^{k-1} (\max_{i=1..m} \frac{w_i^0(l)}{\tilde{c}} - \max_{i=1..m} \frac{w_i^0(l)}{\tilde{c}'})] - H \\
&= (\frac{1}{\tilde{c}} - \frac{1}{\tilde{c}'}) \sum_{l=l^*}^{k-1} E[\max_{i=1..m} w_i^0(l)] - H,
\end{aligned}
\tag{9}
$$

where $\tilde{c}' = c'/c^0$. Let $\mu_i$ and $\sigma_i^2$ be the mean and variance of the scaled workload change $\delta_i^0(\cdot)$. Since $w_i^0(l) = w_0 + \sum_{t=0}^{l-1} \delta_i^0(t)$ and the phase-wise scaled workload changes of each agent $\delta_i^0(\cdot)$ are i.i.d. random variables w.r.t. phases, the central limit theorem of statistics [9] guarantees that as $l$ gets large, the distribution of $w_i^0(l)$ tends to become normally distributed with mean $w_0 + l\mu_i$ and variance $l\sigma_i^2$. Because $\delta_i^0(\cdot)$, for $i = 1..m$, are independent random variables, the scaled workloads $w_i^0(\cdot)$ are also independently distributed. So we have $Pr\{\max_{i=1..m} w_i^0(l) \leq x\} = \prod_{i=1}^{m} Pr\{w_i^0(l) \leq x\}$. Since each $w_i^0(\cdot) \geq 0$, it is clear

$$
\begin{aligned}
E[\max_{i=1..m} w_i^0(l)] &= \int_0^\infty Pr\{\max_{i=1..m} w_i^0(l) > x\}\, dx \\
&= \int_0^\infty [1 - \prod_{i=1}^{m} \int_{-\infty}^{x} f_i(u)\, du]\, dx,
\end{aligned}
\tag{10}
$$

where $f_i(u)$ is the probability density function of normal distribution with parameters $w_0 + l\mu_i$ and $l\sigma_i^2$ for the scaled workload

$w_i^0(l)$. Therefore, we can derive the lower bound of the destination server capacity, as shown in the following theorem.

**Theorem 4.2** *For any server $s$ with capacity $c$ in a virtual machine, suppose the scaled workload changes of agents on the original server, $\delta_i^0(\cdot)$, $i = 1..m$, have means $\mu_i$ and variances $\sigma_i^2$. The minimal capacity that a prospective destination server must have during a service migration at the optimal phase $l^*$, under Assumption 1 and Assumption 2, is*

$$c^* = \max\{c^+, c + \frac{\bar{\mu}}{R} c^0\}, \tag{11}$$

*where $R$ is the overload bound of the expected relative workload in (3) and $c^+$ is the solution to equation:*

$$(\frac{1}{\tilde{c}} - \frac{1}{\tilde{c}'}) \sum_{l=l^*}^{k-1} [\int_0^\infty (1 - \prod_{i=1}^{m} \int_{-\infty}^{x} f_i(u)\, du)\, dx] - H = G, \tag{12}$$

*in which the optimal service migration phases $l^* = (\tilde{c}R - w_0)/\bar{\mu}$ and $k = (\tilde{c}'R - w_0)/\bar{\mu}$ by Theorem 4.1.*

**Proof:** By applying Eq. (10) to the migration gain function, we get the left-hand side part of Eq. (12). And it is clear the resulting gain function monotonously increases as its parameter $c'$ becomes greater. So for a given target gain value $G$, the minimal capacity satisfying $g(c') \geq G$ is the solution to equation $g(c') = G$, denoted by $c^+$.

At the same time, the prospective optimal migration phase $k$ for the new server $s'$ should be greater than phase $l^*$ for server $s$. Otherwise, a new service migration will occur as soon as the previous one completes. We call this phenomena *idle migrations*. So, we have $k \geq l^* + 1$, i.e. $(R\tilde{c}' - w_0)/\bar{\mu} \geq (R\tilde{c} - w_0)/\bar{\mu} + 1$ and obtain $c' \geq c + \bar{\mu}c^0/R$. Therefore, the minimal capacity of a destination server takes the form in the theorem. $\square$

The expected gain function is hard to calculate by Eq. (10). A special case is when the scaled workload changes $\delta_i^0(\cdot)$, for $i = 1..m$ are i.i.d. random variables with the same mean and variance. This is reasonable for the SPMD applications, in which agents execute the same program on their own data sets and they have similar workload change behaviors. For these applications, the minimal destination server capacity can be determined by the following corollary, using the extreme value theory [1].

**Corollary 4.1** *Under the condition of Theorem 4.2, except that the scaled workload changes $\delta_i^0(\cdot)$, $i = 1..m$, have the same mean $\mu$ and variance $\sigma^2$, $c^+$ is the solution to equation:*

$$(\frac{1}{\tilde{c}} - \frac{1}{\tilde{c}'}) \sum_{l=l^*}^{k-1} [w_0 + l\mu + \alpha(m)\sigma\sqrt{l}] - H = G, \tag{13}$$

*in which $\alpha(m) = (2 \ln nm)^{1/2} - (\ln \ln nm + \ln 4\pi)/[2(2 \ln nm)^{1/2}] + \gamma/(2 \ln m)^{1/2}$ and $\gamma$ is Euler's constant $(0.5772\cdots)$.*

We can see the lower bound of the destination server capacity ensures the performance improvement due to a service migration equals to a given target gain in addition to the migration overhead. Since servers make their migration decisions independently, it is possible that two or more servers may decide to migrate to the same destination server according to Theorem 4.2. This phenomena is called *destination conflict* in service migrations. To solve the conflict and reduce migration frequency, we allow the server with the largest prospective next optimal migration timing, determined by Theorem 4.1, to take the destination server. Other servers will try to choose those from the remaining available servers with the least sufficient capacities. After selecting a destination server and completing service migration to it, we update the server sequence of the VM and the capacity distribution sequence $C$. Since then, the renewal process begins a new round of virtual machine computation and each server determines its next migration timing.

## 5 Hybrid Migration Decision

To adapt to the change of server capacities, agents may need to migrate. The decision question is when to migrate and which server the agent should travel to. A locally optimal strategy can be derived if we assume individual agents make their migration decisions independently. But unlike service migration, different agents may migrate to the same server. The interaction among them may cause this migration strategy useless. So, certain global information about the agent or workload distribution is needed. If we consider the global optimization of agent migration, the decision problem is equivalent to the task scheduling in distributed computing. In general, it is a NP-problem to find the globally optimal task distribution. However, in the bulk synchronous computation model for SPMD, agents proceed their computation in phases and they carry out the same task at each phase. It is possible to find a feasible optimal solution to agent migration with some global information. We relate the coordinated decision problem of agent migration to the remapping problem in parallel computing and use dynamic programming to derive a globally optimal solution, similar to the discussion in [16].

An agent may decide to migrate to a server that will perform a service migration to another server at the same phase. So the information, *e.g.* server capacity, for the agent to make decision may be incorrect at the moment of its migration. To avoid this problem, we require service migrations are decided and performed first, and after their completion, agents decide whether to migrate or not with the new system information. Now the agent distribution sequence $M=\langle m_1, m_2, \ldots, m_N \rangle$ of a VM is no longer a constant. Instead, we treat it as a sequence of random variables whose distributions are determined by the dynamic agent migration strategy. At certain computational phase, the residing agents on server $s$ are denoted by $\langle a_1, a_2, \ldots, a_m \rangle$. They may come from different servers via agent migrations. These agents are assigned to their original servers, represented by $\langle s_{(1)}, s_{(2)}, \ldots, s_{(m)} \rangle$, at phase $l = 0$. Entries in this sequence may be identical, which reflects some agents come from the same server. The optimal service migration timing for a server in Theorem 4.1 will be extended by considering the dynamic composition of its agent set. As we can see, it is quite complicated to make optimal decisions with both service and agent migrations for general applications. Here we consider a simplified case where agents on their original servers have the same capacity quota. It can be realized by the task scheduler at the system initiation. The optimal service migration timing with agent migration is described in the following theorem.

**Theorem 5.1** *For any server $s$ with capacity $c$ in a virtual machine, its $m$ agents may migrate from different servers. Suppose these residing agents are, at the initial phase, have equal initial capacity quota $q_0$. Their scaled workload changes, $\delta_i^0(\cdot)$, $i = 1..m$, have the same mean $\mu$. The optimal service migration timing $l^*$ in phase, under Assumption 1 and Assumption 2, is*

$$l^* = \frac{1}{\mu}\left(\frac{cR}{q_0 E[m]} - w_0\right). \quad (14)$$

**Proof:** For a residing agent $a_i$ on server $s$, suppose it originally resides on server $s_{(i)}$, whose capacity and initial number of agents are $c_{(i)}^0$ and $m_{(i)}^0$, respectively. Its initial capacity quota $q_0 = c_{(i)}^0/m_{(i)}^0$. According to the previous discussion, its scaled workload at phase $l$ is $w_i(l) = w_i^0(l)c_{(i)}^0 m/(cm_{(i)}^0) = w_i^0(l)q_0 m/c$. Since $w_i^0(l)$ tends to have a normal distribution with mean $w_0 + l\mu$, we have $E[w_i^0(l)q_0] = (w_0 + l\mu)q_0$. Similarly, the initial scaled workloads of other agents on server $s$ are also normally distributed. The $m$ random variables $w_1^0(l)q_0, \ldots, w_m^0(l)q_0$ are i.i.d. with the same mean $(w_0+l\mu)q_0$. Since $m$ is also a random variable, we have

$$r(l) = \frac{1}{c} \cdot E[\sum_{i=1}^{m} w_i^0(l)q_0] = \frac{1}{c} \cdot E[E[\sum_{i=1}^{m} w_i^0(l)q_0 \mid m]]$$
$$= \frac{1}{c} \cdot E[m]E[w_i^0(l)q_0] = \frac{1}{c}q_0(w_0 + l\mu)E[m].$$

By applying the above equation to $r(l) \le R$, the optimal service migration timing $l^*$ of server $s$ can be derived as in the theorem. $\square$

According to Theorem 5.1, we can see the optimal service migration timing is reversely proportional to the expected value of agent number $m$. This can be explained that as the number of agents on a server increases, its overall workload tends to become greater and this leads to a reduced migration interval. Compared with Theorem 4.1, Eq. (14) is additionally related to the initial capacity quota of each agent due to agent and service migrations. The destination server selection policy in Section 4.2 can also be extended when incorporating agent migration.

## 6 Simulation Results

To verify and analyze results of the migration decision according to our optimal model, we performed experiments to simulate the random processes of agent execution in a reconfigurable distributed VM with 30 agents on each server. Each data point of the simulation results was an average of 200 runs. The 95% confidence interval for each simulation result is also presented to demonstrate the robustness of the estimates.

**Case 1.** In the first experiment, we were to find and verify the optimal computational phase before a service migration according to Theorem 4.1 with the objective of minimizing the migration frequency. The agents on a server were divided into three groups with 10 agents in each one. They might be run in different phases and their initial scaled workload changes obeyed the following distribution functions respectively. where w.p. means

$$\delta_1^0(l) = \begin{cases} 0.1 & \text{w.p. } 0.50, \\ 0 & \text{w.p. } 0.50. \end{cases} \quad \delta_2^0(l) = \begin{cases} 0.1 & \text{w.p. } 0.50, \\ 0 & \text{w.p. } 0.25, \\ -0.1 & \text{w.p. } 0.25. \end{cases} \quad \delta_3^0(l) = \begin{cases} 0.1 & \text{w.p. } 0.25, \\ 0 & \text{w.p. } 0.50, \\ -0.1 & \text{w.p. } 0.25, \end{cases}$$

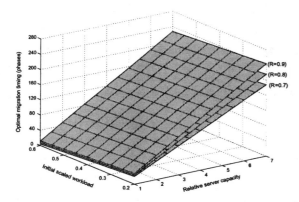

**Figure 1. Optimal service migration timing (numerical results).**

"with probability". The distribution of scaled workload change $\delta_1^0(l)$ implies the total workload of an agent keeps increasing. This is valid in the early phase of some search algorithms, such as the branch-and-bound method [6]. The branching procedure recursively expands a (sub)problem into subproblems such that the size of subproblem set is on the steady increase. Distributions $\delta_2^0(l)$ and $\delta_3^0(l)$ indicate other two phases.

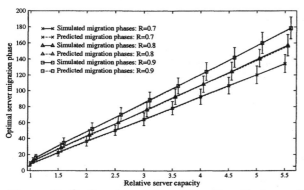

**Figure 2. Optimal service migration timing with $w_0 = 0.5$(simulation results).**

We varied the initial scaled workload $w_0$ from 0.2 to 0.6 and the capacity of each server relative to the original server of its residing agents, $\tilde{c}$, from 1 to 7. The corresponding optimal migration timing changed from the $4^{th}$ to $244^{th}$ phase as shown in Fig. 1. By varying the overload bound $R$ from 0.7 to 0.9, we can see the migration timing increases. Even with $w_0 = 0.5$, $R = 0.7$ and $\tilde{c} = 4$, the optimal migration phase is the $100^{th}$, at which much computation has been performed. So service migration is a feasible approach to realize virtual machine reconfiguration. Fig. 2 shows the migration phases simulated by random processes when the initial scaled workload $w_0$ is 0.5. To prevent the marks from overlapping, we move the curves corresponding to $R = 0.8$ and 0.9 to the right along x-axis by 0.05 unit. This does not affect the experiment results. We can see our migration decision provides an accurate lower bound in determining the service migration timing. The difference between simulated and predicted results tends to decrease as the overload bound $R$ increases. The small confidence interval indicates the robustness of the estimates.

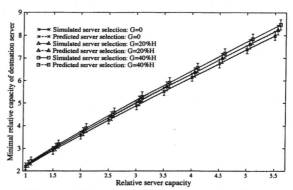

**Figure 3. Destination server selection.**

**Case 2.** The purpose of the second experiment is to verify the accuracy of the destination server selection by Theorem 4.2 for a service migration. The agent composition and distribution functions of scaled workload change were the same as those in Case 1. The initial scaled workload of agents and overload bound were set as $w_0 = 0.5$ and $R = 0.8$ respectively. The service migration overhead was $H = 50$, as 100 times greater than the initial scaled workload. It confirms to our measurements of the runtime overhead of service migration in M-DSA [4].

Fig. 3 plots the minimal capacity that a prospective destination server must have. We varied the capacity of a server from 1 to 5.5 relative to the original server and measured the minimal relative capacity of destination server. We can see the predicted value is either equal to or slightly smaller than the simulated result. This is because our migration decision finds the lower bound of the destination server capacity. The difference is caused by approximating the scaled workload of an agent by a normal distribution according to the central limit theorem. From the figure, we can also see that the minimum value of destination capacity increases at a sub-linear rate. As shown in the figure, if the target gain $G$ is set to 20% of the migration overhead and the relative capacity of a server is 1, the minimal relative capacity of a destination server is about 2.3. Then during the next optimal migration timing, this service will be further migrated to an available server whose capacity should be at least 4.0 times greater than the original server of its residing agents. After migration, the process will be renewed and agent tasks will be executed until the next migration.

**Case 3.** In the third experiment, we repeated the second experiment, but assuming all agents of a server had the same distribution function of the scaled workload change as

$$\delta^0(l) = \begin{cases} 0.1 & \text{w.p. } 0.50, \\ 0 & \text{w.p. } 0.25, \\ -0.1 & \text{w.p. } 0.25. \end{cases}$$

According to Corollary 4.1, the problem of finding the lower bound of the destination server capacity can be approximated by using the extreme value theory.

Fig. 4 shows the accuracy of the prediction approximation. The results in solid line are due to simulation measurements. Compared with the predicted values in Case 2, Corollary 4.1 is a little less accurate in the destination server selection. It is because the extreme value theory provides an upper bound approximation of the expected value for maximal jointly distributed random variables. But, in the figure, we can see the predicted

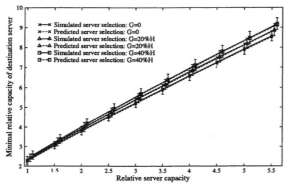

**Figure 4. Destination server selection with extreme value theory.**

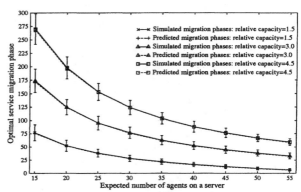

**Figure 5. Optimal service migration timing for hybrid mobility with $w_0 = 0.5$ and $R = 0.8$.**

results are still very close to the simulated ones. The advantage of applying Corollary 4.1 is to simplify calculation of the expected migration gain function.

**Case 4.** To analyze the interplay between agent and service migrations, we conducted the fourth experiment. We applied Theorem 5.1 to extend the optimal service migration decisions in Case 1 and conducted simulations to verify the results. To meet the premise of the theorem, we assigned 30 agents to each server and ensured each agent was allocated the same initial capacity quota. All other settings were equivalent to those in Case 3.

Fig. 5 presents the simulation results. We measured the migration timing for the capacity ratio equal to 1.5, 3.0 and 4.5. We can see the difference between simulated and predicted phases tends to be small around $E[m] = 30$, which is the initial number of agents on each server.

# 7 Conclusions

In this paper, we have studied the decision problem of service and agent migrations for a reconfigurable distributed virtual machine. The optimal service migration policy is derived in both time and space domains for a given overload bound and a target gain value. We note that although the assumption of scaled workload changes remaining the same distributions during migration was assumed in literature, determination of a distribution is non-trivial. This poses a new challenge to the migration decision problem. The present solution to the destination conflict problem is still preliminary. New collaborative approach will be developed for the globally optimal decision. Finally, we will investigate the support of fault tolerance by the hybrid mobility, which is an important application of reconfigurable distributed VM systems.

**Acknowledgement** This work is supported in part by the U.S. National Science Foundation under Grants CCR-9988266 and ACI-0203592.

# References

[1] A. H.-S. Ang and W. H. Tang. *Probability Concepts in Engineering Plannig and Design*, volume II. Rainbow Bridge, 1984.

[2] J. Cao, Y. Sun, X. Wang, and S. K. Das. Scalable load balancing on distributed web servers using mobile agents. *Journal of Parallel and Distributed Computing*, 63(10):996–1005, Oct. 2003.

[3] R. Figueiredo, P. Dinda, and J. Fortes. A case for grid computing on virtual machines. In *Proc. of the 23rd Int'l Conference on Distributed Computing Systems (ICDCS)*, May 2003.

[4] S. Fu, C.-Z. Xu, B. Wims, and R. Basharahil. Distributed shared array: A distributed virtual machine with mobility support for reconfiguration. *Journal of Cluster Computing*, 2004. (accepted).

[5] A. Fuggetta, G. P. Picco, and G. Vigna. Understanding code mobility. *IEEE Transactions on Software Engineering*, 24(5):342–361, 1998.

[6] E. L. Lawler and D. E. Wood. Branch and bound methods, a survey. *Operations Research*, 14:699–719, 1966.

[7] K. Moizumi and G. Cybenko. The travelling agent problem. *Mathematics of Control, Signals and Systems*, 14(3):213–232, 2001.

[8] D. M. Nicol and J. H. Saltz. Dynamic remapping of parallel computations with varying resource demands. *IEEE Transactions on Computers*, 37(9):1073–1087, Sep. 1988.

[9] S. M. Ross. *Introduction to Probability Models*. Academic Press, 6 edition, 1997.

[10] C. P. Sapuntzakis, R. Chandra, B. Pfaff, J. Chow, M. S. Lam, and M. Rosenblum. Optimizing the migration of virtual computers. In *Proc. of the 5th Symposium on Operating Systems Design and Implementation (OSDI)*, Dec. 2002.

[11] E. G. Sirer, R. Grimm, A. J. Gregory, and B. N. Bershad. Design and implementation of a distributed virtual machine for networked computers. In *Proc. of ACM SOSP*, pages 202–216, Dec. 1999.

[12] C. A. Waldspurger and W. E. Weihl. Lottery scheduling: Flexible proportional-share resource management. In *Proc. of USENIX OSDI*, pages 1–11, Nov. 1994.

[13] D. Wang, N. Paciorek, and D. Moore. Java-based mobile agents. *CACM*, 42(3):92–102, Mar. 1999.

[14] C.-Z. Xu, L. Wang, and N.-T. Fong. Stochastic predication of execution time for dynamic bulk synchronous computation. *Journal of Supercomputing*, 21(1):91–103, Jan. 2002.

[15] C.-Z. Xu and B. Wims. A mobile agent based push methodology for global parallel computing. *Concurrency: Practice and Experience*, 14(8):705–726, Jul. 2000.

[16] G. Yin, C.-Z. Xu, and L. Wang. Optimal remapping in dynamic bulk synchronous computations via a stochastic control approach. *IEEE Transactions on Parallel and Distributed Systems*, 14(1):51–62, Jan. 2003.

[17] W. Zhu, C.-L. Wang, and F. C. M. Lau. JESSICA2: A distributed java virtual machine with transparent thread migration support. In *Proc. of the 4th Int'l Conference on Cluster Computing*, Sep. 2002.

[18] X. Zhuang and S. Pande. Compiler scheduling of mobile agents for minimizing overheads. In *Proc. of IEEE ICDCS*, May 2003.

# An Efficient Deadlock-Free Tree-Based Routing Algorithm for Irregular Wormhole-Routed Networks Based on the Turn Model

Yau-Ming Sun, Chih-Hsueh Yang, Yeh-Ching Chung[1], and Tai-Yi Huang
*Department of Computer Science,*
*National Tsing Hua University,*
*HsingChu, Taiwan 300 R.O.C*
*{sym87u, dickyang}@sslab.cs.nthu.edu.tw, {ychung, tyhuang}@cs.nthu.edu.tw*

## Abstract

*In this paper, we proposed an efficient deadlock-Free tree-based routing algorithm, the DOWN/UP routing, for irregular wormhole-routed networks based on the turn model. In a tree-based routing algorithm, hot spots around the root of a spanning tree and the uneven traffic distribution are the two main facts degrade the performance of the routing algorithm. To solve the hot spot and the uneven traffic distribution problems, in the DOWN/UP routing, it tries to push the traffic downward to the leaves of a spanning tree as much as possible and remove prohibited turn pairs with opposite directions in each node, respectively. To evaluate the performance of DOWN/UP routing, the simulation is conducted. We have implemented the DOWN/UP routing along with the L-turn routing on the IRFlexSim0.5 simulator. Irregular networks that contain 128 switches with 4-port and 8-port configurations are simulated. The simulation results show that the proposed routing algorithm outperforms the L-turn routing for all test samples in terms of the degree of hot spots, the traffic load distribution, and throughput.*

## 1. Introduction

The *Up\*/Down\* routing* was the first deadlock-free tree-based routing algorithm for irregular networks. It is simple and easy to be implemented. However, it does not perform well. The reasons are three-fold. First, the so called *hot spots* [5] will occur around the root of a spanning tree. Second, the average length of routing paths is long compared to other tree-based routing algorithms. Third, there may exist two prohibited turns whose directions are opposite to each other on a node. These opposite prohibited turn pairs make the traffic distribution uneven [4].

To overcome the drawbacks of the *up\*/down\* routing*, the *L-turn routing* was proposed in [4] based on the 2D turn model [3]. In the *L-turn routing*, the routing is based

on the *L-R tree*. By carefully setting up the prohibited turns for each node, one can obtain a more even distribution of traffic load and shorter routing paths compared to the *up\*/down\* routing* [4]. However, in the *L-turn routing*, the *tree links* and the *cross links* are considered as the same type of links. They have the same definition on directions. It is possible that the hot spots will still occur around the root under some *L-R trees* and makes traffic load unbalancing.

In this paper, we propose an efficient deadlock-free tree-based routing algorithm, the *DOWN/UP routing*, for irregular wormhole-routed networks based on the turn model. In the *DOWN/UP routing*, the *communication graph* based on the *coordinated tree* of a given topology is used to derive the prohibit turns. There are many ways to construct the coordinated tree of a given topology. Different coordinated trees lead to different performance of a routing algorithm. In this paper, we proposed a better way to construct the coordinated tree such that a better throughput can be obtained when a routing algorithm is performed.

In a communication graph, the tree links and cross links are considered as different links. They have different definitions on directions. This allows us to make the prohibited turn selection more precisely, that is, we can select the prohibited turns between the same or different type of links. Therefore, the traffic flow control by selecting prohibited turns in a communication graph is easier than that in the *L-R tree* used by the *L-turn routing*.

Based on the maximal direction graph, we can construct a maximal *acyclic direction dependency graph* by performing prohibited turn selection process. In the prohibited turn selection process, we careful select the set of prohibited turns such that the traffic can be pushed downward to leaves of a spanning tree as much as possible and a more even distribution of traffic load can be achieved. From the maximal acyclic direction dependency graph, the *DOWN/UP routing* can be derived by applying the same prohibited turns to each node in the communication graph and releasing unnecessary prohibited turns for each node. The *DOWN/UP routing*

---

[1] The corresponding author.

can be directly applied to arbitrary topology with (or without) any virtual channel of wormhole-routed networks.

To evaluate the proposed *DOWN/UP routing*, we compare its performance with that of *L-turn routing*. The hot spots, the traffic load distribution, and throughput are the three key factors for the evaluation. We implemented these two routing algorithms on simulated irregular networks that contain 128 switches with 4-port and 8-port configurations. The simulation results show that the *DOWN/UP routing* has less hot spots, better traffic load distribution, and higher throughput than the *L-turn routing*.

The rest of the paper is organized as follows. In Section 2, a brief survey of related work will be presented. In Section 3, we will introduce notations and terminology used in this paper. Section 4 presents the proposed deadlock-free routing algorithm in detail. The simulation environment and results will be presented in Section 5.

## 2. Related Work

Many deadlock-free routing algorithms for irregular network topologies have been proposed in the literature. In [7], the *up*/down* routing* used in DEC AN1 system was proposed for arbitrary network topologies. This adaptive routing algorithm assigns each network channel an *up* or a *down* direction based on a spanning tree. From the direction definitions, each packets must go through zero or more than one *up* direction channels followed by zero or more than one *down* direction channels to guarantee connectivity and deadlock-free. In [8], the *up*/down* routing* was extended to consider virtual channels or additional physical channels to achieve high-performance routing. In [6], an improved *up*/down* routing* based on depth first search (DFS) spanning tree was proposed. The proposed routing is deterministic source routing that has lower latency and better throughput than the original *up*/down* routing* algorithm.

Ni and Glass [1] proposed the *turn model* to design partially adaptive wormhole routing algorithms without any additional physical links and virtual channels. The idea of this model is to prohibit the minimum number of turns to break all of the cycles so that the routing is deadlock-free. Based on the model, the authors also proposed three partially adaptive routing algorithms, *west-first*, *north-first*, and *negative-first*, for two-dimensional meshes.

In [3] [4], Funahashi *et al.* proposed the *2D turn model* by introducing two-dimensional directions into a spanning tree to solve the traffic unbalancing problem occurred in the *up*/down* routing*. Two adaptive routing algorithms, *left/right routing* and *L-turn routing*, were proposed. The simulation results in [4] have shown that

the *L-turn routing* achieves better performance than the *up*/down* routing*.

## 3. Preliminaries

**Definition 1**: A network with arbitrary switch-based interconnection can be represented as a graph $G = (V, E)$, where $V$ is the set of switches and $E$ is the set of bidirectional links between switches. For each link $e = (v_1, v_2)$ in $E$, it consists of two communication channels $<v_1, v_2>$ and $<v_2, v_1>$ in which $v_1$ can send message to $v_2$ through $<v_1, v_2>$ and $v_2$ can send message to $v_1$ through $<v_2, v_1>$. For each channel $<v_1, v_2>$, $v_1$ and $v_2$ are called *start* and *sink* nodes of the channel, respectively. $<v_1, v_2>$ is called the *output* channel and *input* channel of $v_1$ and $v_2$, respectively. $G$ is called the network topology or the topology of the network.

**Definition 2** (*coordinated tree*): Given $G = (V, E)$, a *coordinated tree* is a breath first search (BFS) spanning tree of $G$. For each node $v$ in a coordinated tree, node $v$ is associated with a two dimensional coordinate $v(x, y)$. We use $X(v)$ and $Y(v)$ to denote the $x$ and $y$ coordinates of node $v$, respectively, that is, $X(v) = x$ and $Y(v) = y$. $X(v)$ is defined as the order of preorder traversal of the coordinated tree starting from the root to node $A$ and $Y(v)$ is defined as the level of node $v$ in the coordinated tree.

Due to two or more children nodes can be selected as the next preorder traversal node, several coordinated trees can be built from the same network topology.

**Definition 3**: Given $G = (V, E)$ and a coordinated tree $CT = (V, E')$ of $G$, $E'$ and $E - E'$ are the sets of *tree links* and *cross links* of $G$ with respect to $CT$, respectively.

**Definition 4**: Given $G = (V, E)$ and a coordinated tree $CT = (V, E')$ of $G$, for each link $e = (v_1, v_2) \in E$, we define

(1) $v_2$ is the *left-up* node of $v_1$ if $X(v_2) < X(v_1)$ and $Y(v_2) < Y(v_1)$,

(2) $v_2$ is the *left* node of $v_1$ if $X(v_2) < X(v_1)$ and $Y(v_2) = Y(v_1)$,

(3) $v_2$ is the *left-down* node of $v_1$ if $X(v_2) < X(v_1)$ and $Y(v_2) > Y(v_1)$,

(4) $v_2$ is the *right-up* node of $v_1$ if $X(v_2) > X(v_1)$ and $Y(v_2) < Y(v_1)$,

(5) $v_2$ is the *right* node of $v_1$ if $X(v_2) > X(v_1)$ and $Y(v_2) = Y(v_1)$, and

(6) $v_2$ is the *right-down* node of $v_1$ if $X(v_2) > X(v_1)$ and $Y(v_2) > Y(v_1)$.

**Definition 5** (*Communication graph (CG)*): Given $G = (V, E)$ and a coordinated tree $CT = (V, E')$ of $G$, the *communication graph* $CG = (V, \vec{E})$ with respect to $G$ and $CT$ is a directed graph, where $\vec{E}$ is the set of all communication channels of $E$. For each channel $\vec{e} = <v_1, v_2> \in \vec{E}$, if $\vec{e}$ is a channel of a tree link, the direction of

$\vec{e}$, denoted as $d(\vec{e})$, is defined as *LU_TREE* and *RD_TREE* if $v_2$ is a *left-up* node of $v_1$ and $v_2$ is a *right-down* node of $v_1$, respectively. If $\vec{e}$ is a channel of a cross link, the direction of $\vec{e}$ is defined as *LU_CROSS*, *LD_CROSS*, *RU_CROSS*, *RD_CROSS*, *R_CROSS*, and *L_CROSS* if $v_2$ is a *left-up* node of $v_1$, $v_2$ is a *left-down* node of $v_1$, $v_2$ is a *right-up* node of $v_1$, $v_2$ is a *right-down* node of $v_1$, $v_2$ is a *right* node of $v_1$, and $v_2$ is a *left* node of $v_1$ respectively.

**Definition 6** (*Turn*): Given a communication graph $CG = (V, \vec{E})$, the directions of $\vec{e}_1$ and $\vec{e}_2$ form a *turn* for $v_2$ if $\vec{e}_1 = <v_1, v_2>$ and $\vec{e}_2 = <v_2, v_3>$. We use $T_{d(\vec{e}_1),d(\vec{e}_2)}$ to denote the turn formed by the directions of $\vec{e}_1$ and $\vec{e}_2$.

**Definition 7** (*Turn cycle*): A *turn cycle* $TC = (T_{d(\vec{e}_1),d(\vec{e}_2)}, T_{d(\vec{e}_2),d(\vec{e}_3)}, \dots, T_{d(\vec{e}_k),d(\vec{e}_{k+1})})$ is a sequence of turns in which the sink node of the first channel is also the sink node of the last channel in the turn sequence, that is, the start node of $\vec{e}_2$ is the sink node of $\vec{e}_{k+1}$.

**Definition 8** (*Direction graph (DG)*): The *direction graph* $DG = (D, \vec{T})$ with respect to a communication graph $CG = (V, \vec{E})$ is a complete directed graph, where $D$ is the set of directions defined in $CG$ and $\vec{T} = \{ T_{d_1,d_2} \mid$ for all $d_1, d_2 \in D$ and $d_1 \neq d_2 \}$ is the set of possible turns that can be defined in $CG$. A $DG$ is called the *complete direction graph* (*CDG*) if $D = \{LU\_TREE, RD\_TREE, LD\_CROSS, RU\_CROSS, R\_CROSS, L\_CROSS, LU\_CROSS, RD\_CROSS\}$.

**Definition 9** (*Direction dependency graph (DDG)*): Given a $DG$, any subset of $DG$ is called the *direction dependency graph* (*DDG*) of $DG$.

**Definition 10** (*Acyclic direction dependency graph (ADDG)*): Given a $CG$, the $DG$ of $CG$, and a $DDG$ of $DG$, for each node $v$ in $CG$, if the edges of $DDG$ are the only available turns allowed at $v$ and no turn cycle can be formed in $CG$, then the $DDG$ is called *acyclic DDG*.

**Definition 11**: Given a $CG$, the $DG$ of $CG$, an $ADDG$ of $DG$ is called the *maximal ADDG* if adding any edge that in $DG$ but not in $ADDG$ to the $ADDG$ will result in turn cycles in $CG$.

**Lemma 1**: Given a $CG$ and a $DDG$ of $CG$, if there is no cycle in the $DDG$, then no possible turn cycle can be formed in $CG$ when the edges of $DDG$ are the only available turns allowed at each node in $CG$.

*Proof* : Assume that there is a turn cycle $TC = (T_{d(\vec{e}_1),d(\vec{e}_2)}, T_{d(\vec{e}_2),d(\vec{e}_3)}, \dots, T_{d(\vec{e}_k),d(\vec{e}_{k+1})})$ in $CG$. The turn cycle $TC$ can be simply represented as $TC'(T_{d_1,d_2}, T_{d_2,d_3}, \dots, T_{d_k,d_1})$ in a $DDG$, where $d_1 = d(\vec{e}_1) = d(\vec{e}_{k+1})$, $d_2 = d(\vec{e}_2)$, $d_3 = d(\vec{e}_3)$, $\dots$, and $d_k = d(\vec{e}_k)$.

$TC'(T_{d_1,d_2}, T_{d_2,d_3}, \dots, T_{d_k,d_1})$ is a cycle in the $DDG$. This contradicts the assumption. $\qquad\square$

We now give examples to explain the above definitions. Figure 1(a) is an example of a switch-based network with irregular interconnection. The corresponding network topology of Figure 1(a) is shown in Figure 1(b). A *coordinated tree* for the network topology shown in Figure 1(b) is shown in Figure 1(c). In Figure 1(c), we have $Y(v_1) = 0$, $X(v_2) = 2$, and $v_3$ is the *right* node, *left* node, and *right-down* node of $v_5$, $v_4$, and $v_1$ respectively. For a link in Figure 1(b), if it is a link in Figure 1(c), then it is a tree link. Otherwise it is a cross link. The $CG$ with respect to Figure 1(b) and Figure 1(c) is shown in Figure 1(d). In Figure 1(d), $d(<v_2,v_4>) = RU\_CROSS$, $d(<v_5,v_2>) = RD\_TREE$, $T_{RD\_TREE,RU\_CROSS}$ is a turn, $TC = ( T_{d(<v_5,v_1>),d(<v_1,v_3>)}$, $T_{d(<v_1,v_3>),d(<v_3,v_5>)}$, $T_{d(<v_3,v_5>),d(<v_5,v_1>)} )$ is a turn cycle, and the set of direction $D = \{LU\_TREE, RD\_TREE, LD\_CROSS, RU\_CROSS, R\_CROSS,$ and $L\_CROSS\}$. In Figure 1(d), the thick links are tree links and thin links are cross links. The corresponding $DG$ of Figure 1(d) is shown in Figure 1(e). Figure 1(f) is an $ADDG$ of Figure 1(d) and Figure 1(e). In Figure 1(f), the $ADDG$ has two nodes, $LD\_CROSS$ and $RD\_TREE$, and two edges (or *turns*), $T_{LD\_CROSS,RD\_TREE}$ and $T_{RD\_TREE,LD\_CROSS}$. The two edges form a cycle in the $ADDG$. However, if each node of $CG$ shown in Figure 1(d) only allows these two *turns*, no turn cycle can be formed in the $CG$. From Figure 1(f), we can see that a cycle in a $DDG$ may not result in a turn cycle in a $CG$.

## 4. The *DOWN/UP Routing*

Given an irregular network topology $G = (V, E)$, the construction of the *DOWN/UP routing* consists of the following three phases.

Phase 1: Construct a $CT = (V, E')$ from $G$ and the $CG = (V, \vec{E})$ with respect to $G$ and $CT$.

Phase 2: Find the *maximal ADDG max_ADDG* $= (D, \vec{T}')$ from the complete direction graph $CDG = (D, \vec{T})$.

Phase 3: Let $PT = \vec{T} - \vec{T}'$ be the set of prohibited turns for each node in $CG$. According to $CG$, remove the redundant prohibited turns for each node and find the possible shortest routing paths for any two nodes based the available turns of each node to form the *DOWN/UP routing*.

In the following, we explain each phase in details.

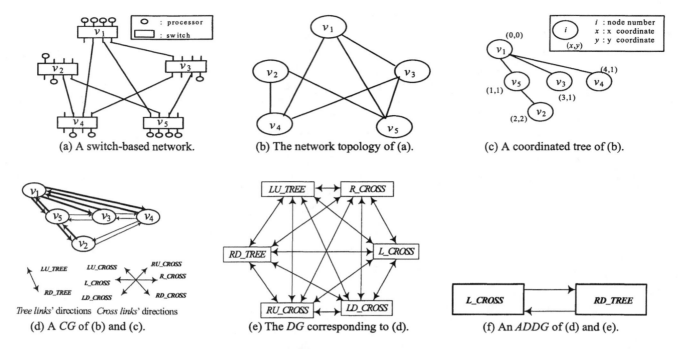

(a) A switch-based network.

(b) The network topology of (a).

(c) A coordinated tree of (b).

(d) A *CG* of (b) and (c).

(e) The *DG* corresponding to (d).

(f) An *ADDG* of (d) and (e).

**Figure 1. Examples for Definitions 1 to 11.**

## 4.1. Phase 1

There are many ways to construct a coordinated tree from a network topology. Different coordinated trees lead to different performance of routing algorithms. How to construct a coordinated tree that leads to a better performance for routing algorithms is an important issue. One of the main contributions of this paper is that we propose a better way to construct a coordinated tree that leads to a better performance of routing algorithms. The construction of a coordinated tree $CT = (V, E')$ is composed of the following steps:

Step 1. Initially, let $Q$ be an empty queue, *Visited* be an array of size $|V|$ initialized with 0, and $E'$ be an empty set.

Step 2. Select $v$ with the smallest node number from $V$. Set *Visited*$[v] = 1$ and insert $v$ to $Q$.

Step 3. Delete $v$ from $Q$.

Step 4. Let $W = \{w_1, w_2, ..., w_k\}$ be the set of nodes adjacent to $v$, where *Visited*$[w_i] = 0$, for $i = 1, ..., k$ and the node number of $w_i$ is less than that of $w_{i+1}$. For $i = 1, ..., k$, insert $w_i$ to $Q$, $E' = E' \cup \{(v, w_i)\}$, and set *Visited*$[w_i] = 1$.

Step 5. If $Q$ is not empty, perform Steps 3 and 4.

Step 6. Traverse the tree in preorder and nodes with smaller node numbers are visited first. Set the values of $X(v)$ and $Y(v)$ of node $v$ as the order of preorder traversal and the level of the spanning tree, respectively.

From Definition 5, the construction of the $CG = (V, \vec{E})$ with respect to $G = (V, E)$ and $CT = (V, E')$ is straightforward.

## 4.2. Phase 2

The complete direction graph contains all eight directions that can be defined in a *CG*, that is, it contains all possible turns that can be found in a *CG*. If we can find a maximal *ADDG* from the complete direction graph, then apply the edges (turns) in the maximal *ADDG* to each node of a *CG* will also result in no turn cycle. There are two issues to find the *maximal ADDG* from the complete direction graph. The first issue is to decide what edges should be removed (prohibited) from the complete direction graph. The second issue is the routing algorithm derived from the found maximal *ADDG* should perform efficiently. For the first issue, we use an incremental method to remove edges step by step from the complete direction graph to obtain a maximal *ADDG*. For the second issue, when removing edges from a *DDG* in each step, we will try to prevent the traffic from flowing to the root of a *CG* and push the traffic downward to the leaves of a *CG*. The process of finding the maximal *ADDG* from the complete direction graph consists of the following four steps:

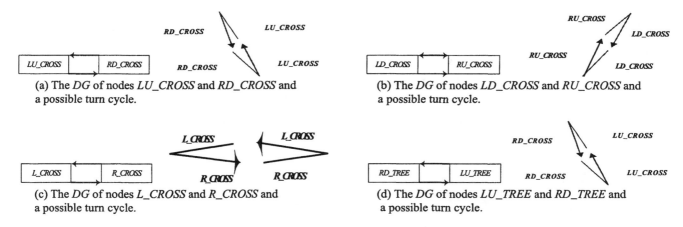

(a) The *DG* of nodes *LU_CROSS* and *RD_CROSS* and a possible turn cycle.

(b) The *DG* of nodes *LD_CROSS* and *RU_CROSS* and a possible turn cycle.

(c) The *DG* of nodes *L_CROSS* and *R_CROSS* and a possible turn cycle.

(d) The *DG* of nodes *LU_TREE* and *RD_TREE* and a possible turn cycle.

**Figure 2. The *DGs* of node pairs and their corresponding possible turn cycles.**

Step 1. Find the maximal *ADDGs* $ADDG_1$, $ADDG_2$, $ADDG_3$, and $ADDG_4$, from *DGs* of nodes *LU_CROSS* and *RD_CROSS*, nodes *LD_CROSS* and *RU_CROSS*, nodes *L_CROSS* and *R_CROSS*, and nodes *LU_TREE* and *RD_TREE* from the complete direction graph, respectively.

Step 2. Combine $ADDG_1$ with $ADDG_2$ by adding edges between nodes in $ADDG_1$ and $ADDG_2$ to form a new *DDG* and find a maximal *ADDG* $ADDG_5$ from the new formed *DDG*.

Step 3. Combine $ADDG_3$ with $ADDG_5$ by adding edges between nodes in $ADDG_3$ and $ADDG_5$ to form a new *DDG* and find a maximal *ADDG* $ADDG_6$ from the new formed *DDG*.

Step 4. Combine $ADDG_4$ with $ADDG_6$ by adding edges between nodes in $ADDG_4$ and $ADDG_6$ to form a new *DDG* and find a maximal *ADDG* $ADDG_7$ from the new formed *DDG*. The found $ADDG_7$ is a maximal *ADDG* of the complete direction graph.

### A. Step 1

In this step, we want to find the maximal *ADDGs* $ADDG_1$, $ADDG_2$, $ADDG_3$, and $ADDG_4$ from *DGs* of nodes *LU_CROSS* and *RD_CROSS*, nodes *LD_CROSS* and *RU_CROSS*, nodes *L_CROSS* and *R_CROSS*, and nodes *LU_TREE* and *RD_TREE* from the complete direction graph, respectively. The reason we choose these node pairs is that the *DG* of each node pair contains edges with opposite directions. These edges form a cycle that may lead to a turn cycle. Figure 2 shows the *DGs* of these node pairs and their corresponding possible turn cycles.

To find the maximal *ADDG* from the *DG* of each node pairs, we must remove one of the two edges of the *DG*. For each node $v$ in a *CG*, the *LU_CROSS* and *RU_CROSS* directions indicate that the traffic flow is going upward from node $v$ to other nodes whose $Y$ coordinate is less

than that of node $v$. The edges (*turns*) $T_{RU\_CROSS,LD\_CROSS}$ and $T_{LU\_CROSS,RD\_CROSS}$ in Figure 2(a) and Figure 2(b), respectively, will make the traffic flow goes upward before downward. In order to push the traffic flow downward to the leaves of the corresponding *CT*, we remove edges $T_{RU\_CROSS,LD\_CROSS}$ and $T_{LU\_CROSS,RD\_CROSS}$ from Figure 2(a) and Figure 2(b), respectively. The maximum *ADDGs* $ADDG_1$ and $ADDG_2$ for the *DGs* shown in Figure 2(a) and Figure 2(b) are shown in Figure 3(a) and Figure 3(b), respectively. For the cycle shown in Figure 2(c), since the removal of either edge leads to the same result, we randomly remove edge $T_{L\_CROSS,R\_CROSS}$ from the *DG*. The $ADDG_3$ is obtained and is shown in Figure 3(c). For each node $v$ in a *CG*, the *LU_TREE* direction indicates that the traffic is flowing from node $v$ to the root of the corresponding *CT*. For the cycle shown in Figure 2(d), in order to prevent the traffic from flowing to the root of a corresponding *CT*, we remove edge $T_{RD\_TREE,LU\_TREE}$ from the *DG*. The $ADDG_4$ is formed and is shown in Figure 3(d).

(a) $ADDG_1$

(b) $ADDG_2$

(c) $ADDG_3$

(d) $ADDG_4$

**Figure 3. The maximal *ADDGs* of *DGs* shown in Figure 2.**

### B. Step 2

In this step, we want to combine $ADDG_1$ with $ADDG_2$ by adding edges between nodes in $ADDG_1$ and $ADDG_2$ to

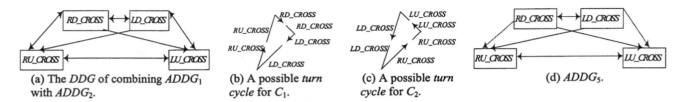

(a) The *DDG* of combining $ADDG_1$ with $ADDG_2$.

(b) A possible *turn cycle* for $C_1$.

(c) A possible *turn cycle* for $C_2$.

(d) $ADDG_5$.

**Figure 4. Combine $ADDG_1$ with $ADDG_2$ to form $ADDG_5$.**

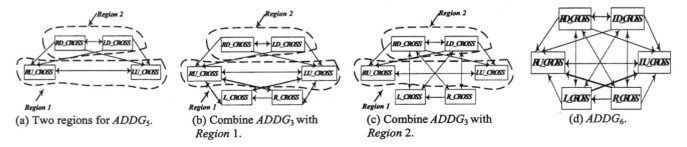

(a) Two regions for $ADDG_5$.

(b) Combine $ADDG_3$ with *Region* 1.

(c) Combine $ADDG_3$ with *Region* 2.

(d) $ADDG_6$.

**Figure 5. Combine $ADDG_3$ with $ADDG_5$ to form $ADDG_6$.**

form a new *DDG* and find a maximal *ADDG* $ADDG_5$ from the new formed *DDG*.

The *DDG* of combining $ADDG_1$ with $ADDG_2$ is shown in Figure 4(a). When adding edges between node *RD-CROSS* in $ADDG_1$ and nodes in $ADDG_2$, a cycle $C_1(T_{RU\_CROSS,RD\_CROSS}, T_{RD\_CROSS,LD\_CROSS}, T_{LD\_CROSS,RU\_CROSS})$ is formed. This cycle may form the turn cycle, shown in Figure 4(b), in a *CG*. When adding edges between node *LU_CROSS* in $ADDG_1$ and nodes in $ADDG_2$, a cycle $C_2(T_{LU\_CROSS,LD\_CROSS}, T_{LD\_CROSS,RU\_CROSS}, T_{RU\_CROSS,LU\_CROSS})$ is formed. This cycle may form the turn cycle, shown in Figure 4(c), in a *CG*. Since the edges (*turns*) $T_{RU\_CROSS,RD\_CROSS}$ and $T_{LU\_CROSS,LD\_CROSS}$ in cycles $C_1$ and $C_2$ will make the traffic flow goes upward before downward, respectively. In order to push the traffic flow downward the leaves of a corresponding *CT*, we remove edges $T_{RU\_CROSS,RD\_CROSS}$ and $T_{LU\_CROSS,LD\_CROSS}$ from the *ADD* shown in Figure 4(a). The $ADDG_5$ is formed and is shown in Figure 4(d).

### C. Step 3

In this step, we want to combine $ADDG_3$ with $ADDG_5$ by adding edges between nodes in $ADDG_3$ and $ADDG_5$ to form a new *DDG* and find a maximal *ADDG* $ADDG_6$ from the new formed *DDG*. For nodes in Figure 4(d), we have the following observations:

**Observation** 1: Any combination of edges (*turns*) from nodes *LD_CROSS* and *RD_CROSS* would not have upward directions in a *CG*.

**Observation** 2: Any combination of edges (*turns*) from nodes *LU_CROSS* and *RU_CROSS* would not have downward directions in a *CG*.

Therefore, we divide $ADDG_5$ into *Region* 1 and *Region* 2 as shown in Figure 5(a). For the $ADDG_3$ shown in Figure 3(c), edge $T_{R\_CROSS,L\_CROSS}$ indicates that the traffic is flowing between nodes in the same level of a corresponding *CT*. To combine the $ADDG_3$ with *Region* 1 or *Region* 2 shown in Figure 5(a), we have the following observations:

**Observation** 3: If we combine $ADDG_3$ with *Region* 1 to form a *DDG* shown in Figure 5(b), no turn cycles can be formed from the *DDG* shown in Figure 5(b).

**Observation** 4: If we combine $ADDG_3$ with *Region* 2 to form a *DDG* shown in Figure 5(c), no turn cycles can be formed from the *DDG* shown in Figure 5(c).

**Observation** 5: If we combine $ADDG_3$ with $ADDG_5$, a possible turn cycle can be formed from node $v$ in *Region* 1 to nodes in $ADDG_3$, *Region* 2, and back to node $v$.

To combine $ADDG_3$ with $ADDG_5$ to form $ADDG_6$, based on Observations 3, 4, and 5, we can first combine Figure 5(b) and Figure 5(c). Then by removing either edges from nodes in *Region* 1 to nodes in $ADDG_3$ or edges from nodes in *Region* 2 to nodes in $ADDG_3$, we can obtain $ADDG_6$. Since any combination of edges (turns) between nodes in $ADDG_3$ and nodes in *Region* 1 would not have downward directions in a *CG*, to keep the traffic flow downward, we remove edges from nodes in *Region* 1 to nodes in $ADDG_3$. We then obtain $ADDG_6$ as shown in Figure 5(d).

### D. Step 4

In this step, we want to combine $ADDG_4$ with $ADDG_6$ by adding edges between nodes in $ADDG_4$ and $ADDG_6$ to form a new *DDG* and find a maximal *ADDG* $ADDG_7$

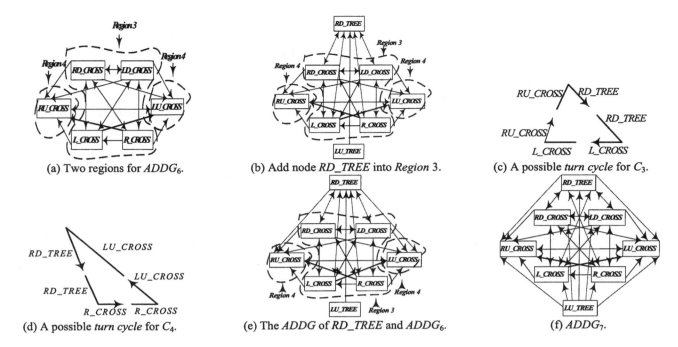

(a) Two regions for $ADDG_6$.

(b) Add node $RD\_TREE$ into $Region$ 3.

(c) A possible *turn cycle* for $C_3$.

(d) A possible *turn cycle* for $C_4$.

(e) The $ADDG$ of $RD\_TREE$ and $ADDG_6$.

(f) $ADDG_7$.

**Figure 6. Obtain a maximal *ADDG* for the complete direction graph.**

from the new formed $DDG$. The found $ADDG_7$ is a maximal $ADDG$ of the complete direction graph.

For nodes in Figure 5(d), we have Observation 2 and the following observation:

**Observation 6:** Any combination of edges (turns) from nodes $LD\_CROSS$ and $RD\_CROSS$, $L\_CROS$, and $R\_CROSS$ would not have upward directions in a $CG$.

Therefore, based on Observations 2 and 6, we divide $ADDG_6$ into $Region$ 3 and $Region$ 4 as shown in Figure 6(a).

When adding edges between node $RD\_TREE$ and nodes in $Region$ 3, no turn cycles can be formed from the $DDG$ and any combination of edges (turns) from the $DDG$ would not have upward directions in a $CG$, that is, the turns defined in the $DDG$ will push the traffic downward to the leaves of a corresponding $CT$. We keep all edges in between node $RD\_TREE$ and nodes in $Region$ 3 and the $DDG$ is shown in Figure 6(b).

Based on Figure 6(b), when adding edges between node $RD\_TREE$ and nodes in $Region$ 4, two cycles $C_3(T_{RD\_TREE,L\_CROSS},\ T_{L\_CROSS,RU\_CROSS},\ T_{RU\_CROSS,RD\_TREE})$ and $C_4(T_{RD\_TREE,R\_CROSS},\ T_{R\_CROSS,LU\_CROSS},\ T_{LU\_CROSS,RD\_TREE})$ are formed. These cycles may form *turn cycles* as shown in Figure 6(c) and Figure 6(d), respectively. Therefore, we remove the two edges $T_{LU\_CROSS,RD\_TREE}$ and $T_{RU\_CROSS,RD\_TREE}$ and the $DDG$ is shown in Figure 6(e).

When adding edges between node $LU\_TREE$ and nodes in $ADDG_6$ based on Figure 6(e), a possible turn cycle can be formed from node $RD\_TREE$ to nodes in $ADDG_6$, $LU\_TREE$, and back to node $RD\_TREE$. For each node $v$ in a $CG$, the $LU\_TREE$ direction indicates

that the traffic is flowing from node $v$ to the root of the corresponding coordinated tree. To prevent the traffic from flowing to the root of a corresponding $CT$, we remove all edges from nodes in $ADDG_6$ to node $LU\_TREE$ to form an $ADDG$ as shown in Figure 6(f). This new formed $ADDG$ is $ADDG_7$, a maximal $ADDG$ of the complete direction graph.

### 4.3. Phase 3

In Phase 2, we have removed eighteen edges from the complete direction graph. These eighteen edges form a set of prohibited *turns* $PT = \{T_{RD\_TREE,LU\_TREE},$ $T_{RD\_CROSS,LU\_TREE},$ $T_{L\_CROSS,LU\_TREE},$ $T_{R\_CROSS,LU\_TREE},$ $T_{RU\_CROSS,LU\_TREE},$ $T_{LU\_CROSS,LU\_TREE},$ $T_{LD\_CROSS,LU\_TREE},$ $T_{RU\_CROSS,LD\_CROSS},$ $T_{RU\_CROSS,RD\_CROSS},$ $T_{LU\_CROSS,LD\_CROSS},$ $T_{LU\_CROSS,RD\_CROSS},$ $T_{LU\_CROSS,RD\_TREE},$ $T_{RU\_CROSS,RD\_TREE},$ $T_{L\_CROSS,R\_CROSS},$ $T_{R\_CROSS,RU\_CROSS},$ $T_{R\_CROSS,LU\_CROSS},$ $T_{L\_CROSS,RU\_CROSS},\ T_{L\_CROSS,LU\_CROSS}\ \}$. Since the $ADDG_7$ found in Phase 2 is a maximal $ADDG$ of the complete direction graph, when the prohibited turns in $PT$ applied to nodes of a $CG$, it is possible that some prohibited turns are redundant for some nodes. For example, for the $CG$ shown in Figure 7, in which the thick lines are the tree links and the thin lines are cross links, the turn from node $v_9$ through node $v_6$ to node $v_8$ ($T_{RU\_CROSS,RD\_TREE}$) and the turn from node $v_4$ through node $v_{11}$ to node $v_5$ ($T_{LU\_CROSS,RD\_TREE}$) are unnecessary prohibited turns for nodes $v_6$ and $v_{11}$, respectively, since these prohibited turns on these nodes do not form turn cycles in the $CG$. In this phase, we want to remove these redundant prohibited turns for each node in *CG* from *PT* and find routing paths from the available turns of each node in *CG* to form the *DOWN/UP routing*.

We propose a *cycle detection* algorithm, which is similar to that in [4], to remove the redundant prohibited turns for each node in *CG* from *PT*. In the cycle detection algorithm, we only consider to release the prohibited turns $T_{LU\_CROSS,RD\_TREE}$ and $T_{RU\_CROSS,RD\_TREE}$ in each node. The reasons are two-fold. First, only the prohibited turns $T_{LU\_CROSS,RD\_TREE}$ and $T_{RU\_CROSS,RD\_TREE}$ in *PT* can help the traffic flow not go upward to the root and push the traffic flow downward to the leaves of a corresponding *CT*. Second, each node in a *CG*, except the leaves of a corresponding *CT*, has the output channel with direction *RD_TREE*. The number of $T_{LU\_CROSS,RD\_TREE}$ and $T_{RU\_CROSS,RD\_TREE}$ may be more than that of other prohibited turns in a *CG*. The algorithm is given as follows:

---

*Algorithm cycle_detection(CG, PT)* /* $CG = (V, \vec{E})$ */
1. Let *in(v)* be the set of input channels of node *v* in *V* whose direction is *LU_CROSS* or *RU_CROSS*.
2. Let *out(v)* be the set of output channels of node *v* in *V* whose direction is *RD_TREE*.
3. $\forall v \in V$, for each pair of ($\vec{e}_1, \vec{e}_2$) **do** /* where $\vec{e}_1 \in in(v)$ and $\vec{e}_2 \in out(v)$ */
4. { Initialize stacks *S* and *D*.
5. Starting from *v*, visit its adjacency node *v'* through $\vec{e}_2$ and mark $\vec{e}_2$.
6. Let *in_channel* = $\vec{e}_2$ and push $\vec{e}_2$ into *D*.
7. **if** (node *v'* has an output channel $\vec{e}' = <v', v''>$ that is not marked and does not form a prohibited turn with *d(in_channel)*) **then** { Push *v''* into *S*, push $\vec{e}'$ into *D*, mark $\vec{e}'$, and *v'* = *v''*. }
     **else if** ($S \neq \varnothing$) **then** { *v'* = pop(*S*), *in_channel* = pop(*D*). }
     **else** { Release the *turn* $T_{d(c_1),d(c_2)}$ of node *v*.
     Check next input and output channel pair of node *v*. }
8. **if** (*v'* = *v* and *in_channel* = $\vec{e}_1$)
     **then** {A turn cycle exists and the prohibited turn in node *v* can not be released.
       Check next input and output channel pair of node *v*. }
9. **Goto** line 7.}
*end_of_cycle_detection*

---

Algorithm *cycle_detection* uses the depth first search (DFS) to check whether a prohibited turn of a node can be released or not. The time complexity of algorithm *cycle_detection* is O($d*|V|^2$), where *d* is the degree of each node in a *CG*. After algorithm *cycle_detection* is performed, the prohibited turns for each node are determined. We then can use the shortest path algorithms based on the prohibited turns to find the routing path between any two nodes. We call the routing algorithm by applying the proposed method as *DOWN/UP routing* since the packet must go downward cross links then go upward cross links.

**Theorem 1**: The *DOWN/UP* routing is deadlock-free and connectivity between each node pair is guaranteed.

*Proof*: Based on Phase 2, there is at least one prohibited turn to break each turn cycle in the maximal *DG*. Therefore, this routing algorithm is deadlock-free. Since the *turn* $T_{LU\_TREE,RD\_TREE}$ is not prohibited for each node in a *CG*, each flit from any source node to it destination node can first go upward their least common ancestor and then goes downward to the destination node. Therefore, connectivity between each node pair is guaranteed. □

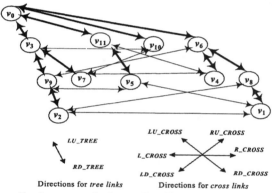

**Figure 7. An example for redundant prohibited turns.**

## 5. Performance Analyses

To evaluate the performance of the *DOWN/UP routing*, we have implemented the proposed method along with the *L-turn routing* on the IRFlexSim0.5 simulator [2], a wormhole technique simulator written in C. To simulate an irregular network, we assume that the network contains 128 switches. Each switch is associated with a processor. The port number of each switch is set to 4 and 8. Each port has an input and an output channels. The packet length is set to 128 flits. The delay of a flit passes through a link is one clock. The delay of a routing header to be routed and arbitrated to the output channel is one clock. A data flit to be transmitted from the input channel to output channel is one clock. A uniform traffic pattern is assumed.

For both 4-port and 8-port configurations, we have randomly generated 10 irregular networks each as test

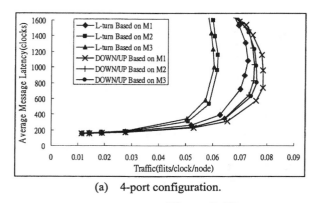

(a) 4-port configuration.

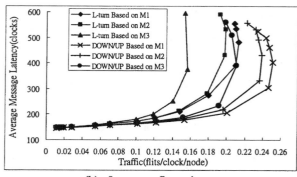

(b) 8-port configuration.

**Figure 8. The average message latency and accepted traffic.**

samples. Since different coordinated trees will lead to different performance, for each test sample, we used three coordinated trees, $M1$, $M2$, and $M3$, to evaluate the performance of the *L-turn routing* and the *DOWN/UP routing*. When perform the preorder traversal to determine the *x*-axis coordinate of a node in a coordinated tree, the next node to be traversed for $M1$, $M2$, and $M3$ is the node with the smallest node number, a randomly selected one, and the node with the largest node number, respectively. The method for $M1$ is the one we proposed in Phase 1 of Section 4. When construct a coordinated tree, we choose the node with the smallest node number as the root a spanning tree. Since the *L-turn routing* and the *DOWN/UP routing* are both non-minimal adaptive deadlock-free routing algorithms, in the simulation, we use the shortest possible paths between all pairs of source and destination nodes to transmit flits. For any two nodes, it is possible that more than one shortest possible path exist. For this case, one of them is selected randomly.

Figure 8(a) and Figure 8(b) show the average simulation results of message latency and accepted traffic for 4-port and 8-port configuration, respectively. The message latency is defined as the time elapsed since the packet transmission is initiated at a node until the packet is received at the destination node. The smaller the message latency, the less the flits delay. The throughput is defined as the accepted traffic measured in flits/clock pernode (flits/clock/node). The higher the throughput, the better the bandwidth offered. From Figure 8, for the same coordinated tree and the same configuration, we observe that the proposed routing algorithm has smaller message latency and higher throughput than that of the *L-turn routing*. For different coordinated trees and the same configuration, we observe that both routing algorithms have the smallest message latency and the highest throughput if $M1$ is used.

In order to analyze the characteristics of both routing algorithms, for each test sample, we also measure the *node utilization*, the *traffic load*, the *degree of hot spots*, and the *leaves utilization* when both routing algorithms

reach their maximal throughputs. Table 1 shows the average simulation results of node utilization for both 4-port and 8-port configurations. The utilization of an output channel of a node is defined as the average number of flits across the node through the output channel during one clock. The node utilization of a node is defined as the sum of utilization of all output channels of the node divided by the number of ports connecting to other switches. The higher the node utilization is, the smoother the traffic flows. From Table 1, for the same coordinated tree and the same configuration, we observe that the node utilization of the proposed routing algorithm is higher than that of the *L-turn routing*. For different coordinated trees and the same configuration, both routing algorithms have the best node utilization if $M1$ is used.

**Table 1. The average simulation results of node utilization.**

|  | *L-turn routing* | | *DOWN/UP routing* | |
|---|---|---|---|---|
|  | 4-port | 8-port | 4-port | 8-port |
| $M1$ | 0.115772 | 0.123159 | 0.123295 | 0.147124 |
| $M2$ | 0.108101 | 0.111653 | 0.121793 | 0.139588 |
| $M3$ | 0.095841 | 0.092198 | 0.120955 | 0.126071 |

Table 2 shows the average simulation results of traffic load for both 4-port and 8-port configurations. The traffic load is defined as the standard deviation of the node utilization of all nodes. The smaller the traffic load, the better the balanced traffic load. From Table 2, for the same coordinated tree and the same configuration, we observe that the traffic load of the proposed routing algorithm is less than that of *L-turn routing*. This indicates that the *DOWN/UP* routing has a more balanced traffic load than the *L-turn routing*. For different coordinated trees and the same configuration, both routing algorithms have the smallest traffic load if $M1$ is used.

**Table 2. The average simulation results of traffic load.**

| | L-turn routing | | DOWN/UP routing | |
|---|---|---|---|---|
| | 4-port | 8-port | 4-port | 8-port |
| M1 | 0.078314 | 0.048727 | 0.077657 | 0.043990 |
| M2 | 0.081115 | 0.050460 | 0.078501 | 0.047316 |
| M3 | 0.083969 | 0.053392 | 0.078047 | 0.049796 |

Table 3 shows the average simulation results of degree of hot spots. The degree of hot spots is defined as the percentage of the node utilization of nodes in levels 0 and 1 of a coordinated tree. The smaller the degree of hot spots is, the less the traffic congests. Table 4 shows the average simulation results of leave utilization. The leave utilization is defined as the average of node utilization of leaves of a coordinated tree. The more the leave utilization, the higher the traffic flow to leaves. From Tables 3 and 4, for the same coordinated tree and the same configuration, we observe that the proposed routing algorithm has less degree of hot spots and higher leave utilization, respectively. For different coordinated trees and the same configuration, we observe that both routing algorithms have the smallest degree of hot spots and the highest leave utilization if $M1$ is used.

**Table 3. The average simulation results of degree of hot spots.**

| | L-turn routing | | DOWN/UP routing | |
|---|---|---|---|---|
| | 4-port | 8-port | 4-port | 8-port |
| M1 | 12.85 % | 13.26 % | 12.00 % | 9.930 % |
| M2 | 14.15 % | 14.90 % | 12.13 % | 10.56 % |
| M3 | 16.18 % | 18.43 % | 12.16 % | 11.25 % |

**Table 4. The average simulation results of leave utilization.**

| | L-turn routing | | DOWN/UP routing | |
|---|---|---|---|---|
| | 4-port | 8-port | 4-port | 8-port |
| M1 | 0.07336 | 0.1065 | 0.082897 | 0.13807 |
| M2 | 0.063953 | 0.093437 | 0.080773 | 0.131578 |
| M3 | 0.050633 | 0.072627 | 0.078453 | 0.111609 |

From Tables 3 and 4, we can see that the *DOWN/UP routing* has less degree of hot spots and better leaves utilization than the *L-turn routing*. These lead to higher node utilization and more balanced traffic load for the *DOWN/UP routing* compared to the *L-turn routing*. That is why the *DOWN/UP routing* has smaller message latency and higher throughput than that of the *L-turn routing*.

## 6. Conclusion Remarks

From the simulation results shown in Section 5, we have the following remarks for the proposed routing algorithm and the *L-turn routing*.

**Remark 1**. The way we construct a coordinated tree ($M1$) leads to the best performance for both *DOWN/UP routing* and *L-turn routing* compare to other methods ($M2$ and $M3$).

**Remark 2**. Since traffic in the *DOWN/UP routing* flows more downward to the leaves of a coordinated tree than that of the *L-turn routing*. Under the same coordinated tree and the same configuration, the *DOWN/UP routing* outperforms the *L-turn routing* in terms of node utilization, traffic load, the degree of hot spots, leaves utilization, message latency, and throughput for all test samples.

## Acknowledgments

This work in this paper was partially supported by Program for Promoting Academic Excellence of Universities under contract 89-E-FA04-1-4.

## References

[1] C. J. Glass and L.M. Ni, "The Turn Model for Adaptive Routing,' *J. ACM,* Vol. 41, No. 5, pp. 874-902, Sept. 1994.

[2] IRFlexSim0.5 is available in" http://www.usc.edu/dept/ceng/pinkston/tools.html"

[3] A. Jouraku, A. Funahashi, H. Amano, and M. Koibuchi, "Routing Algorithms on 2D Turn Model for Irregular Networks," *the Sixth International Symposium on Parallel Architectures, Algorithms, and Networks(I-SPAN),* pp.289-294, May. 2002

[4] A. Jouraku, A. Funahashi, H. Amano, and M. Koibuchi,"L-turn routing: An Adaptive Routing in Irregular Networks," *the International Conference on Parallel Processing,* pp.374-383, Sep. 2001.

[5] G. Pfister and V. Norton, "Hot Spot Contention and Combining in Multistage Interconnection Networks," *IEEE Trans. Computers.* C34 (10):943-948, Oct. 1985.

[6] A. Robles , J. Duato, and J.C. Sancho," A Flexible Routing Scheme for Networks of Workstations," *ISHPC,* pp. 260-267,2000.

[7] M. D. Schroeder et al., "Autonet: A High-Speed Self-Configuring Local Area Network Using Point-to-Point Links," *SRC research report 59,* DEC, Apr. 1990.

[8] F. Silla and J. Duato, "High-Performance Routing in Networks of Workstations with Irregular Topology," *IEEE Transactions on Parallel and Distributed Systems,* Vol.11, No.7, pp. 699-719, July 2000.

# Parallel Network RAM: Effectively Utilizing Global Cluster Memory for Large Data-Intensive Parallel Programs

John Oleszkiewicz, Li Xiao, and Yunhao Liu
Department of Computer Science and Engineering
Michigan State University
East Lansing, MI 48824 USA
{oleszkie, lxiao, liuyunha}@cse.msu.edu

## Abstract

*Large scientific parallel applications demand large amounts of memory space. Current parallel computing platforms schedule jobs without fully knowing their memory requirements. This leads to uneven memory allocation in which some nodes are overloaded. This, in turn, leads to disk paging, which is extremely expensive in the context of scientific parallel computing. To solve this problem, we propose a new peer-to-peer solution called Parallel Network RAM. This approach avoids the use of disk and better utilizes available RAM resources. This approach will allow larger problems to be solved while reducing the computational, communication and synchronization overhead typically involved in parallel applications.*

## 1. Introduction

Many scientific computing applications demand a large amount of processing power, memory space and I/O accesses. One standard approach to alleviate processor and memory load is to parallelize these applications into multiple parallel processes so that the may be run on multiple nodes in a computing cluster. An advantage of this approach is CPU and memory resources are evenly distributed and used. Another advantage is the nature of load balancing in parallel computing. However, these two advantages may not serve the best performance interests of these parallel processes because the balanced workload distribution among processes may result in unbalanced resource utilization in a cluster. Specifically, there are trade-offs between the number of parallel jobs and memory usage.

For a given problem size, in order to ensure each node has enough memory space, the number of parallel processes in a parallel job may be set very high. This results in less

work and more required synchronization per parallel process The CPU on each node may be underutilized. Parallel speedup is very hard to improve as the number of parallel processes increases to a certain value, due to increasing communication and synchronization overhead. Good performance cannot be guaranteed by using a large number of nodes.

On the other hand, if the number of parallel processes is limited, the CPU will be better utilized but nodes may run out of available memory and may be forced to use the local disk as a swapping site. Performance will suffer from frequent page faults since hard disks are orders of magnitude slower than RAM. Research has shown that disk paging results in unsatisfactory performance on parallel platforms and should be avoided [3, 4, 15].

Network RAM [1, 11] has been proposed to schedule sequential jobs in clusters to even memory load and reduce paging overhead. This technique allows applications to allocate more memory than is available on the local machine while avoiding paging to disk by allocating idle memory of other machines over a fast interconnecting network. The remote RAM is treated as a new layer in the memory hierarchy between RAM and disk. Resulting page accesses are slower than RAM, but much faster than disk [11, 23].

Network RAM techniques cannot be directly applied to parallel jobs to achieve satisfactory performance for several reasons. One serious issue is that parallel processes from the same parallel job synchronize regularly. If each node seeks network RAM independently, it is likely that an uneven amount of network RAM will be granted to the nodes. With this uneven allocation, parallel processes will run at different speeds. However, parallel jobs as a whole will only run at the speed of the slowest process, due to synchronization. The nodes with extra network RAM waste it, since their hosted processes will spend most of their time waiting for other processes. Therefore, coordination is required to grant overloaded nodes equal portions of memory to allow hosted processes to run at equal speeds.

Another issue is network congestion. If parallel processes individually seek out network RAM with no coordination among themselves, a potentially large amount of network traffic will result. This may induce congestion on the cluster. Parallel applications require high performance networks to run efficiently. Congestion could seriously impact the performance of jobs on the system.

We propose a new peer-to-peer solution, called Parallel Network RAM (PNR), so parallel jobs can utilize idle remote memory. In this scheme, each node requests memory resources as well as provides memory for others. Requests are indirect in that each node contacts a local manager (super-peer) node and requests that it allocate network RAM on its behalf. Managers coordinate the allocation of network RAM of several nodes and ensure that load is distributed evenly to the nodes hosting parallel processes belonging to the same parallel job. PNR will allow more jobs to execute concurrently without resorting to disk paging. This will lead to decreased average response time and higher system throughput.

We make several contributions in this paper.

- We show that existing techniques cannot maximize the performance gain of parallel jobs in terms of both parallel speedup and execution time given a cluster with unbalanced resource utilization.

- We propose a novel and effective solution to this problem called Parallel Network RAM (PNR). PNR coordinates the allocation of network RAM to overcome limitations of past solutions. This allows CPU cycles to be provided by a small subset of nodes, while the global memory space is open to the memory demand of any parallel job.

- We build a simulator that models a cluster and our proposed PNR algorithms. Conducting trace-driven simulations, we compare the performance of the PNR system to a disk paging-only solution (DP) and a network RAM solution similar to previous work (NR).

The rest of the paper is organized as follows. Section 2 describes background information related to our work. Section 3 presents our proposed PNR algorithms. Section 4 describes our trace-driven simulator and justifies our simulation parameters and metrics. Section 5 presents our performance evaluation. Section 6 discusses the implications of our simulation results and section 7 concludes the paper.

## 2. Background and Related Work

The majority of work in this area has focused on parallel job scheduling. In this section, we describe various parallel job schedulers and previous solutions to the problem of overloaded memory on cluster systems.

## 2.1. Parallel Scheduling Algorithms

The primary duty of the scheduler on a cluster system is to ensure high system throughput and low overall response times of submitted jobs. One simple scheduling system is a space sharing system. Space sharing allows more than one job to be scheduled on the multicomputer at one time. Each node is devoted to one parallel process, and each job runs until completion without preemption. The space sharing model is vulnerable to large jobs monopolizing the system.

Gang scheduling combines both space sharing and time sharing. Each job is alloted a time slot and the job may execute in its time slot. Nodes within each time slot are space shared. When a time quantum has expired, all jobs in the current slot are preempted and replaced with jobs in the next slot. The preemption process is called a Parallel Context Switch (PCS) and involves a certain amount of overhead. There is at most one process running on each node at any given time. The maximum number of time slots allowed is known as the maximum multiprogramming level (MPL). Setting the MPL to a low level is a convenient way to reduce PCS overhead and reduce overall memory load on nodes. A system with an MPL value of one is a simple space sharing system with no time sharing.

There are a variety of processor allocation strategies and variations of gang scheduling. These include first fit, best fit, left-right by size, left-right by slots, load-based allocation strategies, "buddy" systems such as distributed hierarchical control, and migration-based algorithms [8, 24].

## 2.2. Previous Solutions to the Memory Problem

Previous studies agree that unmodified disk paging results in severely reduced performance [4, 18]. Generally speaking, previous solutions to this problem either attempt to avoid disk paging entirely or attempt to reduce its effect.

Various ways to avoid paging by altering the scheduler have been suggested. If no memory information about incoming jobs is known, then the simplest solution is to keep the MPL to a minimum [14]. Another solution attempts to guess memory usage information based on information about the job provided by the user and information contained in the program executable. The solution then uses this information in scheduling decisions [3]. If other information on jobs, such as speedup information, is known ahead of time, then another solution can use that information [15].

One method that is aimed at reducing the disk paging penalty is called block paging. In this scheme, the system groups sets of pages together and acts upon these groups as units. Groups are defined by the system based on memory reference behavior of jobs [20].

Much work has been done for sequential job scheduling with memory considerations. Regarding network RAM implementations, the Global Memory System (GMS) [7] and the Remote Memory Pager [13] attempt to reduce the page fault overhead by using remote paging techniques. DoDo [1] is designed to improve system throughput by harvesting idle memory space in a distributed system. Here, the owner processes have the highest priority for using the CPUs and memory on their workstations. This divides the global memory system into different local regions. A memory ushering algorithm is used in MOSIX for memory load sharing [2]. This solution is a job-migration-based load sharing approach.

Recently, we have developed several load sharing alternatives by considering both CPU and memory resources with known and unknown memory demands [21, 22]. The objective of our designs is to reduce the number of page faults caused by unbalanced memory allocations of distributed jobs so that overall performance can be significantly improved.

# 3. Parallel Network RAM

We propose a novel and effective technique called Parallel Network RAM (PNR) to better utilize the resources of both CPU and memory and minimize communication and synchronization overhead. Our objective is to fundamentally improve the efficiency of large scale scientific computing. Instead of evenly allocating parallel tasks among the nodes, we consider CPU and memory resource allocations separately. Under this non-uniform scheme, the number of CPUs to be assigned to a parallel job will be optimized in order to better utilize increasingly powerful CPU cycles and to minimize the communication and synchronization overhead among cluster nodes. Each job can utilize both the local memory space from the assigned CPUs and the remote memory space in other nodes. With PNR, speedup can be scaled very well as the available remote memory increases, and performance can also be scaled very well as the problem size increases.

It is assumed that the PNR algorithms are implemented as a subsystem or module of each node's kernel. PNR runs as just another part of the virtual memory system. This minimizes disruption to established cluster systems. Parallel applications will not have to be re-compiled with special PNR libraries and the execution of remote paging will be transparent to them. The assumed centralized scheduler of the system will not have to be changed since PNR is not a part of it and will not coordinate with it in any way.

In brief, all nodes host PNR servents. All servents act as PNR clients and servers. Some servents may act as managers. When a new process is started, nodes participating in that job will contact their local PNR client if in need of additional memory resources. Clients will contact their local managers and managers will contact PNR servers on the behalf of multiple clients. Similarly, when a job is stopped, nodes will notify their clients if they no longer need the allocated network RAM. Clients will contact their managers and the managers will contact servers on the clients' behalf.

Previous work, such as [1, 7], has introduced centralized proxies to network RAM allocation and management. However, to our knowledge, the use of distributed proxies to coordinate network RAM allocation for threads within a parallel job is unique.

## 3.1. Architecture Detail

A PNR client attempts to allocate and deallocate network RAM on the behalf of its hosting node. The node treats allocated network RAM as additional virtual memory - just as it would with disk space. When a process starts execution on a node, it allocates the amount of memory it will use during its execution. If the node's PNR client determines that this allocation will lead to disk usage, the client contacts a manager and requests network RAM. Once network RAM is allocated, the client is informed by the manager what machines are serving network RAM. The client may then start sending pages to the server(s) for storage and later retrieval. A similar process is followed for network RAM deallocation.

PNR managers do the majority of allocation and deallocation work. Managers take requests from multiple clients and send requests to PNR servers on the clients' behalf. Managers exist to balance memory requests from multiple parallel processes that belong to one job.

When a new job starts, one of the job's servents volunteers to be a PNR manager. The volunteering is randomized but all clients affected by the new job must agree on which servent is the manager. Managers decide which PNR servers to contact based on local memory load tables. These tables are maintained via extra information sent in by PNR communications. Specifically, every message sent to a manager will also include the sending node's current memory load. Managers record this information and broadcast their updated load tables to all servents after each job start and stop. In this way, all managers will have a general idea of memory allocation on each node. Managers use a randomized worst-fit algorithm for memory allocation and will pick the servers they believe have the largest amount of unallocated memory.

Servers receive requests from managers for network RAM. If the server has more unallocated RAM than a certain threshold, it will grant the network RAM request and allocate the memory to the manager. Currently the unallocated memory threshold is set to a low value - a tenth of a megabyte. This parameter can be changed if memory appears to be consistently overallocated on PNR servers. After the memory is allocated, servers receive requests to read and write the allocated network RAM directly from clients. Servers grant all valid deallocation attempts.

# 4. Simulation Methodology

We have developed a trace-driven simulator to experiment with clusters and their interaction with the proposed PNR algorithms. This section describes the simulator and the experimental environment.

## 4.1. Workload Model

Many workload traces and synthetic workload generators exist for use by simulators. However, no standard memory usage benchmarks currently exist [5]. We decided to use a large trace with memory allocation information that has been assembled and discussed by Feitelson [9]. The trace has been gathered from the CM-5 parallel platform at the Los Alamos National Lab. It contains 201,387 lines, each of which represents information of one parallel job (e.g. number of processors used, CPU seconds, amount of memory allocated, etc.) This information was recorded through the majority of 1996.

We will use a subset of jobs from this well-studied trace. This subset is arbitrarily chosen as the first 5000 jobs of the workload. Since the workload profile at a given site tends to be fairly stable over time [12], using a subset of jobs should be indicative of the load on the system.

## 4.2. System Model

We model a system architecture similar to the CM-5 but change some system parameters where possible to model a more modern cluster architecture. Just as the trace assumes, each node runs at 33 Mhz and has 32 MB of local memory. An addition to the modeled system compared to the CM-5 are hard drives local to each node. It is assumed each disk has an infinite capacity and runs at 7200 RPM with a seek time of 9ms and has a transfer rate of 50 MB/s. It should be noted that these performance figures are representative of current commodity hard drives (example: [17]) and are not performance figures from the time period in which the CM-5 was used. The interconnecting network is assumed to be a simple Ethernet 100 Mbps star topology. Each link has a latency of 50ns and the central switch has a processing delay of 80 microseconds. For the sake of simulator speed, we scale down the trace from its original 1024 nodes to 64 nodes. Job processor usage is scaled down accordingly. Note that other job characteristics, such as memory usage and communication frequency, are held constant.

## 4.3. Scheduler Models

It is assumed there is one centralized scheduler for the system. In our simulations we experiment with two schedulers: a simple space sharing scheduler and a gang scheduler. For both schedulers, we use FCFS as our queuing discipline and a simple best-fit node packing scheme. It is assumed that the scheduler has no knowledge of the memory requirements of jobs.

Each time slice in the gang scheduler runs for a 60 second quantum as suggested by [16]. The time required to perform a PCS is fixed at 4ms [4]. The maximum number of time slices is set to two. This number is conservative and limits paging activity [14]. Alternative scheduling and slot unification are provided.

## 4.4. Job Behavior Model

Each parallel job is composed of multiple parallel processes. It is assumed that each process allocates a static amount of memory at start time. Each process accesses memory at its node independently. Previous studies have shown that parallel scientific applications generate memory references every three to five CPU cycles. They also suggest that the cache hit ratio for these applications ranges from approximately 50% to 65% [6, 19]. We assume that our parallel applications access memory every four CPU cycles and have a cache hit ratio of 50%.

All processes in a job synchronize with each other at regular intervals. The synchronization pattern is a simple master/worker pattern, where multiple workers send and receive messages from one master. In our experiments, we set the time interval between synchronizations to be one CPU second (once every 32 million cycles). This is not a heavy synchronization load. Future experiments should use more complex and more frequent loads.

It is assumed no paging activity will result when all jobs fit into available memory on each node. When more memory is allocated than is available, there is a chance a non-cache memory access will result in a page fault. We use an exponential function that is dependent on both the average memory access rate and the amount of process memory currently paged out to determine the time until the next page fault.

## 4.5. Metrics

There are no universally valid and accepted metrics. In fact, different metrics can give contradictory results [10]. In this section we list and justify the metrics we used.

First is average response time, or total wallclock time from submit to finish. This metric is used very often but can overemphasize large jobs. In parallel workloads, small jobs account for the majority of jobs. [10]

Second, to directly compare DP to PNR, we create another metric: "optimization rate". This metric represents the improvement of PNR over DP.

$$OptimizationRate = \frac{R_{disk} - R_{pnr}}{R_{disk}} \times 100\%$$

Third, we calculate the average and standard deviation of node memory allocation by sampling the memory allocation information of each node every 50,000 simulated time seconds.

# 5. Performance Evaluation

We have defined a set of experiments to evaluate PNR. Specifically, we defined a base experiment and explored variations on this base experiment to gain insight into PNR performance characteristics. We will first describe the results from the base experiment and follow with results from the variations. We compare a system with PNR to a system without PNR that we call "Disk Paging" (DP) since this system's only way of dealing with overallocation is using the disk. We also compare PNR to a system which uses uncoordinated network RAM allocation (NR). In NR, each node will independently seek network RAM. This system is conceptually identical to the system proposed in [13]. By comparing PNR to DP, we demonstrate that PNR has tangible performance benefits over using disk paging alone. By comparing PNR to NR, we demonstrate that the extra coordination used in PNR is essential to improving the performance of network RAM on cluster systems.

## 5.1. Base Experiments

In our base experiment, all parameters are set to the values described in the methodology section. Figure 1 demonstrates that PNR performed comparatively well in terms of response time. DP had an average response time of 60974.8 seconds, NR had an average response time of 65912.1 seconds, and PNR had an average response time of 42226.2 seconds. Optimization rate for PNR is a modest 31% while it is -8.1% for NR!

PNR also made better use of available RAM resources. DP used an average of 17.87 MB (55.8%) per node with a standard deviation of 5.17 MB, NR an average of 16.37 MB (51%) with a standard deviation of 5.75 MB, and PNR an average of 14.71 MB (45.9%) with a standard deviation of 4.98 MB. Average disk usage was also down and more uniform. DP used, on average, 3.51 MB of disk space per node with a standard deviation of 1.51 MB, NR an average of 2.97 MB and standard deviation of 1.92 MB, and PNR an average of 1.91 MB with a standard deviation of 1.13 MB. These results indicate that the overall system load is lower

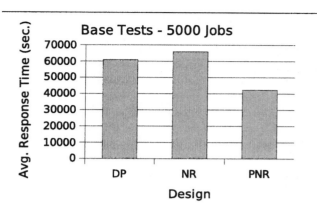

**Figure 1. Response time of base test with 5000 job workload.**

with PNR due to a higher job turnover rate, and that allocation of memory is becoming more uniform - one of the goals of PNR.

PNR experienced only 65% the number of page faults that DP experienced. This can be attributed to the fact that, since PNR jobs will finish faster, they will experience less PCSs. This in turn leads to less page loading due to memory contention by multiple processes.

## 5.2. Network Performance Variations

When we reduce the bandwidth of the links in the standard star topology to 10 Mbps, we observe a dramatic impact on PNR (not shown in figures). For all workloads PNR performs significantly worse than DP. Optimization rate may be anywhere between -10% to -1000%. Response times for PNR reach as high as three million seconds, while the highest DP response times are easily within 100,000 seconds. Significantly, this is the only set of experiments in which PNR is substantially outperformed by DP.

Figure 2 shows that the optimization rate for PNR is consistently superior to DP and NR at high network bandwidths. Interestingly, however, PNR and NR performance decreases at some points as bandwidth increases. The cause of the increased response times is apparently increased disk usage for both NR and PNR. As network performance passes a certain threshold, disk usage goes up. This phenomena makes sense if we consider that if processes are becoming backlogged in this large trace, and if increased network performance results in higher turnover, then longer-running jobs will tend to start running together in greater frequency than under the lower-performing networks. Longer running jobs tend to demand more memory than shorter jobs and when larger jobs start running together more frequently, memory load and response times increase.

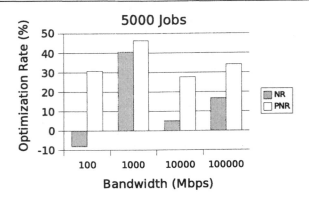

Figure 2. Optimization rate at varying network speeds with 5000 jobs.

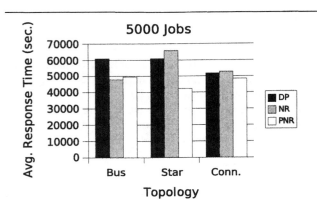

Figure 3. Response time of methods under different topologies.

## 5.3. Network Topology Variations

Figure 3 displays the results over various network topologies. Bus and star behave as expected for both DP and PNR. Interestingly, NR has a slight advantage over PNR in the bus environment. However, with the connected topology, PNR response time rises compared with star while DP and NR experience performance benefits. We believe that the same phenomena which caused the performance penalty in high bandwidth networks is at work here.

## 5.4. RAM Variations

We varied the amount of total RAM available at each node to simulate different memory loads and observe how DP and PNR react. The RAM ratio of the x-axis in Figures 4-6 is a multiplier we apply to the standard amount of RAM

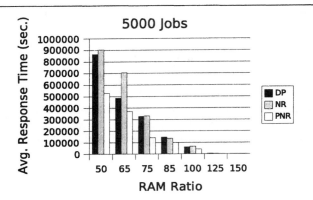

Figure 4. Response time with varying amount of RAM available with 5000 jobs.

available in the base tests. For instance, RAM ratio 1.5 results in nodes with 48 MB of RAM (up from the original 32 MB).

Two observations are obvious: as memory load decreases, PNR, NR, and DP converge to the same performance metrics and as memory load increases, PNR and NR/DP metrics diverge. When no paging activity occurs, all of the methods are equivalent in performance. For instance, we observe in Figure 4 that as the RAM ratio is increased from 0.5 to 1.5, response times for each converge to 1960.6 seconds. This is an important result, since it demonstrates that the extra communication overhead of PNR adds only a negligible amount to response time in situations of light load.

In Figure 5, we see the optimization rates converging when the RAM ratio is at 1.35 and higher. PNR does particularly well as RAM is initially decreased (0.75) and increased (1.15). As the RAM ratio is lowered, however, some of the initial advantage is lost We believe that PNR and DP will eventually converge again as RAM becomes so scarce that it can never be shared via PNR. NR has consistently lower optimization rates compared to PNR

## 5.5. Space Sharing Scheduler Experiments

We repeat the base set of experiments and the RAM variation experiments with a simple space sharing scheduler. For all inputs and for all variations of memory load tested, a pattern emerges. NR has a slight advantage under light memory loads (0.75 RAM ratio) but is consistently and significantly outperformed by PNR at heavier memory loads (see Figure 6).

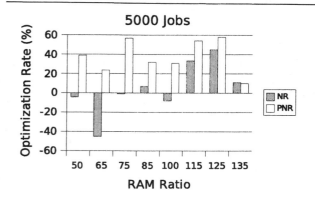

**Figure 5. Optimization rate with varying amounts of RAM with 5000 jobs.**

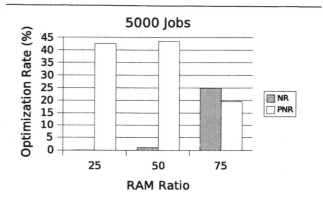

**Figure 6. Optimization rate under simple space sharing scheduler with varying amounts of RAM available.**

## 6. Discussion

Given our observations, it is clear that all designs follow an exponential curve as memory load is changed. As memory load increases, they tend towards infinite response times. As memory load decreases, they will converge on a constant number. PNR's curve is lower than NR/DP's by a constant factor.

This model implies that adding PNR to lightly loaded systems (with high performance networks) will not harm performance and under moderate memory loads PNR can lead to large improvements over disk paging. However, as memory becomes too scarce to share, PNR performance will tend to converge to DP performance.

PNR is very sensitive to network performance. The general shape of results is another exponential curve, where PNR response time tends toward infinity as network ser-

vice time is increased and converges to some constant number as service time decreases.

Since low network performance results in low PNR performance, PNR should not be considered on systems with low bandwidth or high message RTT times. A standard 100 Mbps network or higher should be regarded as the minimum for satisfactory performance.

Network bandwidth and latency appear to be much more important to the performance of PNR than does the topology of the underlying network. Congestion did not appear to play a large role in our experiments. This situation may be different in a larger network. Topology changes should be studied again on a larger scale.

PNR is clearly the superior method under heavy memory loads when using the space sharing scheduler. But, interestingly, NR consistently beats PNR under light memory loads. Apparently, the added communication and coordination overhead of PNR is useful when RAM is very scarce, but the lightweight NR may be sufficient under light load conditions. This may be due to the fact that PCSs are eliminated on this system. This eliminates a large portion of network activity (i.e. the large amount of page faults after a PCS) and lessens the impact of a bad network RAM allocation decision. These results are interesting and should be studied further.

## 7. Conclusion and Future Work

In this paper we identified a novel way of reducing page fault service time and better utilizing memory resources. This method, which we call Parallel Network RAM, uses remote idle RAM as another tier in the memory hierarchy for parallel jobs in clusters. We implement this idea as a set of scalable peer-to-peer algorithms which can be implemented on a variety of multicomputer systems. We discovered that adding PNR to systems with high performance networks will not hurt overall system performance, and will help speed up memory accesses and more evenly spread load.

While average response time figures are favorable for PNR, this paper did not explore the degree to which PNR penalizes processes running on PNR servers. Performance may be compromised on these nodes in favor overall memory balance. Future work should examine the severity of this problem and propose solutions if necessary.

While we believe our PNR algorithm is scalable, this paper does not explore this aspect of PNR. Future work should concentrate on examining the scalability of our PNR algorithm, both in terms of additional CPUs and additional memory. We must study how additional CPUs increase communication overhead of our PNR strategy and at what scale the fundamental limit of virtual memory address space becomes a concern.

Ultimately, PNR should be compared to competing paging avoidance strategies. These include scheduling strategies that attempt to avoid paging, hardware solutions, and others. It is important to know if one strategy is superior, or if several strategies are best used in conjunction.

### Acknowledgments

This research was made possible by a grant from the Michigan Space Grant Consortium and National Science Foundation grant ACI-0325760.

# References

[1] A. Acharya and S. Setia. The utility of exploiting idle memory for data-intensive computations. Technical Report TRCS98-02, 1998.

[2] A. Barak and A. Braverman. Memory ushering in a scalable computing cluster. *Journal of Microprocessors and Microsystems*, 22(3-4):175–182, August 1998.

[3] A. Batat and D. G. Feitelson. Gang scheduling with memory considerations. In *14th Intl. Parallel Distributed Processing Symp.*, pages 109–114, 2000.

[4] D. C. Burger, R. S. Hyder, B. P. Miller, and D. A. Wood. Paging tradeoffs in distributed-shared-memory multiprocessors. *The Journal of Supercomputing*, 10(1):87–104, 1996.

[5] S. J. Chapin, W. Cirne, D. G. Feitelson, J. P. Jones, S. T. Leutenegger, U. Schwiegelshohn, W. Smith, and D. Talby. Benchmarks and standards for the evaluation of parallel job schedulers. In D. G. Feitelson and L. Rudolph, editors, *Job Scheduling Strategies for Parallel Processing*, pages 67–90. Springer-Verlag, 1999. Lect. Notes Comput. Sci. vol. 1659.

[6] G. F. P. F. Darema-Rogers and K. So. Memory access patterns of parallel scientific programs. *Performance Evaluation Review*, 15(1):46–57, 1987.

[7] M. J. Feeley, W. E. Morgan, F. H. Pighin, A. R. Karlin, H. M. Levy, and C. A. Thekkath. Implementing global memory management in a workstation cluster. In *Symposium on Operating Systems Principles*, pages 201–212, 1995.

[8] D. G. Feitelson. Packing schemes for gang scheduling. In D. G. Feitelson and L. Rudolph, editors, *Job Scheduling Strategies for Parallel Processing*, pages 89–110. Springer-Verlag, 1996. Lect. Notes Comput. Sci. vol. 1162.

[9] D. G. Feitelson. Memory usage in the LANL CM-5 workload. In D. G. Feitelson and L. Rudolph, editors, *Job Scheduling Strategies for Parallel Processing*, pages 78–94. Springer Verlag, 1997. Lect. Notes Comput. Sci. vol. 1291.

[10] D. G. Feitelson. Metrics for parallel job scheduling and their convergence. In D. G. Feitelson and L. Rudolph, editors, *Job Scheduling Strategies for Parallel Processing*, pages 188–205. Springer Verlag, 2001. Lect. Notes Comput. Sci. vol. 2221.

[11] M. D. Flouris and E. P. Markatos. *High Performance Cluster Computing*, chapter 16, pages 383–408. Prentice Hall, 1999.

[12] V. Lo, J. Mache, and K. Windisch. A comparative study of real workload traces and synthetic workload models for parallel job scheduling. In D. G. Feitelson and L. Rudolph, editors, *Job Scheduling Strategies for Parallel Processing*, pages 25–46. Springer Verlag, 1998. Lect. Notes Comput. Sci. vol. 1459.

[13] E. P. Markatos and G. Dramitinos. Implementation of a reliable remote memory pager. In *USENIX Annual Technical Conference*, pages 177–190, 1996.

[14] Y. Z. A. S. H. F. J. E. Moreira. Improving parallel job scheduling by combining gang scheduling and backfilling techniques. *IPDPS*, pages 133–142, 2000.

[15] E. W. Parsons and K. C. Sevcik. Benefits of speedup knowledge in memory-constrained multiprocessor scheduling. *Performance Evaluation*, 27/28(4):253–272, 1996.

[16] U. Schwiegelshohn and R. Yahyapour. Improving first-come-first-serve job scheduling by gang scheduling. In D. G. Feitelson and L. Rudolph, editors, *Job Scheduling Strategies for Parallel Processing*, pages 180–198. Springer Verlag, 1998. Lect. Notes Comput. Sci. vol. 1459.

[17] Seagate. Barracuda ata v and barracuda ata v plus technical specifications. http://www.seagate.com/docs/pdf/datasheet/disc/ds_barracudaata5.pdf.

[18] S. K. Setia. The interaction between memory allocation and adaptive partitioning in message-passing multicomputers. In D. G. Feitelson and L. Rudolph, editors, *Job Scheduling Strategies for Parallel Processing*, pages 146–164. Springer-Verlag, 1995. Lect. Notes Comput. Sci. vol. 949.

[19] K. C. Sevcik and S. Zhou. Performance Benefits and Limitations of Large NUMA Multiprocessors. In *Proceedings of Performance '93*, pages 183–204. Elsevier Science Publ, Sept 93.

[20] F. Wang, M. Papaefthymiou, and M. Squillante. Performance evaluation of gang scheduling for parallel and distributed multiprogramming. In D. G. Feitelson and L. Rudolph, editors, *Job Scheduling Strategies for Parallel Processing*, pages 277–298. Springer Verlag, 1997. Lect. Notes Comput. Sci. vol. 1291.

[21] L. Xiao, S. Chen, and X. Zhang. Dynamic cluster resource allocations for jobs with known and unknown memory demands. *IEEE Transactions on Parallel and Distributed Systems*, 13(3):223–240, March 2002.

[22] L. Xiao, S. Chen, and X. Zhang. Adaptive memory allocations in clusters to handle unexpectedly large data-intensive jobs. *IEEE Transactions on Parallel and Distributed Systems*, 15(6), June 2004.

[23] L. Xiao, X. Zhang, and S. A. Kubricht. Incorporating job migration and network RAM to share cluster memory resources. In *HPDC*, pages 71–78, 2000.

[24] B. B. Zhou, D. Welsh, and R. P. Brent. Resource allocation schemes for gang scheduling. In D. G. Feitelson and L. Rudolph, editors, *Job Scheduling Strategies for Parallel Processing*, pages 74–86. Springer Verlag, 2000. Lect. Notes Comput. Sci. vol. 1911.

# Panel Session:
# Grids: Hype, Substance, or Renaissance?

# Keynote Address

# Future Building Blocks for Parallel Architectures

Ulrich Bruening
*University of Mannheim*

Wolfgang Giloi
*Fraunhofer Institute for Computer Architecture and Software Technology*

Early parallel architectures where shared memory systems (UMA, NUMA), which had the disadvantage of the shared memory bottleneck that limited the scalability of the system. In contrast, distributed memory architectures with message passing (NORMAs) provided any desired scalability; however, at the cost of a substantial communication latency. The latency could be reduced by custom communication hardware (examples: SUPRENUM, MANNA) yet since there was still a software routine involved, the remaining latency was in the order of microseconds. Therefore, and because of the simpler programming model of shared memory, it became the trend of the nineties to return to UMAs and NUMAs, employing powerful communication hardware to minimize the remote memory access time. This approach required a complex, highly expensive custom chip set. State-of-the art is to augment the processor hardware on the chip by facilities such as memory controllers, caches, cache-coherent multiple links with switches for NUMA support. This is called "glue-less NUMA," an example being the AMD Opteron. Since one wants to obtain the performance advantages of cache hierarchies with their need for cache coherence mechanisms, the complexity of the additional communication hardware increases exponentially with the number of nodes, thus limiting the scalability severely. Consequently, the demand for scalable, massively parallel systems built with cost-effective COTS (commercial off the shelf) hardware has revived the NORMA architecture, realized with very fast communication devices that are connected to a high-performance IO interface (PCI-X, PCI Express, Hypertransport, ...). Examples for such devices are Myrinet, Infiniband, Quadrix QsNet, or Atoll, which all feature crossbars as interconnects. However, because of the "distance" of such a device from the processor, communication latency is still significantly higher than the local memory access time. This calls for moving as a next step the communication facilities on the chip as multithreading devices, with the interconnect crossbar directly on the die. This will eliminate the multiplexing of the device and the bottleneck of the processor bus. The ever increasing number of transistors on the chip will readily allow such a move. The instruction set of such a processor will be extended by send, receives, remote loads, remote stores, hence providing all the flavors of communication types as machine instruction with a start-up latency of one processor clock tick. The speed-up obtainable with such building blocks will be quantified.

# Session 6A:
# Applications

# Using Tiling to Scale Parallel Data Cube Construction

Ruoming Jin    Karthik Vaidyanathan    Ge Yang    Gagan Agrawal
Department of Computer Science and Engineering
Ohio State University, Columbus OH 43210
{jinr,vaidyana,yangg,agrawal}@cis.ohio-state.edu

## ABSTRACT

Data cube construction is a commonly used operation in data warehouses. Because of the volume of data that is stored and analyzed in a data warehouse and the amount of computation involved in data cube construction, it is natural to consider parallel machines for this operation. Also, for both sequential and parallel data cube construction, effectively using the main memory is an important challenge.

In our prior work, we have developed parallel algorithms for this problem. In this paper, we show how sequential and parallel data cube construction algorithms can be further scaled to handle larger problems, when the memory requirements could be a constraint. This is done by *tiling* the input and output arrays on each node. We address the challenges in using tiling while still maintaining the other desired properties of a data cube construction algorithm, which are, using minimal parents, and achieving maximal cache and memory reuse. We present a parallel algorithm that combines tiling with interprocessor communication.

Our experimental results show the following. First, tiling helps in scaling data cube construction in both sequential and parallel environments. Second, choosing tiling parameters as per our theoretical results does result in better performance.

## 1. INTRODUCTION

Analysis on large datasets is increasingly guiding business decisions. Retail chains, insurance companies, and telecommunication companies are some of the examples of organizations that have created very large datasets for their decision support systems. A system storing and managing such datasets is typically referred to as a data warehouse and the analysis performed is referred to as On Line Analytical Processing (OLAP) [1].

Computing multiple related group-bys and aggregates is one of the core operations in OLAP applications [1]. Jim Gray has proposed the *cube* operator, which computes group-by aggregations over all possible subsets of the specified dimensions [6]. When datasets are stored as (possibly sparse) arrays, data cube construction involves computing aggregates for all values across all possible subsets of dimensions. If the original (or *initial*) dataset is an n-dimensional array, the data cube includes $C_m^n$ m-dimensional arrays, for $0 \leq m \leq n$. Developing sequential algorithms for constructing data cubes is a well-studied problem [10, 9, 11, 12].

Data cube construction is a compute and data intensive problem. Therefore, it is natural to use parallel computers for data cube construction. Recently, many parallel algorithms for data cube construction have been proposed [3, 4, 5, 8].

Both the input and output datasets for data cube construction can be extremely large. The problem of scaling data cube construction for large input datasets has been addressed by the early work in this area [12]. The basic idea to is to divide the input dataset into *chunks*, read one chunk at a time, and update corresponding output values. However, only limited effort has been put on scaling data cube construction for large output datasets. In practice, data cubes are constructed starting from an array that is both sparse and high-dimensional. This can result in output sizes that are larger than the input size. For example, the first level of data cube construction starting from a (potentially sparse) $n^m$ dataset results in $m$ dense arrays of size $n^{m-1}$. Depending upon the relative values of $n$, $m$, and the sparsity of the input array, the output at the first level can easily be larger than the size of the input array.

This paper develops a general approach for scaling data cube construction. We tile input and output arrays and only one tile of an output array is typically allocated and updated at any given time. Using tiling, however, involves a number of challenges. In this paper, we present algorithms and analysis addressing the following:

- How do we incorporate tiling of output arrays in a sequential data cube construction, while preserving other desirable properties, i.e., using minimal parents and maximizing cache and memory reuse ?

- Given a memory constraint, how do we tile to both meet the memory constraint and minimize the overhead associated with tiling, i.e., the cost of rereading and rewriting tiles ?

- How do we develop a parallel algorithm that combines tiling with interprocessor communication, while minimizing both communication volume and tiling overhead ?

We have implemented and evaluated our algorithms. The main observations from our experiments are as follows. First, tiling helps scaling data cube construction in both sequential and parallel environment. Second, choosing tiling parameters as per our theoretical results does result in better performance.

## 2. DATA CUBE CONSTRUCTION

This section further elaborates the issues and challenges in data cube construction. Before that, we also give some general motivation for data cube construction.

Organizations often find it convenient to express facts as elements of a (possibly sparse) multidimensional array. For example, a retail chain may store sales information using a three-dimensional dataset, with item, branch, and time being the three dimensions. An element of the array depicts the quantity of the particular item sold, at the particular branch, and during the particular time-period.

In data warehouses, typical queries can be viewed as *group-by* operations on a multidimensional dataset. For example, a user may be interested in finding sales of a particular item at a particular

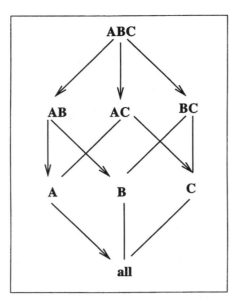

**Figure 1: Lattice for data cube construction. Edges with arrows show the minimal spanning tree when $|A| \leq |B| \leq |C|$**

branch over a long duration of time, or all sales of all items at all branches for a given time-period. The former involves performing an aggregation along the time dimension, whereas the latter involves aggregations along the item and the branch dimensions.

To provide fast response to the users, a data warehouse computes aggregated values for all combinations of values. If the original dataset is $n$ dimensional, this implies computing and storing ${}^nC_m$ $m$-dimensional arrays, for $0 \leq m \leq n$. ${}^nC_m$ is the standard combinatorics function, which is defined as

$$ {}^nC_m = \frac{n \times (n-1) \times \ldots \times (n-m+1)}{m \times (m-1) \times \ldots \times 1} $$

For simplicity, assume that the original dataset is three-dimensional. Let the three dimensions be $A$, $B$, and $C$. The sizes along these dimensions are $|A|, |B|, |C|$, respectively. Without loss of generality, we assume that $|A| \leq |B| \leq |C|$. We denote the original array by ABC. Then, data cube construction involves computing arrays AB, BC, AC, A, B, C, and a scalar value *all*. As an example, the array AB has the size $|A| \times |B|$.

Some of the major issues in data cube construction are as follows.

**Cache and Memory Reuse:** Consider the computation of AB, AC, and BC. These three arrays need to be computed from the initial array ABC. When the array ABC is disk-resident, performance is significantly improved if each portion of the array is read only once. After reading a portion or chunk of the array, corresponding portions of AB, AC, and BC can be updated simultaneously. Even if the array ABC is in main memory, better cache reuse is facilitated by updating portions of AB, AC, and BC simultaneously. The same issue applies at later stages in data cube construction, e.g., in computing A and B from AB.

**Using minimal parents:** In our example, the arrays AB, BC, and AC need to be computed from ABC, by aggregating values along the dimensions C, A, and B, respectively. However, the array A can be computed from either AB or AC, by aggregating along dimensions B or C. Because $|B| \leq |C|$, it requires less computation to compute A from AB. Therefore, AB is referred to as the *minimal parent* of A.

A lattice can be used to denote the options available for computing each array within the cube. This lattice is shown in Figure 1. A data cube construction algorithm chooses a spanning tree of the lattice shown in the figure. The overall computation involved in the construction of the cube is minimized if each array is constructed from the *minimal parent*. Thus, the selection of a *minimal spanning tree* with minimal parents for each node is one of the important considerations in the design of a sequential (or parallel) data cube construction algorithm.

**Memory Management:** In data cube construction, not only the input datasets are large, but the output produced can be large also. Consider the data cube construction using the minimal spanning tree shown in Figure 1. Sufficient main memory may not be available to hold the arrays AB, AC, BC, A, B, and C at all times. If a portion of the array AB is written to the disk, it may have to be read again for computing A and B. However, if a portion of the array BC is written back, it may not have to be read again.

Another important issue is as follows. To ensure maximal cache and memory resue, we need to update AB, AC, and BC, simultaneously. However, if sufficient memory is not available to hold these three arrays in memory at the same time, we need to allocate and update portions of these arrays. Managing this can be quite challenging.

Some of these issues are addressed by a new data structure, aggregation tree which we introduce in the next section.

## 3. SPANNING TREES FOR CUBE CONSTRUCTION

This section introduces a data structure that we refer to as the *aggregation tree*. An aggregation tree is parameterized with the ordering of the dimensions. For every unique ordering between the dimensions, the corresponding aggregation tree represents a spanning tree of the data cube lattice we described in the previous section. Aggregation tree has the property that it bounds the total memory requirements for the data cube construction process.

To introduce the aggregation tree, we initially review *prefix tree*, which is a well-known data structure [2].

Consider a set $X = \{1, 2, \ldots, n\}$. Let $\rho(X)$ be the power set of $X$.

**DEFINITION 1.** $L(n)$ *is a lattice* $(V, E)$ *such that:*

- *The set of nodes* $V$ *is identical to the power set* $\rho(X)$.

- *The set of edges* $E$ *denotes the* immediate superset *relationship between elements of the power set, i.e, if* $r \in \rho(X)$ *and* $s \in \rho(X)$, $r = s \cup \{i\}$, *and* $i \notin s$, *then* $(r, s) \in E$.

The lattice $L(n)$ is also referred to as the *prefix lattice*. The lattice we have shown earlier in Figure 1 is a complement of the prefix lattice, and is referred to as the *data cube* lattice.

A prefix tree $P(n)$ is a spanning tree of the prefix lattice $L(n)$. It is defined as follows:

**DEFINITION 2.** *Given a set* $X = \{1, 2, \ldots, n\}$, *a prefix tree* $P(n)$ *is defined as follows:*

(a) $\phi$ *is the root of the tree.*

(b) *The set of nodes of the tree is identical to the power set* $\rho(X)$.

(c) *A node* $\{x_1, x_2, \ldots, x_m\}$, *where* $m \leq n$, *and* $1 \leq x_1 < x_2 < \ldots < x_m \leq n$, *has* $n - x_m$ *children. These children, ordered from left to the right are,* $\{x_1, x_2, \ldots, x_m\} \cup \{x_m + 1\}, \ldots, \{x_1, x_2, \ldots, x_m\} \cup \{n\}$.

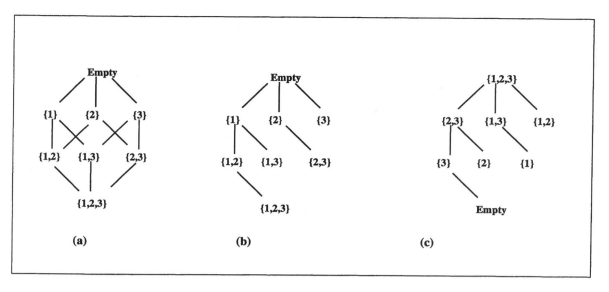

**Figure 2: Prefix Lattice (a), Prefix Tree (b), and Aggregation Tree (c) for n = 3**

```
Construct_Cube(D_1, D_2, ..., D_n)
{
    Evaluate({D_1, D_2, ..., D_n})
}

Evaluate(l)
{
    Compute all children of l
    For-each children r from right to left
        If r has no children
            Write-back to the disk
        Else Evaluate(r)
    Write-back l to the disk
}
```

**Figure 3: Sequential Data Cube Construction Using the Aggregation Tree**

Given a prefix tree $P(n)$, the corresponding aggregation tree $A(n)$ is constructed by complementing every node in $P(n)$ with respect to the set $X$. Formally,

DEFINITION 3. *Given a set* $X = \{1, 2, \ldots, n\}$ *and the prefix tree* $P(n)$ *as defined earlier, an aggregation tree* $A(n)$ *is defined as follows:*

(a) *If* $r$ *is a node in* $P(n)$, *then there is a node* $r'$ *in* $A(n)$, *such that* $r' = X - r$.

(b) *If a node* $r$ *has a child* $s$ *in* $P(n)$, *then the node* $r'$ *in* $A(n)$ *has a child* $s'$.

Figure 2 shows the prefix lattice, prefix tree and the aggregation tree for $n = 3$.

Since an aggregation tree is a spanning tree of the data cube lattice, it can be used for data cube construction. We next present an algorithm that uses the aggregation tree and has minimally bounded memory requirements.

Figure 3 shows this sequential algorithm. Suppose we are computing data cube over $n$ dimensions which are denoted by $D_1, D_2, \ldots, D_n$. The data cube construction algorithm starts by invoking the function *Evaluate* for the root of the aggregation tree.

When the function *Evaluate* is invoked for a node $l$, all children of $l$ in the aggregation tree are evaluated. This ensures maximal cache and memory reuse, since no portion of the input dataset or an intermediate result needs to be processed more than once. After computing all children of a node, the algorithm progresses in a depth-first fashion, starting with the right-most child. An array is written back to the disk only if it is not going to be used for computing another result. Thus, the only disk traffic in this algorithm is the reading of the original input array, and writing each output (or computed) array once. Moreover, each array is written once in its entirety. Therefore, frequent accesses to the disks are not required.

The depth-first traversal, starting from the right-most child in the aggregation tree, creates a bound on the total memory requirements for storing the intermediate results. Consider data cube construction starting from a three dimensional array ABC, where the sizes of the three dimensions are $|A|$, $|B|$, and $|C|$, respectively. After the three children of the root of the aggregation tree are computed, the memory requirements for holding them in main memory are $M = |A| \times |B| + |A| \times |C| + |B| \times |C|$. The design of the aggregation tree and our algorithm ensure that the total memory requirements for holding output arrays during the entire data cube construction process are bounded by $M$. The reason is as follows. Suppose the ordering between the three dimensions is $C, B, A$. After the first step, BC can be written back. Then, the node AC is used for computing the array C. Since $|C| \leq |B| \times |C|$, the memory requirements do not increase above the factor $M$. After computing C, both AC and C can be written back. Then, A and B are computing from AB. Since $|A| \leq |A| \times |C|$ and $|B| \leq |B| \times |C|$, the total memory requirements again do not increase beyond $M$. This result generalizes to an arbitrary number of dimensions [8].

As we had stated in the previous section, one challenging situation arises when sufficient memory is not available to hold AB, AC, and BC in memory at any given time. To handle this, we need to allocate and update portions (or *tiles*) of these arrays at any given time. Since the aggregation tree based approach minimally bounds the memory requirements without tiling, we believe it gives us a good basis for developing tiling approach.

## 4. PARALLEL ALGORITHM WITHOUT TILING

In the previous section, we introduced the aggregation tree based

```
Construct_Cube(D_1, D_2, ..., D_n)
{
    Evaluate({D_1, D_2, ..., D_n}) on each processor
}

Evaluate(l)
{
    Locally aggregate all children of l
    Forall children r from right to left
        Let r' = X - r = {D_{i1}, ..., D_{im}}
        If the processor is the lead processor along D_{i1}, ..., D_{im}
            Communicate with other processors to finalize portion of r
            If r has no children
                Write-back the portion to the disk
            Else Evaluate(r)
    Write-back l to the disk
}
```

**Figure 4: Parallel Data Cube Construction Without Tiling**

sequential data cube construction algorithm. In this section, we develop and analyze a parallel version of this algorithm. In the next section, we show how tiling can be applied to both sequential and parallel algorithms.

Consider a n-dimensional initial array from which the data cube will be constructed. Suppose we will be using a distributed memory parallel machine with $2^p$ processors. Through out this paper, we will assume that the number of processors used is a power of 2. This assumption corresponds well to the parallel processing configurations used in practice and has been widely used in parallel algorithms and partitioning literature.

We partition the dimension $D_i$ along $2^{k_i}$ processors, such that $\sum_{i=1}^{n} k_i = p$. Each processor is given a unique label $\{l_1, l_2, ..., l_n\}$ such that $0 \leq l_i \leq 2^{k_i} - 1$. Since $\sum_{i=1}^{n} k_i = p$, it is easy to verify that there are $2^p$ unique labels. A processor with the label $l_i$ is given the $l_i^{th}$ portion along the dimension $D_i$.

A processor with the label $l_i = 0$ is considered one of the *lead* processors along the dimension $D_i$. There are $2^p/2^{k_i}$ lead processors along the dimension $D_i$. The significance of a lead processor is as follows. If we aggregate along a dimension, then the results are stored in the lead processors along that dimension.

The parallel algorithm is presented in Figure 4.

We explain this algorithm with the help of an example. Consider data cube construction with $n = 3$ and $p = 3$. Let $k_1 = k_2 = k_3 = 1$, i.e., each of the three dimensions is partitioned along 2 processors. Initially, all 8 processors process the portions of $D_1 D_2 D_3$ they own to compute partial results for each of $D_1 D_2$, $D_1 D_3$, and $D_2 D_3$.

Next, consider a processor with the label $\{0, l_2, l_3\}$. This processor communicates with the corresponding processor $\{1, l_2, l_3\}$ to compute the final values for the $\frac{1}{4}^{th}$ portion of the array $D_2 D_3$. Similarly, a processor with the label $\{l_1, 0, l_3\}$ communicates with the corresponding processor $\{l_1, 1, l_3\}$ to get the final value for the $\frac{1}{4}^{th}$ portion of the array $D_1 D_3$.

Consider the computation of $D_1$ from $D_1 D_3$. Only 4 of the 8 processors, i.e., the ones with a label $\{l_1, 0, l_3\}$, perform this computation. These 4 processors process the portion of $D_1 D_3$ they own to compute partial result for $D_1$. Then, 2 of the processors with the label $\{l_1, 0, 0\}$ communicate with the corresponding processor $\{l_1, 0, 1\}$ to each compute the final values for the half portion of the array $D_1$. Computation of $D_2$ and $D_3$ from $D_2 D_3$ proceeds in a similar fashion.

A detailed analysis of the impact of data distribution on the com-

munication volume is presented in our earlier work [8].

# 5. TILING-BASED APPROACH FOR SCALE DATA CUBE CONSTRUCTION

The sequential and parallel algorithm we have presented so far assume that sufficient memory is available to store all arrays at the first level in memory. In general, this assumption may not hold true. In this section, we present sequential and parallel algorithms that use tiling to scale data cube construction.

## 5.1 Sequential Tiling-Based Algorithm

Let the initial multidimensional array from which a data cube is constructed be denoted by $D_1 D_2 ... D_n$. We tile this array, dividing each dimension $D_i$ into $t_i$ tiles, creating a total of $\prod_{i=1}^{n} t_i$ tiles. Suppose we are computing a partial or complete data cube using a given aggregation tree. Consider any node $N$ of the tree $D_{x_1} ... D_{x_{m-1}}$, where $1 \leq x_i \leq n$ and $m < n$. Let the parent of this node in the tree be $D_{x'_1} ... D_{x'_m}$, where

$$\{x'_1, ... x'_m\} = \{y\} \cup \{x_1, ..., x_{m-1}\}$$

Thus, the node $N$ is computed from its parent by aggregating along the dimension $y$.

The array $D_{x_1} ... D_{x_{m-1}}$ computed at the node $N$ comprises $t_{x_1} \times ... t_{x_{m-1}}$ tiles. For scaling the computations of views, we can separately read and write these portions from and to disks. A particular tile of this array is denoted by a tuple $< p_{x_1}, ... p_{x_{m-1}} >$, where $1 \leq p_{x_i} \leq t_{x_i}$.

Dividing each array into tiles adds a new complexity to the process of computing these arrays. A given tile $< p_{x_1}, ..., p_{x_{m-1}} >$ of the node $N$ is computed using $t_y$ different tiles of its parent. This is because the dimension $y$, which is aggregated along to compute $N$ from its parent, is divided into $t_y$ tiles. Since the different tiles comprising the parent array of $N$ can be allocated in the memory only one at a time, a tile of the node $N$ may have to be computed in $t_y$ phases. In each of these phases, one tile of the parent of $N$ is processed and the corresponding elements in $N$ are updated.

Note that a node can have multiple children in the tree. To ensure high memory and cache reuse, when a tile of an array is brought into memory, we update the corresponding tiles of all children of that node. Since these children are computed by aggregating along different dimensions, it is not possible to read all tiles that are used to compute one tile of a child node consecutively. As a result, a tile of a node being computed may have to be written and reread from the disks as it is computed from multiple tiles of its parent node.

To facilitate correct computations using tiling, we associate a table with each node of the tree. For the node $N$ described above, this table is an array with $m - 1$ dimensions, $N.Table[1 ... t_{x_1}, 1 ... t_{x_2}, ..., 1 ... t_{x_{m-1}}]$. An element $Table(< p_{x_1}, ..., p_{x_{m-1}} >)$ has a value between 0 and $t_y$ and denotes the status of the tile $< p_{x_1}, ..., p_{x_{m-1}} >$. A value of 0 means that this tile is currently uninitialized. A value $i$, $0 < i \leq t_y$ means that the elements of this tile have been updated using $i$ tiles of the parent node. If the value is $t_y$, then the elements in this tile have received their final values. In this case, we say that the tile is *expandable*, because it can now be used for starting the computation of its children nodes.

The tiling-based algorithm is presented in Figure 5. We assume that the original array is indexed in such a way that each tile can be retrieved easily. In the algorithm, $Maptile(N, T, C)$ is the tile of $C$ which can be updated using the tile $T$ of $N$, where $N$ is a given node, $T$ is a tile of this node and $C$ is a child of this node. $Reduc\_tiles(N)$ is the number of tiles of the parent of $N$ along the

```
Construct_Views(D_1 D_2 ... D_n)
{
    Foreach tile T of this node
        Expand_tile(D_1 ... D_n, T)
}

Expand_tile(Node N, Tile T)
{
    Foreach child C of N in the tree {
        T' = Maptile(N, T, C)
        C.Table(T')++
        If C.Table(T') == 1
            Allocate and initialize the tile T'
        Else
            Read the tile T' from disk if required
    }
    Foreach chunk of the tile T {
        Read the chunk
        Foreach child C of N
            Perform aggregation operations on the tile Maptile(N, T, C)
    }
    Foreach child C of N {
        T' = Maptile(N, T, C)
        If (C.Table(T') == Reduc_tiles(C))
            Expand_tile(C, T')
        Else
            Write-back the tile T' to disk if required
    }
    If N is not root
        Write-back T to disk
}
```

**Figure 5: A Tiling-Based Algorithm for Constructing Data Cube**

---

dimension that is aggregated to compute $N$, where $N$ is a non-root node.

The function *Expand_tile* takes a tile and a node of the tree, and computes or updates the appropriate portions of the descendants of the tree. Given a node $N$ and a tile $T$, we find the tiles of the children of $N$ that can be updated using the function $Maptile(N, T, C)$. We then use the $Table$ data structure to determine the status of the tiles of children. If they have not yet been initialized, we allocate space and initialize them. If they have been updated previously, they may have to be read from the disks. Once a chunk corresponding to a parent node is brought into memory and cache, all children are updated together.

We next check if the corresponding tile of a child node has been completely updated (i.e. if $(C.Table(T') == Reduc\_tiles(C))$). If so, we expand its children before writing it back to the disks.

Thus, our algorithm ensures that once a tile is in memory, we update all its children simultaneously, and further expand upon the children if possible. In the process, however, a tile of child node may have to be written back and read multiple times. We prefer to ensure high memory and disk reuse of the parent tiles to some possible extent for two important reasons. First, the sizes of arrays decrease as we go down the tree, so it is preferable to write back and read lower level nodes in the tree. Second, if the original array is partitioned along only a few dimensions, $Reduc\_tiles$ will have the value of one for many nodes in the tree. In this case, the node being computed will not need to be written back and read multiple times.

## 5.2 Using Tiling in Parallel Data Cube Construction

While applying our tiling-based algorithm to parallel construction of data cubes, we should note that we have two kinds of par-

titions of a node in the aggregation tree. The first is due to the data distribution among multiple processors. Since each processor has a portion of the original array, interprocessor communication is needed to get final values of this node. The second is due to tiling. The portion on each processor is divided into several tiles and the final values can not be obtained until all tiles of the node are aggregated.

The existence of these two different kinds of partitions adds complexity in deciding whether or not a node is ready for computing its children. For example, consider constructing a data cube from an original four-dimensional array $D_1 D_2 D_3 D_4$ on 8 processors. The aggregation tree is shown in Figure 6. Using the terminology used in the previous section, we do a three-dimensional partition for the original array, which means dimensions $D_2, D_3, D_4$ are partitioned along two processors. Then on each processor, we divide the $\frac{1}{8^{th}}$ portion of the array on this processor into 4 tiles by tiling along dimensions $D_3$ and $D_4$ in half respectively. According to the tiling-based algorithm we introduced above, after computing each tile of the node $D_1 D_3 D_4$, the tile becomes expandable since $D_1 D_3 D_4$ is obtained by aggregating along dimension $D_2$ and $D_2$ is not tiled. But it is not the case since $D_2$ is partitioned along two processors and we have to do the interprocessor communication to get the final values of $D_1 D_3 D_4$ before we can compute its child. Therefore, we can not apply the tiling-based algorithm directly to parallel data cube construction on multiple processors.

A solution to this problem is to apply tiling-based algorithm only to the children of the root node in the aggregation tree. For the computation of other nodes, we follow a similar process as we had presented in the previous section. Considering that the dominant part of computation is at the first level for multidimensional data cube construction, we believe that tiling all nodes at the first level can reduce memory requirements. For simplicity, we use Level One Parallel Algorithm for the computation of lower levels nodes in the aggregation tree. The complete algorithm is shown in Figure 7. In this algorithm, $C.T'$ stands for a tile of values of child $C$. Other notations have the same meaning as in Figures 5 and 4.

Compared with the sequential tiling-based algorithm in Figure 5, we apply the sequential tiling-based algorithm only to the children of the root node. In addition, we do not expand the node even when $C.Table(T') == Reduc\_tiles(C)$. (Actually, we do not check whether $C.Table(T') == Reduc\_tiles(C)$ at all.) We write back every $T' = Maptile(D_1 D_2 ... D_n, T, C)$ to the disk and after all tiles are processed, each child has $t_{total}/t_y$ tiles of values, where $y$ is the dimension along which the child is computed by aggregating its parent, $t_y$ is the number of tiles of dimension $y$ and $t_{total}$ is the total number of tiles of the original array.

As we have mentioned earlier, we can not get the final values of children of the root node until we do interprocessor communication. Therefore, we follow a similar procedure as in Level One Parallel Algorithm to finalize each tile of values of the children. The difference is that we first do the required interprocessor communication to get the final values of the child, and then we aggregate its children. Note that we do not use optimized Level One Parallel Algorithm since memory requirement is our key consideration here.

We use the same example we mentioned at the beginning of this section to describe how this algorithm works for parallel data cube construction. We consider three-dimensional partition of the original array, which means dimensions $D_2, D_3, D_4$ are partitioned along two processors. Then on each processor, we divide the $\frac{1}{8^{th}}$ portion of array on this processor into 4 tiles by tiling along dimensions $D_3$ and $D_4$ in half respectively.

After processing all 4 tiles of $D_1 D_2 D_3 D_4$, each child of $D_1 D_2 D_3 D_4$

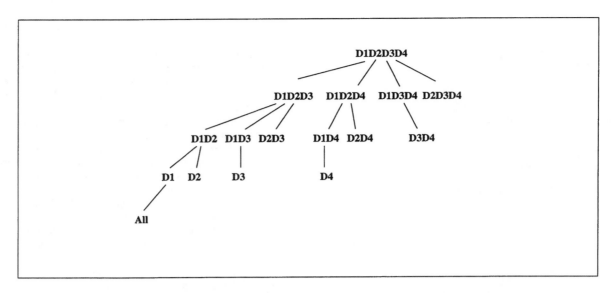

**Figure 6: Aggregation Tree for Four-dimensional Data Cube Construction**

```
Construct_Cube(D_1 D_2 ... D_n)
{
    Foreach tile T of the root node D_1 D_2 ... D_n on each processor{
        Foreach child C of D_1 D_2 ... D_n in the tree {
            T' = Maptile(D_1 D_2 ... D_n, T, C)
            C.Table(T')++
            If C.Table(T') == 1
                Allocate and initialize the tile T'
            Else
                Read the tile T' from disk if required
        }
        Foreach chunk of the tile T {
            Read the chunk
            Foreach child C of D_1 D_2 ... D_n
                Perform aggregation operations on the tile Maptile(D_1 D_2 ... D_n, T, C)
        }
        Write-back the tile Maptile(D_1 D_2 ... D_n, T, C) to disk if required
    }
    Foreach child C of D_1 D_2 ... D_n from right to left
        Foreach tile T' of C {
            Read C.T' from disk if required
            Evaluate(C.T') on each processor
        }
}

Evaluate(C)
{
    Let C' = X - C = {D_{i1}, ..., D_{im}}
    If the processor is the lead processor along D_{i1}, ..., D_{im}
        Communicate with other processors to finalize portion of C if required
        If C has no children
            Write-back the portion to disk if required
        Else
            Locally aggregate all children of C
            Foreach child r from right to left
                Evaluate(r)
    Write-back C to disk if required
}
```

**Figure 7: A Tiling-Based Algorithm for Parallel Data Cube Construction**

has tiles of values stored on each processor. For instance, $D_2 D_3 D_4$ and $D_1 D_3 D_4$ each has 4 tiles of values, $D_1 D_2 D_4$ and $D_1 D_2 D_3$ each has 2 tiles of values. We then consider each tile of $D_2 D_3 D_4$. Since $D_2 D_3 D_4$ is computed by aggregating along dimension $D_1$ which is not partitioned, we do not need to do interprocessor communication and each processor already has a tile of final values of $D_2 D_3 D_4$. $D_2 D_3 D_4$ also has no child, therefore, it is done and can be written back to the disks.

We now consider the first of the 4 tiles of $D_1 D_3 D_4$. Since $D_2$ is partitioned in half, interprocessor communication is needed to get the final values of the tile of $D_1 D_3 D_4$. The communication process is the same as in the parallel algorithm we presented originally. After final values are obtained on lead processors, we compute $D_3 D_4$ from final values of this tile of $D_1 D_3 D_4$. Since there is no need to communicate for $D_3 D_4$ and $D_3 D_4$ has no child, we are done with the first tile of $D_1 D_3 D_4$. For the other three tiles of $D_1 D_3 D_4$, we follow the same procedure as above.

The computation of each tile of $D_1 D_2 D_4$ and $D_1 D_2 D_3$ can be proceeded in a similar fashion, except that we must pay attention to the fact that some offsprings of $D_1 D_2 D_4$ and $D_1 D_2 D_3$, such as $D_1 D_4$, $D_1 D_3$, $D_1 D_2$ and $D_1$, also need interprocessor communication to get final values.

Note that the number of tiles of each child below the first level in the aggregation tree is decided by the number of tiles of its parent. For example, since $D_1 D_3 D_4$ has 4 tiles of values, $D_3 D_4$ also has 4 tiles of values. In contrast, each offspring of $D_1 D_2 D_4$ and $D_1 D_2 D_3$ has only 2 tiles. The number of tiles of children at the first level is determined by $t_{total}/t_y$, as we have stated earlier.

In a related technical report [7], we have derived closed-form expressions for tiling overhead.

## 6. EXPERIMENTAL RESULTS

We have implemented the algorithms we have presented in this paper. In this section, we present a series of experimental results evaluating our algorithms and validating the associated theoretical results (presented in a related technical report [7]). Specifically, we had the following two main goals:

- Evaluating how tiling helps scale sequential and parallel data cube construction and the impact the number of tiles has on execution time.

- Evaluating how the choice of tiling parameters impacts execution time.

## 6.1 Scaling Data Cube Construction

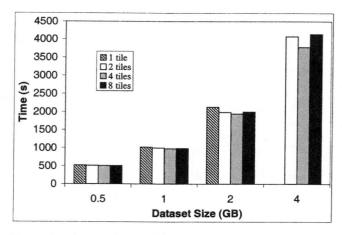

**Figure 8: Scaling Sequential Data Cube Construction with Tiling (8 dimensional datasets)**

We now present results showing how tiling helps scale data cube construction in both sequential and parallel environments.

Our experiments for sequential execution were conducted on a machine with 1 GB memory. We used 4 8-dimensional datasets, which were dense arrays with sizes $8^5 \times 16^3$, $8^4 \times 16^4$, $8^3 \times 16^5$, $8^2 \times 16^6$, respectively. As each element requires 4 bytes, the sizes of these datasets are .5, 1, 2, and 4 GB, respectively. Without the use of tiling, the total memory required for the first level of the tree is 416 MB, 768 MB, 1.4 GB, and 2.5 GB, respectively.

The execution time with 1, 2, 4, and 8 tiles for these 4 datasets are presented in Figure 8. For the .5 GB and 1 GB datasets, sufficient memory was available to execute the algorithm without tiling (or using a single tile). The execution time for these datasets remains approximately the same with the use of 1, 2, 4, or 8 tiles. As all data can fit in main memory, the read and write operations for tiles only involve accessing main memory buffers, and therefore, use of large number of tiles does not result in a slow down.

A more interesting trend is noted with the 2 GB dataset. The use of 2 or 4 tiles results in lower execution time than the use of 1 or 8 tiles. With only 1 tile, memory thrashing causes the overhead. With the use of 8 tiles, the high tiling overhead causes the slow down. As the total memory requirements are large, read and write operations for tiles now require disk accesses. Therefore, the use of larger number of tiles is not desirable.

With the 4 GB dataset, the code cannot even be executed with the use of a single tile. The lowest execution time is seen with the use of 4 tiles. Memory thrashing and tiling overheads are the reasons for slow down with 2 and 8 tiles, respectively. Note, however, because the execution times are dominated by computation, the relative differences are never very large.

We repeated a similar experiment for parallel data cube construction, using a 8 node cluster. We used four 9-dimensional datasets whose size were 4 GB, 8 GB, 16 GB, and 32 GB, respectively. After data partitioning, the size of the array portion on each node was .5 GB, 1 GB, 2 GB, and 4 GB, respectively, similar to the previous experiment. The results are presented in Figure 9 and are similar to the previous set of results. Note that there is some increase in per

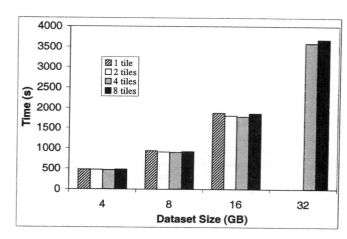

**Figure 9: Scaling Parallel Data Cube Construction with Tiling (9 dimensional datasets on 8 nodes)**

node memory requirements, because memory is needed for communication buffers. Therefore, with the largest dataset, a minimum of 4 tiles are required to complete execution.

Another observation from Figures 8 and 9 is as follows. As we experiment with larger input datasets, the execution time remains proportional to the amount of computation on each node. Thus, the use of tiling and parallelism helps scale data cube construction.

## 6.2 Impact of Tiling Parameters

In this sub-section, we focus on the evaluation of the theoretical results on tiling overhead.

Our first experiment was done on a single processor machine. We experimented on a $128 \times 128 \times 128 \times 128$ dataset with two different levels of sparsity 25% and 5%. We assume that the main memory is not sufficient and divide the dataset into 8 tiles. There are three possible tiling parameters, (0 1 1 1), (0 0 1 2) and (0 0 0 3). We refer these three options as three-dimensional, two-dimensional and one- dimensional tiling, respectively. The results are shown in Figure 10. The versions involving tiling are compared with a version that does not involve tiling.

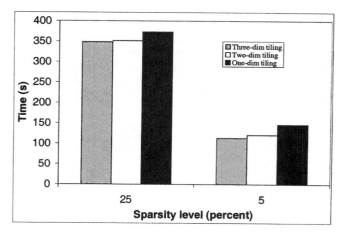

**Figure 10: Impact of Tiling Parameters on Tiling Overhead, $128^4$ dataset, 1 Processor**

We have two observations from these experimental results. First, even as the sparsity is varied, tiling on multiple dimensions has less tiling overhead, which is consistent with our theoretical results. Second, for the same dataset, less sparsity means more tiling overhead due to the smaller computation volume involved in each tile. In our experiments, compared with the tiling-based algorithm with the best tiling parameter (0 1 1 1), the sequential algorithm without tiling is slowed down by 8.41% and 15.92% on 25% and 5% datasets, respectively.

We also evaluated the performance of applying tiling-based algorithm to parallel data cube construction. The experiment was conducted on a $128 \times 128 \times 128 \times 128$ dataset with two different levels of sparsity 25% and 5%. We assume that after data distribution among processors, we still need to partition the portion of the original array on each processor into 4 tiles. Figure 11 shows that given a data distribution, using tiling parameters obtained through the algorithm of choosing tiling parameters can reduce the tiling overhead. The best case with tiling parameter (1 0 0 1) outperforms the case (0 0 0 2) by 4.62% and 6.14% on 25% and 5% datasets, respectively. Note that the execution times of the two cases with tiling parameters (1 0 0 1) and (0 0 1 1) are quite close to each other. This is because these two cases both involve two-dimensional tiling.

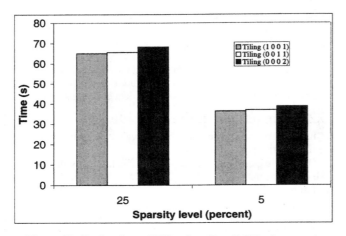

**Figure 11: Evaluation of Tiling in a Parallel Environment**

## 7. RELATED WORK

Since Jim Gray [6] proposed the data cube operator, techniques for data cube construction have been extensively studied for both relational databases [10, 9] and multi-dimensional datasets [12, 11]. Our work belongs to the latter group. Zhao *et. al* [12] use MMST (Minimum Memory Spanning Tree) with optimal dimension order to reduce memory requirements in sequential data cube construction. However, their method requires frequent write operation to the disks. In comparison, our approach of tiling does not require frequent write operations, and can flexibly work with different amounts of available memory. Tam [11] uses MNST (Minimum Number Spanning Tree) to reduce computing cost, with ideas some-what similar to our prefix tree. Again, this method also requires frequent writing back to disks. Also, the MMST and MNST approaches have not been parallelized so far.

Many researchers have developed parallel algorithms for data cube construction. Goil *et. al* [4, 5] did the initial work on parallelizing data cube construction starting from multidimensional arrays. Recently, Dehne *et. al* [3] have studied the problem of parallelizing data cube. They focus on a *shared-disk* model where all processors access data from a common set of disks. None of these efforts have considered combining tiling and parallelization.

## 8. CONCLUSIONS

In this paper, we have shown how sequential and parallel data cube construction algorithms can be further scaled to handle larger problems. This is done by *tiling* the input and output arrays on each node. We have addressed the challenges in using tiling while still maintaining the other desired properties of a data cube construction algorithm, which are, using minimal parents, and achieving maximal cache and memory reuse. We have presented a parallel algorithm that combines tiling with interprocessor communication. In a related technical report [7], we also present a closed form expression for tiling overhead, and have shown how tiling parameters can be chosen to minimize this overhead.

Our experimental results show the following. First, tiling helps in scaling data cube construction in both sequential and parallel environments. Second, choosing tiling parameters as per our theoretical results does result in better performance.

## 9. REFERENCES

[1] S. Chaudhuri and U. Dayal. An overview of datawarehousing and olap technology. *ACM SIGMOD Record*, 26(1), 1997.

[2] Thomas H. Cormen, Charles E. Leiserson, and Ronald L. Rivest. *Introduction to Algorithms*. McGraw Hill, 1990.

[3] Frank Dehne, Todd Eavis, Susanne Hambrusch, and Andrew Rau-Chaplin. Parallelizing the data cube. *Distributed and Parallel Databases: An International Journal (Special Issue on Parallel and Distributed Data Mining), to appear*, 2002.

[4] Sanjay Goil and Alok Choudhary. High performance OLAP and data mining on parallel computers. Technical Report CPDC-TR-97-05, Center for Parallel and Distributed Computing, Northwestern University, December 1997.

[5] Sanjay Goil and Alok Choudhary. PARSIMONY: An infrastructure for parallel multidimensional analysis and data mining. *Journal of Parallel and Distributed Computing*, 61(3):285–321, March 2001.

[6] J. Gray, A. Bosworth, A. Layman, and H. Pirahesh. Data Cube: A Relational Aggregational Operator for Generalizing Group-Bys, Cross-Tabs, and Sub-totals. Technical Report MSR-TR-95-22, Microsoft Research, 1995.

[7] Ruoming Jin, Karthik Vaidyanathan, Ge Yang, and Gagan Agrawal. Using tiling to scale parallel data cube construction. Technical Report OSU-CISRC-5/04-TR??, Department of Computer Science and Engineering, The Ohio State University, May 2004.

[8] Ruoming Jin, Ge Yang, Karthik Vaidyanathan, and Gagan Agrawal. Communication and Memory Optimal Parallel Data Cube Construction. In *Proceedings of the International Conference on Parallel Processing (ICPP)*, October 2003.

[9] K. Ross and D. Srivastava. Fast computation of sparse datacubes. In *Proc. 23rd Int. Conf. Very Large Data Bases*, pages 263–277, Athens, Greece, August 1997.

[10] S.Agrawal, R. Agrawal, P. M.Desphande, A. Gupta, J.F.Naughton, R. Ramakrishnan, and S.Sarawagi. On the computation of multidimensional aggregates. In *Proc 1996 Int. Conf. Very Large Data Bases*, pages 506–521, Bombay, India, September 1996.

[11] Yin Jenny Tam. Datacube: Its implementation and application in olap mining. Master's thesis, Simon Fraser University, September 1998.

[12] Yihong Zhao, Prasad M. Deshpande, and Jeffrey F. Naughton. An array based algorithm for simultaneous multidimensional aggregates. In *Prceedings of the ACM SIGMOD International Conference on Management of Data*, pages 159–170. ACM Press, June 1997.

# A Novel FDTD Application Featuring OpenMP-MPI Hybrid Parallelization

Mehmet F. Su
Dept. of Electrical and Computer Engineering
University of New Mexico
Albuquerque, NM 87131
mfatihsu@ece.unm.edu

Ihab El-Kady
Sandia National Laboratories
PO Box 5800, MS 0603
Albuquerque, NM 87185
ielkady@sandia.gov

David A. Bader
Dept. of Electrical and Computer Engineering
University of New Mexico
Albuquerque, NM 87131
dbader@ece.unm.edu

Shawn-Yu Lin
Sandia National Laboratories
PO Box 5800, MS 0603
Albuquerque, NM 87185
sylin@sandia.gov

## Abstract

*We have developed a high performance hybridized parallel Finite Difference Time Domain (FDTD) algorithm featuring both OpenMP shared memory programming and MPI message passing. Our goal is to effectively model the optical characteristics of a novel light source created by utilizing a new class of materials known as photonic bandgap crystals. Our method is based on the solution of the second order discretized Maxwell's equations in space and time. This novel hybrid parallelization scheme allows us to take advantage of the new generation parallel machines possessing connected SMP nodes. By using parallel computations, we are able to complete a calculation on 24 processors in less than a day, where a serial version would have taken over three weeks. In this paper we present a detailed study of this hybrid scheme on an SGI Origin 2000 distributed shared memory ccNUMA system along with a complete investigation of the advantages versus drawbacks of this method.*

*Keywords: FDTD, Finite Difference Time Domain, OpenMP, MPI, Maxwell Equations, Photonic Crystals.*

## 1 Introduction

Photonic crystals are materials fabricated with a periodicity in index of refraction and specifically designed to affect and control the properties of light (or photons) in much the same way that semiconductors affect and control the properties of electrons. This provides scientists with a completely new dimension in the ability to control and manipulate the properties of light. The key lies in the concept of a photonic band gap — the optical analogue of the electronic band gap in semiconductors. In effect, it allows us to tailor the properties of photons the way we tailor the properties of electrons. Harnessing the broad potential of photonic crystals promises to have enormous technological implications in telecommunications, optical computing, and optoelectronics, as well as in associated imaging applications. One such application is the use of such materials in the lighting technology, where such crystals were suggested to possess the ability to internally recycle the unwanted thermal losses of usual light sources, such as conventional light bulbs, into useful visible radiation in the form of visible light [7]. Recent work has proven that such suggestions are actually possible, and an observation of the novel emission characteristics of such systems has appeared in several publications [13, 10, 11, 12].

Modeling the behavior of these photonic systems is however a very complicated task given the nature of the metal-photon coupled system. Conventional methods based on real-space transfer matrices [14, 6] and Modal Expansion techniques [9, 8], are only capable of producing passive optical properties of such systems such as transmittance, reflectance, and in some cases absorbance. Such methods however lack the ability to produce the real-time behavior and development of the electromagnetic field vectors in the photonic crystal environment. Furthermore, because such methods can at most provide passive optical properties, they are incapable of estimating the emissivity of such systems, and lack the ability to quantify the anisotropy of the emission process.

In this paper we present a finite difference time domain (FDTD) method based on the solution of the second order discretized Maxwell's equations in space and time, and designed specifically for modeling such complicated photonic systems. Because of the frequency dependent metallic properties and the skin-depth effects that arise from light-metal interactions, a very fine meshing of the system is needed. As a result huge data sets are involved and a sluggish computational performance is observed. To alleviate the problem we introduce a novel hybrid parallelization scheme that employs both OpenMP shared memory programming and MPI message passing. The result is a highly performing algorithm capable of handling such complicated physical problems, and paves the way for more efficient algorithms better suited for the new generation of clusters with SMP nodes. With parallel computations, we are able to reduce the time required for a full scale simulation from over three weeks to about one day.

This paper is organized as follows: The next section gives a brief formulation of Maxwell Equations and a specific FDTD method known as Yee's algorithm. The third section discusses the specifics of OpenMP and MPI parallelization schemes and their applications to FDTD. The fourth section shows some experimental results and discusses performance issues. In the fifth and final section, we conclude.

# 2 Maxwell Equations and Yee's Algorithm

## 2.1 Maxwell Equations

Maxwell Equations are a set of coupled vectorial partial differential equations. They govern the world of electromagnetics and optics. The usual compact formulation is:

$$\frac{\partial \vec{B}}{\partial t} = -\nabla \times \vec{E} - \vec{M} \tag{1}$$

$$\frac{\partial \vec{D}}{\partial t} = \nabla \times \vec{H} - \vec{J} \tag{2}$$

$$\nabla \cdot \vec{D} = 0 \tag{3}$$

$$\nabla \cdot \vec{B} = 0 \tag{4}$$

with definitions

$$\vec{D} = \epsilon_r \epsilon_0 \vec{E} \tag{5}$$

$$\vec{B} = \mu_r \mu_0 \vec{H} \tag{6}$$

$$\vec{J} = \vec{J}_{source} + \sigma \vec{E} \tag{7}$$

$$\vec{M} = \vec{M}_{source} + \sigma^* \vec{H} \tag{8}$$

where $\epsilon_r, \mu_r, \sigma, \sigma^*$ are known material parameters, $\vec{J}_{source}, \vec{M}_{source}$ are known properties of electromagnetic sources inside the system and $\epsilon_0, \mu_0$ are defined constants.

$\vec{E}$ is known as the electric field and $\vec{B}$ is known as the magnetic field.

Maxwell Equations have both space and time derivatives. In the above form, space derivatives are hidden in the $\nabla \times$ (curl) and $\nabla \cdot$ (divergence) operators.

## 2.2 FDTD revisited: Yee's algorithm

FDTD is a direct integration method which casts partial derivatives to partial differences on a finite mesh. This mesh contains the material parameters mentioned above, and is actually a representation of the scientific problem to be solved. Then the resulting equation is integrated numerically in space and time by the aid of initial conditions and termination conditions (boundary conditions).

Yee's algorithm is a well known method published in 1966 [17]. It gives a second order (in time and space) correct FDTD solution to Maxwell equations. For reasons of brevity and focus, we shall not attempt to give a full derivation of all the difference equations here, but merely cite the resulting equations. The interested reader is referred to [15].

In Yee's algorithm, the electric and magnetic fields are defined on an intertwined double mesh, where electric field components are circulated by four magnetic field components and magnetic field components are circulated by four electric field components. The first partial space derivative of a field $u$ is defined to be (correct to the second order):

$$\frac{\partial u}{\partial x}(i\Delta x, j\Delta y, k\Delta z, n\Delta t) \approx \frac{u^n_{i+1/2,j,k} - u^n_{i-1/2,j,k}}{\Delta x} \tag{9}$$

and the first time derivative is similarly (again, correct to the second order),

$$\frac{\partial u}{\partial t}(i\Delta x, j\Delta y, k\Delta z, n\Delta t) \approx \frac{u^{n+1/2}_{i,j,k} - u^{n-1/2}_{i,j,k}}{\Delta t} \tag{10}$$

For mathematical reasons, it suffices to apply these transformations to only the first two of the Maxwell equations. The other two equations are satisfied inherently by the formulation of the algorithm. Usage of these difference formulas with simple averaging where necessary yields six explicit time stepping equations. The electric fields and the magnetic fields are updated using [5] equations (11) and (12), respectively.

In these equations, $\hat{i}, \hat{j}, \hat{k}$ refer to space indices $x, y, z$ and their cyclic permutations.

$$\vec{E}_{\hat{i}}\big|_{i,j,k}^{n+1} = \left(\frac{1 - \frac{\sigma_{i,j,k}\Delta t}{2\epsilon_{i,j,k}}}{1 + \frac{\sigma_{i,j,k}\Delta t}{2\epsilon_{i,j,k}}}\right) \vec{E}_{\hat{i}}\big|_{i,j,k}^{n}$$

$$+ \left(\frac{\frac{\Delta t}{\epsilon_{i,j,k}}}{1 + \frac{\sigma_{i,j,k}\Delta t}{2\epsilon_{i,j,k}}}\right) \left(\frac{\vec{H}_{\hat{k}}\big|_{i,j+\frac{1}{2},k}^{n} - \vec{H}_{\hat{k}}\big|_{i,j-\frac{1}{2},k}^{n}}{\Delta \hat{j}} - \frac{\vec{H}_{\hat{j}}\big|_{i,j,k+\frac{1}{2}}^{n} - \vec{H}_{\hat{j}}\big|_{i,j,k-\frac{1}{2}}^{n}}{\Delta \hat{k}}\right) \quad (11)$$

$$\vec{H}_{\hat{i}}\big|_{i,j,k}^{n+\frac{1}{2}} = \left(\frac{1 - \frac{\sigma_{i,j,k}^{*}\Delta t}{2\mu_{i,j,k}}}{1 + \frac{\sigma_{i,j,k}^{*}\Delta t}{2\mu_{i,j,k}}}\right) \vec{H}_{\hat{i}}\big|_{i,j,k}^{n-\frac{1}{2}}$$

$$+ \left(\frac{\frac{\Delta t}{\mu_{i,j,k}}}{1 + \frac{\sigma_{i,j,k}^{*}\Delta t}{2\mu_{i,j,k}}}\right) \left(\frac{\vec{E}_{\hat{k}}\big|_{i,j+1,k}^{n} - \vec{E}_{\hat{k}}\big|_{i,j,k}^{n}}{\Delta \hat{j}} - \frac{\vec{E}_{\hat{j}}\big|_{i,j,k+1}^{n} - \vec{E}_{\hat{j}}\big|_{i,j,k}^{n}}{\Delta \hat{k}}\right) \quad (12)$$

## 2.3 Initial conditions and boundary conditions

The FDTD explicit time stepping requires initial conditions for the field values and boundary conditions at space boundaries. The conventional way to define initial conditions is to initialize all the field values to zero everywhere. It is also possible to save the fields between two consecutive FDTD time steppings and resume such a saved calculation, where saved fields are loaded as an initial condition.

As for boundary conditions, several choices are possible. The electromagnetic energy is reflected at the end of FDTD numerical space since the space is finite. This yields spurious, unwanted energy reflections. The usual way of preventing such reflections is to use Absorbing Boundary Conditions (ABC's) at the space boundaries.

In our application Liao and Uniaxial Perfectly Matched Layer (UPML) boundary conditions [16] were used. Liao ABC is based on a Newton extrapolation polynomial technique. Used at the space boundaries, this extrapolation simulates "endless free space" and absorbs electromagnetic energy, removing reflections. The UPML ABC is a variant of Berenger's Perfectly Matched Layer [3] technique, and it is a slab of artificial material. The properties of the slab are set up so as to absorb all incoming electromagnetic energy. Deeper into a PML absorber slab, the absorbance of the material is increased polynomially or geometrically. We chose to increase the absorbance polynomially.

## 3 Parallel FDTD calculations

### 3.1 FDTD and MPI Parallelization

In this part, details on MPI parallelization for FDTD are given. To make comparisons easier, a serial version of the algorithm is presented first:

The MPI programming paradigm assumes that data structures are not shared, but divided among the multiple processors used. This idea of storage division calls for a domain decomposition technique. Since the field updates

---

Algorithm: Serial-FDTD

Do one time initialization work;
Initialize fields, apply initial conditions;
**for** *t = 1 to tmax* **do**
    **for** *i, j, k = 1 to imax, jmax, kmax* **do**
        Update electric fields using magnetic fields;
        Update magnetic fields using updated electric fields;
        Update fields at boundaries, apply boundary conditions;
    **end**
**end**

**Algorithm 1:** Serial FDTD algorithm.

---

at a mesh point take field values from surrounding points, exchanges are required at domain boundaries. Alg. 2 implements domain decomposition using MPI message passing, and is a modification of the preceding serial FDTD algorithm.

The number of required field components to exchange grows with total surface area of the domains, which is proportional to *both* the total size of the mesh *and* the number of processors (or distinct domains) used in calculation. This is an overhead cost that is brought by domain decomposition.

On the other hand, the MPI parallelization is advantageous not only because it allows one to take advantage of a parallel machine to reduce execution time, but it also has the very important features of distributed allocation and distributed storage allowing for the solution of larger problem instances. With MPI parallelized FDTD, the total storage used is nearly evenly divided between the MPI processes. Hence, the per-process storage is low, and it becomes lower as the number of processes increases. This enables one to calculate with larger meshes and even overcome the 32-bit storage limit problem in the parallel systems built using commodity 32-bit system components.

```
Algorithm: MPI-FDTD

Do one time initialization work;
Initialize fields, apply initial conditions;
for t = 1 to tmax do
    for i, j, k = 1 to imax, jmax, kmax do
        Using MPI message passing, exchange
        magnetic fields with neighbors;
        Update electric fields using magnetic fields;
        Using MPI message passing, exchange up-
        dated electric fields with neighbors;
        Update magnetic fields using updated electric
        fields;
        Update fields at boundaries, apply boundary
        conditions;
    end
end
```

**Algorithm 2:** MPI parallelized FDTD algorithm.

## 3.2 FDTD and OpenMP

Many modern large-scale computer systems are net-works of connected shared memory SMP nodes, using combined distributed and shared memory approaches. In these systems, message passing in a node is emulated on shared memory and message passing between nodes uses actual messages. In order to efficiently harness the computational power of such systems, one has to use both shared and distributed memory approaches together [1].

Inspecting the field update equations, a simple fact is realized: When the electric fields are being *updated*, the magnetic fields are only *read*, and when the magnetic fields are being *updated*, the electric fields are only *read*. As long as the field update loops are kept separate, these calculations can be completed in a multi-threaded environment. There is no risk of a race condition as long as different threads update different field components. There is also no domain distribution overhead problem as long as the storage is shared and accessible by all the threads.

In our approach, we use the OpenMP shared memory parallel programming standard. The FDTD code maps naturally to the OpenMP paradigm, and has the benefits mentioned above. However, there are several down sides of shared memory FDTD:

- OpenMP lacks support for distributed allocation of shared structures, causing bottlenecks on some systems.

- Since the data set is very large, there are many cache misses, affecting performance and scalability severely.

- Optimization of OpenMP constructs is not trivial and requires extensive experimentation and optimization.

To solve the first issue, we use the distributed allocation and automated data relocation features available on an SGI Origin 2000 [4]. SGI's OpenMP implementation accepts several environment variables which affect how the system allocates data and how data is relocated at run-time to optimize access latency. It is possible to make the system allocate data with a first-touch policy, which distributes data properly if the storage is allocated by all the processors in parallel. Since OpenMP does not have such support, the *first-touch* policy is not useful. Another policy is to allocate each page of storage on different regions of the distributed memory, that is, the *round robin* allocation. That way, access latency is not optimized, but any bottlenecks caused by massive usage of a single portion of the physical memory is prevented. The third policy is the usage of a *predetermined storage map*, which requires a separate run to generate the map first. The allocated pages can be relocated by the system automatically to minimize access latency incurred by two processors, according to the usage statistics by each processor, yielding optimal memory placement at run time. For our case, we find round-robin allocation with automatic relocation best.

To solve the second problem, we employ some methods to reduce the total storage requirement (to contain the number of total cache misses) as well as rearrangement of calculations to make better use of caches and prefetch features. To reduce the storage requirement, our implementation uses a lookup table and stores material properties as short one-byte integers referring to this table. Specifically, 12 double complex parameters are replaced per grid point. This approach reduces the storage requirement by almost half and boosts scalability, as shall be discussed in the next section.

Last but not least, algorithm engineering techniques [2] of explicit timings, educated guesses and trial-and-error are used in the rearrangement of FDTD equations to increase prefetch efficiency and to optimize OpenMP options such as whether it would be more efficient to use *SHARED* or *FIRSTPRIVATE* and whether an SGI extension to OpenMP, the *NEST* construct, should be used. The effects of all these optimizations will be discussed in the next section.

## 3.3 Hybrid FDTD: Using OpenMP and MPI together

Shared memory machines do not scale up beyond a certain number of processors as overheads become unbearable. To obtain a more general parallel FDTD application, OpenMP and MPI are used together. In this case, the calculations performed in the MPI storage domains go multithreaded. This gives the option to choose how the processors are shared between MPI processes and how many OpenMP threads are used in each MPI process. It also reduces the MPI domain decomposition overhead, since there will not be as many domains as a pure MPI parallelized FDTD. Where OpenMP is not supported, one can of course use just MPI with only a change in compiler options and no changes in the source code. The hybrid algorithm is:

---

Algorithm: Hybrid-FDTD

Do one time initialization work;
**Using OpenMP multithreading,** initialize fields, apply initial conditions;
**for** *t = 1 to tmax* **do**
    **for** *i, j, k = 1 to imax, jmax, kmax* **do**
        Using MPI message passing, exchange magnetic fields with neighbors;
        **Using OpenMP multithreading,** update electric fields using magnetic fields;
        Using MPI message passing, exchange updated electric fields with neighbors;
        **Using OpenMP multithreading,** update magnetic fields using updated electric fields;
        **Using OpenMP multithreading,** update fields at boundaries, apply boundary conditions;
    **end**
**end**

---

**Algorithm 3:** MPI-OpenMP hybrid parallelized FDTD algorithm.

In the next section, we shall present and discuss the results obtained.

## 4 Results and Discussion

In this section, we shall concentrate on the performance analysis of the OpenMP parallelized FDTD since MPI parallelized FDTD has been around long enough to reach standard university curricula. Performance tests of MPI-based and hybrid FDTD schemes will be discussed in a future work in order to keep this paper concise and focused on the issues with and optimization of OpenMP enhanced FDTD codes. The FDTD application code analyzed here has two versions: The first version implements OpenMP in a straightforward manner, relying mostly on compiler optimizations. The second (a further optimized version) is derived from the first version and includes changes to improve cache usage and reduce memory footprint, as mentioned earlier. Analysis has been made on an SGI Origin 2000 featuring 350 MHz MIPS R12000 processors.

Figure 1 shows the execution times of the two versions of the code for a sample case. For this sample, the mesh contains 188x188x78 grid points, and the calculation was allowed to run for 3000 time steps. The time scale is in seconds, which means the calculation completes in almost

5 hours when run on a single processor. For uses of physics research, the calculation often has to be repeated with a different set of parameters (such as in a sweep of the frequencies emitted by the sources). As a result, the total time required can easily become several weeks when a single processor is employed.

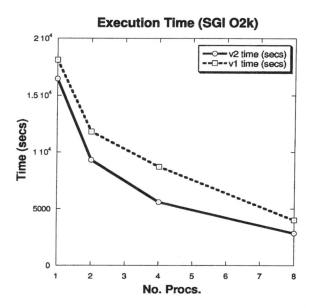

**Figure 1. Execution times on the SGI Origin 2000**

The speedup curves (Figure 2) obtained from the same system make it easier to see that a straightforward OpenMP parallelization does not quite provide an efficient answer for our needs.

Usage of the profiling facilities [4] available on the SGI Origin as a first probe indicates that the program has a problem of cache and prefetch misses. The average reuse rate for L1 cache lines are 10.4, whereas for L2 cache this rate drops to only 3.4 (see Table 1). To appreciate these results as well as the problem itself, a closer look at the profile statistics is necessary.

Without doubt, the most time consuming parts of such an FDTD calculation are the electromagnetic field updates. Formulated in the complex equations (11) and (12), these updates are performed at every grid point for every time step. The main data for these equations are the fields and the constant factors[1]. At every time step, a complete sweep of the space grid (and this data) is performed. Considering that 32-byte *double complex* variables are used for the fields, a small calculation shows a whopping amount of 200 MB is necessary for electromagnetic field data storage alone. As

---
[1]The terms with $\epsilon$ and $\mu$

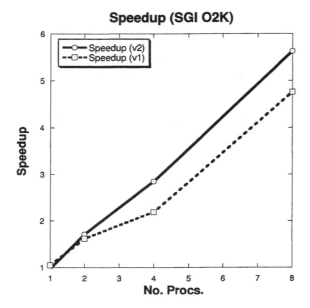

**Figure 2. Speedups on the SGI Origin 2000**

| Categories | Statistics (v1) | Statistics (v2) |
|---|---|---|
| Data mispredict /Data scache hits | 0.003954 | 0.007023 |
| Instruction mispredict /Inst. scache hits | 0.043838 | 0.064697 |
| L1 Cache Line Reuse | 10.412669 | 17.648883 |
| L2 Cache Line Reuse | 3.375819 | 4.589698 |
| L1 Data Cache Hit Rate | 0.912378 | 0.946377 |
| L2 Data Cache Hit Rate | 0.771471 | 0.821099 |
| Time accessing memory /Total time | 0.638376 | 0.576530 |
| Memory BW (MB/s, avg per proc) | 186.573422 | 150.096080 |
| Cache misses/cycle (avg) | 2.572237 | 1.557080 |
| Prefetch cache miss rate | 0.433175 | 0.282235 |

**Table 1. Various statistics for the two versions of the application (SGI Origin 2000, 8 processors)**

the problem size grows, this exceeds current cache sizes except for perhaps the highest-end systems available.

The situation is even more complicated by the form of the field update equations (11) and (12). A closer look indicates that, 27 floating point numbers have to be loaded for every grid point at every time step per each of the two equations: 9 floating point numbers per the 3 spatial components mapped at every grid point. Moreover, the access patterns are far too complicated to allow for any optimizations, and they are even not at a stride to fit into cache.

Hence, there are two different performance problems: one is about the complicated access patterns and the other is about the high number of cache misses. In fact, the first problem somewhat contributes to the second one, since complicated access patterns with large strides often incur cache misses. Both of these problems indicate that our code is memory bound, and its performance will depend on the performance of the memory subsystem.

Our solution to the first problem mentioned above is to merge all the field updates for one grid point into one big loop. Although the access patterns are still complex when the field updates are taken one spatial component at a time, the updates for all three spatial components per grid point per field access close array elements in aggregate. Profiling the code confirms that the rate of prefetch cache misses is reduced from 43.3% to 28.2% (Table 1).

To improve cache usage is to find ways to *slow down*, if not *prevent*, cache flushing as the calculation goes on and new data is read into the cache. Since the data set does not fit into the cache, prevention is not an option for our case. The other option, to slow down, calls for inventing ways to

reduce memory footprint of the data set. Our solution is to implement a lookup table which would keep the few constant factors used in cache. The elements of this table are pointed to by short (1-byte) integers, which replace the old storage of constant factors, which are floating point numbers. In our implementation, 12 constant factors are used per grid point (4 factors per 3 spatial components). By implementing the lookup table, we are able to reduce the overall memory footprint in half, and the cache line reuse rates are improved to 17.7 for L1 cache and 4.6 for L2 cache (Table 1).

The SGI Origin 2000 is a cache coherent, non-uniform memory access (ccNUMA) distributed shared memory platform. Since OpenMP lacks support for distributed allocation of shared storage, an OpenMP parallelized code using default allocation policies allocates storage from a single segment of the distributed memory. This single location bombarded by many processors is bound to become a memory hotspot and a bandwidth bottleneck. Indeed, timings of the second version of the code on 8 processors indicate 4975 seconds for the running time when default allocation policies are used (versus 2828 seconds[2]).

The Origin has facilities to migrate pages of data automatically to a closer position to the processors using them most. To activate this feature, one sets an environment variable named _DSM_MIGRATION. Another environment variable, _DSM_PLACEMENT, affects the policies used to determine the physical location of the pages allocated. The default, named *first touch allocation* causes memory pages become allocated closer to the first processor access-

---

[2]with round-robin allocation and automated data migration

ing to them. This same policy is the culprit that causes an OpenMP parallelized code to allocate all the shared storage from one single location. An alternative, allocating pages in a *round robin* fashion from all available distributed memory locations, is available and can be activated by setting the aforementioned environment variable. During our runs, we activate both of these features.

## 5   Conclusions and Future Directions

To sum up; we have designed, implemented and analyzed an FDTD simulation for a challenging physics problem which takes weeks to compute without parallel calculations. We indicated how an OpenMP based parallel implementation could be improved and gave quantitative indications to support our suggestions. The results suggest that OpenMP parallelization can be used together with an MPI domain distribution scheme to get a high performance, hybrid parallelized FDTD application to harness the power of newer parallel systems constructed out of interconnected SMP nodes.

Another lesson that has been learned is, relatively newer technologies in software and programming (such as OpenMP) can shed a new light to the application areas where the methods are well known and beyond a certain age. It may take time to see how an improved technology or technique could help in probable application areas that look unrelated or impossible at first sight.

As for future work, we will be studying the performance characteristics exhibited by this application under several other architectures, so as to expose details on how to get better performance from these machines. As of the preparation date of this document, analysis is under way on Sun UltraSparc and IBM Power based platforms. The intimate experience gained in optimizing the application on the Origin 2000 and other architectures will be useful as case studies and the knowledge will help the designs of future scientific simulations that achieve the highest performance.

## 6   Acknowledgments

This work was supported in part by: DOE Sandia National Laboratories contract 161449; NSF Grants CAREER ACI-00-93039, ITR ACI-00-81404, DEB-99-10123, ITR EIA-01-21377, Biocomplexity DEB-01-20709, ITR EF/BIO 03-31654; and DARPA Contract NBCH30390004.

## References

[1] D. A. Bader and J. JáJá. SIMPLE: A methodology for programming high performance algorithms on clusters of symmetric multiprocessors (SMPs). *Journal of Parallel and Distributed Computing*, 58(1):92–108, 1999.

[2] D. A. Bader, B. M. E. Moret, and P. Sanders. Algorithm engineering for parallel computation. *Experimental Algorithmics, Lecture Notes in Computer Science*, 2547:1–23, 2002.

[3] J. P. Berenger. A perfectly matched layer for the absorption of electromagnetic waves. *J. Computational Physics*, 114:185–200, 1994.

[4] D. Cortesi, J. Fier, J. Wilson, and J. Boney. *Origin 2000 and Onyx2 Performance Tuning and Optimization Guide*. Silicon Graphics Inc., 2001. Document Number 007-3430-003.

[5] I. El-Kady. *Modeling of photonic band gap crystals and applications*. PhD thesis, Iowa State University, Ames, Iowa, 2002.

[6] I. El-Kady, M. M. Sigalas, R. Biswas, K. M. Ho, and C. M. Soukoulis. Metallic photonic crystals at optical wavelengths. *Phys. Rev. B*, 62(23):15299, 2000.

[7] J. G. Fleming, I. El-Kady, S. Y. Lin, R. Biswas, and K. M. Ho. All metallic, absolute photonic band gap three-dimensional photonic-crystals for energy applications. *Nature*, 417:52, 2002.

[8] Z. Y. Li, I. El-Kady, K. M. Ho, S. Y. Lin, and J. G. Fleming. Photonic band gap effect in layer-by-layer metallic photonic crystals. *Journal of Applied Physics*, 93:38, 2003.

[9] L. L. Lin, Z. Y. Li, and K. M. Ho. Lattice symmetry applied in transfer-matrix methods for photonic crystals. *Journal of Applied Physics*, 94:811, 2003.

[10] S. Y. Lin, J. G. Fleming, and I. El-Kady. Experimental observation of photonic-crystal emission near photonic band-edge. *Applied Physics Letters*, 83(4):593, 2003.

[11] S. Y. Lin, J. G. Fleming, and I. El-Kady. Highly efficient light emission at 1.5microns by a 3D tungsten photonic crystal. *Optics Letters*, May 2003. Accepted.

[12] S. Y. Lin, J. G. Fleming, and I. El-Kady. Three-dimensional photonic-crystal emission through thermal excitation. *Optics Letters*, May 2003. Accepted for publication.

[13] S. Y. Lin, J. G. Fleming, Z. Y. Li, I. El-Kady, R. Biswas, and K. M. Ho. Origin of absorption enhancement in a tungsten, three-dimensional photonic crystal. *J. Opt. Soc. Am B.*, 20(7):1538, 2003.

[14] J. B. Pendry. Calculating photonic band structure. *J. Phys. Cond. Mat.*, 8:1085–1108, 1996.

[15] A. Taflove and S. C. Hagness. *Computational Electromagnetics: The Finite Difference Time Domain Method*, chapter 3. Artech House, Boston, MA, second edition, 2000.

[16] A. Taflove and S. C. Hagness. *Computational Electromagnetics: The Finite Difference Time Domain Method*, chapter 7. Artech House, Boston, MA, second edition, 2000.

[17] K. S. Yee. Numerical solution of initial boundary value problems involving Maxwell's equations in isotropic media. *IEEE Trans. Antennas and Propagation*, 14:302–307, 1966.

# Parallel Software for Inductance Extraction*

Hemant Mahawar[†] and Vivek Sarin
Department of Computer Science
Texas A&M University
College Station, TX 77843-3112

## Abstract

*The next generation VLSI circuits will be designed with millions of densely packed interconnect segments on a single chip. Inductive effects between these segments begin to dominate signal delay as the clock frequency is increased. Modern parasitic extraction tools to estimate the on-chip inductive effects with high accuracy have had limited impact due to large computational and storage requirements. This paper describes a parallel software package for inductance extraction called ParIS, which is capable of analyzing interconnect configurations involving several conductors within reasonable time. The main component of the software is a novel preconditioned iterative method that is used to solve a dense complex linear system of equations. The linear system represents the inductive coupling between filaments that are used to discretize the conductors. A variant of the Fast Multipole Method is used to compute dense matrix-vector products with the coefficient matrix. ParIS uses a two-tier parallel formulation that allows mixed mode parallelization using both MPI and OpenMP. An MPI process is associated with each conductor. The computation within a conductor is parallelized using OpenMP. The parallel efficiency and scalability of the software is demonstrated through experiments on the IBM p690 and Intel and AMD Linux clusters. These experiments highlight the portability and efficiency of the software on multiprocessors with shared, distributed, and distributed-shared memory architectures.*

**Keywords.** Inductance extraction, Parallel computing, Iterative methods, Preconditioning, Mixed mode parallelization.

*This work has been supported in part by NSF under the grants NSF-CCR 9984400 and NSF-CCR 0113668, and by the Texas Advanced Technology Program grant 000512-0266-2001. The AMD Linux cluster at Texas A&M University was acquired through the MRI grant NSF-DMS 0216275. Access to the IBM p690 and Intel Linux clusters was provided by the NCSA, University of Illinois at Urbana-Champaign.

†Corresponding author: mahawarh@cs.tamu.edu.

## 1 Introduction

The design and testing phases in the development of VLSI chips rely on accurate estimation of the signal delay. Signal delay in a VLSI chip is due to the parasitic resistance (R), capacitance (C), and inductance (L) of the interconnect segments. As a result of newer technology, which uses thicker copper wires, the influence of parasitic resistance has decreased. On the other hand, clock rates in the GHz range have increased the effect of the parasitic inductance on signal delay. Fast and accurate inductance extraction techniques are needed for signal delay estimation in the next-generation microprocessors with millions of interconnect segments.

At high frequencies, the physical proximity of interconnect segments leads to strong inductive coupling between neighboring conductors. This coupling arises due to a magnetic field that is created when current flows through a conductor. This magnetic field opposes any change in the current flow within the conductor as well as in the neighboring conductors. Self-inductance is the resistance offered to change in current within a conductor. Mutual inductance refers to the resistance offered to change in current in a neighboring conductor. Inductance extraction refers to the process of estimating self and mutual inductance between interconnect segments of a chip.

To estimate inductance between a set of conductors in a particular configuration, one needs to determine current in each conductor under appropriate equilibrium conditions. The surface of each conductor is discretized by a uniform two-dimensional grid whose edges represent current-carrying filaments. The potential drop across a filament is due to its own resistance and due to the inductive effect of other filaments. Kirchoff's current law is enforced at the grid nodes. This results in a large dense system of equations that is solved by iterative methods such as the generalized minimum residual method (GMRES) [7]. Each iteration requires a matrix-vector product with the coefficient matrix that can be computed without explicitly forming the matrix itself. Matrix-vector products with the dense matrix are computed approximately via hierarchical methods such as the Fast Multipole Method (FMM) [3]. The task of developing preconditioners, which accelerate the rate of convergence of the iterative method, is complicated by the unavailability of the coefficient matrix.

FastHenry [4] is a commonly available software package that uses the above approach for accurate inductance extraction. Matrix-vector products are computed efficiently by using FMM. Preconditioners are obtained by approximating the dense matrix with a sparse matrix that is derived from the FMM hierarchical structure. Since the process of constructing and applying these preconditioners requires large amount of memory and time, the software has found limited use.

This paper presents an object-oriented parallel inductance extraction software package called *ParIS*. The software uses a different formulation in which the current is restricted to the subspace satisfying Kirchoff's law through the use of solenoidal basis functions. The reduced system of equations is solved by a preconditioned iterative solver that uses FMM to compute products with the dense coefficient matrix and the preconditioner. Improved formulation and the associated preconditioning is responsible for significant reduction in computational and storage requirements.

This paper describes a parallel formulation of the algorithm and the performance of the parallel code on a variety of multiprocessors. Section 2 presents the inductance extraction problem and outlines the solenoidal basis method. Section 3 describes the parallel formulation of the algorithm and implementation of the software. Section 4 presents a set of experiments that show the parallel efficiency and scalability of the software on a variety of architectures. The experiments have been conducted on IBM p690, 64-bit Intel Linux cluster, and 64-bit AMD Linux cluster. Conclusions are presented in Section 5.

## 2  Background

For a set of $s$ conductors, we need to determine an $s \times s$ impedance matrix that represents pair-wise mutual inductance among the conductors at a given frequency. The element $(l, k)$ of the matrix equals the potential drop across conductor $l$ when there is zero current in all conductors, except conductor $k$ that carries unit current. The $k$th column is computed by solving an instance of the inductance extraction problem with the right hand side denoting unit current flow through conductor $k$. The impedance matrix can be computed by solving $s$ instances of this problem with different right hand sides.

The current density $\mathbf{J}$ at a point $r$ is related to potential $\phi$ by the following equation [4]

$$\rho \mathbf{J}(\mathbf{r}) + j\omega \int_V \frac{\mu}{4\pi} \frac{\mathbf{J}(\mathbf{r}')}{\|\mathbf{r} - \mathbf{r}'\|} dV' = -\nabla \phi(\mathbf{r}), \quad (1)$$

where $\mu$ is magnetic permeability of the material, $\rho$ is the resistivity, $r$ is position vector, $\omega$ is frequency, $\|\mathbf{r} - \mathbf{r}'\|$ is the Euclidean distance between $\mathbf{r}$ and $\mathbf{r}'$, and $j = \sqrt{-1}$. The volume of the conductor is denoted by $V$ and incremental volume with respect to $r'$ is denoted by $dV'$. Equation (1) can be derived from Maxwell's equations that define the fundamental laws of electrodynamics.

To obtain a numerical solution for (1), each conductor is discretized into a mesh of $n$ filaments $f_1, f_2, \ldots, f_n$. Current is assumed to flow along the filament length. The current density within a filament is assumed to be constant. Filament currents are related to the potential drop across the filaments according to the linear system

$$[\mathbf{R} + j\omega \mathbf{L}]\mathbf{I}_f = \mathbf{V}_f, \quad (2)$$

where $\mathbf{R}$ is an $n \times n$ diagonal matrix of filament resistances, $\mathbf{L}$ is a dense inductance matrix denoting the inductive coupling between current carrying filaments, $\mathbf{I}_f$ is the vector of filament currents, and $\mathbf{V}_f$ is the vector of potential difference between the ends of each filament. The $k$th diagonal element of $\mathbf{R}$ is given by $\mathbf{R}_{kk} = \rho l_k / a_k$, where $l_k$ and $a_k$ are the length and cross-sectional area of the filament $f_k$, respectively. Let $\mathbf{u_k}$ denote the unit vector along the $k$th filament. The elements of the inductance matrix $\mathbf{L}$ are given by

$$\mathbf{L}_{kl} = \frac{\mu}{4\pi} \frac{1}{a_k a_l} \int_{r_k \in f_k} \int_{r_l \in f_l} \frac{\mathbf{u}_k \cdot \mathbf{u}_l}{\|\mathbf{r}_k - \mathbf{r}_l\|} dV_k dV_l.$$

Kirchoff's current law states that the net current flow into a mesh node must be zero. These constraints on current lead to additional equations

$$\mathbf{B}^T \mathbf{I}_f = \mathbf{I}_s, \quad (3)$$

where $\mathbf{B}^T$ is a sparse $m \times n$ branch index matrix and $\mathbf{I}_s$ is the known branch current vector of length $m$ with non-zero values for source currents only. The branch index matrix defines the connectivity among filaments and nodes. The $(k, l)$ entry of the matrix is $-1$ if filament $l$ originates at node $k$, 1 if filament $l$ terminates at node $k$, and 0 otherwise. Since the unknown filament potential drop $\mathbf{V}_f$ can be represented in terms of node potential $\mathbf{V}_n$ by the relation $\mathbf{B}\mathbf{V}_n = \mathbf{V}_f$, one needs to solve the following system of equations to determine the unknown filament current $\mathbf{I}_f$ and node potential $\mathbf{V}_n$

$$\begin{bmatrix} \mathbf{R} + j\omega\mathbf{L} & -\mathbf{B} \\ \mathbf{B}^T & 0 \end{bmatrix} \begin{bmatrix} \mathbf{I}_f \\ \mathbf{V}_n \end{bmatrix} = \begin{bmatrix} 0 \\ \mathbf{I}_s \end{bmatrix}. \quad (4)$$

For systems involving a large number of filaments, it is not feasible to compute and store the dense matrix $\mathbf{L}$. These linear systems are typically solved by iterative techniques such as GMRES. The matrix-vector products with

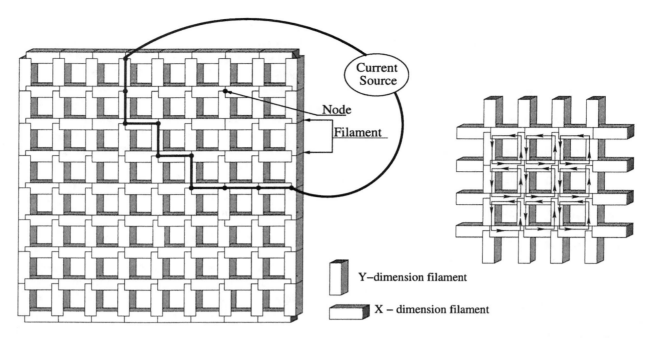

**Figure 1. Discretization of a ground plane with a mesh of filaments (left) and solenoidal current flows in each mesh cell (right). (Reproduced from [6].)**

**L** are computed using fast hierarchical methods such as the FMM. The main hurdle in this matrix-free approach is the construction of effective preconditioners for the coefficient matrix.

### 2.1 The Solenoidal Basis Method

We present a brief overview of the solenoidal basis method for solving (4) (see, e.g., [6] for details). Consider the discretization of a ground plane in Fig. 1. Current flowing through the filaments must satisfy Kirchoff's law at each node in the mesh. Current can be decomposed into two components: constant current along the bold line shown on the left and a linear combination of mesh currents as shown in the partial mesh on the right. This decomposition converts the system in (4) into the following system:

$$
\begin{bmatrix} \mathbf{R} + j\omega\mathbf{L} & -\mathbf{B} \\ \mathbf{B}^T & 0 \end{bmatrix} \begin{bmatrix} \mathbf{I} \\ \mathbf{V}_n \end{bmatrix} = \begin{bmatrix} \mathbf{F} \\ \mathbf{0} \end{bmatrix}. \tag{5}
$$

The main difference between matrix representations in (4) and (5) is that the former uses current boundary conditions and the later uses potential boundary conditions.

Solenoidal functions are a set of basis functions that satisfy conservation laws automatically. As shown in the partial mesh in Fig. 1, unit circular flows defined on mesh cells automatically satisfy Kirchoff's law at the grid nodes. The unknown filament currents can be expressed in the solenoidal basis: $\mathbf{I}_f = \mathbf{P}x$, where $x$ is a vector of unknown

mesh currents and $\mathbf{P}$ is a sparse matrix whose columns denote filament current in each mesh. A column of $\mathbf{P}$ consists of four non-zero entries that have the value 1 or $-1$ depending on the direction of current in the filaments of the cell.

The system (5) is converted to a *reduced* system

$$
\mathbf{P}^T \left[ \mathbf{R} + j\omega\mathbf{L} \right] \mathbf{P}x = \mathbf{P}^T\mathbf{F}, \tag{6}
$$

which is solved by a preconditioned iterative method. The preconditioning step involves product with a dense matrix that represents inductive coupling between filaments placed at the cell centers. This scheme can be implemented using FMM as well, and leads to rapid convergence of the iterative method. On a set of benchmark problems, serial implementation of this software is up to 5 times faster than FastHenry [4], with only one-fifth of memory requirements [6].

### 3 *ParIS*: Parallel Inductance Extraction Software

We have developed an object oriented parallel implementation of the solenoidal basis algorithm for inductance extraction. This software combines the advantages of the solenoidal basis method, fast hierarchical methods for dense matrix-vector products, and highly effective preconditioning scheme to provide a powerful package for inductance extraction. In addition, the software includes an efficient parallel implementation to reduce overall computation time [5] on parallel architectures.

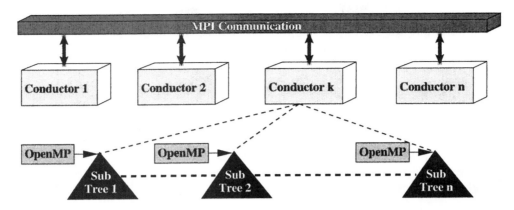

**Figure 2. Two-tier parallelization scheme implemented in** *ParIS*.

The building blocks of *ParIS* are conductor elements. Each conductor is uniformly discretized with a mesh of filaments. The most time-consuming step in the solution of the reduced system involves matrix-vector products with the impedance matrix. This matrix is the sum of a diagonal matrix $\mathbf{R}$ and a dense inductance matrix $\mathbf{L}$. Since the preconditioning step also involves matrix-vector products with a dense matrix that is similar to $\mathbf{L}$, it is worthwhile to reduce the cost of the matrix-vector product with $\mathbf{L}$.

### 3.1 Parallel Dense Matrix Vector Product

The computational complexity of a matrix-vector product with a dense $n \times n$ matrix is $O(n^2)$. This complexity can be reduced significantly through the use of hierarchical approximation techniques. These algorithms exploit the decaying nature of the $\frac{1}{r}$ kernel for the matrix entries to compute approximate matrix-vector products with bounded error. Higher accuracy can be achieved at the expense of more computation. For instance, the Barnes-Hut [1] method computes particle-cluster interactions to achieve $O(n \log n)$ complexity, while the Fast Multipole Method (FMM) [3] computes cluster-cluster interactions to achieve $O(n)$ complexity. *ParIS* uses a variant of FMM to compute approximate matrix-vector products.

FMM is used to compute the potential at each filament due to current flowing in all the filaments. The algorithm divides the domain into eight non-overlapping subdomains, and continues the process recursively until each subdomain has at most $k$ filaments, where $k$ is a parameter that is chosen to maximize computational efficiency. A subdomain is represented by a subtree whose leaf nodes contain the filaments in the subdomain. These subdomains are distributed across processors. The potential evaluation phase consists of two traversals of the tree. During the up-traversal, multipole coefficients are computed at each node. These coefficients can be used to compute potential due to all the filaments within the node's subdomain at a *far away* point.

These multipole computations do not require any communication between processors. During the down-traversal, local coefficients are computed at each node from the multipole coefficients. The local coefficients can be used to compute potential due to *far away* filaments at a point within the node's subdomain. Potential due to *near by* filaments is computed directly.

One can also use other hierarchical multipole-based approximation techniques instead of FMM to compute the dense matrix-vector products. Parallel formulations of multipole-based techniques including the FMM have been developed by several groups. The reader is referred to [2, 8, 9, 10] for a representative set of approaches.

### 3.2 Conductor Level Parallelism

To exploit parallelism at the conductor level, each conductor is assigned to a different processor. The data structures native to a conductor are local to its processor. This includes the filaments in a conductor and the associated FMM tree. With the exception of matrix-vector products, all other computations are local to each conductor.

The matrix-vector product with the inductance matrix involves two types of filament interactions. Interactions between the filaments of the same conductor are computed locally by the associated processor. To get the effect of filaments in other conductors, a processor needs to exchange multipole coefficients with other processors. During a preprocessing step, *ParIS* identifies the nodes in a conductor's tree that are required by other conductors. The cost of this step is amortized over the iterations of the solver. While computing the dense matrix-vector product, communication is needed to translate the multipole coefficients of these nodes to the nodes on other processors. Communication is also needed when computing direct interactions between adjacent nodes that belong to different subtrees. This type of communication is proportional to the number of filaments on the subdomain boundary.

Additional parallelism is available within each conductor. By assigning different processes or threads to all the nodes at a specific level in the FMM tree, one can partition the computation for subdomains between processes. Fewer processes can be assigned to the top part of the FMM tree to further improve parallel efficiency. With different sized conductors, one can have more processes associated with larger conductors. This scheme allows load balancing to a certain extent.

A two-tier approach, as shown in Fig. 2, allows the algorithm to be implemented in hybrid or mixed mode using both MPI and OpenMP. The software can be executed on a variety of platforms ranging from shared-memory multiprocessors to workstation clusters without any change.

## 4  Experimental Results

The software design of *ParIS* has the dual advantage of portability and performance across a variety of platforms. This is achieved through a two-tier parallelization approach that uses MPI processes for conductor level parallelism and OpenMP directives to exploit parallelism within a conductor. This section presents experiments to demonstrate the parallel performance of *ParIS* on multiprocessors with shared, distributed, and distributed-shared memory architectures. Distributed memory platforms such as the 64-bit Intel and AMD Linux clusters allow parallelism to be exploited via MPI processes only. Distributed-shared memory platforms such as the IBM p690 allow mixed mode parallelization with both MPI and OpenMP.

The performance of the code is measured by the efficiency on a set of benchmark problems. In these experiments, a generalized notion of efficiency is used to provide a uniform basis to compare different experiments. Efficiency is defined as follows:

$$E = \frac{BOPS}{p},$$

where $p$ is the number of processors and $BOPS$ is the average number of *base operations* executed *per second*. A base operation involves computing an interaction between a pair of filaments. In general, $BOPS$ should remain unchanged when the number of conductors and the filaments per conductor are varied. With this definition of efficiency, it is possible to compare the performance of the code on different benchmarks that require unequal number of mutual inductance interactions.

Since the multipole degree, $d$, influences the accuracy of the approximate dense matrix-vector product, a fair comparison is possible only when the impedance error is bounded. It was seen that for $d = 4$, the impedance error was always within 1% of a reference value that was calculated using FMM with $d = 8$. The parallel performance of the algorithm is reported for a fixed number of GMRES iterations. The results are identical to the case when the full inductance extraction problem is solved because the dense matrix-vector products account for over 98% of the execution time. It may be noted that the use of higher multipole degree increases the fraction of time spent in the dense matrix-vector product, which in turn improves the parallel effficiency (see, e.g., [5] for details).

The symbols used for the experiments are summarized below.

| | |
|---|---|
| $T$ | Execution time (seconds) |
| $E$ | Parallel efficiency (%) |
| $p$ | Number of processors |
| $P_{OMP}$ | Number of OpenMP processes |
| $P_{MPI}$ | Number of MPI processes |

### 4.1  Shared Memory Parallelization

The benchmark problem presented in this section illustrates the parallel performance of the code on a shared memory multiprocessor. These experiments were conducted on a 32-processor IBM p690 multiprocessor with 1.3GHz processor speed and AIX5.1 operating system. The *ground plane problem* shown in Fig. 1 models the ground plane that is used to provide a uniform ground potential to all the components of a VLSI circuit.

**Table 1. Parallel performance for the ground plane problem on shared memory machine.**

| $p$ | Problem Size | | | | | |
|---|---|---|---|---|---|---|
| | $128 \times 128$ | | $256 \times 256$ | | $512 \times 512$ | |
| | $T$ | $E$ | $T$ | $E$ | $T$ | $E$ |
| 1 | 770 | 100 | 3727 | 100 | 17164 | 100 |
| 2 | 385 | 100 | 1865 | 100 | 8610 | 99 |
| 4 | 193 | 99 | 938 | 99 | 4315 | 99 |
| 8 | 103 | 93 | 483 | 96 | 2203 | 97 |
| 16 | 55 | 87 | 250 | 93 | 1193 | 89 |

The problem requires computing the self-impedance of a 1cm × 1cm ground plane. A uniform two-dimensional mesh is used to discretize the ground plane. A tolerance of $10^{-3}$ was specified for the relative residual norm of the preconditioned GMRES method. Table 1 shows the execution time and efficiency for linear systems of order 32K, 128K and 512K unknowns. For a fixed size problem, a modest decrease in parallel efficiency with increase in the number of processors indicates an efficient parallel implementation. Figure 3 illustrates the scalability of the algorithm. It can be seen that by increasing the problem size, parallel efficiency is maintained when the number of processors are increased.

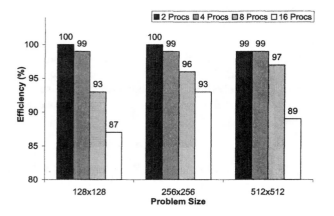

Figure 3. Shared memory parallel efficiency for the ground plane problem.

## 4.2 Mixed Mode Parallelization

The *cross-over* problem shown in Fig. 4 is a standard benchmark problem for inductance extraction. This setup represents a cross-over of interconnect segments. The problem consists of determining the impedance matrix for these segments. The segments are 1cm long and 2mm wide, and are separated by $500\mu$m in the horizontal direction. This problem leads to a non-uniform point distribution for the dense matrix-vector multiplication algorithm.

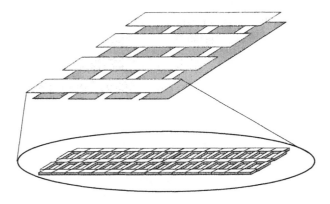

Figure 4. Cross-over problem with a view of a discretized conductor.

Mixed mode experiments were conducted on 16 processors of an IBM p690 at NCSA, Illinois. No more than 16 processors were available due to site restrictions. Various combinations of OpenMP and MPI processes were used to demonstrate the mixed mode parallel efficiency of the software. Each MPI process was responsible for one conductor and OpenMP directives were used to parallelize computation within the conductor.

Table 2. Parallel performance for the cross-over problem with 128 × 640 filaments per conductor.

| $P_{OMP}$ | $P_{MPI}$ | | | | | | | |
|---|---|---|---|---|---|---|---|---|
| | 1 | | 2 | | 4 | | 8 | |
| | $T$ | $E$ | $T$ | $E$ | $T$ | $E$ | $T$ | $E$ |
| 1 | 578 | 100 | 582 | 99 | 597 | 99 | 618 | 98 |
| 2 | 286 | 100 | 292 | 99 | 296 | 100 | 316 | 96 |
| 4 | 150 | 96 | 150 | 96 | 158 | 94 | | |
| 8 | 81 | 88 | 82 | 88 | | | | |
| 16 | 49 | 74 | | | | | | |

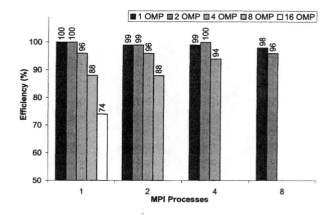

Figure 5. Mixed mode parallel efficiency for the cross-over problem with 128 × 640 filaments per conductor.

Table 2 shows the parallel performance of the software on the *cross-over* problem where each conductor has been discretized by a mesh of size 128 × 640. Figure 5 shows that the parallelism within a conductor is exploited very effectively via the OpenMP directives.

## 4.3 Distributed Memory Parallelization

The parallel performance of the software was studied on the IBM pSeries 690 as well as the Intel and AMD Linux clusters. The experiments were conducted on a 64-bit Intel Itanium cluster at NCSA, Illinois and on a 64-bit AMD Opteron-240 Tensor cluster at Texas A&M University. The Intel cluster consists of 800MHz 64-bit Itanium processors with Redhat-Linux operating system. Intel compilers were used to compile the code. The Tensor cluster consists of 1.4GHz 64-bit AMD Opteron processors with SuSE-Linux operating system. GNU compilers were used on the Tensor cluster for compiling the code.

Table 3 shows the execution time and parallel efficiency

**Table 3. Parallel performance for the cross-over problem on workstation clusters. Each conductor has been discretized by a 128 × 640 filament mesh.**

|  | IBM p690 | | Intel-64 Linux | | AMD-64 Linux | |
|---|---|---|---|---|---|---|
| $p$ | $T$ | $E$ | $T$ | $E$ | $T$ | $E$ |
| 1 | 578 | 100 | 738 | 100 | 300 | 100 |
| 2 | 585 | 99 | 746 | 99 | 301 | 99 |
| 4 | 604 | 98 | 765 | 99 | 310 | 99 |
| 8 | 629 | 97 | 790 | 99 | 320 | 99 |

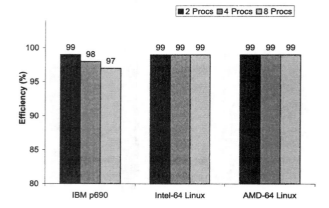

**Figure 6. Parallel efficiency of the software for cross-over problem on different clusters. Each conductor was discretized by a 64 × 320 filament mesh.**

of the software for the *cross-over* problem. Note that the number of conductors is identical to the number of MPI processors. In these cases, the total base operations and the execution time increase with increasing conductors. This is accompanied by a growth in the communication required among the processors. However, the parallel efficiency defined as the average base operations per second per processor is maintained across problem instances. This indicates that the code utilizes each processor efficiently when the load is distributed uniformly across processes.

## 5 Conclusion

This paper presents a high performance parallel software package called *ParIS* for inductance extraction of VLSI circuits. The software is based on a parallel formulation of the solenoidal basis method for inductance extraction. The computational complexity of the algorithm depends on the cost of computing matrix-vector products with dense coefficient and preconditioner matrices. *ParIS* uses an efficient

parallel formulation of a hierarchical approximation scheme that is similar to the FMM algorithm. The software employs a two-tier approach in the mixed mode parallel code that is both portable and efficient on a variety of multiprocessors. Experimental results demonstrate that *ParIS* achieves very high parallel efficiency on shared-memory, distributed-memory, and distributed-shared memory multiprocessors.

## References

[1] J. Barnes and P. Hut. A hierarchical O($n$ $log$ $n$) force calculation algorithm. *Nature*, Vol. 324:446–449, 1986.

[2] A. Grama, V. Kumar, and A. Sameh. Parallel hierarchical solvers and preconditioners for boundary element methods. *SIAM Journal on Scientific Computing*, Vol. 20:337–358, 1998.

[3] L. Greengard. *The Rapid Evaluation of Potential Fields in Particle Systems.* The MIT Press, Cambridge, Massachusetts, 1988.

[4] M. Kamon, M. J. Tsuk, and J. White. FASTHENRY: A multipole-accelerated 3D inductance extraction program. *IEEE Transaction on Microwave Theory and Techniques*, Vol. 42:1750–1758, September 1994.

[5] H. Mahawar and V. Sarin. Parallel iterative methods for dense linear systems in inductance extraction. *Parallel Computing*, Vol. 29:1219–1235, September 2003.

[6] H. Mahawar, V. Sarin, and W. Shi. A solenoidal basis method for efficient inductance extraction. In *Proceedings of the 39$^{th}$ Conference on Design Automation*, pages 751–756, New Orleans, Louisiana, June 2002.

[7] Y. Saad. *Iterative Methods for Sparse Linear Systems.* PWS Publishing Company, Boston, 1996.

[8] F. Sevilgen, S. Aluru, and N. Futamura. A provably optimal, distribution-independent, parallel fast multipole method. In *Proceedings of the 14$^{th}$ IEEE International Parallel and Distributed Processing Symposium*, pages 77–84, Cancun, Mexico, May 2000.

[9] J. P. Singh, C. Holt, T. Totsuka, A. Gupta, and J. L. Hennessy. Load balancing and data locality in hierarchical n-body methods. *Journal of Parallel and Distributed Computing*, Vol. 27:118–141, 1995.

[10] S. H. Teng. Provably good partitioning and load balancing algorithms for parallel adaptive n-body simulation. *SIAM Journal of Scientific Computing*, Vol. 19:635–656, 1998.

# Session 6B:
# Grid: Resource Management

# A Data Scheduling Algorithm for Autonomous Distributed Real-Time Applications in Grid Computing

Mohammed Eltayeb
*The Ohio State University*
*eltayeb@ece.osu.edu*

Atakan Doğan
*Anadolu University*
*atdogan@anadolu.edu.tr*

Füsun Özgüner
*The Ohio State University*
*ozguner@ece.osu.edu*

## Abstract

*Large-scale data intensive applications with real-time requirements are currently emerging in many disciplines of science and engineering. Such applications can benefit from a Grid environment provided that an efficient solution to the following data scheduling problem can be found: Schedule the transfer of a set of large-scale data objects of distributed applications in a Grid environment so as to meet real-time constraints associated with these data transfers. Based on this premise, this paper focuses on the aforementioned problem and proposes a new effective path-selection based scheduling algorithm. The algorithm performs its optimization based on a schedule reflection model; a new cost criterion that takes into account the satisfiability of each application as a whole. We show, by simulation, that our algorithm improves the performance of data intensive real-time applications.*

## 1. Introduction

The *Grid Computing* community seeks to provide a framework for establishing and deploying a massive set of resources to support large-scale applications with scalability, reliability, security and efficiency. For the community, newly emerging distributed applications pose a great challenge due to the fact that the amount of data produced and processed by these applications ranges from hundreds of *gigabytes* to several *petabytes* [1]. In addition, such applications with huge data sets will demand real-time support from the Grid, which further complicates the problem. A variety of motivating applications, which are expected to evolve into data intensive real-time computing, can be found in the fields of distributed medical data systems [2], [3], computer vision [4], distributed defense and surveillance applications [5], and real-time scientific experimentation [6].

Computational Grids and Data Grids must be real-time aware in order to support data intensive real-time computing. By real-time, we mean the ability of a Grid to perform the computation, scheduling and data-transfer operations by specific pre-assigned deadlines. Let us take the example of a distributed application that runs climate simulations online for a storm for the purpose of scientific visualization [7] or some control purposes. Portions of these simulations run on remote locations. This application requires that the frequent output of very large files of successive computations be analyzed by distributed tasks. Massive data movements follow the successive and massive operations. The data need to arrive by specific deadlines; otherwise lose their significance (e.g., real-time tracking of a storm for flight control). Moving huge amount of data for such a real-time distributed computing model is not trivial, particularly for a large number of flights. The Grid must intelligently and efficiently allocate and transfer the data between the distributed components of the application to meet these assigned deadlines. Meeting the assigned deadline of a task is a new factor in allocating data replicas and in scheduling data transfers in a Grid environment.

Many issues related to Grid computing have been studied in detail in the open literature [8], [9]. However, data scheduling and replication for real-time applications in Grid environments have not been thoroughly investigated. The staging algorithms proposed in [5] have first introduced data scheduling within the real-time context of distributed computing. In [5], a number of tasks are assumed to be running on different nodes on the network and each task aperiodically generates requests for data elements (*data-items*). Each of three proposed heuristics in [5], referred to as the PPH, FPH and FPA (Partial Path Heuristic, Full Path Heuristic and Full Path All destinations heuristic, respectively), aims at maximizing an objective function in the framework of a special data transfer mechanism called *data staging*. Staging is moving the data-item in its entirety from one node to intermediate nodes along the path to the final destination node(s).

The three aforementioned heuristics PPH, FPH and FPA schedule only one data-item each time along the shortest path from source to destination. We proposed the *Concurrent Scheduling* (CS) method in a previous paper [10] to allow a communication step to include different data-item transfers simultaneously in an organized fashion. The CS algorithm utilizes and builds on top of the EPP (Extended Partial Path) heuristic which we proposed in [11].

The heuristics provided thus far for data staging are based on greedy algorithms. While these greedy heuristics are successful in maximizing the *satisfiability* (in terms of number or total weight of satisfied requests), in solving the particular problem, it is clear that alternative combinations of requests and path sets for the requests exist and may result in better performance. Achieving an optimum combination is addressed in some communication-oriented algorithms for the path-selection problem [4], [12], [13], [14], [15]. More recent studies have presented the path selection problem for real-time communication in wormhole networks [16], [17]. In [18], a framework is defined for data scheduling in a computational Grid environment. The framework addresses the issue of data replication and proposes a component in a distributed model for keeping track of the popularity of the data and replicates the data to other sites based on a specific algorithm.

This paper proposes a new efficient path-selection based scheduling algorithm. The algorithm performs its optimization based on a schedule *reflection* model; a new cost criterion that takes into account the satisfiability of each application as a whole. In addition to introducing the schedule reflection, this paper proposes a new scheduling method that allows concurrent transfer of data-items from different applications based on perceived blocking delays along the selected paths. We show, by simulation, that our algorithm improves the performance of data intensive real-time autonomous applications.

## 2. System model

The staging system model is composed of a network, end points and data request information (see [5] for details of a similar and comprehensive mathematical model). We assume an irregular network of machines connected by different communication links. The network graph $G = (V, E)$ specifies the connectivity of a set of $n$ vertices $V = \{V_1,...,V_n\}$ and $m$ edges $E = \{E_{i,j}: V_i, V_j \in V$ and there is a communication channel between the vertices\}. Each vertex $V_i$ is a node with a specific processing power and limited storage capacity $C_i$. Each edge $E_{i,j}$ is considered to be a virtual communication link with specific bandwidth and latency. We assume that both machines and links are available throughout the data staging process.

A distributed application $A_j = \{T_{j,1} ,..., T_{j,k_j}\}$ is composed of $k_j$ tasks running on several predetermined processing nodes. Each task produces a set of *requests* to specific data-items of large, fixed sizes at different times during its execution. Let $R_{T_{j,i}} = \{r^j_{i,1},...,r^j_{i,l^j_i}\}$ be the set of $l^j_i$ requests produced by the ith task $T_{j,i}$ of application $A_j$. Each request $r^j_{i,u}$ is associated with one of $\chi$ data-items $I_t$ (t $=1,...,\chi$) to be transferred to a *destination* node $N^j_{i,u}$ where

the corresponding requesting task $T_{j,i}$ resides. It is assumed that the release times for such requests are known once the application arrives at the system and are a function of their tasks release times. If a data-item is stored or produced in a particular machine, the machine is considered a *source* machine for all requests to the specific data-item. Thus, it is possible that multiple source machines may exist for a particular request. In addition, several different tasks from different applications can produce a batch of requests to a particular data-item. Each request $r^j_{i,u}$ is assigned a deadline $Dl(r^j_{i,u})$ by which the data-item must be delivered to its destination. Generally, we assume that the probability that a task meets its deadline is proportional to the number of requests (which are produced by the task) that meet their respective deadlines. Hence, a task is guaranteed to meet its deadline if all of its requests are *satisfied* (i.e., meet their deadlines). Similarly, the application is guaranteed to meet its deadline if all requests of all the tasks in the application are satisfied. The request is also assigned a priority value $Py(r^j_{i,u})$ which is inherited from the application, which includes the task that produced the request. A request $r^j_{i,u}$ is hence summarized by the following tuple: $\left\langle I_t(r^j_{i,u}), N^j_{i,u}, Dl(r^j_{i,u}), Py(r^j_{i,u}) \right\rangle$.

The *achieving* path $P_{r^j_{i,u}}$ of a request $r^j_{i,u}$ is a path that has a network latency less than or equal to the deadline of the request. An achieving path is also assumed to be *node-unique*. A node-unique path between a source $V_S$ and a destination $V_N$ ($V_S \neq V_N$) is given as P = $\{V_S,...,V_i,..., V_j ,..., V_N\}$ and $i \neq j$ for all $V_i, V_j \in P$. The set of achieving paths of a request $P_{r^j_{i,u}}$ is defined as the collection of all achieving paths from all sources of the data-item associated with the request $r^j_{i,u}$.

## 3. Problem statement

Consider a staging system as described above. The data transfer is attained through intermediate nodes while keeping a copy of the data-item locally in the intermediate nodes for a specific period of time. The requested data-items are, hence, made available for access to other potential requests of tasks residing nearby the intermediate nodes. The staging heuristic collectively schedules data transfers for all present tasks of the currently available applications. The staging heuristic exploits the temporal locations of the data in making new scheduling decisions, reducing the latencies of the individual requests. The ultimate goal here is to *satisfy* all requests of all tasks present at any specific point of time. *A request $r^j_{i,u}$ is considered to be satisfied if it reaches the final destination $N^j_{i,u}$ on or before the assigned deadline $Dl(r^j_{i,u})$.* The goal of satisfying all requests, however, collides with the storage limitation of the system especially for large number of requests. An efficient heuristic aims at maximizing the real-time satisfiability via effectively scheduling the limited resources.

We consider that application $A_j$ is *fully satisfied* under schedule $\gamma$ if and only if all associated tasks are satisfied. Based on our definition of the task-request relation, an application is, hence, fully satisfied if and only if all requests generated by all of its tasks are satisfied. Let the set of satisfied applications via $\gamma$ be $W(\gamma) = \{A_j: A_j$ is *satisfied* in $\gamma$, $\forall j\}$. We define the *absolute reflection $R(\gamma)$* (or the *reflection*) of the schedule as,

$$\mathcal{R}(\gamma) = \sum_{A_j \in W(\gamma)} Py(A_j)$$

Here, $Py(A_j)$ is the priority value of application $A_j$. This priority value is assumed to be externally assigned and represents the relative importance of the application in the system. The problem becomes finding $\gamma^*$ which is the schedule that results in the maximum reflection value.

# 4. Blocking analysis concurrent scheduling

The heuristic proposed in this paper employs a *concurrent scheduling* (CS) method and a *blocking analysis* (BA) method (hence the name blocking analysis concurrent scheduling or shortly BACS) for data transfers to solve the data-scheduling problem. By concurrent scheduling, we mean that several data-items will be allowed to stage or transfer along the designated paths, allowing simultaneous service for many requests. By blocking analysis, we mean that the blocking delays for the transferred data-items (due to storage space limitations in the intermediate nodes) are computed and used as an input for the algorithm. Next, we present a general overview of the proposed BACS algorithm.

## 4.1. Overview of the algorithm

It is now clear from our previous discussion that staging large-scale data-items through a path composed of nodes with limited storage capacities results in "blockings" along the path. A blocking occurs when a request competes with another request in one or more of the intermediate nodes along its path. Due to this situation, the proposed algorithm enforces a special *blocking policy*. This policy forces a lower priory requests to "await" before a specific blocking point (a *contention node* on the path) until a space adequate for its data-item is available in the contention node.

In reaching a near-optimal path selection, the algorithm adopts a graphical method (*blocking dependency graph* (BDG)) to compute the exact blocking delays incurred by each request in a specific schedule. These delays are used by the algorithm to determine the feasibility of a solution and hence, the feasibility of the path selection.

The BACS algorithm starts from an initial solution where an achieving shortest path is picked for each request. If all requests are not satisfied due to blocking delays under the initial solution, BACS relies on a heuristic in which the initial solution is altered by choosing other paths for requests than the shortest ones with the hope of maximizing the reflection. BACS stops once a feasible solution is found; otherwise, it returns the best-found solution. The BACS algorithm can be divided into the following phases of operation:

**Phase 1:** *Generating the blocking dependency graph (BDG) of requests for a path set.*

**Phase 2:** *Computing the total blocking delay incurred by each request.*

**Phase 3:** *Modifying the path selection (if phases 1 and 2 do not result in a solution under which all request are satisfied).*

## 4.2. Phase 1: Generating the BDG

The BACS algorithm generates a BDG of the set of requests based on a particular path assignment. This assignment is established initially by the set of the achieving "shortest paths" for all requests. Finding the (achieving) shortest path of each request is accomplished by running a multiple-source version of Dijkstra's shortest path algorithm [19]. To compute the blocking delays of the group of requests, we need to rearrange these requests based on their priorities. This priority-based rearrangement along with the path assignment allows us to apply the aforementioned enforced blocking policy. The BDG for a set of requests is generated in the following steps in this phase:

**Step 1:** Determine the priority assignment for all requests. Since we need to maximize the satisfiability of the application as a whole, we have to consider all of its requests as one unit. In other words, the algorithm must strive to maximize the satisfiability of the requests from a particular application. The priorities assigned to the requests are determined by the priorities of the applications. This assignment results in grouping the requests based on their applications' priorities. i.e., for request $r_{i,u}^j$,

$$Py(r_{i,u}^j) = Py(A_j)$$

After computing the priorities of all requests, these requests are arranged in descending order of their priorities. Then, each request is scheduled along its selected path with respect to this order. During the scheduling process, a higher priority request can block a lower priority request when contending for an intermediate node at the *intersection* of their paths (see Definition 1 in the Appendix). If two requests with an equivalent priority value contend for a node, they will be handled based on a FIFO scheme. This is a very possible scenario since we group the requests into classes of priorities based on the applications' assigned priorities. Any request that is contending with a higher priority request will be awaited at the node before the contention point. This blocking is performed by the scheduler by reserving a space in the intermediate node that is adequate for the data-item.

**Step 2:** Compute the direct blocking delays between all possible request pairs based on Definition 2 in the Appendix. The amount of time a lower priority request will be blocked at a contention point is determined by the time needed for the higher priority request to clear its path (clear the intermediate nodes on the request's path). This time is the time needed to deliver the data-item associated with the higher priority request to its final destination from the current node. Note that, in computing the direct blocking delay between two requests, these two requests are assumed to be the only requests existing in the system. In addition, the total delay encountered by a request is not just the direct blocking since a direct blocking request may encounter other blocking delays from higher priority requests, and so on (see Definition 3 and 4 in the Appendix).

It is important to realize that the dependency between the blocked request and the blocking request is determined also by the sizes of the data-items of both requests as well as the capacity of the node at the blocking point. A blocked request will only be free to proceed if the sum of size of the data-item of the blocking request and the remaining space in the intermediate node (the contention node) is equal to or greater than the size of the blocked data-item. That is, when a blocking request clears out, the new available space at the node must be large enough to store the data-item of the blocked request. Let $\psi_x = \{\zeta_1, \zeta_2, ..., \zeta_w\}$ be a set of "w" higher priority requests contending with a lower priority request $\rho$ with data-item size $|I_t(\rho)|$ at node $V_x$. Consider a special ordered arrangement $\zeta_{k_1}, \zeta_{k_2}, ..., \zeta_{k_w}$ of $\psi_x$ such that $|P_{\zeta_{k_1}}| < |P_{\zeta_{k_2}}| < ... < |P_{\zeta_{k_w}}|$ where $|P_{\zeta_{k_i}}|$ is the length of path $P_{\zeta_{k_i}}$. Let $\psi_{x,B}$ be the set of requests which will directly block request $\rho$. Then,

$$\psi_{x,B}^{\rho} = \left\{ \zeta_{k_i} : \zeta_{k_i} \in \psi_x^{\rho} \text{ and } \left|I_t(\zeta_{k_i})\right| + \left[C_x - \sum_{\zeta_{k_u} \in \psi_x^{\rho}} \left|I_t(\zeta_{k_u})\right|\right] \geq \left|I_t(\rho)\right| \right\} \cup$$

$$\left\{ \zeta_{k_i} : \forall \zeta_{k_i}, \zeta_{k_j} \in \psi_x^{\rho}, (i < j) \text{ and } \sum_{j=1}^{i} |I_t(\zeta_{k_j})| + \left[C_x - \sum_{\zeta_{k_u} \in \psi_x^{\rho}} \left|I_t(\zeta_{k_u})\right|\right] \geq |I_t(\rho)| > \right.$$

$$\left. \sum_{j=1}^{i-1} | I_t(\zeta_{k_j}) | + \left[C_x - \sum_{\zeta_{k_u} \in \psi_x^{\rho}} \left|I_t(\zeta_{k_u})\right|\right] \right\}.$$

The direct blocking incurred on request $\rho$ by $\zeta_{k_i} \in \psi_{x,B}^{\rho}$ on their corresponding achieving paths $P_{\zeta_{k_i}}$ and $P_\rho$ at node $V_x$, which is denoted by $D_{\zeta,\rho}$, is given by:

$$D_{\zeta,\rho} = \left|P_\zeta\right| - \sum_{E_i \in \overline{P}_\rho} | E_i |$$

where $\overline{P}_\rho$ is the non-blocking portion of path $P_\rho$ which is composed of all vertices up to but not including contention point vertex $V_x$ and $|E_i|$ is the length of edge $E_i$ in $\overline{P}_\rho$. Note that we ignored the subscripts in request $\zeta_{k_i} \in \psi_{x,B}^{\rho}$ to simplify the above expression. After computing the direct blocking delays for each pair of requests by using the above equation, the algorithm proceeds to execute Step 3.

**Step 3:** In this step, the algorithm develops the BDG for the requests. Each node in this graph represents a request and each directed edge represents the awaited time incurred on a request by a higher priority request sharing the same path. The direction of the edge indicates a blocking time from a request at the start of the edge to another request at the end of the edge. The developed BDG represents the dependencies between the requests.

*Remark: The result of connecting the set of requests (as nodes) in the given staging system (with the enforced blocking policy) by the computed direct blocking delays (as edges), is a combination of DAG graphs (a group of disconnected DAG may result due to a separate blocking schemes) by which the input nodes represent the highest priority requests and the exit nodes represent the lowest priority requests.*

### 4.3 Phase 2: Computing the total blocking delays

Based on the above remark, it is now possible to compute the total delays of all available requests in the system. This is in basically done by computing the length of the *critical path* of each request in the resultant DAG. The critical path of a request is the longest path to the request from all available nodes in the graph. The length of this path represents the total blocking time which the request will experience due to direct and indirect blockings. The total delay for a request is equal to the sum of the length of the critical path and the length of the selected path of the request.

The Dijkstra's shortest-path algorithm can be modified to solve the longest-path problem for a DAG. With reasonable complexity, the delays of all requests are, hence, determined in this phase of the algorithm. Note that the delays established in this phase depend on the path selection that resulted in the BDG. At the end of this phase, the algorithm is able to determine the set of all unsatisfiable requests due to the deadline constraints. The algorithm then tries to improve the solution by constructing a better path selection for the requests as will be explained in Phase 3.

## 4.4 Phase 3: Modifying the Path Selection

This phase is the core of the algorithm. We provide a heuristic, namely the *Least Contending Shortest Path (LCSP)*, for exploring the most likely parts of the search space to avoid a prohibitively expensive exhaustive search method and to reach our objective quickly. LCSP relies on altering the set of achieving paths for the set of requests to perform the modification phase. LCSP is based on a *Contention Index* (CIX) measure. The CIX is defined as a function of the contention value, contention length of the contention distance (see Definitions 5, 6 and 7). The CIX value indicates the amount of contention that a particular path of a certain request will possess against the other requests. The heuristic computes this value to obtain path alternatives for the group of requests.

The modification phase of the algorithm is performed on a subset of the requests which we call here the set of *candidate* requests. Since our goal is to improve the satisfiability of the application as a whole favoring higher priority applications, the set of candidates includes requests of a particular application. This application is initially selected as the highest-priority application. We use the following formula, referred to here as the *completion factor* of the application, to distinguish the applications with equal priorities. The completion factor of application $A_j$ under schedule $\gamma$ is the ratio of the satisfied requests in the application to the total number of the application's requests.

$$\phi_j^\gamma = \frac{|S_j(\gamma)|}{|A_j|}.$$

The application with the highest completion factor and highest priority is a *candidate application* and determines the candidate requests set. This set includes the requests in the blocking chains of the critical paths of all unsatisfied requests in the candidate application as well as the edges of the chains.

### 4.4.1. Least contending shortest path first.
The BACS employs the LCSP heuristic as an improvement heuristic modifying the path selection. The LCSP iteratively alters the paths for only the request in the set of candidate requests that is produced in Phase 3. The following steps are performed by LCSP until reaching a feasible solution (A feasible solution is one by which all requests in all applications are satisfied):

1) Generate the set of candidate requests (start with the highest priority application with completion factor less than one).

2) Starting with the highest request in the set of candidates[*], LCSP replaces the shortest path with the next shortest for the request. If some paths are of the same length the heuristic selects the "least contending" based on the CIX value. Note that computing the CIX value is performed whenever arbitration between the paths with equivalent length is needed in this step.

3) The algorithm evaluates the total delays of the requests (via Phase 1 and Phase 2) and computes the reflection value (the optimization criterion) as follows:

$$\mathcal{R}'(\gamma) = \sum_{A_j} \left( Py(A_j) \cdot \left[ \phi_j^\gamma \right]^2 \right).$$

We referred to this value as the *normal reflection*. The square term here allows us to pick schedule $\gamma_1$ over $\gamma_2$ if $\gamma_1$ provides better completion ratio for some applications than $\gamma_2$ even though $\gamma_2$ may maximize the sum of the completion ratios over all applications. For example, assume we have only two applications with equivalent priorities of unity; one attains a completion factor of 0.7 and the other 0.2 via schedule $\gamma_1$. Another schedule gives completion factors 0.5 for both. The reflections of $\gamma_1$ and $\gamma_2$ are 0.9 and 1.0 respectively indicating that the second schedule is better. The normal reflections of the two schedules are 0.53 and 0.50 respectively indicating that $\gamma_1$ is a better selection for a schedule. Although this formula depicts an unfair distribution of resources between the two applications, it improves the satisfiability of the system. If no better value is found in this step, the next path for the current request is tested and so on. Once a better normal reflection value is found for this request, the path of

---

[*] The highest request is the request with the highest priority in the set. If all requests have the same priority value the algorithm starts from the highest request in the chain to the lowest.

the particular request is fixed and the algorithm proceeds to Step 3.

4) The algorithm moves to another request in the list of candidates and repeats Step 2 until a feasible solution is found or the candidate requests list is covered. The algorithm exits with the best solution (highest normal reflection) found thus far after visiting all applications.

## 5. Simulation results

In order to test the performance of the BACS algorithm, a requests generator has been constructed in this simulation. This generator randomly creates requests with random source and destination locations. An irregular network topology is created randomly out of 30 machines constituting all nodes in the system. Each machine is assumed of a fixed storage capacity. The data-items are assumed of equal sizes and their number is assumed to vary according to the random generator per iteration. The links connecting the nodes for simplicity are assumed to be uniform and of equivalent in latencies. This assumption tends to be acceptable for the fast proprietary networks required for critical applications. An Internet model allows this assumption to relax, but the proposed algorithm is capable of dealing with such issue given that we use an average latency. Our notion of latencies here includes the time needed by the data-item to be transferred between the nodes in one hop. To assess the performance of the algorithm for the total satisfiability and compare with the reflection, the algorithm is run under different load and deadline conditions. We compared our algorithm with some other proposed algorithms under the same conditions. The load is varied from 100 requests to 600 requests generated for random set of applications. The performance of the system is first presented as the percentage of the satisfiability. The average length of the path is 10 links. The LCSP heuristic uses the CV function of the request's path as the CIX value in this experiment.

Figure 1 shows the performance of BACS, CS/EPP [10] and PPH [5]. BACS shows the best performance under all scenarios. When the deadlines of requests are tight, BACS is slightly better than CS/EPP in improving the number of satisfied requests. When deadlines are relaxed, BACS responds very well since many paths are considered for staging the requests. Figure 2 shows a comparison between the BACS and the CS/EPP when fixing the deadline and altering the load of the system. The deadline is assumed equivalent for all requests and set to be 500 time units (25 times the link latency). BACS shows superiority over CS/EPP especially at the light load situations. Finally, Figure 3 represents our optimization criterion (reflection of the schedule). It is clear that, when using the normal reflection as optimization, BACS enhances the weight of the satisfied applications in the

resulting schedule. This indicates that the schedule pays attention to the high priority applications that are near completions. This is shown by the plot REFLECT_OPTIMIZE. Figure 3 also shows that only optimizing the sum of the priorities of the aggregate requests does not yield high weight of satisfied application as indicated by the plot EFFECT_OPTIMIZE. Note that this sum is defined as the effect of the schedule and is presented as the criterion used for the algorithm proposed in [5] and [10].

## 6. Conclusion

We have addressed the problem of data scheduling in distributed real-time systems with large-scale data communications. The ultimate goal is to satisfy the distributed applications by meeting the assigned deadlines for the data retrievals for their tasks. We developed an objective function that considered the overall satisfiability of the set of applications based on the schedule reflection. We proposed the BACS algorithm, which maximizes the objective based on the simple heuristic LCSP and returns the best schedule based on the normal reflection formula. The performance of the BACS algorithm is shown by simulation to be superior to other staging algorithms in the literature.

The complexity of BACS is higher than these other algorithms since multiple path searches are performed for solving the problem. Let $|V| = \mathcal{M}$, $|E| = \mathcal{E}$, and $\mathcal{R}$ be the number of requests. The time complexity of producing at most $\mathcal{M}$ achieving paths from at most $\mathcal{M}$ different sources to a destination node for a request is $O(\mathcal{M}^2(\mathcal{E} + \mathcal{M} \log \mathcal{M}))$. Thus, for all requests, we have $O(\mathcal{R}\mathcal{M}^2(\mathcal{E} + \mathcal{M} \log \mathcal{M}))$. The time complexity of producing a BDG and computing the blocking delays of all requests are $O(\mathcal{E}\mathcal{R}^2)$ and $O(\mathcal{R}^3)$, respectively. Given that there are at most $\mathcal{M}$ achieving paths for each request, the search space of LCSP is $O(\mathcal{R}\mathcal{M})$. Even though the BACS seems to be a bit costly algorithm than others its high scheduling performance outweigh its cost in sparse network situations. The actual increase in complexity from the other algorithms is due to constructing the BDG, the blocking delay computation phase and the LCSP heuristic. However, for large number of requests and sparse network the cost of these procedures are of $O(\mathcal{R}^2)$, $O(\mathcal{R}^3)$ and $O(\mathcal{R})$ respectively. Hence, the complexity of the combined procedure for sparse network and large number of requests is of $O(\mathcal{R}^6)$. This represents an increase of $O(\mathcal{R}^3)$ from the CS/EPP and $O(\mathcal{R}^4)$ from the PPH. It is important to mention that BACS possesses the ability to optimize the reflection of the schedule in a much better way especially for large number of requests.

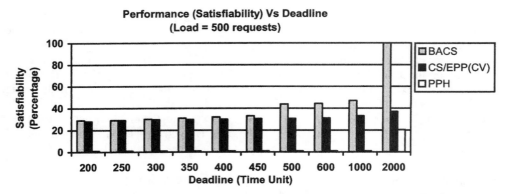

**Figure 1.** The performance of the BACS, CS/EPP (CIX=CV) and PPH algorithms in terms of the percentage of satisfied requests at the load of 500 requests.

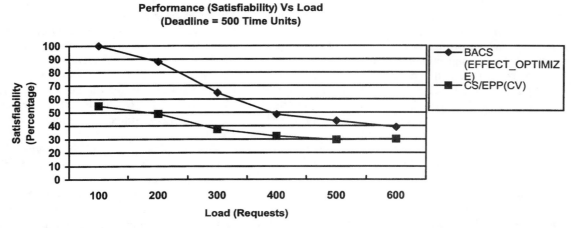

**Figure 2.** The satisfiability performance of the BACS and CS/EPP as a function of the load. The deadlines of all requests are fixed at 500 time units (about 70% of the average path length of the requests).

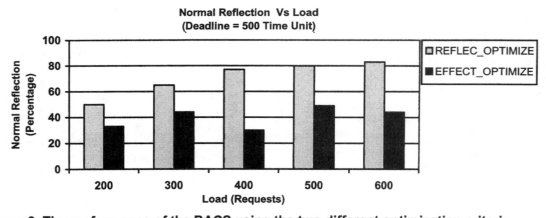

**Figure 3.** The performance of the BACS using the two different optimization criteria.

# Appendix

**Definition 1.** *Two paths $P_\zeta$ and $P_\rho$ of the two requests $\zeta$ and $\rho$ are said to be intersecting if and only if $\exists$ at least a node $V_x$ such that $V_x \in P_\zeta$ and $V_x \in P_\rho$. All $V_x$ such that no storage space is available for both $I_t(\zeta)$ and $I_t(\rho)$ at a specific point of time are called contention points for $\zeta$ and $\rho$ at the point of time or, for simplicity, contention points for $\zeta$ and $\rho$.*

**Definition 2.** *If the two paths $P_\zeta$ and $P_\rho$ of the two requests $\zeta$ and $\rho$ with $Py(\zeta)>Py(\rho)$ are intersecting, then $\zeta$ is said to be directly blocking $\rho$, which is denoted by $\zeta \succ \rho$, if and only if the first contention point for both requests is not the destination of either requests. The amount of time $\zeta$ is directly blocking $\rho$ is called the direct blocking delay between the two requests.*

**Definition 3.** *A blocking chain is said to exist between two requests $\zeta$ and $\rho$ with $Py(\zeta)>Py(\rho)$ if and only if $\exists$ a set of requests $\Sigma = \{\sigma_1, \sigma_2,..., \sigma_z\}$ such that $Py(\sigma_i)>Py(\sigma_{i+1})$, $(i=1,2,...,z)$ and $\zeta \succ \sigma_1 \succ ... \succ \sigma_i \succ ... \succ \sigma_z \succ \rho$. The set $\Sigma$ is called the blocking chain set of the two requests.*

**Definition 4.** *Two requests $\zeta$ and $\rho$ are said to be indirectly blocking if and only if $\exists$ a blocking chain set $\Sigma \neq \phi$ for the two requests. The amount of time $\zeta$ is indirectly blocking $\rho$ is called the indirect blocking delay between the two requests.*

**Definition 5.** *Assume that $P_\zeta$ is an achieving path for request $\zeta$. The Contention Value of $P_\zeta$ denoted by $CV(P_\zeta)$ is the total number of paths which share at least one node with $P_\zeta$ or intersect with $P_\zeta$. If $CV(P_\zeta)>0$, the path $P_\zeta$ is called a contending path for request $\zeta$.*

**Definition 6.** *The Contention Length of path $P_\zeta$ denoted by $CL(P_\zeta)$ is the total number of nodes shared by $P_\zeta$ and other contending paths.*

**Definition 7.** *The Contention Distance for path $P_\zeta$ of request $\zeta$ denoted by $CD(P_\zeta)$, is the total number of nodes before the first contention point in $P_\zeta$ from source to destination.*

# 7. References

[1] Henri Casanova, *"Distributed Computing Research Issues in Grid Computing,"* ACM SIGAct News, vol. 33, no. 3, pp. 50 – 70, 2002.

[2] J. Lee, B. Tierney and W. Johnston, *"Data Intensive Distributed Computing: A Medical Application Example,"* In Proceedings of the High Performance Computing and Networking Conference (HPCN 99), April 1999.

[3] M. Zikos, E. Kadoudi and S. C. Orphanoudakis, *"DIPE: A Distributed Environment for Medical Image Processing,"* In Proceedings of MIE'97, pp. 465-469, Porto Carras, Greece, May 1997.

[4] S. B. Shukla and D. P. Agrawal, *"Scheduling Pipelined Communication in Distributed Memory Multiprocessors for Real-time Applications,"* Int'l Symposium on Computer Architecture, pp. 222-231, 1991.

[5] M. D. Theys, M. Tan, N. Beck, H. J. Siegel and M. Jurczyk, *"A Mathematical Model and Scheduling Heuristic for Satisfying Prioritized Data Requests in an Oversubscribed Communication Network,"* IEEE Transaction on Parallel and Distributed Systems, vol. 11, no. 9, pp. 969-988, Oct. 2000.

[6] B. Tierney, W. Johnston and J. Lee, *"A Cache-Based Data Intensive Distributed Computing Architecture for Grid Applications,"* CERN School of Computing, Sept. 2000.

[7] B. Allcock, I. Foster, V. Nefedova, A. Chervenak, E. Deelman, C. Kesselman, J. Lee, A. Sim, A. Shoshani, B. Drach and D. Williams, *"High –Performance Remote Access to Climate Simulation Data: A Challenge Problem for Data Grid Technologies,"* Proc. of the Int'l Conference for High Performance Computing and Communications (SC2001), Nov. 2001.

[8] Alexander Barmouta and Rajkumar Buyya: GridBank "A Grid Accounting Services Architecture (GASA) for Distributed Systems Sharing and Integration" Proc. 18th Int'l. Parallel and Distributed Processing Symposium PDPS 2003: pp. 245-257.

[9] I. Foster, C. Kesselman, J. Nick, and S. Tuecke *"The Physiology of the Grid: An Open Grid Services Architecture for Distributed Systems Integration,"* Technical report, Open Grid Service Infrastructure WG, Global Grid Forum, June 2002.

[10] M. Eltayeb, A. Doğan and F. Özgüner, *"Concurrent Scheduling for Real-time Staging in Oversubscribed Networks,"* Proc. of the 16th Int'l Conference on Parallel and Distributed Computing Systems, pp. 175-180, Aug. 2003.

[11] M. Eltayeb, A. Doğan and F. Özgüner, *"Extended Partial Path Heuristic for Real-time Staging in Oversubscribed Networks,"* Proc. of the 18 Int'l Symposium on Computer and Information Sciences (ISCIS), pp. 942-951, Nov. 2003.

[12] R. Guerin, S. Kamat, A. Orda, T. Przygienda and D. Williams, *"QoS Routing Mechanisms and OSPF Extensions,"* IETF Draft, Nov. 1996.

[13] Z. Wang and J. Crowcroft, *"Quality of Service Routing for Supporting Multimedia Applications,"* IEEE Journal on Selected Areas in Communications, vol. 14, no. 7, pp. 1228-1234, 1996.

[14] Q. Ma and P. Steenkiste, *"On Path Selection for Traffic with Bandwidth Guarantees,"* Proc. of IEEE Int'l Conference on Network Protocols, Oct. 1997.

[15] D. Kandlur and K. Shin, *"Traffic Routing for Multicomputer Networks with Virtual Cut-Through Capability,"* IEEE Transactions on Computers, vol. 41, no. 10, pp. 1257-1270, Oct. 1992.

[16] S. Lee and J. Kim, *"Path Selection for Message Passing in a Circuit-Switched Multicomputers,"* Journal of Parallel and Distributed Computing, pp. 211-218, July 1996.

[17] S. Lee, K. W. Nam, S. J. Hong, and J. Kim, *"Path Selection for Real-Time Communication in Irregular Wormhole Networks,"* Parallel and Distributed Processing Technologies and Applications (PDPTA-2000), Vol. II, pp. 1071-1075, June 2000.

[18] Kavitha Ranganathan and Ian Foster, *"Decoupling Computation and Data Scheduling in Distributed Data-Intensive Applications,"* Proc. of the 11th Int'l. Symposium on High Performance Distributed Computing (HPDC'02), Edinburgh (Scotland), pp. 352-365, July, 2002.

[19] T. Cormen, C. Leiserson, and R. Rivest, *Introduction to Algorithms.* Cambridge, Massachusetts, MIT Press, 1990.

# Faucets: Efficient Resource Allocation on the Computational Grid

Laxmikant V. Kalé, Sameer Kumar, Mani Potnuru,
Jayant DeSouza, Sindhura Bandhakavi
Department of Computer Science
University of Illinois at Urbana-Champaign
`kale,skumar2,potnuru,jdesouza,bandhaka@cs.uiuc.edu`

## Abstract

*The idea of a "Computational Grid" suggests that high end computational power can be thought of as a utility, similar to electricity or water. Making this metaphor work requires a sophisticated "power distribution" infrastructure. In this paper, we present the Faucets framework that aims at providing (a) user-friendly compute power distribution across the grid, (b) market-driven selection of Compute Servers for each job, resulting in effective utilization of resources across the grid, and (c) improved utilization within individual Compute Servers.*

*Utilization of individual Compute Servers is improved by the notions of* adaptive jobs *and smarter job schedulers. Server selection is facilitated by quality-of-service (QoS) contracts for parallel jobs. Market efficiencies are then attained by a bidding and evaluation system that makes the Compute Servers compete for every job by submitting bids, thus transforming the computational grid into a free market. Job submission and monitoring is simplified by several tools and databases within the Faucets system.*

*We describe the overall architecture of the system. All the essential components of the system have been implemented, which are described in the paper. We also discuss ongoing work and future research issues.*[1]

## 1  Introduction

Over the past decade there has been a dramatic increase in the amount of available computing and storage resources. The emergence of high performance compute clusters has lead to compute power becoming relatively inexpensive and abundant. With high speed networking many geographi-cally distributed resources can be coupled together, thus resulting in the raw infrastructure of the *computational grid*. The presence of powerful parallel machines has fueled the development of large scale and high performance applications. Standardized programming systems such as MPI, collections of libraries such as Linpack, Paramesh[20], Global Array [12], domain specific frameworks[2], and advanced support for irregular and dynamic applications (such as Charm++ [14]) are facilitating development of such applications. The Globus Tool Kit[8] provides middleware to make these applications run on geographically distributed resources.

There are two major hindrances that need to be overcome to fully utilize the *computational grid*. The first problem is that end users of massively parallel applications have the tedious task of discovering available and most suitable resources, uploading files and babysitting their applications (i.e. monitoring progress, restarting from the last checkpoint if the job crashed, and when the machine is about to be taken down, checkpointing the job and moving it to another machine, if possible).

The second problem is that existing supercomputers can remain underutilized because of the nature of parallel applications and the mechanism available for users to submit jobs. The utilization of resources in an environment with multiple users and multiple Compute Servers is affected by external fragmentation as well as internal fragmentation. *External fragmentation* occurs because individual users have access to only a subset of parallel machines. *Internal fragmentation* occurs when a Compute Server schedules existing jobs in such a way that new jobs cannot be scheduled even while many processor resources are idle within the same Compute Server. The following two scenarios illustrate these obstacles.

- *Internal Fragmentation:* Consider a single parallel machine with 1000 processors. A user wants to run an urgent and important job **A** which needs 600 processors. However, the machine happens to be running a rela-

[1]This work was supported in part by the National Science Foundation under Grant NSF NGS 0103645 and the National Institute of Health under Grant NIH PHS 5 P41 RR05969-04.

tively unimportant but long job **B** on 500 processors. So the important job languishes while 500 processors remain idle.

- *External Fragmentation:* Now consider the following scenario: when a user needs to run a parallel application, all the parallel machines that they have accounts on are busy running important jobs. However, there are several other parallel machines that are idle, but cannot be used since the user does not have an account on them.

Such wastage is clearly undesirable, especially with parallel systems becoming profit centers that sell compute power.

In this paper we present the *Faucets* system which is aimed at simplifying the process of submitting and monitoring jobs for the end user and eliminating inefficiencies in resource utilization. The term *Faucets* draws an analogy with the distribution of water as a utility delivered via faucets.

We contend that the underutilization problem can be solved by treating compute power as a commodity, and by unleashing a market economy for the producers and consumers of compute power. The producers would be the Compute Servers which would run applications for the users and charge the users for the runs.

In the scenario we envisage, users authenticated by a central service submit jobs to the "grid". A job runs on some anonymous supercomputer, and may be moved between supercomputers during its life. A few rare large jobs may also run on multiple supercomputers simultaneously. Users can monitor and interact with their jobs via the Web, and input and output files can be appropriately moved from and to the user's computer. Users pay for the compute power used via the billing services, or barter the unused compute power of their own Compute Server via an accounting service that allows Compute Servers to pool their resources effectively. The basic architecture of the Faucets system for supporting this scenario is described in Section 2.

We plan to improve resource utilization in this scenario by two interdependent classes of mechanisms:

1. Optimizing the usage of each individual parallel machine with smart job schedulers, and

2. Providing automatic, scalable and market-efficient matching between jobs and Compute Servers.

To this end, we develop the notion of **quality of service (QoS) contracts** for parallel jobs (see Section 2.1), which specify the job's resource requirements, its behavior over the range of processors it can use, as well as its payoff, i.e. how much the client will pay for running the job.

An important twist we add to this scenario is the introduction of **Adaptive Jobs:** which can change the number of processors allocated to them at runtime on demand[15]. In a previous paper [15], we described how the Charm++ load balancing framework can be extended to create adaptive jobs. Traditional MPI jobs can also be transformed into adaptive ones via our adaptive implementation of MPI (AMPI [3]).

Resource utilization on individual parallel machines can now be optimized by **smart job schedulers** that shrink and expand the processors allocated to their jobs as needed. In the example above, job B can be shrunk to 400 processors to make the remaining 600 processors available for the important job A, thus fully utilizing the system.

While operating as profit centers in the market economy of parallel jobs, such smart schedulers can further tune their processor allocation to maximize their profit by taking complex payoff functions into account, which may specify premiums for early completion and penalties for delays beyond deadlines. Further, the schedulers incorporate **bid generation algorithms** (Section 5.2), which take into account the current commitments and the grid job "weather" (analogous to the network weather systems [25], and/or "futures" market for perishable commodities) to generate bids for jobs submitted by users. The faucets system must scalably select machines that potentially match the requirements of the jobs, and scalably evaluate and select bids on behalf of users.

## 2 Architecture

In the near future the *computational grid* may consist of tens of thousands of Compute Servers each with its distinct way of functioning. Potentially, millions of jobs, each with a QoS requirement, may be submitted to the grid per day. Resource allocation in such a scenario becomes the problem of matching between the jobs with the available Compute Servers in an efficient (both from the point of view of the client as well as the Compute Servers) and scalable manner.

We have developed a prototype *Faucets* system to experiment with the ideas mentioned earlier. Figure 2 shows a simplified overview of the architecture of our Faucets system.

The main components of the system are Central Faucets Server(FS), Faucets Daemon(FD), Adaptive Queueing System aka Scheduler aka Cluster Manager (CM), Faucets Client (FC), AppSpector Server(AS) and Database(DB).

Each Scheduler (CM) represents an individual Compute Server in the system. The Scheduler running on the supercomputer can be a traditional queuing system, or the Adaptive Job Scheduler in Section 4. Each scheduler is associated with a Database(DB) to store the current status of all the running and scheduled jobs on the Compute Server.

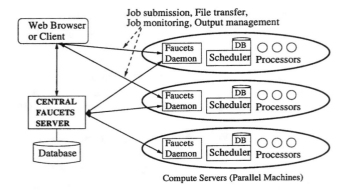

**Figure 1. System Components.**

This Database will be queried for determining the state of the scheduler, based on which the Scheduler has to decide whether to accept a new job or not. Each Scheduler is associated with a Faucets Daemon process which listens on a well-known port. The FD acts like an agent for the Scheduler to communicate with the rest of the Faucets system. At startup each FD registers itself with the Faucets Central Server(FS). The client process sees the FD, but not the actual CM. When FD receives a *bid request* from a client, it queries the CM with that request and receives an appropriate bid which it forwards to the client. The client then chooses the least bid and submits its job to the corresponding FD which in turn starts the job through the CM. In essence to the external world, FD is the representative of the Compute Server to the faucets system.

The Faucets Central Server (FS) is at the heart of the system. It maintains the list of available Compute Servers and refreshes the list by periodically polling the corresponding FDs. The FS also maintains the list of applications clients can run. In addition the FS is also responsible for authenticating the users of the system. It uses a database to store the Users information. This database also stores the directory of available Compute Servers and some information about each one, such as the maximum number of processors it has, the available memory, CPU type, and the address and port number of the FD corresponding to each Compute Server. When the client contacts FS for the list of available Compute Servers, FS returns this directory of FDs.

The user interacts with the system using a web browser or a command-line client or a GUI client by authenticating himself to the Faucets Central Server. To submit a job, the client connects to the Central Server and requests a list of matching supercomputers. The client then connects to each FD and solicits a bid for the desired job. After some interaction between the FD and the Scheduler, the FD either declines the job or replies with a bid. Once the bids are collected, the client chooses a satisfactory bid, and informs

the appropriate FD. At this point the client uploads the input files to the chosen FD and the FD takes over the job and starts it on the Scheduler. Once the job starts, the FD registers the running job with the AppSpector Server(AS). Figure 2 shows our GUI client through which the user specifies the application name, parameters such as minimum (minpe) and maximum (maxpe) number of processors, estimated time, deadline and files to be uploaded to the parallel machine.

AppSpector is the *Job Monitoring* component of the Faucets system. AppSpector server connects to the job through a network connection and buffers the display data so that multiple clients can monitor the job simultaneously. Any authenticated users using the faucets client can connect to their running (or just completed) parallel job using its job-ID via the AppSpector. The AppSpector retrieves dynamic output from the parallel program and provides a graphical representation of the current status to the user, as shown in Figure 3. One section of this display is application specific and the other section generic, providing the processor utilization/throughput of the application on the Compute Server. At any point of the job execution the user can download the output files generated by the job.

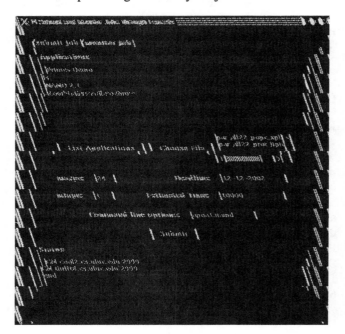

**Figure 2. Faucets Client: Job Submission**

## 2.1 Specifying QOS Requirements

**The Job requirements** portion of the quality-of-service contract must include, at a bare minimum:

- The software environment required by the job. This

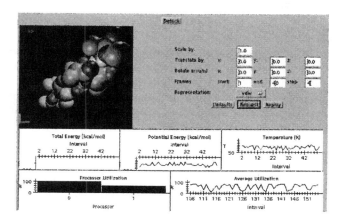

**Figure 3. Faucets Client:AppSpector Display of a NAMD Job**

could include the executable for the job, the host operating system, and the required compilers and libraries.

- The number of processors the job can run on (a single number, a set of numbers, or a range.)

- The amount of time needed to complete the job, and some notion of how this changes with the number of processors.

- The job's payoff; and how this changes with the completion time of the job. Thus a job with a deadline would have a steep post-deadline drop-off in the payoff vs. time function.

In the current implementation, the QoS requirements are simplified to include only the following: the minimum and maximum number of processors, per-processor and total memory requirement, total CPU time, or wall-clock total time, (optionally) the efficiency with minimum and maximum number of processors (with linear interpolation assumed), and a deadline. In addition, an experimental feature includes a payoff function with a soft and hard deadline with specification of relative payoff as a function of time of completion. (payoff at soft deadline, payoff at hard deadline, and penalty after deadline. Linear interpolation is assumed for payoff between soft and hard deadlines).

One of the research issues is to decide the level of detail in the specifications. For example, the completion time as a function of number of processors can be specified by simple linear function (as used above) or more sophisticated models.

Job requirements should also be made machine-independent. So in a scientific application, for example, one might specify the run time as the floating-point operation count times the machine speed divided by the parallel efficiency. An exact answer is, of course, nearly impossible to obtain; but easy to estimate bounds on these quantities are all that are needed.

Other requirements include memory, communication and disk access patterns. For memory, one could list the amount of memory used per processor, as well as some measure of the cache utilization. For communication, one may characterize the number and volume of messages internal to the program, and the communication with outside world, either for continuous interaction or initial/final data transfer. Disk I/O may also be characterized by initial input size, output size, and access pattern during the run itself.[2]

Some applications have distinct phases or components, each with very different requirements. They can potentially be housed on different supercomputers over time. Even when they are running on the same machine, the scheduler may benefit from knowing the shift in performance parameters when the program shifts from one phase to another. The QoS contract will be able to specify such phases and components, and iterative structures around them (if any). Note that to be useful, such a phase must last for several minutes, to justify the overhead of moving the job.

## 2.2 Security Model and Other Considerations

The client authenticates itself to the Faucets Server through a userid, password pair. So every user should obtain an account from the Faucets system. Also the client embeds the userid, password information in any communication with the FS or any FD. But since the FD does not have any accounting information, it contacts the Faucets Central Server again to verify the user's authenticity. In future,the single sign-on feature of the Globus Security Framework(GSI) [10] can be used to avoid these multiple authentication requests to the Faucets Server for the same user.

In many scenarios envisaged in Faucets, the end-user may not have an account with the particular Compute Server that is to run their job. The Faucets system runs the job with a temporary userid. This makes the issue of Compute Server's trust in the client's job more complicated. However, we resolve this issue by identifying classes of secure applications, and allowing each cluster to adopt a different policy and export a different set of applications.

One proposed mechanism is *Mobile Sandboxing*, as described in [17], to trap such untrusted calls and deny service. Also, since each site may have different policies of trust, these Sandboxes have to be configured differently for each Compute Server.

The emergence of JAVA into the realm of high performance computing provides us another alternative class of

---

[2]For example, an out-of-core solver may have extensive online disk usage.

secure applications.

Further, many individual Compute Servers may have their own applications that the administrators trust based on their knowledge of those applications (e.g. locally developed applications). They may include such applications in their list of supported applications. The Faucets Server can then keep track of registered applications from each Compute Server to avoid unnecessary broadcasts of request-for-bids.

In our current prototype, we assume that each parallel machine exports certain "Known Applications" and the user will be able to select one of these available jobs through the Faucets Server. This scheme can be generalized to an auditing-and-certification service for applications. The recent developments and standardization of *WebServices* provides us a better way of doing this. On the lines of the Bayanihan Computing .NET [7], each Compute Server can potentially provide a WebService which allows the *Computational Clients* to choose an application, execute it and retrieve the results. Open Grid Services Architecture (OGSA)[26] describes a standard way of integrating the Grid and Web Technologies. GSI can enable web browsers to single sign-on to multiple Web Servers and also to delegate capabilities to a web server so that the server could act on the client's behalf. Faucets system can significantly leverage the new OGSA enabled Globus Tool Kit components for integration of our system with WebServices.

## 3   Improving Ease of Use

The Faucet systems also aims at simplifying and automating the process of running parallel applications for the end user. For one, users don't need to learn the peculiarities of multiple queuing systems (and their installations) used by different Compute Servers. Input files are uploaded and outputs downloaded automatically. As discussed in the section on Architecture, the web-based Appspector subsystem makes it easy to interact with parallel jobs, irrespective of where they are running. We are also implementing features that allow the system to restart users jobs from their last checkpoint if the system had to stop the job or if the machine had any transient hardware problem. We will also make use of Data Grid [28] components of Globus for managing files, for the purpose of storage and visualizations.

## 4   Improving the Utility of a Server

Individual Compute Servers must be able to maximize their utilization (and profit, in the general case). The job schedulers in Faucets system make use of *adaptive jobs* to this end.

An **adaptive job** is a parallel program that can dynamically (i.e. at run-time) shrink or expand the number of processors it is running on, in response to an external command or an internal event. The number of processors can vary within the bounds specified when the job is started. Typically, the user will specify the bounds taking into consideration memory usage and efficiency of the job on a given number of processors. We have developed adaptive jobs in both Charm++ and MPI. The performance and implementation of adaptive jobs is presented in [15].

### 4.1   Smart Job Scheduling

Once adaptive jobs are feasible, with their characteristics and payoff functions specified in the QoS, they enable the design of intelligent job schedulers that aim at maximizing system utility. Most current production queuing systems are incapable of exploiting the opportunities created by adaptive jobs. We have developed an adaptive job scheduler that can manage such adaptive jobs [15].

The scheduler is triggered when a new job arrives in the system, and when a running job finishes (or requests a change in the number of processors assigned to it). On arrival, the scheduler analyzes the job's resource requirements and deadlines to decide if it can be accepted.

The scheduler would try to maximize a system utility metric. This metric can be system utilization, job response time, or a more complex profit metric, specifying the amount the user pays if his job is finished before the deadline. Hence if a high profit job arrives and has a tight deadline, the low priority jobs can be shrunk and the freed processors can be allocated to the high priority job. The communication topology also needs to be considered because the shrunk jobs should continue to have locality and a contiguous set of processors need to be assigned to the new job. Jobs may also have to be check-pointed and restarted at a later point in time and possibly at another (subcontracted) Compute Server with a different architecture.

Decisions on allocating processors to jobs is taken by a strategy that can be plugged in to the adaptive job scheduler. One of the earliest strategy we implemented is presented in [15]. It is a simple strategy that tries to maximize system utilization by using a variant of equipartitioning: Each job gets a proportionate shared of available processors, while respecting the specified upper and lower bounds on the number of processors for each job.

The utility metric can also be maximizing the payoff function from running a job before its deadline: Such jobs typically have a soft deadline, and a hard deadline. The payoff for the job linearly decreases after the soft deadline, and may have a significant penalty after the hard deadline. In such a scenario, running a new job may delay other jobs and lead to a loss in profit. So the payoff from the new job must at least compensate for the loss mentioned above or the job must be rejected. The strategy must find time windows for the job in its processor-time Gantt chart before the job's deadline. If enough time cannot be allocated for the job it must be rejected. We are currently in the process of developing such a strategy. Our current prototype strategy accepts a job if it is profitable and can be scheduled to run now or at a finite lookahead in future.

## 5 Market-Efficient Server Selection

This section describes the components of the Faucets system that decide which job runs on which Compute Server. For each component, we describe its current implementation and ongoing work. We then also comment on research issues that will arise in scalable implementations in future.

### 5.1 Scalable Identification of Potential Servers

In the current implementation, the client software (but not the end users personally) gets a list of all Compute Servers from the Central Faucets Server (FS) , and broadcasts a request for bids, with QoS requirements, to all of them. Ongoing work involves implementation of simple filtering services at the FS so that static properties (such as number of processors and amount of memory per processor) as well as dynamic properties (e.g. current availability of the Compute Server) are taken into account to eliminate Compute Servers from the broadcast. In future, the broadcast itself will be handled by a distributed Faucets system, making the potential-server selection scale up, even in the presence of millions of jobs submissions a day.

### 5.2 Bid Generation Algorithms

Probably the most research intensive task will be development of algorithms for generating bids for jobs submitted via the request-for-bids broadcasts. These algorithms will run at individual Compute Servers, and will reflect the characteristics of the Compute Server, its orientation to risk and profit. The bidding decisions can be potentially based on local factors, such as how busy the Compute Server is during the time-period covered by the job, and how far into the future is the job's deadline. For example, a simple strategy may be to set a low bid if the job's deadline is in the very near future (e.g. next hour), and the machine is relatively free.

The current strategies we have implemented include a baseline strategy that always returns a multiplier of "1.0" if it can run the job. (The bid is converted to Dollar amount by multiplying the CPU-seconds needed for the job with a normalized cost and the multiplier returned by the bidding algorithm). Another implemented strategy returns a multiplier linearly interpolated between $k(1 - \alpha)$ and $k(1 + \beta)$

depending on what the average system utilization is likely to be between the current time and the deadline of the proposed job. $k$, $\alpha$ and $\beta$ are parameters of this strategy (current values we use are 1, 0.5 and 2.0). We expect $\alpha$ and $\beta$ to be associated with the risk the Compute Server is willing to take to maximize profit, and $k$ with urgency of the job for the cluster. (For the job in the example above, with a near-by deadline, one expects to use a low value of $k$).

In future versions, the bid may also depend on non-local factors, such as "what is the average price of similar contracts in the recent past, in the whole system?" or "how busy is the entire computational grid likely to be during the period covered by the deadline?". For this, bid generators need support from the Faucets system.

#### 5.2.1 Faucets Support for bidding

The Faucets system will provide such global information to Compute Serversand/or their agents running on faucets infrastructure. The particular mechanisms we envisage supporting include: maintaining a history of every individual contract over recent time periods, summaries based on various histogram metrics (e.g., grouping jobs based on the minimum or maximum number of processors they need), trends for future usage based on customer surveys, etc.

### 5.3 Scalable Bid Evaluation and QoS Contract

In the current implementation, each client receives all the bids and selects one of the Compute Servers for the job based on a simple criteria (such as least cost, or earliest promised completion time). We expect this scheme to scale to reasonably large grids (consisting of hundreds of Compute Servers). However, in a larger grid of the future, a scalable mechanism is needed for Compute Server selection for a couple of reasons. Firstly, the large number of Compute Servers will make it impractical for each client to deal with a flood of bids. Secondly, since many bid-requests may be in progress at the same time, a two phase protocol will be needed to get a firm commitment from the selected Compute Server (which may have received a more lucrative job in between).

An issue for future research here is a scalable asynchronous system for bid evaluation and contract confirmation. We envisage a system in which each Compute Server as well as client is represented by several agent processes running on the distributed faucets framework. The server agents communicate with their master Faucet Daemons, as well as with bid commitment algorithms of the Faucets system. The client agents simply specify user-specific selection criteria to evaluation.

We plan to publish a generic interface for the bid-generation algorithm, allowing other researchers to test their bid generation algorithms against each other.

## 5.4 Simulation System

To evaluate the scalability of the framework and to compare the effectiveness of alternative bidding strategies, we have built a simulation framework: each entity in the Faucets system — clients, Compute Servers, Faucets-Server (and its distributed servers in future), job schedulers with their bid-generation algorithms, and application programs — is represented by an object, and discrete-event simulation is carried out over patterns of job submissions under study.

## 5.5 Alternative Contexts for use of the Faucets

The Faucets system can be used in a variety of possibly overlapping contexts, as described below.

### 5.5.1 Pay-for-use system

Clearly, the primary aim of the Faucets system will be in a context in which users will pay for running each job. The bids in this context will be Dollar amounts. It may be necessary to have regulatory mechanisms in place to avoid misuse of markets: limits on how far the bids can be from some notion of "normal" price can be one such mechanism. It may also be necessary to have additional priority to jobs of national importance to prevent denial-of-service attacks on such systems.

### 5.5.2 Academic Applications

How can the current practices in the Science and Engineering academic research transition to a market based economy? This research suggests that management of cycle-providing centers be decoupled from users and handed over to private (for-profit) producers. Users can then be allocated quota in terms of Service-Units (SUs) as before. However, the bids generated by the Compute Servers will now be multipliers to SUs rather than Dollar amounts. ("I will run your job that needs 1000 SUs, but I will charge 1400 SUs for it.", or "I will only charge 750 SUs for it"). This will lead to bringing market efficiency to such centers. Traditional supercomputing centers supported by NSF can still be in the business of providing expert services and consulting for effective parallelization of parallel jobs.

### 5.5.3 Bartering

The Faucets architecture is equally suitable to create co-operative computing environments where a community of individuals share each others' resources. Those who are contributing to a common pool can get access to that pool [23]. We have a reasonably sophisticated accounting system in place for deciding how much resources each contributor can get. Each contributor earns *credit* for sharing his/her resource and can use up the credit when needed. In our architecture the *Faucets Central Server* keeps track of the credits of all the collaborating clusters. Each user belongs to a single *Home Cluster* and normally whenever he tries to submit a job, the system tries to submit the job to the user's Home Cluster. But if the resources on the Home Cluster are not available and the Home Cluster has enough credits the system tries to submit the job to any of the collaborating Compute Servers and the appropriate number of credits are added to the Compute Server that executed the job and equal amount is deducted from the Home Cluster's account. The credits can be amount of the computational units the job has taken to execute or any other function of it. This mode of bartering of computational units is very useful when the participating entities in the Grid have to be both service provides and consumers.

### 5.5.4 Intranets

When a company or a laboratory wishes its Compute Server's resources to be pooled among its users, the Faucets system can be used with some small modifications. Different jobs may have priorities assigned by management. Pre-emption of low priority jobs may be allowed (with automatic restart from a checkpoint later). Further, some elements of the bartering scheme may be incorporated in order to allow individual departments or users from getting "fair usage" from resources, so that high priority jobs do not forever starve a subset of user, who may own some of the resources.

## 6 Related Work

Several projects have studied resource allocation and job management on the Computational Grid. Condor-G [11], Legion [1], SETI@home, Entropia's PC Grid Computing, Parabon's Pioneer, NetSolve [9], Application Level Scheduling (AppLeS)[6], and Bayanihan [16] are distributed and ubiquitous resource allocation frameworks.

Condor-G [11] gives end-users a unified view of all the dispersed resources they are authorized to use. It gathers information about the Grid resources and the job requests from the users in the form of ClassAds and with the help of the Matchmaking framework [24] it tries to determine where to execute user jobs. The ClassAds are similar to the QoS contracts and the Bids generated by the Faucets system. With ClassAds, the system matches jobs to resources; in contrast, with Faucets, choosing the appropriate "bid" (and hence the Compute Server) is up to the client (or Client's Agent). The Condor-G match making algorithms are applicable in our context at the stage of screening the Compute Servers to get a list of potential Compute Servers.

Legion [1] takes an object oriented approach to the problem of resource scheduling by formulating an object placement process model. The Coordinator/Mapper(CM) is responsible for making the mapping decision. Legion concentrates more on providing basic infrastructure for the grid similar to Globus[8]. SETI@home, Entropia's PC Grid Computing, Parabon's Pioneer and Bayanihan [16, 7] employ a master-slave paradigm where a single master server controls the distribution of available work among different worker agents sitting on the users desktops. Net-Solve [9] is a client-agent-server RPC-based system to solve computational problems. Its middleware system provides a computational framework for "task farming" applications with load balancing and scheduling strategies to distribute tasks evenly. NetSolve scheduling strategies do not have the economy model built into them. Both NetSolve and Nimrod concentrate on scheduling master-slave based loosely coupled independent tasks. Faucets, on the other hand, focuses on parallel jobs. AppLeS (Application Level Scheduling)[6] on the other hand takes the approach of developing individual scheduling agents for each application, thus adapting them to the execution-time characteristics of dynamic, distributed environments. The user must provide an application-specific performance model, describing its structure and execution activities, and the application performance criteria.

Many resource allocation frameworks have also studied and incorporated *computational economics* and *computational markets* [18, 19, 22, 4, 27, 5, 13, 21]. Enterprise [27] is one of the earliest decentralized market-like schedulers for load sharing in distributed computational environments. The protocol has *announcement, bid, and award* stages. In the *announcement* stage, a *client* broadcasts a request for bids which includes a description of the task to be run, an estimate of required processing time, and a numeric task priority. Idle *contractors* reply with bids containing estimated completion times for the client's announced task. The client collects bids from responding contractors, evaluates all the bids, and awards its task to the best bidder (with the earliest estimated completion time). Since Enterprise has no concept of market price, the flexibility of the system is inhibited by constraining the criteria by which contractors and clients could make decisions. Also, it is limited to the execution of independent tasks on compatible workstations. Spawn [5] takes a slightly different approach, where a seller executes an *auction* (sealed, second-price auctions) process to manage the sale of his workstation's processing resources, and a buyer executes an application that *bids* for time on nearby auctions. Nimrod/G [22] has a computational economy based distributed scheduling component that tries to select the resources that meet the deadline and minimize the cost of computation. In addition to addressing these issues, *Faucets* system aids resource providers in their price decision process (and hence scheduling), to maximize their profit and to attract more customers.

## 7 Summary and Future Work

We described *Faucets*, a system that supports the notion of compute power as a utility. Faucets is designed for parallel jobs, although it can also be used for sequential jobs. Users submit jobs with their Quality-of-Service requirements to the Faucets system, via clients (command-line, GUI, or Browser based clients are supported and provided). The Faucets system identifies the Compute Servers that may be able to run the job and sends the QoS requirements to them. The Compute Servers themselves run a daemon that interfaces with the Faucets system, and mediates with the local scheduler. The local scheduler may submit a bid for the job. The Faucets system, taking the users-specified selection criteria into account, selects the best bid. User's job files are then uploaded to the system. Although the user doesn't explicitly know which Compute Server is running his job, he can connect to it and examine its output and current status via a web-based server called AppSpector. The output files can be downloaded to the user computer (or other storage on the network).

One unique aspect of the Faucets system is its use of adaptive jobs, which can change the number of processors they use on command. Adaptive Queuing Systems (Schedulers) that take advantage of such jobs have been designed for use within the Compute Servers of the Faucets system. Such Schedulers have a competitive advantage over normal schedulers in the free-market economy of compute power unleashed by the grid via Faucets.

The Faucets system is in operation at the University of Illinois, with two research clusters. Soon, it will be extended to several other clusters, some via a bartering subsystem of Faucets.

We described architecture of the Faucets system, and its components. We also identified research issues for future, which involve more sophisticated bid-generation algorithms and scalable bid-evaluation framework. Further, improvements that simplify parallel job administration for the user are being implemented in the system. As a result, we expect Faucets to be a widely used system for utilizing resources on the computational grid.

## References

[1] A.S.Grimsaw and W.A.Wulf. Legion: A view from 50,000 feet. In *Fifth IEEE International Symposium on High Performance Distributed Computing*, 1996.

[2] Milind Bhandarkar and L. V. Kalé. A Parallel Framework for Explicit FEM. In M. Valero, V. K. Prasanna, and S. Vajpeyam, editors, *Proceedings of the International Conference on High Performance Computing (HiPC 2000), Lecture Notes in Computer Science*, volume 1970, pages 385–395. Springer Verlag, December 2000.

[3] Milind Bhandarkar, L. V. Kale, Eric de Sturler, and Jay Hoeflinger. Object-Based Adaptive Load Balancing for MPI Programs. In *Proceedings of the International Conference on Computational Science, San Francisco, CA, LNCS 2074*, pages 108–117, May 2001.

[4] B.N.Chun and D.E.Culler. REXEC: A decentralized, secure remote execution environment for clusters. In *Communication, Architecture, and Applications for Network-Based Parallel Computing*, pages 1–14, 2000.

[5] C.A.Waldspurger, T.Hogg, B.A.Huberman, J.O.Kephart, and W.S.Stornetta. Spawn: A distributed computational economy. *Software Engineering*, 18(2):103–117, 1992.

[6] D.Zagorodnov, F.Berman, and R.Wolski. Application scheduling on the information power Grid. Technical Report CS2000-0644, 11, 2000.

[7] L.F.G.Sarmenta et.al. Bayanihan computing .NET: Grid computing with XML web services. In *Global and Peer-to-Peer Computing Workshop at CCGrid*, 2002.

[8] I. Foster and C. Kesselman. Globus: A Metacomputing Infrastructure Toolkit. *International Journal of Supercomputer Applications*, 11(2):115–128, 1997.

[9] H.Casanova, M.Kim, J.S.Plank, and J.J.Dongarra. Adaptive scheduling for task farming with grid middleware. *The International Journal of High Performance Computing Applications*, 13(3):231–240, Fall 1999.

[10] I.T.Foster, C.Kesselman, G.Tsudik, and S.Tuecke. A security architecture for computational grids. In *ACM Conference on Computer and Communications Security*, pages 83–92, 1998.

[11] J.Frey, T.Tannenbaum, I.Foster, M.Livny, and S.Tuecke. Condor-G: A computation management agent for multi-institutional grids. In *Tenth IEEE Symposium on High Performance Distributed Computing (HPDC10)*, 2001.

[12] J.Nielocha, R.Harrison, and R.Littlefield. Global arrays: A portable shared-memory programming model for distributed memory computers. In *Supercomputing*, 1994.

[13] J.S.Chase, D.C.Anderson, P.N.Thakar, A.Vahdat, and R.P.Doyle. Managing energy and server resources in hosting centres. In *Symposium on Operating Systems Principles*, pages 103–116, 2001.

[14] L. V. Kale and Sanjeev Krishnan. Charm++: Parallel Programming with Message-Driven Objects. In Gregory V. Wilson and Paul Lu, editors, *Parallel Programming using C++*, pages 175–213. MIT Press, 1996.

[15] Laxmikant V. Kalé, Sameer Kumar, and Jayant DeSouza. A malleable-job system for timeshared parallel machines. In *2nd IEEE/ACM International Symposium on Cluster Computing and the Grid (CCGrid 2002)*, May 2002.

[16] L.F.G.Sarmenta. Bayanihan: Web-based volunteer computing using java. In *Proc. of the 2nd International Conference on World-Wide Computing and its Applications*, 1998.

[17] M.Litzkow, T.Tannenbaum, J.Basney, and M.Livny. Checkpoint and migration of unix processes in the Condor distributed processing system. Technical Report 1346, University of Wisconsin-Madison Computer Sciences, April 1997.

[18] M.S.Miller and K.E.Drexler. Markets and computation: Agoric open systems. *The Ecology of Computation Ed. B. A. Huberman. North-Holland*, pages 133–176, 1988.

[19] M.Stonebraker, R.Devine, M.Kornacker, W.Litwin, A.Pfeffer, A.Sah, and C.Staelin. An economic paradigm for query processing and data migration in Mariposa. In *Third International Conference on Parallel and Distributed Information Systems, Austin, TX*, 1994.

[20] P.MacNeice, K.M.Olson, C.Mobarry, R.deFainchtein, and C.Packer. Paramesh : A parallel adaptive mesh refinement community toolkit. *Computer Physics Communications*, 126:330–354, 2000.

[21] R.Braynard, D.Kostic, A.Rodriguez, J.Chase, and A.Vahdat. Opus: An overlay peer utility service. In *Proceedings of the 5th International Conference on Open Architectures and Network Programming (OPENARCH)*, 2002.

[22] R.Buyya, D.Abramson, and J.Giddy. Nimrod/G: An architecture of a resource management and scheduling system in a global computational grid. In *HPC Asia 2000*, pages 283–289, 2000.

[23] R.Buyya, D.Abramson, J.Giddy, and H.Stockinger. Economic models for resource management and scheduling in grid computing. *The Journal of Concurrency and Computation: Practice and Experience (CCPE), Wiley Press*, 2002.

[24] R.Raman, M.Livny, and M.H.Solomon. Matchmaking: Distributed resource management for high throughput computing. In *HPDC*, 1998.

[25] R.Wolski, N.T.Spring, and J.Hayes. The Network Weather Service: A distributed resource performance forecasting service for metacomputing. *Future Generation Computer Systems*, 15(5–6):757–768, 1999.

[26] S.Tuecke, K.Czajkowski, I.Foster, J.Rey, F.Steve, and G.Carl. Grid service specification, 2002.

[27] T.Malone et al. Enterprise: A market-like task scheduller for distributed computing environments. *In The Ecology of Computation, B.A. Huberman Ed., 40 Amsterdam, North-Holland*, pages 177–205, 1988.

[28] W.Allcock, J.Bester, J.Bresnahan, A.Chervenak, I.Foster, C. Kesselman, S. Meder, V. Nefedova, D. Quesnel, and S. Tuecke. Data management and transfer in highperformance computational grid environments. *Parallel Computing*, 2001.

# A Genetic Algorithm based Approach for Scheduling Decomposable Data Grid Applications

Seonho Kim and Jon B. Weissman
*Dept. of Computer Science and Engineering,*
*University of Minnesota, Twin Cities*
*shkim@cs.umn.edu*

## Abstract

*Data Grid technology promises geographically distributed scientists to access and share physically distributed resources such as compute resource, networks, storage, and most importantly data collections for large-scale data intensive problems. Because of the massive size and distributed nature of these datasets, scheduling Data Grid applications must consider communication and computation simultaneously to achieve high performance. In many Data Grid applications, Data can be decomposed into multiple independent sub datasets and distributed for parallel execution and analysis. In this paper, we exploit this property and propose a novel Genetic Algorithm based approach that automatically decomposes data onto communication and computation resources. The proposed GA-based scheduler takes advantage of the parallelism of decomposable Data Grid applications to achieve the desired performance level. We evaluate the proposed approach comparing with other algorithms. Simulation results show that the proposed GA-based approach can be a competitive choice for scheduling large Data Grid applications in terms of both scheduling overhead and the relative solution quality as compared to other algorithms.*

## 1. Introduction

Grid computing has become a promising technology for providing seamless access to heterogeneous resources and achieving a high performance benefit in wide-area environments [1]. In its early stages, Grid computing research focused mainly on the coordination of geographically distributed compute resources for high performance. However, in many areas of science and engineering such as high-energy physics and aerospace, requirements have emerged for collaborating and sharing huge amounts of widely distributed data as well as sharing high-performance compute resources. For example, in LHC experiments at CERN, huge amounts of data (tera byte or peta byte in scale) collected by observing collisions of particles, are analyzed through different levels of data processing operations [14]. Data Grids have been proposed to address this data requirement [18]. Data Grid technology enables geographically distributed scientists to access and share physically distributed heterogeneous resources such as compute resources, network, storage, and widely distributed datasets for large-scale data intensive problems.

While a Computational Grid achieves high performance mainly by scheduling applications to powerful computing resources, communication and computation should be considered jointly when scheduling Data Grid jobs because of the potential communication bottleneck originating from the massive size and the widely distributed nature of datasets. There have been studies on scheduling computation and communication jointly for Data Grid applications [2][3][4][5]. However, most of them do not reflect a characteristic typical in many data intensive applications, that data can be decomposed into multiple independent sub datasets and distributed for parallel execution and analysis. We exploit the parallelism to achieve desired performance levels when scheduling large Data Grid applications.

When parallel applications require multiple data from multiple data sources, the scheduling problem is challenging along several dimensions – how should data be decomposed, should data be moved to computation or vice-versa, and which computing resources should be used. We can solve the problem optimally by adding some constraints (e.g., decomposing data into sub datasets of the same size). Another approach is to use heuristics such as those based on optimization techniques e.g. genetic algorithm, simulated annealing, and tabu search.

This paper proposes a novel Genetic Algorithm (GA) based approach to address scheduling of decomposable Data Grid applications, where communication and computation are considered at the same time. The proposed algorithm is novel in two ways. First, it automatically balances load, that is, data in our case, onto communication/computation resources and generates a near optimal schedule. Second, it does not require a job to be pre-decomposed - most GA based approaches for scheduling problems have addressed the problem of scheduling $m$ pre-decomposed tasks onto $n$ computing nodes. We examined the relative quality of the solution generated with the GA-based approach as compared to other algorithms (constraint based approaches). We developed a suite of algorithms for comparison: two Divisible Load Theory (DLT)-based algorithms - baseline algorithm and Iterative DLT (IDLT), Constrained DLT (CDLT), and Tasks on Data Present (TDP).

We found that the GA based approach with a good initial population, in general, outperform other algorithms. However, some approaches (IDLT and TDP) perform competitively under certain Grid configurations compared to the GA based algorithms because their scheduling time is much less compared to that of GA based approaches. Since the running time of the GA-based approaches is negligible for large jobs, the proposed GA-based approach can achieve the desired performance level for large jobs - common in Data Grid applications such as CMS experiments [14].

This paper is organized as follows. Some related works are reviewed in Section 2. In Section 3, problem space and models are described. Section 4 presents the proposed GA-based approach. Experimental results are discussed in Section 5. Finally, we conclude and discuss conclusion and future work in Section 6.

## 2. Related Work

In data intensive environments, the location of input data objects should be taken into consideration when selecting resources for a job. Job scheduling in data intensive environments, has recently been studied [2][3][4][5]. [2][5] examines several scheduling heuristics and several data replication strategies. In ChicSim [2], they found that benefits such as good system utilization and low response time can be achieved when jobs are always scheduled where data is located. In Bricks [5], they examined several scheduling mechanisms considering computing resources and location of datasets as well as the impact of data replication. In [4], Park et al. propose a new scheduling model of executing a job on one site while considering both computation and communication in a Data Grid environment. They found that replication of data has considerable impact on enhancing the performance of the scheduler. Orlando et al [3] examined the on-line MCT (Minimum Completion Time) heuristic strategy for scheduling high performance data mining tasks on top of the Knowledge Grid. The most important difference between these works and our work is that the parallelism is not considered in these works. Parallelism significantly complicates the scheduling problem because problem partitioning now becomes an integral part of the scheduling process.

Divisible Load Theory (DLT) has recently emerged as a powerful tool for modeling data-intensive computational problems and allowing tractable performance analysis of systems incorporating communication and computations issues [6][7][8][9]. DLT exploits the parallelism of a divisible application, a model of computation which is continuously divisible into parts of arbitrary size (chunks), by distributing loads in a single source onto multiple computing resources. However, in the real world, DLT is not applicable directly to the problem of finding a globally optimal distribution of load for applications requiring multiple datasets from different distributed data sources because the system of equations is under-constrained. In [8], Ko et al. suggested a two-step approach to address this problem: (1) finding the optimal number of computing nodes (a set) to distribute a particular load, and (2) balancing load over sets. Wong [9] addresses this problem by adding the additional constraint that each worker node receives the same load fraction from each data source. However, any solution provided by these approaches is not globally optimal.

The Genetic Algorithm (GA) has widely been used as a practical and robust optimization and search method in various areas [10][11][13]. GA has recently been applied to many scheduling problems [10][11][17] which are, in general, NP-complete [16]. Most GA based approaches for scheduling problems have addressed the problem of scheduling $m$ pre-decomposed tasks onto $n$ computing nodes. However our approach is different in that we design and apply a novel GA-based approach for the decomposition of a job into multiple sub-tasks while simultaneously considering communication and computation.

## 3. Problem Description and Models

We consider a virtual organization (VO) Grid model that is applicable to numerous distributed science applications such as high energy and nuclear physics, climate analysis, and bio-informatics, to name a few. A VO consists of $n$ virtual sites. We assume virtual sites are connected to the Grid with a relatively low bandwidth network relative to the network within a virtual site. A virtual site may consist of multiple physical sites if they are interconnected by a high bandwidth network. Each site consists of computing resources, storage systems, and large data collections. A virtual site, e.g., in the MONARC [15] context, can be thought of as a "regional center", a composite object containing a number of data servers and processing nodes where all are connected to a LAN. In this paper, we consider scheduling of a single parallel Data Grid application onto a network. Scheduling multiple Data Grid applications competing for shared resources is a subject of future work.

### 3.1 Job and Data Model
We target data intensive applications that can be decomposed into multiple independent subtasks and

executed in parallel across multiple sites without any interaction among sub tasks. We consider job decomposition by decomposing input data objects into multiple smaller data objects of arbitrary size and processing them on multiple virtual sites. For example, in theory, HEP jobs are arbitrarily divisible at event granularity and intermediate data product processing granularity [14]. The physical datasets may represent raw data (collected with detectors) or an intermediate data product stored at different locations. We assume that a job requires a very large logical input data set (D) that consists of m physical datasets and each physical dataset (of size $L_k$) resides at a data source ($DS_k$, k=1..m) of a particular site. The scheduling problem is to decompose D into datasets ($D_i$, i=1..n) across n virtual sites in a VO given its initial physical decomposition. We assume that the decomposed data can be analyzed on any site by applying the same data parallel operation p. Hence a decomposable job J can be modeled as follows:

$p(D_i)$ : an operator p is applied to $D_i$ at site i

$p_{aggr}$: an operator aggregating output data sets

$$J = p(D) = p_{aggr}(p(D_1), p(D_2), \dots p(D_n))$$

$$size(D) = \sum_{k=1}^{m} L_k \quad D = \sum_{i=1}^{n} D_i$$

We assume that the cost of p in processing $D_i$ is linear in the size of data object $D_i$ and that the size of output data generated by p is linear with respect to the size of input data $D_i$. However, both of these assumptions can be easily relaxed.

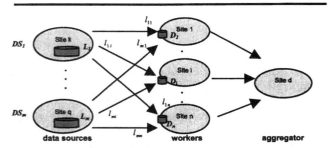

**Figure 1. Data Decomposition and processing**

Figure 1 shows how the logical input data (D) is decomposed onto networks and computing resources. A dataset of size $L_k$ in a data source $DS_k$ is decomposed into $\{ l_{ki} : L_k = \sum l_{ki}$, where i=1..n } and transferred to each worker site. After processing the datasets transferred to site i ($D_i$, where size($D_i$) = $d_i$, $d_i = \sum l_{ki}$, k=1.. m), the output is transferred to the destination site and aggregated. The size of output data is a function of the size of the data ($d_i$).

## 3.2 Cost Model

The execution time of a subtask allocated to the site i ($T_i$) and the turn around time of a job J ($T_{turn\_around\_time}$) can be expressed as follows:

$$T_i = T_{input\_cm}(i) + T_{cp}(i) + T_{output\_cm}(i,d)$$

$$T_{turnaround\_time} = \max_{i=1,\dots,n} T_i$$

The cost ($T_i$) includes input data transfer ($T_{input\_cm}(i)$), computation ($T_{cp}(i)$), and output data transfer to the client at the destination site d ($T_{output\_cm}(i,d)$). The turnaround time of an application is the maximum among all the execution times of the sub tasks.

$$T_{input\_cm}(i) = \max_{k=1\dots m} \{l_{ki} \cdot \frac{1}{z_{ki}}\}$$

$$T_{cp}(i) = d_i \cdot \omega_i$$

$$T_{output\_cm}(i,d) = f(d_i) \cdot z_{id}$$

where $z_{ij}$ : the network bandwidth between site i and j

$\omega_i$ : the computing time to process a unit dataset at site i

$f(d_i)$ : output data size : a function of the size of input data

We assume that data from multiple data sources can be transferred to a site i concurrently in the wide area environment and computation starts only after the assigned data set is totally transferred to the site. The consideration of the data replication and the communication/computation overlapping is out of scope of this paper and a subject of future work.

Hence, the problem of scheduling a divisible job onto n sites can be stated as deciding the portion of original workload (D) to be allocated to each site, that is, finding a distribution of $\{l_{ki}\}$ which minimizes the turn-around time of a job. The proposed GA-based approach uses this cost model when evaluating solutions at each generation.

## 4. GA-based Job Decomposition/ Scheduling

The GA based search methods are rooted from the mechanisms of evolution and natural genetics [10][13]. They search large solution spaces to find near-optimal solutions. A general genetic algorithm consists of three steps: 1) Population initialization 2) Evaluation of the initial population 3) Evolution (selection/ crossover/ mutation/ evaluation). The final step is applied iteratively until stopping condition is met. In this paper, we use the notations and conventions outlined in [13].

### 4.1 Problem Representation for GA

**4.1.1 Chromosome Representation.** To apply the GA approach to an optimization problem, a solution needs to be represented as a chromosome encoded as a set of strings. We designed a representation for our problem as follows. Given **n** sites, a job is decomposed into **n** sub tasks and each task is allocated to one of **n** sites. The job may require multiple input files distributed among **m** data sources. A chromosome consists of **n** genes and each gene is composed of **m** sub-genes as shown in Fig. 2. Each gene in a chromosome matches a task allocated to a site. That is, a gene $g_i$ corresponds to a task $t_i$ assigned to site $S_i$ for $1 \leq i \leq n$. Each sub-gene of a gene is associated with a real value, $f_{ki}$, in the range 0 to 1, where $1 \leq k \leq m$ and $1 \leq i \leq n$. This value represents a portion of workload assigned to task $t_i$ from data source $DS_k$, the $S_k$ containing the required input data. Since $f_{ki}$ is a portion of workload $L_i$ in $DS_i$, $\sum_{i=1}^{n} f_{ki} = 1$, for each **k** from **1** to **m** [Gene-Value Constraint]. In order to associate a sub gene with a float value, a binary string representation of a float is used [12]. We discuss this in more detail when we discuss the mutation operation.

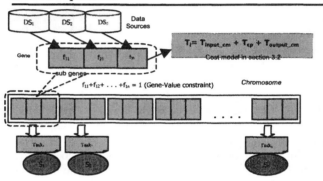

**Figure 2. Chromosome Representation**

**4.1.2 Fitness Function and Evaluation.** Each chromosome is associated with a fitness value evaluated by a fitness function (or objective function) and all chromosomes in the population are ranked by these values. The associated fitness value is the time when the last subtask finishes its execution. The cost model discussed in section 3.2 is used as a fitness function.

**4.1.3 Population Initialization.** In this step, a collection of chromosomes is generated as an initial population. We developed two methods: Random Initialization (GA_Random) and Initialization based on application hint (GA_Hint). GA_Random spawns a pool of chromosomes randomly and selects a predetermined number of chromosomes after evaluating chromosomes according to their fitness values. The basic idea behind the method GA_Hint is using application specific information (e.g. the ratio of computation to communication) to generate a seed chromosome of good quality (high fitness value). Intuitively, computation intensive jobs would be better scheduled on sites with powerful computing resources, while communication intensive jobs on sites with required input data sets to reduce data transfer time. We calculate

$cap_i = comp_i \cdot ccRatio + data_i / ccRatio$ for each site, where $comp_i$ is the normalized computing power of site $i$, $data_i$ represents the normalized portion of required input data sets residing in site $i$ and $ccRatio$ is the non-zero ratio of computation and communication. The value of each gene is, then, set with $cap_i \big/ \sum_{i=1}^{n} cap_i$. Now each sub gene of a gene has the same value. Since data transfers from other data source sites to a data source site are unnecessary, we adjust values of sub genes representing the transfer of input data sets from other data source sites. We use the sigmoid function to smoothly and continuously threshold those values: $value_{adjusted} = \dfrac{value_{current}}{1 + e^{-a \cdot \log(ccRatio)}}$. Finally, a predefined number of slightly different twin chromosomes are generated mutating the seed chromosome. After extensive experiments, we found that a=2 gives the best result. In order to prevent premature convergence, identical chromosomes are not allowed as members of the initial population.

**4.1.4 Selection Methods.** Two selection schemes are implemented and tested: rank-based roulette wheel selection scheme [13] and proportionate selection scheme. The rank-based roulette wheel selection scheme allocates a sector on a roulette wheel to each chromosome. The ratio of angles of two adjacent sectors is a constant. The basic idea of rank-based roulette wheel selection is to allocate larger sector angle to better chromosomes so that better solutions will be included in the next generation with higher probability. A new chromosome for the next generation is cloned after a chromosome as an offspring if a randomly generated number falls in the sector corresponding to the chromosome. Alternatively, the proportionate selection scheme generates chromosomes for the next generation only from a predefined percentage of the previous population.

**4.1.5 Crossover Operation.** In this step, pairs of chromosomes are picked at random from the current population and a uniform crossover operator is applied only if a randomly generated number is less than a predefined crossover rate ($r_x$) (chromosome-level crossover). For each gene in a chromosome, a random number is generated and two genes are exchanged only if the number is less than a predefined gene crossover rate ($r_{gx}$) (gene-level crossover). After crossover, each chromosome is normalized to meet the Gene-Value Constraint. From extensive experiments, we found the proposed GA-based approaches works with $r_x=r_{gx}=0.6$.

**4.1.6 Mutation Operation.** After the crossover operation, chromosomes are subjected to a mutation operation. Each sub gene contains a binary array string representation of a 32 bit floating point number as shown in Fig. 2 and randomly selected bits are flipped from 0 to 1 or vice versa. Since real numbers associated with each sub gene are in the range 0 to 1, the mutation operator flips only bits from the mantissa part. We tested two different mutation schemes: uniform mutation and two points mutation. For both schemes, two parameters are given: mutation rate $(r_m)$ and gene mutation rate $(r_{gm})$. For each chromosome in current population, a random number is generated and the mutation operator is applied only if the random number is less than $r_m$. If a chromosome is subjected to the mutation operation (chromosome-level mutation), then the two points mutation scheme selects two genes randomly and sub genes of one of the two genes are mutated (gene-level mutation). Each bit from the mantissa is flipped only if a random number is less than $r_m$. After mutating one of two genes, the sub-gene values of the other gene are revised as shown in figure 3. On the other hand, in the uniform mutation scheme, all genes in a chromosome that is subjected to chromosome-level mutation are subjected to gene-level mutation in a manner similar to the two-points mutation scheme.

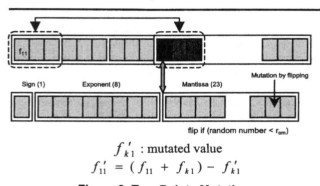

$f'_{k1}$ : mutated value

$$f'_{11} = (f_{11} + f_{k1}) - f'_{k1}$$

**Figure 3. Two Points Mutation**

**4.2.7 Stopping Condition.** We used three criteria as stopping conditions. (1) The evolution stops if the total number of iterations reaches a predefined number of iterations, (2) if the fittest chromosome of each generation has not changed much, that is, the difference is less than $10^{-3}$ over a predefined number, or (3) if all chromosomes have the same fitness values, i.e., when the algorithm has converged.

# 5. Experiment Results

## 5.1 Algorithms

To investigate the effectiveness of the proposed GA approach as compared to other constraint based approaches, we developed two DLT based algorithms (a baseline algorithm and IDLT) and for comparison, we examined another DLT based algorithm (CDLT) discussed in [9] and a simple mapping strategy named TDP (Tasks on Data Present). We compared them with

two different GA approaches: GA_Random and GA_Hint discussed in section 4.1.3. Our intuition is that different approaches may be better in different situations.

**5.1.1 Baseline Algorithm.** The basic idea behind the baseline algorithm is to collect all required input datasets to one site and then apply DLT to get a distribution of load. In this algorithm, one data source is selected from a set of data sources by evaluating and ranking them based on two values: the estimated transfer time of all input data sets from other data sources to the data source site (Data Gathering Time: $DGT_i$) and the estimated execution time ($EET_i$). Since we assume concurrent data transfer, $DGT_i$ is the maximum among all the data transfer times from other data sources to the data source i. Since DLT gives the optimal solution for the single data source case, we apply DLT to get $EET_i$. Finally, we choose a data source with $\min_i \{DGT_i + EET_i\}$ and collect all input data sets into this site and apply DLT to decide the optimal distribution of loads.

**5.1.2 Iterative DLT (IDLT).** For the case of a single data source, DLT finds the optimal distribution of the load by solving equations systematically. However, for the case of multiple sources, DLT cannot get the optimal distribution of load because the system of equations is under-constrained. We developed a near optimal algorithm based on the DLT algorithm: Iterative DLT. In this algorithm, DLT is applied to each data source to find the optimal distribution of workloads for the workload in the data source. Then it allows one-directional data transfer between two data source sites in order to eliminate unnecessary data transfer between data sources.

**5.1.3 Constrained DLT (CDLT).** For the case of $m$ data sources and $n$ sites, we have $n$ equations with $mn$ unknowns ($l_{ki}$'s). In order to solve this under-constrained system, additional constraints need to be added to this system. One possible constraint we tested, suggested in [9], is that each worker node receives the same load fraction from each data source. With this constraint, the system of equations is solvable for a unique solution.

**5.1.4 Task Data Present (TDP).** Since applications in a Data Grid usually deal with huge data sets of tera- or peta- byte scale, running jobs on sites having required data sets might be a better choice than moving data to sites with powerful computing resources. In previous work [2][5], this heuristic was examined with other strategies for non-divisible applications. We modified this heuristic for our job model. This strategy maps tasks only to the sites where required data is present. Each task processes the data sets residing at that site. There is no input data transfer in this case.

## 5.2 Experimental Results

To measure the performance of the proposed GA-based approach against other approaches, randomly generated experimental configurations were used. The estimated expected execution time for processing a unit dataset on each site, the network bandwidth between sites, input data size, and the ratio of output data size to input data size were randomly generated with uniform probability over some predefined ranges. The network bandwidth between sites is uniformly distributed between 1Mbyte/sec and 10Mbyte/sec. The location of $m$ data sources ($DS_k$) is randomly selected and each physical dataset size ($L_k$) is randomly selected with a uniform distribution in the range of 1GB to 1TB. We assume that the computing time spent in a site $i$ to process a unit dataset of size 1MB is uniformly distributed in the range $1/r_{cb}$ to $10/r_{cb}$ seconds, where $r_{cb}$ is the ratio of computation speed to communication speed.

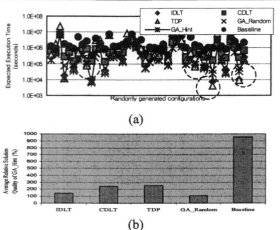

(a)

(b)

**Figure 4. Experiments on 200 randomly generated configurations (a) the expected execution time (b) average relative quality of solutions compared to baseline algorithm**

We examined the overall performance of each algorithm by running them under 200 randomly generated Grid configurations. We set the GA related parameters ($r_x = r_{gx} = 0.6$, $r_m = 0.5$, and $r_{gm} = 0.6$) with values that we found after some preliminary experiments and we varied other parameters: ccRatio (0.001~1000), oiRatio: the ratio of output data size to input data size (0~1), $r_{cb}$ (10~500), n (3~20), m (2~20). Overall, GA_Hint outperforms other algorithms including GA_Random as shown in figure 4 (a) and (b). GA_Hint finds the best solution in general (averagely 45% better solutions compared to IDLT algorithm, 140% for CDLT, 160% for TDP, 13% for GA_Random, and 800% for Baseline algorithm). However, for some configurations(short jobs, ccRatio= 0.001), TDP and IDLT occasionally offer slightly better solutions, as marked in a circle in figure 4(a).We further

examined the impact of various parameters by conducting two different experiments: (1) varying GA-related parameters such as mutation rate, crossover rate, generation number, selection schemes, and population initialization schemes and (2) varying application specific parameters.

**5.2.1 Impact of application related parameters.** Figure 5 and 6 show the impact of application specific parameters on the performance of the algorithms. As shown in figure 5 (a), for communication intensive applications (small ccRatio), TDP, GA-based approaches, and IDLT generate better solutions than other algorithms in general. On the other hand, TDP does not perform well for compute intensive applications (large ccRatio) because applications that fall into this type should be scheduled on sites with powerful computing resources to reduce data transfer overhead. As ccRatio increases, GA based approaches, IDLT, CDLT, and the baseline algorithm show similar performance.

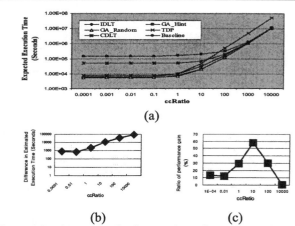

(a)

(b)                    (c)

**Figure 5. Impact of the ratio of computation to communication (a) relative solution quality compared to IDLT algorithm (b) The difference in estimated execution time of solutions between GA_Hint and other algorithms (c) The ratio of performance gain to total execution time**

However, GA_Hint offers more performance gain as ccRatio increases even though the relative solution quality decreases as shown in figure 5 (b). It is because the total execution time also increases. In terms of the ratio of performance gain, GA-based approaches give the best results around ccRatio=10 by at least 40 % as shown in figure 5 (c)

Figure 6 shows the impact of the ratio of output data size to input data size. GA_Hint and TDP perform well for communication intensive applications that generate small output data compared to input data size (low oiRatio) while GA_Random does not perform well because this algorithm starts with a population of poor quality as shown in figure 6 (a). For computation intensive applications, the ratio of output data size to input data size does not affect the performance of the algorithms much.

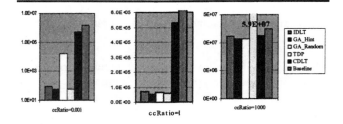

(a) oiRatio = 0

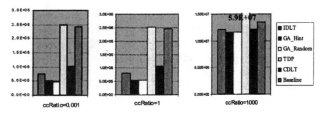

(b) oiRatio > 0.5

**Figure 6. The impact of output data size to input data size (a) oiRatio = 0 : No output or small size of output (b) oiRatio > 0.5**

**5.2.2 Impact of GA related parameters.** Figure 7 shows the performance comparison of two GA related schemes: selection scheme and population initialization scheme. In terms of selection scheme, proportionate scheme outperforms rank-based roulette wheel selection scheme (RW) for non compute intensive jobs while RW works better for compute intensive jobs. From the observation that GA_Hint outperformed GA_Random, we found that heuristic information about system or applications can be used to enhance the performance of the GA-based approach when generating the initial population.

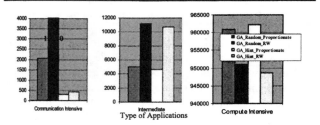

**Figure 7. Comparison of GA related schemes: selection scheme and Initialization scheme**

We examined the impact of the number of iterations on the quality of solutions generated. Figure 8 (a) shows GA_Hint starts converging after about 1500 iterations for communication intensive applications. However, GA_Random converges relatively slowly. Shown in

figure 8 (b) and (c), both GA_Hint and GA_Random converge quickly as ccRatio increases: after about 700 iterations for intermediate type of applications and 300 for compute intensive type of applications.

Finally, we measured the scheduling overhead of the GA-based approach with 1000 iterations to investigate the applicability of the approach. We tried different population sizes from 100 to 10000. The population size represents the total number of genes in population: ($n$ x $m$ x # of chromosomes in population). Figure 9 shows that the GA based approach takes about 3 minutes for 1000 iterations with the configuration of population size 10000. Compared to other algorithms (scheduling time: 50 ~ 100 ms), the running time of the GA-based approach will be much longer.

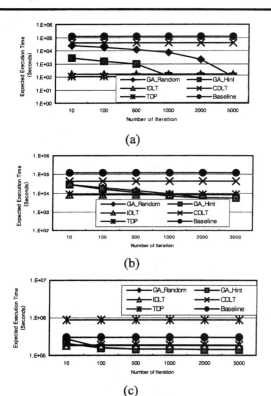

**Figure 8. Impact of number of iteration (a) communication intensive application (ccRatio=0.001) (b) intermediate application (ccRatio=1) (c) compute intensive application (ccRatio=1000)**

However the running time of the GA-based approach is negligible (0.002% ~ 0.5% of total execution time) for large jobs ($10^4$~$10^8$ seconds, as shown in Figure 4 (a)) - the most common case in Data Grid applications. On the other hand, the GA-based approach might not be a good choice for short jobs (10~1000 seconds). This observation suggests that the proposed GA-based approach can be a competitive choice for scheduling large jobs (requiring at least a couple of hours of execution time) common in Data Grid applications such as CMS experiments [14].

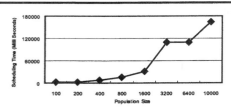

**Figure 9. Running time of GA-based algorithm (CPU: Pentium 4 2.4 GHz dual processors, RAM: 512 MB, OS: Linux)**

In summary, we found the following: (1) In general, GA_Hint outperforms other algorithms over a wide set of parameters. (2) The proposed GA-based approach will be a competitive choice for scheduling large Data Grid applications in terms of both the scheduling overhead and the quality of solutions as compared to other algorithms. (3) Since a good initial population can improve the solution quality and convergence rate (reduced scheduling time), we may use one of the other less expensive algorithms to generate an initial population.

## 6. Conclusion and Future work

In this paper, a novel GA-based approach is proposed to address the problem of scheduling a divisible Data Grid application while considering communication and computation at the same time in wide area data intensive environment. We examined the overall performance of the proposed approach and investigated the impact of various parameters such as ccRatio, oiRatio, selection schemes, population initialization schemes, and the number of iterations. Results show that the proposed GA-based approach outperformed other algorithms in general. The proposed GA-based approach will be a competitive choice for scheduling large Data Grid applications in terms of both scheduling overhead and the quality of solutions as compared to other algorithms. The results from experiments on GA-related parameters suggest that the initialization of population with chromosomes of good quality is critical to GA-based approach in terms of the quality of solution and the convergence rate.

Even though we targeted Data Grid applications as an application model, this approach can be applied to other applications where computation and communication should be considered simultaneously. As a next step, we will extend this work for the case of multiple jobs competing for shared resources.

## Acknowledgements

The authors would like to acknowledge the support of the National Science Foundation under grants NGS-0305641 and ITR-0325949, the Department of Energy's Office of Science under grant DE-FG02-03ER25554, the Minnesota Supercomputing Institute and the Digital Technology Center at the University o f Minnesota

## References

[1] I. Foster and C. Kesselman, The GRID: Blueprint for a New Computing Infrastructure, Morgan Kaufmann, 1999

[2] K. Ranganathan, I. Foster, "Decoupling Computation and Data Scheduling in Distributed Data-Intensive Applications", 11$^{th}$ IEEE International Symposium on High Performance Distributed Computing, 2002

[3] S. Orlando, et al, "Scheduling High Performance Data Mining Tasks on a Data Grid Environment", Proceedings of Int. Conf. Euro-Par 2002

[4] S.M. Park, and J.H. Kim, "Chameleon: A Resource Scheduler in A Data Grid Environment", In Proceedings of the 3$^{rd}$ IEEE International Symposium on Cluster Computing and the Grid (CC-GRID 2003), 2003

[5] A. Takefusa, O. Tatebe, S. Matsuoka, and Y. Morita, "Performance Analysis of Scheduling and Replication Algorithms on Grid Datafarm Architecture for High Energy Physics Applications," Proceedings on the 12 IEEE international symposium on HPDC, 2003

[6] T.G. Robertazzi, "Ten Reasons to Use Divisible Load Theory", IEEE Computer, 63-68, May 2003

[7] V. Bharadwaj, D. Ghose, V. Mani, and T.G. Robertazzi. Scheduling Divisible Loads in Parallel and Distributed Systems. IEEE Computer Society Press, 1996

[8] K. Ko and T.G. Robertazzi., Scheduling in an Environment of Multiple Job Submissions," Proceedings of the 2002 Conference on Information Sciences and Systems, Princeton University, Princeton NJ, March 2002

[9] H.M. Wong, D. Yu, V. Bharadwaj, T.G. Robertazzi., "Data Intensive Grid Scheduling: Multiple Sources with Capacity Constraints," 15$^{th}$ IASTED International Conference on Parallel and Distributed Computing and Systems, Los Angeles, 2003

[10] L. Wang, H.J. Siegel, V.P. Roychowdhury, and A.A. Maciejewski, "Task Matching and Scheduling in Heterogeneous Computing Environments Using a Genetic Algorithm-Based Approach", Journal of Parallel and Distributed Computing 47, 8-22, 1997.

[11] A. Abraham, R. Buyya, and B. Nath., "Nature's Heuristics for Scheduling Jobs on Computational Grids", Proceedings of 8$^{th}$ IEEE International Conference on Advanced Computing and Communications, 2000

[12] L. Budin, M. Golub, and A. Budin., "Traditional Techniques of Genetic Algorithms Applied to Floating-Point Chromosome Representations," Proceddings of the 41st Annual Conference KoREMA, pp.93-96, Opatija, 1996,

[13] M. Srinivas and L.M. Patnaik, "Genetic Algorithms: A Survey," IEEE Computer 27, 617-26, June 1994

[14] K. Holtman, "CMS Requirements for the Grid", in Proceedings of the International Conference on Computing in High Energy and Nuclear Physics (CHEP2001), 2001

[15] "Models of Networked Analysis at Regional Centers for LHC Experiments (MONARC) Phase 2 Report", 2000

[16] M.R. Garey and D.S. Johnson, "Computers and Intractability, a Guide to the Theory of NP-Completeness", W.H. Freeman and Company, New York, 1979

[17] A.Y. Zomaya, F. Ercal, and S. Olariu., "Solutions to Parallel and Distributed Computing Problems", A Wiely-Interscience Publication, 2001

[18] A. Chervenak, I. Foster, C. Kesselman, C. Salisbury, S. Tuecke,., "The Data Grid: Towards an Architecture for the Distributed Management and Analysis of Large Scientific Datasets", Journal of Network and Computer Applications, 2001

# Session 6C:
# Wireless: Mobile Systems

# Application-Aware Service Differentiation in PAWNs

Hanping Lufei, Sivakumar Sellamuthu, Sharun Santhosh, and Weisong Shi

Department of Computer Science
Wayne State University
{*hlufei, siva, sharun, weisong*}*@wayne.edu*

## Abstract

*We have witnessed the increasing demand for pervasive Internet access from public area wireless networks (PAWNs). The diverse service requirements from end users necessitate an efficient service differentiation mechanism, which should satisfy two goals:* end-user fairness *and* maximizing the utilization of wireless link. *However, we found that the existing best-effort based service model is not enough to satisfy either goal. In this paper, we have proposed an application-aware service differentiation mechanism which takes both application semantics and user requirements into consideration. The results show that our proposed method outperforms two other bandwidth allocation approaches,* best effort *and* static allocation, *in terms of both client fairness and wireless link bandwidth utilization, especially in heavy load environments.*

## 1 Introduction

As the rapid growth of the deployment of public area wireless networks (PAWNs) [2], the *diverse service requirements of end users* become an important issue that need to be addressed. A *service differentiation and access control* mechanism is necessary in such an environment to ensure genuine users receive the services they have paid for, to protect them from malicious users, and to efficiently use the network bandwidth resources.

Several access control or bandwidth allocation algorithms have been proposed. RSVP [11] is a signaling protocol to reserve resources at all the routers along the path. Several measurement-based admission control algorithms [8] can provide a soft guarantee. Although these previous results are promising, few of them take the application level information into consideration. The result is either lower link utilization or unfair service differentiation. Therefore, we envision that an efficient service differentiation mechanism should satisfy two goals: *end user fairness*

and *maximization of wireless link utilization.*

To achieve both goals, in our proposed approach *Application-Aware Service Differentiation* (AASD), bandwidth is not allocated to clients statically based on their reserved bandwidth only. Instead, application level information, such as requested object size, available Web server bandwidth, and user reserved bandwidth are taken into consideration comprehensively. Even during the course of processing requests, bandwidth adjustment may be made in accordance with variations in measured Internet path bandwidth. We felt that by adaptively varying the bandwidth allocated to users in the last-mile wireless hop, the network can accommodate more users while at the same time increase the likelihood of admitting users at pre-negotiated service levels. All our results validate this intuition.

The service differentiation algorithm was implemented and evaluated under two different scenarios: *fixed upstream bandwidth* and *dynamic upstream bandwidth*. The results show that in comparison with two other bandwidth allocation approaches, best effort and static access control algorithms, our proposed method outperforms them in terms of both client fairness and wireless bandwidth utilization. For example, when the access point hosts 120 clients with different reserved bandwidths that follow a normal distribution, the utilization of our approach is twice of that of static allocation method and 50% more than best effort approach while at the same time satisfies 90% of clients with 95% of their individual reserved bandwidth. Furthermore, we proposed an exponential weighted queue optimization technique to adapt bandwidth allocation dynamically to bandwidth variations between access points and web servers.

The rest of the paper is organized as follows. Two performance metrics related to service differentiation algorithm are described in Section 2.1. Section 2.2 presents two other access control algorithms for comparison purpose. The design details of the AASD algorithm is presented in Section 3. Section 4 reports the details of performance evaluation, including experimental platforms, performance analysis, and implications. Related work and conclusion remarks are listed in Section 5 and Section 6 respectively.

## 2  Background

A common access scenario in public-aware wireless network includes a set of wireless users sharing one wireless access point. The wireless access point in turn connects to the Internet through wired connection. There are two important metrics to be concerned. First, The investor cares about how many percentage of the wireless resource can be used in order to get the maximal profit. Second, for the end users the matters is the reserved bandwidth they paid can be satisfied to the most extend.

### 2.1  Performance Metrics

**Fairness** — Fairness tries to guarantee that each user should get the bandwidth he deserved no more and no less. Fairness is a relative concept. Assume user A sends out $n$ connections, $bw_i$ is the bandwidth of connection $i$, $BW_{reserv}^A$ is the reserved bandwidth of user A. We define the fairness as following:

$$\text{Fairness of A} = \frac{\frac{\sum_{i=1}^n bw_i}{n}}{BW_{reserv}^A} \qquad (1)$$

**Utilization** — Utilization shows the usage of wireless resources. For a given number of users, say $n$ users, in time interval $T_{interval}$, user $i$ receives $size_i$ bytes in total and the specific wireless link bandwidth of the access point is $BW_{ap}$, we can calculate the utilization by the following equation:

$$\text{Utilization} = \frac{\frac{\sum_{i=1}^n size_i}{T_{interval}}}{BW_{ap}}. \qquad (2)$$

### 2.2  Non-Application Aware Methods

For comparing purpose, we also implement two other service differentiation algorithms: *best effort* and *static allocation*:

1. *Best Effort with no Reservation:* Strictly speaking there is no algorithm. When the access control program receives a request from the client, it just sets up a connection to the destination, then sends back the response to the client. None of the bandwidth allocation algorithms are applied. With increasing number of clients the wireless link resource will finally get saturated and the throughput of each flow will become too small to be tolerated by the users.

2. *Static Access Control with User Reservation:* The main principle of this algorithm is try to statically allocate

the total bandwidth to the clients. In this model an access point serves $n$ client each associated with a reserved bandwidth. Let $B_i$ denotes the reserved bandwidth associated with client $i$ ($i \in [1, N]$), where $N$ is the maximum number of clients. Let $B_{total}$ be the total wireless bandwidth. In order to satisfy each client total wireless bandwidth is allocated statically to the incoming clients. When the total upstream bandwidth is used up the new incoming client will not get served. Thus the following observation holds.

$$\sum_{i=1}^{n+1} B_i \geq BW_{total} \geq \sum_{i=1}^n B_i, \qquad (3)$$

In this approach, the fairness can be satisfied maximally but the utilization is badly affected. Once the bandwidth has been statically assigned to a client, no matter what he does this part can not be used by anyone else even if the client is idle all the time.

## 3  Application-Aware Service Differentiation

Based on the observations of the two previous access control algorithms, we propose an application aware access control with adaptive allocation algorithm. First let us start our discussion with the behavior of wireless users.

### 3.1  User Behavior

Our proposed algorithm is inspired by previous studies on the mobile user behavior of Web surfing. Balachandran *et al.*'s recent study found that major part of the mobile user traffic is HTTP traffic [4]. At the same time, study from Barford and Crovella [5] found that for web surfing not much time is spent on data transfer, on the contrary most of the time the user is idle and this is refereed to as user 'think' time. Borrowed the term from [5], a user equivalent (UE) is defined as a single process in an endless loop that alternates between making requests for online content, and lying idle. Each UE is therefore an ON/OFF process; Statistical models show Active OFF Times follow the Weibull distribution and Inactive OFF Times follow the Pareto distribution. For a given time $\tau = 10$, $\alpha = 1.5$ and $k = 1$ in Pareto distribution.

$$\int_1^\tau \alpha k^\alpha x^{-\alpha+1} dx = 1 - \tau^- 1.5 = 99.68\% \qquad (4)$$

It means 99.68% of users have 1 to 10 average seconds idle time between their clicks, this is users' 'think' time. In the thinking time period the bandwidth allocated to the user is wasted. In order to utilize the wasted bandwidth the application-aware service differentiation algorithm is proposed.

## 3.2 Design

The goal of a service differentiation algorithm would be to efficiently allocate wireless bandwidth to the users, and at the same time to satisfy both the fairness and the utilization metrics.

### 3.2.1 Overview

Our design differs from existing resource allocation and access control algorithms in the following three ways: First, *application-awareness*, application level demands, such as object size, Web server bandwidth etc., are taken into consideration. An acceptance decision is not based only on the user reserved bandwidth but also on the application specific parameters predicted by our application-aware algorithm. Second, *dynamic server bandwidth adaptation*, our algorithm monitors (passively) the current Internet path bandwidth (of different servers) and take bandwidth history for each Web server into consideration to get a more stable and predictable bandwidth value for the next connection. Third, *discrete service differentiation*, the AASD algorithm distinguishes different levels of Web server bandwidth service queues. This method improves the utilization of the total bandwidth dramatically. Theoretically the more differentiation service queues we have the better is the performance.

### 3.2.2 Multiple Service Queues

Usually, the available bandwidth between an access point and a fixed Web server is dynamically changing. Thus, using one queue for multiple clients and multiple servers probably can not fill up the total wireless upstream bandwidth, given the fact of the head of queue blocking effect [13]. Hence, in AASD, we divide total upstream bandwidth into discrete service queues based on different individual bandwidth limits, as shown in Figure 2. However, how to allocate servers into these service queues is a problem.

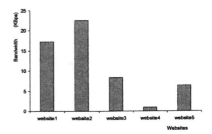

**Figure 1. The top five Web server bandwidth accessed by a medium-size research institution.**

To address this problem, we examined the top five Web servers accessed by the users from a medium-size research institution. Figure 1 shows a snapshot of the available bandwidth of these Web sites. We found that the following observation can be hold: basically, the ratio of bandwidth between Web servers follows exponential distribution [16], and this relationship can be used to decide the allocation of multiple service queues. We call these queues as exponential weighted queues (EWQs). Suppose there are $n$ queues the bandwidth ratio of these queues would be

$$1 : 2 : 2^2 : 2^3 : ... : 2^n$$

Another reason to chose EWQ is to take care of service downgrade dynamically. If the Internet bandwidth of an incoming request later turns out to be much lower than the bandwidth specified by this queue, GetURL module can move this request to an appropriate queue to avoid jamming the following requests in the original queue.

For each individual queue, it is different from the traditional first in first out (FIFO) queue. For any individual client, its request can be inserted into any position in the queue. There is a GETURL module that only takes out the head of queue and processes the request, so that at any instant moment there is only one request is being served for each queue. For each service queue, each entry includes three important elements: $T_{delay}$ is the maximum delay time before serving this request. $T_{download}$ is the estimated download time of the requested object. $URL$ is the location of the object as shown in the Figure 2. The entries are increasingly ordered by $T_{delay}$ so that the following formula holds.

$$T_{delay}^i \leq T_{delay}^{i+1}, i = 1, 2, ..., n \tag{5}$$

Based on the statistical result of web object size distribution most of the web page frame is no more than 20KB [7], with high probability, the following formula holds.

$$T_{delay}^i + T_{download}^i \leq T_{delay}^{i+1} \tag{6}$$

It means downloading object $i$ probably will not delay serving $(i + 1)^{th}$ request. Even if the inequation doesn't hold, the *GetURL* module will dynamically migrate the request to an appropriate lower bandwidth service queue. $T_{delay}^i$ and $T_{download}^i$ are calculated by the following two formulas. $S_{obj}$ is the object size, $B_{user}$ is the user bandwidth and $B_{svr}$ is the Web server bandwidth.

$$T_{delay}^i = \frac{S_{obj}^i}{B_{user}} - T_{download}^i, \tag{7}$$

$$T_{download}^i = \frac{S_{obj}^i}{B_{svr}}, \tag{8}$$

Simply speaking, as long as the queues are not empty the wireless link will be fully utilized. So our application aware algorithm combines multiple loosely loaded user sessions into one (maybe more) tightly heavy loaded service queue to improve utilization and maintain fairness at the same time.

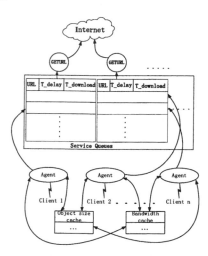

**Figure 2. The basic model of the application-aware service differentiation algorithm.**

### 3.2.3 Two Important Modules

Due to the space limit, we briefly explain two important modules here. More details can be found in the technical version of this paper [10]. The Agent module in Figure 2 handles each client request, checks the request object size and server bandwidth from the cache first, inserts the request in the appropriate position of the proper queue, sends back response and updates the object size and server bandwidth if necessary. For the object size cache studies show that the distribution of Web object size follow the Pareto distribution, most of the html files are below 50KB [7] respectively. The object size cache is maintained to store size information of objects that have already been handled by the agent. The agent searches for the size of the requested URL in the cache. If the size is not known the default size is used and the actual size will be updated to the cache after the *GetURL* module retrieves the object. Next time when the same URL is requested the accurate size value can be obtained.

The GetURL module is in charge of grabbing the head of queue, getting URL object, probing Internet bandwidth etc., as shown in Figure 2. At the beginning a default bandwidth value is used. Later on the Internet path bandwidth will be calculated from the latest bandwidth that each connection observed and the bandwidth value of the immediate

previous connection. The new server available bandwidth ($B_{i+1}$) will be calculated as follows:

$$B_{i+1} = \frac{B_{latest} + B_i}{2}, \qquad (9)$$

where $B_{latest}$ represents the latest bandwidth measured between bandwidth allocation server and the specific Web server. This feedback based adaptive bandwidth measurement mechanism makes the curve of bandwidth more fluent and stable.

## 4 Performance Evaluation and Analysis

In this section, we first briefly describe the experimental platforms, then compare different algorithms in terms of fixed and dynamic Internet bandwidth. After that we will discuss effects of available server bandwidth and queue optimization on our algorithm.

### 4.1 Experimental Setup

We set up four machines and run web servers, allocation algorithms and clients on these machines separately, as shown in Figure 3, where the two Web servers are running on two SUN UltraSparc2 dual-processor running Solaris 5.8, bandwidth allocation server is running on Intel-based Linux box running RedHat Linux 8.0 (P4 2.2GHz with 512 MB SDRAM), clients are emulated on another Linux box with the same configuration. All these four machines are connected by a 100Mbps fast switched Ethernet. Generally our experimental platform consists of the following parts.

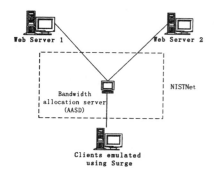

**Figure 3. Experimental setup.**

*Hardware Configuration* — As shown in Figure 3, we set up two Apache [1] web servers with different bandwidths connected to our bandwidth allocation server where our algorithms will be deployed. All the web traffic generated by clients will be processed by the bandwidth allocation server by applying the appropriate bandwidth allocation algorithm. We evaluate different service differentiation algorithms in the context of two scenarios: *fixed upstream bandwidth* and *dynamic upstream bandwidth*. During the experiments, the fixed upstream bandwidth is set to 6Mbps, while the dynamic upstream bandwidth is set by using the available bandwidth extracted from the wireless LAN traces from ACM SIGCOMM'01 [4]. Both the fixed and dynamic upstream bandwidths are emulated by using NISTNet [12], a network emulation package developed by NIST.

*Simulation of User Behavior* — Surge [5] is a realistic Web workload generation tool which mimics a set of real users accessing a server. It generates references matching empirical measurements of server file size distribution, request size distribution, relative file popularity, embedded file references, temporal locality of reference and idle periods of individual users. We use Surge to generate the client requests. The number of clients we simulated using Surge is between 1 to 200.

*Distribution of User Reserved Bandwidth* In the real world, different users have different reserved bandwidths. So in our experiment we use two distributions, one is uniform distribution; all users have the same bandwidth set to 100Kbps. Another one is normal distribution; that most of the users have bandwidth set to 80Kbps or 120Kbps, while small part of users have 40Kbps or 160Kbps reserved bandwidth. All the results below are for normal distribution client bandwidth, for uniform distribution we get more or less similar results.

## 4.2 Fixed Upstream Bandwidth

First, we compare these three service differentiation algorithms in the context of ideal fixed upstream bandwidth case. We set the bandwidth between Web server one (WS1) and the bandwidth allocation server as half of the bandwidth between Web server two (WS2) and the bandwidth allocation server. We also regulate the total wireless bandwidth as 6Mbps, a reasonable approximation of a 802.11b [6] network.

Figure 4 shows the evaluation results of different algorithms in the fixed upstream bandwidth scenario, with the user reserved bandwidth follows a normal distribution. First, let's have a look at the number of accepted clients in Figure 4(a). Although the best effort algorithm will accept any incoming clients without any rejection, the individual user reserved bandwidth suffers. In the static access control algorithm, once the remaining wireless link bandwidth is used up by incoming clients, about 60 clients in our experiment, all new clients will be refused unless one of the previous clients exits from the network. For the AASD, the curve tells us that it serves more clients than the static method although it has to reject new comers when the bandwidth gets saturated.

For the utilization of the wireless link, as shown in Figure 4(b), in the static access control case, the utilization

value doesn't change to much since the number of accepted clients remains unchanged. But for the best effort and the application aware approaches, the utilization curves are both increasing in a similar fashion, which means the application aware access control does almost as good as the best effort in terms of utilization.

As far as the user bandwidth satisfaction is concerned, Figure 4(c) shows that average bandwidth deteriorates dramatically with the increase of client numbers. On the other hand, average bandwidth is abnormally high in light load scenario. In Figure 4 (d) the x axis is the percentage of satisfaction of user reserved bandwidth, defined as *Fairness* in equation 1, while the y is the cumulative number of clients. We can see that in the scenario with 60 clients active involving, the application aware approach performs as good as the static access control, as 90% of clients experience about 95% fairness. In the 160 clients scenario, where the number of clients increase 167%, AASD still can satisfy 60% of clients with 90% fairness. AASD has the potential to hold more users than static access control algorithm, while at the same time guarantees the reserved bandwidth.

Note that we also evaluated these algorithms in the context of other user reserved bandwidth distributions, such as the uniform distribution, and got similar results [10].

In summary, the best effort approach can reach the high utilization of wireless bandwidth but with poor user bandwidth satisfaction. On the contrary, the static access control has the good user bandwidth fairness but with the fair wireless link utilization. The proposed application aware approach takes both advantages so that it can maximally guarantee user reserved bandwidth and improve the utilization of wireless link bandwidth as efficiently as possible at the same time.

## 4.3 Dynamic Upstream Bandwidth

In addition to the fixed upstream scenario, we also evaluate the proposed algorithm under the circumstance of dynamic changing environment, which is collected from ACM SIGCOMM 2001 conference [4]. For simplicity, we calculate the average bandwidth ever 100 seconds, over a 10 minute duration. Totally we have six different upstream bandwidths, as shown in Figure 5.

From Figure 6 it is easy to see that the application aware approach has the potential to accept more clients than fixed upstream bandwidth scenario as shown in Figure 4(a). This is because in most of the time the bandwidth from the trace is greater than the bandwidth used in the fixed bandwidth scenario.

For the utilization of wireless link bandwidth, generally it is less than the fixed Internet bandwidth scenario because most of the time the Internet bandwidth fluctuates below the value of fixed bandwidth. AASD is still able to follow the

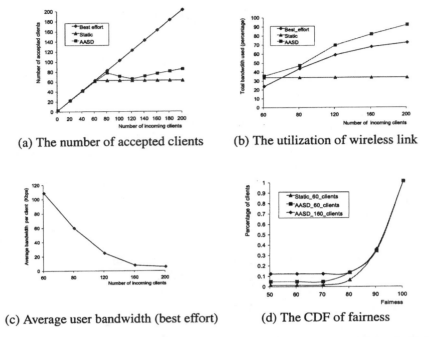

(a) The number of accepted clients

(b) The utilization of wireless link

(c) Average user bandwidth (best effort)

(d) The CDF of fairness

**Figure 4. Evaluation results of different algorithms in the fixed upstream bandwidth scenario, with normal user reserved bandwidth distribution: (a) the number of accepted clients, (b) the utilization of wireless link, (c) the average user bandwidth of the best effort approach, and (d) the CDF of fairness.**

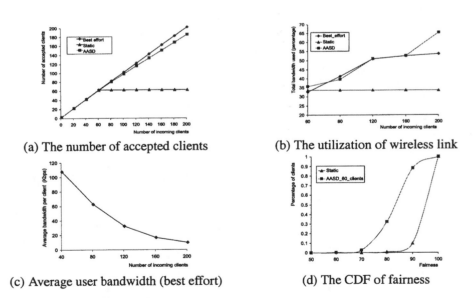

(a) The number of accepted clients

(b) The utilization of wireless link

(c) Average user bandwidth (best effort)

(d) The CDF of fairness

**Figure 6. Evaluation results of different algorithms in the dynamic upstream bandwidth scenario, with normal user reserved bandwidth distribution: (a) the number of accepted clients, (b) the utilization of wireless link, (c) the average user bandwidth of the best effort approach, and (d) the CDF of fairness.**

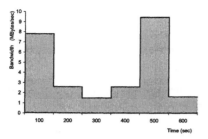

**Figure 5. A discrete 10-minute Internet bandwidth trace from ACM SIGCOMM'01 [4].**

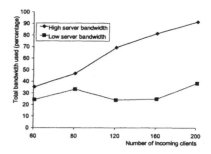

**Figure 7. The utilization of wireless link for different server bandwidths.**

best effort curve closely as can be seen in Figure 6(b).

In terms of user bandwidth fairness, Figure 6(d) shows the application aware approach is a little bit worse than the static access control by about 10%. One of the reason is, if the Internet bandwidth changes fast our approach will exhibit a delay to accommodate the new Internet bandwidth. On the other hand if the Internet bandwidth drops out of the range of a service queue the request have to be transferred to another queue (see the design of AASD 3, which makes results in request thrashing between queues. These factors affect user reserved bandwidth satisfaction. But generally the 10% is in an acceptable range.

Again, we also evaluated these algorithms in the context of the uniform user reserved bandwidth distribution, and got similar results [10].

### 4.4 Effect of Available Server Bandwidth

We also notice that available server bandwidth has great effect on the the utilization of wireless bandwidth, as shown in Figure 7. We compare utilization under two server bandwidth scenarios. The low server bandwidth scenario sets server bandwidth to 2Mbps and 4Mbps for each webserver. While the high server bandwidth scenario sets server bandwidth to 4Mbps and 8Mbps. No matter how hard the algorithm tries, the total utilization is still not high if the Internet server bandwidth is low. An increase in server bandwidth can dramatically improve the total utilization.

### 4.5 Effect of Queue Optimization

As we discussed in Section 3, multiple queues, EWQs in our algorithm, are useful to improve the utilization of upstream stream bandwidth. To show the effect of our design, we set up an experiment which compares EWQ with two other queue algorithms. In our settings, we use $n = 2$, the two other queue algorithms are: *one queue only*, and *two equally distributed queues* (UWQ). We found the EWQ approaches outperforms other two queue algorithms in terms

of the utilization of wireless bandwidth as shown in Figure 8. It is obvious that the performance is improved when two queues are used than that of one queue is used. However, it is worth noting that the performance is not proportional to the number of queues because more queues will definitely add more overhead to the system and in turn put penalty on the total performance. Based on the variation of Web server bandwidths we found two or three queues is the optimal choice in practice.

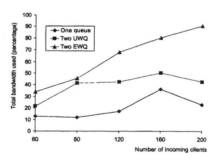

**Figure 8. The utilization of wireless link for different queue implementations.**

## 5 Related Work

Extensive research has been done on the subject of providing quality of service over a network. RSVP [11] is a signaling protocol that reserves resources on all the routers along the path. Though it guarantees quality of service, it exhibits significant scalability problems. Admission control in integrated service (IntServ) architecture: flows must request services from the network and are accepted or rejected depending on the availability of resources. Differentiated services (Diffserv) is another approach to provide QoS. It is based on DS field in the packet header, priority scheduling and buffering. Upon overload in a given service class all flows in that class suffer a degradation of service. End point admission control [8] combines Diffserv superior scalability and IntServ superior quality of service. Measurement based admission control algorithms provide a soft guarantee. Most previous work on wireless QoS work has focused on the MAC layer [14]. All these approaches do not take application-level demands into consideration.

Vaidya, Bahl and Gupta [15] developed a fully distributed algorithm for scheduling packet transmissions such that different flows are allocated bandwidth in proportion of their weights. Qiu, Bahl and Adya [9] evaluated several first-hop allocation schemes using traces collected from a popular Web site. Their results show that the scheme which takes into account both the application data rate and available Internet path bandwidth yields the best performance. But they did not propose their own bandwidth allocation algorithm. Our evaluation results show that adapting to variations in server bandwidth plays an important role in service differentiation, as this scheme gets the best results.

In Balachandran *et al.*'s recent work [3], they proposed a hot-spot releasing approach that when a user requests service from the network in an overloaded region, the wireless network tries to adapt itself to handle the user service request by readjusting the load across its APs. This approach is different from ours: they deal with the load balance between multiple APs, for each AP no special method is proposed, while we try to make one AP serves more clients than usual and each client can still get the reserved bandwidth so they do not need to reluctantly move to other place to get the service. But we believe these two approaches compliment very well, and the combination of them will provide a more comprehensive solution for this kind of questions related to wireless resource utilization and service differentiation.

# 6 Summary and Future Work

This paper proposed an application-aware service differentiation mechanism in public-area wireless network, aiming to satisfy two goals *end user fairness* and *maximization of wireless link utilization*. The unique feature of our algorithm is both the application semantics, client requirements and the varying individual server bandwidths are taken into consideration. The performance evaluation shows that AASD outperforms other algorithms in terms of both performance metrics. Furthermore, an exponential weighted queue optimization technique applied to AASD allows it to adapt to constantly changing bandwidth environments. Our next step is to extend the AASD approach for other non-HTTP based application traffic, such as SSH, Telnet and email.

# References

[1] Apache HTTP Server Project.

[2] P. Bahl, W. Russell, Y. Wang, A. Balachandran, G. Voelker, and A. Miu. PAWNs: Satisfying the need for ubiquitous secure connectivity and location services. *IEEE Personal Communicationsi Magazine*, 9(1):40–48, Feb. 2002.

[3] A. Balachandran, P. Bahl, and G. Voelker. Hot-spot congestion relief and service guarantees in public-areawireless networks. In *Proceedings of WMCSA 2002*, June 2002.

[4] A. Balachandran, G. Voelker, P. Bahl, and V. Rangan. Characterizing user behavior and network performance in a public wireless lan. In *Proceedings of ACM SIGMETRICS 2002*, June 2002.

[5] P. Barford and M. E. Crovella. Generating representative web workloads for network and server performance evaluation. In *Proceedings of Performance '98/ACM SIGMETRICS '98*, July 1998.

[6] IEEE. IEEE std 802.11 — wireless LAN medium access control (mac) and physical layer (phy) specifications, 1997.

[7] B. Krishnamurthy and J. Rexford. *Web Protocols and Practice: HTTP/1.1, Networking Protocols, Caching and Traffic Measurement*. Addison-Wesley, Inc, 2001.

[8] L.Breslau, E.W.Knightly, S.Shenker, I.Stoica, and H.Zhang. Endpoint admission control: Architectural issues and performance. In *SIGCOMM*, pages 57–69, 2000.

[9] L.Qiu, P.Bahl, and A.Adya. The effect of first-hop wireless bandwidth allocation on end-to-end network performance. In *Proceedings of the 12th international workshop on Network and operating systems support for digital audio and video*, pages 85–93, 2002.

[10] H. Lufei, S. Sellamuthu, S. Santhosh, and W. Shi. Application-aware service differentiation in pawns. Technical Report CS-MIST-TR-2003-009, Department of Computer Science, Wayne State University, Aug. 2003.

[11] L.Zhang, S.Deering, and D.Estrin. RSVP: A new resource ReSerVation protocol. *IEEE network*, 7(5):8–?, September 1993.

[12] Nist network emulation tool (nistnet).

[13] L. Peterson, T. Anderson, D. Culler, and T. Roscoe. A blueprint for introducing disruptive technology into the internet. In *ACM First Workshop on Hot Topics in Networks (HotNets-I)*, Oct. 2002.

[14] T.Nandagopal, T.Kim, X.Gao, and V.Bharghavan. Achieving MAC layer fairness in wireless packet networks. In *Mobile Computing and Networking*, pages 87–98, 2000.

[15] N. H. Vaidya, P. Vahl, and S. Gupta. Distributed fair scheduling in a wireless lan. In *Proc. of the 6th ACM SIGMOBILE International Conference on Mobile Computing and Networking (MobiCom'00)*, Aug. 2000.

[16] Z. Zhu, Y. Mao, and W. Shi. Workload characterization of uncacheable web content — and its implications for caching. Technical Report CS-MIST-TR-2003-003, Department of Computer Science, Wayne State University, May 2003.

# Algorithm Design and Synthesis for Wireless Sensor Networks*

Amol Bakshi and Viktor K. Prasanna
Department of Electrical Engineering
University of Southern California
Los Angeles, CA 90089
{amol, prasanna}@usc.edu

## Abstract

*Most of current research in wireless networked embedded sensing approaches the problem of application design as one of manually customizing network protocols. The design complexity and required expertise make this unsuitable for increasingly complex sensor network systems. We address this problem from a parallel and distributed systems perspective and propose a methodology that enables domain experts to design, analyze, and synthesize sensor network applications without requiring a knowledge of implementation details. At the core of our methodology is a virtual architecture for a class of sensor networks that hides enough system details to relieve programmers of the burden of managing low-level control and coordination, and provides algorithm designers with a clean topology and cost model. We illustrate this methodology using a real-world topographic querying application as a case study.*

## 1. Introduction

Wireless sensor networks (WSNs) are ad hoc networks of unattended smart sensors performing in-network collaborative computation and communication to monitor the environment for events of interest. Most of the current research on information processing in WSNs has focused on mostly manual optimization and application-specific customization of the network protocol stack. While this approach has been successful for relatively simple application scenarios, there is now an increasing realization of the need for new programming models and abstractions for algorithm designers and programmers that do not demand an expertise in wireless networking - in addition to a knowledge of the application domain [4, 12].

In this paper, we explore a methodology for algorithm design and synthesis for a class of sensor network applications, with the goal of reducing design complexity. Our methodology enables a domain expert to design and analyze algorithms, and synthesize programs for the virtual architecture, without requiring a knowledge of low level networking aspects of the deployment. While WSNs are approached from a wireless ad hoc networking perspective in most of state of the art, we model them as parallel and distributed systems. However, there are important differences between sensor networks and traditional distributed systems that should be considered while defining models of computation and algorithm design methodologies for WSNs.

Sensor networks are data driven in the sense that data is created in the network (by the sensing interfaces) and the values of sensor data and the application semantics determine the pattern of computation and communication at run time. Also, the computation has to be performed as close to the data as possible, in order to reduce communication energy consumption in the network. This means that the (re)distribution of data and computation to nodes of the network is subject to constraints that arise from application semantics and performance requirements. In traditional parallel and distributed processing, latency and throughput of execution have been the major performance metrics, and the overall objective is to manage the resources efficiently so as to minimize execution time of the computation. In embedded systems such as sensor networks, the application essentially executes in an infinite loop, and the concept of a round of execution is ill defined in many scenarios due to their data driven behavior. Hence, at the system level, minimizing energy consumption of the network as a whole is the dominant concern, sometimes even at the expense of increased latency of some path of execution.

The rest of this paper is organized as follows. Section 2 presents our overall design methodology. Sections 3 and 4 illustrate the process of defining a virtual architecture, algorithm design, and (manual) program synthesis for our case study. Section 5 describes a set of protocols to implement the modeling abstractions at run time. Related work is discussed in Section 6, and we conclude in Section 7.

* This work is supported by the National Science Foundation under award number IIS-0330445.

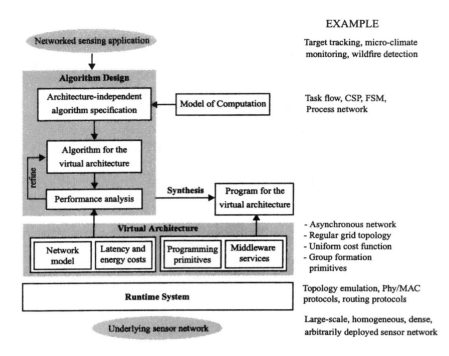

EXAMPLE

Target tracking, micro-climate
monitoring, wildfire detection

Task flow, CSP, FSM,
Process network

- Asynchronous network
- Regular grid topology
- Uniform cost function
- Group formation
  primitives

Topology emulation, Phy/MAC
protocols, routing protocols

Large-scale, homogeneous, dense,
arbitrarily deployed sensor network

Figure 1: Our Proposed Design Methodology

## 2. Our Proposed Methodology

Our methodology is based on a virtual architecture for the sensor network that enables algorithm design and synthesis. A virtual architecture is an abstract machine model for algorithm design and synthesis and a set of primitives that are independent of low level protocols used to implement them in the underlying network. It is important for the end user that the modeling abstractions correspond to mental notions of application behavior on a sensor network system, that a formalism exists to specify such behavior, and that some mechanism exists to map the behavior onto the underlying network such that theoretical performance analysis corresponds to real performance measurements.

**Defining a Virtual Architecture**: The virtual architecture should: (i) facilitate rapid first-order performance estimation of algorithms, (ii) provide suitable primitives to enable translation of the selected algorithm into a program for the underlying network, and (iii) export appropriate middleware services that allow the end user to think in terms of abstract logical entities such as events of a specific type. Key components of our virtual architecture are:

*Network model*: The network model specifies the topology of the deployment that can be assumed at design time. This (virtual) topology can be emulated on the real network deployment in a variety of ways that could be hidden from the algorithm designer. The choice of virtual topology will be influenced by the expected nature of the deploy-

ment, and also by the nature of collaborative computation and collaboration in the target application. Depending on the type of network, the model could support synchronous algorithms (e.g., TDMA), purely asynchronous message-passing paradigms, or a combination of the two [8].

*Programming primitives*: The virtual architecture specifies the computation and communication primitives available to the programmer. These primitives could be for the individual node or for a set of nodes (collective). Communication primitives could range from the simple send() and receive() message passing primitives to more sophisticated ones for group communication. Computation primitives could include summing, sorting, or ranking a set of data values from a set of sensor nodes [5]. The implementation of these primitives could be transparent to the end user who is aware only of their functionality and associated costs.

*Middleware services*: A middleware service implements a high-level functionality that is commonly needed for a certain class of applications [20]. For example, collaborative computation through the formation of logical groups is a very useful concept for a large number of WSN applications, allowing the end user to reason in terms of a follower-leader relationship between nodes in a group. Middleware services are essential in decoupling high-level functional abstractions from their implementation details, and hence are part of our virtual architecture.

*Cost functions and performance metrics*: Computation and communication costs in terms of time and energy are specified for each primitive, as well as for the operations supported by the middleware services. These cost functions, combined with the application representation should provide sufficient information to decide an efficient mapping of application tasks onto sensor nodes and for communication synthesis. The performance metric to be used for evaluating an algorithm will be based on these cost functions, but will depend on the application. For example, total energy, energy balance, total latency of a set of operations, system lifetime, etc., are various performance metrics that can be calculated from the cost model, but which of these to use will depend on the algorithm designer's objective.

**Design Flow**: In Figure 1, the graphical depiction of the major components of our methodology and the design flow is annotated with concrete examples for some of the abstractions. First, the network model and cost model for the target class of sensor networks is defined using a **bottom-up** approach that involves analysis of the expected nature of deployment, characteristics of the node hardware, etc. The end user analyzes alternate algorithms for the desired functionality and selects one with the best performance for that network and cost model. For example, the end user could decide if a divide and conquer approach is better than a centralized approach if, say, total latency of one round of the application is to be minimized. After the algorithm is chosen, a **top-down** approach is required to convert (synthesize) it into the program that executes on each node of the network. In the top-down approach, the algorithm is specified using an architecture-independent application model such as an annotated task graph. The application graph is used as an input to a mapping tool (manual or automatic) that will explore alternate design time and run time role assignments in the network and determine an efficient one. When the roles are assigned (i.e., the tasks are mapped), the actual software has to be synthesized for each node. The structure of the task graph and explicit annotations by the application developer are used to determine which of the available middleware services (if any) are useful. For instance, in a task graph structured as a $k$-ary tree, the interaction between every parent node and its $k$ children can be implemented using a middleware API for group communication if one is available. Further, if logical naming service is supported, the group membership can even be determined at run time. Finally, the program for each node is synthesized, including the appropriate calls to middleware.

## 3. Case Study: Identification and Labeling of Homogeneous Regions

The purpose of this case study is to demonstrate the definition and use of a virtual architecture for an example application scenario. For the problem described in the next subsection, we choose a divide-and-conquer algorithm for in-

network merging of boundary information. This algorithm is represented as a high-level task graph. Using the communication primitives and cost models offered by the virtual architecture, the performance of this algorithm can be analytically estimated. Then we illustrate how this high-level specification is (manually) synthesized into an algorithm for the virtual architecture. This synthesis includes mapping logical entities in the high-level representation to nodes in the (virtual) topology, while satisfying some constraints on the mapping process. We then demonstrate how the architecture-specific algorithm is expressed as a program that executes on the individual node of the (virtual) topology. Finally, in Section 5, we present some protocols that could be used to to implement the modeling abstractions, with a view to preserving the correspondence between the theoretical performance analysis and the actual performance on the underlying network. These protocols are representative of the approaches that can be adopted to implement a virtual architecture.

### 3.1. The Application

*Topographic querying* is the process of extracting data from a sensor network for understanding the graphical delineation of features of interest in the environment. The end user might be interested in visualizing gradients of sensor readings across the region or other queries such as enumeration of regions with sensor readings in a specific range. Application areas where this is useful range from contaminant monitoring to HVAC (heating, ventilation, and air conditioning) applications. Boundary estimation and counting regions of interest can also be used in acoustic monitoring and tracking applications. Querying the properties of sensor node such as residual energy levels is useful for resource management, dynamic retasking, preventive maintenance of sensor fields, etc.

A basic operation that supports a large class of topographic queries is the identification and labeling of *homogeneous regions*. A homogeneous region (or *feature region*) is one where all sensors have the same reading of a phenomenon. Sensor nodes whose readings are of interest to a particular query are called *feature nodes*. For simplicity we assume that a sensor node has a binary status (feature node or not a feature node) for the query. Once this information is gathered and stored in the network, other queries can be answered. For example, a query to count the number of regions of interest can obtain and sum the local counts of each of the distributed storage nodes. Processing and responding to queries could be in most cases decoupled from the actual data gathering and boundary estimation process, which can occur independently.

## 3.2. Our Virtual Architecture

We define the following virtual architecture for algorithm design and synthesis on large scale, homogeneous sensor networks that are arbitrarily and densely deployed on a terrain for purposes of environment monitoring applications such as topographic querying described above.

**The network**: In our application scenario, the end user is interested in monitoring the temperature over the entire terrain with a certain granularity. In other words, the set of locations - or points of coverage (PoCs) - are uniformly distributed over the entire terrain. For a rectangular terrain, the PoCs form a grid with a certain 'cell size' corresponding to each PoC. Note that the locations of the PoCs (in this case, in a grid) is not necessarily related to the pattern of deployment. As long as there is at least one sensor node in each geographic cell, the topology emulation algorithm (Sec. 5) is responsible for overlaying the virtual grid topology over the possibly irregular topology of the underlying network. Other topology creation and maintenance algorithms such as the one proposed in [17] can also be employed.

A grid will be an appropriate choice of virtual topology for uniform node deployment over the terrain. For nonuniform deployments, other virtual topologies such as a tree could be more appropriate. For the purposes of this case study, our virtual architecture in this case study abstracts the underlying network topology as an *oriented, two-dimensional grid*.

**Middleware services:** The concept of a group is central to networked sensing applications. Most in-network collaborative computation is accomplished by temporarily or permanently organizing sensor nodes in terms of groups. The membership in a group can be determined based on different factors such as geographic location, current reading of a sensor, the functionality of the program running on a node, etc. Geographic groups are ones where all nodes that are deployed in a certain geographic region are members of the group. Our virtual architecture incorporates a group formation middleware service specifically tailored for our case study. In a general application scenario, this service can be implemented using a combination of geographically constrained groups and logical naming, but for simplicity of exposition, the service is defined as follows.

The concept of hierarchical groups is supported for the grid topology. At the lowest level of hierarchy (level 0), every node is both a group member and a group leader. At level 1, the grid is partitioned into blocks of $2 \times 2$ nodes. The node in the north-west corner is designated a level 1 leader, and remaining nodes of the block are level 1 followers, and so on. Since every node knows its own grid coordinates, it can also determine its role as leader and/or follower at each level of the hierarchy.

**Communication primitives:** The virtual architecture in this case study supports *send()* and *receive()* message passing primitives that a node can use to communicate with any other node in the network. A *group communication primitive* is also available that can be used by a node to directly address a level $k$ leader as a logical entity.

**Cost functions**: We assume that each node has a short-range, omnidirectional antenna. For such antennas, the reception and transmission energy is of similar magnitude, and depends only on the radio electronics [13]. A *uniform cost function* for energy and time analysis of these systems can be defined – the energy cost for transmission, reception or computation of one unit of data is defined to be one unit of energy. One unit of latency is the time taken to complete $p$ computations or transmit $b$ units of data, where $p$ and $b$ are the processing speed and transmission bandwidth of the node respectively. This simple cost model has been used in most of the recent work related to algorithm design for sensor networks [5, 14, 18]. Whether these cost functions are realistic for a specific network is a decision for the end user. A different set of cost functions can be used if the characteristics of the deployment necessitate it.

## 4. Algorithm Design and Synthesis

### 4.1. Algorithm Specification

Our starting point is an algorithm for topographic querying that runs in $O(\sqrt{v})$ steps for a $\sqrt{v} \times \sqrt{v}$ grid, by using a divide and conquer strategy [3]. A step denotes a round of computation and is used for convenience of analysis. No assumptions are made about the degree of synchronization in the network. This algorithm can be represented as a data flow graph structured as a quad-tree (Figure 2). A leaf node corresponds to a task that is linked to the sensing interface, and interior nodes represent in-network processing on the sampled data. At each level of the tree, every node transmits its information to its parent at the next higher level. Processes at higher levels have greater oversight in terms of the extent of the regions they represent. In terms of groups, nodes at higher levels of the quad-tree are group leaders whose group members are its children in the tree.

A leaf node can compute its status as a feature node by comparing its current reading with a pre-specified threshold. At each level of hierarchy, a node receives data from its four children, containing a description of the boundaries of feature regions contained within the sender's geographic oversight. The boundary information also indicates whether the feature region(s) lie entirely within that extent, or information from neighboring extents is required to identify the true boundary of the feature region.

Again, the choice of application model will depend on the deployment scenario. In this case study, a task graph rep-

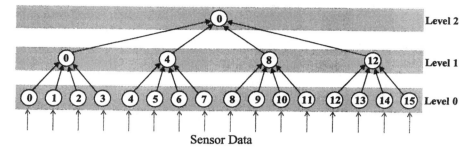

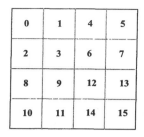

Figure 3: Example mapping

Figure 2: Quad-tree representation of the algorithm

resentation is an appropriate model because we assume that the pattern of computation and communication is known at design time. Leaf nodes sample at a known frequency, and every 'round' of sampling triggers one execution of the entire task graph. This model might not be suitable for event-driven applications such as target tracking where only the sensor nodes in the vicinity of the target (event) perform the sampling and in-network collaborative signal processing. If a task graph model has to be used for this scenario, the frequency of sampling at the leaf nodes could be expressed in probabilistic terms derived from a knowledge of expected events in the network.

The semantics of our application impose the following design time constraints on the task-to-node mapping.

**Coverage**: Each node in the virtual topology corresponds to one point of interest in the terrain and accordingly, the number of leaf nodes in the task graph is equal to the number of nodes in the virtual network graph. The coverage constraint states that each leaf node of the task graph (that represents one sampling task) should be mapped to a distinct node of the virtual topology to ensure the desired level of coverage.

**Spatial correlation**: In our application, the data exchanged between nodes represents boundaries of feature regions. When this data is merged at the parent nodes, the algorithm expects that the information from child nodes represents spatially adjacent geographic extents. That way, maximum data compression can be achieved in terms of representing the results of the processing. Hence, the spatial correlation constraint states that all children of a given node should represent information about a single contiguous geographic extent.

## 4.2. Role assignment

The virtual topology, cost model, and application graph can be provided as input to any of the numerous task mapping algorithms that exist in literature [6]. Since energy is an important consideration for sensor networks, the optimization criteria for the chosen algorithm will have to reflect new performance metrics such as total energy and/or

energy balance. Also, for the mapping to be feasible, constraints such as coverage and spatial correlation will have to be satisfied.

Our virtual architecture exports a grid topology, and a mapping that satisfies both constraints is shown by the labeling of the quad-tree nodes in Fig. 2, which indicates their mapping to the regions of the grid in Fig. 3. As shown in the figures, the terrain of deployment is partitioned into $2 \times 2$ blocks and groups of four level 0 nodes of the quad-tree that share the same parent are mapped onto each block.

Only the leaf nodes perform the actual sampling. Hence, the non-leaf nodes can be mapped anywhere in the grid subject to performance optimization. In general, the algorithm designer can express the *relationship between a parent and child as a leader and follower in a collaborative group*, and leave their mapping entirely to the group formation middleware service of the virtual architecture. Evaluating the relative performance of this algorithm compared to some other approach means that the middleware should provide the associated cost for member to leader communication within the group. With our group formation technique described in Sec. 3.2, the latency and energy of transmitting a data packet from a level $k$ follower to the level $k$ leader is proportional to the minimum number of hops separating them in the virtual network graph, assuming shortest path routing. We do not provide a detailed latency and energy analysis in this paper due to space limitations. Interested readers can refer to [16] for a detailed analysis and high-level simulation results of this algorithm on a sensor network architecture very similar to the algorithm described above.

Using the static group formation provided by the virtual architecture, the mapping that will finally occur is shown by the labels of non-leaf nodes in Fig. 2 and corresponding region labels of the grid in Fig. 3. The root node is mapped to location 0, and the four level 1 nodes are mapped to locations 0, 4, 8, and 12 respectively, which are the leaders of their corresponding groups. The mapping exploits the correspondence between the quad-tree structure, and the idea of recursively dividing the topology into quadrants and merging data within quadrants.

## 4.3. Program Synthesis

The output of the mapping stage is an algorithm specified for a grid topology, which relies on middleware support for group formation, and on communication primitives that can be used by any node to send a message to group leaders at the appropriate level of hierarchy. The next step is to synthesize this algorithm into a program that executes at each node of the grid topology.

We use a reactive, event-driven programming model that is supported by state-of-the-art code generation frameworks [8] and programming languages [10] for sensor networks. An asynchronous data flow model of computation is assumed, which means that a process need not wait for all its input data (incoming messages) before computing on them. This is because latency of message delivery is unpredictable in typical sensor networks and some messages might even be dropped. Therefore, it is advisable to structure the program in such a way that incoming information is incrementally processed wherever possible. In our application, since the information represents region boundaries, it can be incrementally merged into the existing aggregated information at that leader.

A manually synthesized program specification for the algorithm is given in Figure 4. A brief description of the working of this program is as follows. Initially ($start = true$), each node decides if it is a feature node and constructs its local data structure to store the information. It then increments the level of recursion (hierarchy) and transmits the information to the appropriate leader node for merging. For all levels higher than 0, a node can expect to receive 3 messages from group leaders at the next lower level of recursion since the network is partitioned into quadrants at every stage and by virtue of the mapping, one of the four incoming messages in the quad-tree representation is from the node to itself. An array is used for the $msgsReceived$ data structure in consideration of the fact that information can be transmitted and processed at different speed in each quadrant.

In a grid of size $\sqrt{v} \times \sqrt{v}$ where $\log \sqrt{v}$ is an integer, all level $k$ leaders are also level $(k-1)$ leaders. A level $k$ leader can receive messages from other level $(k-1)$ leaders before it completes processing messages from level $(k-2)$ leaders in its own quadrant. Hence, messages contain their level information, and on receipt are merged with other messages at that level of recursion. Once a level $k$ leader that is not also a level $(k+1)$ leader sends a message to a level $(k+1)$ leader, it no longer participates in the aggregation process and its level of recursion does not increase. Only the node which performs the final aggregation reaches $maxrecLevel$, triggers the corresponding Action clause, and exfiltrates the entire boundary information (or stores it locally, depending on the end user requirements).

**State (initial values) :**
start(=*false*), recLevel(=0), maxrecLevel,
  mySubGraph[1..maxrecLevel](=NULL),
myCoords, msgsReceived[1..maxrecLevel](=0)
transmit(=*false*)

**Message alphabet :**
mGraph = {senderCoord, msubGraph, mrecLevel}

**Condition** : start = true
**Action** :  start = false
        compute mySubGraph[recLevel]
            from intra-cell readings
        transmit = true
        recLevel = recLevel + 1

**Condition** : received mGraph
**Action** :  merge(mGraph,mySubGraph[mrecLevel])
        msgsReceived[mrecLevel]++

**Condition** : transmit=true
**Action** : message = {myCoords, mySubGraph, recLevel}
        if (recLevel = maxrecLevel)
            exfiltrate message
        else
            send message to Leader(recLevel+1)
        transmit = false

**Condition** : msgsReceived[recLevel] = 3
**Action** :  transmit=true
        recLevel = recLevel + 1

Figure 4: Synthesized program specification

## 5. The Runtime System

We now briefly describe some protocols for the runtime system designed to accomplish two main functionalities: emulating the grid topology on the arbitrary network deployment, and binding virtual processes of the synthesized program to real nodes of the underlying network.

### 5.1. Topology Emulation

The underlying network consists of $n$ identical sensor nodes deployed over a square terrain of side $l$. Let $G_g = (V_g, E_g)$ denote the virtual network graph (grid). The terrain can be partitioned into non-overlapping equal sized cells each of side $c$ - such that $\frac{l}{c} = \sqrt{v}$, where $v = |V_g|$. Each sensor node has a transmission range of $r$. Let $SN = \{s_0, s_1, \ldots, s_n\}$ be the set of sensor nodes. The real network can therefore be represented by a graph $G_r = (V_r, E_r)$, where vertices correspond to sensor nodes, and $(i, j) \in E_r$ iff $\delta(s_i, s_j) \leq r$, where $\delta$ is the Euclidean distance. We assume $G_r$ is connected. Let $NB_i$ be the set of neighbors of $s_i$, where $s_j \in NB_i$ iff $(i,j) \in E_r$. Each node is aware of its $(x,y)$ coordinates in an absolute or relative co-ordinate system, and also knows the outer boundary of the terrain of deployment in the same co-ordinate system. Let $s_i^x$ and $s_i^y$ be the $x$ and $y$ coordinates of node $s_i$.

Let $MAP : SN \to I \times I$ associate each $s_k \in V_r$ with a pair of grid coordinates $(i,j)$ where $s_{i,j} \in V_g$ is the node to be emulated. Let $CELL_{i,j} = \{s_k | MAP(s_k) = (i,j)\}$, i.e., the set of nodes that collectively emulate the $(i,j)$-th node in the virtual grid. In this paper, we assume that the subgraph of $G_r$ induced by nodes in $CELL_{i,j}$ ($\forall i,j$) is connected.

A simple, cell-based protocol can be used to emulate $G_g$ on $G_r$. We assume that localization and neighbor discovery has occurred and each node can compute $MAP(s_i)$ and knows the number and location of its one-hop neighbors. The routing table at node $s_i$ is a function $RT_{s_i} : DIR \to NB_i \cup \{NULL\}$, where $DIR = \{No, Ea, We, So\}$ is the set of directions in the oriented grid. Some entries of the routing table can be filled in using the initially available information. For example, $RT_{s_i}(No)$ can be associated with $s_j$ if $\exists s_j \in NB_i$ s.t. $s_j \in CELL_{i-1,j}$. If there is no node in $NB_i$ that lies in a neighboring cell, the routing table entry is $NULL$. Now each node $s_i$ now tries to discover multi-hop paths to neighboring cells that are associated with $NULL$ entries in $RT_{s_i}$. Each node $s_i$ initially broadcasts its own (small) routing table to all its neighbors. When a node $s_i$ receives a message from some $s_j \in NB_i$ where $MAP(s_j) \neq MAP(s_i)$, the message is ignored. If $s_j \in NB_i$, $MAP(s_j) = MAP(s_i)$ and $\exists d \in DIR$ such that $RT_{s_j}(d) \neq NULL$ and $RT_{s_i}(d) = NULL$, $s_i$ sets $RT_{s_i} = s_j$. Since new nodes can be added to the network or existing nodes can leave or fail, the above protocol should execute periodically. The user can choose any routing protocol implemented on the oriented grid using the routing table to forward messages between adjacent cells of the grid.

*This topology emulation protocol is time and energy-efficient* because (i) the path setup in all cells occurs in parallel, (ii) messages cross at most one cell boundary before being suppressed, and (iii) the latency is proportional to the maximum, over all cells, of the length of the longest path between pairs of nodes in a cell.

### 5.2. Binding virtual processes to physical nodes

To execute the mapping on the real network, a mechanism is required where the functionality of the $v$ nodes of the virtual topology is somehow mapped onto the $n$ nodes of the underlying, real network. We assume that $n > v$ and describe one way of accomplishing this mapping, using the same cell-based approach as for topology emulation.

Let $gc_{i,j}$ denote the geographic center of cell $i,j$ and $gc_{i,j}^x$ and $gc_{i,j}^y$ denote its $x$ and $y$ coordinates. Since each node $s_i$ knows its own coordinates, the cell size, and the boundary of the terrain of deployment, it can compute $gc_{i,j}^x$ and $gc_{i,j}^y$. Also, it can compute its Euclidean distance to the center of the cell. Each node maintains a flag *leader* initially set to $TRUE$. Each $s_i$ now broadcasts $\delta(s_i, gc_{MAP(s_i)})$ to its neighbors. As in the path setup phase, messages crossing cell boundaries are suppressed. If node $s_i$ receives a value from $s_j \in NB_i$ that is less than its own $\delta$ value, it sets $leader = FALSE$ and broadcasts the updated value to all $s_j \in NB_i$. Eventually, the only node whose $leader = TRUE$ will be the one that has not received $\delta$ values lower than its own from any of its neighbors, and hence is the node closest to the geographic center. This node can start executing the program specified for node $s_{i,j}$ in $G_g$. The choice of the node closest to the center of the cell as leader is an effort to align the problem geometry and the network geometry as closely as possible. Residual energy level or more sophisticated metrics could also be employed depending on the particular application, especially if the role of leader is to be periodically rotated among nodes in the cell.

## 6. Related Work

The state-centric programming framework proposed in [12] has a similar motivation as our work: to define an appropriate mental model that application developers can use to program distributed sensor networks. The framework is based on the concept of collaboration groups which abstract common patterns in application-specific communication and resource allocation. We consider the state-centric framework complementary to our proposed methodology in the sense that it provides programming primitives and a means of implementing the synthesized algorithms on the target network. The UW-API [15] is an example of a communication library for distributed computations in sensor networks, motivated by the MPI library [9]. Similar to MPI, some of the UW-API primitives are to be invoked by a single sensor node and others are for collective communication, to be invoked simultaneously by a group of nodes in a geographic region. All operations take place on regions, which can be created using specific primitives. Even barrier synchronization is supported for the sensor nodes that lie within a region.

There are other efforts in the community that are addressing algorithm development [5, 11], task allocation [7, 21], middleware services [19, 20], and programming models [1, 2] for sensor networks. However, we are not aware of any coherent top-down methodology to simplify and ultimately automate the design and synthesis of networked sensing applications.

# 7. Discussion

End to end application design for large scale sensor networks is a complex process. A significant fraction of this complexity is at the networking layer because a host of interacting low level services and protocols are required for the sensor network to be functional. In addition, the end user is required to coordinate the execution of different tasks at the application level, and their interactions with each other and with the physical world through the sensing interface. System wide energy performance has to be optimized for extending the network lifetime, and issues such as fault tolerance must also be handled. State of the art protocol-centric approaches assume an omniscient end user who has a good understanding both of the application domain and of wireless networking issues, and who is capable of energy efficient and robust cross-layer design and customization of the protocol stack. There is now a growing body of research on high level abstractions and middleware that aim to hide low level networking details from the application developer, and thereby reduce the design complexity.

Design methodologies that employ multiple layers of abstraction to reduce design complexity risk doing so at the expense of performance of the implementation compared to hand-optimized designs. We believe, however, that the obvious and significant benefits of this approach - rapid first-order analysis of algorithms and greatly reduced complexity of programming - outweigh performance considerations, especially where hand-optimization at reasonable cost might not be possible.

# References

[1] T. Abdelzaher, B. Blum, Q. Cao, D. Evans, J. George, S. George, T. He, L. Luo, S. Son, R. Stoleru, J. Stankovic, and A. Wood. EnviroTrack: An Environmental Programming Model for Tracking Applications in Distributed Sensor Networks. In *Proceedings of International Conference on Distributed Computing Systems (ICDCS)*, 2004.

[2] H. Abrach, S. Bhatti, J. Carlson, H. Dai, J. Rose, A. Sheth, B. Shucker, J. Deng, and R. Han. MANTIS: System Support for MultimodAl NeTworks of In-situ Sensors. In *2nd ACM International Workshop on Wireless Sensor Networks and Applications (WSNA)*, pages 50–59, 2003.

[3] H. M. Alnuweiri and V. K. Prasanna. Parallel architectures and algorithms for image component labeling. *IEEE Transactions on Pattern Analysis and Machine Intelligence*, 14(10):1014–1034, 1992.

[4] R. Barr, J. Bicket, D. Dantas, B. Du, T. Kim, B. Zhou, and E. Sirer. On the need for system-level support for ad hoc and sensor networks. In *Operating Systems Review, ACM*, April 2002.

[5] R. S. Bhuvaneswaran, J. L. Bordim, J. Cui, and K. Nakano. Fundamental protocols for wireless sensor networks. In *International Parallel and Distributed Processing Symposium (IPDPS) Workshop on Advances in Parallel and Distributed Computational Models*, April 2001.

[6] S. H. Bokhari. *Assignment Problems in Parallel and Distributed Computing*. Boston: Kluwer Academic, 1987.

[7] B. Bonfils and P. Bonnet. Adaptive and decentralized operator placement for in-network query processing. In *Information Processing in Sensor Networks (IPSN)*, 2003.

[8] E. Cheong, J. Liebman, J. Liu, and F. Zhao. TinyGALS: A programming model for event-driven embedded systems. In *ACM Symposium on Applied Computing (SAC)*, March 2003.

[9] MPI Forum. MPI: A message-passing interface standard. *International Journal of Supercomputer Applications and High performance Computing*, 8(3/4), 1994.

[10] D. Gay, P. Levis, R. von Behren, M. Welsh, E. Brewer, and D. Culler. The nesC language: A holistic approach to networked embedded systems. In *Proceedings of Programming Language Design and Implementation (PLDI)*, 2003.

[11] B. Krishnamachari and S. Iyengar. Bayesian algorithms for fault-tolerant event region detection in wireless sensor networks. *IEEE Transactions on Computers*, 53(3), 2004.

[12] J. Liu, M. Chu, J. Liu, J. Reich, and F. Zhao. State-centric programming for sensor-actuator network systems. In *IEEE Pervasive Computing*, 2003.

[13] R. Min and A. Chandrakasan. Top five myths about the energy consumption of wireless communication. *Mobile Computing and Communications Review*, 6(4), 2003.

[14] K. Nakano, S. Olariu, and A. Zomaya. Energy-efficient routing in the broadcast communication model. *IEEE Transactions on Parallel and Distributed Systems*, 13(2):1201–1210, December 2002.

[15] P. Ramanathan, K. C. Wang, K. K. Saluja, and T. Clouqueur. Communication support for location-centric collaborative signal processing in sensor networks. In *DIMACS Workshop on Pervasive Networks*, May 2001.

[16] M. Singh, A. Bakshi, and V. K. Prasanna. Constructing topographic maps in networked sensor systems. Technical Report CENG-2004-09, Department of EE-Systems, Univ. of Southern California, June 2004.

[17] M. Singh, A. Pathak, and V. K. Prasanna. Constructing and maintaining a clustered mesh topological infrastructure in sensor networks. Technical Report CENG-2004-08, Dept of EE-Systems, Univ. of Southern California, May 2004.

[18] M. Singh and V. K. Prasanna. Energy-optimal and energy-balanced sorting in a single-hop wireless sensor network. In *International Conference on Pervasive Computing and Communications (PERCOM)*, March 2003.

[19] M. Welsh and G. Mainland. Programming sensor networks using abstract regions. In *Proceedings of the First USENIX/ACM Symposium on Networked Systems Design and Implementation (NSDI)*, March 2004.

[20] Y. Yu, B. Krishnamachari, and V. K. Prasanna. Issues in designing middleware for wireless sensor networks. *IEEE Network*, 18(1), 2004.

[21] Y. Yu and V. K. Prasanna. Energy-balanced task allocation for collaborative processing in wireless sensor networks. *(accepted by) Mobile Networks and Applications (MONET)*, special issue on Algorithmic Solutions for Wireless, Mobile, Ad Hoc and Sensor Networks, 2004.

# A Reliable Connection Migration Mechanism for Synchronous Transient Communication in Mobile Codes

Xiliang Zhong and Cheng-Zhong Xu
Department of Electrical & Computer Engg.
Wayne State University, Detroit, Michigan 48202
{xlzhong, czxu}@wayne.edu

## Abstract

*With the increasing popularity of network applications, mobile codes become a promising technology to provide scalable services. Due to their mobile nature, it is a challenge to support synchronous transient communication between mobile objects. This paper presents a reliable connection migration mechanism that allows mobile objects in communication to remain connected during their migration. This mechanism supports concurrent migration of both endpoints of a connection and guarantees exactly-once delivery of all transmitted data. In addition, a mobile code access control model is integrated to ensure secure connection migration. This paper presents the design of the mechanism and a reference implementation, namely NapletSocket, over Java Socket in a mobile agent system. Experimental results show that NapletSocket incurs a moderate cost in connection setup, mainly due to security checking, and marginal overhead for communication over established connections. Furthermore, we investigate the impact of agent mobility on communication performance via simulation. Simulation results show that NapletSocket is efficient for a wide range of migration and communication patterns.*

## 1 Introduction

Mobile codes refer to programs that function as they are transferred from one machine to another. The concept of code mobility represents a promising solution for today's network services for load balancing, fault resilience, system administration, etc. A special form of migration is mobile agent that has the ability to travel autonomously, carrying its code, as well as data and running state. Because of its unique properties, mobile agents have been the focus of much speculation in the past decade.

In mobile agents based computing, it is often necessary for remote agents to communicate with each other to work efficiently. Conventional technologies for remote inter-agent communication is through a mailbox-like *asynchronous persistent* communication mechanism due to the requirement for agent autonomy [1]. That is, an agent can send messages to others no matter its communication parties exist or not. Asynchronous persistent communication plays a key role in many distributed applications and is widely supported by existing mobile agent systems; see [13] for a comprehensive review of location independent communication protocols between mobile agents.

A common asynchronous communication mechanism works in two steps. First a message is sent to an intermediate, such as a proxy or a mail-box. Then the message is forwarded to the receiver. This communication model doesn't guarantee instantaneous message delivery and it is hard for the sender to determine whether and when the receiver gets the message. Thus it is not sufficient for applications that require agents to closely cooperate. For example, in the use of mobile agents for parallel computing [16], cooperative agents need to be synchronized frequently during their lifetime. A *synchronous transient* communication mechanism would keep the agents working more closely and efficiently. TCP socket is a solution for synchronous communication in distributed applications. However, the traditional TCP protocol has no support for mobility because it has been designed with the assumption that the communication peers are stationary. To support message delivery in case of agent migration, a connection migration scheme is desirable so that an established socket connection would migrate with the agent continuously and transparently.

There are recent studies on mobile TCP/IP in both network and transport layers to support the mobility of physical devices in the arena of mobile computing [6, 7, 8, 11, 12]. We refer to this type of mobility as physical mobility, in contrast to logical mobility of codes. Although these protocols provide feasible ways to link mobile devices to network, they have no control over the logical mobility.

Mobile agent systems are usually organized as a middleware. Agent connection migration requires support of session-layer implementations in the middleware. In the past, a few session-layer connection migration mechanisms were proposed [9, 10, 17, 18]. However, none of them was targeted at agent mobility. Agent related connection migration involves two unique reliability and security problems. Reliable agent connection migration needs to have mobility support for exactly-once delivery of all transmitted data, even if the two agents migrate simultaneously. Security is a major concern in agent-oriented programming. Socket is a critical resource and its access must be fully controlled by agent servers. Connection migration is vulnerable to eavesdropper attacks and it is necessary to protect transactions over a connection from any malicious attacks.

In this paper, we present the design and implementation of an integrated mechanism that deals with reliability and security in agent connection migration. It provides an agent-oriented socket programming interface for location-independent socket communication and guarantees exactly-once message delivery. To assure secure connection migration, each connection is associated with a secret session key created during connection setup. We prototyped the mechanism as a NapletSocket component in Naplet mobile agent system. Naplet [14] is a featured mobile agent system we developed in house for educational purposes. It supports a mailbox-based PostOffice mechanism with asynchronous persistent communication. NapletSocket provides a complementary mechanism for synchronous transient communication.

The remainder of the paper is organized as follows. Section 2 and Section 3 give an overview and details of the design of NapletSocket. Section 4 presents experimental results. Section 5 presents a communication performance model and simulation results on the impact of agent mobility. Related work is summarized in Section 6. Section 7 concludes the paper.

## 2 NapletSocket: A Connection Migration Mechanism

### 2.1 NapletSocket Architecture

NapletSocket provides interfaces similar to Java Socket. It comprises of two classes *NapletSocket(agent-id)* and *NapletServerSocket(agent-id)*. They resemble Java Socket and ServerSocket in semantics, except that NapletSocket connection is agent oriented. It is known Java Socket/ServerSocket establish a connection between a pair of endpoints in the form of (Host IP, Port). Due to security reasons, an agent is not allowed to specify a port number for its pending connection. Instead, it is the underlying NapletSocket system that allocates ports to the connection based on resource availability and access permissions. The Naplet system contains an agent location service that maps an agent ID to its physical location. This ensures location transparent communication between agents. Once the connection is

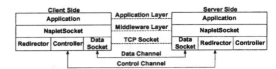

**Figure 1. NapletSocket Architecture.**

| State | Description |
|---|---|
| CLOSED | Not connected |
| LISTEN | Ready to accept connections |
| CONNECT_SENT | Sent a CONNECT request |
| CONNECT_ACKED | Confirmed a CONNECT request |
| ESTABLISHED | Normal state for data transfer |
| SUS_SENT | Sent a SUSPEND request |
| SUS_ACKED | Confirmed a SUSPEND request |
| SUSPEND_WAIT | Wait in a suspend operation |
| SUSPENDED | The connection is suspended |
| RES_SENT | Sent a RESUME request |
| RES_ACKED | Confirmed a RESUME request |
| RESUME_WAIT | Wait in a resume operation |
| CLOSE_SENT | Sent a CLOSE request |
| CLOSE_ACKED | Confirmed a CLOSE request |

**Figure 2. States in NapletSocket transitions.**

established, all communications are through the connection and location service is no longer needed.

To support connection migration, NapletSocket provides two new methods *suspend()* and *resume()*. They can be called either by agents for explicit control over connection migration, or by Naplet docking system for transparent migration.

Figure 1 shows NapletSocket architecture. It comprises of three main components: data socket, controller and redirector. The data socket is the actual channel for data transfer. It is associated with an input buffer to keep undelivered data. The controller is used for management of connections and operations that need access rights to socket resources. The redirector is used to redirect socket connection from a remote agent to a local resident agent. Both the controller and the redirector can be shared by all NapletSockets so that only one pair is necessary in a Naplet server.

### 2.2 State Transitions

The design of NapletSocket can be described as a finite state machine, extended from the TCP protocol. It contains 14 states, as listed in Figure 2. The states in bold are newly added to the standard TCP state transitions. In each state, certain action will be taken when an appropriate event occurs. There are two types of events: calls from local agents and messages from remote agents. Actions include sending messages to remote agents and invoking local functions.

Figure 3 shows the state transitions of a NapletSocket connection. The solid lines show the transitions of clients connecting to servers and the dotted lines are for servers. Details of the open, suspend, resume and close transactions are as follows.

**Open a connection.** Both client and server are initially at the CLOSED state. When an agent does an active open, a

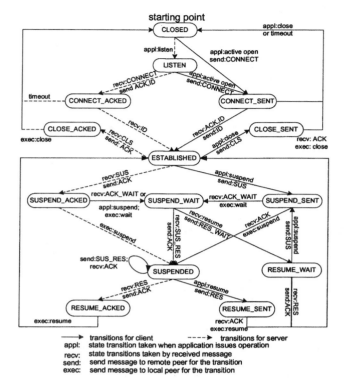

**Figure 3. State transitions diagram.**

CONNECT request is sent to the server and the state of the connection changes to CONNECT_SENT. If the request is accepted, the client side NapletSocket receives an ACK and a socket ID to identify the connection. Then it sends back its own ID and the state changes to ESTABLISHED.

Connection in server side switches to the LISTEN state once an agent does a listen. When a CONNECT request comes from a client, the server acknowledges it by sending back an ACK and a socket ID. The connection then changes to the CONNECT_ACKED state. After the socket ID of the client side is received, the state switches to ESTABLISHED. Now data can be transferred between the two peers as normal socket connection.

**Suspend/Resume a connection.** Either of the two peers may suspend an established connection. When invoked, the suspend operation sends a SUS to the other side. If the request is acknowledged, an ACK is sent back and triggers the action of closing underlying I/O streams and data socket. The connection state then switches to SUSPENDED.

When the other side of NapletSocket receives the SUS message, it sends back an ACK if it agrees to suspend. Then it closes the underlying connection. After that, the connection state for this peer changes to SUSPENDED. No data can be exchanged in this state.

In the SUSPENDED state, when either of the agents decides to resume the connection, it invokes the resume inter-

face. The resume process first sets up a new connection to the remote redirector and sends a RES message. If an ACK is received, it then resumes the connection and the state switches to ESTABLISHED. Once the remote peer in the SUSPENDED state receives a resume request, it first sends back an ACK. Then the redirector hands its connection to the desired NapletSocket and new I/O streams are created. After that, the connection changes to ESTABLISHED.

**Close a connection.** In either the ESTABLISHED or the SUSPENDED state, the close interface can be invoked to close the current connection. A CLS(CLOSE) request is sent to the peer. After acknowledgement, both sides may close the underlying socket and I/O streams. Then the connection state changes to CLOSED.

## 3 Design Issues

### 3.1 Transparency and Reliability

Connection migration needs to be transparent to end users. The main approach is to use a data socket under NapletSocket. During connection migration, the underlying data socket is first closed before migration and updated afterward. It is possible there are in-flight data at the time of migration. To guarantee messages delivery, we add an input buffer to each input stream and wrap them together as a NapletInputStream. To suspend a connection, the operation retrieves all currently undelivered data into the buffer before closing the data socket. The data migrate with the agent. When migration finishes and the connection is resumed at the remote server, a read operation first reads data from the input buffer. It will only read data from the new socket stream after all data in the buffer have been retrieved.

When two agents of a connection move simultaneously, there is a problem since the resume operation only remembers the previous destination. It is not difficult to get information of the new destination. The problem is if an agent migrates frequently, a resume operation may have to chase the agent. To avoid the problem, we provide a simplified solution by delaying one of the migration, which means one agent migrates first and the other must wait for the first one to finish. Therefore agents migrations occur sequentially although they are issued concurrently. But from the viewpoint of high level applications, the underlying sequential migration is transparent.

To delay one of the two simultaneous suspend requests, two states SUSPEND_WAIT and RESUME_WAIT are used. One of the suspend operation is delayed and the connection is put into the SUSPEND_WAIT state. At this state, the operation is blocked until the other agent finishes migration and sends a SUS_RES message. RESUME_WAIT is the state when a resume operation is blocked. After the first migration, the resume operation is invoked and the underlying socket is updated. But the connection needs to be suspended due to

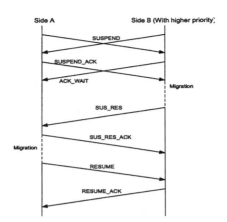

**Figure 4. Sequence of over-lapped migration.**

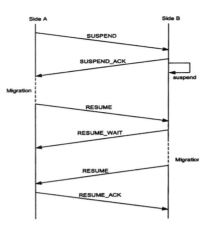

**Figure 5. Sequence of non-overlapped migration.**

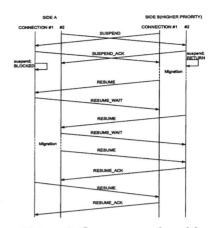

**Figure 6. Sequence of multiple connections migration.**

the second agent migration and the underlying socket may have to be closed. To prevent this extra update, we block the resume operation and change the state of the connection to RESUME_WAIT. The resume operation will get signaled after the second migration and finish.

Depending on the ordering of two suspend operations, we classify the problem into two types. One is over-lapped concurrent connection migration; the other is non-overlapped. In the first case, both SUSPEND requests are issued simultaneously and neither side receives an acknowledgement before the SUSPEND request. Both sides have to decide whether to approve the request. To approve one and only one request, we give higher priority to one of the agents. The priority is decided by unique agent IDs. An agent with a larger ID has a higher priority. A time sequence for this case is in Figure 4, with agent in side B having a high priority. Side B receives a SUSPEND request and since it has also sent a request, it knows this is a concurrent connection migration. Then it sends back an ACK_WAIT to delay the migration. Side A has the same situation. But side A always acknowledges a SUSPEND request since it has a low priority. After that, the state of the connection in side B switches to SUSPENDED and in side A it switches to SUS-PEND_WAIT. The agent in side B migrates and informs side A with a SUS_RES message. Side A can then proceed with normal connection suspend and resume.

In the second case, agent in one side issues a suspend request after a SUSPEND request is acknowledged and the request processing hasn't finished. So no new suspend operation should be issued until the first one finishes. A time sequence is presented in Figure 5 as an example.

### 3.2 Multiple Connections

In the preceding discussions on concurrent connection migration, we focused on one connection. When multiple connections are established, all connections should be sus-

pended before agents migration. During the suspend operations, it is possible for them to be suspended in different orders. For example, suppose there are two connections by agents in side A and B, represented as #1 and #2. Side A may suspend the connections in the order of #2, #1 and side B in the order of #1, #2. During concurrent migration, it is possible for side A to suspend connection #2 while at the same time side B tries to suspend #1. Neither these operations needs to be delayed because they are operating on different connections. Thus both connections are successfully suspended. When suspending the second connection, side A on #1 while side B on #2, both sides will find the connections already suspended. By default a suspend operation simply returns for a suspended connection. Therefore both sides successfully suspend their connections and agents migrations happen at the same time. As a result, neither knows where the other agent is after migration.

To ensure only one agent migrates at a time, we give different responses to a suspend operation when it is operating on a suspended connection. Suspend operations are distinguished by whether they are issued locally, *suspend locally*, or invoked by remote messages, *suspend remotely*. In a suspend operation, if the connection has already been suspended remotely which means there is an on-going agent migration in the other side, we decide whether to continue or block depending on the priority of the agent. If it has a low priority, we block the suspend operation; if it has a high priority, we finish the operation without further actions. The blocked suspend operation will get signaled when the one with high priority finishes migration. Figure 6 gives an illustration of the protocol in the case of two connections.

### 3.3 Security

Security is always a major concern in mobile agent systems. NapletSocket addresses security issues in two aspects. First, the agent should not be able to cause any security problems to the host it resides. Second, the connection should be secure from possible attacks like eavesdropping. More specifically, a connection can only be suspended/resumed/closed by the one who initially creates it.

Regarding the first issue, any explicit requests to create a Socket or ServerSocket from an agent are denied. Permissions are only granted to requests from the NapletSocket system. This can be achieved by user-based access control introduced in the latest JDK security mechanism. It allows permissions to be granted according to who is executing the piece of code (subject), rather than where the code comes from (codebase). A subject represents the source of a request such as a mobile agent or NapletSocket controller. An agent subject has no permission to access local socket resources. When it needs such access, it submits a request to the controller. The controller authenticates the agent and checks access permissions. If the security check passes, a NapletSocket or NapletServerSocket is created and returned to the agent. More details about agent-oriented access control in Naplet system can be found in [15].

Regarding the second issue, connection migration can be realized by the use of a socket ID. However, a plain socket ID couldn't prevent eavesdropping attacks. To this end, we apply Diffie-Hellman key exchange protocol to establish a secret session key between the pair of communicating agents at connection setup stage. Any subsequent operations on the connection must be accompanied with the secret key. Such requests will be denied unless their keys are verified. This protects NapletSocket connections from eavesdropping attacks.

## 4  Experimental Results of NapletSocket

In this section, we present an implementation of NapletSocket and its performance in comparison with Java Socket. All experiments were conducted in a group of Sun Blade 1000 workstations connected by a fast Ethernet. We first show the effectiveness and overhead of the implementation. Then we evaluate the overall communication performance in case of agent migration.

### 4.1  Effectiveness of Reliable Communication

The first experiment gives a demonstration of reliable communication using NapletSocket. A stationary agent keeps sending messages one at a millisecond to a mobile agent. Each message contains a counter, indicating the message order. Reliable communication requires the mobile agent to receive all the messages in the same order as they are sent.

Figure 7 shows a trace of the message counters received by the mobile agent at different time. Agent migration time is omitted for simplicity. The agent migrates at 10th, 20th, 30th milliseconds. The light dots show the messages read from the socket stream and the dark dots are those into or

**Table 1. Cost of open/close operations.**

| Connection Type | Open (ms) | Close (ms) |
|---|---|---|
| Java Socket | 3.7 | 0.6 |
| NapletSocket w/o security | 18.2 | 12.5 |
| NapletSocket with security | 134.4 | 12.6 |

from the NapletSocket buffer. In the first migration point, the agent migrates before it retrieves all the messages in transmission. The undelivered three messages (7, 8, 9) are kept in the buffer. They are transferred together with the agent and delivered to the application after migration by the support of NapletSocket. Similarly, the third agent migration involves transferring of one message.

### 4.2  Cost of Primitive NapletSocket Operations

The second experiment focused on the cost of primitive operations defined in NapletSocket, including connection open, close, suspend, and resume.

We performed open and close operations with and without security checking for 100 times. Table 1 shows the average time for both operations. From the table, we can see that opening a secure mobile connection costs almost 40 times as much as that of a Java socket. A breakdown of the cost shows that more than 80% of the time was spent on key establishment, authentication and authorization. The cost would reduce to 18.2ms without security support.

Similarly, we recorded 27.8ms and 16.9ms for suspend and resume operations, respectively. The costs are mainly due to the exchange of control messages, which makes up about 50% for suspend and 70% for resume.

The benefit of provisioning a reliable connection can be seen by comparing the time required for re-opening a connection with that of suspend/resume. If we close a NapletSocket before migration and reopen a new one afterwards, the total cost involved is 147ms. However, if we use suspend and resume instead, the cost is only 44.7ms. The total time saved increases with the number migration.

### 4.3  NapletSocket Throughput

In the third experiment, we tested NapletSocket throughput by the TTCP [3] measurement tool, in which a pair of TTCP programs is used to communicate messages of different sizes as fast as possible. Figure 8 shows NapletSocket throughput between two stationary agents. The throughput of Java Socket is included for comparison. From the figure, we can see the NapletSocket throughput degrades slightly. This degradation is mainly due to synchronized access to I/O streams. With the increase of message sizes, the performance gap becomes almost negligible.

We then measured NapletSocket throughput with different agent migration frequency (i.e. service time at each hop). We used a *single migration* pattern where one agent

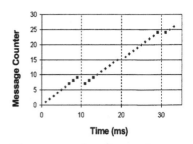

**Figure 7. A trace of message transmissions and deliveries.**

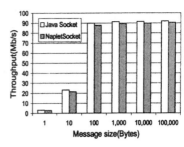

**Figure 8. Throughput of NapletSocket versus Java Socket.**

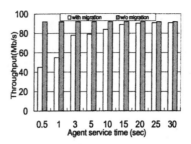

**Figure 9. Impact of migration frequency on effective throughput.**

remains stationary while the other keeps moving at a certain rate. We refer to the total traffic communicated over a period of communication and migration time as *effective throughput*. In this experiment, we assume a constant message size of 2K bytes. Figure 9 shows the results. We can see the throughput is only about 45Mb/s when the service time is 0.5 second. If an agent stays in a host long enough, for example 10 seconds, the effective throughput gets very close to the stationary throughput. This implies that the effect of agent and connection migrations on throughput becomes negligible when an agent migrates at a low frequency.

## 5 Performance Model of Agent Mobility

The experiments in the preceding section assumed agents communicate to each other "as fast as possible". The objective of this section is to investigate the impact of the communication rate as well as the agent migration concurrency on the performance of NapletSocket.

### 5.1 Performance Model

Consider two mobile agents, say A and B, which are connected via a NapletSocket connection. Both agents travel around the network at various rates. Without loss of generality, we assume agent B has a higher priority. At each host, the agents process their tasks for certain time and communicate with each other for synchronization. Then the agents migrate to other hosts. Associated with each agent migration is a connection migration, with a suspend operation before agent migration and a resume operation afterward.

It is known effective throughput of NapletSocket is determined by the cost for connection migration as well as the overhead for agent migration. Since the agent migration overhead is application-dependent (being dependent upon the code and state sizes), we develop a model for connection migration, denoted by $T_{c-migrate}$, instead. Let $T_{suspend}$ and $T_{resume}$ denote the costs for suspend and resume operations, respectively. It follows that $T_{c-migrate} = T_{suspend} + T_{resume}$.

Notice that the costs for suspend and resume operations are related to agent migration concurrency. In the case of

single migration, both $T_{suspend}$ and $T_{resume}$ are constant. When both endpoints of a connection are mobile, both costs are dependent upon the ordering of their requests. Let $t^a_{begin}$ and $t^b_{begin}$ denote the request time of the two agents A and B and their interval $\tau = |t^a_{begin} - t^b_{begin}|$. If $\tau$ is large enough for the first suspend to complete before the second request, it is single migration. Otherwise, it is concurrent migration.

As we discussed in Section 3.1, concurrent migration can be further distinguished by being overlapped or non-overlapped. In the overlapped case, the suspend cost of agent B, $T^b_{suspend}$, is the same as that of a single migration, since it has a higher priority. The suspend operation of agent A couldn't continue until B finishes and sends a SUS_RES message, as shown in Figure 4. From the figure, we can see that the arrival time of SUS_RES at agent A $t_{sus\_res} = t^b_{begin} + T^b_{suspend} + T^b_{a-migrate} + T_{control}$, where $T^b_{a-migrate}$ refers to the migration time of agent B and $T_{control}$ is the latency for delivery of a control message between agent A and B. Consequently, the suspend operation of agent A can be finished within the time of $t_{sus\_res} - t^a_{begin}$. Since B's migration is overlapped with A, the suspend cost for connection of agent A can be approximated as $T_{control} + T^b_{suspend} + \tau$.

In the non-overlapped case, as shown in Figure 5, agent A issues a suspend request earlier than B. A's request gets confirmed and its suspend operation takes the same time as in the single migration. The suspend operation of agent B won't be issued until a RESUME message from agent A is received. The waiting time is equal to $T^a_{suspend} + T^a_{a-migrate} + T_{control} + \tau$. In fact, B's waiting time is overlapped with A's migration. As far as connection migration is concerned, B saves the cost for a suspend operation. Hence, we have $T^b_{c-migrate} = T_{resume} + T_{control} + \tau$.

### 5.2 Simulation Results

The performance model in the preceding section reveals that the cost for connection migration $T_{c-migrate}$ depends on the suspend starting time $t^a_{begin}$ and $t^b_{begin}$ and their interval $\tau$, in addition to the cost for delivery of a control message $T_{control}$ and the cost for suspend and resume opera-

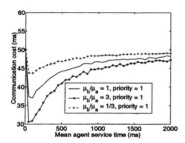

**Figure 10. Connection migration cost for high priority agent.**

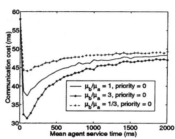

**Figure 11. Connection migration cost for low priority agent.**

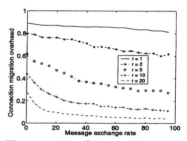

**Figure 12. Connection migration overhead with agent communication**

tions $T_{suspend}$ and $T_{resume}$. The starting time $T_{begin}$ is in turn determined by the agent migration pattern, characterized by migration frequency.

In this simulation, we set $T_{control}$, $T_{suspend}$, and $T_{resume}$ as 10ms, 27.8ms, and 16.9ms, respectively, as we measured in our experiments in Section 4.2. In addition, we set the cost for agent migration $T_{a-migrate}$ as 220ms, measured in Naplet system. We evaluate the impact of migration frequency by modeling it as a random variable following exponential distribution with expectation $\mu$.

Figures 10 and 11 show the cost for connection migration of NapletSocket with the change of mean service time for agent A (i.e., $1/\mu^a$). Plots for different service time for agent B $1/\mu^b$, relative to $1/\mu^a$, are also presented. When two agents migrate with a very high speed (i.e. small service time), there are more chances for concurrent connection migrations. When they migrate with a low speed (i.e. large service time), a single connection migration most likely occurs. In both cases, the cost for connection migration, $T_{c-migrate}$, remains unchanged for the high priority agent. By contrast, the low priority agent experiences a little more delay when both agents migrate at a high speed.

From the figures, we can also see that the lowest latency for both agents happens around the point where $\tau$ is larger than $T_{control}$, but not large enough for a single migration. Given agent A's migration rate, increase of the ratio $\mu^b/\mu^a$ means agent B migrates faster so that when agent A suspends a connection, it has more chances of meeting an ongoing suspend request from B. This leads to a block of agent A's suspend requests and the overall cost for its connection migration gets decreased.

Finally, we examine the impact of message exchange rate on the cost for connection migration in terms of the number of control messages relative to the number of data messages communicated. The message exchange rate, denoted by $\lambda$, refers to the number of data messages transmitted in a time unit. We define $r = \lambda/\mu$ as a relative message exchange rate. Figure 12 shows the connection migration overhead with different combinations of message exchange rates and migration frequencies.

From the figure, we can see that for a fixed ratio $r$, when the message exchange rate is small, the agent issues relatively more control messages to maintain a persistent connection and hence more overhead incurs. As the message exchange rate increases, the overhead is amortized over each communication. When the ratio $r$ decreases to as low as one, which means the agent communicates once in each host, the overhead for persistent connection is always above 80% no matter how large the message exchange rate is.

## 6 Related Work

Communication between mobile agents has long been an active research topic. Agent communication languages like KQML [4] and FIPA's ACL [5] focus on a semantic level of agent communication. In literature, there also exist many protocols in support of asynchronous communication between mobile agents; see [13] for a recent review. A widely-used approach is mailbox-based mechanism [1], in which each agent is associated with a mail-box. A message is either sent directly or forwarded to the mail-box before delivered. In [2], the authors furthered the mailbox mechanism for reliable communication. It is achieved by performing synchronization between delivery and mailbox's migration. This forwarding based mechanism is not suitable for applications that need instantaneous message delivery. Furthermore, if agent involves long migration path, synchronization with mail-box may become a bottleneck.

In the research field of connection migration, there are a number of techniques proposed in different contexts. The conventional technique is from network-layer, using the same IP address even when users change network attachment point. An example of this technique is Mobile IP [7] which works on a concept of home agent associated with the mobile host. Every package destined to a mobile host by its home address is intercepted by its home agent and forwarded to it.

Network layer implementations are not appropriate or sufficient for many applications. There are many studies focusing on transport layer support for mobility. One of the representative work is [11], which uses an end-to-end mechanism to handle host mobility. By extending the TCP protocol with a TCP migrate option, the semantics of TCP remains unchanged. There is other similar work, such as TCP-R [6], M-TCP [12]. Although most of them work well, they require to change OS kernels. This hinders the protocols from wide deployment.

There are some session-layer connection migration mechanisms. In [18], the authors introduced a persistent connections model. They described connection end points in terms of location-independent IDs, which are stored in a centralized host. When an end point changes its attachment point, it notifies the host and then the host notifies all others. In [10], the authors proposed a scheme to preserve upper layer unbroken connections using some OS-specific kernel interfaces to access the system buffer for data not yet delivered. In [9], the authors presented a library solution called MobileSocket on top of Java Socket. They used dynamic socket switch to update connection of MobileSocket and application layer window to keep all in-flight data at user level so that data can be recovered from broken connections. Similarly, in [17], the authors proposed Reliable Sockets (Rocks) that allows TCP connections to support changes in attachment points with emphasis on reliability over mobility. It has support for automatic failure detection and a protocol for inter-operation with end points that do not support Rocks.

## 7 Conclusions

Mailbox-based asynchronous persistent communication mechanisms in mobile agent systems are not sufficient for certain distributed applications like parallel computing. Synchronous transient communication provides complementary services that make cooperative agents work more closely and efficiently. This paper presents a connection migration mechanism in support of synchronous communication between agents. It support concurrent migration of both agents in a connection and guarantees exactly-once message delivery. The mechanism uses agent-oriented access control and secret session keys to deal with security concerns arising in connection migration. A prototype of the mechanism, NapletSocket, has been developed in Naplet mobile agent system. Experimental results show that NapletSocket incurs a moderate cost in connection setup and marginal overhead for communication over established connections. Furthermore, we investigate the impact of agent mobility on communication performance via simulation. Simulation results show that NapletSocket is effective and efficient for a wide range of migration and communication patterns.

### Acknowledgement

This research was supported in part by NSF grants CCR-9988266 and ACI-0203592.

## References

[1] J. Cao, X. Feng, J. Lu, and S. Das. Mailbox-based scheme for mobile agent communication. *IEEE Computer*, 35(9):54–60, 2002.

[2] J. Cao, L. Zhang, J. Yang, and S. Das. A reliable mobile agent communication protocol. In *Proc. 24th Int'l Conf. on Distributed Computing Systems*, March 2004.

[3] Chesapeake Computer Consultants. Tools - Test TCP (TTCP). http://www.ccci.com/tools/ttcp/.

[4] T. Finin, R. Fritzson, D. McKay, and R. McEntire. KQML as an Agent Communication Language. In *Software Agents*. AAAI/MIT Press, 1997.

[5] FIPA. FIPA ACL message structure specification, foundation for intelligent physical agents, 2001. http://www.fipa.org/.

[6] D. Funato, K. Yasuda, and H. Tokuda. TCP-R: TCP mobility support for continuous operation. In *Proc. IEEE Int'l Conf. on Network Protocols, pages 229-236*, October 1997.

[7] J. Ioannidis, D. Duchamp, and G. Q. Maguire. IP-based protocols for mobile internetworking. In *Proc. ACM SIGCOMM*, pages 235–245, September 1991.

[8] D. A. Maltz and P. Bhagwat. MSOCKS: An architecture for transport layer mobility. In *Proc. IEEE Infocom*, pages 1037–1045, September 1998.

[9] T. Okoshi, M. Mochizuki, and Y. Tobe. Mobilesocket: Toward continuous operation for java applications. In *Proc. Int'l Conf. on Computer Communications and Networks*, October 1999.

[10] X. Qu, J. X. Yu, and R. P. Brent. A mobile TCP socket. In *Proc. IASTED Int'l Conf. on Software Engineering*, November 1997.

[11] A. C. Snoeren and H. Balakrishnan. An end-to-end approach to host mobility. In *Proc. ACM MobiCom*, August 2000.

[12] F. Sultan, K. Srinivasan, D. Iyer, and L. Iftode. Migratory TCP: Highly available internet services using connection migration. In *Proc. 22nd Int'l Conf. on Distributed Computing Systems*, July 2002.

[13] P. T. Wojciechowski. Algorithms for location-independent communication between mobile agents. In *Proc. AISB '01 Symposium on Software Mobility and Adaptive Behaviour*, pages 10–19, March 2001.

[14] C.-Z. Xu. Naplet: A flexible mobile agent framework for network-centric applications. In *Proc. of the 2nd Workshop on Internet Computing and e-Commerce (In conjunction with IPDPS)*, April 2002.

[15] C.-Z. Xu and S. Fu. Privilege delegation and agent-oriented access control in naplet. In *Proc. of Int'l Workshop on Mobile Distributed Computing (In conjunction with ICDCS)*, April 2003.

[16] C.-Z. Xu and B. Wims. Mobile agent based push methodology for global parallel computing. *Concurrency: Practice and Experience*, 14(8):705–726, July 2000.

[17] V. C. Zandy and B. P. Miller. Reliable network connections. In *Proc. ACM MobiCom*, September 2002.

[18] Y. Zhang and S. Dao. A persistent connection model for mobile and distributed systems. In *Proc. Int'l Conf. on Computer Communications and Networks*, September 1995.

# Session 7A:
# Algorithms

# Energy-Efficient Scheduling Algorithms of Object Retrieval on Indexed Parallel Broadcast Channels [*]

Bingjun Sun, Ali R. Hurson, and John Hannan
Department of Computer Science and Engineering
The Pennsylvania State University
University Park, PA 16802-6106
{bsun, hurson, hannan}@cse.psu.edu

## Abstract

*With the goal of providing "timely and reliable" access to information in a mobile computing environment, mobile units and the wireless medium operate under constraints on energy, bandwidth, and connectivity. Among these limitations, power limitation of mobile units is one of the key issues.*

*In a mobile computing environment, broadcasting has proved to be an effective method to distribute public data. Efficient methods for allocating and retrieving objects on parallel indexed broadcast channels have been proposed to manage power consumption and access latency. Employment of parallel channels also brings out the notion of conflicts. To minimize the effect of conflicts on both access latency and power consumption, one has to develop schemes to schedule access to the objects that minimizes the number of passes over the parallel channels.*

*This work extends our past efforts and proposes two new scheduling algorithms that can find the minimum number of passes and inside channel switches. The simulation results show that the proposed scheduling algorithms relative to our previous work have a great impact on energy consumption and access latency. The proposed scheduling algorithms are simulated and results are presented.*

**Keywords:** Mobile computing, Energy-aware scheduling, Parallel broadcast channels, object retrieval

## 1. Introduction

Multidatabases (MDB) are capable of allowing timely and reliable global access to large amounts of heterogeneous or homogeneous data sources in an environment that is characterized as "sometime, somewhere" [2]. However, with the rapid expansion of technology, the concept of *mobility* has introduced additional complexities to MDB designers.

Global data sources can be classified as [10]: *private data, public data,* and *shared data.* Broadcasting is an efficient method to make public data available to a large number of users. Previous studies have shown that retrieving data objects from the air channel(s) is a major source of power consumption in mobile units [4, 12, 13]. To manage power consumption, one needs to develop power-aware protocols that run hardware units in different operational modes [3, 5-7]. The literature has suggested several schemes to allocate/retrieve data objects to/from single or parallel broadcast air channel(s) [3-5]. In general, these schemes are based on indexing techniques to reduce the active time of mobile units. Furthermore, when parallel channels are employed, due to the conflicts, proper protocols should be developed to schedule access to the indexed parallel channels to reduce power consumption and response time by reducing the number of broadcast passes and channel switches [12]. Within the scope of indexed parallel broadcast channels, heuristic rules were applied to generate access patterns, during the broadcast cycles, to reduce both the number of passes and channel switching frequency [9, 12-13]. However, these algorithms do not necessarily generate optimal access latency and power consumption in all cases.

This work extends the scope of our earlier investigation. It proposes and examines two new scheduling algorithms that generate access patterns with minimum response time and energy consumption when retrieving objects from indexed parallel broadcast channels. The rest of this paper is organized as follows. Section 2 provides background information related to the broadcasting over parallel channels. Section 3 reviews the general access protocol of object retrieval from indexed parallel air channels, and then proposes several scheduling algorithms. Section 4 presents and analyzes the simulation results. Finally, in section 5, the conclusions are drawn, and future research directions are discussed.

[*] This work in part has been supported by The Office of Naval Research under the contract N00014-02-1-0282 and National Science Foundation under the contract IIS-0324835.

## 2. Background

The multidatabase concept was proposed to manage, share, and integrate the existing "islands of information" into a coherent system in a sometimes, somewhere environment. Recent advances in technology have made mobile computing a reality. However, in a wireless mobile computing environment, one should take technological constraints into consideration.

### 2.1 Wireless Computing

The wireless computing architecture consists of mobile hosts and fixed hosts. The network servers communicate with mobile units through mobile support stations (MSSs). In this environment two types of services are available [7, 9]:

- *Interactive/on-demand service*: The client requests a piece of data on the uplink channel, and the server responds by sending the result to the client - the channels are bi-directional and asymmetric.

- *Broadcasting service*: Periodic broadcasting of data on the channel - the channels are unidirectional from servers to mobile units.

### 2.2 MDAS

Mobile Data Access Systems (MDAS), as an extension to MDBS, was proposed to support wireless communication, with the goal of accessing heterogeneous and autonomous data sources anytime and anywhere [10]. The current limited bandwidth in a wireless environment places an obstacle on the rate and the amount of · conventional two-way communication in a MDAS [3].

### 2.3 Data Broadcasting

Wireless data broadcasting is an efficient method to make public data available to the users while overcoming the technological limitations of the wireless network. In addition, data broadcasting is scalable and the air channel(s) can be assumed as the extended memory of mobile devices [1]. Data on a broadcast channel are read-only and must be accessed sequentially. Data can be broadcast either on a single channel or parallel channels. This work assumes that all parallel channels have the same transfer rate, and data broadcasting will be done in a cyclic manner.

### 2.4 Allocation and Retrieval Methods on Parallel Air Channels

Within the scope of broadcasting, the indexing technique can be used to reduce power consumption. In addition, broadcasting along parallel channels can be used to reduce the broadcast length and hence to reduce the access latency. However, employment of parallel channels introduces conflicts which could enforce multiple passes over the parallel air channels. This increases the power consumption and access latency. Therefore, it would be desirable to schedule the object retrieval during each broadcast cycle with the goal of reducing the number of passes [9, 12].

#### 2.4.1 Indexing Techniques on Air Channels

With indexing techniques, the mobile unit can predict the arrival time of requested objects in order to switch into an energy-saving mode [3]. The advantages of indexing schemes come at the expense of computational overhead and increased broadcast length. Several indexing techniques, such as signature and tree based, have been addressed in the literature [4-9, 12-13]. This work employs the tree-based index techniques.

An index tree is the auxiliary information representing one or several data attributes pointing to the location of a data frame sharing the same common attribute value(s). Nodes at the lowest level of the index tree point to the locations of the data frames on the broadcast. Previous works have studied different indexing allocation schemes (namely, *distributed indexing* and *(1, m) indexing*) [6-8].

*Single-class* indexing and *hierarchical* indexing in single and parallel broadcast channel(s) have been studied in detail. The simulation results showed that the application of an index on the single broadcast air channel can reduce energy consumption drastically with a reasonable increase in response time due to a longer broadcast [3]. In parallel broadcast channels, for the case of single-class scheme, there are several possible layouts to organize index and data. Without loss of generality, this work will employ a layout that is depicted in Figure 1 because of its simplicity and clarity.

#### 2.4.2 Object Retrieval on Parallel Channels

Within the scope of parallel broadcast channels, the mobile unit can switch between different channels and download objects. However, usually not all the requested objects can be accessed in one pass due to the conflicts among requested objects when broadcasting simultaneously and/or during channel switching periods. A general access protocol to retrieve data objects from parallel channels should minimize power consumption and response time [12]. The protocol involves the following steps:

1) *Initial probe*: The client tunes into the broadcast channel to determine when the next index will be broadcast.

2) *Search*: The client accesses the index and determines the offsets of requested objects.

3) *Compute*: The client generates the access patterns for the requested objects using a scheduling algorithm.

4) *Retrieve*: The client, in an active mode, tunes into one of the channels and downloads the required data objects and changes to doze mode if needed.

| $I_H$ | D/c |
|---|---|
| F/s | D/c |
| F/s | D/c |
| F/s | D/c |

| | |
|---|---|
| F/s | Free space |
| $I_H$ | Hierarchical Index |
| D/c | Data on each channel |

**Figure 1:      Broadcast Layout**

During the *compute* step, scheduling algorithms can attempt to minimize the number of passes and the number of channel switches, at a reasonable overhead. There are two kinds of channel switches: Inside switches and outside switches. Inside channel switches are those occurring during a broadcast cycle. Outside switches are channel switches which occur between two successive broadcast cycles.

Several heuristic-based algorithms have been proposed to schedule object retrieval during a broadcast cycle. The solution to the Traveling Salesman Problem, the *Next Object*, and row scan heuristics were used to access objects from the air channels [9]. As reported in [12], three rules were employed to generate the access patterns.

# 3.  Energy-Efficient Scheduling of Object Retrieval

## 3.1 Object Retrieval on Parallel Broadcast Channels

The literature has identified the Access Time, the Tune-in Time, and the number of Channel Switches as the performance metrics to measure the effectiveness of retrieval schemes [5, 7]. We use response time and energy consumption as the performance metrics to evaluate the effectiveness of our proposed methods. The overall power consumption is computed as (assuming that the power consumption for channel switching is 10% of the power consumed in active mode):

*Energy Consumption = (Access Time - Tune-in Time) \* DozeModePower + (Tune-in Time) \* ActiveModePower + TheNumberOfSwitching \*10% \* ActiveModePower.*

## 3.2 Scheduling Algorithms on Indexed Parallel Channels

### 3.2.1 Problem Analysis

In this work, a two-dimensional array of $N \times M$ is used to represent a parallel broadcast, where $N$ is the number of channels and $M$ is the number of pages on a channel. In this array, each cell $C_{i,j}$, $1 \le i \le N$, $1 \le j \le M$, represents a page. Without loss of generality, we assume objects are not fragmented across adjacent pages, and if we request any object in a page, we will retrieve the whole page. A row of cells represents a channel on the broadcast, while a column of cells represents pages transmitted at the same time on parallel channels. For a query requesting a set of objects $S$, if the cell $C_{i,j}$ has a requested object then $C_{i,j} \in S$. Finally, a query requests $K$ objects $O_k$, $1 \le k \le K$. Based on the aforementioned assumptions we have the following definitions with respect to a given query (Figures 2 and 3 are intended to clarify these definitions).

**Definition 1:** *Empty Columns*: A column without any requested objects.

**Definition 2:** *Sparse Columns*: A column containing requested objects without any conflicts.

**Definition 3:** *Dense Columns*: A column that is neither *Empty* nor *Sparse* is *Dense*. With respect to a user request, the minimum required number of passes depends on dense columns.

We define $R_j$ to be the set of rows we need to scan in column $j$ based on objects in columns $j$ through $j+OPR-1$ (OPR stands for overlap page region). This naturally leads to the definition of the cut at column $j$.

**Definition 4:** Let $R_j = \{i \mid \exists j', j \le j' \le j+OPR-1$, such that $C_{ij'} \in S\}$. Then, the *cut* at column $j$ is $|R_j|$.

**Definition 5:** The *maximum cut*, *MAX_cut*, is $max\{cut_j \mid 1 \le j \le N\}$

**Definition 6:** The *total requested channels*, *MAX_total*, is $|\{i \mid \exists j$ such that $C_{ij} \in S\}|$.

We can conclude **MAX_cut = minimum number of passes = MAX_total**.

We define some useful sets of cells:

**Definition 7:** The set of *Empty Cells*, $E$, is $\{C_{i,j} \mid C_{i,j} \notin S\}$.

**Definition 8:** The set of *Restrictive Cells*, $R$, is $\{C_{ij} \mid C_{i,j} \notin S \wedge (C_{i,j+1} \in S \vee C_{i,j-1} \in S)\}$.

**Definition 9:** The set of *Free Cells*, $F$, is $\{C_{i,j} \mid C_{i,j} \in E \wedge C_{i,j} \notin R\}$.

An important concept in our algorithms is the empty block which is a contiguous sequence of empty cells in one row.

**Definition 10:** An *Empty Block*, $B_{i,j}$, is the largest set of contiguous empty cells in row $i$ starting in column $j$.

Given a set of empty blocks all starting in the same column, a *rightmost empty block* is a block in the set that is not smaller than any other block in the set, i.e., no other empty block extends farther to the right of it.

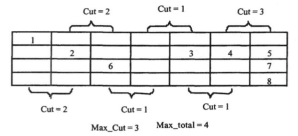

**Figure 2:    cut, MAX_cut and MAX_total**

**Definition 11:** *Overlapped Empty Blocks*: Two empty blocks $B$ and $B'$ overlap each other, iff they contain a cell from some column, i.e., $\exists j$, such that $C_{i,j} \in B \wedge C_{i',j} \in B' \wedge i \neq i'$.

**Definition 12:** The set of *Obstacles*, $O$, is $\{C_{i,j} \mid C_{i,j} \in S \wedge C_{i,j-1} \in E \wedge C_{i,j-2} \in E\}$.

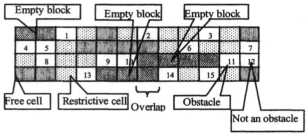

**Figure 3:    Free   cells,   restrictive   cells, overlapped   empty   blocks,   and obstacles**

### 3.2.2 Parallel Object Scan

In this presentation, graphically, lines (access lines) are used to represent the access patterns in different passes. Parallel Object Scan (POS) is a scheduling algorithm that uses *MAX_cut* passes to scan all requested objects on a broadcast. Starting in the first column the algorithm simultaneously (in parallel) constructs *MAX_cut* lines, column by column, working left to right. The algorithm attempts to use access lines to visit all the requested objects in the next column with the fewest switches from the previous column. POS observes which cell $C_{i,j}$ with a line has a less chance to have a requested object in the future on the same channel and uses this line to make an inside switch when necessary. This strategy can minimize the number of inside switches.

**Definition 13:** A Line $l$ is a vector of length $M$ representing one pass through the matrix. The value $l[j]$ is the channel (row #) that the line reads at time (column) $j$.

We define *freeright(i,j)* to be the rightmost column of the *Empty block* containing $C_{ij} \in E$.

**Definition 14:** Let *freeright(i,j)* be the largest $j'$ such that for all $k, j \leq k \leq j'$, $C_{ik} \in E$.

We define *next(j,L)* to be the line in $L$ that reads from the channel with the rightmost empty block in column $j$.

**Definition 15:** Let *next(j,L)* be a line $l \in L$ such that $freeright(l[j],j) = max\{freeright(l'[j],j) \mid l' \in L\}$.

We define *First(i)* to be the column in which a requested object first appears in row $i$.

**Definition 16:** Let *First(i)* be the smallest $j$ such that for all $j'$, $1 \leq j' < j$, $C_{ij'} \notin S$.

Let *Start(m)* be rows $\{i_1,...,i_m\}$ such that for any row $i'$ $\notin \{i_1,...,i_m\}$ $First(i) \leq First(i')$ for all $i \in \{i_1,...,i_m\}$. In other words, *Start(m)* are rows that contain objects before any other rows. These rows will be the starting point for our *MAX_cut* lines, as we obviously do not want to switch a line before it has read any objects on a channel.

The POS algorithm is shown below:

**POS Algorithm:**
```
1.    if (MAX_total = MAX_cut)
2.        use Row Scan;
3.    else
4.        Let m = MAX_cut
5         Create m lines, l₁,...,lₘ
6         Lines = {l₁,...,lₘ}   /* Set containing all the
                                       lines */
7.        l₁[1], ..., lₘ[1] = Start(m)  /* Initialize lines */
8.        for j = 2 to M do {
9.            L = Lines        /* All the lines */
10.           A = Rⱼ /* Required Rows: |A| ≤ |L| */
11.           foreach l ∈ L      /* check for no switch,
                              line reads an object*/
12.               if l[j] ∈ A then l[j] = l[j-1]; A = A-
                              {l[j]}; L = L-{l}
13.               foreach i ∈ A   /* remaining objects,
                                       inside switch */
14.                   l = next(j,L)
15.                   l[j] = i
16.               L=L-{l}
17.           foreach l ∈ L  /* no object to read, no
                                       switch */
18.               l[j] = l[j-1] }
```

The POS algorithm runs in $O(N^2 M)$ time. Observe that all of the required sets and functions except *next* (e.g., $R_j$, $E$, *freeright*, *First*, *Start*) can be computed in $O(NM)$ time. If we pre-compute these once, then any use of them during the algorithm requires just constant time. The function *next* takes $O(N)$ time since the size of $L$ (the number of lines) will be at most $N$. The algorithm consists of an outer loop iterated $M-1$ times. Inside are three inner loops each iterated at most $N$ times (since the sizes of $L$ and $A$ are bounded by $N$). The first and third inner loop bodies take constant time while the second inner loop body takes $O(N)$ time due to the call to *next*.

### 3.2.3 Serial Empty Scan

An alternative to POS is Serial Empty Scan (SES) which examines empty blocks instead of requested objects. The basic idea behind the algorithm is as follows. We construct ($MAX\_total - MAX\_cut$) paths that scan only empty blocks (empty paths). As we do this we also compress the requested objects into $MAX\_cut$ channels. Each of these resulting "logical" channels describes the sequence of requested objects that an access line reads. The action of compressing (copying objects from one channel to another) simulates a switch during a scan.

The SES algorithm is serial because it finds the ($MAX\_total - MAX\_cut$) empty paths one by one. The SES algorithm constructs an empty path by starting with the rightmost empty block $B_{i',1}$ in some row $i'$. The path starts in row $i'$ at column 1 and continues to column $k$, where $k$ is the length of $B_{i',1}$. Next it finds a rightmost overlapping empty block $B_{i'',k}$. The path continues on row $i''$ for the length of this empty block and so forth. Additionally, the SES algorithm begins to create a logical channel by moving all requested objects $C_{i'',a}$, to $C_{i',a}$, for $1 \leq a < k$. Finally it marks the empty cell $C_{i',lk}$ as *no obstacle*, indicating a physical switch occurs at this point in the logical channel. This end marker is used during the construction of subsequent empty paths. By convention, we also define that $\forall i'$, $C_{i',M} = no\ obstacle$, iff $C_{i',M} \in E \wedge C_{i',M-1} \in E$. The SES algorithm repeats this construction of an empty path until it reaches the right end. During subsequent scans, when choosing an overlapping empty block, the SES algorithm chooses the rightmost block ending with the *no obstacle* marker, if one exists. If no such empty block exists, the algorithm simply chooses the rightmost empty block. After every scan, $MAX\_total$ is decremented by 1. The algorithm will terminate when $MAX\_total = MAX\_cut$, and all the requested objects have been moved into $MAX\_cut$ logical channels, on each of which the order of the requested objects gives the access pattern during each broadcast.

Since choosing the next empty block is a fundamental step in the SES algorithm we define it first. Given a set of row indices *Rows* and a column $j$, *nextblock(Rows, j)* returns the appropriate row $i$ to add to the empty path being constructed. To define this function we also define *rightmost(Rows, j)* which returns the row index of the rightmost free block among $B_{ij}$ for $i \in Rows$.

*rightmost(Rows, j)* = $i$ s.t. $i \in Rows$ & $freeright(i,j) = max(freeright(i', j) \mid i' \in Rows)$

*nextblock*(Rows, j) =

let EBs = $\{i \mid i \in Rows$ & $C_j \in E\}$ /* Empty Blocks */

let OBs = $\{i \mid i \in$ EBs & $k = freeright(i,j)$ & $C_{ik} = no\ obstacle\}$

if OBs $\neq \{\}$ then return(*rightmost*(OBs, j)) else return(*rightmost*(EBs,j))

In the SES algorithm, an obstacle on a broadcast may result in an inside switch if the empty block on the left of it is scanned. Those obstacles whose empty blocks on the left are not chosen to scan will not result in a switch. Cells that are not obstacles will not generate inside switches. It should be noted that if the algorithm moves requested objects from channel $A$ to channel $B$, a switch is indicated, but if they are subsequently moved from channel $B$ to channel $C$, it is equal to moving from channel $A$ to channel $C$, and still only one switch occurs. Thus, the strategy of choosing blocks marked no obstacle (in the function *nextblock*) minimizes the number of inside switches. Choosing the rightmost empty block, at each step also contributes to minimizing the number of inside switches of a scan.

**SES Algorithm:**
```
if (MAX_total = MAX_cut)
    use Row Scan;
else
    Rows = {1,...,N} /* Rows we can compress */
    repeat until (MAX_total = MAX_cut) {
        j = 1;
        i = nextblock(Rows,j)
        k = freeright(i,j)   /* free block is Cij to Cik */
        repeat until k=M {
            i' = nextblock(Rows, j)
            k = freeright (i', j)
            Cia = Ci'a for 1 ≤ a < k   /* compress
                    channels */
            Ci'k = no obstacle /* indicate a
                    switch occurs */
            i = i'
            j = k
        }
        MAX_total = MAX_total – 1
        Rows = Rows – {i}      /* delete the
            empty row */
    }
```

The SES algorithm has complexity $O(N^2M)$. The functions *rightmost* and *nextblock* are both bounded by the number of rows, hence they are both $O(N)$. The SES algorithm's outer loop iterates at most $N$ times and its inner loop iterates at most $M$ times. Finally, the body of the inner loop takes $O(N)$ times due to the call to *nextblock*. Consequently, the inner loop has complexity $O(NM)$ and so does the body of the outer loop.

## 4. Simulation Results

### 4.1 Simulation Design

A simulator was developed to verify the behavior of the proposed algorithms and measure their effectiveness against the tree based indexing algorithm proposed in [12, 13]. The simulator assumes a hierarchical inheritance-based indexing as the underlying object organization on the parallel air channels for a retrieval protocol. For the sake of simplicity, the simulator simulates the "Layout 1" configuration as depicted in Figure 1. Finally, to compensate for the execution time of each algorithm, a delay gap of one page is inserted between the index and data objects to avoid missing any requested objects in the first broadcast pass. For each simulation run, user requests are generated requesting $K$ random objects on the broadcast.

The NASDAQ [12] database with 4290 securities is used as the source data for the objects on the broadcast. The simulator assumes some physical parameters as input. These parameters are summarized in Table 1. It should be noted that, for every simulated configuration, the simulator is run 1000 times, and the average number of every estimated performance metric is calculated and represented in this paper.

**Table 1: Input parameters to the simulator**

| Parameter | Value |
|---|---|
| Number of Objects | 4290 |
| Number of Channels | 1-16 |
| Size of Air Page | 512 Bytes |
| Broadcast Data Rate | 1 Mbit/sec |
| Power Consumption (Active Mode) | 130 mW |
| (Doze Mode) | 6.6 mW |
| (Channel Switch) | 13 mW |

### 4.2 Simulation Results

Conceptually, the POS and SES algorithm should generate the same number of passes and inside switches regardless of the simulated configuration. The simulator ran 1000 times for 80 different configurations, and the results verified this point.

#### 4.2.1 Number of Passes

Figure 4 shows the number of passes for the POS, SES, and tree-based algorithms (abbreviated as "Tree" in the figures). As expected, regardless of the number of objects requested and the physical configuration of the simulated environment, the POS, and SES algorithms generate the same number of passes.

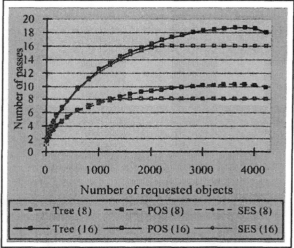

**Figure 4: Number of passes**

When $K$ is relatively small, the tree-based algorithm is as efficient as the POS and SES algorithms. However, as $K$ grows larger, the tree-based algorithm became relatively less efficient. Interestingly, relative to the number of air channels, after a threshold value, the tree-based algorithm requires more passes than *Row Scan* algorithm. Increasing $K$ and/or $N$ increases the number of passes required to pull requested objects from the parallel air channels. An increase in $N$ would increase the probability of conflicts and, consequently, results in a higher *MAX_cut* value. This would increase the number of required passes over the air channels. As $K$ approaches $((M * (N - 1)) + 1)$, *MAX_cut* approaches $N$. At this threshold point, the algorithm behaves as *Row Scan* algorithm since it would be the most cost efficient algorithm to use.

#### 4.2.2 Number of Channel Switches

Figure 5 shows the number of channel switches for different scheduling algorithms. As expected, the POS and SES algorithm require almost the same number of switches regardless of the number of channels and/or the number of objects requested. This is due to the fact that the POS and SES algorithms can find the optimal solution of inside switches. Compared to the POS and SES algorithm, the tree-based algorithm requires more channel switches, especially as $K$ grows larger.

As $N$ and/or $K$ increases, more inside switches are needed Since, more requested objects are distributed over different channels. When $K$ increases beyond some threshold point, the number of channel switches begins to decrease. This is because the number of passes approaching to $N$. As $K$ approaches $((M * (N - 1)) + 1)$, no inside switches are required, since, as noted earlier, at this threshold point the *Row Scan* algorithm would be applied which requires no inside channel switches.

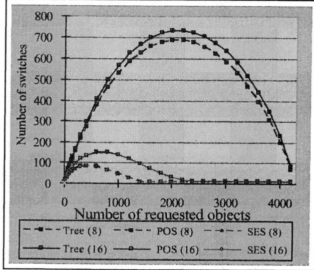

**Figure 5:      Number of switches**

### 4.2.3   Cost of Algorithms

As noted earlier, it was one of our objectives to develop a scheduling algorithm that generates access patterns with reasonable overhead cost. As noted before, the cost of the tree-based algorithm is $O(K^2)$, much more than those of the proposed algorithms, especially when a large number of objects is requested. The cost of the POS and SES algorithms is $O(N^2M)$ in the worst case. The cost of POS and SES algorithms linearly increases when a relatively small number of objects are requested. As the number of requested objects increases, the cost of the algorithms decreases because more and more cases will use the *Row Scan* algorithm. After the threshold point, it is constant since the *Row Scan* algorithm is applied.

### 4.2.4   Response Time

Figure 6 shows the response time of different scheduling algorithms. Response time is directly related to the number of passes. The response time of the POS and SES algorithm is almost the same, while the tree-based algorithm usually requires a longer response time, especially when $K$ is large. Interestingly, we observed that for small $K$, the POS and SES algorithm have a little longer response time than the tree-based algorithm. This is due to the

heuristics employed by the tree-based algorithm - it retrieves as many objects as possible in the earlier passes.

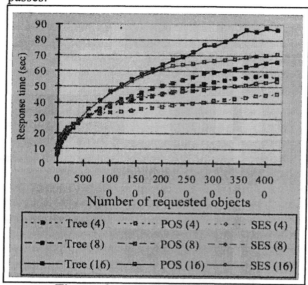

**Figure 6:      Response time**

### 4.2.5   Energy Consumption

Figure 7 shows energy consumption of different scheduling algorithms. The total energy consumption is determined based on the consumed energy: in active mode, in doze mode, and in channel switching phase. Obviously, for different scheduling algorithms, the consumed energy in active mode is almost the same. The energy consumed in doze mode is not much different for different scheduling algorithms. As a result, one can conclude that the energy consumed in switching phase is the dominating factor that distinguishes different scheduling algorithms based on this performance metric. As a result, the shapes of the curves in figure 8 are similar to those of Figure 5.

### 4.2.6   Trade-off between Broadcast Passes and Channel Switches

There is a trade-off between the response time and the number of channel switches (energy consumption). To show this we ran the simulator for a fixed configuration, i.e., the same requested objects and the same number of channels, and observed the number of channel switches and the corresponding response time. The following observation was made: more passes result in longer response time and fewer channel switches. On the other hand, the energy consumption depends on the number of passes and the number of channel switches. In addition, the number of objects requested plays an important role in defining the relationship between energy consumption and the number of passes. For example, for a relatively small number of requested objects, a smaller number of passes consumes less energy and for relatively a large number of requested objects, more passes over the parallel channels consume less energy. Between these two boundaries, a medial number of passes results in the least amount of energy consumption.

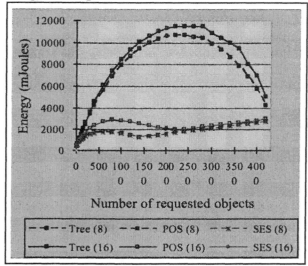

**Figure 7:      Energy consumption**

## 5. Conclusions and Future Directions

Two new scheduling algorithms, namely, the Parallel Object Scan (POS) and Serial Empty Scan (SES), were presented along with their time complexity. The proposed algorithms were simulated and compared against the tree based algorithm proposed in [12, 13] using performance metrics such as the energy consumption, the response time, and the number of channel switches. Simulation results showed that the proposed scheduling algorithms, for a user request, generate access patterns with the minimum number of passes and inside switches at a reasonable overhead cost.

This work can be extended in many directions, including the following:

- To reduce response time and energy consumption further, one can develop a scheme that caches the index in the mobile units locally.

- The simulator can be extended to find the channel layout of allocating the index and data objects that offers the best performance.

- User's profile can be used to bundle multiple potential queries together to reduce the overall power consumption.

## References

[1]   S. Acharya, R. Alonso, M. Franklin, and S. Zdonik, "Broadcast Disks: Data Management for Asymmetric Communication Environments," *ACM SIGMOD Conference on the Management of Data*, 1995, pp. 199-210.

[2]   Bright, M.W., Hurson, A.R. and Pakzad, S. "Automated Resolution of Semantic Heterogeneity in Multidatabases," *ACM Trans. on Database Systems*, 19(2):212-223, 1994.

[3]   Y.C. Chehadeh, A.R. Hurson, L.L. Miller, "Energy-Efficient Indexing on a Broadcast Channel in a Mobile Database Access System," *Conference on Information Technology: Coding and Computing*, 2000, pp. 368-374.

[4]   Y.C. Chehadeh, A. R. Hurson, D. Tavangarian, "Object Organization on Single and Parallel Broadcast Channel," *Proceedings of the International Conference on High Performance Computing*, 2001, pp. 163-169.

[5]   Q.L. Hu, and D.L. Lee, "A Hybrid Index Technique for Power Efficient Data Broadcast," *Distributed and Parallel Databases Journal*, 9(2):151-177, 2001.

[6]   T. Imielinski, S. Viswanathan, and B. R. Badrinath, "Data on Air: Organization and Access," *IEEE Transactions on parallel and distributed systems*, 9(3):353-372, 1997.

[7]   T. Imielinski, and H.F. Korth, "Mobile Computing," *Kluwer Academic Publishers*, 1996.

[8]   T. Imielinski, and B.R. Badrinath, "Mobile Wireless Computing: Challenges in Data Management," *Communications of the ACM*, 37(10):pp. 18-28, 1994.

[9]   J. Juran, A.R. Hurson, and N. Vijaykrishnan, "Data Organization and Retrieval on Parallel Air Channels: Performance and Energy Issues," *ACM Journal of WINET*, 10(2), 2004.

[10]  J.B. Lim, A.R. Hurson, "Heterogeneous Data Access in a Mobile Environment - Issues and Solutions," *Advances in Computers*, Vol. 48, pp.119-178.

[11]  Lim J.B., and Hurson A.R., "Transaction Processing in Mobile, Heterogeneous Database Systems," *IEEE Transactions on Knowledge and Data Engineering*, 14(6):1330-1346, 2002.

[12]  Munoz-Avila A., and Hurson A.R., "Energy-Efficient Objects Retrieval on Indexed Broadcast Parallel Channels," *Conference on Information Resource Management*, pp. 190-194, 2003.

[13]  Munoz-Avila A., and. Hurson A.R., "Energy-Aware retrieval From Indexed Broadcast Parallel Channels," *Advanced Simulation Technology*, pp. 3-8, 2003.

[14]  E. Pitoura, and P.K. Chrysanthis, "Scalable Processing of Read-Only Transactions in Broadcast Push," *Conference on Distributed Computing Systems*, pp. 432-439, 1999.

[15]  K. Stathatos, N. Roussopoulos, and J.S. Baras, "Adaptive Data Broadcast in Hybrid Networks," *International Conference on Very Large Data Bases*, pp. 326-335, 1997.

# The Euler Tour Technique and Parallel Rooted Spanning Tree

Guojing Cong, David A. Bader*
Department of Electrical and Computer Engineering
University of New Mexico, Albuquerque, NM 87131 USA
{cong, dbader}@ece.unm.edu

## Abstract

*Many parallel algorithms for graph problems start with finding a spanning tree and rooting the tree to define some structural relationship on the vertices which can be used by following problem specific computations. The generic procedure is to find an unrooted spanning tree and then root the spanning tree using the Euler tour technique. With a randomized work-time optimal unrooted spanning tree algorithm and work-time optimal list ranking, finding rooted spanning trees can be done work-time optimally on EREW PRAM w.h.p. Yet the Euler tour technique assumes as "given" a circular adjacency list, it is not without implications though to construct the circular adjacency list for the spanning tree found on the fly by a spanning tree algorithm. In fact our experiments show that this "hidden" step of constructing a circular adjacency list could take as much time as both spanning tree and list ranking combined. In this paper we present new efficient algorithms that find rooted spanning trees without using the Euler tour technique and incur little or no overhead over the underlying spanning tree algorithms.*

*We also present two new approaches that construct Euler tours efficiently when the circular adjacency list is not given. One is a deterministic PRAM algorithm and the other is a randomized algorithm in the symmetric multiprocessor (SMP) model. The randomized algorithm takes a novel approach for the problems of constructing the Euler tour and rooting a tree. It computes a rooted spanning tree first, then constructs an Euler tour directly for the tree using depth-first traversal. The tour constructed is cache-friendly with adjacent edges in the tour stored in consecutive locations of an array so that prefix-sum (scan) can be used for tree computations instead of the more expensive list-ranking.*

**Keywords:** Spanning Tree, Euler Tour, Parallel Graph Algorithms, Shared Memory, High-Performance Algorithm Engineering.

## 1  Introduction

Many parallel algorithms for graph problems, e.g., biconnected components, ear decomposition, and planarity testing, at some stage require finding a rooted spanning tree to define some structural relationship on the vertices. The standard approach for finding a rooted spanning tree combines two algorithms: an (unrooted) spanning tree algorithm and rooting a tree using the Euler tour technique, which can be done work-time optimally w.h.p. (see Pettie and Ramachandran [12], and JáJá [8]). In practice, however, there is a gap between the input representations assumed by these two algorithms. For most spanning tree algorithms the input graphs are represented as either adjacency or edge lists, while for the Euler tour technique, a special circular adjacency list is required where additional pointers are added to define an Euler circuit on the Eulerian graph induced by the tree that visits each directed edge exactly once. To convert a plain adjacency list into a circular adjacency list, first the adjacency list of each vertex $v$ is made circular by adding pointers from $v_i$ to $v_{(i+1) \bmod d(v)-1}$ where $d(v)$ is the degree of $v$, and $v_i$ $(0 \le i \le d(v) - 1)$ are the neighbors of $v$. Then for any edge $< u, v >$ there are cross pointers between the two anti-parallel arcs $< u, v >$ and $< v, u >$. Setting up these cross pointers is the major problem. In the literature, the circular adjacency list is usually assumed as "given" for the Euler tour technique. In the case of the rooted span-

*This work was supported in part by NSF Grants CAREER ACI-00-93039, ITR ACI-00-81404, DEB-99-10123, ITR EIA-01-21377, Biocomplexity DEB-01-20709, and ITR EF/BIO 03-31654; DARPA Contract NBCH30390004; and DOE Sandia National Laboratories contract 161449.

ning tree problem, however, as the results of the spanning tree algorithm are scattered among the adjacency or edge list, setting up the cross pointers efficiently is no longer trivial, especially when it is sandwiched between two very fast parallel algorithms.

Natural questions then arise: are there better direct techniques to root a tree and what additional work is required to convert an efficient spanning tree algorithm into one that produces a rooted spanning tree. If we consider the rooted spanning tree problem as a single problem instead of two subproblem steps, a new approach reveals itself. Many existing efficient parallel spanning tree algorithms adapt a graft-and-shortcut approach to build a tree in a bottom-up fashion. We observe that grafting defines a natural structural relationship on the vertices. Thus the required information to root a tree is already largely paid for. In Section 2 we present new approaches for finding a rooted spanning tree directly without using the Euler tour technique. The new algorithms incur little or no overhead over the underlying spanning tree algorithms.

The Euler tour technique is one of the basic building blocks for designing parallel algorithms, especially for tree computations (JáJá [8], and Karp and Ramachandran's survey in [15]). For example, pre- and post-order numbering, computing the vertex level, computing the number of descendants, and finding a centroid, can be done work-time optimally on EREW PRAM by applying the Euler tour technique. In Tarjan and Vishkin's biconnected components algorithm [14] that originally introduced the Euler tour technique, the input is an edge list with the cross pointers between twin edges $< u, v >$ and $< v, u >$ established as given. This makes it easy to set up later the cross pointers of the Euler tour defined on a spanning tree, yet setting the circular pointers needs additional work because now a list tail has no information of where the list head is. An edge list with cross pointers is an unusual data structure from which arises the subtle question as to whether we should include the step of setting the cross pointers in the execution time and whether it is appropriate for other spanning tree algorithms. For more natural representations, for example, a plain edge list without cross pointers, Tarjan and Vishkin recommend sorting to set up the cross pointers. After selecting the spanning tree edges, they sort all the arcs $< u, v >$ with $\min(u, v)$ as the primary key, and $\max(u, v)$ as the secondary key. The arcs $< u, v >$ and $< v, u >$ are then next to each other in the resulting list so that the cross pointers can be easily set. We denote the Tarjan-Vishkin approach as Euler-Sort. Our experimental results show that using sorting to set up the cross

pointers can take more time than the spanning tree algorithm and list ranking combined. Two new efficient algorithms for the construction of Euler tours without sorting nor given circular adjacency lists are presented in Section 3. The first, a PRAM approach, is based on the graft-and-shortcut spanning tree algorithm, and the second, using a more realistic SMP model, computes a cache-friendly Euler tour where prefix-sum (scan) is used for the tree computation.

Section 4 compares the performance of our new rooted spanning tree algorithms (RST-Graft and RST-Trav) over the spanning tree approach, and our two new Euler tour construction approaches (Euler-Graft and Euler-DFS) versus the Tarjan-Vishkin approach (Euler-Sort).

## 2 New Parallel Rooted Spanning Tree Algorithms

In this section we present two new rooted spanning tree algorithms without using the Euler tour technique. Both algorithms compute a rooted spanning tree directly without having to go through the intermediate step of finding an unrooted spanning tree. One of the algorithms is based on the "graft and shortcut" spanning tree algorithm (denoted as RST-Graft), and the other is based on a new graph traversal spanning tree algorithm for SMPs (denoted as RST-Trav).

### 2.1 Rooted Spanning Tree: Graft and Shortcut Approach (RST-Graft)

RST-Graft is based on Shiloach-Vishkin's connected component algorithm (from which a spanning tree algorithm ST-Graft can be derived [1]) that adopts the "graft and shortcut" approach. We observe that ST-Graft can be extended naturally to deal with rooted spanning tree problems. In ST-Graft for a graph $G = (V, E)$ where $|V| = n$ and $|E| = m$ we start with $n$ isolated vertices and $m$ PRAM processors. Each processor $P_i$ ($1 \leq i \leq m$) tries to graft vertex $v_i$ to one of its neighbors $u$ under the constraint that $u < v_i$. Grafting creates $k \geq 1$ connected components in the graph, and each of the $k$ components is then shortcut to a single supervertex. The approach continues to graft and shortcut on the reduced graphs $G' = (V', E')$ with $V'$, the set of supervertices, and $E'$, the set of edges among supervertices, until only one vertex is left.

For a rooted spanning tree algorithm, we need to set up the *parent* relationship on each vertex. Note that grafting defines the *parent* relationship naturally on the vertices. With RST-Graft we set *parent(u)* to *v* each time an edge $e = <u,v> \in E$ causes the grafting of the subtree rooted the supervertex of *u* onto the subtree of *v*. One issue we face with this approach is that for one vertex its *parent* could be set multiple times by the grafting, hence creating conflicts as shown in Fig. 1.

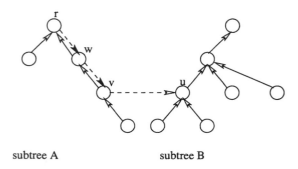

**Figure 1. Setting the parent relationship. The *parent* of *v* was initially set to *w*, then set to *u*.**

In Fig. 1, after the $i^{th}$ iteration, there are two subtrees *A* and *B*, and the white arrows show the current *parent* relationship on the vertices where *parent(v)* is set to *w* in subtree *A*. In the $(i+1)^{st}$ iteration, subtree *A* is grafted onto subtree *B* by edge $<u,v>$ and *parent(v)* is set to *u* as shown by the dashed line with a white arrow. To merge the two subtrees consistently into one rooted spanning tree, we need to reroot subtree *A* at *v* and reverse the *parent* relationship for vertices on the path from *v* to root *r* of subtree *A* as shown by the dashed lines with black arrows.

Existing algorithms for rerooting a tree also use the Euler tour technique. Instead we give our new, faster algorithm that uses pointer-jumping and broadcasting. The basic idea is to find all the vertices that are on the path from *v* to *r* and reverse their *parent* relationship; that is, if $u = parent(v)$, we now set $parent(u) = v$. Note that simply chasing the *parent* pointer from *v* to *r* has $\Theta(H(v))$ complexity where $H(v)$ is the height of *v* and in the worst case could be $\Theta(n)$ where *n* is the number of vertices in the tree.

In our algorithm to reroot a tree from *r* to the new root *r'*, associated with each vertex *u* in the tree is an array *PR* of size $O(\log n)$. All vertices that ever become *u*'s *parent* in the process of pointer jumping are put into *PR*. Fig. 2 shows an example of *PR* for the vertices after pointer jumping.

Information stored in *PR* is useful when we try to find all the vertices that are on the path from *u* and root *r*.

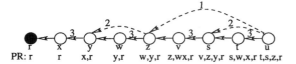

**Figure 2. Illustration of *PR* for each vertex after pointer jumping. The number on each edge shows the step during which the message is broadcasted.**

We find these vertices in a way that is similar to that of broadcasting over a binary tree. Take Fig. 2 as an example. Here we denote the processor assigned to work on vertex *v* processor $P_v$. Except for processor $P_r$ whose vertex is always on some path to *r*, initially only processor $P_u$ knows that its vertex is on the path. In the first step, $P_u$ checks its *PR* array, finds *z* on the path, and *broadcasts* a message to processor $P_z$. In the second step, there are two processors $P_u$ and $P_z$ that are aware that their vertices are on the path, so they both again check their *PR* and broadcast messages to $P_y$ and $P_s$, respectively. In the step that follows, there will be four processors broadcasting, and so on.

**Lemma 1** *Identifying all the vertices on the path from u to root r can be done in $O(\log n)$ time with n processors on EREW PRAM.*

**Proof** *PR* for each vertex *v* is created by recording *v*'s parent during pointer-jumping. Pointer-jumping can be done in $O(\log n)$ time with *n* processors on EREW PRAM. With *PR* available for each vertex *v*, all the vertices on the path from *u* to root *r* can be identified by broadcasting from *v* in $O(\log n)$ time with *n* processors on EREW PRAM. □

**Lemma 2** *Rerooting a tree can be done in $O(\log n)$ time with n processors on EREW PRAM.*

**Proof** By Lemma 1, identify the vertices on the path from *u* to root *r*. This takes $O(\log n)$ time with *n* processors on EREW PRAM. Reversing the pointers can be done in $O(1)$ time with *n* processors by finding a vertex's parent and setting the parent of a vertex's parent to be the vertex itself. □

Alg. 1 in Appendix A is a formal description of our algorithm that reroots a tree from *r* to *u*.

For any of the unrooted spanning tree algorithms that adopts the graft and shortcut approach (e.g., spanning tree algorithms based on Shiloach-Vishkin's and

Hirschberg *et al.*'s connected component algorithm [13, 6], see [1] for a survey and comparison), we can extend it to a rooted spanning tree algorithm with Alg. 1. In our RST-Graft algorithm, whenever an edge $< u, v >$ causes the grafting of one subtree $A$ that contains $u$ onto another subtree $B$ that contains $v$, except when it is the case that $u$ is the root of $A$, our rooted spanning tree algorithm invokes the tree rerooting algorithm to reroot $A$ at $u$. Alg. 2 in Appendix A is the formal description of RST-Graft.

Note that Alg. 1 reroots one subtree, while in each iteration of RST-Graft, multiple graftings can happen and multiple subtrees need to be rerooted. We show that rerooting a forest of subtrees can be done within the same complexity for rooting one subtree.

**Lemma 3** *A forest of subtrees with a total of $n$ vertices can be rerooted in $O(\log n)$ time with $n$ processors on EREW PRAM.*

**Proof** For each subtree $T_i$ with size $n_i$, we can reroot $T_i$ with $n_i$ processors within $O(\log n_i)$ time on EREW by applying the same argument of Lemma 2. With $\sum_i n_i = n$ and $\max_i n_i \leq n$, we can reroot the subtrees within the stated complexity bound. □

**Theorem 1** *RST-Graft computes a rooted spanning tree on CRCW PRAM in $O\left(\log^2 n\right)$ time with $O(m)$ processors.*

**Proof** Steps 1, 2, 3 and 4, of Alg. 2 run in $O(1)$ time with $m$ processors; moreover, Step 2 requires arbitrary CRCW PRAM. Step 5 is the pointer-jumping step that runs in $O(\log n)$ time with $n$ processors. Step 6 is the rerooting step that takes $O(\log n)$ time with $n$ processors. During each iteration the number of (super)vertices is reduced at least by half, and since there are $O(\log n)$ iterations, RST-Graft can be performed on an arbitrary CRCW PRAM with $O\left(\log^2 n\right)$ time using $m$ processors. □

Note that although RST-Graft has an additional $\log n$ factor compared with the best approach in theory, the $\log n$ factor is determined by both the underlying spanning tree algorithm which we found to be more practical than most other spanning tree algorithms with lower running times, and by the tree rerooting algorithm. Our experimental results show that RST-Graft runs almost as fast as ST-Graft.

## 2.2 Rooted Spanning Tree: Graph Traversal Approach (RST-Trav)

Previously we designed a parallel spanning tree algorithm that achieves good speedup over the best sequen-

tial spanning tree algorithm on SMPs [1]. We observe that this algorithm is also a rooted spanning tree algorithm without any further overhead because it builds a spanning tree by finding the *parent* of each vertex. Here we give a brief description of the algorithm, and refer interested readers to our spanning tree papers for details. First a small rooted subtree $T_s$ with size $O(p)$ is created where $p$ is the number of processors. Then each processor picks a unique leaf $l$ from $T_s$ and starts growing a subtree rooted at $l$ by breadth-first traversal. In the process of breadth-first search, a processor will check a vertex's color, and if it is not colored, color it with a color that is associated with the processor, and set its parent. Under the assumption of sequential memory consistency, the algorithm correctly computes a spanning tree by setting up the parent relation for each vertex in the graph. Without further modification, this algorithm also produces a rooted spanning tree algorithm (RST-Trav), so the accompanying experimental results can also be used for rooted spanning tree. One caveat of RST-Trav is that in some very rare cases, there may be a limit to the parallelism of this approach and a detection scheme allows the algorithm fall back to either Shiloach-Vishkin's or Hirschberg *et al.*'s algorithm. As RST-Graft is a rooted spanning tree algorithm based on Shiloach-Vishkin's algorithm, in case of encountering such graphs, we can fall back to RST-Graft.

## 3 Efficient Construction of Euler Tours

In this section we show two new approaches for constructing Euler tours without sorting. The first one is in the PRAM framework that finds the twin edge $< v, u >$ of edge $< u, v >$ in the edge list during the spanning tree algorithm, and the second one uses the more realistic SMP model that instead builds a tour from a rooted tree based on the DFS ordering of the edges. We denote the first approach Euler-Graft, the second Euler-DFS.

### 3.1 Euler Tour Construction: Graft and Shortcut Approach (Euler-Graft)

As with RST-Graft, twin edges can be found with some small overhead during the graft-and-shortcut spanning tree algorithm. The key observation is that for any iteration in the spanning tree algorithm edge $< u, v >$ is inspected and a grafting happens only if $v$'s supervertex is less than $u$'s supervertex and the twin $< x = v, y = u >$ is somewhere else in the edge list. $< x, y >$ would have caused the grafting if the inspection is to compare whether $v$'s supervertex is less than $u$'s supervertex. To identify $<x,y>$ without having to search for it, we re-run the iteration and do the comparison in the other direction. Note that in an iteration we need to find $O(m)$ twin edges. If an edge causes this same grafting as $<u,v>$, we know it is the twin of $<u,v>$. This is true under the condition that in every iteration a supervertex is grafted only by one processor to one other supervertex. To guarantee that this condition holds on CRCW PRAM, basically a tournament is run between the processors that try to graft a certain supervertex $v$, and only the winner gets to graft $v$. The graft and short-cut approach runs with $O(\log n)$ time with $m$ processors on arbitrary CRCW [1, 14].

**Theorem 2** *With $m$ processors using the graft-and-shortcut spanning tree algorithm, the twin pointers for the Euler tour can be set in $O(\log n)$ time on CRCW PRAM.*

**Proof** In each iteration of the graft-and-shortcut spanning tree algorithm two inspection rounds are executed. For edge $<u,v>$, the first round checks whether $v$'s supervertex is less than $u$'s supervertex and if $<u,v>$ causes a grafting, associates with $u$'s supervertex the $<u,v>$ location in the edge list. In the second round for edge $<x,y>$ we check whether $x$'s supervertex is less than $y$'s supervertex, and if true, then associate with $x$'s supervertex the location of $<x,y>$'s twin in the edge list. When the algorithm terminates, each edge in the spanning tree finds its twin. The running time is the same as the spanning tree algorithm, which is $O(\log n)$ time with $m$ processors on arbitrary CRCW. □

After the twin pointer is set, we can construct an Euler tour in $O(1)$ time with $n$ processors. This approach can be easily combined with RST-Graft, so with one single run of a graft-and-shortcut spanning tree algorithm, we have spanning tree, rooted spanning tree, and Euler tour, for the tree.

## 3.2 Euler Tour Construction: DFS Approach (Euler-DFS)

Generally list ranking is needed to perform tree computations with the Euler tour. For an edge $<u,v>$, the next edge $<v,w>$ could be far away from $<u,v>$ in the list with no spatial locality. For any fast implementations on modern computer systems, temporal and spatial locality of the algorithm and the data structures are crucial for good performance. An algorithm with good temporal and spatial locality lends itself to cache-friendly implementations. It is desirable that for an Euler tour the consecutive edges are placed nearby each other in the

list. We present a randomized algorithm under the SMP model that constructs an optimal tour in terms of spatial locality, i.e., consecutive edges in the tour are placed into consecutive memory locations in the list. Under the SMP model, there are two parts to an algorithm's complexity, $M_E$ the memory access complexity (number of non-contiguous memory accesses) and $T_C$ the computation complexity [5]. Parameters of the model include the problem size $n$ and the number of processors $p$. The $M_E$ term recognizes the importance that memory accesses have over an algorithm's performance. Recognizing that $p$ is usually far smaller than $n$, which is true for most actual problems and architectures, has significant impact on the design of algorithms. Euler-DFS is one such example.

Given a rooted spanning tree $T$ with root $r$, the basic idea of our algorithm is first to break $T$ into $s$ tree blocks by randomly choosing $s-1$ vertices (called *rep_vertices*). As $r$ is a natural *rep_vertex* the total number of *rep_vertices* is $s$. The resulting tree blocks are non-overlapping except at the $s$ *rep_vertices*, and the *rep_vertices* form a *rep-tree* (short for representative tree) if we shrink a tree block into a single *rep_vertex*. Fig. 3 illustrates the notion of tree blocks.

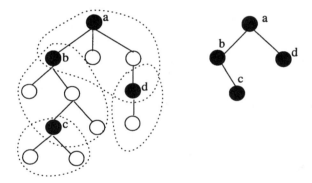

**Figure 3. Illustration of tree blocks. On the left, four *rep_vertices* $a$, $b$, $c$, and $d$, are chosen. Tree blocks are circled by dotted lines. On the right is the *rep-tree*.**

Each of these tree blocks is then traversed in DFS order creating $s$ local Euler tours for the $s$ subtrees. We then combine the $s$ local Euler tours into one global tour for which each local tour is broken up at each *rep_vertex* it encounters to incorporate the local tour of the tree block represented by that *rep_vertex*. To do so for each *rep_vertex* we need to compute where its local tour starts in the global tour for $T$. This is achieved by doing some tree computations on the much smaller *rep-tree*.

We do post-order numbering and DFS numbering on *rep-tree* and record in *local_dfs_num* the DFS numbering of each *rep_vertex* in its parent's tree block. *global_start* is the location in the global tour where *rep_vertex*'s local tour starts, and *g_size* is the size of the subtree (not tree block) rooted at *rep_vertex*. *g_size* can be computed in one post-order traversal of *rep-tree*. Then in the order of DFS numbering, for each *rep_vertex* $v$ with predecessor $u$ and parent $w$, we set $v$'s *g_size* to be $u.global\_start + v.local\_dfs\_num$ if $u = w$, otherwise set $v.global\_start$ to be $w.global\_start + t + v.local\_dfs\_num$ where $t$ is the sum of the *g_size* of the siblings of $v$ listed before $v$ in the DFS ordering.

The pseudo-code of our algorithm is as follows, in which the input is a rooted tree $T$ with $n$ vertices and root $r$, and the output is an Euler tour $\mathcal{E}$ with consecutive edges of the tour stored in consecutive memory locations.

- **(1):** For processor $P_i$ ($0 \leq i \leq p - 1$), if $i\frac{n}{p} \leq r \leq (i+1)\frac{n}{p} - 1$, choose uniformly and at random $\frac{s}{p} - 1$ non-root vertices as *rep_vertices* and add $r$ to the *rep_vertices*; otherwise, choose uniformly and at random $\frac{s}{p}$ vertices as *rep_vertices*. The result is that $T$ is broken into $s$ tree blocks $B_1, \cdots, B_s$, with each processor owning the *rep_vertices* of $\frac{s}{p}$ blocks.

- **(2):** Processor $P_i$ traverses each of its $\frac{s}{p}$ tree blocks rooted at the *rep_vertices* in DFS order, creating $\frac{s}{p}$ local Euler tours of the blocks. With each edge $e$ of the tour is associated a *position* that now records the location of $e$ in the local tour. With each *rep_vertex* is associated a *local_dfs_num* that records the DFS numbering of the *rep_vertex* in its parent's tree block.

- **(3):** Processor $P_0$ computes post-order numbering and DFS numbering of the *rep-tree* formed by the $s$ *rep_vertices*. In one post-order traversal, the subtree size *g_size* rooted at each *rep_vertex* can be computed. For root $r$, $r.global\_start = 0$. In the order of DFS numbering, if a *rep_vertex* $v$ has a predecessor $u$ that is also its parent $w$ ($u = w$), which means from $r$ to $v$ the global tour is the pieces of local tours that have been seen during the DFS traversal, then set $v.global\_start = w.global\_start + v.local\_dfs\_num$; otherwise extra spaces are needed to accommodate other local tours. One way to look at this is $w$'s *global_start* is now available, and we know the DFS numbering of $v$ in $w$'s tree block, so there must have been other *rep_vertices* $S$ visited in DFS order before $v$ (or otherwise $u = v$). Hence,

extra spaces are needed to accommodate the tours of the subtrees (not blocks) rooted at the vertices in $S$, and they are $v$'s siblings. Let $t$ be the sum of the *g_size* of the siblings of $v$ listed before $v$ in the DFS ordering in $w$'s tree block. $v.global\_start = w.global\_start + t + v.local\_dfs\_num$.

- **(4):** For each of the $\frac{s}{p}$ tours defined by the *rep_vertices* on processor $P_i$, for each edge $e$ in the ordering of the appearance in the local tour, if $e = <u, v>$ with $u$ being a *rep_vertex*, add $\delta = u.global\_start$ to *position* of $e$ and all edges following $e$ until the appearance of another *rep_vertex*; if $e = <u, v>$ with $v$ being a *rep_vertex*, increase $\delta$ by $v.g\_size$.

- **(5):** For each of the $\frac{s}{p}$ tours defined by the *rep_vertices* on processor $P_i$, copy each edge $e$ in the tour into location $e.position$ of tour $\mathcal{E}$.

Let $|B|$ be the size of block $B$, that is, the number of vertices in the tree block. We show that the largest tree block $B_i$ has size less than $\frac{cn}{s}$ (where $c$ is some small constant greater than one) with probability at least $1 - e^{-c}$.

**Lemma 4**
$$P\left(|B_i| \geq \frac{cn}{s}\right) \leq e^{-c}.$$

**Proof** Suppose $T_i$ is the smallest subtree of $T$ that contains $B_i$. As each vertex is equally likely to be a *rep_vertex*, the probability that a *rep_vertex* is outside of $T_i$ is
$$\frac{n - \frac{cn}{s}}{n} = \frac{s - c}{s},$$
while the probability that a *rep_vertex* is inside $T_i$ is $\frac{c}{s}$. Let

$\mathcal{A}$ be the event that $|B_i| \geq \frac{cn}{s}$,
$\mathcal{B}$ be the event that no *rep_vertex* splits $T_i$ ($\mathcal{A} \subseteq \mathcal{B}$),
$\Theta_k$ be the event that $k$ *rep_vertices* fall in $T_i$, and
$\Lambda_k$ be the event that $k$ *rep_vertices* fall outside $T_i$.

$$P\left(|B_i| \geq \frac{cn}{s}\right) = P(\mathcal{A}) \leq P(\mathcal{B})$$

$$\leq \sum_{k=1}^{s} P(\Theta_k)P(\Lambda_{s-k})$$

$$= \sum_{k=1}^{s} \left(\frac{s-c}{s}\right)^{s-k} \left(\frac{c}{s}\right)^{k}$$

$$= \left(\frac{s-c}{s}\right)^{s} \sum_{k=1}^{s} \left(\frac{c}{s-c}\right)^{k}$$

$$\leq \left(\frac{s-c}{s}\right)^{s}$$

$$\leq e^{-c}$$

$\square$

The expected size of a tree block is $\frac{n+s-1}{s} \approx \frac{n}{s}$ when $n$ is large. By Lemma 4 the probability that the largest number of vertices visited by a particular processor deviates from $\frac{n}{p}$ by a constant factor of $\alpha$ is bounded by $e^{(-\alpha s)/p}$, which can be bounded by $n^{-\lambda}$ for some $\lambda > 0$ if $\frac{s}{p} \geq \ln n$. Hence with high probability the work is fairly balanced among the processors, and the expected running time of the algorithm is $O(n/p + \ln n)$ with $p$ processors when $n \gg p$ and $s = p \ln n$.

# 4 Experimental Results

This section summarizes the experimental results of our implementation. We compare the performance of ST-Graft and RST-Graft on a variety of input graphs. As for RST-Trav, [1] give a comprehensive experimental study. We test our shared-memory implementation on the Sun Enterprise 4500, a uniform memory access (UMA) shared memory parallel machine with 14 Ultra-SPARC II processors and 14 GB of memory. Each processor has 16 Kbytes of direct-mapped data (L1) cache and 4 MBytes of external (L2) cache. The clock speed of each processor is 400 MHz.

## 4.1 Experimental Data

Next we describe the collection of graph generators that we use to compare the performance of the parallel rooted spanning tree graph algorithms. Our generators include several employed in previous experimental studies of parallel graph algorithms for related problems. For instance, we include the mesh topologies used in the connected component studies of [4, 9, 7, 3], the random graphs used by [4, 2, 7, 3], the geometric graphs used by [2], and the "tertiary" geometric graph **AD3** used by [4, 7, 9, 3].

- **Meshes** Computational science applications for physics-based simulations and computer vision commonly use mesh-based graphs. In the **2D Mesh**, the vertices of the graph are placed on a 2D mesh, with each vertex connected to its four neighbors.

- **Random Graph** We create a random graph of $n$ vertices and $m$ edges by randomly adding $m$ unique edges to the vertex set. Several software packages generate random graphs this way, including LEDA [10].

- **Geometric Graphs and AD3** In these $k$-regular graphs, $n$ points are chosen uniformly and at random in a unit square in the Cartesian plane, and each vertex is connected to its $k$ nearest neighbors. Moret and Shapiro [11] use these in their empirical study of sequential MST algorithms. **AD3** is a geometric graph with $k = 3$.

## 4.2 Performance Results and Analysis

Fig. 4 contains the performance comparison between the rooted spanning tree algorithm RST-Graft, Euler tour construction algorithm Euler-Graft and the spanning tree algorithm ST-Graft. These algorithms are all based on the graft-and-shortcut approach. In the figure the ratios of the running time of RST-Graft/ST-Graft and Euler-Graft/ST-Graft are given. For most input graphs, the overhead of the RST-Graft over ST-Graft is within 25%, and for each input graph, there are cases that RST-Graft actually runs faster than ST-Graft which is caused by the different number of iterations due to the races among the processors. In each iteration of ST-Graft, there are two runs of grafting, the first one is a competition run and the second one actually performs the grafting. In Euler-Graft, a third run is needed to find the twin edges for the tree edges, so we expect to see roughly 50% overhead of Euler-Graft/ST-Graft. This is true for the input graphs shown in Fig. 4. 2D Mesh is an anomaly where Euler-Graft actually runs faster than ST-Graft, because the optimization (compacting edge list) for ST-Graft does not work efficiently for this special input graph.

In Fig. 5 we plot the running times of the two approaches for computing the rooted spanning tree and Euler tour. Euler-DFS is our approach using ST-Trav from [1], and Euler-Sort is based on Tarjan and Vishkin's approach although we replace the spanning tree algorithm with our much faster algorithm ST-Trav. Generally Euler-DFS is 3-5 times faster than Euler-Sort. Note that the comparison result would be more dramatic if we

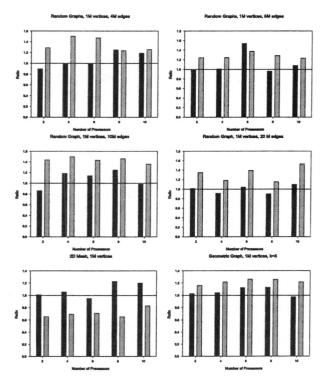

**Figure 4. The performance ratio of the running times of RST-Graft and Euler-Graft over the spanning tree algorithm ST-Graft. In each plot, the left- and right-hand bars correspond to RST-Graft and Euler-Graft, respectively, as compared with ST-Graft.**

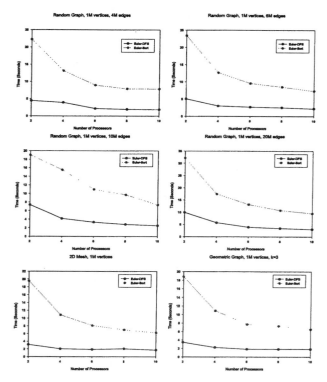

**Figure 5. Comparison of Euler-DFS and Euler-Sort running times for various input graphs.**

compare only the two approaches for rooted spanning tree, our rooted spanning tree algorithm could be an order of magnitude faster than the traditional approach of spanning tree plus Euler tour. In practice this comparison would be fair if after finding a rooted spanning tree the algorithm no longer does any tree computation. If it does, as in the case of Tarjan and Vishkin's biconnected component algorithm, we compare two algorithms that achieve the same functionality, that is, they both compute the rooted spanning tree and Euler tour. In addition to running faster, Euler-DFS tends to be more flexible (only computes Euler tour when needed), simpler (no sorting is involved) and uses less memory (no need to maintain the twin information). One other advantage of Euler-DFS that does not affect the performance but is a useful property is that it takes the straightforward adjacency list representation of the input graphs. While Euler-Sort needs both adjacency list (required by the fast spanning tree algorithm otherwise it is even slower) and

edge list representation, which is clumsy and doubles the memory usage. With Euler-DFS, as the number of processors increases, it is observed that parallel memory writes (e.g., copying tour elements into appropriate locations) start to dominate the execution time. We expect better scalability results of Euler-DFS on platforms with more scalable memory bandwidth.

## 5 Conclusions

We presented new algorithms for rooted spanning trees and rerooting a tree without having to compute the Euler tour. These algorithms have little or no overhead over the underlying spanning tree algorithms, and the technique will greatly reduce the running time and programming complexity of an algorithm if no further tree computations are required. Two new approaches of computing an Euler tour are also discussed when the pointers between twin edges are not given. For all the input graphs we tested, Euler-DFS runs much faster than the sorting approach. As Euler tour is fundamental in tree computations, our results will have impact on the implementation of higher-level algorithms, for example, tree computations, biconnected components, lowest common ancestors, upward accumulation, etc. Our results are also examples that algorithm engineering techniques pay off in parallel computing.

# References

[1] D. A. Bader and G. Cong. A fast, parallel spanning tree algorithm for symmetric multiprocessors (SMPs). In *Proc. Int'l Parallel and Distributed Processing Symp. (IPDPS 2004)*, Santa Fe, NM, April 2004.

[2] S. Chung and A. Condon. Parallel implementation of Borůvka's minimum spanning tree algorithm. In *Proc. 10th Int'l Parallel Processing Symp. (IPPS'96)*, pages 302–315, April 1996.

[3] S. Goddard, S. Kumar, and J.F. Prins. Connected components algorithms for mesh-connected parallel computers. In S. N. Bhatt, editor, *Parallel Algorithms: 3rd DIMACS Implementation Challenge October 17-19, 1994*, volume 30 of *DIMACS Series in Discrete Mathematics and Theoretical Computer Science*, pages 43–58. American Mathematical Society, 1997.

[4] J. Greiner. A comparison of data-parallel algorithms for connected components. In *Proc. 6th Ann. Symp. Parallel Algorithms and Architectures (SPAA-94)*, pages 16–25, Cape May, NJ, June 1994.

[5] D. R. Helman and J. JáJá. Designing practical efficient algorithms for symmetric multiprocessors. In *Algorithm Engineering and Experimentation (ALENEX'99)*, volume 1619 of *Lecture Notes in Computer Science*, pages 37–56, Baltimore, MD, January 1999. Springer-Verlag.

[6] D. S. Hirschberg, A. K. Chandra, and D. V. Sarwate. Computing connected components on parallel computers. *Commununications of the ACM*, 22(8):461–464, 1979.

[7] T.-S. Hsu, V. Ramachandran, and N. Dean. Parallel implementation of algorithms for finding connected components in graphs. In S. N. Bhatt, editor, *Parallel Algorithms: 3rd DIMACS Implementation Challenge October 17-19, 1994*, volume 30 of *DIMACS Series in Discrete Mathematics and Theoretical Computer Science*, pages 23–41. American Mathematical Society, 1997.

[8] J. JáJá. *An Introduction to Parallel Algorithms.* Addison-Wesley Publishing Company, New York, 1992.

[9] A. Krishnamurthy, S. S. Lumetta, D. E. Culler, and K. Yelick. Connected components on distributed memory machines. In S. N. Bhatt, editor, *Parallel Algorithms: 3rd DIMACS Implementation Challenge October 17-19, 1994*, volume 30 of *DIMACS Series in Discrete Mathematics and Theoretical Computer Science*, pages 1–21. American Mathematical Society, 1997.

[10] K. Mehlhorn and S. Näher. *The LEDA Platform of Combinatorial and Geometric Computing.* Cambridge University Press, 1999.

[11] B.M.E. Moret and H.D. Shapiro. An empirical assessment of algorithms for constructing a minimal spanning tree. In *DIMACS Monographs in Discrete Mathematics and Theoretical Computer Science: Computational Support for Discrete Mathematics 15*, pages 99–117. American Mathematical Society, 1994.

[12] S. Pettie and V. Ramachandran. A randomized time-work optimal parallel algorithm for finding a minimum spanning forest. *SIAM J. Comput.*, 31(6):1879–1895, 2002.

[13] Y. Shiloach and U. Vishkin. An $O(\log n)$ parallel connectivity algorithm. *J. Algs.*, 3(1):57–67, 1982.

[14] R.E. Tarjan and U. Vishkin. An efficient parallel biconnectivity algorithm. *SIAM J. Computing*, 14(4):862–874, 1985.

[15] J. van Leeuwen, editor. *Handbook of Theoretical Computer Science.* The MIT Press/Elsevier, New York, 1990.

# A Algorithms

**Input**: 1. A rooted tree $T$ with $n$ vertices, root $r$, and new root $u$

       2. Array $PR_v$ for each vertex $v$

**Output**: Rooted tree $T'$ with root at $u$

**begin**

    **if** $i = u$ **then** On-Path[$i$] $\leftarrow 1$ **else** On-Path[$i$] $\leftarrow 0$ ;

    $j \leftarrow size(PR_i) - 1$ ;

    **for** $h \leftarrow 1$ *to* $\lceil \log n \rceil$ **do**

        **if** *On-Path[i]=1 and* $j \geq 1$ **then**

            On-Path[$PR_i[j]$] $\leftarrow 1$ ;

            $j \leftarrow j - 1$ ;

    **if** *On-Path[i]=1* **then**

        *parent*[*parent*[$i$]] $\leftarrow i$

**end**

**Algorithm 1:** Algorithm for rerooting a tree on processor $P_i$, for $(0 \leq i \leq n-1)$

---

**Input**: Undirected graph $G = (V, E)$ with $n$ vertices, $m$ edges

**Output**: A rooted spanning tree $T$ of $G$

**begin**

    **while** *Number of Connected Component* $> 1$ **do**

        1. **for** $i \leftarrow 1$ *to n in parallel* **do** $D[i] \leftarrow i$;

        2. **for** $i \leftarrow 1$ *to n in parallel* **do**

            **for** *each neighbor j of i in parallel* **do**

                **if** $D[j] < D[i]$ **then**

                    $Winner[D[i]] \leftarrow K$

        3. **for** $i \leftarrow 1$ *to n in parallel* **do**

            **for** *each neighbor j of i in parallel* **do**

                **if** $D[j] < D[i]$ *AND* $Winner[D[i]] = K$ **then**

                    $D[D[i]] \leftarrow D[j]$;

                    $parent[i] \leftarrow j$;

                    Label $i$ as the new root of the old subtree;

        4. j=0;

        5. **for** $i \leftarrow 1$ *to n in parallel* **do**

            **if** $D[i] \neq D[D[i]]$ **then**

                $PR[j] \leftarrow D[i]$;

                $j \leftarrow j + 1$ ;

        6. **for** *each i that is labeled as the new root of a subtree* **do**

            call Alg. 1 to reroot the subtree

**end**

**Algorithm 2:** Algorithm for finding rooted spanning tree on processor $K$

# Optimal Parallel Scheduling Algorithm for WDM Optical Interconnects with Recirculating Buffering

Zhenghao Zhang and Yuanyuan Yang

Department of Electrical & Computer Engineering, State University of New York, Stony Brook, NY 11794, USA

*Abstract*—In this paper we study scheduling algorithms in WDM optical interconnects with recirculating buffering. The interconnect we consider has wavelength conversion capabilities. We focus on limited range wavelength conversion while considering full range wavelength conversion as a special case. We formalize the problem of maximizing throughput and minimizing packet delay in such an interconnect as a matching problem in a bipartite graph and give an optimal parallel algorithm that runs in $O(Bk^2)$, as compared to $O((N+B)^3k^3)$ time if directly applying other existing matching algorithms, where $N$ is the number of input/output fibers, $B$ is the number of fiber delay lines and $k$ is the number of wavelengths per fiber.

## I. INTRODUCTION AND BACKGROUND

In this paper, we consider *optical packet switching* over WDM as it may offer better flexibility and better exploitations of the huge bandwidth of optical systems [7]. We study scheduling problems in WDM interconnects (or switches) which are used to direct the incoming packets to their destinations. Our goal is to resolve output contention, which arises when some packets on the same wavelength are destined for the same output fiber. To resolve output contention, the contending packets can be sent to optical buffers to be delayed until they can be transmitted. If there are wavelength converters in the interconnect, the contention can also be resolved by converting the wavelengths of the contending packets to some idle wavelengths (if there are any) on the output fiber. In this paper we study the combination of these two methods.

In an optical interconnect each output fiber may have its own buffers [7], [6]. However, optical buffers are made of fiber delay lines and are costly and bulky, therefore it is more desirable to share the buffers to reduce the buffer size. We consider recirculating buffering [3] [4] in which the optical buffers are shared. A packet that cannot be sent to the output fiber directly is first sent to a delay line. After being delayed for some time, the packet will come out of the delay line and be at the input side of the interconnect again. It will attempt to be transmitted along with the newly arrived packets, and if fails one more time, the packet will be sent to some delay line again to wait for the next round.

To translate signals on one wavelength to another wavelength, *wavelength converters* are needed. A wavelength converter is *full range* if it is capable of converting a wavelength to any other wavelengths in the optical system, and is *limited range* if it is only capable of converting a given wavelength to a limited number of wavelengths. It was shown [8], [5] that limited range wavelength converters can achieve network performance similar to full range wavelength convert-

This research was supported by the U.S. National Science Foundation under grant numbers CCR-0073085 and CCR-0207999.

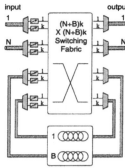

Fig. 1. Optical packet switch with recirculating buffering and wavelength conversion.

ers even when the conversion degree is very small. Thus they are considered to be more realistic and cost-effective and will be the main focus of this paper. However, full range wavelength converters are also considered and will be treated as a special case of limited range wavelength converters.

Fig.1 shows such an interconnect. As in [7] [10] [6], we assume that the duration of an optical packet is one time slot. The traffic pattern considered in this paper is unicast, i.e., each packet is destined to only one output fiber. The interconnect has $N$ input fibers and $N$ output fibers, and inside the interconnect there are $B$ delay lines, each capable of delaying a packet for one time slot. There are $k$ wavelengths on these fibers. The switching fabric is capable of connecting each of the $(N+B)k$ input wavelength channels, $Nk$ from the input fibers and $Bk$ from the delay lines to each of the $N+B$ fibers ($N$ output fibers and $B$ delay lines). Limited range wavelength converters are equipped for these input wavelength channels, which are capable of converting a wavelength to several adjacent wavelengths. The scheduling algorithm decides which wavelength the input signal should be converted to.

Our goal is to find an algorithm that drops as few packets as possible to minimize the packet loss and sends as many packets directly to the output fibers as possible to minimize the packet delay. We formalize the problem as a matching problem in a weighted bipartite graph and show that the optimal scheduling is the optimal matching in the bipartite graph. We then give an efficient parallel algorithm called Parallel Segment Expanding Algorithm to find this optimal matching.

Parallel scheduling algorithms for electronic interconnects have been extensively studied, for example, the iSLIP algorithm [12] for input-buffered interconnects. However, since the recirculating buffer is a shared output buffer, these algorithms do not apply. Parallel matching algorithms for general bipartite graphs were also well studied [11]. However, since the bipartite graph considered in this paper exhibits special properties due to limited range wavelength conversion, we can give new algorithms to greatly accelerate the speed of scheduling. WDM interconnects with dedicated output buffers and full range wavelength conversion were studied and their performances were evaluated with analytical models in [10]. Scheduling in unbuffered WDM interconnects with limited range wavelength conversion were studied in [14] and [9], and [9] gives an optimal scheduling algorithm called the First Available Algorithm. Scheduling in WDM interconnects with dedicated output buffers and limited range wavelength conversion were studied in [6] and [13], and [13] gives an optimal scheduling algorithm called the Scan and Swap Algorithm. The scheduling problem studied this paper is quite different and in some sense more complicated than that in [9] and [13]. This is because first, in the case of no buffer or dedicated buffer, the scheduling can be carried out for each output fiber independently, but when the buffers are shared, the scheduling must be carried out with respect to the whole switch. Secondly, though [9] and [13] also formalized the scheduling problems into matching problem in bipartite graphs, the bipartite graphs are different from the bipartite graphs considered in this paper, because in [9] and [13], the adjacency set of a vertex is always an interval, while in this paper, this property does not hold.

## II. Wavelength Conversion

As mentioned earlier, with limited range wavelength conversion, an incoming wavelength may be converted to a set of adjacent outgoing wavelengths. We define the set of these outgoing wavelengths as the *adjacency set* of this input wavelength. The cardinality of the adjacency set is the *conversion degree* of this wavelength. We also define the *conversion distance* as the largest difference between the index of a wavelength and a wavelength that it can be converted to. We assume the wavelength conversion has the following two properties:

*Property 1:* The wavelengths in the adjacency set can be represented by an interval of integers. The adjacency set of an input wavelength $\lambda_i$ is denoted by $[begin(i), end(i)]$, where $begin(i)$ and $end(i)$ are positive integers and $begin(i) \leq end(i)$.

*Property 2:* For two wavelengths $\lambda_i$ and $\lambda_j$, if $i < j$, then $begin(i) \leq begin(j)$ and $end(i) \leq end(j)$.

Fig.2(a) shows the conversion of a 4-wavelength system. Note that full range wavelength conversion can simply be considered as a special case by letting the conversion degrees for all wavelengths be $k$.

## III. Problem Formalization

As mentioned earlier, the basic design rule of the scheduling algorithm should be: (1) To minimize the packet loss, drop as few packets as possible. (2) To minimize the packet delay, send as many packets directly to the output fiber as possible. This is a typical resource allocation problem and can be formalized as a matching problem. We can draw a bipartite graph, with left side vertices representing arrived

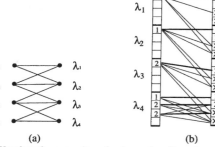

Fig. 2. (a) Wavelength conversion of a 4-wavelength system. (b) Packets and wavelength channels in a switch with $N = 2$, $B = 2$, $k = 4$ and the wavelength conversion as defined in (a).

packets and right side vertices representing wavelength channels. Fig.2(b) shows such a graph when $N = 2$, $B = 2$, $k = 4$ and wavelength conversion as defined in Fig.2(a). In the figure, we put number '1' or '2' in the box representing a left side vertex according to the destination of this packet. In this example, there is one packet on $\lambda_1$, $\lambda_2$ and $\lambda_4$ destined for output fiber 1 and one packet on $\lambda_3$ and two packets on $\lambda_4$ destined for output fiber 2. For right side vertices, there are two types: the output vertices and the buffer vertices. Output vertices represent wavelength channels on the output fibers. Buffer vertices represent wavelength channels on the delay lines. In the figure, an output vertex is labeled '1' or '2' according to the fiber it is on and a buffer vertex is labeled as a cross. Vertices are ordered according to their wavelength indices, smaller indices at higher positions. Vertices on the same wavelength are in an arbitrary order. There is an edge connecting left side vertex $a$ and right side vertex $b$ if and only if the wavelength channel represented by $b$ can be assigned to the packet represented by $a$. Note that if $b$ is a buffer vertex, $b$ is adjacent to all the input packets with a wavelength in its adjacency set, regardless of the destinations of these packets. However, if $b$ is an output vertex, $b$ is only adjacent to the input packets with a wavelength in its adjacency set and also destined to the output fiber where $b$ is in.

In this bipartite graph, let $E$ denote the set of edges. Any scheduling can be represented by a subset of $E$, $E'$, where edge $ab \in E'$ if wavelength channel $b$ is assigned to packet $a$. Under unicast traffic, any packet needs only one output channel and an output channel can be assigned to only one packet. It follows that the edges in $E'$ are vertex disjoint, since if two edges share a vertex, either one packet is assigned two wavelength channels or one wavelength channel is assigned to two packets. Thus, $E'$ is a *matching* in $G$. To maximize network throughput, we should find a maximum cardinality matching in this bipartite graph. However, this might not be enough since we also wish to minimize the total delay. Thus the matching we want to find is a maximum cardinality matching which covers maximum number of output vertices. To do this we can assign weight 1 to the output vertices and weight 0 to the buffer vertices and find the optimal matching in this weighted bipartite graph, where an optimal matching in a weighted bipartite graph is defined as a maximum cardinality matching with maximum total weight. In the example in Fig.2(b) an optimal matching is shown in heavy lines.

## IV. PARALLEL SEGMENT EXPANDING ALGORITHM

### A. *Matroid Greedy Algorithm*

Optimal matching in an arbitrary bipartite graph can be found by the following simple greedy algorithm which can be called the Matroid Greedy Algorithm [1], [2]. The algorithm starts with an empty set $\Pi$. In step $s$, let $a$ be the left side vertex with the $s_{th}$ largest weight. The algorithm checks whether there is a matching covering $a$ and all the previously selected vertices in $\Pi$. If yes, add $a$ to $\Pi$, otherwise leave $a$ uncovered. Update $s \leftarrow s + 1$ and repeat until all vertices have been checked. When finished, $\Pi$ stores left side vertices that can be covered by an optimal matching.

However, the time complexity of the matroid greedy algorithm is $O(n^3)$ for an $n$-vertex bipartite graph, since to check whether a vertex can be covered along with all the previously covered vertices one needs $O(n^2)$ time. For our application in this paper, it will be as high as $O((N+B)^3 k^3)$ time, where $N$ is the number of input/output fibers, $B$ is the number of delay lines and $k$ is the number of wavelength channels. This is apparently too slow since the scheduling must be performed in real time for an optical interconnect. In the following we will give a fast optimal parallel scheduling algorithm called the Parallel Segment Expanding Algorithm that solves the problem in $O(Bk^2)$ time. The algorithm uses the idea of the matroid greedy algorithm, however, the running time is greatly reduced due to the following three reasons.

First, in our bipartite graph, vertices have only two types of weights: output vertices have weight 1 and buffer vertices have weight 0. Therefore to find an optimal matching, according to the matroid greedy algorithm, we can first check all the output vertices since they are of a higher weight, and find a matching that covers the maximum number of them. By doing so, we make sure that the matching has largest weight. After this, we can check all the buffer vertices which are of a lower weight, and augment the matching until it covers as many buffer vertices as possible. The resulting matching will then also have maximum cardinality.

Secondly, we can have easier ways for finding maximum matchings and augmenting matchings by taking advantage of the special properties of the bipartite graph, induced by the properties of wavelength conversion. Lastly, the running time can be further reduced by running the algorithm in parallel.

We will first explain how to cover maximum number of output vertices.

### B. *Covering Maximum Number of Output Vertices*

When trying to cover maximum number of output vertices, buffer vertices need not to be considered since they are of lower priority. Output vertices are only adjacent to left side vertices representing packets destined to this output fiber. Therefore, the entire bipartite graph decomposes into $N$ isolated subgraphs, one for each output fiber. In subgraph $G_i, i \in [1, N]$, the left side vertices represent the packets des-

TABLE 1
FIRST AVAILABLE ALGORITHM

```
for i := 1 to n do
    let a_j be a vertex adjacent to b_i
    not matched yet and is with the smallest index
    if no such a_j exists
        b_i is not matched
    else
        match b_i to a_j
    end if
end for
```

tined for output fiber $i$, and the right side vertices represent the wavelength channels on output fiber $i$. Since the subgraphs are all isolated, the matching we are looking for can be obtained by finding maximum matchings for each of the subgraphs and then combine them together.

We number the left side vertices in $G_i$ as $a_1$ to $a_m$ and number the right side vertices as $b_1$ to $b_n$ according to the wavelength indices, lower index first, and vertices on the same wavelength are in an arbitrary order.

Based on the properties about wavelength conversion, $G_i$ has the following two properties:

*Property 1:* The adjacency set of any left side vertex is an interval.

*Property 2:* Let $[begin(a_i), end(a_i)]$ be the adjacency set of left side vertex $a_i$ and $[begin(a_j), end(a_j)]$ be the adjacency set of left side vertex $a_j$. If $i < j$ then $begin(a_i) \leq begin(a_j)$ and $end(a_i) \leq end(a_j)$.

As in [9], we call a bipartite graph with Properties 1 and 2 *request graph*. Maximum matching in request graphs can be found by First Available Algorithm described in Table 1. This algorithm checks the right side vertices from the top to the bottom. A right side vertex $b_i$ will be matched to its *first available vertex*, which is the adjacent left side vertex with the smallest index and is not matched to other right side vertex yet. The time complexity of this algorithm is $O(n)$, where $n$ is the number of right side vertices, since the loop is executed $n$ times and the work within the loop can be done in constant time.

It can also be shown that in a bipartite graph with Properties 1 and 2 has the following property:

*Property 3:* If edge $a_i b_u \in E$, $a_j b_v \in E$ and $i < j, u > v$, then $a_i b_v \in E, a_j b_u \in E$.

This property can be called the "crossing-edge" property, where we say edge $a_i b_u$ and $a_j b_v$ are a pair of crossing edges if $i < j$ and $u > v$. A matching is "non-crossing" if it does not have any crossing edges. In a non-crossing matching, the $i_{th}$ matched left side vertex will be matched to the $i_{th}$ matched right side vertex.

In addition, the following property can be easily verified:

*Property 4:* The matching found by First Available Algorithm is non-crossing.

Another property of the matching found by the First Available Algorithm, due to the fact that a vertex is always matched to its first available vertex, is

*Property 5:* If $b_u$ is matched to $a_i$, all the left side vertices adjacent to $b_u$ with smaller indices than $a_i$ must be matched to right side vertices with smaller indices than $b_u$.

## C. Covering Buffer Vertices

After covering the maximum number of the output vertices, the matching needs to be augmented to cover the buffer vertices, or, in other words, channels on the ODLs now need to be assigned the packets. The goal is to cover as many buffer vertices as possible while keeping the output vertices covered.

We can check the buffer vertices one by one to see whether it can be covered along with all the previously covered vertices. The checking may start with the $B$ buffer vertices on $\lambda_1$ (one on each ODL), then move to vertices on $\lambda_2, \lambda_3, \ldots$, till $\lambda_k$. After we found that a buffer vertex can be matched to a left side vertex, if that left side vertex represents a packet destined to output fiber $i$, we say the buffer vertex is assigned or added to $G_i$. The optimal scheduling can also be thought as optimally assigning the buffer vertices to different subgraphs, such that maximum number of vertices can be covered.

Any buffer vertex assigned to a subgraph should be inserted to the proper position according to its wavelength, such that, though the buffer vertices may have connections to other subgraphs, the connections within a subgraph still have Properties 1 and 2. As a result, the maximum matchings in the subgraphs can be found by First Available Algorithm. In the following, before checking a buffer vertex, we will assume that the current matching within each subgraph is the matching found by the First Available Algorithm.

## D. Direct Insertion

At first, we can try to match a buffer vertex by each subgraph independently. We will check whether there exists some subgraph $G_i$ in which $b_x$ can be matched while all the right side vertices previously matched in $G_i$ are still matched in $G_i$. If this can be done, the modification of the matching is restricted to $G_i$, and the matchings in other subgraphs need not be changed. Thus we call this "direct insertion". It the case that $b_x$ can be directly inserted in more than one subgraphs, we can arbitrarily pick one.

To see if $b_x$ can be directly inserted is simple. We first place $b_x$ at its proper location in $G_i$. Now consider running First Available Algorithm. By this algorithm, matchings for right side vertices with smaller indices than $b_x$ will remain the same, since they are checked before $b_x$. If $b_x$ can be matched, it will be matched to its first available left side vertex, say, $a_t$, which is the vertex previously matched to the vertex following $b_x$. Thus, to check whether $b_x$ can be directly inserted in $G_i$, one can simply run First Available Algorithm on the subgraph of $G_i$, with left side vertices being those with larger indices than $a_t$ and right side vertices being those with larger indices than $b_x$. $b_x$ can be directly inserted if and only if all the right side vertices in this subgraph of $G_i$ can still be matched. Note that this can be done in parallel for all the $N$ subgraphs and no information exchange is needed.

## E. Searching for Augmenting Path

The problem gets complicated when vertex $b_x$ cannot be directly inserted to any of the $N$ subgraphs. In this case, $b_x$ may still be covered. By graph theory, $b_x$ can be covered if and if there exists an augmenting path for the current matching with one end being $b_x$.

In the previous case when $b_x$ can be directly inserted, this augmenting path is within one subgraph, and we actually do not have to look for the path since we can simply run the First Available Algorithm. When $b_x$ cannot be directly inserted, the augmenting path, if exists, will have to visit more than one subgraphs, and along this path there must be some matched buffer vertex, since only buffer vertices have connections to more than one subgraphs.

Note that by updating the matching according to the augmenting path, we are actually moving some buffer vertices from one subgraph to another. The purpose of this moving can be considered as "making room" for $b_x$ in one of the subgraphs. The searching for the path is in the backwards or upwards direction, because we need to look back to the upper parts of the subgraphs to check whether there are some unused resources (unmatched left side vertices) to be utilized, after we have failed to find any in the lower parts, by direct insertion.

To find an augmenting path, one can search for the *reachable set* of $b_x$ which is defined as all the left side vertices that can be reached by $b_x$ using alternating paths. Denote this reachable set as $R$. If there is an unmatched left side vertex in $R$, $b_x$ can be matched, otherwise $b_x$ cannot be matched.

We will show how to search for this reachable set in parallel. The work done in each subgraph is the same as in all others, hence we describe only one subgraph, $G_1$. The first fact can be used to simplify the search is that we need only to work on a subgraph of $G_1$ with vertex set of $a_1$ to $a_i$ and $b_1$ to $b_u$, where $b_u$ is the right side vertex which is right above $b_x$ and $a_i$ is the vertex matched to $b_u$. This is because if $b_x$ cannot be directly inserted in $G_1$, $b_x$ cannot be matched to left side vertices with larger indices than $a_i$ in any noncrossing matchings. However, to avoid introducing too many notations, we will refer to this subgraph as $G_1$ with the understanding that when searching for the augmenting path $G_1$ means a subgraph of itself.

## F. Identifying Forward and Backward Segments

This subsection presents the main part of the scheduling algorithm. We show that we can find the reachable set more efficiently by identifying the *forward segments* and *backward segments* in the subgraphs. The nice thing about these segment is that, once an alternating path extends to a segment, many of the vertices in the same segment can be added to the reachable set simultaneously. More importantly, this can be done in *constant* time regardless of the number of vertices in the segment, because we can find the segments before starting to extend the reachable set and we can use simple data structures to store the information about the segments. All these make a parallel algorithm possible.

First we define *forward segment*. For notational simplicity, for any matched vertex $a$, we use $mat[a]$ to denote the vertex matched to it. It is important to keep in mind that the matching in the subgraph is found by the First Available Algorithm. Now imagine scanning the right side vertices from $b_1, b_2, \ldots,$ until $b_v$ when one of the following conditions is satisfied: (1) $b_v$ is not adjacent to $mat[b_{v+1}]$; (2) $b_v$ is adjacent to $mat[b_{v+1}]$, but there are some unmatched left side vertices between $mat[b_v]$ and $mat[b_{v+1}]$. If such $b_v$ is found, the subgraph with vertex set of $b_1$ to $b_v$ and all the left side vertices matched to them, plus the unmatched left side vertices adjacent to $b_v$ with smaller indices than $mat[b_{v+1}]$ is called a *forward segment*.

After finding the first forward segment, scan from $b_{v+1}$ to find the second forward segment, then the third until reach $b_u$, the last right side vertex in $G_1$. When a forward segment is found, the following information should be stored: (1) Whether there is an unmatched left side vertex in this segment, if yes, the index of that vertex; (2) The wavelength indices of buffer vertices in the segment.

We have following properties regarding forward segments.

*Property 1:* The index of an unmatched left side vertex in a forward segment is larger than any matched left side vertex in the same forward segment.

**Proof.** This is due to the way we construct a forward segment. When come to an unmatched left side vertex, we will halt the scanning, form a segment, then resume the scanning again. As a result, for two left side vertices, one matched and the other unmatched, if the matched one has a larger index, the two must be in different forward segments. ∎

Therefore, in a forward segment, the matched left side vertices are consecutive. Any unmatched left side vertices will be appended to the end.

*Property 2:* If $a_s$ is a matched left side vertex and is in the reachable set of $b_x$, left side vertices in the same forward segment as $a_s$ with larger indices than $s$ are all in the reachable set.

**Proof.** Suppose $a_s$ is matched to $b_w$ and $b_v$ is matched to $a_q$ where $b_v$ is the last right side vertex in this forward segment. Since the matching is non-crossing, left side vertices in the same forward segment but with larger indices than $a_s$ are the left side vertices matched to $b_{w+1}, b_{w+2}, \ldots, b_v$, plus the unmatched vertices which are adjacent to $b_v$ (if there are any). A possible alternating path is $a_s$ to $b_w$, $b_w$ to $mat[b_{w+1}]$, $mat[b_{w+1}]$ to $b_{w+1}, \ldots, b_{v-1}$ to $a_q$ then $a_q$ to $b_v$ then to all the unmatched vertices . This path visits all the left side vertices in this segment with larger indices than $a_s$. ∎

We say that a right side vertex $b_z$ can be inserted to a forward segment if $b_z$ is adjacent to at least one left side vertices in that segment.

*Property 3:* Consider inserting a right side vertex $b_z$ to a forward segment. $b_z$ can be matched if there is an unmatched left side vertex in this segment. Or, $b_z$ can be matched by moving out a right side vertex with an index no smaller than $b_y$ where $b_y$ is a right side vertex in this segment, if $b_z$ is adjacent to $mat[b_y]$.

**Proof.** This is because each right side vertex in a forward segment is adjacent to the left side vertex matched to the next right side vertex. Suppose $b_z$ is adjacent to $mat[b_y]$. We can shift down the matchings for the right side vertices by one, starting at $b_y$: match $b_y$ to $mat[b_{y+1}]$, match $b_{y+1}$ to $mat[b_{y+2}], \ldots$. If there is an unmatched left side vertex, we can match the last right side vertex to it. Otherwise, one right side vertices must be moved out. ∎

It is also easy to verify that

*Property 4:* Any non-isolated vertex is in exactly one forward segment.

*Property 5:* Non-isolated vertices on the same wavelength are in the same forward segment.

The *backward segment* is defined in a similar way, only the scan direction is now reversed to backwards. Start at $b_u$ where $b_u$ is the last right side vertex in $G_1$, scan back to $b_{u-1}$, $b_{u-2}, \ldots,$ till $b_w$ when $b_w$ is not adjacent to $mat[b_{w-1}]$, the left side vertex matched to $b_{w-1}$. The subgraph with vertex set of $b_w$ to $b_u$ and all the left side vertices matched to them is called a *backward segment*. Note that there are no unmatched vertices in a backward segment. After finding the first backward segment, start scanning from $b_{w-1}$ to find other backward segments. For each backward segment, only the wavelength indices of buffer vertices in this segment are stored. Also note that unlike the forward segments which are numbered from top to bottom, the backward segments are numbered in the reverse direction, or from bottom to top, in accordance to the scanning direction.

Similarly, we can prove the corresponding Properties 1-5 for backward segments and they are omitted due to limited space.

*G. The Parallel Segment Expanding Algorithm*

Now we are ready to present the Parallel Segment Expanding Algorithm shown in Table 2. We store both left side and right side vertices in an array with $k$ entries, denoted by $LS[]$ and $RS[]$ respectively. Each entry stores: (1) the number of vertices on this wavelength; and (2) the index of forward and backward segments these vertices belong to. Forward and backward segments can be represented by intervals of integers, since each type of vertices in a segment, right side vertices, matched left side vertices and unmatched left side vertices are all consecutive. The index wavelengths having buffer vertices can be represented by a $k$-bit register, denoted by $reg_s$ for segment $s$, where a bit is set to '1' if there is a buffer vertex on the corresponding wavelength.

In the following we explain how the algorithm works. At the beginning, the algorithm finds the first backward segment in each subgraph. If $b_x$ is not adjacent to the last left side vertex in the segment nothing needs to be done. Otherwise all the left side vertices in the segment can be added to the reachable set. However, among them there cannot be any unmatched left side vertex, by Property 1 of backward segments. If there is no buffer vertex in this backward segment, any alternating path starting at $b_x$ in this subgraph, say $G_1$, will be confined within $G_1$ and can only reach vertices in this segment. If this is true for all subgraphs, $b_x$ cannot be matched.

If there are buffer vertices in the backward segment, the alternating path can reach left side vertices in other subgraphs. A subgraph then informs other subgraphs about the wavelength range of left side vertices that are adjacent to the buffer vertices in its first backward segment. This would be a set of intervals and we call this "adjacency interval" of this segment. Each subgraph finds its own adjacency interval and the whole adjacency interval is the union of these intervals. We represent it by $[e_1, f_1], [e_2, f_2], \ldots$, which means that left side vertices with wavelengths falling in these intervals are adjacent to some buffer vertex in at least one of the backward segments in the $N$ subgraphs, or can be added to the reachable set. After obtaining these intervals, we say the algorithm finishes step one.

Now step two begins: Each subgraph checks the adjacency intervals obtained in the previous step independently. Basically, when subgraph $G_1$ is checking interval $[e, f]$, it will first look for unmatched left side vertices, and if yes an augmenting path is found; otherwise it will mark the wavelength indices of some buffer vertices it has found for the next step.

To be specific, the subgraph scans the wavelengths in $[e, f]$ one by one, starting at $\lambda_e$. When checking $\lambda_p$ where $e \leq p \leq f$, it will first find the forward segment which left side vertices on $\lambda_p$ belong to. By Property 4 of forward segments, all vertices on $\lambda_p$ belong to the same forward segment. Then it checks whether there is an unmatched left side vertex in this segment, and if yes, by Property 3 of forward segments, an augmenting path is found. Otherwise it marks the wavelength indices of buffer vertices in this forward segment with indices no less than those matched to left side vertices on $\lambda_p$, since these buffer vertices may be used to reach other subgraphs. It then moves to $\lambda_{p+1}$ and find the forward segment which left side vertices on $\lambda_{p+1}$ belong to. It will do the same checking and then move to the next wavelength and so on.

If no unmatched left side vertex can be found after checking all the forward segments, it starts to check the backward segments. No unmatched left side vertices can be found by checking the backward segments. The purpose of this checking is to find the buffer vertices by which to reach other subgraphs. Unlike forward segments, only one backward segment, the one on the top, needs to be checked. To be precise, let $a_l$ be the left side vertex with the smallest index in wavelength range $[e, f]$, then we need only check the backward segment that $a_l$ belongs to and mark the wavelength indices of the buffer vertices in this segment with indices no larger than $mat[a_l]$. This is because, all the vertices that can be reached by alternating paths that have not been found by checking the forward segments but can be found by checking the backward segments must be on smaller wavelengths than $\lambda_e$ for left side vertices and have smaller indices than $mat[a_l]$ for right side vertices.

After finishing checking $[e, f]$, it begins to check the nex-

t interval. After checking all intervals, if no unmatched left side vertex was found, it generates adjacency intervals according to the marked wavelength indices at this step. The $N$ adjacency intervals from the $N$ subgraphs are then "OR"ed, and then this step is repeated again. Each step is called an "expansion". This process ends when: (1) an unmatched vertex is found, or (2) after an expansion, no new wavelength index of buffer vertices is marked.

Suppose after the $I_{th}$ expansion, the algorithm finds an unmatched left side vertex $a_t$ or the augmenting path is found. We will then need to trace back to update the matching.

We say a buffer vertex *finds* a forward or backward segment if it is adjacent to a left side vertex in this segment. Suppose buffer vertex $b_u$ is adjacent to left side vertex $a_t$, and $a_t$ is in forward segment $FS$ and is in backward segment $BS$. We say $b_u$ finds all the left side vertices in $FS$ with indices no less than $a_t$. We also say $b_u$ finds all the left side vertices in $BS$ with indices no larger than $a_t$. If $a_t$ is matched to $b_w$, we say $b_u$ finds all the right side vertices in $FS$ with indices no less than $b_w$. We also say that $b_u$ finds all the right side vertices in $BS$ with indices no larger than $b_w$. In particular, if $b_u$ finds a buffer vertex $b_v$, $b_u$ can be matched in that segment by moving out $b_v$, by Property 3 of forward and backward segments. In the algorithm, every newly discovered vertex was found by a buffer vertex which itself was found in the previous expansion. Vertices found in the first expansion were all found by $b_x$. A vertex may be found by many buffer vertices and we can arbitrarily choose one.

Now suppose $a_t$ was found by $b_u$. We can move $b_u$ to the segment that includes $a_t$. Suppose in the previous step, $b_u$ was found by $b_v$. We know that by moving out $b_u$, $b_v$ can be matched in the segment that $b_u$ was in. We then move $b_v$ to this segment, and this moving is carried on until we reach $b_x$. Totally it takes $I$ steps where $I$ is the number of expansions.

After moving the vertices we can run the Fist Available Algorithm to update the matchings in each subgraph, and at the same time, update the forward and backward segments.

We now prove the correctness of the algorithm.

*Theorem 1:* When the algorithm terminates, it finds either an unmatched left side vertex reachable from $b_x$ or the entire reachable set of $b_x$.

**Proof.** It suffices to show that if the algorithm terminates without reporting an augmenting path, it has found all the left side vertices reachable from $b_x$. We show this by contradiction. If this is not true, there will be a left side vertex $a_t$, either matched or unmatched, that can be reached by an alternating path starting from $b_x$, but the algorithm did not find it. Suppose in the alternating path, $a_t$ is proceeded by $b_u$, and $b_u$ is proceeded by $a_s$. Note that $b_u$ must be matched to $a_s$. We next show that if $a_t$ was not found, so must be $a_s$.

Suppose this is not true, that is, the algorithm has found $a_s$. If it finds $a_s$ it must also find $b_u$ since $b_u$ is matched to $a_s$. If $b_u$ is a buffer vertex, the algorithm would have found $a_t$, since it scans all the vertices adjacent to $b_u$. If $b_u$ is an output vertex, $a_t$ would be in the same subgraph as $a_s$.

## TABLE 2
### PARALLEL SEGMENT EXPANDING ALGORITHM

```
for i := 1 to N do in parallel
    Run First Available Algorithm in G_i with only
    output vertices on the right side.
end for
for x := 1 to Bk do
    for i := 1 to N do in parallel
        Try direct insertion in G_i. If succeed, continue.
    end for
    for i := 1 to N do in parallel
        Find fs, the first backward segment of G_i.
        Set reg_i ← reg_fs if RS[j] > 0 where b_x is on λ_j.
    end for
    Generate adjacency intervals with reg_i, i ∈ [1, N].
    while the adjacency intervals are not empty
        for i := 1 to N do in parallel
            Clear reg_i.
            for each interval [e, f]
                for each wavelength λ_p in this interval
                    If there is a left side vertex on λ_p, find the
                    forward segment it belongs to. Check if there is
                    an unmatched left side vertex in this segment. If
                    yes, exit the while loop. Else find the wavelength
                    indices of the buffer vertices in this segment with
                    indices no less than those matched to vertices on
                    λ_p and "OR" with reg_i.
                end for
                Find a_l, the left side vertex within wavelength
                range [e, f] with the smallest index. Find the
                backward segment it belongs to. Find wavelength
                indices of buffer vertices in this segment with
                indices no larger than mat[a_l] and "OR" with reg_i.
            end for
        end for
        Generate adjacency intervals with reg_i, i ∈ [1, N].
    end while
    if there is an unmatched left side vertex a_t
        Let b_z be the buffer vertex that found a_t.
        Move b_z to the subgraph where a_t is in.
        Let b_y be the buffer vertex that found b_z.
        while b_y is not b_x
            Move b_y to the subgraph where b_z is in.
            b_z ← b_y.
            Let b_y be the buffer vertex that found b_z.
        end while
        for i := 1 to N do in parallel
            Update matching and segments.
        end for
    end if
end for
```

Now if $s < t$, if $a_s$ and $a_t$ are in the same forward segment, the algorithm would have found $a_t$. Thus $a_s$ and $a_t$ must be in different forward segments. But in this case there must be an unmatched vertex between $a_s$ and $a_t$ and it is in the same segment as $a_s$, by the construction of forward segments. Thus the algorithm would have terminated by reporting an unmatched vertex. This is a contradiction. Thus $s$ cannot be smaller than $t$.

But if $s > t$, $a_t$ must be a matched vertex, due to Property 5 in Section IV-B. Since $b_u$ is adjacent to $a_t$, it is not hard to see that $a_s$ and $a_t$ must be in the same backward segment. But if the algorithm finds $a_s$, it must have found all the vertices in the same backward segment as $a_s$ with smaller indices than $a_s$, including $a_t$.

Therefore by the algorithm, in any cases, if it finds $a_s$, it would have found $a_t$. Thus the algorithm did not find $a_s$. Following the same argument we can show that the algorithm also did not find the left side vertex proceeding $a_s$ in the alternating path. This can be carried on until the conclusion that the algorithm did not find any left side vertex in this alternating path. But this contradicts with the fact that the algorithm at least finds all the left side vertices directly adjacent to $b_x$ and any alternating path starting from $b_x$ must visit one of these vertices first. ∎

### H. Complexity Analysis

In this section we give the complexity analysis of this algorithm. We show that by running in parallel on $N$ processing units, the algorithm runs in $O(Bk^2)$ time. It should be mentioned that the $N$ processing or decision making units used in the algorithm can be implemented in hardware to reduce the cost and further speed up the scheduling process.

The first task, covering maximum number of output vertices, is to run First Available Algorithm on each subgraphs with only output vertices. It is done in parallel and takes $O(k)$ time. The initial forward and backward segments can also be found by a linear search in $O(k)$ time.

After this, we need to add buffer vertices to the subgraphs one by one. After buffer vertices were added the number of right side vertices in the subgraphs will exceed $k$. However, note that since vertices on the same wavelength have the same connections and must belong to the same segments, finding maximum matching and the forward and backward segments needs only a linear search on the wavelengths, not on each individual vertex, and can be still done in $O(k)$ time.

When searching a matching for a buffer vertex $b_x$ on wavelength $\lambda_j$, at first we will try direct insertion, which is to run First Available Algorithm on a subgraph of $G_i$ with $k - j$ right side vertices and will take $O(k - j)$ time. If the direct insertion is successful $b_x$ is matched. We then update $RS[]$ by incrementing the number of vertices on $\lambda_j$ by one. Also, the forward and backward segments are updated.

If the direct insertion fails, the algorithm begins to search for an augmenting path. As explained earlier, at each expansion step, each subgraph checks the adjacency intervals to see if there is an unmatched left side vertex. The search is linear and each subgraph has the same running time. Thus, the total time spent on this task is $O(j)$, since in each step the subgraphs only check the new intervals and the total length of the intervals cannot exceed $j$.

Between two expansions, the content of $reg_i$ for $1 \le i \le N$ should be "OR"ed, and the new wavelengths that can be reached should be found and be represented by the adjacency intervals. We can implement this function in hardware, and the total time spent on this task is $O(j)$, since the total number of new wavelengths cannot exceed $j$.

If one unmatched left side vertex is found, we need to trace back to $b_x$ to find the augmenting path. The number of expansions cannot exceed $j$, therefore this will also take $O(j)$ time. When finding the augmenting path we can also simul-

464

taneously move buffer vertices from one subgraph to another or update $RS[]$. After updating $RS[]$, the new matching and new forward and backward segments in each subgraph can be obtained in $O(k)$ time. Overall, it needs $O(k)$ time for a buffer vertex to find a matching. There are $Bk$ buffer vertices. Thus the total running time of the algorithm is $O(Bk^2)$.

## V. Performance Study

We implemented Parallel Segment Expanding Algorithm in software and evaluated the performance of WDM optical interconnects under this scheduling algorithm. The interconnect simulated has 8 input fibers and 8 output fibers with 8 wavelengths on each fiber. We assume that the arrivals of the packets at the input channels are bursty: an input channel alternates between two states, the "busy" state and the "idle" state. When in the "busy" state, it continuously receives packets and all the packets go to the same destination. When in the "idle" state, it does not receive any packets. The length of the busy and idle periods follows geometric distribution. The durations of the packets are all one time slot and for each experiment the simulation program is run for 100,000 time slots.

In Fig.3(a) we show the packet loss probability (PLP) of the interconnect as a function of the number of fiber delay lines. The average burst length is 5 time slots and the average idle period is 1.25 time slots. Therefore the traffic load is 0.8. Two wavelength conversion distances, $d = 1$ and $d = 2$ were tested, along with the no conversion case ($d = 0$) and the full conversion case. As expected, packet loss probability decreases as the number of delay lines increases. However, more significant improvements seems to come from increasing the conversion ability. For example when $d = 0$, the PLP curve is almost flat, which means that without wavelength conversion, there is scarcely any benefit by adding buffer to the interconnect. But when $d = 1$, the PLP drops by a great amount as compared to $d = 0$, and as the number of ODL increases, the PLP will decrease in much faster pace than $d = 0$. We can also see that the PLP for $d = 2$ is already very close to the full wavelength conversion, therefore there is no need to further increase the conversion ability. All this suggests that in a WDM interconnect, wavelength conversion is crucial, but the conversion needs not be full range, and with a proper conversion distance, adding buffer will significantly improve the performance.

In Fig.3(b) we show the average delay of a packet as a function of the number of fiber delay lines. The average delay is actually the average rounds a packet needs to be recirculated before being sent to the output fibers. We can see that a larger conversion distance results in a shorter delay, and the delay for $d = 2$ is very close the delay for full conversion. For a fixed conversion distance, the delay is longer for larger buffer sizes, since when buffer is larger more packets are directed to buffers rather than being dropped.

## VI. Conclusions

In this paper we studied scheduling in WDM interconnects with recirculating buffering and limited range wave-

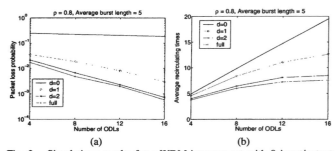

Fig. 3. Simulations results for a WDM interconnect with 8 input/output fibers and 8 wavelengths per fiber under bursty traffic. (a) Packet loss probability. (b) Average packet delay.

length conversion. We formalized the problem of maximizing throughput and minimizing delay as a weighted bipartite graph matching problem. We gave an optimal parallel algorithm called Parallel Segment Expanding Algorithm which runs in $O(Bk^2)$ time, as compared to $O((N+B)^3 k^3)$ time if directly applying other existing matching algorithms, where $N$ is the number of input/output fibers, $B$ is the number of fiber delay lines and $k$ is the number of wavelength per fiber. We also conducted simulations to evaluate the performance of such interconnects under the proposed scheduling algorithm.

## References

[1] E. L. Lawler, *Combinatorial Optimization: Networks and Matroids*, Holt, Rinehart and Winston, 1976.
[2] W. Lipski Jr and F.P. Preparata, "Algorithms for maximum matchings in bipartite graphs," *Naval Res. Logist. Quart.*, vol. 14, pp. 313-316, 1981.
[3] D. K. Hunter and I. Andronovic, "Approaches to optical Internet packet switching," *IEEE Comm. Mag.*, vol. 38, no. 9, pp. 116-122, 2000.
[4] C. Develder, M. Pickavet and P. Demeester, "Assessment of Packet Loss for an Optical Packet Router with Recirculating Buffer," *Optical Network Design and Modeling 2002*, pp. 247-261, Torino, Italy, 2002.
[5] T. Tripathi and K. N. Sivarajan, "Computing approximate blocking probabilities in wavelength routed all-optical networks with limited-range wavelength conversion," *JSAC*, vol. 18, pp. 2123-2129, 2000.
[6] G. Shen, et. al, "Performance study on a WDM packet switch with limited-range wavelength converters," *IEEE Comm. Letters* , vol. 5, no. 10, pp. 432-434, 2001.
[7] L. Xu, H. G. Perros and G. Rouskas, "Techniques for optical packet switching and optical burst switching," *IEEE Comm. Mag.*, pp. 136-142, 2001.
[8] R. Ramaswami and G. Sasaki, "Multiwavelength optical networks with limited wavelength conversion," *IEEE/ACM Trans. Networking*, vol. 6, pp. 744-754, 1998.
[9] Z. Zhang and Y. Yang, "Distributed scheduling algorithms for wavelength convertible WDM optical interconnects," *Proc. of 17th IEEE International Parallel and Distributed Processing Symposium*, Nice, France, 2003.
[10] S.L. Danielsen, et. al, "Analysis of a WDM packet switch with improved performance under bursty traffic conditions due to tunable wavelength converters," *J. Lightwave Technology*, vol. 16, no. 5, pp. 729-735, 1998.
[11] M. Karpinski and Wojciech Rytter, "Fast Parallel Algorithms for Graph Matching Problems," *Oxford University Press*, 1998.
[12] N. McKeown, "The iSLIP scheduling algorithm input-queued switch," *IEEE/ACM Trans. Networking*, vol. 7, pp. 188-201, 1999.
[13] Z. Zhang and Y. Yang, "Scheduling in buffered WDM packet switching networks with arbitrary wavelength conversion capability," *IEEE INFOCOM 2004*.
[14] V. Eramo, M. Listanti and M. DiDonato; "Performance Evaluation of a Bufferless Optical Packet Switch With Limited-Range Wavelength Converters," *IEEE Photonics Technology Letters*, vol. 16 , no. 2, pp. 644-646, 2004.

# Session 7B:
# Embedded Systems

# Partitioning real-time tasks among heterogeneous multiprocessors*

**Sanjoy K. Baruah**
The University of North Carolina at Chapel Hill

**Abstract:** Given a collection of tasks that comprise the software for a real-time system, and a collection of available processing units of different kinds upon which to execute them, the *heterogeneous multiprocessor partitioning problem* is concerned with determining whether the given tasks can be partitioned among the available processing units in such a manner that all timing constraints are met. It is known that this problem is intractable; efficient implementations of sufficient (albeit not necessary) partitioning algorithms are presented here, and proved correct.

## 1  Introduction

As the functionality demanded of embedded systems has increased, it is becoming unreasonable to expect to implement them upon uniprocessor platforms. This fact is particularly true for systems that are aimed at the consumer market, where cost considerations rule out the use of the most powerful (and expensive) processors [24, 21]. Hence embedded systems today are often implemented upon platforms comprised of different *kinds* of processing units, such as CPU's, DSP chips, graphics co-processors, math co-processors, etc., with each kind of processing unit specialized to perform a different function most efficiently. Such platforms are commonly referred to as *heterogeneous* platforms [6, 14, 4].

One important consequence of this processor-specialization in heterogeneous platforms that needs to be taken into account during system implementation is that the *same* piece of code may require different amounts of time to execute upon different processing units. E.g., a process responsible for rendering images may take far less time to execute upon a graphics co-processor than on a CPU, while a number-crunching routine would execute more efficiently upon the CPU. In this research, we explore the issue of implementing real-time systems upon such heterogeneous multiprocessor platforms. We assume that the software comprising the real-time system under analysis can be modelled as a collection of simple tasks, each

of which must be mapped on to a single processor. Given the rates at which these tasks would execute on the different processors, the **heterogeneous multiprocessor partitioning problem** is to determine whether these tasks can be mapped on to the processors without exceeding the computing capacity of any processor. Perhaps not surprisingly, the heterogeneous multiprocessor partitioning problem is intractable — NP-hard in the strong sense. Our major contribution here is an efficient (i.e., polynomial-time) test for solving this problem, for which worst-case performance bounds can be proved. Our sufficient test introduces no new techniques; rather, it is based upon an observation by Potts [17], and some new techniques devised by Lenstra et al. [11], in the context of the non-preemptive scheduling on heterogeneous multiprocessor platforms to minimize makespan (the total schedule duration).

The remainder of this paper is organized as follows. In Section 2, we formally define the problem that we wish to solve, and explain why we are unlikely to be able to solve this problem exactly. In Section 3 we describe how our problem may be mapped on to an equivalent integer linear programming (ILP) problem. In Section 4, we briefly review some properties of linear programs, that will be useful in later sections. In Section 5, we define the *linear program (LP)-relaxation* of the ILP formulation of the partitioning problem, and prove some properties of the resulting linear program. In Section 6, we use the results in Section 5 to derive our approximation algorithm for obtaining approximate solutions to the partitioning problem. We conclude in Section 7, with a summary of the results presented here.

## 2  Problem Statement

Given a collection of software processes ("tasks") that comprise an embedded application, a collection of processing units ("processors") that comprise the hardware upon which these tasks are to execute, and information regarding the rate at which each task executes upon each processor, our goal is to determine

*Supported in part by the National Science Foundation (Grant Nos. ITR-0082866, CCR-0204312, and CCR-0309825).

whether these tasks can be mapped on to the available processors without exceeding the computing capacity of any processor. A heterogeneous real-time system comprised of $n$ tasks to be executed upon a given $m$-processor heterogeneous platform is specified by specifying a **utilization matrix** $\mathcal{U}_{[n \times m]}$. This is an $(n \times m)$ matrix $[u_{i,j}]; i = 1, 2, \ldots, n; j = 1, 2, \ldots, m$ of real numbers. The value of $u_{i,j}$ denotes the fraction of the computing capacity of processor $j$ that is needed in order to completely execute task $i$ (if the $i$'th task cannot be executed upon the $j$'th processor, then $u_{i,j} \leftarrow \infty$).

In the remainder of this paper, we will use the notation $\mathcal{U}_{[n \times m]}$ to denote a heterogeneous multiprocessor system comprised of $n$ tasks to be executed upon $m$ processors. Where necessary, we will use the notation $\Gamma(\mathcal{U}_{[n \times m]})$ and $\Pi(\mathcal{U}_{[n \times m]})$ to denote the set of tasks and the set of processors respectively that comprise this heterogeneous multiprocessor system.

**Assumptions.** We restrict our attention in this paper to *partitioned scheduling*, in which each task is exclusively assigned to a particular processor. Run-time scheduling can be performed efficiently in such systems: the run-time scheduling problem reduces to uniprocessor scheduling, for which efficient optimal algorithms (such as *preemptive earliest deadline first scheduling algorithm (EDF)*) are known. We are also completely ignoring the issue of inter-task communication; in actual systems, outputs produced by certain tasks are consumed by others, and the layout of tasks upon processors should take into consideration the underlying interconnection network among the processors and favor mapping tasks that communicate with each upon proximal processors.

**Problem statement.** Given the specifications $\mathcal{U}_{[n \times m]}$ of a heterogeneous multiprocessor system, our goal, informally speaking, is to determine a mapping of the $n$ tasks among the $m$ processors such that the capacity of any individual processor is not exceeded. We will refer to this design problem as **the heterogeneous multiprocessor partitioning problem**, which we formally specify below. But first, some additional definitions.

**Definition 1** *For any set of tasks $\Gamma'$, let $U_j(\Gamma')$ denote the cumulative utilization of tasks in $\Gamma'$ if they are implemented upon the $j$'th processor:*

$$U_j(\Gamma') \stackrel{def}{=} \sum_{i \in \Gamma'} u_{i,j} \; .$$

**Definition 2** *Let $\chi : \Gamma(\mathcal{U}_{[n \times m]}) \to \Pi(\mathcal{U}_{[n \times m]})$ denote a mapping from the tasks comprising system $\mathcal{U}_{[n \times m]}$ to the processors in system $\mathcal{U}_{[n \times m]}$. Let $\Lambda_\chi(j)$ denote the set of all tasks mapped onto processor $j$ by the mapping $\chi$: $\Lambda_\chi(j) \stackrel{def}{=} \{i \mid \chi(i) = j\}$ . Mapping $\chi$ is a **feasible mapping** if and only if it satisfies the following condition:*

$$\left[ \forall j \; : \; 1 \leq j \leq m \; : \; \Big( U_j(\Lambda_\chi(j)) \leq 1 \Big) \right] \quad (1)$$

That is, a feasible mapping is one in which the capacity of no processor is exceeded.

The **heterogeneous multiprocessor partitioning problem** is now defined as follows: *Given* the utilization matrix $\mathcal{U}_{[n \times m]}$ denoting a system comprised of the $n$ tasks $\Gamma(\mathcal{U}_{[n \times m]})$ and the $m$ processors $\Pi(\mathcal{U}_{[n \times m]})$, *determine* A feasible mapping from $\Gamma(\mathcal{U}_{[n \times m]})$ to $\Pi(\mathcal{U}_{[n \times m]})$, if one exists.

**Related Work.** Most interesting variants of task partitioning problems, including the simpler problem of partitioning a collection of tasks among *identical* multiprocessors, are known to be NP-hard in the strong sense (see, e.g., [19]). Consequently, much prior work on the allocation and scheduling of mutually dependent tasks upon multiprocessors has been based upon heuristic approaches. For example, [13] proposes the use of a genetic algorithm to synthesize multiprocessor embedded systems, while [22, 23] use Constraint Logic Programming (CLP) to represent the synthesis problem by a set of finite domain variables and constraints imposed on these variables. The approach adopted in [7] is to extend the "Algorithm Architecture Adequation" heuristic to the multiprocessor synthesis problem. The algorithm described in [18], like our algorithm, is based upon an integer linear programming (ILP) formulation of the task assignment problem; however, the algorithm in [18] requires that the ILP actually be solved, and hence usually has unacceptably large run-times for non-trivial systems.

**Our result.** Our approach to the heterogeneous multiprocessor partitioning problem differs from the approaches mentioned above in that we make use of some very interesting techniques that were introduced by Potts [17] (and subsequently refined by Lenstra et. al [11]) in the context of the non-preemptive scheduling of jobs without deadlines upon heterogeneous multiprocessor platforms where the goal is to minimize the makespan of the schedule. Our major result is an efficient algorithm for determining a partitioning of any heterogeneous multiprocessor system, that makes the following performance guarantee.

If there exists a partitioning of the tasks among the processors and some constant $u_{\max}$ ($u_{\max} < 1$) such that (i) at most a fraction $(1 - u_{\max})$ of each processor is used, and (ii) no *individual* task occupies more than $u_{\max}$ of the capacity of any processor (i.e., if task $i$ is mapped onto processor $j$ by this partitioning, then $u_{i,j} \leq u_{\max}$)

**then** our feasibility test will determine that the heterogeneous multiprocessor system is feasible, and furthermore will produce a feasible mapping.

However, it is possible that there is a partitioning of the tasks among the processors which do not satisfy the conditions listed above; in that case, our algorithm may fail to find a feasible mapping. Thus, our algorithm is a sufficient, rather than exact, test — given that the heterogeneous multiprocessor partitioning problem is NP-hard, this is only to be expected.

## 3   An ILP formulation

In a integer linear program (ILP), one is given a set of $n$ variables, *some or all of which are restricted to take on integer values only*, a collection of "constraints" that are expressed as linear inequalities over these $n$ variables, and an "objective function," also expressed as a linear inequality of these variables. The set of all points in $n$-dimensional space over which all the constraints hold is called the *feasible region* for the integer linear program. The goal is to find the extremal (maximum/ minimum) value of the objective function over the feasible region.

Suppose that we are given the specifications $\mathcal{U}_{[n \times m]}$ of a heterogeneous multiprocessor system. For any mapping of the $n$ tasks on the $m$ processors, let us define $(n \times m)$ *indicator variables* $x_{i,j}$, for $i = 1, 2, \ldots, n; j = 1, 2, \ldots, m$. Variable $x_{i,j}$ is set equal to one if the $i$'th task is mapped onto the $j$'th processor, and zero otherwise. A mapping of the $n$ tasks upon the $m$ processors would have these variables satisfy the following constraints:

$$x_{i,j} = 0 \text{ or } 1, \qquad (i = 1, 2, \ldots, n; \ j = 1, 2, \ldots, m)$$
$$\sum_{j=1}^{m} x_{i,j} = 1, \qquad (i = 1, 2, \ldots, n)$$

where these constraints restrict that each task be assigned to exactly one processor. We can represent the heterogeneous multiprocessor partitioning problem as the following **integer programming problem**, with the variables $x_{i,j}$ restricted to integer values.

---

**ILP-Feas($\mathcal{U}_{[n \times m]}$).**

---

*Minimize* $\mathbf{U}$, subject to the following constraints:

1. $\sum_{j=1}^{m} x_{i,j} = 1,$      $(i = 1, 2, \ldots, n)$
2. $\sum_{i=1}^{n}(x_{i,j} \cdot u_{i,j}) \leq \mathbf{U},$      $(j = 1, 2, \ldots, m)$
3. $x_{i,j}$ is a non-negative integer,      $(i = 1, 2, \ldots, n;$
                              $j = 1, 2, \ldots, m)$

---

Informally, $\mathbf{U}$ represents the maximum fraction of the capacity of any processor that is used, and is set to be the objective function (i.e., the quantity to be minimized) of the ILP problem. The first constraint asserts that each task be assigned some processor; the second, that at most $\mathbf{U}$ of the $j$'th processor's capacity be used for each $j$, and the third, that it is semantically meaningless to assign negative values to the indicator variables. Let $\mathsf{opt}(\text{ILP-Feas}(\mathcal{U}_{[n \times m]}))$ denote the minimum value of $\mathbf{U}$, obtained by solving of ILP-Feas($\mathcal{U}_{[n \times m]}$). If $\mathsf{opt}(\text{ILP-Feas}(\mathcal{U}_{[n \times m]}))$ is at most one, it is not hard to see that an assignment of non-negative integer values to the variables satisfying these constraints is equivalent to a partitioning of the $n$ tasks upon the $m$ processors. Thus, obtaining a solution to ILP-Feas($\mathcal{U}_{[n \times m]}$) is equivalent to determining whether the heterogeneous multiprocessor task system ($\mathcal{U}_{[n \times m]}$) is feasible. This is formally stated by the following theorem:

**Theorem 1** *The integer linear programming problem ILP-Feas($\mathcal{U}_{[n \times m]}$) has a solution with $\mathbf{U} \leq 1$ if and only if the heterogeneous multiprocessor system ($\mathcal{U}_{[n \times m]}$) is feasible.*

**Proof:** Suppose first that ($\mathcal{U}_{[n \times m]}$) is feasible, and let $\chi$ denote a feasible mapping. It is straightforward to observe that the following assignment to the variables $x_{i,j}$:

$$x_{i,j} \leftarrow \begin{cases} 1, & \text{if } \chi(i) = j \\ 0, & \text{otherwise} \end{cases}$$

is a solution to ILP-Feas($\mathcal{U}_{[n \times m]}$) in which $\mathbf{U}$ is at most 1.

Suppose now that there is a solution to ILP-Feas($\mathcal{U}_{[n \times m]}$) with $\mathbf{U} \leq 1$. Define a mapping $\chi_o$ of tasks onto processors as follows:

$$\chi_o(i) \leftarrow j, \text{ where } (x_{i,j} \equiv 1) \text{ in this solution.}$$

By constraints (1) of ILP-Feas($\mathcal{U}_{[n \times m]}$), each task $i$ is mapped on to exactly one processor by $\chi_o$. By constraints (2) of ILP-Feas($\mathcal{U}_{[n \times m]}$), each processor's total capacity is not exceed by this mapping (since $\mathbf{U} \leq 1$ in this solution). Hence, mapping $\chi_o$ is a feasible mapping. ∎

The result in Theorem 1 above allows us to transform the problem of determining whether a heterogeneous multiprocessor system is feasible to an integer linear programming (ILP) problem. At first sight, this may seem to be of limited significance, since ILP is also known to be intractable (NP-complete in the strong sense [16]). However, some recently-devised approximation techniques for solving ILP problems, based upon the idea of *LP relaxations* to ILP problems, may prove useful in obtaining approximate solutions to the heterogeneous multiprocessor partitioning problem – we explore these approximation techniques in the remainder of this paper.

## 4  Linear Programming

In this section, we briefly review some facts concerning linear programming (LP) that will be used in later sections. In a linear program (LP) over a given set of $n$ variables, as with ILP's, one is given a collection of constraints that are expressed as linear inequalities over these $n$ variables, and an objective function, also expressed as a linear inequality of these variables. The region in $n$-dimensional space over which all the constraints hold is again called the *feasible region* for the linear program, and the goal is to find the extremal value of the objective function over the feasible region. A region is said to be *convex* if, for any two points $\mathbf{p_1}$ and $\mathbf{p_2}$ in the region and any scalar $\lambda, 0 \le \lambda \le 1$, the point $(\lambda \cdot \mathbf{p_1} + (1 - \lambda) \cdot \mathbf{p_2})$ is also in the region. A *vertex* of a convex region is a point $\mathbf{p}$ in the region such that there are no distinct points $\mathbf{p_1}$ and $\mathbf{p_2}$ in the region, and a scalar $\lambda, 0 < \lambda < 1$, such that $[\mathbf{p} \equiv \lambda \cdot \mathbf{p_1} + (1 - \lambda) \cdot \mathbf{p_2}]$.

It is known that an LP can be solved in polynomial time by the ellipsoid algorithm [9] or the interior point algorithm [8]. (In addition, the exponential-time simplex algorithm [5] has been shown to perform extremely well "in practice," and is often the algorithm of choice despite its exponential worst-case behaviour.) We do not need to understand the details of these algorithms: for our purposes, it suffices to know that LP problems can be efficiently solved (in polynomial time).

We now state without proof some basic facts concerning such linear programming optimization problems.

**Fact 1** *The feasible region for a LP problem is convex, and the objective function reaches its optimal value at a vertex point of the feasible region.*

An optimal solution to an LP problem that is a vertex point of the feasible region is called a **basic solu-**tion to the LP problem.

**Fact 2** *Consider a linear program on n variables $x_1, x_2, \ldots, x_n$, in which each variable is subject to the constraint that it be $\ge 0$ (these constraints are called non-negativity constraints). Suppose that there are a further m linear constraints. If $m < n$, then at most m of the variables have non-zero values at each vertex of the feasible region[1] (including the basic solution).*

## 5  LP-relaxation of ILP-Feas($\mathcal{U}_{[n \times m]}$)

By relaxing the requirement that the $x_{i,j}$ variables in the integer linear programming formulation ILP-Feas($\mathcal{U}_{[n \times m]}$) (Section 3) be integers only, we obtain the following linear programming problem, which is referred to as the *LP-relaxation* [20] of ILP-Feas($\mathcal{U}_{[n \times m]}$):

---

**LPR-Feas($\mathcal{U}_{[n \times m]}$).**

*Minimize* $\mathbf{U}$, subject to the following constraints:

1. $\sum_{j=1}^{m} x_{i,j} = 1$, $\qquad (i = 1, 2, \ldots, n)$
2. $\sum_{i=1}^{n} (x_{i,j} \cdot u_{i,j}) \le \mathbf{U}$, $\qquad (j = 1, 2, \ldots, m)$
3. $x_{i,j}$ is a non-negative **real number**, $\quad (i = 1, 2, \ldots, n;$
$\qquad\qquad\qquad\qquad\qquad\qquad j = 1, 2, \ldots, m)$

---

Let $\mathbf{X}$ denote the $n \times m$ variables $x_{i,j}$. Let $\mathbf{X_{OPT}}$ and $\mathbf{U_{OPT}}$ denote the values assigned to the variables in $\mathbf{X}$, and to $\mathbf{U}$, in the basic solution to LPR-Feas($\mathcal{U}_{[n \times m]}$). Recall that opt(ILP-Feas($\mathcal{U}_{[n \times m]}$)) denotes the optimal value of $\mathbf{U}$ obtained by solving of ILP-Feas($\mathcal{U}_{[n \times m]}$). Since LPR-Feas($\mathcal{U}_{[n \times m]}$) is a *less* constrained problem than ILP-Feas($\mathcal{U}_{[n \times m]}$), we have the following result.

**Lemma 1**

$$\mathbf{U_{OPT}} \le \text{opt}(\text{ILP-Feas}(\mathcal{U}_{[n \times m]})) \ .$$

■

The constraints (3) of LPR-Feas($\mathcal{U}_{[n \times m]}$) above are non-negativity constraints; hence, LPR-Feas($\mathcal{U}_{[n \times m]}$) is a linear program on the $(n \cdot m + 1)$ variables (the $n \cdot m$ variables $\mathbf{X}$, and $\mathbf{U}$), with only $(n + m)$ constraints other than non-negativity constraints. By Fact 2 above, therefore, at most $(n+m)$ of the $(nm+1)$ variables have non-zero values at the basic solution; in particular, *at most $(n + m - 1)$ of the values in* $\mathbf{X_{OPT}}$ *are non-zero.*

---

[1] The feasible region in $n$-dimensional space for this linear program is the region over which all the $n + m$ constraints (the non-negativity constraints, plus the $m$ additional ones) hold.

The crucial observation is that each of the $n$ constraints (1) of LPR-Feas($\mathcal{U}_{[n \times m]}$) is on a *different* set of $x_{i,j}$ variables — the first such constraint has only the variables $x_{1,1}, x_{1,2}, \ldots, x_{1,m}$, the second has only the variables $x_{2,1}, x_{2,2}, \ldots, x_{2,m}$, and so on. Since there are at most $(n + m - 1)$ non-zero variables in $\mathbf{X}_{\text{OPT}}$, it follows from the pigeon-hole principle that at most $(m - 1)$ of these constraints will have more than one non-zero value in $\mathbf{X}_{\text{OPT}}$. For each of the remaining (at least) $(n - m + 1)$ constraints, the sole non-zero $x_{i,j}$ variable must equal exactly 1, in order that the constraint be satisfied. Fact 3 follows.

**Fact 3** *For at least $(n - m + 1)$ of the integers $i$ in $\{1, 2, \ldots, n\}$, exactly one of the variables $\{x_{i,1}, x_{i,2}, \ldots, x_{i,m}\}$ is equal to 1, and the remaining are equal to zero, in $\mathbf{X}_{\text{OPT}}$.* ■

As a consequence of Fact 3, it follows that the solution to the LP problem LPR-Feas($\mathcal{U}_{[n \times m]}$) immediately yields a partial mapping of tasks to processors, in which all but at most $(m - 1)$ tasks get mapped. In the remainder of this section, we prove some properties of the optimal basic soluton $(\mathbf{X}_{\text{OPT}}, \mathbf{U}_{\text{OPT}})$, which will permit us to efficiently obtain a mapping for the remaining tasks.

We start with a definition.

**Definition 3** *For any heteregeneous multiprocessor system specification $\mathcal{U}_{[n \times m]}$ and any real number $r$, $0 \leq r < 1$, let $\mathcal{U}_{[n \times m]}^{(r)}$ denote the system obtained from $\mathcal{U}_{[n \times m]}$ by setting all $u_{i,j}$ values in $\mathcal{U}_{[n \times m]}$ that are greater than $r$ equal to $\infty$.* ■

Informally, we obtain system $\mathcal{U}_{[n \times m]}^{(r)}$ from system $\mathcal{U}_{[n \times m]}$ by forbidding the mapping of any task $i$ on to any processor $j$, if $i$ would consume more than a fraction $r$ of processor $j$. (Hence, the original system $\mathcal{U}_{[n \times m]}$ can, in this notation, be represented as $\mathcal{U}_{[n \times m]}^{(1.0)}$.)

Observe that $\mathcal{U}_{[n \times m]}^{(r)}$ also specifies a system comprised of $n$ tasks and $m$ processors just as $\mathcal{U}_{[n \times m]}$ does; hence, **all the properties we proved above about the ILP problem ILP-Feas($\mathcal{U}_{[n \times m]}$) and its LP-relaxation LPR-Feas($\mathcal{U}_{[n \times m]}$), hold, when suitably modified to take care of the different utilization prarmeters, for ILP-Feas($\mathcal{U}_{[n \times m]}^{(r)}$) and LPR-Feas($\mathcal{U}_{[n \times m]}^{(r)}$) as well.**

In a straightforward extension to prior notation, let $\mathbf{X}_{\text{OPT}}^{(r)}$ and $\mathbf{U}_{\text{OPT}}^{(r)}$ denote the values assigned to the variables in $\mathbf{X}$, and to $\mathbf{U}$, in the basic solution to LPR-Feas($\mathcal{U}_{[n \times m]}^{(r)}$). The following definition, and the subsequent lemma (and proof), are essentially from [11].

**Definition 4 (Bipartite graph $G(\mathbf{X}_{\text{OPT}}^{(r)})$)** *Bipartite graph $G(\mathbf{X}_{\text{OPT}}^{(r)})$ is obtained from $\mathbf{X}_{\text{OPT}}^{(r)}$ as follows. $G(\mathbf{X}_{\text{OPT}}^{(r)})$ has one vertex corresponding to each task and one vertex corresponding to each processor: for each such pair $i$ and $j$, $(i, j)$ is an edge in the graph if and only if $\mathbf{X}_{\text{OPT}}^{(r)}$ has $x_{i,j} > 0$.* ■

**Lemma 2** *Each connected component in bipartite graph $G(\mathbf{X}_{\text{OPT}}^{(r)})$ is either a tree or a 1-tree (a tree plus one edge).*

**Proof:** Consider any connected component in $G(\mathbf{X}_{\text{OPT}}^{(r)})$. Let $\Gamma'$ and $\Pi'$ denote the tasks and processors respectively, corresponding to task and processor vertices in this connected component. Let $|\Gamma'| = n'$, and let $|\Pi'| = m'$. Let $\mathbf{Y}$ denote the $n' \times m'$ variables $x_{i,j}$ for which $i \in \Gamma'$ and $j \in \Pi'$, and let $\mathbf{Z} \stackrel{\text{def}}{=} \mathbf{X} \setminus \mathbf{Y}$. Let $\mathbf{Y}_{\text{OPT}}$ and $\mathbf{Z}_{\text{OPT}}$ denote the values assigned in $\mathbf{X}_{\text{OPT}}^{(r)}$ to the variables in $\mathbf{Y}$ and $\mathbf{Z}$ respectively.

Consider the feasible region defined by only the constraints corresponding to the tasks and processors in $\Gamma'$ and $\Pi'$ in LPR-Feas($\mathcal{U}_{[n \times m]}^{(r)}$), i.e., the following $n' + m'$ constraints:

$$
\begin{aligned}
\sum_{j \in \Pi'} x_{i,j} = 1, && \text{for each } i \in \Gamma' \\
\sum_{i \in \Gamma'} (x_{i,j} \cdot u_{i,j}) \leq \mathbf{U}, && \text{for each } j \in \Pi'
\end{aligned}
\tag{2}
$$

We claim that $\mathbf{Y}_{\text{OPT}}$ is a vertex point of this feasible region. To see why, suppose that $\mathbf{Y}_{\text{OPT}}$ were not a vertex point. By the definition of vertex points, there are therefore distinct points $p_1$ and $p_2$ in this feasible region such that $\mathbf{Y}_{\text{OPT}} = \alpha \cdot p_1 + (1 - \alpha) \cdot p_2$. But in that case it must be true that points $q_1 \stackrel{\text{def}}{=} (p_1 \cup \mathbf{Z}_{\text{OPT}})$ and $q_2 \stackrel{\text{def}}{=} (p_2 \cup \mathbf{Z}_{\text{OPT}})$ are in the feasible region for LPR-Feas($\mathcal{U}_{[n \times m]}^{(r)}$), such that $\mathbf{X}_{\text{OPT}}^{(r)} = \alpha \cdot q_1 + (1 - \alpha) \cdot q_2$. However, this contradicts our assumption that $\mathbf{X}_{\text{OPT}}^{(r)}$ is a baisc solution for LPR-Feas($\mathcal{U}_{[n \times m]}^{(r)}$).

Hence, $\mathbf{Y}_{\text{OPT}}$ is a vertex point of the feasible region in $(n' \times m')$-dimensional space (since there are $n' \times m'$ variables in $\mathbf{Y}$), which is subject to the $(n' + m')$ linear Constraints 2 above. By Fact 2, it follows that at most $n' + m'$ of the values in $\mathbf{Y}_{\text{OPT}}$ are non-zero; i.e., that the connected component has at most as many edges as vertices. Since the number of edges in a tree is one less than the number of vertices, it follows that the connected component is either a tree, or a 1-tree. ■

**A mapping algorithm.** In Figure 1, we present Algorithm taskPartition, a 2-step algorithm for obtaining a mapping $\chi$ of tasks to processors from a basic solution to the LP problem LPR-Feas($\mathcal{U}_{[n \times m]}^{(r)}$). In Step 1,

**Algorithm** taskPartition.

**Input:** Heteregeneous multiprocessor system $\mathcal{U}_{[n \times m]}^{(r)}$.

**Output:** Mapping $\chi : \Gamma \to \Pi$, which is obtained as follows:

**Step 0.** Let $\mathbf{X}_{\text{OPT}}^{(r)}$ and $\mathbf{U}_{\text{OPT}}^{(r)}$ denote the values assigned to the variables in $\mathbf{X}$, and to $\mathbf{U}$, in the basic solution to LPR-Feas($\mathcal{U}_{[n \times m]}^{(r)}$). If $\mathbf{U}_{\text{OPT}}^{(r)} > 1$, then declare failure and return. Else, proceed to Steps 1 and 2.

**Step 1.** By Fact 3 above, at least $(n - m + 1)$ of the constraints (1) of LPR-Feas($\mathcal{U}_{[n \times m]}^{(r)}$) have exactly one non-zero $x_{i,j}$ variable in $\mathbf{X}_{\text{OPT}}^{(r)}$, and the value of this $x_{i,j}$ variable is exactly one. These 1-valued $x_{i,j}$ variables define a mapping for the corresponding tasks: if $x_{i,j} = 1$ in $\mathbf{X}_{\text{OPT}}^{(r)}$, then $\chi(i) \leftarrow j$.

**Step 2.** For the remaining tasks, we describe below how the $\mathbf{X}_{\text{OPT}}^{(r)}$ is used to obtain a mapping such that each processor has at most one task mapped on to it. We make use of the bipartite graph $G(\mathbf{X}_{\text{OPT}}^{(r)})$ constructed from $\mathbf{X}_{\text{OPT}}^{(r)}$, discussed above.

  **1.** Each task $i$, for which there is some $j$ such that $x_{i,j} = 1$, has been mapped in the step above; delete all vertices corresponding to such tasks from $G(\mathbf{X}_{\text{OPT}}^{(r)})$. By Lemma 2, $G(\mathbf{X}_{\text{OPT}}^{(r)})$ is comprised of disconnected trees and 1-trees; since removing vertices from a tree or a 1-tree results in trees or 1-trees, it follows that each connected component in the remaining graph is also either a tree or a 1-tree. Furthermore, all task vertices in each such connected component has degree at least two (since for each task vertex $i$, $\sum_j x_{i,j} = 1$ and each $x_{i,j} < 1$).

  **2.** For each 1-tree, identify the unique cycle in the 1-tree. This cycle is comprised of alternating task and processor vertices; hence, choose every alternate edge in the cycle to obtain a mapping of all the tasks in the cycle to unique processors. That is, suppose that the cycle is comprised of the vertices $i_1, j_1, i_2, j_2, \ldots, i_k, j_k$; then $\chi(i_\ell) \leftarrow j_\ell$ for $1 \le \ell \le k$.

  **3.** Delete the cycle after having done so. Now we are left with a forest of trees; in each such tree, there can be at most one task vertex of degree one (which may be created when the cycle is removed from a 1-tree).

  **4.** For each tree (including the ones created in the step above by deleting the cycle from a 1-tree), root the tree at the task vertex of degree one if any, or an arbitrary task vertex otherwise. Starting at the root, match each task-vertex to any one of its children processor vertices. This is a well-defined matching, since (i) each processor vertex is matched to its unique parent in the tree, and (ii) each non-root task vertex has degree at least two; hence, it is guaranteed to have some processor vertex child to which it can be matched.

---

**Figure 1. Algorithm for partitioning tasks.**

this algorithm maps those tasks $i$ for which $x_{i,j} = 1$ for some processor $j$, in the solution $\mathbf{X}_{\text{OPT}}^{(r)}$ to LPR-Feas($\mathcal{U}_{[n \times m]}^{(r)}$); by Fact 3 above, at most $m - 1$ tasks may remain unassigned at this step. In Step 2, the bipartite graph constructed above is used to map the remaining tasks on to the processors such that at most one task is mapped on to each processor at this step.

**Runtime complexity of Algorithm** taskPartition. Given a basic solution to the LP problem LPR-Feas($\mathcal{U}_{[n \times m]}^{(r)}$), Steps 1 and 2 take time polynomial in $n$ and $m$:

**Step 1.** This involves examining all $n \times m$ $x_{i,j}$ variables in the solution $\mathbf{X}_{\text{OPT}}^{(r)}$, and can be done in $\mathcal{O}(n \times m)$ time.

**Step 2.** This involves constructing the bipartite graph $G(\mathbf{X}_{\text{OPT}}^{(r)})$. Graph $G(\mathbf{X}_{\text{OPT}}^{(r)})$ contains $n + m$ vertices; it follows from Lemma 2 that $G(\mathbf{X}_{\text{OPT}}^{(r)})$ contains no more than $n + m$ edges. It is straightforward to observe that Step 2 takes time polynomial in the number of edges in the graph, i.e., polynomial in $(n + m)$.

Steps 1 and 2 crucially depend upon the fact that the solution returned in Step 0 be a *basic* solution. Note that Fact 1 (Section 4) does not claim that all points in the feasible region that correspond to optimal solutions to an LP are vertex points; rather, the claim is that *some* vertex point is guaranteed to be in the set of optimal solutions. For LP problems with a unique optimal solution, it is guaranteed that this unique solution is a basic solution and hence all (correct) LP solvers will return a basic solution; for LP problems that have several solutions, however, the polynomial-time interior-point or ellipsoid algorithms do not guarantee to find a basic solution (although the exponential-time simplex algorithm does). However, there are efficient polynomial-time algorithms (see, e.g, [20]) for obtaining a basic solution given any optimal solution to a LP problem – if the LP-solver being used does not guarantee to return a basic solution, then some such algorithm must be used to convert the optimal solution returned to a basic solution.

## 6 A sufficient feasibility test

In this section, we apply the results of Section 5 to obtain a sufficient test for heterogeneous multiprocessor feasibility analysis, that runs in time polynomial in the representation of the system. To determine the feasibility of system $\mathcal{U}_{[n \times m]}$, this test makes repeated calls to Algorithm taskPartition (Figure 1), on restrictions $\mathcal{U}_{[n \times m]}^{(r)}$ of the system for various different values of $r$.

PROCEDURE optSrch

1    Let $r_1, r_2, \ldots, r_k$ denote the distinct utilization values in $\mathcal{U}_{[n \times m]}$, sorted in increasing order

2    **for** $i \leftarrow 1$ **to** $k$ **do**

3        Call Algorithm taskPartition with input $(\mathcal{U}_{[n \times m]}^{(r_i)})$.

4        **if** $\left( \mathbf{U}_{\text{OPT}}^{(r_i)} \leq 1 - r_i \right)$

5          **then** return the mapping $\chi$ obtained by Algorithm taskPartition on $(\mathcal{U}_{[n \times m]}^{(r_i)})$.

6    return **failure** $\triangleright$ Exited the for loop $(i > k)$ without success

**end** PROCEDURE optSrch

**Figure 2. A sufficient feasibility test.**

For a given heterogeneous multiprocessor task system $\mathcal{U}_{[n \times m]}$, the utilizations $u_{i,j}$ can take on at most $n \times m$ distinct values. Let $r_1, r_2, \ldots, r_k$ denote these distinct utilization values ($k \leq n \times m$), sorted in non-decreasing order ($r_i \leq r_{i+1}$ for all $i$). Consider the execution of Procedure optSrch (Figure 2) on task system $\mathcal{U}_{[n \times m]}$. Theorem 2 below asserts that this procedure determines a feasible mapping for any feasible task system satisfying certain additional properties.

**Theorem 2** *For any system* $(\mathcal{U}_{[n \times m]})$*, if there is a feasible mapping of* $\Gamma(\mathcal{U}_{[n \times m]})$ *to* $\Pi(\mathcal{U}_{[n \times m]})$ *and some constant* $u_{max}$ *($u_{max} < 1$) such that* **(i)** *at most a fraction* $(1 - u_{max})$ *of each processor is used, and* **(ii)** *no individual task occupies more than* $u_{max}$ *of the capacity of any processor* then *Procedure* optSrch *will find a feasible mapping for* $\mathcal{U}_{[n \times m]}$*.*

**Proof:** Suppose that the antecedents of the theorem hold, in that there is a mapping and such a constant $u_{\max}$ for input system $(\mathcal{U}_{[n \times m]})$. Let $r_h$ denote the largest utilization $\leq u_{\max}$ in the utilization matrix of $(\mathcal{U}_{[n \times m]})$. Observe that

- By Theorem 1, this mapping implies the existence of a solution to the ILP program ILP-Feas($\mathcal{U}_{[n \times m]}^{(r_h)}$), for which the objective function opt(ILP-Feas($\mathcal{U}_{[n \times m]}^{(r_h)}$)) has value at most $(1 - u_{\max})$.

- By Lemma 1, this implies that the LP problem LPR-Feas($\mathcal{U}_{[n \times m]}^{(r_h)}$) has a solution with $\mathbf{U}_{\text{OPT}}^{(r)} \leq (1 - u_{\max})$.

- Consider the iteration of the for-loop of Procedure optSrch in which the loop variable $i$ takes on value $h$. The condition in Line 4 is satisfied; hence, the mapping $\chi$ obtained by Algorithm taskPartition (Figure 1), when called during this for-loop iteration from Line 3 with input $(\mathcal{U}_{[n \times m]}^{(r_h)})$ is returned.

- The partial mapping obtained in Step 1 of this call to Algorithm taskPartition uses a fraction of at most $(1 - r_h)$ of each processor, while Step 2 assigns at most

one task to each processor. But in $\mathcal{U}_{[n \times m]}^{(r_h)}$, there is no utilization value greater that $r_h$; hence, each task that is assigned during Step 2 of this call to Algorithm taskPartition can be accommodated on the processor to which it is assigned.

This completes the proof of Theorem 2. ∎

**Run-time complexity.** Since Procedure optSrch makes no more than $n \times m$ calls to Algorithm taskPartition, it is straightforward to observe that Procedure optSrch completes execution in time polynomial in the representation of the task system $\mathcal{U}_{[n \times m]}$ (provided that a polynomial-time LP solver is used within Algorithm taskPartition).

## 7   Context and Conclusions

The partitioning approach to scheduling preemptive tasks upon multiprocessor platforms has been extensively studied, both theoretically and emperically, in the context of identical multiprocessor platforms [15, 12, 1, 2]. With respect to heterogeneous platforms such as the ones considered in this paper, however, most prior work seems to have been in the design of of heuristics that are then experimentally (as opposed to theoretically) evaluated [6, 14, 4, 3, 10] — to our knowledge, there has been no prior theoretical work concerning the scheduling of task systems upon heterogeneous multiprocessor platforms.

In this paper, we have studied the partitioning of task systems upon preemptive heterogeneous multiprocessor platforms, and have designed a polynomial-time approximation algorithm for solving this problem. We reiterate that the technique upon which our algorithm is based — representing a scheduling problem as an integer linear programming (ILP) problem with many more variables than constraints, solving the LP-relaxation of the ILP problem, and then doing some additional work to obtain a near-optimal solution to the ILP problem — is not new: Potts [17] has used this approach in the context of the non-preemptive scheduling of (non-real-time) jobs without deadlines upon heterogeneous multiprocessor platforms where the goal is to minimize the makespan of the schedule, and has devised algorithms for constructing schedules with near-minimal makespan that are polynomial in the number of tasks and exponential in the number of processors. Lenstra et al. [11] subsequently improved this result and obtained an approximation algorithm that is polynomial in both the number of tasks and the number of processors. We have merely applied the method in [11] to our problem of interest – preemptive scheduling of tasks upon heterogeneous multiprocessors, with the goal of meeting all deadlines.

# References

[1] ANDERSSON, B., AND JONSSON, J. The utilization bounds of partitioned and pfair static-priority scheduling on multiprocessors are 50%. In *Proceedings of the EuroMicro Conference on Real-Time Systems* (Porto, Portugal, July 2003), IEEE Computer Society Press, pp. 33–40.

[2] BAKER, T. Multiprocessor EDF and deadline monotonic schedulability analysis. In *Proceedings of the IEEE Real-Time Systems Symposium* (December 2003), IEEE Computer Society Press, pp. 120–129.

[3] BRAUN, T. D., SIEGEL, H. J., AND MACIEJEWSKI, A. A. Static mapping heuristics for tasks with dependencies, priorities, deadlines, and multiple versions in heterogeneous environments. In *Proceedings of the 16th International Parallel and Distributed Processing Symposium* (Fort Lauderdale, FL, April 2002).

[4] BRAUNAND, T. D., SIEGEL, H. J., AND MACIEJEWSKI, A. A. Heterogeneous computing: Goals, methods, and open problems. In *Proceedings of the International Conference on Parallel and Distributed Processing Techniques and Applications* (June 2001), pp. 1–12.

[5] DANTZIG, G. B. *Linear Programming and Extensions*. Princeton University Press, 1963.

[6] FREUND, R. F., AND SIEGEL, H. J. Heterogeneous processing. *IEEE Computer 26* (June 1993), 13–17.

[7] GRANDPIERRE, T., LAVARENNE, C., AND SOREL, Y. Rapid prototyping for real-time embedded heterogeneous multiprocessors. In *International Workshop on Hardware/Software Co-Design (CODES)* (Rome, Italy, 1999), ACM Press.

[8] KARMAKAR, N. A new polynomial-time algorithm for linear programming. *Combinatorica 4* (1984), 373–395.

[9] KHACHIYAN, L. A polynomial algorithm in linear programming. *Dokklady Akademiia Nauk SSSR 244* (1979), 1093–1096.

[10] KIM, J.-K., SHIVLE, S., SIEGEL, H. J., MACIEJEWSKI, A. A., BRAUN, T. D., SCHNEIDER, M., TIDEMAN, S., CHITTA, R.,

DILMAGHANI, R. B., JOSHI, R., KAUL, A., SHARMA, A., SRIPADA, S., VANGARI, P., AND YELLAMPALLI, S. S. Dynamic mapping in a heterogeneous environment with tasks having priorities and multiple deadlines. In *Proceedings of the 12th Hereogeneous Computing Workshop* (Nice, France, April 2003), IEEE Computer Society.

[11] LENSTRA, J. K., SHMOYS, D. B., AND TARDOS, E. Approximation algorithms for scheduling unrelated parallel machines. *Mathematical Programming 46* (1990), 259–271.

[12] LOPEZ, J. M., GARCIA, M., DIAZ, J. L., AND GARCIA, D. F. Worst-case utilization bound for EDF scheduling in real-time multiprocessor systems. In *Proceedings of the EuroMicro Conference on Real-Time Systems* (Stockholm, Sweden, June 2000), IEEE Computer Society Press, pp. 25–34.

[13] MADSEN, J., AND BJORN-JORGENSEN, P. Embedded system synthesis under memory constraints. In *International Workshop on Hardware/Software Co-Design (CODES)* (Rome, Italy, 1999), ACM Press.

[14] MAHESWARAN, M., BRAUN, T. D., AND SIEGEL, H. J. Heterogeneous distributed computing. In *Encyclopedia of Electrical and Electronic Engineering*, J. G. Webster, Ed., vol. 8. John Wiley, New York, NY, 1999.

[15] OH, D.-I., AND BAKER, T. P. Utilization bounds for N-processor rate monotone scheduling with static processor assignment. *Real-Time Systems: The International Journal of Time-Critical Computing 15* (1998), 183–192.

[16] PAPADIMITRIOU, C. H. On the complexity of integer programming. *Journal of the ACM 28*, 4 (1981), 765–768.

[17] POTTS, C. N. Analysis of a linear programming heuristic for scheduling unrelated parallel machines. *Discrete Applied Mathematics 10* (1985), 155–164.

[18] PRAKASH, S., AND PARKER, A. C. Synthesis of application-specific multiprocessor systems including memory components. *Journal of VLSI Signal Processing 8* (1994), 97–116.

[19] SARKAR, V. *Partitioning and scheduling parallel programs for execution on multiprocessors*. MIT Press, 1989.

[20] SCHRIJVER, A. *Theory of Linear and Integer Programming*. John Wiley and Sons, 1986.

[21] SRIRAM, S., AND BHATTACHARYA, S. S. *Embedded Multiprocessors: Scheduling and Synchronization*. Marcel Dekker, Inc., 2000.

[22] SZYMANEK, R. W., AND KUCHCINSKI, K. A constructive algorithm for memory-aware task assignment and scheduling. In *International Workshop on Hardware/Software Co-Design (CODES)* (Copenhagen, Denmark, 2001), ACM Press.

[23] SZYMANEK, R. W., AND KUCHCINSKI, K. Partial task assignment of task graphs under heterogeneous resource constraints. In *International ACM/ IEEE Design Automation Conference (DAC)* (Anaheim, CA, 2003), ACM Press, pp. 244–249.

[24] WOLFE, W. *Computers as Components: Principles of Embedded Computing Systems Design*. Morgan Kaufmann Publishers, 2000.

# Timing Optimization of Nested Loops Considering Code Size for DSP Applications *

Qingfeng Zhuge,    Zili Shao,    Edwin H.-M. Sha
Department of Computer Science
University of Texas at Dallas
Richardson, Texas 75083, USA
{qfzhuge, zxs015000, edsha}@utdallas.edu

## Abstract

*Software pipelining for nested loops remains a challenging problem for embedded system design. The existing software pipelining techniques for single loops can only explore the parallelism of the innermost loop, so the final timing performance is inferior. While multi-dimensional (MD) retiming can explore the outer loop parallelism, it introduces large overheads in loop index generation and code size due to transformation. In this paper, we use MD retiming to model the software pipelining problem of nested loops. We show that the computation time and code size of a software-pipelined loop nest is affected by execution sequence and retiming function. The algorithm of Software PIpelining for NEsted loops technique (SPINE) is proposed to generate fully parallelized loops efficiently with the overheads as small as possible. The experimental results show that our technique outperforms both the standard software pipelining and MD retiming significantly.*

## 1. Introduction

With the advance of the technology, embedded systems with multiple cores or VLIW-like architectures, such as TI's TMS320C6x, Philips' TriMedia, and IA64, etc., become necessary to achieve the required high performance for the applications with growing complexity. To exploit multiple functional units or processors in parallel embedded systems, software pipelining is widely used to explore the instruction-level parallelism in loops [6, 13]. However, software pipelining can greatly expand the code size [14, 16]. Code size is one of the most critical concerns for many embedded processors because the capacity of on-chip memory

modules is still very limited due to the chip size, cost and power considerations. The code size problem has a dramatic effect on nested loops because code size can be expanded in multiple loop levels. Our research shows that the code size of software-pipelined loop nests is greatly affected by the execution sequence and the software pipelining degree chosen by an optimization technique. An example of software pipelining on a nested loop is shown in Figure 1. Figure 1(a) shows the original loop nest. The schedule length of the loop body is 3 control steps. Figure 1(b) and Figure 1(c) are software pipelined loops with the same schedule length of loop body which is 1 control step. However, the code in Figure 1(c) is much more complicated than that in Figure 1(b). The optimization technique generating the code in Figure 1(b) uses a row-wise execution sequence, while the technique generating the code in Figure 1(c) uses a skewed execution sequence which introduces large overheads in code size and loop indexes computation. Because of the space limitation, we do not show the code sections of epilogues which are about the same size as the prologues in this case. Optimization techniques on nested loops need to consider both timing and code size requirements, therefore, becomes a great challenge for parallel compiler.

While software pipelining of single loops has been extensively studied and implemented [2, 3, 6, 13, 14, 16], there is very few work done for the software pipelining problem on nested loops. A few existing techniques that could be applied to nested loop optimization either cannot fully explore the parallelism in a nested loop or do not consider the overheads such as loop indexes and loop bounds computation, and code size expansion due to transformation. The standard software pipelining techniques for single loops focuses on one-dimensional problems. When applied to nested loops, it only optimizes the innermost loop [1, 2, 6, 13]. While nested loops usually exhibit dependencies cross loop dimensions. Therefore, the performance improvement that can be obtained by the standards software pipelining techniques is very limited. Hyperplane schedul-

---

* This work is partially supported by TI University Program, NSF EIA-0103709, Texas ARP 009741-0028-2001, and NSF CCR-0309461

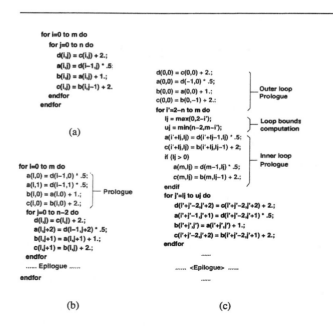

```
for i=0 to m do
    for j=0 to n do
        d(i,j) = c(i,j) + 2.;
        a(i,j) = d(i-1,j) * .5;
        b(i,j) = a(i,j) + 1.;
        c(i,j) = b(i,j-1) + 2.
    endfor
endfor
```

(a)

```
for i=0 to m do
    a(i,0) = d(i-1,0) * .5;
    a(i,1) = d(i-1,1) * .5;
    b(i,0) = a(i,0) + 1.;
    c(i,0) = b(i,0) + 2.;
    for j=0 to n-2 do
        d(i,j) = c(i,j) + 2.;
        a(i,j+2) = d(i-1,j+2) * .5;
        b(i,j+1) = a(i,j+1) + 1.;
        c(i,j+1) = b(i,j) + 2.;
    endfor
    ...... Epilogue ......
endfor
```
— Prologue

(b)

```
d(0,0) = c(0,0) + 2.;
a(0,0) = d(-1,0) * .5;
b(0,0) = a(0,0) + 1.;
c(0,0) = b(0,-1) + 2.;
for i'=2-n to m do
    lj = max(0,2-i');
    uj = min(n-2,m-i');
    a(i'+lj,lj) = d(i'+lj-1,lj) * .5;
    c(i'+lj,lj) = b(i'+lj,lj-1) + 2;
    if (lj > 0)
        a(m,lj) = d(m-1,lj) * .5;
        c(m,lj) = b(m,lj-1) + 2.;
    endif
    for j'=lj to uj do
        d(i'+j'-2,j'+2) = c(i'+j'-2,j'+2) + 2.;
        a(i'+j'-1,j'+1) = d(i'+j'-2,j'+1) * .5;
        b(i'+j',j') = a(i'+j',j') + 1.;
        c(i'+j'-2,j'+2) = b(i'+j'-2,j'+1) + 2.;
    endfor
    ......
endfor
    ...... <Epilogue> ......
    ......
```
Outer loop Prologue

Loop bounds computation

Inner loop Prologue

(c)

**Figure 1. (a) The original code. (b) The software-pipelined code generated by the SPINE technique. (c) The software-pipelined code generated by the chained MD retiming.**

ing [5, 12] tries to convert a nested loop into a single loop using loop unrolling and skewing to reduce the execution time. However, this technique makes code generation extremely difficult, and introduces large overhead in loop index generation. The best effort existing in industry on nested loop pipelining is to overlap the executions of the prologue and epilogue of the innermost loop, called outer loop pipelining [8, 15]. In this method, the dependencies among the outer loop iterations are still not exploited. Hence, the potential parallelism that can be explored is very limited. The only existing method that can fully explore the potential parallelism in multi-dimensional problems is multi-dimensional (MD) retiming [10]. MD retiming can achieve full parallelism of an multi-dimensional problem. That is, all the computations in an MD problem can be executed in parallel. However, MD retiming does not consider some critical issues for nested loop optimization, such as loop index generation and code size. To the authors' knowledge, there is no existent technique that can effectively solve the software pipelining problem for nested loops in embedded systems.

In this paper, we use retiming concept [7] to model the software pipelining on nested loops. The theory of software pipelining for nested loops is derived based on the understanding of the relationship among execution rate, execution sequence, and the retiming function of nested loops.

We prove that the minimum computation time of an iteration without unfolding [4, 9] for a nested loop with given execution sequence can be achieved by choosing an appropriate retiming function (Theorem 3.3). We do not consider the relationship between execution rate and unfolding factor for nested loops in this paper because unfolding duplicates the code size of loop body. Based on the theoretical foundation of software pipelining for nested loops, we propose a Software PIpelining for NEsted loops (SPINE) technique with an efficient algorithm, the SPINE-FULL algorithm. It fully parallelizes a nested loop with the minimal overheads. We conduct experiments on a set of two-dimensional DSP benchmarks to compare the code quality generated by SPINE with that generated by the other two techniques: the standard software pipelining technique, Modulo scheduling [13], and the standard MD retiming technique, the chained MD retiming [11]. Our experimental results show that SPINE out-performs or ties both of the other two techniques on all of our benchmarks.

The rest of the paper is organized as follows: Section 2 gives an overview for the graph representation of nested loops and multi-dimensional retiming model. The limitations of the existing techniques are discussed in Section 2.1. Section 3 presents the theory of software pipelining for nested loops. Section 4 presents the SPINE algorithms with an illustrative example. The experimental results are provided in Section 5. Finally, we conclude the paper in Section 6.

## 2. Basic Principles

In this section, we give an overview of basic concepts and principles related to software pipelining problem for nested loops. These include multi-dimensional data flow graph, multi-dimensional retiming, and software pipelining. We demonstrate that retiming and software pipelining are essentially the same concept.

A *multi-dimensional data flow graph (MDFG)* $G = \langle V, E, \mathbf{d}, t \rangle$ is a node-weighted and edge-weighted directed graph, where $V$ is the set of computation nodes, $E \subseteq V * V$ is the set of edges representing dependencies, $\mathbf{d}$ is a function from $E$ to $\mathbb{Z}^n$, representing the multi-dimensional delays between two nodes, where $n$ is the number of dimensions, and $t$ is a function from $V$ to a set of positive integers, representing the computation time of each node.

Programs with nested loops can be represented by an MDFG with cycles as shown in Figure 2(a). An *iteration* is the execution of each node in $V$ exactly once. Iterations are identified by a vector index $\mathbf{i} = (i_1, i_2, \ldots, i_n)$, starting from $(0, 0, \ldots, 0)$, where elements are ordered from the outermost loop to innermost loop. Inter-iteration dependencies are represented by edges weighted by delay vectors. For any iteration $\mathbf{j}$, an edge $e(u \rightarrow v)$ with delay $\mathbf{d}(e)$ indicates that the computation of node $v$ at iteration $\mathbf{j}$ requires data produced by node $u$ at iteration $(\mathbf{j} - \mathbf{d}(e))$. Intra-iteration dependencies, i.e. dependencies within the same iteration, are represented by edges without delay. A legal MDFG must have no zero-delay cycle. A static schedule must obey intra-iteration dependencies. The *cycle period* of a data flow graph G, denoted by $\Phi(G)$, is defined as the computation time of the longest zero-delay path, which corresponds to the minimum schedule length without resource constraint. We assume the computation time of a node is 1 time unit in this paper. The longest zero-delay paths of the MDFG in Figure 2(a) are from $D \rightarrow A \rightarrow B$ or $D \rightarrow A \rightarrow C$. Thus, the cycle period is $\Phi(G) = 3$.

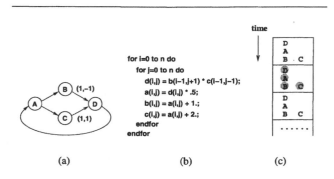

**(a)**

**(b)**

**(c)**

**Figure 2. (a) An MDFG. (b) Code of the nested loop. (c) The static schedule.**

The retiming technique [7] can be applied on a data flow graph to minimize the cycle period in polynomial time by evenly distributing the delays in the graph. The delays are moved around in the graph in the following way: a delay unit is drawn from *each* of the incoming edges of $v$, and then added to *each* of the outgoing edges of $v$, or vice verse. Note that the retiming technique preserves data dependencies of the original DFG. The multi-dimensional retiming (MD retiming) function $\mathbf{r} : V \rightarrow \mathbb{Z}^n$ represents the number of delay units moved through node $v \in V$. Figure 3(a) shows the retimed MDFG of Figure 2(a) with MD retiming function $\mathbf{r}(D) = (0, 1)$. Consider a retimed DFG $G_r = (V, E, \mathbf{d}_r, t)$ computed by retiming $\mathbf{r}$. The number of delays of any edge $e(u \rightarrow v)$ after retiming can be computed as $\mathbf{d}_r(e) = \mathbf{d}(e) + \mathbf{r}(u) - \mathbf{r}(v)$. And the total number of delays remains constant for any cycle in the graph.

When a delay is pushed through node D to its outgoing edge as shown in Figure 3(a), the actual effect on the schedule of the new MDFG is that the $\mathbf{i}^{th}$ copy of D is shifted up and is executed with $(\mathbf{i} - (0, 1))^{th}$ copy of nodes A, B, and C. Because there is no dependency between node D and nodes A, B, and C in the new loop body, node D

and node A can be executed in parallel in the new schedule. The schedule length of the new loop body is then reduced from three control steps to two control steps as shown in Figure 2(c) and Figure 3(c). In fact, every retiming operation corresponds to a software pipelining operation [16]. Some nodes are shifted out of the loop body to become prologue and epilogue. We can measure the exact code size of prologue and epilogue [16] using retiming function $\mathbf{r}$.

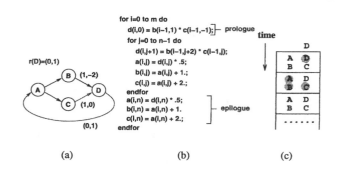

**(a)**

**(b)**

**(c)**

**Figure 3. (a) The retimed MDFG $G_r$ of MDFG in Figure 2(a) with $r(D) = (0, 1)$. (b) Code of the retimed MDFG.**

### 2.1. Limitations of Existing Techniques

There are several techniques can be applied to optimize nested loops. However, they all have limitations in terms of performance improvement, code size, or complexity of code generation. By analyzing the limitations of the existing techniques, the issues of nested loop optimization becomes clear.

The standard software pipelining techniques for one-dimensional loops are well developed [13]. However, when they are applied to optimize nested loops, the performance improvement is very limited. Consider the MDFG in Figure 4(a) with cycle period $\Phi(G) = 3$. The best result can be achieved by the standard software pipelining techniques, such as Modulo scheduling, is $\Phi(G) = 2$, as shown in Figure 4(b). Actually, the MDFG can be fully-parallelized. Figure 4(c) shows the retimed MDFG by using our SPINE technique which exploit the outer loop dependencies. The detailed SPINE algorithms will be presented later.

Another interesting example is shown in Figure 5(a) which has two orthogonal delay vectors $\mathbf{d}(B \rightarrow C) = (0, 1)$ and $\mathbf{d}(D \rightarrow A) = (1, 0)$. A cell dependency graph (CDG) clearly shows the execution sequence of the loop nest [10] as shown in Figure 5(b). The cell dependency graph of an

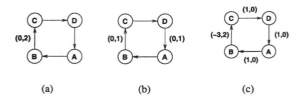

(a)                    (b)                    (c)

**Figure 4. (a) An MDFG. (b) The retimed MDFG using the standard software pipelining technique. (c) A fully-parallelized MDFG using SPINE technique.**

MDFG is a directed acyclic graph showing the dependencies between copies of nodes representing the MDFG. A node in CDG is a computational cell that represents a complete iteration. The CDG of a nested loop is bounded by the loop indexes. A *schedule vector* $\mathbf{s}$ is a normal vector for a set of parallel hyper-planes that defines a sequence of execution in a CDG. A legal MDFG $G = \langle V, E, \mathbf{d}, t \rangle$ is realizable if there exists a schedule vector $\mathbf{s}$ for the cell dependency graph with respect to $G$, i.e., $\mathbf{s} \cdot \mathbf{d}(e) \geq 0$, for all $e \in E$, and no cycle exists in the CDG [10]. The CDG shown in Figure 5(b), can be executed by a row-wise execution sequence, i.e., the schedule vector $\mathbf{s} = (1, 0)$.

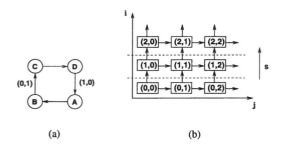

(a)                              (b)

**Figure 5. (a) An MDFG. (b) The cell dependency graph.**

For the MDFG shown in Figure 5(a), the standard software pipelining techniques can do nothing to optimize the loop. However, it can be fully parallelized using MD retiming techniques, such as the chained MD retiming [10]. The chained MD retiming [10] can fully parallelize a MDFG $G = \langle V, E, \mathbf{d}, t \rangle$ by selecting a legal schedule vector $\mathbf{s}$ such that $\mathbf{s} \cdot \mathbf{d}(e) > 0$, for all $e \in E$, and a retiming vector $\mathbf{r}$ such that $\mathbf{r} \perp \mathbf{s}$. To achieve a realizable MDFG after retiming, the legality condition, $\mathbf{s} \cdot \mathbf{d_r}(e) \geq 0$, has to be satis-

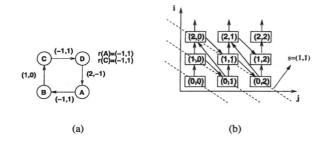

(a)                              (b)

**Figure 6. (a) A fully-parallelized MDFG using chained MD retiming. (b) The cell dependency graph.**

fied, and there should not exist any cycle in the cell dependency graph of the MDFG. For the example in Figure 5(a), a fully-parallelized solution using the chained MD retiming is shown in Figure 6(a). However, the original row-wise execution sequence is skewed by using the chained MD retiming. The schedule vector becomes $\mathbf{s} = (1, 1)$ as shown in Figure 6(b). The skewed execution sequence generates the code with large overheads as shown in Figure 1(c). The dramatically large overheads are produced due to the following reasons: First, prologue and epilogue are produced for multiple loop levels. Second, the computation of new loop bounds and loop indexes becomes much more complicated than using a row-wise execution sequence. Extra computation for executing the iterations along the loop boundary makes the final code even more complicated as indicated by the "Inner Loop Prologue" in Figure 1(c). And third, the original data locality is disrupted because of the skewed execution sequence. As a result, address generation becomes very complicated. Therefore, MD retiming is not suitable for software pipelining of nested loops.

## 3. Theory of Software Pipelining for Nested Loops

In this section, we show that the lower bound of the computation time of a nested loop is affected by schedule vector and retiming function. We present the theoretical foundation of software pipelining for nested loops with two loop levels based on retiming concept. Although the theorems are derived for two-dimensional, unit-time MDFGs, they can be generalized to multi-dimensional, general-time cases. First, we will introduce definitions and assumptions that are necessary for the understanding of the theorems.

**Definition 3.1.** *Given a schedule vector* $\mathbf{s}$ *and a retiming function* $\mathbf{r}$. *Let* $\ell$ *be a cycle in an MDFG* $G$. *The minimum* *cycle time of cycle $\ell$, $C_{min}(\ell)$, is the minimum execution time of $\ell$ with schedule vector $\mathbf{s}$ via MD retiming.*

We also make the following assumptions: 1) We assume all the elements of a schedule vector are nonnegative integers. 2) If there are delay vectors orthogonal to $\mathbf{s}$, we assume that only the ones on the right hand-side of $\mathbf{s}$ are the legal ones in order to avoid cycles in cell dependency graph. For instance, the given schedule vector is $\mathbf{s} = (0, 1)$. Delay vectors $\mathbf{d} = (1, 0)$ and $\mathbf{d} = (-1, 0)$ produce cycles in cell dependency graph. According to our assumption, only the delay vector $\mathbf{d} = (1, 0)$ is legal, which is corresponding to a loop counter with an increasing value.

We start with the simplest case with schedule vector $\mathbf{s} = (1, 0)$ and retiming function $\mathbf{r} = (0, 1)$. The following theorem derives the achievable minimum cycle time, and show that the minimum cycle time $C_{min}(\ell) = 1$ is not always achievable with given $\mathbf{s}$ and $\mathbf{r}$.

**Theorem 3.1.** *Given a unit-time MDFG $G = \langle V, E, \mathbf{d}, t \rangle$, a schedule vector $\mathbf{s} = (1, 0)$, and a retiming function $\mathbf{r} = (0, 1)$. Let $\ell$ be a cycle in G.*

1. *The minimum cycle time $C_{min}(\ell) = 1$ can be achieved via MD retiming, if $\sum_{e \text{ in cycle } \ell} \mathbf{d}(e) = (i, j)$, for $i > 0$,*

2. *If $\sum_{e \text{ in cycle } \ell} \mathbf{d}(e) = (0, k)$, for $k > 0$, then the minimum cycle time $C_{min}(\ell) = \lceil T(\ell)/k \rceil$ can be achieved, where $T(\ell) = \sum_{v \text{ in cycle } \ell} t(v)$.*

Theorem 3.1 states that a cycle can always be fully parallelized using a row-wise execution sequence when the total delay of the cycle is $\mathbf{d}(\ell) = (i, j)$, $i > 0$. The total delay vector after retiming is $\mathbf{d_r}(\ell) = \mathbf{d}(\ell) + \mathbf{r}(u) - \mathbf{r}(v) = (i, j) + (0, k) - (0, l) = (i, j + k - l)$, and $i > 0$. Therefore, the legality condition of MD retiming is always satisfied. In other words, a nested loop with outer-loop carried dependency can always be fully parallelized via MD retiming using a row-wise execution sequence.

For the nested loops without outer-loop carried dependency, the total delay of a cycle has a formula of $(0, k)$. We call this kind of cycle a (0,k)-cycle. Then, the full parallelism may not be achievable. For example, the minimum cycle time of the (0,2)-cycle in Figure 4(a) is 2, as shown in Figure 4(b), using a row-wise execution sequence.

Theorem 3.1 indicates that we need to consider the total delay of a cycle to decide whether a cycle can be fully parallelized with given schedule vector and retiming vector. We propose an idea of merging delays via MD retiming based on this theorem. Let's re-consider the example in Figure 5(a). The standard software pipelining technique such as Module scheduling cannot do any optimization for this kind of loop. While the chained MD retiming can fully parallelize the loop nest, but use a skewed schedule vector $\mathbf{s} = (1, 1)$, which expands the code size dramatically. While we suggest that the MDFG needs to be

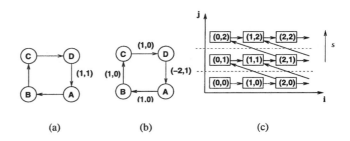

**Figure 7. (a) Merging delays. (b) The fully parallel MDFG via retiming $\mathbf{r}(A) = (3, 0)$, $\mathbf{r}(B) = \mathbf{r}(C) = (2, 0)$, and $\mathbf{r}(D) = (1, 0)$. (c) The cell dependency graph.**

transformed before software pipelining by merging the delays in a cycle. The resultant MDFG shown in Figure 7(a) has only one delay vector $\mathbf{d}(D \rightarrow A) = (1, 1)$, using retiming $\mathbf{r}(C) = \mathbf{r}(D) = (0, 1)$. Then, we can fully parallelize the loop via another MD retiming with schedule vector $\mathbf{s} = (1, 0)$ and retiming vector $\mathbf{r} = (0, 1)$. Thus, the row-wise execution sequence can be preserved, which is critical for obtaining the final code with small overheads. The final code of the retimed MDFG in Figure 7(b) is shown Figure 1(b). The final code size is substantially reduced. Loop bounds and loop indexes can be easily computed according to retiming functions. The data locality is also maintained. The cell dependency graph with row-wise execution sequence is shown Figure 7(c).

To further understand the timing property of an MDFG with given schedule vector and retiming function, Theorem 3.2 derives the achievable minimum cycle time by generalizing the result of Theorem 3.1 to any given schedule vector $\mathbf{s}$ and a retiming $\mathbf{r}$ that is orthogonal to $\mathbf{s}$.

**Theorem 3.2.** *Given a unit-time MDFG $G = \langle V, E, \mathbf{d}, t \rangle$, a schedule vector $\mathbf{s}$, a retiming function $\mathbf{r}$ and $\mathbf{r} \perp \mathbf{s}$. Let $\ell$ be a cycle in G.*

1. *The minimum cycle time $C_{min}(\ell) = 1$ can be achieved via MD retiming if $\exists e \in \ell$, $\mathbf{d}(e) \not\parallel \mathbf{r}$.*

2. *If $\mathbf{d}(e) \parallel \mathbf{r}$, $\forall e \in \ell$, then, $C_{min}(\ell) = \lceil T(\ell)/D(\ell) \rceil$, where $T(\ell) = \sum_{v \text{ in cycle } \ell} t(v)$, and $D(\ell) \times \mathbf{r} = \sum_{e \text{ in cycle } \ell} \mathbf{d}(e)$.*

The result of Theorem 3.1 is generalized based on the understanding that if only there exists a delay vector in a cycle that is not parallel to retiming $\mathbf{r}$, then the total delay of the cycle will not be parallel to retiming $\mathbf{r}$. Thus, the MDFG can be fully parallelized using retiming $\mathbf{r}$. On the other hand, if the summation of the delay vectors in a cycle is parallel to $\mathbf{r}$, all the delay vectors in the cycle must be parallel to **r**. In this case, the full parallelism may not be achievable.

To fully understand the timing property of any loop nest, we further derive the minimum cycle time for any given **s** and **r** such that **s** $\not\perp$ **r**. The minimum cycle time can be computed as $C_{min}(\ell) = \lceil T(\ell)/D(\ell) \rceil$, where $T(\ell) = \sum_{v\ in\ cycle\ \ell} t(v)$, and $D(\ell) = min(g(\ell), T(\ell))$, where $g(\ell) = \lceil \frac{s\cdot d(\ell)}{s\cdot r} \rceil + \delta$, and $\delta$ can be computed as follows: If $\lceil \frac{s\cdot d(\ell)}{s\cdot r} \rceil \neq \frac{s\cdot d(\ell)}{s\cdot r}$, $\delta = 0$. If $\lceil \frac{s\cdot d(\ell)}{s\cdot r} \rceil = \frac{s\cdot d(\ell)}{s\cdot r}$, and $d(\ell) \cdot x - \lceil \frac{s\cdot d(\ell)}{s\cdot r} \rceil \cdot (r \cdot x) \leq 0$, $\delta = 0$. Otherwise, $\delta = 1$. Due to the space limitation, we do not show the formal theorem and its proof. They can be easily verified on MDFGs.

The above theorems show that the minimum cycle time $C_{min}(\ell)$ of a cycle $\ell$ is affected by retiming function **r** and schedule vector **s**. In the following theorem, we show that a retiming function $\vec{r}$ that is orthogonal to $\vec{s}$ is the best choice for timing optimization. Due to the space limitation, we omit the formal proof of the theorem, but the correctness of the theorem can be easily verified.

**Theorem 3.3.** *Given MDFG* $G = \langle V, E, d, t \rangle$, *and a schedule vector* **s**. *Let* $\ell$ *be a cycle in G. Let* **r** *and* **r**′ *be two retiming functions such that* **r** $\perp$ **s** *and* **r**′ $\not\perp$ **s**. *The minimum cycle time of* $\ell$ *via MD retiming using retiming function* **r** *is always less than or equal to that using* **r**′.

Based on the theory of software pipelining for nested loops, we propose a Software PIpelining for NEsted loops (SPINE) technique. The principals of SPINE technique can be summarized as follows: (1) There must exist a schedule vector **s**, and a retiming function **r** orthogonal to **s**, such that the retimed loop is fully parallelized. (2) We should pick **r** $\perp$ **s**, so that it gives the shortest schedule. (3) If we fix **s** = $(1, 0)$ and use **r** = $(0, 1)$, SPINE will find the retimed MDFG of the input program with the minimum computation time. The computation cost due to loop transformation and the code size overhead of the software-pipelined loop is minimal.

## 4. SPINE Algorithm

In this section, we present the algorithm of software pipelining for nested loops. The SPINE-FULL algorithm generates fully-parallelized nested loops with computation and code size overheads as small as possible. It will be interesting to see that the chained MD retiming becomes a special case of the SPINE-FULL algorithm. Although the algorithm is presented for two-dimensional loops, multi-dimensional problems can be solved in a similar way.

We employ the idea of delay merge but transform it into a more efficient technique in our SPINE algorithm. According to retiming theory, DAG can always be retimed such that any edge has at least one delay. After the (i,j)-delay

---

**Algorithm 4.1** SPINE-FULL Algorithm

**Input:** MDFG $G = \langle V, E, d, t \rangle$
**Output:** A fully parallel MDFG $G_r = \langle V, E, d_r, t \rangle$ with the smallest possible overheads.
  **if** SPINE((1,0), G, 1) == 1 **then**
    **Return: s** = $(1, 0)$
  **else if** SPINE((0,1), G, 1) == 1 and $d(e) \cdot (0, 1) \geq 0$ **then**
    **Return: s** = $(0, 1)$
  **else if** SPINE((1,1), G, 1) == 1 and $d(e) \cdot (1, 1) \geq 0$ **then**
    **Return: s** = $(1, 1)$
  **else**
    Choose a **s** such that SPINE(**s**, G, 1) == 1, $s \cdot d(e) \geq 0, \forall e \in E$, and $|s_x| + |s_y|$ is as small as possible.
    **Return: s**
  **end if**

---

**Algorithm 4.2** Procedure of SPINE(G, s, c)

**Input:** MDFG $G = \langle V, E, d, t \rangle$, schedule vector **s**, a desired cycle period c.
**Output:** Retiming function **r**, retimed graph $G_r$, and cycle time c if it is feasible; otherwise, return 0.
  /* Check the legality of schedule vector **s**. */
  **if** $s \cdot d(e) \not\geq 0, \forall e \in E$. **then**
    Error: Illegal schedule vector.
  **end if**
  Choose retiming vector such that **r** $\perp$ **s**
  /* Remove the edges that are not parallel to **r**. */
  Construct graph $G' = \langle V, E', d', t \rangle$, such that $E' \longleftarrow E - \{e \mid d(e) \not\| r, \forall e \in E\}$, and $d'(e) \longleftarrow d(e)/r, \forall e \in E'$
  /* The feasible clock-period test algorithm */
  Compute $D(u, v)$ and $T(u, v)$ for any two nodes $u, v \in V$.
  Construct the constraint graph with the desired cycle period c.
  Use the shortest path algorithm to find a solution.
  **if** There exists a retiming solution $r'(v)$ such that $\Phi(G'_{r'}) \leq c$ **then**
    /* Update the retimed graph */
    Retime G with $r'(v) \cdot r, \forall v \in V$.
    **Return:** c
  **else**
    Error: Unfeasible cycle period.
    **Return:** 0
  **end if**

---

edges are removed, a cycle with (i,j)-delay edges becomes a DAG. Thus, we can directly apply one-dimensional retiming to minimize the cycle period without actually doing delay merge.

Algorithm 4.1 shows the procedure of SPINE-FULL Algorithm. The major function of the algorithm is SPINE(G, **s**, c) which is shown in Algorithm 4.2. The inputs of SPINE function are schedule vector **s**, MDFG G, and a desired cycle period c. The function produces a retiming of G with cycle period at most c, and returns c, if such a retiming exists; otherwise, it returns 0. The procedure first checks the legality of a given schedule vector **s**, and chooses a retiming **r** that is orthogonal to **s**. Then, it removes all the edges with delay vectors not parallel to **r**. In order to apply 1-D retiming, the delay vectors are converted to the delay units with respect to $\mathbf{r}$. To apply the feasible cycle-period test algorithm [7], the total number of delays of the critical path between any two nodes $D(u, v)$, and the total computation time of the critical path $T(u, v)$ are computed. If the desired cycle period c is achievable, the MD retiming will be performed on the MDFG G, and the value of c is returned. Otherwise, the function reports error and returns 0.

Given an MDFG $G = \langle V, E, d, t \rangle$ and a desired cycle period c, this algorithm produces a retiming r of G such that the cycle period of the retimed graph $\Phi(G_r) \leq c$, if such a retiming exists. The shortest path algorithm, such as Bellman Ford algorithm, can be used to find the solution of a set of constraint inequalities which is formulated from the following legality and feasibility conditions of retiming:

1. Legality: $d_r(e) = d(e) + r(u) - r(v) \geq 0 \implies r(v) - r(u) \leq d(e), \forall e(u \rightarrow v) \in E$.

2. Feasibility: $r(v) - r(u) \leq D(u, v) - 1, \forall u, v \in V$ such that $T(u, v) > c$.

where $D(u, v)$ is the minimum number of delays on any path from node u to node v. The path $u \rightsquigarrow v$ with the delay number $= D(u, v)$ is called the critical path from u to v. The value of $T(u, v)$ is the maximum total computation time on any critical path from u to v.

The SPINE-FULL Algorithm shown in Algorithm 4.1 aims to achieve a fully parallelized loop. Therefore, the desired cycle period c is set to be 1 for unit-time MDFG. First, the algorithm tries to use row-wise execution sequence, i.e. schedule vector $\mathbf{s} = (1, 0)$, to fully parallelize the MDFG G. If it is not achievable, the algorithm tries the schedule vector $\mathbf{s} = (0, 1)$ if it is a legal schedule vector. The schedule vector $\mathbf{s} = (0, 1)$ represents an column-wise execution and can be transformed to row-wise execution by loop index interchange. The schedule vectors $(1, 0)$ and $(0, 1)$ are the ones that produce the smallest code size expansion and the least loop index and bounds computation. If these two schedule vectors are not achievable, the algorithm chooses a legal schedule vector such that $|\mathbf{s}_x| + |\mathbf{s}_y|$ is minimal. In fact, the schedule vector $\mathbf{s} = (1, 1)$ is always tried before choosing other candidates. When the chosen schedule vector satisfies $\mathbf{s} \cdot \mathbf{d}(e) > 0$, i.e., $\mathbf{s}$ is not parallel to any delay vectors, the final result is equivalent to that produced by the chained MD retiming which becomes a special case of SPINE-FULL algorithm.

Consider the example shown in Figure 4(a), SPINE algorithm uses a column-wise execution sequence to optimize the computation time as shown in Figure 4(c). While the chained MD retiming can choose schedule vector $\mathbf{s} = (1, 1)$. Remember that the chained MD retiming has to use a schedule vector such that $\mathbf{s} \cdot \mathbf{d}(e) > 0$ for any non-zero delay vector in the MDFG. Therefore, the schedule vector $\mathbf{s} = (0, 1)$ is not even considered because of the existence

of delay vector $(0, 2)$. By using schedule vector $\mathbf{s} = (1, 1)$ the row-wise execution sequence cannot be maintained anymore, and the final code will have large overheads.

## 5. Experiments

In our experiments, we compare software-pipelined loops generated by three different approaches: the standard software pipelining technique, Modulo scheduling ("Modulo"), the standard MD retiming technique, chained MD retiming ("Chained"), and the SPINE-FULL algorithm ("SPINE"), on a simulated system without resource constraint. Our benchmarks include a set of 2-D nested loops: Wave Digital filter ("WDF"), Differential Pulse-Code Modulation device ("DPCM"), Two Dimensional filter ("2D"), Floyd-Steinberg algorithm ("Floyd"), a small multi-dimensional data flow graph example ("MDFG"), and its 2-by-2 unfolded graph ("MDFG22"). Three metrics are compared in our experiments: cycle period of a MDFG, execution time of a software-pipelined loop, and code size of a pipelined loop. We use the count of instructions in the compiled code to measure the code size.

| Bench | Node | Cycle Period | | | Execution Time | | |
|---|---|---|---|---|---|---|---|
| | | SPINE | Modulo | Improv | SPINE | Modulo | Improv |
| WDF(1) | 4 | 1 | 3 | 66.7% | 2600 | 7500 | 65.3% |
| WDF(2) | 12 | 1 | 6 | 83.8% | 2750 | 15000 | 81.7% |
| DPCM | 16 | 1 | 4 | 75.0% | 3838 | 10150 | 62.2% |
| 2D(1) | 4 | 1 | 4 | 75.0% | 2650 | 10000 | 73.5% |
| 2D(2) | 34 | 1 | 3 | 66.7% | 2850 | 7800 | 63.5% |
| MDFG | 8 | 1 | 3 | 66.7% | 2650 | 10000 | 73.5% |
| MDFG22 | 32 | 1 | 3 | 66.7% | 2650 | 7650 | 65.4% |
| Floyd | 16 | 1 | 10 | 90.0% | 2950 | 25000 | 88.2% |

**Table 1. Compare cycle period and execution time of software-pipelined nested loops generated by SPINE and Modulo scheduling.**

Table 1 compares the cycle period and execution time of the pipelined loops using the Modulo scheduling and the SPINE-FULL algorithm. Column "Node" shows the number of nodes in a loop. Column "Improve" shows the percentage of the improvement on cycle period of loops by using the SPINE-FULL algorithm. The experimental results show that the cycle period of the pipelined loop generated by SPINE is one time unit for all the benchmarks. While the Modulo scheduling cannot achieve full parallelism for all the cases. It indicates that the potential parallelism that can be explored by the standard software pipelining techniques on nested loops is very limited. The improvement on cycle period by using SPINE is 73.8% on average. The improvement on execution time of the whole loop is 71.7%.

| Bench | Retime | Code Size | | | Execution Time | | |
|-------|--------|-------|---------|--------|-------|---------|--------|
| | | SPINE | Chained | Improv | SPINE | Chained | Improv |
| WDF(1) | 2 | 21 | 70 | 70.0% | 2600 | 3759 | 30.8% |
| WDF(2) | 5 | 81 | 474 | 82.9% | 2750 | 3996 | 31.2% |
| DPCM | 3 | 312 | 312 | 0% | 3838 | 3838 | 0% |
| 2D(1) | 3 | 25 | 98 | 74.5% | 2650 | 3838 | 31.0% |
| 2D(2) | 7 | 281 | 2240 | 87.5% | 2850 | 4194 | 32.0% |
| MDFG | 3 | 41 | 166 | 75.3% | 2650 | 3838 | 31.0% |
| MDFG22 | 3 | 137 | 574 | 76.1% | 2650 | 3838 | 31.0% |
| Floyd | 9 | 169 | 1646 | 89.7% | 2950 | 4312 | 31.6% |

**Table 2. Compare code size and execution time of software-pipelined nested loops generated by SPINE and Chained MD Retiming.**

Table 2 compares the code size and execution time of the software-pipelined loops generated by the SPINE-FULL algorithm and the chained MD retiming. Column "Retime" shows the retiming times. For most of the benchmarks, SPINE achieves full parallelism using schedule vector $\mathbf{s} = (1, 0)$, while the chained MD retiming needs to skew the execution sequence using schedule vector $\mathbf{s} = (1, 1)$. For the DPCM program, $(0,k)$- cycles of the MDFG cannot be removed. In this case, SPINE-FULL uses schedule vector $\mathbf{s} = (1, 1)$. Therefore, the code sizes and execution rates are the same as the chained MD retiming. The code size is reduced by 69.5% on average by using SPINE. The average improvement on execution time is 27.3%.

## 6. Conclusion

The existing techniques cannot optimize nested loops effectively for many embedded systems with strict timing and code size requirements. The standard software pipelining techniques only explore the parallelism in one-dimension. Multi-dimensional retiming can fully parallelize a nested loop, but does not consider timing and code size overheads due to loop transformation. In this paper, we present the theory of Software Pipelining for NEsted loops (SPINE) based on the fundamental understanding of the properties of the software-pipelined nested loops using retiming concept. An efficient SPINE algorithm is developed to fully parallelize a nested loop with the minimal overheads. The experimental results show that our SPINE technique outperforms the standard software pipelining techniques, such as Modulo scheduling, for all our benchmarks. It is also superior to MD retiming technique for most of the cases in terms of the ex-

ecution time and the code size of software-pipelined loop nests.

## References

[1] R. Bailey, D. Defoe, R. Halverson, R. Simpson, and N. Passos. A study of software pipelining of multi-dimensional problems. In *Proc. 13th Int'l Conf. on Parallel and Distributed Computing and Systems*, pages 426–431, Aug. 2000.

[2] L.-F. Chao, A. S. LaPaugh, and E. H.-M. Sha. Rotation scheduling: A loop pipelining algorithm. *IEEE Trans. on Computer-Aided Design of Integrated Circuits and Systems*, 16(3):229–239, Mar. 1997.

[3] L.-F. Chao and E. H.-M. Sha. Static scheduling for synthesis of DSP algorithms on various models. *Journal of VLSI Signal Processing*, 10:207–223, 1995.

[4] L.-F. Chao and E. H.-M. Sha. Scheduling data-flow graphs via retiming and unfolding. *IEEE Trans. on Parallel and Distributed Systems*, 8(12):1259–1267, Dec. 1997.

[5] A. Darte and Y. Robert. Constructive methods for scheduling uniform loop nests. *IEEE Trans. on Parallel and Distributed Systems*, 5(8):814–822, Aug. 1994.

[6] M. Lam. Software pipelining: An effective scheduling technique for VLIW machines. In *Proc. SIGPLAN'88 ACM Conf. on Programming Language Design and Implementation*, pages 318–328, June 1988.

[7] C. E. Leiserson and J. B. Saxe. Retiming synchronous circuitry. *Algorithmica*, 6:5–35, Aug. 1991.

[8] K. Muthukumar and G. Doshi. Software pipelining of nested loops. In R. Wilhelm, editor, *CC 2001*, LNCS 2027, pages 165–181. Springer-Verlag, Berlin Heidelberg, 2001.

[9] K. K. Parhi. *VLSI Digital Signal Processing Systems: Design and Implementation*. John Wiley & Sons, 1999.

[10] N. L. Passos and E. H.-M. Sha. Achieving full parallelism using multi-dimensional retiming. *IEEE Trans. on Parallel and Distributed Systems*, 7(11):1150–1163, Nov. 1996.

[11] N. L. Passos, E. H.-M. Sha, and S. C. Bass. Loop pipelining for scheduling multi-dimensional systems via rotation. In *Proc. 31st ACM/IEEE Design Automation Conf. (DAC)*, pages 485–490, 1994.

[12] J. Ramanujam. Optimal software pipelining of nested loops. In *Proc. 8th Int'l Parallel Processing Symposium*, pages 335–342, Apr. 1994.

[13] B. R. Rau. Iterative modulo scheduling: An algorithm for software pipelining loops. In *Proc. 27th IEEE/ACM Annual Int'l Symp. on Microarchitecture (MICRO)*, pages 63–74, Nov. 1994.

[14] B. R. Rau, M. S. Schlansker, and P. P. Tirumalai. Code generation schema for modulo scheduled loops. In *Proc. 25th IEEE/ACM Annual Int'l Symp. on Microarchitecture (MICRO)*, pages 158–169, Dec. 1992.

[15] R. Scales. Nested loop optimization on the TMS320C6x. Application Report SPRA519, Texas Instruments, Feb. 1999.

[16] Q. Zhuge, Z. Shao, and E. H.-M. Sha. Optimal code size reduction for software-pipelined loops on dsp applications. In *Proc. IACC Int'l Conf. on Parallel Processing (ICPP)*, pages 613–620, Aug. 2002.

# Architecture and Implementation of Chip Multiprocessors: Custom Logic Components and Software for Rapid Prototyping

Naraig Manjikian, Huang Jin, James Reed, and Nathan Cordeiro
Department of Electrical and Computer Engineering
Queen's University
Kingston, Ontario, Canada K7L 3N6
nmanjiki@ee.queensu.ca

## Abstract

*This paper describes components and software tools in support of rapid prototyping in programmable logic for research on chip multiprocessors. Contemporary programmable logic chips offer considerable on-chip logic and memory resources. Prototyping of systems in programmable logic chips is faster and less costly than full-custom chip design. The first contribution that is described in this paper is a collection of original research-oriented logic components that provides processor, memory, and interconnect functionality for rapid prototyping. Because these are original components, and not proprietary vendor-supplied components, they may be arbitrarily extended and modified to suit research needs. The second contribution is a set of enhanced software tools for generating executable code. The third contribution is user-configurable software for testing and evaluating prototype chip multiprocessor implementations in hardware. In addition to describing these contributions, this paper provides results from implementing and testing prototype components and complete chip multiprocessors, including simulation waveforms, logic chip resource utilization, and observations of hardware operation.*

## 1  Introduction

Parallel computer architectures are useful in a variety of applications, and shared-memory multiprocessors, in particular, provide an easy-to-program parallel architecture. Microelectronics technology improvements have enabled increased chip-level integration, leading to single-chip multiprocessors. Nonetheless, further research is still appropriate, particularly for application-specific enhancements in parallel embedded systems.

Architectural simulation is often used in parallel systems research to explore the design space and assess new ideas. Simulation models, however, require assumptions and simplifications that may obscure implementation-related issues. Furthermore, executing a detailed simulation may be computationally expensive. To more fully address implementation issues, rapid prototyping in programmable logic chips can be pursued as a fast, low-cost alternative to full-custom chip design.

This paper describes contributions in support of research on chip multiprocessor architecture and implementation through rapid prototyping in programmable logic. A collection of original architectural components has been developed for prototyping, including single-issue and superscalar processors with caches, bus interconnects, and memory units. Software tools have also been developed or enhanced for code generation and system testing. This paper describes the components and tools, then provides implementation results.

## 2  Related Work

Related research for chip multiprocessors includes, among others, the Stanford Hydra project [9] and the Compaq Piranha project [4]. Similar research often relies on architectural simulation to assess potential performance or other aspects of interest [8]. Related commercial developments include the Lucent Daytona architecture [1] and IBM Power4 microprocessor [7].

Vendors of programmable logic devices now offer proprietary embedded processor components such as the Altera Nios processor [2] for integration with other components in a logic chip. Such components are valuable in commercial settings, but they may not always be suitable for research experimentation. For example, commercial embedded processor designs may only provide write-through data caches without cache coherence support. For prototyping of cache-coherent chip multiprocessor architectures, however, write-back data caches with coherence support are desirable.

Integration of processing and high-capacity memory is another related area. It is exemplified by commercial products such as the Mitsubishi M32R/D [14]. There has also been considerable research to explore architectures based on this type of integration [11, 17].

This paper describes support for prototype implementation of chip multiprocessors that can be integrated with components such as multibank embedded memory units, specialized processing engines, or specialized input/output interfaces. Such support enables unrestricted experimentation to directly answer initial questions about implementation complexity and functionality.

## 3 Target Prototyping Platform

The target platform in this paper is a Rapid Prototyping Platform (RPP) based on the Integrator/AP system from ARM Limited that incorporates a separate ARM microprocessor and a user-programmable Xilinx XCV2000E logic chip [3]. The Xilinx chip has 19,200 configurable logic blocks and 160 separate 4-kbit SRAM memory units called BlockRAMs. Figure 1(a) depicts a complete prototyping environment at Queen's University consisting of a Sun workstation, a PC workstation, a Tektronix logic analyzer, and the RPP. The Sun workstation hosts the CAD software for logic designs. The PC workstation is used to develop code for the ARM processor and to download logic configurations or ARM code to the RPP. The logic analyzer enables observation of nearly 100 signals on the pins of the user-programmable logic chip, as shown in detail in Figure 1(b). The block diagram in Figure 1(c) shows the interconnection between the two modules of the RPP. An external 1-Mbyte SRAM chip is attached to the user-programmable Xilinx chip.

## 4 Components for Rapid Prototyping

### 4.1 Processors with Caches

This section describes two original processor components that have been developed for unrestricted experimentation in rapid prototyping of multiprocessors.

#### 4.1.1 Single-Issue Pipelined Processor

A single-issue 32-bit pipelined processor has been designed with separate instruction/data caches, a cache controller, and a bus interface. As shown in Figure 2(a), the design is based on a five-stage pipelined architecture [15]. The assembly language instruction set is derived from the MIPS architecture [10]. Although it is

(a) RPP and supporting components

(b) RPP modules and logic analyzer probes

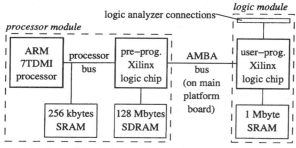

(c) Simplified block diagram of RPP modules

**Figure 1. Rapid Prototyping Platform for implementing chip multiprocessors**

MIPS-derived, this original processor is not compatible with, nor is it intended to compete with, any licensed commercial implementation; it is purely an internal implementation for research purposes only. Most typical integer instructions are implemented, but floating-point instructions are excluded, as are unaligned load half-word instructions, unaligned store half-word instructions, and special co-processor instructions. All other memory access, arithmetic/logic, jump, and branch instructions are included, for a total of 52 instructions. Unlike the MIPS architecture, this implementation has

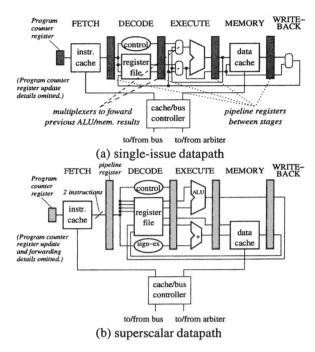

**(a) single-issue datapath**

**(b) superscalar datapath**

**Figure 2. Simplified block diagrams of pipelined processor datapaths**

no delay slots. Control logic in the decode stage generates all necessary control signals for subsequent pipeline stages. Forwarding resolves data hazards and a one-cycle pipeline stall handles load-use hazards [15].

The prototype implementation of this processor in the Xilinx logic chip utilizes the on-chip BlockRAM components for the register file and the caches. The cache capacity is initially limited to 2 kbytes with a one-word (4-byte) block size in the baseline implementation, but larger cache blocks and larger caches are possible. The data cache uses a writeback scheme in order to better support cache coherence.

### 4.1.2 Two-way Superscalar Pipelined Processor

In order to provide a more aggressive processor implementation for prototyping purposes, a two-way superscalar pipelined processor has also been developed that permits issuing an ALU or branch instruction in parallel with a memory access instruction [15]. A software tool has also been developed to ensure that the appropriate pairing of instructions preserves program semantics in such a datapath. The superscalar processor uses the same MIPS-derived (but not MIPS-compatible) instruction set as the single-issue processor in Section 4.1.1.

The superscalar datapath uses a five-stage pipeline, as shown in Figure 2(b). Two instructions are fetched

as a pair from the instruction cache, and with two additional instructions in each subsequent stage, ten instructions may be in progress at any time. Superscalar execution requires writing two results to the register file in the same cycle; the register file accommodates this requirement. The superscalar implementation uses a larger cache block size of 8 bytes for fetching two instructions simultaneously. Both caches use this block size, hence doubling the width of the caches for superscalar execution leads to a larger 4-kbyte baseline cache capacity. The data cache for the superscalar datapath also uses a writeback scheme in support of cache coherence.

### 4.2 Multiprocessor Support

Both processor implementations have a cache controller and a bus interface to support multiprocessor data cache coherence. The data caches use a writeback/invalidate scheme for cache coherence that is enforced through bus snooping using an MSI protocol [6]. Duplicate tags for snooping are implemented within the single-level data cache in both implementations.

Both processor implementations include load-linked (LL) and store-conditional (SC) instructions in order to provide an atomic read-modify-write capability for multiprocessing [6]. Each processor has a link address register and a link flag bit register for supporting these instructions. The memory stage of the pipeline and the cache controller interact in order to correctly implement the required functionality for these instructions.

### 4.3 Bus Interconnects for Multiprocessing

Two different components have been developed to provide either a simpler atomic bus or a more sophisticated split-transaction bus that can provide higher throughput. Both buses include support for enforcing cache coherence.

### 4.3.1 Atomic Bus

A simple atomic bus is one in which there are no intervening bus transactions between a request and its corresponding response. This approach reduces complexity at the cost of potentially lower bus utilization. An atomic bus with multiplexed address/data lines, command lines, additional lines for supporting cache coherence (such as a memory-inhibit line), and a round-robin arbiter has been developed for implementation in the Xilinx logic chip. For the single-issue processors that use a one-word (4-byte) cache block size, a 32-bit instance of the bus is used. For the superscalar processor that uses two-word (8-byte) cache blocks, a 64-bit instance of the bus is used; only half of the 64 multiplexed lines are used

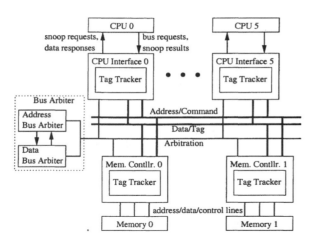

**Figure 3. System with split-transaction bus**

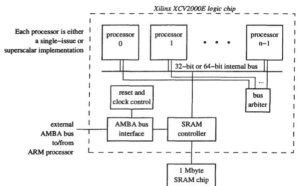

**Figure 4. Block diagram of multiprocessor with dual-access shared memory**

when this bus is carrying address information. When either bus is instantiated with multiple processors connected to it, the cache/bus controller for each processor provides support to snoop all requests that appear on the bus for cache coherence.

### 4.3.2 Split-Transaction Bus

A split-transaction bus permits a request and its corresponding response to be decoupled so that other requests and responses may use the bus during otherwise idle periods. Such a bus increases throughput, especially for multiple memory units to service requests concurrently.

For prototyping purposes, a split-transaction bus component with non-multiplexed address/data lines has been developed. Non-multiplexed lines require more sophisticated bus arbitration, particularly for handling writebacks that require the simultaneous use of both portions of the bus [16]. An additional complication stems from the decoupling of requests from responses. A mechanism is required to match the responses to their requests. One approach is to assign and maintain a unique tag for each active request, and provide the tag information on the bus at the same time as the response [6]. Thus, command and address lines are used for requests, and tag and data lines are used for responses. A device that has issued a request can recognize the tag for its response. Additional hardware in the form of a request tag tracking table for each device can provide the necessary support. Figure 3 illustrates the organization of a system built around this split-transaction bus.

### 4.4 Shared Memory Controller

A cache-coherent multiprocessor system requires a shared memory component. For the target platform de-

scribed in Section 3, the vendor provides a design example with a memory controller that permits the ARM microprocessor in Figure 1(c) to access the 1-Mbyte SRAM chip through the programmable Xilinx chip. This design has been significantly enhanced to serve as the shared memory controller for chip multiprocessor implementations in the Xilinx logic chip. One enhancement is support for the memory-inhibit line on the bus for cache coherence. An additional enhancement is providing two access ports to the SRAM chip, one for the on-chip multiprocessor and the other for the external ARM microprocessor. Concurrent accesses are not supported because the SRAM chip has only one set of address/data connections. The enhanced controller gives higher priority to the on-chip multiprocessor.

### 4.5 Complete Multiprocessor Subsystems

With the components described to this point, complete multiprocessor subsystems can be implemented within the Xilinx chip of the prototyping platform. Figure 4 illustrates the connection of multiple processors to the atomic bus, and the enhanced memory controller that serves requests from the on-chip multiprocessor and the external ARM microprocessor.

### 4.6 Prototyping Embedded Memory

Current microelectronics technology allows embedding substantial amounts of dynamic random-access memory (DRAM) with processing components in the same chip. Compared to on-chip SRAM and commodity DRAM chips, embedded DRAM provides wider on-chip interfaces, lower power consumption, and customizable capacities. To explore the design space for embedded DRAM architectures, particularly for chip multiprocessors, we have developed a multibank mem-

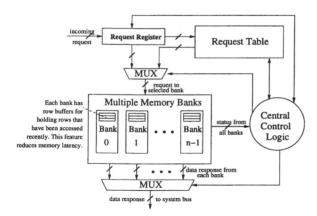

**Figure 5. Embedded memory architecture**

ory prototype in programmable logic. Each bank contains a *pseudo*-DRAM array that is emulated by a collection of BlockRAM components on the Xilinx chip. For instance, each 4-kbit BlockRAM is organized in a $256 \times 16$ array, and 16 such BlockRAMs can be combined to form a $256 \times 256$ pseudo-DRAM array with appropriate control to emulate DRAM I/O and access latencies.

As shown in Figure 5, our memory architecture consists of multiple banks with a central controller that distributes memory requests from one or more sources. Each bank contains several row buffers to hold recently-accessed rows from the pseudo-DRAM array. Each bank has its own internal control for read or write accesses. The row buffers are checked, and the increased latency for accessing the main array on row buffer misses is emulated by a delay when the requested data is not found in the row buffers. The address and data input lines are shared among all banks, whereas data output lines are separate and multiplexed to the system bus.

## 5 Software Support for Rapid Prototyping

Components for prototype hardware implementation of chip multiprocessor architectures must be complemented with appropriate software tools for simulation, code generation, and testing. This section outlines the tools that have been developed in support of these tasks.

### 5.1 Architectural Simulators

Architectural simulation enables exploration of the design space prior to committing effort to a prototype implementation. In support of such efforts, appropriate tools have been enhanced and developed. The starting point for our tools is the SimpleScalar tool set [5]. SimpleScalar provides an instruction-level simulator that

supports a derivative of the MIPS instruction set architecture [10]. The software tools that are provided with the simulator include an adaptation of the GNU compiler and related software for generating executable code.

The original version of SimpleScalar supports only uniprocessor simulation. In earlier work, enhancements were made to SimpleScalar for supporting multiprocessor simulation [12]. The enhancements include management of multiple thread contexts and the necessary library support for simulated application code to create and synchronize multiple threads of execution. Subsequently, the multiprocessor-enhanced version of SimpleScalar has been used as a front-end instruction-level simulator to feed an original object-oriented back-end system-level simulator called *Quasar* for Queen's University Architectural Simulation Archive [13].

The front-end SimpleScalar simulator can be modified to support interpretation of new instructions. The back-end Quasar simulator can also be modified to model the system-level behavior associated with such new instructions. Thus, new hardware features can be readily investigated with architectural simulation prior to committing to a detailed prototype implementation.

### 5.2 Code Generation Tools

As indicated in the previous section, the SimpleScalar tool set includes compiler and other support from the GNU tool chain for code generation. Various enhancements have been made to the code generation tools in support of research efforts. One key enhancement is related to the assembler. In order to easily support any number of new application-specific instructions, the enhanced assembler can read the details for new instructions from a text file at run time. This information is then used to properly interpret and process assembly-language code that includes any new instructions. This approach avoids the need for researchers to directly modify and recompile the assembler source code for each new instruction that is to be considered. Other enhancements include a run-time library for multiprocessing. Figure 6 shows the flow of code generation for either simulation or for a prototype implementation.

### 5.3 User-Configurable Testing Software for Target Platform

Once a logic configuration for a prototype implementation has been generated by the appropriate CAD tools, it is programmed into the Xilinx logic chip for testing. User-configurable software has been developed in order to support evaluation and testing of prototype chip multiprocessor implementations. The software is called *Qualm* for Queen's University Adaptable Logic Monitor

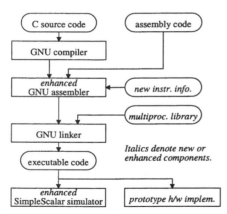

**Figure 6. Code generation tool flow for simulation or execution in hardware**

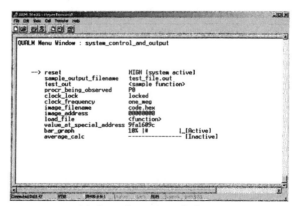

(a) Sample menu window

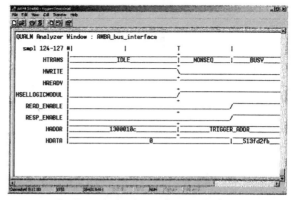

(b) Sample logic analyzer window

**Figure 7. Configurable windows displayed by *Qualm* testing software**

and it provides features for controlling and monitoring custom logic under test.

*Qualm* executes on the ARM processor in the target rapid prototyping platform (RPP) discussed earlier in Section 3. It interacts with the custom logic under test, such as a prototype chip multiprocessor implementation, through the bus connection to the programmable Xilinx chip shown earlier in Figure 1(c). This arrangement is yet another level of parallel processing on the target platform: processors implemented within the logic chip execute concurrently with the ARM processor that is executing the *Qualm* testing software.

*Qualm* interacts with the user through serial communication with a standard $80 \times 24$ terminal device or terminal emulator on an attached desktop PC computer. Up to two such terminals may be connected for *Qualm* to use because the RPP provides two serial ports. The user specifies the desired appearance and behavior of on-screen windows in a configuration file. Predefined window types include a command-line interface, a menu window, and a logic analyzer waveform window. The contents of a menu window and waveforms to display on the analyzer window are entirely user-configurable. Multiple windows can be defined for display on up to two terminals, and simple keyboard commands are provided to switch between different windows.

Figure 7 provides samples of a menu window and a logic analyzer window. The logic analysis capability is supported by integrating a custom analyzer component with the system under test within the programmable logic chip. The signals of interest are connected internally to the analyzer component, which uses Block-RAMs to sample those signals. The *Qualm* software uses the bus connection between the ARM microprocessor and the programmable logic chip to control the analyzer and collect sampled data for waveform display.

*Qualm* has been conceived with predefined features to provide a reusable, reconfigurable tool for evaluation and testing without requiring custom code. Because it is a research tool, however, it is possible to modify *Qualm* or to integrate more specialized code into the base software where necessary. This ability can be used to define more specialized windows and related evaluation/test functionality. For example, a separate console window has been defined to support character input/output for chip multiprocessor implementations. New features can be made available for specification in the configuration file in the same manner as the existing features.

## 6 Prototype Implementation Results

The architectural components described in Section 4 have been implemented in the VHDL language for detailed logic simulation and for logic synthesis. This section provides results for these components in terms of simulation waveforms, logic chip resource utilization, and observations of components operating in the pro-

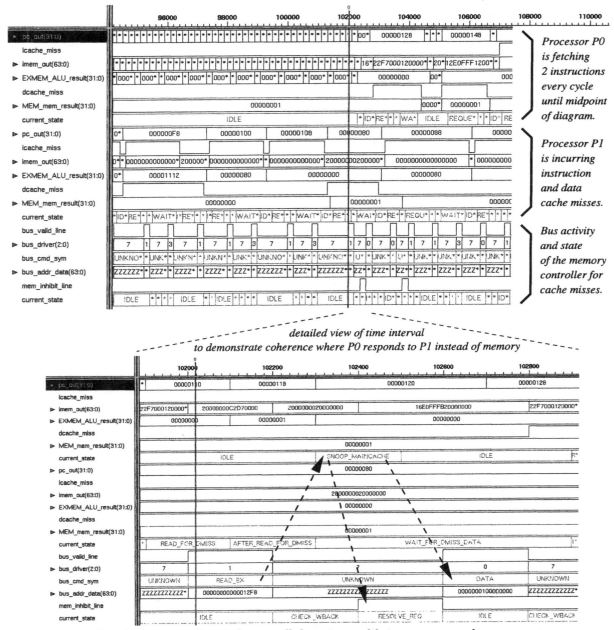

**Figure 8. Simulation waveforms for parallel system with two superscalar processors**

grammable logic chip.

## 6.1 Logic Simulation Results for Superscalar Multiprocessor

For implementing chip multiprocessor subsystems in VHDL, logic simulation is used for initial verification prior to programming the logic chip. Figure 8 provides two annotated simulation waveform diagrams obtained with Synopsys CAD tools for two superscalar processors on an atomic bus executing a parallel program that

was generated by the tools described in Section 5. The top waveform diagram in Figure 8 shows a period of time in which superscalar processor P0 is successfully fetching and processing two instructions in every cycle. Meanwhile, superscalar processor P1 is incurring cache misses. The bus and memory controllers are active to service each of these cache misses. The bottom waveform diagram in Figure 8 shows an expanded view for a short interval of simulated time from the top waveform diagram. The miss by processor P1 for a store to address 0x12F8 causes a read-exclusive request on the bus.

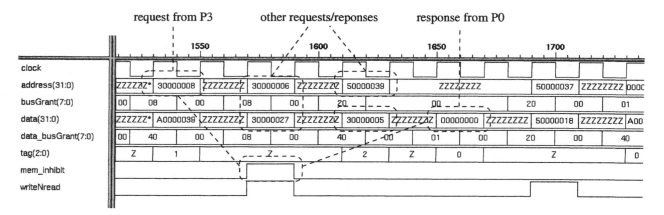

**Figure 9. Simulation waveforms for split-transaction bus operation**

The cache controller for the other superscalar processor P0 performs snooping on that request, then asserts the memory inhibit signal because P0 will respond instead of memory. The response from P0 is then placed on the bus for P1 to accept.

## 6.2 Logic Simulation Results for Split-Transaction Bus

The added complexity of a split-transaction bus implementation requires appropriate testing. Sample simulation results from a special test configuration are shown in Figure 9 to highlight split-transaction bus capabilities with cache coherence. A request from processor 3 causes processor 0 to assert the memory inhibit signal and provide the response instead of memory. Until the response appears, the bus is granted to processor 3 to perform a pending writeback to memory.

## 6.3 Logic Chip Resource Utilization

The target platform for prototype chip multiprocessor implementations includes a Xilinx XCV2000E logic chip, as discussed in Section 3. The chip provides 19,200 configurable logic blocks, each of which contains two 4-input lookup tables for implementing combinational logic and two flip-flops. The chip also provides 160 BlockRAMs with 4 kbits of storage in each one.

Chip multiprocessor implementations consisting of single-issue processors or superscalar processors on the atomic bus have been synthesized for the Xilinx logic chip using Synopsys and Xilinx CAD tools. The external 1-Mbyte SRAM chip provides the shared memory. Figure 10 depicts floorplans generated by the CAD tools for two such implementations on the Xilinx XCV2000E chip that has a 240 × 80 grid of logic blocks. The clustering of utilized blocks directly reflects the processors. The six vertical channels on the left and right sides of

each floorplan hold the BlockRAMs that are used for register files and caches. Four single-issue processors along with the bus and memory control components utilize 35% of the logic resources and 52% of the Block-RAM units. Two superscalar processors utilize 23% of the logic resources and 41% of the BlockRAMs. In both cases, there are considerable logic resources and on-chip memory available to implement additional processors and other components.

## 6.4 Observations of Multiprocessor Operation in Hardware

Figure 11 shows the operation of a chip multiprocessor with single-issue processors on an atomic bus as observed with the Tektronix logic analyzer shown earlier in Figure 1. The internal signals of processor P0 are shown along with activity on the shared internal bus. In Figure 11(a), processor P0 misses in its instruction cache and the memory responds when the read request appears on the bus. Immediately after that, however, P0 misses again, but P1 is granted the bus for a read request. The cache controller for P0 snoops this request, but allows the memory to respond to P1 in this case. In Figure 11(b), however, a miss in P1 is for data that P0 has in a modified cache block. In this case, the memory is inhibited and P0 provides the data response.

## 6.5 Observations of Multibank Memory Operation in Hardware

The prototype implementation of the multibank embedded memory component discussed in Section 4.6 has been tested in hardware with its own test configuration. A test state machine generates memory requests to different memory locations and collects the responses from the memory. The memory access pattern that is used by the test machine enables verification of functionality and

490

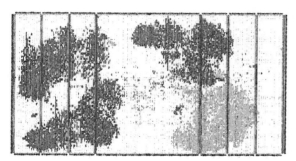

(a) 4 single-issue processors

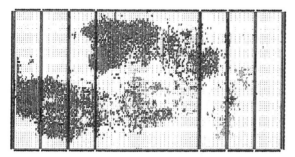

(b) 2 superscalar processors

**Figure 10. Logic chip resource utilization of multiprocessor implementations**

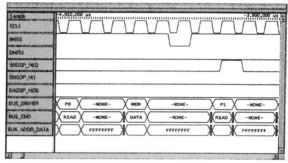

(a) Response from memory

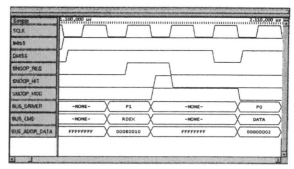

(b) Response from another processor

**Figure 11. Observations of prototype chip multiprocessor operation in hardware**

demonstrates concurrency across multiple banks. Figure 12 shows observations using the logic analyzer for a sequence of 4 write requests followed by 4 read requests. The waveforms show the concurrency of the memory with all four banks active in performing the writes and then the reads. Annotations highlight two memory accesses to address 0x0080, which is in Bank#0. The first access is a write for which a row buffer miss occurs, and the second access is a read that retrieves the data 0x00000100 from the row buffers with reduced access latency.

## 7 Conclusion

Research on chip multiprocessor architectures stems from microelectronics technology improvements that enable increased on-chip integration. Architectural simulation for exploring the design space should be complemented by implementation wherever possible in order to fully explore hardware/software considerations for such systems. Contemporary programmable logic chips provide considerable on-chip logic and memory resources that can be effectively exploited for rapid prototyping of chip multiprocessors.

This paper has described architectural components for prototyping chip multiprocessors, including single-issue and superscalar processors with caches, bus interconnects, and memory units. Software tools have also been developed to aid in simulation, code generation, and testing for prototype multiprocessor implementations. Results have indicated logic chip resource utilization and demonstrated component and system functionality in logic simulation and in actual hardware operation.

Future work includes the development of additional components for prototyping parallel embedded systems. Examples include network processing and other specialized processing engines, specialized input/output interfaces, and other types of interconnect topologies. Other directions for future work include the development of software to aid in automating the instantiation and integration of customized architectural components. With such a framework of components and software tools, further research on architecture and implementation of chip multiprocessors will be well-supported.

## Acknowledgements

This research was supported by the Natural Sciences and Engineering Research Council of Canada (NSERC), Communications and Information Technology Ontario

491

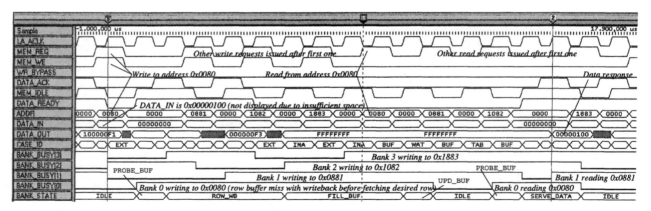

**Figure 12. Operation of prototype 4-bank memory component in hardware showing concurrency**

(CITO), and Queen's University. The Rapid Prototyping Platform and associated CAD tools were provided by the Canadian Microelectronics Corporation. Gratitude is also extended to the Microelectronics and Computer Systems Laboratory at McGill University in Montreal and the System-on-Chip Laboratory at the University of British Columbia in Vancouver for granting Naraig Manjikian access to similar instances of the Rapid Prototyping Platform during his visits to those institutions.

# References

[1] B. Ackland et al. A single-chip, 1.6-billion, 16-b MAC/s multiprocessor DSP. *IEEE J. of Solid State Circuits*, 35(3):412–424, March 2000.

[2] Altera Corp. *Nios Embedded Processor 32-bit Programmer's Reference Manual*, January 2003. Document No. MNL-NIOS32PROG-3.1. Further details are available at http://www.altera.com.

[3] ARM Limited. *Integrator/AP ASIC Development Motherboard User Guide*, April 2001. Document No. ARM-DUI-0098B. Further details are available at http://www.arm.com.

[4] L. A. Barroso et al. Piranha: A scalable architecture based on single-chip multiprocessing. In *Proc. 27th Int'l Symp. on Computer Architecture*, pages 282–293, Vancouver, British Columbia, June 2000.

[5] D. Burger and T. M. Austin. The SimpleScalar tool set, version 2.0. Technical Report 1342, Computer Science Department, University of Wisconsin-Madison, June 1997.

[6] D. E. Culler and J. P. Singh. *Parallel Computer Architecture: A Hardware/Software Approach*. Morgan Kaufmann, San Francisco, California, 1999.

[7] K. Diefendorff. Power4 focuses on memory bandwidth: IBM confronts IA-64, says ISA not important. *Micro Processor Report*, 13(13), October 1999.

[8] M. Ekman and P. Stenstrom. Performance and power impact of issue-width in chip-multiprocessor cores. In

[9] L. Hammond et al. The Stanford Hydra CMP. *IEEE Micro*, 20(2):71–84, March/April 2000.

[10] G. Kane and J. Heinrich. *MIPS RISC Architecture*. Prentice Hall, Englewood Cliffs, NJ, 1992.

[11] X. Li and N. Manjikian. A performance study of system-on-chip network processor architecture. In *Proc. 2003 Symp. on Perf. Eval. of Computer and Telecommunications Systems*, Montreal, Quebec, July 2003.

[12] N. Manjikian. Multiprocessor enhancements of the SimpleScalar tool set. *ACM Computer Architecture News*, 29(1):8–15, March 2001.

[13] N. Manjikian et al. Evolution and research applications of an objected-oriented framework for architectural simulation. In *Proc. 2003 IEEE Pacific Rim Conf. on Communications, Computers and Signal Processing*, pages 684–687, Victoria, British Columbia, August 2003.

[14] Y. Nunomura, T. Shimizu, and O. Tomisawa. M32R/D–integrating DRAM and microprocessor. *IEEE Micro*, 17(6):40–48, November 1997.

[15] D. A. Patterson and J. L. Henessy. *Computer Organization and Design: The Hardware/Software Interface*. Morgan Kaufmann, San Francisco, CA, 2nd edition, 1998.

[16] J. Reed and N. Manjikian. A dual round-robin arbiter for split-transaction busses in system-on-chip implementations. In *Proc. 2004 IEEE Canadian Conf. on Electrical and Computer Engineering*, Niagara Falls, Ontario, May 2004.

[17] L. Wang and N. Manjikian. A performance study of chip multiprocessors with integrated dram. In *Proc. 2003 Symp. on Perf. Eval. of Computer and Telecommunications Systems*, Montreal, Quebec, July 2003.

*Proc. 32nd Int'l Conf. on Parallel Processing*, pages 359–368, Kaohsiung, Taiwan, October 2003.

# Session 7C:
# Wireless: Ad Hoc Networks

# RMAC: A Reliable Multicast MAC Protocol for Wireless Ad Hoc Networks

Weisheng Si and Chengzhi Li

*Department of Computer Science, University of Virginia*

*Email: {ws4u, cl4v}@cs.virginia.edu*

## Abstract

*This paper presents a new MAC protocol called RMAC that supports reliable multicast for wireless ad hoc networks. By utilizing the busy tone mechanism to realize multicast reliability, RMAC has the following three novelties: (1) it uses a variable-length control frame to stipulate an order for the receivers to respond, such that the problem of feedback collision is solved; (2) it extends the traditional usage of busy tone for preventing data frame collisions into the multicast scenario; and (3) it introduces a new usage of busy tone for acknowledging data frames. In addition, we also generalize RMAC into a comprehensive MAC protocol that provides both reliable and unreliable services for all the three modes of communications: unicast, multicast, and broadcast. Our evaluation shows that RMAC achieves high reliability with very limited overhead. We also compare RMAC with other reliable multicast MAC protocols, showing that RMAC not only provides higher reliability but also involves lower cost.*

## 1. Introduction

To date, most MAC protocols for wireless networks do not provide a reliable multicast service. For example, IEEE 802.11 [9], the widely-used wireless MAC protocol today, only supports reliability for unicast with the RTS/CTS/DATA/ACK scheme; and for multicast or broadcast, it simply transmits the data frames once without any recovery mechanism. In recent years, however, the provision of multicast reliability at the MAC layer has received increasing attention due to the following two observations.

First, mechanisms solely at the network layer cannot provide highly reliable multicast for wireless ad hoc networks in an efficient way. So far, many network layer multicast protocols have been proposed, such as [6], [15], [21], [3], [12], and [5]. They can be classified into tree-based protocols ([6], [15], [21], [3]) and mesh-based protocols ([12], [5]). Unfortunately, both types of protocols encounter problems in achieving multicast reliability. In tree-based protocols, where a tree is used to do multicast, severe packet loss occurs due to the scarce connectivity of the tree. As manifested by [5] and [13], if one node in the tree does not receive a multicast packet, then all its downstream children cannot receive the packet. On the other hand, mesh-based protocols overcome the problem of the tree by forwarding multicast packets with a mesh, such that a node can receive the packets from several upstream nodes. However, mesh-based protocols are inefficient in that they introduce redundant packet transmissions and nodes need to be able to distinguish previously-received packets in some way.

Second, in the perspective of functionality provisioning in the protocol stack, the MAC layer is a proper place to provide the reliability for wireless ad hoc networks. Unlike the wired networks where, with almost error-free links, reliability can only be implemented at the end-to-end level (e.g., TCP), wireless networks are characterized by error-prone links, so it is worthwhile to perform local recovery at each hop. As shown in [4], adding local recovery at the MAC layer can greatly improve the end-to-end performance for unicast in wireless networks. For multicast, we believe that the same effect will be produced if MAC layer reliability is provided.

For the implementation of multicast reliability, two basic technologies exist: Forward Error Correction (FEC) and Automatic Repeat reQuest (ARQ). In FEC, redundant data are transmitted for error recovery and no feedback is needed from the receivers. The advantage of FEC is that it scales to a large number of receivers and its disadvantages are that it involves encoding/decoding overhead and the sender cannot know whether full reliability has been achieved. In ARQ, retransmission is used for error recovery and feedback is needed from the receivers. The advantage of ARQ is that it can achieve full reliability and its disadvantage is that it cannot scale to a large number of receivers due to the feedback implosion problem [19].

In this paper, we focus on using ARQ to implement the MAC layer reliable multicast for wireless ad hoc networks where the number of one-hop multicast receivers is not large. In applying ARQ to multicast for wireless ad hoc networks, two problems have to be solved: (1) how to reserve the wireless channel for multiple receivers so as to increase the successful transmissions and (2) how to collect the feedback from multiple receivers. Several existing ARQ-based multicast MAC protocols (to be described in Section 2) try to solve these two problems by extending the IEEE 802.11 RTS/CTS/DATA/ACK scheme to the multicast scenario. Observing that these IEEE 802.11 based protocols are not efficient, in this paper we present the RMAC protocol which solves these two problems by the introduction of the busy tone mechanism. Besides supporting multicast reliability, RMAC is also generalized into a comprehensive MAC protocol that provides both reliable and unreliable services to the upper layer, with each service covering three modes of communications: unicast, multicast, and broadcast. Our evaluation shows that RMAC can achieve high reliability with very limited overhead.

## 2. Related work

The current ARQ-based reliable multicast MAC protocols, including [11], [17], and [16], all extend the RTS/CTS/DATA/ACK scheme in IEEE 802.11 Distributed Coordination Function (the ad hoc mode) to provide the reliable multicast service. Generally, while maintaining the use of RTS and CTS to reserve the wireless channel and the use of ACK to acknowledge the DATA frames, they augment the use of these frames into the multicast scenario. Also, some new control frames are introduced in [11] and [16].

In the Leader Based Protocol (LBP) proposed by Kuri and Kasera [11], a "leader" selected by the multicast receivers takes the responsibility to reply CTS and ACK to the sender, such that no multiple CTSs or ACKs are generated by the receivers. Although LBP avoids the multiple acknowledgments, selecting and maintaining a "leader" by multicast receivers are not easy tasks.

In [17], Tang and Gerla proposed the Broadcast Medium Window (BMW) protocol that only adds the reliable broadcast service to the IEEE 802.11. Basically, BMW (Figure. 1 (a)) realizes the reliable broadcast by using a unicast to each of the one-hop neighbors with the RTS/CTS/DATA/ACK scheme. The gain of BMW lies in that during each unicast to a neighbor, other neighbors try to overhear the DATA frame. When a unicast is successful, the sender increases the sequence number of the DATA frame and switches to the next neighbor. If a neighbor does not receive a DATA frame, it replies to the

sender a CTS with the sequence number being expected when the sender sends it an RTS, then the sender will retransmit the DATA frame with that sequence number. BMW is advantageous in its simplicity; however, it can introduce arbitrary long delays for DATA frame receptions. For example, in Figure. 1 (a), when the sender transmits DATA frame 1 to receiver 1 and all receivers except receiver $n$ obtain the DATA frame, receiver $n$ needs to wait for each receiver $i$ ($i = 1, 2, \cdots, n - 1$) to successfully obtain DATA frames from 1 to $i$ before it can have a chance to ask for the retransmission of DATA frame 1.

In [16], Sun et al. proposed the Batch Mode Multicast MAC (BMMM) protocol to add the reliable multicast service to the IEEE 802.11. Basically, BMMM (Figure. 1 (b)) introduces $n$ pairs of RTS/CTS frames and $n$ pairs of RAK (Request for ACK)/ACK frames for the reliable transmission of a DATA frame to $n$ receivers, with RTS and RAK being transmitted to solicit CTS and ACK respectively from each receiver. The advantages of BMMM are that (1) it does not cause arbitrary long delays and (2) as shown in [16], the number of contention phases involved to complete the reliable multicast transmissions is much less than that of BMW. Here we point out the drawback of BMMM is its high control overhead: $2n$ pairs of control frames are introduced for a single DATA frame. According to the IEEE 802.11b [10], each frame transmission involves two types of overhead at the physical layer: *physical layer preamble* (having a length of 72 bits, required to transmit at 1 *Mbps*) and *physical layer header* (having a length of 48 bits, required to transmit at 2 *Mbps*). Thus, these two types of overhead together introduce a transmission delay of 96 $\mu s$, a delay even longer than the transmission delay of a control frame itself. For example, the transmission of an ACK frame (14 bytes) only takes 56 $\mu s$ if transmitted at 2 *Mbps*. Considering both physical layer and MAC layer transmission delays, $2n$ pairs of control frames in BMMM (with RTS being 20 bytes and CTS, RAK, and ACK being 14 bytes) totally cost $632n$ $\mu s$, which is a very large overhead even for a moderate $n$.

Overlapping with our work, a new protocol called "802.11MX" that also uses the busy tones to realize multicast reliability was recently proposed by Gupta et al. [7]. Though we propose the same idea, our employments of this idea in designing reliable MAC protocols have fundamental differences. First, 802.11MX is targeted as an extension to the current IEEE 802.11, having the advantage of being compatible with the existing standard. However, we believe the introduction of the busy tones can radically change the behavior of

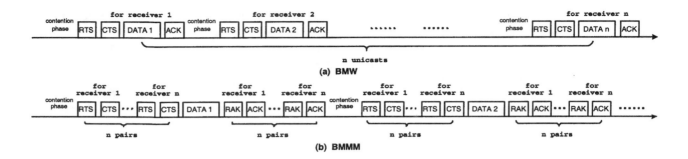

Figure 1: BMW and BMMM.

the IEEE 802.11, so we design our protocol as an independent protocol that completely exploits the busy tones to prevent the data frame collisions, discarding the virtual carrier-sense mechanism used by IEEE 802.11. As a result, RMAC can provide higher reliability and is more efficient. Second, 802.11MX is a receiver-initiated protocol (using negative feedback), while RMAC is a sender-initiated protocol (using positive feedback). Being receiver-initiated, 802.11MX is efficient in processing feedback, but its sender cannot know whether full reliability is achieved, since a receiver will not enter the state to send a negative feedback if it fails to receive the initial transmission request from the sender. On the other hand, being sender-initiated, RMAC is capable of achieving full reliability, but it has to pay the price of dealing with multiple feedback. So here we note that, happening in parallel, 802.11MX and RMAC embody different directions in applying the busy tone idea to implement a reliable multicast MAC protocol.

## 3. The RMAC protocol

### 3.1. Background on busy tone

A "busy tone" is a signal transmitted over a narrow-bandwidth channel with enough spectral separation from the data channel [1]. With a narrow bandwidth, a busy tone can only be sensed as being present or non-present. The busy tone mechanism has been used in several research efforts such as [18], [20], and [8]. It is believed that the temporal overhead caused by control can be considerably saved with the separation of data channel and control channel.

Basically, all the three aforementioned approaches ([18], [20], and [8]) use busy tones to address the hidden-node or the exposed-node problems in the wireless environment for the unicast scenario. In [18], Tobagi and Kleinrock first introduced the busy tone mechanism to eliminate the hidden-node problem in a wire-

less environment with a central station. Their basic idea is that during the reception of a frame, the receiver turns on the busy tone; other nodes that sense the busy tone cannot start new transmissions, thus the frame reception at the receiver will experience no collision. In [20], Wu and Li extended the same usage of busy tone into the wireless environment with time-slotted channels to address the hidden-node problem. Recently in [8], Haas and Deng proposed the Dual Busy Tone Multiple Access (DBTMA) protocol, which solves both the hidden-node and the exposed-node problems in a wireless ad hoc environment by using two busy tones: the transmit busy tone ($BT_t$) and the receive busy tone ($BT_r$). Concretely, they let the receivers set up $BT_r$ while receiving data frames, thus solving the hidden-node problem; on the other hand, they let the senders set up $BT_t$ while transmitting RTS frames, thus other nodes can sense $BT_t$ instead of the data channel to avoid sending RTSs simultaneously. By using both $BT_r$ and $BT_t$, DBTMA completely exempts nodes from the operation of sensing the data channel, such that the exposed-node problem is also solved.

### 3.2. Basic ideas of RMAC

Due to the inefficiency of reliable multicast in the IEEE 802.11 based solutions described in Section 2, we propose to utilize busy tones to realize multicast reliability at the MAC layer. We altogether introduce two busy tones (each with its own narrow-bandwidth channel) in our RMAC protocol: the Receiver Busy Tone (RBT) and the Acknowledgment Busy Tone (ABT).

RBT is used the same way as suggested by Tobagi and Kleinrock to eliminate the hidden-node problem, and we extend its use to multiple receivers, letting every receiver set up the RBT during the data reception. Using RBT to address the hidden-node problem is superior to the the RTS/CTS mechanism in that (1) the data reception is guaranteed to be collision-free, thus the number of retransmissions is greatly reduced; recall that the RTS/CTS mechanism cannot completely avoid frame collisions; and (2) RBT exempts nodes from maintaining the Network Allocation Vector (NAV) variable needed in the RTS/CTS mechanism, thus simplifying the protocol.

ABT is used to acknowledge the data frames, i.e., the receiver will reply an ABT to the sender if a data frame is correctly received. Using ABT to do acknowledgments has the following two advantages over using frames: (1) an ABT does not need the physical layer preamble and header prepended to a frame as described in Section 2, so it can be very short, only having to be long enough to be detected; (2) an ABT does not suffer from collisions or bit errors.

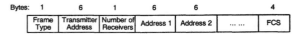

Figure 2: MRTS format. *Number of Receivers* contains the number of receiver MAC addresses included. *FCS (Frame Check Sequence)* contains a 32-bit cyclic redundancy code.

To distinguish ABTs from multiple receivers, we introduce a new control frame called Multicast Request-To-Send (MRTS) to lay down an order for the receivers to respond. With a variable length, the MRTS frame (Figure. 2) mainly contains a sequence of the MAC addresses of the intended receivers. The order of the receivers' appearance in this sequence is used by the receivers to reply ABTs to the sender. The advantage of our condensing control information into a single MRTS frame, instead of using multiple control frames as BMMM does, is that the control frame overhead is greatly reduced: (1) each receiver only costs six bytes in MRTS instead of costing an entire control frame and (2) the physical layer overhead associated with the frame transmissions is also reduced accordingly. Note that in our protocol, MRTS is also used in the case of reliable unicast or broadcast by putting the unicast receiver address or all the one-hop neighbor addresses into the MRTS address sequence.

## 3.3. RMAC description

The RMAC protocol is a comprehensive MAC protocol that provides both reliable and unreliable transmission services to the upper layer, with each service covering three modes of communications: unicast, multicast, and broadcast. We call the two services in RMAC *Reliable Send* and *Unreliable Send* respectively. Specifically, *Reliable Send* implements the reliable transmission of data frames to the receivers with the use of

MRTS, RBT, and ABT; and *Unreliable Send* only performs one transmission of data frames without any recovery mechanism. We distinguish the data frames in *Reliable Send* and *Unreliable Send* into "reliable data frames" and "unreliable data frames" by labeling the frames with different frame types.

**3.3.1. Procedure of the *Reliable Send* service.** The *Reliable Send* service provides reliability to three modes of communications: unicast, multicast, and broadcast. All three modes essentially follow the same procedure. The only difference is that the MRTS frame includes the MAC address(es) of the unicast receiver, the multicast receivers, or the entire one-hop neighbors in its address sequence depending on the communication mode. The symbols and timers used in the procedure description are as follows:

- $n$: the number of intended receivers.
- $\tau$: the maximum one-way propagation delay. We set $\tau = 1\,\mu s$, assuming that the maximum radio range is less than $300\,m$.
- $\lambda$: the duration needed to detect a busy tone. We use $\lambda = 15\,\mu s$ according to the Clear Channel Assessment time in physical layer of IEEE 802.11b [10].
- $T_{wf\_rbt}$: a timer set up by the sender right after the MRTS transmission. The RBT should be detected before the expiration of this timer. Its period $|T_{wf\_rbt}|$ is set to $2\tau + \lambda$.
- $T_{wf\_rdata}$: a timer set up by the receiver right after the reception of the MRTS frame. The first bit of the data frame should arrive before its expiration. Its period $|T_{wf\_rdata}|$ is set to $2\tau + \lambda$.
- $i$: the location index of a receiver in the address sequence in MRTS. For example, the first receiver in the sequence has $i = 0$, and the second receiver has $i = 1$, etc.
- $l_{abt}$: the duration of ABT. We set $l_{abt} = 2\tau + \lambda$, which guarantees the ABT detection in consideration of propagation delay.
- $T_{tx\_abt}$: the timer used to trigger the response of ABT at the receiver. Its period $|T_{tx\_abt}|$ is set to $i \times l_{abt}$.
- $T_{wf\_abt}$: the timer used to sense an ABT at the sender. Its period $|T_{wf\_abt}|$ is set to $2\tau + \lambda$.

The procedure of the *Reliable Send* service is as follows (Figure. 3):

1. The sender transmits an MRTS to the intended receivers.

2. Upon receiving the MRTS, a node checks whether its MAC address is contained in the address sequence of MRTS. If it is, it memorizes its index $i$ in the address sequence and turns on the RBT.

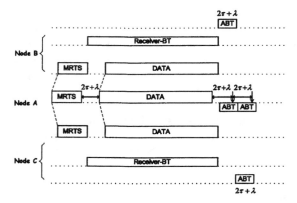

Figure 3: Procedure of the *Reliable Send* service. In this figure, Node A is the sender, which has two multicast receivers, Node B and Node C.

3. After the transmission of MRTS, the sender begins to sense the RBT and sets up the timer $T_{wf\_rbt}$. Upon the expiration of $T_{wf\_rbt}$, if there is RBT detected during the timer period, the sender transmits the reliable data frame; otherwise, the sender enters the backoff procedure to retransmit.

4. When turning on the RBT, a receiver also sets up the timer $T_{wf\_rdata}$. If the first bit of data frame arrives before $T_{wf\_rdata}$ expires, it cancels the timer and the RBT continues until the end of the data frame reception; otherwise, it stops the RBT upon the expiration of $T_{wf\_rdata}$. If the data frame is correctly received, the receiver sets up the timer $T_{tx\_abt}$ with $|T_{tx\_abt}| = i \times l_{abt}$. When $T_{tx\_abt}$ expires, it turns on the ABT for the duration of $l_{abt}$.

5. After the data frame transmission, the sender sets up the timer $T_{wf\_abt}$, which will cycle $n$ times. During each timer period, an ABT from one of the receivers is sensed. At the end, if all the intended receivers are found to have responded with an ABT, the transmission is successful. Otherwise, the sender constructs a new MRTS frame which contains those receivers for which no ABTs are detected and enters the backoff procedure to retransmit.

Note in this procedure: (1) there is a limit for the number of retransmissions associated with a frame; if this limit is exceeded, the frame will be dropped; (2) the reason for setting $|T_{wf\_rbt}| = 2\tau + \lambda$ is because $2\tau + \lambda$ is the minimum time required to guarantee the detection of all the possible arriving RBTs, since the duration for detecting a busy tone is $\lambda$ and the maximum round trip delay for a receiver is $2\tau$.

**3.3.2. Procedure of the *Unreliable Send* service.** The

*Unreliable Send* service simply performs one transmission of the unreliable data frame over the data channel. It covers the three modes of communications (unicast, multicast, and broadcast) by setting the receiver address in the unreliable data frame to the intended unicast address, multicast address, or broadcast address respectively. The procedure of the *Unreliable Send* service is as follows:

1. The sender senses both data channel and RBT channel. If both are idle, the sender transmits the unreliable data frame. If either channel is busy, the sender enters the backoff procedure; when the backoff procedure comes to the end, it transmits the frame.

2. During the transmission of the unreliable data frame, the sender keeps sensing the RBT channel. If RBT is sensed, it will simply abort the current transmission, which is to guarantee the collision-free data reception in the *Reliable Send* service.

3. Upon receiving an unreliable data frame, a node checks the receiver address in the frame. If the frame is destined for the node in cases of unicast, multicast, or broadcast, the node accepts it; otherwise, the node discards it.

## 4. Evaluation

RMAC is implemented and evaluated under Glo-MoSim [22], a widely-used simulator in wireless networking research. Our evaluation on RMAC focuses on two aspects: *reliability* and *overhead*, with each aspect evaluated under several metrics. For each metric, we also compare RMAC with BMMM [16]. The reasons for choosing BMMM for comparison are that (1) BMMM is the most recent reliable multicast MAC protocols (except 802.11MX) known by us and (2) Ref. [16] has shown that BMMM is better than BMW in terms of reliability and efficiency. To make comparison under the same environment, we also implemented BMMM under GloMoSim.

### 4.1. Experiment setup

**4.1.1. Experiment environment.** We use multi-hop wireless ad hoc networks to evaluate RMAC and BMMM, since the busy tone mechanism or the RTS/CTS/DATA/ACK scheme can affect nodes that are within two hops of each other. The networks used in our experiments contain 75 nodes randomly placed on a $500\,m \times 300\,m$ plain. The radio propagation range for each node is $75\,m$ and the transmission bit rate at each node is $2\,Mbps$.

To test the performance of RMAC and BMMM, we use a multicast application that forwards packets along

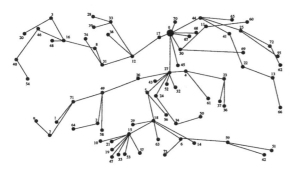

Figure 4: An tree topology example.

a single source tree to all the 75 nodes in the network. At each hop, the packets are transmitted from the parent node to the child nodes using the reliable multicast services provided by RMAC or BMMM at the MAC layer. The single source tree is obtained by a simplified version of the BLESS protocol [14]. In this simple protocol, the node with ID=0 is always designated as the root node (which is to be used as the source node by the multicast application); and the tree is formed by only one operation — a periodical one-hop broadcast of the routing messages. This broadcast is performed by the unreliable services of RMAC or BMMM accordingly.

An example of the tree topologies formed in our experiments is shown in Figure. 4. Our experiments on such tree topologies show that (1) the average and 99 percentile number of hops to root in these tree topologies are 3.87 and 10 respectively and (2) the average and 99 percentile number of children for a non-leaf node are 3.54 and 9 respectively.

**4.1.2. Experiment method.** To evaluate RMAC in both static and mobile networks, we altogether conduct experiments in the following three scenarios: (1) *Stationary:* no node is moving. (2) *Moving at speed 1:* nodes are moving under the random waypoint model [2]. In random waypoint, a node first randomly selects a destination from the physical plain, then moves toward that destination in a speed uniformly distributed between MIN-SPEED and MAX-SPEED. After reaching the destination, the node stays there for INTER-PAUSE time. In this scenario, we use MIN-SPEED = 0 $m/s$, MAX-SPEED = 4 $m/s$, and INTER-PAUSE = 10 $s$. (3) *Moving at speed 2:* nodes are also moving under the random waypoint model. However, the parameters are different: we use MIN-SPEED = 0 $m/s$, MAX-SPEED = 8 $m/s$, and INTER-PAUSE = 5 $s$.

In each of the scenario above, we conduct eight kinds of experiments with the source node transmitting pack-

ets at rates of 5, 10, 20, 40, 60, 80, 100, 120 packets/second respectively. All these packets have a length of 500 bytes and in each experiment the source node transmits 10000 packets in total. To make the experimental results independent of the network topologies, in each kind of experiments, we conduct a set of ten experiments with different random node placements (i.e., different tree topologies). And in the plots to be presented, each data point except the maximum and 99 percentile values represents the average result of a set of ten experiments. To compare RMAC with BMMM, each set of ten experiments is done for RMAC and BMMM respectively with identical node placements.

## 4.2. Reliability

In the reliability evaluation of RMAC, we measured data on the following two metrics: the packet delivery ratio and the packet drop ratio.

**4.2.1. The packet delivery ratio.** We define the packet delivery ratio (denoted by $R_{delv}$) in a multicast experiment as the total number of packets received by all nodes versus the total number of packets supposed to be received by all nodes. Figure. 5 plots $R_{delv}$ in each kind of our experiments for RMAC and BMMM respectively. From this figure we see that (1) when the nodes are stationary, $R_{delv}$ for RMAC is very close to 1, showing that RMAC can achieve very high reliability for a stationary network and (2) when the nodes are moving, $R_{delv}$ for RMAC drops to around 0.75, but it remains much higher than that of BMMM. Here we note that the apparent decrease of reliability in mobile networks is because nodes move out of range of the previous parents. Since the MAC layer is only responsible for one-hop communications, the issue of out-of-range nodes should be dealt with by upper layer protocols.

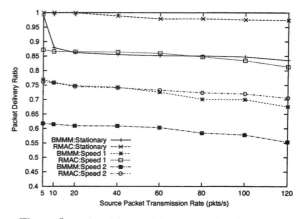

Figure 5: Packet delivery ratio in RMAC and BMMM.

**4.2.2. The packet drop ratio.** We define the packet drop ratio (denoted by $R_{drop}$) at a node as the total number of packets dropped by that node versus the total number of packets to be transmitted by that node. Recall that in *Reliable Send*, the only reason for a receiver to lose a packet is because its sender drops the packet after certain number of failed transmissions, so packet drop has a direct relationship with reliability.

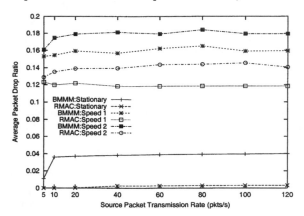

Figure 6: Average packet drop ratio in RMAC and BMMM.

Figure. 6 plots the average $R_{drop}$ over all non-leaf nodes in the network in each kind of our experiments. Note that for a leaf node, since it forwards no packets, it drops no packets. From Figure. 6 we see that (1) when the nodes are stationary, RMAC has very few packet drops: e.g., under the highest source traffic rate 120 pkts/sec, the $R_{drop}$ for a non-leaf node is only about 0.0032 on average; (2) when the nodes are moving, the average $R_{drop}$ in RMAC increases considerably, since mobility often causes that nodes cannot be reached by their previous parents until the new parents are discovered; (3) for all the three scenarios, RMAC has less packet drops than BMMM.

## 4.3. Overhead

In the overhead evaluation of RMAC, we measured data on the following two metrics: the packet retransmission ratio and the transmission overhead ratio.

**4.3.1. The packet retransmission ratio.** Retransmission is a major overhead involved in the ARQ-based reliable networking protocols. To evaluate the retransmission overhead of RMAC, we use a metric called the "packet retransmission ratio" (denoted by $R_{retx}$), which is defined as the total number of retransmissions conducted by a node versus the total number of packets to be transmitted by that node.

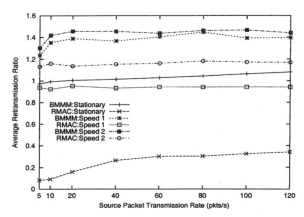

Figure 7: Average packet retransmission ratio in RMAC and BMMM.

Figure. 7 plots the average $R_{retx}$ over all non-leaf nodes in the network in each kind of our experiments. From this figure we see that (1) when the nodes are stationary, $R_{retx}$ for a non-leaf node in RMAC on average is no more than 0.32, a very low retransmission ratio for the multicast scenario; (2) when the nodes are moving, $R_{retx}$ for RMAC increases to around 1; however, RMAC still has less $R_{retx}$ than BMMM. In general, the above results reflect that the protection of RBT really helps to reduce the number of retransmissions.

**4.3.2. The transmission overhead ratio.** We define the "transmission overhead ratio" (denoted by $R_{txoh}$) at a node as the total time spent in transmitting/receiving control frames and checking ABTs versus the total time spent in transmitting the reliable data frames. $R_{txoh}$ can be similarly defined for BMMM, except that no time spent in checking ABTs is included.

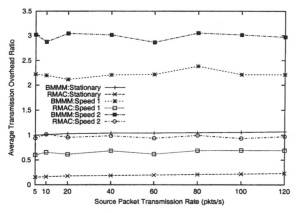

Figure 8: Average transmission overhead ratio in RMAC and BMMM.

Figure. 8 plots the average $R_{txoh}$ over all non-leaf

nodes in the network in each kind of our experiments. From this figure we see that (1) when the nodes are stationary, $R_{txoh}$ for RMAC increases slowly from 0.16 to 0.23, which is quite low compared with $R_{txoh}$ for BMMM (ranging from 1.0 to 1.1) and (2) when the nodes are moving, the values of $R_{txoh}$ for both RMAC and BMMM rise significantly, but RMAC can still achieve an $R_{txoh}$ below 1.1. It can be concluded from this figure that the use of MRTS and ABT generates very limited transmission overhead.

## 5. Conclusion

In this paper, we presented a new MAC protocol for wireless ad hoc networks called RMAC that implements the reliable multicast service at the MAC layer using the busy tone mechanism. In addition, we generalize RMAC into a comprehensive protocol that supports both reliable and unreliable services for all the three modes of communications: unicast, multicast, and broadcast. Evaluation is done on RMAC and comparison is also made with BMMM, an example of other ARQ-based reliable multicast MAC protocols. The evaluation and comparison showed that RMAC achieves high reliability with very limited overhead.

## References

[1] D. Bertsekas and R. G. Gallagher. *Data Networks, Second Edtion.* Prentice-Hall, 1992.

[2] C. Bettstetter. Mobility modeling in wireless networks: categorization, smooth movement, and border effects. *ACM SIGMOBILE Mobile Computing and Communications Review,* 5(3):55–66, 2001.

[3] E. Bommaiah, M. Liu, A. McAuley, and R. Talpade. AMRoute: Ad hoc multicast routing protocol. Internet Draft, IETF, Aug 1998.

[4] D. Eckhardt and P. Steenkiste. Improving wireless LAN performance via adaptive local error control. In *Proc. IEEE ICNP'98,* 1998.

[5] J. Garcia-Luna-Aceves and E. Madruga. The core-assisted mesh protocol. *IEEE Journal on Selected Areas in Communications,* 17:1380–1394, Aug 1999.

[6] M. Gerla, C.-C. Chiang, and L. Zhang. Tree multicast strategies in mobile multihop wireless networks. *ACM/Balzter Mobile Network and Applications Journal,* 4:193–207, 1999.

[7] S. Gupta, V. Shankar, and S. Lalwani. Reliable Multicast MAC Protocol for Wireless LANs. In *Proc. IEEE ICC'03,* May 2003.

[8] Z. Haas and J. Deng. Dual busy tone multiple access (DBTMA): A multiple access control scheme for ad hoc networks. *IEEE Transactions on Communications,* 50:975–985, June 2002.

[9] IEEE. Part 11: Wireless LAN Medium Access Control (MAC) and Physical Layer (PHY) Specifications. ANSI/IEEE Std 802.11, 1999 Edition, 1999.

[10] IEEE. Part 11: Wireless LAN Medium Access Control (MAC) and Physical Layer (PHY) Specifications: Higher-Speed Physical Layer Extension in the 2.4 GHz Band. ANSI/IEEE Std 802.11b, 1999 Edition, 1999.

[11] J. Kuri and S. K. Kasera. Reliable multicast in multi-access wireless LANs. *Wireless Networks,* 7(3):359–369, 2001.

[12] S. Lee, W. Su, and M. Gerla. Ad hoc wireless multicast with mobility prediction. In *Proc. IEEE ICCCN'99,* Boston, MA, Oct. 1999.

[13] S. Lee, W. Su, J. Hsu, M. Gerla, and R. Bagrodia. A performance comparison study of ad hoc wireless multicast protocols. In *Proc. IEEE INFOCOM'00,* Tel Aviv, Israel, Mar. 2000.

[14] P. Levis and D. Culler. Mate: A virtual machine for tiny networked sensors. In *Proc. ACM Conference on Architectural Support for Programming Languages and Operating Systems,* pages 207–218, San Jose, CA, Oct. 2002.

[15] E. M. Royer and C. E. Perkins. Multicast operation of the ad hoc on-demand distance vector routing protocol. In *Proc. ACM MobiCom'99,* pages 207–218, Seattle, WA, Aug. 1999.

[16] M. T. Sun, L. Huang, A. Arora, and T. H. Lai. MAC layer multicast in IEEE 802.11 wireless networks. In *Proc. the International Conference on Parallel Processing (ICPP) 2002,* 2002.

[17] K. Tang and M. Gerla. MAC reliable broadcast in ad hoc networks. In *Proc. IEEE MILCOM 2001,* pages 1008–1013, Oct. 2001.

[18] F. Tobagi and L. Kleinrock. Packet switching in radio channels: Part II —the hidden terminal problem in carrier sense multiple-access and the busy-tone solution. *IEEE Transactions on Communications,* Com-23:1417–1433, Dec 1975.

[19] D. Towsley, J. Kurose, and S. Pingali. A comparison of sender-initiated and receiver-initiated reliable multicast protocols. *IEEE Journal on Selected Areas in Communications,* 15:398–406, Apr. 1997.

[20] C. Wu and V. Li. Receiver-initiated busy-tone multiple access in packet radio networks. In *Proc. ACM SIGCOMM'87,* pages 336–342, 1987.

[21] C. Wu and Y. Tay. AMRIS: A multicast protocol for ad hoc wireless networks. In *Proc. IEEE MILCOM'99,* Atlantic City, NJ, Nov 1999.

[22] X. Zeng, R. Bagrodia, and M. Gerla. GloMoSim: a library for parallel simulation of large-scale wireless networks. In *Proc. The 12th Workshop on Parallel and Distributed Simulations,* Alberta, Canada, May 1998.

# On-Demand Location-Aided QoS Routing in Ad Hoc Networks *

Chun Huang, Fei Dai, and Jie Wu
Department of Computer Science and Engineering
Florida Atlantic University
Boca Raton, FL 33431

## Abstract

*With the development and application of position devices, location-based routing has received growing attention. However, little study has been done on QoS routing with the aid of location information. The existing location-based routing approaches, such as flooding-based routing schemes and localized routing schemes, have their limitations. Motivated by ticket-based routing, we propose an on-demand location-aided, ticket-based QoS routing protocol (LTBR). Two special cases of LTBR, LTBR-1 and LTBR-2, are discussed in detail. LTBR-1 uses a single ticket to find a route satisfying a given QoS constraint. LTBR-2 uses multiple tickets to search valid routes in a limited area. All tickets are guided via both location and QoS information. LTBR has lower overhead compared with the original ticket-based routing, because it does not rely on an underlying routing table. On the other hand, LTBR can find routes with better QoS qualities than traditional location-based protocols. Our simulation results show that LTBR-1 can find high quality routes in relatively dense networks with high probability and very low overhead. In sparse networks, LTBR-2 can be used to enhance the probability of finding high quality routes with acceptable overhead.*

## 1 Introduction

An ad hoc network is a temporary network composed of wireless mobile hosts (nodes), where wireless links are setup or destroyed whenever one node moves in or out of transmission ranges of other nodes. Routing in ad hoc networks is challenging due to this dynamic nature. Existing routing protocols in ad hoc networks are either *proactive* or *on-demand*. Proactive protocols pre-compute and store paths to all possible destinations for each node in a routing table, and during the routing process, each intermediate node simply sends data to the next hops based on the

routing table. On-demand protocols compute the path upon each route request. Proactive protocols have low routing discovery overhead, however, they need to maintain routing information. On-demand protocols avoid the huge expense of updating routing tables, however, as flooding is always used to search paths, the routing overhead is high.

*Quality-of-Service (QoS) routing* has been motivated by multimedia applications, such as voice channels, live videos, and document transfer. QoS routing selects paths based on QoS metrics to satisfy specific requirements, such as end-to-end delay, delay jitter, bandwidth, and packet loss probability. These metrics can be classified into three classes [11]: additive, multiplicative, and concave. QoS routing is much more complicated than regular routing in that routing under multiple constraints is needed under many circumstances. Wang and Crowcroft [11] have shown that the problem of finding a path subject to constraints on two or more additive and multiplicative metrics is NP-complete. In ad hoc networks where the network topology changes arbitrarily, QoS routing is even more challenging.

With rapid development of positioning techniques, location-aided routing has received wide attention. Previous study shows that location information can effectively assist the routing process [1, 5, 6, 8, 9, 10]. However, existing location-based routing protocols have their limitations. Both localized algorithms and flooding-based algorithms have either unsatisfactory success rate or undesirable routing overhead. In addition, previous solutions are designed to deal with best-effort data traffic, giving no consideration to optimizing the QoS properties. The ticket-based probing scheme (TBP) [3] is a novel heuristic approach for solving QoS routing problems. In TBP, a ticket represents a permission for searching a path. The total number of tickets is determined at the start of routing and controls the exploring scope in the routing process. TBP has been shown to achieve as high a success rate as flooding, while incurring as low a routing overhead as single path routings. However, TBP is a proactive protocol where periodical update is applied to maintain the routing tables, which makes it deficient and unscalable.

*This work was supported in part by NSF grants CCR 0329741, ANI 0073736 and EIA 0130806. Contact address: jie@cse.fau.edu

Motivated by location-aided routing and ticket-based routing, we present a new QoS routing protocol called location-aided ticket-based routing (LTBR). By combining the low overhead nature of location-based routing and QoS awareness of ticket-based routing, LTBR can find high quality routes with relatively low maintenance overhead. Two special cases of LTBR are examined in this paper. LTBR-1 uses a single ticket to find a route that satisfies a given QoS constraint. This single ticket is guided by a location and QoS aware metric called progress-over-cost (i.e., progress toward the destination in unit cost). At each step of the probing, the ticket is relayed from one node to the next node that maximizes the progress-over-cost. In addition, a technique called backward checking is used to further enhance the QoS measure of a discovered route. LTBR-2 allows limited ticket duplication. That is, each node can send at most two copies of a received ticket to the selected successors. The two successors are selected within a certain range of directions, so that the dissemination of the tickets is restrained in a small area. On the other hand, the angle between two successors is larger than a minimum value, so as to avoid excessive redundancy within the searching area. Simulation results show that LTBR-1 has similar success ratio and overhead to single path location based protocols, such as GEDIR and MFR, and the found paths have better QoS measures. LTBR-2 has similar overhead and path quality to location based protocols using limited flooding, such as LAR, and achieves higher success ratio.

Contributions of this paper include the new location and QoS aware metric that guides the dissemination of tickets, the backward checking mechanism that enhances the route quality, and techniques to use multiple tickets searching a limited area. The effectiveness of those mechanisms are also confirmed by the simulation study.

## 2 Related Work

**Location-based routing.** Stojmenovic [8] classified location-based routing schemes into two categories: *localized* approaches and *flooding-based* approaches.

Localized approaches are marked by single path strategy and greedy principle. In the routing process, one node always selects *one* neighbor as the successor to forward the message, based on the locations of the destination, the current node and the neighbors. MFR (Most Forward within Radius) [10], GEDIR (GEographic DIstance Routing) [9] and DIR (Compass Computing) [6] are three typical protocols. In MFR, a node always sends the packet to the neighbor with the greatest progress. In GEDIR, the packet is sent to the neighbor which is the closest to the destination. In DIR, a node selects a neighbor, such that the angle constructed by the selected neighbor, the source and the destination will be minimized.

Flooding-based approaches are marked by a flooding-based strategy, where messages are flooded through the whole network area or a portion of the network. LAR (Location-Aided Routing) [5] and DREAM (Distance Routing Effect Algorithm For Mobility) [1] are two flooding-based protocols. LAR has two schemes. In LAR1, messages are sent to neighbors within the request zone, which is defined as the minimum rectangle that contains the source and the expected zone, a circular area centered at the destination with radius $v(t_1 - t_0)$, where $v$ is the velocity. In LAR2, messages are sent to neighbors which are closer to the destination than the current node. In DREAM, a direction range is selected at the source and every intermediate node, in such a way that the probability of finding the destination in this range is higher than a given threshold, and only neighbors of the current node within such direction range will receive the message.

The localized approach has the advantage of low routing overhead, but it cannot achieve a satisfactory success rate under some circumstances, such as in sparse networks. The flooding-based approach has relatively higher success rate. However, it is accompanied by high routing overhead. Besides, LAR1, LAR2 and DREAM do not have competitive performances in sparse networks, where it is not uncommon that the neighbors of a node are out of the predefined request zone or the direction range. Furthermore, in LAR1 and DREAM, the request zone or the directional range is primarily determined by the mobility of the destination. Other factors, such as the likelihood that intermediate nodes may deviate from this area, are ignored. This reduces the possibility of finding paths under certain circumstances. For example, when the destination is still, the direction range in DREAM will be a line segment connecting the source and the destination. Similarly, in LAR1, if the destination is still and has the same $x$ or $y$ coordinate with the source, the request zone also becomes a line segment. Overall, there is no existing location-based routing protocol that can achieve satisfactory performance in both low routing overhead and high success rate.

Boukerche et al [2] proposed using location information to reduce the flooding cost in on-demand route discovery processes. When the route request message for source $s$ arrives at an intermediate node $v$, the angle $\angle svx$ will be calculated for each neighbor $x$. Only neighbors with the angle $\angle svx$ larger than a given *screening angle* are selected as successors. The number of successors can be reduced significantly with a larger screening angle. However, this approach still selects many successors in dense networks, and the selection of successors is not guided by the destination location.

**Ticket-based probing.** *Ticket-based probing scheme* (TBP) [3] is a distributed routing scheme to solve two QoS routing problems. One is the delay-constraint least-cost routing problem (referred to as the DCLCR problem), which is to find a path that satisfies the delay constraint and has the least cost among all qualified paths. Another one is the bandwidth-constraint least-cost routing problem (referred as the BCLCR problem), which is to find a path that satisfies the bandwidth constraint and has least cost among all qualified paths. In TBP, an imprecise state model is first set up based on the distance vector scheme, then end-to-end state information for all destinations is stored and periodically updated in each node's routing table. For example, to solve DCLCR problem, node $i$ keeps (*next-hop*, $D_i(d)$, $\Delta D_i(d)$) for each destination $d$, where *next-hop*, $D_i(d)$, $\Delta D_i(d)$ respectively represent the next hop, the end-to-end delay and expected maximum change of delay of the least-delay path from $i$ to $d$. In the routing process, $D_i(d) + \Delta D_i(d)$ and $D_i(d) - \Delta D_i(d)$ are respectively used to estimate the worst and best expected end-to-end delay from $i$ to $d$.

For a route request to node $d$ with delay constraint $D$, source $s$ first determines total number of tickets, $N_0$, by the following rules: request is rejected if the possibility to find a feasible path is too low (i.e., $D < D_s(d) - \Delta D_s(d)$); $N_0$ is set to a small constant if such possibility is high enough (i.e. $D > D_s(d) + \Delta D_s(d)$). Otherwise, $N_0$ is set to a value between 1 and a constant such that for a more stringent QoS requirement, a larger $N_0$ is assigned. Then $s$ distributes $N_0$ tickets among its neighbors in a way such that a neighbor with lower estimated end-to-end delay to the destination will be given more tickets. Then, $s$ sends a probe with assigned number of tickets to each selected neighbor. Each probe contains information of the QoS route request and the path the ticket travels along. Any node receiving a probe will distribute its received tickets among the neighbors in the same way as $s$, except it finds the ticket violates the QoS constraints. Thus a probe arriving at the destination contains a path that satisfies the QoS constraints. Note that, at anytime in the routing process, the total amount of tickets contained in all probes for this request is $N_0$.

TBP is one of the few routing protocols that can achieve a high success ratio while producing low routing overhead. However, TBP is a proactive protocol where the routing relies on the pre-computed QoS state information, which is expensive to be maintained. Therefore, TBP is not scalable.

# 3 Protocol Overview

## 3.1 System model

We focus on QoS routing where an additive metric such as delay is used. Let $d(l)$ be the QoS metric of a link $l$ and $\bigoplus$ the additive operation, the QoS measure of path $p = (l_1, l_2, \ldots, l_n)$ is $d(p) = d(l_1) \bigoplus d(l_2) \bigoplus \ldots \bigoplus d(l_n)$. For example, when delay is used as the QoS metric, $d(l_i) \bigoplus d(l_j) = d(l_i) + d(l_j) + c$. $c$ is the constant processing time

at each node. To simplify the discussion, $c$ is assumed to be 0. A QoS routing request is a triple $Q(s, d, D)$, where $s$ is the source, $d$ is the destination, and $D$ is a QoS constraint. A QoS routing protocol accepts such a request and finds a path $p = (s = l_1, l_2, \ldots, l_n = d)$ such that $d(p) \leq D$.

For simplicity, we assume that each node in the network is aware of its geographical location. Each node $v$ knows its neighbor set $N(v)$ and locations of its neighbors. In on-demand routing protocols, it is a challenging task for each node to obtain and maintain the location information of other nodes. Several proactive solutions exist for this *location management problem*. DREAM [1] maintains a location table at each node via controlled flooding. GLS (Grid Location Service) [7] and DLM (Distributed Location Management) [12] have location servers to answer location queries.

In our protocol, we use a simple on-demand location management scheme similar to the route discovery process in DSR [4]. When the location information of the destination is needed, the source broadcasts a location query message. On receiving the location query, the destination sends a location reply message back to the source. In order to reduce the flooding overhead, each node maintains a location cache that contains a list of known locations, and issues a location query only when the demanded location is missing in the location cache. Two techniques in DSR, expanding ring search and reply with cache, can be used to further reduce the overhead. The location information is also piggypacked in each normal packet for location cache update. In the following discussion, we assume the source and intermediate nodes in the QoS routing process know the location of the destination, and this location information is accurate enough to guide the route search.

## 3.2 Location-aided ticket-based routing

We propose location-aided ticket-based routing (LTBR), an on-demand and localized QoS routing protocol that combines location-based routing and ticket-based routing. In LTBR, a ticket is a special control message for searching QoS paths. A ticket contains the information of the QoS routing request and traversed path. In the routing process, one ticket is originally generated at the source and sent to neighbors selected by certain ticket assignment rules. Any intermediate node receiving a ticket either ignores it or sends tickets to successors selected in the same way as the source. A ticket will be forwarded until reaching the destination, or stopped at an intermediate node if it violates the QoS constraints. A ticket arriving at the destination indicates the success in finding a path.

The routing mechanism of LTBR resembles the ticket-based routing process in TBP [3], with two differences: (1) LTBR uses location information to guide ticket forwarding

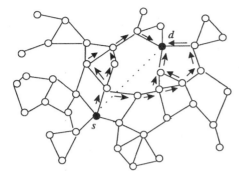

**Figure 1. Location-aided ticket-based routing.**

and does not need the underlying routing table in TBP; (2) LTBR allows issuing multiple tickets in the intermediate nodes to improve the success rate with controllable overhead. As shown in Figure 1, in the routing process for source $s$ to destination $d$, each intermediate node uses certain ticket assignment rules to select successors. The selection is based mainly on QoS metrics of adjacent links, and locations of the destination $d$, current node, and neighbors of the current node. By such rules, the tickets are guided toward the destination. Hopefully one or more tickets will arrive at the destination after exploring different paths.

The routing process can be described briefly as follows. Upon QoS routing request $Q(s, d, D)$, the source $s$ constructs a ticket that contains the QoS routing request and traversed path, and sends it to one or more neighbors selected by certain *ticket assignment rules*. An intermediate node $v$ receiving a ticket $t$ for $Q$ will first check whether QoS constraints are violated and ignore it if they are. If $t$ is the first ticket $v$ receives for $Q$, $v$ selects successors and forwards $t$ to all of the successors after adjusting the traversed path information in the ticket.

When destination $d$ receives the first ticket for $Q$, it waits for a period of time to receive all possible tickets for $Q$. If at least one received ticket fulfills the QoS requirements, $d$ picks one ticket $t_1$ from all received tickets which has the best QoS measure, constructs a route reply $r$ and sends it to the source. The route reply contains field *returnPath*, which is copied from reversed $t_1.traversedPath$ and guides the reply route to the source. Any node receiving route reply $r$ updates the remaining part of $r.returnPath$ with the path information stored in the optimal ticket, and relays it to the next hop along $r.returnPath$. If a route reply is not received by the source after a certain period of time, this routing process is viewed failed.

The effectiveness (i.e., success ratio) and efficiency (i.e., routing overhead) of LBTR is determined by the ticket assignment rule that decides the number and selection of suc-

cessors in forwarding tickets. We focus on two ticket assignment schemes: one-ticket LBTR where a single ticket is used for each QoS request, and two-ticket LBTR where each intermediate node (including the source) can send at most two tickets to two neighbors.

## 4  Special Cases

### 4.1  One-ticket LTBR

One-ticket LTBR (LTBR-1) is a single path routing protocol, where at each step at most one successor is selected. LTBR-1 resembles GEDIR and MFR in that every node selects a successor based on the location information. However, with two enhancements, a hybrid metric called *progress-over-cost* and an optimization mechanism called *backward checking*, it improves QoS properties of the found paths significantly, which is confirmed by our simulation results.

---

**Algorithm 1** ASSIGN-ONE-TICKET $(u, v, d)$

---

1: **if** $d \in N(v)$ **then**
2:     **return** {d}
3: **else**
4:     $N_1(v) \leftarrow N(v) - \{u\}$
5:     **if** $N_1(v) \neq \emptyset$ **then**
6:         $x_1 \leftarrow$ BEST$(v, N_1(v), d)$
7:         **return** {$x_1$}
8:     **else**
9:         **return** $\emptyset$

---

Algorithm 1 describes the ticket assignment rule of LTBR-1. When the source or an intermediate node $v$ has a ticket to destination $d$, it first checks if $d$ is in its neighbor set $N(v)$. If it is, the ticket is sent directly to the destination (steps 1–2). If $v$ has at least one neighbor other than the predecessor $u$ ($u$ is empty if $v$ is the source), it selects the "best" neighbor $x_1$ as its successor and forwards the ticket to $x_1$; otherwise no successor is selected, and the ticket is dropped (steps 4–9). $v$'s selection of the "best" successor from the set of candidates $N_1(v)$ ($N(v)$ by excluding predecessor $u$) with respect to the destination $d$ is based on the hybrid metric described in the next subsection.

### 4.2  A location and QoS aware metric

In localized location-based routing protocols, every intermediate node selects the successor by applying greedy principle on a certain metric. In LTBR, a metric called progress-over-cost is used, which combines the consideration for both location and QoS metrics. Given the current node $v$, destination $d$, and $v$'s neighbor $x$, the *geographic progress* $p(v, x, d)$ of successor $x$ is the projection of line $vx$ onto line $vd$. For example, in Figure 2,

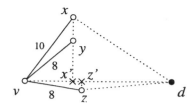

**Figure 2. Progress-over-cost.**

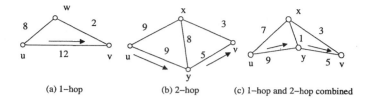

(a) 1-hop     (b) 2-hop     (c) 1-hop and 2-hop combined

**Figure 3. Backward checking.**

$p(v, x, d) = p(v, y, d) = |vx'|$ and $p(v, z, d) = |vz|$. The progress-over-cost of successor $x$ is defined as

$$p_d(v, x, d) = \frac{p(v, x, d)}{d(v, x)}$$

where $d(v, x)$ is the additive QoS metric of link $(v, x)$.

Progress-over-cost is easy to understand. By viewing the QoS metric as the cost we must pay to move to the destination, the 1-hop progress/cost ratio can be considered as the progress toward the destination in unit cost. Naturally, neighbors with greater progress/cost ratio are preferred. In Figure 2, node $v$ has three neighbors $x$, $y$, and $z$. Since $p_d(v, x, d) < p_d(v, y, d) < p_d(v, z, d)$, $z$ is most preferred in selecting successor for $v$. In Algorithm 1, BEST $(v, N_1(v), d)$ simply returns the node $x$ in $N_1(v)$ with the maximum progress-over-cost $P_d(v, x, d)$.

### 4.3 Backward checking

Backward checking is a technique to find paths with better QoS properties. Consider a QoS routing request $Q(u, v, 11)$ in Figure 3 (a). Suppose $u$ selects $v$ as the only successor. The routing fails, although there exists a path $(u, w, v)$ that satisfies the QoS constraint. It fails because node $u$ knows only $d(u, v)$ and $d(u, w)$ but not $d(w, v)$ when it makes the decision. However, the failure could be avoided by doing a simple check when the ticket arrives at $v$, which has knowledge of $d(w, v)$. We propose the 1-hop backward checking technique as follows. Each ticket memorizes neighbor set $N(u)$ of the last traversed node $u$. After a ticket arrives at a successor $v$, $v$ checks if there is a node $w \in N(u) \cap N(v)$, such that $u \to w \to v$ has less QoS measure than path $u \to v$. If such a node $w$ is found, it adjusts the traversed path of the ticket by replacing $u \to v$ with $u \to w \to v$. If multiple nodes exist, select one with the best QoS metric. In order to increase the probability of finding a path with better QoS property, 2-hop backward checking can also be used. That is, each ticket contains neighbor sets $N(u')$ and $N(u)$ of the last two traversed nodes $u$ and $u'$, and the successor $v$ also checks a better path $(u', w, v)$ that has a better QoS property than the traversed path $(u', u, v)$.

Figure 3 (a) illustrates the 1-hop backward checking. When ticket $t$ arrives at $v$, $v$ finds that path $(u, w, v)$ has a smaller QoS measure, and adjusts $t$'s traversed path by replacing $(u, v)$ by $(u, w, v)$. Figure 3 (b) illustrates the 2-hop backward checking. After ticket $t$ travels from $u$ to $y$ to $v$, $B$ finds that path $(u, x, v)$ is better than path $(u, y, v)$, and adjusts $t$'s traversed path by replacing $(u, y, v)$ by $(u, x, v)$. Figure 3 (c) gives a more complicated example. $u$ first selects $y$ as the only successor and sends it ticket $t$. When $t$ arrives at $y$, $y$ changes the path in $t$ from $(u, y)$ to $(u, x, y)$ by applying 1-hop backward checking. Then $y$ forwards $t$ to its successor $v$. When $t$ arrives at $v$ carrying path $(u, x, y, v)$, $v$ changes path to $(u, x, v)$ by applying 2-hops backward checking.

Backward checking can effectively make up for the weaknesses of localized routing. As the successors are selected based on the knowledge of 1-hop neighborhood, the decision may be "shortsighted". Backward checking examines multiple paths while traversing only one path, and makes better decisions based on a broader view beyond its 1-hop neighborhood. Backward checking can be also applied in other localized routing protocols such as GEDIR and MFR.

### 4.4 Two-ticket LTBR

Two-Ticket LTBR (LTBR-2) lies between flooding and single path routing, where at most two successors are allowed to be selected at each step. LTBR-2 uses an extra ticket at each step, thus the routing process could explore more paths, and both the success ratio and QoS properties could be enhanced. It has been observed that the effect of using a second ticket is significant in sparse networks. The ticket assignment algorithm of LTBR-2 (Algorithm 2) selects at most two successors, and has two implementation parameters $\alpha$ and $\beta$ that control the directions of the ticket dissemination.

The first parameter $\alpha$ controls the $\angle xvd$, the angle between the destination $d$ and the successor $x$, with respect to the current node $v$. A neighbor $x$ satisfying $\angle xvd \leq \alpha$ is called a *preferred neighbor*. Usually, only preferred neighbors are considered in ticket assignment. Non-preferred neighbors are considered only when the preferred neighbors

**Algorithm 2** ASSIGN-TWO-TICKETS $(u, v, d, \alpha, \beta)$

1: **if** $d \in N(v)$ **then**
2:     **return** $\{d\}$
3: **else**
4:     $N_1(v) \leftarrow \{i \mid i \in N(v) \wedge \angle ivd \le \alpha\}$ - $\{u\}$
5:     **if** $N_1(v) = \emptyset$ **then**
6:         $x_1 \leftarrow \text{BEST}(v, N_1(v), d)$
7:         $N_2(v) \leftarrow \{j \mid j \in N_2(v) \wedge \angle x_1 vj > \beta\}$
8:         **if** $N_2(v) \ne \phi$ **then**
9:             $x_2 \leftarrow \text{BEST}(v, N_2(v), d)$
10:             **return** $\{x_1, x_2\}$
11:         **else**
12:             **return** $\{x_1\}$
13:     **else** {if the preferred neighbor set is empty}
14:         $N_1(v) \leftarrow N(v) - \{u\}$
15:         **if** $N_1(v) \ne \emptyset$ **then**
16:             $x_1 \leftarrow \text{BEST}(v, N_1(v), d)$
17:             **return** $\{x_1\}$
18:         **else**
19:             **return** $\emptyset$

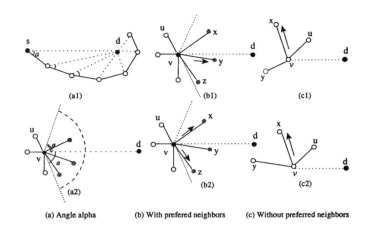

**Figure 4. Ticket assignment in LTBR-2.**

are unavailable. For example, the three gray nodes in Figure 4 (a2) are node $v$'s preferred neighbors. Using such a parameter is based on one assumption. That is, a good path (the one with good QoS measure) from node $s$ to $d$ is not far away from line $sd$. Such a path has smaller hop counts than a path which has traversed far from line $sd$, and usually has smaller end-to-end QoS measure. Therefore, by limiting the exploring scope to a small area around line $sd$, we can find good paths with relatively low overhead. It is also observed that, if at each step the successor $x$ satisfies $\angle xvd \le \alpha$, the whole exploring scope of the routing process will be limited to a small area around $sd$, as shown in Figure 4 (a1).

The second parameter $\beta$ controls the $\angle x_1 vx_2$, the angle between the first successor $x_1$ and the second successor $x_2$. When selecting $x_2$, we expect $\angle x_1 vx_2$ to be greater than a proper threshold $\beta$, so that the exploring scope of the two tickets will not share a large common area. Thus, their combined exploring scope is large and the possibility of finding a good path is high. Theoretically, a large $\alpha$ allows a node to send tickets to neighbors in a wide range, and a large $\beta$ allows a node to split the tickets into two different directions thus a large scope of the network area can be explored. Therefore, large $\alpha$ and $\beta$ increase the success ratio, as well as produce high routing overhead. In dense networks, relatively small $\alpha$ and $\beta$ should be used to minimize overhead. In sparse networks, large $\alpha$ and $\beta$ are necessary for a high success ratio.

The ticket assignment rules of LTBR-2 are as follows: (1) If the destination $d$ is a neighbor of the current node $v$', $d$ is the only successor. (2) If $v$ has no neighbor except the predecessor $u$, no successor will be selected. (3) If $v$'s preferred neighbor set $N_1(v)$ is not empty, $v$ picks the preferred neighbor $x_1$ with the best metrics as the first successor. If $v$

has other preferred neighbors satisfying $\angle x_2 vx_1 > \beta$, $v$ selects the best $x_2$ as the second successor. (4) If $v$'s preferred neighbor set is empty, the best non-preferred neighbor is selected as the only successor.

Figure 4 gives examples for this algorithm, where node $d$, $v$, $u$ are respectively the destination, the current node and the predecessor. Figure 4 (b) shows the scenarios when the preferred neighbor set is not empty and $\beta = 60^\circ$. In Figure 4 (b1), when $y$ is selected as the first successor, no other successor is selected since $\angle xvy$ and $\angle zvy$ are less than $\beta$. In Figure 4 (b2), when $x$ is selected first, $z$ is also selected since $\angle zvx$ is greater than $\beta$. Figure 4 (c) shows the scenarios when the preferred neighbor set is empty and $\beta = 60^\circ$. In this case, only one successor $(x)$ will be selected, whether the angle between two non-preferred neighbors is larger than $\beta$, (as in Figures 4 (c1)) or not (as in Figures 4 (c2)).

## 5 Simulation

We have developed a simulator that implements various routing protocols, including Flooding (FLD), LTBR-1 (LTB1), LTBR-2 (LTB2), GEDIR (GDR), MFR, LAR1, and LAR2. We conduct the simulations in static ad hoc networks. Each network is randomly generated by deploying 500 nodes in a $60 \times 60$ area following the uniform distribution. All nodes in the network have the same transmission range $r$. Each wireless link is assigned a random QoS metric within $(3, 21)$. All protocols are simulated with the same set of QoS routing requests. To eliminate the disturbance on evaluation from the definitions of QoS constraints (i.e., if the QoS constraints are set too tight, all routing protocols may fail, and vice versa), we let all route requests have unlimited QoS constraints.

Among implemented protocols, Flooding uses no location or QoS information to guide the dissemination of tickets. LTBR-1 and LTBR-2 use progress-over-cost in selecting successors to forward tickets. GEDIR, MFR, LAR1 and LAR2 use location information only. The following performance measures are compared: (1) $SuccRa$: $\frac{100n}{n_0}$, where $n$ is the number of successful routings in a certain protocol, and $n_0$ is the success number in Flooding. (2) $QoSMea$: the average end-to-end QoS measure of the found paths. (3) $MsgSnt$: the average number of messages sent per routing process. (4) $MsgRec$: the average number of messages received per routing process. (5) $AvgHop$: the average hop number of found paths. The simulations are repeated until 95% confidence intervals of all average values are within ±5%.

**LTBR vs. Flooding.** We first compare LTBR with several existing protocols. As shown in the following table, compared with Flooding, LTBR-1 achieves high success ratio with very low overhead (in terms of MsgSnt and MsgRec) in dense networks ($r = 6$). In sparse networks ($r = 4$), LTBR-2 has a high success ratio, while its overhead is still one magnitude lower than Flooding. Flooding can always find the optimal path, but the quality of the found paths (in terms of QoSMea and AvgHop) are very close for all three protocols. The only drawback of LBTR-1 is that it has a low success ratio in sparse networks. Since LBTR-1 has the lowest overhead, we suggest using LBTR-1 in dense networks and LBTR-2 in sparse networks. The selection of $\alpha$ and $\beta$ in LTBR-2 are different in different networks, as will be discussed later in this section.

|        | $r = 6$ | | | $r = 4$ | | |
|--------|-----|------|------|------|------|------|
|        | FLD | LTB1 | LTB2 | FLD | LTB1 | LTB2 |
| SuccRa | 100 | 98   | 99   | 100  | 38   | 92   |
| QoSMea | 51  | 63   | 55   | 93   | 104  | 97   |
| MsgSnt | 499 | 9    | 56   | 449  | 11   | 144  |
| MsgRec | 6142| 9    | 105  | 2169 | 11   | 253  |
| AvgHop | 9   | 9    | 9    | 11   | 11   | 11   |

**LTBR-1 vs. GEDIR and MFR.** The following table compares the performance of LTBR-1 with two single path protocols GEDIR and MFR. All three protocols have similar success ratio and overhead. On the other hand, paths found by LTBR-1 have better (lower) QoS measures than the other two protocols. Obviously, using the QoS-aware metrics and backward checking in LTBR-1 increases the chances of finding "high quality" paths.

|         | $r = 6$ | | | $r = 4$ | | |
|---------|-----|-----|------|-----|-----|-----|
|         | GDR | MFR | LTB1 | GDR | MFR | LTB |
| SuccRa  | 98  | 98  | 98   | 38  | 40  | 38  |
| QoSMea  | 98  | 98  | 63   | 131 | 130 | 105 |
| MsgSnt  | 7   | 7   | 9    | 10  | 10  | 11  |
| MsgRec  | 7   | 7   | 9    | 10  | 10  | 11  |
| AvgHops | 7   | 7   | 9    | 10  | 10  | 11  |

**LTBR-2 vs. LAR.** We compare LTBR-2 with two location-based protocols using limited flooding: LAR1 and LAR2.

As shown in the following table, LTBR-2 has lower overhead than LAR in dense networks, and higher success ratio in sparse networks. The quality of the found paths are close for different protocols. In our simulation, only limited flooding is used in both LAR1 and LAR2; that is, the failure of finding a valid route will not trigger a global flooding.

|        | $r = 6$ | | | $r = 4$ | | |
|--------|------|------|------|------|------|------|
|        | LTB2 | LAR1 | LAR2 | LTB2 | LAR1 | LAR2 |
| SuccRa | 99   | 75   | 99   | 84   | 24   | 55   |
| QoSMea | 55   | 58   | 53   | 125  | 128  | 125  |
| MsgSnt | 59   | 84   | 175  | 97   | 75   | 62   |
| MSgRec | 112  | 918  | 1142 | 172  | 348  | 187  |
| AvgHop | 9    | 9    | 9    | 14   | 14   | 14   |

**$\alpha$ and $\beta$ in LTBR-2.** Now we check the effects of several parameters that affect the performance of LTBR. The following tables show the effect of two parameters $\alpha$ and $\beta$ in LTBR-2 in (1) dense networks ($r = 6$)

| $\alpha$ | 60 | 90 | 90 | 135 | 135 | 135 | 180 | 180 | 180 |
|-----------|-----|-----|-----|-----|-----|-----|-----|-----|-----|
| $\beta$   | 30 | 30 | 60 | 30  | 60  | 90  | 30  | 60  | 90  |
| SucRa    | 99  | 99  | 99  | 100 | 100 | 100 | 100 | 100 | 100 |
| QoSMea   | 60  | 58  | 59  | 58  | 59  | 60  | 58  | 59  | 61  |
| MsgSnd   | 51  | 67  | 83  | 70  | 98  | 155 | 70  | 100 | 177 |
| MsgRec   | 94  | 126 | 157 | 133 | 186 | 289 | 132 | 188 | 327 |
| AvgHop   | 9   | 10  | 10  | 10  | 10  | 10  | 10  | 10  | 10  |

and (2) sparse networks ($r = 4$)

| $\alpha$ | 60  | 90  | 90  | 135 | 135 | 135 | 180 | 180 | 180 |
|-----------|-----|-----|-----|-----|-----|-----|-----|-----|-----|
| $\beta$   | 30  | 30  | 60  | 30  | 60  | 90  | 30  | 60  | 90  |
| SuccRa   | 46  | 63  | 64  | 78  | 82  | 84  | 81  | 89  | 93  |
| QosMea   | 125 | 121 | 121 | 120 | 121 | 121 | 121 | 121 | 123 |
| MsgSnd   | 30  | 45  | 47  | 63  | 76  | 87  | 75  | 112 | 204 |
| MsgRec   | 47  | 77  | 82  | 113 | 136 | 154 | 137 | 200 | 357 |
| AvgHop   | 13  | 14  | 14  | 14  | 14  | 14  | 14  | 14  | 14  |

Simulation results show that, in dense networks, LTBR-2 achieves desirable success ratio and QoS properties of discovered paths for all listed parameter combinations. In sparse networks, there is not an ideal combination of $\alpha$ and $\beta$. The selection must be made based on specific requirements. $(180^o, 90^o)$ is the best choice for seeking best success ratio. When the message overhead is also a concern, $(135^o, 60^o)$, $(135^o, 90^o)$ or $(180^o, 60^o)$ are better choices. Through this section, we set $(\alpha, \beta)$ to $(75^o, 30^o)$ in networks with $r \geq 6$, $(135^o, 30^o)$ when $r = 5$, and $(180^o, 90^o)$ when $r \leq 4$.

**Backward checking.** The following table compares the average QoS measures of the found paths using different routing protocols with backward checking (C) or without (N). Column R is the reduced ratio $((N-C)/N)$.

|      | $r = 6$ | | | $r = 5$ | | | $r = 4$ | | |
|------|-----|-----|------|-----|-----|------|-----|-----|------|
|      | N   | C   | R    | N   | C   | R    | N   | C   | R    |
| GDR  | 98  | 71  | 0.28 | 129 | 100 | 0.23 | 130 | 107 | 0.18 |
| MFR  | 98  | 71  | 0.28 | 128 | 100 | 0.22 | 129 | 107 | 0.17 |
| LTB1 | 71  | 63  | 0.11 | 105 | 94  | 0.11 | 116 | 104 | 0.10 |
| LTB2 | 59  | 55  | 0.07 | 96  | 90  | 0.06 | 132 | 125 | 0.05 |

Simulation results show that, backward checking does improve QoS properties of found paths. Note that, the improvement is higher in networks with higher densities. The improvement in non-QoS-aware routing protocols, such as GEDIR and MFR, is greater than that in LTBR. The improvement for LTBR-1 is also greater than LTBR-2. This is because the paths found by LTBR already have quite good QoS properties. In LTBR-2, the routing process has already searched multiple paths, leaving less room for improvement.

**All enhancements.** At last we evaluate the benefit of three proposed enhancements: progress-over-cost, backward checking and the ticket-based parallel routing scheme. The following table shows reduced ratios of the average QoS measure when these enhancements are applied to GEDIR. Columns (PoC) and (BkChk) are the results when progress-over-cost and backward checking are separately applied. Column (Both) described the results when both of them are applied (equivalent to LTBR-1). Column (ALL) describes the results when all the three enhancements are applied (equivalent to LTBR-2).

| $r$ | PoC | BkChk | Both | All |
|---|---|---|---|---|
| 7 | 0.32 | 0.31 | 0.40 | 0.48 |
| 6 | 0.28 | 0.28 | 0.36 | 0.44 |
| 5 | 0.15 | 0.23 | 0.28 | 0.36 |
| 4 | 0.11 | 0.18 | 0.20 | 0.26 |
| 3 | 0.06 | 0.12 | 0.13 | 0.14 |

Simulation results show that the quality of found paths are improved by using progress-over-cost, backward checking, or parallel routing. The effect is more significant in dense networks. In addition, those three enhancements can be combined together to achieve the best result.

## 6 Conclusion

In this paper, we have proposed the generic mechanism of location-aided, ticket-based QoS routing (LTBR) and its two special cases, LTBR-1 and LTBR-2. Our approach differs from the traditional location-based routing protocols in that two important enhancements to localized QoS routing, the location-and-QoS-aware metric and backward checking, are introduced, and a parallel routing scheme is implemented. Our approach differs from the original ticket-based probing scheme in its on-demand feature. The tickets are dynamically generated based on timely position and QoS information; no routing table maintenance is needed. Simulation results show that, with the two enhancements, LTBR-1 beats existing localized location-based routing protocols in finding a path with better QoS properties. LTBR-2 achieves performance close to flooding with lower routing overhead in networks with any density. Moreover, in LTBR-2, by adjusting parameter $\alpha$ and $\beta$, tradeoff is allowed between the success ratio and the routing overhead.

Currently, our focus is the performance of LTBR in static networks, and routing with single additive QoS metric. It would be interesting to find out if LTBR still maintains its high success ratio in mobile ad hoc networks, where the destination location is inaccurate due to node movement. Our future work includes the performance evaluation of LTBR in dynamic networks and location-aided routing with multiple QoS constraints. In addition, an adaptive routing scheme will be explored, where the number of tickets issued at each node is adjusted dynamically to balance the success ratio and routing cost under different network density and mobility situations.

## References

[1] S. Basagmo, I. Chlamtac, V. R. Syrotiuk, and B. A. Woodward. A distance routing effect algorithm for mobility (DREAM). *Proceedings of MOBICOM*, pages 76–84, 1998.

[2] A. Boukerche and S. Rogers. GPS query optimzation in mobile and wireless ad hoc networks. *Proceedings of IEEE Symposim on Computers and Communications*, pages 198–203, 2001.

[3] S. Chen and K. Nahrstedt. Distributed quality-of-service routing in ad hoc networks. *IEEE Journal Selected Areas in Communication*, 17(8):1488–1505, Aug 1999.

[4] D. B. Johnson, D. A. Maltz, Y. C. Hu, and J. Jetcheva. The dynamic source routing protocols for mobile ad hoc networks (DSR). *Internet Draft*, Feb. 2002.

[5] Y. B. Ko and N. H. Vaidya. Location-aided routing (LAR) in mobile ad hoc networks. *Proceedings of MOBICOM*, pages 66–75, 1998.

[6] E. Kranakis, H. Singh, and J. Urrutia. Compass routing on geometric networks. *Proceedings 11th Canadian Conf. Computational Geometrym*, Aug 1999.

[7] J. Li, J. Jannotti, D. S. J. D. Couto, D. R. Karger, and R. Morris. A scalable location service for geographic ad hoc routing. *Proceedings of MOBICOM*, pages 120–130, March 2000.

[8] I. Stojmenovic. Position-based routing in ad hoc networks. *IEEE Communications Magazine*, 39(2):142–148, Feb. 2001.

[9] I. Stojmenovic and X. Lin. GEDIR: Loop-free location based routing in wireless networks. *Proceedings IASTED Int'l Conf. Parallel and Distriuted Computing and Systems*, pages 1025–1028, Nov. 1999.

[10] H. Takagi and L. Kleinrock. Optimal transmission ranges for randomly distributbed packet radio terminals. *IEEE Transactions on Communications*, 32(3):246–257, 1984.

[11] Z. Wang and J. Crowcroft. Quality-of-service routing for supporting multimedia applications. *IEEE Journal on Selected Areas in Communications*, 14(7):1228–1234, Sep. 1996.

[12] Y. Xue, B. Li, and K. Nahrstedt. A scalable location management scheme in mobile ad-hoc networks. *Proceedings LCN 2001. 26th Annual IEEE Conference on Local Computer Networks, 2001*, pages 102–111, 2001.

# PDAgent: A Platform for Developing and Deploying Mobile Agent-enabled Applications for Wireless Devices

Jiannong Cao, Daniel C.K. Tse, and Alvin T.S. Chan
*Internet and Mobile Computing Lab*
*Department of Computing*
*Hong Kong Polytechnic University*
*Hung Hom, KLW, Hong Kong*

## Abstract

*Mobile agents (MAs) can support mobile computing by carrying out tasks autonomously for a mobile user temporarily disconnected from the network. In this paper we describe PDAgent, a lightweight and highly portable platform for developing and deploying mobile agent-enabled applications on wireless handheld devices. Our approach offers the following advantages: (i) It does not require installing MA server on handheld devices and supports the adoption of any kind of mobile agent system at network hosts, while at the same time allow mobile users to have control of mobile agent activities; (ii) It supports dynamic downloading of MA-enabled applications which can be made aware of and adaptive to the user's current context, and deploying the application to perform various tasks on behalf of the user over the wired network; (iii) It requires the minimum network connectivity and cost for users to deploy their applications. PDAgent provides APIs which allow developers to build new mobile applications on top of PDAgent. Example applications have been developed for PDAgent. We will report on and discuss the results of experimental performance evaluations of PDAgent.*

*Key words: Mobile agent, mobile computing, mobile network access, wireless devices*

## 1. Introduction

Wireless handheld devices, such as cellular phones and PDAs, are becoming increasingly popular. In the past few years, many mobile computing applications have been developed for handheld devices including m-commerce, mobile office, and mobile service/information access applications. However, these applications running on mobile devices in a wireless network still suffer from limited computing, battery power and storage capability, low bandwidth, greater latency, as well as having high network connection costs.

Mobile agent technology has been proposed as one way to overcome the limitations of connectivity, latency and bandwidth [5, 4, 7]. Mobile agents can move through the network of sites to search for, filter, and process information they need to accomplish their tasks [10, 18]. They can also cooperate with each other by sharing and exchanging information and partial results, and collectively making decisions [1, 2]. Mobile agents have also been used to develop middleware for mobile computing [15].

In this paper, we focus on mobile agent support of mobile computing by carrying out tasks for a mobile user temporarily disconnected from the network. The mobile user can dispatch a mobile agent to perform these tasks autonomously over the network. Once the agent is dispatched, the user can disconnect from the network. Later on the user reconnects to the network to collect the result returned by the mobile agent. To provide this support requires a suitable MA platform and tools for mobile users to deploy mobile agents and manage their execution from wireless handheld devices.

We describe a general approach and a lightweight and highly portable platform, called *PDAgent*, for developing and deploying mobile agent-enabled applications from wireless handheld devices. Although MA platforms have been developed for small devices [11, 12, 16], our approach has a number of advantages:

(i) Most of the existing approaches to deploy mobile agents on wireless devices are bound to one specific mobile agent platform. PDAgent, however, does not require the installation of any MA server on the wireless handheld devices and supports the adaptation of any kind of mobile agent system at the network host as the underlying runtime platform. This feature makes mobile applications highly portable across handheld devices and networks with different MA servers.

(ii) It provides mobile users reliable and efficient mobile computing services in a low-bandwidth mobile network environment, with the minimum network latency and cost. In our approach, the user downloads the MA code for an application and then deploys the application by passing the code with appropriate parameters to a proxy gateway. Then the user can disconnect from the network. The gateway serves as a middle-tier to manage the mobile agent dispatched from the mobile user. It provides a more powerful processing capability that can reduce the CPU loading within the wireless devices. It also helps to provide a reliable network connection to the Internet so that when the user goes offline, it can communicate and retract the mobile agent. For interoperability, both the agent code and the parameters are encoded with XML.

(iii) It supports dynamic downloading and deployment of MA-enabled mobile applications, which can be made aware of and adaptive to the current user's context.

PDAgent's APIs provide function primitives for programming mobile agent-enabled activities, such as downloading mobile agent code, dispatching mobile agent, disposing a mobile agent, and managing the mobile agent operations. Using the APIs, the programmer can develop various new applications on the PDAgent platform.

The rest of this paper is organized as follows. Section 2 describes related work, comparing various approaches for mobile users to access information and run applications in wired networks. We also review research on mobile agent platforms adapted to handheld devices and compare them with the design of PDAgent. Section 3 presents the design of the PDAgent platform. Chapter 4 describes the implementation and performance evaluation of PDAgent with sample applications. Chapter 5 concludes the paper with the discussion of our future work.

## 2. Related work

In the past several years, researchers have been seeking efficient solutions to the problem of providing reliable Internet service to users with wireless devices. Various approaches have been proposed. The major ones as illustrated in Figure 1, including the client-server-model, client-agent server model, and mobile agent server model.

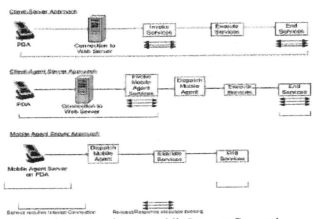

Figure 1. Approaches to mobile Internet Computing

The *Client-Server* approach makes use of the traditional Client-Server model, in which a mobile client communicates with the web-server to invoke Internet services. In this approach, the mobile user has to keep the connection with the wired network until the service is completed and the result is obtained [6].

The *Client-Agent Server* approach makes use of an Agent Server, which is a combination of a web server and a mobile agent server. The mobile user does not need to maintain the Internet. Instead, the mobile user only needs to submit the service request to the server and can then disconnect from the network. The agent server will determine and launch a mobile agent to execute the requested network services without having any interaction or communication with the mobile client. The mobile agent will later bring back the execution result and temporarily store it at the agent server. Afterwards, the mobile client can collect the execution result by reconnecting to the agent server [17]. This approach has a limitation that a mobile user is provided with only MA-based applications which must have been installed on the agent server.

The *Mobile Agent Server* approach makes use of a Mobile Agent Server installed on the mobile client device. Mobile users can program mobile agents and store them on their handheld devices. No middle-tier server is needed to launch the mobile agent application in order to access network services, assuming network sites are capable of hosting the specific forms of mobile agents. All the preprocessing can be done on the handheld device without being connected to the Internet. The connection is needed only when the mobile client wants to dispatch or retract the mobile agent [11, 12, 16].

Compared with the client-server and client-agent approaches, the Mobile Agent Server approach provides a better way for mobile access to Internet services because it allows the mobile user to store and launch mobile agent-enabled applications, and reduces network connection time and the amount of message-passing between clients with servers. Reducing network connection time also decreases the possibility of network errors. However, developing and installing a mobile agent platform on wireless handheld devices is not an easy job; there are limitations on storage capacity and processing power. Another major problem with this approach is the difficulty of achieving interoperability between the proprietary platform on the handheld device and the mobile agent servers located in network sites.

In this paper we propose an alternative approach called the *Agent-Proxy-Server* approach, as illustrated in Figure 2. In this approach, no mobile agent server needs to be installed on the handheld device. Instead, it can be adapted to use any kind of mobile agent server supported by hosts in the target service network (e.g., either Intranet or a VPN over the Internet). A gateway acts as the middle-tier service bridge. The code for mobile agent-enabled applications are downloaded and stored in the handheld devices. The mobile user can launch the application by deploying the code with necessary parameters, both are encoded in XML for interoperability, to the gateway, which accepts and interprets the mobile agent code, wraps it into a mobile agent in a form supported by the network sites, and dispatches the mobile agent on behave of the mobile user. The handheld device acts as remote server controller, with the capability to perform all the mobile agent functions and to administer the mobile agent server to manage the mobile agent operations.

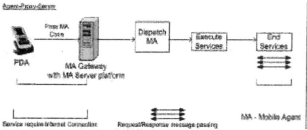

Figure 2. Overview of Agent-Proxy-Server
Approaches

Our approach has the advantages of the previous approaches while at the same time solves both problems of resource limitations and dependency on any specific proprietary mobile agent system. More importantly, it provides a potential to address MA interoperability problem by facilitating a standard MA code format (e.g., specified using XML) which can be understood and interpreted by gateways and different MA servers. In addition, by providing a mechanism for downloading and deployment of MA-enabled applications, it supports the development of context-aware and adaptive mobile applications. MA programs can be designed in a way that can be parameterized, either manually or automatically, to reflect the current user's context. The mobile user can pre- or dynamically download the MA code to be used in a particular context, and further customize the code by specifying appropriate parameters, before launch the application. This approach has been advocated recently by researchers because it is believed that applications may have valuable information that could enable the middleware system on the wired network to deliver services more efficiently [3]. We observe that for most mobile applications, the MA code is of a size ranging from 1KB to 8KB, and can be compressed before download into the wireless device. Therefore, it should not cause big problems in terms of storage capacity and network latency.

## 3. Design of PDAgent

Based on the proposed Agent-Proxy-Server approach described in the last section, we have developed a lightweight and highly portable platform, called PDAgent. Figure 3 shows the operating environment of PDAgent. There are several important issues to consider in the

design of PDAgent:

- *Mobility* – the mobile user can access network services in different locations from all wireless devices that support the PDAgent platform.
- *Being lightweight* – The PDAgent platform should be able to run on resource-constrained devices.
- *Adaptability* – the PDAgent platform should support mobile agents that can run on the different kinds of mobile agent servers located in network sites.
- *Network Connectivity* – Wireless handheld devices are not permanently connected to the network and can often be disconnected for long periods of time. Even if the wireless device is connected, the connection often suffers with low bandwidth and high latency. The PDAgent platform should provide mobile users with reliable and efficient network access minimizing network connection. It should also minimize the size of information packages transmitted during the running of applications when interacting with network services.

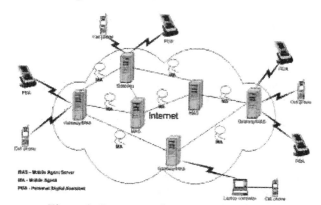

Figure 3. System environment of PDAgent

The overall system structure of PDAgent consists of three main parts: a *PDAgent Platform* on wireless devices, the *Gateway*, and the *Mobile Agent Server*. The Mobile Agent Server can be any kind of Mobile Agent Server located on a high-end desktop in a network site. Figure 4 shows the architectures of the PDAgent system and the Gateway.

The PDAgent Platform is the main component, which provides functions to mobile users for downloading of mobile agent code, internal mobile agent administration, and agent launching and management. The components of the PDAgent Platform are separated into UI and System API. UI is the interface via which mobile users submit service requirements and administer mobile agent activities both internally and externally. System API separates the a background process running inside the PDAgent platform that facilitates tasks such as dispatching mobile agents, disposing mobile agent and managing internal Database.

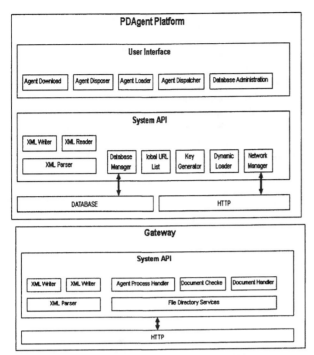

Figure 4. System Architecture of PDAgent Platform and Gateway

Gateway is a middle-tier communication and operation bridge. It is responsible for transferring information between the mobile agent platform located in wireless devices and the mobile agent server located in Gateway.

To support interoperability, XML is used to encode the MA code and the parameter/result data transferred between the PDAgent platform on handheld devices and the Gateway. The PDAgent platform also offers secure design by encrypting MA code and data during wireless transmission. As described in the next section, PDAgent implementation uses an opened source lightweight XML API called 8 for XML conversion and interpretation. The size of kXML [8] API is very small. PDAgent collects client request and converts it into XML document by using kXML API. The XML document is compressed within the wireless devices before being transferred to the gateway. This minimizes the size of the transferred packet and thus reduces the transmission time. Using simple text compression algorithms, the compression process requires only small amount of CPU time.

In the remaining part of this section, we will describe the main functions that PDAgent provides for acquiring services, and for providing reliable services and security.

### 3.1. Service Subscription

A mobile user can subscribe network services to downloading the service mobile agent code from the nearest trusted Gateway (see Figure 5). Upon downloading, the PDAgent platform will store the mobile

agent code into its database on the wireless device. Each MA code downloaded will be assigned a unique id by the platform for the purpose of authorization in later execution. Once the service agent code is present in PDAgent's database, the subscription is no longer needed.

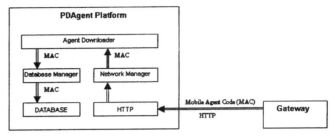

Figure 5. System Architecture of service subscription

### 3.2. Service Execution

Figure 6 shows the interactions that take place between system components when invoking a service. To deploy an application, the application interface is loaded within the wireless device. The mobile user enters service parameters using the application interface without being connected to the network. The Agent Dispatcher will collect the agent code and parameters, generate a unique key from the assigned code id, encode them into a XML document, and pass it on as a single package, called "Packed Information" (PI), to the Network Manager. The Network Manager is responsible of uploading the packed information to the Gateway through a HTTP connection.

When the Gateway receives the packed information, it will pass the information to the Agent Dispatch Handler. The Agent Dispatch Handler will separate this information into modules and pass them on to the XML Writer, Agent Handler, and Document Handler for further extraction. The XML Writer will read the xml document and parse all the user requirement parameters. The Agent Creator will generate mobile agent classes from the information if the supplied unique key is valid. The Document Creator will create different files from information for the Mobile Agent Server to collect later on. Once the document and classes are ready, the File Directory will allocate a space for storing these document and classes, and then it will signal the Mobile Agent Server to create a mobile agent from the user's uploaded classes and dispatch it to the Internet.

### 3.3. Service Result Collection

In our current design, the mobile agent will return to the Gateway where it is dispatched after the service execution is completed. The result it brings back will be wrapped in XML format. The mobile user can download the XML document from the Gateway by reconnecting to the Internet. The PDAgent platform on the wireless handheld device will extract the XML document and display it on the user interface.

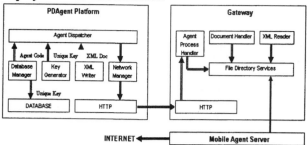

Figure 6. System Architecture of service execution

## 3.4. Information Security Management

One of the important issues that PDAgent addresses is that of providing secure information. Although implementing a comprehensive security service is beyond the scope of this paper, we have attempted to handle as much as possible security issues in developing the PDAgent platform.

First, the design of PDAgent advocates the provision of MA service code for mobile users to download from trusted gateways. This, to certain degree, will solve the traditional security problem of mobile agent. Second, data submission in PDAgent is secured since it is done without connecting to the Internet. However, the mobile user is required to send packed information to the Gateway via a HTTP connection during code dispatching and result collection. At this point, data may be stolen and/or altered. PDAgent provides security control which is based mainly on the existing Internet security model, using "Asymmetric Key Encryption" to identify the PDAgent user and encrypt the data during the dispatching process (see Figure 7). PDAgent will encrypt user's information using a public key [14] and then wrap it into XML format, generating the so called Packed Information. Once the Gateway receives the Packed Information, it will use MD5 [14] to verify whether the Packed Information is valid if so. It will then extract the mobile agent code and the mobile client's requirements by using its private key to decrypt the Packed Information.

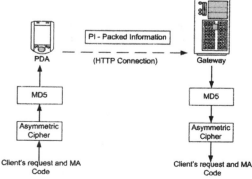

Figure 7. PDAgent's Security Model

## 3.5. High Performance Service Management

Reducing network connection time and network error is an important issue in designing the PDAgent platform. In order to provide high performance services, PDAgent executes a service mobile agent on behalf of the mobile user, thereby making use of the Gateway to reduce the network connection time. Furthermore, to ensure that communication between the wireless device and the Gateway will not affect overall operational performance, PDAgent will find the nearest Gateway for sending the Packed Information.

Initially, PDAgent will download a list of gateway addresses from the central server. This list will be used until the Round Trip Time (RTT) from the nearest gateway found in the list exceeds the pre-defined threshold. In this case, the PDAgent will request for a new address list from central server or through one the gateways.

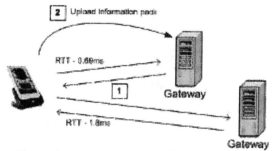

Figure 8. PDAgent's High Performance Service Management Model

As shown in Figure 8, the PDAgent platform will find the nearest Gateway by sending 1-bit data to all the gateways on the address list and calculating which Gateway takes the shortest Round Trip Time (RTT). The PDAgent platform will send the Packed Information to the Gateway with the shortest RTT. Assuming that the network bandwidth and the size of Packed Information is the same, this can minimize data transfer time, with the minimum transfer time being dependent on the shortest RTT from the wireless device to the Gateway.

## 3.6. Mobile Agent Management

The mobile user can manage the mobile agent from the PDAgent's platform on the wireless device. The concept is the same as managing mobile agent activity from a mobile agent server located on a high-end desktop. For example, the mobile user can invoke functions to clone an agent, retract an agent, dispatch an agent, and view agent status.

PDAgent provides a set of APIs that help application developers to build their own mobile applications. The API contains primitives for dispatching mobile agents, monitoring mobile agent activities, retracting mobile agents from the Internet, and disposing mobile agents. In addition to these core functions, PDAgent APIs also provide functions for internal system management and network management. System management allows the programmer to write code for generating unique keys, and reading and writing XML documents. Network management is responsible of managing all the activities that require wireless network connections from wireless devices to gateways, such as downloading mobile agent code and upload packed information.

Because PDAgent supports any kind of mobile agent system as the underlying operating environment on the gateways and on network hosts, the developer can use development tools provided by the underlying mobile agent system (e.g., Aglets, Voyager etc) to build their applications.

## 4. Implementation and evaluation of PDAgent

A prototype of PDAgent has been implemented. As with the design, the implementation is in three main parts: *PDAgent platform* on wireless devices, *Gateway,* and *Internal mobile agent manager.*

The PDAgent platform was implemented using Java CLDC / MIDP [20] in the J2ME technology [19]. J2ME is a lightweight VM supporting Java applications on wireless devices. It addresses the problems of storage capacity and low processing power on wireless devices. For XML encoding and parsing, kXML [8], a light-weigh XML API package for J2ME technology, is used. The kXML API supports DOM, DTD and generic XML parsing functions. The database located inside the PDAgent platform on the handheld devices was implemented using J2ME's Record Management System (RMS). RMS is a persistent storage mechanism modeled from a simple record-oriented database. Figure 10 shows some screen captures for PDAgent's main functions. The PDAgent platform is very lightweight. To store the PDAgent platform together with the kXML package within the wireless devices requires only 120KB storage space.

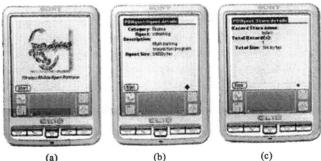

(a)        (b)        (c)

Figure 9  a. Platform Main Screen; b. Mobile Agent Management; c. Internal Database Management

A web server is installed inside Gateway for request/response though a HTTP connection. We used Tomcat as the Gateway web server because Tomcat is well known and widely used in most business sectors. The Gateway's functional component was implemented using Java Servlet.

IBM Aglets [9], a well known Java-based mobile agent system, is used as the Mobile Agent Server. It is worth noting that any mobile agent system can be used. We chose IBM Aglets because it is stable and easy to use.

To experiment and test the performance of PDAgent, we have developed several example applications, for example, Food Search Engine, E-Banking etc. The results of the experiments described here have been collected from running an "e-banking" application, in which a mobile client makes transaction requests from one bank site to another bank site.

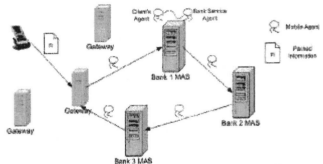

Figure 10. Runtime environment of E-Banking application

Figure 10 illustrate the runtime environment of the e-Banking application. The mobile user submits the transaction information (Figure 11b) from the wireless device without connecting to the Internet. PDAgent Platform collects client transaction information and mobile agent code wrapped as Packed Information (PI), and sends it to the nearest Gateway. The platform will also display the dispatched agent ID (Figure 11c). The Gateway will dispatch mobile agent to execute the service on behalf of the mobile client. In this application, there is a Mobile Agent Server (MAS) with a Service Agent within each bank. When the client's agent arrived at each bank, it will execute the transaction by communicating with the Service Agent. If the transaction is completed, the Service Agent will return transaction details to the client's agent, which will dispatch itself to other banks to continue the transaction execution. At last, the client's agent will return to Gateway and create a XML document containing all the transaction details. Later on, the mobile user can view the transaction result (Figure 11d) by downloading the XML document from the Gateway.

Performance is evaluated by running the same application and comparing the performance with other two approaches: a client-server and a web-based approach – accessing Internet services through a web browser on a high-end desktop. Performance metrics used are the Internet connection time and the variances of network latency.

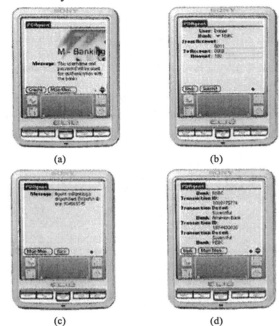

(a)                              (b)

(c)                              (d)

Figure 11 a. E-Banking Login Screen; b. Submit Transaction Information,;    c. Dispatched Mobile Agent ID; d. Obtain Transaction Results

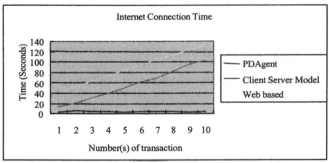

Figure 12. Internet connection times: three different approaches

We can see from Figure 12 that increasing the number of transactions submitted affects the Internet connection time for both the client-server and the web-based approaches. The Internet connection time increases roughly in a constant manner against the increasing number of transactions. This is because the mobile client has to maintain the network connection – beginning when the request for Internet services is made and until the service is completed. In contrast, PDAgent's Internet connection time is not affected by any increase in the number of transactions. This is because the user's requirement for all the transactions is submitted without

the need to connect to the network. PDAgent requires an Internet connection only when sending the PI and collecting the result documents from the Gateway. As a result, internet connection time is less than the other two approaches no matter how many transactions it makes.

An experiment was also conducted to compare the variance of latency in wireless network access and its effect on the Internet connection times of both the PDAgent approach and the client-server approach. Four test runs were conducted to determine the variance in network latency. The results are expressed in terms of the effect of variances on transaction completion times. It was observed that network latency in server request/response is the dominant factor affecting transaction completion times, assuming that the time for submitting a transaction is the same for every single trial with same number of transactions. The transaction complete time is calculated as follows:

- *Client-server-platform* - time for submitting transaction information (offline) + time for requesting server (online) + time for obtaining the server response (online)
- *PDAgent* - time for sending "Packed information" (online) + time for downloading result (online)

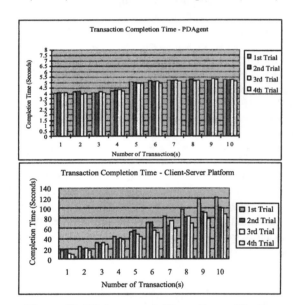

Figure 13. PDAgent and Client-Server Platform: Transaction completion times

As we can observe from Figure 13, variances in network latency in the client-server approach are greater than for PDAgent. Ideally, the completion time should be roughly the same for different trials if the network latency is stable. However, we found that as the number of transaction increased, the completion time of the client-server approach became more unstable.

The completion time of PDAgent was little affected by

network latency, which remained quite stable for all of the trials. This is because PDAgent uses a network connection only when it sends PI and downloads the result documents from the Gateway, while the client-server approach requires that many network connections be made between the client and the server before the Internet service can be completed.

## 5. Conclusions

In this paper, we have described a lightweight and highly portable platform, called PDAgent, for developing and deploying mobile agent-enabled applications from wireless devices. It has several advantages over existing solutions in providing support for the development of highly portable, efficient, and reliable mobile applications.

PDAgent provides efficient and reliable network services to mobile users with handheld devices without requiring a large amount of resources. Yet, it has low network latency and low network connectivity costs. This is achieved by providing a lightweight platform for running mobile agents that can execute services autonomously on the Internet on behalf of the user. The mobile user can go offline after submitting the execution plan to the Mobile Agent, thereby reducing network connection times. PDAgent also reduces the use of resources within wireless devices by 1) using the Gateway as a middle-tier for deploying and managing mobile agent to the Internet, and 2) compressing the agent code before storing it in the device's database. PDAgent is platform independent. It supports the adoption of different mobile agent systems located in high-end desktops on Internet sites. It is implemented using JAVA and allows developers to build PDAgent applications without being bound to a specific type of mobile devices. Performance of PDAgent has been evaluated and compared with other approaches. The results show that the PDAgent is not only lightweight but very efficient in terms of network connectivity and latency.

The work described in this paper is a part of a larger project in developing a middleware for mobile agent-enabled mobile applications. In our future work, we will further enhance the functionality and performance of the PDAgent platform as well as developing more practical applications, including m-commerce and mobile workflow management. Further experiments for performance evaluation will also be carried out.

## 6. Acknowledgment

This research is partially supported by the Hong Kong Polytechnic University under PolyU ICRG grant G-YD63 and grant A-PD54.

## 7. References

[1] J. Cao, X. Feng, J. Lu, and S. K. Das, "Mailbox-based Scheme for Mobile Agent Communications", IEEE Computer, Vol. 35, No. 9, Sept. 2002. pp. 54-60.

[2] J. Cao, X. Wang, J. Wu, "A Mobile Agent Enabled Fully Distributed Mutual Exclusion Algorithm", Proc. 6th IEEE International Conference on Mobile Agents (MA'02), Oct. 2002, Barcelona, Spain. Lecture Notes in Computer Science, Vol. 2535, pp.138-153.

[3] L. Capra, W. Emmerish, and C. Mascolo, "CARISMA: Context-Aware Reflective Middleware System for Mobile Applications", to appear in IEEE Transactions on Software Engineering, Nov. 2003.

[4] P. Dasgupta, N. Narasimhan, L.E. Moser, and P.M. Melliar-Smith, "MAgNET: Mobile Agents for Networked Electronic Trading", IEEE Trans. On Knowledge and Data Engineering, Vol. 11, No. 4, July/Aug. 1999. pp. 509-525.

[5] L. Hagen, M. Breugst, and T. Magedanz, "Impact of Mobile Agent Technology on Mobile Communications System Evolution", IEEE Personal Comm., Aug. 1998. pp.56-69.

[6] J. Jing, A. Helal, and A. Elmagarmid, "Client-Server Computing in Mobile Environments", ACM Computing Surveys, Vol. 31, No. 2, June 1999.

[7] D. Kotz and R.S. Gray, "Mobile Agents and the Future of the Internet", ACM Operating Systems Review, 33(3), Aug. 1999. pp.7-13.

[8] kXML, http://kxml.org

[9] D.B. Lange and M. Oshima, "Programming And Deploying Java Mobile Agents With Aglets", Addison Wesley, 1998.

[10] D. B. Lange and M. Oshima, "Seven Good Reasons for Mobile Agents", Communication of the ACM, Vol. 42, No. 3, March 1999. pp. 88-89.

[11] LEAP – Lightweight Extensible Agent Platform 5th Framework Project Contract: IST-1999-10211 http://leap.crm-paris.com/index.html

[12] Qusay H.Mahmoud, "MobiAgent: A Mobile Agent-based Approach to Wireless Information Systems". Proceedings of the 3rd International Bi-Conference Workshop on Agent-Oriented Information Systems, Montreal, Canada. May, 2001.

[13] C. Mascolo, L. Capra, and W. Emmerich, "Mobile Computing Middleware", Lecture Notes in Computer Science, Vol. 2497. 2002, pp.20-58.

[14] Internet RFC/STD/FYI/BCP Archives – RFC1321 http://www.faqs.org/rfcs/rfc1321.html

[15] P. Bellavista, A. Corradi, and C. Stefanelli, "Mobile Agent Middleware for Mobile Computing", IEEE Computer, March 2001. pp.73-81.

[16] Patik Mihailescu, Walter Binder and Elizabeth A. Kendall, "MAE: A Mobile Agent Platform for Building Wireless M-Commerce Applications", Proc. 8th ECOOP Workwhop on Mobile Object Systems, Málaga, Spain, June 2002.

[17] S. Papastavrou, G. Samaras and E. Pitoura, "Mobile Agents for World Wide Web Distributed Database Access", IEEE Transactions on Knowledge and Data Engineering, 12(5), pp 802-820, 2000

[18] V. A. Pham and A. Karmouch, "Mobile Software Agents: An Overview", IEEE Communications Magazine, July 1998. pp. 26-37.

[19] Java 2 Platform Micro Edition (J2ME) Technology for Creating Mobile Devices White Paper. May 19, 2000.

[20] Mobile Information Device Profile (JSR-37) JCP Specification Java 2 Platform, Micro Edition, 1.0a.

# Session 8A:
# Programming Methodologies

# Architectural Support for System Software on Large-Scale Clusters*

Juan Fernández[1,2]

[1]Departamento de Ingeniería y
Tecnología de Computadores
Universidad de Murcia
30071 Murcia (Spain)
{peinador}@ditec.um.es

Eitan Frachtenberg[2], Fabrizio Petrini[2],
Kei Davis[2] and José C. Sancho[2]

[2]CCS-3 Modeling, Algorithms, and Informatics
Computer and Computational Sciences Division
Los Alamos National Laboratory
Los Alamos, NM 87545 USA
{eitanf,fabrizio,kei,jcsancho}@lanl.gov

## Abstract

*Scalable management of distributed resources is one of the major challenges in deployment of large-scale clusters. Management includes transparent fault tolerance, efficient allocation of resources, and support for all the needs of parallel computing: parallel I/O, deterministic behavior, and responsiveness. Meeting these requirements with commodity hardware and operating systems is difficult because they were not designed to support global management of a large-scale system. In this paper we propose a small set of hardware mechanisms in the cluster interconnect to facilitate the implementation of a simple yet powerful global operating system. This system, inspired by concepts from the BSP and SIMD computational models, allows commodity clusters to grow to thousands of nodes while still retaining the usability and responsiveness of the single-node workstation. Our results on a software prototype show that it is possible to implement efficient and scalable system software using the proposed set of mechanisms.*

*Keywords: Cluster computing, cluster operating system, network hardware, debuggability, resource management, fault tolerance.*

## 1 Introduction

Although workstation clusters are a common platform for high-performance computing (HPC), they remain considerably more difficult to manage than single-node systems or symmetric multiprocessors. Furthermore, as cluster size increases, the role of the system software—essentially all of the code that runs on a cluster other than the applications—becomes increasingly more important. The system soft-

ware's main components include the communication library, resource manager, parallel file system, system monitor, and the infrastructure to implement fault tolerance. The quality of the system software not only affects application performance but also the cost of ownership of such machines.

System software design for high-performance clusters traditionally relies on an abstraction that views the network simply as a mechanism for moving information with a performance expressed by latency and bandwidth. The success of this interface relies on the implicit assumption that any performance improvement in the network is directly inherited by the system software. On the other hand, abstract interfaces may change to exploit new hardware capabilities. For example, in the last decade this basic abstract interface has been augmented to exploit distributed shared memory. A global, virtually addressed shared memory which enables remote direct memory access (RDMA) is now a common feature in networks as Infiniband [18] or Quadrics [19].

In this paper we try to answer question of *what hardware features, and thus which abstract interface, should the interconnection network provide to the system software designers?* We argue that the efficient and scalable implementation of a small set of network primitives that perform global queries and distribution of data is sufficient to support most system software and user applications. These primitives can be easily implemented in hardware with current technology and can greatly reduce the complexity of most system software. In a sense they represent the least common denominator of the various components of the cluster software, and the backbone to integrate a collection of local operating systems (OS) into a single, global OS.

This paper makes the following contributions. First, it makes the case for the importance and the potential of having these primitives for global coordination fully implemented in hardware. Second, a series of case studies shows how the system software can benefit from these primitives.

*This work is partially supported by the spanish MCYT under grant TIC2003-08154-C06-03 and the U.S. Department of Energy through Los Alamos National Laboratory contract W-7405-ENG-36.

519

We provide experimental evidence that resource management and job scheduling can can be implemented on thousands of nodes and achieve the same level of responsiveness as a dedicated workstation, without any significant increase in complexity. Finally, we describe how a popular communication library, the Message Passing Interface (MPI), can be implemented with these global coordination primitives. The proposed implementation is so simple that it can run almost entirely on the network interface card (NIC) as fast as the production-quality MPI.

The rest of the paper is organized as follows. The next section describes some of the system tasks required on clusters and the problems that need to be addressed to achieve responsive and scalable environments. Section 3 details the core primitives and mechanisms that constitute the building blocks of our proposed scalable system software. Section 4 presents several case studies and reports several experimental results obtained on our software prototype. Section 5 concludes and offers directions for future research.

## 2. Challenges in the Design of System Software

Many of today's fastest supercomputers are composed of commercial off-the-shelf (COTS) symmetric multiprocessor (SMP) servers connected by a fast interconnect. These nodes typically use commodity operating systems such as Linux to provide a hardware abstraction layer to programmers and users. These OSes are quite adequate for the development, debugging, and running of applications on independent workstations and small clusters. However, such a solution is often insufficient for running demanding HPC applications in large clusters.

Common cluster solutions include middleware extensions on top of the workstation operating system, such as the MPI communication library [22] to provide some of the functionality required by these applications. These components tend to have many dependencies and their independent designs may lead to redundancy of functionality. For example, both the communication library and the parallel file system used by the HPC applications implement their own communication protocols. Even worse, some desired features such as multiprogramming, garbage collection, or automatic checkpointing are either not supported at all or are very costly in terms of both development costs and overall performance degradation. Consequently, there is a growing gap between the services enjoyed on a workstation and those provided to HPC users, forcing many application developers to complement these services in their application. Table 1 overviews several of these gaps in terms of the basic functionality required to develop, debug, and effectively use parallel applications. Next we discuss some of the gaps in detail.

**Job launching.** Virtually all modern workstations allow simple and quick launching of jobs, thus enabling interactive tasks such as debugging sessions or visual applications. In contrast, clusters offer no standard mechanism for launching parallel jobs. Typical workarounds rely on shell scripts or custom middleware. Job launching times can range anywhere from seconds to hours and are usually far from interactive. Many solutions have been suggested, ranging from the use of generic tools such as rsh and NFS, to sophisticated programs such as RMS [9], GLUnix [12], Cplant [3], BProc [13], and SLURM [15]. However, because of their reliance on software mechanisms, with larger clusters (thousands of nodes) these systems may be expected to take many seconds or minutes to launch parallel jobs.

**Job scheduling.** In the workstation world it is taken for granted that several applications can be run concurrently using time sharing, but this is rarely the case with clusters. Most middleware used for parallel job scheduling use simple versions of batch scheduling (or gang-scheduling at best). This affects both the user's experience of the machine, which is less responsive and interactive, and the system's utilization of available resources. Even systems that support gang scheduling typically revert to relatively high time quanta to hide the high overhead costs associated with context switching a parallel job [11, 14, 23].

**Communication.** User processes running in a workstation communicate with each other using standard interprocess communication mechanisms provided by the OS. While these may be rudimentary mechanisms that provide no high-level abstraction, because of their low synchronization requirements they are adequate for serial and coarse-grained distributed jobs. Unlike these jobs, HPC applications require a more expressive set of communication tools to keep the software development effort manageable.

The prevailing communication model for modern HPC applications is message passing, where processes use a communication library to send synchronous and asynchronous messages to each other. Of these libraries, the most commonly used is MPI [22]. These libraries offer standards that facilitate portability across various cluster and MPP architectures. However, in order to improve the latency and bandwidth for single messages, much effort is required to tune these libraries to different platforms. Another problem is that these libraries offer low-level mechanisms that force the software developer to focus on implementation details, and make modeling application performance difficult. In order to simplify and abstract the communication performance of applications, various performance models have been suggested [6, 24].

**Table 1. System tasks in workstations and clusters**

| Characteristic | Workstation | Cluster |
|---|---|---|
| Job Launching | Operating system (OS) | Scripts, middleware on top of OS |
| Job Scheduling | Timeshared by OS | Batch queued or gang scheduled with large quanta (seconds to minutes) using middleware |
| Communication | OS-supported standard IPC mechanisms and shared memory | Message Passing Library (MPI) or Data-Parallel Programming (e.g. HPF) |
| Storage | Standard file system | Custom parallel file system |
| Debuggability | Standard tools (reproducibility) | Parallel debugging tools (non-determinism) |
| Fault Tolerance | Little or none | Application / application-assisted checkpointing |

**Determinism.** Serial applications are much easier to debug than their parallel counterparts: their inherent determinism makes many problems easy to reproduce. In contrast, for a large parallel program a trace of message passing may have a practically unbounded number of correct orderings; the difficulty of debugging an inherently non-deterministic, asynchronous system is exacerbated by interference by the debugging tool itself by imposing constraints on execution order (reduces non-determinism).

**Fault tolerance.** Non-determinism also makes fault tolerance using checkpointing challenging because the application is rarely known to be in a state wherein all processes and in-transit messages are synchronized. Fault tolerance on workstations is not considered a major problem and thus rarely addressed by the OS. On large clusters, however, where the high number of components results in a low mean time between failures, and the amount of computation invested in a single execution of an application can be significant, fault tolerance becomes one of the most critical issues. Here there is no standard solution available, and many of the existing solutions rely on modifying applications or introduce a considerable application slowdown [2].

## 2.1 Designing a Parallel Operating System

The design, implementation, debugging, and optimization of system middleware for large-scale clusters is far from trivial, and potentially very time- and resource consuming. System software is required to deal with one or more parallel jobs comprising thousands of processes each. Furthermore, each process may have several threads, open files, and outstanding messages at any given time. All these elements result in a large and complicated global machine state which in turn increases the complexity of the system software. The lack of global coordination is a major cause of the non-deterministic nature of parallel systems. The lack of synchronization also diminishes application performance, for example, when non-synchronized system dæmons introduce computational holes that can severely skew and impact fine-grained applications [20].

To address these issues, we promote the idea of a simple, global cluster OS that makes use of advanced network resources, just like any other HPC application. Our vision is that a cluster OS should behave like a SIMD application, performing resource coordination in lockstep. We argue that performing this task scalably and at sub-millisecond granularity requires hardware support realizable by a small set of network mechanisms. Our goal in this study is to identify and describe these mechanisms. Using a prototype system on a network that supports most of these features, we present experimental results that indicate that a cluster OS can be scalable, powerful, and relatively simple to implement. We also discuss the gaps between our proposed mechanisms and the available hardware, and suggest methods for overcoming these limitations.

## 3 Core Primitives and Mechanisms

In this section, we characterize the primitives and mechanisms that we consider essential in the development of system software for large-scale clusters. We then explain how to use these mechanisms to overcome the challenges raised in the previous section.

## 3.1 Suggested Mechanisms

The proposed architectural support consists of just three hardware-supported network primitives:

XFER-AND-SIGNAL Transfer (PUT) a block of data from local memory to the global memory of a set of nodes (possibly a single node). Optionally signal a local and/or a remote event upon completion. By global memory we refer to data at the same virtual address on all nodes. Depending on implementation, global data may reside in main or network-interface memory.

TEST-EVENT Poll a local event to see if it has been signaled. Optionally, block until it is.

COMPARE-AND-WRITE Arithmetically compare a global variable on a node set to a local value. If the condition is true on *all* nodes, then (optionally) assign a new value to a (possibly different) global variable.

Note that XFER-AND-SIGNAL and COMPARE-AND-WRITE are both atomic operations. That is, XFER-AND-SIGNAL either PUTs data to *all* nodes in the destination set (which could be a single node) or (in case of a network error) *no* nodes. The same condition holds for COMPARE-AND-WRITE when it writes a value to a global variable. Furthermore, if multiple nodes simultaneously initiate COMPARE-AND-WRITEs with identical parameters except for the value to write, then, when all of the COMPARE-AND-WRITEs have completed, all nodes will see the same value in the global variable. In other words, XFER-AND-SIGNAL and COMPARE-AND-WRITE are *sequentially consistent* operations. TEST-EVENT and COMPARE-AND-WRITE are blocking operations, while XFER-AND-SIGNAL is non-blocking. The only way to check for completion is to TEST-EVENT on a local event that XFER-AND-SIGNAL signals. These semantics do not dictate whether the mechanisms are implemented by the host CPU or by a network co-processor. Nor do they require that TEST-EVENT yield the CPU (though it may be advantageous to do so).

### 3.2 Implementation and Portability

The three primitives presented above assume that the network hardware provides global, virtually addressable shared memory and RDMA. These features are present in several state-of-the-art networks like QsNet and Infiniband and their functionality has been extensively studied [18, 19]. While the physical implementation aspects of these primitives are outside the scope of this paper, we note that some or all of them have have already been implemented in several other interconnects, as shown in Table 2. They were originally designed to improve the communication performance of user applications. To the best of our knowledge their usage as an infrastructure for system software was not explored before this work.

Hardware support for multicast messages sent with XFER-AND-SIGNAL is needed to guarantee scalability for large-scale systems. Software approaches, while feasible for small clusters, do not scale to thousands of nodes. In our case, QsNet provides hardware-supported PUT/GET operations and events so that the implementation of XFER-AND-SIGNAL is straightforward.

COMPARE-AND-WRITE assumes that the network is able to return a single value to the calling process regardless of the number of queried nodes. Again, QsNet includes a hardware-supported global query operation that allows the implementation of COMPARE-AND-WRITE.

Table 2 shows the expected performance of the mechanisms that are already implemented by several interconnect technologies. While several networks already support at least some of these mechanisms, we argue that they should become a standard part of every large-scale interconnect. We also stress that their implementation must exhibit scalability and high performance (in terms of bandwidth and latency) for them to be useful to the system software.

### Table 2. Measured/expected performance of the core mechanisms for $n$ nodes

| Network | COMPARE ($\mu s$) | XFER (MB/s) |
|---|---|---|
| Gigabit Ethernet [21] | $46 \log n$ | Not available |
| Myrinet [4, 5] | $20 \log n$ | $\sim 15n$ |
| Infiniband [18] | $20 \log n$ | Not available[1] |
| QsNet ([19]) | $< 10$ | $> 150n$ |
| BlueGene/L [1] | $< 2$ | $700n$ |

### 3.3 System Software Requirements and Solutions

Next we examine the areas where current system software is lacking and explain how the proposed mechanisms can simplify the design and implementation of practical solutions. Table 3 summarizes these arguments.

**Job Launching** The traditional approach to job launching, including the distribution of executable and data files to cluster nodes, is a simple extension of single-node job launching: data is transmitted using network file systems such as NFS, and jobs are launched with scripts or simple utilities such as rsh or mpirun. These methods do not scale to large machines where the load on the network file system, and the time it would take to serially execute a binary on many nodes, make them inefficient and impractical. Several solutions have been proposed for this problem, all focusing on software tricks to reduce the distribution time. For example, Cplant and BProc both use their own tree-based algorithm to distribute data with latencies that are logarithmic in the number of nodes [3, 13]. While more portable than relying on hardware support, these solutions are significantly slower and not always simple to implement [10].

Decomposing job launching into simpler sub-tasks makes more clear that it needs only modest effort to make the process efficient and scalable:

- Executable and data distribution are no more than a multicast of packets from a file server to a set of nodes, and can be implemented using XFER-AND-SIGNAL.

---

[1]Multicast is an optional operation in the Infiniband standard.

## Table 3. Network mechanisms usage

| Characteristic | Requirement | Solution |
|---|---|---|
| Job Launching | Data dissemination | XFER-AND-SIGNAL |
| | Flow control | COMPARE-AND-WRITE |
| | Termination detection | COMPARE-AND-WRITE |
| Job Scheduling | Heartbeat | XFER-AND-SIGNAL |
| | Context switch responsiveness | Prioritized messages / Multiple rails |
| Communication | PUT | XFER-AND-SIGNAL |
| | GET | XFER-AND-SIGNAL |
| | Barrier | COMPARE-AND-WRITE |
| | Broadcast | COMPARE-AND-WRITE + XFER-AND-SIGNAL |
| Storage | Metadata / file data transfer | XFER-AND-SIGNAL |
| Debuggability | Debug data transfer | XFER-AND-SIGNAL |
| | Debug synchronization | COMPARE-AND-WRITE |
| Fault Tolerance | Fault detection | COMPARE-AND-WRITE |
| | Checkpointing synchronization | COMPARE-AND-WRITE |
| | Checkpointing data transfer | XFER-AND-SIGNAL |

We may use COMPARE-AND-WRITE for flow control to prevent the multicast packets from overrunning the available buffers.

- Actual launching of a job can be achieved simply and efficiently by multicasting a control message to all the nodes that are allocated to the job by using XFER-AND-SIGNAL. In response the system software on each node would then fork the new processes and wait for their termination.

- The reporting of job termination can incur much overhead if each node sends a single message for every process that terminates. This problem can be solved by ensuring that all the processes of a job reach a common synchronization point upon termination (using COMPARE-AND-WRITE) before delivering a single message to the resource manager (using XFER-AND-SIGNAL).

**Job Scheduling.** Interactive response times from a scheduler are required to make a parallel machine as usable as a workstation. This in turn implies that the system must be able to perform preemptive context switching with the same latencies we have come to expect from single processor systems, that is, on the order of a few milliseconds. Such latencies are virtually impossible to achieve without hardware support: the time required to coordinate a context switch over thousands of nodes can be prohibitively large in a software-only solution. A good example of this is the SCore-D software-only gang scheduler of Hori *et al.* [14]. There the time for switching the network context on a relatively small Myrinet cluster is more than two thirds of the total context switch time. Furthermore, the context switch

message is propagated to the nodes using a software-based multicast tree, increasing in latency as the cluster grows. Finally, even though the system is able to efficiently context switch between different jobs, the coexistence of application traffic and synchronization messages in the network could unacceptably delay response to the latter. If this occurs even on a single node for even just a few milliseconds it will have a detrimental effect on the system responsiveness.

To overcome these problems the network should offer capabilities to the software scheduler for preventing these delays. The ability to maintain multiple communication contexts alive in the network securely and reliably, without kernel intervention, is already implemented in some state-of-the-art networks like QsNet. Job context switching can be easily achieved by simply multicasting, using XFER-AND-SIGNAL, a control message to all the nodes in the network. One method of guaranteeing quality of service for synchronization messages is to have support for message prioritization. The current generation of many networks, including QsNet, does not yet support prioritized messages in hardware, so a workaround must be found to keep the system messages' latencies low. In our case, we exploit the fact that some of our clusters have dual networks (two rails), and use one rail exclusively for system messages so that they do not compete with application-induced traffic.

**Determinism and fault tolerance.** Even when a single application is running (one network context, no preemption), messages can still be en route at different times and the system's state is not deterministic. When the system globally coordinates all the application processes, parallel jobs can be led to evolve in a controlled manner. Global coordination can be easily implemented with XFER-AND-

SIGNAL, and can be used to perform global scheduling of all the system resources. Determinism can be enforced by taking the same scheduling decisions between different executions. At the same time, the global coordination of all the system activities helps to identify the states along the program execution in which it is safe to checkpoint the status.

**Communication.** Most of MPI's, TCP/IP's, and other communication protocols' services can be reduced to a rather basic set of communication primitives, e.g. point-to-point synchronous and asynchronous messages and multicasts. If the underlying primitives and the protocol reductions are implemented efficiently, scalably, and reliably by the hardware and cluster OS, respectively, the higher level protocol can also inherit the same benefits of scalability, performance, and reliability. In many cases, this reduction is simple and can eliminate the need for many of the implementation quirks of protocols that need to run on a variety of network hardware. To illustrate this strategy we have implemented a small subset of the MPI library, called BCS-MPI [8], which has sufficient functionality to support real applications. As shown in the next section these applications have similar performance using BCS-MPI as using production-quality versions of MPI, but have the potential to benefit from the simplicity, determinism and scalability of BCS-MPI.

# 4. Case Studies

To demonstrate our thesis that these mechanisms can be exploited by a scalable global OS we built a prototype resource-management system, called STORM, and tested it on three architectures. In all cases we used the Quadrics *Elan3* network as our interconnect because it supports most of the mechanisms described in Section 3. In this section we review the performance and scalability that can be obtained with these mechanisms on three tasks: job launching, job scheduling, and deterministic communication.[2]

## 4.1. Software Environment

Our prototype resource-management system is composed of a set of dæmons that run on the compute nodes and management node of a cluster [10]. It contains a network abstraction layer that uses the described mechanisms for executing tasks such as job launching, process coordination (e.g. gang scheduling), and resource accounting. Although currently implemented as user-mode dæmons, we plan to fully incorporate the core functionality of STORM

---

[2]In [10] we study in detail other properties of STORM's job scheduling and job launching abilities, and model their scalability.

with the Linux kernel to obtain optimal performance and latencies. The code is relatively small at around 10,000 lines of C for the core functionality.

In addition to resource management, the core primitives can be used to implement almost any communication protocol while still retaining the advantages of performance and determinism. Here we have implemented the previously mentioned BCS-MPI. To use BCS-MPI applications simply need to be re-linked against the new libraries without any code modification. However, to achieve the best performance of BCS-MPI it can be beneficial to replace blocking communication calls such as MPI_Send() and MPI_Recv() with their non-blocking counterparts. This allows BCS-MPI to aggregate several communication calls together within the same timeslice whenever possible, so improving the possibility of interleaving communication and computation.

In the following case studies we used both synthetic and real HPC applications. The applications SWEEP3D and SAGE are representative of two hydrodynamics codes from the ASCI workload [16, 17].

## 4.2. Hardware Environment

For the experimental evaluation we used two different clusters at LANL/CCS-3 to test our mechanisms on different processor architectures. The clusters are called *Crescendo* and *Wolverine*. All clusters used a 128-port Quadrics Elite switch and Quadrics software library version 1.5.0-0. Table 4 summarizes the hardware comprising each cluster.

## 4.3. Job Launching

In this set of experiments we study the cost associated with launching jobs with STORM and analyze STORM's scalability with the size of the binary and the number of PEs on Wolverine. We use the approach taken by Brightwell *et al.* in their study of job launching on Cplant [3], which is to measure the time it takes to launch run a program of size 4 MB, 8 MB, or 12 MB that then terminates immediately.

STORM logically divides the job-launching task into two separate operations: the transmission of the binary image, and the actual execution, which includes sending a job-launch command, forking the job, waiting for its termination, and reporting back to the machine manager (MM). For the transmission of the binary images the MM uses XFER-AND-SIGNAL for multicasting chunks and COMPARE-AND-WRITE for flow control. To reduce nondeterminism the MM can issue commands and receive the notification of events only at the beginning of a timeslice. Therefore, both the binary transfer and the actual execution will take at least one timeslice. To minimize the MM

### Table 4. Cluster Description

| Component | Feature | *Crescendo* cluster | *Wolverine* cluster |
|---|---|---|---|
| Node | Number×PEs | 32×2 | 64×4 |
| | Memory/node | 1GB | 8GB |
| | I/O buses/node | 2 | 2 |
| | Model | Dell PowerEdge 1550 | AlphaServer ES40 |
| | OS | Red Hat Linux 7.3 | Red Hat Linux 7.1 |
| CPU | Type (speed) | Pentium-III (1GHz) | Alpha EV68 (833MHz) |
| I/O bus | Type | 64-bit/66MHz PCI | 64-bit/33MHz PCI |
| Network | NIC model | 1×QM-400 Elan3 | 2×QM-400 Elan3 |
| Software | Compiler | Intel C/Fortran v5.0.1 | Compaq's C Compiler |

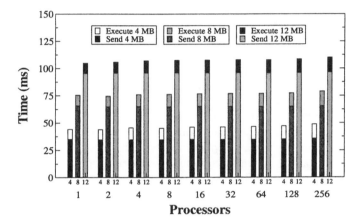

**Figure 1. Send and execute times for several file sizes on an unloaded system (Wolverine)**

overhead and expose maximal protocol performance, in the following job-launching experiments we use a small time quantum of 1 ms.

Figure 1 shows the time needed to transfer and execute a do-nothing program of sizes 4 MB, 8 MB, and 12 MB on 1–256 processors. Observe that the send times are proportional to the binary size but grow only slowly with the number of nodes. This is explained by the scalable algorithms and hardware mechanism that are used for the send operation. On the other hand, the execution times are quite independent of the binary size but grow more rapidly with the number of nodes. The reason for this growth is the skew, mainly due to the OS, that is accumulated by the processes of the job. In the largest configuration tested a 12 MB file can be launched in 110 ms, a remarkably low latency.

**Scalability Issues** These job launching results are comparable to other systems in the literature for clusters of up to a few hundreds of nodes (see Table 5). Our premise is that one of the main advantages of using hardware mecha-

### Table 5. A selection of job-launch times (in seconds) found in the literature

| Software | Job-launch time / program size | |
|---|---|---|
| rsh | 90 | Minimal job on 95 nodes [12] |
| RMS | 5.9 | 12 MB job on 64 nodes [10] |
| GLUnix | 1.3 | Minimal job on 95 nodes [12] |
| Cplant | 20 | 12 MB job on 1,010 nodes [3] |
| BProc | 2.7 | 12 MB job on 100 nodes [13] |
| SLURM | 4.9 | Minimal job on 950 nodes [15] |
| **STORM** | 0.11 | 12 MB job on 64 nodes [10] |

nisms is that the resource manager can inherit the scalability features of the hardware layer. To verify this property, we have elsewhere presented a detailed model of STORM's job-launching scalability [10]. In that work we have also extrapolated the expected job-launching performance of the software-based methods found in the literature. Not surprisingly, the hardware-supported mechanisms of STORM provide at least an order of magnitude better performance on very large clusters. In fact, it is the only system that is expected to deliver sub-second performance on thousands of nodes.

### 4.4. Job Scheduling

STORM supports a variety of job scheduling algorithms including various batch and time-sharing methods. Some of the time-sharing methods require a global synchronization message (strobe), which STORM implements using XFER-AND-SIGNAL. We have chosen to focus our evaluation specifically on gang scheduling [7], which is one of the most popular coscheduling algorithms. In particular we have studied the effect of timeslice on overhead. Smaller timeslices yield better response time at the cost of decreased throughput (due to scheduling overhead that cannot be amortized). To measure this overhead, we use

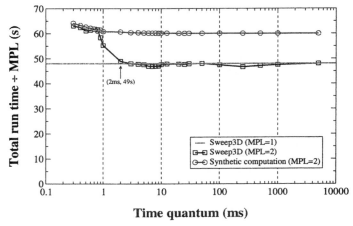

**Figure 2. Effect of time quantum with a multi-programming level (MPL) of 2 on 32 nodes**

SWEEP3D and a do-nothing synthetic program, and run two copies of each concurrently, with different timeslice values. Figure 2 shows the average run time of the two jobs for timeslice values from $300\,\mu s$ to 8 seconds, running on the entire Crescendo cluster. The smallest timeslice value that the scheduler can handle gracefully is $\sim 300\,\mu s$, any less than which the node cannot process the incoming strobe messages at the rate they arrive. With a timeslice as short as 2 ms STORM can run multiple concurrent instances of SWEEP3D with virtually no performance degradation over a single instance of the application.[3] This timeslice is an order of magnitude smaller than the local Linux scheduler's quanta, and is significantly smaller than the smallest time quanta that conventional gang schedulers can handle without significant performance penalties [9]. This, together with brisk job launching, allows for workstation-class system responsiveness on a large parallel system.

### 4.5. Communication Library

In the following experiments we demonstrate the performance of BCS-MPI. Of interest here is the impact of BCS-MPI's global synchronization of all the nodes in order to schedule communication requests issued by the application processes. We also provide and analyze some results comparing the performance of BCS-MPI to that of Quadrics MPI, a production-quality implementation of MPI.

With BCS-MPI a global strobe is sent to all the nodes (using XFER-AND-SIGNAL) at regular intervals. This tightly couples all the system activities by requiring that they occur at the same time on all nodes. Both computation

---

[3]This result is also influenced by the poor memory locality of SWEEP3D—the lack of a small memory working set implies minimal extra penalty for a context switch.

and communication are scheduled and the communication requests are buffered. At the beginning of every timeslice a partial exchange of communication requirements, implemented with XFER-AND-SIGNAL and TEST-EVENT, provides the information needed for scheduling the communication requests issued during the previous timeslice. After that all of the scheduled communication operations are performed by using XFER-AND-SIGNAL and TEST-EVENT.

The BCS-MPI communication protocol is implemented almost entirely in the network interface card (NIC). By running on the NIC's processor, BCS-MPI is able to overlap the communication with the ongoing computation. The application's processes directly interact (transparently via the BCS-MPI library) with threads running in the NIC. When an application process invokes a communication primitive, it simply posts a descriptor in a region of NIC memory that is accessible to a NIC thread. This descriptor includes all the communication parameters which are needed to complete the operation. The actual communication is performed by a set of cooperating threads running in the NICs (using XFER-AND-SIGNAL). In QsNet, these threads can directly read/write from/to the application process memory space (no copies to intermediate buffers are required). Moreover, the posting of the descriptor is a lightweight operation, making the entire overhead of the BCS-MPI call even lower than that of the Quadrics MPI.

The communication protocol is divided into microphases within every timeslice and its progress is also globally synchronized. To illustrate how BCS-MPI primitives work, two possible scenarios for blocking and non-blocking MPI primitives are described in Figure 3(a) and Figure 3(b), respectively. In Figure 3(a), process $P_1$ sends a message to process $P_2$ using MPI_Send and process $P_2$ receives a message from P1 using MPI_Receive: (1) $P_1$ posts a send descriptor to the NIC and blocks. (2) $P_2$ posts a receive descriptor to the NIC and blocks. (3) The transmission of data from $P_1$ to $P_2$ is scheduled since both processes are ready (all the pending communication operations posted before timeslice $i$ are scheduled if possible). (4) The communication is performed (all the scheduled operations are performed before the end of timeslice $i + 1$). (5) $P_1$ and $P_2$ are restarted at the beginning of timeslice $i$. (6) $P_1$ and $P_2$ resume computation. Note that the delay per blocking primitive is 1.5 timeslices on average. However, this penalty can be usually be avoided by using non-blocking communications or by scheduling a different job in timeslice $i + 1$. Figure 3(b) shows the same situation for non-blocking MPI primitives. In this case, communication is completely overlapped with computation with no performance penalty.

In Figure 4(a) the runtime of SWEEP3D for both BCS-MPI and Quadrics MPI is shown for various numbers of processes on the Crescendo cluster. The effective overlap between computation and communication along with the

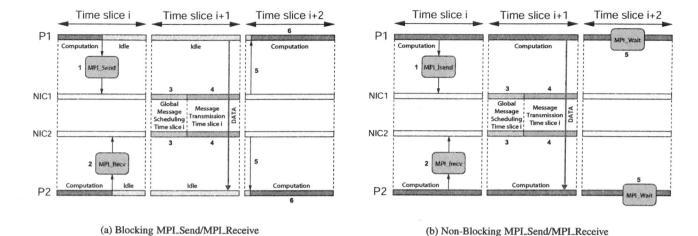

(a) Blocking MPI_Send/MPI_Receive

(b) Non-Blocking MPI_Send/MPI_Receive

**Figure 3. Blocking and Non-Blocking MPI_Send/MPI_Receive Scenarios in BCS-MPI**

low overhead of its primitives allow BCS-MPI to slightly outperform Quadrics MPI, with speedups of up to 2.28%.

**Scalability Issues** To complete the application study and to gain a better understanding of BCS-MPI's scalability, we show SAGE's performance on Crescendo with Quadrics and BCS-MPI. Unlike SWEEP3D, which requires square configurations, SAGE can run on any number of nodes. Figure 4(b) shows the run time of SAGE on varying both the number of nodes and the problem size, up to 62 (one node is reserved for the MM). Both versions perform similarly because SAGE uses mostly non-blocking point-to-point communication. Most notably, BCS-MPI performs slightly better than Quadrics MPI for the largest configuration, which indicates that the scalability of SAGE is not an issue with BCS-MPI and this cluster size.

## 5. Conclusions and Future Work

In this paper we proposed a new abstraction layer for large-scale clusters. This layer, which can be implemented by as few as three communication primitives in the network hardware, can greatly simplify the development of system software. In our model the system software is a tightly-coupled parallel application that operates in lockstep on all nodes. If the hardware support for this layer is both scalable and efficient the system software inherits these properties. Such software is not only relatively simple to implement but can also provide parallel programs with most of the services they require to make their development and usage efficient and more manageable. In particular, we discuss how this abstraction layer can be used for the implementation of efficient, deterministic communication libraries, workstation-class responsiveness, and transparent fault tolerance. We

have presented initial experimental results which demonstrate that scalable resource management and application communication are indeed feasible while making the system behave deterministically. Our future work will expand to incorporate transparent fault tolerance into the system software. We also plan to explore other possible benefits of a global operating system, such as coordinated parallel I/O and debugging. Lastly, we plan to migrate our code into the Linux kernel. Such an integration should also improve further the performance of the cluster operating system.

## References

[1] Challenges in developing scalable scalable software for Bluegene/L. In *Scaling to New Heights Workshop*, Pittsburgh, PA, May 2002.

[2] G. Bosilca, A. Bouteiller, F. Cappello, S. Djailali, G. Fedak, C. Germain, T. Herault, P. Lemarinier, O. Lodygensky, F. Magniette, V. Neri, and A. Selikhov. MPICH-V: Toward a Scalable Fault Tolerant MPI for Volatile Nodes. In *Proceedings of IEEE/ACM Supercomputing 2002 (SC'02)*, Baltimore, MD, November 2002.

[3] R. Brightwell and L. A. Fisk. Scalable parallel application launch on Cplant. In *Proceedings of IEEE/ACM Supercomputing 2001 (SC'01)*, Denver, CO, November 10–16, 2001.

[4] D. Buntinas, D. Panda, J. Duato, and P. Sadayappan. Broadcast/multicast over Myrinet using NIC-assisted multidestination messages. In *Workshop on Communication, Architecture, and Applications for Network-Based Parallel Computing (CANPC '00), High Performance Computer Architecture (HPCA-6) Conference*, Toulouse, France, January 2000.

[5] D. Buntinas, D. Panda, and W. Gropp. NIC-based atomic operations on Myrinet/GM. In *SAN-1 Workshop, High Performance Computer Architecture (HPCA-8) Conference*, Boston, MA, February 2002.

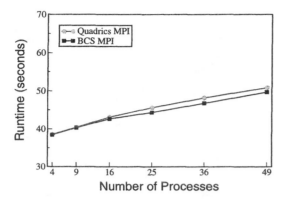

(a) Non-Blocking SWEEP3D (Crescendo)

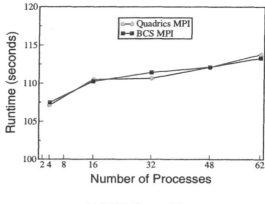

(b) SAGE (Crescendo)

[6] D. E. Culler, R. M. Karp, D. A. Patterson, A. Sahay, K. E. Schauser, E. Santos, R. Subramonian, and T. von Eicken. LogP: Towards a realistic model of parallel computation. In *Proceedings of ACM SIGPLAN Symposium on Principles and Practice of Parallel Programming*, pages 1–12, 1993.

[7] D. G. Feitelson and L. Rudolph. Gang scheduling performance benefits for fine-grain synchronization. *Journal of Parallel and Distributed Computing*, 16(4):306–318, December 1992.

[8] J. Fernandez, F. Petrini, and E. Frachtenberg. BCS MPI: A New Approach in the System Software Design for Large-Scale Parallel Computers. In *Proceedings of IEEE/ACM Supercomputing 2003 (SC'03)*, Phoenix, AZ, November 2003.

[9] E. Frachtenberg, F. Petrini, S. Coll, and W. chun Feng. Gang scheduling with lightweight user-level communication. In *Proceedings of the 30th International Conference on Parallel Processing (ICPP'01), Workshop on Scheduling and Resource Management for Cluster Computing*, Valencia, Spain, September 2001.

[10] E. Frachtenberg, F. Petrini, J. Fernandez, S. Pakin, and S. Coll. STORM: Lightning-Fast Resource Management. In *Proceedings of IEEE/ACM Supercomputing 2002 (SC'02)*, Baltimore, MD, November 2002.

[11] H. Franke, P. Pattnaik, and L. Rudolph. Gang Scheduling for Highly Efficient Distributed Multiprocessor Syetems. In *Proceedings of the 6th Symposium on the Frontiers of Massively Parallel Computation (FRONTIERS '96)*, pages 1–9, Annapolis, MD, October 1996.

[12] D. P. Ghormley, D. Petrou, S. H. Rodrigues, A. M. Vahdat, and T. E. Anderson. GLUnix: a global layer Unix for a network of workstations. *Software—Practice and Experience*, 28(9):929–961, July 25, 1998.

[13] E. Hendriks. BProc: The Beowulf distributed process space. In *Proceedings of the 16th Annual ACM International Conference on Supercomputing (ICS '02)*, New York, NY, June 22–26, 2002.

[14] A. Hori, H. Tezuka, and Y. Ishikawa. Overhead analysis of preemptive gang scheduling. In D. G. Feitelson and L. Rudolph, editors, *Job Scheduling Strategies for Parallel Processing*, pages 217–230. Springer Verlag, 1998.

[15] M. A. Jette, A. B. Yoo, and M. Grondona. SLURM: Simple linux utility for resource management. In D. G. Feitelson and L. Rudolph, editors, *Job Scheduling Strategies for Parallel Processing*, pages 37–51. Springer-Verlag, 2003.

[16] D. Kerbyson, H. Alme, A. Hoisie, F. Petrini, H. Wasserman, and M. Gittings. Predictive Performance and Scalability Modeling of a Large-Scale Application. In *Proceedings of IEEE/ACM Supercomputing 2001 (SC'01)*, Denver, CO, November 2001.

[17] K. R. Koch, R. S. Baker, and R. E. Alcouffe. Solution of the first-order form of the 3-D discrete ordinates equation on a massively parallel processor. *Transactions of the American Nuclear Society*, 65(108):198–199, 1992.

[18] J. Liu, J. Wu, D. K. Panda, and C. Shamir. Designing clusters with Infiniband: Early experience with Mellanox technology. Submitted for publication.

[19] F. Petrini, W. Feng, A. Hoisie, S. Coll, and E. Frachtenberg. The Quadrics Network: High-Performance Clustering Technology. *IEEE Micro*, 22(1):46–57, January/February 2002.

[20] F. Petrini, D. Kerbyson, and S. Pakin. The Case of the Missing Supercomputer Performance: Achieving Optimal Performance on the 8,192 Processors of ASCI Q. In *Proceedings of IEEE/ACM Supercomputing 2003 (SC'03)*, Phoenix, AZ, November 2003.

[21] P. Shivam, P. Wyckoff, and D. Panda. EMP: Zero-copy OS-bypass NIC-driven Gigabit Ethernet message passing. In *Proceedings of IEEE/ACM Supercomputing 2001 (SC'01)*, Denver, CO, November 10–16, 2001.

[22] M. Snir, S. Otto, S. Huss-Lederman, D. Walker, and J. Dongarra. *MPI: The Complete Reference*, volume 1, The MPI Core. The MIT Press, Cambridge, Massachusetts, 2nd edition, September 1998.

[23] Thinking Machines Corporation. *NI Systems Programming*, 1992. Version 7.1.

[24] L. G. Valiant. A Bridging Model for Parallel Computation. *Communications of the ACM*, 33(8):103–111, August 1990.

# Preemption-Based Avoidance of Priority Inversion for Java

Adam Welc
welc@cs.purdue.edu

Antony L. Hosking
hosking@cs.purdue.edu

Suresh Jagannathan
suresh@cs.purdue.edu

Department of Computer Sciences
Purdue University
West Lafayette, IN 47906

## Abstract

*Priority inversion occurs in concurrent programs when low-priority threads hold shared resources needed by some high-priority thread, causing them to block indefinitely. Shared resources are usually guarded by low-level synchronization primitives such as mutual-exclusion locks, semaphores, or monitors. There are two existing solutions to priority inversion. The first, establishing high-level scheduling invariants over synchronization primitives to eliminate priority inversion a priori, is difficult in practice and undecidable in general. Alternatively, run-time avoidance mechanisms such as priority inheritance still force high-priority threads to wait until desired resources are released.*

*We describe a novel compiler and run-time solution to the problem of priority inversion, along with experimental evaluation of its effectiveness. Our approach allows preemption of any thread holding a resource needed by higher-priority threads, forcing it to release its claim on the resource, roll back its execution to the point at which the shared resource was first acquired, and discard any updates made in the interim.*

*The compiler inserts code at synchronization points, permitting rollback of thread execution, and efficient revocation of interim updates. Our design and implementation are realized in the context of IBM's Jikes RVM, a high-quality compiler and runtime system for Java. Our performance results show that throughput of high-priority threads using our scheme can be improved by 30% to 100% when compared with a classical scheduler that does not address priority inversion.*

## 1 Introduction

Modern programming languages (*eg*, ML, Java, C++, and Modula-3) support concurrent programming, either through built-in language primitives, or via a set of external libraries. In general, the basic units of concurrent execution are *threads*. Threads can interact by accessing and modifying objects in their shared address space, synchronizing their actions via mutual exclusion *locks*.

The resulting programming model is reasonably simple, but unfortunately unwieldy for large-scale applications. A significant problem with using low-level, lock-based synchronization primitives is priority inversion. We propose a new solution for priority inversion that exploits close cooperation between the compiler and the run-time system. Our approach is applicable to any language that offers the following mechanisms:

- Multithreading: concurrent threads of control executing over objects in a shared address space.

- Synchronized sections: lexically-delimited blocks of code, guarded by dynamically-scoped monitors. Threads synchronize on a given monitor, acquiring it on entry to the block and releasing it on exit. Only one thread may execute within a synchronized section at any time, ensuring exclusive access to all monitor-protected blocks. Monitors are usually implemented using locking, with acquisition of a mutual exclusion lock on entry, and release of the lock on exit.

- Exception scopes: blocks of code in which an error condition can change the normal flow of control of the active thread, by exiting active scopes, and transferring control to a handler associated with each block.

The advantages of multithreading, for I/O-bound applications, human interfaces, distributed and parallel systems are established and well-understood. However, the difficulties in using locking with multiple threads are also widely-recognized.

A low-priority thread may hold a lock even while other threads, which may have higher priority, are waiting to acquire it. *Priority inversion* results when a low-priority thread $T_l$ holds a lock required by some high-priority thread $T_h$, forcing the high-priority $T_h$ to wait until $T_l$ releases the lock. Even worse, an unbounded number of runnable *medium*-priority threads $T_m$ may exist, thus preventing $T_l$ from running and making unbounded the time that $T_l$ (and hence $T_h$) must wait. Such situations can play havoc in real-time systems where high-priority threads demand some level of guaranteed throughput.

The ease with which even experienced programmers can write programs that exhibit priority inversion makes it worthwhile to explore transparent solutions that dynamically resolve priority inversion by reverting programs to consistent states when it occurs, while preserving source program semantics. For real-world concurrent programs with complex module and dependency structures, it is difficult to perform an exhaustive exploration of the space of possible interleavings to statically determine when priority inversion may arise. For such applications, the ability to transparently redress undesirable interactions between scheduling decisions and lock management is very useful.

In this paper, we propose a scheme to deal with priority inversion for monitor-based prorgrams that differ from existing solutions such as *priority ceiling* and *priority inheritance*. These latter techniques, although useful for certain applications, suffer from several significant drawbacks. Priority ceiling requires a programmer to manually specify the ceiling (the highest priority of any thread that uses the lock) for every lock, and is therefore not transparent to applications. Although priority inheritance does not exhibit this particular problem, it has several other notable disadvantages [25] that encourage us to explore alternative approaches: (a) It is non-trivial to implement; (b) Because it is a transitive operation, it may lead to unpredictable performance degradation when nested regions are protected by priority inheritance locks; (c) The existence of non-inheriting blocking operations (*eg*, synchronous inter-thread communication) may lead to unbounded inversion delay.

## 1.1 Our contribution: Monitor rollback

Our approach is to combine compiler techniques with run-time detection and resolution of priority inversion. Having detected priority inversion, the run-time system selectively revokes the effects of the offending thread within a synchronized section in order to resolve the problem. The compiler provides support by injecting *write barriers* to log updates to shared state performed by threads active in synchronized sections and generating code that allows interruption and revocation of the active thread. Note that this means *all* compiled code needs at least a fast-path test on every non-local update to check if the thread is executing within a synchronized section, with the slow path logging the update if it is. Compiler analyses and optimization may elide these run-time checks when the update can be shown statically never to occur within a synchronized section.

Detection of priority inversion (either at lock acquisition, or periodically in the background) by the run-time system triggers revocation of the relevant critical section for its associated thread. The run-time system interrupts the target thread, revokes the updates for the section, and transfers control for the thread back to the beginning of the section for retry. Externally, the end effect of the rollback is as if the low-priority thread never executed the section.

The process of revoking effects performed by a thread within a synchronized section is illustrated in Figure 1, where wavy lines represent threads $T_l$ and $T_h$, circles represent objects $o_1$ and $o_2$, updated objects are marked grey, and the box represents the dynamic scope of a common monitor guarding some (set of) synchronized section(s) executed by the threads. In Figure 1(a) low-priority thread $T_l$ is about to enter the synchronized section, which it does in Figure 1(b), modifying object $o_1$. High-priority thread $T_h$ tries to acquire the same monitor, but is blocked by low-priority $T_l$ (1(c)). Here, a priority inheritance [21] approach would raise the priority of thread $T_l$ to that of $T_h$ but $T_h$ would still have to wait for $T_l$ to release the lock. Instead, our approach preempts $T_l$, undoing any updates to $o_1$, and transfers control in $T_l$ back to the point of entry to the synchronized section (1(d). Here $T_l$ must wait while $T_h$ now enters the monitor, and updates objects $o_1$ (1(e)) and $o_2$, before leaving (1(f)). At this point the monitor is released and $T_l$ will gain re-entry.

Note that the same technique can also be used to detect and resolve *deadlock*. Deadlock results when two or more threads are unable to proceed because each is waiting on a lock held by another. Such a situation is easily constructed for two threads, $T_1$ and $T_2$: $T_1$ first acquires lock $L_1$ while $T_2$ acquires $L_2$, then $T_1$ tries to acquire $L_2$ while $T_2$ tries to acquire $L_1$, resulting in deadlock. Generally, deadlocks may occur among more than two threads, and deadlocking programs are often difficult to diagnose and fix. As a result, many deployed applications may execute under schedules in which deadlock may occur. Using our techniques, such deadlocks can be detected and resolved automatically, permitting the application to make progress. Of course, applications that deadlock are intrinsically incorrect; our approach is not intended to mask such errors. However, for mission-critical applications in which running programs cannot be summarily terminated, our approach provides an opportunity for corrective action to be undertaken gracefully. Note that while deadlocks can be handled using our technique, without taking additional precautions a sequence of deadlock revocations may result in livelock.

The remainder of this paper details design choices and modifications made to IBM's Jikes Research Virtual Machine (Jikes RVM) to implement our approach. Section 2 outlines the design. Section 3 details several implementation choices for efficiently implementing rollbacks. Performance results are given in Section 4. Related work is discussed in Section 5.

## 2 Design

One of the main principles underlying our design is a *compliance requirement*: programmers must perceive all programs executing in our system to behave exactly the same as on all other existing platforms implemented according to the specification of a given language. In order to achieve this goal we must adhere to the execution semantics of a given language and follow the memory access rules defined by the language.

Our work is couched in terms of the Java language. In Java, every object can act as a *monitor*. A thread holding a

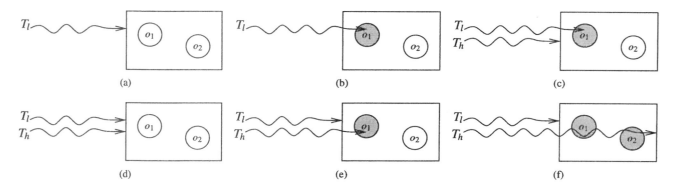

**Figure 1. Revoking synchronized sections**

monitor may enter another synchronized section guarded by the same or a completely different monitor. This action may be repeated an arbitrary number of times thus permitting monitors to be arbitrarily nested dynamically.

We fulfill the compliance requirement by *logging* all updates to shared data performed by a thread executing within a monitor. We use the information from the log to *roll back* updates whenever the monitor is revoked to permit a higher priority thread to run. In effect, synchronized sections execute speculatively, and their updates may be revoked at any time until the section exits. However, the introduction of revocable synchronized sections requires a careful consideration of the interaction between revocation and the Java Memory Model (JMM) [16].

## 2.1 The Java memory model

The JMM defines a *happens-before* relation (written $\xrightarrow{hb}$) among the actions performed by threads in a given execution of a program. For single-threaded execution the happens-before relation is defined by program order. For multi-threaded execution a happens-before relation is induced between an unlock $u_M$ (release) and a subsequent lock $l_M$ (acquire) operation on a given monitor $M$ ($u_M \xrightarrow{hb} l_M$). The happens-before relation is transitive: $x \xrightarrow{hb} y$ and $y \xrightarrow{hb} z$ imply $x \xrightarrow{hb} z$. The JMM shared data visibility rule is defined using the happens-before relation: a read $r_v$ is *allowed* to observe a write $w_v$ to a given variable variable $v$ if $r_v$ does not happen before $w_v$ and there is no intervening write $w'_v$ such that $r_v \xrightarrow{hb} w'_v \xrightarrow{hb} w_v$ (we say that a read becomes *read-write dependent* on the write that it is *allowed* to see). As a consequence, it is possible that partial results computed by some thread $T$ executing within monitor $M$ become visible to (and are used by) another thread $T'$ even before thread $T$ releases $M$ if accesses to those updated objects performed by $T'$ are not mediated by first acquiring $M$. However, a subsequent revocation of monitor $M$ would undo the update and remove the happens-before relation, making a value seen by $T'$ appear "out of thin air" and thus the execution of $T'$ inconsistent with the JMM.

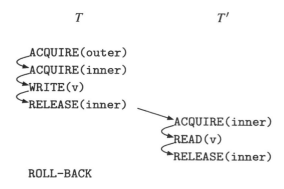

**Figure 2. Bad revocation: nesting**

An example of such an execution appears in Figure 2: thread $T$ acquires monitor `outer` and subsequently monitor `inner`, writes to a shared variable v and releases monitor `inner`. Then thread $T'$ acquires monitor `inner`, reads variable v and releases monitor `inner`. The execution is JMM-consistent up to the rollback point: the read performed by $T'$ is *allowed* but the subsequent rollback of $T$ would violate consistency.

A similar problem occurs when *volatile* variables are used. The Java Language Specification (JLS) [8] states that updates to volatile variables immediately become visible to all program threads. Thus, there also exists a happens-before relation between a volatile write and all subsequent volatile reads of the same (volatile) variable. For the execution presented in Figure 3 `vol` is a volatile variable and edges depict a happens-before relation. As in the previous example, the execution is JMM-consistent up to the rollback point because a read performed by $T'$ is *allowed*, but the rollback would violate consistency. We now discuss possible solutions to these JMM-consistency preservation problems.

## 2.2 Preserving JMM-consistency

Several solutions to the problem of partial results of a monitored computation being exposed to other threads can

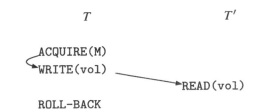

Figure 3. Bad revocation: volatile access

```
static boolean v=false;
```

| $T$ | $T'$ |
|---|---|
| synchronized(outer) {<br>  synchronized(inner) {<br>    v=true;<br>  }<br><br>  // ROLL-BACK<br>} | while (true) {<br>  synchronized(inner) {<br>    if (v) break;<br>  }<br>} |

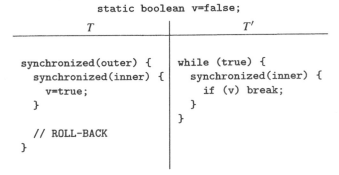

Figure 4. Impossible re-schedule

be considered. We might trace read-write dependencies among all threads and upon rollback of a monitor trigger a cascade of rollbacks for threads whose read-write dependencies are violated. An obvious disadvantage of this approach is the need to consider *all* operations (including non-monitored ones) for a potential rollback. In the execution of Figure 3 the volatile read performed by $T'$ would have to be rolled back even though it is not guarded by any monitor. Furthermore, to apply this solution, the full execution context of program threads would have to be logged in addition to shared data operations performed by the threads. Consider a situation based on the example of Figure 2 where thread $T'$ *returns* (from the current method) after releasing monitor inner but before thread $T$ is asked to roll back the execution of monitor outer. Without the ability to restore the full execution context of $T'$, the subsequent rollback of monitor inner by that thread becomes infeasible.

Another potential solution is to re-schedule the execution of threads in problematic cases. In both of the examples presented above, if thread $T'$ executes fully before thread $T$, the execution will still be JMM-consistent. The rollback of $T$ does not violate consistency since none of the updates performed by $T$ are visible to $T'$. Besides the obvious question about the practicality of this solution (some knowledge about future actions performed by threads would be required), there also remains the issue of correctness. While correct in some cases, this solution is not necessarily correct in others. Consider the Java program presented in Figure 4. We cannot re-schedule thread $T'$ to execute fully before thread $T$ because of semantic constraints: termination of $T'$ depends on thread $T$ performing the operation v=true.

The solution that does seem flexible enough to handle all possible problematic cases, and simple enough to avoid using complex analyses and/or maintaining significant additional meta-data, is to disable the revocability of monitors whose rollback could create inconsistencies with respect to the JMM. As a consequence, not all instances of priority inversion can be resolved. We mark a monitor $M$ *non-revocable* when a read-write dependency is created between a write performed within $M$[1] and a read performed by another thread. We believe this solution does not severely penalize the effectiveness of our technique. Intuitively, programmers guard accesses to the same subset of shared data using the same set of monitors; in such cases, there is no need to force non-revocability of any of the monitors (even if they are nested) since mutual-exclusion induced by monitor acquisition prevents generation of problematic dependencies among these threads. Determining the precise impact of this design choice on the effectiveness of our technique is an integral part of future research.

There exist other Java constructs that affect revocability of the monitors. Calling a native method within a monitor also forces non-revocability of the monitor (and all of its enclosing monitors if it is nested), since the effects of a native method cannot generally be revoked (*eg*, printing a message to the console is irrevocable). The same applies to executions where a *wait* method is invoked within a nested monitor.[2] A revocation of the wait call would result in a situation where a respective *notify* call (that "woke up" the waiting thread) "disappears" (*ie*, does not get delivered to any thread) which would violate the Java execution semantics. A call to notify does not enforce the irrevocability of the enclosing monitors: Java VM implementations are permitted [16] to perform "spurious wake-ups" so a rolled back notification can be considered as such.

## 3 Implementation

In order to demonstrate the validity of our approach, we base our implementation on a well-known Java execution environment with a high-quality compiler. We use IBM's Jikes RVM [2], a state-of-the-art research virtual machine (VM) for Java with performance comparable to many production VMs. Java bytecodes in Jikes RVM are compiled directly to machine code using either a low-cost non-optimizing "baseline" compiler or an aggressive optimizing compiler.

When discussing the details of our approach, we concentrate on what we believe is the main contribution of this paper, namely *how* to resolve a priority inversion problem once detected (though later parts of the paper also briefly discuss how the VM determines *when* a priority inversion situation occurs and needs to be resolved). In other words

---

[1] The write may additionally be guarded by other monitors nested within M.

[2] A monitor object associated with the receiver object is released upon a call to wait and reacquired after returning from the call. In the case of a non-nested monitor a potential rollback will therefore not reach beyond the point when wait was called.

we concentrate on the description of necessary compiler and run-time support that allows the VM to interrupt execution of synchronized sections at arbitrary points without inducing any observable effects on an application's execution behavior. In subsequent sections, we describe how to implement the re-execution procedure itself: transparently return control from an arbitrary point during a synchronized section's execution to that section's starting point, restore the state of the VM, and re-execute the synchronized section's code.

## 3.1 Our strategy

Our implementation uses bytecode rewriting[3] to save program state (values of local variables and method parameters) for re-execution and to return control to the beginning of the synchronized section. We modify the compiler and run-time system to suppress generation (and invocation) of undesirable exception handlers during a rollback operation, to insert write barriers for logging, to revert updates performed during the unfinished execution of a synchronized section, and to augment context-switch code invoked at yield points[4] to check also whether a rollback action must be initiated.

### 3.1.1 Bytecode transformation

There exist two different synchronization constructs in Java: synchronized methods and synchronized blocks. To treat them uniformly, we transform synchronized methods into non-synchronized equivalents whose entire body is enclosed in a synchronized block. For each synchronized method we create a non-synchronized wrapper with a signature identical to the original method. We fill the body of the wrapper method with a synchronized block enclosing invocation of the original (non-synchronized) method, which has been appropriately renamed to avoid name clash. We also instruct the VM to inline the original method within the wrapper to avoid performance penalties related to the additional method invocation. This approach greatly simplifies the implementation,[5] is extremely simple, robust, and also efficient, because of inlining directives.

Each synchronized section (bracketed by *monitorenter* and *monitorexit* operations) is wrapped within an exception scope that catches a special type of *rollback exception*. The rollback exception is thrown internally by the VM (see below), but the code to catch it is injected into the bytecode. Since a rollback may involve a nested synchronized section,

each rollback exception catch handler invokes an internal VM method to check if it corresponds to the synchronized section that is to be re-executed. If it does, then the handler releases the monitor associated with its synchronized section, and returns control to the beginning of the section. Otherwise, the handler re-throws the rollback exception to the next outer synchronized section.

There is an additional complication related to the return of control to the beginning of the section. The contents of the VM's operand stack before executing a *monitorenter* operation must be the same at the first invocation and at all subsequent invocations resulting from that section's re-execution. However, according to the Java VM specification [14], the run-time system erases the operand stack of the method activation that will catch the exception. To handle this, we inject bytecode to save the values on the operand stack just before each rollback-scope's *monitorenter* opcode, and to restore the stack state in the handler before transferring control back to the *monitorenter*.

### 3.1.2 Compiler and run-time modifications

The rollback operation is initiated by throwing the rollback exception (as described in the previous section). However, we cannot rely on the default exception handling mechanism to propagate the rollback exception up the activation stack to the synchronized section being rolled back, since it will also run "default" exception handlers in nested exception scopes as it unwinds the stack up to the rollback scope. Such "default" handlers include both `finally` blocks, and `catch` blocks for exceptions of type `Throwable`, of which all exceptions (including *rollback*) are instances. Running these intervening handlers would violate our semantics that an aborted synchronized block produces no side-effects.

To handle this, the augmented exception handling routine ignores all handlers (including `finally` blocks) that do not explicitly catch the *rollback* exception, when one is thrown. The default behavior still applies for all other exceptions, to preserve the standard semantics. We are careful to release monitors as necessary wherever the Jikes RVM optimizing compiler releases them explicitly in its implementation of synchronized blocks.

We also modified both compilers to inject write barriers before every store operation (represented by the bytecodes: `putfield` for object stores, `putstatic` for static variable stores, and `Xastore` for array stores). The barrier records in the log every modification performed by a thread executing a synchronized section. We implemented the log as a sequential buffer. For object and array stores, three values are recorded: object or array reference, value offset and the (old) value itself. For static variable stores two values are recorded: the offset of the static variable in the global symbol table and the old value of the static variable.

If the execution of a synchronized section is interrupted and needs to be re-executed then the log is processed in reverse to restore modified locations to their original values. The procedure to do this is invoked before a thread that has been interrupted releases any of its locks. Since partial re-

---

[3]We use the Bytecode Engineering Library (BCEL) from Apache for this purpose. Note that our solution does not preclude the use of languages that do not have a similar intermediate representation – we could use source-code rewriting instead.

[4]Threads in the Jikes RVM are pseudo-preemptive: thread context-switches can happen only at pre-specified yield points inserted by the compiler.

[5]We need only handle explicit *monitorenter* and *monitorexit* bytecodes, without worrying about implicit monitor operations for synchronized methods.

sults of a computation performed by a thread executing the interrupted synchronized section are reverted before any of the locks are released, they do not become visible to any other thread, in accordance with Java execution semantics.

## 3.2 Discussion

Rather than using bytecode transformations, we note that an alternative strategy would implement the re-execution procedure entirely at the VM level (*ie*, all the code modifications necessary to support rollbacks would only involve the compiler and the Java run-time system). This approach simply requires that the current state of the VM (*ie*, contents of local variables, non-volatile registers, stack pointer, *etc*) be remembered upon entry to a synchronized section, and restored when a rollback is required. Unfortunately, this strategy has the significant drawback that it introduces implicit control-flow edges in the program's control-flow graph that are not visible to the compiler. Consequently, liveness information necessary for the garbage collector may be incorrectly computed, since a rollback action may require stack slots to remain live that would ordinarily be marked dead. Resolving these issues would entail substantial changes to the compiler and runtime system.

A second alternative we considered (and discarded) was a fully portable user-level implementation that would not require any modifications to the VM or the compiler. Instead, this solution would take advantage of language-level exceptions and use bytecode rewriting techniques exclusively to provide all the support necessary to perform a rollback operation. Unfortunately, in the absence of any compiler modifications, the built-in exception handling mechanism may execute an arbitrary number of other user-defined exception handlers and finalizers, violating the transparency of the design. Moreover, inserting write-barriers at the bytecode level to log changes would require optimizations to remove them to be re-implemented at this level as well, since existing optimizations are currently implemented internally by Jikes on a different intermediate representation.

The middle-ground approach that we adopted fulfills all our design requirements and was relatively easy to implement. We also managed to keep the number of modifications to the virtual machine and the compilers small, and they are mostly machine independent.[6] Thus, our implementation is easily portable.

## 4 Experimental evaluation

We quantify the overhead of the mechanism using a detailed micro-benchmark. We measure programs that exhibit priority inversion to verify if the increased overheads induced by our implementation are mitigated by higher overall throughput of high-priority threads.

Our algorithm to detect priority inversion is reasonably simple. A thread acquiring a monitor deposits its priority in the header of the monitor object. Before another thread can attempt acquisition of the same monitor, it checks whether its own priority is higher than the priority of the thread currently executing within the synchronized section. If it is, the scheduler initiates a context-switch and triggers rollback of the low priority thread at the next yield point. After the low-priority thread rolls back its changes and releases the monitor, the high-priority thread acquires control of the synchronized section. If the incoming thread's priority is lower, it blocks on the monitor and waits for the other thread to complete execution of the synchronized section.

The Jikes RVM does not include a priority scheduler; threads are scheduled in a round-robin fashion. This does not affect the generality of our solution nor does it invalidate the results obtained, since problems solved by the mechanism proposed in this work cannot be solved simply by using a priority scheduler. However, in order to make the measurements independent of the random order in which threads arrive at a monitor, we implemented prioritized monitor queues. A thread can have either high or low priority. When a thread releases a monitor, another thread is scheduled from the queue. If it is a high-priority thread, it is allowed to acquire the monitor. If it is a low-priority thread, it is allowed to run only if there are no other waiting high-priority threads.

## 4.1 Benchmark program

The micro-benchmark executes several low and high-priority threads contending on the same lock. Regardless of their priority, all threads are compiled identically, with write barriers inserted to log updates, and special exception handlers injected to restart synchronized sections. Our benchmark is structured so that only low-priority threads will actually employ this functionality.[7] Every thread executes 100 synchronized sections. Each synchronized section contains an inner loop executing an interleaved sequence of read and write operations. We emphasize that our micro-benchmark has been constructed to gauge overheads inherent in our technique (the costs of re-execution, logging, *etc*) and not necessarily to simulate any particular workload of a real-life application. We strived to avoid biasing the benchmark structure toward our solution by artificially extending the execution time using benign (with respect to logging) operations (*eg*, method calls). Therefore, we decided to make the execution time of a synchronized section directly proportional to the number of shared data operations performed within that section. We fixed the number of iterations of the inner loop for low-priority threads at 500K, and varied it for the high-priority threads (100K and 500K). The remaining parameters for our benchmark include:

- the ratio of high-priority threads to low-priority threads – we used three configurations: $2 + 8$, $5 + 5$, and $8 + 2$, high-priority plus low-priority threads, respectively.

---

[6]The exception is the insertion of the barriers in the baseline compiler, which had to be implemented in assembly language.

[7]However, updates of both low-priority and high-priority threads are logged for fairness, even though in the case of this micro-benchmark high-priority threads can never be rolled back.

- the ratio of write to read operations performed within a synchronized section – we used six different configurations ranging from 0% writes (*ie*, 100% reads) to 100% writes (*ie*, 0% reads)

Our benchmark also includes a short random pause time (on average equal to a single thread quantum in Jikes RVM) right before an entry to the synchronized section, to ensure random arrival of threads at the monitors guarding the sections.

Our thesis is that the total elapsed time of high-priority threads can be improved using the rollback scheme, at the expense of longer elapsed time for low-priority threads. Improvement is measured against a priority scheduling implementation that provides no remedy for priority inversion. Thus, for every run of the micro-benchmark, we compare the total time it takes for all high-priority threads to complete their execution for the following two settings:

- An *unmodified* VM that does not allow execution of a synchronized section to be interrupted and revoked: when a high-priority thread wants to acquire a lock already held by a low-priority thread, it waits until the low-priority thread exits the synchronized section. The benchmark code executed on this VM is compiled using the Jikes RVM optimizing compiler without any modification.

- A *modified VM* equipped with the compiler and runtime changes to interrupt and revoke execution of synchronized sections by low-priority threads: when a high-priority thread wants to acquire a lock held by a low-priority thread, it signals its intent, resulting in the low-priority thread exiting the synchronized section at the next yield point, rolling back any changes to shared data made from the time it began executing inside the section. The benchmark code executed on this VM is compiled using the modified version of the Jikes RVM optimizing compiler described in Section 3.1.2.

To measure the total elapsed time of high-priority threads we take the first time-stamp at the beginning of the run() method of every high priority thread and the second time-stamp at the end of the run() method of every high-priority thread. We compute the total elapsed time for all high-priority threads by calculating the time elapsed from the earliest time-stamp of the first set (*ie*, start times) to the latest time-stamp of the second set (*ie*, end times). We also present the impact that our solution has on the overall elapsed time of the entire micro-benchmark, including low-priority elapsed times; this is a simple generalization of the above description, with time-stamps taken at the beginning and end of the run() method for all threads, regardless of their priority.

The measurements were taken on an 800MHz Intel Pentium III (Coppermine) with 1024MB of RAM running Linux kernel version 2.4.20-13.7 (RedHat 7.0) in single-user mode. We ran each benchmark in its own invocation of the VM, repeating the benchmark six times in each invocation, and discarding the results of the first iteration, in which the benchmark classes are loaded and compiled, to eliminate the overheads of compilation. We report the average elapsed time for the five subsequent iterations, and show 90% confidence intervals in our results. Our system is based on Jikes RVM 2.2.1 and we use a configuration where both the Jikes RVM (which is itself implemented and bootstrapped in Java) and dynamically loaded classes are compiled using the optimizing compiler. Even in this configuration there remain some methods (*eg*, class initializers) that are still baseline compiled, in both the original and modified VMs alike.

## 4.2 Results

Figures 5 and 6 plot elapsed times for high priority threads executed on both the modified (solid line) and unmodified (dotted line) VM, normalized with respect to the configuration executing 100% reads on an unmodified VM. In Figure 5 every high priority thread executes 100K internal iterations; in Figure 6 the iteration count is 500K. In each figure: the graph labeled (a) reflects a workload consisting of two high-priority threads, and eight low-priority threads; the graph labeled (b) reflects a workload consisting of five high-priority and five low-priority threads; and, the graph labeled (c) reflects a workload consisting of eight high-priority threads and two low-priority ones.

If the ratio of high-priority threads to low-priority threads is relatively low (Figures 5-6 (a)(b)), our hybrid implementation improves throughput for high-priority threads by 25% to 100% over the unmodified implementation. Average elapsed-time percentage gain across all the configurations, including those where the number of high-priority threads is greater than the number of low-priority threads, is 78%. If we discard the configuration where there are eight high-priority threads competing with only two low-priority ones, with larger numbers of high-priority threads than low-priority ones, the average elapsed time of a high-priority thread is twice as fast as in the reference implementation.

Note that the influence of different read-write ratios on overall performance is small; recall that all threads, regardless of their priority, log all updates within a synchronized section. This implies that the cost of operations related to log maintenance and rollback of partial results is also small, compared to the elapsed time of the entire benchmark. Indeed, the actual "workload" (contents of the synchronized section) in the benchmark consists entirely of data access operations – no delays (method calls, empty loops, *etc*) are inserted in order to artificially extend its execution time. Since realistic programs are likely to have a more diverse mix of operations, the overheads would be even smaller in practice.

As expected, if the number of write operations within a synchronized section is sufficiently large, the overhead of logging and rollbacks may start outweighing potential benefit. For example, in Figure 6(c), under a 100% write configuration, every high priority thread writes, and thus logs, approximately 500K words of data in every execution of a synchronized section. We believe that synchronized sec-

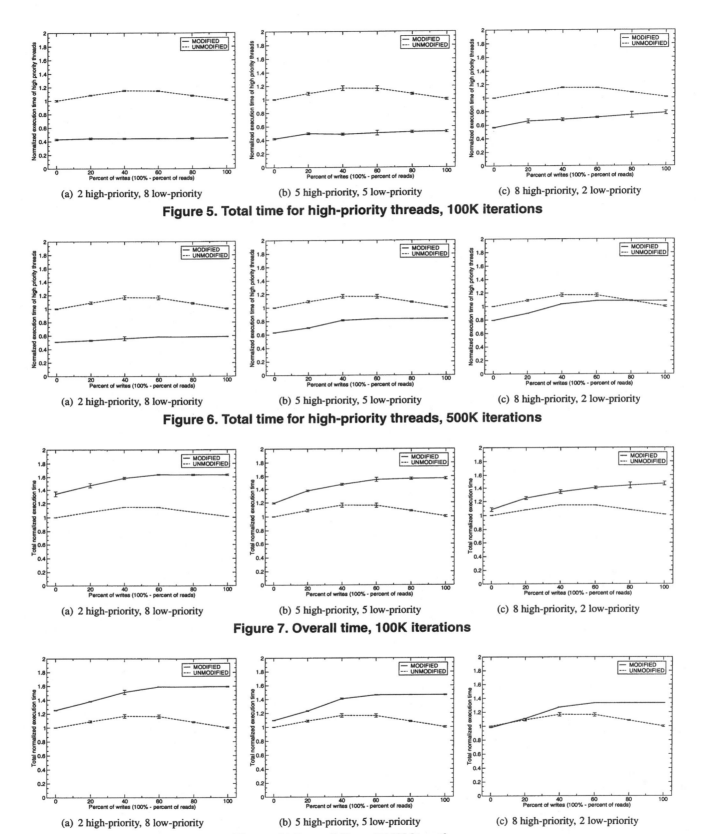

(a) 2 high-priority, 8 low-priority          (b) 5 high-priority, 5 low-priority          (c) 8 high-priority, 2 low-priority

**Figure 5. Total time for high-priority threads, 100K iterations**

(a) 2 high-priority, 8 low-priority          (b) 5 high-priority, 5 low-priority          (c) 8 high-priority, 2 low-priority

**Figure 6. Total time for high-priority threads, 500K iterations**

(a) 2 high-priority, 8 low-priority          (b) 5 high-priority, 5 low-priority          (c) 8 high-priority, 2 low-priority

**Figure 7. Overall time, 100K iterations**

(a) 2 high-priority, 8 low-priority          (b) 5 high-priority, 5 low-priority          (c) 8 high-priority, 2 low-priority

**Figure 8. Overall time, 500K iterations**

536

tions that consist entirely of write operations of this magnitude are relatively rare.

As the ratio of high-priority threads to low-priority threads increases, the benefit of our strategy diminishes (see Figures 5(c) and 6(c)). This is expected: since there are relatively fewer low-priority threads in the system, there is less opportunity to "steal" cycles from them to improve throughput of higher priority ones. We note, however, that even when the rollback-enabled VM has weaker performance than the unmodified implementation, the average difference in execution time is only a few percent.

Figures 7 and 8 plot overall elapsed times for the entire application executed on both modified (solid line) and unmodified (dotted line) VMs. These graphs are also normalized with respect to a configuration executing 100% reads on the unmodified VM. Note that the overall elapsed time for the modified VM must always be longer than for the unmodified VM. If we disallowed revocability of synchronized sections, threads executing on both VMs would need exactly the same amount of time to execute their workloads (modulo costs related to the implementation of our mechanism for the modified VM: barriers, log maintenance, etc). However, if the execution of synchronized sections can be interrupted and revoked, low-priority threads executing on the modified VM will re-execute parts of their synchronized sections thus lengthening overall elapsed time. Since our focus is on lowering elapsed times of high priority threads, we consider the impact on overall elapsed time (on average 30% higher on the modified VM) to be acceptable. If our mechanism is used to resolve deadlocks then these overheads may be an even more acceptable price to pay to obtain progress by breaking deadlocks.

## 5 Related work

Priority inversion is a well-studied problems in concurrent programming. Avoiding priority inversion is especially important in mission critical or real-time applications [15, 20, 21]. Priority inheritance and priority ceiling are two well-known protocols that attempt to avoid priority inversion. The priority ceiling emulation technique raises the priority of any locking thread to the highest priority of any thread that ever uses that lock (ie, its priority ceiling). This requires the programmer to supply the priority ceiling for each lock. In contrast, priority inheritance will raise the priority of a thread only when holding a lock causes it to block a higher priority thread. When this happens, the low priority thread inherits the priority of the higher priority thread it is blocking. Yet another alternative is to have privileged threads, for example those executing on behalf of the operating system. They can often disable interrupts or preemption that effectively prevents lower-priority threads from acquiring critical resources. Regardless of the approach, once a thread enters a synchronized section its locks cannot be summarily relinquished without potentially violating synchronization invariants. In contrast, our use of compiler-assisted rollbacks provides a *dynamic* approach to

resolving priority inversion issues. Since the overheads to perform rollbacks are charged only to low-priority threads, our scheme biases throughput in favor of threads that actually require it.

Our use of rollbacks to redo computation inside synchronized sections as a result of an undesirable scheduling is reminiscent of optimistic concurrency protocols first introduced in the 1980's [13] to improve database performance. Given a collection of transactions, the goal in an optimistic concurrency implementation is to ensure that only a serializable schedule results [1, 9, 23]. Devising fast and efficient techniques to confirm that a schedule is correct remains an important topic of study.

Transactional techniques such as the kind proposed here have also been applied to a broader setting. For example, researchers have investigated lock-free data structures [18, 12] and transactional memory implementations [11, 22, 10] which generalize transactional protocols for database systems, to any concurrent system. Our solution differs from these efforts in that it is not limited to support for specific lock-free data structures, requires no hardware support and relies only on limited transactional support (requiring no resolution of conflicts between data accesses, deadlock-related situations, etc). It is also transparent to the programmer since it modifies only the implementation of the language and not its semantics.

Rinard [19] describes experimental results using low-level optimistic concurrency primitives in the context of an optimizing parallelizing compiler that generates parallel C++ programs from unannotated serial C++ source. His approach does not ensure atomic commitment of multiple variables. In the case of our solution, in contrast to a low-level facility, the code protected by monitors may span an arbitrary dynamic context.

There has been much recent interest in data race detection for Java. Some approaches [6, 3, 4] present new type systems using, for example, ownership types [5] to verify the absence of data races and deadlock. There has also been recent work on generalizing type systems to reason about higher-level atomicity properties of concurrent programs that subsume data race detection [7]. Other techniques [24] employ static analysis, such as escape analysis, along with runtime instrumentation that meters accesses to synchronized data.

The approach presented here shares similar goals with these efforts but differs in some important respects. In particular, our implementation does not rely on global static analysis (although it may benefit from it), programmer annotations, or alternative type systems. Instead, our use of rollback permits discarding effects of undesirable schedules.

## 6 Conclusions

We have presented a revocation-based priority inversion avoidance scheme and demonstrated its utility in improving throughput of high priority threads in a priority scheduling environment. The solution proposed is relatively simple to implement, portable, and can be adopted to solve other types of problems (*eg*, deadlocks). Our techniques use compiler support that insert barriers on read and write operations to log accesses and updates to shared data, and runtime modifications to implement revocation when a preemption event occurs.

Although our preliminary experiments are encouraging, we believe there are numerous opportunities to improve the performance of our design by incorporating compiler optimizations to eliminate overheads currently incurred to deal with logging and commits. For example, read barriers on code not protected by locks could be removed if such regions were identified. We also intend to evaluate the performance of our technique for real-world applications to precisely measure the impact of our enforced non-revocability of monitors.

**Acknowledgments** This work is supported by the National Science Foundation under grants Nos. CCR-9711673, STI-0334141, IIS-9988637, and CCR-0085792, by the Defense Advanced Research Program Agency, and by gifts from Sun Microsystems, IBM, and NEC.

# References

[1] ADYA, A., GRUBER, R., LISKOV, B., AND MAHESHWARI, U. Efficient optimistic concurrency control using loosely synchronized clocks. *ACM SIGMOD Record 24*, 2 (June 1995), 23–34.

[2] ALPERN, B., ATTANASIO, C. R., BARTON, J. J., COCCHI, A., HUMMEL, S. F., LIEBER, D., NGO, T., MERGEN, M., SHEPHERD, J. C., AND SMITH, S. Implementing Jalapeño in Java. In *Proceedings of the ACM Conference on Object-Oriented Programming Systems, Languages, and Applications* (Denver, Colorado, Nov.). *ACM SIGPLAN Notices 34*, 10 (Oct. 1999), pp. 314–324.

[3] BOYAPATI, C., LEE, R., AND RINARD, M. C. Ownership types for safe programming: preventing data races and deadlocks. In *Proceedings of the ACM Conference on Object-Oriented Programming Systems, Languages, and Applications* (Seattle, Washington, Nov.). *ACM SIGPLAN Notices 37*, 11 (Nov. 2002), pp. 211–230.

[4] BOYAPATI, C., AND RINARD, M. A parameterized type system for race-free Java programs. In OOPSLA'01 [17], pp. 56–69.

[5] CLARKE, D. G., POTTER, J. M., AND NOBLE, J. Ownership types for flexible alias protection. In *Proceedings of the ACM Conference on Object-Oriented Programming Systems, Languages, and Applications* (Vancouver, Canada, Oct.). *ACM SIGPLAN Notices 33*, 10 (Oct. 1998), pp. 48–64.

[6] FLANAGAN, C., AND FREUND, S. N. Type-based race detection for Java. In *Proceedings of the ACM Conference on Programming Language Design and Implementation* (Vancouver, Canada, June). *ACM SIGPLAN Notices 35*, 6 (June 2000), pp. 219–232.

[7] FLANAGAN, C., AND QADEER, S. Types for atomicity. In *Proceedings of the 2003 ACM SIGPLAN International Workshop on Types in Language Design and Implementation* (New Orleans, Louisiana, Jan.). 2003, pp. 1–12.

[8] GOSLING, J., JOY, B., STEELE, JR., G., AND BRACHA, G. *The Java Language Specification*, second ed. Addison-Wesley, 2000.

[9] HERLIHY, M. Apologizing versus asking permission: Optimistic concurrency control for abstract data types. *ACM Trans. Database Syst. 15*, 1 (1990), 96–124.

[10] HERLIHY, M., LUCHANGCO, V., MOIR, M., AND SCHERER, III, W. N. Software transactional memory for dynamic-sized data structures. In *Proceedings of the Annual ACM Symposium on Principles of Distributed Computing* (Boston, Massachusetts, July). 2003, pp. 92–101.

[11] HOSKING, A. L., AND MOSS, J. E. B. Object fault handling for persistent programming languages: A performance evaluation. In *Proceedings of the ACM Conference on Object-Oriented Programming Systems, Languages, and Applications* (Washington, DC, Sept.). *ACM SIGPLAN Notices 28*, 10 (Oct. 1993), pp. 288–303.

[12] JENSEN, E. H., HAGENSEN, G. W., AND BROUGHTON, J. M. A new approach to exclusive data access in shared memory multiprocessors. Tech. rep., Lawrence Livermore National Laboratories, 1987.

[13] KUNG, H. T., AND ROBINSON, J. T. On optimistic methods for concurrency control. *ACM Trans. Database Syst. 9*, 4 (June 1981), 213–226.

[14] LINDHOLM, T., AND YELLIN, F. *The Java Virtual Machine Specification*. Addison-Wesley, 1999.

[15] LOCKE, D., SHA, L., RAJIKUMAR, R., LEHOCZKY, J., AND BURNS, G. Priority inversion and its control: An experimental investigation. In *Proceedings of the second international Workshop on Real-time Ada issues* (Moretonhampstead, Devon, England, June). 1988, pp. 39–42.

[16] MANSON, J., AND PUGH, W. JSR133: Java memory model and thread specification, 2004.

[17] *Proceedings of the ACM Conference on Object-Oriented Programming Systems, Languages, and Applications* (Tampa, Florida, Oct.). *ACM SIGPLAN Notices 36*, 11 (Nov. 2001).

[18] RAJWAR, R., AND GOODMAN, J. R. Transactional lock-free execution of lock-based programs. In *Proceedings of the ACM International Conference on Architectural Support for Programming Languages and Operating Systems* (San Jose, California, Oct.). *ACM SIGPLAN Notices 37*, 10 (Oct. 2002), pp. 5–17.

[19] RINARD, M. Effective fine-grained synchronization for automatically parallelized programs using optimistic synchronization primitives. *ACM Trans. Comput. Syst. 17*, 4 (Nov. 1999), 337–371.

[20] SCHMIDT, D. C., MUNGEE, S., FLORES-GAITAN, S., AND GOKHALE, A. S. Alleviating priority inversion and non-determinism in real-time CORBA ORB core architectures. In *IEEE Real Time Technology and Applications Symposium* (Denver, Colorado, June). 1998, pp. 92–101.

[21] SHA, L., RAJKUMAR, R., AND LEHOCZKY, J. P. Priority inheritance protocols: An approach to real-time synchronization. *IEEE Trans. Comput. 29*, 9 (Sept. 1990), 1175–1185.

[22] SHAVIT, N., AND TOUITOU, D. Software transactional memory. In *Proceedings of the Annual ACM Symposium on Principles of Distributed Computing* (Ottawa, Canada, Aug.). 1995, pp. 204–213.

[23] STONEBRAKER, M., AND HELLERSTEIN, J., Eds. *Readings in Database Systems*, third ed. Morgan Kaufmann, 1998.

[24] VON PRAUN, C., AND GROSS, T. R. Object race detection. In OOPSLA'01 [17], pp. 70–82.

[25] YODAIKEN, V. Against priority inheritance. http://www.fsmlabs.com/articles/inherit/inherit.html.

# Session 8B:
# Multimedia

# 16-bit FP sub-word parallelism to facilitate compiler vectorization and improve performance of image and media processing

Daniel Etiemble *, Lionel Lacassagne**
*LRI, ** IEF, University of Paris Sud
91405 Orsay, France
{ de@lri.fr , lionel.lacassagne@ief.u-psud.fr }

## Abstract

*We consider the implementation of 16-bit floating point instructions on a Pentium 4 and a PowerPC G5 for image and media processing. By measuring the execution time of benchmarks with these new simulated instructions, we show that significant speed-up is obtained compared to 32-bit FP versions. For image processing, the speed-up both comes from doubling the number of operations per SIMD instruction and the better cache behavior with byte storage. For data stream processing with arrays of structures, the speed-up mainly comes from the wider SIMD instructions.*

## 1. Introduction

Graphics and media applications have become the dominant ones for general purpose microprocessors and have led to the introduction of specific instruction set extensions such as the SIMD multimedia extensions now available in most ISAs. Graphics and media applications either use integer or FP computation. While some applications need the dynamic range and accuracy of 32-bit FP numbers, a general trends is to replace FP by integer computations for better performance when hardware resources are limited (embedded applications). However, many integer computations must deal with several integer formats, which forbid the compiler to use SIMD instructions. Using "intrinsics" or assembly language is tiresome and time consuming or even impossible with integer formats. In this introduction, we discuss the motivation for introducing 16-bit floating point operations and instructions in general purpose microprocessors.

### 1.1 16-bit floating point formats

16-bit floating formats have been defined for some DSP processors, but rarely used. Recently, a 16-bit floating point format has been introduced in the OpenEXP format [1] and in the Cg language [2] defined by NVIDIA. This format, called "half", is presented in figure 1. A number is interpreted exactly as in the other IEEE FP formats. The exponent is biased with an excess value of 15. Value 0 is

reserved for the representation of 0 (Fraction =0) and of the denormalized numbers (Fraction ≠ 0). Value 31 is reserved for representing infinite (Fraction = 0) and NaN (Fraction ≠ 0). For 0<E<31, the general equation for calculating the value in a floating point number is $(-1)^S$ x (1.fraction) x $2^{(\text{Exponent field}-15)}$. The range of the format extends from $2^{-24} = 6 \times 10^{-8}$ and $(2^{16}-2^5) = 65504$. In the remaining part of this paper, the 16-bit floating point format will be called *half* or F16. The "half" FP format is justified both by ILM, which developed the OpenEXP graphics format, and NVidia as a trade-off between precision, dynamic range and storage cost.

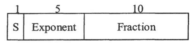

**Figure 1: NVIDIA "half" format**

### 1.2 Data format for image and media processing

Image processing generally need both integer and FP formats. For instance, vImage [3], which is the Apple image processing framework, proposes four image types with four pixel types: the first two pixel types are unsigned byte (0 to 255) and float (0.0 to 1.0) for one color or alpha value and the two other pixel types are a set of four unsigned char or float values for Alpha, Red, Green and Blue. Convolution operations with byte inputs need 32-bit integer formats for the intermediary results. Geometric operations need floating point formats. In many cases, using the "half" format would be a good trade-off: the precision and dynamic range of 32-bit FP numbers is not always needed and 16-bit FP computations are compatible with byte storage if efficient byte to/from half format is available. As input and output operands of floating point operations have the same format, the floating point computation has another potential advantage with SIMD instructions: it is far easier for the compiler to vectorize.

For media processing, the debate between integer and FP computing is also open. In [4], G. Kolly justifies "using Fixed-Point Instead of Floating Point for Better 3D Performance" in the Intel Graphics Performance Primitives library. Techniques for automatic floating-point to fixed-point conversions for DSP code generations have been presented [5]. On the other hand, people propose lightweight floating point arithmetic to enable FP signal processing applications in low-power mobile applications [6]. Using IDCT as benchmark, the authors show that FP numbers with 5-bit exponent and 8-bit mantissa are sufficient to get a Peak-Signal-to-Noise-Ratio similar to the PSNR with 32-bit FP numbers. These results illustrate one case for which the "half" format is adequate. If this debate first concerns the embedded applications, it is worth considering the interest of the "half" format for general purpose microprocessor as an extension for the SIMD instructions.

With the same SIMD register set of the currently available SIMD extensions, using SIMD F16 instructions doubles the number of parallel operations compared to SIMD 32-bit integer or FP instructions or provide the same number of parallel operations as the SIMD 16-bit integer instructions but with a larger dynamic range.

## 1.3 Integer, FP and compiler use of SIMD instructions

The choice between integer or FP data doesn't only depend on dynamic range and accuracy of computed values. As a matter of fact, using SIMD instructions and optimizing data accesses to improve cache performance are the two principal techniques that a programmer and/or a compiler can use to significantly reduce execution time. Compiler capabilities to vectorize are a key issue to improve performance. Presently, automatic compiler vectorization impact is generally disappointing even if compiler techniques improve steadily. One reason is that integer and FP instructions don't have the same features for compiler vectorization. Integer arithmetic operations have different input and output formats: adding two N-bit numbers provide an N+1-bit number while multiplying two N-bits numbers provide a 2N-bit number. This property leads to specific characteristics in the SIMD extensions. Saturating arithmetic (by definition) and 2's complement arithmetic discard carry outputs and cannot be used for arithmetic operations for which output dynamic range is greater than the input one. SIMD multiplications generally provide either the lower part or the higher part of the 2N-bit result for N-bit inputs. In IA-32 SIMD extension, the only instruction to get round the issue is the multiplication-add instruction (PMADDWD) that multiplies 4 or 8 signed short integers to deliver 32-bit intermediate results and horizontally adds two partial products to deliver 2 or 4 32-bit results (when using 64-bit or 128-bit SIMD registers). It is a specific exception with different input and output formats. A compiler can hardly find the opportunity to use such an instruction, which has obviously been defined for the dot product of 16-bit vectors widely used in signal processing. Such instructions are ad-hoc ones. The PSABDW instruction is the most

famous example. Computing the sum of absolute values of differences between adjacent bytes, its only use is for motion estimation for which it has been defined. On the other hand, FP SIMD instructions have the same input and output formats and can be easily used by compilers. To optimize portable programs (without using assembly language or intrinsics), FP formats exhibit a significant advantage.

## 1.4 Organization of this presentation

In this paper, we only focus on the performance evaluation of the 16-bit FP operations and the vectorization issues. We don't discuss the precision and dynamic range issues for graphics and media applications, which are the programmer's responsibility. We will show that the proposed F16 format has performance close to the performance of the SIMD 16-bit integer version (whether this version has or not enough dynamic range) and more or less than two times the performance of the 32-bit FP version because the number of SIMD operations is double and of the smaller cache footprint. The second characteristic is the easy vectorization, which is similar to "float" or "double" compiler vectorization while different integer formats generally prevent any vectorization.

After this introduction motivating the introduction of 16-bit FP operations, section II presents the methodology that has been used including the benchmarks and the technique to "simulate" the execution of 16-bit FP operations on general purpose microprocessors and measure the execution time of the benchmarks. Section III presents the microarchitectural assumptions and the defined 16-bit operations on a Pentium 4 and on a PowerPC G5. Section IV presents the performance evaluation for the different benchmarks both for the Pentium 4 and the Power PC G5. Section V presents a preliminary evaluation of the chip area for the 16-bit FP operators compared to the actual chip area of the 64-bit FP operators used in general purpose microprocessors.

## 2. Methodology

In this section, we describe the benchmarks and the simulation methodology that have been used.

### 2.1. Description of benchmarks

For image processing, we first consider convolution operators: the horizontal and horizontal-vertical versions of Deriche filters [7] and a gradient: these filters operate on 2D arrays of pixels (*unsigned char*), do some computation by using integers and deliver byte (or integer) results. They are representative of spatial filters and have a relatively high computation to memory accesses ratio. The two next benchmarks are variants of scan algorithms. Given an associative operator o, and a vector v(x), the scan operation returns a vector w(x) such as w(x) = v (0) o v (1) o ... o v(x). For example, the +scan returns for every pixel the 2D accumulation of the "previous" pixels of an image. The first benchmark implements a 2D accumulation and focuses on memory bandwidth limitation; the second one is based on a new segmentation algorithm proposed by Mérigot [8]. The classical image segmentation algorithm uses a quad tree computation based on the region's average and the variance (split and merge algorithm) [9]. Mérigot uses a +*scan operation to optimize both the speed and the quality of the segmentation. This +*scan operator accumulates the sum and the sum of the squares of the pixel area. These two last benchmarks have a lower computation to memory access ratio than our first set of benchmarks. For intermediate results, they need a dynamic range that implies floating point data.

For media processing, we consider the OpenGL data stream case study presented by Intel in [10]. The benchmark considers an OpenGL stream of triangles and computes the smallest box that bounds each triangle. We only considered the stream for which the triangle data are arranged in a tri-strip format (Figure 2) where the starting triangle is represented with all three vertices, but for each additional triangle that shares an edge with the triangle, only the third new vertex is stored (for N triangles, N+2 vertices are stored). Intel original assembly code has been converted into "intrinsics" code for the reference version to compare to the F16 version.

The code for all the benchmarks is provided in [11].

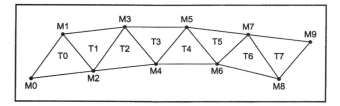

**Figure 2: Triangle in tri-strip format**

## 2.2. Simulation technique

Instead of using a software simulator, we have used a "hardware" one by measuring the execution time of the simulated instructions on actual hardware (Pentium 4 /PowerPC G5) for which the instructions are defined. The graphics and media benchmarks that we use have a nice specificity: the kernel computation consists in loop nests which are not data dependant (the loop iterations only depend on the loop bounds that are defined at compile time). In this situation, the "simulated" instructions can be

replaced by any "actual" instruction with given latency and throughput figures. There are basically three constraints: a) the cache accesses should be the same for the simulated and actual memory instructions. b) The data dependencies should be strictly enforced. c) As it is no longer possible to check the results, we must carefully check that the compiler generates all the required instructions according to the data dependencies. With a Pentium 4, the SIMD MULPS (packed floating point multiplication) can be used to simulate a MULF16 (packed *half* multiplication with the same latency (6 cycles) and throughput (2 cycles). The drawback of this technique is that there is less degrees of freedom to choose latency and throughput values than with a software simulator. But one can easily argue that these values, corresponding to the actual values of the Pentium 4 instructions are more realistic of VLSI technical constraints than the values generally assumed in software simulators. By using the same latency and throughput figures for F16 instructions as the Pentium 4 single (and double) precision ones, we get an upper bound of the execution time for the F16 instructions. Using realistic lower latency figures for the F16 instructions give a good insight of possible improved results. The situation is the same for the Altivec instructions of the PowerPC.

## 2.3. Measures

For each benchmark, the execution time has been measured at least 10 times and we have taken the averaged value. For the Pentium 4, we have used a 2.4 GHz processor with 768 MB memory running Windows 2000. We have used the Intel C++ 8 compiler The QxW option generates specialized code for the Pentium 4. The execution time has been measured with the RDTSC (read-time stamp counter) instruction available with IA-32. All the measures have been done with only one running application (Visual C++). For the PowerPC, we have used a 1.6 GHz PowerPC G5 with 768 MB DDR400 running Mac OS X.3. The programs have been compiled with the Xcode programming environment including gcc 3.3.

For all the image benchmarks, the results are presented as the number of cycles per pixel (CPP) which is the execution time of the overall benchmark divided by the number of pixels. For the OpenGL stream case study, the results are presented as the number of cycles per triangle. For all image benchmarks, we have followed the same approach. First, the naïve integer version has been transformed into an optimized integer SIMD version when this version can be implemented. Otherwise, it has been transformed into a float version for which each pixel is represented by a float. Then we have written another float version with Intel intrinsics which performance is equivalent or better than the compiler version. The SIMD integer or float versions with intrinsics have then been converted into an F16 version that operates on 16-bit FP data after conversion from the original byte array layout. This version is compared with the best optimized SIMD integer version and the best SIMD float version.

# 3. ISA and microarchitectural assumptions

As the reference processor, we considered the presently available version of the Pentium 4. As the MMX instructions are somewhat special by sharing the MMX registers with the x87 FP instructions, we only considered the XMM register set with 128-bit integer and SP FP instructions.

We assume the currently available 128-bit XMM register set. Extending to 256 bits would be a dramatic change on many aspects of the architecture: data cache access, doubling the number of functional units for all the SIMD operations, etc. With 128-bit registers and data path, the number of functional units for each SIMD F16 operation is 8. The issues to solve are: the conversions between bytes to/from F16 data, the type of FP operators and the permutation and formatting operations that must be added for the F16 format.

Byte to F16 conversion means converting 8 packed bytes into 8 packed F16 "half". IA32 ISA having a (2,1) instruction format, the source operand can be either a register or a memory operand. One could define a conversion from a 64-bit memory operand (or the lower part of an XMM register) into an XMM register. The other option consists in defining two different byte-to-F16 conversion instructions. After loading the XMM register with a 16-byte memory access, the first conversion instruction would convert the lower part of the XMM register into 8 packed F16 in another register and the second one would convert the higher part. This second conversion instruction is not absolutely necessary, but avoids an intermediate move/shift from the upper part to the lower part of the source register. These conversion instructions are register only instructions. The opposite F16 to byte conversion are needed. The second option looks more efficient. It implicitly unrolls two times any loop (the lower 8-byte operands first, then the higher ones). It avoids the alignment issues when dealing with byte accesses such as X[i][j] and X[i][j+1] which are easier to treat within the XMM registers.

To deal with the complete F16 format, the FP operators that are needed are the same as the ones that are available for single and double precision formats: the packed F16 addition/subtraction, multiplication, division and square root operators. Bitwise logical operations are the same for F16 formats as for any other format. Shuffle and pack/unpack instructions can be more efficiently executed on the original byte data before conversion for byte stored arrays, but they are needed for "half" stored arrays. When

F16 data are stored, all the shuffle or packing/unpacking instructions that are now available for 16-bit data can be used but these operations should be extended to the 8 different slots, which raise a small difficulty. The shuffle or packing/unpacking operations are defined by an 8-bit immediate in the IA-32 ISA, which is OK with four slots as each couple of bits controlling one out of four slots. Keeping an 8-bit immediate with eight slots would need a coding of the different operations on the eight slots.

**Table 1: 16-bit FP instructions for Pentium 4**

| Instruction | Latency | Meaning |
|---|---|---|
| ADDF16 | 4 | Xmmd <= Xmmd+Xmms |
| SUBF16 | 4 | Xmmd <= Xmmd-Xmms |
| MULF16 | 6 | Xmmd <= Xmmd * Xmms |
| MAXF16 | 4 | Xmmd <= Xmmd max Xmms |
| MINF16 | 4 | Xmmd <= Xmmd min Xmms |
| CBL2F16 | 4 | Xmmd <=I8toF16 (Xmms low) |
| CBH2F16 | 4 | Xmmd<= I8toF16 (Xmms high) |
| CF162BL | 4 | Xmmd low<= F16toI8 (Xmms) |
| CF162BH | 4 | Xmmd high<= F16toI8(Xmms) |
| SHUFF16 | 4 | Xmmd <= shuffle (8 slots) Xmms |

Table 1 lists the different F16 IA-32 instructions that we used in our benchmarks. All the proposed instructions have a throughput value of 2. *Short* from/to *half* conversions are also needed. Load and store packed instructions for *half* data are similar to the already packed integer instructions.

**Table 2: G5 instruction latencies**

| Execution Unit: | cycles |
|---|---|
| IU (+, -, logical, shift) | 2-3 |
| IU (multiplication) | 5-7 |
| FPU (+, -, *, MAF) | 6 |
| LSU (L1 hit) to GPR, FPR, VR | 3,5,4-5 |
| LSU (L2 hit, loads only) | 11 |
| VPERM | 2 |
| VSIU (part of VALU) | 2 |
| VCIU (part of VALU) | 5 |
| VFPU (part of VALU) | 8 |

We also considered the presently available G5 processor with Altivec extension and the instruction latencies [12] given in Table 2. As the Altivec extension is rather complete, we only need to add the vector F16 instructions and the byte to/from F16 conversion instructions. All the packing/unpacking and permutation instructions are already available for *short* integer operands. The simulated conversion instructions have a latency of 2, which may be a little bit optimistic. The F16 multiplication-accumulation instruction, which is used for F16 add, mul and mul-add, has a latency of 5. Compared to our Pentium 4 simulation of F16 instructions that are pessimistic, our G5 simulation are slightly optimistic.

## 4. Measured results

### 4.1. Deriche benchmarks

Both the horizontal (H) and horizontal-vertical (HV) versions of Deriche filters and the Deriche gradient can use one or two arrays. In the first case, the original array is replaced by the final array. The results presented in Table 3 for the Pentium 4 and Table 4 for the PowerPC G5 correspond to only one array. The measures have been done with 512x512 images for which the image fits in the 512-KB L2 cache of Xeon or G5 with byte pixels, but doesn't fit with 32-bit FP pixels.

Both tables give the best scalar and the best SIMD versions for 16-bit integer and 32-bit FP formats together with the F16 version. The crossed out values correspond to integer versions for which it is necessary to first check the coefficient values to avoid overflow (as detailed below for Deriche filters) or for which overflow can occur (gradient). F16 versions assume the instructions latencies previously defined in Tables 1 and 2.

The horizontal filter exhibits a loop-carried dependency. The best integer scalar version unrolls 3 times the inner loop and 2 times the outer loop. The best float scalar version unrolls 4 times the outer loop. There are two obstacles to manual vectorization with intrinsics: first the loop-carried dependency and second the dynamic range of the results when multiplying pixels by b0, a0 and a2 coefficients. The loop-carried dependency is suppressed by transposing the initial array before applying the filter and transposing back the resulting array. A 16 x 16 byte block transposition can be implemented with SIMD unpack instructions. To reduce the cache misses, we transpose a horizontal tile of 16 x 16 byte blocks into a vertical tile of 16 x 16 byte blocks, apply the filter on this vertical buffer and transpose back the resulting column into the initial horizontal tile. Vectorizing the multiplications is possible if coefficient values are known. If all coefficients values are less than 256, then multiplying a coefficient by a pixel value fits in a 16-bit value and using the Pentium 4 SIMD

multiplication on 16-bit inputs and the lower 16-bit of the 32-bit output is OK. As it turns out that 2 coefficients are positive while the third one is negative, the inner loop can be implemented as a subtraction followed by an addition to avoid any overflow. If one coefficient is greater than 256, the expression computed in the inner loop can be transformed to become similar to the previous case. For instance, if $256 < b0 < 512$, then $b0 * X[i][j] >> 8 = X[i][j] + (b0 - 256) b0 * X[i][j] >> 8$ and the multiplication of the pixel value by $b0 - 256$ is similar to the previously described case, and so on. We only give these details to outline that using SIMD integer instructions generally needs a detailed knowledge of the application including the dynamic range of the different coefficients. With 16-bit or 32-bit FP values, after the horizontal tile to vertical tile transposition, the inner loop easily vectorizes.

**Table 3: Execution time (CPP) on a 512x512 image on a Pentium 4**

| Benchmark | Scalar integer | Scalar F32 | SIMD integer | SIMD F32 | F16 |
|---|---|---|---|---|---|
| Deriche H | 35.5 | 30 | ~~9.1~~ | 19.7 | 9.3 |
| Deriche HV | 33.3 | 17 | ~~6.1~~ | 16.9 | 7 |
| Gradient | 17 | 11 | ~~4.1~~ | 6.8 | 3.5/5.3 |

**Table 4: Execution time (CPP) on a 512x512 image on a PowerPC G5**

| Benchmark | Scalar integer | Scalar F32 | SIMD integer | SIMD F32 | F16 |
|---|---|---|---|---|---|
| Deriche H | 27.7 | 10.3 | ~~4.2~~ | 13.8 | 5 |
| Deriche HV | 25 | 23 | ~~2.2~~ | 11.1 | 2.6 |
| Gradient | 17.6 | 73.6 | ~~2.4~~ | 5.7 | 2.5 |

For the two processors, the 16-bit integer or FP versions for filters and gradient outperform the 32-bit scalar integer and FP versions. The 16-bit integer and FP versions have similar performance, as memory accesses are the same and the conversions are similar (byte to short by unpacking with zero expansion, byte to F16 by actual conversion). The performance differences come from the difference in integer or F16 operation latencies.

For the Pentium, the F16 version is slightly slower than the 16-bit integer version as the additions (latency of 4 for F16 versus 2 for int16) are more frequent than the multiplications (latency of 6 for F16 versus 8 for int16). However, the integer versions are specific and depend on the coefficient values when the F16 version is generic. The

F16 versions exhibit a speed-up close to 2 versus the float versions for two reasons: there are 8 operations per instruction instead of 4, and storing byte instead of float reduces the cache footprint. There are two values for the F16 version in Table 3: the first one supposes one specific FABS16 instruction to compute the absolute value while the second one has not this instruction that doesn't exist in the IA-32 SIMD float instructions.

For the G5 processor, the speed-up between F16 and 32-bit FP versions ranges from 2.2 to 4.2. It comes from the number of operations per instruction, the cache footprint plus smaller latency values (F16 arithmetic operations have a latency of 5 instead of 8 and the latency of conversion instructions is 2, which is less than the latency of integer to float conversion for the G5 processor).

The best scalar version of the horizontal-vertical Deriche filter unrolls two times the inner loop. This filter has no dependency, but the same coefficient problems as the horizontal one. The only difference between the horizontal filter and the horizontal vertical execution times comes from the transposition execution times.

## 4.2. Scan benchmarks

The scan benchmarks have a lower computation to memory access ratio than the previous benchmarks: the +scan has two additions for three memory accesses. Because of the accumulation, the accumulator must be large enough to avoid any overflow. 32-bit integers or floats are typically used for large images and 16-bit integer for small images. For the +*scan, the 32-bit integer format has not enough range: a $2^{34}$ range is needed for a 512x512 image and a $2^{36}$ one for a 1024x1024 image. Either the *half* or the *float* format is needed. The outputs can be stored in two separated matrices of floats, or interleaved in a single matrix. The F16 version was simulated from an integer *short* version and adding extra code for square computations and accumulations. The +scan (horizontal add) within a 128-bit register was implemented with 3 couples of addition/shift instructions.

The results for copy, +scan and +* scan are given in Table 5 for the Pentium 4 and in Table 6 for the PowerPC G5. The crossed out values correspond to versions for which the dynamic range is insufficient to get correct results.

It turns out that the +scan has performance that is close to the performance of the copy benchmark, which mean that the +scan is clearly memory-bounded. It is quite obvious in that situation that using FP formats cannot bring any advantage and that simply using integer formats is the best solution.

**Table 5: Execution time (CPP) for the +*scan on a 512 x 512 image on a Pentium 4**

| Data formats | I8-I16 | I8-I16 | I8-F32 | F32-F32 | I8–F16 |
|---|---|---|---|---|---|
| Scalar Copy | 4.9 | 9.4 | 9.5 | 13.6 | |
| SIMD Copy | 4.7 | 9.2 | 9.4 | 12.5 | |
| Scalar +scan | 5.6 | 9.6 | 10 | 15.3 | |
| SIMD +scan | 7.2 | 10.5 | 10.6 | 17.5 | 7.8 |
| Scalar +*scan | | 18.8 | 19 | 17 | |
| SIMD +*scan | 9.9 | 18.7 | 18.7 | 21.3 | 10.5 |

**Table 6 : Execution time (CPP) of the +scan for a 512 x 512 image on a PowerPC G5**

| Data formats | I8-I16 | I8-I16 | I8-F32 | F32-F32 | I8–F16 |
|---|---|---|---|---|---|
| Scalar Copy | 5.5 | 9.3 | 62.4 | 10.4 | |
| SIMD Copy | 4.5 | 6.7 | 7 | 7.6 | |
| Scalar +scan | 24.3 | 10.4 | 95 | 18 | |
| SIMD +scan | 5.1 | 7 | 7.7 | 15 | 5.1 |
| Scalar +*scan | | 17.7 | 26.7 | 18.5 | |
| SIMD +*scan | 7.8 | 13 | 15 | 15.8 | 7.8 |

For the +* scan, the F16 version on the Pentium 4 has a speed-up slightly less than 2, which is easily explained by the same reasons as previously. The best 32-bit integer version, which has not enough range, would run at 12.1 CPP versus 7.5 for the F16 version. We outline that the SIMD instructions are not suitable to implement the + scan and +* scan operations as each result correspond to the sum (or sum of squares) of all the previous results: this typical recurrence situation prevents automatic vectorization. A significant number of SIMD instructions are needed to accumulate the previous sums into a SIMD register. With the Pentium 4, the SIMD version is always slower than the scalar one. Only the F16 version is faster than the scalar 32-bit FP version. The F16 version of +* scan has 1.3 times the execution time of the fastest copy with 16-bit integers, which is the lower bound. The overhead comes from the bookkeeping instructions and the significant number of copy instructions that results from the two-operand format of IA-32 ISA (when destination operand must be preserved, it should first be copied into another operand). Going further to improve performance means improving the memory bandwidth and/or reducing the instruction overhead for loop nests, as suggested by the MediaBreeze architecture [19].

With the G5, F16 delivers a 1.5 speed-up versus the 32-bit FP format and 1.4 versus the 32-bit integer format for the +scan. For the +*scan, the speed-up is 1.9 versus the 32-bit FP format. Opposed to the Pentium 4, the SIMD versions are better than the scalar ones. As the Altivec extension is far more complete than the SSE/SSE2 extension, it is far easier to manually vectorize the scan benchmarks, which leads to better performance.

### 4.3. OpenGL benchmark

For the OpenGL stream case study, the reference version has vertices with float coordinates and stores each bounded box coordinates as 3 10-bit values packed into a 32-bit integer. The Pentium 4 execution time of the function is 195 cycles per triangle, which correspond to CPI=7. The F16 version has vertices with F16 coordinates and store each bounded-box coordinates as a 64 word (3 x F16 + padding). The execution time is 107.5 cycles per triangle and the CPI is 5. The speed-up is 1.8 and results from the eight parallel operations per SIMD instruction.

The PowerPC G5 execution time of the original version is 21.5 cycles per triangle versus 10.5 cycles per triangle for the F16 version. The speed-up (2.0) is close to the Pentium speed-up, but the G5 uses 9 times less cycles because it uses half the number of instructions of the Pentium to transform the initial input data structure into a structure suitable for SIMD operations and because the CPI is better (For the initial 32-bit FP version, the G5 CPI equals 1.6 versus 7 for the Pentium 4). There are several reasons for this huge difference. First, the Altivec Vector Permute Unit behaves as a crossbar able to permute both regular and irregular patterns from 2 vectors. Fewer instructions are needed to reformat data with Altivec compared to SSE2. Second, the 3-operand instruction format of Altivec avoids many copies that results from the 2-operand IA-32 instructions. Finally, we directly used the code provided in [10] for the OpenGL case study with IA-32 while the PowerPC code is slightly more optimized by factorizing the computation of the bounding box of one triangle with partial results computed for the previous triangle.

While the overall result is very different, the relative performance between F16 and 32-bit FP versions are very similar.

### 6. Chip area evaluation of F16 functional units

Only a VLSI implementation in the framework of the actual microprocessor (Pentium 4 or G5) could provide significant figures to estimate the area, power and timing features of the 16-bit floating point functional units. To get a rough preliminary approximation, we used VHDL models of floating point operators and a 0.18 μm cell-based library from ST (HCMOS8D technology). The same approach has been used by Talla et al [13] to evaluate the hardware cost of the MediaBreeze architecture. The VHDL models have been developed by J. Detrey and F. De Dinechin [14]: they include non pipelined and pipelined versions for the addition, the multiplication, the division and the square root operation. The adder uses a close path when the exponent values are close and a far path when their difference is large. The divider uses a radix-4 SRT algorithm while the square root operator uses a radix-2 SRT algorithm. In Table 7, we show the chip area of the different operators that is estimated by the Cadence 4.4.3 synthesis tool before placement and routing. For eight such 16-bit FP functional units, the chip area would be less than 11% than the chip area for the four 64-bit FP functional units that are implemented in the general purpose microprocessors (we assumed that the same FP units are used both for single and double precision FP numbers, as the corresponding instructions have the same latency). In our evaluation, the 16-bit FP adder is rather large compared to the other 16-bit operators. The dual path approach that gives the best results for 64-bit addition is probably unnecessary for 16-bit addition. A smaller 16-bit FP adder with a straightforward approach could be used as mentioned in [6].

**Table 7: Estimation of chip area (mm$^2$) for non pipelined FP operators in a 0.18$\mu$m CMOS technology**

| Op. | Add. | Mul. | Div. | Sqrt | Overall |
|-----|------|------|------|------|---------|
| 16-bit | 0.019 | 0.016 | 0.047 | 0.027 | 0,110 |
| 64-bit | 0.097 | 0.276 | 1.008 | 0.679 | 2,059 |
| Ratio | 19.90% | 5.91% | 4.64% | 4.04% | 5.33% |

### 7. Concluding remarks

For graphics applications on CPUs and GPUs, there is a common trade-off between precision and dynamic range on one hand and cost of storage on the other hand. Many graphics applications have better performance with floating point formats than with integer ones. One reason is that using FP formats make easier compiler or manual vectorization as FP operations have the same input and output formats. However, the single precision floating point format uses four times more memory as a byte format. When it provides enough precision and dynamic range, the 16-bit floating point format defined by ILM for the OpenEXP format and NVIDIA seems a good trade-off.

In this paper, we have considered a limited set of 16-bit FP operations and a set of conversion instructions between byte and 16-bit FP format for two common general purpose microprocessors. We have measured the execution time of different versions of typical graphics benchmarks (Deriche filters, Gradient, scan) with integer, float and "half" formats. For this last format, we have simulated the "half" instructions by using actual Pentium 4 or PowerPC G5 instructions having the same latency and throughput as the simulated instructions. For the compute bounded benchmarks that can be vectorized, the speed-up is greater or less than 2 (but close to 2) compared to the best "float" version. For the +*scan that needs floating point formats, the speed-up is greater than 2.

A very preliminary evaluation of the chip area shows that for eight 16-bit FP functional units, the chip area should not exceed 11% of the chip area currently devoted to the FP functional units in a Pentium 4 or a G5.

This work will be completed by considering a more significant lot of graphics and media applications. For graphics or media applications that are compute-bounded, F16 speed-up is close to 2 versus 32-bit FP versions. For graphics applications with byte stored pixels, the F16 versions have performance close to 16-bit integer versions, but have two significant advantages: compiler vectorization is greatly facilitated and the dynamic range is larger for intermediate results. Even when significant differences between the two considered SIMD extensions (SSE/SSE2 and Altivec) can lead to significant differences in performance figures (clock cycles per pixel), the performance gain between F16 and 32-bit FP versions are consistent for the two processors for all the benchmarks.

### 8. Acknowledgements

A. Dupret and J.O. Klein, from the IEF laboratory (University Paris Sud) have provided us the chip area evaluations using the Cadence synthesis tool with the 0.18 μm ST technology. Their help was greatly appreciated. F. Tourant, from Apple France Edu, provided us for a couple of weeks the Dual 2GHz PowerPC G5 which allows starting experiments on G5.

## 9. References

[1] OpenEXP, http://www.openexr.org/details.html

[2] NVIDIA, Cg User's manual, http://developer.nvidia.com/view.asp?IO=cg_toolkit

[3] Apple, "Introduction to vImage", http://developer.apple.com/documentation/Performance/Conceptual/vImage/

[4] G. Kolli, "Using Fixed-Point Instead of Floating Point for Better 3D Performance", Intel Optimizing Center, http://www.devx.com/Intel/article/16478

[5] D. Menard, D. Chillet, F. Charot and O. Sentieys, "Automatic Floating-point to Fixed-point Conversion for DSP Code Generation", in International Conference on Compilers, Architectures and Synthesis for Embedded Systems (CASES 2002)

[6] F. Fang, Tsuhan Chen, Rob A. Rutenbar, "Lightweight Floating-Point Arithmetic: Case Study of Inverse Discrete Cosine Transform" in EURASIP Journal on Signal Processing, Special Issue on Applied Implementation of DSP and Communication Systems

[7] R. Deriche. "Using Canny's criteria to derive a recursively implemented optimal edge detector". The International Journal of Computer Vision, 1(2):167-187, May 1987.

[8] A. Mérigot, Revisiting image splitting, 12th International Conference on Image Analysing and Processing, pp 314-319, ICIAP 2003.

[9] S. Horowitz, T. Pavlidis. Picture segmentation by a tree traversal algorithm. Journal of the ACM, 22:368-388, 1976.

[10] A. Kumar, "SSE2 Optimization – OpenGL Data Stream Case Study", Intel application notes, http://www.intel.com/cd/ids/developer/asmo-na/eng/segments/games/resources/graphics/19224.htm

[11] Sample code for the benchmarks available: http://www.lri.fr/~de/F16/codetsi

[12]Apple Developer Connection, "G5 performance programming", http://developer.apple.com/hardware/ve/g5.html

[13] D. Talla, L.K.John and D. Burger, "Bottlenecks in Multimedia processing with SIMD Style Extensions and Architectural Enhancements", in IEEE Transactions on Computers, Vol 52, N° 8, August 2003, pp 1015-1031.

[14] J. Detrey and F. De Dinechin, "A VHDL Library of Parametrisable Floating Point and LSN Operators for FPGA", http//www.ens-lyon.fr/~jdetrey/FPLibrary

# OSCAR – An Opportunistic Call Admission Protocol for LEO Satellite Networks

Stephan Olariu, Rajendra Shirhatti

*Department of Computer Science*
*Old Dominion University*
*Norfolk, VA 23529, U.S.A.*
*{olariu rshirhat},@cs.odu.edu*

Albert Y. Zomaya

*School of Information*
*The University of Sydney*
*Sydney, NSW 2006, Australia*
*zomaya@it.usyd.edu.au*

## Abstract

*The main contribution of this work is to propose OSCAR - - an OpportuniStic Call Admission pRotocol that provides a simple and robust solution to call admission and handoff management in LEO satellite networks. One of the features that sets OSCAR apart from existing protocols is that it avoids the overhead of reserving resources for users in a series of spotbeams along predicted user trajectories. Instead, OSCAR relies on a novel opportunistic bandwidth allocation mechanism that is very simple and efficient and does not involve maintaining complicated data structures or making expensive reservations. Extensive simulation results have shown that OSCAR achieves results comparable to those of Q-Win: it features very low call dropping probability, thus providing for reliable handoff of on-going calls, low call blocking probability for new call requests, and high bandwidth utilization.*

## 1. Introduction

In response to the increasing demand for truly global coverage needed by Personal Communication Services (PCS), a new generation of mobile satellite networks intended to provide *anytime-anywhere* communication services was proposed in the literature [Aky97, Bar03,Del00,Jam01,Lug99,MMJ03]. Low Earth Orbiting (LEO) mobile satellite networks, deployed at altitudes ranging from 500km to 2000km, are well suited to handle bursty Internet and multimedia traffic and to offer *anytime-anywhere* connectivity to mobile users. These satellite networks offer numerous advantages over terrestrial networks including global coverage and low cost-per-minute access to end-users equipped with hand-held devices. Since LEO satellite networks are expected to support real-time interactive multimedia traffic they must be able to provide their users with Quality-of-Service (QoS) guarantees [Far00,Hua98].

While providing significant advantages over their terrestrial counterparts, LEO satellite networks present protocol designers with numerous challenges, including handoff, mobility and location management [Com97,Del95,Fos03,Ngu00]. Because LEO satellites are deployed at low-altitude, Kepler's third law implies that these satellites must traverse their orbits at a very high speed. The coverage area of a satellite – a circular area of the surface of the Earth - is referred to as its *footprint*. For spectral efficiency reasons, the satellite footprint is partitioned into slightly overlapping cells, called *spotbeams*. As their coverage area changes continuously, in order to maintain connectivity, end-users must switch from spotbeam to spotbeam and from satellite to satellite, resulting in frequent intra-satellite and inter-satellite handoffs. For example, in the IRIDIUM satellite system the average spotbeam diameter is 425km and the rotational period is about 110min, implying that the time interval between two consecutive handoffs is about 65sec [Del95,Del00]. Due to the large number of handoffs experienced by a typical connection during its lifetime, resource management and connection admission control are very important tasks if the system is to provide fair bandwidth sharing and QoS guarantees. A successful handoff provides continuation of the call that is vital for the perceived QoS. Thus, a reliable handoff mechanism is needed to maintain connectivity and to minimize service interruption to on-going connections, as end-users roam about the system. An important QoS parameter is the *call blocking probability* (CBP), denoting the likelihood that a new connection request will be denied admission into the network. A similar situation arises when an established connection in one cell attempts to migrate into a neighboring cell (i.e. a handoff is attempted). If the new cell cannot support the level of resources required by the connection, the handoff is denied and the connection is dropped. The *call dropping probability* (CDP) expresses the likelihood that an existing connection will be forcibly terminated during a handoff between cells due to a lack of resources in the target cell. The CBP and CDP together offer a good indication of a network's quality of service in the face of mobility. An additional important consideration is the degree to which the network makes an effective use of bandwidth -- unquestionably its scarcest resource. This parameter, referred to as *bandwidth utilization*, expresses the ratio between the amount of bandwidth used by various applications admitted into the network and either the total bandwidth requested or the total bandwidth available, whichever is smaller. Keeping the CBP and CDP low, while at the same time maximizing bandwidth utilization is one of the most challenging tasks facing protocol designers [Lev97,Oli98,Pei99,Wer97]. In the remainder of this work we concern ourselves with intra-satellite handoffs, referred to, simply, as handoffs.

Our main contribution is to propose OSCAR - an opportunistic call admission protocol that provides a simple and robust solution to call admission and handoff management in LEO satellite networks. OSCAR was designed with efficiency and scalability in mind. Instead of maintaining priority queues and making resource reservations in a number of cells that the user is likely to visit, OSCAR relies on a novel bandwidth allocation mechanism that uses a number of virtual windows to make an opportunistic decision for admission of new users. Even though it adds up more processing time, the overhead of maintaining queues during heavy traffic is avoided and hence makes this algorithm more simple and less dependable on buffers. Moreover, the processing time is transparent to the mobile hosts, being absorbed by the on-board processing capabilities of the satellite. Consequently, our scheme scales to a large number of users.

The performance of OSCAR is compared to that of Q-Win and SILK, two recent schemes proposed in the literature. Extensive simulation results have shown that OSCAR outperforms SILK, achieving results comparable to those of Q-Win: it features a very low call dropping probability, low call blocking probability and high bandwidth utilization.

## 2. Related work

In wireless mobile networks the radio bandwidth is shared by a large number of users. An important property of the network is that a user would change its access points several times. This fact causes technical problems in which fair sharing of bandwidth between handoff connections and new connections is required. Resource allocation and call admission control (CAC, for short) are very important tasks that need to be performed efficiently in order to achieve high bandwidth utilization and QoS provisioning in terms of low dropping probability for handoffs and reasonably low blocking probability for new connections.

In the remainder of this section we survey a number of call admission algorithms proposed in the literature. We refer Table 1 for an at-a-glance comparison between several resource allocation strategies and CAC algorithms for LEO satellite networks found in the literature.

| Papers | * | ** | *** | + | ++ | +++ |
|--------|---|----|----|---|----|----|
| [Del95] | No | FCA | DCA | Handoff residual time | Local | No |
| [Mer97] | Yes | Fixed per connection | FCA | Handoff residual time | Local | No |
| [Uzu99] | No | No | FCA | User location | Threshold | Yes |
| [Cho00] | No | Adaptive | DCA | User location | Local | No |
| [Elk01] | Yes | Time-dependent probabilistic | FCA | Handoff residual time | Local and non-local | Yes |
| [Tod02] | Yes | Predictive | DCA | Handoff residual time | Local and non-local | Yes |
| [Ola03] | Yes | Adaptive | DCA | User location | Local and non-local | Yes |

\* Multi-services, \*\* Reservatin strategy, \*\*\* Resource allocation, + Necessary information, ++ CAC criteria, +++ QoS issues

**Table 1: A synopsis of recent resource allocation and admission control strategies**

Quite recently, Olariu *et al.* [Ola03] proposed Q-Win, a novel admission control and handoff management strategy for multimedia LEO satellite networks. A key ingredient in Q-Win is a novel predictive resource allocation protocol. Extensive simulation results have confirmed that Q-Win offers low CDP, acceptable call blocking probability (CBP) for new call attempts, and high bandwidth utilization. Q-Win involves some processing overhead. However, as the authors show, this overhead is transparent to the mobile hosts, being absorbed by the on-board processing capabilities of the satellite. Their simulation results show that Q-Win scales to a large number of users.

## 3. Mobility model and traffic parameters

Although several mobility models exist for LEO satellites [Jam01,Ngu02] it is customary to assume a one-dimensional mobility model where the end-users move in straight lines and at a constant speed, essentially the same as the orbital speed of the satellite [Del95,Del00,Ngu02]. We assume an orbital speed of 26,000Km/h. All the spotbeams (also referred to as cells) are identical in shape and size. Although each spotbeam is circular, we use squares to approximate spotbeams (we note that some authors use regular hexagons instead of squares). The diameter of a cell is taken to be 425Km [Del95,Del00]. Further, mobile hosts traverse each cell along its maximum diameter. Thus, the time $t_s$ it takes a mobile host to cross a cell is roughly 65 seconds.

Referring to Figure 1, assume that a connection $C$ was accepted in cell $N$ at time $t_C$. The connection remains in cell $N$ for $t_f$ time, where $t_f$ is uniformly distributed between 0 and $t_s$. Thus, $t_f$ is the time until the first handoff request, assuming that the call does not end in the original cell. After the first handoff, a constant time $t_s$ is assumed between subsequent handoff requests until call termination.

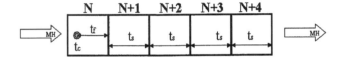

**Figure 1. Illustrating the mobility and cell parameters**

The traffic offered to the satellite may be real-time multimedia traffic, such as interactive voice and video applications, and non real-time data traffic, such as email or ftp. When a mobile user requests a new connection $C$ in a given cell, it provides the following parameters:

- $M_C$ the desired amount of bandwidth for the connection, and
- the minimum acceptable amount of bandwidth, $m_C$, that the source requires in order to maintain acceptable quality, e.g. the smallest encoding rate of its codec.

The stated goal of the opportunistic bandwidth allocation scheme that defines OSCAR is to minimize the likelihood of a connection being dropped. This is due to the fact that blocking a handoff request is, generally, considered less desirable from a user's point of view than blocking a new call.

## 4. OSCAR: the call admission strategy

Connection admission control is one of the fundamental tasks performed by the satellite network at call setup time in order to determine whether a connection request can be accepted into the system without violating prior QoS commitments. The task is non-trivial since the traffic offered to the system is a heterogeneous mix of new call attempts and handoff requests.

Consider a request for a new connection $C$ in cell $N$. Very much like SILK [Tod02] and Q-Win [Ola03], OSCAR bases its connection admission control on a novel scheme that combines the following two criteria:

- *Local availability:* The first call admission criterion, which is *local* in scope, ensures that the originating cell $N$ has sufficient resources to provide the connection with its desired amount of bandwidth $M_C$.

- *Short-term guarantees:* The second admission control criterion, which is *non-local* in scope, attempts to minimize the chances that, once accepted, the connection will be dropped later due to a lack of bandwidth.

However, unlike both SILK and Q-Win that look at a distant horizon and maintain complicated data structures, OSCAR looks ahead only one cell. As our simulation results indicate, this short horizon works well when supplemented by an opportunistic bandwidth allocation scheme. OSCAR's second admission criterion relies on a novel idea that is discussed in full detail in Subsection 4.1.

### 4.1. The details

Consider a request for a new connection $C$ in cell $N$ at time $t_C$ and let $t_f$ be the estimated residence time of $C$ in $N$. Referring to Figure 2, the key observation that inspired our second criterion is that when $C$ is about to handoff into cell $N+1$, the connections resident in $N+1$ are likely to be those in region $A$ of call $N$ and those in region $B$ of cell $N+1$. More precisely, these regions are defined as follows:

- A connection is in region $A$ if at time $t_C$ its residual residence time in cell $N$ is less than or equal to $t_f$.
- A connection is in region $B$ if at time $t_C$ its residual residence time in cell $N+1$ is larger than or equal to $t_f$.

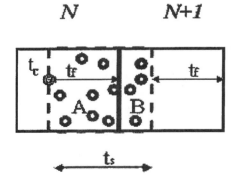

**Figure 2. Illustrating the sliding window concept for call admission.**

In general, the satellite does not know the exact position of a new call request in generic cell $N$. This makes the computation of the bandwidth committed to connection in areas $A$ and $B$ difficult to assess. In what follows we describe a *heuristic* that attempts to approximate the bandwidth held by the connections in A and B. For this purpose, we partition the union of cells $N$ and $N+1$ into $m+1$ virtual windows $W_0, W_1, ..., W_m$ each of width $t_s$. In this sequence, $W_0$ is the *base* window, and its left boundary is normalized to 0. For every $i$, $0 \leq i \leq m$, window $W_i$ stretches from

$$\frac{i \times t_s}{m} \text{ to } t_s + \frac{i \times t_s}{m}. \qquad (1)$$

In particular, by equation (1), window $W_0$ coincides with cell $N$, and window $W_m$ coincides with cell $N+1$. We refer the reader to Figure 3 for an illustration, with $m = 5$. All the virtual windows have the exact shape and size of a cell (for clarity purposes, they are drawn differently in Figure 3).

For later reference, we partition a generic window $W_i$ into a *left* sub-window $W_i^N$ and a *right* sub-window $W_i^{N+1}$ denoting, respectively, the intersection of $W_i$ with cells $N$ and $N+1$ (refer to Figure 4 for an illustration).

We distinguish between mobile hosts that have experienced a handoff (that will be refereed to as *old*) from those that have not (referred to as *new*). As we are about to describe, mobile hosts may or may not be assigned *timers*. Specifically, each old mobile host is assigned a timer $\theta$; no timer is assigned to new mobile hosts. Upon entering a new cell, $\theta$ is set to $t_s$ (the time it takes to traverse a cell). Every time unit, $\theta$ is decremented by one, making it close to zero by the time it is about to reach the next handoff. For illustration purposes, we note that in Figure 3, since $m = 5$, $W_1^N$ contains the old users in cell $N$ with $\theta \leq 65 - \frac{65}{5} = 52$; likewise, $W_1^{N+1}$ contains the old users in cell $N+1$ with $\theta \geq 52$. $W_2^N$ contains the old users in cell $N$ with $\theta \leq 65 - 2 \times \frac{65}{5} = 39$, and so on.

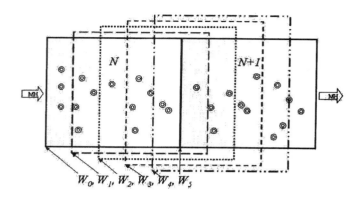

**Figure 3. Illustrating the virtual windows**
$$W_0, W_1, ..., W_m$$

Let $B_i$ and $D_i$ denote, respectively, the total amount of bandwidth in use by the old and new mobile hosts in window $W_i$. Notice that the amount of bandwidth $B_i$ is easy to compute by the satellite since, by virtue of timers, the position of old mobile hosts, up to the granularity of a virtual window, is known.

The location of new mobile hosts (i.e. newly accepted ones that have not yet experienced their first handoff) is unknown. It is, therefore, difficult to determine $D_i$ exactly. However, it is reasonable to assume that, within each of the cells $N$ and $N+1$, these mobile hosts are uniformly distributed. Notice that this does not imply a uniform distribution of new mobile hosts across the union of cells $N$ and $N+1$. Let $n_N$ and $n_{N+1}$ stand, respectively, for the number of new mobile hosts in cells $N$ and $N+1$. As illustrated in Figure 4, the assumption of uniform distribution of new mobile hosts in cell $N$ implies that the expected number of mobile hosts in $W_i^N$ is $n_N\left(1 - \frac{i}{m}\right)$. Likewise, since the new mobile hosts are uniformly distributed in cell $N+1$, the expected number of new mobile hosts in $W_i^{N+1}$ is $n_{N+1} \times \frac{i}{m}$. Thus, by a simple computation we obtain the following approximation for $D_i$:

$$D_i = \left(1 - \frac{i}{m}\right)n_N + \frac{i}{m}n_{N+1}. \qquad (2)$$

Let $M$ stand for the total bandwidth capacity of a cell. Using $B_i$ and the value of $D_i$ from equation (2), the virtual window $W_i$ determines the residual bandwidth $R_i = M - B_i - D_i$. If $R_i \geq M_C$, $W_i$ *votes* in favor of accepting the new request $C$ with desired bandwidth $Mc$; otherwise it *votes* against its admittance. After counting the votes, if the majority of the virtual windows had *voted* in favor of admittance, the new connection request is admitted into the system. Otherwise, it is rejected. Once admitted, the desired bandwidth of connection $C$ is allocated in the current cell.

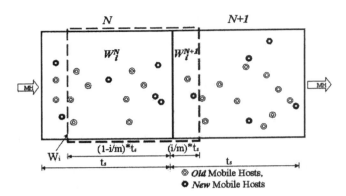

**Figure 4. *Illustrating the computation of $D_i$.***

# 5. OSCAR: The Handoff Management Scheme

A well-known strategy for reducing handoff failure is to reserve bandwidth for the exclusive use of handoff connections [Cho00,Del95,Mer97,Oli98]. In the *fixed reservation* approach, a fixed percentage of the available bandwidth in a cell is permanently reserved for handoff. It is well known that the fixed reservation strategy is either wasteful of bandwidth or outright ineffective depending on the amount of bandwidth reserved. In the *predictive reservation* strategy, bandwidth is reserved dynamically using a probabilistic approach [Elk01,Lev97,Nag96,Tod02,Ola03].

In OSCAR handoff calls fall into one of the two types discussed below:

- *Type 1*: those which are still not assigned a timer i.e. these are newly admitted calls that are about to make their first handoff

- *Type 2*: those which are assigned a timer i.e. the calls which have already made one or more handoffs.

It is important to observe that by virtue of our call admission scheme that is looking at both the originating cell and the next one along the mobile user's path, handoffs of Type 1 succeed with high probability. We are, therefore, only showing how to manage Type 2 handoffs. The details of this scheme are discussed in Subsection 5.1.

## 5.1 The details

Each cell in the network dynamically reserves a small amount of bandwidth specifically for handoffs of Type 2. When a Type 2 handoff request is made, the algorithm will first try to satisfy the request by allotting the bandwidth from the reserved channel. If the reserved channel is already full, the request will be allotted the bandwidth from the remaining available bandwidth of the cell. Otherwise, the handoff request is dropped.

Let the maximum amount of bandwidth that could be reserved be $\beta_{max}$ -- a small percentage of total available bandwidth. The amount of bandwidth reserved for Type 2 handoffs dynamically varies between 0 and $\beta_{max}$ depending on the relative position of the *average load line* in the previous neighboring cell.

To explain the concept of average load line, consider a cell $N$, and refer to Figure 5. Assume that cell $N-1$ contains $k$ Type 2 handoff calls with *residual* residence times in cell $N-1$ denoted by $t_1, t_2, ..., t_k$ such that $t_1 \le t_2 \le ... \le t_k$ and let the corresponding amounts of bandwidth allocated to the calls be $b_1, b_2, ..., b_k$. Write

$$B = \sum_{j=1}^{k} b_j.$$ The average load line $L$ is defined as

$$L = \frac{t_i + t_{i+1}}{2}$$ where $i$ is the *smallest* subscript for which the inequality (1) below holds.

$$\sum_{j=1}^{i} b_j \ge \left\lceil \frac{B}{2} \right\rceil \qquad (1)$$

We note that form a computational standpoint determining the average load line $L$ is a simple instance of the parallel prefix sums problem and can be handled easily by the satellite.

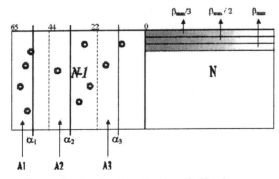

**Figure 5. Illustrating the handoff scheme.**

The dynamic channel reservation scheme in cell $N$ can be explained as follows. Since cell $N$ knows about its neighbors, it can track all the Type 2 handoff calls in cell *N-1* as shown. A1, A2 and A3 represent equal sized areas of a cell *N-1*. Average line will always fall into one of these three areas depending upon the distribution of Type 2 handoff calls. $\alpha_1$, $\alpha_2$ and $\alpha_3$ represent the positions of the *average line*. The bandwidth for Type 2 calls in cell N is reserved depending upon the position of the *average line*.

If the position of average load line *L* is at $\alpha_1$ in area A1, then it can be inferred that roughly half of the bandwidth required by Type 2 handoff calls is concentrated in area A1. Since *L* far away from cell *N*, a minimum bandwidth of $\beta_{max}/3$ is reserved for Type 2 handoff calls in cell *N* as shown so that more bandwidth is available for other call requests. If the average load line *L* is at $\alpha_2$ in A2, then a moderate bandwidth of $\beta_{max}/2$ can be reserved in cell *N*. If the average load line *L* is at $\alpha_3$ in A3, then a maximum bandwidth of $\beta_{max}$ is reserved for Type 2 calls in cell *N*.

## 6. Performance Evaluation

The main goal of this section is to analyze the performance of OSCAR through simulation. We begin by describing the simulation model and then we go on to present the results of our simulation. For comparison purposes we have implemented OSCAR, SILK and Q-Win. A detailed performance comparison of the three protocols is presented in Subsection 6.2.

### 6.1 Simulation model

Based on the description of call admission and handoff management schemes, we have developed a simulation program to evaluate their performances. Each spotbeam consists of a server and bandwidth with a part of it for Type 2 calls, shown in Figure 6.

**Server functions:**
The server functions implemented are: monitor the amount of available bandwidth in each of the spotbeams, reserve bandwidth required by individual connections, accept or reject new call requests, and accept or reject Type 1 and Type 2 requests.

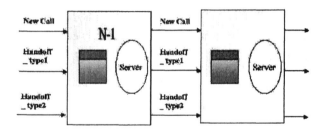

**Figure 6. The simulation model**

The system parameters used in our simulation experiments are described in Table 2. New call arrival rate follows a Poisson distribution and holding times are exponentially distributed.

| Spotbeam Parameters | | |
|---|---|---|
| Radius | Capacity | Speed |
| 212.5km | 30000KBit | 26000 km/h |
| Service Parameters | | |
| Mean duration (s) | 180 | 300 | 600 |
| Maximum bandwidth (kbps) | 30 | 256 | 1000 |
| Minimum bandwidth (kbps) | 30 | 256 | 6000 |

**Table 2: Simulation parameters**

We define three types of services with different QoS requirements and assume equal mean arrival rate for each service type and fixed bandwidth capacity in each spotbeam.

### 6.2 Simulation results

The simulation results are shown in Figures 7-9. We compare the CDP, CBP and bandwidth utilization performances of algorithm with those of Q-Win [Ola03] and SILK [Tod02].

Figure 7 shows that OSCAR has almost the same CBP as Q-Win and much better than SILK. The results for OSCAR and Q-Win can be seen more comprehensively in Figure 8.

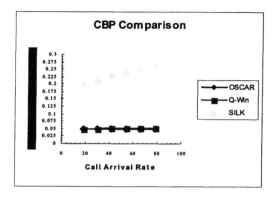

**Figure 7. Illustrating Call Blocking Probability**

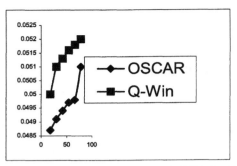

**Figure 8. A detailed comparison of CBP in OSCAR and Q-Win**

Figure 9 shows that the CDP of OSCAR is little higher than Q-WIN but is fair enough to conclude that the handoff management scheme yields almost the same results as SILK and Q-WIN.

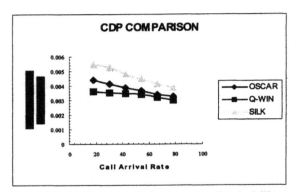

**Figure 9. Illustrating Call Dropping Probability**

It is well known that the goals of keeping the call dropping probability low and that of keeping the bandwidth utilization high are conflicting. It is easy to ensure a low CDP at the expense of bandwidth utilization and similarly, it is easy to ensure a high bandwidth utilization at he expense of call dropping probability. The challenge, of course, is to come up with a handoff management protocol that strikes a sensible balance between the two. As Figure 10 indicates, OSCAR features high bandwidth utilization in addition to keeping the call dropping probability low.

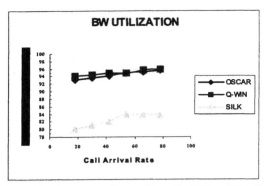

**Figure 10: A comparison of bandwidth utilization**

# 7. Concluding Remarks

LEO satellites are expected to support multimedia traffic and to provide their users with the appropriate QoS. However, the limited bandwidth of the satellite channel, satellite rotation around the Earth and mobility of end-users makes QoS provisioning and mobility management a challenging task. The main contribution of this work was to propose a new call admission and handoff management scheme for LEO satellite networks. Our scheme was specifically tailored to meet the QoS needs of multimedia connections where real-time and non-real-time service classes were differently treated. With our call admission scheme and handoff management scheme, better overall performance is achieved without knowledge of the exact location of mobile hosts. Our simulation results showed that OSCAR offers low CDP, good CBP for new calls and high bandwidth utilization.

**ACKNOWLEDGEMENT:** This work was supported, in part, by NATO grant PST.CLG979033. The first author is grateful to Alex Markhasin, Petia Todorova and Nam Nguyen for many discussions on LEO satellite networks.

# References

[Aky97] I. F. Akiyldiz and S. H. Jeong, Satellite ATM networks: A survey, *IEEE Communications*, 35(7), 1997.

[Bar03] S. J. Barnes and S. L. Huff, Rising sun: iMode and the wireless Internet, *Communications of the ACM*, 46(11), 2003, 79-84.

[Cho00] S. Cho, Adaptive dynamic channel allocation scheme for spotbeam handover in LEO satellite networks, *Proc. IEEE VTC 2000*, 1925-1929.

[Com97] G. Comparetto and R. Ramirez, Trends in mobile satellite technology, *IEEE Computer*, 1997, 44-52.

[Del95] E. Del Re, R. Fantacci, and G. Giambene, Efficient dynamic channel allocation techniques with handover queuing for mobile satellite networks, *IEEE*

*Journal of Selected Areas in Communications*, 13(2), 1995, 397-405.

[Del00] E. Del Re, R. Fantacci, and G. Giambene, Characterization of user mobility in Low Earth Orbiting mobile satellite systems, *Wireless Networks*, 6, 2000, 165-179.

[Elk01] M. El-Kadi, S. Olariu and P. Todorova, Predictive resource allocation in multimedia satellite networks, *Proc IEEE, GLOBECOM 2001*, San Antonio, TX, November 25-29, 2001.

[Far00] J. Farserotu and R. Prasad, A survey of future broadband multimedia satellite systems, issues and trends, IEEE Communications, 6, 2000, 128-133.

[Fos03] I. Foster and R. G. Grossman, Data integration in a bandwidth-rich world, *Communications of the ACM*, 46(11), 2003, 51-57.

[Hua98] A. Huang, M-J. Montpetit and G. Kesidis, ATM via satellite: A framework and implementation, *Wireless Networks*, 4, 1998, 141-153.

[Jam01] A. Jamalipour and T. Tung, The role of satellites in global IT: trends and implications, *IEEE Personal Communications*, 8(3), 2001, 5-11.

[Lev97] D. Levine, I. F. Akyildiz and M. Naghshineh, A resource estimation and call admission algorithm for wireless multimedia networks using the shadow cluster concept, *IEEE/ACM Transactions on Networking*, 5, 1997, 1-12.

[Lug99] M. Luglio, Mobile multimedia satellite communications, *IEEE Multimedia*, 6, 1999, 10-14.

[Mer97] I. Mertzanis, R. Tafazolli, and B. G. Evans, Connection admission control strategy and routing considerations in multimedia (Non-GEO) satellite networks, *Proc. IEEE VTC*, 1997, 431-436.

[MMJ03] Mobile Media Japan, Japanese mobile Internet users: http://www.mobilemediajapan.com/, January 2004.

[Nag96] M. Naghshineh and M. Schwartz, Distributed call admission control in mobile/wireless networks, *IEEE Journal of Selected Areas in Communications*, 14, 1996, 711-717.

[Ngu02] H. N. Nguyen, S. Olariu, and P. Todorova, A novel mobility model and resource allocation strategy for multimedia LEO satellite networks, *Proc. IEEE WCNC*, Orlando, Florida, March 2002.

[Ngu00] H. N. Nguyen, J. Schuringa, and H. R. van As, Handover schemes for QoS guarantees in LEO satellite networks, *Proc. ICON'2000*.

[Ola03] S. Olariu, S. A. Rizvi, R. Shirhatti, and P. Todorova, Q-Win -- A new admission and handoff management scheme for multimedia LEO satellite networks, *Telecommunication Systems*, 22(1-4), 2003, 151-168.

[Oli98] C. Oliviera, J. B. Kim, and T. Suda, An adaptive bandwidth reservation scheme for high-speed multimedia wireless networks, *IEEE Journal of Selected Areas in Communications*, 16, 1998, 858-874.

[Pei99] H. Peyravi, Medium access control Protocol performance in satellite communications, *IEEE Communications Magazine*, 37(3), 1999, 62 -71.

[Tod02] P. Todorova, S. Olariu, and H. N. Nguyen, A selective look-ahead bandwidth allocation scheme for reliable handoff in multimedia LEO satellite networks, *Proc. ECUMN'2002*, Colmar, France, April 2002.

[Uzu99] H. Uzunalioglu, A connection admission control algorithm for LEO satellite networks, *Proc. IEEE ICC*, 1999, 1074-1078.

[Wer97] M. Werner, C. Delucchi, H.-J. Vogel, G. Maral and J.-J. De Ridder, ATM-Based Routing in LEO/MEO Satellite networks with inter-satellite links, *IEEE Journal on Selected Areas in Communications*, 15(2), 1997, 69-82.

# Session 8C:
# Proxy in Wireless Systems

# Dynamic, Power-Aware Scheduling for Mobile Clients Using a Transparent Proxy

Michael Gundlach, Sarah Doster, Haijin Yan, David K. Lowenthal, Scott A. Watterson
Dept. of Computer Science, The University of Georgia
Athens, GA, 30606
Email:{gundlach,sdoster,yan,dkl,saw}@cs.uga.edu

Surendar Chandra
Dept. of Computer Science and Engineering, The University of Notre Dame
Notre Dame, IN, 46556
Email: surendar@cse.nd.edu

## Abstract

*Mobile computers consume significant amounts of energy when receiving large files. The wireless network interface card (WNIC) is the primary source of this energy consumption. One way to reduce the energy consumed is to transmit the packets to clients in a predictable fashion. Specifically, the packets can be sent in* bursts *to clients, who can then switch to a lower power* sleep *state between bursts. This technique is especially effective when the bandwidth of a stream is small.*

*This paper investigates techniques for saving energy in a multiple-client scenario, where clients may be receiving either UDP or TCP data. Energy is saved by using a transparent proxy that is invisible to both clients and servers. The proxy implementation maintains separate connections to the client and server so that a large increase in transmission time is avoided. The proxy also buffers data and dynamically generates a global transmission schedule that includes all active clients. Results show that energy savings within 10-15% of optimal are common, with little packet loss.*

## 1  Introduction

The wireless network interface card (WNIC) often causes the largest power drain in a mobile client. This is especially true in (1) streaming multimedia applications and (2) ftp or HTTP file downloads. In both situations, packets arrive frequently (though not always predictably) requiring the WNIC to remain in *idle* or *receive* mode, both of which use significant amounts of energy. Fortunately, a proxy may buffer packets for a client and then send them to the client in *bursts* at regular intervals. This allows the client to keep its WNIC in *sleep* mode while not receiving data; this mode consumes an order of magnitude less power. This is especially effective when the bandwidth of the stream is low, in which case a large fraction of the overall energy can be saved.

There are many challenges in the implementation of such a scheme. Ideally, the proxy should be transparent, so that clients can save energy with only minor modifications. It should also avoid parsing packet data, so that it can support any protocol. Furthermore, the proxy should be able to support multiple clients, as well as multiple connection types (e.g., multimedia, HTTP, ftp, etc.) simultaneously among those clients. This is important because it is common for multiple clients to share a single wireless access point. Currently, however, only single-client, proxy-based solutions exist[4, 3, 14]. Multiple clients present additional challenges. An example (shown in [3]) is that data can arrive at the access points for different clients at the same time—because the wireless medium is shared between clients, an energy-aware scheme must involve clients agreeing on a global schedule. Finally, a scheduling policy must be developed that can adapt to both regular and bursty behavior.

Our implementation addresses these concerns. We have designed a scheduling policy that bursts packets to clients; it is implemented in a transparent proxy that resides between clients and servers, which both believe connections to each other are direct. Our proxy uses *address spoofing* for transparency and separate connections to the client and server to implement this abstraction efficiently. We allow any protocol to be used, and we support multiple clients as well as different types of connections from those clients. The number of clients supported is dependent only on the the effective bandwidth of the network. All clients save energy by receiving data in bursts from a wireless access point.

In this paper we investigate dynamic scheduling of multiple clients, using both UDP and TCP traffic. Our results show that energy savings within 10-15% of optimal are common. For example, when multiple clients viewing 56kbps UDP streams are connected to the proxy, they save over 75% energy compared to a naive client (one who keeps its WNIC in high-power mode exclusively). This is within 15% of the theoretical optimal. In addition, with mixed UDP and TCP traffic, clients downloading either or both were able to achieve good energy savings. Furthermore, this is usually done with few missed packets (typically less than 2%) on the clients.

The rest of the paper is organized as follows. Section 2 discusses related work. Section 3 describes the design and implementation of our proxy as well as its scheduling policy, and Section 4 describes our experiments and discusses the results. Finally, Section 5 summarizes the paper.

## 2  Related Work

The idea of a transparent proxy has been previously studied. These can be used to improve TCP throughput [13]. Another way they can be used is to partition the Internet into distinct regions [8]. Also, *connection splicing* can be used with a proxy, which can improve latency within the proxy [16]. The primary difference with using a transparent proxy in our setting is that we must buffer packets in the proxy. This means that a transparent proxy will increase round-trip times from the point of view of both sender and receiver, potentially decreasing the TCP window size and hence increasing the transmission time. Our proxy handles this problem by using transparent double connections along with source address spoofing (see Section 3). Our implementation is similar in spirit to that of Indirect TCP [1] and Snoop [2]. The former splits a TCP connection at the base station and the latter modifies the link layer; both are intended to optimize for wireless networks. The differences between these two protocols and our transparent proxy are that (1) they are optimizing for performance, whereas we are scheduling for reduced WNIC energy, and (2) our proxy handles both UDP *and* TCP traffic, as opposed to only TCP traffic (which causes some implementation difficulties), and (3) we are not modifying the access point or any other part of TCP.

A body of closely related work to ours provides energy savings for a single multimedia client. This has been done by [14] as well as [4, 3]. The former includes transcoding, conversion of a variable bit rate stream to a constant bit rate stream, and client side prediction. The latter provides energy savings for a single multimedia client for Quicktime, Real, and MS Media. However, while it effectively saves energy for a single client, the scheduling policy developed in that work caused high rates of collision and packet loss

for multiple clients. Our work is distinct in that it supports multiple concurrent clients.

Our work uses a particular scheduling algorithm for both UDP and TCP data. It schedules each client on the same frequency, so all clients share the total bandwidth; this is similar to TDMA [7]. Others have also worked on wireless scheduling algorithms (e.g., [5]).

Other related approaches are to use the energy-saving mechanisms defined by 802.11b. However, it is not a good match for multimedia [4]. One improvement to 802.11b is the Bounded Slowdown Protocol [9], which uses minimal energy given a desired maximum increase in round trip time. However, like 802.11b, this protocol is aimed at long periods of inactivity followed by small amounts of data received (e.g., web pages). Our work is focused on multimedia streams, which by their nature have packets arriving for a long period of time. Finally, there has been work done on reducing idle energy in the network interface [15].

## 3  Implementation

This section describes our implementation. Section 3.1 gives an overview, and Section 3.2 describes our scheduling policy and its implementation, including *address spoofing* to achieve transparency without unduly increasing the transmission time. Section 3.3 describes *delay compensation* algorithms used on clients to adjust to routing delays in the wireless access point.

### 3.1  Overview

Our implementation is within a proxy that is interposed between servers and clients. It buffers data from the servers, and transmits it at regular intervals as a burst to the appropriate client. This way, the access point will not have to make scheduling decisions between clients, because only one client will be receiving at a time. Clients can request arbitrary types of data, though in our experiments we use UDP and TCP.

We collect a trace of the wireless-side activity using a packet sniffer running on a mobile computer known as the *monitoring station*. This trace is read by a simulator post-mortem in order to determine energy used per client. This is compared to the total energy used by a naive client, which keeps its WNIC in high-power mode for the duration of the trace. The overall architecture is shown in Figure 1.

We assume that a wireless network interface card (WNIC) can be in *sleep*, *idle*, *receive*, or *transmit* mode. *Sleep* mode uses a very small amount of power, and during this time no data can be received or transmitted. The remaining modes use a relatively large amount of power, with *receive* and *transmit* modes somewhat larger than that used by *idle* mode [17, 6]. We therefore refer to *sleep*

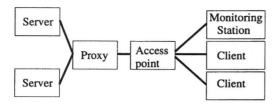

**Figure 1. System architecture.**

mode as *low-power mode* and all other modes as *high-power mode* for the remainder of the paper. A client saves energy by transitioning its WNIC between high- and low-power modes according to our scheduling policy, which is described next.

## 3.2 Scheduling Policy

This section describes the design and implementation of our energy-conserving scheduling policy. We use a proxy placed between the server and the wireless access point to carry out this policy. Section 3.2.1 discusses the design of our policy, and Section 3.2.2 details our implementation of the policy.

### 3.2.1 Design

Our primary design goal is to transform ordinary data streams into bursty streams, scheduling bursts so that each client receives a fair share of the bandwidth. We implement this policy through a transparent proxy, which is described below. The scheduling policy (see Figure 2) works as follows. The proxy broadcasts a schedule message as a UDP packet to all active clients at well-defined intervals. We define the *scheduler rendezvous point* (SRP) as a moment in time at which the proxy agrees to send the schedule. The schedule describes the length of each client's data burst and the order of the bursts, so that client $i$ is assigned rendezvous point $CRP_i$. At point $CRP_i$, client $i$ transitions its WNIC to high-power mode. At the same time, the proxy transmits data from the packet queue for client $i$ to that client in a burst, marking the type-of-service bit in the IP header of the last packet so that the client knows when to transition its WNIC back to low-power mode. The time period between schedule broadcasts is known as a *burst interval*. Each schedule is valid for exactly one burst interval, and then a schedule for the next burst interval is sent at the next SRP[1]. In the example in Figure 2, in fact, there is another client that receives traffic during the second burst interval.

Schedules are determined immediately before being broadcast. We allow the size of a schedule to be variable

---

[1]While the information sent to each client could be done individually at the end of its burst, complete information is available after *all* clients have received their data for a burst interval. This allows fairness between clients as well as schedules with variable burst intervals (see Section 4).

or fixed. If schedules are of varying size, a new schedule is determined by examining a snapshot of the packet queues for all clients. The schedule is constructed such that each client can empty its packet queue during the next burst interval. The schedule will also contain the time at which the following schedule will be broadcast. If the schedule is a fixed size, however, the proxy gives each client a fraction of the available burst interval proportional to the amount of data in its packet queue. At present, we do not perform admission control at the proxy and so do not handle overload; to solve this problem we could leverage off of the significant amount of work in this area (e.g., [18]).

Our proxy is transparent, meaning that neither clients nor servers are aware of its involvement in any data transfer. A transparent proxy is desired for generality, as application protocols such as RTSP, HTTP and ftp can be supported without explicitly understanding the protocol semantics. To initiate a connection, the client contacts the server, which responds by opening a connection (as usual). After the connection is established, the server will simply send data to the client as normal. The client, on the other hand, sees data being transmitted from the server in a bursty manner. The client must also read the UDP broadcast packet from the proxy, which contains its rendezvous point as well as the arrival time of the next schedule. The client can turn off its WNIC until its rendezvous point is reached, at which point it transitions the WNIC to high-power mode. After the client receives its burst, it transitions the WNIC back to low-power mode until the next schedule packet is due. The modifications to the client to allow this are straightforward and could be implemented with a simple daemon. Note that the client may want to itself buffer multimedia packets and locally deliver them to the multimedia player at a regular pace. Such buffering introduces its own energy requirements, which we are not modeling.

### 3.2.2 Implementation

The proxy is implemented using the Linux 2.4.18 bridging mechanism [10]. We use the bridging code in the Linux 2.4.18 kernel, as well as the `brctl` utility, to do this. The proxy uses *IPQ*, a packet filter built into iptables, to catch all incoming or outgoing packets. The proxy is implemented using multiple threads: an *IPQ* thread, which catches and possibly modifies all incoming or outgoing packets; a bursting thread, which bursts data to clients; and a queuing thread, which moves packets between queues for the clients and servers.

Because the proxy is transparent, the clients and servers believe that they are connected to each other directly. However, as described above, to avoid a large increase in transmission time, there must be separate connections between (1) the client and the proxy and (2) the proxy and the server.

Figure 3 describes the steps taken when a client connects

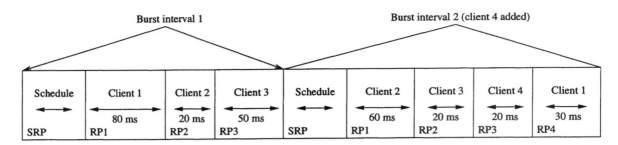

| Burst interval 1 | | | | Burst interval 2 (client 4 added) | | | | |
|---|---|---|---|---|---|---|---|---|
| Schedule | Client 1 | Client 2 | Client 3 | Schedule | Client 2 | Client 3 | Client 4 | Client 1 |
| ← → | ← 80 ms → | ← 20 ms → | ← 50 ms → | ← → | ← 60 ms → | ← 20 ms → | ← 20 ms → | ← 30 ms → |
| SRP | RP1 | RP2 | RP3 | SRP | RP1 | RP2 | RP3 | RP4 |

**Figure 2. Example scheduling policy with four clients. Client 4 has traffic during the first burst interval and so joins the schedule for the second burst interval.**

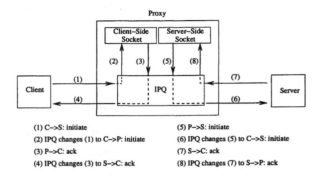

(1) C->S: initiate      (5) P->S: initiate
(2) IPQ changes (1) to C->P: initiate      (6) IPQ changes (5) to C->S: initiate
(3) P->C: ack      (7) S->C: ack
(4) IPQ changes (3) to S->C: ack      (8) IPQ changes (7) to S->P: ack

**Figure 3. Picture of the steps taken on a TCP connection from client (C) to server (S) with a transparent proxy (P).**

to the server. In step 1, the client sends an initiate request (SYN packet) to the server. This request is caught by *IPQ*, which creates a receiving socket (the "client-side" socket) and changes the header of the message so that the request is from the client to the proxy, then "re-injects" the packet to be routed (step 2). The proxy responds to this by first acknowledging the client (returning a SYN ACK packet) (step 3); this acknowledgement is caught by *IPQ*, which changes the header to indicate it is from the server (step 4). The proxy also creates a server-side socket and initiates a connection to the server (step 5); *IPQ* catches the message and changes the header to indicate that the message is from the client (step 6). Finally, the server sends back an acknowledgement to the the client (step 7), which *IPQ* changes so that the destination is the proxy (step 8). Similar steps are taken to handle the acknowledgement of the SYN ACK packet, as well as transmission of packets from the server to the client.

While the basic idea is given above, there are important low-level details required for its implementation. These include handling unexpected packet orderings, correctly marking the last packet of a client's burst, and handling bandwidth limitations. We describe each of these in turn.

**Packet Ordering** The proxy transmits both UDP and TCP data and sends out a new schedule after all clients have received their data for the previous schedule. Because UDP is unreliable, packets can arrive at the client in a different order than they were sent from the proxy. Specifically, the schedule message (which is UDP) for burst interval $B$ can actually arrive at a client when the client is (1) still receiving data for burst interval $B - 1$ or (2) already receiving data packets for burst interval $B$. In other words, in practice the schedule can arrive slightly before or slightly after the next burst. To handle (1), clients must ignore the new schedule until they receive a marked packet that indicates the end of the previous burst (or until another schedule is received, if the marked packet is dropped). To handle (2), clients must accept data that comes before a schedule.

**Packet Marking** Recall that a burst is terminated with a marked packet. While this idea is simple in principle, in practice it is somewhat more difficult for TCP packets. This is because we mark these packets in the *IPQ* thread, but we determine what data should be marked in the bursting thread. We accomplish this by having the bursting thread communicate via shared variables as to which is the last byte in a burst. Specifically, there are three shared variables per client-side socket $C$: $B_c$, $I_c$, and $M_c$. Variable $B_c$ stores the number of bytes sent by the bursting thread, and $I_c$ stores the number sent by the *IPQ* thread; the invariant is $B_c >= I_c$. Variable $M_c$, which represents the byte number to be marked, is initialized to $-1$. When the bursting thread sends the last packet in a burst, it copies $B_c$ into $M_c$. The *IPQ* thread then marks a packet when $I_c = M_c$ and resets $M_c$ to $-1$. This scheme is further complicated by potential retransmissions from the proxy to the client, which are handled by the proxy by comparing sequence numbers. For this case, $B_c$ would not be incremented.

**Bandwidth Constraints** The schedule developed for a burst interval contains a set of client IP addresses and their associated transmission start and end times. However, the proxy must be careful to accurately estimate the amount of data that can be sent to a client during its reception period. The proxy can transmit data to the access point faster than the access point can transmit to the client. If the proxy sends data to a client (through the bursting thread) during the whole period, some of that data may actually be forwarded by the *IPQ* thread *after* the end of the interval, due to the limited wireless network bandwidth. If this happens, the data for that client may take longer to transmit than the time allotted, meaning that subsequent clients will not receive their data as scheduled. This leads to wasted energy on those clients. Furthermore, if the proxy sends too few packets, bandwidth is wasted.

To address this problem, we executed a set of microbenchmarks to create a model of send overhead and latency on our wireless network. From these, we developed a linear cost function based on the message size. The proxy uses this to estimate how much data can be sent in a given time period.

**Proxy memory requirements** In our experiments, the memory buffer required on the proxy is not large. The proxy requires the maximum space when the entire wireless bandwidth is in use. With an effective bandwidth of 4Mbps, this means that even if one second of data (to all clients) had to be buffered, 512KB would be sufficient.

### 3.3 Delay Compensation Algorithms

A client's WNIC must be transitioned to high-power mode to receive the schedule and then again to receive its burst. If the client transitions early, some energy will be wasted while waiting for the packets to arrive; if the client transitions late, packets will be missed. The goal is to minimize the wasted energy, while avoiding missing packets. If the client could perfectly predict when a packet would arrive based on the information in the schedule, this would not be a problem. However, while the proxy usually sends the schedule as well as data bursts with better than millisecond accuracy, delay may at times be observed by the client. Even though the proxy is as close to the client as possible, all packets must pass through the access point. This, as well as the multithreaded nature of the proxy, can cause a packet to arrive earlier or later than expected. Another possibility is that the clocks on the proxy and a client may not be perfectly synchronized. For this reason, we use an adaptive *delay compensation algorithm* on each client to determine when to transition the WNIC out of low-power mode.

The intuition behind it is as follows. If a schedule packet arrives earlier or later than expected, it is likely a change in access point delay between the proxy and the client, and several subsequent schedule packets will arrive according to the same pattern. Adaptive delay compensation algorithms therefore set each transition point a fixed amount after the *arrival time of the previous schedule*. In order to reduce

missed packets, the amount is slightly less than a burst interval; we refer to the difference as the *early transition amount*. While this synchronization strategy is simple, we found it to be effective in practice.

## 4 Performance

This section describes our experiments and presents our results. Section 4.1 describes the experimental setup. Section 4.2 describes the experiments performed and gives the results. Finally, Section 4.3 analyzes the results.

### 4.1 Experimental Setup

In each experiment, clients either (1) requested a video in Real format or (2) downloaded either HTTP or ftp. The results obtained from the Real format video should apply to any streaming data (e.g. Quicktime, MS Media); while there are some differences in the streaming patterns, all streaming data should be handled similarly. The monitoring station and clients were various laptops using 11Mbps Orinoco PCMCIA WNICs. The monitoring station ran tcpdump to capture data about each packet on the wireless network. We ran RealServer 8.01 as our video server, and each client laptop ran RealOne 2.0. The multimedia server, web server, and access point were connected over 100Mbps Fast Ethernet. The multimedia clients requested a 1:59s trailer for the movie *The Wall*, encoded by Adobe Premier 6.0 at 56kbps, 128kbps, 256kbps, or 512kbps. Because the encoder could not perfectly match the requested bitrates, the effective bitrates of these streams are 34kbps, 80kbps, 225kbps, and 450kbps respectively. For video experiments, requests were spaced roughly one second apart in order to spread traffic; transmitting identical multimedia streams simultaneously could cause large spikes of activity during high bitrate periods. The streams were unicast to the clients, so that the total bandwidth used was roughly equal to the sum of the individual streams (i.e., no streams were multicast).

We used a simulator to read the tcpdump trace postmortem, calculating (1) how much time a client's WNIC has spent in high- and low-power mode, (2) how many bytes its WNIC has transmitted and received, (3) how many packets are lost (UDP) or packets dropped (TCP) for each client, and (4) how much energy the client would use by transitioning its WNIC between modes according to a given delay compensation algorithm. This is compared to the naive client, which keeps its WNIC in high-power mode. The card simulated is 2.4Ghz WaveLAN DSSS, which uses 1319 mJ/s when idle, 1425 mJ/s when receiving, 1675 mJ/s when transmitting, and 177mJ/s when sleeping [17, 6]. Also, we model the energy cost of transitioning the WNIC from *sleep* to *idle* mode as 2 ms in *idle* time [9].

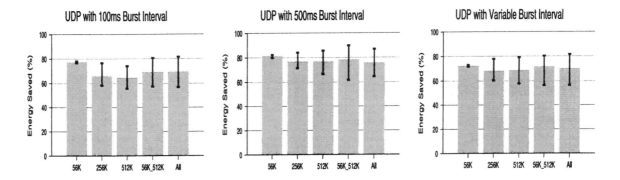

**Figure 4. Results with ten clients viewing UDP (video) streams with 100ms, 500ms, and variable burst intervals. Average, minimum, and maximum energy usage for the clients are represented by the bar and error lines, respectively. The first three bars (56K, 256K, 512K) show the experiments where each client viewed an identical stream, while the last two bars represent cases where the clients viewed streams of different fidelity.**

## 4.2 Experiments

We performed three different sets of experiments. The first set investigated a scenario where all clients view video streams. This shows how well our system generalizes from prior work done with a single video client [3, 14]. Next, we performed experiments with all clients downloading HTTP data. This is a more realistic scenario, as web access is the most common activity on wireless devices. Third, we performed experiments where a subset of the clients view video streams and the rest download TCP data (either HTTP or ftp). These experiments are intended to investigate potential interactions between the two types of data.

For each type of experiment, we tested three burst interval sizes: fixed burst intervals of 100ms and 500ms as well as a variable burst interval. This is intended to determine the tradeoffs involved in scheduling. We discuss the results of our experiments below. In Section 4.3 we analyze the results.

**Multiple video clients**  The first set of experiments involved each client receiving only a video stream. Figure 4 shows the average, minimum, and maximum energy usage for each experiment (represented by the bar and error lines, respectively). There were five types of client access patterns. The first three involved each client viewing an identical bitrate stream; we tried 56Kbps, 256Kbps, and 512Kbps. The results show that the average energy saved is 77% for the 56Kbps streams, 66% for the 256Kbps streams, and 53% for the 512Kbps streams.

The fourth type involved five clients viewing a 56Kbps stream and the other five viewing a 512Kbps stream. The final type involved five clients viewing a 56Kbps stream

and the remaining five clients viewing different fidelities ranging at 56Kbps, 128Kbps, 256Kbps, and 512Kbps. The dynamic nature of our scheduler allows the energy savings to average about 69% in both experiments. As expected, lower fidelity streams save more energy because they use less bandwidth, giving them more opportunity to transition the WNIC to *sleep* mode.

**Multiple TCP clients**  The next set of experiments involves each client browsing the web, which generates multiple concurrent TCP streams per client. For each experiment, we used a script (which was generated prior to the experiments) to ensure that the traffic pattern remained identical across different experiments. We used burst intervals of 100ms and 500ms as well as a variable interval. Due to space limitations a graph is not shown, but the results showed that as with the video experiments, the clients save significant amounts of energy compared to a naive client (between 70 and 80%).

**Video and TCP traffic**  We next examined our system when handling a combination of video and TCP traffic. Four experiments were run; each one has seven clients viewing video and three clients browsing the web. Figure 5 shows the results of our tests. The first three bars show all video clients viewing a specific quality stream, 56Kbps, 256Kbps, and 512Kbps respectively. The fourth test (labeled *All/TCP*) had the video clients view a variety of fidelities. The energy savings varies from just over 50% to just under 90%. One interesting point is that the best-case energy savings among the video clients is similar among different fidelities. This is discussed further in Section 4.3.

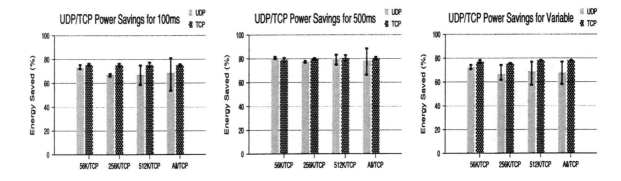

**Figure 5. Results with ten clients with some viewing UDP (video) streams and others downloading TCP (HTTP) data with 100ms, 500ms, and variable burst intervals. The left bar is for the UDP clients and the right one for TCP clients.**

### 4.3 Analysis of Results

This section analyzes the results. We first compare our results to the theoretical optimal. Next, we discuss packet loss. We then compare our results to those that could be obtained using a static schedule. Finally, we discuss the worst-case client.

**Comparison to optimal** One important metric to consider is how close the energy saving for a client is to the theoretical optimal. The optimal energy saved for a stream can be computed by the formula:

$$E_{opt} = \frac{(T_r \times P_r) + ((T_p - T_r) \times P_s)}{(T_n \times P_i) + P_b}.$$

Here, $T_r$ is the time to receive the entire stream if it were sent all at once, $P_r$ is the energy cost per second to receive, $T_p$ is the time for the download using the proxy, $P_s$ is the energy cost per second to sleep, $T_n$ is the time for the download without the proxy, $P_i$ is the energy cost per second in idle mode, and $P_b$ is the energy cost per byte. This is based on the idea that optimally, the WNIC is in high-power mode only to receive the data and in *sleep* mode at all other times, while a naive client is idle when not receiving data. Using this formula, the optimal energy saved for the 56Kbps, 256Kbps, and 512Kbps streams from the video-only experiments is 90%, 83%, and 77% respectively, compared to our results (from Section 4.2) of 77%, 66%, and 53% for the same streams.

In the mixed video/web experiments, generally, the median client energy savings is within 15% of optimal. However, there are some outlying cases; for example, with 512Kbps video files, the best case client saves over 80% of the WNIC energy compared to a naive client. As stated above, the optimal energy savings is 77% for a 512Kbps

stream. The reason for this anomaly is that the peak bandwidth required to transfer 10 512Kbps streams exceeds the effective wireless network bandwidth. This causes RealServer to believe that the connection is lossy, and the stream is adapted to a lower-quality, lower-bandwidth one. This is a problem inherent to exceeding bandwidth limitations rather than a problem introduced by the proxy. The TCP clients have a lower variance in energy savings, which is because adaptation does not occur.

The reason the 100ms burst interval performs worse than the 500ms burst interval in all experiments is because the WNIC is transitioned five times more often. As there is an early transition amount (see Section 3.3) each time the WNIC is transitioned to high-power mode (to avoid missing packets), this penalty is significant. For example, in our experiments, we used 6ms as the early transition amount for the 100ms experiments. In general, our experiments showed a factor of four increase in this penalty, on average from 3 seconds to 11 seconds of time the WNIC must be in high-power mode, between using a 500ms and 100ms burst interval. To investigate this further, we tried different early transition amounts for a 100ms burst interval, transitioning 0, 2, 4, 6, 8, and 10ms early. The ideal value is the one that minimizes wasted energy due to transitioning the WNIC early while avoiding missed packets. The latter degrades performance in two ways: first, it makes video stream quality poor and causes TCP data retransmission, and second, if a schedule is missed, a client must keep the WNIC in high-power mode until the next schedule arrives. Figure 6 shows the amount of wasted energy on a single client caused by early transitioning of the WNIC. As the early transition amount decreases, the overhead for transitioning to high-power mode early decreases, but the number of missed schedules increases. In this case, 6ms is the best value to choose. The other dimension is missed packets;

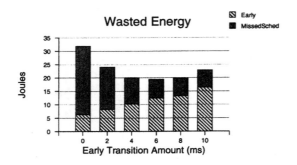

**Figure 6. The effect of different early transition amounts on wasted energy.**

this ranged from 0.97% (10ms early) to 1.83% (0ms early). Variable burst intervals appear to have energy savings in between the 100ms and 500ms interval. This is because the minimum burst interval is 100ms, and the maximum is less than 500ms unless several streams have high bandwidth.

**Packets lost or dropped** Packets lost (UDP) or packets dropped (TCP) are usually less than 2% with a few outliers, indicating that generally, the data is sent according to the schedule issued by the proxy.

It is difficult to analyze the effect on UDP streams of dropping up to 5% of the packets. Obviously, in the case of a video, the video will appear worse to the user. However, while we believe that missing a few packets is acceptable, this is fundamentally an human perception issue. We leave this to researchers in that area.

On the other hand, dropping TCP packets in reality causes retransmissions. In our tests, we actually receive packets that would be dropped and compute what would be dropped postmortem. (This is primarily because most of our clients are running Windows, where we do not know how to drop packets when necessary.) To estimate the effect of drops, we ran separate experiments with one client and Netfilter [11], which we configured so that if the client was in *sleep* mode, packets are actually dropped. We found that the effect of dropping packets was small (no more than a 10% increase in transmission time, which would have the corresponding effect of an expected increase in in energy consumed of no more than 5%[2]). We repeated an experiment using DummyNet [12], configuring a 4Mb/s network with a 2ms round-trip time and 5% drop rate. Similar results were observed. Essentially, the low round-trip time between proxy and client means that dropping packets is not severe.

---

[2]The extra energy is consumed because the transmission time is longer; however, most of the extra time would be time the WNIC is in *sleep* mode.

**Comparison to static schedules** For the subset of experiments above where all clients view streams of equal fidelity, a static schedule (rather than our dynamic one) can be used. In other words, the proxy can simply broadcast a single (permanent) burst interval for each client. This should save energy compared to our dynamic approach in that there is no early transition necessary to receive the schedule. If all clients are receiving approximately the same amount of data, it is also sufficient (i.e. no bandwidth is wasted by assigning a client a fixed-size amount of time for receiving) because on average, each client is receiving data at approximately the same rate. Hence, we implemented a static schedule for comparison, using a 100ms burst interval and ten clients viewing (identical) video streams of 56Kbps, 256Kbps, and 512Kbps. We found that both average energy usage and variance is lowered by using a static schedule.

However, a static schedule is insufficient in the case that the fidelity of the videos vary per client or TCP traffic is involved. An example is shown in more detail in Figure 7, which contains the results from using fixed-sized slots for both TCP and UDP data. During TCP slots, all TCP data is sent to the appropriate clients, and during UDP slots, UDP data is sent. However, the burst interval was 500ms, and the TCP and UDP slots were varied so that for each traffic pattern (light, medium, and heavy), we ran experiments where the TCP slot size was larger than, smaller than, and roughly equal to the size necessary to support the TCP traffic. (We show only the medium traffic pattern.) In these experiments, during the TCP slot, all clients must have their WNIC in high-power mode, so that the latency increase is restrained. It is not possible to simply minimize the TCP slot size, as TCP data will not be able to travel through the proxy: as the slot size decreases, the end-to-end latency of background traffic increases. The larger the slot size, the more energy that is wasted. For example, while the energy use for the UDP clients is lowest with a small TCP slot, the added latency of the TCP stream is significant.

Instead, our dynamic schedule handles this seamlessly; recall from Figure 4 the following experiments: (1) five clients viewing a 56Kbps stream and the other five viewing a 512Kbps stream, and (2) different clients viewing different fidelities ranging at 56Kbps, 128k, 256Kbps, and 512Kbps. The dynamic nature of our scheduler allows the energy savings to average about 69% in both experiments.

**Worst-case client** In the case of the worst-performing client (as shown by the error bars in Figure 4), examination of the traces shows that missed schedules are the primary cause. In particular, this client generally happens to miss the broadcast *and* at the same time misses its data. This means that it does not receive a marked packet (and the WNIC remains in high-power mode); on the other hand, other clients that miss the broadcast may receive some or all of their burst and then transition the WNIC to *sleep* mode.

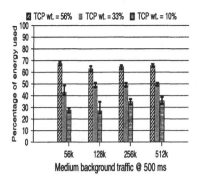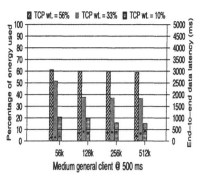

**Figure 7. On the left, the average, minimum, and maximum energy usage for ten multimedia clients with TCP traffic on the network, using a static schedule. On the right, the TCP client is analyzed; both energy usage (bars, left y-axis) and transmission latency (dots, right y-axis).**

## 5 Summary and Future Work

This paper has described a novel scheme to save energy for multiple mobile clients. We have designed a scheduling policy, capable of adapting to steady and bursty traffic. Our policy is implemented in a transparent proxy that bursts packets to clients. This allows clients to transition to low-power mode between bursts, saving energy. Our proxy uses *address spoofing* for transparency, which allows clients and servers to appear to communicate directly. It also maintains separate transparent TCP connections to the client and server in order to reduce transmission times

Results showed that energy savings within 10-15% of optimal were common with a low missed packet rate—typically less than 2%. For low-bandwidth streams, clients saved over 75% energy compared to a naive client. Our proxy was able to support multiple concurrent clients downloading both UDP and TCP data.

One avenue for future research is reducing the energy wasted by requiring the client to transition to high-power mode at both the schedule and burst rendezvous points. If the schedule does not change from one burst interval to the next, the proxy may inform the client that it will use the same schedule again for the next burst interval. The client can then transition to high-power mode only at its burst rendezvous point, avoiding the energy cost of receiving the schedule from the proxy.

## References

[1] A. Bakre and B. R. Badrinath. I-TCP: Indirect TCP for mobile hosts. *15th International Conference on Distributed Computing Systems*, 1995.

[2] H. Balakrishnan, S. Seshan, and R. H. Katz. Improving reliable transport and handoff performance in cellular wireless networks. *ACM Wireless Networks*, 1(4), 1995.

[3] S. Chandra. Wireless network interface energy consumption implications of popular streaming formats. In *Multimedia Computing and Networking (MMCN '02)*, Jan 2002.

[4] S. Chandra and A. Vahdat. Application-specific network management for energy-aware streaming of popular multimedia formats. In *USENIX Annual Technical Conference*, 2002.

[5] S. Damodaran and K. M. Sivalingam. Scheduling algorithms for multiple channel wireless local area networks. *Computer Communications*, 2002.

[6] P. J. M. Havinga. *Mobile Multimedia Systems*. PhD thesis, Univ. of Twente, Feb 2000.

[7] IEC. www.iec.org/online/tutorials/tdma/.

[8] B. Knutsson and L. Peterson. Transparent proxy signalling. *Journal of Communications and Networks*, 2001.

[9] R. Krashinsky and H. Balakrishnan. Minimizing energy for wireless web access with bounded slowdown. In *Mobicom 2002*, Atlanta, GA, September 2002.

[10] Linux Bridging. http://bridge.sourceforge.net/.

[11] Netfilter. http://www.netfilter.org.

[12] L. Rizzo. Dummynet: A simple approach to the evaluation of network protocols. *ACM Computer Communications Review*, 27(1), Jan. 1997.

[13] P. Rodriguez, S. Sibal, and O. Spatscheck. TPOT: translucent proxying of TCP. *Computer Communications*, 24(2):249–255, 2001.

[14] P. Shenoy and P. Radkov. Proxy-assisted power-friendly streaming to mobile devices. In *Proceedings of the 2003 Multimedia Computing and Networking Conference*, Santa Clara, CA, January 2003.

[15] E. Shih, P. Bahl, and M. Sinclair. Wake on wireless: An event driven energy saving strategy for battery operated devices. In *Mobicom 2002*, Atlanta, GA, September 2002.

[16] O. Spatscheck, J. S. Hansen, J. H. Hartman, and L. L. Peterson. Optimizing TCP forwarder performance. *IEEE/ACM Transactions on Networking*, 8(2):146–157, 2000.

[17] M. Stemm, P. Gauthier, D. Harada, and R. H. Katz. Reducing power consumption of network interfaces in hand-held devices. In *Proc. 3rd International Workshop on Mobile Multimedia Communications*, Sept. 1996.

[18] H. M. Vin, A. Goyal, and P. Goyal. Algorithms for designing multimedia servers. *Computer Communications*, 18(3):192–203, 1995.

# MobiGATE: A Mobile Gateway Proxy for the Active Deployment of Transport Entities

Yongjie Zheng      Alvin T. S. Chan

*Department of Computing*
*The Hong Kong Polytechnic University*
*Hung Hom, Kowloon*
*Hong Kong, SAR, China*
*{csyzheng, cstschan}@comp.polyu.edu.hk*

## Abstract

*Using gateway proxies is one important approach to facilitating adaptation across wireless and mobile environments. Importantly, augmented service entities deployed within the gateway proxy residing on the wired network can be composed and deployed to shield mobile clients from the effects of poor network characteristics. The usual approach to the static composition of service entities on the gateway proxy is to have these service entities interact with each other by explicitly invoking procedures on the named interface. The tight coupling of interfaces inhibits the flexible composition and adaptation of the service entities to the dynamic operating characteristics of wireless networks. In this paper, we present a __Mobi__le __GATE__way for the __A__ctive deployment of __T__ransport __E__ntities or MobiGATE (pronounced as Mobi-Gate) for short. MobiGATE is a mobile middleware framework that supports the robust and flexible composition of transport entities, known as streamlets. The flow of data traffic is subjected to processing by a chain of streamlets. Each streamlet encapsulates a service entity that serves to adapt the flow of traffic across the wireless network. To facilitate the dynamic reconfiguration of the streamlets, we advocate applying the concept of coordination as the unifying approach to composing these transport service entities. Importantly, MobiGATE delineates a clear separation of interdependency parts from the service-specific computational codes of those service entities by using a separate coordination language to describe the coordination among streamlet service entities. To this end, we have defined a compositional language called MobiGATE Coordination Language (MCL) that provides rich constructs to support the definition of compositions, with constrained type validation and checking.*

## 1. Introduction

Ubiquitous access to data is becoming a reality due to the large-scale deployment of wireless communication services and advances in mobile computing devices. However, mobile computing environments exhibit operating conditions that differ greatly from their wired counterparts. In particular, the application must be able to tolerate the highly dynamic channel conditions that arise as users move about the environment. Moreover, the computing devices used by participants often vary in terms of display characteristics, processor speed, memory size, and battery lifetimes. To enable these applications to be operated effectively and optimally in such environments, the communication-related software must be able to adapt to these dynamic conditions at runtime [3].

One way to meet these challenges is by using a proxy-based gateway approach to adaptation, in which augmented network services placed between mobile clients and gateway servers perform aggressive computation and storage on behalf of clients [4]. With such architecture, applications are built from some interconnected building blocks and deployed at proxy stations. Each building block, or service entity, specializes in a specific task in processing the flow of data. For example, the task could involve the scaling/dithering of images in a particular format, or conversion between specific data formats, or even suitable caching to minimize the traffic transiting across the wireless network. As such, the development of mobile applications may extend beyond the end-host process to include the composition of service entities to adapt to variations in networks and client resources.

A common approach to implementing the adaptation of service at the gateway proxy is to have the service entities statically interact with each other by explicitly invoking procedures on a named interface. The result will be that the system integration code will inevitably become intermixed with the application-specific codes. Any replacement or modification of a service entity requires the updating not only of the code for the new service entity to be integrated to the system, but also of the code of those entities that have a direct relation with the old service entity. The tight coupling of service entities in terms of the strong coordination dependency translates into the need for manual modifications when the transport service entities are deployed into a new environment. In a wireless network, which exhibits highly dynamic network conditions, the adaptation of service entities in the form of dynamic composition and reconfiguration is considered the norm rather than the exception.

In this paper, we present the architecture of a **Mobi**le **G**ATEway for the **A**ctive deployment of **T**ransport **E**ntities, or MobiGATE (pronounced as Mobi-Gate) for short. MobiGATE is a mobile middleware framework that supports the robust and flexible composition of transport entities, known as *streamlets* (In this paper, we use the terms streamlets, service entities and transport entities interchangeably). The flow of data traffic is subjected to processing by a chain of streamlets. Each streamlet encapsulates a service entity that serves to adapt the flow of traffic across the wireless network. To facilitate the dynamic reconfiguration of the streamlets, we advocate the application of the concept of coordination [8] as the unifying approach to composing these transport service entities. Importantly, MobiGATE delineates a clear separation of interdependency parts from the service-specific computational codes of those service entities by using a separate coordination language to describe the coordination among streamlet service entities. To this end, we have defined a compositional language called *MobiGATE Coordination Language (MCL)* that provides rich constructs to support the definition of compositions, with constrained type validation and checking. In the description of the coordination, each service entity is regarded as a black box with well-defined interfaces. MCL enables the core functional pieces of an application to be clearly separated from its application-specific patterns of interdependencies. MCL does this by supporting two distinct language elements: *streamlets*, for representing core functional service entities; and *channels*, for representing relationships of interconnection among streamlets. Each implementation-level entity is represented in MCL as optional attributes of streamlets and channels. This approach has a number of advantages, ranging from the ability to reuse common communication service entities, to offering flexible dynamic reconfiguration where transport entities can be inserted, removed, and reordered at run time without recompilation or redefinition.

The MobiGATE middleware system directly supports composition using the MCL and, addresses the design and implementation of middleware services for dynamic, heterogeneous environments. A major goal of the MobiGATE architecture is to provide such an environment, where programmers can develop new mobile applications through combining some active service entities (streamlets), while the configuration structure of the application is completely separated from

the computational activities of individual entities. The architecture has the advantages of supporting ease of dynamic reconfiguration through the runtime reflective configuration of MCL and of promoting the re-usability of service entities across applications. The MobiGATE execution environment is comprised of a coordination plane for controlling MCL coordination activities and an execution plane for managing the execution of various computational service-specific processes, including streamlets.

The rest of the paper is organized as follows: Section 2 describes some background knowledge on adaptation using gateway proxies in mobile computing, together with a brief introduction of the coordination model and languages. Section 3 details the architecture of MobiGATE, with an emphasis on some of the core modules driving the system. Section 4 describes the design of our coordination language MCL, including its language constructs and some refinement work. Finally, the paper concludes with a discussion of future work and some relevant issues.

## 2. Background and Related Work

This section begins with an introduction to gateway proxies, which represents an important architecture for introducing augmented services across a mobile and wireless environment. This is followed by a review of some related works on the coordination model and languages to enable "plug-and-play" in the composition and evolution of services.

### 2.1. Gateway Proxy Services

Today's Internet clients vary widely with respect to both hardware and software properties. As a result, it has become increasingly difficult to hide the diverse variations at the network level, making application-level techniques necessary. On-the-fly adaptation by transformational proxies is a widely applicable, cost-effective, and flexible technique for addressing all of these types of variations. It mainly consists of the following two network components that reside between the wireless end-points:

1) A wired-side gateway called the server proxy that is commonly deployed at the edge of a wired network.

2) A peer client-side proxy called the client proxy that is deployed within the mobile host (MH).

The two components operate at a peer-to-peer level to implement service entities that aim to adapt and optimize the flow of data across the wireless environment.

The architecture supports augmented wireless network services by allowing adaptation-based service entities to be deployed at both server and client proxies to shield clients from all kinds of variances. Importantly, the architecture inherits the principle of interoperability, in which innovative and exciting services can be rapidly deployed within the existing networking environment without causing changes to the infrastructure. The kinds of service entities that may be applied to adapt the flow of data include transformation (filtering, format conversion, etc.), aggregation (collecting and collating data from various sources), caching (both original and transformed content), and customization (maintenance of a per-user preferences database). Studies in this area have focused primarily on applying fixed specific service entities to the gateway proxy to introduce specific adaptation to data flowing across the wireless environment. In [4], a service entity based on image transcoding was been applied to convert images on-the-fly so that the bandwidth requirement could be reduced and the images displayed on a display-constrained device such as a PDA. Text-compression, XML streaming and caching service entities have been similarly experimented with and deployed based on the architecture of the gateway proxy. The central motivation behind our work is to address more generally the complex challenges related to the design, implementation, and deployment of service entities that are highly composable and reconfigurable, and that promote service adaptations that react to the dynamic operating conditions of wireless and mobile networking.

## 2.2. Coordination Model and Languages

Coordination is a new class of model that has recently been developed to describe concurrent and distributed computations. In the area of Programming Languages, coordination is defined as the process of building programs by gluing together active pieces. Thus, a coordination model can be regarded as the glue that binds separate activities into an ensemble [7]. A coordination language is the linguistic embodiment of a coordination model, offering facilities for controlling the synchronization, communication, creation, and termination of computational activities.

The most prominent advantage of the coordination model is that we have a complete separation of coordination from computational concerns, which is usually achieved by defining a new coordination language to describe the architecture of the composition. With recent advances in this field, a number of such coordination languages have become available, such as PCL, Conic, Darwin, and Manifold. These languages share many common characteristics. In particular, the system generally consists of two kinds of processes: coordination and computation. Computational processes are treated as black boxes, while processes communicate with their environment by means of clearly defined interfaces, usually referred to as *input* or *output* ports. Producer-consumer relationships are formed by setting up

channel connections between the output ports of producers and the input ports of consumers. While these languages support primitive constructs to enable a connection to be established between coordinating processes in the form of a high-level architectural description, they lack the linguistic support to capture the input and out types associated with the ports. As a result, interconnected processes must be manually established to ensure compatibility of type as messages are exchanged between the respective input and output ports. Computing architecture that requires the coordination of process to be dynamically composed and reconfigured at runtime requires the intrinsic support of typed messages that allow the programmer to capture the intended compatibility between input-output ports, and to exercise runtime safety checks.

In this paper, we present the MCL language that possesses some attractive characteristics to support the composition and reconfiguration of flexible service entities in MobiGATE. First, the language supports the capturing of flow types between service entities at the conceptual level and allows strong type compatibility checks in the composition activities. MCL employs MIME (Multipurpose Internet Mail Extensions) specifications to model streamlet interfaces and message types. MIME is an official Internet standard that specifies how messages are formatted and interpreted across email systems. Since its inception, it has been extended and applied to diverse applications, including the adoption of the standard to the World Wide Web. Importantly, MIME posses a flexible and extensible format that easily accommodates well-known message types such as text, images, video, sound, or other application-specific data. Second, MCL supports the notion of recursive compositions of coordinated entities. In other words, a composition of streamlets can itself be organized as a composite streamlet. The recursive structuring of streamlet compositions can be nested to an arbitrary level to promote modularization and re-usability.

## 3. An Overview of the Architecture

In MobiGATE, there exists a clear distinction between activities of coordination and computation. Figure 1 shows the architecture of MobiGATE, which is organized into two executing planes. The streamlet executing plane is responsible for scheduling streamlet instances for computation, while the coordination plane is responsible for maintaining the interaction and relationship between the coordinated streamlets. The Coordination Manager maintains a configuration table for each instance of streamlet composition. The configuration table serves to contain meta-information on the composition of streamlets, message type constraints, ports connections, and routing constraints. The table is derived from the compilation of the MCL script, which the Coordination Manager uses to control the generation of the stubs and the channel objects and to facilitate the exchange of messages among the streamlets. In short, the coordination plane can be viewed as a routing plane, where activities of coordination and interaction are abstracted from the codes of the streamlets. This leads to a highly reconfigurable system where interconnections and relationships between service entities can be composed dynamically in a non-intrusive way.

On another plane, the Streamlet Manager controls the execution of instances of streamlet. During the setup process, the manager is required to locate the classes of streamlets and allocate necessary computational resources for execution. The Event Manager is responsible for generating system events in reaction to different conditions. Finally, there will also be a Streamlet Directory, where the streamlet providers can advertise their services. This directory provides code-level implementations of streamlets at runtime. We discuss in detail various components of the MobiGATE architecture below.

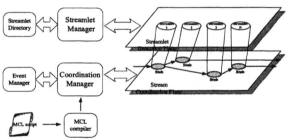

Figure 1. Architecture of MobiGATE

**Coordination Manager.** The Coordination Manager controls the generation of stubs and channel objects and facilitates the exchange of messages among the streamlets. It maintains a configuration table for each running coordination stream, defining the specific message flow route in these streams. From the perspective of networking, the role of the Coordination Manager is somewhat similar to that of a router, while the configuration table acts as the routing table. Another important function of the Coordination Manager is to filter events coming from the Event Manager and broadcast them among coordination streams, which may invoke dynamic actions of reconfiguration if necessary.

**Stream Coordination Plane.** The Stream Coordination Plane is the layer where coordination activities happen. In the plane, a stream object is modeled as streamlet stubs connected by channels, with the composition structure defined by the configuration table held by the Coordination Manager. Stubs do not contain any service logic. Instead, they implement whatever

operations are necessary to forward the request to streamlet instances and receive the result. The exchange of data among the stubs is currently done through channels. The channels transport data using a very frequently used method called *carrier resource*, where a *repository* or *carrier resource*, accessible to both producer and user stubs, is created. Producer stubs write the data to the shared carrier. User stubs read the data from the shared carrier. The carrier resources can be read only after they have been written.

**Streamlet Manager.** The Streamlet Manager manages the execution of various streamlets. It intercepts service requests from the Stream Coordination Plane, passes the incoming message to the corresponding streamlet instance for processing, and finally returns the result message. If the requested streamlet has not yet been initiated, the manager will create an instance for it from the Streamlet Directory; otherwise the manager will directly deliver the message to the Streamlet Execution Plane.

**Streamlet Execution Plane.** All of the computation activities take place in the Stream Execution Plane. In this plane, individual streamlets run independently of the others and focus on imposing services on the incoming messages. We distinguish two kinds of streamlets, *Stateless* and *Stateful*, depending on whether they keep state information for the requesting coordinator processes.

One of the fundamental benefits of using the MobiGATE architecture is that it is able to handle a heavy workload while maintaining a high level of performance. There is a relationship between the number of streams and the number of streamlets that are required to service them. As the stream population increases, that is, as the number of applications increases, the number of streamlets required increases correspondingly. At some time, the increase in the number of streamlets will have an impact on performance and diminish the throughput. MobiGATE explicitly supports a mechanism called *streamlet pooling* that makes it easier to manage large numbers of streamlets in the Streamlet Execution Plane.

The concept of pooling resources is not new. A commonly used technique is to pool database connections so that the business objects in the system can share access to the database. This mechanism reduces the number of database connections that are needed, which reduces the consumption of resources and increases throughput. The MobiGATE Streamlet Execution Plane also applies resource pooling to streamlets; this technique is called streamlet pooling. Streamlet pooling reduces the number of instances of streamlet, and therefore, the resources needed to service requests from the Stream Coordination Plane. It is also less expensive to reuse pooled streamlet instances than to frequently create and destroy instances.

Streamlet pooling is applicable to streamlets that are considered stateless. In other words, since stateless streamlets are never associated with a specific stream, there is no fundamental reason to keep a separate copy of each streamlet for each instance of stream. Thus, the system can keep a much smaller number of streamlets, reusing each instance of streamlet to service different requests. By this means it greatly reduces the resources actually needed to service all of the requests for service.

**Event Manager.** The Event Manager is responsible for generating system events in reaction to different conditions. These events may be caused by client requests, changes to the system environment, or by exceptions in executions of streamlet. Coordinating the publication of events is fundamental to the realization of adaptive processing in a mobile middleware system such as MobiGATE.

**MCL Complier.** The MCL Compiler controls the compilation of the MCL coordination script and generates the necessary configuration tables to define the message flow routes in coordination streams. It is also responsible for any compile-time validation work such as compatibility checks. In case there are any incompatible connections in the script, the compiler should return with a detailed error message.

**Streamlet Directory.** The Streamlet Directory serves as the repository where streamlet providers can advertise their services. In addition, it serves as a central storage for streamlet codes in which the Streamlet Manager may locate the relevant streamlets and create instances for execution. Note that it is possible for a streamlet itself to be represented as an MCL coordination script, which defines a recursive composition of other native streamlets.

## 4. MobiGATE Coordination Language

The MobiGATE Coordination Language (MCL) provides a declarative specification of the composition and coordination of streamlets through various construct abstractions. The language is not concerned with the operational logic of the streamlet but seeks to capture the streamlet's high-level abstract characteristics such as interfaces through the abstraction of input-output ports and the types of data associated with the messages. The coordination and relationship between the streamlets are captured through the abstraction of channels.

### 4.1. Language Elements

The MCL language is comprised of several important abstractions including streamlets, channels, and streams. Collectively, the abstractions, labeled constructs, constrained typing, and definitions form the building blocks for describing the composition of the streamlets and their architectural description.

**Streamlet.** Streamlets represent the main functional pieces of an application. They own a set of ports, through which they interconnect with the rest of the system. Interconnections among streamlets are explicitly represented as separate language elements, called channels. Streamlets must always connect to one another through channels. As a consequence, every streamlet port must be connected to a compatible channel port based on the definition of MIME type. Within the context of a streamlet, ports play the role of placeholder, which means they will not be affected by the computation of the streamlet. Streamlets read/write messages from/to their associated input/output ports by using **read/write** primitives, without the explicit need to know the real source/destination of messages. The separation and externalization of the interconnections of the streamlets promote the independence of streamlets from their environment and their reusability.

**Channel.** Channels describe relationships of interconnection and constraints among streamlets. Traditional programming languages do not support a distinct abstraction for representing such relationships and implicitly encode support for component interconnections inside their abstractions for components. In contrast, MCL requires that all interconnections among streamlets be explicitly represented using channels. Like streamlets, channels own ports. Channel ports must be connected to compatible streamlet ports.

**Stream.** A stream is a purely composition script, also known as a coordination script, running at the coordinator side. It is within a stream that different streamlet and channel instances are created, network topologies are constructed, and actions in response to different events are specified. On the one hand, streams can be viewed as streamlets connected by channels with the ability to perform adaptations. On the other hand, a stream can also be viewed as a "streamlet" with input/output ports, which come from the stream's inner streamlet ports that are not concerned with any inner connections. Dynamic reconfiguration is another important task that needs to be addressed in the description of stream. In MCL the interaction model is *event-driven*. That is, a coordinator process waits to observe an occurrence of some specific event that triggers it to enter a predefined state and perform some actions. These actions typically consist of setting up or breaking off connections of ports and channels. The coordinator then remains in that state until it observes the occurrence of some other interested event.

### 4.2. Case Example

In this section, we present a pragmatic example of the composition of service entities based on MCL to illustrate and highlight the robustness of the language in regulating complex adaptations in response to evolving wireless and mobile operating environments. We make use of the

Datatype-Specific Distillation application that was deployed at U.C. Berkeley [4], together with some of our own modifications, as an example for illustration. The service entities used in this example are listed below.

- *Switch*: Dividing the incoming message based on the semantic type of the data;
- *Image down sampling*: Lossy compression of an image by reducing the sample rate;
- *Map to 16 grays*: Reducing images to 16 grays to support shallow grayscale displays;
- *PostScript-to-text*: Discarding some information on format and converting documents to rich-text supported by most devices;
- *Text compress*: A generic text compressor;
- *Merge*: Integrating different types of information into a whole body;
- *Power Saving*: A power-saving mechanism as discussed in [1].

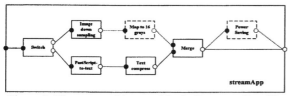

Figure 2. The composition model of a Datatype-Specific Distillation application

Figure 2 is the composition model of this application. In the figure, rectangle boxes represent the service entities modeled as streamlets associated with input ports (black points) and output ports (white points). Lines between different ports embody intermediate channel objects. Note that the dashed parts are optional, which means they will be included into the architecture only when some specific events happen. For example, the power-saving entity is invoked on the condition that the system subscribes and correspondingly receives the *low energy* signal from the hardware abstraction driver. Containing the composition of the streamlets is the abstraction of the stream application *streamApp*, which exercises recursive composition. The composite streamApp streamlet has its own input/output ports that are derived from those internal ports that are not satisfied by any internal connections. Therefore, from the outside the streamApp can also be regarded as a streamlet object and be graphically represented in the form of an encapsulated box and ports to be reused in other stream applications. We will have a detailed discussion about this recursive composition later in this paper.

Below is the description of individual streamlets in MCL. Considering the large size of this image information, we specifically create a channel with a buffer of 1024 Kbytes to connect image-related streamlets, while others still use the default 100 Kbytes-sized channel.

```
streamlet switch{
    port{
        in pi     : multipart/mixed;
        out po1 : image;
        out po2 : application/PostScript;
    }
    attribute{
        type = STATELESS;
        library = "/general/switch.class" ;
        description =
            "Divide incoming message based on
            the semantic type of the data." ;
    }
}
streamlet img_down_sample{
    port{
        in pi     : image;
        out po  : image;
    }
    attribute{
        type = STATELESS;
        library = "/image/downSample.class" ;
        description =
            "reduce sample rate of the image" ;
    }
}
streamlet map_to_16_grays{
    port{
        in pi     : image;
        out po  : image;
    }
    attribute{
        type = STATELESS;
        library = "/image/mapGrays.class" ;
        description =
            "To support clients with shallow
            grayscale displays" ;
    }
}
streamlet powerSaving{
    port{
        in pi     : multipart/mixed;
        out po  : multipart/mixed;
    }
    attribute{
        type = STATEFUL;
        library = "/general/powerSaving.class" ;
        description =
            "Power saving mechanism." ;
    }
}
```

```
streamlet postscript2text{
    port{
        in pi     : application/PostScript;
        out po  : text/richtext;
    }
    attribute{
        type = STATELESS;
        library = "/text/p2t.class" ;
        description =
            "Convert PostScript material to
            richtext document." ;
    }
}
streamlet text_compress{
    port{
        in pi     : text;
        out po  : text;
    }
    attribute{
        type = STATELESS;
        library = "/text/Compressor.class" ;
        description =
            "a generic text compressor." ;
    }
}
streamlet merge{
    port{
        in pi1     : image;
        in pi2     : text;
        out po  : multipart/mixed;
    }
    attribute{
        type = STATELESS;
        library = "/general/merge.class" ;
        description =
            "Merge messages together." ;
    }
}

channel  largeBufferChan{
    port{
        in     : image;
        out   : image;
    }
    attribute{
        type = ASYN;
        category = KB;
        buffer = 1024 Kbytes;
    }
}
```

Figure 3. Streamlet and channel descriptions

Based on these streamlet descriptions, the final composition script for the stream *streamApp* is written as shown in Figure 4.

```
stream streamApp{
    streamlet s1 = new-streamlet (switch);
    streamlet s2 = new-streamlet (img_down_sample);
    streamlet s3 = new-streamlet (map_to_16_grays);
    streamlet s4 = new-streamlet (powerSaving);
    streamlet s5 = new-streamlet (postscript2text);
    streamlet s6 = new-streamlet (text_compress);
    streamlet s7 = new-streamlet (merge);

    channel c1, c2, c3 = new channel (largeBufferChan);

    connect (s1.po1, s2.pi, c1);
    connect (s1.po2, s5.pi);
    connect (s2.po, s7.pi1,c2);
    connect (s5.po, s6.pi);
    connect (s6.po, s7.pi2);

    when(LOW_ENERGY){
        connect (s7.po, s4.pi);
    }
    when(LOW_GRAYS){
        disconnect(s2.po, s7.pi1);
        connect(s2.po, s3.pi, c2);
        connect(s3.po, s7.pi1, c3);
    }
}
```

Figure 4. Stream description

### 4.3. Design Issues

The design of MCL is greatly influenced by a set of core design issues. These issues, in a way, differentiate MCL from existing and general coordination languages, with specific focus as an underlying coordination language to facilitate robust composition and support for dynamic reconfiguration in a mobile and wireless environment.

**4.3.1. Checking Compatibility.** In a manner analogous to the checking of type in programming languages, it is desirable to be able to perform the limited static checking of compatibility when connecting or transforming the composition of service entities. Such controls facilitate the construction of correct and consistent architectures while helping designers focus their attention on more complex issues. MCL provides such a mechanism, based on the matching of streamlet port types.

MCL imposes several semantic restrictions and constraints on the ability of streamlets to connect to each other. The two most important restrictions are:

- Streamlet ports can only be connected to channel ports (and vice versa).
- Sink ports can only connect to source ports that are equal to or a specialization of the sink ports.

It is desirable to encode such restrictions and constraints, so that a number of compatibility tests can be automatically performed by the language at the time of compilation. Since all MCL connections are between ports, it is desirable to be able to perform compatibility checks at the port level.

The first restriction is relatively easy to validate by language. Before establishing a connection, MCL checks the source of two ports. If both of them come from streamlets, or channels, the connection is considered illegal. For the second restriction, MCL bases its checking of compatibility on types of port. Multiple associated direct subtypes or supertypes can be assigned to a port type. These subtype/supertype relations are used to specify the second restriction on compatibility. To establish a connection, MCL performs a match of port types: if the type of source port is equal to or a subtype of a type of sink port, the connection is considered legal. In the application shown in figure 2, the connection between the *PostScript-to-text* output port and the *Text compress* input port is valid, since the source port type *text/richtext* is a subtype of the sink port type *text*.

**4.3.2. Recursive Composition.** As mentioned above, the stream and streamlet processes are indistinguishable in terms of their abstraction as boxes with associated input/output ports. Thus, a stream object can logically be regarded as a streamlet written in native MCL

composition languages and reused in another stream application. This is known as recursive composition. In addition, we include a key word **main** to indicate the highest-level stream object in a coordination script. As such, the system can start to execute an MCL application by locating a stream object that is labeled **main** in the coordination script.

To support this recursive composition, we need to compose a separate description of streamlets associated with each stream object. Based on these descriptions, the system instantiates instances of streamlet and sets up connections to each streamlet, just as it does for common streamlets. For example, we can reuse the example stream discussed above as follows.

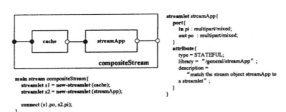

Figure 5. Recursive Composition

As shown in Figure 5, the composite stream is oblivious in the internal structure of the stream *streamApp*. From the view point of the composite stream, this stream object is just a common streamlet that is implemented in MCL. In a similar manner, this composite stream can also be reused in another higher-level stream object as a common streamlet object.

The support of the recursive composition model corresponds to the spirit of coordination theory in facilitating organized composition. As MobiGATE evolves, coupled with the proliferation of streamlets, we envisage a need to provide a coordinated and structured organization of streamlets to promote ease of use and management. This is reflected in MCL through the support of the hierarchical modeling of streamlet composition based on recursive coordination.

**4.3.3. Streamlet Sharing.** Another important contribution of our work is the concept of *streamlet sharing*. As each streamlet is only concerned with imposing its computation on incoming messages and producing response messages, it is oblivious of the source or destination of the messages. The complete decoupling of coordination from computation makes it possible to share instances of streamlet between different streams.

The issue is: how to distribute messages to their corresponding stream when the messages are generated on the output ports of the shared instances of streamlet? In other words, how can we differentiate between messages belonging to different instance of stream?

As introduced previously, streamlets exchange messages based on MIME. In MIME message format, there exists a header called the *MIME-extension-field* for applications to define their own application-specific headers. Taking advantage of this feature, we define a new field in the message header to identify messages from different streams.

*session ::= "Content-Session" ":"session-id*

Before executing a coordination stream, the system will automatically generate a unique session ID for each instance of stream. Subsequently, all of the messages belonging to this stream will be labeled with the assigned session ID in their "Content-Session" field. By this means, the system can easily differentiate messages from different streams.

## 5. Conclusions

This paper presents a novel coordination language called MCL, supported by MobiGATE architecture, to describe the composition of proxy services in a wireless environment. The services offered in MobiGATE are composed of streamlets that are chained together in the form of a stream that adapts to the flow of data traffic to alleviate the poor characteristics of a wireless environment. The dynamic changing characteristics of a mobile and wireless environment mean that MobiGATE needs to support the dynamic reconfiguration of services through the evolutionary composition of a mix of streamlets. This is achieved by separating the interactions among streamlets from their computation through the abstraction of a coordination plane. In particular, the complexity of directly coding the flow of interactions among streamlets is captured via the abstraction of a new coordination flow language called MCL. The novel features of MCL include the modeling of service interfaces based on a MIME media type system, support for a check on the compatibility of the compositions, support for recursive compositions, the concept of streamlet sharing, and a complete separation of coordination from computation activities in the MobiGATE architecture.

So far, we have completed the definition of the MCL coordination language and the supporting MobiGATE architecture. The complete infrastructure of this architecture is being implemented on a Java execution platform, which supports a highly portable system to operate across heterogeneous environments. In particular, in the future, we are planning to port the Java implementation of the MobiGATE client proxy to operate on resource-constrained devices such as PDAs, and mobile phones executing on a J2ME platform. The complete setup of the experimental platform will provide us with the unique opportunity to truly exercise and validate the operations of MobiGATE and to collect empirical results on the performance of the system. Initial experiments conducted with the system have revealed promising results and will be the subject of our future publications.

## 6. References

[1] Giuseppe Anastasi, Marco Conti, and Willy Lapenna "A Power-Saving Network Architecture for Accessing the Internet from Mobile Computers: Design, Implementation and Measurements", The COMPUTER JOURNAL, Vol. 46, No. 1, 2003.

[2] F. Arbab, "The IWIM Model for Coordination of Concurrent Activities", First International Conference on Coordination Models, Languages and Applications (Coordination '96), Cesena, Italy, 15-17 April, 1996, LNCS 1061, Springer Verlag, pp. 34-56.

[3] Alvin T.S. Chan and Siu Nam Chuang, "MobiPADS: A Reflective Middleware for Context-Aware Computing", IEEE Transactions on Software Engineering, vol. 29, no. 12, Dec 2003, pp. 1072-1085.

[4] A. Fox, S. Gribble, Y. Chawathe and E. Brewer, "Adapting to network and client variation using infrastructural proxies: lessons and perspectives" IEEE Personal Communications, Vol. 5, No. 4, (Aug. 1998), pp. 10-19.

[5] N. Freed, "Multipurpose Internet Mail Extensions, (MIME) Part Two: Media Types" RFC 2046, November 1996.

[6] David Garlan and Mary Shaw "An Introduction to Software Architecture" Carnegie Mellon University Technical Report CMU-CS-94-166, January 1994.

[7] George A. Papadopoulos, Farhad Arbab "Coordination Models and Languages" Advances in Computers, Marvin V. Zelkowitz (ed.), Academic Press. Vol. 46, August, 1998, 329-400.

[8] T. W. Malone and K. Crowston, "The Interdisciplinary Study of Coordination", ACM Computing Surveys 26, 1994, pp. 87-119.

# Notes

# Author Index

# Notes

# Notes

# Notes

# Notes

# Notes

## Press Operating Committee

---

### IEEE Computer Society Publications

The world-renowned IEEE Computer Society publishes, promotes, and distributes a wide variety of authoritative computer science and engineering texts. These books are available from most retail outlets. Visit the CS Store at *http://computer.org* for a list of products.

### IEEE Computer Society Proceedings

The IEEE Computer Society also produces and actively promotes the proceedings of more than 160 acclaimed international conferences each year in multimedia formats that include hard and soft-cover books, CD-ROMs, videos, and on-line publications.

For information on the IEEE Computer Society proceedings, please e-mail to csbooks@computer.org or write to Proceedings, IEEE Computer Society, P.O. Box 3014, 10662 Los Vaqueros Circle, Los Alamitos, CA 90720-1314. Telephone +1-714-821-8380. Fax +1-714-761-1784.

**Additional information regarding the Computer Society, conferences and proceedings, CD-ROMs, videos, and books can also be accessed from our web site at *http://computer.org/cspress***

---

Revised: May 6, 2004